MANAGEMENT
A PACIFIC RIM FOCUS

Fourth Edition

McGraw-Hill
Irwin

National Library of Australia Cataloguing-in-Publication Data

Management: a Pacific rim focus.

    4th ed.
    Bibliography.
    Includes index.
    ISBN 0 07 471419 8.

    1. Management. 2. Management – Pacific Area.
    I. Bartol, Kathryn M.

658.4

Published in Australia by
McGraw-Hill Australia Pty Limited
Level 2, 82 Waterloo Road, North Ryde, NSW 2113, Australia
Senior Sponsoring Editor: Ailsa Brackley du Bois
Developmental Editor: Melina Deliyannis
Publishing Services Manager: Jo Munnelly
Project Editors: Amber Cameron, Graham Watson
Permissions Editors: Colette Hoeben, Jane Brimacombe
Senior Marketing Manager: Susan Talty
Director of e-Learning: Cameron Craig
Editor: Christine Connor
Cover and Internal Design: Modern Art Production Group
Cover Image: George Lepp/The Image bank/Getty Images
Typesetter: Anne McLean
Proofreader: Tim Learner
Indexer: Frances Paterson
Printed by Pantech Limited, Hong Kong

MANAGEMENT
A PACIFIC RIM FOCUS
Fourth Edition

KATHRYN BARTOL, University of Maryland
MARGARET TEIN, RMIT University
GRAHAM MATTHEWS, RMIT University
DAVID MARTIN, American University

McGraw-Hill Irwin

Boston Burr Ridge, IL Dubuque, IA Madison, WI New York
San Francisco St. Louis Bangkok Bogotá Caracas Kuala Lumpur
Lisbon London Madrid Mexico City Milan Montreal New Delhi
Santiago Seoul Singapore Sydney Taipei Toronto

DEDICATION

A woman of valor who can find, far beyond pearls is her value
Proverbs 31:10:31

To the women of valor in my life:
In memory of Joyce Matthews
for Shoshana Cutter
Callie Tein
Ellen Ester Tein
Madeleine Shira Tein

For another blessing in our lives Jay Benjamin Cutter

Margaret Tein & Graham Matthews

PREFACE

This stunning fourth edition of **Management: A Pacific Rim Focus,** complete with accompanying CD-ROM and on-line resources, continues to equip students with the skills they need to become informed and effective managers. The text and package does so by offering the most stimulating, diverse and original content of any management text available today.

Our experience tells us that one of the most challenging things for lecturers in this field is to teach students to think critically and strategically about theories, and to develop decision-making and analytical skills of their own. To that end, this edition extends each chapter of the text by providing ten new critical thinking questions, as well as application exercises and true/false and multiple choice questions. These questions invite students to carefully evaluate contemporary management debates in a regional and global context, and inspire the development of analytical and decision-making skills.

We believe that diverse case studies and vignettes are essential for providing students with a foundation from which to develop the decision-making and analytical skills that they will need to deal effectively with managerial challenges. That is why, in this edition, we provide even more interesting and relevant new case studies. These ensure the most current coverage available on gender issues, SMEs, globalisation or engineering situations. Each case features real people, real organisations and real strategies and decisions, and is accompanied by critical discussion questions.

The preface to previous editions began with the statement 'Management is about people'. To us, this is self-evident. Ironically, of late our students have begun to question the relevance of a personal approach to management, perceiving that it is being replaced by technology. They see electronic messaging taking the place of verbal communication, e-commerce replacing the need for front-line interactions with customers or suppliers, and computer software performing many of the planning and control functions previously completed by managers.

The popularity of technology might lead students to believe that success will evade them unless they use and master such tools. However, while we maintain that the tools are relevant and that it would be foolish to disregard their value, they are, nonetheless, only tools. This is why we maintain the stance that management is about people. The use of current technology puts the competence of managers at risk, because it is too easy to rely on it, thereby ignoring the potency of the person-to-person interactions that result in true management excellence. We would like to stress that any electronic supplements are only tools; it is the content and concepts that you study and how you apply them that will make the difference to your effectiveness and success.

This book was conceived based on the philosophy that management is about human endeavour and people achieving results, and, in spite of many changes appearing in society, our convictions remain the same. As you work your way through this text, you will observe that our emphasis is still on the applications of theory to produce a culture and environment in which success is possible. If the use of tools determines the degree of success, this can be achieved by any individual or organisation with the skills to do so. How then, do organisations and individuals differentiate themselves when both have the resources to acquire, and the skills to use, the tools?

The key differences are found in examples of leadership; how individuals in organisations treat one another, their clients, their suppliers and their competitors—in other words, how people are managed. If business enterprise is about people and their aspirations to succeed, then it is the ability to direct the human energies generated in fulfilling these aspirations that constitutes the key to good management.

Margaret Tein & Graham Matthews

Welcome to McGraw-Hill's

It's all about flexibility. Today. You want to be able to teach your course, your way. McGraw-Hill offers you extensive choices in content selection and delivery backed by uncompromising service.

Your course: Connect your students with leading texts and study guides, websites, online readings, online cases, online course materials and revision programs. To assist you in teaching your course, McGraw-Hill provides you with cutting edge resources, including online testing and revision, instructor's manuals and guides, test banks, visual resources and PowerPoint slide shows. Your McGraw-Hill Academic Sales Consultant is trained to help match your course with our content, today.

Your way: Your McGraw-Hill Academic Sales Consultant, our instructional designer, and our E-learning team are trained to help you customise our content for your existing or new course. We carefully examine and match your course to our content and then discuss what, how, and when you would like it to be delivered — online or in print. It is that easy.

Your guarantee: Our programs are backed by our unique service guarantee. If you are a loyal McGraw-Hill customer, we will convert your course to our content each time your course changes — we use only qualified instructional designers or we consult with your own academic staff. Ask about our Course Conversion Program today!

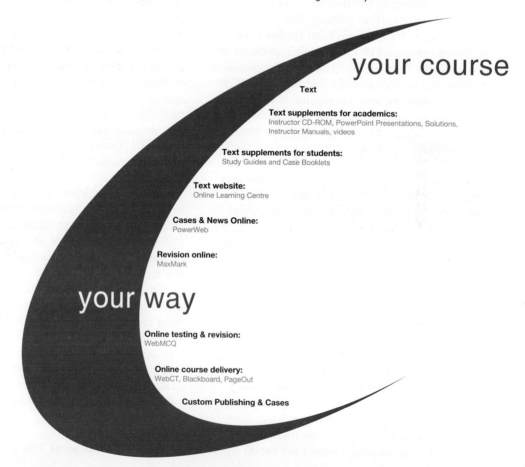

your course

Text

Text supplements for academics:
Instructor CD-ROM, PowerPoint Presentations, Solutions, Instructor Manuals, videos

Text supplements for students:
Study Guides and Case Booklets

Text website:
Online Learning Centre

Cases & News Online:
PowerWeb

Revision online:
MaxMark

your way

Online testing & revision:
WebMCQ

Online course delivery:
WebCT, Blackboard, PageOut

Custom Publishing & Cases

www.mcgraw-hill.com.au/contenttoday

CONTENTS IN BRIEF

CONTENTS IN DETAIL

CHAPTER 3   UNDERSTANDING INTERNAL AND EXTERNAL ENVIRONMENTS 62

MaxMARK   **POWERWEB**

CHAPTER 4   SOCIAL RESPONSIBILITY AND ETHICS IN MANAGEMENT 94

MaxMARK   **POWERWEB**

PART 2 PLANNING AND DECISION MAKING 129

MaxMARK   *POWERWEB*

CHAPTER 7   FOSTERING AN INNOVATIVE ORGANISATION — 218

MaxMARK   **PowerWeb**

PART 3 ORGANISING — 251

CHAPTER 8   ORGANISATION STRUCTURE — 252

MaxMARK   **PowerWeb**

MaxMARK **POWERWEB**

MaxMARK **POWERWEB**

PART 4 LEADING · 363

CHAPTER 11 · MOTIVATION · 364

MaxMARK **POWERWEB**

CHAPTER 12 · LEADERSHIP · 398

MaxMARK **POWERWEB**

MaxMARK   **POWERWEB**

MaxMARK   **POWERWEB**

PART 5 CONTROLLING   497

CHAPTER 15   CONTROLLING THE ORGANISATION   498

MaxMARK   **POWERWEB**

Supplement 1 to Chapter 15   Managerial control methods   533

Supplement 2 to Chapter 15   Operations management   547

Supplement 3 to Chapter 15   Management information systems   563

CHAPTER 18   THE REGIONAL CONTEXT 650

(MaxMARK)   POWERWEB

HIGHLIGHTS OF THIS EDITION

1 Retains a strong overview of management processes as it focuses on the manager's activities, skills and knowledge required for effectiveness.

2 Examines the roots of contemporary approaches to management.

3 Links the characteristics of the internal organisation culture and practices to the demands of a changing external environment.

4 Examines the complex issues associated with business ethics and corporate social responsibility in the context that organisations, in order to be ethical and socially responsible, must be made up of ethical and responsible individuals.

5 Incorporates creativity as an important factor in decision making in a business context that increasingly demands more efficient and effective ways of doing things.

6 Presents an amalgamated overview of the planning process and how it can be carried forward in to the practices required, allowing senior managers to manage strategically and successfully implement those plans.

7 Examines the balance between integrating the planning process with strategies to enhance the energies and capabilities of staff achieving results required to meet the demands of the market.

8 Looks at an organisation's structure as the primary tool for achieving the goals of the organisation.

9 Examines the strategic approaches to structuring the organisation for the best fit in the contemporary environment.

CONTENTS IN BRIEF

10 Gives an up-to-date overview of human resources as a strategic tool for effectively achieving the goals and outcomes of the organisation. This chapter has all new cases.

11 Looks at an increasingly educated and sophisticated workforce that demands more effective motivation strategies on the part of managers.

12 Presents leadership as a set of skills which can be learned and taught, embedded in the processes of personal influence.

13 Continues to explore the different types of communication channels that lead to effective organisations.

14 Encourages the power inherent in group activities, one of the key strategies of the effective manager.

15 Examines how successful organisations pay close attention to how they are doing; taking swift action when problems arise and changing direction as needed.

16 Looks at people being the key to successful change. They need to believe that they can make a difference across organisations, both large and small.

17 Focuses on the need for cross-cultural understanding as an increasing number of organisations enter trans-national enterprises.

18 Highlights some of the differences about doing business with our key regional partners. It points out the challenges which will need to be faced by managers in dealing with different cultures and mind sets.

TEXT AT A GLANCE

Management: A Pacific Rim Focus 4e is a pedagogically rich learning resource. The features laid out on these pages are especially designed to encourage and enhance your acquisition of the principle tenets of management.

CHAPTER OPENER

Chapter Openers present a summary of the subheadings in the chapter you are about to study and a list of Learning Objectives that set out what you should be able to achieve after completing that chapter.

STRIVING FOR EXCELLENCE

Each Chapter opens with a BRW profile that showcases a successful manager who has made an impact on the industry in which they operate.

KEY TERMS

Key terms supplied in the margin allow you easy access to the language of management. They are highlighted in the text and also presented in an alphabetical glossary at the end of the book.

BOXED FEATURES

CASE IN POINT

These short cases bring to life key concepts explained in the text. They invite you to diagnose particular management problems and identify the specific decisions, models and processes that are represented in each example.

GENDER FACTOR

Gender Factor cases examine the changing roles of men and women in business and the new workplace realities that these create. These cases challenge you to think about the impact of gender-related issues within the context of each chapter topic.

MANAGERIAL DILEMMAS

These cases describe a course of action managers have had to make in response to various threats and opportunities. Reflect on the possible outcomes of the management decisions presented and use the theory you have learned so far to offer strategies you may have followed instead.

MANAGING THE E-CHALLENGE

How is technology impacting on business? How are organisations harnessing electronic tools to further themselves? Managing the e-Challenge cases examine the various electronic activities of organisations to increase customer reach and productivity.

MANAGEMENT SKILLS FOR A GLOBALISED ECONOMY

These practical exercises help you to develop the basic skills critical to being a successful manager, for example, creativity, self-analysis, entrepreneurship, quality assurance, and negotiation and delegation skills. Work through these skill-building activities and apply your newfound wisdom to your professional and student life.

xxii

GAINING THE EDGE

Take a critical look at an organisation whose management practices are exemplary in some way, and identify why they are successful. These short, inspiring examples enliven your learning and broaden your view of how management applies to your everyday life.

FOCUS ON PRACTICE— STRATEGIES FOR IMPROVING

Apply theory to everyday practice with these practical applications. Undertake and perform the variety of tasks requested and gain a better understanding of the theories presented within each chapter.

REFLECTIVE PRACTITIONER

This feature focuses on one manager, Kimberley Turner, Business Woman of the Year 2002, and her thoughts and practices about every aspect of her developing organisation, Aerosafe.

END-OF-CHAPTER MATERIAL

MANAGEMENT EXERCISES

Actively build the management skills you need to succeed as a manager by working through these rigorous applications. These exercises encourage you to think independently, as well as operate in a group.

CHAPTER SUMMARY

The Chapter Summary recaps the key themes of the chapter topic. Use these summaries as a reliable pre-exam revision tool.

Once you have read the chapter summary, get ahead of the class with MaxMark, a self-paced online assessment tool that contains thirty interactive questions per chapter. To access please see the registration card at the front of this book.

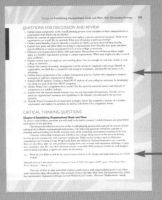

QUESTIONS FOR DISCUSSION AND REVIEW

These short-answer discussion questions give you an opportunity to think about and discuss different situations directly related to the chapter you have just read.

CRITICAL THINKING QUESTIONS

Over 100 critical thinking questions challenge you to diagnose specific management issues so that you learn to analyse problems and make decisions. These questions aim to improve your ability to think at a higher level and hone your critical abilities.

ON THE RIM CASE

These end-of-chapter cases look closely at the management activities of different organisations conducting business on the Pacific Rim. They are important because they highlight the management behaviours of Australia's main trading partners. Business conduct varies markedly in different parts of the Asia-Pacific region, particularly in terms of motivation and reward.

The PowerWeb icon appears here as a reminder that you may search for more related articles and cases online. To access please see the registration card at the front of this book.

FURTHER READING RECOMMENDATIONS

At the end of every chapter a list of Further Reading is provided that encourages and steers you to extend your reading on the theme of that particular chapter.

END-OF-PART MATERIAL

GRADUATE GLIMPSE

This new feature examines the many and varied paths which graduates in management have taken. Read and be inspired by their career trajectories and the endless future possibilities that a management degree may offer you.

GOING GLOBAL CASE

These extended end-of-part cases focus on companies that are doing something notable on the world stage, be they Pacific Rim organisations with an international focus or overseas multinationals operating in the region. Read the case and build your critical thinking skills by undertaking the activities for discussion, analysis and further research.

CASE MATRIX

Customise your case focus! Locate specific case studies in the text by matching the case type to the chapter theme you require in the matrix below.

CASE TYPE	1	2	3	4	5	6
CASE IN POINT	page 18	page 37	page 68	page 104	page 139	page 181
GENDER FACTOR	page 21	page 49	page 80	page 109	page 149	page 199
MANAGERIAL DILEMMA	page 20	page 40	page 71	page 107	page 143	page 190
MANAGING THE E-CHALLENGE	page 15	page 51	page 76	page 102	page 148	page 193
MANAGEMENT SKILLS FOR A GLOBALISED ECONOMY	page 8	page 50	page 70	page 112	page 152	page 186
GAINING THE EDGE	page 22	page 53	page 84	page 116	page 154	page 206
REFLECTIVE PRACTITIONER	page 24	page 54	page 85	page 117	page 155	page 206
ON THE RIM	page 28	page 60	page 91	page 123	page 161	page 214
GOING GLOBAL				page 126		

7	8	9	10	11	12	13	14	15	16	17	18
page 224	page 257	page 291	page 323	page 370	page 405	page 438	page 469	page 509	page 583	page 634	
page 235	page 271	page 307	page 332	page 382	page 418	page 447	page 474	page 516	page 589	page 624	
page 228	page 263	page 300	page 326	page 372	page 410	page 443	page 471	page 503	page 586	page 617	
page 230	page 268	page 301	page 329	page 377	page 416	page 449	page 478	page 512	page 594	page 622	
page 236	page 268	page 308	page 335	page 383	page 408	page 442	page 477	page 507	page 597	page 630	
page 238	page 275	page 310	page 347	page 385	page 420	page 451	page 481	page 520	page 600	page 639	
page 239	page 277	page 311	page 349	page 386	page 421	page 452	page 482	page 522	page 601	page 640	
page 244	page 283	page 317	page 355	page 386	page 427	page 458	page 490	page 530	page 607	page 646	
page 248			page 360				page 494		page 610		page 676

E-STUDENT

www.mhhe.com/au/bartol4e

ONLINE LEARNING CENTRE

The Online Learning Centre that accompanies this text is an integrated online product to assist you in getting the most from your course. This text provides a powerful learning experience beyond the printed page.

The Premium content areas, which are accessed by registering the code at the front of this text, provide you with powerful online resources. After registration, you will have seamless access to International PowerWeb articles, and the MaxMark revision program. Each component of the Online Learning Centre is described below and can be found in both the *student edition* and the *instructor edition*.

MAXMARK

Maximise your Marks with this unique online self-assessment tool, exclusive to McGraw-Hill Australia. With MaxMark, thirty multiple choice questions per topic are available for self-paced revision on each of the key concepts in the chapter.

Importantly, you will receive extensive 'Feedback' and 'More Information' from the text to help you in your understanding. You can randomise the questions and set yourself time limits, track your progress throughout the semester, and thoroughly test your knowledge before exams.

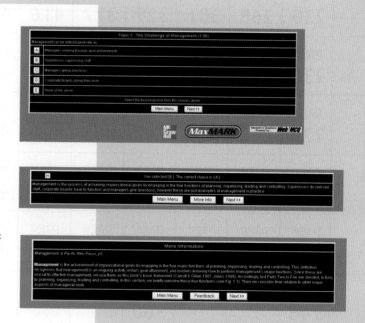

POWERWEB

Unique to McGraw-Hill, PowerWeb provides you with full text international articles on Management, published in International journals and magazines. These articles are updated annually and are organised to each chapter of the text.

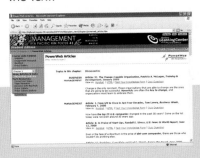

AUTOLIV RUNNING CASE STUDY

This progressive case from the third edition, featuring car manufacturer Autoliv Australia, shows you first-hand how an organisation puts the chapter theories into practice. Judge for yourself whether Autoliv's business strategies could have been managed differently to achieve better outcomes.

WEBLINKS

Links to management organisations, news services and interesting regional and global companies are provided here. Use these to investigate the management practices of leading organisations and to explore the variety of management resources available to you.

STUDY GUIDE

A Study Guide providing an extensive range of exercises and problems to help you develop critical managerial skills and provide relevant revision for exams is available with this text. This may be packaged together with your text or sold separately at your bookshop.

NEW ZEALAND MANAGEMENT SUPPLEMENT

The *New Zealand Management Supplement* by Geare, Campbell-Hunt, Ruwhui and Bull specifically addresses management issues of direct relevance to the New Zealand business environment.

STUDENT VIDEO CD

Packaged together with this book is a local video suite on CD which covers content from Australia, New Zealand and South-East Asia. These clips contextualise the part themes within the text. They are accompanied by online case notes which relate their relevance to part themes. They provide an alternative learning tool for you to understand the functioning of management practice in real-life situations.

E-INSTRUCTOR

www.mhhe.com/au/bartol4e

INSTRUCTOR MANUAL

The Instructor Manual features comprehensive lecture notes, teaching ideas, additional case studies and examples, and suggested solutions to discussion questions and case problems. An ideal resource for busy lecturers, the Instructor Manual can be used in conjunction with the PowerPoint slides as part of a powerful teaching package.

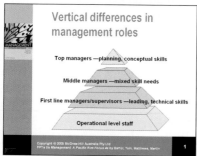

POWERPOINT SLIDES

This text comes with a full suite of colour PowerPoint slides that distil key concepts from each chapter of the book. Present these slides in lecture theatres to reinforce management principles to your class, and distribute them as lecture notes.

TEST BANK

More than 900 multiple-choice questions are available which may be used in WebMCQ's powerful and flexible online quizzing format with tracking and reporting capabilities. Exclusive to McGraw-Hill, WebMCQ allows you to deliver your own online revision quizzes or tests and adapt them to suit your individual or class needs. The Test Bank is also available in WebCT or Blackboard format.

CASE SOLUTIONS

Suggested solutions for cases appearing in the text are available at the Instructor site.

ARTWORK FILES

All artwork, including figures and tables is available in PowerPoint slides on the Instructor Resource CD.

GLOSSARY

Unsure about the meaning of a management term? The glossary contains a quick reference to key terms and definitions.

STUDENT RESULTS

The integrated MaxMark tool that accompanies this text provides you with diagnostics on the performance of your class as your students revise the key concepts in each chapter of the text. (See E-Student to find out more about MaxMark.) You can even compare the performance of your class with the performance of an aggregated group of other institutions teaching with this text.

INSTRUCTOR RESOURCE CD

As one complete package, the Instructor Manual, PowerPoint slides, Test Bank, Case Solutions and Artwork files are all available on CD.

COURSE MANAGEMENT SYSTEMS

Course Management Systems (CMS) allow you to deliver and manage your course via the Internet. McGraw-Hill can provide online material to supplement your existing material for your chosen CMS.

Page Out is McGraw-Hill's exclusive tool for creating websites quickly and easily. It is designed for people with little or no HTML experience. Page Out allows you to create a website using your own materials and your choice of McGraw-Hill's online content. See your McGraw-Hill representative for details.

LOCAL VIDEO SUITE

A suite of local video clips—available on CD or VHS—contextualise the part themes within the text. These are ideal for use within lectures or tutorials. These are also available to students as part of the book package. Students are able to refer back to them, at home or in department labs, in their own time. Video case notes accompanying each clip explain how the footage relates to part material.

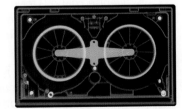

ACKNOWLEDGMENTS

Just as teams are crucial to effective management in business, so too have they been essential to the creation of the fourth edition of this text. We are extremely proud to acknowledge the contributions made by our diverse author team, case contributors and reviewers of this new edition.

Content contributors to the fourth edition

We would like to extend our thanks to Colin Innes (University of Technology, Sydney) for his work on writing our chapter on human resource management. Elizabeth Hall (University of Otago) has patiently read through the new edition and added relevant New Zealand content wherever appropriate. Matene Love (Victoria University of Wellington) has further enriched the relevance of this edition to New Zealand by adding pertinent material on Maori issues in business.

We gratefully acknowledge Julian Teicher and Jo-anne Tui McKeown (Monash University) for their exceptional work on the critical thinking questions. The depth of their research has given this book an additional dimension, and one that further challenges students to think critically and intelligently about management in a real world context.

Case contributors to the fourth edition

We are grateful to our latest case contributors to come on board:

- Peter Woods (Griffith University)
- George Sansbury (La Trobe University)
- Joel Mendelson (Curtin University)
- Denise Faifua (University of Tasmania)
- Allison James (Australian Maritime College)
- Matene Love (Victoria University of Wellington)

Special thanks go to Kimberley Turner from Aerosafe Risk Management whose enthusiasm and unflagging energy often left us breathless.

We would like to thank all our Graduate Glimpse participants for giving generously of their time to tell their story so that students hopeful for a career in management may be inspired: Chris Blanksby, Beverley Schubert, Anthony Ross, Nicole Underwood, Paul Vorbach, Linda Duncombe, Martinique Visser, Bob van de Kuilen, Mark Simpson, Carolyn Dickie, Claire Besanvalle, Ben de Beyer and James Gray.

Ongoing case contributors to the fourth edition

- André M. Everett (University of Otago)
- John Paynter (University of Auckland)
- Ken Dooley (Central Queensland University)
- Ravindra Bagia (University of Technology, Sydney)
- Glenice Wood (University of Ballarat)
- Ella Henry (Unitec Institute of Technology)
- Elizabeth Hall, Virginia Phillips, Karen Henderson and Jodyanne Kirkwood (University of Otago)
- John Krasnostein (Murdoch University)
- Michael Schaper (University of Newcastle)
- Stephen Choo (Curtin University of Technology)
- Ross Milne (Auckland University of Technology)
- Elizabeth Hall (University of Otago)

Reviewers of the fourth edition

Our appreciation also goes to the reviewers from institutions around Australia and New Zealand who took the time to offer constructive criticism on the fourth edition during its development.

- Clancey Covington (Charles Sturt University)
- R. Pathak (University of the South Pacific)
- Alan Simon (University of Western Australia)
- Joseph Beer (University of Auckland)
- Greg Patmore (University of Sydney)

- Imke Fisher (Australian Catholic University)
- Robert Macklin (Charles Sturt University)
- Julie Douglas (Auckland University of Technology)
- Gordon Campbell (Victoria University)
- Pamela Mathews (Charles Sturt University)
- David Morgan (University of New South Wales)
- Philip Ritson (University of Adelaide)
- Jenny Devine (Edith Cowan University)
- Nicola McNeil (Deakin University)
- Bishnu Sharma (University of the Sunshine Coast)
- Kerry Pedigo (Curtin University)
- Lorene Gottschalk (Ballarat University)

Instructor resource authors

In addition, we would like to acknowledge those authors who developed the supplementary material that accompanies this edition:

- Instructor Manual—Mario Fernando (University of Wollongong)

- Test Bank—Imke Fischer (Australian Catholic University)

- MaxMark—Ken Dooley (Central Queensland University)

- PowerPoint slides—George Sansbury (LaTrobe University)

- Video Case Contributors—Peter Woods (Griffith University) and Alan Simon (University of Western Australia)

Thanks also go to Pamela Mathews (Charles Sturt University) who has once again done a fabulous job on the Study Guide.

We thank our colleagues, both at RMIT and other universities around the Pacific Rim, for their suggestions and encouragement.

For their time and interest in this book we are grateful to Christine Connor, our freelance editor, the first thing we asked for when we were told that yet another edition was to be written—thank you for putting up with us for this long; to Jennifer Thompson, our administrative officer at RMIT for her endless support at times when we ready to scream and run away; the friends and colleagues who stopped asking us how the book was going; and finally Kerry Franklin, our IT person who kept us sane when we wanted to throw the computer out the window.

Finally, there are a number of people at McGraw-Hill without whom completion of this fourth edition would not have been possible. Our special thanks go to Ailsa Brackley du Bois and Melina Deliyannis for their on-going dedication. The McGraw-Hill production team also deserves our sincere thanks: Jo Munnelly, Amber Cameron, Graham Watson, Colette Hoeben, Jane Brimacombe and Rachel Jelley.

Margaret Tein & Graham Matthews

PREVIOUS CONTRIBUTORS

Throughout the life of this book many other people have provided ongoing and generous support.

Numerous case study contributors deserve our gratitude for enriching the vitality of the text throughout its life: Murray Ainsworth; Tony Cvorkov; Phillippe Cahill; L. Nash; Lindsay Nelson; Peter Holland; K. Walters; Tom Batley; J. Kirby; S. Dhume; C. Dawson; P. Switzer; S. Lloyd; P. Harmsen; Andrew Hutt; M.G. Harvey; Q. Hardy; A. Gome; Alexander Sibbald; K. Lee; J. Gordon; A.T. Cheng; Graham Elkin; Mark Weston Wall; C. Deutsch; N. Way; W.E. Deming; D. James; R. Garran; S. Elegant; M. Hiebert; Bob Franklin (Managing Director) and Cheryl Woodland of Autoliv Australia.

We remain appreciative to past reviewers without whose constructive comments our book would not have taken the form it has today. Special thanks go to John Dugas (University of Newcastle), Andrew Sense (University of Wollongong), Tony Jolley (management consultant), John Rodwell (Deakin University) and Clive Oliver (Edith Cowan University) for their comments.

We would also like to acknowledge Rae Dorai, who was invaluable in writing the answers to the case study questions that appear in the text for the third edition Instructor Manual; Loretta Inglis (Monash Graduate School), who wrote the third edition of the Test Bank; David Meacheam (University of Newcastle), who authored the original PowerPoint slides; Ken Dooley (Central Queensland University), who wrote the rigorous self-assessment questions for the original MaxMark. We also thank Stephanie Miller (Victoria University) for authoring the online management newsletters that accompanied the third edition of this book and Timothy Bartram (LaTrobe University) for writing video cases to accompany the original clips presented in the enhanced third edition.

Margaret Tein & Graham Matthews

PART 1

INTRODUCTION

As we move into the twenty-first century, management is at a significant stage. Global competition is a way of life. Technology, international activities, business practices and changes in organisational social responsibility mean managers must reconsider their methods and goals, and increasingly emphasise innovation. In this section we consider some applications of basic management principles in this rapidly changing environment.

CHAPTER 1 overviews the management process. It focuses on managers' actual activities and on skills and knowledge needed to be effective and innovative. However, any innovative practice does not emerge in a vacuum; it is built on the best ideas about management that have developed.

CHAPTER 2 analyses the roots of current approaches to management: the scientific, behavioural, quantitative and contemporary perspectives.

As CHAPTER 3 shows, effective managers require knowledge of both the organisation's environment and its internal culture. Successful managers can deal with external and internal factors in ways that support organisational goal achievement.

CHAPTER 4 explores organisational social responsibility and managerial ethics. Taking a broad perspective, it also considers the debate about how much social responsibility an organisation should assume relative to shareholders, employees, customers, community and the larger society.

CHAPTER 1

THE CHALLENGE OF MANAGEMENT

CHAPTER OUTLINE

Management: An overview
What is management?
The management process

What managers actually do
Work methods
Managerial roles
Managerial work agendas

Managerial knowledge, skills, and performance
Knowledge base
Key management skills
Performance

Managerial job types
Vertical dimension: Hierarchical levels
Differences among hierarchical levels
Promoting innovation: The entrepreneurial role
Horizontal dimension: Responsibility areas

Managing in the twenty-first century
Managing change and innovation
Managing diversity: The workforce of 2000 and beyond
Developing a global perspective
The quest for total quality and continuous improvement

LEARNING OBJECTIVES

After studying this chapter, you should be able to:

- Explain four functions of management and other major elements in the management process.
- Describe three common work methods managers use and their 10 major roles.
- Identify the main factors influencing work agendas and how managers use such agendas to channel their efforts.
- Delineate three major managerial skill types.
- Distinguish between effectiveness and efficiency in regard to organisational performance.
- Explain how managerial jobs differ by hierarchical level and responsibility area.
- Explain how managers at different hierarchical levels can use the entrepreneurial role to foster innovation.
- Describe how management education and experience prepare managers.
- Identify four significant twenty-first century management trends.

Erica King: CEO Focus Dental Management

Ever been frustrated by a dentist running behind schedule? Try creating a consultancy based on changing the business habits of dentists. Erica King, 38, has spent close to 15 years pushing and cajoling dentists into trying her ideas for making more money. It has been tough but her consultancy, Focus Dental Management, is growing fast and has reached annual revenue of $5 million. King's entrepreneurial flair and strong drive developed during her childhood. Her parents owned a catering business, and by the age of 12 King was serving drinks and food and spending her weekends peeling prawns. 'By 16, I would walk into a kitchen somewhere in the city with my portable equipment and whip up a fabulous lunch for executives. I learnt that if you want something from life, grab it.'

At university, King did her thesis on tribal communication and lived for 18 months in the highlands of Papua New Guinea, at times sleeping in huts next to pigs. She left university with a degree in psychology and soon started her own business. It was based on a friend's throwaway line about TV stars having trouble handling fame. 'I learnt early how to project myself and decided to show others', she says. At 21, she started a small consultancy, Creating a Positive Image, to coach film and TV stars in dealing with fame and was soon freelancing for Ten Network, and later for Seven Network.

But King kept searching for an opportunity that was unique and had the potential to grow. 'I always wanted to grow a big business. I saw my big strength as helping people make changes to achieve their goals.' Her big idea came on a visit to her dentist. ('I had a phobia about dentists,' she says.) Her dentist, Jon Kozeniauskas, complained about his 35 staff, so King developed a management program for him. She then helped him with a presentation to his colleagues. 'I took the principles I had been teaching and applied them to dentists. We decided that he could do presentations to dentists and I should do them for staff.'

In 1989, Focus Dental Management started from King's lounge room, with King and Kozeniauskas owning 50 per cent each. The typical client was the average suburban dentist, usually male and conservative, with a poor concept of service. 'Dentists, doctors, surgeons do not understand that it is arrogant to keep people waiting.'

But King knew little about the dentistry industry. Telling dentists they were arrogant was not going to get her in the door. Nor was an upfront offer to save them money. 'That was too snake oily.' Instead she would sit down with the dentists and listen. 'I want to understand where dentists are at, what motivates them and what their goals are. Then I want to know how many more years they want to work and where they are now.' She also promised that if she did not increase the dentist's profit by a set amount they would not have to pay for her consulting services. Once in the door, she worked hard on impressing administration staff in the dental clinics. As they became more positive, so did the dentist. 'Dentists are so influenced by their teams.'

continued

STRIVING FOR EXCELLENCE *continued*

King found big differences in attitudes among dentists. She describes those in their 30s as 'wannabe millionaires'; in their 40s, as defeated by dashed expectations and expensive lifestyles; and in their 50s, panicked by the realisation they may not have enough money to retire. Some dentists she visited were struggling financially.

King then drew up growth plans for her clients. The dentists hired more staff and King advised on office management, including hiring and firing, coaching and managing of staff, running the appointment book, budget control, education and improving communication with clients. Her business began growing by 20 to 30 per cent a year, mainly through dentists' referrals. By 1997, revenue reached $1 million and King had two staff. By 2000, it had grown to $3.2 million with five staff. But the growth was too slow for King. 'The dentists would say, "We think it works but we don't want to pay".' (An 18-month program can cost $60 000.) King began presenting the financial success in a visual form. She increased the frequency of updates to monthly and made sure she presented them in person. That resulted in such a large jump in dentists' referrals that revenue took another leap. Now the business is turning over

$5 million, has 14 staff and is profitable, she says. Next year, turnover is expected to be about $6.5 million. King says that of the 350 clients, 98 per cent have made at least $200 000 more from efficient organisation and attracting and retaining patients.

King says she has 1 per cent of the market of 7000 dentists in Australia and that growth potential is enormous. But the business has competition. In 1995, Kathleen McKellar arrived from the United States, where she had been working in dental management outsourcing for years. McKellar says: 'I was astonished to find only one company (Focus Dental Management) doing it.' Now there are 25 companies and franchises offering these services, including the US-based Pride Institute and McKellar's company, Dental Development Services. However, King is highly competitive and regularly re-invents the business. She has just launched a brand, Dental Clinics of Australia, which 50 dentists have joined. 'If you want exceptional service, latest technology and skills and not to be whizzed in and out, you can select one of those clinics.' The first 50 dentists will not pay to belong but the next 50 will each pay a $30 000 fee.

Source: Gome, A. (2003).

This book examines many organisations in looking at critical management approaches to modern organisational success.

To do this, we highlight several significant managerial themes. For one, we will examine techniques found effective to manage change and promote innovation. These techniques help explain how a company can develop many new products. For another, we explore why forward-looking companies emphasise developing quality and initiating total quality management systems. Yet another theme is the value of building and managing a diverse workforce. Statistics show the population profile is changing, with women and minority groups increasing in the 21st-century workforce. Finally, we will highlight the need to take a global perspective, as managers work in an increasingly international context. We will return to these themes across the book as we explore management.

First, the current chapter overviews the nature of management and basic processes involved. Then what managers actually do is discussed by describing their work methods, different roles played and work agendas guiding their actions. We also examine the knowledge base and skills managers need for high performance. We explore two major dimensions along which managerial jobs differ, and we consider how the entrepreneurial role at different management levels fosters innovation. Finally, we investigate how effective management demands understanding future trends and issues.

MANAGEMENT: AN OVERVIEW

Management is a challenging process. Unfortunately managers largely receive little formal training in this complex process, picking up ideas and techniques from observation or modelling. Management involves a number of skills, with the most basic being reflection.

Reflection means the manager stands back from the experience and examines it, relating it to theories and models to develop an understanding of it (Gosling & Mintzberg 2004). This book presents a wide selection of models and theories for you to link to your experiences as you move through your organisational careers.

Also bear in mind that even though many models have been developed over the years, you will find links between the different models. You will also find organisation members displaying behaviours which can be explained in different ways.

Organisations are important in our daily lives. By **organisation**, we mean two or more persons engaged in a systematic effort to produce goods or services. We deal with organisations when we come to class, bank money, buy clothing or see a movie. Organisations impact indirectly on our lives through their products (Schermerhorn 2002).

What is management?

Management is achievement of organisational goals through the major functions of planning, organising, leading and controlling. This definition shows management as an ongoing activity, entailing goal attainment, and knowing how to carry out management's major functions. These functions are crucial to effective management, so they provide this book's basic framework (Carroll & Gillen 1987; Jones & George 2003). Accordingly, text Parts 2 to 5 deal with, in turn, planning, organising, leading and controlling. Here, we review briefly these four functions (see Fig. 1.1). Then we consider them in relation to other major managerial work aspects.

Planning

Planning is the management function involving goal setting and deciding how to achieve goals best.

Organising

Organising is the management function focusing on allocating and arranging resources, both human and non-human, so plans can succeed. Through their organising function managers determine tasks needed to be done, how to best combine these tasks into specific jobs, and how jobs can be grouped into units to form the organisation's structure. Staffing jobs to carry out plans successfully is also part of the organising function.

organisation

Two or more persons engaged in a systematic effort to produce goods or services

management

The process of achieving organisational goals by engaging in the four major functions of planning, organising, leading and controlling

planning

The process of setting goals and deciding how best to achieve them

organising

The process of allocating and arranging human and non-human resources so that plans can be carried out successfully

FIGURE 1.1 The functions of management

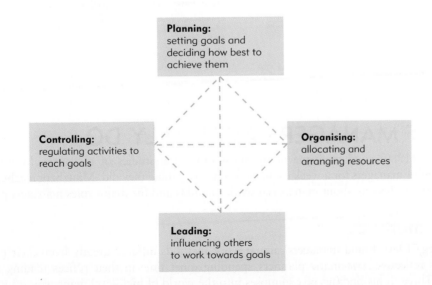

Leading

leading

The process of
influencing others to
engage in the work
behaviours necessary to
reach organisational
goals

Leading is the management function where others are influenced to engage in work behaviours to reach organisational goals. Leading includes communicating with others, helping to outline a vision of what can be achieved, giving direction, and motivating members to put forth necessary effort. This function also includes encouraging needed levels of change and innovation.

Controlling

controlling

The process of regulating
organisational activities
so that actual
performance conforms to
expected organisational
standards and goals

Controlling is the management function regulating organisational activities so actual performance conforms to expected standards and goals (Newman 1975). To regulate, managers monitor ongoing activities, compare results with expected standards or progress toward goals, and take any corrective action necessary.

The management process

**not-for-profit
organisation**

An organisation whose
main purposes centre on
issues other than making
profits

While the four major management functions form the basis of the managerial process, there are other key elements. Carroll and Gillen (1987) reviewed major studies of managerial work and identified these elements. As Figure 1.2 shows, work methods and managerial roles, as well as work agendas, feed management's core functions. A manager's knowledge base and key management skills contribute to high performance (goal achievement). We look at these in the next two sections of this chapter. Remember, management process applies to both organisation types, profit-making and not-for-profit (Lachman 1985). A **not-for-profit organisation** (or a non-profit organisation) has its main purposes centred on issues other than profit. Government organisations (the federal government), educational institutions (your university or college), cultural institutions (a theatre company), charitable institutions (Red Cross) and many health-care facilities (a large public hospital) are common examples.

FIGURE 1.2 An extended model of the management process (adapted from Carroll & Gillen 1987, pp. 38–51)

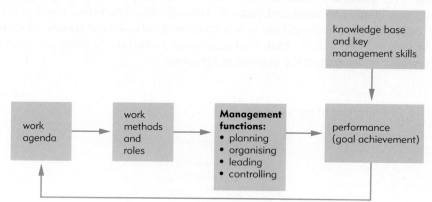

WHAT MANAGERS ACTUALLY DO

Mintzberg (1980) conducted one of the most influential studies of managers, by following several senior managers for a week each, recording everything they did. Mintzberg reached some interesting conclusions about managerial work methods and the major roles managers play.

Work methods

Mintzberg (1980) found managers' actual work methods differed greatly from their popular image as reflective, systematic planners spending quiet time in their offices reading formal reports. Three of his findings give glimpses into the world of high-level managers.

Unrelenting pace

The managers studied by Mintzberg (1980) started work in the morning as they arrived at the office and continued until they left at night. Rather than taking coffee breaks, managers usually drank coffee while in an average of eight meetings each day. Lunches were generally eaten during formal or informal meetings. When not meeting, managers handled on average 36 pieces of mail per day, as well as other written and verbal communications. Any free time was quickly filled by subordinates wanting to speak with the boss.

Brevity, variety and fragmentation

Mintzberg found managers handled a wide range of issues through the day, from a retirement presentation to discussing a bid on a multi-million-dollar contract. Many activities were brief: about half the activities Mintzberg recorded took less than nine minutes, and only 10 per cent took more than an hour. Telephone calls tended to be short, averaging six minutes. Work sessions at a manager's desk and informal meetings averaged 15 and 10 minutes respectively. Managers were continually interrupted by telephone calls and subordinates, often stopping their deskwork to make calls or ask subordinates to drop by. Leaving meetings in progress was common. Due to fragmentation and interruptions, many top managers saved their major brainwork for time beyond the normal workday.

Verbal contacts and networks

Managers in Mintzberg's (1980) study strongly preferred verbal communication either by phone or meetings, rather than written communication such as memos and formal reports. For getting and sending information, they relied heavily on networks. A **network** is a set of co-operative relationships with those whose help the manager needs to function effectively. The contact network in Mintzberg's study included superiors, subordinates, peers and other organisation members, as well as many outsiders. Some were personal contacts, such as friends and peers. Others were professionals, such as consultants, lawyers and insurance underwriters. Still others included trade association contacts, customers and suppliers.

network

A set of co-operative relationships with individuals whose help is needed in order for a manager to function effectively

Implications of Mintzberg's findings

Although Mintzberg's study focused on top-level managers, his findings apply to many managers (Kurke & Aldrich 1983; Gibbs 1994). For example, a study of factory supervisors found they undertook between 237 and 1073 activities within a workday—or more than one activity every two minutes (Guest 1956). Such research supports the need for managers to develop a major network of contacts to have influence and operate effectively (Luthans 1988). To explain the development of such contacts as a manager, see 'How to build networks'.

Managerial roles

To organise his data, Mintzberg (1980) categorised managers' various activities into ten roles. A **role** is an organised set of behaviours associated with a particular office or position (Mintzberg). Positions may entail multiple roles. For example, a salesperson position in a retail shop might include roles of information giver, stock handler and cashier.

role

An organised set of behaviours associated with a particular office or position

Three general types of role Mintzberg observed were interpersonal, informational and decisional. Interpersonal roles grow directly from managerial position authority and involve developing and maintaining positive relationships with significant others. Informational roles relate to receiving and sending information so managers can act as their organisational unit's nerve centre. Decisional roles involve making major organisation decisions. Within these role types, Mintzberg outlined 10 more specific roles managers play (see Table 1.1).

Mintzberg's categorisation of managerial activities into roles gives insight into what managers actually do during their workday. The roles also give us clues about the kinds of skills managers need to carry out their work effectively.

Mintzberg's role approach is a different view of management from the four management functions. At first, it might seem Mintzberg's findings do not match with the view that

How to build networks

Building influence networks involves the principle of reciprocity. This means people generally feel they should be given something back for things they do and one good (or bad) turn deserves another. An immediate return or a specific type of return is not necessarily expected; 'close enough is usually good enough'. As people anticipate a reimbursement for their actions, influence and networking can occur.

Viewing oneself as a 'trader' is a way to apply the reciprocity principle in networking, using the metaphor of 'currencies' for the exchange process. Just as the world uses many currency types, there are many different kinds of organisational currencies. People often only think of money, promotions and status, but there are many other possibilities.

Some possible currencies

Some currencies you might have available include the following:

- Resources: budget increases, personnel, space, etc.
- Assistance: help with projects or unwanted tasks
- Information: furnishing organisational and/or technical knowledge
- Recognition: acknowledging effort, accomplishment or abilities
- Visibility: providing the chance to be known by higher-ups
- Advancement: giving tasks to aid in promotion
- Personal support: providing personal and emotional backing
- Understanding: listening to others' concerns

How to use currencies

In using currencies, it helps to consider four steps:

1. Think of each person you deal with as a potential ally or network member. If you want to gain organisation influence and get the job done, you must create internal network members or allies. Even a difficult person is a potential network member.

2. Get to know the potential network member's world, including the pressures they have, as well as their needs and goals. An important factor influencing behaviour is how performance is measured and rewarded. If you ask someone to do things which may be seen as poor performance within their work unit, they are likely to resist.

3. Be aware of your own strengths and potential weaknesses as a networker. Networkers may underestimate the range of currencies they have available. List potential currencies and resources you offer. Then think about your own preferred interaction style. Would-be networkers often cannot see how their preferred interaction style fits or doesn't fit with the potential ally's preferred style. For instance, does the potential ally like to socialise first and work later? If so, they may find it difficult to deal with someone who likes to solve the problem first and then talk about weather, family or office politics. Skilled networkers adapt their own style to others in dealing with potential allies.

4. Gear your exchange transactions so both parties can win. Organisational transactions are rarely one-time events. Parties usually need to deal with one another again, perhaps often. In fact, that is the idea of networks—to have contacts to call on as needed. The implication is that in most exchange relationships there are two outcomes that make a difference. One is achieving the task goals. The other is enhancing the relationship so contact remains viable. With networking, it is better to lose the battle than to lose the war.

Source: Cohen & Bradford 1989; Baker 1994.

planning, organising, leading and controlling are an important part of management. However, Mintzberg's study did not consider why managers were engaging in different roles. When the why is taken into account, it is clear management functions are an important blueprint to help managers channel their role behaviours to lead to goal achievement (Kotter 1982). For

TABLE 1.1 MINTZBERG'S 10 MANAGERIAL ROLES

Role	Description
Interpersonal	
Figurehead	Performs symbolic duties of a legal or social nature
Leader	Builds relationships with subordinates and communicates with, motivates and coaches them
Liaison	Maintains networks of contacts outside work unit who provide help and information
Informational	
Monitor	Seeks internal and external information about issues affecting organisation
Disseminator	Transmits information internally obtained from either internal or external sources
Spokesperson	Transmits information about the organisation to outsiders
Decisional	
Entrepreneur	Acts as initiator, designer and encourager of change and innovation
Disturbance handler	Takes corrective action when organisation faces important, unexpected difficulties
Resource allocator	Distributes resources of all types including time, funding, equipment and human resources
Negotiator	Represents the organisation in major negotiations affecting the manager's areas of responsibility

Source: Based on Mintzberg (1980).

example, information transmission through a disseminator role or representing the organisation in the negotiator role have little meaning unless linked to a purpose such as a management function. But how do managers tie various activities and roles to the planning, organising, leading and controlling needed to reach goals? Part of the answer is suggested by another study, conducted by Kotter.

Managerial work agendas

Kotter's (1982) study focused on 15 general managers in nine companies from a wide range of industries. General managers are typically responsible for a major section of an organisation. From his findings, Kotter suggested managers focus their efforts through work agendas.

Nature of work agendas

A **work agenda** is a loosely linked set of tentative goals and tasks a manager attempts to accomplish. In their first six months on a new job, managers develop and continually reassess work agendas due to evolving events and new opportunities. Such agendas address immediate and long-term job responsibilities supported by formal organisational plans. Kotter (1982) found that to set up their work agendas, general managers established the extensive networks Mintzberg identified.

By using work agendas and networking strategies, managers in Kotter's (1982) study could still accomplish their missions while engaging in short, seemingly disjointed conversations. Consider the following interaction. Peter Barr is the New South Wales state sales manager and is preparing to chair the monthly review meeting of his sales team. His senior account executive, Harry, arrives at the meeting early.

> 'By the way, Peter, those figures on the 23 are rather good, aren't they?'
> 'They sure are. I hope we can match them again this month. And beat the Northern Region, as well. Did you pick up on that call Irene passed on to you?'
> 'Actually, Peter, I passed that on to Roxanne. You remember, we talked about giving her a first small account. Now about those guidelines …'
> 'Harry, not now. I want to hear what your three musketeers come up with first.'

work agenda

A loosely connected set of tentative goals and tasks that a manager is attempting to accomplish

The above dialogue may seem somewhat disjointed to an outsider. That perception comes from unfamiliarity with what has gone before and specific business and organisational knowledge shared by the managers. For example, an outsider could not identify Peter Barr, know that his business is food distributorship as the wholesale arm of a large food manufacturer and that item 23 is a range of soups. An outsider could not explain why beating the Northern Region, which is subtropical, on selling soups is important to the state sales office. In fact, the Northern Region is Queensland and for the past six years Queensland has sold more soups than New South Wales. Another puzzling item is who the three musketeers are and why Peter would want to know what they had to say before listening to Harry's comments.

However, the interchange had many worthwhile consequences. Peter learned that:

Harry is aware of the figure on item 23.
Harry has remembered to pass on an account to Roxanne, and which account it is.
Harry is concerned with the guidelines for restructuring the state's regions.

Peter has also passed on the following information:

He is concerned about the figures for the following month and he really wants them to show an increase over the Northern Region.
He wanted to ensure action was taken over the call Irene had passed on.
He wished to let the team given the task of working out guidelines for the restructure do it, and he did not wish to have this pre-empted by Harry.

This discussion shows how pace, brevity, variety and fragmentation are characteristic of a manager's workday. It also demonstrates use of verbal contacts and networks identified in Mintzberg's study. Read the conversation again. Can you identify where Peter used the monitor role in seeking information, the disseminator role in providing information, and the entrepreneur role to follow up on issues which could affect plans for the state? His words had purposes ultimately related to reaching his goals.

Without a work agenda (the manager's own working plan), similar discussions could actually be quite random and inefficient. Even with an agenda, managers must ensure they work within its guidelines. Work agendas give rough guidelines for managers to orient their various activities and roles. But what factors influence work agenda content?

Factors influencing work agendas

According to Stewart (1982) three main factors impact on a manager's work agenda: demands, constraints and choices.

Job demands are activities a manager must do in a job. For example, managers' responsibilities usually relate to significant major organisation goals and plans (such as increasing sales 10 per cent).

Job constraints are factors, inside and outside the organisation, which limit what a manager can do. Constraints include resource limitations, legal restrictions, union activities, technological limitations and how much a manager's work unit is defined.

Job choices are work activities a manager can do but does not have to do. For example, without being directed, a manager might initiate a proposal to develop a computerised customer service tracking system. Work agendas therefore tend to reflect individual managers' personal preferences and career objectives.

MANAGERIAL KNOWLEDGE, SKILLS AND PERFORMANCE

Managers need a sound knowledge base and key management skills to develop work agendas, act out roles and engage in planning, organising, leading and controlling. In this section, we consider these essential management process elements and their relationship to performance.

Knowledge base

Managers can switch between companies in different industries, but they may have a problem if they lack a relevant, fairly extensive knowledge base for their particular managerial job. This knowledge base can include detail on an industry and its technology, company policies and practices, company goals, plans, company culture, key organisation member personalities, and significant suppliers and customers. For example, Kotter (1982) found general managers could accomplish much in short time periods because they took action based on small bits of information. Their extensive knowledge base meant they could attach appropriate meaning to these information fragments.

Key management skills

In addition to having a knowledge base, managers need skills for various management functions. A skill is the ability to engage in a set of functionally related behaviours, leading to a desired performance level in a given area (Boyatzis 1982). Three skill types are necessary for managers: technical, human and conceptual.

Technical skills

Technical skills involve both an understanding of and a proficiency in a specialised field. For example, a manager may have technical skills in accounting, finance, engineering, manufacturing or computer science.

Human skills

Human skills, also known as people skills, are associated with a manager's ability to work well with others, both as a group member and as a leader who gets things done through others. Managers with effective human skills are good at communicating with others and motivating them to develop and perform well in pursuit of organisational goals.

Conceptual skills

Conceptual skills relate to the ability to see the organisation as a whole, to identify relationships between organisational parts, and to see how it fits into the wider industry, community and global contexts. Conceptual skills, combined with technical skills, human skills and a knowledge base, are important elements in organisational performance.

Performance

What constitutes high performance in an organisation? Drucker (1967) says performance achieved through management comprises two important dimensions: effectiveness and efficiency.

Effectiveness

Effectiveness is the ability to choose appropriate goals and achieve them. An organisation is effective when managers choose appropriate goals and then achieve them. Some years ago, for example, McDonald's decided to provide breakfast service to gain more customers. This was smart, as breakfast food sales now comprise over 30 per cent of McDonald's revenues (Jones 2000). Thus McDonald's illustrates what Drucker (1988) means when he points out that effectiveness is doing (accomplishing) the right things. Very recently McDonald's has moved into sales of 'healthy fast food' due to community concerns about fat levels.

Efficiency

Efficiency is the ability to use available resources best in achieving goals. Organisations are efficient when managers minimise input resources (labour, raw materials and components) or the time needed to produce a given output or services. For example, McDonald's developed a more efficient fat fryer that reduces (by 30 per cent) the amount of oil used in cooking but also

---

technical skills

Skills reflecting both an understanding of and a proficiency in a specialised field

human skills

Skills associated with a manager's ability to work well with others, both as a member of a group and as a leader who gets things done through others

conceptual skills

Skills related to the ability to visualise the organisation as a whole, discern interrelationships among organisational parts, and understand how the organisation fits into the wider context of the industry, community and world

effectiveness

The ability to choose appropriate goals and achieve them

efficiency

The ability to make the best use of available resources in the process of achieving goals

shortens french fry cooking time. Through such means, McDonald's illustrates Drucker's (1988) point that efficiency is doing things right.

In essence, organisations must be both effective (doing the right things) and efficient (doing things right) to perform well. As these dimensions are so closely linked, we generally use the term 'effectiveness' in this book to refer to both effectiveness and efficiency. We do this for simplicity and readability.

MANAGERIAL JOB TYPES

Managerial jobs vary on two important dimensions. One is a vertical dimension, focusing on different hierarchical organisation levels. The other is a horizontal dimension, addressing variations in managers' responsibility areas. We explore these dimensions and their implications in this section. Because of its impact in fostering innovation, we pay special attention to the entrepreneurial role at different hierarchical levels (refer to Table 1.1).

Vertical dimension: Hierarchical levels

Along the vertical dimension, managerial jobs fall into three categories: first-line, middle and top management. The categories represent vertical differentiation among managers as they involve different organisation levels, as shown in Figure 1.3.

First-line managers

first-line managers/supervisors

Managers at the lowest level of the hierarchy who are directly responsible for the work of operating (non-managerial) employees

First-line managers (or **supervisors**) operate at the lowest hierarchical level and are responsible for operational (non-managerial) employee work. Common titles include the word 'supervisor'. First-line managers are vital to organisation goal success as they are responsible for smooth daily operations.

Operating between management and the rest of the workforce, first-line supervisors often face conflicting demands. First-line supervisor power has been eroded due to factors such as union influence, increased worker education levels, setting up of work teams and computers tracking activities that were formerly first-line managerial activities. In future, first-line

FIGURE 1.3   Types of managers by hierarchical level and responsibility area

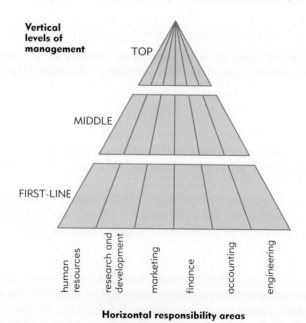

supervisors' jobs will involve more emphasis on internal human relations and being the unit's external face.

Middle managers

Middle managers are managers below the top hierarchical levels and directly responsible for lower-level managerial work. They may be directly responsibility for other middle managers or first-line managers. They may supervise operating staff such as administrative assistants and specialists (e.g. engineers or financial analysts). Middle managers' titles include 'manager', 'director of', 'chief', 'department head' and 'division head'. They are mainly responsible for implementing overall organisational plans to achieve organisational goals.

Large organisations traditionally had many layers of middle managers. For example, General Motors had 14 or 15 management levels. This was a post–World War II trend of adding middle-management layers to co-ordinate expanding activities. By the 1980s, the trend was reversed as companies cut managerial levels to lower costs, reduce decision-making layers and aid communication (Labich 1989).

Reducing middle-management layers brings challenges and opportunities. A common result is that remaining middle managers become more autonomous and have greater responsibilities. Pressure on middle managers also grows (Wysocki 1995). Over half the respondents to one survey reported increased work hours for middle managers in their organisations, and a quarter said more weekends were spent in the office (Zemke 1988; Fisher 1992). For those losing their jobs due to downsizing, dislocation can be hard until another job is found (Grossman 1996; Cascio 1993; Parker, Wall & Jackson 1997).

Though fewer middle managers may be needed, Kanter (1989) argues that distinctions between managers and managed are decreasing. She sees less emphasis on hierarchical level and greater weight on horizontal influence and peer networks, greater access to information and more control over assignments at lower levels. As middle managers take on more responsibility, many of their current duties will move to lower management levels, as the importance of these positions grows.

Top managers

Top managers are at the very top hierarchical levels and responsible for the whole organisation. There are few and their titles include 'chief executive officer' (CEO), 'president', 'general manager' and 'director'. Top-level managers are called executives, although the term can also include upper-middle managers. Top managers are responsible for the upper layer of middle managers. They typically oversee overall organisation planning, work with middle managers to implement the planning, and maintain control over the organisation's progress.

Differences among hierarchical levels

Although the same managerial process applies at all hierarchical levels, the emphasis is different. Major differences come from the importance of the four management functions, the skills needed for effective performance, the emphasis on each level's managerial roles, and the use of the entrepreneurial role.

Functions of management

The importance of planning, organising, leading and controlling differs by managerial level (Mahoney, Jerdee & Carroll 1965; Gomez-Mejia, McCann & Page 1985). As indicated in Figure 1.4, planning is more important for top managers than for middle or first-line managers. This is because top managers set the organisation's overall direction, which needs extensive planning.

Similarly, organising is more important for top and middle managers than for first-line managers. This stems from top- and middle-management levels being mainly responsible for allocating and arranging resources, though first-line supervisors also do this.

In contrast, leading is more important for first-line supervisors than higher-level managers. Since first-line supervisors are in charge of producing goods or services, they use more communication, motivating, directing and supporting—all associated with leading.

middle managers

Managers beneath the top levels of the hierarchy who are directly responsible for the work of managers at lower levels

top managers

Managers at the very top levels of the hierarchy who are ultimately responsible for the entire organisation

FIGURE 1.4 Use of management functions at different hierarchical levels

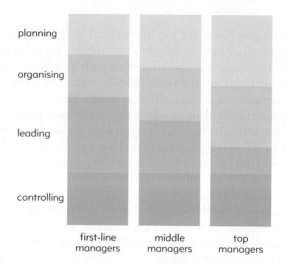

Finally, the management function common across all levels is controlling. This shows a common emphasis on monitoring activities and taking corrective action.

Management skills

The three management levels also differ in the importance of key skills raised before: technical, human and conceptual (see Fig. 1.5) (Katz 1974). Generally top management most needs conceptual skills. These managers must see the organisation as a whole, understand how its parts relate to each other, and link it to the outside world (Maruca 1994).

In contrast, first-line managers have the greatest need for technical skills, as they supervise most non-managerial technical and professional employees. Yet middle managers, too, often need technical skills to communicate with subordinates and recognise major problems (Torrington & Weightman 1987). Even top managers must have some technical skills, when technology is important to their organisation's products or services. Otherwise, upper-level managers cannot foster innovation, allocate resources efficiently, or devise strategies to beat the competition.

FIGURE 1.5 Use of key management skills at different hierarchical levels

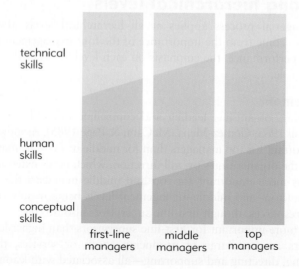

Not surprisingly, all three management levels need strong human skills as they all must get things done through people (Pavett & Lau 1983). Ironically, promotions to first-level management are often based on good technical skills, with little consideration given to human skills. Managers with poor human skills have serious difficulties dealing with those both inside and outside their work units. In fact, studies focusing on reasons executives derail suggest human skills are major factors (see Table 1.2). Derailed executives are those who reach relatively high levels but then find little chance of further advancement due to insufficient personal skills (Van Velsor & Leslie 1995).

TABLE 1.2 CAUSES OF EXECUTIVE CAREER DERAILMENT

1. Problems with interpersonal relationships

2. Failure to meet business objectives

3. Inability to build and lead a team

4. Inability to develop or adapt

Source: Adapted from Van Velsor & Leslie (1995, p. 64).

Managerial roles

Although Mintzberg (1980) argued that his 10 managerial roles apply at all management levels (see Table 1.1), he did note differences in emphasis at various levels. Later research suggests that figurehead and other roles such as liaison and spokesperson become more significant as a manager rises. On the other hand, the leader role appears more critical at lower levels, a result supporting the idea that the leading function is more important to lower-level managers than higher ones (Pavett & Lau 1983).

In a study of the importance of various roles, all levels of managers gave very high ratings to the entrepreneurial role (Pavett & Lau 1983). Several innovation experts argue that the entrepreneurial role varies in some ways by managerial hierarchical level (Kanter 1982; Pearson 1988). Because of the importance of innovation to organisation success, we explore the differences below.

MANAGING THE E-CHALLENGE

Technology and fraud

While we would all wish that technological developments were used for the benefit of mankind, there are those among us (including our own staff) who would use it to defraud others. In a show of ingenuity, a waiter who was part of an organised gang carried out a scam on a restaurant in Hong Kong. Customers at the restaurant began to complain that they were being billed on their credit cards for outlandish expenditure in exotic places. The common thread of evidence was that the cards were used at the restaurant in Hong Kong only hours before the illegal usage took place in other countries such as Japan and Taiwan. Investigators from the merchant banks and the card companies involved were able to ascertain that when credit card transactions took place in the restaurant, gang members overseas were supplied with all the information contained on the card that was normally used to verify the authenticity of the transaction.

The merchant banks and card companies checked their own staff and systems and established that the scam was based only on cards used at the restaurant. However, management at the restaurant was able to show the investigators that the card transactions were carried out only by 'trusted' staff under management supervision.

After a lengthy investigation, which was very unpleasant for the restaurant owners, it was discovered that the customers whose cards were defrauded had attended the restaurant on nights that coincided with the roster for one of the casual waiters. The waiter was clearly a 'mole' for the gang. But how did this waiter—in full view of patrons and management—obtain information stored on the customers' cards?

A stakeout was set up in the restaurant and it was observed that as the waiter carried the card from the customer at their table to the cashier for processing, he swiped the card inside his coat pocket. His coat was fitted with a swipe reader (a skimmer) connected to a mobile phone that transmitted the details stored on the card to partners in places such as Taiwan and Japan. These partners were then able to make purchases using the information, buying portable luxury items that could easily be sold for cash.

As a result, card companies have set up controls to stop the use of cards in different countries within a short period of time. If a transaction is attempted too soon after a previous transaction in a different country, it is not approved. Nonetheless a problem still exists, and it is no secret that card fraud is a major problem worldwide. Just as serious a problem is the fact that staff can now use technology to defraud their employers. Management must be aware of this and take steps to introduce controls that limit the potential for workplace fraud involving technology. Management must also understand and keep up with technology.

Unfortunately there is a code of silence among the card companies and banks, who avoid publicising details of card fraud for fear that customers will lose confidence in the cards. The real dilemma is that attempts by business to make it easier for customers to use cards to purchase goods over the telephone and on the Internet simply make it easier to carry out card fraud.

Source: Contributed by Ken Dooley; Belson K.(2000).

Websites:

www.theinvestigatoronline.com/
http://fraud.org/forconsumers.htm
www.fraud.org/internet/99final.htm

Activities for discussion, analysis and further research

1. 'Management' can be defined as achieving organisational goals through people. While we understand that people can be difficult, we at least expect our employees to be honest. In cases such as this, what lessons about human nature are there for those who intend to become managers?

2. What skills are required to detect dishonest workers? What attitude should a manager adopt towards staff who carry out fraud in the workplace?

3. How does a manager avoid becoming cynical and treat all staff as potentially dishonest? Should managers treat their staff with suspicion?

4. Visit one or more of the sites listed below and report back to your fellow students on the information gained. Evaluate it in terms of its interest and its value as an aid to management.

Promoting innovation: The entrepreneurial role

innovation

A new idea applied to initiating or improving a process, product or service

An **innovation** is a new idea involving initiating or improving a process, product or service (Kanter 1983). The innovation process is closely related to the entrepreneurial role, as this role relates to finding and exploiting new opportunities. In fact, innovative activities are often referred to as entrepreneurship in organisations. Those engaging in entrepreneurial roles in organisations are called **intrapreneurs**. This differentiates innovators working inside existing organisations from those who innovate by creating new organisations (often called entrepreneurs). Similarly, innovating in an existing organisation is referred to as **intrapreneurship**.

intrapreneurs

Individuals who engage in entrepreneurial roles inside organisations

Encouraging organisational innovation is hard. Successful innovations are rarely one person's work. The innovative process usually needs people at different levels to fulfil three entrepreneurial roles: idea generator or champion, sponsor and orchestrator (Galbraith 1982).

intrapreneurship

The process of innovating within an existing organisation

Idea champion

An **idea champion** generates a new idea or believes in its value and supports it despite many potential barriers. Such people are called entrepreneurs, inventors, creative individuals or risk takers. They usually operate at lower organisation levels, see a problem and help develop a solution. First-line supervisors are idea champions when they develop innovative ideas, nurture them in others, and fight to help make them a reality. However, as idea champions are at low levels in the hierarchy, they often lack the power and status to get their innovations accepted. This situation creates the need for the next type of role.

Sponsor

A **sponsor** is an individual, usually a middle manager, who recognises an idea's significance, helps get funding needed to develop the innovation, and facilitates implementation. Sponsors tend to be middle managers where their higher-level position lets them give the backing needed for an innovation to survive. While organisational innovation is unlikely to occur without a sponsor, innovations also need someone to fill a third role.

Orchestrator

An **orchestrator** or high-level manager shows the need for innovation, funds innovating activities, creates incentives for middle managers to sponsor new ideas, and protects idea people. Because innovation often challenges established ways of operating, those happy with or having an interest in the status quo often resist. (For example, an expert in a process may resist a change and this makes it outmoded.) An orchestrator balances power so new ideas can be tested despite negative responses. By acting as orchestrator, top managers encourage innovation.

Without all three roles, major innovations are much less likely.

Horizontal dimension: Responsibility areas

In addition to vertical differences, managerial jobs differ on a horizontal dimension related to the nature of the responsibility area involved (see Figure 1.3). In horizontal differentiation, there are three major managerial job types: functional, general and project.

Functional managers

Functional managers are responsible for a specific organisation area (or a functional area) and supervise those with appropriate expertise and training. Common functional specialisations include finance, manufacturing or operations, marketing, human resource management, accounting, quality assurance and engineering.

General managers

General managers are responsible for a whole organisation or a substantial subunit including most of the common specialised areas. In other words, a general manager presides over several functional areas (hence the term 'general'). General managers have several titles such as 'division manager' and 'president', depending on the situation. A small company normally has just one general manager, who heads the whole organisation. Depending on how it is organised, a large company may have several general managers (as well as the chief executive officer), each presiding over a major division.

Project managers

Project managers co-ordinate the efforts of people in different units working on a particular project. As individuals report to managers in their specific work units as well as their project manager, these managers must have very strong interpersonal skills to keep things smooth (we discuss this further in Chapter 11). Project managers are common in aerospace and other high-technology firms that co-ordinate projects, such as aeroplane or computer project development. They are also used in consumer-oriented companies to launch or stay on top of market development for specific products, such as biscuits or margarine (Stanley & Davis 1977).

idea champion

An individual who generates a new idea or believes in the value of a new idea and supports it in the face of numerous potential obstacles

sponsor

A middle manager who recognises the organisational significance of an idea, helps obtain the necessary funding for development of the innovation, and facilitates its actual implementation

orchestrator

A high-level manager who explains the need for innovation, provides funding for innovating activities, creates incentives for middle managers to sponsor new ideas, and protects idea people

functional managers

Managers with responsibility for a specific, specialised area of the organisation who supervise mainly individuals with expertise and training in that area

general managers

Managers with responsibility for a whole organisation or a substantial subunit including most of the common specialised areas

project managers

Managers with responsibility for co-ordinating efforts involving individuals in several different organisational units all working on a particular project

C & D Clothing—Making dreams happen

For David Stewart and Chris Carr, starting their own company was a long-held dream. They shared the same motivations: the satisfaction of seeing their clothes worn in the streets, the opportunity to push past the salary ceiling that came with working for someone else, and greater control over their own lives. On 15 May 1997, they did just that. Leaving their previous employer, they launched C & D Clothing which trades as Henley Clothing Company.

The plan for their range of casual men's wear was simple: better quality, quicker turnaround, lower prices. The pair had a network of customers and suppliers and were experienced in the clothing industry.

Their start-up vision was to run a business with a $5 million turnover a year. Kicking off without orders in hand meant that they needed to purchase raw materials using their cash reserves and this entailed taking a risk. The partners, however, were fairly confident that they could rapidly turn this risk into advantage. With an initially conservative start, they contracted an overseas supplier to make samples for a small range which sold very quickly.

The decision they were faced with entailed the development of a strategic focus. Their plan was to pre-sell. This meant that they would hold very little, if any, stock. Ranges would be designed, samples made, shown and orders taken which would then be manufactured. This strategy worked very well and soon Chris and David were faced with more orders than could easily be filled on their current base.

What they needed was extra financial backing to set them up the way they needed to be in order to reach their goals and vision. Discussion with them revealed that at the time they saw themselves as having three options to achieve this:

The first option was to invite a past colleague, Ron Tenabel, who had been searching for investment opportunities, to join them. Their second option came from one of their off-shore suppliers who wanted to bank roll them in exchange for a share of the business. Finally, extended family members were prepared to assist. Upon consideration of these options, David and Chris decided to accept Tenabel's offer . This decision

was based on an analysis of the advantages this brought to the partnership. Ron Tenabel was located in Melbourne and brought warehousing expertise to the organisation. This expertise left the two partners free to concentrate on those areas which would make a significant impact on the success of the venture. This is encapsulated in their philosophy: 'We wanted to run a business with a better quality garment produced faster than the competition', says Chris. 'The market place wants a quick turnaround. People are no longer prepared to wait six months for your range to reach their stores.'

The strength of the organisation is based on maintaining a small operating base keeping expenses low but able to produce a better garment at a lower cost. Business has grown to the extent that sales people have been employed full time and administrative backup has been provided to production. This enables Chris and David to look at the bigger picture and work on key accounts. Over the past three years staff has grown from five to eleven and turnover has doubled to over $10 million. This includes both an increase on the return on sales as well as an increase in the volume of sales.

When asked about the key reasons for this success, David explains the strategies that he and Chris have tried to maintain:

'We do not get locked into one particular customer. No one customer is more than 10 per cent of the business. This means that you have a wide customer base to work from and are not overly reliant on one source of orders.'

'Business still follows the 20–80 rule, in that we get 80 per cent of our turnover from 20 per cent of our customers, but we feel we have a good spread of bigger customers and that gives us good margins.'

'We now tend to do a lot more ranges. The trade has moved away from having one range per season. Successful wholesalers offer two or three injection ranges per season. This requires a smaller range of garments which enables you to take advantage of the current flavour and capitalise on what sells well in a particular area. In that instance turnaround is crucial. We now airfreight stock in to cut the turnaround time.'

'We deal directly with owners of businesses. These people spend time in the stores and know what moves. Satisfying them builds the relationship and therefore builds your business. Working closely with retailers means you can stock to suit the demography.'

'We give retailers the differentiation they want to make them unique—so things like the print on a garment, the colours, labels to have their own look. Our growth has been two-fold—on one hand we have grown as our customers have grown, such as Man to Man which has gone from 20 stores to 50 stores since we have been supplying them. On the other hand we have expanded our customer base, and one way to do that has been involvement in the Fashion Fairs which take place twice a year. There we have gained customers from West Australian stores or from Northern Queensland where we are less likely to travel.'

Given their growth, Chris and David can no longer interact with every customer as closely as they used to, but have appointed full-time staff who are trained to manage the relationships in a personal manner. This expansion has had another impact on the way business is done at C & D

Clothing. With the growth in customer base came the requirement to pay even closer attention to quality. Consequently, the company employs a full-time Quality Assurance person in India and has all stock from China checked by a third party before it is shipped. These measures mean that problems, if any, can be addressed at the source.

So next time you buy a garment from Jay Jays of the Just Jeans Group, or Hizz Men's Wear, consider that you are actually wearing a customised garment produced by C & D Clothing.

Source: M. Tein; interviews with Chris Carr and David Stewart.

Activities for discussion, analysis and further research

1. Identify the manner in which the managerial functions and responsibilities are being divided in the above organisation.
2. Identify the Mintzberg roles as they are evidenced by the above organisation.
3. Find another and larger clothing manufacturer's website (for example, Austin, where Chris and David used to work) and find evidence of the differences in philosophy of conducting business.

MANAGING IN THE TWENTY-FIRST CENTURY

Successful managers must watch future trends likely to impact on the actions they must take to keep their organisations moving. As we mentioned at the beginning of this chapter, important themes are emerging from studies of trends related to managing in the twenty-first century. We expand on these four themes, explaining how they will be addressed through the book to help you become a successful twenty-first-century manager.

Managing change and innovation

As we move into the twenty-first century, effective change and innovation management is increasingly critical. Change is an alteration to the status quo to which a company must respond. Innovation is a new idea used to initiate or improve a process, product or service. Most firms face serious competitive challenges due to increasingly rapid and unpredictable technological change. Information technology change will be significant for the twenty-first century. Firms face many pressures, such as competitor strategies, shifts in economic condition, or changes in customer preference (Seiders & Barry 1998). Companies will only survive to prosper if managers guide

MANAGERIAL DILEMMAS

When the unexpected hits

Consider the following process in an organisation the author is familiar with but is not at liberty to name.

This organisation for a number of years has been running a very successful offshore manufacturing facility. As a result of the financial crisis in South-East Asia, its export market all but disappeared. This was later compounded by the SARS epidemic which aggravated the issue by preventing sales staff from travelling on business. However, when the budget forecasts were done, the expected income from exports had been included. This meant that the organisation stood to make an enormous loss.
Source: M. Tein.

Decision point

1. If you were the general manager of this organisation what would you do? Why?

Reflection points

1. Senior management decided that what they would do is retrench all the team leaders, as they were the most expensive staff in the factory. What do you think happened? Why? What would you now do to overcome the resulting difficulties?
2. With the aggravated situation, experienced sales staff who normally handle that lucrative territory were transferred to other smaller territories where younger and sometime less experienced representatives were invited to take a cut in commission. Most left for other jobs. Six months later, the SARS epidemic was over. How do you think the organisation was placed to address the new environment? What would you have done in their place?

the change process so their organisation makes the adaptations needed as conditions alter (Anderson 1997). But they must do more. Increasingly, successful firms emphasise innovation opportunities (Lengnick-Hall 1992; Bower & Christensen 1995).

We devote an entire chapter to issues relating to managing change and innovation (see Chapter 9). In addition, we will often refer to organisational examples of successful change and innovation management.

Managing diversity: The workforce of the twenty-first century

To effectively use all resources, organisations recognise the need to capitalise on managers' and employees' country-specific or continent-specific knowledge. For example, Coca-Cola uses its diverse foreign workforce's knowledge to develop marketing campaigns in its major global markets. At senior levels too, Coca-Cola uses global diversity, employing diverse managers as leaders. Former Coca-Cola chairman Roberto Goizueta came from Cuba; other senior managers are from France, Brazil and Spain.

Many other companies rely on their diverse workforce's talents. For example, Jac Nasser, Ford's CEO from 1998 to 2001, was born in Lebanon and headed Ford's Australian operations. Alex Trotman, former Ford US chairman and pioneer of Ford's global restructure, is English. Trotman got his knowledge of European customers' needs while leading Ford's European operations. This is important as managers who value their employees' diversity invest in developing these employees' skills and capabilities and link available rewards to their performance. They are managers who succeed in promoting long-term performance (Cox & Blake 1991). More and more organisations realise people are indeed their most important resource and that developing and protecting human resources is crucial to manage in a globally competitive environment.

A survey showed over 70 per cent of *major* American organisations have diversity management programs. A further 16 per cent are developing programs or have initiatives at division levels (Society for Human Resource Management 1995). Most countries in the Pacific Rim region, including Australia, are still lagging on this issue. Why do organisations set up diversity programs? Motivations behind the efforts are various. For one, companies are concerned about attracting and retaining the best talent. Firms with positive reputations for diversity management are likely to have a competitive advantage in gathering talented people. For another, the customer base of most companies is increasingly diverse.

Essentially managers themselves must reflect this emerging diversity and need to effectively utilise an increasingly diverse workforce. We discuss diversity further in the Managing diversity sections in several chapters and we focus on important organisational efforts through the use of Managing diversity boxes.

Developing a global perspective

With diversity initiatives, organisations must take a global perspective for three main reasons. First, businesses have more global competition. Second, more companies will be operating in other countries. Third, businesses are increasingly globalised in that they are operating as one company, despite far-flung operations. As these trends imply, managers' knowledge of international business in the twenty-first century must be greater. Accordingly, we devote a chapter to international management (see Chapter 17) and have international material in many other chapters. In addition, we often use international companies as examples so you can learn more about such organisations and how they operate.

GENDER FACTOR

Second skin at the cutting edge

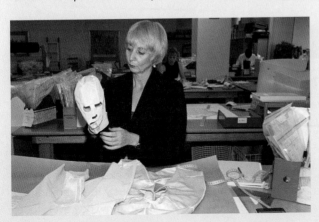

In 1988, Jenni Ballantyne set up a small manufacturing business with three employees in a suburb of Perth, Western Australia. The business—Second Skin—produced pressure garments for burns victims. These garments had previously been manufactured and imported, often with considerable delays, from the United States. Jenni, who worked as an occupational therapist in the hospital, heard surgeons complaining about this, and questioned why no one was producing the garments locally. Jenni's business is based on two primary product ranges: pressure suits that promote healing and reduce scarring, and are worn by people with severe burns; and lycra-based, dynamic splints that re-educate the limbs, and are designed for patients whose movements have been affected by tonal changes within muscles because of acquired brain injuries, strokes or other neurological disorders. Her innovative designs have been incorporated into a range of 'world first' products that have significantly improved the quality of life and the medical management of clients and patients who wear them.

Many of the innovations have been simple but ingenious, and have their origins in Jenni's ability to accurately observe what is required, and then change the design to suit. For example, many children who wear pressure socks over long periods (sometimes several years) had problems with the traditional design, which tended to restrict growth.

Jenni designed a toe gusset into a sock that would allow for growing feet. She combines commitment to the care of her clients with a dedication to finding the most appropriate clinical solution possible, and believes this underpins the culture at Second Skin. Jenni has a passionate commitment to her work and a desire to live life to the full, rather than 'saving things for tomorrow'. Her philosophy can be summed up as 'do it well today'. She was always confident of success, but admits that her confidence was tested at various times. 'As long as you can cope with the little rejections and frustrations and not see them as signs of personal failure, you can hang in there long enough to do well', she advises.

It sounds like good advice. Her business has now grown to the extent that it supplies Australia, New Zealand and the United Kingdom with her products, has offices in Brisbane, Sydney and the United Kingdom, and plans to commence exporting to other European countries in the near future.

Source: Contributed by Glenice Wood; adapted from Second Skin promotional material and *The West Magazine* (1995).

Activities for discussion, analysis and further research

1. In terms of Mintzberg's categorisation of managerial activities, do you consider gender is a factor in Jenni Ballantyne's performance? In which areas do you feel she excels?
2. Is Jenni Ballantyne an entrepreneur or an intrapreneur? Explain your answer.
3. Consider the four themes discussed under 'Managing in the twenty-first century'. In groups, discuss one theme per group, and make a judgment about how effectively Jenni Ballantyne is performing on each of these future trends to allow her organisation to continue to move forward.
4. Go to the website: www.secondskin.com.au/index3.htm and look up the mission statement of the company. What does this suggest to you about the commitment Jenni Ballantyne has to her organisation, her staff and her product?

The quest for total quality and continuous improvement

Due to global competition, particularly from Japanese companies, many organisations have emphasised quality and embraced concepts of continuous improvement. Commonly these programs are known as total quality management (TQM). Total quality management is a management system integrated with an organisation's strategy, aimed at continually improving the quality of products and services to achieve high customer-satisfaction levels and build customer loyalty (Bounds, Yorks, Adams & Ramney 1994; Riecheld 1996).

Many companies benefit from emphasising TQM; however success needs company-wide commitment. So we refer to quality issues in several chapters and cover this topic extensively in Supplement 1 to Chapter 15 on quality and other managerial control methods.

In this chapter, we have overviewed the basic management challenge and glanced at trends likely to influence how managers work in the future. Remember always that the challenge of management lies in the ability to reflect on experience and filter it through the models and theories from this area of study. In the next chapter, we look back at the pioneering ideas which shaped our knowledge of management today.

GAINING THE EDGE

The challenge of management—Fremantle Port

The Port of Fremantle is Western Australia's major general-cargo port. It is a sheltered, all-weather port situated on the west coast some 20 kilometres from the state capital, Perth. Fremantle Ports, as a West Australian Government trading enterprise and as strategic port manager, is responsible for ensuring that port services and facilities are provided in a reliable, competitive and efficient manner.

Few of us will ever be confronted with a management challenge as problematic as that facing the newly appointed chief executive officer (CEO) of Fremantle Ports (previously the Fremantle Port Authority) in the 1990s. We may, however, face

management opportunities that involve dynamics that are just as complex. The progress achieved by Kerry Sanderson, CEO, demonstrates how a management style optimises efficiency and effectiveness.

A century-old tradition of 'worker versus boss' makes it tough to improve effectiveness, efficiency and customer focus. Fremantle Port's customers—ship owners and shippers—saw the port as an inaccessible 'ivory tower'. One described the culture as a 'long-established command-control culture'. The Sanderson style is something the port had not seen till then. Five years after Sanderson's arrival following an $11.5 million loss, the port had doubled container trade and posted a $7.5 million profit. In 2002/03, the container trade was three times the level a decade before and Fremantle Ports recorded an after-tax profit of $12.4 million.

So how was this change achieved? What is different about her management style? What gives this port an 'edge'? Why all this talk about change and the new twenty-first century manager? Do contemporary managers really need new competencies?

In the 'traditional' managerial approach, the 'chain of command' was instituted with clear lines of authority. Distinct functional divisions evolved. Communication and reporting lines were established. 'Traditional' competencies such as decisiveness, results-orientation, strategic thinking, task-orientation, assertiveness and bottom-line and customer focus were considered desirable.

Sanderson realised that a new approach to managing required a complex series of interactions between the leader, followers and the situation—the change in each of these gave leading and managing the port its special characteristics.

Sanderson advocates an 'inclusive' style of management—understanding and taking into account the claims of all stakeholders to build competitive advantage. The inclusive style implies an overall holistic approach in both strategic and operational decision making for stakeholders both within and outside the organisation.

Sanderson has been noted for her ability to develop a strategy, map out a vision and articulate it in such a manner that the participants—staff and port customers and the community—feel 'included'. It is this sense of inclusion of stakeholders that she has nurtured from the outset of the changes.

Sanderson noted 'that the "feel good" work would be ineffective without the strategic framework of corporate planning'. This suggests that contemporary managers require a range of skills, both strategic and interpersonal, to guide their people in an international marketplace. Part of her 'armoury' included the concepts of continuous improvement, integrated management systems and long-term corporate planning. In 2003, Fremantle Ports was recognised at award level by Business Excellence Australia.

'Inclusivity' is a term used to describe how executives freely communicate their ideas to better engage and inform the workforce and stakeholders. Through the utilisation of a wider range of sources, Fremantle achieves a greater awareness of the community's concerns toward the port as well as providing policies that will effectively cultivate stakeholder contributions. Having a greater awareness of community environmental, social or financial priorities provides Fremantle Ports with useful information to be taken into account in strategic planning. Strategies can be created to prevent or rectify negative situations while issues receiving positive feedback may be marketed. Additionally, inclusivity provides a base to become more accountable.

Source: Contributed by Allison James (details of sources are listed on p. 735).

Activities for discussion, analysis and further research

1. Explain the diversity of a manager's role, functions, abilities and the scope of skills required to operate successfully in a contemporary management position. Use examples from Fremantle Port to illustrate your understanding.
2. Explain clearly the difference between effectiveness and efficiency. Use an example from Fremantle Port to explain.
3. Define 'inclusive management' and explain the importance to contemporary management.

REFLECTIVE PRACTITIONER

KIMBERLEY TURNER

AEROSAFE
RISK MANAGEMENT

I guess my start in business was actually back in 1996, when there was a major military accident with the Blackhawk helicopters who were training on a counter-terrorism exercise in the lead-up to the Olympics. This significant accident saw the loss of 18 Defence personnel and two helicopters in that special forces area. I was researching at university at the time and put up my hand to do some free flight-safety research, and got involved in what I guess was the aftermath of the accident. I was invited to help them design their risk-management program.

They didn't really know what risk management was; they didn't know the scope of it at all. It was really interesting—they just knew that they needed it. I started to work with the Australian Army Aviation Corps to help them set up their operational risk-management program.

From a business perspective, I started to get invitations to go and talk with an airline, talk with an airport, talk with other people in industry about what we had done and I guess that was where I identified that there was a much broader need within industry.

In designing the program for Army Aviation, the first thing I did was look around to see what other people were doing, and when I was talking with the chief pilots, managing director and operations managers of aviation companies, nobody seemed to have what I was looking for. So when I started to get invitations to go and brief other people in the industry, I thought: 'Hey, there is a real need here, an untapped market. The trend in the flight-safety and risk-management area was certainly going that way and there was lot of work to be done.'

So when I went and briefed an airline, I did some business cards and I thought, I would not go and present to them in the capacity of working as a part-time Defence member. From there I registered a company name and saw this field continue to grow and grow. Within about three years we had seven staff in Sydney and we were starting to build our client base both within the aviation and defence sectors. I knew we were about three years ahead of the market and had to quickly establish ourselves as a reputable leader in this field.

FOCUS ON PRACTICE

Strategies for improving

1. Discuss with a manager you know how much time they spend on each of the four categories of functions: planning, leading, organising and controlling. Based on the theory you have studied, is this proportion appropriate?
2. Ask this manager to rate his or her performance on Mintzberg's 10 managerial roles. Which roles are being performed adequately? Why?

3. What steps would you suggest to this manager to ensure he or she possesses the skills appropriate to the management level?

Source: Jones et al. (2000).

SUMMARY

- Management is the achievement of organisational goals by engaging in the four major functions of planning, organising, leading and controlling. These functions are the basis of the managerial process, however several other elements contribute to our understanding of how managers actually operate. For instance, work methods and managerial roles, as well as work agendas, feed into management functions aimed at performance. A manager's knowledge base and management skills are also important in reaching performance targets.

- Mintzberg's study of top managers found their work methods were characterised by unrelenting pace, brevity, variety, fragmentation and heavy use of verbal contacts and networks. To make sense of the data he collected while observing managers, Mintzberg isolated three major categories of roles: interpersonal, informational and decisional. Within these categories, he identified 10 specific roles: figurehead, leader, liaison, monitor, disseminator, spokesperson, entrepreneur, disturbance handler, resource allocator and negotiator. To a large extent, these work methods and roles are characteristic of managers at other organisational levels.

- On the basis of his research on general managers, Kotter found managers channel their various efforts through work agendas, or loosely connected sets of tentative goals and tasks a manager seeks to accomplish. Work agendas usually develop from demands, constraints and choices associated with a manager's job.

- For managers to develop work agendas, act out roles and engage in planning, organising, leading and controlling, they also need a knowledge base and key management skills. The key skills fit into three categories: technical, human and conceptual. These skills, and other elements in the process, impact performance. Performance has two important dimensions: effectiveness and efficiency. Effectiveness is the ability to choose appropriate goals and achieve them, while efficiency is the ability to make best use of available resources in the process of achieving goals.

- Managerial jobs differ by hierarchical level (a vertical dimension) and responsibility areas (a horizontal dimension). They are generally divided into three hierarchical levels: first-line, middle and top. Managers at these levels vary in the emphasis they place on planning, organising, leading and controlling. They also differ in the importance placed on key management skills and the degree to which they use different types of managerial roles. Although managers at all levels rate the entrepreneurial role as very important, how they use this role to encourage innovation depends on their hierarchical level, as follows: idea champion (first-line), sponsor (middle) and orchestrator (top). In contrast, horizontal managerial job differences focus on responsibility area and involve three major managerial types: functional, general and project.

- According to several surveys, managerial work in future is very likely to be affected by greater need to manage change and innovation, growing workforce diversity, expanding globalisation of business, and mounting concern with quality and continuous improvement issues.

QUESTIONS FOR DISCUSSION AND REVIEW

1. Describe each major management function: planning, organising, leading and controlling. For a campus or other organisation to which you belong, give an example of a manager engaging in each of these functions. What implications are there if one or more of the functions are absent?
2. List three common managerial work methods Mintzberg identified. How could a manager misuse these work methods to the extent they would lead to poor performance?
3. Explain the three general types of roles and 10 specific roles managers play. Suppose you opened a ski-and-surf shop near campus carrying clothing, skis and other accessories for recreation at ski resorts and beaches. Assume you have six employees. How might you use the 10 roles in managing your shop?
4. Outline three major sources of managerial work agendas. How do work agendas help managers channel their efforts to appropriate performance levels?

5. Contrast effectiveness and efficiency as they apply to organisational performance. What happens when you have one without the other?
6. Describe how managerial jobs vary by hierarchical level. What are the managerial implications?
7. Outline how managers at different hierarchical levels use the entrepreneurial role. What is likely to happen if the entrepreneurial role is missing from middle or top organisation levels?
8. Indicate how managerial jobs vary by responsibility area. What are the managerial implications?
9. Identify the four themes mentioned in the chapter as important to managing in the twenty-first century. How can learning more about these trends help you manage more effectively?

CRITICAL THINKING QUESTIONS

To answer some of these questions you will need to do further research. Useful references are given below each section of the questions.

This chapter presented an overview of the management process by focusing on the actual activities, knowledge and skills that managers require to be effective and innovative. The evolution of management ideas of Mintzberg and Kotter have been a key theme of the chapter. This section uses an article by Andrews (2003) on the need for innovation in our views of managerial styles to ensure that the skills learnt in the past are adapted to meet the demands of the twenty-first century organisation.

1. The best managers can change their style to suit the need but, however they work, Andrews (2003) suggests that good management of time is the key to effective control. Recent research suggests that executives who take longer to consider and consult before making a decision eventually earn higher salaries than those who made quick decisions with a limited amount of information. Why?

Andrews draws on the work Michael Driver (a professor of industrial-social psychology at the Marshall School of Business at the University of Southern California) and Kenneth Brousseau (Driver's business partner in management consultancy firm, Decision Dynamics), who have developed categories of management styles. 'Decisive style' managers tend to use a minimum amount of information to respond rapidly to a situation, and they can seem impressive simply because they make decisions at speed. Driver and Brousseau's analysis of managers' salaries in the US shows that managers who identify themselves as 'decisive' earn higher salaries than their counterparts, even when employed at the junior levels of a company. However, as they move into more senior positions, on average their salaries are overtaken by managers who take more time with their decisions.

2. How does a manager's level within the organisation affect decision making?

3. How do managers go about making this transformation in decision-making styles as their careers progress?

4. An important problem identified was the ability to effectively manage meetings. How do meetings become 'time-killers' for managers and what can they do about it?

5. Emails were also identified as another form of communication 'time-killers' for managers. What can managers do to control this problem?

The higher up a manager moves in an organisation, the longer the hours spent in the office dealing with people. It is an essential component of the job and a time-consuming one. The key to success is using time effectively and efficiently. Andrews concludes his article with three very relevant insights:

- When Mintzberg carried out his seminal 1973 study, *The Nature of Managerial Work*, he found that managers typically spent about 15 minutes per task without interruption. When he repeated the study in the 1990s, he found the time had been almost halved.
- Today, the effective use of time is critical to a manager's career, and time wasters, such as meetings and emails, in particular, need to be monitored.

- As managers progress up the career ladder, they must constantly reassess how they are using their time. While middle managers may be able to make quick decisions, this is often possible because the issues they are dealing with are often short term. In contrast, senior managers need to use more reflective and contemplative decision-making styles, incorporating a greater spread of information, as the decisions they are involved in generally have strategic, longer-term impact on the business.

(Material relevant to these questions may be found in Andrews, B. 2003, Masters of Time, *Business Review Weekly*, Australia, 20 November, p. 134.)

MANAGEMENT EXERCISES

Exercise 1 Management exercise: Producing the new binding machine

You are a first-line supervisor in the production department of a local manufacturer of a range of office products such as staplers, binders and cellotape holders. Recently, the research department developed an innovative small machine which binds reports in one easy operation. According to market research and early sales figures, demand for the new machine (on which the company holds the patent) is expected to be strong because the machine produces good-looking reports at a reasonable price. Because sales of the machine are already brisk, the company has decided to add a new production unit. A new first-line supervisor will be hired to head the unit.

You, your boss (who heads the production department) and a few other first-line supervisors who report to your boss are having a working lunch in a small room off the company cafeteria. The purpose of the meeting is to discuss the basic requirements of the new job and the details to be explained to job candidates. It is likely many candidates will not have management experience and may be unfamiliar with the nature of managerial jobs.

Using your knowledge of management process and types of managerial job, list the kinds of information the group might provide to candidates.

Exercise 2 Skill building: Identifying management functions

You have just accepted a job as manager of a local pizza shop. You are reviewing management activities you will need to perform. You are aware they will be part of one of the four major management functions. Indicate which function (or functions) would normally include each activity listed in the chart below.

Identifying management functions	Planning	Organising	Leading	Controlling
1. Decide whether to open a second pizza shop				
2. Assign job duties				
3. Check register slips to ensure proper prices are being charged				
4. Provide incentives for employees				
5. Check that pizzas are prepared on time				
6. Decide what new menu items to offer				
7. Hire experienced cooks				
8. Determine profit margins to be achieved for the year				
9. Institute an employee suggestion program				
10. Monitor the pizza shop opening and closing times as compared to the schedule				

END-OF-CHAPTER CASE: ON THE RIM

Getting the timing right

CCK Financial Solutions is a wholly Australian-owned designer and developer of treasury solutions and services. Established in 1981, it now has offices in Australia, Malaysia and Singapore.

Its chairman and CEO, Joe Wong, has discovered that good business ideas never fade, but it sometimes just takes time to win a market. More than 20 years ago he designed treasury software that was obviously ahead of its time. This world-class treasury management system had been gathering dust until demand caught up with his work.

Today, Joe Wong, 50, sells his treasury systems to some of the biggest companies in Australia and is poised to go global and list on the Stock Exchange. His company had its origins as Campbell Cook and King (the original name of CCK), where Wong worked as an actuary. The treasury systems now so much in demand date back to 1978 when Joe Wong was asked, as part of his actuary work, to write a system for the merchant bank Westralian International. He did and it worked, but it was probably too advanced for its time, and Westralian disappeared from the merchant banking world.

CCK Financial Solutions has carved out a niche by offering a service that adds value to the work of banks, corporate treasurers and fund managers. Its software handles complex questions of dealing in money, shares, foreign exchange and the many derivatives that are being created almost daily.

'Our software enables the dealer to analyse his portfolio and run what-if scenarios and simulate deals', Wong says. 'It helps them look at changed market conditions on their portfolios. That is just one facet of the system. It is a fully integrated system that handles the front office where the deals are done, the middle office where risk is managed, and the back office processing.'

Only Wong, his staff of 60 and the client users have the time, and inclination, to understand how the software works. The best way for the casual observer to grasp the value of the work lies in CCK's customer list which, in Australia, includes Westpac, Merrill Lynch, Deutsche Bank, AMP, Foster's Brewing Group, Unilever and Telstra. In Asia, the customer list includes Bank Negara Malaysia, Land Bank of the Philippines, and Far East Bank and Trust. Each has signed with the Perth-based CCK because it is selling a unique niche product.

'I put it in the bottom drawer and it gathered dust', Wong says. That was until a friend working for the Philadelphia National Bank in Sydney called and asked what had happened to the old Westralian treasury management system. Wong's program, suitably upgraded, was back in business. After that first call, a request came from Australia's most infamous merchant bank, Rothwells.

Wong laughs when talking about Rothwells, a business that failed spectacularly in 1987, but it was that job that convinced him he could make a business out of CCK. He continued with his actuarial work, merging Campbell Cook and King into William M. Mercer and Co and becoming a principal of William M. Mercer. These days, Wong's time is largely devoted to building CCK, which has an annual turnover of $5 million. He is aiming much higher as international clients take a closer look at his business and its products. Earlier this year, Wong took CCK to the European trade fair and conference of SIBOS, an arm of the Swift international bank settlement organisation.

While exhibiting at SIBOS, Wong was visited by a senior Australian banking executive—a man who for years had been unreachable in Australia. ('Before that we never even got to first base', Wong says.) The banker was so impressed with what he saw in the CCK system that he has asked for a full demonstration back in Australia.

Wong is now planning to choose a partner to take CCK products into the global marketplace. The costs of global expansion and continued product development (including new risk management software) will be met through a planned float of the business 'later this year'.

In January of 2000, CCK obtained its first Singaporean client. RHB Bank Bhd will be implementing CCK's INFINITY treasury management system in its Singapore branch. With an established client base in Malaysia and the Philippines, CCK is forging ahead to becoming a regional player.

Sources: Adapted from Treadgold, T. (1999); www.cck.com.au.

Activities for discussion, analysis and further research

1. Identify what roles Joe Wong takes on at CCK. How do you think those roles have changed over the past 20 years? Why have they done so?
2. Log on to CCK's web page at www.cck.com.au and find out what other activities the company has been active in during the past year. Have a look at the profile of its management team. Do you detect a pattern of specialisation? Examine their listed credentials and draw some conclusions about them.

FURTHER READING

Chou, T-J. and Chen, F-T. C. 2004, Retail pricing strategies in recession economies: The case of Taiwan, *Journal of International Marketing*, 12, 1, pp. 82–103.

Euroweek 2003, China climbs to top of Asian debt tree as upgrade, spaceshot power demand, 10/24, 826, pp. 1–3.

Momaya, A.A. 2004, Competitiveness of firms: Review of theory, frameworks, and models, *Singapore Management Review*, 1st Half, 26, 1, pp. 45–62.

Saville, H. 2003, Asia Pacific specifics, *In-Store Marketing*, pp.17–20.

Schwarz, A. and Villinger, R. 2004, Integrating Southeast Asia's economies, *McKinsey Quarterly*, 1, pp. 36–49.

CHAPTER 2

PIONEERING IDEAS IN MANAGEMENT

LEARNING OBJECTIVES

After studying this chapter, you should be able to:

- Identify several early innovative management practices and explain the evolution of basic management theory.
- Trace preclassical contributions to the field of management.
- Explain major approaches within the classical viewpoint of management.
- Describe major developments contributing to establishing the behavioural viewpoint.
- Explain major approaches within the quantitative management viewpoint.
- Discuss the relevance of systems theory and contingency theory to the field of management.
- Explain how management in Japan influenced the Theory Z management viewpoint.
- Explain how current knowledge about management results from innovative processes involving many management pioneers.

STRIVING FOR EXCELLENCE

Kirsty Dunphey—Director, M & M Real Estate. Age: 24. Staff: 11

Most 15-year-old girls see a nice piece of silver jewellery and think about buying it for themselves. An entrepreneur thinks differently. Kirsty Dunphey asked about wholesaling opportunities and planned to sell the jewellery at a local market. 'I always knew I wanted to run my own business', says Dunphey. At 21, she took out a $10 000 personal loan (ostensibly for a car) to establish M & M Real Estate. She and her two business partners, both in their 40s, set up in a two-bedroom apartment in Launceston. Dunphey had just received her real-estate licence and had some experience in an estate agency. Her two business partners brought a wealth of real-estate sales experience to the business.

On the first day of M & M Real Estate, not even the phone or internet were connected. Two years later, the M & M team had sold $65 million of property in a town where the average house was worth $108 000. 'We paid back the loan in the first three months', says Dunphey. Turnover in the first year was just over $500 000.

Despite a population of only 140 000 and just 27 000 households, there were 20 real-estate agents in the greater Launceston area. Competition was fierce. Dunphey, now a vivacious 24-year-old, is the antithesis of the real-estate 'bloke'. Her marketing strategy includes reality-TV renovation makeovers. Dunphey says her agency's approach includes a strong internet presence and a 'slicker' feel than the local competitors.

Dunphey says her modest background has been an inspiration. 'We did it pretty tough', she says. 'That financial struggle was not something that appealed to me.' Now she is paying for her brother's schooling, her mother works in the business and Dunphey has just settled on her ninth investment property. She drives around Launceston in a yellow four-wheel-drive (buying, rather than leasing). 'I'm just trying to set myself up', she says.

What also helped has been her network of mentors, a real-estate agent who is the director of a Melbourne firm, and e-mailing people such as Julia Ross, the founder of Julia Ross Recruitment, and Katrina Allen, the Du Jour Tampon entrepreneur, for support and advice. 'It is so important to have mentoring, it pushes you to that next level.'

Dunphey's success has made her a role model in her home town. 'Well, there is me and our 27-year-old female mayor', she says. A Telstra Young Business Woman of the Year award in 2002 has given her a national profile that has led to a string of speaking engagements. When Dunphey spoke at a recent real-estate conference in Sydney, she was the youngest person ever to address the group. She received 500 emails in the first 48 hours after the speech. 'There is no reason why more women can't do what I'm doing', she says. 'They just need drive, ambition and can't be afraid of failure.'

Source: Gome, A. & Ross, E. (2003).

Throughout this book, we discuss leading-edge approaches to management. New ideas, however, do not arise in a vacuum. They normally arise from a foundation of established ideas, as well as an awareness of the shortcomings of those ideas.

Thus, in this chapter, we explore the birth of management ideas. We examine approaches of the preclassical contributors, those pioneers who predated modern management thinking but laid the groundwork. We consider classical management ideas, covering scientific, administrative and bureaucratic approaches. Next we analyse three major management viewpoints: the behavioural, quantitative and contemporary perspectives. Finally, we summarise the contributions of major viewpoints to modern management.

THE BIRTH OF MANAGEMENT IDEAS

The evolution of management theories

While examples of management practice can be found across several thousand years—including the Assyrians, Egyptians and Romans and other early civilisations as they developed large infrastructure projects—management as a field of knowledge has developed only recently. Much pressure to develop management theories and principles came from the industrial revolution and factory growth during the early 1800s. With factories came a need to co-ordinate many people in producing goods (Rue & Byars 2003).

Some people began to think about running factories more effectively. Eventually known as preclassical management contributors, they developed techniques to solve specific problems (see Fig. 2.1). Then came individuals who developed the broader principles and theories that formed the bases of the major management viewpoints, or schools: classical, behavioural,

FIGURE 2.1   Major viewpoints in the development of modern management

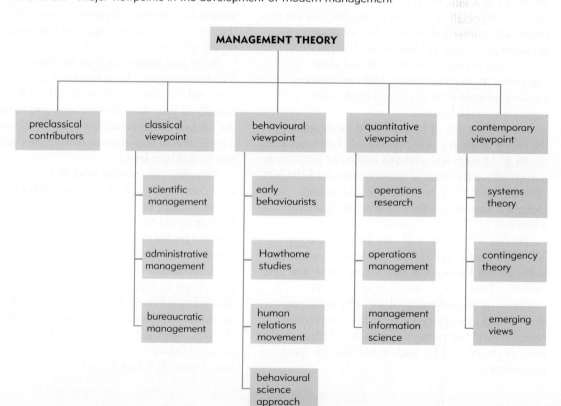

quantitative and contemporary. Several approaches contributed to developing each viewpoint (see Fig. 2.1). We examine them after briefly first focusing on preclassical contributors.

PRECLASSICAL CONTRIBUTORS

During the preclassical period of the middle and late 1800s, several people offered ideas that formed the basis for later, broader inquiries into the nature of management. Principal contributors were Robert Owen, Charles Babbage and Henry R. Towne (see Table 2.1).

Robert Owen

Robert Owen (1771–1858), a successful British entrepreneur, was ahead of his time in seeing how important were human resources. While running a cotton mill in New Lanark, Scotland, he became concerned with his employees' working and living conditions As was common, the mill employed 400 to 500 young children, who worked 13-hour days including 90 minutes off for meals. Although his business partners resisted some of his ideas, Owen worked to improve employees' living conditions by upgrading streets, houses, sanitation and the educational system in New Lanark. At the time, Owen was seen as a radical, but today his views are widely accepted. His ideas laid the groundwork for the human relations movement, discussed later in this chapter (Wren 1994; Duncan 1989).

Charles Babbage

Charles Babbage (1792–1871), an English mathematician, is called 'the father of modern computing'. His projects produced the world's first practical mechanical calculator and an 'analytical engine' with basic elements of modern-day computers (Duncan 1989). Difficulties with his many projects led him to look at new ways of doing things and to contribute to management theory.

Work specialisation, or how much work is divided into specific jobs, excited Babbage (1832). (Work specialisation is discussed in Chapter 8.) He saw that both physical and mental work could be specialised. In this sense, he foresaw specialists, such as accountants who limit their practice to either personal or corporate taxes.

Babbage also set up a two-part profit-sharing plan: a bonus for useful suggestions and a portion of wages based on factory profits. His ideas foreshadowed some modern-day group incentive plans, such as the Scanlon Plan, where workers suggest how to improve productivity, then share in resulting profits.

Henry R. Towne

Henry R. Towne (1844–1924), President of the Yale and Towne Manufacturing Company and a mechanical engineer, argued for management to be a separate field like engineering. He wrote a paper titled 'The engineer as an economist', delivered in 1886 to the American Society of Mechanical Engineers in Chicago. He saw that good engineering skills and business skills rarely occurred in the same person, but both were needed for an effective organisation. The paper argued for the establishment of a science of management and the development of management principles. Although the engineering society was not a significant contributor in developing

TABLE 2.1 THE PRECLASSICAL CONTRIBUTORS AND THEIR PIONEERING IDEAS

Contributor	Pioneering ideas
Robert Owen	Advocated concern for the working and living conditions of workers
Charles Babbage	Built the first practical mechanical calculator and a prototype of modern computers; predicted the specialisation of mental work; suggested profit sharing
Henry R. Towne	Outlined the importance of management as a science and called for the development of management principles

management knowledge, Frederick Taylor, who was present at Towne's presentation, was influential later in the development of management as a field (Towne 1886; Noble 1977; Wren 1994). The paper also ignited engineers' interest in addressing business problems (Rue and Byars, 2003).

Assessing preclassical contributors

While these early pioneers explored several avenues related to management, their efforts were unco-ordinated. They focused on developing specific techniques to solve particular problems. For example, as a guide to running orderly meetings, Henry Robert wrote Robert's Rules of Order, a preclassical-era document still used to run large, formal meetings.

> #### *Robert's Rules* bring order
>
> *In the late 1800s, Henry Martyn Robert, a US brigadier general, frequently attended meetings with people from many backgrounds during his military career as a civil engineer. He often needed to preside over these meetings.*
>
> *He quickly discovered running meetings was a challenge when the first he presided over, with a group of Baptist ministers, ended in total chaos. Robert was puzzled because nothing was settled or resolved. He had prepared his subject well and took advice on how to conduct a meeting. He decided he would never again face such an encounter.*
>
> *Over the next seven years, he collected information on meeting conduct and produced a 176-page book titled* Pocket Manual of Rules of Order for Deliberative Assemblies. *The book set out a set of parliamentary rules for conducting meetings.*
>
> *He promoted the book, which he published, by sending 1000 copies to United States politicians, including governors, legislators, the vice president and some lawyers, for comment. After receiving enthusiastic responses and suggestions, he edited the text, changing the title to* Robert's Rules of Order. *The book is a classic source of guidance for running large, formal meetings and is used by many legislative bodies, government councils, associations and other organisations where decisions are made by member vote. First published in 1876, the book is still in print. Over four million copies have been sold across the English-speaking world. It has also been published in Braille (Sampson 1988).*
>
> *Early pioneers were generally from technical backgrounds and did not see management as a separate field until Towne's (1886) paper. Still, they were innovators laying foundations for later major management thinkers. Their ideas have endured.*

CLASSICAL VIEWPOINT

classical viewpoint

Perspective on management emphasising finding ways to manage work and organisations more efficiently

Henry Towne's call to establish management as a separate field resulted in the major approach known as the **classical viewpoint**. This viewpoint emphasises efficiently managing work and organisations. It comprises three management approaches: scientific, administrative and bureaucratic. The viewpoint is called 'classical' as it includes early works and contributions comprising the core of the management field (Bluedorn 1986).

Scientific management

scientific management

Approach emphasising the scientific study of work methods to improve worker efficiency

Scientific management is an approach in classical management theory focusing on the scientific study of work methods to improve worker efficiency. Representatives of this approach include Frederick Winslow Taylor, Frank and Lillian Gilbreth and Henry Gantt.

Frederick Winslow Taylor

soldiering

Deliberately working at less than full capacity

Frederick Winslow Taylor (1856–1915), called 'the father of scientific management', was born into a fairly wealthy Philadelphia family. Taylor worked as an apprentice pattern maker and machinist at a local firm before going to Midvale Steel. At Midvale, rising from labourer to chief engineer over six years allowed him to tackle a serious problem he saw—soldiering by workers (Duncan 1989). **Soldiering** is deliberately working below full capacity. Taylor thought workers did this for three main reasons. First, they feared greater productivity would mean they or other workers would lose their jobs. Second, management's wage systems encouraged workers to operate slowly. For example, some firms cut incentive pay when standards were exceeded, so workers did not want to excel. Third, general methods of working and rules of thumb were often inefficient (Staudenmaier 1994; Benyon 1975).

Taylor believed soldiering could be avoided through a science of management based on four principles, shown in Table 2.2. This required scientific methods to determine how tasks should be done rather than relying on past experience. Specifically, Taylor pioneered time-and-motion study (he called it a time study). This involved breaking a task into elements or motions, eliminating unneeded ones, deciding how best to do the job, and then timing each motion to find the expected daily production level (allowing for delays and rest periods) (Taylor 1985).

Where wage systems encouraged soldiering, Taylor supported using wage incentive plans. He argued that workers should be paid between 30 and 100 per cent more for using scientifically developed work methods and reaching daily standards (Locke 1982).

At Bethlehem Steel, Taylor studied shovelling. Until he introduced scientific management, workers used their own tools on the job. Taylor saw that workers used the same shovel for both iron ore and ashes, though the relative weights of the materials were very different. From his studies, Taylor found that 9.5 kilograms was the optimum shovelling weight. He argued that it was sensible to have shovels of different sizes for different materials so the weight of what was being shovelled was about 9.5 kilograms. Implementing his plan with company-owned shovels demonstrated that the average tonnes shovelled per worker per day grew from 16.3 to 60.2. Meanwhile the average earnings per worker per day grew from $1.15 to $1.88, and the average cost of handling a tonne dropped from $0.072 to $0.033. Taylor's plan included additional worker incentive pay and benefits for the company (Locke 1982). Some managers, Bethlehem citizens and others opposed Taylor, arguing that he exploited workers by increasing their production, resulting in large workforce reductions at Bethlehem Steel.

A subsequent strike at the Watertown (Massachusetts) Army Arsenal (1911–12), where some of Taylor's ideas were being tried, led to a congressional investigation. The investigation found no evidence of worker abuse by 'Taylorism'. Nevertheless, the publicity slowed the growth of scientific management (Wren 1994).After World War I scientific management, aided by many French management experts, spread across Europe and was eventually applied in very diverse locations such as English chocolate factories, Icelandic fisheries, German paper mills and Swedish typewriter factories (Breeze 1986; Wregge & Perroni 1974; Wregge & Stotka 1978; Fry 1976; Locke 1982).

When the methods were applied at the Ford Company, overall assembly times dropped to 13 per cent of previous levels, with similar improvements for all other subassemblies (Bateman & Snell 2004). More recently, in Australia the ShearExpress, a mobile mechanical sheep-shearing unit, demonstrated the continuing application of scientific management principles (Clancy 2003). In the ShearExpress there are separate specialised stations in the shearing process, sheep move between the stations, and there are performance quotas to meet.

TABLE 2.2 TAYLOR'S FOUR PRINCIPLES OF SCIENTIFIC MANAGEMENT

1. Scientifically study each part of a task and develop the best method for performing it.

2. Carefully select workers and train them to perform a task using the scientifically developed method.

3. Co-operate fully with workers to ensure they use the proper method.

4. Divide work and responsibility so management is responsible for planning work methods using scientific principles and workers are responsible for executing work.

Taylor's ideas are still applied today. As we will see in Chapter 8, scientific management can lead to over-specialised jobs, worker resentment, monotony, poor quality, absenteeism and turnover.

The Gilbreths

Other major scientific-management advocates were the husband and wife team of Frank (1868–1924) and Lillian (1878–1972) Gilbreth. Though Frank qualified for admission to the Massachusetts Institute of Technology, he become a bricklayer because the profession was so important at the time. As Frank helped train young bricklayers, he noticed that experienced workers handed on inefficiencies.

He suggested using motion studies to streamline the process of laying bricks. Frank designed special scaffolding for different job types, and developed precise directions for mortar consistency. On the basis of these ideas and others, Frank cut bricklaying motions from $18\frac{1}{2}$ to 4. As a result, workers increased bricks laid per day from 1000 to 2700 with no greater physical effort (Wren 1994).

Frank married Lillian Moller, who worked with him while finishing a doctorate in psychology. The two continued to study the elimination of unneeded motions, expanding their interests to explore the reduction of task fatigue. Part of their work was the isolation of 17 basic motions, each a therblig ('Gilbreth' reversed, with the 't' and 'h' transposed). Therbligs were motions such as select, position and hold—motions the Gilbreths used to study tasks across industries. The Gilbreths also pioneered motion picture technology use to study jobs (Locke 1982). They applied many of their ideas to different aspects of their own domestic life (Kinicki & Williams 2003).

Lillian's (Gilbreth 1914) doctoral thesis, published as *The Psychology of Management*, applied psychology's findings to the workplace. The publisher insisted that she be listed as L. M. Gilbreth to disguise the fact that the author was a woman. Lillian was interested in the human implications of scientific management, arguing that it should help people develop their skills and abilities to reach their maximum potential (Wren 1994).

In 1924 Frank died from a heart attack, leaving Lillian with 12 children aged from 2 to 19. She continued their innovative studies and consulting, finally becoming a management professor at Purdue University (Wren 1994). Lillian Gilbreth is the first woman prominent in the development of management as a science.

Henry L. Gantt

Henry Gantt (1861–1919) was one of Taylor's closest associates, working with him in several firms including Midvale Steel and Bethlehem Steel (Wren 1994; Duncan 1989). Gantt later made his own contributions. The Gantt chart is the best known. It is a planning, scheduling and control graphic aid that is still used. (The supplement to Chapter 5 shows a Gantt chart.) He developed a unique incentive pay system which raised workers' pay on reaching a standard in the allotted time and gave supervisors bonuses when workers reached the standard. This system encourages supervisors to coach workers who have difficulties.

Bureaucratic management

bureaucratic management

Approach emphasising the need for organisations to operate in a rational manner rather than relying on owners' and managers' arbitrary whims

Another branch of the classical viewpoint is **bureaucratic management**, which saw the need of an organisation to operate rationally rather than relying on the arbitrary whims of owners and managers. The bureaucratic management approach is based largely on prominent German sociologist Max Weber's work.

Weber (1864–1920) was born to a wealthy, politically and socially well-connected family (Wren 1994; Eisen 1978; Duncan 1989). He worked as a consultant, professor and author. Among his major management contributions were his ideas on the need of organisations to operate more rationally.

Weber reacted to general norms of class and nepotism. For example, only aristocrats could become officers in the Prussian Army or reach high-level government and business jobs. Weber saw this as unfair and believed that it wasted significant human resources. He also thought that running companies on the basis of who one knew, not what one knew, and allowing nepotism (hiring of relatives regardless of competence) made organisations less effective.

To visualise how large organisations evolving from the industrial revolution might operate ideally, Weber laid out the characteristics of an 'ideal bureaucracy' (see Table 2.3). He coined the word 'bureaucracy' (based on the German *büro*, or 'office') to identify large rational

TABLE 2.3 MAJOR CHARACTERISTICS OF WEBER'S IDEAL BUREAUCRACY

Characteristic	Description
Specialisation of labour	Jobs are broken down into routine, well-defined tasks so members know what is expected of them and can become very competent at their particular task subset.
Formal rules and procedures	Written rules and procedures specify behaviours wanted from members, facilitating co-ordination and ensuring uniformity.
Impersonality	Rules, procedures and sanctions are applied uniformly regardless of individual personalities and personal considerations.
Well-defined hierarchy	Multiple levels of positions, with carefully determined reporting relationships among levels, provide supervision of lower offices by higher ones, a means of handling exceptions and the ability to establish accountability of actions.
Career advancement based on merit	Selection and promotion is based on members' qualifiations and performance.

CASE IN POINT

The only person in the company without a computer

The managing director of Perth's James Brown & Associates is an eclectic practitioner. He specialises in finance advice for the smallest end of the listed sector. Among his business venues he lists China, New Zealand and even Port Moresby, where his clients are likely to bring in their accounts in a shoe box.

He believes in coming in at the inception of a venture so that he can be involved in deciding how to tackle it. This prevents having to compete in a tender process which saves time and money for both himself and the client. He sees his role as doing something imaginative for the project, not only running the numbers. His greatest difficulty is the recruitment of staff, for which he competes against larger firms.

In spite of the growing size of the company, James Brown refuses to have a computer on his desk, believing he gets better value from time spent in telephone discussions.

Source: Adapted from Thomas, T. (1999a).

Activities for discussion, analysis and further research

1. Imagine that you are one of James Brown's employees. Describe the type of management processes which might best be used to effectively manage this company. Why?

2. Imagine yourself in his role. What other reasons might you have for not wishing to have a computer on your desk?

3. Contact a senior manager of your acquaintance and ask them for their opinion of such a practice. Are they supportive or is their view different? Why?

organisations. Weber knew his ideal bureaucracy did not really exist. In fact, he did not mean his ideas to be used as guidelines for managers. Rather, he wanted to present his ideas as a starting point to understand organisations (Weiss 1983; Stern & Barley 1996; Scott 1996). However, when translated into English late in the 1940s, many scholars used his ideas as a guide to effective organisation management.

When Weber's ideas were carried to excess, the term 'bureaucracy' was used negatively to mean red tape and excessive rules. However, clearly Weber's bureaucratic characteristics do have advantages.

Administrative management

administrative management

Approach focusing on principles used by managers to co-ordinate the organisation's internal activities

While scientific management's supporters worked to develop principles to help, most effectively, organise individual worker tasks and Weber struggled with the idea of bureaucracy, another branch within the classical viewpoint developed. The **administrative management** approach focused on principles for managers to co-ordinate organisations' internal activities. Major contributors include Henri Fayol and Chester Barnard, both executives of large firms. Their work laid the foundation for the concept of management as a professional field (Bateman & Snell 2004).

Henri Fayol

French industrialist Henri Fayol (1841–1925) was born to a middle-class family near Lyon, France (Wren 1994; Duncan 1989). Trained as a mining engineer, he joined a coal-and-iron company as an apprentice, rising to managing director by 1888. He moved the company from severe financial problems to a strong position before retiring at 77. The company today is part of LeCreusot-Loire, a large mining and metallurgical group in central France.

Based on his top-level managerial experiences, Fayol believed management theories could be developed then taught to those with administrative responsibilities. His theories were published in a monograph titled *General and Industrial Management* (1916).

Fayol worked to isolate the main activity types in industry or business. Under 'managerial activities', he identified five major functions: planning, organising, commanding, co-ordinating and controlling. This is the functional management approach. You may see Fayol's functions are similar to the four management functions (planning, organising, leading and controlling) used as this book's framework. Many modern management texts use some version of the functional approach with roots in Fayol's work.

Fayol laid out principles (see Table 2.4) that he found helped in running his large coal-and-iron firm. Although later research found some exceptions to his principles (discussed in later chapters), they are still valid (Eccles & Nohira 1992).

Chester Barnard

acceptance theory of authority

Theory arguing that authority does not depend as much on 'persons of authority' who give orders as on the willingness to comply of those who receive the orders

Chester Barnard (1886–1961) was a major contributor to administrative management. Born in Massachusetts, he attended Harvard without completing his degree (Duncan 1989). After joining AT&T as a statistician, he rose rapidly to become president of the New Jersey Bell Telephone Company in 1927. Barnard recorded his observations on effective administration in a book, *The Functions of the Executive*, in 1938.

One of Barnard's best-known contributions is his **acceptance theory of authority**. This theory argues that authority depends less on 'persons of authority' who give orders, than on those who receive the orders being willing to comply. Thus, in Barnard's view, it is really employees who decide whether or not to accept orders and directions from above. Practically, Barnard felt managers can exert daily authority because each person has a 'zone of indifference' within which they accept orders and directions without much questioning.

On the basis that authority flows from the bottom to the top, Barnard argued that employees more readily accept directions from a manager if they (1) understand the communication, (2) see the communication as consistent with organisational purposes, (3) believe the actions asked for suit both their needs and the needs of other employees and (4) see themselves as able mentally and physically to comply.

TABLE 2.4 FAYOL'S GENERAL PRINCIPLES OF MANAGEMENT

1. Division of work	Work specialisation can result in efficiencies and applies to both managerial and technical functions. Yet there are limitations to how much that work should be divided.
2. Authority	Authority is the right to give orders and power to exact obedience. It comes from the formal authority of the office and personal authority based on factors like intelligence and experience. With authority comes responsibility.
3. Discipline	Discipline is absolutely vital for an organisation's smooth running, but the state of discipline depends on its leaders' worthiness.
4. Unity of command	An employee should receive orders from one superior only.
5. Unity of direction	Activities aimed at the same objective should be organised so there is one plan and one person in charge.
6. Subordination of individual interest to general interest	The interests of one employee or group should not prevail over the organisation's interests and goals.
7. Remuneration	Compensation should be fair to both employee and employer.
8. Centralisation	The proper amount of centralisation or decentralisation depends on the situation. The objective is optimum use of personnel capabilities.
9. Scalar chain	A scalar (hierarchical) chain of authority extends from top to bottom of an organisation and defines the communication path. However, horizontal communication is also encouraged as long as managers in the chain are kept informed.
10. Order	Materials should be kept in well-chosen places to facilitate activities. Similarly, due to good organisation and selection, the right person should be in the right place.
11. Equity	Employees should be treated with kindness and justice.
12. Stability of personnel tenure	Because time is required to become effective in new jobs, high turnover should be prevented.
13. Initiative	Managers should encourage and develop subordinate initiative to the fullest.
14. Esprit de corps	Since union is strength, harmony and teamwork are essential.

Source: Adapted from Fayol (1949, pp. 19–42).

Barnard helped integrate concern with authority, which grew from the administrative and bureaucratic approaches, with emphasis on worker needs, which was developing within the behavioural viewpoint. He also knew about early behaviourists and the Hawthorne studies, a primary force in developing the behavioural viewpoint, to which we turn next (Wolf, cited in Wren 1994; Barnard 1968).

BEHAVIOURAL VIEWPOINT

Classical theorists saw people as production mechanisms. They were largely interested in finding how organisations could use people efficiently. Despite Barnard's views, the idea that an employee's behaviour might be changed by internal reactions to different aspects of job situations was widely seen as irrelevant to increasing efficiency. By contrast, the **behavioural viewpoint** focused on the need to understand the effect of different factors on human behaviour in organisations. To understand this viewpoint, we look at four aspects of its development: early behaviourists' contributions, the Hawthorne studies, the human relations movement and the more recent behavioural science approach.

behavioural viewpoint

Perspective on management emphasising the importance of attempting to understand various factors affecting human behaviour in organisations

Which theory is that?

You are beginning to be exposed to the development of management theory. The closest example of this that you might have at the moment is how your lecturer manages your class. Consider which theory your lecturer is practising, then interview your lecturer and consider whether your perception of their practice is congruent with their statement.

Decision points

Consider these issues:

1. What is your lecturer's theory of learning (how people learn)?
2. What are your lecturer's views on the question of evaluation?
3. What is their role in the classroom?
4. Do you think that your lecturer's attitude to the students is affected by stereotypes of them? What are the stereotypes? Why did you come to that conclusion?

Reflection points

1. Discuss and compare your answers to the last section with those of a couple of your peers. In what ways were they similar? Why do you think this was so? Are you prepared to give your lecturer some feedback? If so, how? If not, why?
2. If possible, interview a lecturer in another discipline area. Compare the two sets of responses. What do you think are the determining factors for these differences? Does the discipline in which these people teach affect the way they manage the class? Why?

Early behaviourists

With interest in management growing, individuals with other backgrounds began to offer options to the engineering focus of scientific management. Two early behaviourists, psychologist Hugo Münsterberg and political scientist Mary Parker Follett, contributed pioneering ideas that helped make the behavioural perspective a major viewpoint.

Hugo Münsterberg

Hugo Münsterberg (1863–1916), born and educated in Germany, earned both a PhD in psychology and a medical degree. At Harvard in 1892, he set up a psychological laboratory studying practical applications of psychology. His attention soon turned to industrial applications, leading him, in 1913, to publish a major book, *Psychology and Industrial Efficiency*. The book argued that industry could be helped by psychologists in three major ways. The first was linked closely to scientific management: psychologists could study jobs and identify individuals best suited to particular jobs. The second way psychologists could help was by identifying psychological conditions where people will tend to do their best work. The third was developing strategies to influence employees to behave in ways that fit management's interests. Münsterberg's ideas and examples led to the establishment of the field of industrial psychology, or the study of human behaviour in a work context. Thus, Münsterberg is known as 'the father of industrial psychology' (George 1972; Landy 1977).

Mary Parker Follett

Mary Parker Follett (1868–1933) was another well-known early behaviourist. Born in Boston and educated in political science at what became Radcliffe College, Follett was a social worker interested in employment and workplace issues.

Follett gave much greater importance to group functioning in companies than supporters of the classical management view. She argued that organisation members are always influenced by groups within which they operate (Parker 1984). In fact, she believed that groups could control themselves and their own activities, a re-emerging view due to growing interest in self-managed teams.

Another of Follett's ideas was her belief that firms should operate on the principle of 'power with' rather than 'power over'. Power, to her, was a general ability to influence and produce change (Graham & Follett 1995). She argued that power should be jointly developed and co-operative, where employees and managers work together, rather than a coercive concept based on hierarchical influence. Though her views probably influenced Barnard's acceptance theory of authority, Follett advocated power sharing while Barnard emphasised appropriate responses encouraged from below (Barnard 1968; Duncan 1989).

Follett suggested fostering the 'power with' concept by conflict resolution through integration. By integration she meant finding a solution satisfactory to all. She gave an example of a dairy co-operative which almost broke down due to a disagreement over the pecking order in milk-can unloading. The creamery was located part-way down a hill, and those who came downhill and those who came uphill both thought they should unload first. The situation was frozen until an outsider showed that changing the loading dock's position meant both groups could unload their cans at once. Follett noted, 'Integration involves invention, and the clever thing is to recognise this, and not to let one's thinking stay within the boundaries of two alternatives that are mutually exclusive' (Metcalf & Urwick 1940, p. 32). Her integration ideas are echoed in modern methods of conflict-resolution (see Chapter 15).

Follett emphasised integrative unity, where the company works as a functional whole with all interrelated parts working to effectively achieve organisational goals. She saw the process of working together as a dynamic process, because environmental factors demand change. As we will see, her ideas anticipated the systems view of management (Wren 1994; Parker 1984; Linden 1995). A contemporary reviewer argued that its significance 'rivals the long-standing influence of such giants as Taylor and Fayol' (Parker 1984, p. 738). A new book of her ideas was published by Harvard Business School Press (1995).

Hawthorne studies

While Follett was working, other researchers, including Elton Mayo, were involved in the **Hawthorne studies**. These were carried out at Western Electric's Hawthorne plant in the late 1920s and early 1930s, and led to the human relations view of management, a behavioural approach emphasising concern for the worker. To understand their importance, we must trace the studies from the start.

Initially, the Hawthorne studies reflected scientific management's tradition of seeking to increase efficiency by improving tools and methods of work—in this case, lighting. General Electric wanted to sell more light bulbs so, with other electric companies, it paid for studies by the National Research Council on links between lighting and productivity. The tests were held at the Hawthorne Works (Chicago) of the Western Electric Company, an equipment-producing subsidiary of AT&T (Greenwood & Wrege 1986). Three sets of studies were conducted.

First set of studies

The first set of studies, or the Illumination studies, occurred between 1924 and 1927 carried out by several engineers. In one study, light was gradually reduced for the experimental group (the group for whom lighting changed), while light levels were kept the same for the control group (a comparison group working in another area). Both groups' performance increased, though lighting for the experimental group became so dim that workers complained they could not see. At that point, the experimental group's performance finally declined (see Fig. 2.2). Researchers realised that factors beyond lighting were at work (as both groups' performance increased), and ended the project (Greenwood & Wrege 1986). However, the experimental and control groups may have been in contact and competed with each other.

Second set of studies

Interested in the positive productivity changes, some engineers and company officials wanted to find the causes. So a second set of experiments was run between 1927 and 1933. The most

Hawthorne studies

Group of studies conducted at the Hawthorne plant of the Western Electric Company during the late 1920s and early 1930s, the results of which ultimately led to the human relations view of management

FIGURE 2.2 Actual versus expected results for experimental and control groups in one of the Hawthorne Illumination Studies

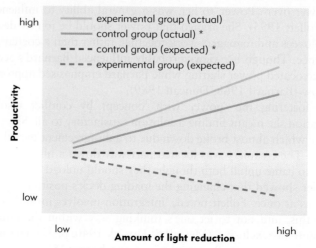

* lighting remained at the same level in the control group

famous study had five women assembling electrical relays in the Relay Assembly Test Room, where they were apart from other workers so researchers could alter work conditions and evaluate results. Beforehand, researchers were concerned about possible negative responses from participants. To reduce possible resistance, researchers altered arrangements so there was no official supervisor. Instead, workers operated under the general direction of the experimenters. Workers were given privileges, including being able to leave their workstation without permission, and received a lot of attention from experimenters and management (Adair 1984). The study aimed to explore the best combination of work and rest periods, but other aspects were also changed (sometimes at the same time), such as pay, work-day length and provision of free lunches. Over the study productivity generally increased, no matter how elements changed (Greenwood & Wrege 1987).

A Harvard University research group (involved in result assessment) decided changes to supervision were the main reason for productivity increases in the Relay Assembly Test Room study and two related studies with other work groups. Researchers felt that physical changes, including rest periods, free lunches and shorter hours, as well as group incentive pay plans, were less significant (largely because some negative changes did not seem to decrease performance).

As researchers had changed supervisory arrangements before the study began, this change was not one of the study factors and was not expected to affect results. One result was identification of a famous concept eventually known as the **Hawthorne effect.** The Hawthorne effect is the possibility that the performance of those being studied may improve due to the researchers' attention, not due to any specific factors being tested (Rice 1982).

More recent research suggests the Hawthorne-effect concept is a simplistic explanation of the studies and the concept is flawed. Possibly the Hawthorne plant results came from workers and researchers seeing what happened differently (rather than that workers simply reacted positively due to researchers' attention). Workers probably saw the supervision changes as a positive work environment change, though this was not the researchers' intention (Adair 1984).

Third set of studies

The third set of Hawthorne studies built on the second's findings. It included the famous Bank Wiring Observation Room study (1931–2), with a group of male workers. Studying the group gave information about informal social relations and use of norms to restrict output when the group sees this as worthwhile (Wren 1994; Bramel & Friend 1981).

Hawthorne effect

Possibility that individuals singled out for a study may improve their performance simply because of the added attention received from researchers, rather than because of any specific factors being tested

Impact of the Hawthorne studies

Due to the Hawthorne studies, the focus of management study changed greatly. In contrast to the classical approach's impersonality, the Hawthorne studies showed how much a job's social aspects impact on productivity, especially the effects of supervisors' attention and group-member relationships. As one writer put it, 'No other theory or set of experiments has stimulated more research and controversy nor contributed more to a change in management thinking than the Hawthorne studies and the human relations movement they spawned' (Adair 1984, p. 334; Carey 1967; Shepard 1971; Bramel & Friend 1981; Greenwood, Bolton & Greenwood 1983; Sonnenfeld 1985).

Human relations movement

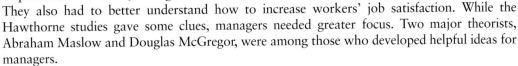

However faulty, the Hawthorne research raised great interest in the organisation's social dimension. From a managerial view the key to productivity seemed to be to show greater concern for workers to increase their satisfaction with their jobs and willingness to produce more. Building more collaborative and co-operative supervisor-and-worker relationships was emphasised. As a result, managers needed social skills as well as technical skills. They also had to better understand how to increase workers' job satisfaction. While the Hawthorne studies gave some clues, managers needed greater focus. Two major theorists, Abraham Maslow and Douglas McGregor, were among those who developed helpful ideas for managers.

Abraham Maslow

Abraham Maslow (1908–70) received his doctorate in psychology from the University of Wisconsin, eventually becoming chairman of Brandeis University's psychology department. He developed a theory of motivation based on three assumptions about human nature. First, human beings have needs that are never totally satisfied. Second, humans aim to fulfil unsatisfied needs. Third, needs fit into a relatively predictable hierarchy, going from basic, lower-level needs at the bottom to higher-level ones at the top (Duncan 1989). Maslow's hierarchy has five need levels: physiological (lowest), safety, belongingness, esteem and self-actualisation (highest). Self-actualisation needs refer to the need to develop our capabilities and reach our full potential (Maslow 1954).

Maslow's work showed managers that workers have needs beyond a basic drive to earn money to put a roof over their heads. This idea conflicted with scientific management, which focused on the importance of pay. Among management-related theories, Maslow's theory of hierarchy of needs is probably the best known to modern managers.

Douglas McGregor

Douglas McGregor (1906–1964) drove the move to have managers see workers differently. McGregor gained a doctorate at Harvard then spent most of his career as a professor of industrial management at the Massachusetts Institute of Technology. During six years as president of Antioch College he realised that simply aiming to have everyone like the boss (i.e. maintaining good relations with workers) was a poor guide for managers.

He explored managerial assumptions about workers by developing the concept of Theory X versus Theory Y. McGregor thought managers' activities were influenced by these assumptions. Theory X managers (see Table 2.5) assume workers are lazy, must be coerced, have little ambition and focus largely on security needs. By contrast, Theory Y managers assume workers do not inherently dislike work, can display self-control, creativity and innovation, and generally have higher-level needs often unmet on the job.

McGregor believed that managers with Theory X assumptions set up elaborate controls and try to motivate entirely with economic incentives. As a result, workers' responses will reinforce the manager's assumptions.

TABLE 2.5 THEORY X AND THEORY Y MANAGERIAL ASSUMPTIONS

Theory X Assumptions

1. The average person dislikes work and will try to avoid it.

2. Most people must be coerced, controlled, directed and threatened with punishment to get them to work toward organisational goals.

3. The average person wants to be directed, shuns responsibility, has little ambition and seeks security above all.

Theory Y Assumptions

1. Most people do not inherently dislike work; the physical and mental effort involved is as natural as play or rest.

2. People will exercise self-direction and self-control to reach goals they are committed to; external control and punishment threats are not the only way to get effort toward goals.

3. Commitment to goals is a function of available rewards, particularly those satisfying esteem and self-actualisation needs.

4. When conditions are favourable, the average person learns not only to accept but also to seek responsibility.

5. Many people have a capacity to exercise a high degree of creativity and innovation in solving organisational problems.

6. The intellectual potential of most individuals is only partly used in most organisations.

In contrast, managers with Theory Y assumptions integrate individual and organisational goals. McGregor believed this occurs when managers give workers latitude to perform tasks, encourage them to be creative and innovative, minimise use of control and try to make work more interesting and satisfying for higher-level needs. The result of Theory Y, according to McGregor, was that 'The limits of collaboration in the organisational setting are not limits of human nature but of management's ingenuity in discovering how to realise the potential represented by its human resources' (Jones, George & Hill 2000, p. 45). A manager's task was to grow commitment to organisational goals and, by creating appropriate work settings, give workers the chance to be creative, exercising initiative and self-direction. McGregor (1960) knew that immature, dependent workers might need greater control to build the maturity needed for a Theory Y approach.

As with Maslow's hierarchy, McGregor's Theory X and Theory Y helped managers develop a broader view of workers' nature and how to interact with them. It also helped avoid the phenomenon of the self-fulfilling prophecy. This is where the manager's expectations of a subordinate's behaviour become their perceived behaviour (Kinicki & Williams 2003). The ideas appealed to managers wanting to operate most effectively. These theories became very popular and are widely used.

Behavioural science approach

behavioural science

Approach emphasising scientific research as the basis for developing theories about human behaviour in organisations, that is used to establish practical guidelines for managers

Maslow, McGregor and others building the human relations viewpoint tried to show options to the classical school's rational-economic view of workers. They showed workers as social creatures, with varied needs to be met on the job. But they drew a fairly general basic picture, that often left managers unsure what to do and what would result from their actions. The need for a richer view of the work situation led to the behavioural science perspective.

The **behavioural science** approach uses scientific research to develop theories on human behaviour in organisations. The theories help give practical managerial guidelines. This approach draws on many disciplines, such as management, psychology, sociology, anthropology and economics. Concepts are tested in companies or laboratories before being offered to managers. Behavioural science's aim is ultimately to develop theories to guide managers to assess different situations and choose the best action. Since humans and their interactions are complex, the challenge is to understand organisations and their members.

An example of behavioural science is the idea that people perform better when faced with challenging but attainable goals, than without them. Of course, goals have to be specific and measurable ('I want to get an A this semester in my management subjects'), not vague ('I want to do well this semester in my course'). The idea of goal-setting helping performance stems from the research of Edwin A. Locke and others (Locke, Shaw, Saari & Latham 1982; Pritchard, Jones, Roth, Stuebing & Ekeberg 1988). We look at goal setting's motivational aspects in Chapter 6.

QUANTITATIVE MANAGEMENT VIEWPOINT

During World War II the quantitative management viewpoint emerged. Due to the war effort's sheer size, Allied military forces used quantitative methods to decide how to use resources effectively. For example, the allocation of scarce pilots and planes during the Battle of Britain was optimised in this way (Kinicki & Williams 2003). Later the US Navy used quantitative studies to replace the 'catch-as-catch-can' method aeroplanes used searching for enemy ships. Quantitative analysis showed a search pattern which cut search-plane numbers needed for a given area and provided better coverage. Scarce resources were saved and more enemy ships and valuable cargo in the South Atlantic were seized, helping Allied efforts (Gaither 1986). This and other vital applications of quantitative methods drew business attention, as quantitative experts found work in civilian organisations after the war.

The quantitative management viewpoint focused on mathematics, statistics and information aids supporting managerial decision making and organisational effectiveness (Miller & Feldman 1983). Three main branches have evolved: management science, operations management and management information systems.

Management science

Management science increases decision effectiveness by using mathematical models and statistical methods. (Caution: The term is not synonymous with 'scientific management', discussed before.) Another name for management science is **operations research**. Increased computer power has simplified the use of management science's mathematical and statistical tools. For example, Avon, maker of beauty, health-care and fashion jewellery products, used management science. Group Vice President for Planning and Development, Robert W. Pratt, used statistical methods to find what effects would flow from altering the company's normal practice of giving heavy discounts to generate larger orders. His results showed the firm could greatly boost profits by cutting discounts, even if average orders dropped (Waldon 1985). In the Supplement to Chapter 5, we discuss tools for operations research, including linear programming; queuing or waiting-line models; and routing or distribution models.

Operations management

Operations management is responsible for production and delivery management of products and services (Sawaya & Giauque 1986). It includes inventory management, work scheduling, production planning, facility location and design, and quality assurance. Manufacturing areas often use operations management for production aspects such as production process design, raw materials purchase, employee work scheduling, and final product storage and shipping. Operations management can be used for service delivery too. We look at some methods in the Supplement to Chapter 5 and explore operations management in Chapter 16.

Management information systems

The term **management information systems** refers to the management field focused on design and implementation of computer-based management information systems. These systems turn

management science

Approach aimed at increasing decision effectiveness through use of sophisticated mathematical models and statistical methods

operations research

Another name used for management science

operations management

Function or field of expertise primarily responsible for managing production and delivery of an organisation's products and services

management information systems

Field of management focused on designing and implementing computer-based information systems for use by management

raw data into information for many management levels. They are powerful competitive weapons for industries to manage large information volumes. We discuss computer-based information systems for management further in Chapter 16.

CONTEMPORARY VIEWPOINTS

While classical, behavioural and quantitative approaches still help management, others have emerged. These are contemporary or recent management thinking innovations. Two important contemporary viewpoints are systems and contingency theories. At any time, emerging ideas influence the development of management thinking, without yet having the status of enduring viewpoints.

Systems theory

systems theory

Approach based on the idea that organisations can be visualised as systems

Systems theory is based on viewing organisations as **systems** (Kast & Rosenzweig 1972). A system is a set of interrelated parts working as a whole in pursuit of common goals. The systems approach is founded on biological and physical sciences (Bertalanffy 1951; Katz & Kahn 1978; Boulding 1956). In this section, we consider major systems components, open versus closed systems and open system characteristics.

Major components

system

Set of interrelated parts operating as a whole in pursuit of common goals

According to the systems approach, an organisation system has four major components (see Fig. 2.3). **Inputs** are the human, material, financial, equipment and information resources needed for goods and services production. **Transformation processes** are a firm's managerial and technological abilities used to change inputs into outputs. **Outputs** are organisational products, services and other outcomes. **Feedback** is information on results and organisational status relative to the environment (Ramaprasad 1983).

inputs

Various human, material, financial, equipment and informational resources required to produce goods and services

The systems approach gives many benefits. First, it can analyse systems at different levels (Asmos & Huber 1987). For example, Miller developed a typology of hierarchical levels of living systems, ranging from an individual human cell including atoms and molecules, to a supranational system of two or more societies (Miller 1978). Usually, managers look at the

transformation processes

An organisation's managerial and technological abilities used to convert inputs into outputs

FIGURE 2.3   A systems view of organisations

outputs

Products, services and other outcomes produced by the organisation

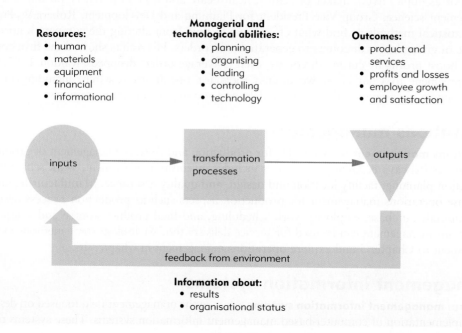

feedback

Information about results and organisational status relative to the environment

organism (individual), group, organisation and society levels, although greater global emphasis means the supranational level is growing in importance. Second, the systems view forms a framework to assess interaction between organisation parts. Third, it shows change in one system part affects others. To think about interrelationships between organisation parts, you need to imagine them joined by rubber bands. Pulling on one part changes the others' positions. Fourth, the systems approach considers an organisation's interaction with its environment— outside factors impacting it. To properly consider the environment, an organisation must operate as an open system.

Open versus closed systems

Systems can be open or closed. An **open system** interacts with its environment continually. By these interactions the system gains new inputs and learns how its outputs are viewed by external elements. In contrast, a **closed system** does not interact with its environment and gets little feedback. Companies are always somewhat open, since a firm cannot operate for long with no environmental interaction. Still, organisations differ greatly in their place on the open–closed continuum. If an organisation operates too close to the closed end, it might miss significant environmental factors until major problems emerge (Kast & Rosenzweig 1974).

Characteristics of open systems

Organisations operating near the open end of the continuum share characteristics that help them survive and prosper. Two major open-system characteristics are negative entropy and synergy (Kast & Rosenzweig 1972; Katz & Kahn 1978).

Entropy refers to the tendency of systems to decay over time. In contrast, **negative entropy** is the ability of open systems to delay or arrest entropy by bringing in new energy from the environment in the form of inputs and feedback.

A second major open-system characteristic is **synergy**, the ability of the whole to equal more than the sum of its parts. This means a firm can achieve its goals more effectively and efficiently than if parts operate separately.

According to the systems viewpoint, managers operating their units and firms as open systems tuned in to significant environmental factors will be more successful. We discuss environmental factors more closely in Chapter 3.

Contingency theory

Classical theorists, such as Taylor and Fayol, tried to find 'the one best way' for managers to operate. If universal principles could be found, then a good manager would need to learn these principles and their applications. Sadly, it was not so simple. Researchers found some classical principles, such as Fayol's unity of command (each person should report to one boss), could be violated without harm. As a result, **contingency theory** developed. This theory argues that

FIGURE 2.4 The contingency managerial viewpoint

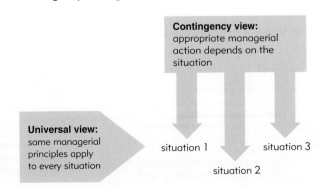

---

open system

System operating in continual interaction with its environment

closed system

System doing little or no interacting with its environment and receiving little feedback

negative entropy

Ability of open systems to bring in new energy, in the form of inputs and feedback from the environment, to delay or arrest entropy

synergy

Ability of the whole to equal more than the sum of its parts

contingency theory

Viewpoint arguing that appropriate managerial action depends on the particular parameters of the situation

appropriate managerial action depends on a situation's parameters. Thus, instead of universal principles for every situation, contingency theory identifies actions to take depending on situational characteristics (see Fig. 2.4) (Luthans 1973; Lee, Luthans & Olson 1982).

To be sure, Fayol and other classical theorists realised judgment was needed in applying their principles. Still, they focused on universal rules and became vague about exceptions (Lorsch 1979; Tosi & Slocum 1984).

Throughout this book are theories and concepts relating to the contingency viewpoint—that is, areas where applications of management ideas depend on situational factors. The contingency approach is applicable to environmental factors, strategy, organisational design, technology and leadership.

Theory Z

Japanese management

Approach focusing on aspects of management in Japan that may be appropriate for adoption in other countries

A more recent perspective is known as the **Japanese management** approach, since it looks at Japanese management aspects appropriate for use elsewhere. There is interest due to Japanese firms' success, particularly in manufacturing, including televisions, videocassette recorders and computer printers (Keys 1994).

From his studies of both American and Japanese management approaches, Ouchi set out **Theory Z**. Theory Z combines American and Japanese management elements into a approach to enhance US managerial effectiveness consistent with American society and culture norms and values (see Fig. 2.5). Theory Z means giving workers job security; making them part of decision-making structure; emphasising group responsibility; raising quality; setting up gradual-advancement policies, more informal controls and broader career paths; and showing increased concern for employees' work and non-work well-being. Firms such as General Motors, Ford Motor Company, Hewlett-Packard and Intel have adopted Theory Z aspects, particularly the involvement of workers in decision making, establishing more informal controls and helping group members accept responsibility for their unit's work.

Theory Z

Concept combining positive aspects of American and Japanese management into a modified approach aimed at increasing managerial effectiveness while remaining compatible with the norms and values of American society and culture

The total quality philosophy

Pursuing quality's competitive benefits, some firms have taken another approach. This is **total quality management** (TQM), an approach focused on collective responsibility for product and service quality, encouraging people in different but related departments (e.g. product design and manufacturing) to work together to improve quality. First called total quality control (TQC), the approach involves overall cross-organisation commitment, quality efforts integrated with company goals, and including quality in performance appraisals (Port 1987; Schroeder 1989).

total quality management

Approach highlighting collective responsibility for product and service quality, and encouraging individuals to work together to improve quality

TQM is a change in perception of quality. The traditional view of quality is in terms of deviation from specified standards, products and services. In contrast, TQM aims for zero defects, with the workforce working to make their product or service conform exactly to specified quality standards (Schroeder 1989).

FIGURE 2.5   Characteristics of theory Z management (adapted from Ouchi & Jaeger 1978, pp. 308, 311)

(American)	TYPE Z (modified American)	TYPE J (Japanese)
short-term employment	long-term employment	lifetime employment
individual decision making	consensual decision making	consensual decision making
individual responsibility	individual responsibility	collective responsibility
rapid evaluation and promotion	slow evaluation and promotion	slow evaluation and promotion
explicit, formalised control	implicit, informal control with explicit, formalised measures	implicit, informal control
specialised career path	moderately specialised career path	non-specialised career path
segmented concern	holistic concern, including family	holistic concern

Tall poppy

Poppy was eighteen when she started her business in 1992, with capital of just $40 000. Her first foray into the commercial world was with a range of lipsticks called 'Seven Virtues'. She produced one thousand samples of seven colours and, in less than three years, built her cosmetic business into an empire with an $8 million annual turnover.

It appeared that Poppy King could do no wrong, and she became a household name in Australia during this period. In 1995, her entrepreneurial skills were recognised when she was named 'Young Australian of the Year'. In 1996, she held the position of Managing Director of Poppy Industries, and was also a member of the federal government's Small Business Council. However, in 1997, turnover fell from $6 million to $4 million and pre-tax losses neared $1 million. This dramatic change was put down to the appearance on the market of copy-cat brands of the distinctive matte, long-lasting, vividly coloured lipsticks. Additional capital was brought in when Tab and Eva Fried acquired a half share in the business and injected $3.5 million, but the business continued to decline, with the partners unable to agree on the direction they should take to break into the American market.

By July 1998, the dispute between the partners was beyond resolution. In August 1998, an audit by the accounting firm of Grant Thornton found that the business was 'on its last legs'. The Frieds resigned as directors and Poppy continued to run the business on her own, while launching new products in Melbourne. In September 1998, the Kings asked that the business be placed in the hands of the receiver. Adam Trescowthick subsequently acquired it in 1998 for $1.3 million,

and Poppy King was reinstated as CEO of the company.

Poppy remained as CEO of Poppy Industries until 2002. During that time the business was stabilised and continued to sell its products throughout major department stores in Australia. The range was expanded to include other cosmetic product categories. In 2002 Poppy Industries was sold to the Estee Lauder Corporation and Poppy King was relocated to New York City as Vice President of Creative Marketing for Prescriptives (an Estee Lauder brand). Poppy products were discontinued and the brand has ceased operation in order for Poppy to concentrate on her new corporate role where she is responsible for development of products under the Prescriptives label.

Source: Contributed by Glenice Wood (details of sources are listed on p. 735).

Activities for discussion, analysis and further research

1. Was Poppy King's business operated as an open or closed system? Explain your view.
2. Describe the contingency theory viewpoint (p. 47), and say whether you feel Poppy King's business operated under these principles.
3. Consider Table 2.6 on p. 52. What major viewpoints may have contributed to the way Poppy King thought about and behaved in her organisation? In a group, discuss whether gender would influence an individual's ability to draw significantly from any of these major viewpoints. If so, how?
4. Go to Google.com and type in Poppy King to read the latest information on Poppy King and more history.

Japanese firms are often seen as pioneering TQM, however the idea was originally American. After being ignored in America in the late 1940s, W. Edwards Deming took his ideas on statistical quality improvement methods to Japan. He promoted employee and company unit engagement in quality efforts, outlining his philosophy in 14 points. Japanese industry welcomed his ideas; appreciating them so highly they set up the Deming prize, an annual award for excellence in quality control. In the 1950s Juran, another American, also aided Japanese TQM efforts (Garvin 1987; Juran 1988). For ideas on raising quality, see the Management skills for a globalised economy discussion on 'Deming's 14 points on how to improve quality'.

Deming's 14 points on how to improve quality

In the course of his work, Deming developed 14 points outlining what he believes managers, especially at upper levels, must do to produce quality products:

1. Make a long-term commitment to improve products and services, with the aim of becoming competitive, staying in business and providing jobs.
2. Adopt the new philosophy of concern for quality. We are in a new economic age. Western management must awaken to the challenge, learn its responsibilities and take on leadership for change.
3. Cease dependence on mass-inspection to achieve quality; build quality into the product in the first place.
4. End the practice of awarding business on the basis of price. Instead minimise total cost. Move to a single supplier for any one item, building a long-term relationship of loyalty and trust.
5. Constantly improve the system of production and service so quality and productivity also constantly improve and costs decrease.
6. Institute on-the-job training.
7. Institute leadership. The aim of supervision should be to help people, machines and gadgets do a better job.
8. Drive out fear so everyone may work effectively for the company.
9. Break down barriers between departments so people work as a team.
10. Eliminate slogans, exhortations and targets asking the workforce for zero defects and new levels of productivity. Such exhortations create adversarial relationships because most causes of low quality and low productivity can be traced to the production system and lie beyond the workforce's power.
11. Eliminate work standards (quotas) and use of numerical goals on the factory floor. Substitute leadership instead.
12. Remove barriers robbing workers of the right to take pride in their work. Change the emphasis from sheer numbers to quality.
13. Institute a vigorous program of education and self-improvement.
14. Put everybody in the organisation to work on accomplishing the transformation. The transformation is everybody's job.

Source: Adapted from Deming (1986).

An important aspect of TQM is its emphasis on the cost of quality, the cost of not doing things right the first time (Monks 1987).

More recently, there has been a move away from TQM or TQC as an improvement or control tool, and towards adopting quality as a managerial philosophy. This often becomes a search for continuous incremental improvements in all company processes rather than simply a bean-counting strategy to reduce manufacturing defects.

The learning organisation

This approach is allied to more recent uses of TQM. It argues for viewing an organisation as a learning system, where organisational approaches and systems are focused on retaining and building on knowledge and organisational learnings. These learnings then form the basis of organisation change and variation in adapting to new events and conditions (Bateman & Snell 2004).

The learning organisation uses data and facts, looking for opportunities, checking outcomes, seeking out organisations to model on, then sharing the learnings across all members systematically.

Web on menu at McDonald's

Now you can have McDonald's and be on-line too. Finding a natural match between fast food and the Internet, the central Dunedin (New Zealand) McDonald's restaurant introduced its Cyber Café in June 2001—the first in Australasia and possibly the first in any McDonald's worldwide. The demographics in Dunedin are perhaps ideal for such an experiment. The restaurant is popular with high school, polytechnic and university students, who constitute a significant portion of both the city's population and the local McDonald's patronage. They are comfortable with the concepts of the Web and shared-access terminals, since they regularly use computer labs at school. Usage studies have shown that these two groups are the dominant users of the Cyber Café, supplemented by tourists (many of whom are from overseas) and 'older' local residents.

Initially, twelve terminals were installed. All that was needed to kick-start usage was a combination of free single-session 'promo' cards given away with $5 purchases, posters and flyers at the three local restaurants, and some enthusiastic free radio news coverage. Six additional terminals were added a few months later, with further expansion possible. Use is charged at NZ$5 per hour, via a rechargeable Cyber Card.

The Cyber Café occupies one-third of the restaurant's frontage on George Street (the city's main shopping street). The other two-thirds are taken by the main entry and McCafé, another innovation at urban McDonald's restaurants throughout Australia and New Zealand. New Zealand was the second country in the world to open one.

Corporate executives from the United States and South America, who visited the Dunedin facility, now say the concept may go global. Dunedin McDonald's owner/operator, Peter Shepherd says, 'It is working out very well. We are finding our McCafé patrons enjoy having a great coffee, surfing news sites and catching up with friends via email'. Introducing the Cyber Café earned his restaurant the McDonald's New Zealand 2001 Innovation Award.

A second McDonald's Cyber Café opened at a restaurant in Tel Aviv, Israel, later in 2001, and Auckland trials started in early 2002. In May 2002, the Japanese branch announced plans to provide broadband Web service in all 4000 of its restaurants. Unlike Dunedin's Cyber Café (where computer terminals are provided) the Japanese restaurants will feature a wireless network allowing customers to bring their own mobile devices, including laptops, to surf while they eat.

*   *   *

Rated as one of the world's most recognised brands since 1966, McDonald's has a presence in over 120 countries—some of which have websites with links to the parent company's site. The Australian and New Zealand sites target consumers, potential employees, and those interested in franchising information. Although neither site features Cyber Cafés at the time this was written, it is likely that they will when the concept becomes more established (and when McDonald's wishes to promote their presence). The McDonald's New Zealand site won an 'Outstanding Website' award at the international Web Marketing Association's 2001 annual WebAwards—the only NZ site to win such an award, out of 800 worldwide entries.

Source: Contributed by Andre Everett (details of sources are listed on p. 735).

Weblinks:
www.mcdonalds.com/
links to Australian and New Zealand sites:
(www.mcdonalds.com.au and
www.mcdonalds.co.nz)

Activities for discussion, analysis and further research

1. Why was Australasia's and possibly the world's first McDonald's Cyber Café introduced in Dunedin? How much research should a company conduct before introducing a new service or product? How do the demographics and the relative isolation of Dunedin fit the needs for trialling an innovation?

2. How can information be disseminated within a company? How does the size of the organisation affect this? What are the implications of information dissemination relative to innovations?

3. Should other restaurants introduce Web access? How well does Web culture 'fit' with various types of restaurants? What disadvantages can you see for McDonald's and for other restaurants? Find other cyber cafés, locally or on-line, as well as some restaurants without cyber cafés, and test your theories

PROMOTING INNOVATION: CONTRIBUTIONS OF THE MAJOR VIEWPOINTS

Each major viewpoint has added to current management knowledge and changed managers' thoughts about organisations and behaviour in them (Hill & Jones 1995). The major contributions of these viewpoints are shown in Table 2.6.

While it would be easy to dismiss these contributions as 'history' and irrelevant to today's organisations, this would be shortsighted. During your time in industry you will find many examples of people using or applying these models/approaches on a regular basis. Understanding the models gives you a clear advantage in those interactions.

TABLE 2.6 MAIN INNOVATIVE CONTRIBUTIONS OF MAJOR VIEWPOINTS

Viewpoint	Innovative contributions
Classical	Highlights the need for a scientific approach to management Points out work methods can often be improved through study Identifies a number of important principles useful in running organisations efficiently Emphasises pay's potential importance as a motivator
Behavioural	Spotlights managerial importance of factors such as communication, group dynamics, motivation and leadership Articulates practical applications of behavioural studies Draws on several disciplines such as management, psychology, sociology, anthropology and economics Highlights organisation members' importance as active human resources rather than as passive tools
Quantitative	Provides quantitative aids to decision making Develops quantitative tools to assist in providing products and services Pioneers new computer-based information systems for management
Contemporary (systems and contingency)	Emphasises organisations can be visualised as systems of interrelated parts Points out the potential importance of the environment and feedback to organisational success

Ford Motor charges ahead and into globalisation

Right around the world, through the mid-1980s, the automotive industry was experiencing a downturn. This state of affairs did not exclude Australia, nor did it exclude the Ford Motor Company. In fact, as a whole, the Ford Motor Company was haemorrhaging. Between 1979 and 1982, the company lost $3 billion. It had managed to acquire a reputation for producing cars designed for yesterday's consumers, and—worse—the quality was poor.

Cutting costs and raising quality were clear priorities. By the mid-1980s, the company had reduced its hourly workforce, cut back on white-collar workers and shut down eight plants in the US. The remaining 81 plants were revamped and upgraded technologically to make the work as efficient as possible. Computerised robots and upgraded inventory control were part of the massive changes. At the same time, Ford tied its efficiency and cost-cutting efforts in search of quality. It adopted the Japanese management view that

higher quality ultimately means lower costs. Such changes reduced costs by $5 billion by the mid-1980s, with another $5 billion in savings by the early 1990s.

The company also redirected the design of its cars. Whereas in the past the tendency had been to follow the competition, top management now told designers to 'design the kind of cars you would like to drive'. With the new approach, Ford has produced a number of models that have sold well.

Some of the less visible changes at Ford related to its new approach to internal management. Once considered to have the most autocratic managers in the automotive industry, the company launched a program called Employee Involvement that has pushed decision making to lower levels, including the assembly line. For example, assembly-line workers are now authorised to stop the line if they see a problem. Ford emphasises teamwork and uses the team concept to involve individuals from

various areas such as design, engineering and manufacturing in the development of new models. Ideas come from the bottom of the company as well as from the top.

The company is continuing to further dismantle the old corporate pyramid and place more emphasis on a matrix-type organisation structure, in which many parts of the organisation work together but retain their autonomy. As one part of the change, Ford eliminated separate North American and European engineering operations in favour of moving 15 000 employees into five worldwide product-development centres—four in Dearborn and one in Europe. Under this arrangement, instead of developing separate Escort-size cars for sale in Europe, the United States and Australia, the European centre would develop a basic design that could be modified for use in various markets. The other centres would be responsible for basic designs for other types of vehicles—for example, large cars and minivans or trucks. Through such an approach Ford had hoped to create excellent products within a shorter time period with increased efficiency so that vehicles could be sold at an affordable price. Within a year, though, the company was paring the number of centres back to three, an arrangement somewhat similar to the original one. Ford found that having so many centres was leading to confusion, duplicate work and turf battles. Purchasing was also to be globally integrated, but Ford is still struggling to make the approach work. Meanwhile, Ford has encountered price resistance to its cars, which are loaded with desirable new features but have hefty price tags. The company is quickly shifting gears, working on efficiencies in order to deliver the features desired by today's sophisticated customers at much more competitive levels.

A major challenge facing Ford is to sell its products in more markets. Ford has targeted China and India as high-priority countries for expansion. Indonesia, Thailand and Vietnam also are important. In addition, the company is expending major efforts to build a greater presence in Latin America, particularly in Argentina, Brazil and Venezuela.

As the century turned, Ford hoped to be much more efficient. One of the issues facing the company is industrial safety. A philosophy of health and happiness was the driving force behind a radical new approach Ford Australia has taken to occupational health and safety since the early 1990s. For this, Ford Australia received the 1998 Victorian WorkCover awards which recognised Ford's 'Process safety review', an innovative approach to ergonomics and safety risk assessment which was introduced at the earliest design stages of new vehicle programs.

Safer, more ergonomically comfortable work practices on the assembly line have been designed into the product—a process which goes back to the moment the first designer puts pen to paper on a new vehicle.

This award was a tribute to the teamwork and relentless commitment to safety improvement by many people throughout the company.

Source: Autoweb Pty Ltd and Web Publications.

Activities for discussion, analysis and further research

1. Identify influences from the classical, behavioural and quantitative viewpoints in the way the Ford Motor Company is managed today.
2. Use systems theory to contrast the way the Ford Motor Company operated at the time the Edsel was introduced with the way the company is currently operating, including its worldwide emphasis. You may need to visit the Ford web site to get some more information.
3. Explain the influence of Japanese management (Theory Z) on current management at the Ford Motor Company.
4. Identify some of Ford's competitors and log on to their web sites. Determine whether those organisations also went through similar evolutions. Why do you think that might have happened? Is Ford doing things better than they are? How do you know?

KIMBERLEY TURNER

AEROSAFE
RISK MANAGEMENT

I think there are two different things in management. One is the management function within the organisation and the second one is being a manager. And management is one of those fundamentals of business that in my mind is a combination of good business acumen, leadership and the ability to administer a range of functions. When you actually get that combination right you can run an organisation well and it runs smoothly, effectively, and it performs well. In terms of the function of management, different theories tell you different things, but in my mind, it's probably having an organisation that is cohesive, focused, well orchestrated and coordinated; where resources are actually identified and appropriately allocated. This sets up the framework or the infrastructure around your company, whereas to be a manager is actually to make sure all those things happen and to work

within a framework to get the results. So, if I think about what the difference is between management and being a manager, I believe it's the people aspect. Management is the structure and the framework whereas to be a manager you need to actually implement things within that framework in order to get results, and those are generally around people. My role as a manager has been quite interesting because all of my life I thought I'd love to end up in a management role and I've ended up there by default and a lot quicker than I imagined.

I think for me now, in our business, in our area of expertise, to be a good manager is to be an effective project manager, be an effective leader of people, an effective entrepreneur and an effective subject-matter advisor, and to effectively work within that framework that I was talking about.

I've formed some theories about the relationship between management, leadership and administration. Working in the Defence sector—command, leadership and management for them is bundled in to a suite of attributes and competencies captured in the one area. One aspect actually gives you the authority to be in charge, another is the influence to lead and the third is that structure and the actual discipline of management. So, if you can strike the balance with the combination of those areas, you can really become an effective manager.

The relationship between management and leadership is one which I do not believe is explored enough. That is very much about your ability to influence, and to achieve results within a structured and sustainable framework. If you don't have that framework you can get people to a certain place and then they'll flounder.

Strategies for improving

1. Select an organisation you know and determine to what degree Fayol's 14 principles apply.
2. To what degree does this organisation fit Weber's ideal bureaucracy model?
3. If this organisation has a long history, investigate whether the management style has evolved. How

closely does it follow the evolution of management theory generally? What social and environmental factors impacted on management style changes in this organisation?

Source: Jones et al. (2000).

SUMMARY

- While management practices can be traced to ancient times, the industrial revolution and the need for better ways to run emerging factory systems led to the development of management theories and principles. The initial ideas of preclassical writers such as Robert Owen, Charles Babbage and Henry R. Towne resulted in the identification of management as a significant field of inquiry. From this, four major viewpoints developed: classical, behavioural, quantitative and contemporary.

- The classical viewpoint seeks ways to more efficiently manage work and organisations. It includes three approaches. Scientific management, represented by the work of Frederick Winslow Taylor, Frank and Lillian Gilbreth, and Henry Gantt, focuses on improving worker efficiency by scientific study of work methods. The bureaucratic approach, pioneered by Max Weber, centres on the need for organisations to operate on a rational basis, rather than relying on whims of owners and managers. The administrative management approach, supported by Henri Fayol and Chester Barnard, explores principles used by managers to co-ordinate internal organisation activities.

- The behavioural viewpoint tries to understand factors affecting organisational behaviour. Hugo Münsterberg and Mary Parker Follett were early behaviourists. The Hawthorne studies showed that workers were not just production tools. These studies, although flawed, gave insights leading to the human relations movement, emphasising concern for the worker. Abraham Maslow's hierarchy of needs theory and Douglas McGregor's Theory X and Theory Y gave managerial guidance but were still general. The behavioural science approach, emphasising scientific research, built more specific theories about behaviour in organisations, to give practical managerial guidelines.

- The quantitative viewpoint focuses on mathematics, statistics and information aids in support of managerial decision making and effectiveness. It has three main branches. Operations research uses sophisticated mathematical and statistical methods to raise decision effectiveness. Operations management manages production and delivery of a firm's products and services. Management information systems design and implement computer-based information systems for management.

- Contemporary viewpoints are newer innovations in management thought. They include systems and contingency theories and more recent views. The systems theory approach sees firms as systems, with inputs, transformations, outputs and feedback. Contingency theory says the best managerial action depends on a situation's specific parameters. More recent views include approaches which may become major viewpoints if research supports them. Another view is Theory Z. This theory combines aspects of American and Japanese management into a modified approach appropriate to America. Another important view is total quality management.

- All major viewpoints contribute to management innovation. Other viewpoints will come as the field develops.

QUESTIONS FOR DISCUSSION AND REVIEW

1. Explain how preclassical contributors helped set the stage for the development of management as a science. Identify where you have used the guidelines in *Robert's Rules of Order* or seen them used. Why have the rules been so popular over time?

2. Contrast the three major approaches within the classical viewpoint: scientific management, bureaucratic management and administrative management. Give examples of how these approaches are reflected in a familiar company.

3. Review Frederick Taylor's scientific management principles. How effective do you think these principles would be in eliminating soldiering? What might be some disadvantages of his approach? What did Frank and Lillian Gilbreth add to Taylor's approach?

4. Summarise Mary Parker Follett's contributions. For each, give an example showing how relevant her ideas are today.

5. Explain the development of the behavioural viewpoint. How could a set of flawed studies—the Hawthorne studies—help bring about the behavioural viewpoint of management?
6. Differentiate between the three major approaches within the quantitative management viewpoint. How have computers aided the development of this viewpoint?
7. Explain the major ideas underlying the systems viewpoint. Use this viewpoint to analyse your college or university. To what extent would you consider it to be an open system? Give reasons for your view.
8. Describe the reasoning behind the contingency viewpoint. Why did it emerge? What implications are there for managerial education?
9. Explain the Theory Z approach to management. Under which system would you prefer to work: American (Type A), Japanese (Type J) or modified American (Type Z)? Why? Which system would work best in the following work environments: research, production, mining, agriculture, service?
10. Show how current management knowledge results from innovative processes involving many management pioneers. What can we learn about innovation from studying these people's ideas?

CRITICAL THINKING QUESTIONS

To answer some of these questions you will need to do further research. Useful references are given below each section of the questions.

This chapter reviews the roots of current approaches to management, ranging from the scientific, behavioural and quantitative to the contemporary. This section addresses issues facing managers today, concluding with a brief review of some of the so-called 'management fads' of the last two decades in order to discover how the cynical reaction to many of today's organisational innovations is related to the evolution of the art of management.

1. What can the manager of today learn from the study of 'management classics' such as those listed below?

   Machiavelli, Niccolo 1988, *The Prince*, Cambridge University Press (first published 1513).

   Burns, T. and Stalker, G.M. 1994, *The Management of Innovation*, Oxford University Press (revised edn).

   March, J.G. and Simon, H.A. 1958, *Organisations*, John Wiley & Sons.

   Katz, D. and Kahn, R.L. 1978, *The Social Psychology of Organisations*, John Wiley & Sons (2nd edn).

   Taylor, F.W. 1967, *The Principles of Scientific Management*, W.W. Norton (first published 1912).

   Lawrence, P.R. and Lorsch, J.W. 1986, *Organisation and Environment: Managing differentiation and integration*, Harvard Business School Press, (revised edn).

   Thompson, J.D. 1967, *Organisations in Action: Social science bases of administrative theory*, McGraw-Hill.

   Woodward, J. 1980, *Industrial Organisation: Theory and practice*, Oxford University Press, (2nd edn).

   One of the most famous sets of experiments in management history were the Hawthorne studies (see pp. 41–3).

2. The history of management thinking is partly about developing understanding about the norms of behaviour in the workplace. How did the findings of the Hawthorne experiments contribute to this?

Innovation and adaptability are key words for current organisations. According to Hayward (2002), one of the best books to find inspiration, advice and insights is Diffusion of Innovation by Rogers

(1962). This book appears quite dry and theoretical when placed alongside more contemporary offerings, such as Hamel's (2000) Leading the Revolution, which deals with the painful side of change that many other writers ignore. Part of the strength of modern management ideas probably stems from the fact that the management literature of today has become more accessible to the public as a whole.

3. What are some of the management theories from the last 20 years that are either declining in popularity or have seen their day?

4. Does this support the notion that management theories are just fads and that people only use the word 'guru' because, as Peter Drucker once claimed, 'charlatan' is too long?

(Material relevant to questions 3 and 4 may be found in Hayward, R. 2002, *Manage Your Reputation: How to Plan Public Relations to Build and Protect the Organization's Most Powerful*, Kogan Page, London; Rogers, E. 1962, *Diffusion of Innovation*, Free Press, New York; Hamel, G. 2000, *Leading the Revolution*, Harvard Business School Press, Boston.)

In his recent book, *Change Without Pain* (2003), Columbia Business School professor Eric Abrahamson suggests that 'make do and mend' is the new message for managers, and that organisations reinvent themselves by building on what they have. While management in the 1990s was characterised by the slash-and-burn rhetoric of business process re-engineering, Abrahamson suggests that the past three or four years has seen a turn in the intellectual tide. This has been manifest in the success of books such as Zook's (2003) *Beyond the Core* and Hargadon's (2003) *How Breakthroughs Happen*. The single greatest feature of all these works is the adoption of a conservative approach to the management of change.

5. How and why do you think that this new conservatism has arisen?

Professor Abrahamson suggests many organisations have now become addicted to change—and suffer accordingly with symptoms ranging from barely controlled chaos to employee anxiety, burnout and cynicism. The cure, he argues, is to introduce some stability and continuity. Instead of 'rip-and-replace', managers should adopt the attitude of 'make do and mend'.

6. What does this mean in practice?

Management fads and fashions will continue to come and go, some enjoying spectacular success under given conditions while others sink into relative obscurity. The main task of managers, and the reason they are paid the money they are, is to make the best judgment possible to ensure the success and continuation of the organisation.

(Material relevant to questions 5 and 6 may be found in Abrahamson, E. 2003, *Change Without Pain: How managers can overcome initiative overload, organisational chaos, and employee burnout*, Harvard Business School Press, Boston; Zook, C. 2003, *Beyond the Core*, Harvard Business Publications, Boston; Hargadon, A. 2003, *How Breakthroughs Happen*. Harvard Business Publications, Boston).

MANAGEMENT EXERCISES

Exercise 1 Management exercise: Problems at the ice-cream plant

You are manager of a plant producing a special type of extra-creamy ice-cream. Sales had increased every quarter for the past four years, until last quarter. During that quarter sales slipped 17 per cent; production was about 15 per cent below projections; absenteeism was about 20 per cent higher than in the previous quarter; and lateness increased steadily. You believe the problems are management-related, but you are unsure about the causes or steps to take to correct them. You decide to call in consultants to help determine what to do next. The consultants tell you they wholeheartedly support scientific management and usually look at problems from that point of view.

They mention other consultants in the area who tend to take other views. To get the fullest idea of what should be done at your plant, you call in five other consultants, each of whom supports one of the following approaches: administrative management, bureaucracy, human relations, quantitative management and systems theory.

Form a group with two classmates. Have each member select two of the six management approaches mentioned above. Ensure all approaches are included. Each member plays the role of a consultant for one approach they have selected and then repeats the process for their second role. The person should analyse likely problems at the ice-cream plant and offer solutions from the point of view of the management approach they represent. The other group members critique explanations presented by the consultant.

Exercise 2 Self-assessment exercise: What kind of a manager am I?

Select the response best describing how you would manage a group of employees.

What kind of manager am I?		
1 = Strongly disagree	3 = Neither agree nor disagree	5 = Strongly agree
2 = Somewhat disagree	4 = Somewhat agree	

_____ 1 I would normally give explicit instructions concerning both what is to be accomplished and how it is to be done.

_____ 2 I would make sure subordinates know they could lose their jobs if they do not produce well.

_____ 3 I would motivate mainly through an incentive awards program based on individual output.

_____ 4 I would measure individual contribution based strictly on economic efficiencies.

_____ 5 I would make an effort to recognise and develop individual skills.

_____ 6 I would install a detailed monitoring system to ensure everyone follows proper procedures.

_____ 7 I would attempt to arrange organisational and personal goals so both could be accomplished simultaneously.

_____ 8 I would intervene immediately, at will, to modify an employee's behaviour to reach the organisation's goals.

_____ 9 If I had to choose between using an employee for something today or having that employee gain experience for the future, I would emphasise output for today.

_____ 10 I would rely on my subordinates' imagination and creativity to solve organisational challenges.

Hills finds millions in the backyard

The great Australian backyard is rarely thought of as a seedbed of innovative business ideas. In 1946, the spreading branches of Lance Hill's orange trees were making it difficult for his wife to hang out the clothes on the washing line strung between two poles. Lance built a 'weird contraption' to solve the problem, unwittingly creating the prototype for the internationally successful Hills rotary clothes hoist. Lance and his brother-in-law Harold Ling turned the South Australian backyard innovation into a laundry product manufacturing operation that expanded through organic growth and acquisitions to become Hills Industries. Today the global diversified industrial company employs over 2500 people in Electronics, Building and Industrial, and Home and Hardware business units.

POWERWEB

International articles related to this topic are available at the Online Learning Centre at www.mhhe.com/au/bartol4e

Gaining market share through innovation has remained a constant emphasis of Hills Industries. The company pioneered a research and development program in 1955, and were able to capture a niche in the developing television market through designing and producing a range of television antennae. Today they are the largest antenna producer in Australia and the company continues to invest in research and development to develop new products, upgrade existing products, and to improve production performance and efficiency.

The company retains market share by providing high-quality products, achieved through an emphasis on total quality management (TQM) throughout the organisation. When a problem with quality emerges, it is not just the senior management or professionals who attack the problem. In the company's UK operation, management shut down a production line that had been printing defective labels on plastic pressure vessels. The operators rather than the engineers were asked to produce a solution, and the instructions, training and operating diagrams they produced solved the problem. The production line was closed for 20 days, but management felt that the costs outweighed the benefits as the process

sent an invaluable message to workers that quality is both a serious issue and a mutual responsibility.

Hills Industries keeps its employees motivated through a number of programs that accommodate both the classical and the behavioural management viewpoints. The company sets remuneration according to market surveys conducted by independent national remuneration consultants. The majority of staff (60 per cent) are participants in a profit-sharing scheme. Employees are also eligible to join an employee share scheme after working for the company for one year. The company encourages non-monetary motivators with formal social clubs at larger workplaces that provide social events and discounts on a range of products and services.

The management philosophy of the company plays a key role in the company's success. Leadership and responsibility is devolved where possible, with senior managers operating business units autonomously within a framework of financial control, a focus on customer satisfaction through better and innovative products, and an emphasis on job satisfaction for employees. Managers must be approachable and visible, and the family origins of the company influence the idea that families are an important part of Hills Industries' culture. One of the senior management will dress as Santa at annual Christmas picnics, and other family days are also part of the organisational culture.

The story of the Hills Industries' backyard origin and the rotary clothes hoist as a recognisable icon of innovation have become not only part of the company's organisational culture, but also an important part of Australian business history.

Source: Contributed by Peter Woods (details of sources are listed on p. 735).

Activities for discussion, analysis and further research

1. What management practices of Hills Industries could be attributed to the classical viewpoint?
2. How have management practices attributable to the behavioural viewpoint helped Hills Industries?
3. How have contemporary management viewpoints contributed to the success of Hills Industries?

FURTHER READING

Euroweek 2003, China climbs to top of Asian debt tree as upgrade, spaceshot power demand, 10/24, 826, pp. 1–3.

Houston, D.J. and McKean, J.K. 2002, Quality management in New Zealand: A critical review, *Total Quality Management*; September, 13, 6, pp. 749–59.

Sila, I.E.M. 2003, Examination and comparison of the critical factors of total quality management (TQM) across countries, *International Journal of Production Research*; 1/20, 41, 2, pp. 235–69.

Yadong L. 2002, Capability exploitation and building in a foreign market: Implications for multinational enterprises, *Organization Science: A Journal of the Institute of Management Sciences*; January/February, 13, 1, pp. 48–64.

Yu, Z. and Jun, L.Z. 2002, Responsibility cost control system in China: The Han Dan experience, *Asia Pacific Business Review*; Autumn, 9, 1, pp. 59–79.

CHAPTER 3

UNDERSTANDING INTERNAL AND EXTERNAL ENVIRONMENTS

CHAPTER OUTLINE

Types of external environments
Mega-environment
Task environment

Analysing environmental conditions
Views of the organisation–environment interface
Characteristics of the environment

Managing environmental elements
Adaptation
Favourability influence
Domain shifts

The internal environment: Organisational culture
Nature of organisational culture
Manifestations of organisational culture
Promoting innovation: An adaptive, entrepreneurial culture
Changing organisational culture
How leaders influence cultural change

LEARNING OBJECTIVES

After studying this chapter, you should be able to:

- Explain the concept of mega-environment and outline its major elements.
- Distinguish between the concepts of task environment and mega-environment and describe major task environment elements.
- Contrast population ecology and resource dependence views of the organisation–environment interface.
- Explain how environmental uncertainty and bounty impact on organisations.
- Describe the major methods organisations use to manage their environments.
- Explain the nature of organisational culture and its major manifestations.
- Contrast entrepreneurial and administrative cultures as means of promoting innovation.
- Explain how organisational cultures can be changed.

Vince Gauci, chief executive, MIM Holdings

Ask a chief executive to talk about his greatest achievement and the chances are he will talk about an acquisition or a new project. Ask Vince Gauci, the managing director of MIM Holdings, and he talks about the closure of a smelter. More to the point, he talks about the fair treatment of the workers losing their jobs and the commitment made to rehabilitate the site.

Gauci believes that how you treat employees is a critical element in a corporation's culture. 'It is important,' he says. 'It is an important part of management culture, and an important part of winning the support of your people. It's a natural thing to do.'

Doing the right thing and being close to shop-floor workers has been a hallmark of Gauci's career. It stems from his roots as fourth-youngest in a family of 16 growing up in Broken Hill where his father, Larry, spent 40 years as an underground zinc-mine worker. And it expresses itself in his open-neck, standard-issue blue worker's shirt, complete with company logo on his left breast, badging him as an MIM worker. It is hard to imagine many other chief executives in their city offices dressed as if ready for a shift down a mine.

It is just as hard to picture this nuggetty little man as the boss of a business that once claimed the title of Australia's biggest listed company. That was for a few weeks in 1983 when the copper price was booming and MIM was seen as a contender to displace a lacklustre BHP as Australia's top mining company. But, almost from the time it hit top spot, MIM started a spectacular decline as a series of bad management decisions destroyed billions of dollars in shareholder wealth.

Seven years ago, the reformation began at MIM with the appointment of Nick Stump as chief executive. Stump brought with him a team that included Gauci, a mining engineer by training whose corporate career had included time with Rio Tinto, Denehurst and Pancontinental. The stable-cleaning that followed led to MIM quitting most of its non-core, non-performing assets. Management was overhauled. Suits were replaced by blue collars. Ties were out, badged workshirts in.

In theory, this is classic management by walking around, talking to the workers on the shop floor and leading by example.

The company is also benefiting from stripping out non-core operations and from a dramatic improvement in its coal business. The next big items on Gauci's agenda are expanding the Mount Isa copper business, possibly through the development of a big open-pit mine; repairing the hedge book; and introducing a new zinc processing technology to convert losses into profits.

Gauci has to do this while carrying the burden of past failures, the spectre of an Xstrata takeover, and the potential for investors to finally lose faith and sell out. Despite his rough edges and lack of city sophistication, Gauci may be just the man to keep MIM as one of Australia's few independent big miners.

The defensive moves are being made without fanfare: they are quiet and effective. It is what should be expected from a man who prides himself more on

continued

STRIVING FOR EXCELLENCE *continued*

getting things done than on being seen to be doing something. 'We're all pretty ordinary, coming from Broken Hill', says Gauci in a typically self-deprecating way. It is a comment made to divert attention, just as he avoids talking too much about himself, and always comes back to a common theme of praising the workforce and damning management as the cause of any corporate problems.

'There are no poor workforces in this country', he says. 'You have to provide the leadership.' Gauci, a fitness fanatic who, at 60, could pass for 50, falls back on sporting analogies as a way of explanation. 'Have a look at the Australian cricket team and look at how well it is managed. Leadership makes all the difference.'

Gauci says everyone responds to good leadership if they respect the leader. 'It's not about popularity, it's about respect. All of our general managers talk directly with the workforce throughout the year. In the big operations it might be once a quarter. At Mount Isa that means talking to 2000 people in groups of 60 or 70.'

Gauci's office tells a bit more about the man. It is spartan. There is a large photograph of a youthful Sir Donald Bradman on one wall, and mine-site mementos on the window ledges. There is also a wire-mesh outward mail tray that could easily have seen service at Broken Hill 40 years ago. There are no flash fittings in Gauci's world.

This is how Gauci works, with the team in mind, and a total commitment to doing the right thing and getting a result.

Source: Based on Treadgold, T. (2003).

Update: Despite the public protestations of Vince Gauci regarding the offered share price, MIM Holdings was acquired by Xstrata plc in a high-profile takeover in June 2003. Vince Gauci has since joined a number of his MIM executives and Nippon Mining and Metals to form a new private mining venture called Gallipoli Mining which now operates out of Brisbane.

---

external environment

Major forces outside the organisation with potential to influence significantly the likely success of a product or service

internal environment

General conditions existing within an organisation

organisational culture

System of shared values, assumptions, beliefs and norms uniting members of an organisation

An organisation's effectiveness is influenced by its **external environment**—the major forces outside the organisation able to impact on the success of its products or services. In addition, organisations which could be successful are unable to be unless their **internal environment**, or general internal conditions, is compatible with the external environment. The organisation's internal environment includes members, their interactions and physical setting. The term **organisational culture** is often applied to an organisation's internal environment. Organisational culture is a system of shared values, assumptions, beliefs and norms uniting an organisation's members (Smircich 1983; Kilmann, Saxton & Serpa 1986; Bateman & Snell 2004).

In this chapter, we first look at an organisation's external environment. We consider the mega-, or general, environment within which an organisation functions, and the more specific elements which comprise the task environment. We also explore the relationship between an organisation and its environment, considering significant environmental characteristics. Next we look at the management of environmental elements. Finally, we examine the internal environment by looking at how an organisation's culture can influence success. Our discussion also considers how innovation and entrepreneurial culture are related.

TYPES OF EXTERNAL ENVIRONMENTS

The Warren Featherbone Company had a problem—it could see the ebb of a lucrative market. Over a century ago the company built a thriving business around a patented product, the featherbone. Stiffening corsets, collars, bustles and gowns, the featherbone was made of finely split turkey quills woven into a cord. Though the company survived the Great Depression, technological changes such as plastic were emerging. By 1938 the company started making plastic baby pants to cover nappies, just as featherbone demand fell. It then made a shaky move into baby clothing. Happily, its baby clothing became established by the mid-1960s, as the disposable nappy was developed and destroyed demand for plastic pants (Morgenthaler 1989). As the Warren Featherbone Company's history shows, an organisation's environment is crucial. Organisations must be ready to change and innovate.

Systems theory shows the importance of the environment to organisations. According to this view, an organisation will be more successful if it operates as an open system interacting with, and getting feedback from, its external environment (see Chapter 2). This means managers must understand their organisation's external environment. An external environment comprises two segments: the mega-environment, or general environment, and the task environment. Figure 3.1 shows these segments and their elements. (The internal environment, in terms of organisational culture, is also shown. Organisational culture is discussed later in this chapter.)

Mega-environment

The **mega-environment**, or general environment, is the external environment segment reflecting broad conditions and trends in societies within which an organisation operates. The mega-environment has five major elements: technological, economic, legal-political, sociocultural and international (see Fig. 3.1) (David 1987; Hall 1987). Because these reflect major external trends and conditions, a single organisation's ability to affect or alter them directly, at least short-term, is limited. The Xerox Corporation's mega-environment is shown in Figure 3.2.

Technological element

The **technological element** reflects current knowledge about product and service generation. Although specific technical knowledge and patents give an organisation a competitive edge for a time, eventually technological progress affects all, positively or negatively.

Research in the minicomputer, cement and airline industries shows technological development has periods of incremental change punctuated by breakthroughs which either build or destroy the competence of firms in an industry (Tushman & Anderson 1986; Barnett 1990). For example, in 1947 Nobel prize-winning Bell Laboratory physicists invented the transistor, opening the computer age. Later development of microchips changed businesses and

mega-environment

The broad conditions and trends in societies in which an organisation operates

techological element

Current state of knowledge regarding production of products and services

FIGURE 3.1   The internal and external environments of the organisation

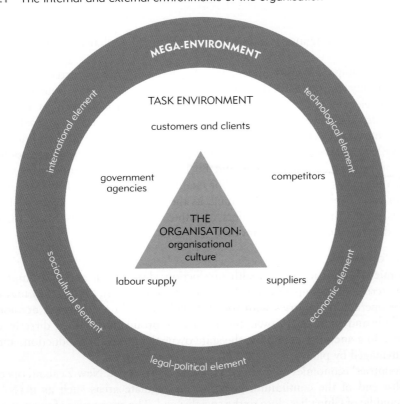

FIGURE 3.2   Elements of the mega-environment of the Xerox Corporation

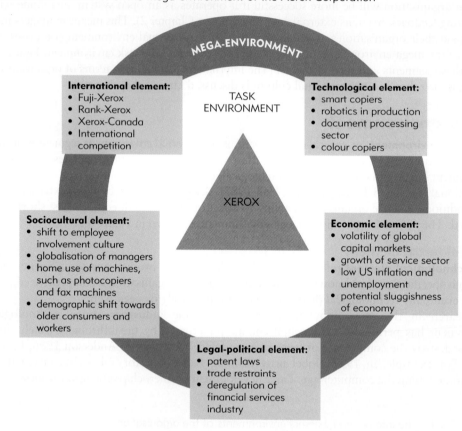

products in industries ranging from automobile and small-appliance manufacturing to home building.

Competitive companies must understand the developments in current technology which affect their ability to offer needed products and services. Many sources give data on environmental elements. These include major business journals (such as *Business Review Weekly*, *Forbes*, *Asia Week* and *Fortune*), specific industry trade journals, government publications, business services (including Dun & Bradstreet indexes), and on-line services (such as LEXIS/NEXIS, a service accessing a range of publications and information sources).

In the competition between Airbus and Boeing there were a number of instances where technological elements were significant. For example, the cockpits of all Airbus models are designed for ease of pilot transition training, as they are consistent in control placement and layout. This means the training of pilots on other Airbus models is easier than transition training on different Boeing aircraft models.

Economic element

The **economic element** involves wealth production, distribution and consumption systems. Firms in Western countries operate largely in capitalist economies, though they may do business with and/or operate in countries with socialist economies. In a **capitalist economy**, market forces operate and individuals own the means of production, either directly or through corporations. In a **socialist economy**, the state owns the means of production, and economic activity is managed by plan.

Most countries' economies are hybrid. Though Australia and New Zealand operate close to the capitalist end of the continuum, governments regulate areas such as mass media. The People's Republic of China lies close to the socialist end. The economies of most countries, such

---

economic element

Systems of producing, distributing and consuming wealth

capitalist economy

Economy in which economic activity is governed by market forces and the means of production are owned by individuals

socialist economy

Economy in which means of production are owned by the state and economic activity is co-ordinated by plan

as Singapore, Thailand and Indonesia, fall between the extremes. Third-world countries (poor countries with low per capita income, little industry and high birthrates) have different patterns as they struggle to decide to follow capitalist or socialist models.

Due to these differences, organisations operating in several countries face many different economic ground rules (Standard & Poor 1993). Within any economic system, of course, firms face economic factors they cannot control, such as inflation, interest rates and recessions.

In China, overseas education providers are attempting to move into the highly regulated compulsory education sector. One significant blockage is that ministry approvals are only granted on one day a year, and if a submission is unsuccessful, an amended submission cannot be made for a further 12 months.

Legal-political element

The **legal-political element** refers to legal and governmental systems within which an organisation operates. Legislative trends, legal decisions, politics and government regulation are significant legal-political environment aspects.

For example, organisations work in a general legal framework for each country they operate in, and face many laws regulating their operations (Salpukas 1994; Snow 2003). These include Acts focused on pollution control and occupational health and safety. Organisations face growing lawsuits filed both by employees and clients. These have been driven by juries awarding large sums, especially in product-liability cases (Finn 1987; Skrzycki 1989; Kesner & Johnson 1990).

The legal system is also influenced by political processes. Government regulation may come from political issues. For instance, share market scandals result in political pressure on regulatory bodies for computerised tracking and criminal prosecutions of illegal stock trading by 'insiders'. Insider trading involves stock transactions by people who have information affecting stock prices, such as company officers or investment bankers.

> **legal-political element**
>
> Legal and governmental systems within which an organisation must function

Sociocultural element

The **sociocultural element** includes attitudes, values, norms, beliefs, behaviours and typical regional demographic trends. Sociocultural variables are important when considering different countries. Sociocultural differences influence multinational companies' competitive success. McDonald's has recognised this, insisting that its foreign franchisees stick to operating procedures, but allowing varied marketing methods or a few menu modifications. For example, in Brazil McDonald's sells a soft drink made from an Amazonian berry, and in Malaysia menus have milk shakes flavoured with durian, a South-East Asian fruit believed to be an aphrodisiac (Deveny 1986).

Because sociocultural aspects change, managers must monitor new opportunities or threats. Changes in sociocultural trends mean demand can shift across product types. Among current changes affecting regional markets are delayed marriage, more single-parent households, greying baby-boomers, an increasingly diverse workforce, longer lifespans requiring more elderly care, company downsizings and the growing influence of minorities in business, politics and community life (Bell 1987; Davies 1995).

> **sociocultural element**
>
> Attitudes, values, norms, beliefs, behaviours and associated demographic trends characteristic of a given geographic area

International element

The **international element** of the mega-environment includes changes in countries other than the organisation's home country which can impact on the company. The international element's influence is generally significant and growing in importance.

International issues affect how an organisation conducts business overseas. For example, currency fluctuations influence a firm's global competitiveness. When the domestic currency's value is high against foreign currencies, the international competitiveness of domestic companies is restricted and options reduced. Conversely, when the local currency drops against foreign currencies, new production or market options emerge.

An illustration of this is aviation fuel, typically priced in US dollars. When conversion rates change, airlines find their profits under pressure and may write forward contracts to protect themselves against those currency movements.

> **international element**
>
> Developments in countries outside an organisation's home country with potential to influence the organisation

Free trade agreements such as the North American Free Trade Agreement (NAFTA) (Canada, Mexico and the United States) offer long-term growth options. Goods, services and funds typically move more freely between members, as tariffs and other trade barriers drop. These agreements produce major changes in the competitiveness of individual businesses (Bhagwati 1988). Thus managerial efforts are directly affected by international factors largely beyond an organisation's control.

CASE IN POINT

Customer Service Institute of Australia

Within any organisation operating in today's competitive global business environment, consumers are constantly bombarded with products and services that seem the same in terms of their use, quality and delivery, and they often have similar prices. How then do organisations involved in the delivery of products or services make themselves shine out from the rest? The answer, according to many, is a commitment to excellent customer service.

Finding out about organisations that provide excellent customer service has often meant choosing a firm based upon word-of-mouth reports from colleagues, friends or family, or relying upon the reports of the companies themselves. However, in 1997 the Customer Service Institute of Australia was formed to be 'dedicated to the professional development of organisations and individuals in customer service'.

Seeing that a major problem for consumers is evaluating customer service in an impartial and uniform manner across industries, the Customer Service Institute created a universal accreditation system. The implementation of the International Customer Service Standard has meant that businesses can apply to be scrutinised by the Institute and, if they meet the rigorous criteria, can be awarded this competitive international standard. This standard, as the Institute states, 'aim(s) to help shift the business focus from Product or Service OUT to Customer IN. This means creating an environment where customer input is largely responsible for determining the product or service output, rather than where the supplier or service-giver attempts to

force their product or service on the customer in the hope that it will meet customer needs and generate loyalty'.

It is also the intention of the Institute to have as many firms as possible endeavour to attain the award, and thus take an outward-in look at their own business's customer service standards and improve them. The Customer Service Institute of Australia also provides consultation and assistance to any organisation, bringing an extensive combined knowledge-base which allows the Institute not only to act as a regulatory body, but also as a peak customer service improvement consultant. If high-quality customer service is internationally regarded as crucial for long-term business growth, development and success, then an increasing number of businesses may turn to organisations such as the Customer Service Institute of Australia for assistance in bringing them up to the international standard.

Source: Contributed by Joel Mendelson; Customer Service Institute of Australia website www.csia.com.au/.

Activities for discussion, analysis and further research

1. Why do you think there has been a global increase in the standard of customer service demanded by individuals and organisations?

2. Go into an organisation or retail outlet which you often visit and observe the customer service techniques. Make a list of ways in which you think they could improve their customer service, and ways in which you think they are already effectively serving their clients.

3. In a small group choose an industry and establish which types of clients you are going to target and what you think their needs will be. Based upon this, outline the service techniques that you would implement in order to be seen as internationally competitive in terms of customer service.

Task environment

The **task environment** is the external environment segment comprising the specific external elements an organisation faces. This environment depends on the products, services and locales where an organisation operates. Any organisation has difficulty influencing the mega-environment, but may affect its task environment. The major task environment includes customers and clients, competitors, suppliers, employees and government bodies. Each organisation must assess its own situation to determine its specific task environment. Elements of the Xerox Corporation's task environment are shown in Figure 3.3.

Customers and clients

An organisation's **customers and clients** are people and firms buying its products and/or services. Many organisations work to be close to the customer, particularly attending to service and quality, and listening to customers to try to serve them better (*New York Times* 1995; Erlick 1995; Wyman 1996; Howarth 2003).

Competitors

An organisation's **competitors** are other firms offering or potentially offering rival products or services. Organisations must focus on known competitors and monitor for potential new entrants (Kuntz 1995).

Organisations must be aware of competitors' activities. For example, Xerox benchmarks competitor activities and costs. To understand Kodak's distribution and handling costs, for instance, Xerox managers ordered Kodak copiers, noting details such as the shipping source and methods, even the packaging (McComas 1986). For ideas on how companies get competitor information, see the Management skills for a globalised economy section, 'Keeping tabs on competitors'.

task environment

Specific outside elements with which an organisation interfaces in the course of conducting its business

customers and clients

Individuals and organisations purchasing an organisation's products and/or services

competitors

Other organisations either offering or with a high potential for offering rival products or services

FIGURE 3.3 Elements of the task environment of the Xerox Corporation

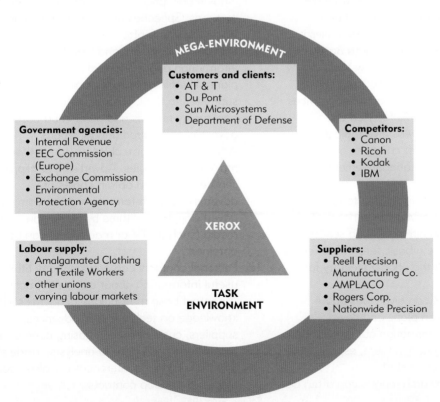

Suppliers

suppliers

Organisations and individuals supplying resources an organisation needs to conduct its operations

An organisation's **suppliers** are companies and people providing resources (including raw materials, products or services) to conduct operations. Traditionally, having many suppliers was seen as desirable to reduce dependence on any one. Global competition changes this. Firms find they can lower costs with fewer contracted suppliers. In 1980, Xerox worldwide had 5000 vendors of parts and components. Now with fewer vendors, Xerox has tougher quality standards, gets better prices, and builds more co-operative supplier relationships (Byrne 1987).

Labour supply and the importance of managing diversity

labour supply

Individuals potentially employable by an organisation

An organisation's **labour supply** is people employable by the organisation. Being able to attract, motivate and retain human resources to provide products and services is crucial (Pyatt 1986). Employers can expect to recruit from a more diverse labour supply (*Economist* 1990). For example, a breakdown of the Australian labour force by birthplace for 1998–9 is shown in Table 3.1.

MANAGEMENT SKILLS FOR A GLOBALISED ECONOMY

Keeping tabs on competitors

Here are 10 legal ways to track what your competitors are doing:

1. Commercial databases are an easy way to get information. Databases contain published articles from newspapers, magazines and trade publications, as well as stock analyst reports, patent applications, biographical information, etc. The information can be accessed by computer. Information on various databases is found in the Directory of Online Data Bases, published by Cuandra/Elsevier (New York). Many firms have web sites with information on new products, special promotions and other activities.

2. Specialty trade publications focused on industries and product areas give topical information on major staff changes, product advertising, new product announcements, trade show notices and so on.

3. Local newspaper news clippings often give specific information unavailable in national publications. You can hire a clipping service. Clipping services have a basic fee, with a fee for each clipping. Check the phone directory for clipping services.

4. Advertised vacancies can give clues about competitors' expansion plans and new technologies, even information about financial status may be embedded in them, especially in advertisements for senior staff.

5. Published market-research reports can often be useful.

6. Stock reports give information about public companies (stock is publicly traded) and any subsidiaries through analysis by securities analysts at brokerage firms.

7. Trade shows and product literature supplied at them are good information sources on product innovations, price changes and marketing methods. Speeches and presentations given at trade shows are often helpful as well.

8. Public filings (federal and state) often give information about financial data and future plans. The filings include public company reports submitted to the Corporate Affairs Commission, bankruptcy records and other court cases and government-required annual reports.

9. Advertisements give clues on competitors' marketing strategies. Advertising or clipping services can often obtain copies of advertisements. Information about competitors' advertising expenditures by product in various media (such as TV or magazines) can be obtained.

10. Personal contacts can provide many titbits of useful information about competitor activities. A contact base may include academics with knowledge on technological advances, suppliers, customers, purchasing agents, service technicians and financial analysts. Trade shows and professional conferences are also good places to develop contacts.

Source: Fuld 1989; 1988.

AYS Stevedoring—Changing corporate culture

You may recognise the situation described under anonymous terms in the following exercise. If you do, look up information and newspaper reports of the incidents. Do you think the organisations concerned made appropriate decisions considering the circumstances of the environment they were operating in?

Assume there is a port where three companies carry out most of the stevedoring work. The companies are Stevedoring A, Stevedoring B and AYS Stevedoring (AYS is an acronym for At Your Service). AYS Stevedoring are a new entrant to the market. Stevedoring A and B had long-lasting, well-established contracts with little or no outside competition (or so they thought) and tended to give little thought to future customers or outside influences. In both Stevedoring A and Stevedoring B the culture was one of complacency.

The complacent cultures of Stevedoring A and B led them to believe that the new company would not be a threat, the market was considered 'closed' and the new competitor would not gain enough work to survive. They thought that the small contracts that the new competitor obtained would not be of great consequence. They were incorrect. In a short time AYS Stevedoring grew from strength to strength and gained many additional contracts on the way.

The factors that have contributed to the success of AYS Stevedoring are:

Customer service—They had a positive attitude to work and were helpful towards both internal and external customers. Their outlook towards current and future business clients was highly professional. The ship owners, freight forwarders and numerous other port users were eager to trial the new company in an effort to increase their productivity, save money and improve their customer service.

Responsiveness—Response times for the new company for most tasks requested were well in front of the competitors'. This further highlighted a lack of enthusiasm from existing competitors.

Price—As the company grew and acquired contracts, it maintained a level of professionalism while offering competitive prices. This combination of professional service and competitive pricing has proved to be a powerful incentive to importers and exporters.

Personal contact—The level of personal contact from senior management and supervisors helped to cement relationships and ensure customers were confident with the dealings of the company.

Source: Allison Powell, Australian Maritime College.

Activities for discussion, analysis and further research

1. The general manager of Stevedoring A seeks your advice as to how to improve the situation. What steps should be taken to change organisational culture? What can be done to embed and maintain the cultural change?
2. The manager of AYS Stevedoring asks you what can be done to ensure that they retain and increase market share in the changing environment. How can they ensure that the organisation will hang on to its market share? What steps can they take to increase their market share?

These figures show some of the variation in life experiences of Australia's workforce. Local migration patterns will also impact on the workforce diversity of many regional countries.

In combination, diversity and the baby boomers are significantly impacting workforce make-up. However, the influence of diversity will grow and the baby-boomer impact will drop. Researchers have identified trends based on Australian Bureau of Statistics (ABS) data. Currently 75 per cent of workers are Australian born and about 60 per cent from Australian-born parents. Others come from many countries, the majority still being from mainly English-speaking countries. The rate of increase of women in the labour force is slowing; six out of ten working-age women are in the labour force. This is approaching men's labour-participation

TABLE 3.1 AUSTRALIAN LABOUR FORCE BY BIRTHPLACE 1998–9

	Total
Birthplace	
Born in Australia	7 083 000
Born outside Australia	2 316 000
Total	**9 399 000**
Country of origin	
Oceania	284 100
Europe and former USSR	1 217 200
Middle East and North Africa	97 500
South-East Asia	284 500
North-East Asia	136 200
Northern America	53 300
Other	243 200
Total	**2 316 000**
Language	
Main English-speaking countries	987 300
Other countries	1 328 700
Total	**2 316 000**

Source: Adapted from ABS (2000).

rate, although more women are in part-time employment than men. Minority workforce participation is growing, in part due to higher rates of minority-group immigration and labour participation increases by minority-group women. The labour force is still growing, but more slowly than over the 1970s and 1980s, when baby boomers entered it in increasing numbers. Overall, by 2050, Australia's population is expected to pass 23 million, compared with 18.9 million in 1998 (http://www.immi.gov.au/facts/13pop.htm; http://www.immi.gov.au/facts/11fifty.htm; http://www.statistics.gov.au/websitedbs/c311).

The New Zealand population reached 4 million in 2003. At the time of the 2001 Census, people from European ethnicity comprised 80 per cent of the resident population, those identifying as Maori comprised 14.7 per cent, the Pacific People ethnic group (including Samoan, Tongan, Cook Island, Maori and Fijian) 6.5 per cent, Asian group 6.5 per cent, and Other (including Arab, Iranian, Somali and Latin American) comprise 0.7 per cent of the New Zealand population. (The percentage total is greater than 100 because people can identify with one or more occupational group.) (Statistics New Zealand 2002)

Baby boomers have dominated the workforce for two decades, but this is diminishing. By 2005 they will be less than half the labour force, down from about 55 per cent in the mid-1980s. The first baby boomers were 55 years old in 2001, and by 2005 many more baby boomers will move into the older-worker category. Older workers will be about 14.7 per cent of the workforce by 2005, rather than 12.3 per cent in 1998.

This is why many firms have set up programs to help organisation members value and use a more diverse workforce.

With growing globalisation, workers (especially better-educated ones) will move to countries needing their skills, despite migration laws discouraging the moves (Johnston 1991; Eisenhardt & Brown 1998). Labour supply issues are discussed in Chapter 10.

Government agencies

Various **government agencies** provide services and monitor compliance with laws and regulations at local, state or regional, and national levels. Usually the task environment requires interactions with representatives of different government agencies (e.g. tax, consumer affairs, police, health, and workers' compensation).

government agencies

Agencies providing services and monitoring compliance with laws and regulations at local, state or regional, and national levels

ANALYSING ENVIRONMENTAL CONDITIONS

Though most researchers agree the environment is influential, views differ on how organisations and their environments are related. In this section, we examine two major views of the organisation–environment interface, then explore major environmental characteristics.

Views of the organisation–environment interface

Among major approaches explaining the interface are the population ecology and resource dependence models (Hall 1987; Ulrich & Barney 1984).

Population ecology model

The **population ecology model** focuses on populations or groups of organisations, arguing that environmental factors cause those with appropriate characteristics to survive and others to fail. Thus, firms can survive whether particular environmental conditions suit them or not. This is also known as the **natural selection model**. Since organisations change slowly, the view is that managers have little chance to affect their company's fate (Hannan & Freeman 1977; Bennon & Dress 1985).

On its 70th anniversary in 1987 *Forbes* magazine published a study of environmental results. Forbes looked at which of the 100 largest companies (in asset terms) in 1917 were among the largest 100 companies 70 years later. Only 22 of the firms were still on the list in 1987. Of these, 11 had the same name as in 1917 (American Telephone & Telegraph; Eastman Kodak; E. I. Du Pont de Nemours; Ford Motor; General Electric; General Motors; Pacific Gas & Electric; Procter & Gamble; Sears, Roebuck; Southern California Edison; and Westinghouse Electric). Another 11 had changed names. The 78 departures from the list had varied fates. Some grew too slowly; some were acquired; some faltered and faded. At the defunct Baldwin Locomotive, for example, executives believed steam locomotives would not be replaced by new technology. Atlantic Gulf & West Indies Steam Ship Lines had lost ships (*Forbes* 1987). Could anything have helped these firms prosper? Supporters of the population ecology model do not think so. However, the resource dependence model sees the situation differently.

population ecology

Model focusing on populations or groups of organisations and arguing that environmental factors cause organisations with appropriate characteristics to survive and other to fail

natural selection model

Term sometimes used for the population ecology model

Resource dependence model

The **resource dependence model** sees organisations as being dependent on the environment for resources, arguing that they manipulate their environment to reduce dependence (Pfeiffer & Salancik 1978; Ulrich & Barney 1984). In this view, organisations cannot generate all resources needed (e.g. financing, materials and services). For example, the Ford Motor Corporation buys many parts rather than make them. Forming relationships helps solve many organisation resource problems. However, these build dependency and reduce flexibility in decision making and action. So organisations seek independence by controlling critical resources or developing alternatives.

For example, IBM developed the PS/2 personal computer and contracted Microsoft to develop the OS/2 operating system. By doing this, IBM sped up the introduction of its new computer. However, Microsoft developed the IBM system and also a better one called Windows. Windows could run on older IBMs, simplifying their use. Microsoft developed Windows to avoid being too dependent on the PS/2. Ironically, Windows slowed sales of IBM's new PS/2 computer. IBM developed its own software then, but too late to beat Windows (Zachary 1989; Burgess 1992). This shows how resource needs and dependence interrelate as organisations manage their environments.

resource dependence model

Model highlighting the organisation's dependence on the environment for resources and arguing that organisations attempt to manipulate the environment to reduce dependence

Compared to population ecology, which sees managerial actions as limited in dealing with the environment, resource dependence argues that managers have strategic choices, or options, and these influence organisational success. Managers have choices in both their reactions and their options in trying to influence their environment (Pfeiffer & Salancik 1978; Rue & Byars 2003). Hence, in the *Forbes* study, Baldwin Locomotive may have survived if managers had considered environmental change. Even Atlantic Gulf & West Indies Steam Ship Lines could have put some resources into safer ventures.

Reconciling the differing models

Managers find both population ecology and resource dependence models useful. The population ecology model shows that organisations have little control over influential environmental factors and that their success may be based more on luck.

The resource dependence model shows that managers can influence environmental aspects, including inter-organisational relations. Therefore they must monitor, understand and influence environmental elements, and realise major organisational impacts can come from unexpected elements.

Characteristics of the environment

Accurately assessing the environment is hard. An organisation's environment can be seen as objective reality—a set of measurable conditions where managers get complete information. However, managers are more likely to act on their perceived environment. Thus, the environment may be better seen as subjective reality within managers' minds (Weick 1995). As managers act on these perceptions they must verify through other information sources (perhaps others' opinions, as well as objective data) (Boyd, Dess & Rasheed 1993).

In analysing the organisation's environment, two key concepts are useful: environmental uncertainty and environmental bounty or capacity. Although task environment is the focus, some mega-environment trends must be considered.

Environmental uncertainty

environmental uncertainty

Condition in which future environmental circumstances affecting an organisation cannot be accurately assessed and predicted

Environmental uncertainty is when an organisation's future environment cannot be accurately assessed or predicted (Pfeiffer & Salancik 1978). As environmental uncertainty increases, managers must monitor, assess and act if needed. Two major factors influence the level of environmental uncertainty: complexity and dynamism (Dess & Beard 1984).

Complexity

environmental complexity

Number of elements in an organisation's environment and their degree of similarity

Environmental complexity is the number of elements in an organisation's environment and their degree of similarity. Where there are a few similar items environments are homogeneous. By contrast, heterogeneous environments have many dissimilar items. As environments become more heterogeneous, managers face more variables.

Dynamism

environmental dynamism

Rate and predictability of change in the elements of an organisation's environment

Environmental dynamism is the rate and predictability of change in the elements of an organisation's environment. When change is slow and fairly predictable, environments are stable. Conversely, where change is fast and fairly unpredictable, environments are unstable. As environmental elements become less stable, managerial challenge increases.

Assessing environmental uncertainty

The concepts of complexity and dynamism can help assess the degree of environmental uncertainty. This can be done by looking at important task-environment elements and major potential mega-environment influences (see Fig. 3.4). As cell 1 in Figure 3.4 suggests, uncertainty is low where both dynamism and complexity are low. This occurs in the funeral industry, with slow change and a steady stream of customers with similar needs. In cell 2 there is low dynamism but high complexity, and uncertainty is moderately low. This is typical of the insurance industry, where firms serve a diverse set of customer needs with slowly changing

FIGURE 3.4 Assessing the degree of environmental uncertainty (adapted from Duncan 1979, p. 63)

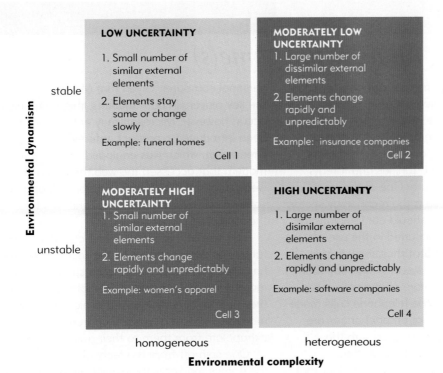

competitive elements. In cell 3, high dynamism but low complexity gives moderately high uncertainty. This characterises the women's clothing industry, where customers and retailers make up fairly homogeneous market segments but where fashion trends move rapidly. Finally, cell 4 has both high dynamism and high complexity, giving high uncertainty. The computer-software industry has high environmental uncertainty, where conditions change rapidly and many environmental factors (technological change, many diverse customers and hard competition) exert strong heterogeneous pressures.

Conditions of uncertainty may change. For example, a homogeneous and stable environment may gradually change to a more uncertain one. Then managers must reassess their situation.

Environmental bounty

Another important environmental element is **environmental bounty**: how much the environment supports sustained growth and stability (Aldrich 1979; Dess & Beard 1984). The range of environmental bounty goes from relatively rich to relatively lean, depending on organisational resource levels available (Castrogiovanni 1991). Firms in rich environments can build an internal resource cushion, such as capital, equipment and experience. High internal resource levels fund innovations and expansions to help a company keep its position, and weather leaner times. Unfortunately, other organisations are attracted to rich environments. An example of this is the continuing introduction of low cost airlines such as Virgin Blue, Paradise Air, Pacific Blue and Jet Star, and Freedom Air in New Zealand.

environmental bounty

Extent to which the environment can support sustained growth and stability

MANAGING ENVIRONMENTAL ELEMENTS

While managing environmental factors has limits, some writers (e.g. resource dependence model supporters) feel environmental elements respond to managerial action, advocating proactive measures. Carnival Cruise Lines for example, the largest cruise operator in the world,

Keeping up with the game(s)

The challenge for management is not only to follow technology trends but to actually lead in their application if possible. One way is to analyse the external environment of the organisation and to systematically trawl for opportunities and threats, keeping a keen eye on opportunities and threats that may emerge in the future. One of the most significant sources of these is the technology sector.

For example, managers should contemplate the amazing growth that has occurred in the use of email and mobile phones. Statistics show that in 2002 there were more emails sent in one day than in the whole of 1995, and more phone calls made on mobile phones than all the telephone calls made in the whole of 1985. So what other changes are possible? How do managers keep up with the changes and try to take advantage of them?

Apart from the telephone, another product that provides lessons in the potential for growth in the use of technology is the computer game. Howarth (2002) has this to say:

'Once dismissed as children's toys, video-game consoles are now challenging the movie and personal computing industries in terms of revenue. Last year the video-game industry turned over US$9.4 billion in the United States, compared with total box-office receipts of US$8.4 billion in cinemas.'

The release of the Nintendo Gamecube in the US grossed US$5 million more than the Harry Potter movie in its first week. Australians are spending approximately $450 million on games this financial year, which Microsoft is forecasting will grow to $678 million in the next financial year. In the UK the long-awaited Sony Play Station 2 was such a success even before its launch that Sony had to maintain secrecy on its rollout plans, as organised gangs targeted truckloads of the games. This was not a joke; two drivers were murdered by gangs that hijacked their trucks.

In companies involved with personal computers, management must consider whether game consoles will grow in sophistication and applications so as to merge with, and in some cases to replace, the personal computer. Given that Microsoft is one of the key players in both markets, this is unlikely to occur; however, Microsoft may not have all the say. Sega introduced a product, referred to as Dreamcast, which was equipped with an internal modem that accessed the web through a dedicated web portal. The product failed, for lack of game software for alternative games, and was taken off the market.

The size of the market—and confidence in its future—is demonstrated by the fact that Microsoft has allocated US$1 billion to be spent over eighteen months just to launch and promote Xbox. Even if they are not directly involved in high-tech products, managers should observe such trends and extrapolate from them to their own industries.

One spin-off from the technology developed for the games market is the availability of the same technology for training purposes. Firms are finding that there are ways of using interactive computing, graphics and artificial intelligence to provide realistic simulations of the workplace. An example of this is a CD that provides training in first aid. Real-life situations are featured on the CD and, by interacting with these situations in various tests, the trainee can actually gain a certificate without contact with another person—either trainer or subject!

Games technology could be harnessed in other applications, for instance allowing customers to 'test drive' a car before purchase without even sitting in it.

Source: Contributed by Ken Dooley (details of sources are listed on p. 735).

Websites:

www.nintendo.com
www.microsoft.com
www.sony.com

Activities for discussion, analysis and further research

1. The growth in the use of computer games is well known to many teenagers, but how much do

they really know? What do you know about the use of computer games? How much do you use them? Do you know others who use them? If so, how much do they use them and how much has this usage grown or declined?

2. Forecasting usage is not easy. Suggest reasons why the growth in computer games has been so dramatic. What arguments would you have offered against a growth in usage? What are the limits on their growth? What would you need to

know to make an estimate of their growth?

3. What possibilities do you see for games technology, in terms both of the games market and of its application in assisting management?

4. Check out the websites for Nintendo, Microsoft and Sony (see below) to evaluate their promotions and obtain an idea of the claims being made. Give some reasons why mature-age managers may miss the opportunities presented by these sites.

attracts passengers by targeting the mass market. Carnival's new cruises allow use of resort amenities at a reasonable cost (Booth 1992). There are three managerial options: adapt to environmental elements, try to make the environment more favourable and/or shift the operating domain from threatening environmental elements to more beneficial ones (Thompson 1967; Kotter 1979; Walters 2003). Major implementation methods are shown in Table 3.2. The situation depends on their feasibility, but prospects are better in a high-bounty environment or if the firm has built a cushion of resources.

Adaptation

The adaptation approach involves changing internal operations and activities to make the organisation and its environment more compatible. This strategy accepts the existing environment as a given and seeks to develop a rational process for adjusting to it. Four common organisation methods to adapt to environmental fluctuations are buffering, smoothing, forecasting and rationing (Thompson 1967).

Buffering

Use of **buffering** involves stockpiling inputs or outputs from a production or service process to overcome environmental variations. Buffering by input stockpiling is used when reliable input sources are hard to find, such as supplies. Conversely, buffering by maintaining finished product inventories is used when wide market demand fluctuations make it hard to produce outputs efficiently (Roberts 2003). Buffering may not be feasible due to high cost, perishable materials, or difficulty of service stockpiling, such as a restaurant's customer service. Further, substantial buffering of inputs and finished products risks obsolescence before they are used or sold.

buffering

Stockpiling either inputs into or outputs from a production or service process to cope with environmental fluctuations

TABLE 3.2 APPROACHES TO MANAGING ENVIRONMENTAL IMPACTS

Approach	Methods
Adaptation	Buffering, smoothing, forecasting and rationing
Favourability influence	Advertising and engaging in public relations, boundary spanning, recruiting, negotiating contracts, co-opting, establishing strategic alliances, joining trade associations and engaging in political activity
Domain shifts	Changing domain completely or diversifying into some new areas

Smoothing

smoothing

Taking actions aimed at reducing the impact of fluctuations, given the market

While buffering accommodates market fluctuations, **smoothing** means acting to reduce market fluctuation impact. For example, electricity firms discount rates at weekends to encourage energy use in slow-demand periods. Department stores run sales over slow months. Restaurants make offers on normally slow weekday nights. Such actions avoid expanding to meet peak demand while resources are underused in non-peak periods.

Forecasting

Environmental fluctuations can be managed by forecasting, or predicting conditions and future events to affect a firm's business. As far as future conditions can be accurately predicted, it may be possible to manage fluctuations. For example, grocery stores hire part-time staff to assist during expected busy periods. For times such as this, forecasts based on previous customer patterns may help. When environmental fluctuations are based on more complex dynamic factors, such as economic trends, more sophisticated techniques are needed. Firms may employ economists and/or subscribe to economic forecast services based on sophisticated econometric models.

Rationing

rationing

Providing limited access to a product or service in high demand

Environmental fluctuations may also be managed by **rationing**, or limiting access to a high-demand product or service. For example, universities may limit places in popular areas by demanding prerequisites, such as a particular first-year average. Rationing allows an organisation to avoid capacity expansion to meet temporary increases in demand. This is good, as many costs of capacity expansion (e.g. plant, equipment or classrooms) remain when demand drops. Rationing helps when demand exceeds forecasts or new production expands slowly (due to heavy costs and risk if demand does not grow). Rationing has a down side though. By denying users a product or service, the firm turns away potential business (Fuhrman 1988).

Favourability influence

As opposed to adaptation strategies, favourability influence means altering environmental elements to fit them better to organisation needs. Rather than accept environmental elements as givens, this approach holds that the organisation can change some environmental aspects.

Organisations can influence major environmental elements in many ways. These include advertising and use of public relations, boundary spanning, recruiting, negotiating contracts, co-opting, establishing strategic alliances, joining trade associations and engaging in political activities (Kotter 1979; Harcourt 2003).

Advertising and public relations

The environment can be influenced by advertising, using mass media to gain publicity for products and services. Aligned with advertising is public relations, using mass media and related activities to create a favourable public view of the firm. Together, advertising and public relations can promote positive feelings towards a firm. For example, as well as normal advertising, major companies may sponsor the Olympics, take part in charitable activities such as the Starlight Foundation, or donate time and money to groups including universities.

Boundary spanning

boundary spanning

Creating roles within the organisation interfacing with important elements in the environment

Another way to influence the environment is **boundary spanning**, creating roles in the organisation to interface with major environment elements. People in these roles perform two functions (Aldrich & Herker 1977; Tushman & Scanlan 1981). The first is an information-processing function: they collect environmental information, then filter and transmit it to organisation members to act on. The second is an external representation function, spreading information about the organisation to outsiders. Boundary spanners include salespeople, purchasing specialists, personnel recruiters, admissions officers, shipping and receiving agents, receptionists, lawyers and scientists with close ties to developments in their fields.

Recruiting

Another method of environmental influence is recruiting, or finding and attracting candidates capable of filling job vacancies. This helps influence the environment when firms seek job candidates with knowledge of, and close ties to, a major environmental element. For example, organisations often hire executives from specific companies or industries due to their environmental knowledge and links. Many executives of computer firms began their careers at IBM.

Negotiating contracts

In some cases, influence can come from negotiating contracts, or seeking favourable agreements on significant issues. Specific customer and supplier agreements can create environmental favourability.

Co-opting

Another method of influence is **co-opting**, or absorbing key members of important environmental elements into an organisation's leadership or policy-making structure. A common example of co-opting is adding key people to the board of directors. For instance, most universities have prominent individuals on their councils. These people help deal effectively with environmental elements, particularly raising funds. However, powerful, influential outsiders may question organisational practices and threaten current management (Mizruchi 1983; Lesly 1995).

co-opting

Absorbing key members of important environmental elements into an organisation's leadership or policy-making structure

Strategic alliances

Organisations increasingly form a **strategic alliance**, where two or more organisations form a co-operative partnership to gain mutual advantage (Miller & Dess 1996; Yoshino & Rangan 1995). Often strategic alliances involve joint ventures. A **joint venture** is an agreement between two or more firms to produce a product or service through a jointly owned enterprise. Strategic alliances usually occur because some mutual advantage for organisations involved would be hard to achieve if each acted alone. These alliances are increasingly common because cost, market and technological factors often encourage resource pooling for greater effectiveness (Anderson 1990). For example, Toys 'R' Us and McDonald's (which owns 20 per cent of the stores in Japan) formed a joint venture to set up a chain of toy stores in Japan, with McDonald's food outlets on some of the premises. Within a few years the venture had 6 per cent of the Japanese toy market, making it number one (Potts 1989; Discount Store News 1996). Unfortunately, 7 of 10 joint ventures do not meet expectations or are abandoned. Mainly this is because the technology or market doesn't materialise, a partner's objectives change, or managers cannot work together (Levine & Byrne 1986).

strategic alliance

Arrangement where two or more independent organisations form a co-operative partnership to gain mutual strategic advantage

joint venture

Agreement involving two or more organisations arranging to produce jointly a product or service

Trade associations

Trade associations are organisations of individuals or firms with common business concerns. Trade associations include manufacturers, distributors, importers, brokers and retailers of a product or product group. They may also be those who supply, transport, or use an industry's goods or services (Washington 1986). As they pool the resources of many individuals or organisations, trade associations can run public relations campaigns, influence legislation by lobbying and improve environmental favourability for members.

trade associations

Organisations composed of individuals or firms with common business concerns

Political activity

The environment can also be affected by political activity, in which organisations try to better their competitive situations by influencing legislation and/or the behaviour of regulatory agencies. Political activities can be carried out by a single company for itself or by several organisations or associations for collective well-being.

Domain shifts

Another approach to managing environmental elements is to make **domain shifts**, or changes in the product and service mix offered, so an organisation will interface with more favourable

domain shifts

Changes in the product and service mix offered so an organisation will interface with more favourable environmental elements

elements. One way is to move away from a current product, service or geographic area and into a more favourable domain. Another way is to diversify, or expand products and services to expand current domains.

GENDER FACTOR

Pumpkin Patch

Pumpkin Patch is a New Zealand-based company established by Sally Synnott, a female entrepreneur who resigned from her job as a group product manager for Kmart in 1990 to set up a mail order clothing company in 1991. Pumpkin Patch originally catered for infants, children, and maternity clothes for expectant mothers. However, due to the local success and the high demand for fashionable children's clothing, the company entered the Australian market in 1994 with a mail order catalogue. This was followed in 1997 by the opening of the Urban Angel girls clothing brand store. Pumpkin Patch is now a thriving business that has hundreds of thousands of its customers on its data bases. By 2004 it employed 1700 workers and had become 'the largest speciality kids wear retailer in Australia and New Zealand with more than 80 stores, including nine stores which have opened since 2000 in the United Kingdom (http://www.pumpkinpatch.co.nz/patch_info.cfm, accessed 26 May 2004).

Sally was inspired to become self-employed by a Victoria's Secret lingerie catalogue that she saw while on holiday in Hawaii. She had formal training in apparel design and work experience in clothing and retail, and saw the potential for a Kiwi mail order business for clothing. At the time the company was established there was a gap in the children's clothing market in New Zealand. Much of what was readily available fitted children only up to age four. Because clothing items were manufactured in Asian countries, they were often too small for New Zealand children. The quality of this clothing was also often poor. Sally and her team designed, made and marketed robust and fashionable clothes for infants and children and produced a colour catalogue using children and expectant mothers as models.

In the early days of its business operation Pumpkin Patch was inundated with orders. They had trouble keeping up with the demand for clothing and their computer system crashed. In order to keep the business operating, a manual system of order and dispatch for the first season was used until a specialised computer system was designed for the company. Extra people were employed, including friends and family, to meet the first orders. Initial setbacks including lost sales and high staff costs meant that Sally discovered the hard way the best business advice she had been given, 'to do an extremely detailed cost budget before you start and then triple it' (Sye 1999, p. 9).

Sally's tips for women entering business include the following:

- Treble your estimated costs.
- Contract out telemarketing and order fulfilment to save costs and then take it back when you know your business is a success.
- Make customer service a real priority.
- Be honest with your customers when you 'stuff up'.
- Fill your team with talented people and look after them well.
- Make your catalogue original, creative and stunning.

Source: Contributed by Elizabeth Hall (details of sources are listed on p. 735).

Activities for discussion, analysis and further research

1. Do an analysis of the task and mega environment for Pumpkin Patch. What forces in the environment do you think will have the most impact for the company in the future?
2. What strategies should the company use to manage its environment in the future?
3. What do you think is the greatest threat to the continued success of the company?

THE INTERNAL ENVIRONMENT: ORGANISATIONAL CULTURE

In this section, we examine the concept of culture more fully, considering its nature and how it can be used to help promote innovation.

Nature of organisational culture

As noted already, organisational culture is a system of values, assumptions, beliefs and norms that members share (Smircich 1983; Kilmann et al. 1986; Bateman & Snell 2004). Culture reflects common views about 'how things are done around here'. Organisational culture is **corporate culture** when the concept is applied to the internal environment of major corporations. Organisational culture describes conditions in not-for-profit organisations too, including government agencies, charities and museums. Culture is important as members act on shared values and other culture aspects, so their behaviours can impact organisational effectiveness.

corporate culture

Term sometimes used for organisational culture

Organisational culture has many sources (Kilmann 1985). As new organisations form, cultures develop that reflect the imagination and drive of those involved. Strong founders, too, can have a major cultural impact. For example, McDonald's founder, Ray Kroc, believed in 'quality, service, cleanliness and value', which is still the corporate creed. When reward systems, policies and procedures are set up, they influence culture by specifying desired behaviour. Then, critical incidents, such as rewarding or firing someone for pushing a major innovation, add to people's view of internal norms. Environmental changes, such as new competitors, may force firms to revisit norms in areas such as quality.

Three aspects of organisational culture are important in analysing cultural impact on an organisation: direction, pervasiveness and strength (Kilmann et al. 1986; Martin 1992; Schein 1992). Direction is the degree to which a culture supports, instead of interferes with, achieving organisational goals. Pervasiveness refers to how widely a culture is, or is not, held among members. Strength shows how much members accept values and other culture aspects.

A culture impacts positively on effectiveness when it supports organisational goals, is widely shared by organisation members, and is deeply internalised (Barney 1986). For example, consistently emphasising innovation has meant 3M produces a stream of new products while improving existing ones. However, culture can impact negatively when it is widely shared and well internalised but influences behaviour to interfere with organisational goals. Mixed situations have less effect: for example, unevenly distributed and weakly held culture has far less impact (positive or negative), regardless of direction.

symbol

Object, act, event or quality serving as a vehicle for conveying meaning

Manifestations of organisational culture

An interesting feature of organisational culture is that the values, assumptions, beliefs and norms making up a particular culture are largely unseen. Rather, the nature of a culture is inferred through symbols, stories, rites and ceremonials (Smircich 1983; Trice & Beyer 1993; Kinicki & Williams 2003).

Symbols

A **symbol** is an object, act, event or quality which conveys meaning. For example, an explicit symbol supporting an organisational value is Corning Inc.'s use of a 'quapple', a pin combining the shape of the letter 'Q' and an apple. Members get the pin after their initial training course in quality improvement, and wear it to show their commitment to quality (Dubashi 1987).

Stories

A **story** is a narrative based on true events, which may be elaborated to strengthen the value. One 3M story is about a worker fired after continuing with a new product idea after the boss said stop. Despite being fired, the employee still came to work, pursuing the idea in an unused office. Eventually he was rehired, the idea became a huge success, and he was made vice-president. The story shows a significant value for 3M's innovative culture—persist if you believe in an idea (Deal & Kennedy 1982).

Rites and ceremonials

A **rite** is an elaborate, dramatic, planned set of activities communicating cultural values to participants and an audience. A **ceremonial** is a system of rites performed at one occasion or event.

Promoting innovation: An adaptive, entrepreneurial culture

Successful organisations foster adaptive, entrepreneurial cultures. The organisation opportunity matrix (see Fig. 3.5) classifies firms by how much a firm's culture supports a desire for change and a belief in its capacity to influence the competitive environment (Stevenson & Gumpert 1985; Kotter & Heskett 1992).

As the matrix shows, adaptive, entrepreneurial organisations tend to have staff who see growth and change as desirable and believe they can affect the competitive environment to their advantage. Hewlett-Packard is seen as an adaptive organisation. For example, the firm changed its competitive environment by halving the time needed for design and production. The change let the company produce a matchbox-sized disk drive, the Kittyhawk, ahead of the competition (Hof 1992). Conversely, members of bureaucratic and lethargic organisations prefer the status quo and have little faith in their ability to influence the competitive environment.

In mixed situations, cultures may support a desire for change but foster little belief in the ability to change competitive situations. These cultures are common in reactive planner organisations, where managers try to plan for environmental change but are not proactive in environmental influence. Finally, cultures oriented to very slow change, while believing they can affect the competitive environment, produce complacent organisations. These firms may be successful, but only while the environment changes slowly. For example, Baldwin Locomotive, identified before, succeeded until technological change made its main product, the steam engine, obsolete.

FIGURE 3.5 Organisation opportunity matrix (adapted from Stevenson & Gumpert 1985, p. 93)

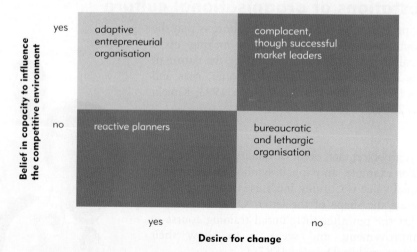

The organisational culture continuum (see Table 3.3) separates cultures on several variables. At one continuum end are characteristics of adaptive, entrepreneurial cultures. With such a culture, the firm anticipates and responds to environmental change. At the other end are characteristics of organisations with administrative cultures. These firms are less likely to make changes needed as the environment shifts.

Culture, it is thought, may span a whole industry, such as the car industry. An interorganisational macroculture occurs when organisation-linked beliefs are held by managers across firms in a whole industry or one segment (Abrahamson & Fombrun 1994; Chatman & Jehn 1994). If an industry has a macroculture and is more toward the continuum's administrative culture end than the adaptive, entrepreneurial end, the entire industry may be slow to innovate and change.

Changing organisational culture

Because they involve fairly stable values, assumptions, beliefs and norms, organisational cultures can be hard to change (Lorsch 1986). One process of changing organisational culture has five main steps (Kilmann 1985):

1. **Surfacing actual norms.** Members list actual norms (expected organisation behaviours) they think influence their attitudes and actions. In a workshop setting a representative employee group meets, or many employee groups meet, depending on the setting. Where the organisation culture's impact on effectiveness is negative, norms emerge such as 'Don't rock the boat', 'Don't enjoy your work', and 'Don't share information with other groups'.
2. **Articulating new directions.** Next, members discuss the organisation's present direction, and behaviours needed for organisational success.
3. **Establishing new norms.** Then, members develop a list of new norms with a positive impact on organisational effectiveness.
4. **Identifying culture gaps.** Following this, areas are identified where a major difference (culture gap) exists between actual norms and those influencing organisational effectiveness positively.
5. **Closing culture gaps.** Finally, new norms are agreed on and ways to reinforce them are developed, such as developing reward systems encouraging members to follow new cultural norms.

While this process is useful to change organisational culture, leaders may want specific cultural changes.

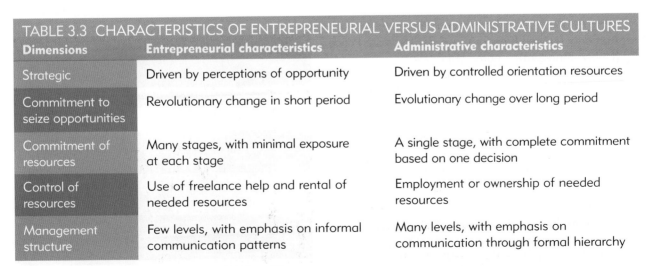

Dimensions	Entrepreneurial characteristics	Administrative characteristics
TABLE 3.3 CHARACTERISTICS OF ENTREPRENEURIAL VERSUS ADMINISTRATIVE CULTURES		
Strategic	Driven by perceptions of opportunity	Driven by controlled orientation resources
Commitment to seize opportunities	Revolutionary change in short period	Evolutionary change over long period
Commitment of resources	Many stages, with minimal exposure at each stage	A single stage, with complete commitment based on one decision
Control of resources	Use of freelance help and rental of needed resources	Employment or ownership of needed resources
Management structure	Few levels, with emphasis on informal communication patterns	Many levels, with emphasis on communication through formal hierarchy

Source: Adapted from Stevenson & Gumpert (1985, p. 89)

How leaders influence cultural change

Despite inherent difficulties, senior managers can achieve specific cultural changes critical to organisational success (Kotter & Heskett 1992; Bateman & Snell 2004). They typically convince members a crisis has occurred or is likely. Next, they communicate a vision of a new organisation direction or strategy. Finally, they motivate others to lead implementing the vision and corresponding strategy, including cultural changes needed.

Further approaches to achieve organisational change are presented in Chapter 11. The issue of organisation values, beliefs and norms is also important to the topic of the next chapter, which is about organisational social responsibility and managerial ethics.

GAINING THE EDGE

Turbosoft—Innovation and customer focus

Turbosoft started as the research and development section of a systems integration company in 1984. In 1988 it became an independent company which focused on developing communications software. Its flagship product, TTWIN is a terminal emulation package. Terminal emulation is a technology that allows a personal computer (PC) to act as a terminal and in doing so, have the ability to communicate with host systems such as mainframe computers. This technology is used primarily by businesses and corporations of all sizes.

Some of Turbosoft's clients in Australia include the whole of ACT government, Big W, Carlton & United Breweries, Deloitte Touche Tohmatsu, the Department of Defence, Diners Club International, the RACV, and the Reserve Bank of Australia. International clients include Fidelity Information Services, MGM Mirage Hotels & Casinos (Worldwide), National City Corporation (North America) , Foxwoods Resort and Casino (USA), Toyota Motor Sports (Germany), B & S Card Services (Germany), the National Planning Authority (United Kingdom) and Bedfordshire Police (United Kingdom) to name but a few.

Turbosoft prides itself on the further development of existing products as well as the investment in new products which meet customers' changing needs. Phil Stenson, the Turbosoft managing director, has overseen the development of all Turbosoft products from day one. Phil admits that the close relationship that Turbosoft has with its customer base has ensured that the software it produces is accurate, relevant and in some cases unique to their needs. Through Phil's vision, Turbosoft, unlike many of its competitors, has been able to cater to the specific development

needs of not only large customers but smaller ones as well.

Turbosoft endeavours to achieve customer satisfaction at all times. It encourages feedback from customers and user groups to fuel the drive for product development, as well as setting the direction for new project innovation.

An outstanding example of Turbosoft's determination to provide total customer satisfaction is the 24-hour, seven-day-a-week technical support service that the company provides to its clients or potential clients. This global sales and support system, which is available via international free-call numbers or the internet, was created by the Turbosoft sales and marketing director Arthur Haddad and helped Turbosoft win the 1998 New Exporter of the Year award. Having this global office in place has enabled Turbosoft to provide customers with local service without the need to open offices across the globe which can be an extremely expensive excerise. In all cases, the level

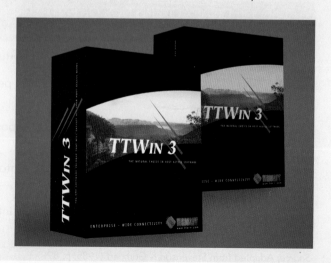

of support that Turbosoft provides has been regarded to be as good as, if not better than, competitors with offices local to its customers. Additionally, with its use of international free-call numbers and 24 by 7 support, it is not uncommon for customers on the otherside of the globe to think that Turbosoft has an office in their region.

Turbosoft insists that if a customer has a problem or query with its software, the issue should be given attention and a prompt and appropriate solution be presented to the customer. Innovative use of technology has enabled Turbosoft to maximise client access on a global basis and decrease its response time.

The company mananging director, Phil Stenson, has ensured that Turbosoft gains a strong reputation for providing both a high-quality product flexible to the needs of the market, and an unmatched level of customer service and support. Turbosoft's three key focus areas are quality product, quality support and quality management. The company is a firm believer in the total quality management philosophy and is constantly developing all areas of the organisation including development, design, production, marketing, sales and support of its own terminal emulation software and protocol software.

The thrust towards working in teams has been identified as the reason for Turbosoft's success

both in Australia and abroad. The team includes distributors and resellers, both locally and around the world, to ensure that needs are recognisef and met. Turbosoft's mission statement highlights this: 'To expand local and international marketd for our connectivity solutions, through developing relationships with established quality, highly focused distribution channels in targeted markets'.
Source: Contributed by Tony Cvorkov; based on information from Turbosoft and www.ttwin.com.

Activities for discussion, analysis and further research

1. Consider Turbosoft's mission statement and determine what factors the organisation should be taking into consideration to meet its own goals.
2. Log on to the Turbosoft web site on www.turbosoft.com.au and check the company's complete mission statement. Look at other pages on the site and consider the external environment issues Turbosoft contends with.
3. Turbosoft takes a unique approach to marketing in that, from first contact, it works one-on-one with clients to respond to specific needs and requirements. In what way is this commitment in tune with current external environment demands? Consider the internal environment issues this might give rise to.

REFLECTIVE PRACTITIONER

About three years ago, one of my staff came to me and said: 'Kimberley I'm not sure if we've got an organisational culture', and I thought, what do you mean by that? In their mind, they didn't actually see that there was something to identify with, or a way things were done around the company. Being a relatively new organisation, it takes time to develop your stamp or imprint which defines the culture and reflects the environment and behaviours that are evident in the organisation. When you are working in a small or large team—people need something to belong to, and be a part of, and that goes much deeper than their job function.

I thought it was really interesting to have a staff member say that because to me our organisational culture was quite defined and was quite noticeable.

So how do I navigate around that? Well, it is definitely about putting forth your ethos, putting forward your principles and the underpinning philosophy that makes your business tick, and for us the thing we want to develop and hold close to our hearts is the integrity of our work. We want to be leaders in an emerging field, our industry and on the international platform—to be 'the premier provider of risk management services globally'. To be the premier provider is about being the best—it is about providing all the things that all the others provide but doing it with that something special which sets you apart. So it's about combining the integrity of our work with innovation, so we are not just doing what everyone else is doing. Having quality in terms of our client work, having a depth of expertise and

KIMBERLEY TURNER

AEROSAFE
RISK MANAGEMENT

ability to apply this knowledge which supersedes competitors, believing in what we do and having a demonstrated passion and enthusiasm for what we do and what it can offer is what I believe sets our company apart. Those are the things which need to be reflected in our organisational culture and represent the underpinning values of who we are.

To generate that culture internally, I need to flick that switch in our staff, to make them believe or help them to believe. Some join the organisation with that belief already there, others don't and need to develop it. The challenge is to maintain that belief

and develop it into action that delivers results.

As our business has diversified over the past three and a half years, we are working in some quite different industries. In the aviation sector, the professional culture is quite different to Defence, is different from not-for-profit or from the medical industry. We need to have the ability to adapt and be relevant to those other industries—so those are the skill sets that we need to develop. All of our staff need to be able to adapt their style. For me, I need to be able to let go of what might be important to me in order to work within industries which have different priorities. It is remarkably different, and if we don't adapt our style, we won't be successful in other fields. Part of what I am trying to do is to enable my staff to understand that and actually be willing to change and accommodate, and even take the leadership role in that accommodation.

Some of the industries we now deal in are extremely conservative, whereas others are very aggressive in business and innovation. This impacts on their requirements for risk management support, frameworks or systems. For example, take a new start-up airline in the aviation industry. They are young, innovative, entrepreneurial and are aggressive in gaining market share. This external environment is very different from the medical research area of the pharmaceutical industry where we now provide our services. Medical research needs to be conservative, evidentially based, tested and cautious. For our team to be able to take the same theory and methodology into either of these two situations and be successful we need a strong ability to adopt our approach.

FOCUS ON PRACTICE

Strategies for improving

1. Consider the organisation you work for, or your university if you do not work. Examine the task environment forces which impact upon it the most. Are they going to require changes in how the organisation operates? How will the changes affect the organisation?

2. Repeat the above in terms of the general environment.

Source: Jones et al. (2000).

SUMMARY

- Organisations are affected by the external environment, the outside forces potentially influencing the success of products or services. Broad society conditions and trends within which an organisation operates make up an organisation's mega-environment. The mega-environment has five major elements: technological, economic, legal-political, sociocultural and international. Generally, an organisation cannot alter directly the mega-environment elements, at least short-term.

- The task, or operational, environment consists of the specific external elements an organisation interacts with in operating. The task environment depends on the firm's specific products and services, and locations where it does business. An organisation may be more successful in affecting its task environment than the mega-environment. Major organisational task-environment elements include customers and clients, competitors, suppliers, labour supply and government agencies.

- Two important, but diverse, perspectives on the relationship between organisations and their environments are the population ecology and resource dependence models. Managers can analyse their organisation's environmental situation using two key concepts: environmental uncertainty and environmental bounty or capacity. Environmental uncertainty is how much future conditions affecting an organisation can be accurately assessed and predicted. Environmental bounty is how much the environment can support sustained growth and stability. The degree of environmental uncertainty is a function of two factors, complexity and dynamism.

- Three major approaches to managing environmental elements are adaptation, favourability influence and domain shifts. Adaptation involves changing internal operations and activities to make an organisation more compatible with its environment. Adaptation methods include buffering, smoothing, forecasting and rationing. Favourability influence focuses on changing environmental elements to make them fit with the organisation's needs. The resource dependence perspective argues that the environmental areas that organisations try to influence are those on which they are most dependent. Major methods of favourability influence include advertising and engaging in public relations, boundary spanning, recruiting, negotiating contracts, co-opting, setting up strategic alliances, joining trade associations and engaging in political activities. Domain shifts are changes in product and service mix so a firm will face more favourable environmental elements. One domain-shift method is moving out of a current product, service or geographic area and into a more favourable domain. Diversification is another method of expanding product and service.

- Organisational culture is a system of shared values, assumptions, beliefs and norms uniting members. A particular firm's culture is assessed through the use of concrete elements, such as symbols, stories, rites and ceremonials. Entrepreneurial cultures encourage innovation, with members viewing growth and change as good and believing they can affect the competitive environment. Changing organisational culture can be hard and is likely to be a multistep process. Top managers often try to produce cultural change that will build organisational prospects for success.

QUESTIONS FOR DISCUSSION AND REVIEW

1. Outline major elements forming the mega-environment. Identify an important trend in each element influencing the organisation in which you or some family member works.

2. Identify major elements making up the typical task environment of an organisation. Use these elements to develop an outline of the task environment of a firm in which you or a family member works.

3. Contrast population ecology and resource dependence views of the organisation–environment interface. Identify a situation where environmental change caused an organisation to fail. What possible actions, if any, might management have taken to avoid the firm's demise?

4. Explain how environmental uncertainty affects organisations. How would you assess environmental uncertainty for R.M. Williams, the Australian clothing maker?
5. Describe how environmental bounty influences organisations. How would you assess environmental bounty for R.M. Williams?
6. Outline the major methods to help organisations adapt to environmental elements. For each, give an example based on a familiar organisation.
7. Enumerate major methods to help organisations influence their environments favourably. For five of these, give an example based on a familiar organisation.
8. Explain how domain shifts can help organisations cope with their environments. Give an example of an organisation making a major domain shift. Was the shift beneficial? Why, or why not?
9. Explain organisational culture and list its principal manifestations. Give an example of each indicating the culture at your university or college. Briefly describe your perception of the culture at your university or college.
10. Explain the difference between an entrepreneurial and an administrative culture.

CRITICAL THINKING QUESTIONS

To answer some of these questions you will need to do further research. Useful references are given below each section of the questions.

This chapter demonstrates how effective managers require knowledge about an organisation's internal and external environments. The central theme is that successful managers deal with both sets of environmental factors in ways that support organisational goal achievement.

In a recent article, Ruthven (2003) reviews the dramatic rise of small and medium-sized businesses in Australia that are taking advantage of innovation and outsourcing. In a brief review, he identifies the checks and balances driving this move.

1. What are some of the advantages and disadvantages for the aspiring Australian entrepreneurial organisation today?

2. Where do new products and industries come from?

3. While Ruthven finds that all enterprises tend to be winners at present, he suggests that small to medium-sized businesses are winning the most. Why is this?

4. How does a small or medium-sized enterprise manage to expand rapidly and then remain successful?

As Ruthven concludes, the Australia Fast 100 demonstrates most of the winning characteristics and are 'in a pack of their own'.

(Material relevant to questions 1 to 4 may be found in Ruthven, P. 2003, Fast and furious business, *Business Review Weekly*, Australia, 23 October, p. 50.)

While Geert Hofstede's assertion that national cultures differ along five dimensions is well known, less well known are his writings on the universal fact of inequality in every society. In his 1997 book, *Cultures and Organization: Software of the mind*, Hofstede reasserts the five dimensions as the degree of integration of individuals within groups; differences in the social roles of women versus men; ways of dealing with inequality; degree of tolerance for the unknown; and the trade-off between long-term and short-term gratification of needs. However, he also adds that a key feature of the difference between organisational and national culture is the fact that organisational cultures are more manageable and actually have the ability to bridge national cultures. There is inequality in any society. Even in the most simple hunter-gatherer band, some people are bigger, stronger, or smarter than others. Today, having a tertiary education tends to place individuals in the middle class.

5. Given Hofstede's five dimensions, what are some of the problems they create and how are these manifested?

Intercultural communication can be taught, but the work of researchers like Hofstede also clearly identifies the fact that national and organisational characteristics will impact on the ability and readiness of individuals to be open to different ideas. Further, even within national and organisational cultures, some individuals will always be more able to learn than others, and those with characteristics such as low personal tolerance for uncertainty, or extreme political or religious views, will probably be poor candidates for training.

(Material relevant to question 5 may be found in Hofstede G. 1997, *Cultures and Organization: Software of the mind*, McGraw-Hill, New York.)

What do individuals within an organisation actually experience as 'company culture'? Recent research has discovered a 'yawning gap between top management's view of what the company culture looks like and how employees actually experience it' (Jayne 2003, p. 43).

6. Why is this happening?

7. The problem of saying one thing and doing another is age old. How do we close the gap between the sort of organisation we apparently want and the one we get?

8. The research also raises an important issue of definition. What is a constructive culture and how is it measured?

In summary, in the words of organisational development consultants Human Synergistics International's (HSI) Wellington chair, Shaun McCarthy, 'Say an organisation has a particular set of values—it frames them and puts them on the office walls in the belief this will cause people to behave that way. The flaw in that approach is that where people actually look for their behaviour clues is in what goes on day-to-day'. The value in a tool such as the Organisational Effectiveness Inventory is that it helps identify the best levers for change and, as Jayne (2003, p. 43) points out, 'not every company follows through—oddly enough Enron was one that failed to act on a cultural survey that highlighted some of the ethical issues that later proved its undoing'.

(Material relevant to questions 6 to 8 may be found in Jayne, V. 2003, The executive disconnect, *New Zealand Management*, September, pp.43–5.)

MANAGEMENT EXERCISES

Exercise 1 Management exercise: Assessing a ski-shop environment

Your best friend's sister and brother-in-law run a ski shop near your campus, but they have recently bought another type of business elsewhere in town. They want you and your friend to manage the ski shop. If you run it successfully, you and your friend will gradually be given substantial equity in the shop and eventually would own the whole business.

So far, the shop has been only marginally profitable. Although the shop carries ski equipment and clothing, it often runs out during the peak ski season. Extra merchandise ordered to meet demand often arrives so late it cannot be sold until the next season, if at all. In addition, the shop does very little business from October to April.

Due to a dispute over the size and prominence of an outside sign displaying the shop's name, the relationship with local government is poor. Tact and diplomacy are not major strengths of your friend's brother-in-law. As a result, the shop gets more than its share of inspections, and a recent effort to gain permission to expand the parking lot was turned down.

So far, other than minimal advertising, nothing has been done to make inroads on campus. Yet the campus should be lucrative. The student population includes many avid skiers, since good skiing is about an hour and a half drive away. Unfortunately, many buy their ski equipment and clothing at the lodges. In part this is because lodges tend to have good arrangements for ski equipment repair and maintenance.

Your initial assessment is that, so far, the ski shop has not tried to deal with its environment. There have been persistent rumours another ski shop may open nearby next year, creating a competitor. You and your friend (and possibly some others willing to give you advice) plan to get together soon to try to develop approaches to help manage the ski shop's environment better. This analysis is crucial to your decision about whether to manage the shop. Also, your friend's sister and brother-in-law want to hear your ideas.

First, outline the major elements in the ski shop's task environment. Then prepare a proposal showing how you would attempt to better manage the shop's environmental elements.

Exercise 2 Self-assessment exercise: The kind of organisation I would manage

Select the response which best reflects the culture you would work to instil in an organisation you managed.

The kind of organisation I would manage

1 = Strongly disagree   4 = Somewhat agree
2 = Somewhat disagree   5 = Strongly agree
3 = Neither agree nor disagree

_____ 1   For many projects, I would prefer to obtain needed additional professional human resources on a part-time or contract basis.

_____ 2   I would prefer to indicate my support for a program/project by committing all resources required when I approve it.

_____ 3   I believe change is often best accomplished by making major changes within a short time frame.

_____ 4   Programs/projects usually are improved by many reviews through the chain of command.

_____ 5   Current resource availability should dictate the size and type of long-term programs and projects attempted.

_____ 6   I would be inclined to have very few levels of management.

_____ 7   I would base resource commitments on successes at several points in a program/project.

_____ 8   I would prefer owning all resources for a project/program so they would be immediately available when needed.

_____ 9   Normally it is relatively easy to recognise opportunities arising and to plan for them well in advance.

_____ 10 Most communication regarding programs/projects under development is best handled through the formal hierarchy.

END-OF-CHAPTER CASE: ON THE RIM

Creating fun

South-east Queensland has become a little-known hub for the rapidly emerging and highly profitable computer-gaming industry in Australia. One company in the hub is 'Fuzzyeyes Studios', based in Brisbane. Sonny Lu started Fuzzyeyes in 2001 as a young entrepreneur with a vision to build a successful multimedia software development company focusing on PC and PS2 games development. Fuzzyeyes' products focus on light-hearted fun and they include Aussie Adventure, OzFighter, Battle Wombat, Super Oz Kart, Crazy Fire Fighters and NHLA (New Human Liveable Atmosphere, HotDogs HotGals). The philosophy of Fuzzyeyes is 'we create fun' and this is reflected in the creation of games that are easy to play, stress free and entertaining.

Fuzzyeyes has found that its main markets are in the US and Europe, rather than in Australia. The company takes on larger US competitors by cooperating with other games developers in Australia through associations such as the Game Developers Association (GDAA) of Australia and Electronic Games Queensland (EGQ). The GDAA helps to coordinate the Australian game industry's presence at major international trade shows and also helps to develop the industry through conferences, conventions and government lobbying. As a small-to-medium sized enterprise (SME), Fuzzyeyes also copes with the challenges of the external environment through involvement with Queensland Games Developers, a cooperative group that works together with local and state governments to promote the talent and skills of firms internationally and win new

business. The external environment, however, is full of promise, with interactive entertainment software sales of over US$6 billion, currently exceeding movie box-office turnover in the United States. The industry is also regarded as being relatively 'recession-proof', with no slowdown in industry growth from the 1980s to today.

The company's internal environment is characterised by an organisational culture where innovation, creativity and passion are rewarded. The company has a flat management structure where the chain of command evolves to adapt the changing needs of different projects. Sonny says: 'we are sort of a cell, with lots of bubbles acting in their own functions and the company is like a big bubble putting them altogether'. Hierarchy is replaced with the chain of command similar to the reactions of a biochemical pathway occurring inside a cell. Sonny says that 80 per cent of people work in the industry because they are interested in the work and they find it fun, rather than just for monetary rewards. Workers in Fuzzyeyes are rewarded for their efforts, however, with a bonus pay system rewarding hard-working and creative staff. Sonny gives credit to his parents who taught him to empower and trust his employees, especially when it comes to decision-making in management. The company's website warmly proclaims, 'we take pride in our creative and innovative staff members who work passionately on inventive and original game concepts'. With such a positive work environment and motivated staff, Fuzzyeyes is poised to continue producing games that are both educational and lots of fun.

Source: Contributed by Peter Woods.

International articles related to this topic are available at the Online Learning Centre at **www.mhhe.com/au/bartol4e**

Websites:

http://www.fuzzyeyes.com/
http://www.gdaa.asn.au/
http://www.qldgamedev.com/

Activities for discussion, analysis and further research

1. What are the characteristics of the external environment that Fuzzyeyes operates in?
2. How does Fuzzyeyes cope with the competitive aspects of the external environment?
3. How would you describe the internal environment of Fuzzyeyes?

FURTHER READING

Gosling, J. and Mintzberg, H. 2003, The five minds of a manager, *Harvard Business Review*, November, 81, 11, pp. 54–64.

Hale, D. and Hughes Hale, L. 2003, China takes off, *Foreign Affairs*, November/December, 82, 6, pp. 36–54.

Im, S., Nakata, C., Park, H. and Ha, Y-W. 2003, Determinants of Korean and Japanese new product performance: An interrelational and process view, *Journal of International Marketing*, 11, 4, pp. 81–103.

Smith, J. 2003, The Asian conundrum, *Food Logistics*, November/December, 64, p.14.

Zhang, Y., Zhang, Z., Men, X. and Huang, S. 2004, Determinants of structural change to sequential foreign direct investment across China: A synthesised approach, *Singapore Management Review*, 1st Half, 26, 1, pp. 63–81.

CHAPTER 4

SOCIAL RESPONSIBILITY AND ETHICS IN MANAGEMENT

CHAPTER OUTLINE

Organisational social responsibility
Major perspectives
Social responsibilities of management
Social stakeholders
Does social responsibility pay?
Promoting innovation: vanguard
    companies

Organisational social responsiveness
Monitoring social demands and
    expectations
Internal social response mechanisms

Being an ethical manager
Types of managerial ethics
Ethical guidelines for managers
Ethical career issues

Managing an ethical organisation
Situational factors influencing ethical
    behaviour
Mechanisms for ethical management

LEARNING OBJECTIVES

After studying this chapter, you should be able to:

- Explain three major perspectives on corporate social responsibility and identify major stakeholder groups often mentioned in conjunction with social responsibility.
- Assess the extent to which organisational social responsibility pays.
- Explain the characteristics of vanguard companies.
- Outline approaches used to monitor social demands and expectations.
- Describe internal social response mechanisms available to organisations.
- Contrast three major types of managerial ethics.
- Outline ethical guidelines for managers and explain actions they can take to handle ethical situations and avoid ethical conflicts.
- Describe situational factors influencing ethical behaviour and outline mechanisms for ethical management.

Andrew Liveris

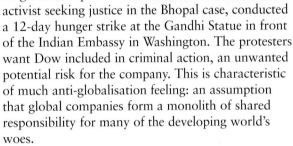

To survive in the global economy, you have to love what you do and you have to make exceptional judgments. They are two features of the world inhabited by Andrew Liveris, president and chief operating officer of Dow Chemicals, one of the largest companies in the United States. An Australian of Greek background, born in Darwin and schooled in Queensland, Liveris heads a division that produces more than US$6 billion in revenue and employs 7500 staff. Some analysts regard Liveris, the manager of Dow's largest division, as the company's next chief executive. If this happens, Liveris will easily be one of Australia's most powerful business people.

In an international company, managing requires focus and breadth of understanding: focus to streamline the company's operations and connect with the market, and breadth to interpret an often chaotically complex international environment. Most of all, it requires passion. 'What makes me tick is that I love business and I love deal-making and I love the human dimension of business and I love the creativity', says Liveris. 'That is my passion. Change is something I live with every day. I want that. I think I have that in common with much of business leadership. That is what we do, that is our job.'

Rising hostility to the phenomenon described as globalisation has meant that large companies such as Dow are routinely demonised, even depicted as economic and social despots. The attacks can be indiscriminate. In some forums, Dow has been attacked for the Bhopal chemical disaster in India in 1984, which killed 8000 people, yet Dow's only sin was to acquire Union Carbide, the company responsible for the catastrophe. In May, two women

survivors of the accident and a long-time Bhopal activist seeking justice in the Bhopal case, conducted a 12-day hunger strike at the Gandhi Statue in front of the Indian Embassy in Washington. The protesters want Dow included in criminal action, an unwanted potential risk for the company. This is characteristic of much anti-globalisation feeling: an assumption that global companies form a monolith of shared responsibility for many of the developing world's woes.

Faced with diminishing returns from productivity and disinflation, there is one main management option for a knowledge and asset-intensive company such as Dow. Be creative. 'I have got to tell you, it is an overused word, but it is the only answer. You have to innovate your way out of it. If you can't innovate and meet the business model requirements of the discontinuities that are out there, and handle the risk, and make the right business decisions, and invest appropriately and cheaply—moving yourself out of the depression—then you will be squeezed to the point that your survival is at risk.'

Dow, like the other big chemical companies, will be an early, and centrally placed, participant in the life-sciences revolution. Liveris clearly senses the beat of history in the scientific and business challenge. 'Between myself and our top R&D guy, and one other guy, we will be steering Dow in this direction. I think it does need an alliance structure to mitigate risk. Not just with other companies, but also universities and government institutions and the countries that are interested in investing in this. It is

continued

STRIVING FOR EXCELLENCE *continued*

so early, you will only understand its impact in 10 to 15 years, and look back and say "I recognised its emergence in the early part of this decade".'

A once-in-a-century convergence of biology, chemistry and physics is transforming science and innovation, Liveris says. From this, unparalleled intellectual property is emerging. 'All this new science is coming out of those new interfaces: the collisions that a hundred years ago came out of maths and chemistry, and 200 years ago from the collision of maths and physics to create astronomy. This current collision, which has IT as its enabler, this is multi-interface science.'

Lessons of recent history

After the disappointments of the digital revolution, any claims that business will be transformed by new technology are customarily greeted with intense scepticism. The history of large corporations punting on biotechnology or related scientific innovation is also patchy. In the late 1990s, Novartis, AstraZeneca and Monsanto all pulled back from pursuing the generic life-sciences industry positioning—initially believed to be a new form of industry convergence—because they found it difficult to create sound businesses.

Dow has only six organisational layers between the lowest employee and the chief executive. 'That means you have a wide span of control, which means you don't do the traditional "manager managing managers" routine. So what you really have to do is push hard at leadership at all levels. The notion of a leader now is not the top person running things.

The notion is that at every level of every job you exert leadership: peer leadership, group leadership, team-based leadership. All you need from a layer above you and a layer above that is alignment, and that is done through strategy and a balanced scorecard.'

One result is a greater stress on the importance of integrity. The backlash is working to the benefit of the older corporations, which have tended to suffer from fewer abuses. Liveris says auditing is now more rigorous. 'You'd better have ethics as your backbone, because if you don't, you are going to be found out. Ethics compliance, ethics committees that report to the board directly, ethics officers, corporate auditors, who your auditors are, what sort of background they have, what are their track records—all of that has ramped up to another degree.

'If the pendulum was at one extreme before, it has probably moved away from an equilibrium point to another extreme. But you need jolting to cause the equilibrium point to move. There is probably a little bit of over-reaction, but who would have imagined two years ago that an Enron or a WorldCom would have been possible? We are in a transition mode, we have to re-earn public trust, we have to examine these outrageous salaries that people earn with no due regard to performance.'

Still determinedly loyal to Australia, Liveris says he keeps in touch with local business conditions. He believes Australian companies have been late entrants to globalisation, and have suffered from the tyranny of distance. But Australian managers, he believes, have something distinctive to offer global companies. 'There are a lot of Australians in global enterprises that have adapted and have become very impressive in their successes. Australians, as a country and individuals and business leaders, call it straight. We are straight talkers and we get it done. I think that is very valued.'

Source: James, D. (2003).

---

managerial ethics

Standards of conduct and moral judgment used by managers of organisations in carrying out their business

Society is increasingly focused on the social responsibility of organisations and the ethics of their managers. For example, in one poll 58 per cent of respondents saw the ethical standards of business executives as only fair or poor (Wildstrom 1987). Ethics are standards of behaviour and moral judgment differentiating right from wrong (Post, Frederick, Lawrence & Weber 1996). **Managerial ethics** are standards of conduct and moral judgment managers use in their business. In this chapter, we explore the nature and extent of organisations' social responsibilities. We look at ways organisations fulfil their social responsibilities, and at managers' ethics. Finally, we examine the challenge of managing an ethical organisation.

ORGANISATIONAL SOCIAL RESPONSIBILITY

Organisational social responsibility refers to an organisation's obligation to act to protect and improve society's welfare as well as its own interests. Organisational social responsibility is often called **corporate social responsibility** when the concept is applied to business firms. Views differ on how much organisations need to consider social responsibilities in their operations (Bahree 1995), although it is becoming more visible as a significant issue (Ryan 2003).

Major perspectives

Concern for organisational social responsibility is fairly recent. In America, for example, social responsibility as an issue emerged in the late 1800s when organisations grew larger. Anti-competitive activities (e.g. kickbacks and price-fixing) led to pressures from government and labour. Concern grew through the Great Depression, and after the stock market crash much business regulation was set up. By 1936 the CEO of Sears, General Robert E. Wood, argued for managerial, not only governmental, actions on social concerns. Social movements (e.g. civil rights, women's liberation and environmentalism) during the 1960s drew more attention to organisational social responsibilities (Carroll 1980). Examples of recent corporate misbehaviour domestically, regionally and globally, such as HIH Insurance, OneTel, and Enron, have refocused attention on these responsibilities (Kinicki & Williams 2003).

These historical forces led to three contrasting views of corporate social responsibility: the invisible hand, the hand of government, and the hand of management (Goodpaster & Matthews 1982).

The invisible hand

Milton Friedman is the chief supporter for the invisible hand, or classical, perspective of corporate social responsibility, but it can be traced to Adam Smith in the eighteenth century. The **invisible hand** view holds that the corporation's social responsibility may be seen as 'make profits and obey the law'. Thus, each corporation works to increase legal profits. In this way, corporate responsibility is guided by the invisible hand of free-market forces, eventually ensuring resource allocation for the betterment of society. Otherwise, business executives will allocate resources, gaining excessive power with little decision accountability. Friedman (1962) also argues that the charitable activities of firms are not socially responsible because, in making such contributions, stockholders cannot make decisions about disposal of funds.

The hand of government

Under the **hand-of-government** perspective, corporations' role is to be profitable within the law. However, this view argues that society's interests are best served by having the regulatory hands of the law and political process, rather than the invisible hand, guide corporations' work (Galbraith 1962; 1975). The hand of government controls the possible negative actions of firms regarding employees (minimum wage, safety and equal employment opportunity legislation), customers (product safety and advertising control) and the larger community (hazardous chemical and pollution control). Neither the invisible hand nor the hand of government approach allows corporate leaders latitude on social issues.

The hand of management

The **hand-of-management** perspective says corporations and managers must act to protect and improve society's welfare while advancing corporate economic interests (Post et al. 1996). Typically three arguments are raised in support of organisational social responsibility (Tuleja 1985). The **anti-freeloader argument** holds that businesses benefit from a better society, and should bear some costs of improvement by working toward solutions to social problems. The **capacity argument** states that the private sector, with its considerable economic and human resources, must make up for government cuts in social programs. The **enlightened self-interest argument** holds that businesses exist at society's pleasure and, for their own legitimacy

---

organisational social responsibility

The obligation of an organisation to seek actions protecting and improving society's welfare along with its own interests

corporate social responsibility

A term used in reference to the concept of organisational social responsibility as applied to business organisations

invisible hand

A view holding that the entire social responsibility of a corporation can be summed up as 'make profits and obey the law'

hand of government

A view arguing that the interests of society are best served by having the regulatory hands of the law and the political process, rather than the invisible hand, guide the results of corporations' endeavours

hand of management

A view stating that corporations and their managers are expected to act in ways that protect and improve society's welfare as a whole as well as advance corporate economic interests

anti-freeloader argument

An argument holding that since businesses benefit from a better society, they should bear part of the costs by actively working to bring about solutions to social problems

capacity argument

An argument stating that the private sector, because of its considerable economic and human resources, must make up for government cutbacks in social programs

enlightened self-interest argument

An argument holding that businesses exist at society's pleasure and that, for their own legitimacy and survival, businesses should meet the public's expectations regarding social responsibility

iron law of responsibility

A law stating that 'in the long run, those who do not use power in a manner that society considers responsible will tend to lose it'

and survival, they must meet public social-responsibility expectations or suffer financially (Stevens 1995). This relates to the **iron law of responsibility**, which states that 'in the long run, those who do not use power in a manner that society considers responsible will tend to lose it' (Post et al. 1996, p. 32). Generally, society's expectations of the social responsibilities of business are growing. For example, one *Business Week*/Harris poll showed most people believe business has social responsibilities beyond shareholder profits (See Table 4.1) (Tuleja 1985). Thus, the relevance of the hand-of-management approach is increasing (Carton 1995).

TABLE 4.1 PERCEPTIONS OF BUSINESS RESPONSIBILITY

Question: Which of the following statements do you agree with more strongly?	% responding
US corporations should have only one purpose—to make the most profit for their shareholders—and their pursuit of that goal will be best for America in the long term. Or	5
US corporations should have more than one purpose. They also owe something to their workers and the communities in which they operate, and they should sometimes sacrifice some profit for the sake of making things better for their workers and communities.	95

Source: Business Week (11 March 1996, p. 65).

Social responsibilities of management

The idea that managers have social responsibilities comes, in part, from greater inter-dependencies. These interdependencies have built ties of common interest between corporations and their communities. This broad view of management's social responsibility involves economic, legal, ethical and discretionary issues, as shown in Figure 4.1 (Carroll 1979; Gatewood & Carroll 1991). Proportions shown in the figure suggest the size of each responsibility for corporate leaders.

FIGURE 4.1 Social responsibilities of management (adapted from Carroll 1979, p. 499)

Economic and legal responsibilities

Management's economic and legal responsibilities are recognised by all three corporate responsibility perspectives—the invisible hand, the hand of government and the hand of management. These responsibilities involve making a profit and obeying the law (Zeigler 1995).

Ethical and discretionary responsibilities

The hand-of-management perspective recognises ethical and discretionary responsibilities, as well as the economic and legal responsibilities dictated by the invisible-hand and hand-of-government views. Ethical responsibilities include behaviours and activities society expects of business. For example, in the 1980s, public pressure, and managerial concerns about apartheid, meant many firms closed their South African activities though not legally required to (Post et al. 1996). Ethical responsibilities are ill-defined, often controversial and changeable. This is why business leaders can find it hard to identify such responsibilities.

On the other hand, discretionary responsibilities include voluntary activities not necessarily expected of business by society. While firms would not be seen as unethical if they did not take part, some part of society may see these activities as desirable. Discretionary activity examples are philanthropic contributions, sponsoring AIDS clinics and training the economically disadvantaged. For instance, Merck provided the drug Ivermectin free to millions of people in Africa, South America and the Middle East to protect them from the parasitic disease 'river blindness'. This cost the company millions of dollars in forgone profits (*Business Week* 1988).

Social stakeholders

If corporations and managers are to be socially responsible, to whom they are to be responsible is important. Six overlapping groups are identified: shareholders, employees, customers, the local community, general society (regional and national) and the international community (Tuleja 1985; Donaldson & Preston 1995). They are social stakeholders, as corporations' business activities can affect them for better or worse.

Shareholders

Despite perceptions of the obligations of business to several constituencies, it is still agreed that the main management role of public firms is to earn profits and shareholder dividends (Post et al. 1996). Shareholders provide capital for the companies to survive and grow.

Managers see themselves as responsible for the firm's survival, to develop and expand it, balancing stakeholders' demands so multiple demands do not result in failing to achieve company goals. Different shareholder and management perspectives may lead to conflict, especially over dividend levels (versus reinvestment allocations) or paying for executive benefits such as stock options and club memberships.

Shareholders may pressure management to change their social stance. Currently, shareholders are concerned about CEOs being paid millions while their companies perform poorly. Top managers rarely disclose their full compensation. In America, AT&T CEO Robert E. Allen was criticised for taking a supplementary stock option of almost $11 million while announcing layoffs of 40 000 workers—other important stakeholders (Byrne 1996). Less extreme examples are common.

Employees—Managing diversity

Organisations must at least honour specific employee agreements and obey relevant employee–employer relationship laws. Laws and regulations specify employer responsibilities on equal employment opportunity, pensions and benefits, and health and safety. Recognition of workforce diversity and public feelings about abuses by employers has led to greater regulation (Robinson & Dechant 1977).

While top managers often refer to employees as 'family', employee treatment is quite variable. An extreme lack of concern for employees was shown by Film Recovery Systems, Inc.

Officials from the Chicago plant were convicted of murder after an employee died, poisoned by cyanide. The death came when workers, largely non-English-speaking immigrants, were not warned cyanide was used to extract silver from film scraps and only given basic safety equipment (Trost 1985).

At the other end of the scale of social concern for employees, Du Pont works to help employees balance family and work pressures. For example, over three years it spent $1.5 million to build and renovate child-care centres near company sites. Du Pont also has a generous leave policy for birth, adoption or family illness. Employees have six weeks on full pay and up to six months of unpaid leave with full benefits (Weber 1991).

Du Pont's actions show efforts to effectively manage diversity. Diversity management is planning and instituting systems and practices to maximise employee potential to contribute to organisational goals and develop employee capabilities unhindered by group identities (such as gender, race or ethnic group) (Cox 1994). It is arguable that managers should effectively manage diversity because it is socially responsible. However, socially responsible actions are good business. As Table 4.2 shows, social responsibility is one argument for building competitive advantage by effectively managing diversity.

Customers

Though many businesses' motto was once caveat emptor ('let the buyer beware'), consumers now expect more. Two current consumer areas of social concern are health and safety, and quality issues.

Product liability suits are increasing, which impact business prospects. For example, Bic Corporation's stock dropped when there were several law suits claiming exploding Bic lighters had led to severe injuries and death (Potts 1987). Increasing liability cases mean many firms find liability insurance harder to find. As the social responsibilities of business have been questioned, the pendulum may have swung too far to the consumer. It is argued that a manufacturer should be liable for product safety only if they 'knew, or should have known, about its dangers'. However, this is risky, as it can be hard to determine what research a manufacturer needs to do to ensure consideration of all safety contingencies. A 100 per cent standard may mean products would take years to reach the market—if at all—and be expensive. Thus businesses caring about consumers compromise by trying to be 99 per cent certain a product is safe, taking out large insurance policies and hoping.

Quality's importance as a consumer issue has grown. Keeping up with the competition is important and some have linked quality to social responsibility. For example, when Harley-Davidson's quality dropped over the 1970s, customers were upset and the company's

TABLE 4.2 ARGUMENTS IN FAVOUR OF MANAGING DIVERSITY FOR COMPETITIVE ADVANTAGE	
Socially responsible	Managing diversity can protect and improve society's welfare while advancing corporate economic interests.
Cost effective	Attracting workers is costly; firms effectively managing diversity can attract and retain good workers.
Enhances prospects for customer satisfaction	A workforce mirroring customer-base diversity provides unique insight into customer needs, and enhances prospects for customer satisfaction.
Encourages innovation	Innovations are more likely to emerge when diversity of thinking is applied to business problems.
Facilitates globalisation	Openness to other cultures and ways of doing things helps doing business around the globe.

reputation suffered. It took great effort to fix the situation. Richard Teerlink, Harley-Davidson's CEO, noted: 'We are living proof that you can win your reputation back. But it's not easy' (Caminiti 1992, p. 76). Perrier learned the hazards of quality issues and social responsibility when it removed its mineral water from sale in 1990 due to benzene contamination. Though the benzene levels were harmless, the company was trying to protect its reputation with consumers. Unfortunately, four months were needed to fix the problem and many consumers changed brands. Nestlé acquired the company, and Perrier struggled to regain its prominence (Brown 1991; Browning 1992; 1993).

The Australian Competition and Consumer Commission (ACCC) has defended the use of misleading 'country of origin' labelling, by taking action against National Chemical for selling Chinese-sourced eucalyptus oils as 'Australian' (Costa 2003). The increasing focus on Customer Relationship Management (CRM) demonstrates that many organisations realise the need to focus on the customers' needs (Howarth 2003).

Local community

In regard to social responsibility, the organisation's community is its local area of business influence (Post et al. 1996). Needs of most communities extend beyond available resources. Thus, businesses are asked for more assistance than they can provide, requiring priorities to be set.

While communities often want business aid, firms need various forms of community support. Forms of support include adequate transport, fair taxes, sufficient school and recreational facilities, and public services, including police, fire services, sewage, water, gas and electricity. Through these needs, businesses and communities are interrelated and may function more effectively with mutual support (see Fig. 4.2) (Moskowitz 1989).

Society

Social responsibility at a societal level involves regional and national issues. For example, many business leaders are involved in educational reform to prepare future labour-pool members. Aetna Insurance trains up to 700 employees a year in basic reading, writing and mathematics (Segal 1992; Bernstein 1992). When links between corporate social expenditures and business-related results are weak, supporters of the invisible hand view of social responsibility will object. Conversely, the hand-of-government view favours government regulation of social expenditures, after higher corporate taxes allow governmental funding allocations.

FIGURE 4.2 Possible levels of business and community mutual support (Frederick et al. 1988, p. 342)

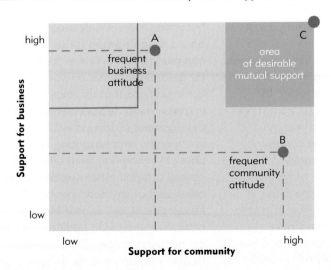

International community

International issues can impact social responsibilities. The Union of International Associations in Brussels listed 10 000 global problems, in categories including international tensions, scarce resources and growing pollution (Cornish 1990). Many firms responded by changing their practices (Ortega 1995).

Does social responsibility pay?

One interesting question is the impact of social responsibility on financial success. Studies are difficult as it is hard to measure accurately one firm's social responsibility against another's. This makes a definite answer impossible; however, research has found no clear relationship

MANAGING THE E-CHALLENGE

Rural women claim the internet

Community-of-interest groups around the world have awakened to the potential of the internet to reach far-flung individuals—neighbours in space or neighbours in thought, sharing common interests—and meld them into a community. One site, created by such a community, serves people who are technically neighbours in both space and interest but who may never meet, due to the scale of local distance and the ongoing commitments required by a rural lifestyle.

Founded in April 1999, 'Not Just Gumboots & Scones' was established by and for rural women in the southern half of the South Island of New Zealand. It would take a whole day's driving to cross this sparsely-populated area, where fewer than 20 000 people live outside the urban centres. The intended target market for this site is obviously small, yet it has attracted worldwide attention, featuring at a Brussels conference called Global Community Networking 2000.

The specific needs that Not Just targets are felt by communities everywhere: sharing information about upcoming events, providing a forum for discussion, identifying opportunities to learn more (including training in information technology) and generally building and supporting the community. Initial funding came from the Community Employment Group, but the majority of time and effort is donated (the webmaster, Anne Elliot, is described as 'either an underpaid worker or a little-rewarded volunteer'). Some businesses have sponsored specific pages, and Central Otago Rural Education Activities Programme (REAP) provided

administrative support for the first three years, with Dunedin Rural Development replacing it at the beginning of 2004.

Key aspects of the site are links to relevant support organisations (Women in Self-Employment (WISE) is an example) and links to sites promoting and explaining diversification of rural business activities (e.g. Australian Olives Ltd). There are overviews of key rural issues (such as New Zealand's new national weed control policy) and links to sources of legal information and advice, educational opportunities, potential funding sources and useful publications. Given the voluntary nature of the organisation, nearly all of the information is provided through links instead of being reproduced or originated on the site.

Not Just has survived its first four years and is becoming more widely recognised as a community-based support group for all members of the rural community (not only the computer nerds). It hopes for greater emphasis on consultation within the community so that its voice may be more influential in government decision making. Personal development of the individuals within the community, who have long felt isolated by their physical separation from urban education centres as well as each other, will also be emphasised. It is believed that the new sponsor, Dunedin Rural Development, will enable Not Just to expand its network and provide additional information and connection services. Simultaneously, Not Just has to deal with an increase in 'spam' (unsolicited email to members) and unpaid advertisements for commercial websites that are somewhat relevant to rural life.

Source: Contributed by Andre Everett (details of sources are listed on p. 735).

Website:

www.notjust.org.nz/

The focus of the Not Just Gumboots & Scones website is to facilitate information sharing and communication, leading to greater interaction, awareness and community activism. Most of the site consists of links to other sources of information, education and funding.

Activities for discussion, analysis and further research

1. What perceived 'gap in the market' is Not Just Gumboots & Scones attempting to fill? Why does this gap exist? Whose responsibility is it to meet this need? Who else could fill the gap, and why do they not already do so?

2. Is it possible to earn an income from sites such as this? How? (*Hint:* Look for page sponsors on the Not Just website.) How would the attempt to earn revenue from sites such as this be received by the communities they are intended to serve? If such sites cannot earn revenues, how should they be financed and managed?

3. Examine a variety of community services websites, including official sites (local, regional and national government), charitable organisations (e.g. Red Cross, Salvation Army), educational institutions and relevant portions of corporate sites. How do people hear about these sites? How can they be promoted to increase their awareness, given their acknowledged resource restrictions? Compare their stated intentions, goals or missions. How effective do you believe they are in achieving them?

between degree of social responsibility and financial success in the short term (Arlow & Gannon 1982; Aupperle, Carroll & Hatfield 1985; McShane & Travaglione 2003).

Research suggests a firm's financial performance is a good predictor of its social responsibility, not a result of it. Successful organisations may be prepared to take on socially responsible activities. Firms also engage in social responsibility to build stable stakeholder relationships and help reduce the chances of legal action and government fines (McGuire, Sundgren & Schneeweis 1988).

Research has found that announcements of illegal corporate action lower a firm's stock price, though long-term impacts are unclear (Davison & Worrell 1988). Ironically, research suggests generous charitable donations may help perceptions of companies as socially responsible, even if the company is behaving illegally (Wokutch & Spencer 1987). Corporate contributions for charitable and social responsibility purposes are called **corporate philanthropy**.

To balance conflicting expectations of stakeholders who support socially responsible behaviour and those favouring concentration on profit, many firms focus on socially responsible activities that affect their profit. Dick Hubbard is the founder of Hubbard's Foods Limited, a company based in New Zealand that produces a range of 23 breakfast cereals targeted towards the middle to high price ranges in the cereal market. Dick believes that there are a number of key stakeholders who have an interest in the business, including shareholders, employees, customers, suppliers and the community. He also believes in sharing his financial success with those outside the company. For over ten years he has supported Outward Bound (a charitable trust aimed at improving social and emotional learning through physical and mentally challenging activities). A donation of 50 cents is made to the Trust for every packet of the 'Outward Bound' cereal that is sold. The company is a member of the New Zealand Business Council for Sustainable Development (NZBCSD) and Dick is on its executive board. The NZBCSD is a branch of the World Business Council for Sustainable Development, and Hubbard's follows campaign of reducing waste, informing and educating customers and producing innovative products that conform to the precepts of sustainable development (Kirkwood & Ruwhiu 2003).

corporate philanthropy

Corporate contributions for charitable and social responsibility purposes

Promoting innovation: Vanguard companies

Though there may not be a direct relationship between social responsibility and financial performance (at least short-term), several firms score highly on both social responsibility and success. O'Toole (1985) calls these 'vanguard' corporations. His examples include John Deere, Honeywell, Levi Strauss and Motorola. There are four common characteristics of vanguard organisations:

1. **They try to satisfy all their stakeholders.** The basic idea is that shareholders' interests are best served in the long term when firms work to satisfy legitimate concerns of all stakeholders. These companies work hard to resolve conflicts and find ways to serve all constituencies at once.

CASE IN POINT

Who takes responsibility for ethics?

In the high-risk world of financial trading, ethical practices are more of a necessity than an option based on social responsibility. Individuals responsible for trading shares, futures or currency on behalf of banks have been subject to extensive and continuous checks since the derivatives trader Nick Leeson squandered nearly $1.4 billion of Barings Bank's money through unauthorised trading in 1995. As a consequence of the collapse of Barings, banks throughout the world strengthened their risk management policies and procedures, and strengthened the ethical standards that traders must adhere to.

In 2004, the term 'rogue transactions' hit the headlines again when the National Australia Bank announced that it had lost $360 million due to a series of unauthorised foreign exchange deals. The bank had been working to further improve its risk management practices since February 2003, when the Australian Prudential Regulation Authority (APRA) expressed its concern in this regard, and the bank established a risk management committee in August 2003. These improvements took place in the context of a company that had made serious efforts to be socially responsible, with equitable employment practices, a triple bottom-line performance evaluation, environmentally friendly policies and practices, extensive community partnerships and best-practice corporate governance structures. Adhering to ethical practices, however, is not just about committees, company image, special projects, written guidelines or regular checks. The huge bonuses from banks paid to individual traders for apparent trading profitability can

become incentives for traders to create illusionary profits. Ethical behaviour must be rewarded and a shared sense of responsibility for ethical practices must stretch across the whole organisation.

In the wake of the loss, the Chairman of the Board and the CEO both resigned. The responsibility for ethical behaviour and good risk management appeared to extend right to the top of the organisation. Since the scandal, the bank has made efforts to create an open culture and organisation and to renew their Board with more experienced bankers. The bank has paid dearly for a weakness in its management of ethics; however, its radical surgery has put it back on the road to a healthier future.

Source: Contributed by Peter Woods.

Websites:

http://www.nabgroup.com/
http://www.national.com.au/
http://www.abc.net.au/news/business/

Activities for discussion, analysis and further research

1. What practices identified in the case study would you label as either immoral management, amoral management or moral management?
2. How does this case illustrate the costs and benefits of social responsibility and ethics in management?
3. Why would the Chairman and CEO resign even though they apparently did not authorise the loss-making transactions?

2. **They are committed to a higher purpose.** These corporations see their role as giving society needed goods and services, employment and wealth creation in profits, to increase the general standard of living and quality of life. In this sense, profit is the means, not the end, of corporate efforts.
3. **They value continuous learning.** These companies see flexibility, change and responsiveness as vital to organisational survival. As a result, they monitor environmental changes, assessing the applicability of their own strategies and practices.
4. **They aim high.** They are dedicated to being best in all they do. As a result, they emphasise innovation to help them reach high goals.

Through commitment to these principles, vanguard companies have managed high-level social responsibility and been financially successful too.

ORGANISATIONAL SOCIAL RESPONSIVENESS

While managers hold a view of their organisation's social responsibilities, it becomes more concrete when managers actually respond to social responsibilities. **Organisational social responsiveness** refers to the development of organisational decision processes where managers anticipate, respond to, and manage social responsibility areas. Organisational social responsiveness is also called **corporate social responsiveness** as it is often applied to business organisations. However, other organisations find social responsiveness to be important too (Bateman & Snell 2004). For example, not-for-profit schools and hospitals must monitor various stakeholders' changing expectations and respond to them.

Two processes are basic to the development of organisational social responsiveness. First, methods must be set up to monitor the external environment's social demands and expectations. Second, internal social response mechanisms need to be developed.

Monitoring social demands and expectations

Means to assess social demands and expectations related to organisations include social forecasting, opinion surveys, social audits, issues management and social scanning.

Social forecasting

Social forecasting is the systematic identification of social trends, evaluation of the organisational importance of those trends, and integration of them into an organisation's forecasting program. One approach is using **futurists**, individuals who track important environmental trends and try to predict their organisational impact, usually 10 or more years ahead. Others use consultants and research institutes specialising in social forecasting.

Opinion surveys

Associations and business publications conduct surveys on social issues. These often identify different groups' views of social responsibility. One poll, for example, showed that only 31 per cent of people saw business executives as having good moral and ethical standards (also see Table 4.1) (*USA Today* 1992).

Social audits

A **social audit** is the systematic study and evaluation of social, rather than economic, organisation performance. It includes assessment of the social impact of a firm's activities, evaluation of programs with social goals, and identification of areas to be actioned. Social audits are difficult because disagreements can arise about what to include, results can be intangible and/or difficult to measure, and opinions may vary about what makes adequate or good social performance. Nevertheless, firms increasingly assess their performance by social audits (Post et al. 1996).

---

organisational social responsiveness

A term referring to the development of organisational decision processes where managers anticipate, respond to, and manage areas of social responsibility

corporate social responsiveness

A term used in reference to the concept of organisational social responsiveness as applied to business organisations

social forecasting

The systematic process of identifying social trends, evaluating the organisational importance of those trends, and integrating these assessments into the organisation's forecasting program

futurists

Individuals who track significant trends in the environment and attempt to predict their impact on the organisation

social audit

A systematic study and evaluation of the social, rather than economic, performance of an organisation

Issues management

As applied to social responsiveness, **issues management** is the identification of a small number of emerging social issues relevant to the organisation, analysing possible impacts, and developing effective responses. Identifying 10 to 15 issues is usual, depending on organisational events. Issues management seeks to reduce 'surprises' from environmental forces and facilitate a proactive approach to environmental change (Fleming 1981; Wartick & Cochran 1985). At Monsanto, for example, the Executive Management Committee, chaired by the president, worked with different parts of the company to identify 170 social issues. The list was culled to five critical issues in the business environment: fair trade, biotechnology regulation, intellectual property rights, agricultural policy, and hazardous waste and public compensation. Through issues management, the firm led greater co-operation between industry and environmental groups.

Social scanning

Social scanning is general surveillance of task-environment elements to find evidence of impending changes affecting organisational social responsibilities. Unlike issues management, social scanning is more informal and unsystematic. Executives use their own experience of issues likely to affect the organisation, but may rely on systematic assessments, as discussed before (Daft, Sormunen & Parkes 1988).

After assessing American social expectations, Sadahei Kusumoto, Minolta's president and CEO, urged the subsidiaries of Japanese companies to attend to US standards of corporate social responsibility. Subsidiaries had not engaged in corporate philanthropy in the United States, as Japanese tax incentives were lower and corporate giving was rare. Kusumoto argued that Japanese subsidiaries in the United States must become more active or risk being branded as 'irresponsible outsiders' and 'dim their prospects for the future'. Thus Kusumoto was important in environment scanning and noting trends impacting Japanese companies working in the United States. When Japan doubled corporate tax deductions for foreign charitable gifts, Japanese corporate giving doubled globally (Kusumoto 1989; Schroeder 1991). While social demands and expectations must be monitored, organisations must also develop appropriate response mechanisms (Rue & Byars 2003).

Internal social response mechanisms

An organisation's internal social response mechanisms include departments, committees and human resources impacting its responsiveness to social environment changes (Strand 1987). The common social responses of an organisation include individual executives, temporary task forces, permanent committees or departments or combinations of these (Holmes 1978; Post et al. 1996).

Individual executives

Using individual executives as a social response mechanism means either appointing or allowing individuals to handle critical social issues as they happen. This is more common in small rather than larger firms.

Temporary task forces

This involves forming a committee of several people for a limited time to deal with a critical social issue. After taking action, the committee or task force disbands. Temporary task forces are very effective when an important social issue suddenly needs input from various parts of the organisation.

Permanent committees

There are many types of permanent committees. Almost 100 of the *Fortune* 500 companies have special committees on the board of directors to deal with social issues. These may be called public policy, public issues, social responsibility and corporate responsibility committees (Lovdall, Bauer & Treverton 1977). Permanent committees of executive-level members, committees of members across management levels, or division-level committees funnelling critical issues to higher-level committees may be used.

Permanent departments

Many firms have a permanent department to co-ordinate social responsibilities, and identify and recommend policies for new social issues. This is often called the **public affairs department**. It may co-ordinate government and/or community relations with other external activities. In a study of large and medium-sized firms, 361 of 400 respondents had a public affairs unit, one-third set up since 1975. The trend to having such departments continues (Post, Murray, Dickie & Mahon 1983; Post et al. 1996).

Combination approaches

In practice, organisations use a combination of mechanisms to build social performance (Bhambri & Sonnenfeld 1988). For example, division-level committees or a public affairs department may make recommendations to an executive-level committee or to certain key executives. Levi Strauss, which has a good reputation for social responsiveness, pioneered a novel use of permanent committees. The program involves employees across the organisation and is co-ordinated by regional and corporate community affairs departments.

public affairs department

A permanent department that co-ordinates various ongoing social responsibilities and identifies and recommends policies for new social issues

MANAGERIAL DILEMMAS

Aye, captain—Aye, captain: Managing ethical quandaries

Values define a person's beliefs. Ethics are concerned with what is right, what is wrong and with moral duty to your employees, your organisation and society. A situation may be further complicated by the fact that moral standards change with time, and by the complexity of conducting business in a multicultural environment. Ethics is very much concerned with the management of physical resources and operations, underpinned by human factors such as attitude and behaviour.

Consider the following situation:

A motor vessel was towing a barge from Singapore to Indonesia and had difficulty getting past Customs. The paperwork was in order but clearance was not given. It was hinted that a sum of money was the 'custom'. The Australian captain considered this to be morally incorrect and, being prepared to stand by his principles, went against the 'custom'. Consequently, the ship was held up for four days. The Company demanded an explanation for the delay. The payment of a sum of money was a known and accepted 'custom/norm' and several people ridiculed the captain's decision for going against the norm.

Source: Allison Powell, Australian Maritime College.

Decision point: The central question of right conduct

Although the outcome resulted in a financial and operational 'cost' in that the ship was held over and the sailing schedule was disrupted, the captain's intentions and underlying motives were good. Generally we tend to judge a person's character by the deeds they perform. A 'good' person, we normally think, is one who tries to do or habitually does what is 'right'. In the managerial context, ethical decisions frequently require us to make careful judgments of character. Therefore a manager has a moral duty to select employees whose moral integrity can be relied upon.

Reflection points

1. What are the ethical issues involved in the above situation?
2. If you were the Australian captain and it was hinted that a personal payment would ease the process, what would you do? Why? What do you think you should do and why?

BEING AN ETHICAL MANAGER

Company social responsibility and responsiveness are based on managers' ethical standards. Media articles about ethical problems in business are common. In a study using simulated business situations, 47 per cent of top executives, 41 per cent of controllers and 76 per cent of graduate-level business students surveyed were prepared to commit fraud by understating write-offs, reducing the value of certain assets. The write-offs would lower profit levels that were soon to be reported (Brief, Dukerich, Brown & Brett 1996). Faced with these problems, many firms are clarifying ethical standards. To help employees internalise company standards, Citicorp and Lockheed Martin Corp. designed games with cards containing situations and issues employees could face. Players move by selecting an option for handling a scenario. They gain or lose points based on how their choices match company standards. Some items from the Lockheed Martin game in the *Grey Matters* book are included in an exercise at the end of this chapter (*Wall Street Journal* 1989; Myers 1992).

In Australia, corporate governance guidelines have been established by the Australian Stock Exchange, for publicly listed companies (Walters 2003).

One issue is growing white-collar crime (fraud or embezzlement, by a business person, government or not-for-profit organisations, or professional) (*Webster's New World Dictionary* 1984). By US estimates, street crime costs $4 billion a year, and white-collar crime about $40 billion, eventually paid by consumers and taxpayers. The rise results from the current emphasis on materialism and competitive pressures. Women, rarely in the past involved in white-collar crime, are increasingly taking part in it (Koepp 1987; Bowen 1987; Burrough 1987).

Business ethics problems raise three significant issues about being an ethical manager: the types of managerial ethics, the ethical guidelines a manager might adopt, and ethical career issues one may face.

Types of managerial ethics

Managerial ethics, as noted, are standards of conduct or moral judgment that managers use in their work. The standards come from society's general norms and values; an individual's experiences in family, religious, educational and other institutions; and interpersonal interactions. Thus, managerial ethics differ between people (Post et al. 1996; Lee 1994; *Business Week* 1995) (see Fig. 4.3). Carroll (1987) notes that three major levels of moral, or

FIGURE 4.3 Extract from *Business Week*/Harris Poll (Business Week 1995)

BUSINESS WEEK/HARRIS POLL: IS AN ANTI-BUSINESS BACKLASH BUILDING?	
Q. How would you describe your own attitude toward business in this country ... very favourable, somewhat favourable, somewhat unfavourable, or very unfavourable?	**A.** Very favourable .... 18% Somewhat favourable .... 54% Somewhat unfavourable .... 18% Very unfavourable .... 6% Not sure 4%
Q. How would you rate the ethical standards of business executives ... excellent, pretty good, only fair, or poor?	**A.** Excellent .... 2% Pretty good .... 38% Only fair .... 46% Poor .... 12% Not sure 2%
Q. Do you think white-collar crime is very common, somewhat common, not very common, or not common at all?	**A.** Very common .... 49% Somewhat common .... 41% Not very common .... 7% Not common at all .... 2% Not sure 1%

ethical, judgment characterise managers: immoral management, amoral management and moral management.

Immoral management

In business 'immoral' and 'unethical' may be synonymous. Thus **immoral management** lacks ethical principles, actively opposing ethical behaviour. There is exclusive concern with profit and success at any cost, readiness to treat others unfairly, viewing laws as obstacles, and an inclination to 'cut corners'. Immoral management's key principle is: 'Can we make money with this action, decision or behaviour?' Implicit is the view that other considerations matter little, if at all.

Carroll (1987) cites an example of immoral management involving plant managers at a GM truck plant. In violation of the work contract, managers used a secret control box to override a control panel setting the assembly line's speed. Plant managers, pressured by higher-level managers after missed deadlines, met production targets and were praised by their bosses. When it was uncovered, workers won compensation.

Amoral management

Amoral management is neither immoral nor moral but ignores or is oblivious to ethical issues. There are two amoral management types: intentional and unintentional. Intentionally amoral managers exclude ethical concerns from decisions and actions as they think general ethical standards are not applicable to business. Unintentionally amoral managers are inattentive or insensitive to moral implications of their decisions and actions and ignore ethical issues. Overall, amoral managers may be well-meaning, but give little attention to their behaviour's impact as they chase profitability. They allow other managers to behave as they will unless the behaviour generates notoriety or pressure. Amoral management's basic principle is: 'Within the letter of the law, can we make money with this action, decision or behaviour?'

Nestlé's decision to market baby formula in third world countries is one example of amoral management. The Swiss company did not anticipate the results of impure water, poverty and illiteracy on mothers and babies when marketing formula there. Its lack of concern led consumers worldwide to boycott Nestlé products.

immoral management

An approach not only lacking ethical principles but actively opposed to ethical behaviour

amoral management

An approach that is neither immoral nor moral, but ignores or is oblivious to ethical considerations

GENDER FACTOR

Christine Nixon is the force

Christine Nixon has been in the police force for thirty years, and is the first female Chief Commissioner of Police in Victoria. Her route to the top has not always been smooth, and along the way she learnt two very important lessons: policies relating to policing could be unjust and pedantic; and the power of senior officers was absolute. She has felt the brunt of that political power when she was sidelined to a posting in Wollongong, effectively blocking her career path. After moving to Melbourne she was appointed by the government to her current position, and has since developed a reform program that is expected to set new directions for the police force well into the next decade.

Forty internal working parties, set up to deal with a range of police matters, have generated approximately 500 recommendations for change; 95 per cent of these will be adopted. Nixon is committed to crime-squad reform and believes it is imperative to have people who are trustworthy and above reproach in these crucial areas. She wants to have the ability to dismiss unsuitable members of the force and plans to appoint an external police authority to add independence to the process of police discipline. She states: 'People involved in the system may not like the outcome but they should believe they have been dealt with fairly.'

Nixon believes consultation is the best way to bring about reforms, but she has made it clear that some issues, such as alcohol and drug-testing of police, are not open for negotiation. Her key focus will be on the four core issues that affect people's lives: stolen vehicles; burglaries; the road toll; and domestic violence and sexual assault.

Although she has shown she can make tough decisions, Nixon also has a capacity to make those around her feel comfortable. She speaks to community groups on at least three days each week, and travels widely to meet her officers. In addition, she encourages police to email her if they have problems or suggestions. These communications indicated that there were morale problems, with employees feeling a lack of support. Morale is now improving—police resignations have dropped from 60 per month to 12—and this is attributed to Nixon's open management style and personality, and her understanding of natural justice and fairness. Christine Nixon appears to be a person of her word. She personally responded to a rumour about her returning to New South Wales before the end of her term with the following email: 'I would like everyone to know that I gave a commitment to you and the Victorian community to serve my full term with Victoria Police, and I intend to fulfil that promise.'

Source: Contributed by Glenice Wood; adapted from Silvester, J. (2002).

Activities for discussion, analysis and further research

1. In terms of organisational social responsiveness, how has Christine Nixon monitored social demands and expectations in the Victorian police force? Discuss.
2. What level of ethical management characterises Christine Nixon: immoral management, amoral management or moral management? Explain your view.
3. Do you believe Christine Nixon has put in place appropriate mechanisms for ethical management practices in the Victorian police force? Consider the seven mechanisms listed on pp. 111–2, and discuss what Nixon has implemented to create an ethical climate.
4. Log on to the website: www.victoriapolice.net. This is the official Victoria Police Force website. Explore this site and consider if the information contained therein creates a sense of confidence in the police force and demonstrates an ethos of social responsibility for the community. Consider this in the light of a visible code of ethics, a concept adopted by an estimated 90 per cent of major corporations.

Moral management

moral management

An approach that strives to follow ethical principles and precepts

In contrast to both immoral and amoral management, **moral management** follows ethical principles and precepts. While moral managers want to succeed, they do so only within ethical standards and ideals of fairness, justice and due process. As a result, moral managers pursue twin business objectives of profit making and engaging in legal and ethical behaviours. They follow both the law's letter and the law's spirit, realising that moral management means working above legally mandated levels. The core principle is: 'Is this action, decision or behaviour fair to us and all parties involved?'

One example of an organisation taking ethical leadership involved the chainsaw manufacturer, McCulloch Corporation, displaying moral management. Statistics showed that chainsaws were involved in 123 000 injuries a year. Despite the statistics, the Chain Saw Manufacturers Association fought mandatory safety standards, arguing they were inflated and did not justify mandatory standards. Displaying moral leadership, McCulloch put chain brakes on all its saws. Later, the firm left the association after repeated attempts failed to have higher safety standards adopted.

Carroll (1987) believes amoral management dominates today. He argues that a moral management stance is likely to be in the best long-term interests of organisations.

Ethical guidelines for managers

Ethical standards vary. For example, 43 per cent of respondents to an *INC.* (1992) survey saw paying suppliers within 60 days as acceptable, while expecting accounts receivables to be paid in 30 days. Of respondents, 16 per cent saw it as acceptable to make dealers take more product than needed. As situations vary, it is hard to write hard-and-fast rules for all options. Ambiguities abound with many grey areas. For example, when is a 'token gift' from a supplier a bribe? (Tuleja 1985; Rue & Byars 2003). To help staff with this issue, General Motors has a policy on 'gifts, entertainment and other gratuities', outlined in a 12-page booklet with scenarios with fictional players. One scenario, demonstrating the use of General Motors' policy, is shown in Table 4.3.

Despite problems in setting specific ethical standards, guidelines can be useful to understand the ethical implications of managerial decisions and behaviours. The guidelines below fit the principle of enlightened self-interest (O'Toole 1985).

Obey the law. A basic social responsibility and managerial ethics tenet is obedience to the law, preferably in both letter and spirit.

Tell the truth. Telling the truth is vital to build stakeholders' trust. The Digital Equipment Corporation (DEC) was asked by an employee group to look at a seemingly high miscarriage rate among female workers on semiconductor assembly lines; DEC commissioned a study. The study found the semiconductor area had miscarriage rates of 39 per cent in contrast to 18 per cent in other company areas and the wider population. DEC gave employees the results, passing them to the Semiconductor Industry Association (Moskowitz 1987).

Show respect for people. Treating people with respect has deep roots in the study of ethics. Respect for the individual is a central aspect in the move to valuing diversity.

Stick to the Golden Rule. The Golden Rule, 'Do unto others as you would have others do unto you', is a standard for measuring the ethical dimensions of business decisions. In business

TABLE 4.3 GENERAL MOTORS' REVISED GRATUITIES POLICY

Guidelines for a specific scenario as set out in the GM Revised Policy on Gifts, Entertainment, and Other Gratuities

Scenario:	A distinguished investment banking firm has successfully concluded a major acquisition for GM and invites, at the firm's expense, all the GM employees who worked with it to a dinner in New York at which each will be given a nice mantle clock, appropriately inscribed, as a memento of the successful venture.
Policy:	The dinner and clock should be politely declined. While 'thank you' gestures are a nice custom socially, they can create wrong appearances if they are lavish or extravagant. Firms that provide high-value services should be rewarded by being considered for future work. There is no need or expectation that they 'thank' individual GM employees with gifts, entertainment or other gratuities. Consistent with business custom and management approval, items of no or nominal commercial value commemorating significant accomplishments or expressing appreciation for past GM support, such as a Lucite block, certificate or baseball cap, may be accepted from suppliers on an infrequent basis.

Source: Reprinted from the *Wall Street Journal* (1996).

terms, it means treat people fairly, as managers would want the firm treated if it were a person (Tuleja 1985). When Cummins Engine closed a components plant in Darlington, England, British trade union leaders went to the firm's head office in Columbus, Indiana, to get the decision changed. Cummins held to their decision but offered to have 500 redundant workers retrained for new jobs. Union leaders praised the firm for its concern (Moskowitz 1987).

Above all, do no harm (*Primum non nocere*). Some writers see this principle—the first rule of medical ethics—to be the bottom-line ethical concern and easily adopted by business. H. J. Heinz told fruit and vegetable growers for its baby foods that products could not be treated with chemicals under study by federal agencies as health dangers. This decision was made although the chemicals were still legal (Moskowitz 1987).

Practise participation, not paternalism. This principle is aimed at finding stakeholders' needs, rather than deciding what is best for them. Weyerhaeuser, a forest-products firm, built a reputation among environmentalists by asking their views before finalising plans for land or facility development.

Always act when you have responsibility. Managers are responsible to act when they have capacity or resources. Managerial action is vital if someone is in need and a manager is the only one who can help. For example, Merck pledged free supplies of Ivermectin to combat river blindness in third world countries, but couldn't find an effective distribution system. So Merck set up a committee for distribution of the drug.

For managerial guidance in these principles, see the discussion under Management skills for a globalised economy, 'Questions to facilitate ethical business decisions'.

Ethical career issues

Like most managers, you will have ethical dilemmas across your career. These generally arise in grey areas, where a situation can be interpreted variably. As well as considering their social responsibilities, managers must reflect on their personal values and self-protection in deciding

MANAGEMENT SKILLS FOR A GLOBALISED ECONOMY

Questions to facilitate ethical business decisions

When faced with an ethical dilemma, you may find it helpful to work through the following questions. These can help clarify your thinking and decide on an action.

1. Have you accurately defined the problem?
2. How would you define the problem if you stood on the other side of the fence?
3. How did this situation occur in the first place?
4. To whom and to what do you give your loyalty as a person and as a member of the company?
5. What is your intention in making this decision?
6. How does this intention compare with the likely results?
7. Whom could your decision or action injure?

8. Can you discuss the problem with affected parties before you make your decision?
9. Are you confident your position will be as valid over a long period of time as it seems now?
10. Could you disclose, without qualm, your decision or action to your boss, your CEO, the board of directors, your family, or society in general?
11. What is the symbolic potential of your action if understood? If misunderstood?
12. Under what conditions would you allow exceptions to your stand?

Source: Nash (1981). Reprinted by permission of *Harvard Business Review.*

how to deal with these situations. They must consider anticipating and avoiding ethical conflicts (Bhambri & Sonnenfeld 1987).

Assessing values and protecting yourself

When facing an ethical dilemma, three steps are important. First, seek expertise and support from a wide network of trusted people. At times others may see a practice as ethical but you will be unsure. In such cases, check with trusted friends, former classmates, peers and/or experts. This clarifies your values on the issue and helps you decide if further action is needed. Second, if necessary, take internal actions to achieve change. As a manager, get the facts straight before suggesting behaviour is inappropriate or illegal. Then bring the issue to your superiors and try to persuade them to take corrective action. If the dilemma persists, move on to the third step, which is to take internal actions to protect yourself. As a manager in the chain of command, you may be scapegoated for actions implicitly or explicitly condoned by higher ups. Claiming to be following orders will not excuse you if you have broken the law. Instead, write a memo for the file, outlining your objections and discussions. Talk with other staff about your concerns. Seeking a new job is another step to consider seriously. Above all, do not engage in illegal activities. These actions together provide evidence you tried to halt the ethical problem.

Anticipating ethical conflicts

Although it can be hard to predict how likely ethical conflicts are, there are some possible steps to help. First, when seeking employment, check for signs of potential conflict. Ask your family, friends and teachers about the firm. Check the web for articles and background information. Use job interviews to understand company operations. Try to meet those you would work with. Try to detect signs of serious dissatisfaction and dissension that might signal ethical conflicts. Second, check industry practices. Stable industries may develop informal networks encouraging competitor collusion. Industries with easy entry, a highly competitive environment, and severe market pressures may face ethical problems. Third, avoid even small ethical compromises: they can escalate. To prevent being trapped in a situation where compromises are hard to avoid, save some of your earnings in a backup account so you will be able to leave a job if it becomes untenable.

MANAGING AN ETHICAL ORGANISATION

Although others can be blamed, people are responsible for their own actions. An important challenge for managers is to operate a firm where business is done ethically. To do this, managers must know the external and internal conditions which make unethical behaviour likely. They can also use mechanisms to aid ethical behaviour.

Situational factors influencing ethical behaviour

Research on ethical versus unethical behaviour in organisations largely focuses on law breaking. The studies suggest several organisational environment factors can encourage illegal, unethical behaviour (see Table 4.4) (Finney & Lesieur 1981; Baucus & Near 1991). Of course, managers' values also influence whether people actually engage in unethical behaviour, though some situations make it more likely.

For example, *environmental competitiveness* encourages unethical behaviour. Industries with common price-fixing, including the motor industry, paper cartons, plumbing fixtures and heavy electrical equipment, have strong competition, similar products, frequent price changes and negotiations. Competition in not-for-profit organisations can foster unethical behaviour too. This behaviour includes illegal athlete payments, illegal political contributions, and the proportion of charitable contributions actually received by the needy (Bateman & Snell 2004).

TABLE 4.4 SITUATIONAL FACTORS INFLUENCING ETHICAL BEHAVIOUR

External factors	Internal factors
Environmental competitiveness	Pressure for high performance
Environmental munificence	Labour dissatisfaction
Extreme dependency	Delegation
	Encouragement of innovation

Low and high *environmental bounty* may also encourage unethical behaviour. If low, success opportunities are limited. Struggling for financial success in this environment may result in firms behaving unethically. The second-largest US baby food manufacturer, the Beech-Nut Nutrition Corporation, demonstrated this. Beech-Nut executives ignored chemists' cautions that the apple concentrate bought at below-market prices was probably being extensively altered. Two executives were jailed and fined for their part in selling the totally synthetic juice, labelled as '100 per cent fruit juice'. The scandal damaged the company's baby food products sales. The executives ignored warnings as the firm was almost broke (Welles 1988; Queenan 1988).

High bounty may lead to unethical activities as firms try to grow quickly and gain from a favourable situation. For example, an executive of Halsey Drug Co., a Brooklyn, New York, generic drug maker, was sentenced to 18 months jail for conspiring to add ingredients unapproved by the Food and Drug Administration (FDA) to generic drugs for irregular heartbeats, meningitis and hyperthyroidism (Pereeira & Rebello 1995). The official was attempting to boost the drugs' effectiveness to benefit from growing markets for generics that were cheaper but assumed to be therapeutically equivalent to brand-name drugs. Another example involves the South Australian Olive Corporation and Inglewood Olive Processors who misrepresented the origins of their extra virgin olive oil. The oil was advertised as being made in Australia, when in reality as much as 50 per cent was from overseas sources (Costa 2003).

A third external factor influencing unethical behaviour is *extreme dependency* of one organisation on another. These dependencies create pressures for bribes and payoffs (Ingersoll 1989).

Internal organisational factors can also make unethical behaviour more likely. *Pressure for higher performance* and output impels people to take 'shortcuts' including price fixing, speeding up an assembly line secretly or releasing unsafe products (Eichenwald 1992; *Economist* 1995).

Labour dissatisfaction may also lead to unethical behaviour as anger replaces logical, rational behaviour. Ironically, *delegation of authority* and *encouragement of innovation* gives greater latitude and creativity and may increase unethical behaviour. For example, at Adam Opel AG, General Motors' German subsidiary, three senior board members and several employees resigned after accusations that they had accepted free work on their homes, or engaged in a kickback scheme involving contract awarding. Opel chairman David Herman said that, in becoming 'leaner', the company may have cut too many financial checks and balances. He warned, 'This is a word to the wise in other companies' (Kurylko 1995, p. 36).

Since external factors and internal pressures increase the incidence of unethical activity, managers must monitor with care. Under these conditions, managers must work harder to convey how important ethical behaviour is to staff.

A study suggests middle- and lower-level managers may feel greater ethical pressure than upper-level managers (Posner & Schmidt 1984). This means upper-level managers may be unaware of the experience of middle- and lower-level managers of these pressures, and do not act to counter them.

Mechanisms for ethical management

An important question is how can managers foster ethical organisational behaviour? Behaviour is not easy to influence; however, managers can create an ethical climate. Mechanisms include the following (Post et al. 1996).

Increasing awareness of diversity

You normally view others from your own viewpoint, using your own attitudes, feelings, thoughts and experiences to guide interactions. Diversity, however, demands awareness of attitudes and experiences of others. Diversity-awareness programs seek to raise participants' awareness of (1) their own attitudes, biases and stereotypes and (2) disparate viewpoints of managers, subordinates, co-workers and customers. The common goals of these programs include (Carnevale & Stone 1994):

- provide participants with accurate information on diversity
- uncover stereotypes and personal biases
- assess personal beliefs, attitudes and values
- overturn inaccurate stereotypes and beliefs
- develop an atmosphere where people can share perspectives and viewpoints
- improve understanding of those who are different

Top-management commitment

Managers can show their commitment through several mechanisms set out below and the positive examples of their own behaviours (Jones 1995). Vernon R. Loucks Jr, president and CEO of Baxter Travenol Laboratories Inc., argues that staff will attend more to your actions than to your words.

Codes of ethics

It is estimated 90 per cent of major corporations have written **codes of ethics**. A code of ethics is a document prepared to guide organisation members in encountering ethical dilemmas. While almost all firms with a code say it helps maintain staff's ethical behaviour, a study showed only 36 per cent issue their code to all staff and only 20 per cent display it widely (Otten 1986). Only about 40 per cent of firms in a comparative study in Britain, France and what was then West Germany had codes of ethics, and with great variation between countries based on political, legal and sociocultural variations (Langlois & Schlegelmilch 1990).

Ethics committees

According to an Ethics Resource Centre survey, about a third of *Fortune* 1000 companies have ethics committees. An **ethics committee** is a group which helps set up policies and resolve major ethical questions facing company members at work. The committee may oversee ethics training programs. Often the committee has members from top management and/or the board of directors.

Ethics audits

Some firms conduct **ethics audits**—systematic efforts to assess conformity to organisational ethical policies, aid understanding of these policies, and identify serious breaches needing remediation. Even so, ethical problems can be hard to identify. For example, Dow Corning, with a model ethics program and ethics audits, was enmeshed in a serious ethical crisis. In Australia an external measure, Reputec, is used increasingly, although it has met with mixed reception from industry (Ryan 2003).

code of ethics

A document prepared for the purpose of guiding organisation members when they encounter an ethical dilemma

ethics committee

A group charged with helping to establish policies and resolve major questions involving ethical issues confronting organisation members in the course of their work

ethics audits

Systematic efforts to assess conforming to organisational ethical policies, aid understanding of those policies, and identify serious breaches requiring remedial action

Ethics hot lines

ethics hot line

A special telephone line established to enable employees to bypass the normal chain of command in reporting grievances and serious ethical problems

An **ethics hot line** is a special telephone line set up to allow employees to bypass the normal chain of command, report grievances and serious ethical issues. The line is normally managed by an executive assigned to investigate and work to resolve reported issues. A hot line aids internal problem handling and reduces the incidence of whistle-blowing employees. A **whistle-blower** is an employee who reports a real or perceived wrongdoing under the control of their employer to those able to take needed action. When a whistle-blower goes outside the organisation, bad publicity, investigations and lawsuits are common (Dozier & Miceli 1985; Near & Miceli 1995).

Ethics training

whistle-blower

An employee who reports a real or perceived wrongdoing under the control of their employer to those able to take appropriate action

Many organisations use ethics training to encourage ethical behaviour. Training can focus just on ethical issues or be integrated into training on many other issues. Clarifying expectations and ethical standards helps reduce unethical behaviour (Michael, Daniel, Hopper, George-Falvey & Ferris 1996; Garland 1998). Understanding company standards better leads to appropriate organisation member decision, the subject of the next chapter.

GAINING THE EDGE

Meeting the challenge of labour shortage: An innovative and socially responsive approach

One of the biggest challenges facing Australian organisations is labour market shortage. As globalisation attracts skilled workers to overseas jobs, and/or skilled workers leave the workforce earlier, the pool of available workers in Australia is becoming smaller. According to ABS statistics (cited in *Business Review Weekly* 2003), between 1993 and 2002 growth in the age-group 20 to 44 fell 6 per cent, and growth between 2003 and 2012 is estimated to be less than 2 per cent.

Australia Post is one of the few organisations adopting an innovative and socially responsive approach to this problem. In the current human resource environment, building a business case for employing older workers makes financial and social sense. Not only does this approach provide a means of dealing with current demographic changes in the pool of labour supply, it actively readdresses one of the key categories of workplace discrimination, namely age discrimination or the tendency to overlook older workers (*Human Rights and Equal Opportunity Commission Act 1986* (Cwlth)).

Australia Post recognises the untapped skills available through older workers and has developed a set of innovative human resource initiatives. These initiatives include encouraging workers to maintain their skill currency over a working life, the redesign of work environments for older workers through ergonomic assessment and the implementation of occupational health and safety standards, and the development of new career paths (*People Management* 2003).

This approach marks a reversal in the trend not to employ older workers but it brings with it a set of new human resource challenges. Organisations will need to develop recruitment and selection processes that successfully target older workers. They will need to actively build cultures that value the skills and experience older workers bring to the organisation.

Source: Contributed by Denise Faifua (details of sources are listed on p. 735).

Activities for discussion, analysis and further research

1. With respect to anti-discrimination law, would you describe Australia Post as behaving in a socially responsible or socially responsive manner? Explain your answer.

2. Do you believe Australia Post's motivations are financial or social, amoral or moral?

3. What arguments, if any, could be used to build a culture that values the skills and experience of older workers?

KIMBERLEY TURNER

AEROSAFE
RISK MANAGEMENT

In my opinion, corporate social responsibility is about both giving something back and maintaining integrity in our approach to business. Sometimes the giving back part may be in pure dollar terms; at times it may be providing our services for somebody who may not be able to afford it or to get the quality which is needed in that area, and other times it may be something a little more personal such as sponsoring the development of a school in a village overseas or getting out on a Friday night as a team and feeding the homeless.

This is something which has become more real to us. We made this commitment about three years ago to give something back to the community. So each year, the whole staff sits down to discuss and select an area of the community that we would like to give back to. One year we sponsored a village in East Timor by contributing a percentage of our

annual turnover to its development. We have supported the Salvation Army by providing our services in setting up their risk-management program in their retail arm 'The Salvo Stores'. For next year, we have selected an aviation project in which we will help establish the safety and risk-management system for over a dozen community helicopter providers in the country. This project is part-government funded, part-funded by the community and our contribution. We are contributing the majority of developmental work and for us that is a substantial financial commitment as well as the provision of intellectual property.

Ethics is important to me. I find it strange that it needs to be a form of discipline in business. In my view it should just be. You shouldn't need to formalise it. To me, being a good manager and being a sound organisation with integrity is what constitutes good corporate governance. Ethics is the heart of good corporate governance—a key to business ethics is accountability. Being accountable for your people, your product, your finances, your clients, your shareholders, your assets, your reputation, your processes, your environment, being accountable for the good management and good business practice of running an organisation. For me in my organisation, it is about honesty, integrity, valuing people and appreciating the good work that they do. This is critical to building solid ethics of the organisation and it comes down to leading by example. Something as small as providing clients with accurate estimates and honest calculations of the work that you have done through to invoicing procedures, fair tendering, proper staff recruitment and following through on rewarding your team when a good job is done. Ethics is about being honest and telling the truth, respecting your staff and appreciating them when they do put in over and above. I see all of this as bundled up in the ethics basket. I think it is a way of living—a way of managing rather than something that you have to do.

Internal ethics is one thing, yet this practice needs to extend to your external relationships to clients, industry, regulatory and partner organisations that you may be teaming with. Respecting intellectual property, competition, playing fair and honestly, and not cutting corners unethically to secure an advantage. Let the advantages you win be on merit, a solid foundation, and not one that could easily be unravelled if challenged or investigated. I sit on the Australian Standard Committee for Corporate Governance and we describe good governance as the alignment of responsibility, accountability and resourcing.

Strategies for improving

1. Does your organisation have a code of ethics? If not, how would you go about convincing your organisation they need to develop one?
2. Develop a strategy to implement development of a code of ethics in an organisation which has not seen they require one.
3. How would you ensure managers in your organisation treat people equitably, rather than based on familiarity with their backgrounds?
4. Develop a plan for helping managers in your organisation understand and avoid stereotypes.

Source: Jones et al. (2000).

SUMMARY

- Organisational, or corporate, social responsibility refers to a firm's obligation to act to protect and improve society's welfare jointly with their own interests. Three major contrasting views on the nature of corporate social responsibility are the invisible hand, the hand of government and the hand of management. Due to expanding social expectations about social responsibility of business and other organisations, the relevance of the hand-of-management view to managers is increasing. The iron law of responsibility suggests socially responsible behaviour may have a positive long-term effect on organisational success.

- Management's social responsibility focuses on six main stakeholder groups: shareholders, employees, customers, the local community, the wider society and the international community. Studies show no clear links between a firm's social-responsibility level and its short-run financial success. However, it is possible to be both socially responsible and financially successful. More organisations are orienting their socially responsible activities into areas which can affect their bottom line and eventually give a competitive edge.

- Corporate social responsiveness refers to development of organisational decision-processes where managers anticipate, respond to, and manage social-responsibility areas. Two processes usually are vital. First, methods of monitoring social demands and expectations must be established. Major means are social forecasting, opinion surveys, social audits and issues management. Second, internal social response mechanisms must be developed. These include use of individual executives, temporary task forces, permanent committees, permanent departments, or combinations of these elements.

- Ultimately, questions of corporate social responsibility and social responsiveness depend on managers' ethical standards. Three types of managerial ethics are immoral, amoral and moral. While amoral behaviour prevails, moral management is likely to be in the organisation's best long-run interests. Ethical guidelines for managers include: obey the law; tell the truth; show respect for people; stick to the golden rule; above all, do no harm; practise participation, not paternalism; and always act when you have responsibility. Ethical career issues for managers may involve assessing their own values and protecting themselves, as well as considering how they can anticipate and avoid ethical conflicts.

- A major management challenge is operating an organisation so members conduct their business ethically. To do so, managers must know what environmental and organisational conditions increase the chances of unethical behaviour. They should also use mechanisms facilitating ethical behaviour, such as top-management commitment, codes of ethics, ethics committees, ethics audits, ethics training and hot lines.

QUESTIONS FOR DISCUSSION AND REVIEW

1. Explain the three major perspectives on corporate social responsibility. What criteria might you use to determine whether a company's management subscribes most closely to the invisible-hand, hand-of-government, or hand-of-management view?
2. Identify at least one regulation in each hand-of-government control category for your local area. In what ways do these direct companies' actions or responsibilities?
3. Identify an organisation fulfilling some discretionary activities in your local area. In what ways will this impact on the community's perceptions of the firm?
4. Identify, from your local business press, one example of shareholders' pressure changing management's social stance. Will this make further changes more likely? Why?
5. Identify six stakeholder groups often mentioned with social responsibility. To what extent do these groups apply to your college or university? What other stakeholders might you add?
6. Evaluate the extent to which organisational social responsibility can pay off financially. Universities are often recipients of corporate philanthropy. Identify two ways such philanthropy has helped your college or university. How might contributors benefit from such donations?

7. Identify the major approaches used to monitor social demands and expectations. Choose an organisation with which you are familiar and suggest how it might use these methods to monitor relevant social issues.

8. Explain several internal social response mechanisms available to organisations. Identify two mechanisms used by your college or university.

9. Distinguish between three major types of managerial ethics. Use *Business Review Weekly* or *Asia Inc* to identify an example of one of these types.

10. Enumerate the ethical guidelines for managers discussed in the chapter.

11. A number of organisations are assessing their 'triple bottom line'. Using a familiar organisation explain how this will impact their performance.

12. Suggest some steps you could take when seeking employment to help you detect potential ethical problems. To what extent do your friends consider these issues when seeking jobs?

13. Describe the situational factors likely to influence ethical behaviour.

14. Which ethical force do 'carbon credits' support?

15. Outline the basic mechanisms for ethical management. Suppose you have just been appointed to a top-level position with a major contractor. How would you use these mechanisms to help prevent some ethical difficulties, such as misrepresenting costs on contracts, that are plaguing other contractors?

CRITICAL THINKING QUESTIONS

To answer some of these questions you will need to do further research. Useful references are given below each section of the questions.

This chapter dealt with the difficult issues of organisational social responsibility and managerial ethics. While few would argue that the traditional role of business has been making profit, it seems that it is also increasingly important to be socially responsible and to practice corporate ethics—in essence, to be a good 'corporate citizen'. This section will examine some of the drivers of this change—as well as questioning the depth of what is really occurring.

Reyes (2003) suggests that the 'do-well-by-doing good' philosophy has been around since the 1950s, moving beyond the then-acceptable standard of corporate contributions to charities to a wider view of a role within society.

1. What are the factors driving corporate citizenship initiatives?

2. One of the key social problems facing the Philippines, but familiar to many developing countries around the world is the issue of child poverty. What are some of the problems and why should they be a target for corporate citizenship initiatives?

3. Given the above focus on child poverty as a key target for intervention, what sort of initiatives would you expect to find being undertaken by volunteer aid groups funded through private organisations, such as Children's Hour Philippines, Inc.?

(Material relevant to questions 1 to 3 may be found in Reyes, I.M. 2003, Good corporate citizenship practices: A cycle of life for the business sector, *Business World*, 19 December, p.18.)

Although there have been some very positive outcomes of corporate social responsibility, this does not imply that such initiatives are universal and altruistic. An eight-country study across the Asia-Pacific by public relations firm Edelman Worldwide in 2003 (McIntyre 2003) found that 'soft issues' such as corporate ethics and integrity rated as among the least important drivers of business reputation. The result? Edelman, which had been a leading global advocate for corporate altruism as the basis for future growth prospects, has become one of its newest detractors!

4. If corporate social responsibility strategies are a waste of time, what are the foundations for a solid business reputation?

Edelman's regional chief, Alan VanderMolen, believes it is important to make the distinction between corporate philanthropy and being a responsible corporate, and then take into account the impact these have on the business.

(Material relevant to question 4 may be found in McIntyre, P. 2003, Corporate philanthropy nice if everybody profits, *Australian*, 11 December, p. B11.)

VanderMolen's advice resonates well with the message of a recent book on the demise of Arthur Andersen. After nearly 80 years as one of the top of accounting firms in the world, Toffler and Reingold (2003) explain in *Final Accounting: Ambition, Greed, and the Fall of Arthur Andersen*, how this firm came to live out its final days mired in disgrace. (Note—one of the authors, Toffler, was partner-in-charge of the ethics and responsible business practices group at Andersen from 1995 to 1999). While the popular media view is that Anderson's downfall followed directly from its misdeeds at Enron, Toffler sees it as just the last nail in the coffin. The Arthur Andersen case provides a good example of the short-term, spectacular organisational death well-documented by the media—which generally results in calls for greater corporate social responsibility—versus the much slower and less spectacular collapse of an organisation through inflexible corporate culture.

5. Given that Arthur Anderson has been one of the Western world's most high-profile and respected accountancy firms for decades, what do you think may have been among some of the long- and short-term problems identified at Arthur Andersen by the 2002 US federal jury?

6. Given the rather more pessimistic approach to corporate social responsibility demonstrated here, what do you think is the way to go about creating genuine commitment to it?

(Material relevant to questions 5 and 6 may be found in Toffler, L. and Reingold, J. 2003, *Final Accounting: Ambition, Greed, and the Fall of Arthur Andersen*, Broadway Books, New York.)

MANAGEMENT EXERCISES

Exercise 1 Skill building: Business ethical dilemmas from Lockheed Martin's ethics game

Use the questions in the discussion in Management skills for a global economy ('Questions to facilitate ethical business decisions') to help you choose what to do in each of the following situations taken from *Grey Matters: The Ethics Game* (Lockheed Martin 1992).

Situation 1

Since program funds are short, you have been directed by your supervisor to charge your time to an account you know to be improper. What do you do?

Potential answers to situation 1 (choose one):

A Explain to your supervisor that mischarging on a government contract is fraud.

B Refuse to mischarge.

C Mischarge as directed by your supervisor.

D Ask finance for an overhead number to charge your time to.

Situation 2

A company-sponsored training course in your field is being held in Orlando, Florida. You have no interest in the training but you are ready for a vacation and have never been to Disney World. What do you do?

Potential answers to situation 2 (choose one):

A Even though you have no interest in the training, ask your supervisor if he thinks it will benefit you.

B Obviously, or maybe not so obviously, it will be of some benefit to you, so you sign up.

C Reluctantly decline to go.

D Suggest that someone else go who has both a need and the interest.

Situation 3

On the bus going home at night, the woman sitting next to you mentions that she is being sexually harassed by one of her fellow employees. Although she does not work for you, you both work for the same company. You are a manager in the company. What do you do?

Potential answers to situation 3 (choose one)

A Listen politely, but since she doesn't work for you, stay out of it.
B Suggest she speak to her supervisor about it.
C Suggest she speak to either your company's equal-opportunity office or ethics officer.
D You contact your company's equal-opportunity officer or ethics officer.

Exercise 2 Management exercise: A question of ethics

After earning an undergraduate degree in history and an MBA in finance, Roberta was offered a job with a medium-sized real-estate development firm in her home town. She was pleased as the job involved working in the firm's 'community projects' area, where she would oversee the books for the company's construction of low-cost housing projects.

The opportunity to work in finance while also aiding public good appealed to Roberta. She had been interviewed for other jobs in finance and real estate, but she didn't like the competitive atmosphere at larger firms, where size of salaries and bonuses seemed to be the overriding concerns of most new employees.

After a few weeks, Roberta discovered a discrepancy in the books of one of her firm's projects. Six separate cheques for $10 000 each had been written by Roberta's boss over the past year, each made payable to cash with no further explanation. When Roberta approached her boss, she was told they were just another cost of doing business and she should inflate the costs of other items to cover the payments.

On further investigation, Roberta learned the cheques were paid to inspectors so they would overlook use of substandard material. Roberta again protested to her boss, who responded with obvious irritation. He said such payments were common and the use of substandard material wouldn't affect safety.

The boss implied that significant cost savings on materials were necessary if the firm was to build low-cost housing profitably. He noted that the cost of each unit would increase by only $2000 to cover the payments and the owners would probably expect to upgrade their units eventually anyway.

Roberta knows that, at the least, replacement or repairs would be needed after only two or three years because of substandard materials. Concerned a wrong was committed and fearful she might personally become entangled in the mess, Roberta protested to her boss's supervisor. The supervisor told Roberta he 'would look into it'. Roberta hasn't heard anything in three weeks and has just discovered that a seventh $10 000 cheque payable to cash has come through. What should Roberta do now?

Source: Adapted from *National Business Employment Weekly* (1987).

END-OF-CHAPTER CASE: ON THE RIM

Transit New Zealand v. the Mystic Taniwha

Under current New Zealand law (particularly under the *Resource Management Act 1991*), in order to obtain a resource consent for a major development or change of use of resources in New Zealand, the local authority (for example, the City Council) responsible for the issuing of the consent will require the applying party to 'consult' with and work through any issues and/or objections to the development with local communities and affected parties. On many occasions the issuing authority will also require the applying party to consult with local iwi (Maori of the area) to identify any cultural or significant historical issues that need to be addressed or mitigated. Authorities are often reluctant to issue consents until all issues and/or objections to a development with local communities and affected parties have been worked through or a compromised reached. The *Resource Management Act 1991* accords 'special status' to Maori interests, including the relationship of Maori with their ancestral lands and 'taonga' (treasures). It also provides for the recognition of Maori values and traditional practices and strongly encourages involving Maori in resource-management decision-making processes and the management of environmental resources.

Often, a stalemate situation is reached between a developer and Maori as to how to decide which cultures, philosophy and values should take precedence over the others.

In November 2002, Transit New Zealand, the organisation responsible for the building and maintaining of the state highways in New Zealand, planned to upgrade a stretch of road just south of Auckland. This part of State Highway One was a notorious 'black spot' and had claimed many lives over the years. Part of the upgrade involved digging out and straightening a section of the 'sacred' Waikato River. Before development started, Transit New Zealand duly consulted with the local iwi (Maori of the area) and were advised that two taniwha (mystical guardians/water monsters) lived on the stretch of river to be developed and that the development

could disrupt and awaken the taniwha.

After discussions between Transit New Zealand and local iwi, a compromise was reached as to how to best deal with the situation, and thus construction started. During the course of the development, local iwi identified another taniwha that was going to be imminently and significantly affected by the works. Transit New Zealand immediately suspended work at the site and once again entered into consultation with representatives of the local iwi. After some discussion, Transit New Zealand agreed to modify its development plans so as to protect the area where the taniwha resided, a compromise that, while costing slightly more, ensured a workable and amiable solution was achieved by both parties.

The case made national and international headlines.

While many Pakeha in New Zealand found the idea of a 'mystical creature' having a serious impact upon a major national development laughable, Maori leaders such as Dr Ranginui Walker, Head of Maori Studies at Auckland University, made the point that the belief in mystical or 'abstract' characters is not unique to Maori. The Irish believe in leprechauns, many Europeans believe in ghosts, goblins and trolls, Catholics believe in God, saints and angels, many parents tell their children about Santa Claus and the Easter Bunny, Maori leaders claimed.

While Transit New Zealand acted responsibly and did everything right under its obligations within the Resource Management Act, many saw this case as a dangerous precedent as they believe Maori could and will hold public and private developers to ransom, should they not be entirely happy with a proposal or if there is financial gain to be made for the iwi by opposing a development.

Source: Contributed by Matene Love.

POWERWEB

International articles related to this topic are available at the Online Learning Centre at **www.mhhe.com/au/bartol4e**

Activities for discussion, analysis and further research

1. Do you think Maori should have the right to have their traditional beliefs and values recognised in today's society even though their arguments may be based on past beliefs and values such as the abstract, mystical creature in this case?

2. Can you think of any other cases similar to this one where the values and beliefs of one culture clashed with that of another? What was the outcome?

3. Do you believe that it is possible for two cultures to live side by side and legally acknowledge each other's beliefs and values even though their philosophies and cultural values may be fundamentally different?

FURTHER READING

Barela, M.J. 2003, Executive insights: United colors of Benetton—From sweaters to success: An examination of the triumphs and controversies of a multinational clothing company, *Journal of International Marketing*, 11, 4, pp. 113–29.

Cary, C., Wen, H.J. and Mahatanankoon, P. 2003, Data mining: Consumer privacy, ethical policy, and systems development practices, *Human Systems Management*, 22, 4, pp. 157–69.

Doh, J.P., Rodriguez, P., Uhlenbruck, K., Collins, J. and Eden, L. 2003, Coping with corruption in foreign markets, *Academy of Management Executive*, August, 17, 3, pp. 114–28.

Soon, L.G. 2003, Differences in ethical judgement between Chinese and Singaporeans: Individual reactions to self and organizational interest considerations, *Singapore Management Review*, 2nd Half, 25, 2, pp. 1–25.

Toth, O. 2003, The ethical progression, *Media Asia*, 5/30 Supplement, pp. 42–4.

GRADUATE GLIMPSE

CHRIS BLANKSBY

Chris Blanksby graduated from the Aerospace Engineering/Business Administration double degree program at RMIT University in 1996.

Why did you decide to undertake a double degree instead of just a straight engineering degree?

The decision to enter into this program was pretty arbitrary—I was a bit interested in science and engineering so I thought aerospace might be fun, and since business was offered, I decided to try that too. Once the lessons being delivered through the business degree started to sink in (about half-way through the program), I was extremely happy for the decision I made. While my prime interest remained in the engineering/scientific discipline, I began to clearly recognise the value of the business education, in almost every facet of education, work and even personal life.

What have you done since graduation?

Since graduating from the program, I worked for two years at a small business named Roaduser

International, specialising in advanced engineering for safety and performance of heavy road vehicles (trucks). I advanced rapidly in this organisation, thanks largely to my business skills providing an extra dimension to my contribution to the company.

I then decided to pursue further education, with the objective of getting into the space industry, which had become a major area of interest for me. I returned to RMIT University to undertake a PhD, which I completed in 2001. I have since been employed at RMIT University as a lecturer and senior research fellow. During this time, I have won several national and international awards for my research, and been project manager for several research projects of strategic importance to the university.

Currently, I am supervising nine PhD and masters students. The leadership and management skills I developed through the business degree have been invaluable in inspiring these high-performing individuals and coordinating their efforts towards team goals.

BEVERLEY SCHUBERT

Beverley Schubert has a Bachelor of Commerce with a double major in management and accounting from Murdoch University. She works for Ernst & Young as a consultant in the entrepreneurial services division.

What does your job entail?

Our client base is the small-to-medium enterprises and emerging growth markets. My role includes consulting with clients to discuss management issues and performing strategic reviews and business planning. I develop financial models and financial analysis to assist clients in resolving financial issues, and I also perform a limited amount of compliance work.

How have your university studies assisted you in your career?

My university studies gave me an advantage in gaining my current position within the firm and the

consulting team. My management major has been invaluable in the consulting arena.

How do you use your knowledge of management principles in the day-to-day functions of your position?

My knowledge of management principles assists me in delivering a quality outcome to my clients in terms of understanding their issues and providing relevant, focused solutions. Through this knowledge I have a deeper understanding of the issues businesses face and of the wider environment in which they operate. This understanding gives depth to the solutions I can propose as I am able to take into account all these issues.

From gifts to wishes

A corporate need coupled with a bright idea launched Rachael Pickworth's million dollar corporate gifting business. When Rachael started her Melbourne-based company, 'Gifted', in 1996, operating from the lounge room on $6000 start-up capital borrowed from her mother, she did not envisage an average annual growth of 400 per cent. Rachael's inspiration came from listening to corporate motivational speakers who promoted the idea of encouraging staff with rewards. In those days, organisations wanting to reward the loyalty of their staff or customers had their choices limited to a hamper of some description. Rachael, who had always wanted to run her own business, thought the hamper market lacked style and taste. Recognising a gap in the market, she came up with the idea of selling gifts to companies that wanted to reward their staff, and decided to take on giftware retailers by emphasising flexibility and care when making up gift packages for clients.

The company flourished. In her first year of operations, Rachel entered her business idea in the Operation Livewire Program, and walked away with

first prize for 'best business idea', and a start-up grant of $5000. Her vision was hinged on a basic principle: apply a new spin to a tired industry. Using that logic, her business grew rapidly. Another benefit of the award was the ensuing publicity, which resulted in a 500 per cent surge in turnover for 1997–98, primarily through mail order.

Growth proved to be the source of the company's two biggest headaches: the lack of opportunity to train new staff to build sales, and the difficulty of budgeting with a lopsided revenue stream. Time management also created problems. When Rachael started out, she found her time was being consumed by bookkeeping and budgeting, for which she was not formally trained. In May 1998, she took on Kym Crosbie, a friend and an accountant, as a partner. The pair split management and financial tasks between them. Nonetheless, Kym found herself constantly helping Rachael with customers and in filling orders.

The partners quickly expanded into retail, opening their first store in Collins Street, Melbourne, that same year. This set Gifted on track to double its turnover for 1998–99. The retail outlet, combined with the mail-order operation, which was now experiencing its third Christmas sales boom, together achieved a turnover of $750 000 for that financial year. The business then launched executive gift wholesaling and retailing. This enabled them to offer their clients (including ANZ, Australia Post, National Mutual, IOOF and Telstra) an attractive alternative to hampers. Their hard work was rewarded when they were selected for the finals of the 1999 Telstra Small Business Awards. One of their big challenges was to educate the market about the value of consistent rewards for employees and customers. A change in focus from rewarding staff to rewarding customer loyalty was a natural step, given the growing trend among real-estate agents and car sales firms to present customers with a gift upon purchase.

Driven by a desire to become a major force in the corporate gifting market, Rachael and Kym decided to develop an e-commerce strategy.

Recognising the synergies achievable through a relationship with an established on-line gift retailer that shared the same commitment to customer service, they made the decision to align their company with wishlist.com.au, Australia's leading on-line gift e-tailer. Wishlist, an Australian-owned and -operated company, was launched in July 1999 with the first-ever Australian website dedicated to online gifting. Combining Gifted's quality products with the convenience of the Internet and a cutting-edge approach to a previously manual market, wishlist.com.au offered the perfect solution for businesses. Joining forces with Wishlist would make Gifted a much larger force in the corporate gifting market.

Wishlist has demonstrated innovative leadership in e-commerce and on-line retailing ever since launching their first business division, wishlist.com.au. Wishlist Holdings now comprises three business divisions: wishlist.com.au (for on-line consumer and corporate retail), Excelio (online reward and recognition solutions) and evoucher.com.au. In April 2001, Wishlist launched a new web-based product, the Corporate Rewards and Incentives Program, to help its corporate clients achieve their business objectives more effectively. This innovation was twelve months in the planning, and offers businesses smart, efficient and cost-effective solutions to encourage profitable behaviour in their customers, employees and suppliers and has since metamorphosed into the Excelio business stream.

Rewards can be a powerful and cost-effective tool in business improvement. They have traditionally been applied in marketing, to increase customer loyalty; in human resources, to improve people's performance; and in direct sales, to drive increased sales. However, these programs have been costly to administer and sometimes inappropriately applied, and their effectiveness has not been fully realised. Wishlist's then CEO, Huy Truong, proposed a complete on-line business solution for rewarding and providing incentives for staff and customers, while lowering the administration costs associated with traditional rewards and incentives programs. Wishlist established a dominant corporate gifting service from a merchandise and fulfilment perspective, and wanted to add value to their clients through helping them better manage their programs for increased return on investment. A significant number of companies did not really understand what they were trying to achieve with rewards, and often had high cost centres associated with them. Wishlist's technology and infrastructure teams developed a solution that would allow companies to recognise and reward business improvement in a simple and cost-effective manner.

The core elements of the Excelio solution are a customised website, hosting services, marketing and communications package and thousands of unique reward ideas powered by the retailing arm of wishlist.com.au. This solution has been developed to help companies identify, measure and reward those who have contributed to improving their business and increasing profitability. With the success of the business-to-consumer (B2C) e-commerce business, the corporate division of Wishlist successfully secured a position in the market as a provider of smart solutions by facilitating cost-effective, time-saving and innovative solutions for many Australian companies wishing to increase loyalty from customers, suppliers and employees. The successful integration of two corporate hamper businesses—Gifted and Sydney-based The Gourmet Merchant—further accelerated the growth of corporate e-services.

E-business places great demands for speed and efficiency on organisations. Unlike traditional companies, e-businesses cannot and should not wait years to implement operating improvements. E-commerce companies have no choice but to be lean organisations. Ever conscious of the importance of customer service, Wishlist addressed the issues of isolation and ease of access. In August 2000, Wishlist customers were able to order gifts on-line and have them delivered for pick-up to the BP convenience store of their choice. This clicks-and-bricks alliance was designed to solve the dilemma many customers faced when ordering gifts. The convenient 24 hour, seven-day pick-up and return option meant no waiting around for couriers.

In a further innovation, Wishlist acquired Australia's leading women's lifestyle site, theLounge.com.au. This acquisition further develops the Wishlist e-commerce strategy and provides a platform for theLounge to grow its customer offerings with integration of content and e-commerce for a loyal community of Australian women.

Wishlist has received a number of awards, including Australian Internet Awards for e-commerce and the most entrepreneurial, recognising the company's unique business model reflected in alliances with old-economy players.

Source: Margaret Tein.

Activities for discussion, *analysis and further research*

1. Log on to the Wishlist website, www.wishlist.com.au, and examine the diversity of offerings.
2. How does the availability of such a service link to organisation structure and design?
3. Discuss the factors which may have influenced Rachael Pickworth and Kym Crosbie as they made the decision to link with Wishlist.
4. Consider Wishlist as a large system. Identify how customer organisations interact with and are acted upon by this large system.

 Please insert the CD-ROM that is packaged with this book to view video clips that correspond to this Part theme.

PLANNING AND DECISION MAKING

The management function of planning involves setting goals, then deciding how best to reach them. It includes consideration of what will encourage needed levels of change and innovation, as well as providing a basis for the other major management functions (organising, leading and controlling) by mapping the course and providing the steering mechanism. This section, then, is geared to gaining a basic knowledge of the planning function.

CHAPTER 5 focuses on the kinds of problems managers try to resolve through decision making, as well as appropriate steps to take in the decision process. This chapter also addresses creativity, a vital component of innovation.

CHAPTER 6 examines the overall planning process and explores how setting goals facilitates organisational performance. It will become clear that goals and related plans necessary to achieve them vary in important ways by organisational level. One of the most important aspects of planning is strategic management. Chapter 6 also explores how managers formulate and implement large-scale action plans called strategies to gain a competitive edge for the organisation.

CHAPTER 7 probes ways managers can effectively facilitate needed innovation and change, as innovation in organisations must be an integral part of the planning process.

PART 2

CHAPTER 5

MANAGERIAL DECISION MAKING

CHAPTER OUTLINE

The nature of managerial decision making
Types of problems decision makers face
Differences in decision-making situations

Managers as decision makers
The rational model
Non-rational models

Steps in an effective decision-making process
Identifying the problem
Generating alternative solutions
Evaluating and choosing an alternative
Implementing and monitoring the chosen solution

Overcoming barriers to effective decision making
Accepting the problem challenge
Searching for sufficient alternatives

Recognising common decision-making biases
Avoiding the decision-escalation phenomenon

Managing diversity: Group decision making
Advantages and disadvantages of group decision making
Enhancing group decision-making processes
Computer-assisted group decision making

Promoting innovation: The creativity factor in decision making
Basic ingredients
Stages of creativity
Techniques for enhancing group creativity

LEARNING OBJECTIVES

After studying this chapter, you should be able to:

- Explain major types of problems facing decision makers and describe variations between programmed and non-programmed decisions.
- Contrast rational and non-rational models of managers as decision makers.
- Describe the steps in an effective decision-making process.
- Explain how to overcome barriers associated with accepting a problem challenge and searching for sufficient alternatives.
- Describe how to recognise common decision-making biases and avoid the decision-escalation phenomenon.
- Assess the advantages and disadvantages of group decision making.
- Explain three basic ingredients and four stages of creativity.
- Describe major techniques for enhancing group creativity.

STRIVING FOR EXCELLENCE

The regular guy: Chip Goodyear

Chip Goodyear rides his bike to work and goes bowling with his executives. After recent turmoil, the new boss of BHP Billiton is minimising the heroics and maximising the team. The analysts will tell you that so far Chip Goodyear looks like the kind of guy who won't blow up the company. Which is good news, given that the 45-year old American is six months into the job of running the world's biggest mining house.

A Wharton MBA hired in as chief financial officer four years ago, Goodyear in January became the miner's third boss in just six months. First there was Paul Anderson, then there was Brian Gilbertson, then there was Chip. To say the market is interested in what makes him run is an understatement.

But this low-key operator keeps them wondering— wondering whether he is just a safe pair of hands, or an entrepreneur who will really 'capitalise on the money cascading from his business', as one fund manager put it.

His predecessors quickly established their place in Australian business. Both dominant personalities, they had a style that the market found easy to read. Goodyear is different, exhibiting none of the ego that is almost a prerequisite for CEOs. Is it a deliberate strategy, or just the way he operates?

Personable and able to work different audiences, Goodyear has all the assurance of a Wall Street banker, without the front. He has a remarkably casual style, exemplified by his habit of riding his pushbike to work every day, and he does the management thing of bonding with the executive team over bowling and throwing paint balls about.

When questioned about his young age of 45, he responds: 'If you look at our executive committee, it has an average age of around 48, which I would say is the youngest around by some significant amount. What we want to create, and I think we are very much doing so, is a meritocracy. This is not an issue about how long you've been here or what boxes you have to check; it's really based on performance.

'And I think the result of that is you find young people around. There's no doubt that we not only want to have, but encourage, a diverse workforce. There are all kinds of reasons for that. Our customers are spread around the world, with 30 per cent of our markets in East Asia, 28 per cent in Europe, 17 per cent in North America.

'We deal with 35 nationalities in the marketing section, and one country, one region alone doesn't have all the best ideas. In a meritocracy you reward people for making a positive, solid contribution, and that is irrespective of race, religion, creed—whatever you want to say, and if we don't do that we're not doing the right job.'

As the chief executive, what role does he play? 'I'd much rather have people think the face of BHP Billiton is the executive committee, because the organisation is so large and has 100 assets around the world. It's a big aircraft carrier and it takes a lot of people to make that work, and so there's plenty of opportunity to give those people the opportunity to get out and talk about their business and do that.

'I'd much rather spend the evenings at home and give all that glory to other people, but it really is mainly based on the idea that we should empower

continued

people—let's give them the chance to take the action that's necessary, and then you go out and talk about it.'

Goodyear describes his management style in this fashion: 'It's really management by walking around. I think that if you get out to see the people that day-to-day are doing the job you have a much better sense of what's going on.

'I think you're providing more motivation to those people because they recognise it's not six layers between them and, in this case, the chief executive. It's their work that is presented and they are there to defend it. You often find that people doing the work are the ones who are best able to answer the questions.

'On a recent trip to the Katali mine in South Africa, a bunch of us were walking around and I said to the mine manager, "There's no railing between the grate and the water and somebody could fall, twist an ankle or something", and he just said, "I'd never thought about it", and I said, "You know you ought to think about it".

'The next day I get a message that says: "We talked about it yesterday, we realised that it's even more dangerous in the winter". And they sent me pictures of five guys putting the railing up across the stream. Now there are 8000 people in the operation who say, "This guy is serious" because of that.'
Source: Durie, J. (2003).

decision making

The process by which managers identify organisational problems and try to resolve them

In this chapter we explore the nature of managerial **decision making**, including types of problems and decision-making situations managers can face. We evaluate managers as decision makers and consider steps in an effective decision-making process. We examine overcoming barriers to effective decision making, and weigh the advantages and disadvantages of group decision making. Finally, we show how managers can promote innovation by using creativity in decision-making processes.

THE NATURE OF MANAGERIAL DECISION MAKING

Managers make many work decisions. While lower-level managers might not make decisions such as changing a revered product's formula, smaller decisions at lower levels have a cumulative effect on company effectiveness. For example, Motorola's reputation for high quality and innovation (in semiconductors, electronic pagers and mobile phones) was built partly through having staff from design, manufacturing and marketing departments involved early in making decisions for new projects (Therrien 1989). Good decision-making processes are vital at all levels.

Effective decision making usually includes four steps, as in Figure 5.1 (Elbing 1978). Some refer to the four steps as 'problem solving', and use 'decision making' for the first three steps up to, but not including, implementation and follow-up (Huber 1980; Bateman & Snell 2004). Here 'decision making' and 'problem solving' are used interchangeably for the process shown in Figure 5.1. This is because use of 'decision making' is more common in business, and it is

FIGURE 5.1 Steps in the decision-making process (adapted from Huber 1980, p. 8)

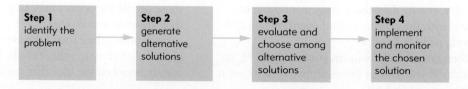

| Step 1 identify the problem | Step 2 generate alternative solutions | Step 3 evaluate and choose among alternative solutions | Step 4 implement and monitor the chosen solution |

clear when it is being used more narrowly. We analyse the four steps in the process in more detail later. First, though, it helps to look at major types of problems managers encounter and to consider the differences in managerial decision-making situations.

Types of problems decision makers face

Managerial decision making centres on three types of problems: crisis, non-crisis and opportunity problems (Mintzberg, Raisignhani & Thoret 1976; Nutt 1985).

Crisis

A **crisis problem** is a difficulty serious enough to need immediate action. An example of a crisis is a discovery of a severe cash-flow deficiency, potentially a serious loss. The National Australia Bank is facing a crisis due to a series of foreign exchange losses. Currently this is $360 million and could become much greater (Baker 2004). Coca-Cola's crisis occurred when there were protests about their changing classic Coke formula to produce New Coke. This tampering with an icon caused customers to react strongly against the company. New Coke is Coke II in some markets, but is just one-tenth of one per cent of carbonated beverage volume (Collins 1995).

crisis problem

A serious difficulty requiring immediate action

Non-crisis

A **non-crisis problem** is an issue needing resolution but without the importance and immediacy of a crisis. Many managerial decisions involve non-crisis problems. Non-crisis problems are significant problems, but do not immediately threaten the viability of the organisation. Examples are a factory needing to meet new anti-pollution standards over the next three years and a staff member often late for work. Another example is when Coke's food division, which produced Minute Maid juices, experienced poor earnings. This was resolved when a new president and CEO was appointed to the division and things improved significantly (Morris 1987).

non-crisis problem

An issue requiring resolution but without the simultaneous importance and immediacy characteristics of a crisis

Opportunity

An **opportunity problem** is a situation with potential organisational gain if the right actions are taken. Typically these problems involve new ideas and directions, and are major innovation opportunities. Melbourne-based company Lochard has developed a nose for noise, developing software to track noise pollution at Sydney and Brisbane airports. This is an increasingly important issue as passenger numbers double roughly every 10 years, driving demand for better noise monitoring to minimise the impact of air transport (Walker 2003a). Opportunities involve ideas for use, not problems for resolution. Non-innovative managers focus on crisis and non-crisis problems, neglecting opportunities. In a study of 78 managerial decision-making situations, 13 per cent were crisis problems, 62 per cent were non-crisis problems, and 25 per cent were opportunity taking (Nutt 1984). As well as these three problem types, managers face different decision-making situations.

opportunity problem

A situation offering strong potential for significant organisational gain if appropriate actions are taken

Differences in decision-making situations

Decision making can overwhelm managers if they view every problem as a totally new situation. Fortunately, it is not so. Decision situations fall into two categories: programmed and non-programmed. Table 5.1 shows examples of both.

TABLE 5.1 TYPES OF MANAGERIAL DECISION-MAKING SITUATIONS

Type of organisation	Programmed decision	Non-programmed decision
Fast-food restaurant	Determine supplies to be reordered	Identify location for new franchise
University	Decide if students meet graduation requirements	Choose new academic programs
Car-maker	Determine work rates	Select new car design

Programmed decisions

programmed decisions

Decisions made in routine, repetitive, well-structured situations by use of predetermined decision rules

Programmed decisions are for routine, repetitive, well-structured situations using predetermined decision rules. These can result from habit, computational techniques or policies and procedures (Kinicki & Williams 2003). Such rules usually use prior experience or technical knowledge about what works. For example, most organisations have policies and procedures for basic employee discipline. These are guided by the country's law related to employment (see Chapter 10).

Programmed decisions fit routine, well-structured situations, but can be very complex. Computers have made sophisticated programmed decision making easier, as they can collect and analyse vast amounts of data to help this. For example, when someone uses a credit card, a computer makes a programmed decision authorising the purchase. However, if an unusually large charge or one over the account limit is tendered then the purchase will not be routinely authorised. Instead, a human will make a programmed decision based on policies and procedures.

Most first-line managers' decisions and many middle managers' decisions are programmed. Top-level managers face few programmed decisions (see Fig. 5.2).

Non-programmed decisions

non-programmed decisions

Decisions for which predetermined decision rules are impractical due to novel and/or ill-structured situations

Non-programmed decisions occur when predetermined decision rules are impractical due to novel and/or relatively unstructured situations (Bazerman 1986). Most major management decisions are non-programmed. Non-programmed decisions, therefore, usually mean considerable **uncertainty**, where the decision maker selects a course of action without being completely sure what the effects will be.

uncertainty

A condition in which the decision maker must choose a course of action with incomplete knowledge of consequences following implementation

Decisions made under uncertainty involve **risk**, the chance an action chosen could yield losses rather than the results desired (Taylor 1984). Uncertainty flows from many sources, so unpredictable or uncontrolled environmental elements can affect a decision's success. Cost and time constraints limit information collection. Social and political issues, such as poor inter-unit communication, make collecting needed information hard. Situations change rapidly, so current information becomes obsolete (Weisman 1989). For example, Woolworths is shown over 25 000 new lines annually and will only take up 2000, after careful consideration (Shoebridge 2003).

risk

The possibility a chosen action could lead to losses rather than intended results

The frequency of managers' non-programmed decisions grows by organisational level (see Fig. 5.2). As these decisions need effective decision-making skills—and, often, creativity—they are the most challenging managerial decision-making type. This chapter focuses mainly on non-programmed decisions.

FIGURE 5.2 Relationship of decision-making situation to management level in organisations (adapted from Daft & Steers 1986, p. 440)

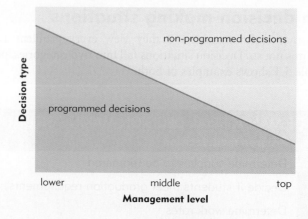

MANAGERS AS DECISION MAKERS

As managers' decisions impact organisation success, their approaches to decision making have been widely researched. In this section, we describe two major models of how managers make decisions: rational and non-rational.

The rational model

The rational model of managerial decision making, popular early in the twentieth century, is based on economic theory of the firm. In developing theories of business firms' economic behaviour, economists made the basic assumption that managers would make decisions in their firms' best economic interests. At first this was accepted by many management theorists. According to the **rational model**, managers use totally rational decision processes, make optimal decisions, and have and understand all information needed for decisions when making them (including all possible alternatives, potential outcomes and ramifications). If you have recently bought an item such as a personal computer or a car, you will have found it hard to get perfect information and make an 'optimal' or best decision. So the serious flaws in the rational model of managerial decision making will not surprise you (Simon 1955; 1956). Nevertheless, it forms a reference point for comparing actual managerial decision-making patterns.

Non-rational models

In contrast to the rational view, **non-rational models** of managerial decision making suggest that information-gathering and processing limitations make optimal decisions hard. Within the non-rational framework, researchers have identified three major decision making models: satisficing, incremental and rubbish bin.

Satisficing model

During the 1950s Herbert Simon studied managerial decision makers' behaviour. From his studies, Simon developed the **bounded rationality** concept as a framework to understand actual managerial decision making (Bazerman 1986). Bounded rationality means that managers' ability to be perfectly rational in decision making is limited by factors such as cognitive capacity and time constraints. The concept suggests some factors commonly limit how much managers make perfectly rational decisions:

- Decision makers may have inadequate information about the nature of the issue to be decided and also about possible alternatives and their strengths and limitations.
- Time and cost factors often limit the amount of information gathered for a particular decision.
- Decision makers' perceptions about the relative importance of various pieces of data may cause them to overlook or ignore critical information.
- The part of human memory used in making decisions retains only a relatively small amount of information at one time.
- The calculating capacities associated with intelligence limit how much decision makers can determine optimal decisions, even assuming perfect information has been gathered (Huber 1980).

Rather than optimising decisions, Simon argued, managers follow the **satisficing model**, which suggests that managers seek options only until they find one which looks satisfactory. Satisficing is best when the cost of delaying a decision or searching for a better alternative outweighs the likely payoff. One other difficulty comes from decision makers looking for information which supports their preferences (McShane & Travaglione 2003). For example, if you are driving on an unfamiliar road with little fuel, it might be better to choose the petrol station you first see than wait for your preferred brand. On the other hand, managers may habitually use a simplistic satisficing approach even when the cost of searching further for alternatives is justified given possible gain (Gupte 1988).

rational model

Model suggesting managers engage in completely rational decision processes, ultimately make optimal decisions, and possess and understand all information relevant to their decisions at the time they make them

non-rational models

Models suggesting information-gathering and processing limitations make it difficult for managers to make optimal decisions

bounded rationality

Concept suggesting the ability of managers to be perfectly rational in making decisions is limited by factors such as cognitive capacity and time constraints

satisficing model

Model stating managers seek alternatives only until they find one which looks satisfactory, rather than seeking an optimal decision

incremental model

Model stating managers make the smallest response possible to reduce the problem to at least a tolerable level

rubbish-bin model

Model stating managers behave in virtually a random way in making non-programmed decisions

Incremental model

Another decision-making approach is the **incremental model**, which holds that managers make the smallest possible response to reduce a problem to a tolerable level (Huber 1980). This approach is geared to short-run problem alleviation rather than to decision making toward a long-term goal. Like the satisficing model, the incremental model frees managers from processing a lot of information in order to take action. One researcher said that incrementalising is like a situation where a home owner may use various multi-outlet adaptors instead of having more electrical power sockets installed in the house. Eventually, the incremental decisions fail, as extra appliances (e.g. VCRs and personal computers) overload the electrical circuits and may blow fuses (Cohen, March & Olsen 1972; Grandori 1984).

Rubbish-bin model

The **rubbish-bin model** of decision making says managers act randomly in non-programmed decision making. In other words, outcomes occur by chance, depending on those involved, problems they are presently concerned with, opportunities they stumble across, and favoured solutions available for a problem to solve. The rubbish-bin strategy is most likely when managers have no goal preferences, unclear means of achieving goals, and/or decision-making participants change rapidly (Weiner 1987; Kindel 1988; O'Neal 1988; *Economist* 1988). Sometimes desirable outcomes can be reached with this strategy, but there can be serious problems.

Thus, while the rubbish-bin approach can help managers take up unexpected opportunities, it can also lead to severe problems. The rubbish-bin approach is often used in the absence of strategic management. (See Chapter 6 for a strategic management discussion.)

STEPS IN AN EFFECTIVE DECISION-MAKING PROCESS

descriptive decision-making models

Models of decision making attempting to document how managers actually make decisions

normative decision-making models

Models of decision making attempting to prescribe how managers should make decisions

organisational problems

Discrepancies between a current state or condition and what is desired

Managerial decision making models outlined above are called **descriptive decision-making models** as they try to explain how managers make actual decisions. In contrast, models as outlined in Table 5.2 are referred to as **normative decision-making models**, as they specify how managers should make decisions. Experts note managers will be more effective decision makers if they follow the general approach in Table 5.2. Although these steps do not guarantee all decisions will give desired outcomes, they make success more likely (Cowan 1986). While managers control few factors affecting decision success, they do control the process used to make decisions. In this section, we discuss the four-step decision-making process more fully.

Identifying the problem

The first step in decision making is problem identification. Part of problem identification, of course, is realising there is one. **Organisational problems** are discrepancies between a current state or condition and that desired. This step has three general stages: scanning, categorisation and diagnosis (Studer 1992; Fuhrman 1992).

Scanning stage

The scanning stage involves monitoring the work situation for changing circumstances signalling an emerging problem. At this point, a manager may only be vaguely aware an environmental change could lead to, or that a present situation is, a problem. For example, in the 1970s, Swiss watchmakers saw inexpensive watches emerge from Japan and Hong Kong (Taylor 1984).

Categorisation stage

The categorisation stage entails trying to understand and verify any discrepancy between the current state and that desired. Here the manager has to categorise the situation as a problem

TABLE 5.2 STEPS IN AN EFFECTIVE DECISION MAKING PROCESS

Step	Activities
Identify the problem	Scan the environment for changing circumstances
	Categorise the situation as a problem (or non-problem)
	Diagnose the problem's nature and causes
Generate alternative solutions	Restrict criticism of alternatives
	Freewheel to stimulate thinking
	Offer as many ideas as possible
	Combine and improve on ideas
Evaluate and choose an alternative	Evaluate feasibility
	Evaluate quality
	Evaluate acceptability
	Evaluate costs
	Evaluate reversibility
	Evaluate ethics
Implement and monitor the chosen solution	Plan the implementation of the solution
	Be sensitive to the decision's effects on others
	Develop follow-up mechanisms

or a non-problem, though it may be hard to specify the nature of the situation exactly. For example, a discrepancy would have occurred in the 1970s when sales dropped of relatively expensive Swiss watches.

Diagnosis stage

The diagnosis stage involves collecting further information and specifying the problem's nature and causes. Without diagnosis, success is difficult in the remainder of the process. The problem is to be stated in terms of the gap between current conditions and those desired, and causes of the discrepancy must be specified. Watchmakers first thought cheaper watches were only a temporary fad. By 1983, however, conditions had not improved, and Switzerland's two largest watchmakers, SSIH and Asuag, were deep in debt. The two firms controlled many of the world's best-known watch brands—Omega, Longines, Tissot and Rado. Clearly cheaper watches from Japan and Hong Kong were a serious threat. The banks for SSIH and Asuag called in Zurich-based management consultant Nicolas G. Hayek to help find a solution.

Generating alternative solutions

The second step in decision-making is developing alternative solutions. This leads to better-quality solutions (Osborn 1963), particularly when creative and innovative ones are needed. Alternative development can be aided by **brainstorming**, a creativity-enhancing technique which encourages group members to generate as many novel ideas as possible on a topic without evaluation. Four principles are involved:

1. Don't criticise ideas while generating possible solutions. Criticism during the idea-generation stage inhibits thinking. Also, as discussion tends to get bogged down when early ideas are criticised, only a few are generated.
2. Freewheel. Offer even seemingly wild and outrageous ideas. Though they may never be used, they may trigger usable ideas from others.

brainstorming

Technique encouraging group members to generate as many novel ideas as possible on a given topic without evaluating them

3. Offer as many ideas as possible. Pushing for a high volume of ideas increases the likelihood some will be effective.
4. Combine and improve on ideas already offered. Often the best ideas come from combinations of others (Maier 1963).

Although normally brainstorming is a group activity, individuals can use the principles too. For example, the manager jots down several possible solutions, including far-fetched ones, works to generate a large number of ideas, and combines or builds on them. Brainstorming and other idea-generating methods will be further considered when we discuss creativity later.

It is important that many options are generated during the decision-making phase. For example, Hayek, the bankers, and the watch companies' heads developed several options, including liquidation, diversification, and merging companies to mount an offensive against the overseas threat.

Evaluating and choosing an alternative

This step involves carefully considering each option's advantages and disadvantages before selecting one. Each is to be systematically evaluated by six general criteria: feasibility, quality, acceptability, costs, reversibility and ethics.

Feasibility

The feasibility criterion refers to the extent to which an option can be achieved within organisational limitations, such as time, budgets, technology and policies. Options which do not meet the feasibility criterion should be cut. The watch companies, for instance, at first did not see fighting the overseas threat as feasible.

Quality

The quality criterion refers to how effectively an option solves the problem. Options which partly solve the problem or are questionable are cut now.

Acceptability

This criterion refers to how much decision makers and others affected by implementation of an option will support it. Acceptability is seen as an important criterion to assess decisions (Gittler 1985).

Costs

The costs criterion refers to both needed resource levels and the extent to which options may have negative side effects. Thus 'costs' are not only direct financial issues but also intangible issues such as competitor retaliation.

Reversibility

This criterion refers to whether an option can be reversed. When the Coca-Cola Company had problems with its new formula for Coke, it reversed the decision, bringing back the old formula as Coke Classic. Other decision types may be less reversible (*Forbes* 1995). In these cases, options must be considered carefully beforehand. For example, reversing liquidating the watchmakers would have been difficult. Instead, the group merged the two firms, forming the Swiss Corporation for Microelectronics and Watchmaking (or SMH), with Hayek as chairman. SMH then launched an inexpensive, innovative plastic Swatch watch, assembled on a fully automated low-cost assembly line. By 1995, over 150 million Swatch timepieces had been sold, competing with Hattori Seiko of Japan to be the world's number-one watchmaker. Unlike the Japanese firms, SMH also makes both medium-priced and luxury watches (Stepp 1991a; 1991b).

Ethics

The ethics criterion refers to how well an option fits with the firm's social responsibilities and managers' ethical standards. For instance, Hayek is considered a Swiss hero for saving the watchmaking industry and many jobs.

Brewing up a storm

Dome Coffees operates 67 café outlets by direct ownership, joint venture or franchising. The chain was launched in Perth in 1990, and expanded rapidly overseas to Singapore, Malaysia, Indonesia, the Philippines and the Middle East. Dome was founded by Phil May and Patria Jafferies. May, who was the director of international business, taught himself how to roast and prepare coffee. Jafferies, who served as the managing director, handled the marketing and presentation package of the franchise division, which became the hallmark of Dome's appeal.

Dome's reputation—and its success—was based on an outstanding range of fine coffees presented in stylish, high-quality packaging. The original Dome Café concept was developed in order to showcase the coffees. It was designed to create the ambience of an old-world style European café to serve as a 'shop window' for Dome products, especially the sale of freshly roasted coffees, supported by a range of quality gourmet foods.

There are an estimated 6000 cafés throughout Australia. The industry is highly fragmented, with most businesses operated by sole proprietors. The biggest retail chain, Coffee Club, has 47 outlets. A coffee war began when Starbucks, the world's biggest coffee-shop chain, opened its first café in Sydney in 2000. Subsequently, Starbucks has opened 12 stores and has an ambitious expansion program with a target of 50 stores by the end of 2002. Not to be left behind, Dome went about raising new capital for further expansion into eastern Australia.

In 2000, the Sydney-based venture capitalist GS Private Equity injected A\$10 million into Dome, in return for a 50 per cent stake in the business. Jafferies and May had no choice but to give up a sizeable portion of the ownership and control of the business for the much-needed capital. The company also has an A\$8.5 million debt facility with the National Bank of Australia. With a fund of A\$18.5 million, Dome accelerated its expansion along Australia's east coast with an aggressive acquisition program, a plan to rapidly develop another 50 outlets and plans to list the company on the Australian share market.

The next phase in Dome's growth strategy is to forsake franchising and rely totally on company-owned stores. 'We tried franchising in our early days because we wanted to expand and didn't have our own capital', says Jafferies. 'There is a role for franchising but we brought in an equity partner to help facilitate the growth of company-owned stores.' However, sluggish economic growth, the goods and services tax (GST) and rising levels of competition have slowed these ambitious plans and delayed Dome's plans for a public float by at least 12 months. Furthermore, slower growth has resulted in senior management changes. Jafferies (winner of the 2000 Telstra Businesswoman of the Year award) and May have been relegated to non-executive consultant positions following a management review headed by the company's new 50 per cent shareholder, GS Private Equity.

When the *Business Review Weekly* interviewed Jafferies, she denied that other board members (including two executives from GS Private Equity) have sidelined her. 'I'm still very much involved with running the Dome business', she says. 'What I have done is cut back from 100 hours a week to 20. This is a business which must survive its founders and the only way that can happen is for the new managers to come through. I am still a director, shareholder and consultant to the company.'

Source: Contributed by Stephen Choo.

Update: Patria Jafferies is no longer with the company.

Websites:

www.domecoffees.com.au/ (Dome Coffees Australia)
The company's homepage provides you with some background information on the firm's history, concept and philosophy.

www.avcal.com.au/ (Australian Venture Capital Association Limited) The association's website provides a virtual network of venture capitalists and companies seeking funding. It provides resources for matters relating to the sourcing of venture capital in Australia.

www.v-capital.com.au/ (Venture Capital Marketplace)
This website is an internet-based venture-capital listing and matching service that assists companies to find investors all around the globe. It also provides useful information relating to the myriad sources of finance that are available to small businesses.

Activities for discussion, analysis and further research

1. When small retailers decide to expand, they can increase the number of outlets either by owning or franchising new stores. Critically evaluate each option.

2. Use the rational model of decision making to generate alternative sources of finance that could be available to Dome for expansion, and evaluate them. List the pros and cons of each option. Select two viable alternatives and give reasons. You can begin this exercise by looking at the above websites. Be complete in your answer.

3. You have been hired as the new managing director. The board of directors has asked you to present a five-point action plan to improve sales. You are told that the current strategy is not working; the stores in the eastern states are not profitable, customer service is poor and the stores are losing customers to their competitors. Be complete in your answer.

Implementing and monitoring the chosen solution

For decision-making success, managers must think deeply about implementing and monitoring the chosen option. A 'good' decision may follow the first three steps and the process still fail due to problems at the final step.

Implementing the solution

Successful implementation depends on two main factors: careful planning and sensitivity to those involved in the process and/or affected by it.

Minor changes may need only a little planning, but major changes may need greater planning such as written plans, coordination with internal and external units, and special funding arrangements. In general, the harder a solution is to reverse, the more planning is needed for effective implementation.

Implementation is also smoother when decision makers consider reactions of those impacted by a decision.

Monitoring the solution

Managers must monitor decision implementation to see progress goes as planned and the problem triggering the decision-making process is resolved. The more important the problem, the greater the need for follow-up. This is vigilance.

OVERCOMING BARRIERS TO EFFECTIVE DECISION MAKING

As non-rational managerial decision-making models suggest, managers rarely follow the four-step process. Despite support for this general approach, managers may be unaware of it. As well, there are barriers to effective decision making. In this section, we discuss overcoming four key decision-making barriers: accepting the initial problem challenge, searching for enough options, recognising common decision-making biases, and avoiding the decision-escalation phenomenon.

Accepting the problem challenge

Researchers have found four basic patterns in people's behaviour when facing a problem in the form of a difficulty or an opportunity. The first three—complacency, defensive avoidance and panic—are effective decision-making barriers. The fourth—deciding to decide—is a more effective approach for decision makers (Keinan 1987).

Complacency

Complacency occurs when people either do not see or ignore the danger or opportunity signs. With complacency, failing to detect signs usually flows from poor environmental scanning. Ignoring signs is the 'ostrich' effect—sticking your head in the sand and hoping the danger or opportunity will go away or fix itself. Complacency can occur even if there is a response. For example, someone may quickly accept a job offer that seems a good opportunity, without giving time or effort to assess the situation properly.

Defensive avoidance

With **defensive avoidance**, individuals deny a danger or an opportunity is important or deny responsibility for action. Defensive avoidance has three forms: rationalisation ('It can't happen to me'), procrastination ('It can be taken care of later'), or buck-passing ('It's someone else's problem'). When Barings Bank's London officials ignored signs that their Singapore-based derivatives trader, 28-year-old Nicholas Leeson, was taking unwarranted risks which led to over $1 billion of losses and the bank's collapse, all three forms occurred. Investigation showed bank officers had 'failed to follow up on a number of warning signals over a prolonged period'. Among the signals were unrealistically high profitability levels; unusually high funding to finance the Singapore office's trades; and earlier auditing reports that were never acted upon due to warring factions within the bank, showing lax controls. Leeson was sentenced to $6^1/_2$ years jail on two fraud charges (Barbash 1995; *Washington Post* 1995).

Panic

With **panic** or panic-like reactions, people get upset, seeking frantically for a way to solve a problem. They seize a quickly formulated option without seeing its severe problems and not considering other, possibly better, options. Panic is more common with crisis problems (Nutt 1984).

Deciding to decide

With a **deciding-to-decide** response, decision makers accept the challenge of deciding what to do about a problem and follow effective decision-making processes. Deciding to decide is important in a legitimate problem situation. Of course, managers cannot check all potential problems that appear, no matter how minor and remote. Some guidelines are shown in Table 5.3.

Searching for sufficient alternatives

For many decision situations, especially non-programmed ones, decision makers cannot identify all potential options assessing all possible pluses and minuses. Information collection, due to time and money, is limited. There are costs even if information gathering is just checking with other members or holding a meeting. So, decision makers must decide how much time, effort and money to invest gathering information to help their decision (Walker 2003b).

Figure 5.3 shows this information-gathering dilemma. The horizontal axis shows potential decision information, from 0 to 100 per cent. The vertical axis depicts the value and cost of additional information. As line *a* indicates, as a decision maker collects more and more information, the value of that information levels off. At the same time, as line *b* shows, additional information cost during the initial search is not high but gets higher as one moves to gaining perfect information. As a result marginal, or incremental, value of additional information

complacency

Condition in which individuals either do not see signs of danger or opportunity or ignore them

defensive avoidance

Condition in which individuals either deny the importance of a danger or an opportunity or deny any responsibility for taking action

panic

Reaction in which individuals become so upset they frantically seek a way to solve a problem

deciding to decide

Response in which decision makers accept the challenge of deciding what to do about a problem and follow an effective decision-making process

TABLE 5.3   GUIDELINES FOR DECIDING TO DECIDE

Appraise credibility of information
Is the source in a position to know the truth?
If so, is the source likely to be honest?
Is there any evidence, and how good is it?

Ascertain importance of threat or opportunity
How likely is a real danger or opportunity?
If a threat, how severe might losses be?
If an opportunity, how great might gains be?

Determine the need for urgency
Is the threat or opportunity likely to occur soon?
Will it develop gradually, or is sudden change likely?
If some action is urgent, can part be done now and the rest later?

Source: Adapted from Wheeler & Janis (1980, pp. 34–5).

FIGURE 5.3   The cost of additional information (adapted from Harrison 1987, p. 47)

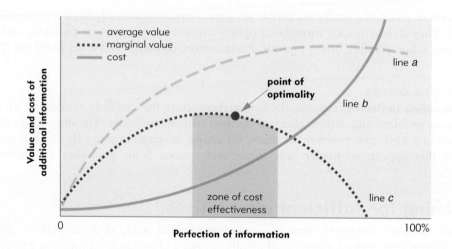

(line *c*) rises to an optimal point then drops as cost exceeds value for more information. The optimal information gathering area is shown.

Decision makers' efforts tend to fall below the cost effectiveness zone for identifying possible alternatives. One study of 78 decision-making situations found that in 85 per cent, there was little or no search for viable alternatives. Instead, another person's solution was copied, an off-the-shelf solution accepted, or an idea of unknown or uncertain value was seized on and support sought. In 15 per cent of cases where developing alternatives was attempted, the search process ceased after a few options were found as decision makers became fatigued or avoided exposing their preferred choice to scrutiny (McKean 1985). Skipping or abandoning a search for alternatives stifles innovation. Some approaches to generating decision alternatives will be dealt with later when discussing creativity. Of course, managers may not see putting time and effort into identifying multiple options as valuable.

Tough decisions in a time of crisis

The implosion of the insurer HIH in March 2001 had a widespread effect on the insurance industry in Australia. The collapse held both promise and dangers for the managers of rival insurance brokers and insurance underwriters. The hope for capturing the customers who were now without adequate insurance services was offset by the danger that collapse could also befall their own company. Insurance underwriters reassessed their ability to cover claims, and the subsequent rise in premiums meant that many customers could no longer afford insurance. More onerous legislation would govern the insurance industry in the wake of the royal commission responsible for investigating the HIH collapse. In the midst of the insurance crisis, some insurers would emerge as winners, and some as losers.

One company that has emerged as a 'winner' between 2001 and 2004 has been the listed group OAMPS. OAMPS is known as a specialist in the provision of insurance services to Australian businesses and selected markets, with operations in insurance broking, underwriting and financial services. Its 2003 Annual Report records a 53 per cent increase in company sales to $644.9 million and that net profit after tax increased by 57 per cent to $18.1 million over the course of the financial year. This growth is the result of careful management decisions in the midst of the insurance crisis.

OAMPS correctly analysed that the industry problems typified by HIH were related to poor profitability rather than a problem with obtaining insurance underwriting market share. In generating alternative solutions, however, OAMPS chose an inclusive strategy where it aimed to selectively increase market share as well as increasing profitability through increasing premiums. As a broker, OAMPS is very selective in building strategic alliances with only the most well-respected and secure suppliers and underwriters. Its market share has rapidly increased though a voracious appetite for acquisitions, with 17 broking operations acquired in the 2001 financial year, 21 in 2002 and 23 in 2003. Its buying power gives it a greater pool of options than many competitors, including direct access to Lloyd's of London, and it has snared market dominance in a number of industries.

In generating alternative solutions to deal with the insurance crisis, OAMPS as a broker built on its strength as a company that could recognise the specific requirements of particular industries. It further strengthened its commitment to personalised service and continuity of staff, and is now surfing on a wave of success, rather than drowning in a sea of failure.

Source: Contributed by Peter Woods (details of sources are listed on p. 736).

Activities for discussion, analysis and further research

1. What did OAMPS identify as the problem with the insurance industry that contributed to the HIH collapse, and how did it respond to this problem?
2. What were some of the alternatives that OAMPS generated to deal with the insurance crisis?
3. How would you characterise the type of problem and the type of decision required from OAMPS and how would this have influenced its decision-making process?

Recognising common decision-making biases

Kahneman and Tversky, investigating decision making operations, identified several typical information processing biases (Dunegan 1993; Slovic 1995). These biases are framing, representativeness, availability, and anchoring and adjustment. A related issue is decision makers' tendency to over-confidence. These biases affect decision makers' evaluation of alternatives, but also influence identifying problems and alternatives. Consider the following:

Faced with a superior enemy force, an army's general faces a dilemma. Intelligence officers say an ambush of his soldiers awaits and unless he uses one of two routes 600 will die. If he takes the first, 200 soldiers will be saved. If he takes the second, there's a one-third chance 600 soldiers will be saved and a two-thirds chance none will be saved. Which route should he take?

Like most, you will chose the first alternative, as the general should save 200, not risk even higher losses. Suppose the situation is as follows:

Again, the general has to select one of two escape routes. But this time his aides say if he takes the first, 400 soldiers will die. If the second, there's a one-third chance no soldiers will die and a two-thirds chance 600 soldiers will die. Which route should he take?

In this situation, most argue the general should take the second route. Their rationale being that with the first route, 400 will die. With the second there is at least a one-third chance no one will die, and casualties will only increase 50 per cent if the scheme fails.

Curiously, people draw one conclusion from the first problem and the reverse from the second. In the first problem, people choose the first option 3 to 1; in the second problem, they select the second option 4 to 1. Careful examination reveals that the problems are identical: just stated differently. The first refers to lives saved, the second to lives lost. This tendency to decide differently depending on how the problem presents is called **framing**.

To explain the paradoxic decision pattern shown by the general's dilemmas, Kahneman and Tversky (Bundescu & Weiss 1987; Fagley & Miller 1987; Neal, Huber & Northcraft 1987; Rachlin 1989; Jegers 1991) developed **prospect theory**. Based on the idea that decision makers tend to be 'loss averse', prospect theory argues the prospect of an actual loss is more painful than the possibility of losing a gain. Some companies seem to apply prospect theory. They offer 'cash discounts' rather than 'credit surcharges' for credit card use in making a purchase. Prospect theory suggests customers may be less happy with a charge for credit card use (an actual loss) than missing out on a cash discount (a potential gain). Even so, credit customers complain about the system (Southerland 1994).

Linda is 31, single, outspoken, very bright and majored in philosophy at university. As a student, she was concerned with discrimination and other social issues, joining anti-war demonstrations. Which statement is more likely?

1. Linda is a bank teller.
2. Linda is a bank teller and active in the feminist movement.

Most people decide Linda is a bank teller and a feminist. But it is in fact less likely that she is both a bank teller and a feminist. The laws of probability suggest an occurrence (bank teller) is more likely alone than in conjunction with another (bank teller and feminist). The Linda problem shows a common decision shortcut called **representativeness**, the tendency to be overly influenced by stereotypes in judging the likelihood of occurrences. We increase decision-making difficulties when judgments ignore laws of probability.

In a typical English text, is the letter 'K' more often the first letter in a word or the third?

People generally believe the letter 'K' will more often be the first letter in a word though it is almost twice as often in the third position. This shows the bias of **availability**, the tendency to judge chances of an occurrence on the basis of how many like instances or occurrences can be easily recalled. In this case, it is easier to recall words starting with the letter 'K' than words with 'K' as the third letter. Availability also shows in tendencies to inflate likelihood of deaths due to vividly imaginable causes such as aeroplane crashes, fires and murder, and underestimate more common, but less spectacular, causes such as heart disease, cigarette smoking, cancer, lack of physical exercise, emphysema and stroke (Lichtenstein, Slovic, Fischoff, Layman & Combs 1978). Managers can fall victim to availability bias. They may, for example, base subordinates'

---

framing

Tendency to make different decisions depending on how a problem is presented

prospect theory

Theory positing that decision makers find the prospect of an actual loss more painful than giving up the possibility of a gain

representativeness

Tendency to be overly influenced by stereotypes in making judgments about the likelihood of occurrences

availability

Tendency to judge the likelihood of an occurrence on the basis of the extent to which other like instances or occurrences can easily be recalled

annual performance appraisals on recent, easily recalled performances. Others may assess performance of competitors' products by how much they are seen in use, and may gauge employee morale based on views of immediate subordinates.

A newly hired engineer for a computer firm in the Sydney metropolitan area has four years' experience and good general qualifications. When asked to estimate an initial salary for this person, a chemist with little knowledge of the profession or industry guessed an annual salary of $27 000. What is your guess? (Bazerman 1986).

Most people do not think their estimate is impacted by the chemist's guess. Yet higher salary estimates emerge when the chemist's estimate is $60 000 instead of $27 000. The tendency to be influenced by an initial figure, even if irrelevant, is **anchoring and adjustment**. Employers, for example, ask a job candidate their current salary then base their offer on this, even though they may be under- or over-paid. Remembering that the salary figures in the previous example are no longer current, what would you guess would be the differences in salary if the job were in New Zealand, Singapore, Hong Kong?

These information-processing biases mean decision makers must be cautious about the accuracy of their estimates about event likelihood. Decision makers may become **overconfident**, tending to be more sure of judgments about a future event's likelihood than is supported by actual predictive accuracy (Bazerman 1986). Ironically, overconfidence is most likely when decision makers operate in unfamiliar areas (Schine 1995; Kinicki & Williams 2003). This comes from failing to fully understand the potential pitfalls. Managers may fall prey to overconfidence when planning moves into new, unfamiliar business areas (Koriat, Lichtenstein & Fischoff 1980).

Managers can avoid some information-processing biases by considering how their judgments can be affected (Barney & Griffin 1992). Becoming fairly well versed on associated issues by gathering enough information on major decisions helps. Decision makers should also think why their judgments might be wrong or off target. Contradictions and inaccuracies can be found through such thinking. Decision making is influenced by factors such as emotions, habits and motivation (Keren 1996). This chapter's supplement presents some quantitative methods for decision makers.

Avoiding the decision-escalation phenomenon

When a manager makes a decision, it is often only one of a series. More decisions may be needed, based on earlier results. For example, you hire a new employee and expect them to perform. However, several months later their performance is still unacceptable. Should you fire them? Of course, you have put time and money into training them, and they may still be learning the job. So you give more time and more training. Even with these extra inputs, two months later their performance is still unacceptable. What do you do now? There is more reason to 'cut your losses'; however, you also have invested even more to make them productive. When do you stop your 'investment'? (Bazerman 1986).

Managers face a dilemma in decision situations like this. There have been major costs, and later actions can either reverse the situation or compound initial losses. These are **escalation situations**, as they signal a strong possibility of commitment escalation and greater losses (Ross & Staw 1993).

Studies show when costs are incurred for an initial decision, managers may then put more resources into the situation even when prospects of improvement are dim. This pattern of behaviour leads to non-rational escalation situations. **Non-rational escalation**, or the escalation phenomenon, is the tendency to increase commitment to a previously selected course of action beyond the level expected if the manager followed an effective decision-making process (Bowen 1987). As economists and accountants warn, previously incurred costs (e.g. time and money) are **sunk costs**. Incurred costs are not recoverable and must be excluded from later actions. Yet decision makers often allow prior costs to influence them if they personally made the early decisions.

anchoring and adjustment

Tendency to be influenced by an initial figure, even when the information is largely irrelevant

overconfident

Tending to be more certain of judgments regarding the likelihood of a future event than one's actual predictive accuracy warrants

escalation situations

Situations signalling a strong possibility of escalating commitment and accelerating losses

non-rational escalation

Tendency to increase commitment to a previously selected course of action beyond the level expected if the manager followed an effective decision-making process; also called escalation phenomenon

sunk costs

Costs which, once incurred, are not recoverable and should not enter into considerations of future courses of action

One reason for the escalation phenomenon is that decision makers are loss-averse and reluctant to write off sunk costs. This may relate to prospect theory. Decision makers may also fear that altering a course of action may allow others to see the original decision as a mistake or even failure. Avoiding non-rational escalation requires setting advance limits on how far to extend commitment, challenging further commitment, reviewing costs, and monitoring escalation situations to avoid commitment traps (Rubin 1980; Brockner 1992).

MANAGING DIVERSITY: GROUP DECISION MAKING

Major organisation decisions are generally made by groups to gain from diverse outlooks (Gentile 1994). For instance, Gencorp Automotive set up its new reinforced plastics plant to run with just three levels: plant manager, team leaders, and 25 teams of 5 to 15 production workers. Rather than being run by managers who do not work at an operational level, each team makes most decisions about its work area (Fowler 1988). In this section, we consider group decision making's advantages and disadvantages, as well as enhancement of group decision-making processes (Huber 1980; Maier 1989).

Advantages and disadvantages of group decision making

Group decision making has many advantages over individual decision making (Table 5.4). A study of over 200 project teams in management-education courses showed that groups outperformed their best member in 97 per cent of cases. In a group, many different ideas are usually focused on a problem (Michaelsen, Watson & Black 1989).

Despite its advantages, group decision making has potential disadvantages in contrast to individual decision making (Table 5.4). One—groupthink—needs to be further discussed.

Groupthink

Tendency of cohesive groups to seek agreement about an issue at the expense of realistically appraising the situation

Groupthink describes the tendency that cohesive groups have to seek agreement about an issue before assessing the situation realistically (Janis 1982). According to groupthink theory, members avoid causing disagreements or giving information that might unsettle discussion because they do not want to disturb the cohesion of the group. National Aeronautics and Space Administration (NASA) officials and others blamed groupthink for the Challenger tragedy. Despite dissent, upper-level officials at NASA and at Morton Thiokol, the maker of the solid rocket boosters, continued with the mission. They ignored information from Morton Thiokol engineers and others about possible problems due to very cold weather. Sadly, all seven crew died in the launch explosion (Kruglanski 1986). Some research suggests groupthink occurs even without highly cohesive groups, if the leader states at the outset a particular preference (Aldag & Fuller 1994; Mullen, Anthony, Salas & Driskell 1994). Other researchers think the groupthink concept is faulty, arguing that group decision making is more complex than groupthink suggests (Watson, Kumar & Michaelson 1993). Still, the groupthink idea may highlight the need for groups to follow an effective decision-making process.

Enhancing group decision-making processes

Managers can take steps to help avoid the major pitfalls of group decision making and to gain the benefits. One step is to involve the group in decisions when the group's information and knowledge are important to decision quality. That way, the time taken by group decision making can be justified.

TABLE 5.4 ADVANTAGES AND DISADVANTAGES OF GROUP DECISION MAKING

Advantages

1. More information and knowledge is focused on the issue.
2. A greater number and diversity of alternatives can be developed.
3. Better understanding and acceptance of the final decision is likely.
4. Members develop knowledge and skills for future use.

Disadvantages

1. Usually it is more time-consuming.
2. Disagreements may delay decisions and cause hard feelings.
3. One or a few group members may dominate discussion.
4. Groupthink may cause members to overemphasise getting agreement.

Group design or composition is another element in enhancing group decision making. For example, membership diversity appears to improve group performance. In one study, culturally homogeneous groups (members all with the same national and ethnic background) performed better initially than culturally heterogeneous ones (members with different national and ethnic backgrounds) (Ancona & Caldwell 1992; Jackson & Associates 1992). Eventually, heterogeneous groups caught up, then surpassed, homogeneous groups' performance. Data showed heterogeneous groups at first could not interact effectively, but gradually learned to use their diverse group perspectives (Zaheer 1995). With growing workforce diversity and globalisation, managers must be able to handle group dynamics to gain diversity's benefits (this is discussed further in Chapter 15) (Watson et al. 1993).

Another way to aid group decision-making involves other aspects of group composition. For example, including members who are likely to focus on major company goals can help overcome the tendency to self-interest (Browning 1994; Tredgold 2003). Having someone skilled at encouraging others' ideas can minimise the effect of dominant members.

Another way to facilitate group decision making is to set up mechanisms to avoid groupthink. For one, managers may appoint one or more **devil's advocates**—individuals who are not afraid to speak up and, by raising concerns and asking probing questions, ensure negative aspects of attractive decision alternatives are considered. Managers can also encourage a group to use **dialectical inquiry**, where a decision situation is approached from two opposite points (Wheeler & Janis 1980; Schwenk 1990; Schwenk & Valacich 1994).

Computer-assisted group decision making

Information technology advances can help group decision making. Teleconferencing, or simultaneous communication among groups by telephone or computer with special software, is one way (Laudon & Price 1994). Such software is **groupware**, designed to support group members' collaborative efforts, such as scheduling or holding meetings, project collaboration and document sharing. Group decision making can be aided by specialised computer-based information or group decision-support systems, which help members work together on poorly structured problems. (See Chapters 13 and 18.) Groupware helps member communication, where group decision-support systems focus more on the group making the decision.

Computer assistance for decision making has not been well researched yet (Hollinghead & McGrath 1995; Guzzo & Dickson 1996). The suggestion is that computer-assisted groups interact and exchange less than face-to-face groups, and are slower to complete their task. The impact seems to depend on the task. Computer assistance seems to lead to better ideas.

devil's advocates

Individuals assigned the role of making sure negative aspects of any attractive decision alternatives are considered

dialectical inquiry

Procedure in which a decision situation is approached from two opposite points of view

groupware

Software designed to support collaborative efforts among group members, such as scheduling meetings, holding meetings, collaborating on projects and sharing documents

The Amazon.com experience

Amazon.com is the outstanding success story amidst the many dot com disasters of the new millennium. This is the example par excellence of the 'virtual' store. The basis upon which amazon.com was built was that in order to sell books there was no need for expensive stores in prime CBD real estate, no need for warehouses filled with books which might never be sold. Customers would order their books (and in time other media) online, Amazon.com would order the books from the publishers and ship them direct to the customer, thus making significant savings. Amazon.com would hold no stock and hence never be left with unsold stock—the bane of the book-selling industry (check out the discount bins in any retail book store). Given the resulting lower costs they were then able to sell at prices which were significantly lower than retail in-store prices.

However, the success of Amazon.com is not due solely to the idea of selling books on line. It is also due to intelligent and creative management. Customers who have sourced the books and other media on the web in extra-quick time, and from the comfort of their lounge rooms, are not then going to wait forever for their purchases to arrive. They also realise that sourcing and delivering the items purchased is not a simple task and they are prepared to wait, providing they are told how long they have to wait and that their expectations are met. Amazon.com found that publishers were not always reliable suppliers. In other words, Amazon.com, having received an order for a book, would then want to place an electronic order with a publisher and have the book delivered to the customer in a predetermined time. However, because some publishers proved unreliable and in some cases were unable to accept electronic orders, in order to be able to guarantee a reasonable delivery time Amazon.com have had to resort to building a warehouse to hold stocks—so much for the 'virtual' store! Nonetheless because their business is truly virtual they were able to locate the warehouse in a location where the price of land was low and where access to all forms of transport was excellent. Hence they have been able to retain their competitive edge on two fronts—lower costs and superior service.

Source: Contributed by Ken Dooley.

Activities for discussion, analysis and further research

1. What difficulties would you expect in making the decision to build a warehouse, given the basis of the company was to have a 'virtual' business, i.e. to avoid physical infrastructure?
2. Visit the Amazon.com website and explain the concept of the 'virtual' store.
3. What are the advantages/disadvantages of the Amazon.com experience from the point of view of the customer?
4. Given access to the web and a credit card, would you use Amazon.com? Explain your answer.

Face-to-face groups by contrast seem to be better at solving difficult problems and resolving major conflicts. Analysis of 13 computer-aided group decision-making studies suggest consensus decreases, as does satisfaction with the process. Face-to-face meetings may be better when there are major opinion differences among group members and where commitment of group members is critical to successful result implementation. This could change with improvements in groupware and group decision-support systems, and studies assessing computer assistance (McLeod 1996).

Computer assistance seems to aid production of creative ideas, helping in decision-making phases where creativity is needed. Creativity is basic to decision-making as it generates new options leading to innovation, fostering novel perspectives on the nature of problems. Next, we discuss encouraging individual and group creativity.

PROMOTING INNOVATION: THE CREATIVITY FACTOR IN DECISION MAKING

Creativity is the cognitive process of developing an idea, concept, commodity or discovery viewed as novel by its creator or a target audience (Bazerman 1986). Creativity is identified by results (Amabile 1983). In fact, Amabile (Kohn 1987, p. 54) argues, 'Creativity is not a quality of a person; it is a quality of ideas, of behaviours, or products'. Creativity is crucial to problem solving which yields organisational innovations. Increasing global competition emphasises creativity. Japan is working to overcome a copycat reputation through greater creativity.

Try the classic creativity problem in Figure 5.4. Then look at Figure 5.5 for some solutions. Solving the nine-dot problem can be difficult if the assumption is that lines cannot go outside the dots. As the problem shows, both convergent and divergent thinking are needed for creativity. **Convergent thinking** means starting with a problem then moving to a solution logically. Convergent thinking can be thought of as digging an ever bigger and deeper hole to search for oil (de Bono 1968). **Divergent thinking** is solving problems by generating new ways of viewing them and searching for novel alternatives. Rather than digging in the same hole, a divergent thinker digs in various places to generate new perspectives. In creativity, convergent thinking helps define a problem and evaluate possible solutions. Divergent thinking helps develop alternate views of problems and seek new ways to manage them. In this section, we examine the basic elements of creativity, describe stages in the creative process, and provide techniques for enhancing group creativity.

creativity

Cognitive process of developing an idea, concept, commodity or discovery viewed as novel by its creator or a target audience

convergent thinking

Effort to solve problems by beginning with a problem and attempting to move logically to a solution

divergent thinking

Effort to solve problems by generating new ways of viewing a problem and seeking novel alternatives

GENDER FACTOR

Wai Ata Productions

Rhonda Kite (Te Aupouri) hails from one of the poorest rural communities in Northland, New Zealand. She was raised in Otara, a working-class suburb that was created in the 1960s and accommodated an increasing number of Maori families who migrated to Auckland during the industrial boom that spearheaded economic development in New Zealand at that time.

Ten years ago, Rhonda was made redundant from her job. She borrowed money from her family and bought a share in a recording studio. Through her experiences in the business and her exposure to the music industry, Rhonda became interested in film and television production. Today, Rhonda owns Eden Terrace Audio, a post-production company, and Wai Ata Productions, a company that produces Maori language versions of children's animation and documentaries. She is 50-per-cent owner of Kiwa Productions, which specialises in documentary production, and owns 82 per cent of VoiceQ International, a software development company. In 1996 Rhonda won the Maori Businesswoman of the Year Small Business Award. In 2001 Rhonda won

three of the five coveted Maori businesswomen's awards.

Some members of Rhonda's family, including her English-born father, husband Mark and a few of her nine brothers and sisters, work in her companies. For Maori, the whanau or family is the centre-post of identity and community. Rhonda describes her leadership style as 'whanau-leadership'.

'I am a late starter to business (she was 38) and one of the main challenges I face is keeping up with the changing cultural and social face of New Zealand and the world', Rhonda states. 'I am the mother of this family. More often than not the disciplinary discussions end up as counselling sessions. I also like to think I lead by example. I think the industry I am in requires more one-on-one interaction. In order to allow the creative process to flow a person must feel they are in a safe environment; they can be at their most vulnerable when being creative. In the creative environment people find a tension between creating their "baby" and then "selling" it. Being Maori encourages me to make decisions based on what is good for the tribe.

I am constantly weighing up whether this is good for us all. While I think my whanau-style is important, it can be seen as "soft" by those who simply do not want to be part of the whanau, they just want a job!'

Rhonda has learned that sometimes 'nice' people have a hard time surviving in business. She has overcome her naiveté and accepted that one needs to be strong, regardless of gender or ethnicity.

Source: Contributed by Ella Henry.

(It is customary for Maori people, when introducing themselves or others, to state their tribal affiliation. Ms Kite's genealogy includes the Te Aupouri tribe.)

Activities for discussion, analysis and further research

1. Go to the website: www.edentce.co.nz and review their program credits. In what way might Rhonda's ethnicity and gender have influenced the programs her company has worked on?
2. How might a background of working-class disadvantage affect decision-making?
3. How might that, in turn, affect management and leadership style?

FIGURE 5.4 The nine-dot problem. Without lifting your pencil from the paper, draw no more than four straight lines that will cross through all nine dots

Basic ingredients

According to Amabile (1983), creativity needs the following three basic ingredients.

Domain-relevant skills

These skills result from expertise in a relevant field. They include related technical skills or artistic ability, talent in the area and factual knowledge.

Creativity-relevant skills

These skills include a cognitive style, or method, of thinking that involves exploring new directions; awareness of ways to generate novel ideas; and a work style helpful to developing creative ideas. A creative work style includes the ability to focus attention and effort for long periods of time; the ability to abandon unproductive avenues; persistence and high energy levels.

FIGURE 5.5 Some possible solutions to the nine-dot problem (based on Adams, reprinted from Papalia & Olds 1985, p. 297)

This puzzle is difficult to solve if the imaginary boundary (limit) enclosing the nine dots is not exceeded. A surprising number of people will not exceed the imaginary boundary, for often this constraint is unconsciously in the mind of the problem-solver, even though it is not in the definition of the problem at all. The overly strict limits are a block in the mind of the solver. The widespread nature of this block is what makes this puzzle classic (Adams 1980, p. 24).

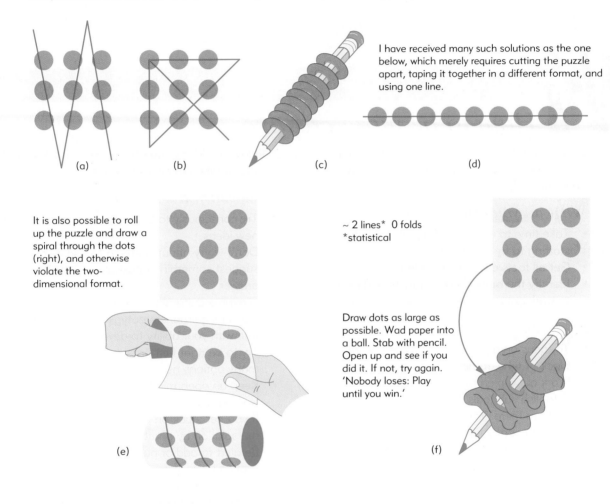

I have received many such solutions as the one below, which merely requires cutting the puzzle apart, taping it together in a different format, and using one line.

(a)   (b)   (c)   (d)

It is also possible to roll up the puzzle and draw a spiral through the dots (right), and otherwise violate the two-dimensional format.

~ 2 lines* 0 folds
*statistical

Draw dots as large as possible. Wad paper into a ball. Stab with pencil. Open up and see if you did it. If not, try again. 'Nobody loses: Play until you win.'

(e)   (f)

30 May, 1994
6 Rowan Road
Frankston, Vic
Dear Prof. James Adams,
    My dad and I love doing Puzzles from 'Conceptual Blockbusting'. We were mostly working on the dot ones, like ⁞⁞⁞ My dad said a man found a way to do it with one line. I tried and did it. Not with folding, but I used a fat line. It doesn't say you can't use a fat line.
    Like this
                        Sincerely,
                        Cathy Bush
                        age 10
PS actually you need a very fat writing apparatus

(g)

1 line 0 folds
Lay the paper on the surface of the Earth. Circumnavigate the globe twice + a few centimetres, displacing a little each time so as to pass through the next row on each circuit as you 'Go West, young man'.

(h)

Task motivation

The individual must be truly interested in a task for itself, not just for any available external reward, such as money. A primary concern for external rewards can inhibit creativity. For example, the creativity of a researcher developing a new drug to obtain a bonus or prize will probably be lower than someone whose interest is focused on uncovering a promising new idea (Amabile 1983). For a creativity boost, see the discussion below in 'How to be more creative'.

MANAGEMENT SKILLS FOR A GLOBALISED ECONOMY

How to be more creative

Some of the following, based on research and thinking on creativity, may build your creativity in work and daily life.

What do you want to do?

- Take time to understand a problem before starting to try to solve it.
- Get all facts clear in your mind.
- Identify the most important facts before you try to work out a detailed solution.

How can you do it?

- To focus on a problem, set aside a worthwhile block of time, rather than scattered sessions.
- Work out a plan to attack the problem.
- Establish subgoals. Solve part of the problem and go from there. You don't have to do it all at once. Record your thoughts. This means you can catch important points and return later. It also means you can look for patterns.
- Visualise yourself acting out the problem. Actually act out the problem.
- Think of a similar problem you've solved before and build on the strategy you used.
- Use analogies when possible. See if you can generalise from a similar situation to your current problem.
- Use many problem-solving strategies—verbal, visual, mathematical, acting. Diagram the problem to help visualisation, or talk to yourself aloud, or 'walk through' a situation.
- Look for relationships among facts.
- Trust your intuition. Take a guess and see if you can back it up.

- Play with ideas and possible approaches. Look at the situation in different ways.

How can you do it better?

- Try consciously to be original, to come up with new ideas.
- Don't worry about seeming foolish if you say or suggest something unusual or if you find a wrong answer.
- Eliminate cultural taboos from your thinking (such as gender stereotyping) which might interfere with your ability to develop a novel solution.
- Try to be right first time, but if not, explore as many options as needed.
- Keep an open mind. If the first approach doesn't work, ask if you made any faulty assumptions.
- If you get stuck on one approach, try to get to the solution by another.
- Be alert to odd or puzzling facts. If you can explain them, your solution may be close.
- Think of odd ways to use objects and the environment. Look at familiar things as if you've never seen them before.
- Consider taking a detour, which delays your goal but eventually leads to it.
- Discard habitual approaches, and make yourself develop new ones.
- Do some brainstorming with other people. This is trying to produce as many new and original ideas as possible, without evaluating any until the end of the session.
- Strive for objectivity. Evaluate your own ideas as you would those of a stranger.

Source: Reprinted from Papalia & Olds (1988).

Stages of creativity

The creativity process has several stages. One commonly used creativity model has four stages (Haefele 1962; Bazerman 1986), shown in Figure 5.6 and described below.

Preparation

This stage involves gathering initial information, defining the problem or task needing creativity, generating alternatives, and seeking and carefully analysing related data. At this stage, the person immerses themselves in every problem aspect. For complex technical problems, this may take months or years.

Incubation

This stage of creativity involves subconscious mental activity and divergent thinking to explore unusual alternatives. In this stage, the person generally does not focus on the problem consciously, letting their subconscious work on a solution.

Illumination

At this stage, a new insight is gained, often with a sudden breakthrough in 'eureka' fashion.

Verification

This stage has ideas tested to check the insight's validity. Here, convergent, logical thinking evaluates the solution. If it is not feasible, cycling back through all or some earlier stages may be needed.

Techniques for enhancing group creativity

While the preceding discussed individual creative efforts, this section turns to group creativity techniques. Two major techniques are brainstorming and nominal group technique. (We discuss two other ways to enhance group creativity, the Delphi method and scenario analysis, in the following Supplement.)

Brainstorming

The brainstorming technique has group members generate as many novel ideas as they can on a topic without evaluation. The four basic rules—do not criticise during idea generation, freewheel, offer many ideas, and improve on ideas already offered—were raised before. Research suggests computer-assisted brainstorming is better than face-to-face for idea generation. This seems to be because more time is available for idea production as members can offer ideas together rather than listening to others or wait for them to stop speaking before offering an idea (Gallupe, Cooper, Grise & Bastianutti 1994).

Nominal group technique

The **nominal group technique (NGT)** enhances creativity and decision making by integrating individual work and group interaction within ground rules. The technique fosters both individual and group creativity and overcomes the criticism of offered ideas.

nominal group technique (NGT)

Technique integrating both individual work and group interaction within certain ground rules

FIGURE 5.6 Stages of creativity

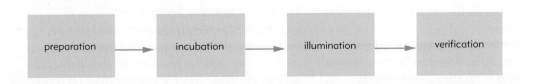

NGT's ground rules, or steps, are as follows:

1. Individual members independently prepare lists of their ideas on a problem.
2. Each member presents their ideas in a round-robin session (one at a time in turn) without discussion. Ideas are recorded so all can see them. If one idea triggers another, the new idea is added to a member's list to offer on a future turn.
3. When all individual ideas are put on the group list, members discuss them to clarify and evaluate.
4. Members silently and independently vote on the ideas, by rank-ordering or rating. The final result comes from pooling individual votes (Delbecq, Van de Ven & Gustafson 1975; Huber 1980).

Evidence generally shows NGT is effective in developing many options while maintaining group satisfaction. It is possible NGT may be more effective than brainstorming for idea generation in face-to-face groups, but less so than computer-assisted brainstorming (Van de Ven & Delbecq 1974; Dennis & Valacich 1994).

Thus there are many ways managers can build creativity and innovation at work. This chapter has focused on various aspects of the organisational decision process, while its supplement provides specific tools to assist planning and decision making.

GAINING THE EDGE

Reach for the clouds

The ushering in of the information age holds great promise for involving even more stakeholders in the process of management decision-making. Some stakeholders, however, are locked out of the decision-making process due to the now infamous 'digital divide'. The digital divide is characterised by the exclusion of stakeholders from informational and decision processes as they don't have access to a computer or the internet, they don't know how to use a computer, or they are unfamiliar with the predominant language of communication in an area. Infoxchange Australia, a not-for-profit social enterprise company, initiated and coordinated a project to bridge this divide among the people of inner Melbourne's Atherton Gardens High Rise Estate. This is a large public housing estate comprising 800 apartments in four towers. The project called 'Reach for the clouds', was chosen in 2001 as a finalist in the education category of the prestigious annual Stockholm Challenge Awards for pioneering IT projects. Infoxchange Australia focuses on community development using information technology as the primary tool to create positive social change.

The 'Reach for the clouds' project sought to provide all residents of the Atherton Gardens estate with free access to a PC in their own home, to establish a local community computer network (intranet), to provide access to internet communications (internet), to train residents in computer use, to enable community management of the network and establish social enterprise opportunities. The community intranet provided vital community service information (including job opportunities and online shopping) and discussion board interaction in English and community languages. The project was funded by a number of organisations including the Victorian government and 'Green PC', another Infoxchange social enterprise where redundant computers and peripherals are donated for refurbishment and distribution to low-income communities, individuals and community organisations.

The development of the project involved residents at every step of the decision-making process. Community project meetings provided the opportunity for language groups to meet with a translator to discuss decisions. The intranet contains information in English, Chinese and Vietnamese. The project is managed by a committee of stakeholders including residents of the estate. Importantly, the project provided the training, support and tools for residents so that they could actively participate in the decision-making processes of the project. The success of the project in producing a better informed and empowered community demonstrates that involving stakeholders in management decision-making is a process of crossing many bridges so that disadvantaged people can ultimately traverse the digital divide.

Source: Contributed by Peter Woods.

Websites:

http://www.infoxchange.net.au/
http://www.atherton.org.au/
http://www.challenge.stockholm.se/
http://www.wired.infoxchange.net.au/

Activities for discussion, analysis and further research

1. What barriers to decision-making are evident in this case?
2. How were these barriers overcome?
3. What advantages to the community would there be from this type of group decision-making?

REFLECTIVE PRACTITIONER

KIMBERLEY TURNER

AEROSAFE
RISK MANAGEMENT

How do I make decisions in the company? Certainly, in decision making there are a couple of different layers that I am looking at. When I started the company, I was an individual with the belief that I could make something happen. Part of the process of me being positioned to make good business decisions was all about having access to the right information. When I talk about various aspects in my business, people often ask: 'How do you actually know that?' It's all about going out there and finding

out, going out and researching. I need to package up my ideas and validate them against the information that I have received from somebody that I respect.

With reference to the different layers that I mentioned before, well—the strategic direction of the company is something that I share with two advisors who I respect in that capacity. I share with them the strategic thoughts of where I'd like to take the business, and really seek their input and their guidance. This gives me effectively a pseudo-advisory board. I am a sole director and sole company owner so I don't have a board of directors. So I have selected people who act in that honorary capacity.

In terms of decisions on a day-to-day operational level, I have made a conscious choice to take a step back from the day-to-day decisions and try to delegate authority to members of our team. I saw my company evolve and develop to the stage where people have almost been stifled and not had the ability or empowerment to make decisions, or not feel that they've got the authority to make those decisions. Consequently I have made a conscious effort to try to support people in making their own decisions and backing them up as long as they provide that justification. So at the operational level, I would say that I would still probably make 40 per cent of the decisions but I'd like to really change that proportion so it's more at the 25 per cent level. We've got various structures in place that support the decision-making process. We have put in place a communication strategy and a reporting structure over the last three years which facilitates that. What that means is that there is a vehicle for the flow of information and validation process. This aids in making decisions in a more timely fashion.

One of the key things that has been important for me is having our organisation and the staff in the organisation recognise when it is a decision that is very much able to be made within the delegated level of authority and when things need to be escalated to the higher level of decision making. There isn't any right or wrong answer to that. You feel your way through it and you work out when you need to spend more time or more focus on assisting and coaching someone. So I need to determine whether I just make the decision myself and give a directive, or allow the person to work beyond their capacity and encourage them to make the decision anyway and support it. I can then use that as a coaching opportunity. I think that I have had the combination of all of those with different staff taking into consideration that different people are at different levels in their ability to make decisions or of their comfort level with the responsibility.

My responsibility as a manager is to watch out for the individual who is over-confident in making decisions without all the information at hand. I need to be aware of what is going on there and assist where I can. My style can be very much authoritarian when it needs to be. When things are very cut and dried and significant to the business, I can be quite direct in the decision or the guidance that is provided. On the other hand, if it is something that has the ability to expand, grow or be more like a learning process, I will adopt a very consultative style. In some cases, it can be perceived as indecision. I'd like to involve people in contributing since at the end of the day, if a decision impacts on another staff member's area of responsibility, they need to have ownership in the decision that is made.

That links very much with the culture that we want. I want people to believe in what they're doing and not just jump through the hoops so that means that people have to be involved and contribute. Depending on the staff member or the manager I am working with, they may only see one side of my management style. When my consultative style is adopted it really demonstrates a trust in the person I am dealing with. So I have two styles that I will activate and employ as I think appropriate.

FOCUS ON PRACTICE

Strategies for improving

1. Develop a strategy that will convince managers it is not always possible to make optimal decisions, and that they must focus on making the best decision for the circumstances.
2. How would you encourage lower-level managers to focus on generating as many options as possible as part of problem-solving processes?
3. Work with a group to get them to identify the impact of their preferences and interests on the options they have generated and the decisions ultimately made.
4. What strategies can you use to try to eliminate biases from alternative generation and decision-making processes?

Source: Jones et al. (2000).

SUMMARY

- Decision making is the process managers use to identify organisational problems and try to resolve them. Managers deal with three problem types: crisis, non-crisis and opportunity. Opportunity problems are major vehicles for organisational innovation. As opportunities involve ideas to be used, rather than problems to be resolved, they may get too little attention.
- Managerial decision situations generally come in two categories: programmed and non-programmed. Due to their nature, non-programmed decisions usually involve significant uncertainty and risk.
- Two models types have been developed to better understand how managers make decisions. The rational model suggests managers are almost perfect information handlers, making optimal decisions. By contrast, non-rational managerial decision-making models, including satisficing, incremental, and rubbish-bin models, suggest that information-gathering and processing limitations make it hard for managers to make optimal decisions.
- An effective decision-making process has four major steps: (1) Identifying the problem involves scanning, categorisation and diagnosis stages. (2) Generating alternative solutions emphasises the importance of alternatives in reaching a high-quality solution. (3) Evaluating and choosing an alternative means feasibility, quality, acceptability, costs, reversibility and ethics must be considered. (4) Implementing and monitoring the solution focuses on careful planning, sensitivity to those involved in implementation and/or affected by it, and design of follow-up mechanisms.
- As non-rational models of managerial decision making suggest, managers may not follow effective decision-making processes. This is due to four major decision barriers they face. Managers must be familiar with how to overcome each. The first entails accepting a problem challenge. This means deciding to decide, rather than reacting with complacency, defensive avoidance or panic. The second involves searching for enough alternatives. The third focuses on identifying common decision-making biases, such as framing, representativeness, availability, anchoring and adjustment, and overconfidence. The fourth centres on avoiding the escalation phenomenon, or non-rational escalation. This is the tendency to greater commitment to a course of action previously selected beyond the expected level if the manager followed an effective decision-making process.
- Group decision making has advantages and disadvantages. The advantages are that more information and knowledge is focused on the issue, a greater number and range of options can be developed, greater understanding and acceptance of the final decision is likely, and members develop knowledge and skills for the future. The disadvantages are group decisions are usually more time-consuming, disagreements may delay decision making and cause hard feelings, one or a few group members may dominate discussion, and groupthink may cause members to overemphasise gaining agreement. Managers can take several steps to minimise disadvantages including taking advantage of group diversity.
- A major aspect of promoting innovation is creativity. Creativity involves both convergent and divergent thinking. Basic ingredients of the creative process are domain-relevant skills, creativity-relevant skills and task motivation. The creativity process has four stages: preparation, incubation, illumination and verification. Creativity enhancing techniques include brainstorming and nominal group technique.

QUESTIONS FOR DISCUSSION AND REVIEW

1. Outline major problem types managers are likely to confront. Give an example of each, which has occurred or could occur at your university.
2. Explain differences between programmed and non-programmed decision situations. Choose a familiar organisation and identify two programmed and two non-programmed decision situations.

3. Contrast rational and non-rational models of managers as decision makers. Think of a recent non-programmed decision situation you have seen handled in an organisation (perhaps a student group or association to which you belong). Which of the following models best describes the decision process involved: rational, satisficing, incremental or rubbish bin? Explain why.

4. Describe each step in an effective decision-making process. We sometimes witness serious unresolved organisational problems, such as poor quality products or services. What are some potential managerial reactions to problem situations, which might account for the persistence of such problems?

5. Explain the main decision barriers involved in accepting the problem challenge and searching for sufficient alternatives. How can these barriers be overcome?

6. Give an example of each common decision-making bias. Explain how these might influence evaluations of alternative solutions.

7. Explain conditions under which the escalation phenomenon is likely to occur. What steps can a manager take to minimise the possibility of falling prey to non-rational escalation?

8. Assess group decision making's advantages and disadvantages. Give an example of (a) a situation in which you felt the advantages outweighed the disadvantages, and (b) one in which you felt the opposite was true. In the latter, what could have been done to prevent the decision-making difficulty? Could effectively managing diversity have helped?

9. Explain the main ingredients of creativity.

10. Suppose you are chairing a task force in a finance company asked to develop new ideas to enhance customer service. What approaches might help the flow of creative ideas? Which would you pick, and why?

CRITICAL THINKING QUESTIONS

To answer some of these questions you will need to do further research. Useful references are given below each section of the questions.

This chapter dealt with the decision-making processes managers utilise when dealing with workplace issues. The challenge of ensuring that appropriate decision-making processes are in place while, at the same time, providing room for creativity is investigated in this section.

1. As work increasingly moves to online formats, organisations are finding the computer-based environment is changing the structure of decision making. What are some of the possible internal challenges to managers' decision-making processes?

2. Budd (2001) argues that e-business also means that organisations have to change their internal decision-making behaviours in order to manage external customers and suppliers well. Why is this?

(Material relevant to these questions may be found in Budd, S. 2001, Keeping a happy hive, *Management*, Auckland, 3 January, pp. 40–4.)

A recent book by Jeremy Hope and Robin Fraser (2002) called *Beyond Budgeting* suggests that budgets, and the annual performance measures they are tied to, provide major hurdles to achieving effective change. Rather than the standard 'toolkit' approach taken by many management guides, Hope and Fraser present an alternative management model based on the decision-making needs of first-level managers.

3. How do you think the model would work?

4. What features would you expect to see in the decision-making processes for the new performance-management climate to flourish?

5. While all the above may sound revolutionary, the fact is that the new performance-management processes will still involve goal setting, rewarding employees, planning action, resources and coordination. How would a manager go about goal-setting in the 'beyond budget' environment?

6. How could managers be rewarded in the new process?

Hope and Fraser believe the value of their model is the way it allows managers to actively engage in strategic planning—because it provides freedom to be innovative and deliver value rather than being confined to focusing on numbers and adhering to preset plans. With the senior management team determining the overall values, direction and boundaries of the organisation, day-to-day decision-making moves to the frontline with only major capital expenditure proposals and resource requirements generally being referred upwards.

7. Apart from the above, what is the major decision-making role for senior management in the 'beyond budget' model?

(Material relevant to questions 3 to 7 may be found in Gould, S. 2003, Working without budgets, *New Straits Times*, Malaysia, 25 October, p.6–EX; Hope, J. and Fraser, R. 2002, *Beyond Budgeting*, Harvard Business School Press.)

The omission of innovation as a possible feature within the small-to-medium organisation is nothing new and begs the question as to whether it is only the large companies who can afford to develop new products.

8. Rodriguez (2003) suggests that when small businesses do actually launch new products, they can often do so in half the time and effort than a big firm takes. How?

Another aspect of the 'hands on' approach typical in small enterprises is illustrated by Loreta Rafisura, managing director of Cagayan de Oro-based Salay Handmade Paper Products, Inc. Rafisura encourages the creativity of her staff and customers in developing new products (Rodriguez 2003).

9. How do you think Ms Rafisura motivates her workers and customers to be involved in the creative decision process required to develop new products?

10. Another example given by Rodriguez of a small business utilising innovative decision-making methods is Ramon Castillo, a Metro Manila-based manufacturer of electronic equipment and gadgets. He utilises computer technology to achieve agility in innovation. How can technology be used to further the innovation process for small business?

The clear message for small-to-medium businesses is that they can be dynamic and nimble and this adds up to more rapid innovation.

(Material relevant to questions 8 to 10 may be found in Rodriguez, M. 2003, Diversification: A possible dream for SMEs, *Philippine Daily Inquirer*, 20 October, p. 2.)

MANAGEMENT EXERCISES

Exercise 1 **Skill-building exercise: Effective decision making**

You own the Happy Hamburger chain of 10 restaurants in your local area. Two weeks ago the competitor in your area has introduced 'funny' hamburgers in different shapes and sizes. These have been very popular with teenagers. You notice sales at several of your restaurants dropped, and managers tell you they are serving fewer teenagers. Yesterday you became aware of a device to cut ground meat into hamburgers of specific weights and several shapes (e.g. round, cars, yachts and bicycles). You realise this could give you the capability to compete with the other restaurant. Further, your employees are currently making hamburgers by hand. These are round in shape and weigh about 150 grams. The hamburger cutter can be rented or purchased. Refer to the following table to determine which of the considerations would be included in each step of the decision-making process.

Considerations in making the decision about hamburger shapes				
Consideration	**Identify the problem/ opportunity**	**Generate alternative solutions**	**evaluate/ choose alternatives**	**Implement/ monitor solution**
1. Could rent device				
2. Provides variety; competitor has device				
3. Device would save some money by precise weighing				
4. Could continue making present round shapes by hand				
5. If device is rented, could opt out				
6. Evaluate sales, costs and satisfaction monthly				
7. Could purchase device				
8. New shapes would appeal to younger buyers				
9. Costs $300 each per month to rent and $1750 each to buy				
10. Schedule an electrician to install the necessary wiring				

Exercise 2 Management exercise: Brainstorming

Objectives
- To learn how the brainstorming technique for stimulating creativity operates
- To gain experience in generating ideas in a brainstorming session

Instructions
1. Select a problem of common interest to group members. If the group has difficulty selecting a problem, try one of these:
   a. How can students be more involved in developing your university's policies (e.g. new programs, admissions and transfers, and electives)?
   b. What kind of game could be developed to help learn how to make better decisions?
   c. What features would you like cars to have 10 years from now?
   d. What new approaches could recent graduates use in developing job leads?
2. Spend 30 minutes brainstorming alternative solutions. Someone in the group should record all ideas. Even if the group runs out of steam after 15 minutes or so, keep brainstorming. Usually, the best ideas occur later in the session. Freewheel. Offer ideas even if they seem wild and impractical. Remember, no criticising is allowed during the brainstorming phase.
3. Go over the list and select the 10 best ideas. Evaluation is allowed in this phase of the process.
4. Narrow the list to the five best ideas, and then select the best idea.
5. Be prepared to discuss your top five ideas with the class as a whole.

END-OF-CHAPTER CASE: ON THE RIM

Decision making at ChocCo

The setting is by a tranquil river bend, with a golf course nearby and splendid mountain views as a backdrop. ChocCo enjoys a tranquil life away from the hurly-burly of large cities, even though the factory is part of a multinational group spanning the world. It employs some 200 factory workers (70 per cent are female) and supporting staff, and has been in its present location since the 1920s. The factory is geared to a continuous process operation in which production spans 24 hours daily, every day of the week. The plant is unionised.

The tranquillity of the surroundings has transferred to the management team, which was caught unprepared for a grass-roots movement among its employees wanting a change in their shift patterns. Traditionally they had worked a daily pattern of three 8-hour shifts but, in some parts of the plant, pressure was applied to management for a move to two 12-hour shifts. The proposal was for three weekly rotating shifts of 12-hours, framed around a six-day fortnight. As far as management could determine, workers were attracted by the idea of having more days off under this regime than the traditional shift pattern. Such a pattern of shifts suited women in particular with respect to their non-work-life activities. Management therefore did not initiate the change in shifts and had no agenda in mind except that of attempting to please its employees.

Although management did not initiate the proposal, it wished to be responsive to workers' desires and so agreed. The main difficulty was that not all sections in the factory were suited to 12-hour shifts. For example, seasonal production processes are not stable and therefore not conducive to 12-hour shifts. Initially, only those in the milk-processing area and the boiler house were granted a change to 12-hour shifts, but the idea soon spread to other areas of the plant, and management was besieged with demands to implement them on a universal basis. Management responded by granting 12-hour shifts to all workers. At no stage in its deliberations did ChocCo consult with outside parties, such as the unions.

After 12 months ChocCo management was unhappy with several aspects of the shiftwork changes. However, since their employees had been working the new shifts for such a lengthy time, in some cases for more than 12 months, the company felt unable to retreat from the new shifts. Management was aware by now that to rescind the arrangement would result in an adverse reaction by employees and for this reason was not prepared to revoke the 12-hour shifts. Moreover, since there was no change in productivity levels or staff turnover, ChocCo felt there were insufficient grounds to claim that the company was 'disadvantaged' to the extent that it was prepared to make an industrial issue of 12-hour shifts and run the risk of a major union dispute.

Management admits that the factory processes are noisy, repetitive and boring for employees. For this reason it is felt that the welfare and wishes of workers are important and should not be ignored or easily dismissed. ChocCo expressed the view that it was 'between a rock and a hard place' with respect to the present situation. On one hand it was deeply concerned about health and safety issues, but on the other hand realised that to withdraw 12-hour shifts at this point would be unacceptable to employees. Chief among the concerns was that the 12-hour regime extended by 50 per cent the 'normal' shift period, contributing significantly to fatigue, stress and accidents. In essence, workers were simply spending too much time on the factory floor, increasing their exposure to adverse work conditions. Accidents had increased, as had the incidence of stress claims and general absenteeism. The stress claims in particular were a matter of considerable concern and appeared to be solely due to the long-term effects of employees working for extended shifts in a noisy and stressful environment.

A further issue related to the rehabilitation of previously injured workers. Whereas returning to work, even on light duties, can be both desirable

POWERWEB

International articles related to this topic are available at the Online Learning Centre at **www.mhhe.com/au/bartol4e**

and possible in an 8-hour shift situation, this is difficult or even impossible where 12-hour shifts are involved, because of the dramatic increase in the length of shift. The fatigue factor over 12 hours compared with 8 hours was found to be excessive and workers were unable to continue at their stations for such a period of time. In another case, this time involving stress, the employee was only able to work for short bursts, a situation that is incompatible with 12-hour shifts.

The union was not involved with management discussions prior to the trials, but was aware of the mooted changes, and advised management to exercise caution before agreeing to 12-hour shifts. In fact neither the union nor management were supportive of the change but both felt that the ground-swell of opinion among workers was too strong to resist. According to union sources, management at ChocCo has a record of poor planning and decision making and it is regarded as a place 'where things just happen'.

The present situation is that ChocCo has a shift regime it does not want and neither does the union. However, the workers are strongly in favour and the company feels at a loss as to how to extricate itself from the present shift patterns, even though it notionally has union support. For its part, the union can see the folly in opting for 12-hour shifts, but is duty bound to support the wishes of its members. It is therefore most unlikely that the union would openly support any initiative by management to move back to 8-hour shifts. ChocCo is worried about the escalation in accidents and workers' compensation claims and the apparent adverse affect upon absenteeism, and is in a quandary as to what it should do next.

Source: Written by Lindsay Nelson and Peter Holland.

Activities for discussion, analysis and further research

1. Describe the decision-making process at ChocCo. Who were the parties involved? Who should have been involved? Why? How might you have ensured that they all were?
2. How could the decision-making process be made more effective?
3. What lessons can be learned from the experience at ChocCo? What would you do differently if you were to be a party to the process?

FURTHER READING

Chi, S-C. and Lo, H-H. 2003, Taiwanese employees' justice perceptions of co-workers' punitive events, *Journal of Social Psychology*, February, 143, 1, pp. 27–43.

Chi-Ya, C.B. 2003, The development of virtual collocation strategies in information technology for small businesses: A Taiwanese case study, *International Journal of Management*, December, 20, 4, pp.523–35.

Hofstede, G., Van Deusen, C.A., Mueller, C.B. and Charles, T.A. 2002, What goals do business leaders pursue? A study in fifteen countries, *Journal of International Business Studies*, 4th Quarter, 33, 4, pp. 785–804.

Hutchings, K. and Murray, G. 2003, Family, face, and favours: Do Australians adjust to accepted business conventions in China? *Singapore Management Review*, 2nd Half, 25, 2, pp. 25–50.

Souchon, A.L., Diamantopoulos, A., Holzmuller, H.H, Axinn, C.N., Sinkula, J.M., Simmet, H., Durden, G.R. 2003, Export information use: A five-country investigation of key determinants, *Journal of International Marketing*, 11, 3, pp.106–28.

SUPPLEMENT TO CHAPTER 5

PLANNING AND DECISION AIDS

Management science (also called operations research) is a management perspective using sophisticated mathematical models and statistical methods to increase decision-effectiveness. (Management science is explained in Chapter 2.) Management science has a variety of quantitative techniques to help managers plan for and make decisions about complex situations. There are a number of aids available to help managers be competitive through innovations in planning and decision making areas (Halloran & Burn 1986; Labich 1987; *World Airlines News* 1995).

Generally, managers using management science tools do not need in-depth mathematics and computer knowledge. Rather, they need to understand the major tools so they can apply these tools. Sometimes, managers need expert assistance. With packaged software increasingly available, many techniques are accessible. Thus, planning and decision-making aids are increasingly important.

In this supplement, we describe several major planning and decision-making aids. We consider some forecasting methods, including one valuable for promoting innovation. We also examine project planning and control tools and explore useful quantitative planning techniques. Finally, we investigate aids for quantitative decision-making.

FORECASTING

Forecasting is predicting changing organisation conditions and significant future events. Forecasting is important to planning and decision making as each relies on assessing future conditions. Forecasting is used in many areas, such as production planning, budgeting, strategic planning, sales analysis, inventory control, marketing planning, logistics planning, purchasing, material-requirements planning and product planning (Mentzer & Cox 1984). There are three categories of forecasting methods: quantitative; technological or qualitative; and judgmental (Wheelwright & Makridakis 1989).

Quantitative forecasting

Quantitative forecasting uses numerical data and mathematical models to predict future conditions. Two main quantitative forecasting method types are time-series and explanatory methods.

Time-series methods

Time-series methods use historical data to forecast the future. Time-series models assume patterns or pattern combinations recur. These models base future projections on patterns identified in extensive historical data, such as weekly sales figures.

Some patterns identified by time-series methods are shown in Figure 5s.1. A trend is a long-range general up or down movement. For example, while coffee-house chains like Starbucks Coffee Co. are growing rapidly, the market could saturate as coffee consumption drops, particularly among those aged in their 20s, who average less than one cup per day (Mathews 1994). A seasonal pattern shows changes occurring at particular times in a year, such as seasons. A cyclical pattern involves changes in a time-span of over a year. For example,

forecasting

Process of making predictions about changing conditions and future events that may significantly affect the business of an organisation

quantitative forecasting

Type of forecasting that relies on numerical data and mathematical models to predict future conditions

time-series methods

Methods using historical data to develop future forecasts

FIGURE 5S.1 Examples of patterns identified by time-series methods (adapted from Gallagher & Watson 1980, p. 116)

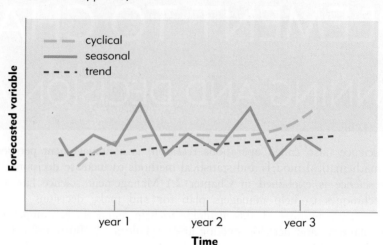

sunspot intensity varies over an 11-year cycle and affects agriculture (Gallagher & Watson 1980).

As time-series methods are based on historical data, they are less useful for predicting the impact of present or future actions managers might take to produce change. They are well suited to predicting broad environmental factors, such as general economic prospects, employment levels, general sales levels or cost trends, influenced by past events. There are time-series analysis methods, many very sophisticated and needing computers. Time-series methods try to predict the future by identifying patterns, and are not concerned with causes of the patterns.

Explanatory, or causal, models

explanatory, or causal, models

Models attempting to identify major variables related to or causing particular past conditions and then using current measures of those variables (predictors) to predict future conditions

Explanatory, or **causal**, **models** try to identify major variables related to or causing particular past conditions, then use current measures (predictors) to predict future conditions. Such models lead to better understanding of forecast situations than time-series models. Explanatory models allow the assessment of the possible impact of changes in predictors. For example, a manager may estimate how future sales will change if sales personnel or shelf space are increased. Generally, explanatory models are more useful than time-series models to assess the impact of managerial actions on variables.

Three major explanatory model types are regression models, econometric models and leading indicators. **Regression models** are equations expressing fluctuations in the variable being forecast, in terms of fluctuations in one or more other variables. An example of simple regression, in which one variable (a predictor) helps predict a future level of another (forecast) variable, is shown in Figure 5s.2. Here, a firm selling burglar alarm systems for homes attempts to predict demand (forecast variable) by the number of information leaflets (predictor variable) the public requests. Leaflets are offered in an advertisement. Data points plotted in Figure 5s.2 show leaflets requested and sales within a month of the request. A simple regression states the relationship between predictor and forecast variables mathematically. The form is $y = a + bx$, where y is the forecast variable, x the predictor variable, a is a constant representing the point where the regression line crosses the vertical axis, and b shows how much y's value changes when the value of x changes by 1 unit. A statistical technique is used to develop the straight line best fitting data points and giving values for a and b. Future projections substitute different values for x in the equation and determine the impact on y. For example, if our equation showed $y = 1.5 + 0.07x$, then substituting 350 leaflets for x would predict alarm system sales of 26.

regression models

Equations expressing fluctuations in the variable being forecast in terms of fluctuations in one or more other variables (predictors)

FIGURE 5S.2 Data points and regression line for number of leaflets requested and number of burglar alarm systems sold (adapted from Gallagher & Watson 1980, p. 134)

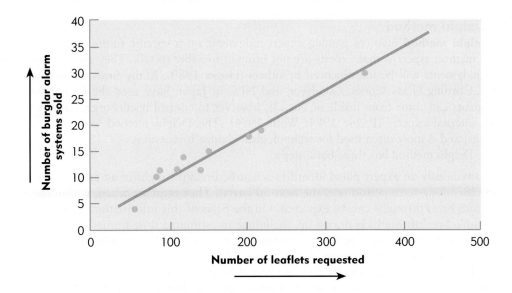

More complex regression models with multiple predictor variables are also used for forecasting.

The second major explanatory model category is **econometric models**. This refers to multiple regression equations with several predictor variables to identify and measure economic relationships or interrelationships.

These models try to predict the economy's future directions and the impact that changes such as tax legislation may have on different economy segments. Econometric model development is complex and expensive. As a result, models are outside the scope of most managerial jobs, and all but the largest firms. However, subscriptions to econometric forecasting services are available. This gives the benefits of econometric forecasting at less cost than developing a model.

The third major explanatory model category is **leading indicators**, variables correlated with the phenomenon of interest but generally occurring prior to the phenomenon. Generally using leading indicators is simple, with complex analytic methods. For example, the semiconductor industry uses book-to-bill ratio as a key leading indicator. This is a comparison of orders to shipments. A ratio therefore of .78 means, of every $100 of products shipped, only $78 were ordered. Compared with a previous month's ratio of .79, this shows a sales decline. However, a trend may take months to establish (Fisher 1996). The difficulty is to identify a leading indicator giving accurate predictions.

Promoting innovation: technological, or qualitative, forecasting

Technological, or **qualitative**, **forecasting** aims to predict long-term technology trends. Technology is emphasised, as companies' innovativeness and competitiveness relates to opportunities from technological change (Ihrcke 2000). Technological, or qualitative, forecasting differs from quantitative approaches as it focuses on longer-term issues less suited to numerical analysis. Instead of relying on quantitative methods, technological forecasting uses qualitative issues such as expert knowledge, creativity and judgment. This forecasting type helps participants think innovatively due to its future focus. Problems of accurate prediction

econometric models

Systems of simultaneous multiple regression equations using several predictor variables used to identify and measure relationships or interrelationships existing in the economy

leading indicators

Variables tending to be correlated with the phenomenon of major interest but also to occur in advance of that phenomenon

technological, or qualitative, forecasting

Type of forecasting aimed primarily at predicting long-term trends in technology and other important, environmental aspects

are clear, and predictors often overlook major shifts, such as global competition's size and rate of increase. While technological, or qualitative, forecasting approaches have been developed, two prominent ones are the Delphi method and scenario analysis.

The Delphi method

Delphi method

Structured approach to gaining judgments of a number of experts on a specific issue relating to the future

The **Delphi method** involves gaining expert judgments on a specific future issue. A unique Delphi method aspect is that experts are not brought together to talk. They are kept apart so initial judgments will be uninfluenced by others (Huger 1980). Many firms, including IBM, AT&T, Corning Glass Works, Goodyear, and NEC in Japan have used the Delphi method. Participants can come from inside or outside, however to control results organisations prefer to use internal experts (Preble 1984; Wolff 1996). The Delphi method looks for creative solutions; and is most often used for technological change forecasting.

The Delphi method has three basic steps:

1. Anonymously an expert panel identifies scientific breakthroughs in an area over a specified long-term period (e.g. the next 50 years). They estimate when, within the period, breakthroughs can be expected. On the basis of this information, a list of possible breakthroughs is drawn up, including an estimated time-frame for each.
2. The list is returned to the panel, to estimate (often on a 50–50 basis) whether each will come before the average estimated time frame. They may specify they do not believe the breakthrough will occur during the time period (e.g. 50 years).
3. Experts are provided with a new list of information gathered in step 2. If there is general agreement, those who disagree must explain. If participants differ widely in their views, they may be asked to justify them. They can alter their estimates then. If substantial divergence still exists, step 3 is repeated to reassess previous explanations.

The Delphi method follows these basic steps; however, minor alterations can be made by companies to suit their circumstances.

Scenario analysis

scenario analysis

Approach that addresses a variety of possible futures by evaluating major environmental variables, assessing likely strategies of other significant actors, devising possible counter-strategies, developing ranked hypotheses about the variables, and formulating alternative scenarios

Developed in France and used widely in Europe, **scenario analysis** (called scenario planning or La Prospective) argues that futures depend on issues such as actor interactions, whether current trends continue, regulatory and other constraints, and actors' relative power (Schoemaker 1995; Clemons 1995). Organisations must thus consider alternative futures, try to make decisions and take actions without limiting further choices. Major problems may flow from rigid, irreversible actions if forecasts are wrong. Scenario analysis addresses many futures by assessing environmental variables and strategies that significant actors may develop (e.g. other organisations), devising counter-strategies, developing ranked hypotheses about variables, and devising alternative scenarios. Scenarios outline future events, including paths leading to these conditions. Use of scenario analysis is increasing (Schoemaker 1995).

Judgmental forecasting

judgmental forecasting

Type of forecasting relying mainly on individual judgments or committee agreements regarding future conditions

Judgmental forecasting relies on individual judgments or committee agreements about future conditions. While judgmental forecasting is the method most widely used, this approach relies on informal opinion gathering and is the least systematic forecasting method. Judgmental forecasting, as a result, is susceptible to common decision-making biases discussed in Chapter 5 (Wheelwright & Makridakis 1989). Two major approaches are the jury of executive opinion and sales-force composites.

The jury of executive opinion

jury of executive opinion

Means of forecasting in which organisation executives hold a meeting and estimate, as a group, a forecast for a particular item

The **jury of executive opinion** is a forecasting method where executives meet and estimate, as a group, a forecast. However, since estimators are in contact, group power and personality factors may weight outcomes. The process can be improved by giving executives background material beforehand.

Sales-force composites

The **sales-force composite** is a means of forecasting used to predict future sales and involves getting opinions from various salespeople, sales managers, and/or distributors about sales outlook. While salespeople and distributors are close to the customer, they often are unaware of broad economic factors affecting future sales. On the other hand, when sales management make forecasts, the process may face the same difficulties met by a jury of executive opinion. The process can be improved by giving salespeople and distributors economic trend information before they start.

sales-force composite

Means of forecasting used mainly to predict sales and typically by obtaining views of various salespeople, sales managers, and/or distributors regarding the sales outlook

Choosing a forecasting method

Criteria for selecting a forecasting method and each method's general characteristics are outlined in Table 5s.1. As this suggests, managers must consider factors such as time horizon desired, type of accuracy needed, ease of understanding, and development costs. Each has advantages and disadvantages, depending on the forecasting situation's needs.

TABLE 5S.1 CRITERIA FOR CHOOSING A FORECASTING METHOD

Criteria	Quantitative	Technological	Judgmental
Time horizon*	short to medium	medium to long	short to long
Time required	short if method developed; long otherwise	medium to long	short
Development costs	often high	medium	low
Accuracy in identifying patterns	high	medium	medium to high
Accuracy in predicting turning points	low for time series; medium for other methods	medium	low
Ease of understanding	low to medium	high	high

*Short term = one to three months; medium term = three months to two years; long term = two years or more

Source: Adapted from Makridakis & Wheelwright (1981, p. 132).

PROJECT PLANNING AND CONTROL MODELS

Managers may manage projects—one-time sets of activities with a clear beginning and ending. For example, a manager may have to design and implement a new computer system, build a new manufacturing plant, or develop a new product. Projects are unique, though the manager may have been responsible for similar projects before. For large and complex projects, managers may need a planning and control model to effectively manage the project. Two planning and control models are the Gantt chart and PERT.

Gantt charts

One of the earliest and most flexible project planning tools is the **Gantt chart**, a specialised bar chart Henry L. Gantt developed (see Chapter 2), which shows every major project activity's current progress relative to needed completion dates. A simple Gantt chart is shown in Figure 5s.3.

A project, in this case finishing a management course, is divided into major activities listed on the chart's left side. The entire project's time frame is indicated at top or bottom. A bar

Gantt chart

Specialised bar chart developed by Henry L. Gantt showing current progress on each major project activity relative to necessary completion dates shows each activity's duration and scheduling, and each is shaded to show how complete the activity is. Thus each activity's status relative to project deadlines can be determined easily. You can construct a Gantt chart to help plan and control activities needed to complete a course or a whole semester. Checking the chart in Figure 5s.3 for 'Today' shows the individual has chosen a topic for a paper, has researched it, and is ahead of schedule writing the paper. However, they are a bit behind in studying for the mid-semester examination and need to catch up.

Gantt charts are popular, and software packages are widely available to help plan and control projects (Hack 1989). While Gantt charts are useful in many cases, they do have a weakness. They do not show the interrelationships of various activities. For small projects, these are clear. For complex projects, more sophisticated methods are needed.

PERT

program evaluation and review technique (PERT)

Network planning method for managing large projects

During the 1950s, in developing Polaris, the first submarine to launch long-range ballistic missiles while remaining submerged, the US Navy had to coordinate 11 000 contractors. The Defense Department, with Lockheed, invented the **program evaluation and review technique (PERT)**, a method of network planning for large projects. Meanwhile, Du Pont, with Remington-Rand, developed another network approach called Critical Path Method (CPM) (Dilworth 1993). Network planning involves breaking projects into activities and determining the time needed for each, but goes beyond Gantt charts by specifically considering the interrelationships of activities.

Setting up PERT to manage a major project involves six main steps:

1. All project activities must be clearly specified.
2. Sequencing requirements among activities must be identified (i.e. which activities must precede others).
3. A diagram reflecting sequence relationships must be developed.
4. Time estimates for each activity must be determined.
5. The network must be evaluated by calculating the critical path. Various activities can be scheduled.

FIGURE 5S.3 Partial Gantt chart for completing a management course

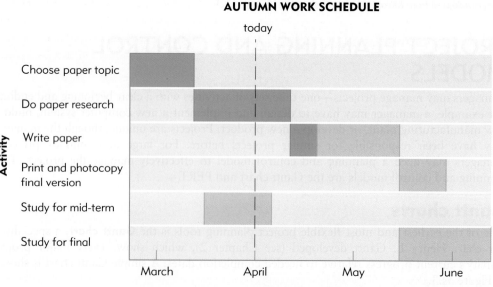

6. As the project progresses, actual activity times must be recorded so any schedule revisions and adjustments needed can be made (Adam Jr & Ebert 1992).

To understand how PERT works, we will use a simple example. Suppose a firm providing nursing-home care, Good Care Inc., wants to expand and upgrade its services. Due to regulations the organisation must build a new facility. First, Good Care Inc.'s administrator must list the major project activities and determine which must precede others (see Table 5s.2).

The next step is constructing a **network diagram** depicting interrelationships among activities graphically. A network diagram for the Good Care project is shown in Figure 5s.4.

On the diagram an **activity**, or work component, is shown by an arrow. Activities take time. A **node**, or **event**, is an indication of network activities beginning and/or ending. It shows a single time point. Nodes are numbered for easy identification, usually in tens (e.g. 10, 20, 30) so additions do not require renumbering. The diagram shows various activities' interrelationships. In Figure 5s.4, for example, building the facility (A) precedes safety inspection (B), and recruiting staff (E) precedes training staff (F). However, as the diagram shows, building and safety inspection processes (A, B) can be accomplished while recruiting and training staff (E, F).

Developing the diagram may include giving initial time estimates for each activity's duration. Unless times are well established, optimistic (t_o), pessimistic (t_p) and most likely (t_m) times needed to complete each activity are estimated. Each activity's expected, or average, time is then calculated using the following formula, which gives heavy weight to the most likely time for activity completion:

$$t = (t_o + 4t_m + t_p)/6$$

Each activity's expected time (in weeks) is shown next to its respective arrow on the network diagram.

The next step is identifying the **critical path**, the network path taking longest to complete. This network has three different paths: 10-20-40-50-60, 10-20-50-60, and 10-30-50-60. By adding up expected times for each path, we can determine the path 10-20-50-60 will take longest (40.8 weeks) and is, therefore, the critical path. This means a delay in any activity on this path delays project completion. The manager must therefore pay particular attention to this path. As well, allocating further resources to this path may shorten time taken for project completion. For example, if time needed to install equipment could be shortened by two weeks, completion time could be reduced to 38.8. When activity times are shortened significantly, another path may become critical. This could happen if activity C (20-50) was cut to eight

network diagram

Graphic depiction of interrelationships among activities

activity

Work component to be accomplished

node, or event

Indication of beginning and/or ending of activities in the network

critical path

Path in the network taking the longest to complete

TABLE 5S.2 MAJOR ACTIVITIES, PREDECESSOR ACTIVITIES, AND TIME ESTIMATES FOR GOOD CARE INC.

Activity	Predecessor activity	Time estimates (weeks) t_o	t_m	t_p	Expected time, T_e
A Build facility	None	20	24	30	24.3
B Conduct safety inspection	A	2	3	4	3.0
C Install equipment	A	8	10	20	11.0
D Decorate interior	B	3	5	9	5.3
E Recruit staff	None	2	2	3	2.1
F Train staff	E	4	5	6	5.0
G Perform pilot	C, D, F	4	5	9	5.5

Source: Adapted from Adam Jr & Ebert (1992, p. 342).

FIGURE 5S.4 Network diagram, critical path and expected time for each activity in the Good Care Inc. project (adapted from Adam Jr & Ebert 1992, p. 343)

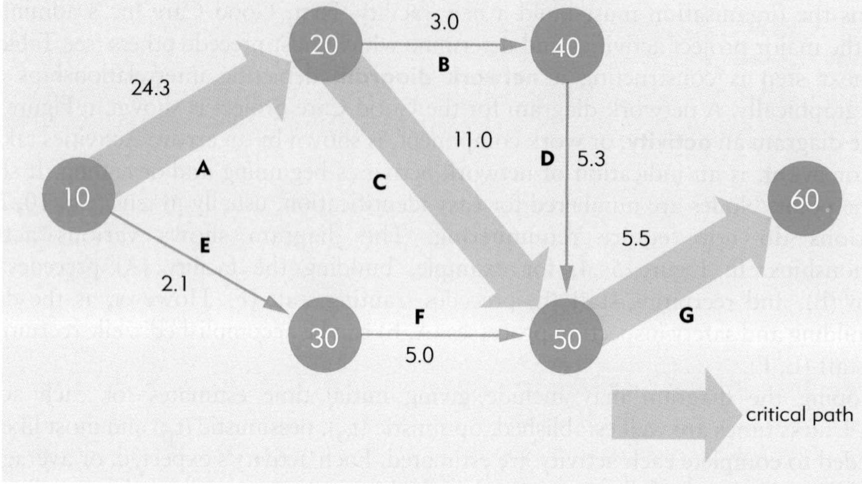

weeks. Then the path 10-20-40-50-60 becomes the critical path. On non-critical paths, there is latitude about when activities can be started without risking the entire project's completion date. This is referred to as **slack**.

Once the critical path is developed, actual time taken for various activities is recorded periodically and then the implications reviewed. For example, when critical path activities take longer than estimated, action must be taken to correct the situation. Otherwise, the entire project may be delayed. Similarly, if activity on a non-critical path takes much longer than expected, the critical path may change. Thus PERT helps managers plan and also control projects. (Control issues are discussed further in Chapters 15 to 18.) Individual managers' ability to use PERT to plan and control both small and large projects has increased greatly due to relatively easy-to-use software packages.

slack

Latitude about when various activities on the non-critical paths can be started without endangering the entire project's completion date

OTHER PLANNING TECHNIQUES

Other quantitative planning techniques can assist managers. Some prominent ones include use of linear programming; queuing, or waiting-line, models; routing, or distribution, models; and simulation models. We discuss each of these briefly. Typically, using these techniques effectively requires a management science expert's help.

Linear programming

linear programming (LP)

Quantitative tool for planning how to allocate limited or scarce resources so a single criterion or goal (often profits) is optimised

Linear programming (LP) is a quantitative tool for planning allocation of limited or scarce resources to optimise a single criterion or goal (often profits). It is a widely used quantitative planning tool. Linear programming can be used when a single objective (maximising profits) must be achieved, constraints exist, and variables are related linearly to the objective (Davis & McKeown 1984). A variable is linearly related to an objective when increasing (or decreasing) the variable leads to a proportional objective increase (or decrease) in the objective. For example, a linear relationship applies if one chair (variable) produced can be sold for $30 profit (objective), four chairs for $120 profit, and six chairs for $180 profit. The technique has been applied to situations including minimising chicken-feed cost while keeping proper nutritional balance, finding the most profitable manufacturing product mix, and maximising oil refinery capacity (Pinney & McWilliams 1982).

Queuing, or waiting-line, models

Managers are often responsible to provide services where persons or units needing service must wait in lines, or queues. **Queuing**, or **waiting-line**, **models** are mathematical models describing queuing situation characteristics. Different models exist for different queuing situations (such as a single window at a small post office versus multiple service points in getting a driver's licence). Unlike linear programming, queuing, or waiting-line, models do not provide optimal solutions. Rather, they let managers vary situation parameters and assess probable effects.

Routing, or distribution, models

Organisations may distribute a product or service to multiple customers. **Routing**, or **distribution**, **models** are tools to assist managers planning effective, economical approaches to distribution problems. The development and use of these models is network optimisation analysis.

Simulation models

Simulation is a mathematical imitation of reality. The technique is used when the situation of interest is too complex for narrower methods such as linear programming or queuing theory. Rather than a standardised set of formulas applicable to a broad set of problems, simulations are usually custom-made for a situation (Pinney & McWilliams 1982). As a result, they can be expensive to develop. Simulations let managers change parameters to evaluate different assumptions and/or approaches. Simulations have been used in production, inventory control, transportation systems, market strategy analysis, industrial and urban growth patterns, environmental control and many other areas (Huber 1980).

QUANTITATIVE AIDS FOR DECISION MAKING

Although aids discussed so far are considered planning tools, they can help managers make decisions during the planning process. A number of aids aim specifically to help managers with particular decisions. Two well-known aids for decision making are payoff tables and decision trees.

Payoff tables

One helpful way to frame managerial decision situations is a payoff table. The **payoff table**, a two-dimensional matrix, lets decision makers compare different future conditions likely to affect outcomes of two or more decision choices. The payoff table is referred to as a **decision matrix**. Typically decision alternatives are row headings in the matrix, and possible future conditions are column headings. The values where row and column intersect represent the **payoff**, the amount of decision-maker value from a particular decision alternative and future condition. An example will help clarify these concepts (Harrison 1981).

Assume you are a decision maker at a college where enrolments may increase but where existing classroom capacity is fully used. Three alternatives are found to increase space: construct a new building, expand an old one, or rent or lease another. These alternatives are row headings in Table 5s.3. There are three possible conditions. Student enrolments may go up, down, or be unchanged. These are column headings in the table. Potential payoffs for each combination are shown at the intersections. If future events were clear then the simple solution would be to select the alternative with the highest payoff. Unfortunately, it is not possible to know which outcome will occur. However, on past experience, current enrolment trends, and personal judgment, the decision maker can assign probabilities to possible future outcomes. A probability is a decision maker's best estimate whether a future condition will occur. These

TABLE 5S.3 PAYOFF TABLE FOR CLASSROOM SPACE PROBLEM

Alternatives	Possible future conditions			Expected value
	Student enrolments up [.50]*	Student enrolments down [.25]	Student enrolments unchanged [.25]	
Construct new building	$500 000	($200 000)†	($100 000)	$175 000
Expand old building	$400 000	$100 000	$100 000	$250 000
Rent or lease another building	$400 000	($100 000)	$200 000	$225 000

*Numbers in brackets are probability estimates for possible future conditions.

†Numbers in parentheses represent losses.

Source: Adapted from Harrison (1987, p. 375)

estimates are usually put as a percentage. For example, as shown, the decision maker estimates a 50 per cent probability that enrolments will increase, while probabilities they will drop or remain unchanged are each estimated at 25 per cent. Which alternative should the decision maker select?

Experts recommend choosing the highest expected value alternative. A given alternative's **expected value** is the sum of payoffs times respective probabilities for that alternative. For example, expected value (EV) for redeveloping an old building is as follows:

expected value

Sum of payoffs times respective probabilities for a given alternative

$$EV = 0.50(400\,000) + 0.25(100\,000) + 0.25(100\,000) = \$250\,000$$

Likewise, expected value for constructing a new building is (notice when the payoff is a loss, a minus sign is used):

$$EV = 0.50(500\,000) - 0.25(200\,000) - 0.25(100\,000) = \$175\,000$$

Similar calculations show for renting or leasing another building an expected value of $225 000.

Therefore, the alternative with the highest expected value in this case is to expand an old building.

The value of payoff tables is that they help decision makers evaluate situations where outcomes of various alternatives depend on the likelihood of future conditions. As such, payoff tables help when a decision maker can determine major relevant alternatives, can quantify payoffs, and make reasonably accurate judgments about future probabilities (Huber 1980; Ferguson & Selling 1985). For example, payoff tables help decide which new products to introduce, which real-estate investments to select, crops to plant, and needed restaurant staff levels (Barron 1985). Managers at Hallmark, the greeting-card company, use payoff matrixes to set production levels of unique products, such as a special Muppet promotion including albums, plaques, gift wrap, stickers, patterns and other items (Ulvila 1987).

Decision trees

decision tree

Graphic model displaying structure of a sequence of alternative courses of action and usually showing payoffs associated with various paths and probabilities associated with potential future conditions

A **decision tree** is a graphic model showing a series of alternative actions. These are usually payoffs associated with various paths, and probabilities associated with each potential event.

A decision tree is shown in Figure 5s.5. Here, the manager faces a decision about building a large or a small manufacturing plant, given uncertain future product demand. If a large plant is built and demand is high, the company will make $12 million profit. However, if demand is low, it will make a $2 million profit (low profit because of overhead on the large plant). This is less profit than made with a small plant when demand is either high or low ($8 million and $5 million, respectively). To help with the decision, each alternative's expected value is computed. The large-plant alternative's expected value is $8 million [(0.60 × $12 million) + (0.40 × $2 million)]. The small-plant alternative's expected value is $6.8 million [(0.60 × $8 million) + (0.40 × $5 million)]. This suggests the large plant should be considered seriously.

The decision tree can be used as a graphic alternative to a payoff table. However, the decision tree's major advantage is that it considers complex alternatives. For example, a small plant may be built initially, then expanded as demand grows. In our example in Figure 5s.5, a small plant would raise the possibility of a second decision point later, when a manager could choose from possibilities ranging from a large plant expansion to no expansion. These can be considered and the values expected can be calculated using decision trees with many decision points. Decision trees help identify options, and consider the potential impacts of alternative branches (Adam Jr & Ebert 1992).

FIGURE 5S.5 Decision tree and expected values for building a large or a small manufacturing plant

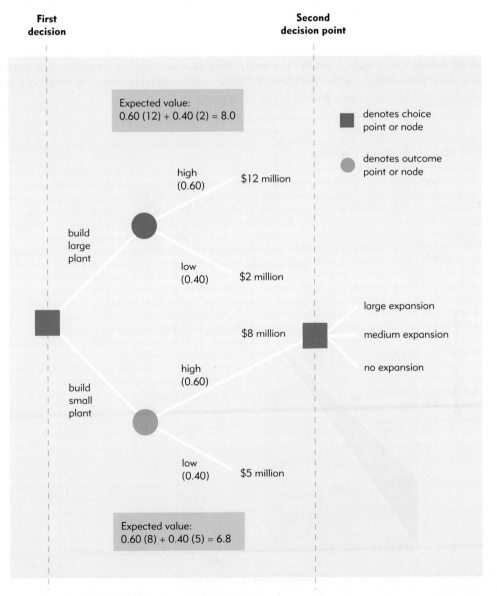

Break-even analysis

break-even analysis

Graphic model helping decision makers understand relationships between sales volume, costs and revenues in an organisation

Break-even analysis is a technique to help decision makers understand the relationships between organisation sales volume, costs and revenues (Brealey & Myers 1991). Break-even analysis is often graphical, as in Figure 5s.6 and it also can be mathematical (Meecham 1995). The technique allows determination of the break-even point—the sales volume at which total revenues equal total costs. The break-even point is where the organisation neither loses nor makes money; it just breaks even. This point is important because only with greater sales volume can an organisation make a profit.

The break-even analysis shown in Figure 5s.6 has several elements. Fixed costs are costs staying the same no matter what output volume is (e.g. costs of heating, lighting, administration, mortgage and insurance). Fixed costs in Figure 5s.6 are shown by the horizontal line at $600 000. Variable costs vary by output level (e.g. raw material, labour, packaging and transport costs). In this situation, variable costs are $40 per unit on a unit selling for $60. These data can be used to draw lines on the graph for total costs (fixed plus variable costs) and total revenues. The break-even point is 30 000 units. Fixed costs of $600 000 plus variable costs of $1 200 000 [30 000 × $40 (variable costs per unit)] are $1 800 000. Revenues are also $1 800 000 [30 000 × $60 (sale price per unit)]. Hence the firm breaks even at 30 000 units.

Break-even analysis can help determine how many product or service units the organisation must sell before it can make a profit. The analysis helps assess the impact of cost cutting when profits start. For example, if the firm lowered fixed and/or variable costs, the total cost line in Figure 5s.6 would drop, lowering the break-even point.

FIGURE 5S.6 Break-even analysis

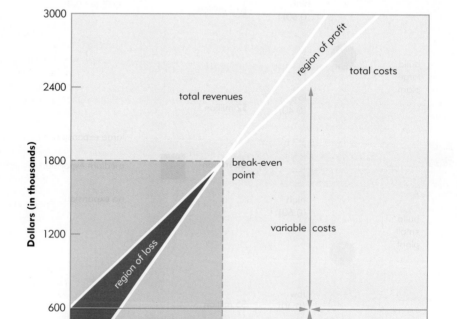

Airlines often use break-even analysis in assessing fare discount levels (Meecham 1995).

Break-even analysis makes some simplifying assumptions. For instance, it assumes the same price will be charged for all units (while some customers may get discounts) and fixed costs will remain the same across many outputs. Such assumptions show the technique is useful for rough analyses, rather than fine-tuning volumes, costs and revenues. More complex break-even analysis types are available if greater precision is needed (Powers 1987).

CHAPTER 6

ESTABLISHING ORGANISATIONAL GOALS AND PLANS, THEN DEVELOPING STRATEGY

CHAPTER OUTLINE

The overall planning process
Major components of planning
Organisational mission

The nature of organisational goals
Benefits of goals
Levels of goals

How goals facilitate performance
Goal content
Goal commitment
Work behaviour
Other process components
Potential problems with goals

Linking goals and plans
Levels of plans
Plans according to extent of recurring use
Time horizons of goals and plans
Promoting innovation: The role of the
    planning process
Potential obstacles to planning

Management by objectives
Steps in the MBO process
Strengths and weaknesses of MBO
Assessing MBO

The concept of strategic management
The strategic management process
Importance of strategic management
Levels of strategy

**The role of competitive analysis in
    strategy formulation**
Environmental assessment
Organisational assessment

Formulating functional-level strategy

Strategy implementation
Carrying out strategic plans
Maintaining strategic control

LEARNING OBJECTIVES

After studying this chapter, you should be able to:

- Describe the major components in the overall planning process.
- Explain the concept of organisational mission and purposes of a mission statement.
- Outline the major benefits of goals and explain how they differ according to organisational level.
- Explain how plans differ by organisational level and extent of recurring use.
- Explain the concept of strategic management and identify three main levels of strategy.
- Describe Porter's competitive strategies for the business level.
- Explain the role of strategies at the functional level.
- Outline the process of strategy implementation.

STRIVING FOR EXCELLENCE

Catherine Livingstone, chairman, CSIRO

Catherine Livingstone's office at the CSIRO North Ryde campus is Spartan, immaculate. She is surrounded by neat piles of work and shelves of Minutes from CSIRO meetings, and a large geology poster adorns the otherwise bare walls. Her desk overlooks a patch of bushland and the final stages of building renovations.

Despite her role as chairman of the CSIRO and positions on the boards of Telstra, Goodman Fielder and Rural Press, Livingstone has never courted publicity. Carefully composed, intensely private, the Nairobi-born chartered accountant physically cringes at the idea of talking about anything other than her work. Gossip, attention-seeking and self-promotion are not her style. 'She is definitely not into small talk', says a colleague.

Many other business identities would have been tempted to exploit the position of running a spectacularly successful public company—during Livingstone's six-year tenure as managing director of Cochlear, the company's share price rose from $2.50 to $28, increasing market capitalisation to $1.5 billion. For a time, Livingstone was also the only female chief executive of a top-100 company.

Livingstone is a highly sought-after business mind, voted number five on BRW's recent list of the 20 most powerful women in Australian business. Described by an executive recruiter as one of the 'magic three' women in Australian boardrooms, along with Margaret Jackson and Carolyn Hewson, Livingstone is regarded by her peers as a master strategist. One colleague says: 'She can fence swords with the highest of minds.'

Her working life has taken Livingstone from chartered accountant to chairman of the CSIRO. She points to her 1983 appointment as group coordinator of the computer implementation program at the medical technology company Nucleus as the turning point that enabled her to combine business skills with a strong interest in science and research and development. 'I was so lucky to have the experience at Nucleus', she says. 'The real benefit was understanding more how innovation actually works and the extent to which it is not a linear process.' She believes that, sometimes, innovation is chaotic, a chance alliance of ideas.

During her six years running Cochlear (1994–2000), Livingstone led a team that successfully took a groundbreaking bionic-ear implant to market. In the 1999/2000 financial year, in which she left Cochlear, the company had revenue of $144 million, up from $72 million in 1995/96, when the company was floated.

Livingstone resigned in March 2000, insisting that it was not due to the demands of her young family (she has three children). It was simply time for a different leader for the company, 'a strategic discontinuity'. A string of non-executive positions followed. Livingstone joined the boards of Rural Press in October 2000 and Telstra and Goodman Fielder the following month. In January 2001, she joined the CSIRO board and became its chairman in November of the same year. 'It is very humbling to be a part of CSIRO', she says. 'There is so much impressive work and so many impressive people.'

She now has to consider the interests of an organisation with 6500 staff (1850 have PhDs) and 60 sites.

She says the CSIRO takes up 25 to 50 per cent of her working time. For Livingstone, there is no such thing as a typical working day—and she enjoys the diversity. 'It is a different way of working. When you are a director dealing with a number of different companies, you have to very consciously switch on to that company and those issues, and immerse yourself. When you are in a company, the highs are high and the lows are low. There is a lot of volatility of experience, minute-by-minute, day-by-day, whereas, as a director, you are dealing with a different time horizon because the board is not management; it is focused on the strategic.'

Livingstone prepared for her new role at the CSIRO by 'reading, talking to people and being constantly alert' and by visiting CSIRO laboratories. 'I would not presume a knowledge of science that is in any way deep', she says. One of the larger projects she has been involved with is the epic national flagship program that is aligning CSIRO research projects with national issues, among them health care, communications and environment. Among the weighty goals of the program are plans to foster economic growth, new industries and employment opportunities and to improve the health of Australians and the environment.

Livingstone is a self-confessed 'champion for innovation', seeing it as a critical issue, not just for business but for all parts of society. Her great fear is that, at a critical time, business, the community and policy makers are becoming too impatient with research and development. 'Innovation occurs over long time frames and, within those time frames, there will be successes and failures', she says. 'We are working in an environment where, apparently, we have less and less tolerance for risk, when, in fact, what is needed is a higher tolerance for risk and to be prepared to manage a higher level of risk.'

Livingstone says that, as a leader, it is important to minimise her own bias. 'In making a decision, I like to be very well informed', she says. 'I believe in the need to make decisions and move forward.'

Rather than being in the engine room of a company, where the chief executive operates, Livingstone sees the non-executive role as providing support, being a sounding board and sometimes playing devil's advocate as the management team develops its business strategies.

Source: Ross, E. (2003).

Without planning, organisations are driven by the winds of environmental change, unable to use the currents, to choose their own direction. Thus, an organisation without planning is like a rudderless yacht. The management function of planning, setting goals and deciding how best to achieve them is crucial to organisational survival. The function includes considering how to achieve levels of change and innovation needed. Planning is the foundation of the other major management functions—organising, leading and controlling—by setting the course and steering.

In this chapter, we examine the overall planning process, including organisational mission development. We also consider the nature of organisational goals and examine a model which helps explain how goals aid performance. Next we probe the link between goals and plans, checking how plans differ by level, the extent of recurring use, and time horizon, and we examine the role of goals and plans in promoting innovation.

Strategic goals and plans are vital to the managerial planning function as they give overall company direction. So, we look at strategic-level planning issues, and how firms are managed strategically. We examine the concept of strategic management. Then we consider how competitive analysis allows development of effective strategies to gain a competitive edge. We next analyse policy formulation at all levels. Finally, we probe the process of strategy implementation.

THE OVERALL PLANNING PROCESS

It is important to an organisation's success to have a good idea of its overall mission, as well as more specific, written goals and carefully developed plans. In this section, we introduce these major planning process components.

Major components of planning

One could argue that organisations cannot function without some goals and plans. A **goal** is a future target or end result an organisation wishes to achieve. Managers and researchers often interchange the terms 'goal' and 'objective'. Others see 'goal' as broader, covering a longer time horizon, and use 'objective' for narrower targets and shorter time frames (Rue & Holland 1989; Bateman & Snell 2003). For simplicity we interchange the two. When the two concepts need differentiation, the context will clearly show whether the scope is broad or narrow or the time frame is long or short.

Where a goal is an end result a firm wants to achieve, a **plan** is the means for trying to reach the goal. Planning, then, is the management function of setting goals and deciding how best to achieve them. In the planning function, managers use decision-making skills extensively, as well as planning and decision aids (see Chapter 5 and the supplement to Chapter 5). The process is overviewed in Figure 6.1. Goal setting and plan development lead to goal attainment and, eventually, to organisational efficiency and effectiveness. As the diagram shows, the planning process is based on the organisation's mission.

Organisational mission

Planning builds on the organisation's **mission**, its purpose or fundamental reason for existence. A mission statement is a broad statement distinguishing the organisation from others of its type by its unique purpose and scope of operations (Pearce & Robinson 1988). For example, the mission statement of the Inland Revenue Department of New Zealand is 'Te Tari Taake' ('To be fair') and the Department of Labour's mission is 'Wired for work and wellbeing'. A **mission statement** has many purposes. For managers, it is a benchmark to evaluate success. For employees, a mission statement defines common purpose, nurtures organisational loyalty, and fosters a sense of community. For external parties such as investors, government agencies and the public, it gives insight into organisational values and future direction (Nash 1988). In some organisations, the mission is a formal written document. In others, the statement is implicit. Of course, in the latter case, members may have different views of the mission, without realising it (Want 1986; Morrisey 1988). It is not unchanging and will need to be revisited on a regular basis as the competitive environment changes (Roberts 2003).

Over 90 per cent of *Fortune* 500 firms have written mission statements (Grede 2001). Mission statements from 75 firms in the *Business Week* 1000 comprise some or all of these nine components (David 1989):

1. Customers. Who are the organisation's customers?
2. Products or services. What are the organisation's major products or services?
3. Location. Where does the organisation compete?
4. Technology. What is the firm's basic technology?
5. Concern for survival. What is the organisation's commitment to economic objectives?
6. Philosophy. What are the organisation's basic beliefs, values, aspirations and philosophical priorities?
7. Self-concept. What are the organisation's major strengths and competitive advantages?

goal

Future target or end result an organisation wishes to achieve

plan

Means devised for attempting to reach a goal

mission

The organisation's purpose or fundamental reason for existence

mission statement

Broad declaration of the basic, unique purpose and scope of operations distinguishing the organisation from others of its type

FIGURE 6.1 The overall planning process

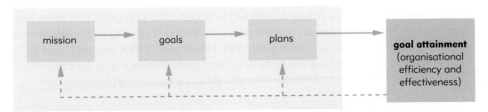

8. Concern for public image. What are the organisation's public responsibilities, and image desired?
9. Concern for employees. What is the organisation's attitude toward its employees?

Mission statement excerpts matching each of these components are shown in Table 6.1. Nash (1988, p. 156) studies mission statements, and reports that her favourite hangs, yellowing, on the wall of a Boston shoe-repair shop. It reads: 'We are dedicated to the saving of soles, heeling and administering to the dyeing'.

TABLE 6.1 MAJOR COMPONENTS OF SAMPLE EXCERPTS

Major component	Sample excerpt
Customers	The New Zealand Department of Labour's purpose is to link social and economic issues to enable people to develop and use their potential for the advantage of themselves and New Zealand. To deliver quality welfare service to New Zealanders in the most cost-effective way and in accordance with the policies of the government. (New Zealand Department of Labour) The purpose of Motorola is to honourably serve the needs of the community by providing products and services of superior quality at a fair price to our customers. (Motorola)
Products or services	We will become a world leader in defining and delivering valued telecommunications services by setting new levels of excellence in service, quality and productivity, and through the application of leading-edge technology. (Optus) We deliver service of an international standard in a professional and personalised way. (ANA Hotel, Singapore)
Location	Sara Lee Corporation's mission is to be a leading consumer marketing company in the United States and internationally. (Sara Lee Corporation)
Technology	Du Pont is a diversified chemical, energy and speciality products company with a strong tradition of discovery. Our global businesses are constantly evolving and continually searching for new and better ways to use our human, technological and financial resources to improve the quality of life of people around the world. (Du Pont)
Concern for survival	To serve the worldwide need for knowledge at a fair profit by gathering, evaluating, producing and distributing valuable information in a way that benefits our customers, employees, authors, investors and our society. (McGraw-Hill)
Philosophy	It's all part of the Mary Kay philosophy—a philosophy based on the golden rule. A spirit of sharing and caring where people give cheerfully of their time, knowledge and experience. (Mary Kay Cosmetics)
Self-concept	Crown Zellerbach is committed to leapfrogging competition within 1000 days by unleashing the constructive and creative abilities and energies of each of its employees. (Crown Zellerbach)
Concern for public image	The company feels an obligation to be a good corporate citizen wherever it operates. (Eli Lilly & Company)
Concern for employees	The Warehouse New Zealand is a values-based organisation. The company has three key values: it puts people first; it focuses on ensuring that everyone shopping at the Warehouse gets a bargain and provides a money-back guarantee for all goods that are sold; and it places a high emphasis on protecting the natural environment (for example, by carefully recycling packaging and aiming to eliminate waste). (http://www.thewarehouse.co.nz/ accessed 27 January 2004)

Source: Adapted from David (1989, pp. 92–3).

CASE IN POINT

Searching for the Holy Grail of modern medicine

Can a company survive on goals and plans without profits? Not in the long-term, but Ventracor has been thriving on goals and plans with no profits for a number of years. Ventracor is the company developing, manufacturing and marketing the revolutionary artificial heart 'VentrAssist'. VentrAssist is an Australian invention that holds promise for dominating the multibillion-dollar market for successful and commercially viable artificial hearts. Although engaged in successful clinical trials throughout 2004 and earlier, Ventracor expects to sell its first artificial heart only in 2005. The company then hopes to ride the 'J' curve of profitability that characterises medical innovations, where slow adoption of the innovation is soon followed by widespread acceptance and a subsequent steep increase in sales.

The company is built on the long-term vision to be the world's pre-eminent supplier of cardiac assist systems. The vision is backed by 12 month rolling milestones such as clinical trials in Australia and Europe and a submission for approval by the US Food and Drug Administration (FDA). These milestones point the way on the company's roadmap, which informs staff of what they need to do to progress the company towards its ultimate destination. The milestones are broken down to give the approximately 90 staff a range of individual and team short-term tasks. These tasks give employees 'ten degrees of focus', so that they can concentrate their daily work on achievable results, rather than be distracted by the many paths within the overall complex roadmap.

The plans and goals for Ventracor are developed through wide consultation with doctors, regulators and external stakeholders. This requires careful balancing of the competing pressures of ethical medical trials of the product with patients, the constraints of an effective commercial pathway for the product, approval from government regulators such as the FDA in the US and CE Mark in Europe and maintaining the confidence of shareholders. This balancing act, however, is performed within the context of a race with at least two other similar products to be the first to produce a commercially viable artificial heart. With careful plans and clear goals, Ventracor hopes to win the prize that has been dubbed the 'Holy Grail' of modern medical technology.

Source: Contributed by Peter Woods.

Website:

http://www.ventracor.com/

Activities for discussion, analysis and further research

1. What role does the company's vision play in the day-to-day operation of Ventracor?
2. What are the competing pressures on the goal commitment of Ventracor staff and how could the company build goal commitment?
3. How does Ventracor use a 'roadmap' to set goals?

THE NATURE OF ORGANISATIONAL GOALS

As we have seen, organisational goals are a major element in the overall planning process. In this section, we assess major benefits of goals and examine how they differ by organisational level.

Benefits of goals

Using goals has many benefits (Locke & Latham 1984; Richards 1986; Washington 2003). For one, performance increases. When challenging goals are set, performance increases range from 10 to 25 per cent, sometimes more. Increases occur across employee groups, such as clerical, maintenance, production, sales, managers, engineers and scientists (Pritchard, Roth, Jones, Galgay & Watson 1988).

Another benefit of goals is they help clarify expectations. With goals, members understand major outcomes required (Hammer & Champy 1993). Members lack direction without goals. Even when all work hard, they may accomplish little collectively—as a group rowing the same boat in different directions and making little progress.

Goals also aid control by giving benchmarks to assess progress so corrective action can be taken if needed. Thus goals help staff gauge their progress and assist managers control organisational activities (Siler 1989). Programmed Maintenance Services (PMS) uses an interesting strategy demonstrating the environmental-control value of goal setting. PMS provides a service in both Australia and England, of long-term painting contracts, where a yearly flat charge is made instead of a 'per job' fee (Walker 2003).

Another benefit of goals is enhanced motivation. Meeting goals, feeling a sense of achievement, and gaining recognition and other rewards for reaching targets all build motivation.

Goal setting's benefits are shown by an interesting study by Latham and Locke (1979). It involved unionised truck drivers of a forest-products firm in the western United States. They were concerned that if their trucks were overloaded with logs, the highway department might fine them and they could be fired. Trucks were rarely filled over 63 per cent of capacity. The company had not set goals regarding expected load levels.

A plan was coordinated with the union, with the goal of achieving 94 per cent of legal truck-load capacity. Under the agreement, no-one would be reprimanded if the goal was not met. No incentives such as money or fringe benefits were offered. Verbal praise was given when load levels increased. Over the first month, trucks were at 80 per cent of capacity, more than ever before. In the second month, performance dropped to 70 per cent of capacity. Interviewing drivers showed they were testing management to see what actions would be taken against those who did not reach the goal. When drivers saw no action was taken, loads grew. Loads were over 90 per cent in the third month and stayed that way for more than seven years. During the nine-month study over $250 000 was saved (Latham & Locke 1979). Expectations were clarified by goals, motivation increased, there was a standard to assess progress against, and performance improved. This and many other studies support goal-setting's organisational value (Lee, Locke & Latham 1980).

Levels of goals

Organisations typically have three levels of goals: strategic, tactical and operational, as shown in Figure 6.2. (Also shown are three parallel levels of plans, discussed later in this chapter.)

Strategic goals

strategic goals

Broadly defined targets or future results set by top management

Strategic goals are broadly defined targets or future results set by top management. Typically they address whole organisation issues and are stated in fairly general terms. Top management formally states strategic or official goals (Perrow 1961; Richards 1986).

Drucker (1974) suggests organisations set goals in at least eight major areas (shown in Table 6.2). These areas encompass aspects important to the health and survival of most profit-making organisations (Morrisey 1996).

Tactical goals

tactical goals

Targets or future results usually set by middle management for specific departments or units

Tactical goals are targets or future results usually set by middle management for specific departments or units. Goals at this level spell out what various departments must do to achieve results outlined in strategic goals. Tactical goals are stated more measurably than strategic goals.

FIGURE 6.2 Levels of goals and plans (Drucker 1974, pp. 103–17, with permission from Elsevier)

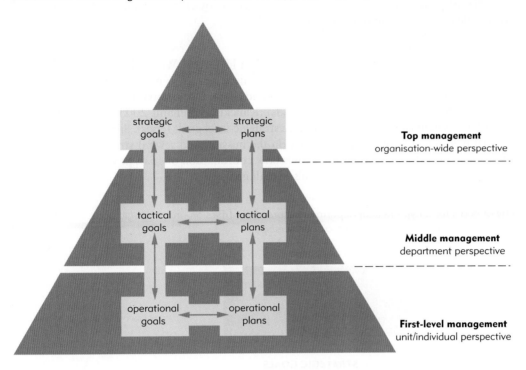

TABLE 6.2 EIGHT MAJOR AREAS FOR STRATEGIC GOALS

Major area	Descriptive
Market standing	Desired share of present and new markets, including areas in which new products are needed, and service goals aimed at building customer loyalty
Innovation	Innovations in products or services, as well as innovations in skills and activities required to supply them
Human resources	Supply, development and performance of managers and other organisation members; employee attitudes and development of skills; relations with unions, if any
Financial resources	Sources of capital and how it will be utilised
Physical resources	Physical facilities and how they will be used in the production of goods and services
Productivity	Efficient use of resources relative to outcomes
Social responsibility	Responsibilities in such areas as concern for community and maintenance of ethical behaviour
Profit requirements	Level of profitability and other indicators of financial well-being

Source: Drucker 1974, pp. 103–17, with permission from Elsevier

Operational goals

Operational goals are targets or future results set by lower management addressing specific measurable outcomes required from lower levels.

Hierarchy of goals

The three levels of goals can be seen as forming a hierarchy. With a hierarchy, goals at each level must be synchronised so all efforts are focused on achieving the organisation's major goals. In this way, levels of goals form a means-end chain. Operational-level goals (means) must be achieved to reach tactical-level goals (ends) (Kinicki & Williams 2003). Tactical-level goals (means), in turn, must be reached to achieve strategic-level goals (ends). Similarly, in Figure 6.3, a partial hierarchy of annual goals, based on the mission and several strategic objectives of a hypothetical department store chain, shows how coordination of goals at various levels creates a united effort to reach the organisation's overall goals.

FIGURE 6.3 Hierarchy of goals for a hypothetical department store chain (mission and strategic goals based on the J. C. Penney publication *Management in the Tradition of Partnership*)

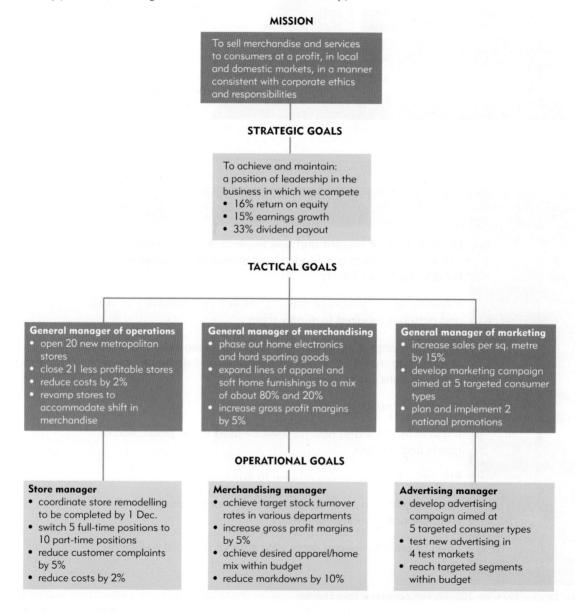

MISSION

To sell merchandise and services to consumers at a profit, in local and domestic markets, in a manner consistent with corporate ethics and responsibilities

STRATEGIC GOALS

To achieve and maintain:
a position of leadership in the business in which we compete
- 16% return on equity
- 15% earnings growth
- 33% dividend payout

TACTICAL GOALS

General manager of operations
- open 20 new metropolitan stores
- close 21 less profitable stores
- reduce costs by 2%
- revamp stores to accommodate shift in merchandise

General manager of merchandising
- phase out home electronics and hard sporting goods
- expand lines of apparel and soft home furnishings to a mix of about 80% and 20%
- increase gross profit margins by 5%

General manager of marketing
- increase sales per sq. metre by 15%
- develop marketing campaign aimed at 5 targeted consumer types
- plan and implement 2 national promotions

OPERATIONAL GOALS

Store manager
- coordinate store remodelling to be completed by 1 Dec.
- switch 5 full-time positions to 10 part-time positions
- reduce customer complaints by 5%
- reduce costs by 2%

Merchandising manager
- achieve target stock turnover rates in various departments
- increase gross profit margins by 5%
- achieve desired apparel/home mix within budget
- reduce markdowns by 10%

Advertising manager
- develop advertising campaign aimed at 5 targeted consumer types
- test new advertising in 4 test markets
- reach targeted segments within budget

HOW GOALS FACILITATE PERFORMANCE

To use goals effectively, managers must understand how performance can be facilitated by goals. The major elements in enhancing performance are shown in Figure 6.4.

In this section, we consider these components, highlighting particularly goal content, goal commitment, work behaviour and feedback aspects.

Goal content

In channelling effort to achievement at strategic, tactical and operational levels, effective goals have five major attributes. Goals should be challenging, attainable, specific and measurable, time-limited and relevant.

Challenging

Research shows that, within some limits, challenging, difficult goals give better performance. Assuming goals are accepted, people try harder when they face a challenge. Interestingly, if asked to do their 'best', people do not perform as well as with specific, challenging goals.

Attainable

Although goals must be challenging, they work best when attainable. If people are making the most use of their skills and abilities, they cannot perform at higher levels. Setting difficult, but attainable, goals is more likely to produce sustained performance than asking people constantly to do the impossible (Locke & Latham 1984; Howarth & Thomson 2003). Still, research shows performance is better with difficult goals than with easy ones.

Specific and measurable

Effective goals must be specific and measurable so people understand expectations and know when a goal is achieved. Goals should also be quantitative. Quantitative goals use easily verified objective numerical standards. At Rubbermaid Inc., which has a reputation for innovative products, a quantitative goal is for 30 per cent of sales to come from products less

FIGURE 6.4 How goals facilitate performance (adapted from Lee, Locke & Latham 1989, pp. 291–326)

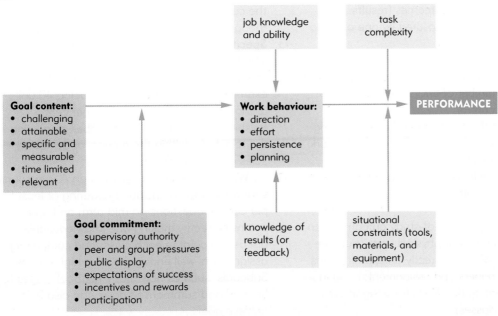

than five years old. Sometimes, though, qualitative goals are more appropriate. Qualitative goals use subjective judgment about whether a goal is reached. A Rubbermaid qualitative goal is to develop an idea and prototype for a new useful, long-lasting, inexpensive plastic desk accessory (Wright & Kacmar 1994; Mathews 1995).

Time-limited

Goals must also be time-limited; that is, there should be a set time period within which the goal is to be achieved. Goals have little meaning otherwise, since people can keep deferring them. In many cases, goals are set annually but reviewed perhaps quarterly (Latham & Wexley 1981).

Relevant

Goals are more likely to be supported when clearly relevant to the organisation's major work and a specific department or work unit.

For guidelines on goal setting, see the discussion in Management skills for a globalised economy, 'How to set goals'.

MANAGEMENT SKILLS FOR A GLOBALISED ECONOMY

How to set goals

There are six main steps in setting goals to obtain optimal results:

1. **Specify the goal to be reached or tasks to be done**. What do you want to accomplish? Do you want to increase sales? Reduce costs? Improve quality? Boost customer service? Maybe you are thinking you would like to get an A in one course this semester (perhaps the one involving this textbook).

2. **Specify how performance will be measured**. Some outcomes are more easily measured than others (e.g. number of units sold and dollar volume of sales). Work outcomes (results achieved) are typically measured by one of three parameters:

   Physical units: For example, production quantity, market share, number of errors, number of rejects (quality control)
   Time: For example, meeting deadlines, servicing customers, completing a project, coming to work each day, punctuality
   Money: For example, profits, sales, costs, budgets, debts, income

   Similarly, many course-of-study outcomes can be measured in terms of physical units (number of questions answered correctly on examinations and grades on papers and assignments) and in time terms (meeting deadlines for assignments and attending classes).

Some outcomes are hard to measure because of the cost or when factors beyond an individual's control affect outcomes. In such cases, behaviours or actions may need to be measured rather than outcomes. For example, if a manager's goal to overcome worker resistance to planned changes will be affected significantly by the actions of others, crucial activities may need to be measured instead of outcomes. Such activities might include whether the manager clearly explains the need for change, outlines how the change will affect others, and listens to the concerns of employees. When possible, though, goal-setting should focus on outcomes.

3. **Specify the standard or target to be reached.** This builds on the measurement type chosen in step 2 by spelling out the result wanted. For example, a target might be producing 40 units an hour, reducing errors by two per cent, finishing a project by 15 December, answering the telephone within three rings, or achieving sales growth of 10 per cent.

   With the objective of getting an A in a course, your targets might include answering at least 90 per cent of questions on mid-term and final exams correctly, making one knowledgeable discussion point in each class, and completing assignments well enough to earn high grades. Subgoals, such as how many textbook pages to be read and summarised daily, can also help achieve goals.

4. **Specify the time span involved.** To impact performance positively, goals must have a time span for completion. In a production context, a goal may be in terms of production per hour or day. In a service context, a goal may be the time to deliver a service. For example, a photocopier repair service's goal may be to respond to customer calls within two hours. Other goals, such as major projects, may have time spans of months or even years. For instance, your goals for the semester may cover a few months, while goals about getting your degree and developing your career may span several years.

5. **Prioritise the goals.** With multiple goals, as are present in most jobs, they must be prioritised so effort and action can be directed in proportion to each goal's significance. Otherwise, individual effort can be focused poorly. For example, suppose for the course where you want to obtain an A, examinations are worth 70 per cent, a paper 20 per cent, and class discussion is 10 per cent of the grade. In this case, an examination goal should be given first priority, while paper and class discussion goals should be second and third priority, respectively.

6. **Determine coordination requirements.** Before finalising a set of goals, check if goal achievement depends on other people's co-operation and contributions. If so, coordination may be needed. Vertical coordination is usually easy in organisations,. It may be harder, but still important, to coordinate horizontally, especially if some staff report to managers from other work units.

In the case of the course you want to excel in, you may need to coordinate with your boss (if employed) so your work schedule allows exam study time. If you plan ahead, parents, spouse or friends may help out at crucial times during semester, such as right before exams, so you have time to review.

Source: Locke & Latham (1984)

Goal commitment

A critical element in effective use of goals is getting individuals and/or work groups to be committed to goals they must carry out. **Goal commitment** is one's attachment to, or determination to reach, a goal (Locke, Latham & Erez 1988). Without commitment, setting specific, challenging goals will not impact performance. How, then, can managers foster commitment to important organisational goals? They can draw on five major factors influencing goal commitment positively: supervisory authority, peer and group pressure, public display of commitment, expectations of success, and incentives and rewards. A sixth factor, participation, is sometimes helpful.

goal commitment

One's attachment to, or determination to reach, a goal

Supervisory authority

Individuals and groups often commit to a goal when the goal and reasons for it are laid out by someone with supervisory authority. With this approach, goals are assigned by a supervisor, who explains the reasons for the goals to staff and gives needed instructions. Explanation and instructions are more effective with a supportive supervisor, not an authoritative one. Rather than simply telling subordinates to meet goals, a supervisor must encourage and offer question opportunities. This is relevant to diversity management, where real change comes from accountability of employment practices, not by simply setting out a company policy (McColl 2003).

Peer and group pressure

Pressure from peers and work-group members builds goal commitment by focusing everyone's efforts. Enthusiasm is infectious. Successful individuals act as role models. However, if goals are seen as unfair, peer and group pressure can cut goal commitment.

Public display

Recent evidence suggests commitment is greater to difficult goals with public commitment (made in front of others) than with private.

Expectations of success

Individuals or groups are more likely to be committed to goals when they have high expectations of success. That is, commitment is higher when they believe they have a good chance of performing well on tasks needed to reach the goal. If they believe they cannot accomplish the tasks, commitment to the goal is less likely.

Incentives and rewards

Incentives and rewards build goal commitment. During goal-setting, incentives are offered, while rewards occur on goal achievement. Some are tangible, such as money; others intangible, such as job challenge, anticipation of or positive feelings about accomplishment, feedback, competition (only if constructive) and recognition for goal attainment.

While positive outcomes foster commitment, negative ones inhibit it. So, if workers fear production increases will mean layoffs, commitment to high production goals will be low. Goal achievement must not become associated with unfavourable outcomes.

Participation

Participation has been shown not to be needed for goal commitment, however where the individual participates in goal-setting commitment is higher. Participation aids in plan development for goal implementation. Managers therefore often include subordinates in goal setting and then planning how to achieve the goals (Locke et al. 1988; Bateman & Snell 2004).

Work behaviour

Given goals and commitment, how ultimately does goal-setting influence behaviour? Goal content and commitment affect a person's work behaviour through four factors: direction, effort, persistence and planning.

Direction

Goals focus attention and action on activities related to goals, rather than other activities. So, when people are committed to specific goals, this helps improve choices of activities to undertake.

Effort

As well as directing tasks, goals to which individuals are committed increase effort by mobilising energy. Individuals try harder for difficult goals than for easy ones.

Persistence

Persistence means direction and effort are maintained in reaching a goal. Persistence may be needed long-term. Goal commitment means persistence is more likely.

Planning

As well as their effects on work behaviour in direction, effort and persistence, goals indirectly influence planning. Those committed to difficult goals will develop plans or methods to attain those goals. Easy goals may need little planning.

Other process components

The impact of goals on job performance is influenced by other components. For one, job knowledge and ability affect an individual's work behaviour and prospects for goal attainment, even where commitment is strong. For another, task complexity affects the influence of goal-directed work behaviour on job performance. Related studies show that goals have higher impact on performance for simple tasks (such as basic arithmetic, toy assembly tasks or basic typing) than more complex ones (such as supervision or engineering projects) (Wood, Meant & Locke 1987). It seems the effects of goals on direction, effort, work behaviour persistence and planning are diluted in a complex task.

Situational constraints also influence the impact of goals on performance. Proper tools, materials and equipment are needed to reach difficult goals. Finally, knowledge of results or feedback of progress toward goals is particularly influential in goal effectiveness. While goals set the target, knowledge of results influences goal achievement by allowing the assessment of progress (Locke, Shaw, Saari & Latham 1981). Thus, goal setting is important to increase productivity and quality. It must be used properly though.

Potential problems with goals

Although goal use in organisations can yield many positive aspects, pitfalls exist (Locke & Latham 1984; 1990). These problems and their solutions are summarised in Table 6.3.

LINKING GOALS AND PLANS

Goals and plans are closely related. An organisation may set strategic, tactical and operating goals, which are meaningless unless the actual process is considered. While goals are desired ends, plans are the means to achieve them. The value of plan development is clear if you remember there may be many ways to reach any goal. Plans differ by organisational level and by extent of recurring use.

Levels of plans

As there are levels of goals, plans also differ by organisational level (see Fig. 6.2). Thus there are strategic, tactical and operational plans (Locke & Latham 1984).

Strategic plans

Strategic plans are detailed action steps laid out to reach strategic goals. These address issues such as responses to changing conditions, resource allocation, and needed actions to create unified and powerful organisation-wide effort to achieve strategic goals (Thompson & Strickland 1987). Top management consults with the board and middle management to develop strategic plans. Typically these have a time horizon of three to five years or more. An example of a longer strategy is that of the New Zealand Ministry of Housing which sets out a vision and strategic direction for housing over the next 10 years. It outlines ways that central and local government, iwi/Maori, Pacific groups and the wider housing sector can work

strategic plans

Detailed action steps mapped out to reach strategic goals

Potential problem	Possible remedies
Excessive risk taking	Analyse risk; avoid careless or foolish risks
Increased stress	Eliminate unnecessary stress by adjusting goal difficulty, adding staff and offering training in necessary skills
Undermined self-confidence	Treat failure as a problem to be solved rather than a signal to punish (due to failure)
Ignored non-goal areas	Make sure goals encompass key areas.
Excessive short-run thinking	Include some long-term goals.
Dishonesty and cheating	Set example of honesty, avoid using goals punitively, offer help in overcoming difficulties, give frequent feedback, and be open to information indicating goals are inappropriate.

TABLE 6.3 POTENTIAL GOAL-SETTING PROBLEMS AND POSSIBLE SOLUTONS

Source: Based on Locke & Latham (1984, pp. 171–2)

Cuisine: Fast-food style

Cuisine Courier claims to be the world's largest multi-restaurant home-delivery company. The company, established in 1986, has more than 500 restaurants participating. It offers more than 100 different styles of cuisine from these restaurants. The company used to depend on a call centre to take orders efficiently and ensure the process was carried through and the orders despatched.

Exploring ways to expand their service, the logical extension was the establishment of an internet site. This improved the call-centre response time and has had the added bonus of allowing the company to offer their call-centre and delivery infrastructure to other businesses that require goods delivery.

In July 2002 Mr Delivery (another restaurant delivery service) bought Cuisine Courier and now operates both brands successfully. Cuisine Courier operates in Sydney, Melbourne & Canberra and will be opening in every major city. Restaurant delivery service is offered to homes, businesses, serviced apartments and hotels. The new managing directors are Ryan Catzel and Marlon Segal.

Source: Adapted from Banagham, M. (1999); further information supplied by the company.

Decision points

1. If you were the managing director of Cuisine Courier, what are the factors that you might have wanted to consider before you committed yourself to such an expansion?
2. Connect to their website at www.cuisinecourier.com.au and consider what could be improved to make the site more user-friendly and facilitate service to customers.

Reflection point

1. In your opinion, is fast food home delivered via the internet a good idea? Why?

together to develop housing policy with the aim of achieving quality, affordable and sustainable housing for all. Its development is being led by Housing New Zealand Corporation and involves the key elements of the housing sector, including the building industry, lending and finance, real estate, landlords and tenants. (http://.minhousing.govt.nz, accessed 28 January 2004)

The strategic plans of organisations often include the mission and goals, as these are the basis for action steps. We discuss issues related to strategic planning later.

Tactical plans

tactical plans

Means charted to support implementation of the strategic plan and achievement of tactical goals

Tactical plans support strategic-plan implementation and tactical-goal achievement. These focus on intermediate time frames, usually one to three years. Generally more specific and concrete than strategic plans, tactical plans outline the major steps towards tactical goals. Middle managers consult with lower-level managers in developing them, before making commitments to top-level management. Managers may consider many possibilities in tactical-plan development, before deciding on a final plan (the plan is subject to change, should things turn out differently). Tactical plans are important to strategic-plan success. This is demonstrated by the move of Korean and Japanese shipbuilders to develop 'jumbo container' ships, capable of carrying 7700 units, instead of the previous 6000. This has helped in part to cushion the increased demands for shipping capacity generated by growing trade markets (Ihlwan 2003).

Operational plans

operational plans

Means devised to support implementation of tactical plans and achievement of operational goals

Operational plans support tactical-plan implementation and operational-goal achievement. These plans usually involve time frames of up to a year, such as a few months, weeks or even days. Lower-level managers consult with middle managers to develop operational-level plans. They spell out what must be accomplished over short time periods to achieve operational goals. Unless operational goals are achieved, tactical and strategic plans will fail and goals at those levels will not be achieved.

Plans according to extent of recurring use

Plans can be categorised by their frequency of use. There are two types of plans: single-use plans and standing plans (see Fig. 6.5).

Single-use plans

Single-use plans aim to achieve a specific goal which, once reached, is unlikely to recur. Programs and projects are the major single-use plan types.

A **program** is a comprehensive plan coordinating a set of activities for a major non-recurring goal. Programs usually involve several organisation units, comprise several projects, and take a year or more to finish. Programs usually have six basic steps: (1) dividing what is to be done into major parts, or projects, (2) determining relationships between parts and developing a sequence, (3) deciding who will be responsible for each part, (4) determining how each part will be completed and resources needed, (5) estimating time required for completing each part, and (6) developing a schedule for implementing each step (Newman & Logan 1981). Programs often have their own budgets. A budget is a statement of the financial resources needed for various program activities.

A **project** is a plan coordinating a set of limited-scope activities not needing to be divided into major components to reach an important non-recurring goal. Projects, like programs, can have their own budgets. Several projects may comprise a program.

Standing plans

Standing plans guide the performance of recurring activities. Three main standing-plan types are policies, procedures and rules (Rue & Holland 1989).

A **policy** is a general guide specifying broad parameters for the activities of organisation members pursuing organisational goals. Specific actions are not normally dictated; rather, boundaries are given for general action. For example, policies spell out important limitations. Retail-store policy generally states that returned merchandise requires a sales receipt. Similarly, policies may outline desirable actions (Sellers 1988; McShane & Traviaglione 2003).

A **procedure** is a set series of steps to be taken in certain recurring circumstances. Well-established, formalised procedures are standard operating procedures (SOPs). Unlike fairly general policies, procedures give detailed, step-by-step instructions. They do not allow flexibility or deviation. For example, banks have SOPs specifying how tellers handle deposits. As they specify desired recurring actions, SOPs are good for training new employees.

A **rule** is a statement spelling out specific actions to be taken or not taken in a situation. Unlike procedures, rules do not specify a series of steps. Instead, they dictate exact action, without flexibility or room for deviation.

FIGURE 6.5 Plans according to extent of recurring use

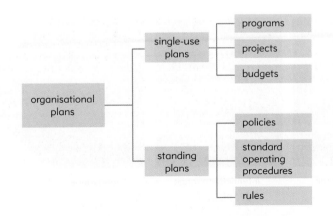

---

single-use plans

Plans aimed at achieving a specific goal which, once reached, will most likely not recur in the future

program

Comprehensive plan coordinating a complex set of activities related to a major non-recurring goal

project

Plan coordinating a set of limited-scope activities which do not need to be divided into several major projects to reach a major non-recurring goal

standing plans

Plans providing ongoing guidance for performing recurring activities

policy

General guide specifying broad parameters within which organisation members are expected to operate in pursuit of organisational goals

procedure

Prescribed series of related steps to be taken under certain recurring circumstances

rule

Statement spelling out specific actions to be taken or not taken in a given situation

Time horizons of goals and plans

Different levels of goals and plans relate to different time horizons (see Fig. 6.6). Strategic goals and plans address long-range issues over five years or more. The time frame depends on the industry. In fluid environments, long-range planning may deal with less than five years. In stable environments (such as the power industry), long-range planning includes 10 to 20 years. Tactical goals and plans cover intermediate-range issues with periods between one and five years. Operational goals and plans involve short-range issues over one year or less.

Promoting innovation: The role of the planning process

The planning process is vital to organisational innovation through the mission, goals and plans. Amabile (1988) argues an organisation's basic view of innovation comes from the highest levels. The CEO sees a future based on innovation and communicates this to organisation members. The mission statement signals innovation's value, and raises general areas to emphasise innovation. The mission statement's vision shows innovation's importance and motivates staff to innovate.

The goals planning component also supports innovation. For example, translating a mission into strategic goals might result in this statement: 'Within five years, the organisation will be the number-one provider of state-of-the-art semiconductor chips in a [specified broad] area'. The 'state-of-the-art' designation signals a need for product innovation. A matched tactical-level goal might be: 'Within two years, the programmable logic devices division will introduce 20 new products'. Finally, operationally, a work unit's goal might be: 'Within one year, the unit will have a working prototype meeting following general specifications...' So each goal level encourages innovation.

The plans component of planning also has an innovation role. While goals seeking innovative outcomes can be put generally, actual plans (e.g. new products) are often looser than those for predictable situations. Greater flexibility is required due to the difficulty of specifying exactly what should be done when seeking innovative breakthroughs and nurturing new ideas, particularly in product or service development. Of course, the possibility of innovative goal achievement is enhanced if managers ensure organisational conditions foster innovation (Hill & Jones 1995). We discuss several of these conditions, such as organisational structure, resource levels, communication patterns and leadership, in later chapters.

FIGURE 6.6 Time horizons for goals and plans

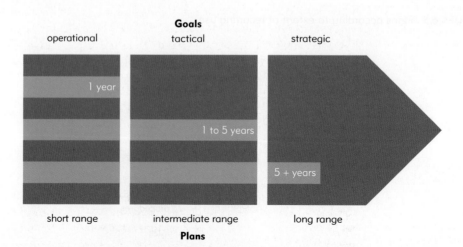

Doctor Global plans a possible future

The Doctor Global website was first launched in May 1999, with 12 online clinics offering consultations with Doctor Global accredited medical practitioners. A Clinical Advisory Board was established, and privacy policy and internet medical guidelines were drafted. The success of this pilot stage demonstrated the need to underpin the service with an online health record, built on a relational database, that allowed processes such as online consultations and health monitoring.

The development of the Doctor Global Electronic Health Record began in July 2000. The record was developed to provide a tool that met the world's best practice standards for the design and deployment of electronic health records. It was also specifically designed to facilitate and broaden the product offerings then currently available from Doctor Global.

Later that year guidance was sought from leading preventative medicine practitioners and from academic advisors on how this record could be used to provide real value to clients, and the record design was again broadened to include this functionality.

Doctor Global positioned the application as a multi-party online communication platform to help established healthcare organisations meet the increasing demand from customers who were turning to the internet to find health-related information and content to manage their health status.

This new focus led to the development of the *e-Care for Life* disease-management platform allowing healthcare organisations to monitor more effectively and manage their chronic patients out in the community, capitalising on the power of the internet to improve the communication and dissemination of information and knowledge between the healthcare provider and the patient community.

The initial development of the Doctor Global product offerings was funded from Venture Capital, with NZ$2 million in venture capital from No.8 Ventures and $1 million from Endeavour Capital Ltd. Three years on, revenue between $1 and 1.5 million is forecast for 2002, derived from users in the Commonwealth and the USA who pay for medical advice and for maintenance of, and access to, their records. A new service, the MyLifeSaver Card, has proven to be popular. This is a web-based medical records service that allows the subscriber (or anyone else to whom they give their card) to access their own medical file, using a unique login code printed on the card.

Medical consultations online may be only the tip of the iceberg for Doctor Global. It has become apparent that the key to giving proper medical diagnoses and prescriptions over the internet lies in accurate and rapid access to critical information about a patient's condition, allergies, blood type, and medical history. Doctor Global created an internet-based medical records system that serves these needs, and this has attracted the attention of a major US medical consortium that includes Hewlett-Packard and the founder of the Visa card system. The consortium has commenced negotiations to use Doctor Global's records system—provided that the tiny New Zealand company fronts up with a US$1 million 'entry fee' to join the consortium. Doctor Global's existing venture funding providers aren't in a position to invest any more, but an Australian technology investor appears ready to provide the needed funding.

The CEO of Doctor Global, Roger Gower, believes that the consortium will boost his company's revenues 100-fold. He claims that if even only 1 per cent of the hospitals and physicians joining the consortium buy a Doctor Global product, it would 'generate revenue that will blow your mind'.

Source: Contributed by Andre Everett (details of sources are listed on p. 736).

Website:

www.doctorglobal.com
Doctor Global's home on the web provides background information about the organisation, its medical staff and its services. The home page typically features a new or popular service such as MyLifeSaver Card. Consultations with medical staff can be arranged and conducted over the web, while

other services (such as MyLifeSaver Card) are designed to be entirely self-serviced via the web. 'Cool tools' provide free access to essential health support information such as a body mass index and a baby-due-date calculator.

Activities for discussion, analysis and further research

1. How should an organisation plan for the future when a single event can propel it towards either worldwide success or obscurity?
2. If the potential Australian investor does provide the 'entry fee' to join the consortium, how will

this affect the goals, plans and management structure of Doctor Global?

3. Examine a variety of health-related websites, including a prescription service and a local hospital. Contrast their services with those provided by Doctor Global. Attempt to ascertain their goals and plans from their websites and   any other information available to you. What factors drive these organisations, and how do they differ from Doctor Global? How does their use of the web differ? How well does their web activity fit with their goals and plans?

Plans can help achieve goals which do not have innovative outcomes but use innovative means. Even when a goal focuses on a traditional outcome, such as cost cutting or quality improvement, plan development can lead to innovative strategies (Ramanujam & Varadarajan 1989; Scheifer & Vishny 1994). Thus, emphasis is on developing innovative ways to reach goals not stated in terms of innovative outcomes.

Potential obstacles to planning

The ability to develop effective plans has several potential obstacles. One is a rapidly changing environment, when planning grows harder. Another obstacle is managers believing planning is not needed. This occurs when they have a general idea of future directions and how to reach company goals (*INC* 1989; Stensholt & Gome 2003). Another potential planning barrier is managers' daily work pressures. Even if they see planning as good, daily stress can distract them from planning (Mintzberg 1980). Yet another obstacle is line-managers with poor planning knowledge and skills. Finally, if staff specialists dominate the process, effective planning may be thwarted. This results in low managerial involvement by those who will apply the plans (Grey 1986).

Organisations can reduce planning obstacles. One step is top-management showing strong support for the planning process. Top-level managers display commitment by personal involvement in the process and by their interest in plan implementation. Lower-level managers are encouraged to engage in and support planning. Another step is ensuring that the role of planning staffs, or corporate planners, is helping, not actually planning. **Planning staff** aid top-level managers develop planning-process components. Typically such staff help monitor internal and external environments to generate data for top management's strategic decisions. They also propose organisation mission, goal and plan changes. Corporate planners' influence grew from the 1960s to early 1980s, often dominating the process and leaving line managers with minor roles. The role of planning staff has reduced since then (Rue & Holland 1989). Thus, when John F. Welch Jr became General Electric chairman, he cut corporate planning staff from 58 to 33, eliminating them across the firm (*Business Week* 1984).

GE's moves are another step firms can take reducing planning obstacles. Top management can actively involve managers who have to carry out the plans. In part, this means training them in planning. Managers must be encouraged to review plans often, especially in fluid environments. Managers can also use **contingency planning**. Contingency planning is developing alternative plans for use if environmental conditions evolve suddenly, making original plans unwise or infeasible.

planning staff

Small group of individuals who assist top-level managers in developing various components of the planning process

contingency planning

Development of alternative plans for use in the event that environmental conditions evolve differently than anticipated, rendering original plans unwise or infeasible

MANAGEMENT BY OBJECTIVES

One method organisations use to help link goals and plans is management by objectives. **Management by objectives (MBO)** is a process where specific goals are set collaboratively for the whole organisation and every unit and individual within it. These goals are then used for planning, managing organisational activities, and assessing and rewarding contributions. MBO uses high levels of managerial and subordinate participation in setting goals.

MBO's origins are unclear, while General Electric seems to have implemented the process first, and Peter Drucker is credited with writing about it first (Drucker 1954; Greenwood 1981; Rue & Byars 2003). MBO has been used by many firms to aid coordination of goal-setting and planning processes at all levels so members' collective efforts support organisational goals ultimately. Organisations using MBO include Black & Decker, Texas Instruments, Boeing and Westinghouse (Raia 1974; Richards 1986).

Steps in the MBO process

How MBO is used in different organisations can vary considerably, with most viable MBO processes having the following six steps (see Fig. 6.7) (Raia 1974; Richards 1986):

1. **Develop overall organisational goals.** At this stage goals are based on organisational mission, and address achievement of the whole organisation's targets (e.g. a certain rate of return for a given period or a specific increase in market share). Essentially these are strategic goals set by top management.
2. **Establish specific goals (or objectives) for various departments, subunits and individuals.** In this step, coordinating goals are set for various organisational levels so each goal helps reach the overall goals set in step 1. This stage opens when upper-level managers develop specific objectives they plan to accomplish, for their own departments or responsibility areas (such as marketing or production). These goals are usually developed in collaboration with the next lower-level managers. For example, a head of a marketing department, with regional sales managers, may set a goal of building a product's sales volume to 100 000 during the coming year. Then regional sales managers confer with district managers in setting goals at regional levels. In the eastern region, for instance, a sales manager and district managers may decide on a goal of growing sales volume to 25 000 for a product, contributing to the 100 000 national-level goal. The process, called cascading goals, continues until all units at different levels have specific goals for next year. At each level, typically goals are set in key areas, with critical results for organisation success.

   Many organisations use the top-down process outlined; however, others use a bottom-up approach, where goal setting starts at lower levels. These levels set their goals based on what they believe they can achieve. Tactical-level goals are then developed based on the proposed operational-level goals. The tactical goals are next proposed to the strategic level. Even a bottom-up approach to goal setting will have some general guidelines developed by the strategic level. With MBO, there is always some give-and-take across levels before goals at various levels are finalised.
3. **Formulate action plans.** Once goals are set, action plans are developed focused on methods or activities to reach particular goals. An action plan is a description of what is to be done, how, when, where and by whom to achieve a goal. Action plans help reach goals, aid problem-area identification, assist spelling out areas where resources and assistance are needed, and help search for efficient and effective ways to reach objectives. Subordinates and their supervisors usually develop such plans.
4. **Implement and maintain self-control.** MBO's basic idea is that once goals are set and action plans laid-out, individuals should be allowed latitude in their activities. The rationale is that individuals know what they need to achieve, have plans mapped out and can check their progress against set goals. A supervisor thus needs to be less involved in an individual's day-to-day activities than they might be without goals and

---

management by objectives (MBO)

Process through which specific goals are set collaboratively for the organisation as a whole and every unit and individual within it; the goals are then used as a basis for planning, managing organisational activities, and assessing and rewarding contributions

action plans. The idea of self-control is very true for managers. Supervisors have to be told about progress and unexpected problems. They may also need to coach and support subordinates if they have difficulties.

5. **Review progress periodically.** Periodic reviews are important to ensure plans are implemented as expected and goals will be met. These are a good way to check performance to date, to identify and remove obstacles, solve problems, and alter action plans not getting results expected. Reviews make it possible to assess continuing appropriateness of goals and to change them or add to them as needed. How often reviews occur depends on situational change speed, but quarterly is common.

6. **Appraise performance.** At the end of a goal-setting cycle, typically a year, a manager meets with each subordinate to appraise performance over the cycle. This typically focuses on how much goals were met, shortfalls, their reasons, and actions to prevent the same problems in future. The appraisal session includes praise and recognition of areas where the subordinate has done well, as well as discussing areas benefiting from future development of knowledge and skills. Goals and plans for the next cycle may also be discussed.

As Figure 6.7 shows, feedback from each step may lead to revising prior goals or setting future ones. While constant goal revision defeats MBO's purpose, some may be needed after changes in major circumstances. The purpose of goal-setting and planning processes is to coordinate efforts toward important organisational goals. If those goals need changing, then efforts probably do too; so goals at various level should be changed.

Strengths and weaknesses of MBO

Management by objectives has a number of major strengths. On the other hand, MBO has several weaknesses. MBO's main strengths and weaknesses are shown in Table 6.4 (Carroll & Tosi 1973; Raia 1974; Leonard 1986; Richards 1986).

FIGURE 6.7 Steps in the MBO process

1. Develop overall organisational goals

2. Establish specific goals for various departments, subunits, and individuals

3. Formulate action plans

4. Implement plans and maintain self-control

5. Review progress periodically

6. Appraise performance

TABLE 6.4 STRENGTHS AND WEAKNESSES OF MBO

Strengths	Weaknesses
1 Aids coordination of goals and plans from top management	1 Tends to falter without strong, continual commitment
2 Helps clarify priorities and expectations	2 Necessitates considerable training of managers
3 Facilitates vertical and horizontal communication	3 Can be misused as a punitive device
4 Fosters employee motivation	4 May cause overemphasis on quantitative goals

Assessing MBO

With these weaknesses, MBO has often not reached its potential. By one estimate, almost half the *Fortune* 500 companies have used MBO, but only about 20 to 25 per cent successfully (Muczyk 1979). MBO system failures seem to stem from a lack of top-management support and poor goal-setting and communication skills among managers who must implement the system. According to a recent study, however, when top management commitment to the MBO program and processes was high, the average productivity gain was 56 per cent (Rodgers & Hunter 1991). Hence, how managers implement MBO impacts its effectiveness.

THE CONCEPT OF STRATEGIC MANAGEMENT

Most well-run organisations try to develop and follow **strategies**, or large-scale action plans for interacting with the environment to reach long-term goals (Jauch & Glueck 1988; Pearce & Robinson 1988). An organisation's strategic plan states its strategies, mission and goals (Thompson & Strickland 1992). To learn their source and how they are put into place, we must examine the planning aspect of strategic management.

Strategic management involves managers developing and implementing strategies to achieve strategic goals, under present conditions (Thompson & Strickland 1992; Rue & Holland 1989). Thus strategic management is oriented to reaching long-term goals, weighing environmental aspects, considering major internal organisation characteristics, and involving specific strategy development. Strategic management is important to the planning process.

The strategic management process

There are several major components in the strategic management process (shown in Figure 6.8). First an organisation's mission and strategic goals are identified. This requires competitive situation analysis, with recognition of external environment and organisational factors. To reach strategic goals managers then develop strategies. **Strategy formulation** needs mission and strategic goal identification, competitive analysis, and specific strategy development. **Strategy implementation**, by contrast, is carrying out strategic plans and controlling their operation (Thompson & Strickland 1992; Atherton 2003). Strategy-implementation is vital to strategic management because a brilliantly formulated strategy will fail if implementation is ineffective.

strategies

Large-scale action plans for interacting with the environment to achieve long-term goals

strategic management

Process through which managers formulate and implement strategies geared to optimising strategic goal achievement, given available environmental and internal conditions

strategy formulation

Process of identifying mission and strategic goals, conducting competitive analysis, and developing specific strategies

strategy implementation

Process of carrying out strategic plans and maintaining control over how those plans are carried out

FIGURE 6.8   The strategic management process

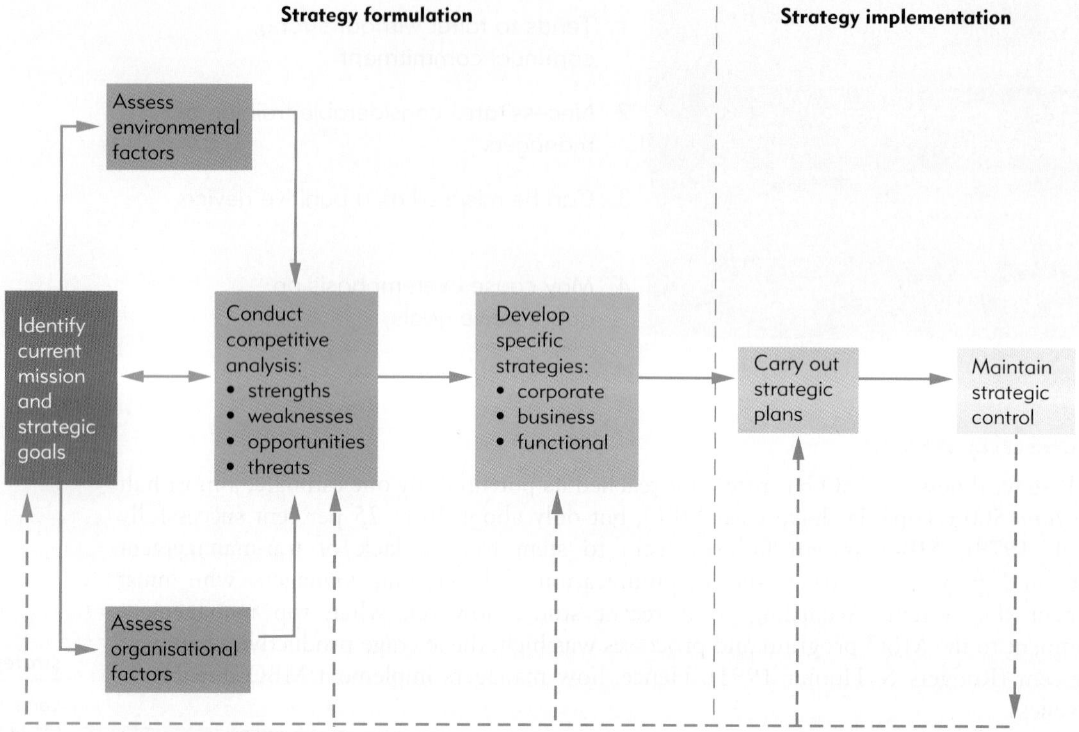

Strategy formulation | Strategy implementation

Assess environmental factors

Identify current mission and strategic goals

Conduct competitive analysis:
- strengths
- weaknesses
- opportunities
- threats

Develop specific strategies:
- corporate
- business
- functional

Carry out strategic plans

Maintain strategic control

Assess organisational factors

Importance of strategic management

Strategic management is important for many reasons (Thompson & Strickland 1992). For one, the process helps organisations identify and develop a **competitive advantage**, or a significant edge in dealing with competitive forces (Porter 1985).

Strategic management is also important because it directs organisation members as to where to put their efforts. Without a strategic plan, managers may concentrate on day-to-day activities, only to find a competitor has gained an advantage by taking a longer-term view of strategic directions.

Strategic management can also show a need for innovation, giving an organised approach for encouraging new ideas related to strategies (Schilit 1987). In addition, the process can involve managers at various levels in planning, making it more likely they will understand plans and be committed to them.

Levels of strategy

Many organisations develop three different levels of strategy: corporate, business and functional. The three levels are shown in Figure 6.9 (Thompson & Strickland 1992).

Corporate-level strategy

Corporate-level strategy addresses the businesses an organisation will operate, how the strategies of those businesses will be coordinated to strengthen the overall competitive position, and how resources will be allocated among businesses. Strategy here is typically developed by top management, often with strategic planning personnel, at least in large organisations. For example, the New Zealand Water & Wastes Association Board Strategic Plan 2000 is guided by a mission statement that is reviewed every five years. The corporate plan includes an annual

competitive advantage

Significant edge over competition in dealing with competitive forces

corporate-level strategy

Type of strategy addressing what businesses the organisation will operate, how strategies of those businesses will be coordinated to strengthen the organisation's competitive position, and how resources will be allocated among businesses

Funky flowers

Gill set up her business in response to changed personal circumstances following her divorce. She moved from Auckland, a major city in New Zealand, to Alexandra, a small country town of 10 000 people in Central Otago, which is in the lower half of the South Island. Because she had not been in full-time paid employment for a number of years and she had custody of her five children (aged 5 to 17 years), she had to rely on state welfare for short-term financial support. When her divorce settlement money came through after six months and she and her children had settled in to the new neighbourhood, she found herself in a position to buy a florist's shop and plant nursery without taking out a mortgage on the property. The former owner had recently retired, and the shop was run down with seriously depleted plant stocks, but it had previously been very successful. It was the only florist shop in town and had a good reputation for service and quality. However, a number of supermarkets and trades shops also offered plants for sale.

Gill had always been interested in flowers; she had a reputation for designing 'funky' and attractive arrangements, and had previously worked part-time (up to 30 hours per week) arranging flowers for a hotel chain. Her previous employers had always relied on her to work at the last minute, often at short notice. Even though it often meant that she had little sleep, she always agreed to do extra work at the hotel, especially for weddings or functions. Basically, she admitted to herself, she was afraid to say no, in case she lost her job. Being in paid employment was very important to Gill's self-esteem; she had come from a family of 'dominating' men who thought that a woman's place was to look after the children and run the household. Her former husband had often expressed this view when he said things such as: 'I don't want you working full-time and having a career—part-time is enough.' After her divorce, Gill took stock of her life. She finally recognised what others had always told her but she had never chosen to believe: that she was a competent, successful professional who was capable of running her own business.

Gill went through waves of excitement, fear and despair at the thought of setting up her own business and sometimes the challenge of it seemed overwhelming. She felt that she lacked the self-confidence and knowledge that was required to run a business, even though she had a Diploma in Business Studies and more than twenty years of experience. She had already encountered negative attitudes towards her as a 'solo mother' when she had gone to the local bank and opened an account for her welfare money to be paid into. The bank manager had made her wait for 15 minutes while he talked on the phone, and she felt humiliated by the experience. However, since she had adequate funds to set up her business, she had taken the opportunity to change banks and now had a personal banker who was a woman. She already felt inspired by the different business relationship that had resulted from this change.

Gill's task as an owner-manager was to take over an existing business in a small rural township. Female-owned businesses were not common, but there were many businesses that were owned by husband-and-wife partnerships. The factor that encouraged her most was that she would be working in a job that she loved and one where her skills as a woman—with an eye for something different and creative—would be valued. She was confident that this was the sort of town where being a woman owner of a flower shop would be acceptable to the locals.

Alexandra is on the main tourist route to Queenstown, which is less than an hour's drive away. Queenstown has an international airport and many big hotels, and it caters for a large tourist population. Gill planned to grow and develop her business by sourcing local flower-growers as her suppliers and then providing a florist service for the Queenstown hotels. She also wished to re-stock the plant nursery, emphasising native plants that would grow well in the tough local conditions. Her long-term plan was to develop an export side of her business, sending fresh and dried flowers to the lucrative Asian, North American and European markets.

Source: Contributed by Elizabeth Hall.

Activities for discussion, analysis and further research

1. Describe the steps that Gill must go through in order to plan her business from scratch.
2. Modify a hierarchy of goals like the one in Figure 6.3 and identify the key challenges and threats to Gill's business.
3. What must Gill do to make sure that she has a business plan that will succeed?
4. Research the export market for fresh and dried flower markets. What are the critical factors in successfully operating in this business environment? Try worldwide fruit, vegetable, or flower search engines and the following addresses as examples: www.dfat.gov.au/regionalexporters/adehills_fleurieu.html www.pathfastpublishing.com/qr27/qr27expstats.htm.

FIGURE 6.9 Levels of strategy (adapted from Pearce II & Robinson Jr 1988, p. 9)

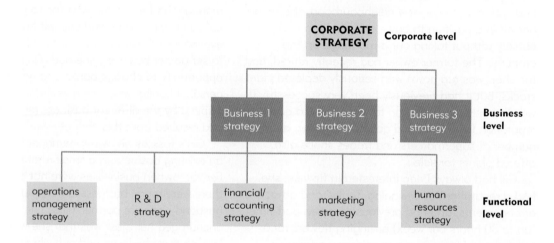

business plan that is prepared each year by the chief executive. This plan is aligned with the strategic initiatives of the organisation and includes performance measures approved by the board of directors. (http://www.nzwwa.com, accessed 24 January 2004)

The board of directors aids in corporate-level strategy development, although participation levels vary. Within the strategic management process, directors can suggest growth directions, major strategy changes needed, and timing of major investments (Mueller 1979; Atherton 2003).

Business-level strategy

Many organisations include strategic business units. A **strategic business unit (SBU)** is a distinct business, with its own competitors, managed independently of others in the organisation (Rue & Holland 1989). **Business-level strategy** concentrates on one business and supports corporate-level strategy. Strategies aim to decide the type of competitive advantage to build, determine responses to changing environments and competitive conditions, allocate unit resources, and coordinate functional-level strategies. Often, business-unit heads develop business strategies, subject to top management's approval. When an organisation is only one business, corporate- and business-level strategies are identical. Thus the corporate- and business-level distinction applies only to firms with separate divisions competing in different industries.

---

strategic business unit (SBU)

Distinct business, with its own set of competitors, which can be managed relatively independently of other businesses within the organisation

business-level strategy

Type of strategy concentrating on the best means of competing within a particular business while also supporting corporate-level strategy

Functional-level strategy

Functional-level strategy focuses on plans for managing a functional area in a business to support business-level strategy. Strategies here address main directions for each major functional business area, including manufacturing or operations, marketing, finance, human resource management, accounting, research and development, and engineering. Functional-level strategies reflect strong functional competencies supporting competitive advantage.

Coordinating strategy levels

Coordinating strategies across levels is critical to building strategic impact. Business-level strategy is better when functional-level strategies support it. Similarly, corporate-level strategy's impact is greater when business-level strategies complement each another (Thompson & Strickland 1992; Thomson 2003a). Thus the three levels must be coordinated as part of strategic management.

THE ROLE OF COMPETITIVE ANALYSIS IN STRATEGY FORMULATION

Before an effective strategy for getting a competitive edge can be devised, managers must analyse a firm's competitive situation. This means assessing environmental and organisational factors influencing ability to compete. Assessment can use SWOT analysis. **SWOT analysis** is a way to analyse an organisation's competitive situation by assessing organisational strengths (S) and weaknesses (W), environmental opportunities (O) and threats (T). Identification of strengths and weaknesses requires internal characteristics to be assessed, while detection of opportunities and threats requires evaluation of environmental factors.

For a SWOT analysis, a *strength* is an internal characteristic which can better an organisation's competitive situation. In contrast, a *weakness* is an internal characteristic where the organisation is vulnerable to competitors' strategic moves. An *opportunity* is an environmental condition giving significant hope for organisational situation improvement. Conversely, a *threat* is an environmental condition with significant prospects of undermining organisational competitiveness.

Environmental assessment

In analysing opportunities and threats, managers must consider general, or mega-environment, elements which can, for good or ill, influence organisational ability to reach strategic goals. These are broad factors such as technological, economic, legal-political, sociocultural and international influences. Managers must assess major task-environment elements, including specific external elements an organisation interfaces while doing business. These include customers, competitors and suppliers. General and task-environment elements are detailed in Chapter 3.

Porter's five competitive forces model

Porter developed the **five competitive forces model** to analyse competition's nature and intensity in terms of five major forces. The forces are rivalry, bargaining power of customers, bargaining power of suppliers, threat of new entrants, and threat of substitute products and services. These affect business profit potential, or long-term return on investment. Major reasons for lower profit potential are outlined in Table 6.5.

Rivalry is how much competitors jockey for position by price competition, advertising battles, product introductions, and increased customer service or warranties. All these cut competitor profits by lowering prices or by raising business costs. This illustrates Porter's view that greater rivalry causes lower profit potential for an industry.

The *bargaining power of customers* is how much customers can force prices down, bargain for higher quality or better service at the same price, and play competitors against each other. Customers are powerful when purchases are large compared to a seller's total sales, when

---

functional-level strategy

Type of strategy focusing on action plans for managing a particular functional area within a business in a way that supports business-level strategy

SWOT analysis

Method of analysing an organisation's competitive situation involving assessing organisational strengths (S), weaknesses (W), environmental opportunities (O) and threats (T)

five competitive forces model

Porter's approach to analysing the nature and intensity of competition in a given industry in terms of five major forces

TABLE 6.5 PORTER'S FIVE COMPETITIVE FORCES MODEL

Competitive forces	Reasons for lower profit potential
Rivalry	Various competitive tactics among rivals lower prices that can be charged or raise costs of doing business.
Bargaining power of customers	Customers force price reductions or negotiate increases in product quality and service at the same price.
Bargaining power of suppliers	Suppliers threaten price increases and/or reductions in quality of goods or services.
Threat of new entrants	New entrants bid prices down or cause incumbents to increase costs to maintain market position.
Threat of substitute products or services	Availability of substitutes limits the prices that can be charged.

Source: Based on Porter (1980, pp. 3–28).

products or services are a major part of customer costs, or when standard items are needed (Alster 1989; Taylor 1994). When customers' bargaining power is higher, an industry's profit potential is lower.

The *bargaining power of suppliers* is how much suppliers exert industry power by threatening to raise prices or cut quality of goods and services. Suppliers have power when only a few sell to many users in an industry, when there are no product or service substitutes, or when critical to a buyer's business. When suppliers' bargaining power is higher, an industry's profit potential is lower.

For example, French champagne makers have a problem due to a lack of grape-growing land in France's Champagne region. The region is famous for producing grapes ideal for the popular sparkling wine. Grape suppliers command premium prices. To remedy the shortage, Moët and other French champagne makers, such as Pommery et Greno and Laurent-Perrier, have bought suitable wineries and land in Australia, Spain, the United States, Latin America and elsewhere. However, the virtues of grapes grown in France versus those from other locations are argued. Some producers feel top-quality wine needs grapes from France's Champagne region, meaning area growers have much supplier power (Toy 1989).

The *threat of new entrants* is how easily new competitors can enter the same product or service market. New entrants add capacity and resources. Price wars and/or costs increase for existing businesses, and raise outlays (additional advertising, larger sales force, better service, etc.) to retain market position. Entry threat relates to how hard a market is to break into.

Barriers are high if starting a business needs large capital investments (as in the steel industry) or when economies of scale mean new entrants find it hard to start small and gradually build volume (as with television manufacturing). Barriers are high when competitors have products or services seen as unique (e.g. a brand-name perfume).

With high barriers, existing competitors will give new entrants a vigorous reaction, and threat of new entrants is low (Siler 1989). Where barriers are low and existing competitors will give new entrants a mild reaction, there is a high threat of new entrants and industry profit potential is low.

Threat of substitute products or services is how much other products can be substituted. For example, artificial sweeteners can substitute for sugar, electricity can substitute for gas in energy production, and paint can substitute for wallpaper. Available substitutes limit prices firms in an industry (such as the coffee industry) can charge, as price rises encourage customers to switch to substitutes (such as cola drinks) (Mathews 1994). Availability of substitute products or services lowers an industry's profit potential.

Organisational assessment

While SWOT analysis needs in-depth assessment of environmental opportunities and threats, it also needs evaluation of internal strengths and weaknesses. The resource-based strategic view is an approach to internal assessment, focused on evaluating organisational internal resources and competitive implications of its capabilities (Miller & Shamsie 1996; Barney 1995).

Organisational resources and capabilities include financial, physical, human and other assets for production of goods and services. Financial resources include debt, equity, retained earnings and related issues. Physical resources include buildings, machinery, vehicles and other material. Human resources include skills, abilities, experience and other work-related characteristics of people in the organisation. Organisational resources include group history, relationships, trust levels, and associated culture dimensions, as well as the formal reporting structure, control and compensation systems. This means staff selection becomes a crucial element in organisation success for firms such as Seek Communications (Roberts 2003a) who supply online employment advertising and staff provision in Australia.

To assess the competitive implications of resources and capabilities relative to their environments, organisations must question four major factors. These are critical to organisational ability to build competitive advantage using internal resources and capabilities.

The first critical factor is value. A resource or capability adds value to the extent it allows capitalisation on opportunities and/or nullification of threats. For example, Sony Corp. has specialised expertise in designing, manufacturing and marketing miniaturised electronic technology. Sony uses this expertise in many products, such as portable tape and portable disc players, and easy-to-handle video cameras, before competitors.

The second significant factor is rareness. A resource or capability is rare to the extent that it is uncommon among competitors. For example, Natural History New Zealand is a small television production company based in Dunedin, New Zealand. It is located in a geographical region that is home to one of the world's most important albatross colonies and many other sources of animal and bird wildlife. A knowledge of local conditions and access to these resources give the company a unique competitive advantage in making natural history documentaries for the international market. Typically a valuable competitor resource or capability is a source of competitive parity—that is, it is needed to match competitors on a given dimension. Partially because Sony maintains and builds expertise by large research and development spending, the depth of expertise is uncommon among competitors.

The third pivotal factor is degree of imitability. A resource or capability that is hard for competitors to duplicate or substitute has low imitability. When a competitor builds the same type of resources or capabilities as the organisation being imitated, duplication occurs. Substitution comes when an equivalent resource or capability no more costly to develop is created. While competitors can quickly reverse-engineer their new products and develop alternatives, Sony's ability to gain high profits by being first with a stream of innovative new products maintains the company's competitive advantage.

The fourth important factor is organisation. Organisational competitive advantage relies on the value of its resources and capabilities, rareness and imitability. Setting this competitive advantage up, however, means a firm must organise maximum usefulness of its resources and capabilities. Company components, such as formal reporting structures, control systems and reward systems, are complementary resources with limited ability to create competitive advantage. They can be merged with other resources and capabilities for maximum competitive advantage. Thus, Sony's collaboration across units which were expert in miniaturised electronic technology (such as tape recorders and earphones) helped leverage their expertise producing innovative products. As Sony moved into the digital era, the company had problems with organisational issues. It has struggled with competitive advantage by combining hardware expertise with a growing software-related entertainment empire including Sony Music Entertainment (formerly CBS Records) and Sony Pictures Entertainment (formerly Columbia Pictures) (Brull & Gross 1996).

Competitive advantage cannot be sustained solely through environmental-factor analysis and developing businesses with favourable competitive forces. Sustaining competitive advantage also needs valuable, rare and difficult-to-imitate resources and capabilities. A valuable, rare and difficult-to-imitate resource or capability is a **distinctive competence**. Factors using effective distinctive competencies are critical to build competitive advantage. (Note this resource-based strategic view connects to the resource dependence model in Chapter 3. The resource dependence model, though, aims to reduce environmental dependence by controlling critical resources. On the other hand, the resource-based strategic view emphasises a need to develop internal resources and capabilities to sustain competitive advantage. Thus the perspectives are complementary, helping managers focus on important issues of organisation resources and effectiveness.)

distinctive competence

Unique strength competitors cannot easily match or imitate

FORMULATING FUNCTIONAL-LEVEL STRATEGY

Functional-level strategies spell out how functional areas can bolster business-level strategy. For example, under a product differentiation strategy, an R&D department might accelerate innovation to provide new products before competitors. Similarly, to support new product lines, marketing might plan for premium prices, distribution in prestigious locations, and a special promotion scheme targeting market segments. Operations, being responsible for actual production, might build a functional strategy based on excellent raw materials, using the latest technology, and subcontracting some components to produce a premium product.

In essence, functional-level strategies can be important in support of business-level strategy. Functional areas typically develop distinctive competencies giving potential competitive advantages. Such competencies rarely just happen. They must be carefully conceived and may take a long time to develop.

STRATEGY IMPLEMENTATION

While strategy formulation is important to strategic management, strategies will not have the intended impact unless implementation is effective. Strategy implementation involves management activities to put the strategy in place, set up strategic controls to monitor progress, and ultimately achieve organisational goals (see Fig. 6.10).

Carrying out strategic plans

Galbraith and Kazanjian (1986) suggest several major internal aspects of an organisation may need synchronising to put a strategy into place. Principal factors (shown in Fig. 6.10) are technology, human resources, reward systems, decision processes and structure. Factors are interconnected, so changing one means changing others.

Technology

Technology is organisation knowledge, tools, equipment and work techniques used to deliver product or service. Technology is important to strategy implementation as technological emphasis must fit strategic thrust. Organisational strategy, at all levels, must consider the

FIGURE 6.10 The strategy-implementation phase of the strategic-management process

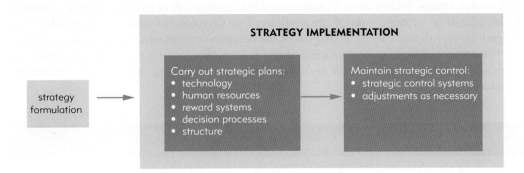

technical business functions. For example, if an organisation has a low-cost strategy, technology changes may help cut costs. A differentiation strategy may need technological change to develop and/or produce enhanced products or services. An example is the AirPork brand using rapid logistics and trading on the Asian market's perceptions of Australian produce as clean and uncontaminated (Roberts 2003b).

Human resources

Human resources are organisation staff. Having people with necessary skills in appropriate positions is a prerequisite for effective strategy implementation. This is managed by strategic human-resource planning, which links human-resource needs to strategies. As well, an organisation's human-resource skills and experience often provide competitive advantage.

A skilled workforce usually can reduce costs or produce new products or services better than less experienced staff. We discuss human resources in more detail in Chapter 10.

Reward systems

Reward systems include bonuses, awards or promotions, and intangible rewards such as personal achievement and challenge. Carefully developed reward systems are an important motivation source supporting a given strategy. We discuss motivational issues further in Chapter 11.

Decision processes

Decision processes include means of resolving questions and problems in organisations. Resource-allocation issues are important to strategy implementation as strategic plans are more successful when needed resources are available. Decision-making processes can help resolve specific problems and issues arising in implementing the plan. We discussed managerial decision making in Chapter 5.

Structure

Organisation structure is the formal interaction and coordination pattern that management designs to link individual and group tasks to achieve organisational goals. These patterns help organisation parts coordinate efforts. An organisation chart shows the organisation's broad outline. Research suggests strategies succeed when structure supports strategic direction. We discuss this further in Chapter 8.

MAINTAINING STRATEGIC CONTROL

In carrying out strategic plans many factors must be considered, and managers must monitor progress. They use strategic control to do so. This means monitoring critical environmental factors affecting strategic-plan viability, assessing the effects of organisational strategic actions, and ensuring strategic plans are implemented as intended. Instituting strategic control includes designing information systems providing feedback on how strategic plans are carried out, as well as their effects. Such systems let managers adjust strategic-plan implementation, as needed. Issues related to strategic control are considered in Chapters 15 and 16. Supplement 3 to chapter 16 investigates various management information systems used for strategic control.

The strategy implementation process, of which strategic control is part, requires change and innovation. In the next chapter, we give special attention to the basic elements of organisation structure.

GAINING THE EDGE

Coming back to call back

Some time ago, call-back centres were said to be doomed in Singapore. Today, thanks to technology advances and a partial lifting of advertising legislation, the business is poised to make an unprecedented boom. With International Direct Dial phone rates declining, it was envisaged that call-back operations were a dying enterprise. However, these organisations, which use computer technology to provide a cheaper alternative to IDD, are enjoying a new lease of life.

Advances in technology have lowered the barriers to entry, and a partial lifting of advertising restrictions by the Infocomm Development Authority of Singapore (IDA) are a boon to operators. With such a huge revenue potential, the process is relatively simple. The tools of the trade include a computer which must have a Pentium 111, 500 MHz chip, a PPMS or pre-paid, post-paid management

software which manages inbound and outbound calls and an ISDN card.

12U is one such operator in Singapore that started out with a base investment of S$100 000 which is expected to be returned within the year.

While such operations are legitimate, they are competing with SingTel but are unlikely to put a major dent in its annual IDD revenue.

Source: Written by Alexandra Hayes.

Activities for discussion, analysis and further research

1. Carry out some research on call-back centres and compare their rates with those of Telstra for IDD calls. In what ways are call centres a successful competitor to long-distance providers?
2. Would you consider them to be a threat? Why?

REFLECTIVE PRACTITIONER

One of the things that I have been very pleased with in our organisation is that from day dot, I have always put a strong emphasis on taking an approach to business planning, setting goals and then looking at really practical strategies to achieve those things. In business and in management, you can have those people who are visionaries and who are the strategic thinkers but not necessarily have the skills or abilities to make it happen and I think my management style very much sits middle of the road. I love the strategic thinking, I love the visionary side of the business that is so essential to growth. Certainly, I can cultivate new ideas, but one of the other strengths that is required is to calculate

what we need in order to cultivate the ideas into results and ultimately increased financial performance.

So how do we plan? In our business, we have actually got a structure and a hierarchy of business plans. We have established a number of different departments within the organisation. We have four departments—risk management, training, research and development and corporate services. So those four departments all actually have a business plan that is a structured yet relatively simple document that is reviewed on a monthly basis. At the beginning of the year, I will sit down with the sponsor of that business plan, which is normally the

KIMBERLEY TURNER

manager in charge of that area, and we will set targets. Going back to the decision-making style I was describing earlier, sometimes I will actually prescribe the targets and the objectives; at other times it will be more of a consultative approach and seeking the advice of that manager as to where they would like to take the aspect of that business. Those targets, goals and objectives are all fairly defined and are tangible and performance can be measured against that. Then it actually flows through. The company-wide business plan level, which is the strategic piece, flows down into the operational piece (department business plans) and reflects how we actually achieve our goals. The resource plan, the HR plan, the activity schedule, the professional development plan for the staff who fall within that department, the marketing approach, the sales strategy, the budget and the finance requirements are all detailed in the business plans. What's our reporting framework within that section? Some of the departments will have a reporting framework which will run right down to the weekly level and some will just report on a monthly basis depending on the scope and the size of that part of the company. With those four business plans, I then review them on a quarterly basis with

the sponsor. This review then provides the foundation for the revision and updating of the company plan and realignment of future direction if it is required. This process of establishing organisational goals and the relationship to the planning process continually flows up and down the company and is cognisant of market demands and trends. Overall progress of our actual achievement against the plans is reported back to my advisory board which includes my accountant, and a legal advisor and the two members of the executive team.

As a sole director there is no obligation or regulatory requirement for me to plan or report in that way, but I have chosen to do that to keep myself accountable. As I prepare each quarter for these reports, it a fantastic tool to assist in taking stock of where we have been, where we are and where we want to go. Reporting and refocusing is integral to effective business planning. It is a real reality check when you have to present your results to someone else who you have selected and opening yourself up and saying: 'This is the progress of the business and I am either happy or not happy about it and this is what I am going to do about it'. The structure we have established in our business planning goes out three to five years— obviously it's quite detailed for the first twelve months to three years and more general for the balance of the five years. That five-year glimpse looks at the general type of direction that we as a company would like to go in and captures our assessment of future markets.

One day some years ago in sorting out my office during the Christmas break, I found a one-page A4 piece of paper that had categories of things that I wanted the company to achieve. I sat back and just ticked the things off—work with this type of clients, do this type of work, run a conference, write a publication. It was quite rewarding to sit back and say that we have actually achieved all of those things. At this stage we had achieved all we had set out to do and the business plan had actually run out. It dawned on me at this time and I had to realise that this cycle of setting organisational goals and plans is an ongoing, reiterative process that evolves and develops. If you are determined, set goals and achieve them, and it should come as no surprise that you will need to repeat this process when you get to the end of one plan!

I had to learn not to be frightened to change and amend a plan. That is something that has been really important to us. If you are sitting back and realise that you have missed the mark, been too ambitious in setting goals, it's OK to change. I have tried to impart to my managers that instead of not achieving, let's change the goal posts, and that's OK. If this does need to occur, it needs to be done through a structured approach to ensure success next time and we learn from the lessons of that situation.

Sometimes that is driven by what the market dictates, not because the staff aren't performing, and it is crucial to take that into account. Sometimes the proportion of earnings that we forecast at the beginning of the year for various departments just doesn't come off because the market wants something different, and we need to adjust to that and take advantage of what is out there. Some of those things are outside our control and we need to realign the expectations in our planning. That needs to be communicated and resources need to be realigned accordingly.

Perception and reality are two different things. In starting up a company where you are the key subject-matter expert and everybody wants you, there is certainly still an element of perception that I am the company. However, from day one I actively tried to really profile our other staff to give them opportunity to give them profile within their own sphere of influence and their own area of expertise.

There are two kinds of staff within our company. Those who understand that the company is bigger than Kimberley Turner, and those who think the business is Kimberley Turner, and that really affects their behaviours and the way in which they conduct themselves at work. Those who understand that the company is bigger than me certainly step up to the mark and take on more responsibility and take ownership of their area because they believe in it as much as I do and see the results. Those who think the company is Kimberley Turner may actually hold back and wait for me to step in and to rectify or to pull the job over the line, because in their mind it's about me and not necessarily about them and their area. That is a big challenge in itself because it is not an effective utilisation of my resources if the work just continues to come back to me and is reliant on just one person within the company. One

of the tests for me has been to see if I can actually leave the business for four to six weeks and still have it tick over and function.

I went through that about five years ago and it became clear back then that the company was still reliant on myself. To overcome that I have looked on how I can formalise processes in the business so that it is not reliant on me and what is in my mind. Just finalising our accreditation of ISO 9000. Once we have that in place there is no reason why that manual set of processes cannot provide guidance to the staff on the how to. Providing confidence in our staff to the client that the staff can deliver as well if not better than I can is an area that I have been really focusing on. To a certain degree, it is really both embarrassing and rewarding to say 'I'm not really the best person for this job—however, one of my staff is. They have the expertise to provide a solution and support you much better than I can'. So we need to instil that confidence in our clients. I can do that quite effectively with staff who I trust and know can deliver the results.

The strategic management aspect of risk management is my assessment of where the industry is going and the decision of where we want to be positioned in order to capitalise on where the industry is going. I spend a lot of time in this area of my business. Because our company vision and statement is to really be the leaders in this field, we need to be not only at the forefront but we need to be predicting the direction and the future of the industry. The by-product of that is that our company's strategic planning will complement and fit nicely within that. So I take a role in various positions within the industry professional bodies. For instance, I am currently the chair of the education committee and the professional development committee for the Risk Management Institute of Australasia. In that role I've got the opportunity and ability to shape qualifications and licensing of the risk management discipline, to shape where the field is actually going as a profession. That provides me with the stimulation in the planning to say, 'OK, if that's where industry is going, how as a business can we now service that industry, or drive it, or lead it?' We tap that into the strategic planning for the company and it is very closely aligned with the profession and its directions.

I am constantly thinking three to five years out and beyond. We have some products and services that have been developed as a result of being linked with the strategic direction of industry and they're sitting on the shelf because industry is not ready for them. They're premature. We are at a stage where we have development that is about two to four years ahead of what people are ready for. Now, that's great but it means that resources have been spent in order to do that development and that has not already matched with the assessment of the market—the futuristic market but not necessarily where it's at right this moment. And that lag is actually shrinking in some aspects and growing in others. So that has an impact on the finances in that we need to consider how much we have in reserve in order to invest in the developmental side and the packaging of intellectual property. This means that we can stay ahead of the industry's needs and not get caught out when the time comes.

FOCUS ON PRACTICE

Strategies for improving

1. Reflect on some plans which you made and which did not get implemented. Why did that happen? In what ways were those plans no longer appropriate and how did you go about changing them?
2. Monitor the planning processes in your organisation at all levels and develop ways of rewarding managers who plan and implement processes to action those plans and review them.
3. Develop a process which will ensure a SWOT analysis is an automatic part of the planning process.
4. Develop a strategy to ensure your staff understand the difference between planning and strategic management.
5. Find an old strategy that was analysed and implemented. Discuss any cost–benefits analysis which may have been performed and repeat it with the present outcomes in mind. To what degree was the analysis correct? What might have been done to increase the accuracy levels?

Source: Jones et al. (2000).

SUMMARY

- The organisation's mission, goals and plans are the major components of the overall planning process. The mission is the organisation's purpose or fundamental reason for existence. The mission statement, a broad declaration of the basic, unique purpose and scope of operation separating the firm from others of its type, has several purposes. The statement can be a benchmark to measure success against; a way to define a common purpose, nurture loyalty and foster a sense of community among members; and a signal of values and future directions. A goal is a future target or end result an organisation wishes to achieve. A plan is a method for attempting to reach the goal.

- Goals have several potential benefits. They can increase performance, clarify expectations, facilitate the controlling function and help increase motivation. Organisations typically have three levels of goals: strategic, tactical and operational. These levels of goals can be conceptualised as a hierarchy of goals.

- Several key components help explain how goals facilitate performance. Goal content is one component. Goals should be challenging, attainable, specific and measurable, time-limited and relevant. Goal commitment is another key component. Commitment can be influenced positively by supervisory authority, peer and group pressure, public display of commitment, expectations of success, and incentives and rewards. Participation may also generate goal commitment. Work behaviour is a major component too. Goal content and goal commitment influence direction, effort, persistence and planning aspects of work behaviour. Other major components are job knowledge and ability, task complexity and situational limitations. Several potential goal-setting problems must be avoided.

- As there are levels of goals, plans also differ by organisation level. Thus there are strategic, tactical and operational plans. Plans can also be categorised by frequency of use. Single-use plans are used once and include programs and projects. Standing plans are used on a recurring basis and include policies, procedures and rules. Different goal and plan levels use different time horizons. Strategic goals and plans usually focus on long-range issues five years or more away, tactical goals and plans are aimed at intermediate-range issues one to five years in the future, and operational goals and plans to a year or less. Research suggests the planning process can help build innovation in several ways. These include phrasing the mission statement to signal the importance of innovation, setting goals with innovative outcomes, and developing loose plans that allow latitude in the innovation process or focus on innovative ways to reach goals. Managers must work to reduce or avoid several obstacles to plan development.

- Management by objectives includes the following steps: develop overall organisational goals; establish specific goals for various departments, subunits and individuals; formulate action plans; implement and maintain self-control; review progress periodically; and appraise performance. MBO has several strengths and weaknesses. Failures of MBO systems seem to stem from poor top-management support and goal-setting and communication skills among managers who implement the system.

- Strategic management is a process where managers formulate and implement strategies for optimising strategic-goal achievement. Strategy formulation is the part of strategic management including identifying mission and strategic goals, conducting competitive analysis and developing specific strategies. Strategy implementation is the part involving carrying out strategic plans and controlling how they are carried out. The overall process helps organisations identify and develop a competitive advantage, a significant edge over the competition.

- Before devising an effective strategy, managers must assess both environmental and organisational factors influencing an organisation's competitive ability. One method is SWOT analysis, which involves assessing organisational strengths (S), weaknesses (W), environmental opportunities (O) and threats (T). Porter's five competitive forces model helps analyse the nature of competition and its intensity in terms of five major forces: rivalry, bargaining power of customers, bargaining power

of suppliers, threat of new entrants and threat of substitute products or services. The resource-based strategic view helps organisations assess internal resources and capabilities in terms of value, rareness, imitability and organisation.
- At the business level, use of Porter's competitive strategies, including cost leadership, differentiation and focus strategies, is the best-known approach. Functional-level strategies specify major ways functional areas can bolster business-level strategy.

QUESTIONS FOR DISCUSSION AND REVIEW

1. Outline major components in the overall planning process. Give examples of these components in an organisation with which you are familiar.
2. Define the concept of organisational mission and explain a mission statement's purpose. Think of an organisation you would like to establish. What type of mission would you develop?
3. Outline major benefits of goals. Describe a situation in which you have observed these benefits.
4. Explain how goals and plans differ according to organisational level. Describe how goals and plans may be different at various management levels at your college or university.
5. Delineate several potential problems with goal setting. Discuss how two of these problems might apply in a familiar organisation (perhaps a campus organisation). What steps might you take to avoid such problems?
6. Explain various types of single-use and standing plans. Give an example of each type of plan at your college or university.
7. Explain the concept of strategic management and the notion of competitive advantage. Identify an organisation you think has a competitive advantage in its industry, and describe the nature of its advantage.
8. Outline major components of the strategic management process. Explain why engaging in strategic management will have organisational benefits.
9. Explain SWOT analysis. Conduct a brief SWOT analysis of your college or university by developing two items for each of the four SWOT categories.
10. Outline Porter's five competitive forces model. Use the model to assess the nature and intensity of competition in a familiar industry.
11. Explain how the resource-based strategic view can aid organisational assessment. Use the view to assess an organisation's resources and capabilities in the industry you analysed in the previous question.
12. Describe Porter's business-level competitive strategies. Assess the competitive strategy of a familiar organisation and explain its usefulness in dealing with Porter's five competitive forces.

CRITICAL THINKING QUESTIONS

To answer some of these questions you will need to do further research. Useful references are given below each section of the questions.

This chapter provided an overview of the overall planning process and explored how the process of setting goals facilitates organisational performance. The following questions extend the concepts of planning and goal-setting and briefly examine some of the interesting innovations occurring in the area.

Customer relationship management (CRM) is increasingly being touted as the secret to driving revenue growth, productivity and customer satisfaction. While success stories—such as Malaysian organisations the Genting Group, Hong Leong Bank and Malaysia National Insurance—are common, there are also those who run into problems ranging from cost overruns and integration challenges to poor user-acceptance. Just like any other planning process, successful CRM strategies need to be well designed and executed to produce a significant return on investment.

1. What do you think would be the critical success factors in the design and implementation of a CRM system?

(Material relevant to this question may be found in Chan, T. 2003, Ten steps to CRM success, *New Straits Times Press*, Malaysia, 7 May, p. 12.)

The issue of how to align individual employee performance with organisational goals is one where some innovative ideas often emerge. One example of this is the Max New York Life Insurance Ltd, which has implemented a Japanese technique termed 'Hoshin Kanri' matrix. The term 'Hoshin Kanri' simply means 'compass needle' and, in the business context, suggests that, just as a compass needle points precisely in the direction of the magnetic field, the Hoshin Kanri process will precisely break down an organisation's long-term strategy into yearly cumulative targets.

2. While the terminology may sound exotic, the principles behind the Hoshin Kanri matrix are likely to be familiar to any first-year management student in terms of implementation. Given this, how do you think the matrix would be implemented in an organisation such as Max New York Life Insurance Ltd?

3. While the idea of setting out and selecting goals may sound fairly self-explanatory, there are clearly a number of important parameters included in the Hoshin Kanri philosophy which significantly add to organisational success. What do you think they might be?

Max New York Life Insurance believes that the Hoshin Kanri technique has led to the development and implementation of a clear business program. Further, in terms of people management, the technique has enabled the organisation to align functions to strategic goals while very visibly defining accountability to all employees within the strategic chain. Hoshin Kanri thus appears to have the ability to help organisations define realistic, measurable goals that can be attained while driving business forward.

(Material relevant to questions 2 and 3 may be found in Anon. 2003, 'Pointing a new way to organisational goals', Global News Wire—Asia Africa Intelligence Wire, 27 January.)

According to Kenny (2003, p. 43), the word 'strategy' is overused, misused and misunderstood but he also argues that it is important managers answer the question: 'What really is competitive strategy?'.

4. Why is this question so important?

5. What actually is competitive advantage?

6. What is the value for an organisation in taking the different approach suggested by Kenny?

David Jones is household name with 35 department stores across Australia and is probably best summed up in the public's mind as the 'quality' department store. It is also highly likely most would view David Jones's last five years as a story of mixed success. On one hand is its department store success, but this is nearly overshadowed by its Foodchain and online website failures. Competitive strategy and strategic factors can be used to explain both how the department store got it right and how Foodchain got it wrong.

7. What do you think the strategic factors of the success of David Jones's department stores would be?

Peter Wilkinson, David Jones's CEO until 2002, revealed the influence Porter has had on their strategy as the key question the management team asked was whether they should differentiate themselves on the strategic factor of price, product range or customer service and whether it should be a broad target market or a narrow one. While David Jones's core business clearly got this right, the Foodchain arm did not.

Foodchain was established in 1999 as part of a strategy to achieve growth as well as provide a buffer against the cyclical nature of department-store retailing. The stores were developed as standalone gourmet food outlets in Australia's major capital cities, and by 18 September 2002 David Jones had to write down $19.5 million on Foodchain (*Sydney Morning Herald*, weekend edition, 21–2 September 2002, cited in Kenny 2003).

8. With the traditional nature of David Jones customers in mind, why do you think Foodchain failed to reach potential?

(Material relevant to questions 4 to 8 may be found in Kenny, G. 2003, Strategy burnout and how to avoid it, *New Zealand Management*, August, p. 43.)

MANAGEMENT EXERCISES

Exercise 1 Skill building: What type of goal is it?

You are reviewing goals for the chain of ice-cream stores your family operates across several suburbs. You are aware of levels of goals used by organisations. Today you want to classify these goals according to the normal hierarchy:

What type of goal is it?

1 = strategic

2 = tactical

3 = operational

Classify the following:

_____	1.	Increase sales at least 18 per cent each year for the next two years.
_____	2.	Reduce staff turnover to 10 per cent in all stores during the next financial year.
_____	3.	During the next five years 40 per cent of revenues will come from our brand of products.
_____	4.	Improve customer service 15 per cent in all stores in the region.
_____	5.	Increase visibility of stores in the region.
_____	6.	Decrease shrinkage to 5 per cent in store X.
_____	7.	Achieve minimum stock turnover ratio of once each month at all stores within two years.
_____	8.	Remodel store Y by April.
_____	9.	In five years be the ice-cream/frozen yoghurt industry leader in these suburbs.
_____	10.	Achieve profits equal to $2000 monthly per employee in all stores this fiscal year.

Exercise 2 Management exercise: Developing a strategy for a country school, NSW

You are an extremely successful restaurant manager. It is your ambition to eventually open up a restaurant of your own, but you do not have the necessary funds to do so. It has come to your attention the state government is in the process of closing some small country schools and selling the buildings. One of the schools for sale is one you attended as a young student. You are excited by the prospect that you might, by entering into a partnership with some of your old classmates, purchase the property and develop it in some way.

The school has six large classrooms, three offices and a medium-sized all-purpose room. The property also has a two-bedroom timber house on the grounds. You have had dinner with a group of your old classmates and some have indicated a willingness to participate in a joint venture if you could demonstrate some gain for them in doing so.

1. Jillian is a general practitioner working in a clinic in a harbourside suburb of Sydney who believes in holistic, preventative medicine. She would be able to invest approximately 20 per cent of the funds required to buy the property. Her comments indicate she might be persuaded to get involved beyond a simple investment.

2. Eric is a primary-school teacher at a large school in Wollongong. He thinks back fondly to the days of small schools and small classes and has indicated he is able to invest about 10 per cent of funds required to buy the property.

3. David is an accountant with a flair for giving his clients advice on creative business ventures. He does not wish to be directly involved in the enterprise but would be willing to assist in the development of it.

4. Joyce and Erica are sisters who own and operate two very successful beauty salons on Sydney's North Shore. They don't know how they could be of use but are willing to invest time and effort if it's appropriate as they do not have any funds available at the moment.

You can raise about 50 per cent of the purchase price yourself and really want to have a go at something. Develop a grand strategy for developing the school property and use a portfolio-strategy approach to analyse various business alternatives. Then use Porter's generic strategies to choose a strategy for each alternative you develop. Be prepared to explain the reasoning behind your choices.

END-OF-CHAPTER CASE: ON THE RIM

Strategy or strategic planning

What is 'strategy'? Is this different from 'strategic planning'? The following story may help address these questions.

There was a business called GoAhead Enterprises that made miniature metal toys. They had a strong national brand and had built up a very good manufacturing plant located in a small rural community. A reasonably loyal workforce, a good range of skills and quality manufacturing equipment had been accumulated over the years. The business was profitable, but a range of cheaper, inferior imported toys had become available and the marketplace was increasingly competitive. GoAhead was inevitably forced to cut margins to stay competitive.

One morning the managers were sitting around with coffee discussing what they should do about the changing landscape of the marketplace. Joe, who was skimming through *Business News*, saw an advertisement for a seminar on improving business profitability. 'Maybe we should go to this seminar,' said Joe. 'It's been a while since we introduced any new thinking around here.' 'Maybe it's time for a change', mused Phil, the accountant. 'Wouldn't hurt', said Bruce. 'It'd be a chance to have a change of scenery for a while. We'll do it!' he said decisively. 'Joe, can you get Susie to arrange for the four of us to go? At the same time we may as well make a night of it so book us into the Central while you're at it.'

Four weeks later, Joe, Phil, Wayne and Bruce seated themselves at the front table in the seminar and eagerly waited to hear how to improve their business profitability. On the table was a blank sheet of butcher's paper and a black felt pen. The presenter, Mike, got up and asked them to write

POWERWEB

International articles related to this topic are available at the Online Learning Centre at **www.mhhe.com/au/bartol4e**

down on the paper what they thought they were in business for.

'To make money of course!' muttered Bruce. When the tables all displayed their signs, this was a common response. 'So what are you doing about it?' asked Mike. 'Or more importantly, what should you being doing about it!' Mike raised his voice slowly. They were hooked. 'I think we're on to a winner here', Wayne said enthusiastically.

Mike paused for a moment. Then, squaring his shoulders, he proceeded straight into his presentation. 'Well, first we must ask ourselves this question. What business are we in?' And so the morning proceeded. Mike showed videos and tools for them to use to undertake their own strategic planning process, to analyse the external environment and to develop their strategy for increasing profitability.

That afternoon, filled with enthusiasm, the four of them scratched out a framework for the future success of GoAhead Enterprises. They identified their goals and did an initial SWOT analysis. They quickly lost track of the time. 'Let's continue this tomorrow when we've got access to all the costs', said Phil, looking anxiously at his watch. 'Yeah, I agree with Phil', Wayne quickly replied. 'This has been thirsty work!' he quickly added, eyeing up the minibar. 'Okay! I get the hint', said Bruce, standing up and stretching. 'But I wouldn't like to lose the momentum we've had today. Let's break and we'll use the next couple of days to really work out where we're heading.'

And the result? GoAhead Enterprises wound down their manufacturing operation and Wayne, Bruce, and Joe moved their offices to The Big City to market the metal toys they now sourced from overseas manufacturers. The workforce was reduced from 85 to 12. Sales volumes remained static; Bruce was looking around for a buyer for the plant left at the factory. They were making money. And the future looked full of roses. Until the situation changed . . .

What is the point of this story?

Often the implicitly assumed objective in any business strategy is to deliver sustained, superior performance. To outperform its rivals, a firm must be—and remain—different from its competitors. Because similar firms in the same industry perform in the same way, a sustainable, competitive advantage requires some form of differentiation.

In formulating strategy the resources and capabilities of a firm should be the central considerations. They are the primary sources of the firm's profitability. The key to strategy formulation is understanding the relationships between resources, capabilities, competitive advantage and profitability. Sustaining a competitive advantage requires an understanding of the mechanisms by which the firm's unique characteristics can be exploited to maximum effect.

The power of manufacturing to create competitive advantage is now broadly understood. Manufacturing has the potential to create difficult-to-imitate and competitively significant capabilities. What GoAhead Enterprises failed to understand was that by closing down their manufacturing capability they were giving up their complexity. They became merely a marketing and distribution company, and therefore easier to imitate. By reducing their workforce they had also altered the marketplace. But that's another story.

Source: Contributed by Ross Milne.

Website:

One of the authors mentioned in question 4 below has a website: www.decisionprocesses.com/ associated with strategy and strategic thinking. If you are interested in researching this topic further this is a good place to start.

Activities for discussion, analysis and further research

1. Go Ahead Enterprises changed from being a manufacturer to a marketer of metal toys. Initially this change was successful. Unfortunately the situation changed. What do you think induced this change? Discuss this from both the environmental and the organisational perspective.
2. In the case study it is suggested that the objective of business strategy should be to deliver 'sustained, superior performance'. What does this mean?
3. You are interested in starting your own business. Many small businesses do not survive. What would you do to ensure that you could reduce the risk of this happening to you?
4. McGraw–Hill publish many good business books about strategy by such authors as Kenichi Ohmae and Michel Robert. Visit the McGraw-Hill website: www.mcgraw-hill.com/ and find out what is available.

FURTHER READING

Idris, F., Abdullah, M., Idris, M.A. and Hussain, N. 2003, Integrating resource-based view and stakeholder theory in developing the Malaysian excellence model: A conceptual framework, *Singapore Management Review*, 2nd Half, 25, 2, pp. 91–110.

Murray, J. 2003, Engines in the Orient, *Aircraft Economics*, November/December, 72, pp.18–22.

Pan, F., & and Zhang, Z. 2004, Cross-cultural challenges when doing business in China, *Singapore Management Review*, 1st Half, 26, 1, pp. 81–91.

Young, I. 2003, Chemical industry drives recovery in Singapore, *Chemical Week*, 7/30, 165, 27, pp. 31–3.

Young, S. 2003, Hot on the trail, *NZ Marketing Magazine*, October, 22, 9, pp. 32–7.

CHAPTER 7

FOSTERING AN INNOVATIVE ORGANISATION

CHAPTER OUTLINE

The nature of change and innovation
Distinguishing between change and
   innovation
Forces for change and innovation

Organisational life cycles
Four life-cycle stages
Organisational termination

**The change management and innovation
   process**
An eight-step model
Organisational development
Innovation for competitive advantage
Product development principles
Intrapreneurship

Key organisational change components
Structural components
Technological components
Human resource components
Cultural components
Interrelationship among components

LEARNING OBJECTIVES

After studying this chapter, you should be able to:

- Distinguish change from innovation and identify major forces for change and
  innovation.
- Enumerate four organisational life-cycle stages and discuss revitalisation and
  termination.
- Explain the eight-step change and innovation model.
- Explain the meaning of organisational development and techniques used in
  interventions.
- Specify four factors needed to link innovation and competitive advantage.
- Describe common aspects of intrapreneurs and factors inducing them to pursue new
  ideas in established organisations.
- Outline key organisational components usually needing to be altered in implementing
  major changes and innovations.

STRIVING FOR EXCELLENCE

Success is skin deep: Dennis Paphitis

In 1987, Dennis Paphitis was running a hair salon in the Melbourne suburb of Armadale. He was unhappy with the hair products available, so he started looking into the potential of developing his own natural range. Using capital from his salon, Paphitis found a laboratory in Los Angeles to develop a gentle scalp-cleansing shampoo that was an instant hit with clients. Based on essential oils and sold in amber bottles, the shampoo became a best-seller.

From there the Aesop range evolved, gathering a strong following. Soon, David Jones and other retailers began stocking Aesop products. Paphitis found himself re-invented as an entrepreneur with international demand for his products.

In 1991, Paphitis sold the salon to concentrate on the Aesop business, which has enjoyed 30 per cent average annual growth since its inception. The Aesop brand now includes 50 hair and skin products stocked in 200 outlets globally, and estimated sales of $15 million in 2002/03. Exports account for 60 per cent of turnover. 'Offshore retailers sought us out; this has not been an engineered strategy on our part', Paphitis says.

Aesop has become a cult brand, its reputation built on word-of-mouth, editorial coverage and prestige stockists. Carefully chosen outlets such as Colette in Paris and Luisa in Florence (which previously had not sold skin-care products) reinforce Aesop's status. Paphitis understands the mentality of the customer attracted to such places: 'To a large degree, it is our irreverence towards conventional cosmetic-industry approaches that makes Aesop desirable to our customers.'

Paphitis forecasts growth of 40 per cent for the privately held company in 2004, boosted by the opening in December of the first two Aesop retail stores, in Melbourne. There are plans to open stores over the next year in Hong Kong, Taipei, Sydney and Singapore. Paphitis says the signature stores will add another dimension to Aesop, giving the retailer total control over the shopping experience. Better access to customer feedback is a motive too, and Paphitis recognises the advantages that a retail outlet offers for communicating with customers and monitoring product sales in specific areas.

Paphitis, who averages 10 overseas trips a year, regards travel as a privilege rather than a necessary evil. 'The world informs what you do', he says. At the same time, Paphitis recognises a creative advantage from Australia's geographic isolation. 'It pushes people further. Everything can be explored from a completely different perspective.'

Stockists hold Paphitis in high esteem, remarking upon his sense of aesthetics and left-of-centre creativity. The Aesop range now includes a best-selling dog shampoo and an outrageously opulent ointment that retails for $42 500. A shaving cream made of Moroccan neroli oil and a fragrance will be launched later this year.

Andrea Birnie, the director of the leading Melbourne cosmetics retailer Kleins Perfumery, has stocked Aesop since 1995, and says it is her leading line. Birnie jokingly calls Aesop 'the new Vegemite' because of the high number of mail orders from

continued

Australians overseas craving their special fix from Aesop's dark glass jars.

The understated Paphitis maintains a low profile, working from Aesop's headquarters in inner-city Melbourne. Each product that leaves the on-site warehouse is individually inspected. 'Controlled and planned growth is what we're about', Paphitis says. 'Every gesture is a long-term one, every decision a thoroughly evaluated one.'

Source: Ross 2003.

In this chapter, we consider the nature of change and innovation, including major forces on organisations to change. We examine effects of organisational life cycles on the need for change and innovation management. We also consider the process of change and innovation management, and consider how innovation can build competitive advantage. We then outline key organisational components useful in change implementation.

THE NATURE OF CHANGE AND INNOVATION

Increasingly fierce domestic and foreign competition emphasises organisational innovation and change (*Business Week* 1984; Jones et al. 2000). The video cassette recorder (VCR), for example, which US manufacturers did not develop into a successful product, was designed by US companies Ampex and RCA in the 1960s. Japanese companies eventually succeeded, monopolising the entire VCR market (Resberger 1987). Events such as this have driven change and innovation. In this section, we look closely at these concepts, and consider major forces pressuring change and innovation in organisations.

Distinguishing between change and innovation

change

Any alteration of the status quo

innovation

New idea applied to initiating or improving a process, product or service

It is useful, in considering change and innovation, to differentiate the two terms. **Change** is an alteration to the status quo, while **innovation** is more specialised. Innovation is a new idea used in initiating or improving a process, product or service (Kanter 1983; Ihrcke 2000). So long as those involved see an idea as new, it is considered to be an innovation, though outside observers may think it already exists elsewhere (Zaltman, Duncan & Holbek 1973; Van de Ven 1986). All innovations imply change; but not all change is innovation, since some changes may not use new ideas or be major improvements—and may cause problems (for example, storm damage to a factory).

Innovations encompass radical breakthroughs (laser technology) and small improvements (a better computer-printer paper tray). Both are valuable (Gersick 1991). Japanese companies are known for product and service enhancements with a series of small, incremental changes. For example, at Matsushita Electric Industrial Company, 100 technicians, PhD scientists and factory engineers spent eight years on a lens for projection televisions and laser-based products, including video disc systems and compact disc players. The new lenses were 90 per cent cheaper than existing ones. So a modest goal—improving a component—led to Matsushita's lenses gaining market share, particularly in compact disc players (Gross 1989).

Innovation combines particular features, as management guru Rosabeth Moss Kanter notes. For one, innovation includes uncertainty, as progress and results may be hard to predict. For another, it is knowledge-intensive, at least during development, as parties to the innovation may have

most situational knowledge. Still another feature is that innovation can be controversial, as resources for innovation could be used elsewhere. Finally, innovation may cross boundaries, as development and implementation often involve more than one business unit, increasing complexity. So managers must understand the major aspects of change and plan for the special needs of the innovation process (Sinclair 2003; McCallum 2003).

Competitive pressure changes, global and domestic, demand nimble innovative organisations. This means organisations must use change management—where managers make organisations more proactive in changing and innovating for competitive advantage. Throughout this chapter, we use the word 'change' to indicate an alteration to the organisational status quo, including an innovation. 'Innovation' is used more narrowly as a new idea for improvement.

Forces for change and innovation

Many forces influence change and innovation in organisations. Some stem from external factors, while others stem from factors largely within organisations.

External forces

Organisations' external forces drive a need for change and innovation (see Chapter 3's discussion of environment). For example, insurance companies must consolidate and innovate faster due to many forces—from earthquakes and hurricanes, to greater government regulation and competition. One response to these forces is to increase employees' flexibility in their work. Technology has enabled this change, and some field representatives now work from home with company-supplied laptops, fax machines and mobile phones (Funk 1996). In another case Austrade is developing alliances to raise the number of small and medium-sized firms moving to export. These alliances include accounting firms, law firms and banks (Andrews 2004). Thus, while external forces can lead to undesirable organisation change, the application of innovative ideas may occur to improve the outcome of change (Haveman 1992; Bateman & Snell 2004).

Internal forces

Many forces lead to internal change and innovation. Forces include strategy and planned changes, ethical difficulties with employee behaviours, change and innovation decisions, culture shifts, restructures, technological and leadership changes (Machan 1991; Ihrcke 2000). Anchor Foods, a venerable West Australian company, is working to move its image from an old fashioned firm to more modern perceptions. Its perception problems have emerged since management and ownership changes focused more attention on its operations. So new packaging, systems and visibility are needed to lift its image (Tredgold 2004d). Successful firms have workers open to new and varied ideas, a clear vision of the future, permission to take risks and be unconventional (see Fig. 7.1).

Of course, many internal changes come from environmental factors. Some needs for internal change for organisations are predictable, as they follow certain life cycles.

ORGANISATIONAL LIFE CYCLES

Life cycles are typical stages of organisation development. Evolving through each stage requires organisation change to survive and grow. Otherwise, **organisational termination**, or ceasing to exist in an identifiable way, may occur.

life cycles

Predictable stages of development organisations typically follow

organisational termination

Process of ceasing to exist as an identifiable organisation

FIGURE 7.1 Cultural barriers (Ihrcke 2000, p. 14; Droege & Co. AG).

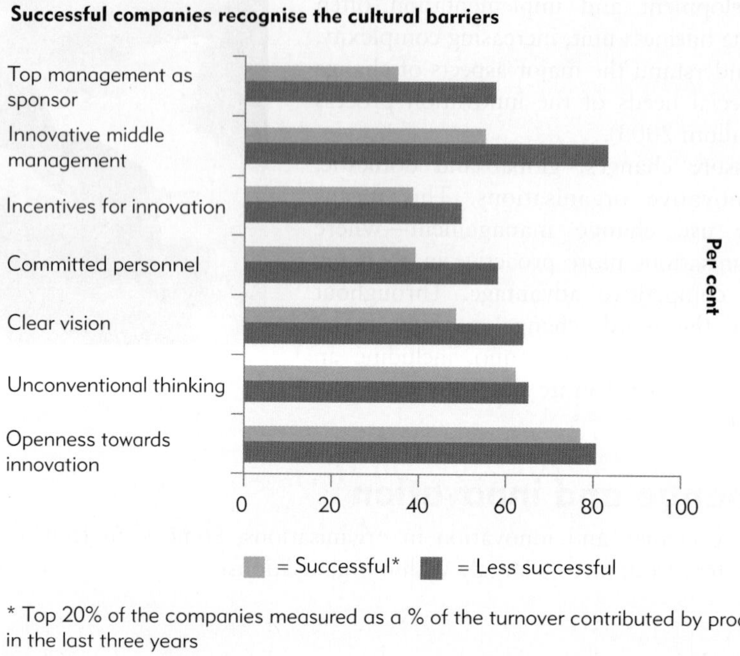

Successful companies recognise the cultural barriers

* Top 20% of the companies measured as a % of the turnover contributed by products introduced in the last three years

Company terminations are common. Many businesses fail in their first five years. Thinking about your local shopping centre or business district, you could name several firms which started then failed.

Four life-cycle stages

Organisations move through four stages (Siler & Atchison 1991). Table 7.1 shows the stages and their characteristics. Each needs operating-method changes for survival and prosperity. Oddly, unless managers plan for and encourage innovation, these same changes may well stop further innovation. Figure 7.2 shows the potential impact of the four life-cycle stages on innovation.

Entrepreneurial stage

In the entrepreneurial stage, a new firm is created, supporting an invention or innovation. It is formed from a single individual's initiative and is a one-person show, though others may be involved. Since the organisation is in its infancy, little planning and coordination occur. Decisions are made by the prime inventor, or entrepreneur. It is non-bureaucratic (Kinicki & Williams 2003).

Needing resources without them being readily available, such as a shortage of cash, usually results in a crisis. Then the entrepreneurial enterprise fails or moves to the next stage. For example, Howard Head, metals expert, ski enthusiast and Head ski inventor, worked for three years to develop a metal ski. Ski professionals were acutely sceptical of his attempts, often returning from the ski slopes with mangled skis. When the firm ran out of money, he had a resource crisis. Investor funds saved the company in return for 40 per cent ownership. Perfecting the design took a few more years, and the skis were so good they were called 'cheaters' (Quinn 1979). Involving investors and helpers took the Head company to the next development stage.

TABLE 7.1   CHARACTERISTICS ASSOCIATED WITH THE FOUR LIFE-CYCLE STAGES

Characteristic	Entrepreneurial stage	Collectivity stage	Formalisation and control stage	Elaboration of structure stage
Structure	Little or none	Informal	Functional; centralisation	Self-contained; decentralisation
Focus	Survival; seeking resources	Growth	Efficiency; coordination	Restructuring
Innovation	Invention	Enhancement	Implementation	Renewal
Planning	Little or none	Short range	Long range	Long range; opportunistic
Commitment	Individual sense	Group sense	Complacency	Recommitment
Managers	Entrepreneurs	Entrepreneurs and early joiners	Professional managers	Professional managers and orchestrators

Source: Based on Greiner (1972) and Quinn & Cameron (1983).

FIGURE 7.2 Potential effects of the four life-cycle stages on innovation

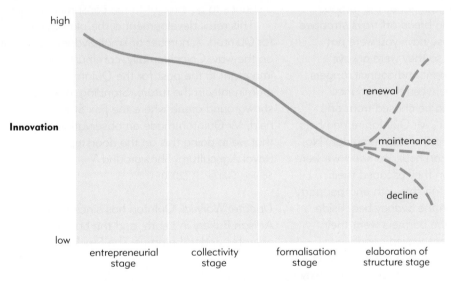

Collectivity stage

At the collectivity stage, others believers join the entrepreneur. The organisation has a youthful and energetic characteristic. Group identification and a sense of mission is strong. Members work long hours, show high levels of commitment, often getting relatively worthless, as yet, stock or shares in the company. But better days are to come. Structure and communication are informal; the group takes part in major decisions. Innovation is still high.

Increasing growth leads to a crisis and informal management systems lead to poor leadership and control. The entrepreneur is often not suited in temper or ability to manage a bigger firm, so they use professional managers. To be Apple's president, John Sculley came from

Dough innovations

When you take a business from an apartment in Sydney's eastern suburbs to a mountain location employing 26, you would suspect that the owners are really rolling in dough. Warwick Quinton literally is rolling dough, with a bread-making business that consumes three-and-a-half tonnes of flour a week and has an annual turnover of almost $1.5 million.

Not bad for someone who got into baking bread simply because he kept telling friends that he made better bread in his Waverley flat than you could find in the shops.

'Dallas bread was one of the first well-accepted organic breads people were buying', Mr Quinton said. 'But I kept telling friends that I made better. So, they said put your money where your mouth is.'

In his early days in the late 1980s he and his wife Vanessa used to run the gauntlet at the famous Paddington Markets selling bread off trays strapped around their necks. In those days you were not allowed to sell food there so they were always evading market management and council rangers. 'In fact, the markets sit between three council boundaries and we used to be chased from one council area into the other', Mr Quinton remembers.

Was this difficult start rather discouraging? 'No, after selling 120 loaves in an hour, we knew we were in the right business.' Soon they escaped their apartment, going into partnership with another party to run Heaven's Leaven in the Sydney beachside suburb of Clovelly. After the partners went their separate ways, the Quintons waved goodbye to Sydney to head up to the Blue Mountains to start Quintons' Bakery Café at Leura, a town on the way to a tourist revival.

'Six years ago when we opened up as a bakery and café there were five food places in Leura and now there are 35', Quinton explained. When asked about the reason for their success, this self-taught baker thought it was his desire to combine his love of organic bread and gourmet food to produce a more consumer-friendly product. 'When I started there were a lot of farmers with organic grain who were dying to supply bakeries but there wasn't the volume', he said.

'I suggested to some of them that they should mill a lighter flour and that has made the difference to the bread I make.' Two of his bakers are from Switzerland and Germany and together with the Quintons, they have produced a bread with a 'Euro–San Francisco' taste.

His latest innovation is to join up with people he hails as some of the best producers in NSW to supply produce for the Growers Market at Fox Studios. 'It's a very competitive market with specialty small retailers and restaurants as key customers—but you can be knocked off by new producers, so the markets give us a chance to go straight to the consumer', he said.

This retail development is the plan of the future for Quinton. A number of small Sydney outlets are on the way. Coincidentally, communal markets were important in the past for the Quintons and will figure prominently in the future. Standing in the old showground arena where the Fox Studio markets are held, Mr Quinton made an observation: 'It's ironic that we're doing this on the doorstep of the old Royal Agricultural Showground.'

Source: Switzer, P. (2000).

Update: Warwick Quinton has since sold Quinton's Artisan Bakery in Leura, and the business now operates under the name The Stockmarket Café.

Activities for discussion, analysis and further research

1. Identify the innovations the Quintons have come up with.
2. How have the Quintons managed their innovative processes?
3. Make suggestions for their next set of innovations.

Pepsi-Cola because Apple's cofounder, Stephen Jobs, felt the company's problems were better handled by an experienced manager rather than doing it himself. Jobs was subsequently fired from his then position as executive vice-president of Macintosh (Apple became Macintosh) two years later by Sculley, after delays and development problems (Uttal 1985).

Formalisation and control stage

Next the organisation's structure becomes more formal. Departments are organised into major specialisation areas such as finance, manufacturing or marketing. Efficiency and market-share maintenance is emphasised. To coordinate, rules and procedures are established and control is centralised. With the company moving to adulthood, this stage helps it consolidate, improve direction and grow further. A conservative stance replaces innovation, deterring risk taking and more innovation. As growth continues, coordination becomes harder.

In this stage, competitive challenges, technological change and other factors increase the information-processing needs, slowing responses. A crisis comes when members are tied by red tape and centralised control. Levi Strauss, for example, did so well they could not meet demand for their product. However, growth period procedures meant the jeans giant reacted slowly to the changes in the jeans market and a move to more fashionable options. One former employee said they had 'enough staff and organisation to run General Motors' (*Business Week* 1983, p. 56). Now, an organisation is ready for the next stage.

Elaboration-of-structure stage

At the elaboration-of-structure stage, managers streamline bureaucratisation from the formalisation and control stage. Decision making is decentralised, often set round specific products or services. Coordinating individuals at similar levels in different work units is emphasised. This requires temporary or continuing groups for cross-departmental issues (discussed in Chapter 15). In the structure change, managers try to cut costs, re-emphasising promising strategic options.

The chief point of the elaboration-of-structure stage efforts is **revitalisation**, or the renewal of the organisation's innovative vigour (Galbraith 1982). Not all try or succeed at revitalisation. Stabilisation and maintenance may be fleeting. Others decline, despite this, and still fail (Gray & Ariss 1985). These organisations may suffer dysfunctions, becoming less manageable (Cameron et al. 1987). Table 7.2 explains these dysfunctions, which can make renewal and revitalisation harder.

revitalisation

Renewal of innovative vigour of organisations

Organisational termination

Recently we have seen the termination of many organisations. These business failures occur when firms have problems then stop operating as discrete entities. Termination occurs for many reasons (see Table 7.3).

TABLE 7.2 DYSFUNCTIONAL CONSEQUENCES OF ORGANISATIONAL STABILISATION AND DECLINE	
Consequence	**Explanation**
Curtailed innovation	No experimentation is conducted; risk aversion is prevalent and scepticism exists about activities unrelated specifically to current major directions.
Scapegoating	Leaders are blamed for pain and uncertainty.
Resistance to change	Conservatism and turf protection lead to rejecting new alternatives.
Turnover	The most competent leaders tend to leave first, causing leadership anaemia.
Conflict	Competition and infighting for control predominates where resources are scarce.

Source: Adapted from Cameron, Whetten & Kim (1987).

TABLE 7.3 METHODS OF ORGANISATIONAL TERMINATION	
Bankruptcy	An organisation unable to pay its debts can seek protection from creditors while it tries to regain financial stability; if the problems continue, its assets will be sold in order to settle debts with creditors.
Liquidation	The sale or dissolution of an entire organisation for reasons associated with serious business difficulties and seemingly insurmountable obstacles.
Merger	The combining of two or more organisations into one.
Acquisition	The purchase of all or part of one organisation by another.
Take-over	The purchase of a controlling share of voting stock in a publicly traded company.

Organisations terminate when they cannot innovate and change quickly enough. Termination can happen at any life-cycle stage. Managers must consider where in the life cycle their organisation is. This determines the changes needed to move the firm to the next development stage.

THE CHANGE MANAGEMENT AND INNOVATION PROCESS

reactive change

Change occurring when one takes action in response to perceived problems, threats or opportunities

Change management and innovation involving major new ideas are hard. Managers face two change types. **Reactive change** is when action is taken in response to perceived problems, threats or opportunities. As one is reacting, the situation is hard to properly assess and a considered response difficult to develop. In the early 1980s, Johnson & Johnson for example had seven people die after taking cyanide-laced Extra-Strength Tylenol capsules. Thirty-one million bottles of pain reliever were recalled at a cost of $100 million. Then, after losing market-share, J&J raised advertising over 30 per cent. The company's market share almost returned to normal, in 'one of the greatest marketing feats in our industry' (*Business Week* 1984, p. 137). The Tylenol story shows managers cannot anticipate every problem and events may force a reaction.

planned change

Change involving actions based on a carefully thought-out process anticipating future difficulties, threats and opportunities

However, situations may allow **planned change**, involving actions based on a carefully crafted process anticipating possible difficulties, threats and opportunities. For example, although the Tylenol crisis was hoped to be an isolated incident, J&J changed to using a tamper-resistant container. Four years later, after another death from a cyanide-laced Tylenol capsule, J&J showed they anticipated another crisis. Chairman James E. Burke was on television almost at once, announcing abandonment of the capsule, and a move to a capsule-shaped tablet he called a 'caplet', and showing a large model caplet. The decision cost millions of dollars and the company's offer to replace all capsules with caplets a further $150 million. The speed and forthrightness of action showed J&J's managers had planned for another crisis and developed an action plan, including implementation (Siwolop & Ekhund 1986). Although clearly not all issues can be planned for, as some union organisers found in the West Australian Pilbara region (Way 2003a). Rio Tinto drove a wedge through a joint union strategy by moving to be covered by more managerially-friendly federal industrial legislation and reaching a pre-emptive agreement with the most accommodating of the four allied union groups.

When managers operate reactively, the chances of serious mistakes increase, as changes are made without proper planning. Effective managers engage in planned, or managed, change and innovation when possible.

An eight-step model

Managers will achieve change and innovation more effectively if they follow the process outlined in Figure 7.3 (Kotter 1995; Zaltman et al. 1973; Maidique 1980). The process has eight basic steps.

1. **Gain recognition of an opportunity or a problem.** Major changes and innovations begin when someone sees a problem situation or an opportunity. Problems are easy to see when things go poorly. For example, when IBM spun its printer operations off, everyone saw the business had been doing poorly and change was needed (Flanagan 1994). When Roberto Goizueta became Coca-Cola's CEO, the firm seemed to be succeeding. Goizueta found its fountains business (retail outlet sales, like McDonald's, use systems called fountains to dispense Coca-Cola) was earning below the cost of capital (running at a loss). He got managers to look at returns from other company parts. They too, were losing money. Goizueta says a company-wide belief that the soft-drink industry was mature meant managers overlooked growth options (*Fortune* 1995). It was easy to miss opportunities for other drink products, such as bottled spring water.

   Peter Drucker argues managers may not be innovative due to the tendency to look at immediate problems and ignore opportunities. Drucker has strategies for raising awareness and changing the focus to opportunities. He notes managers in most firms expect a monthly operations report. Typically, the first page shows areas where performance is not as expected. Drucker (1985) suggests a second 'first page' be added listing things that are better than expected, and identifying possibilities. Another of Drucker's ideas is to have three or four managers report a couple of times each year on entrepreneurial activities going well that others might adopt.

2. **Line up powerful sponsor(s).** Change and innovation need powerful individuals' support to get needed resources and influence others for support. Major renewals need several sponsors in coalition.

3. **Develop and communicate a vision.** To achieve change and innovation, it is important to develop a picture of the future that is easy to communicate and appealing to those who must change or support the process (Ettorre 1995).

4. **Empower others to act out the vision.** Managers must embolden employees to act on the vision. Managers must remove employee obstacles. At Lexmark, teams were asked to find production efficiencies and quality improvements. One assembly-worker team redesigned laser printer production completely.

5. **Prepare to overcome resistance.** That one group, even if it is top management, decides to change does not guarantee support. At Lexmark, when the assembly-worker team showed their new laser-printer production process to their boss for approval, he said all

FIGURE 7.3 The change management and innovation process

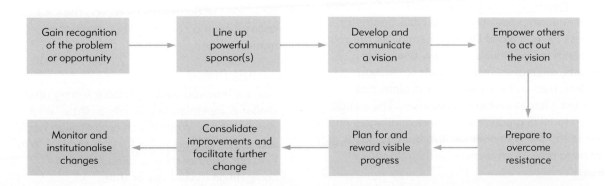

members must sign the plans before he would. The team were hesitant to take the responsibility of empowerment. After a month they presented a design all would sign. (Later, we describe reasons employees resist change, and how to overcome resistance.)

6. **Plan for and reward visible progress.** Major change and innovation takes time, and people can lose focus or give up. One way to keep momentum is to have some projects or phases likely to succeed in 12 to 24 months. Celebrations, recognitions and other rewards show change is important and the vision needs focus (Fisher 1995).

7. **Consolidate improvements and facilitate further change.** With change processes and the search for innovation, it is easy to stop after finding clear improvements. Lexmark's first goal was profit. Competition meant costs had to be cut further and product improved. To do that, Lexmark management focused on worker empowerment, and they still do. Worker teams still seek production, inventory and shipping improvements.

8. **Monitor and institutionalise changes.** Renewal and innovation can revert quickly unless integrated into corporate culture. Thus, the need for new behaviours and their connection to company success must be emphasised until they are integrated into the culture (Ettorre 1995). Innovative firms, such as 3M and Hewlett-Packard, build innovation cultures as part of their competitive advantage.

Organisational development

organisational development (OD)

Change effort planned, focused on an entire organisation or a large subsystem, managed from the top, aimed at enhancing organisational health and effectiveness, and based on planned interventions

Organisational development (OD) is a change effort to improve interpersonal working relationships and organisational effectiveness through strategies using a change agent or third party who is well versed in behavioural sciences (Beckhard 1969; Beer 1980; Kinicki & Williams 2003). The change agent, or consultant, has a fresh view and behavioural science knowledge, and acts as a catalyst to help people and groups approach old problems in new or innovative ways. This may be an external consultant, a company OD specialist, a new manager, or one able to look beyond the traditional.

OD was first used for large-scale organisational change; however, focus has moved to improving work relationships. As such, OD efforts fit the change management and innovation process raised already. OD has three major steps: diagnosis, intervention and evaluation (see Fig. 7.4) (French & Bell 1978; Huse & Cummings 1985; Mohrman, Mohrman, Ledford, Cummings, Lawler & Associates 1989).

MANAGERIAL DILEMMAS

Business idea competition

The annual Best Business Idea competition, which has been running since the early 1990s, encourages creative thinking and shrewd enterprise. The contest is organised by the National University of Singapore Entrepreneurship Society and the NUS Centre for Business Research and Development. Over the years the search for individuals with new services or products, or creative improvements to existing products, backed by sound business plans has attracted a large number of responses. The search is open to NUS graduates and undergraduates and aims to tap the pool of innovative business ideas as well as to provide an avenue for them to market ideas.

Reflection points

1. Why do you think such a competition was initiated?

2. What kind of organisations do you think might sponsor such a contest? What would their motivation be?

Decision points

1. Discuss how you might go about setting up a similar competition in your city or state. Who should host it? Why? Which organisation would you see as approachable for sponsorship? Why?

2. Find out whether there is already such a competition in your city or state.

FIGURE 7.4 The organisational development process

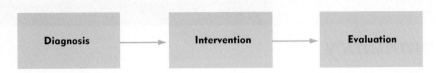

Diagnosis

The first step, diagnosis, often draws attention to beliefs, values and norms members share which may impede effectiveness. Change agents, and others helping the process, collect data by many methods, such as interviews, questionnaires, employee-behaviour observation, and internal documents and reports (Reibstein 1986). Walker (2004c) discusses this in terms of exporting a franchise internationally and understanding the unique strengths and advantages of the business.

Intervention

After diagnosis comes intervention. OD interventions, or change strategies, are designed and implemented with the help of the change agent. While there are many OD change strategies, four techniques of OD specialists are described below (French & Bell 1978; Huse & Cummings 1985).

Process consultation focuses on a work group's interpersonal relations and dynamics. The OD change agent, or consultant, watches the group, identifying any problems in communication patterns, conflict handling and decision making. The goal is to help develop members' skills in identifying and resolving issues of group dynamics.

Team building helps work groups develop effective task accomplishment. Like process consultation, it has OD consultant feedback on communication and conflict resolution. The consultant also helps assess group tasks, member roles, and work-task achievement strategies.

Third-party intervention helps people, groups or departments resolve serious conflicts on specific work issues or caused by poor interpersonal relations. The OD consultant helps parties resolve difficulties by problem solving, bargaining and conciliation.

Technostructural activities help improve work technology and/or organisational structure. In this approach, the OD consultant helps members increase work effectiveness by showing them how to evaluate and make changes in work methods, task design and organisation structure.

Evaluation

Evaluation is step three. As with any change, OD efforts' effectiveness must be checked. The ability to evaluate OD intervention effects depends on how well the diagnosis stage identified areas needing change, and specified results desired.

Innovation for competitive advantage

Innovation does not guarantee commercial success. For innovation to be a competitive advantage, four factors are needed (Lengnick-Hall 1992; Ihrcke 2000). First, so competitors cannot easily match innovations, they must be hard to copy. Second, innovations should meet significant customer needs. For example, staff of Fresh International Corporation took several years to develop and patent a bag to keep ready-to-eat salads fresh on grocery shelves. The product was immediately successful (Lubove 1995). Third, innovations should allow an organisation to exploit a particular industry's timing characteristics. This is clear from the experience of Boral in setting up a plasterboard factory when there was a clear gap between production and use in a building development boom (James 2003). The first with an innovation may have an advantage. This is true in brand-name situations when consumers commit to a product or service before competitors respond. In other situations, cost benefits may come to

Our Community

When Denis Moriarty got together over dinner with his good friend Rhonda Galbally and bemoaned the situation in which the NGO (non-government organisation) sector in Australia found itself, little did he suspect how this concern would grow into a thriving organisation. Because of their backgrounds in health and government both Denis and Rhonda knew that the sector was fragmented, isolated and looking for support.

Despite the billions of dollars in turnover that the NGO sector represents, tens of thousands of community organisations, from bowling clubs to neighborhood houses, were operating in isolation from each other. What if, they wondered, there was a way to bring together these disparate organisations so that they could share important community and funding information, pool their resources when buying equipment, access the latest research and speak for the sector in a unified way? From this conversation 'Our Community' was founded, an organisation dedicated to the myriad of community organisations scattered across Australia's countryside and cities.

The first major problem that they faced was to find a way to provide a common forum for these scattered organisations. This they resolved by creating a website (www.ourcommunity.com.au) through which they could communicate, transmitting valuable data and information. From the outset they decided they would provide services and support that the sector had been asking for, and this they did with innovative products such as newsletters containing information about private and government grants; a purchasing service that pooled the buying power of the sector; and special banking arrangements through one of the major banks. To this range of services they added texts on administrative and management skills, volunteer

coordination services and an on-line donation service. Emboldened by the success of these initial efforts, they proceeded to expand the relationship between the sector, business and government, by providing state, municipal and federal training programs and initiatives to their portfolio—such as the Prime Minister's 'Community Business Partnership'.

Denis and Rhonda exploited the capabilities of the website technology to provide full and instant information in an interactive fashion, with the site architecture providing services such as several newsletters, a management training centre, a leadership centre, an on-line donation centre, and a financial centre.

Their success, they feel, is due to their innovation in finding a way to bring together these many geographically dispersed organisations through their use of the website, providing a means by which the sector could find a common voice. Crucially, they also feel that the services that they provided, both financial and informational, met a need within the sector that had previously been unmet.

Source: Contributed by George Sansbury.

Activities for discussion, analysis and further research

1. Attempt to identify instances of the 'four factors of innovation to promote competitive advantage', as discussed in this chapter.
2. Success breeds imitation! If you were managing 'Our Community', how would you go about retaining your competitive advantage?
3. Visit the 'Our Community' website (www.ourcommunity.com.au) and consider why an isolated community group in north Queensland may find it useful.

early followers. For example, soon after designer clothes are shown on fashion runways or in chic boutiques in Milan, Paris and New York, copies are made. Sometimes, copies appear before stores get the originals. Fourth, innovations use capabilities and technologies the firm can easily access, but competitors cannot.

Product development principles

Managers can build company ability to innovate new goods and services, increasing competitive advantage. They can organise and control product development to cut time, improve fit with customer needs, maximise quality, manufacturability and efficiency. This can be done using four principles (Jones et al. 2000):

Principle 1: Establish a stage-gate development funnel: A mistake managers make in product development is starting too many new projects at once (Clark & Wheelwright 1989). The result is resources are spread thinly over too many projects, so no project has the resources to succeed.

Given this, managers need a process to evaluate product-development proposals and decide which to support and which to reject. A common method is to set up a stage-gate development funnel, a planning model forcing a choice between competing projects so resources are not spread thinly (Clark & Wheelwright 1989). The funnel gives control over product development and lets managers intervene as needed (see Fig. 7.5).

At Stage 1, the funnel has a wide mouth, so employees can be encouraged to develop many new product ideas. Managers can reward those with ideas. Firms can run 'bright idea programs', rewarding employees whose ideas are adopted.

New product ideas are presented as brief proposals. A cross-functional team evaluates the proposal at Gate 1. The team checks whether the proposal fits with organisation strategy and feasibility. Proposals which fit with strategy and viewed as technically feasible go through Gate 1 into Stage 2.

The goal of Stage 2 is a detailed draft product-development plan. This gives all needed information to make the decision about mounting a full-blown effort. The plan has strategic and financial objectives, potential product-market analysis, a desired-features list, technological-needs lists, as well as financial and human-resource needs, a detailed development budget, and a time-line with specific milestones.

FIGURE 7.5 A stage-gate development funnel

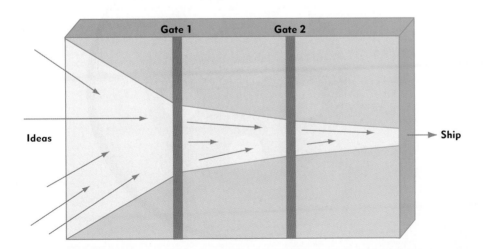

This takes about three months. When it is completed, a committee at Gate 2 (see Fig. 7.5) checks it. Plan details are considered to see if the proposal is attractive (market potential) and viable (if there are enough technological, financial and human resources for development). Senior managers must think about all other product-development efforts. At this point one goal is to ensure effective use of limited company resources.

At Gate 2 projects are rejected, sent for revision, or passed into Stage 3, the development phase. Product development starts with formation of a cross-functional team responsible for product development.

The Stage 3 development effort takes from six months to 10 years, depending on industry and product type.

Principle 2: Establish cross-functional teams: A smooth-running cross-functional team is critical to successful development. Others besides core members work on the project as the need arises, but core members (generally from three to six) stay with the project from inception to completion of development (see Fig. 7.6).

A cross-functional team assures high-level coordination and communication among managers from various functions, enhancing group cohesiveness and performance.

Principle 3: Use concurrent engineering: Traditional product development involves five steps: opportunity identification, concept development, product design, process design and commercial production (see Fig. 7.7a). Opportunity development occurs at Stage 1 of the funnel (see Fig. 7.5), commercial production at Stage 3, and others at Stage 2. The problems with sequential product development are long product-development times, poor quality and high manufacturing costs if there is no direct communication between marketing managers developing the concept, engineering or R&D managers designing the product, and manufacturing managers. In many cases engineers in R&D design a product then 'throw it over the wall' to manufacturing. The result can be costly to manufacture. If solving this requires redesign, manufacturing sends the product back to design, lengthening development time.

FIGURE 7.6 Members of a cross-functional product-development team

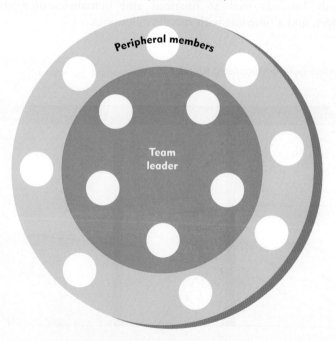

FIGURE 7.7 Sequential and partly parallel development processes

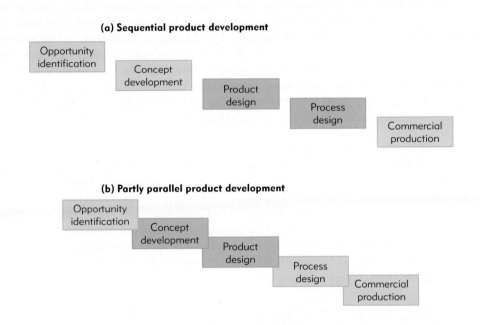

Cross-functional teams help make the process partly parallel, not sequential. In partly parallel product development, each step begins before the prior is finished, and managers from any function are familiar with what goes on in others (see Fig. 7.7b). The goal is facilitating concurrent engineering, the simultaneous design of product and manufacturing process (Heartly 1992). The usual result is an easy-to-manufacture product. Concurrent engineering cuts costs and raises product quality. The other benefit of a partly parallel process is reduced development time, for two reasons. Concurrent engineering reduces costly time-consuming product redesigns and the whole process is compressed.

Principle 4: Involve both customers and suppliers: Many new products fail in the marketplace as they were designed with no attention to customer needs. Product development requires inputs from more than organisation members; inputs from customers and suppliers are needed too (Avishai & Taylor 1989; Sounder 1988; Zinger & Maidique 1990).

In sum, managers must see that successful product development cuts across roles and functions, needing high-level integration. They should recognise how important common values and norms are to promote high levels of cooperation and cohesiveness to build an innovation culture. They must carefully reward successful innovators, making heroes of employees and teams developing new products. Finally, managers should use four product development principles for the process.

Intrapreneurship

To foster innovation, some firms encourage people into entrepreneurial roles, such as idea generator or champion, sponsor and orchestrator (see Chapter 1). These are referred to as intrapreneurial roles when carried out by those inside established companies.

Although people in any of the three roles are intrapreneurs, most often the idea champion is known as an intrapreneur. This is because the idea champion is responsible for turning an idea into reality (Pinchot 1985). The idea champion generates a new idea or realises its value and supports it despite obstacles.

Characteristics of intrapreneurs can be learned, at least partly. For one, they tend to visualise what they want to create. Their vision comes from thinking about an idea over time. Intrapreneurs are action-oriented, dedicated, and willing to do mundane tasks to avoid project delays. They set goals beyond those asked of them, have high internal work standards, and recover from mistakes and failures. For example, Phil Palmquist worked at 3M on reflective coatings even when told to stop. He eventually produced the reflective coating for roads which is over 100 times brighter than white paint, working four nights a week from 7 to 10 pm (Pinchot 1985). Of course, part of a good intrapreneur's task is choosing a good idea. For guidelines on recognising a good intrapreneurial idea and what to do if it is rejected, see the discussion in Management skills for a globalised economy, 'Checklist for choosing intrapreneurial ideas'.

Why would people follow an entrepreneurial idea in a firm (i.e. be intrapreneurs) instead of starting their own business? Existing firms, especially big ones, have a strong technological base (proprietary knowledge and scientific resources), marketing resources (a known name, sales staff and advertising funds), a network of people, established production facilities, and in-house finance. Intrapreneur Art Fry, who championed 3M's Post-it note pads, sees it this way: 'I have only so much time in my life and I want to do as much as I can. I can do things faster here as part of 3M and so I get to do more things' (Pinchot 1985). In turning ideas into reality, intrapreneurs assume official or unofficial management tasks and, like managers, must understand organisation change management.

KEY ORGANISATIONAL CHANGE COMPONENTS

Significant change or innovation usually means changing one or more of the key components of structure, technology, human resources and culture (see Fig. 7.8) (Leavitt 1964; Huse & Cummings 1985). Since these are interrelated, change in one requires adjustment in others.

Structural components

Organisation structure is the interaction patterns and coordination linking individual and group tasks. Structure includes job definition, how jobs are clustered into work units, and mechanisms to facilitate vertical and horizontal communication (e.g. delegation and interdepartmental

FIGURE 7.8 Key components for implementing change (adapted from Leavitt, in Cooper, Leavitt, & Shelly 1964, p. 56)

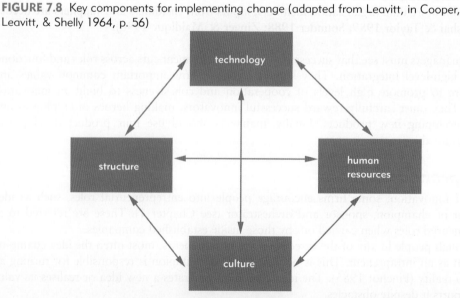

Happy hens

Started in 1984 from humble beginnings, Happy Hens is now a company with an annual turnover of about $750 000–$1 million, and substantial room for growth. The core product of the company is hand-painted clay hens. Yvonne Sutherland, the founding owner of the company, was an art teacher at a local high school who had a self-confessed 'eye for pattern and colour, and an interest in history'. When she heard older folk talking about the hens they used to keep, she did some research and found that there was a huge variety of colourful birds that had been largely forgotten. From this and her interest in hens, she developed a range of colourful ceramic hens which are sold as novelty or decorative items or, increasingly, as collectors' pieces. The company employs nine part-time workers and produces approximately fifteen varieties of hen, which sell for between NZ$14 and NZ$22 on the internet and at the factory, and slightly more in   retail outlets. Yvonne praises the dedication of her predominantly female staff and describes her 'value-added, labour intensive, and export oriented' business as a fun place to work. Happy Hens also licenses the trade name and images to a cross-stitch kit manufacturer and a paper-towel manufacturer. The latest addition is Happy Hen fabric.

The gift market is an increasingly lucrative sector and Yvonne has successfully managed her business, which has gone from strength to strength. However, in the past Yvonne found that the industry was not taken seriously. Her lucky break came when she asked herself the question: 'Why can't we be in there with the big boys?' She joined a delegation of local exporters who travelled to Osaka, Japan, as part of a local Dunedin city business promotion. She also exhibited in Otaru, which is Dundedin's sister city.

As a result of this visit she was able to enter with very little effort what was, at the time, the most difficult export market in the world. She now exports to Australia, Singapore, Canada, the United Kingdom and the United States of America. She has exhibited in the International Gift Fair in New York. Despite her international success, however, she finds that some people still hold the attitude that the gift market is 'women's work', providing women with 'pocket money'. These attitudes may in part stem from the fact that for many years Happy Hens had a strong appeal to female customers, although this trend has changed over time.

Yvonne has to manage many roles within the business, including entrepreneur, artist and creator, day-to-day manager and mother. She is still the major artistic influence in the business, thinking up new ideas for designs and products. She likes to keep things simple, and still manages the company on a day-to-day basis as well as at a strategic level. Yvonne works in the mornings managing the office, and spends the afternoon concentrating on her passion: being creative. Yvonne's family plays a significant role in the business too. Her employees include her husband, who works in an accounting role, one of her five adult children and two of her daughters-in-law. Yvonne recognises it would have been extremely difficult to build the business without the support of her family.

Yvonne does not particularly enjoy the administrative side of the business but doesn't feel comfortable handing it over to a manager at this stage. She likens it to leaving a baby with a stranger or someone whom you didn't trust. She hopes one of her children will succeed her and take over in the future. If this does not eventuate and an outside manager has to be appointed, Yvonne would probably choose a woman manager. She feels she would be more trusting of, and have more rapport with, a woman. She also feels some men tend to focus more on money, and this is not her primary motivation for being in business.

Source: Contributed by Elizabeth Hall (details sources are listed on p. 736).

Website:

www.theframeworkshop.com/gifts.cfm

Activities for discussion, analysis and further research

1. What stage of the business life cycle do you think that Happy Hens is at? Use Table 7.1 to justify and explain your answer.

2. Most small businesses, which are usually the seeding grounds for innovative ideas, fail within their first year of operation. Why has this family-owned business been successful?

3. What are the key factors that explain the success of Yvonne's business, and what do you see as the major threats and opportunities? Use the following websites for information about the business: www.happyhens.co.nz/ and www.visit-dunedin.co.nz/happyhens.html.

4. Why do you think that being a woman manager is important to this business operation?

5. What do you think would be the likely outcome of Happy Hens becoming a large and formal organisation? Explain your reasoning.

6. Another successful business in Dunedin is Jan McLean Originals which produces porcelain and resin art dolls. This now internationally successful business was founded by another creative businesswoman. Use the website: www.janmcleandolls.com/ to explore the similarities and differences in these two businesses.

MANAGEMENT SKILLS FOR A GLOBALISED ECONOMY

Checklist for choosing intrapreneurial ideas

Good intrapreneurial ideas must meet three kinds of needs: yours, the customer's and the firm's. Otherwise, the intrapreneurial endeavour will fail. To test an idea, you can use the following checklist.

Fit with your skills and experience:
- Do you believe in the product or service?
- Does the need it fills mean something to you personally?
- Do you like and understand potential customers?
- Do you have experience in this type of business?
- Do the basic success factors of this business fit your skills?
- Are the tasks of the intrapreneurial project ones you could enjoy doing?
- Are people who would work on the project ones you will enjoy working with and supervising?
- Has the idea begun to take over your imagination and spare time?

Fit with customers and the market:
- Is there a real customer need?
- Can you get a price giving you good margins?
- Would customers believe in the product coming from your company?
- Does the product or service you propose give a clearly perceivable customer benefit significantly better than that provided by competing means of satisfying the same basic need?
- Is there a cost-effective way to get the message and product to the customer?

Fit with the company:
- Is there a reason to believe your company could be very good at the business?
- Does it fit the company culture?
- Can you imagine who might sponsor it?
- Does it look profitable (high margin, low investment)?
- Will it lead to larger markets and growth?

What to do if your idea is rejected

Frequently, as an intrapreneur, you will find your idea has been rejected. There are a few things you can do:

1. Give up and select a new idea.
2. Listen carefully, understand what is wrong, improve your idea and presentation, and try again.
3. Find someone else to whom you can present your idea by considering:
   a. Who will benefit most if it works, and can they be a sponsor?
   b. Who are the potential customers, and will they demand the product?
   c. How can you get to people who really care about intrapreneurial ideas?

Source: Pinchot III, G. (1985).

teams) (Child 1977). As structures must adapt to changing circumstances, reorganisations are common. Reorganisations influence change by altering interaction and coordination patterns (Russell 1987). (Specific structures are discussed in Chapters 8 and 9.) Minor structural changes are common, though many 'fine-tune' earlier changes. Research suggests reorganisations of a quantum nature—concerted and dramatic change—lead to higher performance than piecemeal, incremental changes (Miller & Friesen 1982; Romanelli & Tushman 1994). However, interactions between structural and other components are very important (Trinca 2003).

Technological components

Technology is the knowledge, tools, equipment and work techniques an organisation uses to deliver products or services. Technological changes come in new products and services (e.g. computer scanners and Internet connections) and enhancements to current products and services. For international competition technological change is vital. When Yamaha Motor and Honda Motor competed for the Japanese motorcycle market, Yamaha said it would beat Honda. Sadly for Yamaha, Honda flooded the market with new models, up to one per week. Forced to continually discount obsolete models, Yamaha Motor lost $300 million over two years (Tanzer 1987).

Technological innovations change work methods. Thus, word-processors and personal computers mean documents need not be retyped after correction. Data banks give doctors, engineers, educators and research scientists better information. In biotechnology, robot apprentices help researchers study deoxyribonucleic acid (DNA), the raw material of genes, taking hours for tests which required weeks or months for a trained chemist (Chase 1986). Technological changes can impact staff levels and skill types needed.

Human resource components

Changing workers involves altering knowledge, skills, perceptions and behaviours needed. Change relies on training and development activities, with performance appraisal and reward systems supporting needed behaviours. Often, recruitment and selection systems must change, reflecting the need for members with many skills. Having people with knowledge and skills to handle changing circumstances needs careful planning. For example, Motorola is well known for extensive employee training. One of its programs, the Vice-President Institute (VPI), helps vice-presidents learn and practise innovation and leadership skills. Sustaining Motorola's growth requires vice-presidents with these skills. The program helps Motorola manage diversity, since vice-presidents from many countries and cultures can build networks (Eller 1995). Chapter 10 discusses effective human resource systems. These changes build the value of changes in other components, such as structure and technology.

Cultural components

Organisational culture is the shared values, assumptions, beliefs and norms linking members (Sathe 1983; Smirchich 1983; Kilmann, Sexton & Serpa 1986). Many firms, such as McDonald's, Hewlett-Packard, Pacifica, Dick Hubbard's and The Warehouse, attribute their success to distinctive cultures based on founders' values, reinforced by top executives (Huse & Cummings 1985; Goldsmith 1995). Others have changed culture based on their leader's vision or survival threats. For example, British Airways was a money-losing, state-owned body unconcerned with customers, costs or productivity. Then strong leadership changed the culture to emphasise customer focus, productivity and initiative. Meanwhile the carrier was privatised and became a major global airline. Culture change was needed for the successful transformation (Kotter & Heskett 1992; Dwyer 1992). Major organisational change often needs culture change (see Chapter 3).

Interrelationship among components

While minor change may relate to just one change component, major change may encompass all four. This is because a major change in one component impacts on others. You might visualise components as being connected by rubber bands. If one component changes, tensions are created in others until they are adjusted.

Of course, major innovation and change efforts also need in-depth understanding of people's motivation. In the next chapter, we explore motivational processes and see how managers can motivate others effectively.

GAINING THE EDGE

The value of knowledge

Globalisation is changing the rules of commerce, and what managers bring to an organisation will no longer be enough to furnish an enterprise with competitive advantage. Management skills have become a necessary but not sufficient condition for survival. Managers who do not look outside their discipline are at risk in the global economy.

Such are the thoughts of the authors of 'Funky Business', Jonas Ridderstrale and Kjell Nordstrom. They state that management is on the way out and many external certainties are evaporating. They make the claim that workers own the means of production—knowledge. It is, however, questionable whether knowledge can be owned. It cannot be divested, lost or sold. Perhaps this means that knowledge assets are not the possession of knowledge but the conversion of that knowledge into information, or business processes, or customer relations.

Many of the boundaries which characterised the industrial era are dissolving. To make sense of such a high-degree change requires an ability to cross-reference different areas of activity without

necessarily having a detailed knowledge of them. Enterprises are starting to employ staff for their attitudes rather than their skills. This is underpinned by the belief that individuals will be able to acquire the required skills as they need them. While efficient production is important, it is no longer enough. Motivation and connection with the customer is more vital and this requires a motivated workforce.

Source: Adapted from James, D. (2000).

Activities for discussion, analysis and further research

1. In what ways do innovation and change assist an organisation to adapt to global business requirements?
2. What kind of institutions suit the global economy?
3. Herb Kelleher of South West Airlines says that he recruits for attitude and then trains for skills. This is especially true for industries where knowledge is perishable. Find examples of industries where this is appropriate.

KIMBERLEY TURNER

AEROSAFE
RISK MANAGEMENT

When the company was first started we didn't actually have a detailed list of products or services—we just worked. Our product was our advice and how we turned that advice into activities that helped the organisation we were working with to implement that advice. Over the last seven years, I have really focused on taking that intellectual property and packaging it into products and services that match industry's needs and are easily identifiable to those that don't know what they don't have.

Industry is after training courses, implementation models, executive risk coaching, policy development, base-lining and conducting a needs analysis or a review of their work against industry best practice, and we have actually had the opportunity to package a lot of our methodology down to the level of consultant's guides as to how to provide the service in a consistent and proven way. A lot of that is our own work, and when it is validated against theory and best practice that's presented in industry forums, it's a great validation that we're on the right track. In my mind this verifies and validates the linkage with the strategic planning and the business management and the design work.

As a person, I am very intrinsically motivated. A lot of my motivation is self-generated. But that double-checking and that validation spurs me on even further because it really gives me the confidence that I am on the right track. Purely because of the nature of the work that we do, we need to be an organisation where innovation and new work is at the centre of what we do. People either have that streak or don't have that streak. My job is to identify and nurture those that do, and cultivate an environment that allows them to be innovative and really design and create. Those people who don't fall into that basket are really good at checking, validating, refining and providing the extra detail. But they may not be people who can design the concepts. So the real challenge is getting the balance between those two groups of people and not try to put a square peg in a round hole, but identifying who works well in what areas and providing that environment.

Maintaining the energy and feeding it is often the result of self-driving as it is internally generated, but the importance of double checking against the work of other people in industry is high.

Strategies for improving

1. Discuss strategies for encouraging employees to take risks and become more innovative, and consider how to implement these strategies.
2. Consider strategies for avoiding a culture of risk aversion in your organisation.
3. Develop up-to-date usage skills for information-management systems to ensure high-quality data for innovative decision making.

Source: Jones et al. (2000).

SUMMARY

- Due to competition, management of change and innovation is more important to organisation survival and prosperity. Change is an alteration to the status quo, while innovation is a new idea applied to initiating or improving a process, product or service. Change forces can be external or internal. As they grow, firms go through four life cycles, or development stages: entrepreneurial, collectivity, formalisation and control, and elaboration of structure. Moving through the stages means changing operating methods, but these may inhibit innovation unless managers plan and encourage it. Failure to adapt to changed conditions may lead to organisational termination through bankruptcy, voluntary liquidation, and merger, acquisition or take-over.

- Although managers may have to react to unpredictable situations, effective managers try to plan for major changes and innovations when possible. They typically follow an eight-step process: (1) gain recognition of problem or opportunity, (2) line up powerful sponsor(s), (3) develop and communicate a vision, (4) empower others to act out the vision, (5) prepare to overcome resistance, (6) plan for and reward visible progress, (7) consolidate improvements and facilitate further change, and (8) monitor and institutionalise changes.

- Organisational development (OD) is a change effort aimed to enhance interpersonal working relationships and organisational effectiveness by planned interventions made with a change agent well versed in behavioural sciences. Organisational development has three major stages: diagnosis, intervention and evaluation. Intervention techniques used by OD specialists include process consultation, team building, third-party intervention and technostructural activities.

- To gain competitive advantage by innovation, four factors are important. Innovations should be hard to copy, reflect market realities, exploit industry timing characteristics, and rely on readily accessible organisation capabilities and technologies. Intrapreneurship's importance in organisations is increasing, and intrapreneurs' characteristics are learnable, such as being visionary, action-oriented, and willing to set goals associated with new ideas.

- Major changes require adjustment to one or more key organisational change components: structure, technology, human resources and culture. Components are interrelated, so changing one requires adjustment in others to achieve successful change and innovation efforts.

QUESTIONS FOR DISCUSSION AND REVIEW

1. Explain differences between change and innovation. Think of some changes you have noticed on campus in the past year. In each case, explain the extent to which forces for change were external or internal. Which changes would you classify as innovations? Why?

2. Describe the four organisation life-cycle stages. Choose a familiar organisation and determine its stage in the organisational life cycle. On the basis of your analysis, what changes are likely to be needed in the future?

3. Explain the eight-step model of change and innovation process. Use this model to develop a plan for getting a student group to take advantage of an unexploited opportunity.

4. Explain the concept of organisational development. Suppose you are helping with an OD project at your college or university. What major steps will be involved? What data-collection methods would you suggest for the diagnosis step?

5. Delineate the major intervention techniques used by OD specialists.

6. Specify how an organisation can use innovation to bring about competitive advantage. What possibilities for using innovation as a competitive-advantage tool appear to exist at your college or university?

7. Describe some common characteristics of intrapreneurs. Assuming the characteristics are learnable, how might you go about acquiring them?

8. Enumerate key organisational components needing to be adjusted in implementing major changes and innovations. Identify a recent change at your college or university aimed mainly at one of these components. To what extent did the change in that component alter the rest?

CRITICAL THINKING QUESTIONS

To answer some of these questions you will need to do further research. Useful references are given below each section of the questions.

This chapter proposed that innovation should be an integral part of the planning process and set about examining ways in which managers can effectively facilitate innovation and change within organisations. The following questions examine innovation in small and large companies and look at the problems of one Australian entrepreneur.

The application of knowledge management as an aid to innovation is a new development that is resulting in a completely different perspective that helps managers prevent a crisis before it happens.

1. What is the link between innovation and crisis prevention?

While most organisations, regardless of size, are well versed in knowledge techniques, overseeing processes from the identification and distribution of knowledge, through to issues of protection, application and destruction, the aim in fostering innovation in crisis management is to adopt an approach analogous to completing a jigsaw. Pieces of organisational information are rearranged in innovative patterns to complete a puzzle which adds knowledge and, if this new perspective is acted upon, may prevent a crisis.

2. What knowledge capabilities would an organisation require to allow this innovative use of information to occur?

3. Desouza (2003) suggests that it is in the first step, the generating of knowledge about a potential or impending crisis, where most organisations go wrong. Why?

4. While the link between successful crisis management and knowledge management is the support of innovative thinking, it is very difficult to implement. How can employees be encouraged to generate original ideas?.

Underlying the ability to seek out and identify knowledge that is relevant are efficient search and retrieval systems—systems that are capable of different forms of analysis, from exploitation to exploration. Desouza (2003) argues that it is the ability to strike the right balance between the tasks of exploitation (the refinement of knowledge within existing domains) and exploration (searching for knowledge in fresh areas) which ultimately determines the organisation's capability to identify crises. Too much focus on exploiting existing knowledge can leave an organisation ill-equipped to deal with unconventional problems, and organisations may concentrate too much on exploration that has little or no value.

5. How should an organisation go about effectively seeking knowledge of impending crises?

6. Once information has been gathered, the organisation must effectively distribute this information to gain a return on investment. How should an organisation go about both distributing and applying knowledge?

7. Knowledge, once distributed and understood, must be turned into actions. Organisations commonly fail at this point. Why?

8. The last task in knowledge innovation for crisis management is for organisations to destroy the knowledge they have developed. What is the importance of this last step?

(Material relevant to questions 1 to 8 may be found in Desouza, K. 2003, Don't just manage crises—avoid them, *New Zealand Management*, 50, 8, September, pp. 51–2.)

Now we move to an area traditionally neglected in terms of studies of knowledge innovation—the small business sector. As Gome (2002, p. 41) writes, this sector is dominated by the home-based worker who accounts for nearly two-thirds of small business. Australian Bureau of Statistics figures reveal that, between 1999 and 2001, the number of home-based businesses grew by 26.5 per cent, from 615 000 to 778 000. Home-based businesses now represent 67 per cent of all small businesses, are operated by 998 800 people (as many are operated as husband/wife and other partnership arrangements) and represent 63 per cent of all small-business owners.

9. What are some of the factors that may be responsible for this dramatic growth in home-based businesses?

10. Given these factors, what demographic profiles would you expect to see?

One of the key problems associated with innovation is that new products and new ideas often cross boundaries in unexpected ways, and legal boundaries in particular are breached. This is certainly the case with home-based business. Although 68 per cent of home-based businesses have no employees and are operated just by an owner or owners, the number employing between one and four people increased from 205 000 in 1999 to 218 000 in 2001, a rise of 6.3 per cent. The number with between five and 19 employees grew 50 per cent, from 16 400 to 24 600.

11. What is the problem with this?

(Material relevant to questions 9 to 11 may be found in Gome, A. 2002, Australia becomes a nation of home offices, *Business Review Weekly*, 6 June, p. 41.)

Innovation is just as much a part of ongoing competitive advantage for the large organisation as it is for the small one. Kacher and Jennings (2002) illustrate this in their review of developments at the vehicle manufacturer BMW where, while not about to reinvent the wheel, they are questioning why we need four of them to get around our cities.

12. What are the pressures for such innovation within a well-respected, prestige company?

13. How does an organisation go about minimising the risks associated with such a radical innovation?

(Material relevant to questions 12 and 13 may be found in Kacher, G. and Jennings, B. 2002, On your trike, *Sun Herald*, 6 September, p. 4.)

Paul Rizzo, former Dean of Melbourne Business School, recently advocated the need for more to be done to find political and business leaders who can speak powerfully to the nation and set an inspiring example to the entire community, not just to sectional interests. It is a view of innovation which moves beyond the organisation to focus on the state—so that encouragement is given to ideas-based leadership that creates new thinking and proposes new solutions to Australia's problems in areas such as the environment, energy and pollution, water and land degradation, population, education and training, science, technology and innovation, the relationship between businesses and the community, and structural improvements to our economic base (Rizzo 2002, p. 28).

14. What does innovation mean in the context of a nation?

(Material relevant to question 15 may be found in Rizzo, P. 2002, Ideas leadership wanted, *Business Review Weekly*, 6 June, p. 28.)

The notion of a self-satisfied smugness and complacency ties in the last area of this examination of innovation. Horin's (2002) review of a new book by Michael Gilden (*Secrets of the Super Rich*) reveals that succession planning is a burning issue for our aging entrepreneurs. She cites Rodney Adler's fall from grace as a timely reminder of the pitfalls of nepotism and just how quickly corporate dynasties can unravel when the second generation takes the reins. The FAI Insurance Company was founded and run by Rodney's immigrant father, Larry, from 1955 till his death in 1988. Now all visible traces of it are gone. Within 10 years of taking the helm, Adler had sold FAI and, within three years, it was all over and a disgraced Adler was banned from being a company director for 20 years.

Q.15   What are the problems of family succession that appear to plague Australia's aging post-war business tycoons?

(Material relevant to question 14 may be found in Horin, A. 2002, Pity the poor kids who inherit curse of the rich, *Sydney Morning Herald*, 6 August, p. 31; Gilden, M. 2002 *Secrets of the Super Rich*, Harper Collins, Sydney.)

MANAGEMENT EXERCISES

Exercise 1 Skill building: Strategies for innovation

Peter Clyde has recently been appointed as CEO to Edgemount Industries. He is 41 years old and interested in finding new ways to do things. Edgemount Industries is a family company in business for 83 years. In this generation, no family member is able or willing to take on management of the organisation. Consequently, Peter Clyde has been appointed.

Over the past three months, Peter has discovered some alarming facts. Average employee age is 54 and average length of service is 22 years. While things have been ticking over comfortably, the company has had no real growth in nine years and its products have shown no change in almost 20 years. Peter Clyde has decided to introduce a culture of innovation. Make suggestions as to strategies he could use.

Exercise 2 Skill building: Attitudes to innovation scale

Indicate the extent to which each statement below describes the way you are, or intend to be, on the job. Use the following scale for your responses:

Attitudes to innovation scale	
5 = Almost always true	2 = Seldom true
4 = Often true	1 = Almost never true
3 = Not applicable	

_____	1.	I discuss with my boss how to get ahead.
_____	2.	I try new ideas and approaches to problems.
_____	3.	I take things or situations apart to see how they work.
_____	4.	I welcome uncertainty and unusual circumstances related to my work.
_____	5.	I negotiate my salary openly with my supervisor.
_____	6.	I can be counted on to find new uses for existing methods or equipment.
_____	7.	Among my colleagues and co-workers I will be first, or nearly so, to try out new ideas or methods.
_____	8.	I translate communications from other departments for my work group.
_____	9.	I demonstrate originality.
_____	10.	I will work on a problem that causes others great difficulty.
_____	11.	I provide critical input toward a new solution.

(continued)

_____	12.	I provide written evaluations of proposed ideas.
_____	13.	I develop contacts with experts outside my firm.
_____	14.	I use personal contacts to manoeuvre myself into valued work assignments.
_____	15.	I make time to pursue my own pet ideas or projects.
_____	16.	I set aside resources for pursuit of risky projects.
_____	17.	I tolerate people departing from organisational routine.
_____	18.	I speak out in staff meetings.
_____	19.	I work in teams to solve complex problems.
_____	20.	If my co-workers are asked, they will say I am funny.

Scoring To determine your score, total the numbers associated with your responses to the items. Then compare the score to the following norm group (comprised of graduate and undergraduate business school students, all in full-time employment).

Score	Percentile*
39	5
53	16
62	33
71	50
80	68
89	86
97	95

*Percentile indicates the percentage of people expected to score below you.
Source: Adapted from Erlie & O'Keefe (1982).

END-OF-CHAPTER CASE: ON THE RIM

Uncharted territory

POWERWEB

International articles related to this topic are available at the Online Learning Centre at **www.mhhe.com/au/bartol4e**

After years of weak earnings, Japanese electronics-maker Pioneer finally looks like having bet on a winner. The company has emerged as a leading designer and maker of DVD players—a format for showing movies in the home that's proving a hit in markets as diverse as China and the United States, and is tipped to supersede video-cassette players.

Already, Pioneer has managed to carve out a 20 per cent share of the global DVD, or digital video disc, market—

currently worth about ¥88 billion ($800 million) a year—and is expected to grow almost five-fold by 2003. And it has even bigger plans. 'Our goal is to be industry leader by 2005', says Kaneo Ito, the company's president.

This is not the first time Pioneer has put a video-disc technology at the heart of its ambitions, and it has paid a high price for its previous involvement. The company clung to the unwieldy laser-disc format, which got off to a promising start in 1981 before sales stalled and eventually collapsed in the mid-1990s in the face of the persistent popularity of video cassettes. This time the threat comes not from other formats but from other industry rivals: South Korean firms that are building cheaper players, and Sony whose new PlayStation 2 console comes with a built-in DVD player.

Pioneer has 'very, very good technology, but the problem is their profitability', says Masahiro Ono, an analyst at Warburg Dillon Read. On its own, he believes DVD 'won't make them much money' because competition is already bringing down the price of players.

That's where Pioneer has an ace up its sleeve. It recently launched the world's first recordable DVD system—a player that enables the user to record movies just as they do on video cassettes, or even to edit TV programs or home videos.

Still, it's pursuing a risky strategy by putting so much of its focus on DVD technology. As Ono explains, Pioneer, unlike industry giants like Sony and Matsushita, simply hasn't got the deep pockets or diverse product line-up to soften the blow if its DVD plans don't work out.

For now, investors seem willing to buy Pioneer's strategy and have pushed up its stock price by about 30 per cent in the past year, matching the percentage gains in shares of Matsushita and Sony and the benchmark Nikkei 225 stock index.

Pioneer has spent 25 years refining its optical-disc research, which Ito says gives the company an edge over its rivals. That could be the key to protecting its share of the DVD market, one of the fastest growing segments of the consumer electronic business.

Pioneer is counting on its DVD business to help it recover from a ¥1.9 billion group loss in the half year to September 1999. Thanks in part to the strong demand for DVD players overseas, the company expects to hit its full year net profit forecast of ¥5 billion—a five-fold gain from the previous year. Worryingly though, DVD prices have been falling nearly as fast as the market has been expanding. South Korean players sell in the United States for as little as $299, about $100 less than Pioneer's cheapest model and around half of what they were selling for not too long ago.

Of course, lower prices should boost sales, but Japanese manufacturers must reduce their costs in order to remain competitive. Pioneer and Matsushita are racing to move production off-shore to plants in China and South-east Asia. 'It's really unfortunate that manufacturing of such high-value-added product is being shifted overseas so soon after its introduction, but we really don't have a choice', says Yoichiro Maikawa, manager of the corporate planning office at Matsushita Electric Industrial, which already makes 10 per cent of its players in China.

Another challenge comes from Sony which appears willing to write off its own DVD-player business to spur sales of the PlayStation 2 home video game. The PS2 console, which sells for ¥39 800 in Japan, includes a DVD player that Sony says matches the quality of much more expensive stand alone DVD units sold by Matsushita and Pioneer. Officials at these companies insist that the DVD market is too big to be swallowed whole by the PS2, and say the game player might even help by making more DVD-compatible software available. But some analysts aren't so sure. 'DVD players will be forced to compete with the PlayStation 2', says Dresdner Kleinworth Benson analyst Kimihide Ttakano. 'This will kill the DVD market.'

Pioneer's answer to the PS2 is the DVR-1000, the world's first DVD capable of recording like a standard video-cassette recorder. The player was introduced in Japan in December, and the company hopes it will encourage holdouts to abandon the VCR for the cheaper image and crisper sound of DVD.

'We've finally created an optical disc which can be used over and over again to record', boasts Pioneer's Ito. 'It's like a dream come true.' The ¥250 000 price tag means it won't be on too many shopping lists in the near future, but Pioneer hopes to increase the current output of 10 000 players a month to cut production costs through economies of scale. One way to do that is by starting sales in foreign markets such as the US, where the technology has been held up by wrangling about the methods used to protect copyrighted works from illegal duplication. Pioneer officials say they hope to have the issue resolved later this year.

By getting a jump on the competition, Pioneer hopes to set the de facto industry standard for recordable DVDs. But as analyst Ono points out, 'Pioneer has had no success in the past setting de facto standards'. And with two other groups also trying to be the industry's standard setters—one led by Sony and Philips, the other by Matsushita and Toshiba—Pioneer is unlikely to find the going any easier in the future. None of these formats are compatible with each other, raising the spectre of the sort of battle seen in the VCR market in the 1980s between the Betamax and VHS.

But Pioneer is already looking beyond that battle and working on the next generation of DVDs, which will use blue lasers in quadruple storage capacity on individual discs.

Having decided last year to drop the second half of its old name, Pioneer Electronic, and revamp its logo to reflect its 'devotion to the spirit of the next millennium', Pioneer seems determined to show it has learned from its mistake of sticking with the laser disc in the face of falling sales. It has come up with a new business plan called 'Vision 2005' that outlines its strategy to become the leading company in DVDs, and further expand its production of plasma display panels for wall-hung TVs, advanced cable-TV set top boxes and car navigation systems. Ito says his company is also working with Sony to develop Memory Stick technology for new devices that can download data such as music and films directly onto computer chips instead of intermediate media such as disks.

Longer-term, Pioneer is developing a system code-named 'Agent' that aims to link all major consumer electronics through a voice-activated computer network. This would allow a user, for instance, to instruct his DVD player over a mobile phone to record a favourite movie.

'We want to allow anyone to watch anything, anytime', says Ito. With so much riding on its recordable DVD plans, that may in the end be Pioneer's only sure-fire strategy.

Source: Dawson, C. (2000).

Activities for discussion, analysis and further research

1. Outline the factors required in an organisation which will encourage innovation. Do you think Pioneer possesses those characteristics? Why? Do you identify any weaknesses? What are they? How may they be overcome?

2. Log on to the Pioneer home page and explore their company objectives. How do those reflect an innovative culture?

3. Blue laser technology was developed by a Japanese engineer called Shuji Nakamura while working for Nichia Chemical Industries. Do some literature research to discover why Nakamura has left Japan to take on a research position at the University of California at Santa Barbara. Can you identify which of the factors promoting an innovative culture his original employers were disregarding?

FURTHER READING

Ambastha, A.M. 2004, Competitiveness of firms: Review of theory, frameworks, and models, *Singapore Management Review*, 1st Half, 26, 1, pp. 45–61.

Hedrick, N. and Bridson, K. 2003, A focus on Australian retailers adoption of experiential retailing practices, *European Retail Digest*, June, 38, pp. 1–4.

Lee, S.M. 2003, South Korea: From the land of morning calm to ICT hotbed, *Academy of Management Executive*, May, 17, 2, pp. 7–19.

Ramos, A.D. 2003, The China syndrome, *CFO*, October, 19, 13, pp. 74–8.

Sawhney, M., Balasubramanian, S. and Krishnan, V. 2004, Creating growth with services, *MIT Sloan Management Review*, Winter, 45, 2, pp. 34–54.

GRADUATE GLIMPSE

ANTHONY ROSS

Anthony Ross has a Bachelor of Business majoring in catering and hotel management from Victoria University of Technology. He is the general manager of The Sentosa Resort and Spa in Singapore.

What does you job entail?

I am responsible for the efficient use of the facility to maximise guest and staff satisfaction and the return on investment to the owners. This is achieved through the traditional functions of marketing, human resources, finance and operations. The property features 214 rooms, suites and villas, a 2000-square-metre spa, two restaurants, two bars and a conference centre.

How have your university studies assisted you in your career?

The primary advantage of university is that it teaches you to think broadly and research deeply before making decisions. My course was very specific to my eventual career and I use the analytical, marketing and accounting tools learnt during my degree every day. Some lessons I learnt at university have become internalised so that I no longer recognise where I gained the knowledge, but on reflection a lot of it comes from my formal education.

What is an important management principle that you draw upon frequently in your role?

Any management role involves working with people to achieve results. People tend to be the same all over the world. The most important principle in my opinion is to establish a platform of mutual respect and trust with any team you manage. Once that is established great things can be achieved.

NICOLE UNDERWOOD

Nicole Underwood has a Bachelor of Management with a major in marketing and a minor in human resources from the University of South Australia. She is the general manager of Entrée Recruitment.

What does your job entail?

I have overall responsibility for the profitability and strategic direction of Entrée Recruitment. I ensure that our operational and financial processes are aligned with our vision and strategy in order to achieve continued growth. My other responsibilities include leading and coaching a team of consultants and administration staff, writing and presenting new tender bids, business planning, strategic development, marketing and new business development.

My achievements have included setting up the business from inception and leading it into its third year of operation, being short-listed for the for the Telstra Young Business Woman of the Year Awards in 2002 and over-achieving the sales and profit budgets for the first financial year billing in excess of $1.2 million.

How have your university studies assisted you in your career?

My university studies have assisted me in my career through providing me with the knowledge and management concepts to be successful in business. University also taught me practical skills such as networking, presenting to large groups of people and formal communication skills.

What is an important management principle that you draw upon frequently in your role?

People are your number one asset. After reading Richard Branson's autobiography a few years ago, I became very clear that people come first, customers second and then the profits will take care of themselves.

CTAM Pty Ltd

With the advent of the internet and other advancements in information technology, the information stored on our computers has rapidly become one of the most important areas for increased security. In organisations such as departments of defence and world governments this is especially the case, with information held on their computer databanks around the globe ranging from the location of enemy strongholds to personal information about their staff. Thus, the issue of network security and stability is paramount among governmental priorities. All this seems a world away from the inner south-eastern Melbourne suburb of Ashburton. However, CTAM Pty Ltd, a firm delivering specialised high-speed network security products, has rapidly built up to be a world leader in the field.

Established in 1997, CTAM Pty Ltd began as a small firm devoted to the production of high-quality, high-speed data-encryption devices and other network security devices. Within three years of its initial inception, and with the assistance of the federal government's research and development program, CTAM was supplying high-end data-encryption and information-security equipment to such organisations as the Australian Tax Office, the Australian Federal Police and Defence Science and Technology Organisation.

Through the development of CypherCell, a world-leading high-speed data-encryption solution, CTAM has set the standard in data encryption solutions for commercial and governmental sectors across the globe. This technology provides access control and authentication between secured sites, and confidentiality of transmitted information by cryptographic mechanisms. It is the only such technology to be accredited to both FIPS 140-1 (a high-level US government accreditation) and Common Criteria (international Western government accreditation).

On the domestic front, CTAM's growth was further enriched by a contract secured with Australia's largest telecommunications company,

Telstra, in which their CypherCell technology was adopted on the Telstra asynchronous transfer mode (ATM) network. CTAM's managing director, Dr Roger Knight, said: 'Having worked with Telstra on a number of projects to secure government networks, we are pleased to see our leading security solution meeting the needs of the Australian commercial sector using Telstra's advanced network. This order is significant in the growth of CTAM, not only for the substantial revenue but also for demonstrating the commercial interest and uptake in CTAM's range of high-speed encryption products.' (http://www.ctam.com.au/company-news.htm#investment)

So well received was the small Melbourne IT company, that on the 5 May 2000, the company announced that, after a period of negotiation, Senetas Corporation Ltd (a Melbourne-based enterprise-information solutions company specialising in providing and securing enterprise information) completed its acquisition of a 51 per cent interest in CTAM Pty Ltd. This merger of sorts created $1.5 million and issue of 3 416 667 shares in Senetas to the existing shareholders of CTAM together with a further subscription of $1 million for shares in CTAM Pty Ltd by Senetas. In addition, it allowed CTAM to take advantage of the Senetas link into the United States through their subsidiary firm ComCryp Inc.

In November 2002, the company announced perhaps one of its greatest achievements to date. Through a partnership with an international global technology group, the CyberCell technology was selected by a leading United States defence agency to secure its asynchronous transfer mode (ATM) communications network. The United States government, and its defence agencies in particular, is considered to be the world leader in security-stem use, with the highest standards and requirements. For CTAM to be selected to have its technology used for such a task highlights its position on the world stage.

The following is quoted from the CTAM website interviews:

'The Australian Minister for Communications, Information Technology and the Arts, Senator the Hon. Richard Alston welcomed the announcement, congratulating CTAM, a past recipient of support through the federal government's R&D Start Grant program, on winning such an important contract ahead of international competition: "It is a great result for CTAM, demonstrating what can be achieved by Australian companies on a world stage with the right technology and commercial approach." Senator Alston added that: "What is especially pleasing is that the adoption by this key US defence agency of the CTAM technology demonstrates that Australian companies can successfully aim to be at the leading edge of communications and IT security technology."'

Source: Contributed by Joel Mendelson;
http://www.ctam.com.au; http://www.senetas.com.au.

Activities for discussion, analysis and further research

1. What barriers to market entry do you think CTAM faced when entering the IT security market? How do you think that the company overcame these barriers?

2. In groups of three or four discuss why you think that the security of information is so important within an organisation. Which other areas do you think the CTAM technology has the possibility of entering? Bring your experience of places where you have worked or studied into this discussion.

3. We have seen large Australian multinational corporations (MNCs) such as Newscorp enter the global arena, and then move offshore in order to cope with their international demand. Do you think that CTAM would have to move from their Melbourne offices to the United States or United Kingdom in order to remain a global player?

Please insert the CD-ROM that is packaged with this book to view video clips that correspond to this Part theme.

ORGANISING

Planning, as we saw before, is a crucial management function for setting organisational direction. Nevertheless, even carefully devised strategic, tactical and operational plans mean little if they cannot be carried out effectively. That is where organising is important. To perform the organising function, managers allocate and arrange human and other resources to achieve plans successfully. In the process, the organising function fosters innovation and facilitates needed change.

CHAPTER 8 shows basic elements of organisation structure. Organisation charts, job design, departmentalisation types, and methods of vertical and horizontal coordination are important to a well-structured organisation.

As CHAPTER 9 notes, the way one successful organisation is structured may not suit the needs of another equally successful one. Managers must take a strategic approach to organisation design, assessing alternatives and considering contingency factors influencing structural choice effectiveness.

CHAPTER 10 looks at the strategic use of human resources to enhance the effectiveness of an organisation's workforce through human resource planning, staffing, development, evaluation and compensation. Organising, though, is not just the development of charts and means of coordination: people are the core of any organisation structure.

PART 3

CHAPTER 8

ORGANISATION STRUCTURE

LEARNING OBJECTIVES

After studying this chapter, you should be able to:

- Describe the four elements making up organisation structure.
- Explain the importance of organisation charts and the chain-of-command concept.
- Outline the main approaches to job design, including the principal alternatives to traditional work schedules.
- Explain the five major methods of vertical coordination, including formalisation, span of management, centralisation versus decentralisation, delegation, and line and staff positions.
- Explain how slack resources and information systems can be used to coordinate horizontally.
- Describe the major types of lateral relations and explain their usefulness in facilitating horizontal coordination.

Clear the decks

Shane Flynn arrived to take over the chief executive's role at Flight Centre on 29 July 2002, just one month after the travel retailer closed the books on one of the most extraordinary years in its 21-year history.

Almost a year after September 11 and the collapse of Ansett Australia crippled the tourism and travel industry, Flight Centre told the investment market its pre-tax profit would increase 30 per cent for 2001/02 (the company reports its profit result on 29 August). It is also pressing on with plans to expand in the depressed United States travel market, where early in August the country's seventh-largest airline, US Airways Group, filed for court-protected bankruptcy.

Flynn, who was executive general manager of Flight Centre's South African business, has taken over the day-to-day running of the company from its founder and 20 per cent shareholder, Graham Turner, working in the company's unpretentious Brisbane head office. Turner will remain managing director, concentrating on strategy and acquisitions.

Even in an unstable international travel market, Flynn sees expansion as the only way forward for the company. 'Last year, the total airfare spend in South Africa was US$2 billion, while the total spend (from) the Los Angeles airport was US$7 billion', he says. 'You only need 0.5 per cent market share there and you can do extremely well.'

Flight Centre has grown rapidly from 280 stores and business units in 1996 to more than 970 in 2002 in Australia, New Zealand, South Africa, the US, Canada and Britain. The consensus of three stockbrokers that lodge their forecasts with Multex

Global Estimates is for net profit growth of 38.6 per cent, to $59.6 million, for 2001/02, and a rise of 26 per cent, to $75.1 million, in 2002/03.

One of the company's key challenges is how to manage rapid growth. Analysts have questioned whether it can maintain service levels and manage human resources demands as it continues to expand through acquisitions and opening new outlets.

Flynn says his biggest challenge will be human resources. 'We could open 1000 shops tomorrow if we wanted to, but the key thing would be who is going to run them', he says. 'So we are focused on selecting and developing the right people.'

Flynn says the company's diversification strategy underpinned its strong profit growth in 2001/02 (the only time the company has not increased profits was during the Gulf War in 1990/91). 'The reason that affected us so much is we had one brand and we were based only in Australia and New Zealand', he says. 'We may not have come out of last year as well as we did if we didn't have brand and geographical diversification.'

The company's rapid growth prompted the recent management restructure. '(Turner) had 16 people reporting to him and it's unmanageable', Flynn says. 'It doesn't matter who you are, you can't effectively lead that amount of people, especially when geographically they are so spread out.'

Under the new structure, Turner has six executives reporting to him and will focus on strategy, information technology and internal

continued

business such as office leasing and publishing. He is also responsible for some smaller brands (such as Student Flights and Overseas Working Holidays) and new acquisitions such as the corporate travel agent ITG, which was bought in January for $40 million, and the sports tour operator The Fanatics, with which Flight Centre formed a joint venture in July.

Flynn will manage the company's businesses in Australia, South Africa and Britain, the Flight Centre brand and other brands such as Corporate Traveller and Stage & Screen, along with finance and human resources.

Flight Centre's expansion plan is centred on the US, where it set up in 1999. The US division lost $3 million in 2000/01, hit by start-up costs and the depressed state of the US travel market. Flynn says it

took five years for Flight Centre's British business, which was established in 1995, to become profitable, and he says the US business is likely to follow a similar path. Flight Centre is considering opening outlets in New York, Denver and Chicago.

Flynn also sees opportunities for growth in Australia, where Flight Centre handles 22 per cent of all air-fare sales. The company's goal is a market share of 40 per cent, which Flynn says it can only achieve through further brand diversification.

Source: Condon, T. (2002).

Update: Flight Centre in 2004 has 1400 stores and business units including some in Hong Kong as well as the countries mentioned above. In the US there are now outlets in Chicago as well as Los Angeles.

Organising is important to managers because it is how they match work with resources so organisational plans and decisions (discussed in Part 2) can be made and effectively achieved.

An organising approach effective in one situation may be less so if the situation changes. As a result, organising is a constant management activity. Managers must consider organising issues to maintain company focus. In the first chapter of Part 3, we look at the nature of organisation structure. We explore major considerations in dividing work to energise individuals to perform best. Then we review major ways to group jobs and units to build an organisation's structure. We next investigate several ways to coordinate efforts across the hierarchy. Finally, we examine methods of horizontal coordination to assist departments and units synchronise efforts while encouraging innovation.

THE NATURE OF ORGANISATION STRUCTURE

Like most people, you may have faced a problem and wanted to talk with a supervisor or someone from the next organisational level. If you were told no-one knew who was supervising, or who handled complaints, you would be surprised. We expect firms to work through these issues to survive. In essence, we expect the development of reasonably effective organisation structures.

Organisation structure defined

organisation structure

Formal pattern of interactions and coordination designed by management to link the tasks of individuals and groups in achieving organisational goals

Organisation structure is the formal interactions and coordination patterns management designs to link tasks of individuals and groups to achieve organisational goals. The word 'formal' refers to structures management creates for a specific purpose, and are official, or formal, results of the organising function. Organisations have informal structures, or interaction patterns, that management does not design but that come from common interests or friendship. We discuss informal interaction patterns when looking at groups in Chapter 14.

Organisation structure has four elements (Child 1977):

1. assignment of tasks and responsibilities defining jobs of individuals and units
2. clustering individual positions into units and units into departments and larger units to form an organisation's hierarchy

3. various mechanisms facilitating vertical (top-to-bottom) coordination, such as how many people report to any given manager and the degree to which authority is delegated
4. various mechanisms fostering horizontal (across departments) coordination, such as task forces and interdepartmental teams

The process of developing organisation structure is **organisation design**. The organisation chart is an aid to visualise structure. This chart needs to be described before analysing the four main organisation structure elements more fully.

organisation design

Process of developing an organisation structure

The organisation chart

The **organisation chart** is a line diagram showing organisation structure in broad outline. Details differ, but charts show major positions or departments. They also indicate their grouping into specific units, reporting relationships from lower to higher levels, and official communication channels (Bateman & Snell 2004). Some charts show position titles, as well as occupants. An organisation chart of major managerial positions and departments in the Acacia Mutual Life Insurance Company, based in Washington DC, is shown in Figure 8.1.

These charts give a visual map of the **chain of command**. The chain of command is the unbroken authority line linking each person to the top of the organisation through a managerial position in each layer (Duncan 1989). The basic idea is that each person in an organisation should be able to identify their boss and trace the line of authority across the organisation to the top. In designing organisations managers must follow one basic principle— that the chain of command must be kept to a minimum—that is, the hierarchy must always have the fewest number of levels to effectively and efficiently use its human resources (Jones et al. 1999)

Most organisations of more than a few members have charts showing the chain of command and basic structure. These give a broad view but not all details. For example, organisation charts rarely give information about specific jobs. Yet, as noted, job design is a major structural aspect, and it is that subject we turn to.

organisation chart

Line diagram depicting broad outlines of an organisation's structure

chain of command

Unbroken line of authority ultimately linking each individual with the top organisational position through a managerial position at each successive layer in between

JOB DESIGN

Different job types can involve very different activities. A buyer's job for Grace Brothers, the Sydney-based department store chain, may involve supplier contact in an area (such as shoes), new range previews, in-house brand source development, and consumer taste trend studies. By contrast, a salesperson's job includes learning a department's new items, tidying displays, helping customers and registering sales. The different activities for buyer and salesperson reflect **work specialisation**, the degree to which work to achieve organisational goals is divided into various jobs. Most organisations could not operate without specialisation. This is because all members would need every skill to run an effective organisation.

Conversely, jobs may involve very different activities but have similar titles. For example, an administrative assistant's job may require typing, filing and photocopying, or meeting and travel coordination, problem investigation, and decision-making on many matters. What any job includes depends on **job design**, or specified task activities associated with a particular job.

Job design is important to organising for two reasons. One is the logical grouping of task activities. It may be hard for organisation members to function efficiently otherwise. The other is that the configuration, or design, of jobs influences employee motivation. (We discuss motivation further in Chapter 11.) When designing jobs managers must consider efficiency and motivational issues to achieve effective performance.

work specialisation

Degree to which work necessary to achieve organisational goals is broken down into various jobs

job design

Specification of task activities associated with a particular job

Approaches to job design

There are four major job-design approaches: job simplification, job rotation, job enlargement, and job enrichment (Milkovich & Glueck 1985).

FIGURE 8.1 Organisation chart for the Acacia Mutual Life Insurance Company

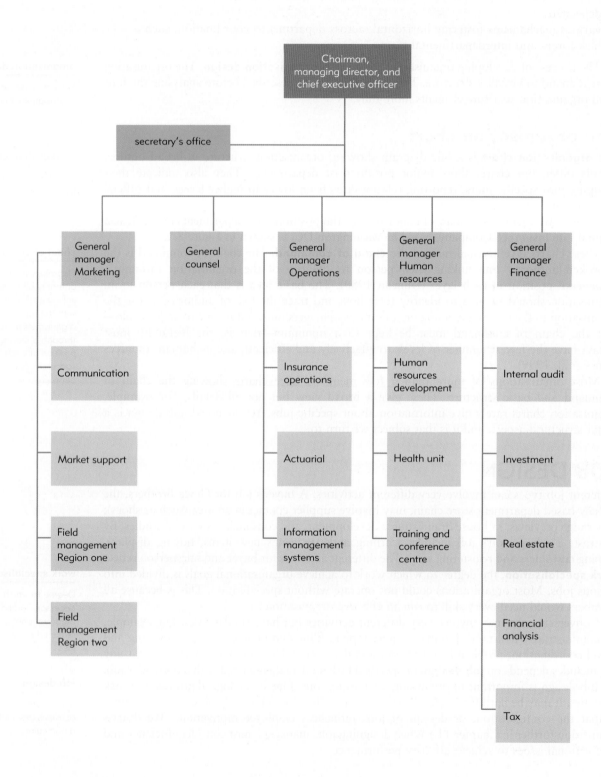

Franchising: A structure for success

Gerry Harvey is Australia's most recent billionaire and the chairman of Harvey Norman Holdings Limited. Harvey started a partnership in Arncliffe in 1961 with cofounder Ian Norman, when they opened their first electrical store, Norman Ross Electrics. The decision by businessman Mr Alan Bond to sack them both, on his acquisition of the Norman Ross company in the 1980s, proved a disaster for the company. Under the control of Bond it went broke and Ian and Gerry formed Harvey Norman, which became one of the most successful retail chains in the country.

Apart from the sale of homewares and electrical goods, other principal activities of Harvey Norman Ltd include Franchisor, a subsidiary that handles provision of advertising and advisory services to Harvey Norman franchisees, provision of consumer finance, property investments and lessor of premises to Harvey Norman franchisees. The company is listed on the Australian Stock Exchange and has averaged an annual rate of return to shareholders of 46.5 per cent over the last ten years. If you had invested $1000 in the company in 1994 it would now be worth over $6000.

Luck plays no part in the layout of a Harvey Norman store. From the selection of the site demographically, to the final design of the store, it is all carefully planned by senior management. The Marion store, in South Australia, is a good example of this. With a total floor area of 1000 square metres, the store contains four departments, bedding, furniture, computers and electrical, and it also has a large on-site carpark and warehouse.

Demographically, this store is situated on a main traffic route and close to a very large Westfield shopping complex. Being situated on the main road is one obvious advantage. Another is its ability to attract curious or unsatisfied Westfield shoppers through its doors. Design of the store is carefully planned. Shoppers are required to walk through the furniture and bedding sections, which are pleasantly merchandised, before entering the computer and electrical departments. With this floor plan, the company is able to get a lot of mileage for their advertising dollar. Why? The store design encourages browsing. A customer responding to a computer advertisement seen on television the night before might be seen walking out with a few other purchases made in other departments. The company promises a big range and it delivers that promise with large, impressive showrooms. This set-up responds to the customer who 'needs it now' with interest-free finance and, in the case of computers and electrical goods, stock on hand.

To the untrained eye, a Harvey Norman store looks like a big shop selling many things, and it is. However, there are actually four businesses under one roof. Not only are store location and design strong success strategies, but these are built upon by the synergy and sense of community that is created within individual departments.

A crucial part of the Harvey Norman jigsaw is the structural path of franchising the company. But don't come knocking with a bag of money, as stores cannot be bought. Only suitably qualified people, generally from within the organisation, get the chance to become proprietor of a Harvey Norman store. As Harvey says, 'the people-management side of the business is more important than anything else . . . there is nothing more important for me than picking the right people and spending a lot of time with them'. This enables senior management to focus on grand plans while still maintaining control.

The responsibility for the operation of individual departments is put in the hands of that particular department's owner. In other words operational duties such as managing staff, merchandising and, of course, motivating the sales force are challenges the proprietor of each section needs to meet. For proprietors, the hours are long, the days are demanding, and dealing with the public can sometimes be difficult. However, it may just be worth your while, considering the average proprietor is capable of earning between $300 000 and $400 000 per annum. By delegating the operational tasks to department proprietors, senior management are then 'freed up' to continue with the group's corporate-level strategy. A part of that strategy is the search for and selection of suitable sites to continue the store roll outs.

The economic conditions of the past few years have been good for retailers in general, with low interest rates and minimal inflation. This often means people are more comfortable spending money. With an advertising budget 'in excess of $30 million a year' and a simple advertising slogan on television which contains a 15 second voice over 'You want it we got it, at Harvey Norman', people are invited to spend at the store. Sales revenues that jumped from around $33 million in 1997 to over $69 million in 1998 indicate that the advertising is extremely effective. Not only is it effective in bringing shoppers in, it has shown itself as extremely cost effective on a store-by-store basis. The company takes advantage of 'economies of scale'. Retailing is an extremely competitive business and what sets these businesses apart is competitive advantage, and preferably a distinct competence.

To identify one for this company would be like trying to choose a colour from a kaleidoscope—there are many. One hundred and one visible stores across the country is one major benefit. As people relocate from other states they already know of a company that can help them 'set-up' home again. This size compared to others in the market place offers other advantages too. Besides competitors' awareness of the chain, manufacturers and suppliers see the company as a way to grow their own businesses as a result of the high-volume sales the company generates. Manufacturers enthusiastic to do business with Harvey Norman need to meet some tough measures, generally relating to price and advertising subsidies. There is no doubt who holds the strong bargaining lever.

Harvey Norman is set to take advantage of the changes that are occurring in technology and in consumer spending due to the changes in taxation law. Sales of computers for the company have been boosted due to the increased usage of the internet. Sales of electrical products are expected to increase with the federal government reducing wholesale sales tax to 10 per cent in July 2000 and the introduction of digital TV the following year. Perhaps foolish to think otherwise, senior management at Harvey Norman have adopted a growth strategy. The acquisition of the Joyce Mayne stores in 1998 will provide a vehicle for the company to concentrate its efforts in a different market. These will be renamed Doymane and will involve a new lifestyle concept in retailing, offering homewares and furniture with a focus on high-spending shoppers.

With the growth of the internet and the stories of millions made on it by retail-type investors, Harvey Norman is cautious. In a recent interview with Channel 9, Gerry Harvey was pessimistic about the use of the internet as another market for the company to pursue. 'Everyone's on this internet thing, you know, and how wonderful it is and how much money they're going to make out of it … but I don't see proof of that.' Harvey, still not a believer in the possibilities of profits on the internet, feels he had better 'keep his toe in the water' to avoid claims from other commentators that he is 'a dinosaur and out of touch'. Despite this, plans are already under way for the opening of the Harvey Norman 'Supersite' store, possibly before Christmas. The directors of the company are aware that the growth the company has achieved in recent times will not continue for ever. Besides continued store roll-outs in Australia, management is looking into countries in South-East Asia as possible locations for future expansion.

Source: Contributed by Andrew Hutt (details of sources are listed on p. 736).

Activities for discussion, analysis and further research

1. Using the theory studied in this chapter, identify the structure of this organisation.
2. Identify another organisation which franchises its stores. Determine the conditions for the franchisees and compare them to the ones Harvey Norman uses. Which of the two would you prefer to join? Why?

3. Consider the structure of the store and the management issues which result from it.
4. Locate the closest Harvey Norman store and make an appointment with the manager to interview them.

5. Discover the issues they feel are primary concerns to the success of their venture.

Job simplification

Job simplification is the designing of jobs with only a narrow range of activities (see Fig. 8.2a). Adam Smith, almost a century ago, identified the benefits of work specialisation and simplification. With an example involving pins, Smith (1910), while he was not the first to identify the benefits of specialisation, noted that a lone worker could make 20 pins a day, while 10 who specialised could make 48 000 pins a day (McShane & Travaglione 2003). Frederick Taylor further popularised simplification through scientific management, focusing on reducing jobs to narrow tasks and training workers in how best to do them (see Chapter 2).

Because jobs involved in simplification are simple and repetitive, workers are undifferentiated, so training new workers is easy. The clearest job simplification example is an assembly line. In a chocolate factory, workers may only do one task, such as melting the chocolate edges on chocolate shells and sticking the two parts together to make a hollow chocolate Easter egg. Jobs can, however, be too simplified, such as an assembly line worker tightening just one nut on the wheel of a car, so they become narrow and repetitive. The negative effects of such jobs include boredom, low job satisfaction, absenteeism, turnover, sabotage and inflexible customer service (Hackman & Oldham 1980).

Job rotation

Job rotation is periodic movement of workers through a set of jobs in sequence (see Fig. 8.2b). The approach tries to cut the boredom of job simplification through task variety (Kinicki & Williams 2003). Rotation cross-trains workers (training them on tasks in several jobs), allowing more flexible job assignments. While job rotation helps with monotony and boredom, it may only be short term. Employees quickly learn new simple jobs and get bored again.

Job rotation has more value in employee development. In this approach, employees increase their capabilities and job assignment flexibility, building their grasp of many organisation aspects as they rotate through more challenging jobs (Waterman 1988). Rotation through different units or geographic locations may aid innovation through exchange of ideas. One study suggests job rotation opportunities are desirable as they improve promotion, pay and other career benefit opportunities (Campion, Cheraskin & Stevens 1994). Unfortunately, departments may see those rotating as temporary help (giving them trivial things to do) and doubt their loyalty to the department.

Job enlargement

Job enlargement is allocation of a wider range of similar tasks to a job to increase challenge (see Fig. 8.2c) (Kilbridge 1960). Enlargement increases **job scope**, the number of different tasks an employee performs in a job. Although this is an improvement over job specialisation, the increase in employee motivation by job enlargement is limited. This is because a few added similar tasks do not raise challenge and stimulation sufficiently. So while a Subway food server's job has a wider task range than one at McDonald's, boredom may not be lowered or motivation raised (Jones et al. 1999). In fact overdone job enlargement cuts job satisfaction, efficiency and mental overload, increases errors and reduces customer satisfaction (Campion & McClelland 1993).

Job enrichment

Job enrichment is the upgrading of the job–task mix to increase potential for growth, achievement, responsibility and recognition. Herzberg (1966) pioneered enrichment by

job simplification

Process of configuring jobs so job-holders have only a small number of narrow activities to perform

job rotation

Practice of periodically shifting workers through a set of jobs in a planned sequence

job enlargement

Allocation of a wider variety of similar tasks to a job to make it more challenging

job scope

Number of different tasks an employee performs in a particular job

job enrichment

Process of upgrading the job-task mix in order to increase significantly potential for growth, achievement, responsibility and recognition

FIGURE 8.2 Major approaches to job design

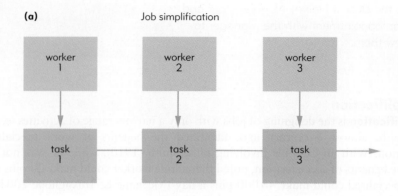

(a)   Job simplification

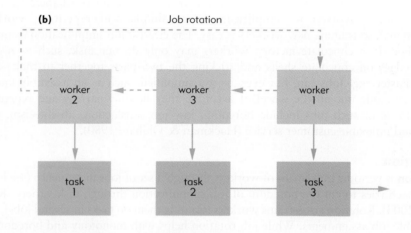

(b)   Job rotation

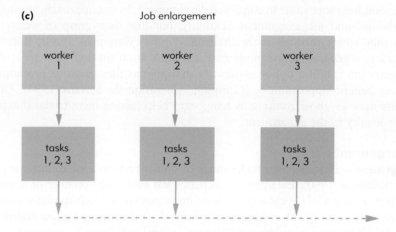

(c)   Job enlargement

job depth

Degree to which individuals can plan and control work involved in their jobs

job characteristics model

Model developed to guide job-enrichment efforts including consideration of core job characteristics, critical psychological states, and outcomes

showing the value of job content as a major motivator. Job enrichment increases **job depth**, how much individuals plan and control their work.

As a job enrichment guide, Richard Hackman and Greg Oldham (1980) developed the **job characteristics model**. The model, in Figure 8.3, has three main elements: core job characteristics, critical psychological states, and outcomes. There are five core job characteristics:

1. **Skill variety** is the extent to which a job entails a number of activities needing different skills.
2. **Task identity** is the degree to which a job allows completion of a major identifiable piece of work, rather than just a fragment.
3. **Task significance** is the extent to which the worker sees job output as having an important impact on others.
4. **Autonomy** is the amount of discretion allowed in determining schedules and work methods for achieving required output.
5. **Feedback** is the degree to which the job provides for clear, timely information about performance results.

The more these core characteristics are reflected in jobs, the more motivating they are likely to be.

These characteristics' motivational value comes from workers experiencing three critical psychological states: feeling work is meaningful, knowing they are responsible for outcomes, and finding out about results. According to the model, these lead to outcomes (listed in Figure 8.3) that include increased work motivation, growth-need satisfaction, job satisfaction and work effectiveness. Raised work effectiveness usually comes from increased work quality, although quantity may increase, due to improved work flow.

Workers react differently to changes in core job characteristic (see moderators in Fig. 8.3). People will be more motivated by job changes if they have knowledge and skills to succeed in redesigned jobs, if they have high **growth-need strength** (how much they need personal growth and development on the job), and if other job context aspects satisfy (such as supervision, pay, coworkers, job security) (Lohner, Noe, Moeller & Fitzgerald 1985; Griffin 1991).

Checking job content is one way to organise work to meet company and worker needs; another is use of alternative work schedules.

skill variety

Extent to which the job entails a number of activities requiring different skills

task identity

Degree to which the job allows completion of a major identifiable piece of work, rather than just a fragment

task significance

Extent to which a worker sees job output as having an important impact on others

autonomy

Amount of discretion allowed in determining schedules and work methods for achieving required output

feedback

Degree to which the job provides for clear, timely information about performance results

growth-need strength

Degree to which an individual needs personal growth and development on the job

FIGURE 8.3 Job characteristics model (reprinted from Hackman & Oldham 1980, p. 90)

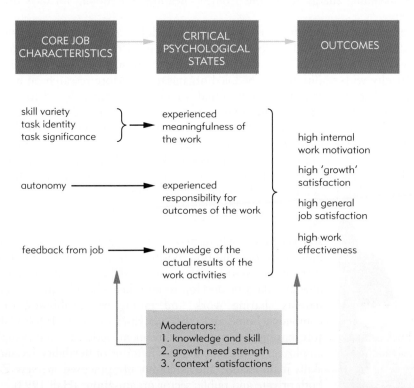

Managing diversity: Alternative work schedules

Related to job design is setting **alternative work schedules**, based on adjusting work schedules instead of content or activities. The approach increases workers' job satisfaction and motivation by setting schedules favouring work-force flexibility by balancing work and personal life. Alternative work schedules help workers juggle work and family responsibilities, and give other benefits too. Flexitime, compressed workweek, and job sharing are three major alternative work schedules.

alternative work schedules

Schedules based on adjustments in the normal work schedule rather than in the job content or activities

Flexitime

Flexitime specifies core hours when people must be on the job, with flexible starting and finishing times as long as required total hours are worked. For example, core hours may be 10 am to 3 pm (with an hour for lunch). Workers then choose a schedule, such as 7 am to 4 pm or 10 am to 7 pm, making eight hours of work a day, including core hours. One study (Hogarth, Hasluck & Pierre with Winterbotham & Vivian 2001) showed the most popular core to be school hours. This is not surprising given that these hours are the hours that mothers and caregivers choose to work.

Flexitime results in improved employee morale, working parents' needs being accommodated, and reduced lateness and traffic congestion as some workers avoid peak times. Absenteeism and turnover are often lower too. Major problems include a lack of supervision at times, unavailability of key people, understaffing, and if some employees' outputs are inputs for others, coordination challenges. Also, tracking several schedules may increase administration. Generally, flexitime has been successful, and increasingly common (Golembiewski & Proehl 1978; Ronen & Primps 1981; Dalton & Mesch 1990; Trost 1992; Poelmans, Chinchilla & Cardona 2003).

flexitime

Work schedule specifying certain core hours when individuals are expected to be on the job and then allowing flexibility in starting and finishing times as long as individuals work the total number of required hours per day

Compressed work-week

The **compressed work-week** is a schedule with four 10-hour days or a similar combination, rather than the normal five 8-hour days. Some firms close three days a week. This allows many economies, including energy reductions from no heating and cooling for days off (*Business Week* 1989).

Other organisations open five days a week by scheduling employees. The basic idea of a compressed workweek, or 4/40 workweek, is to enhance job attractiveness with three (typically consecutive) days a week off. Downsides include fatigue, productivity losses, and accidents, as well as difficulty with traditionally scheduled organisations. More research on a compressed workweek's effects is needed. One study found a compressed schedule led to increased job satisfaction and performance, but after two years positive effects had disappeared (Ivancevich & Lyon 1977). Another (Baughman, DiNardi & Holz-Eakin 2003) found a highly significant correlation between the application of a compressed workweek and employee turnover. Many firms like a 9/80 schedule. In this case, employees work a nine-hour day Monday to Thursday and an eight-hour day on alternate Fridays, so they can have the other Friday off. Employees then get a free Friday in each two-week period (Genasci 1995).

compressed work-week

Work schedule whereby employees work four 10-hour days or some similar combination, rather than the usual five 8-hour days

job sharing

Work practice in which two or more people share a single full-time job

Job sharing

Job sharing is where two or more people share one or sometimes more than one full-time position. In job sharing, one person may work in the morning, the other in the afternoon, or they can work alternate days or develop some other schedule. Job sharers may be parents sharing work and family responsibilities, or mothers combining home and work activities (Thomas 1987; Cohn 1995). Job sharing is a mutually convenient option for both employer and employee. It yields advantages in terms of flexibility, recruitment and skills maintenance and is commonly practised in New Zealand in both private and public sector organisations (Hall 1993).

Structural disease can be deadly

Some organisational structures breed unhealthy practices within companies with sometimes-fatal consequences. Over the past 30 years, the world's biggest accounting firms found that an increasing proportion of their earnings came from management consulting, rather than from the more traditional areas of accounting services. When contracted to provide consulting and auditing for the same firm, the potential for a conflict of interest between these two areas emerges when the consulting unit promises increased profit performance through implementing their recommendations and the auditing unit assesses the accounting standards used in assessing profitability.

The accounting firm Ernst & Young took action to avoid this conflict in 2000 when the organisation restructured by hiving off its consulting division to the French company Cap Gemini. Selling off a promising area of business would seem like foolhardy and radical surgery; however, Ernst & Young has survived the amputation and remain one of the world's biggest accounting firms.

Arthur Andersen was a company that resisted such radical surgery with disastrous consequences. The related firms of Andersen Consulting (Accenture) and Arthur Andersen (accounting services) found themselves competing for the same lucrative consulting business. The organisational structure created a jurisdictional ambiguity that could not be successfully resolved. A bitter court battle between the two Andersens ensued, with a formal separation between the firms being recognised on 1 January

2001. Arthur Andersen's reputation took further blows in 2001, as its auditing competence and independence came under fire in the wake of the failure of its clients HIH in Australia and Enron in the USA.

Ironically, it was the surgically scarred Ernst & Young that merged with the embattled Arthur Andersen (Australia) in May 2002. The merger created a new divisional structure that helped to remove the ambiguities and potential conflicts of interest that played a part in Arthur Andersen's injuries. Ernst & Young is now structured into the three main service divisions of assurance and advisory business services (formally called 'audit'), corporate finance, e-commerce and tax and law. With clearer lines of responsibility and a clearer business focus, Ernst & Young is poised to grow further beyond their position as Australia's second largest professional services firm.

Source: Contributed by Peter Woods (details of sources are listed on p. 736).

Activities for discussion, analysis and further research

1. What organisational structure problems contributed to the demise of Arthur Andersen?
2. What methods of horizontal coordination could have been utilised to solve the structural problems encountered by Arthur Andersen?
3. What methods of vertical coordination could help Ernst & Young avoid falling into similar organisational conflicts?

TYPES OF DEPARTMENTALISATION

How individual jobs are arranged is an important dimension of organisation structure, and another is departmentalisation.

Departmentalisation is grouping individuals into units, and units into departments and larger units to achieve organisational goals. Different patterns of departmentalisation are called organisation designs.

Functional, divisional, hybrid and matrix are four common departmentalisation patterns (Duncan 1979; Robey & Sales 1994). Functional structure units are based on expertise, skill, and similarity of work activities (e.g. marketing, accounting, production or operations, and human resources) (Bounds 1995). Divisional structures in contrast use product or market

departmentalisation

Clustering of individuals into units and of units into departments and larger units to facilitate achieving organisational goals

similarity (e.g. separate divisions for each of several products). Hybrid structures combine aspects of functional and divisional form, with some activities grouped by function and others by products or markets (Jones 1998; Rue & Byars 2003). Finally, matrix structures superimpose, or overlay, horizontal divisional reporting relationships over a hierarchical functional structure. We discuss these methods of departmentalisation, or organisation design, in detail in Chapter 9.

For all designs, managers must focus on vertical and horizontal coordination to make the structure effective. In the next section, we discuss vertical coordination methods.

METHODS OF VERTICAL COORDINATION

vertical coordination

Linking of activities at the top of the organisation with those at the middle and lower levels to achieve organisational goals

While functional, divisional and hybrid departmentalisation types give a basic structure for organisational activities, other mechanisms keep vertical coordination effective. **Vertical coordination** is linking activities at the top of the organisation to those at middle and lower levels to achieve organisational goals. Without coordination, organisation parts cannot work together. Five major methods for effective vertical coordination are formalisation, span of management, centralisation versus decentralisation, delegation, and line and staff positions (Daft 1998; Child 1984).

The role of formalisation

formalisation

Degree to which written policies, rules, procedures, job descriptions and other documents specify what actions are (or are not) to be taken under a given set of circumstances

Formalisation is a common way to achieve vertical coordination. **Formalisation** is the written policies, rules, procedures, job descriptions and other documents specifying actions to take, or not to take, in a set of circumstances (Hall 1996; Child 1984). Vertical coordination is helped by formalisation specifying appropriate behaviours (Moutkheiber 1995). For example, policies give members general guidelines for activities; procedures spell out actions for recurring events; and rules specify what should or should not be done in a situation (see Chapter 6). Job descriptions detail a job's tasks and activities (see Chapter 9).

Most organisations are formalised. For example, major student groups, such as the Otago University Student Union, have written policies on qualifications for office, as well as procedures on the conduct of elections. Without such formalisation, decisions on these issues would be needed each year, taking time that could produce inequities. On the other hand, too many rules and procedures can stifle and discourage needed change and innovation (Marcus 1988; Brown 1998).

When organisations are small, they can be informal, with few written policies and procedures. As they grow, organisations need to increase formalisation to coordinate the increased numbers. The challenge is to avoid becoming too formalised.

Span of management: The trend to downsizing

span of management or span of control

Number of subordinates who report directly to a specific manager

Span of management, or **span of control**, is the number of subordinates reporting to a specific manager. Span of management affects vertical coordination because it defines how much managers interact with, and supervise, subordinates. With too many subordinates, overloaded managers find coordination difficult, and cannot control their work unit's activities. On the other hand, managers with too few subordinates are underused and tend to over-supervise, allowing little discretion (Child 1984; Bateman & Snell 2003).

Factors influencing span of management

Spans of management generally can be wider under the following conditions (Dewar & Simet 1981; Van Fleet 1983; Barkdull 1963; Child 1984):

- **Low interaction requirements** Managers can supervise more people when work is such that subordinates can operate without frequent interaction with each other and/or with their superiors.
- **High competence levels** Managers can handle more subordinates when high job-related skills and abilities of managers and/or subordinates make it possible.

- **Work similarity** When employees in a given unit do similar work, a manager finds it is easier to give adequate supervision than when their work varies widely.
- **Low problem frequency and seriousness** When problems, especially serious ones, are infrequent, managerial attention is less needed.
- **Physical proximity** When subordinates are located close to each other, managers can more easily coordinate activities.
- **Few non-supervisory duties of manager** Managers can handle more subordinates when they have to perform few non-supervisory duties, such as doing part of the work themselves.
- **Considerable available assistance** Managers can supervise more subordinates when they have considerable additional help, such as assistant and secretarial support.
- **High motivational work possibilities** When work offers a high challenge, subordinates are more likely to increase performance levels due to opportunities to exercise discretion, making continual managerial involvement less necessary.

Levels in the hierarchy

Spans of management for various managerial positions directly influence the number of organisational hierarchy levels. A **tall structure** has many levels and narrow spans of control. In contrast, a **flat structure** has few levels and wide spans of control.

To understand span of control's links to the number of levels, compare two hypothetical organisations in Figure 8.4. Organisation A has seven levels, while organisation B has five. Assuming a span of control of four in organisation A, then manager numbers (from the top) would be 1, 4, 16, 64, 256 and 1024, for a total of 1365 (levels 1 to 6). At the seventh (bottom) level, there would be 4096 non-managerial employees. Then, assuming organisation B has a span of control of eight, then manager numbers (from the top) would be 1, 8, 64 and 512, for a total of 585 (levels 1 to 4). Organisation B also has 4096 employees in its bottom level, which is level 5. Thus organisation A needs 811 more managers than organisation B (Robbins 1990).

tall structure

Structure with many hierarchical levels and narrow spans of control

flat structure

Structure with few hierarchical levels and wide spans of control

FIGURE 8.4 Contrasting spans of control (reprinted from Robbins 1990, p. 88)

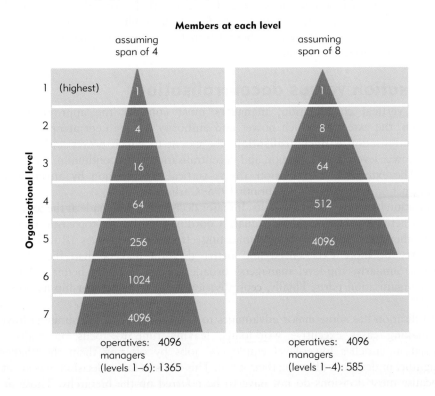

Members at each level

If you wanted to cut the number of hierarchical levels in organisation A without reducing employees at the bottom, you would increase spans of control. Of course, in a real organisation, spans of control vary across the organisation, as in Figure 8.4. Still, the idea is the same. With narrow average spans of control, the organisation is tall. Very tall organisations raise administrative overheads (more managers employed, needing office space, etc.); result in slow communication and decision making (due to many levels); make it harder to track responsibility for various tasks; and encourage dull, routine jobs.

Due to the problems with tall structures, and influenced by the need to cut staffing costs, many firms have downsized. **Downsizing** is the significant cutting of middle management layers, growing spans of control, and shrinking workforce size for greater organisational efficiency and effectiveness (Smallwood & Jacobsen 1987; Bailey & Szerdy 1988; Freeman & Cameron 1993). 'Downsizing' is synonymous with 'restructuring'. **Restructuring** is a major change in organisation structure by reducing management levels and possibly changing some major organisation components through divestiture and/or acquisition (Horton 1988; Bailey & Sherman 1988). Again, the idea is boosting efficiency and effectiveness. Restructuring often means workforce cuts.

In one case of downsizing, Ford Motor Company cut its 12 layers of management levels after finding Toyota had seven (Nienstedt & Wintermantel 1987). Ford's was a competitive disadvantage as the extra levels were an overhead a major competitor did not have. More levels meant the company was less nimble in a situation that was becoming increasingly competitive. Soon after Ford cut management levels, Toyota did too (White 1989; Ono & Brauchli 1989; Reitman 1995; Winberg 1996).

During the 1990s many Japanese organisations have restructured, generally without major layoffs typical of Western firms (Sugawara 1996). In contrast many Western companies downsize by laying off many workers. Downsizing can keep a business viable in recessions or severe competition. Done well, it can cut costs significantly, speed up decision making, energise employees with more challenging jobs, reduce redundancies and increase innovation. If it is poorly done, valuable employees are lost (they are either sacked or leave), survivors demoralised, and there is a drop in short-term productivity as employees assume more responsibilities (Nienstedt 1989; Knox 1992; Burne 1994). Prolonged downsizing destroys employee loyalty and commitment, with serious long-term results (we discuss this in Chapter 10). This is called corporate anorexia, where a firm focuses on downsizing so much it loses resources or the will to grow (Wysocki 1995).

Centralisation versus decentralisation

To improve vertical coordination, managers must consider the appropriate level of **centralisation**, the extent to which power and authority will be kept at upper levels. The reverse of centralisation is **decentralisation**, the extent to which power and authority are delegated to lower levels. Centralisation and decentralisation are a continuum, with degrees of delegation. The extent of centralisation affects vertical coordination by affecting decision making at upper and lower levels (Galbraith 1995; Carlisle 1974).

Centralisation has some positive results. If major decisions are all made at the top, it is easier to coordinate activities of units and individuals. Coordination from the top ensures units do not copy each other's activities, avoiding duplicating effort and resources (Rubel 1996). Top managers may be more experienced and better decision makers than their lower level counterparts. Similarly, top-level managers' broader perspective can better balance needs of different organisation parts. Finally, centralisation helps strong leadership as power stays at the top.

Decentralisation has some major advantages too (Carlisle 1974). Encouraging lower-level decision making eases executive workloads, leaving time to focus on major issues. Decentralisation enriches lower-level employees' jobs by offering them the challenge of making significant decisions affecting their work. This leads to faster decision making at lower levels, because most decisions do not have to be referred up the hierarchy. Those at lower

---

downsizing

Process of significantly reducing middle-management layers, increasing spans of control, and shrinking workforce size

restructuring

Process of making a major change in organisation structure often involving reducing management levels and possibly changing components of the organisation through divestiture and/or acquisition, as well as shrinking workforce size

centralisation

Extent to which power and authority are retained at the top organisational levels

decentralisation

Extent to which power and authority are delegated to lower levels

levels may be closer to the problem and better placed to make decisions. Finally, decentralisation can allow independent units, such as divisions, whose output is easier to measure than functional units. Divisional structures are not synonymous with decentralisation. Some divisional structures still keep power and authority at the top, with most major decisions referred to executive levels.

How can top management decide the balance of centralisation and decentralisation, given the benefits of both approaches? Four main factors tilt the scale from centralisation's end of the continuum, toward decentralisation (Child 1984; Jones 1998):

- **Large size** Top-level managers of large organisations rarely have time or knowledge to make all major decisions.
- **Geographic dispersion** It can be impossible for top executives to keep up with operational details at various locations.
- **Technological complexity** Upper management can find it difficult to keep up technologically.
- **Environmental uncertainty** Top management's ability to assess situations quickly is complicated by rapid change.

Delegation

Another vertical coordination method closely related to centralisation–decentralisation is delegation. For example, you are a new manager of one restaurant in a chain. With nine others you report to a district manager. When you started, you expected to have **responsibility**, the obligation to carry out duties and achieve relevant goals. Your responsibilities might be to keep the restaurant open over certain hours, see food is served, ensure customers are satisfied, and make a certain profit. You also expected to be given **authority**, the right to make decisions, act and direct others in matters related to their duties and goals. As manager, you expected to be able to hire staff, assign jobs, and order food and supplies. You also expected **accountability**, to be able to give good reasons for major changes to duties or expected results.

Carrying the story further, you found the district manager interfered in your decisions, such as hiring new staff, frequently over-ruling them. Then at month's end when you did not reach the profit margin expected (largely because of the district manager's interference), you were held accountable for the result. You might feel you had been given the responsibility but not the authority to do the job.

In this case, the district manager has poorly used **delegation**, the assignment of some managerial tasks to others, with the responsibility and authority to achieve expected results. Delegation means that decision-making authority and responsibility moves from one organisational level to the next lower. Delegators are still responsible for results and accountable to their own managers. Delegation aids vertical coordination as it allows the hierarchy to have work done at the lowest level possible to increase efficiency and effectiveness (Duncan 1989). Delegation also develops subordinates for future managerial positions, ensuring adequate vertical coordination. Generally, delegation is more common with decentralised structures than centralised ones. Although even within a centralised structure, top managers do some delegating. They cannot do everything themselves.

While all theorists emphasise the need to delegate, many managers may find it hard. Some fear blame if subordinates fail, feel they lack time to train subordinates, or want to hold onto their authority and power. Others avoid delegating as they enjoy doing tasks subordinates could do, feel threatened by competent subordinates and fear they may make the manager look poor by comparison, or simply want to ensure work is properly done (Leana 1986; *Management Review* 1995). The result of not delegating may be middle managers untrained for upper-level positions, overloaded managers and demotivated junior staff (Bateman & Snell 2004).

Not delegating may harm managerial careers. For example, a Centre for Creative Leadership study showed that over-managing, or inability to delegate and build a team,

responsibility

Obligation to carry out duties and achieve goals related to a position

authority

Right to make decisions, carry out actions, and direct others in matters related to the duties and goals of a position

accountability

Requirement to provide satisfactory reasons for significant deviations from duties or expected results

delegation

Assignment of part of a manager's work to others, along with both responsibility and authority necessary to achieve expected results

Guidelines for effective delegating

These will help you be an effective delegator:

- The secret is finding what each member of a work unit can do. Choose the subordinate for the project carefully. It will usually be someone immediately below you in the corporate hierarchy. If you want to go down two ranks, work through the person's supervisor.
- Next, decide if you want the subordinate to pinpoint the problem or propose a solution. If the latter, should they act or just give you alternatives? And do you choose the solution together or alone?
- Once your goals are defined, consider whether the person you have chosen can handle the responsibility. Will the task be a challenge but not so hard that the subordinate gets frustrated? According to one expert, the art of managing is to work out what each person can do, then set assignments within their reach, or just above, so they can learn.
- Do not spell out in detail how the subordinate should approach the task. Give clear objectives, though, because some people will fear looking ignorant if they ask questions. Encourage

questions. To build a sense of purpose, explain the task's importance. If it is something that seems menial or insignificant, note that other more important assignments will follow.

- Ensure the subordinate has time, budget, and data or equipment needed to meet the deadline. If they need training, make the investment. Yes, you could do the job in the time needed to train them, but the time training the individual will be recouped many times over in the future. Unless it is a simple project, set up specific checkpoints to review progress so the two of you can ensure work is progressing as planned. That way you can give help, if needed, before the project is in serious trouble. If things are progressing, you can let the subordinate know your appreciation.
- Be prepared to live with an imperfect result. Let subordinates know you will support the outcomes of their efforts, good or bad. Take responsibility for occasional blunders, says an expert, and you will have loyal followers for life.

Source: Adapted from Baum (1987).

RFID

The introduction of radio frequency identification (RFID) is set to revolutionise many systems now used for the purposes of automatic machine-read identification (for example, to identify products). RFID involves the attaching or inserting of a microchip into a product. This microchip emits a low-strength radio signal which can be read by a scanner located near to the chip. The technology is such that chips can now be as small as two millimetres across and can also incorporate sensory systems which can detect changes in temperature, and significant impacts (for example, a container

being dropped on a wharf). Standards are being set down so that the radio frequencies being used are controlled and the strength of the signals being emitted are limited so that, for example, they are not able to interfere with navigation equipment in cargo planes carrying items inserted with the chips.

The usage of the chips has been extended to include the identification of animals, and in fact RFID has been used for some years now in the identification of cattle. A small chip was placed under the skin of the beast and this emitted a low radio signal which was read providing the beast was in close proximity to the reader. As the chip technology improved to withstand harsh treatment the chip can now be placed (clipped) on the ear of the beast and hence can be easily retrieved and reused.

One identification system that is being replaced in many areas by RFID is the barcoding system, though at present more and more items are being identified using barcoding. In other words, the identification of items for all sorts of reasons is an area of great innovation.

In time it is predicted that many grocery items will be inserted with chips. Ideally this would mean that shoppers would be able to wheel their trolley full of groceries past a checkout point, have all items in the trolley 'read' and their bank account automatically deducted by the amount of their purchases. At the same time, shop lifting could be reduced as the offenders would have to find the chips and remove them to avoid detection, so they could not simply hide the item on themselves. However, this is not practical with many items, such as fresh food stuffs. Also, although the cost of the RF chips has gradually been reduced, the cost of the chip must still be very small relative to the cost of the item, so there are many areas where it will not be practical to use RF chips.

The key point is that although the new technology has many exciting possibilities, any such usage requires innovation and the introduction of new applications has to be managed.

Source: Contributed by Ken Dooley.

Activities for discussion, analysis and further research

1. What advantages do you see with RFID, especially over the common barcoding systems now frequently used?
2. What problems do you see with the use of RFID?
3. It is possible that chips could be inserted into humans to facilitate personal identification. What problems do you see with this application?
4. How do you see RFID being introduced? In other words, what processes of innovation should be used in the development and application of this new technology?

was one 'fatal flaw' derailing fast-track executives (McCall & Lombardo 1983). See the discussion in Management skills for a globalised economy, 'Guidelines for effective delegating'.

Line and staff positions

Another issue related to vertical coordination is configuration of line and staff positions. A line position has authority and is responsible for reaching an organisation's major goals. A staff position's primary purpose is giving line positions specialised expertise and assistance. Sometimes the term 'staff' refers to those assisting a particular position as needed (e.g. administrative assistant to a division head).

Positions and departments seen as line or staff vary between organisations. For example, in a grocery chain, line departments might be store operations, pharmacy, and food (directly linked to major organisational goals); staff departments might be human resources and consumer affairs (indirectly related to major goals). For a manufacturer, production and sales are often line departments, and purchasing and accounting staff departments. In many firms, staff departments include human resources, legal, research and development, and purchasing. However, firms must be assessed in terms of their own major goals to differentiate line and staff (Nossiter 1979). For instance, in a law firm, legal function would be line, despite being a staff department in other organisations.

line authority

Authority following the chain of command established by the formal hierarchy

functional authority

Authority of staff departments over others in the organisation in matters related directly to their respective functions

The value of distinguishing line from staff is clear in the variations between line and staff authority. Line departments have **line authority**, or authority following the chain of command set by the formal hierarchy. Staff departments by contrast have **functional authority**, or authority over others in issues related directly to their own function. For example, in the bank's structure shown in Figure 8.5, line departments' authority flows from the chain of command leading to the managing director. The bank's staff departments have functional authority related to other departments; that is, authority in their area of staff expertise. Staff departments help vertical coordination with needed expertise, not through a strict chain of command.

Conflict can still arise when staff departments grow, overseeing departments they should assist. Before cuts, staff at Xerox second-guessed managers until new-product development took two years instead of two to four weeks due to continual staff unit reviews (*Business Week* 1983). Conflict is not inevitable, though, if responsibility areas are clear and line and staff personnel operate as a jointly accountable team for final results.

FIGURE 8.5 Line and staff departments of a bank

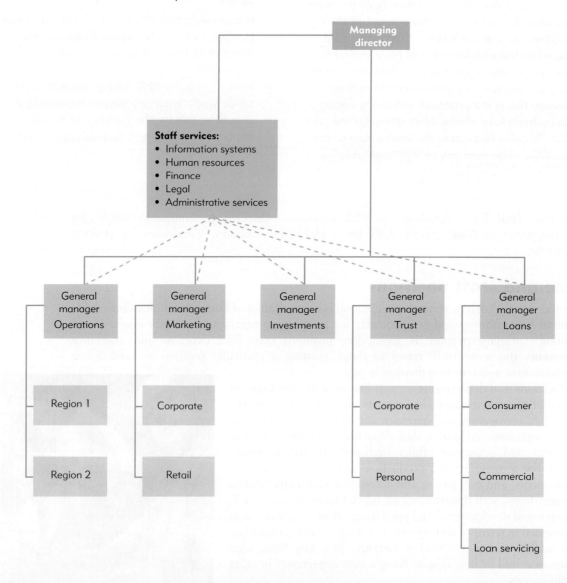

Nola Nails

Nola Nails Salon is a nail and beauty salon offering the services of acrylic and gel nails, manicures and pedicures, and waxing for everyday grooming and for special occasions. Waxing provides a higher return than nails, acrylic, gel or natural work, due to the faster servicing of clients and price margins. Nola's clientele is comprised of regulars—younger career women who like reliable and chic nails and fast appointments that fit around the work day, and clients who enjoy the whole social activity that centres on the salon. Nola's salon has a client-base of 370 regular patrons. Approximately 200 clients visit on a fortnightly basis and it is due to Nola's commitment that she manages to find time to see 100 each week when the schedule for the operating hours is 90 clients over the four days with half-hourly appointments. Nola regularly skips lunch, morning and afternoon tea and she would like to get back to having additional staff so that she can focus on running and promoting the business. Last year, Nola had a part-time technician for three days a week. Jacqui was a vibrant staff member who recently left to have her second child.

Nola is a recognised trainer for sculptured nails. Until very recently she trained at least one new technician a year until her most recent graduates resulted in direct competition rather than expansion of her own business.

Nola strongly believes that the way forward is to offer excellence with product and service, and to expand her business capacity. Nola would like to attract more younger career women and maintain her current clientele, and expand into the waxing and grooming needs of the male market that is currently underserved. Ideas of expansion promote thoughts of how best to staff her business. Overseas, male technicians are respected, working with major success in the beauty industry. Additionally, a male technician might be attractive to men who want professional waxing as part of their grooming regime. This raises questions of how to best expand without risking her current salon. Currently Nola Nails is a women's haven for conversation, a network of relationships where, if you lose one client you run the risk of losing three or four as women visit with booking overlap, making it a social event. If the conversation was inhibited due to the presence of male clientele then Nola might lose one component of her competitive advantage.

Nola can see two options. She could expand, hire staff, probably three or four over the next year, and run a team of specialised technicians. This would likely involve moving to a larger salon somewhere close to her current location. Or she could hire a part-time technician for Nola Nails & Salon; maintain her current facility known as Nola Nails, and set-up a new entity for the male services niche in the adjacent rooms which become available in the next quarter, with personnel who could work part-time in the new venture and part-time at Nola Nails.

Source: Contributed by Virginia Phillips.

Activities for discussion, analysis and further research

1. Discuss the strategic choices Nola faces. How can Nola use organisational structure and branding to improve service and expand her business?
2. In today's environment, it is prosed that an organisation should remain organic in nature. Discuss this concept with reference to an organisation which alters the range of products or services it offers.
3. Prepare a proposal for Nola, outlining the steps to achieve better vertical and horizontal coordination and encourage expansion of the client base.
4. What other skills might Nola need to be able to manage a team and move from being a sole operator?

There is an increasing trend to cut corporate-level staff personnel, as firms try to reduce costs and improve decision making. Small central offices monitor budgets, cash flow, and overall activities (Moore 1987). Improving vertical coordination is a structural matter; promoting horizontal coordination is another.

PROMOTING INNOVATION: METHODS OF HORIZONTAL COORDINATION

You buy a television set at a department store and are told it will arrive in three days, but it does not. You call to ask about the delay, and your call moves up the hierarchy until you are talking with the store chain's regional manager. You will wonder about a firm where a regional manager is drawn into a routine sales and shipping transaction. If all problems were handled vertically, organisations would be paralysed.

horizontal coordination

Linking of activities across departments at similar levels

Instead, organisations facilitate **horizontal coordination**, linking activities across departments at similar levels. Horizontal coordination helps organisational information processing (Capowski 1993). Galbraith (1977) argues that the more companies must process information to produce their product or service, the more horizontal coordination is needed. Organisations must process more information when facing complex and/or changing technology, environmental uncertainty, and increased size. (We discuss these again in Chapter 9.) For example, William H. Wilson set up Pioneer/Eclipse Corporation, a small firm specialising in a floor-cleaning system, with a traditional functional structure and doing most of the coordination himself. As the firm grew, due to poor horizontal coordination it lost money. In one case, the sales department had a promotion then found manufacturing and purchasing were unaware of it, lacking materials and stock for orders. In another, the credit department denied credit to a major account before the sales department could fix the problem. 'The left hand', said one observer, 'did not know what the right hand was doing' (Rodes 1988).

As horizontal coordination helps process information across the organisation, it also encourages innovation (Tushman & Tushman 1986; Kanter 1988). There are three reasons for this. First, new ideas are more likely when many views exist. Second, problem and opportunity awareness sparks creative ideas. Third, involving others in developing ideas often makes them more willing to help implement them (see Chapter 10). Corporate Express is demonstrating some stirrings of innovation, moving first to smaller customers and then to support services (Roberts 2003).

Horizontal coordination mechanisms augment the basic hierarchy and other vertical coordination methods by aiding information exchange across units at similar levels. Three major means to help promote horizontal coordination are slack resources, information systems, and lateral relations (see Fig. 8.6) (Galbraith 1977).

Slack resources

slack resources

Cushion of resources that facilitates adaptation to internal and external pressures, as well as initiation of changes

An interesting support to horizontal coordination is use of **slack resources**, a cushion of resources helping adaptation to internal and external pressures, as well as change initiation (Bourgeois 1981). You will have slack resources in your own life. For example, in your family, a slack resource might be an extra car or television set, or mobile telephone. Through coordination and tight schedule programming, your family might manage with less, but this would take effort and make quick changes of plan hard. Because organisations face similar choices, they, too, often use slack resources, such as extra people, time, equipment and inventory, to reduce the need for constant inter-unit coordination and allow some flexibility in resource use.

Slack resources can help foster creativity and innovation (Bourgeois 1981). For example, 3M researchers spend 15 per cent of their time on projects of their own with long-term payoff potential (the company calls this 'bootlegging'). This promotes slack resource use (time, equipment and materials) to enhance chances for innovation.

FIGURE 8.6 Horizontal coordination methods for increasing information-processing capacity as needed

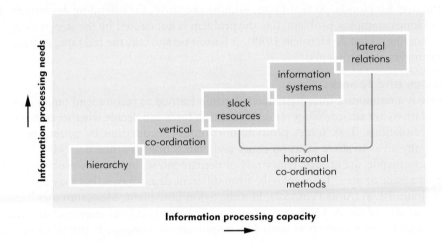

Information systems

A growing horizontal coordination method is information systems, largely computerised ones, to coordinate company parts (Marcia 1995). For example, Mitsubishi Motors Australia is moving to use suppliers already linked to its parent companies' electronic systems, in order to fully utilise gains from the larger corporation's information systems (Thompson 2003). (Computerised information systems are discussed again in Chapter 15.)

Lateral relations

Another increasingly common approach to horizontal coordination is **lateral relations**. Instead of referring issues up the hierarchy for resolution, this is coordination of efforts by communicating and problem solving with peers in other departments or units. Collaboration produces innovative solutions and helps with creative responses to events. Direct contact, liaison roles, task forces, teams and managerial integrators are major lateral relations methods (Galbraith 1977).

Direct contact

One lateral relations method is **direct contact**, or communication between two or more staff in different work units at similar levels, to coordinate tasks and solve problems. Direct contact means issues can be resolved at middle and lower levels without involving upper-level managers. Problems, in fact, can often be handled better by lower-level managers as the issues are more familiar.

Liaison roles

A **liaison role** is a role to which someone is appointed to facilitate communication and issues resolution between two or more areas. Liaison roles are used where continuous coordination between departments for effective functioning is needed. An example is appointing an engineer to set up contact between engineering and manufacturing departments (Reynolds & Johnson 1982).

Liaison roles for businesses and major customers are increasingly common. The liaison person builds horizontal coordination by working with departments and the customer, to satisfy customer needs. A steel company executive's comments (who wished to remain anonymous) showed the benefits of liaison roles in customer dealings. The company has a full-time liaison person on site at Honda's Marysville, Ohio, plant. He explained that if there was no liaison person and a problem emerged with stamping steel for body panels, the following

lateral relations

Coordination of efforts through communicating and problem solving with peers in other departments or units, rather than referring most issues up the hierarchy for resolution

direct contact

Communication between two or more persons at similar levels in different work units to coordinate work and solve problems

liaison role

Role to which a specific individual is appointed to facilitate communication and resolution of issues between two or more departments

scenario would occur. Honda people affected by the problem would go to the purchasing department. Purchasing would contact the steel company's salesperson. The salesperson would complain to their product office. The product office would pass the issue to the department making the steel for Honda. At that point, said the executive, the offending department argues that 'it's a Honda stamping problem' (i.e. the problem is not caused by the steel making but by Honda's stamping) (Flint & Heuslein 1989). A liaison person cuts the red tape, dealing directly with departments and problems.

Task forces and teams

A task force is a temporary interdepartmental group formed to recommend on an issue. These recommendations are advice. Whoever set up the task force can decide whether or not to follow the recommendations. Task forces promote horizontal coordination by getting people from many company areas to share ideas on issues and plan actions (Farnham 1994).

Teams, meanwhile, are groups, temporary or permanent, set up to solve problems and apply solutions on a issue or area. Teams may be from different departments, but may come from the same unit (Jones 1998). At its Pensacola, Florida, nylon fibre plant, Monsanto uses liaison roles and teams in its Adopt A Customer program, to offer excellent customer service. Here, Monsanto matches top customers with key employees as liaisons. If problems appear, the liaison person is a 'resource team leader', helping resolve problems quickly. For example, if a customer says yarn is breaking, the liaison person is then an internal resource team leader. They notify technical salespeople, quickly assembling a team with expertise and resources to solve the problem and offer innovative solutions. 'The whole idea of Adopt A Customer is to give top priority to that problem not in three days, but on day one, with the first phone call from our customer', says Monsanto's manager of technical sales (Flint & Heuslein 1989). We discuss teams and task forces further in Chapter 14.

Managerial integrators

A managerial integrator, another means of lateral relations, is a separate manager who coordinates related work across several functional departments. They have titles like 'project manager', 'product manager' or 'brand manager' and do not belong to departments whose activities they help coordinate. Project managers usually coordinate a project until it is finished. Aerospace, defence and construction industries use them where large, technically complex projects must finish on schedule and at the price contracted (*Supervisory Management* 1995). Product managers launch new products and services and may continue coordinating interdepartmental work on them. Brand managers coordinate company work on brand name products, in soap, food and toiletries industries. Brand managers devise and implement brand strategies and plans, monitor results and correct problems. Managerial integrators are horizontal coordinating agents (Child 1995). They allow rapid reaction to environmental change and efficient resource use as they move between projects; they can also sponsor innovative ideas.

Managerial integrators typically have no line authority, so they must work with functional managers, who control resources (Denton 1995). They compete with those (e.g. managerial integrators for other projects) who also want functional departments to help make their projects, products or brands successful. Thus, managerial integrators must use knowledge, competence,

personality, group skills and persuasion to work with functional managers and their departments assigned to their project (Adams & Kirchof 1984; Vlasic & Kerwin 1996). They can also aid in initial company development. Benjamin (2003) explains the value of a Business Review Group (BRG) in ensuring that the diverse factions involved in set up are melded into a coherent group.

In this chapter, we discussed several major organisation structure elements, including vertical and horizontal coordination methods. In the next, we explore links between strategy and organisation structure in enhancing organisational effectiveness.

Achieving competitive advantage through new patterns of work: The Williamstown Naval Dockyard

Flexible patterns of work have emerged as a key factor in enhancing organisational efficiency and competitiveness. In Australia this has been of particular interest as the globalisation of the marketplace has further increased competitive pressure. The ability of an organisation to respond in a flexible manner to increasing competition and uncertainty through more effective and efficient use of resources, particularly human resources, is becoming increasingly important. This has made the management of human resources a key element in developing competitive organisations. The development of flexible patterns of work can be wide and varied, depending upon the needs of the organisation. It can mean the development of a wider range of skills for the workforce, to allow employees to be deployed according to demand. It can also mean a greater variation in the employment relationships with the outsourcing or subcontracting of non-core production or services.

The Williamstown Naval Dockyard (WND) is Australia's premier naval shipbuilding facility. For many years the efficiency and performance of the dockyards had been a constant problem. Through the 1980s, productivity loss attributed to industrial unrest, and cost over-runs led to a Royal Commission of Inquiry. The Committee reported that the dockyard had fallen into a state of shambles. This led to the dockyard being given the nickname of the 'iron-lung' and described as Australia's worst worksite. The continued losses and lack of international competitiveness, underpinned by archaic work practices and antagonistic industrial relations, forced the federal government to announce the sale of the Williamstown Naval Dockyard in 1987. This was to be the first major privatisation of a public utility in Australia.

Significantly, trade unions at the dockyard and the peak union body, the Australian Council of Trade Unions (ACTU), agreed to cooperate with the sale process. The ACTU position was that it was not opposed to the privatisation of the dockyard because of its poor industrial record and despair in almost all quarters at resolving the problems. In December 1987 the federal government announced the sale of the dockyard to the Australian Marine Engineering Corporation (AMEC). The purchase of the dockyard by AMEC, a private consortium, took place on 4 February 1988. At the same time a restructuring of AMEC itself was in train. By September 1988 the Transfield Group, trading under the name AMECON, had acquired total ownership of the dockyard. The development of a competitive shipbuilding industry meant the removal of highly regulated and restrictive work patterns, the multiplicity of trade unions and the conflictual approach to industrial relations at the dockyard. Prior to the sale of the dockyard, the workforce of 2400 employees was represented by 23 trade unions and 30 industrial awards. Demarcation was endemic and there were 390 work classifications. In addition to these classifications, there were a further 180 allowances. Work practices at the dockyard were further entrenched by policies which took no account of workload demands. This manifested itself in idle time for many employees stretching to more than 12 months.

The major focus for the new dockyard owners was the development of human resource management policies to increase efficiency. The key area that management sought to restructure was work patterns and practices. The first process in AMECON management's raft of reform was the modification of rules and regulations of work practices. Provision for an enterprise agreement (the first in Australia) was agreed upon with the ACTU. This agreement was the platform for further reforms that management wished to implement in order to create a marine engineering centre able to compete with the best in the world. The key aspect of this new agreement was the development of dispute-avoidance mechanisms, skill-enhancement provisions, the use of subcontracting and elimination of restrictive work practices—in other words, a demarcation-free workplace with full flexibility in work allocation. The focus on the removal of lines of demarcation and on skills-enhancement policies within the industrial agreement, and the need to involve unions relevant to the marine engineering industry, logically meant a reduced number of trade unions representing dockyard employees. This policy was supported by the ACTU and the federal government as it was part of a wider agenda to develop a modern trade union movement of 20 industry-based unions. Despite initial industrial unrest, AMECON argued that for the dockyard to increase productivity it was essential that the number of trade unions be reduced to those that were relevant to the dockyard's core work. The ACTU demarcation panel agreed upon three manufacturing-specific trade unions.

The ACTU and the dockyard management also negotiated new work practices into the enterprise agreements. A central theme in the development of an efficient and competitive dockyard for management was a labour force that would be responsive and adaptable to the needs and demands of a market-driven environment. With the enterprise agreement and three unions representing the workforce, the climate in which to undertake these reforms was in place. The first step in the development of new patterns of work was the restructuring of job structures and classification. The process began with the reduction of work classifications from 390 to 2 (tradesperson and non-tradesperson), which immediately eliminated many lines of demarcation. AMECON also invested heavily in training and development, through its training board, which comprised management and employee representatives. The major development of this group was the establishment of the Skill Enhancement Program, which provided employees with the opportunity to develop a broad-based spectrum of skills linked to career progression. The board oversaw the design, development and evaluation of these programs.

The development of total quality management and team-based programs were also part of the board's brief from management to develop an adaptable, multiskilled workforce. In addition, a Management Development Program for dockyard managers was developed in conjunction with local education institutions. A key aspect in the more efficient utilisation of human resources is the ability to adjust the size of the workforce to the level of economic activity at short notice and with relative ease. The traditional model of recruitment at the dockyard had constrained work being undertaken outside the dockyard or by subcontractors. Consequently, recruitment was geared to peak workloads. This combined with the extensive and complex lines of demarcation led to extensive 'idle time'.

The enterprise agreement provides for the use of contractors to facilitate work in the dockyard as and when required. The integration of subcontractors focuses on the need to supplement normal procedures or to provide specialised work. The need to have the option of using external labour allows for whole sections of work to be subcontracted. This maintains a compatible level of activity on-site and enables subcontractors to carry out activities that cannot be economically performed by the company's employees on site. The integration of these work practices allows recruitment to be geared to program troughs rather than peaks. To further develop and maximise the use of the 'core' workforce, variations in work time are also provided for in the enterprise agreement. While work hours are specified within the agreement, incremental variations within the period specified (between one and four weeks) allow a maximum of 10 hours per day, with special provision to work up to 12 hours per day subject to the ACTU Code of Conduct on 12 hour shifts and in accordance with Occupational Health & Safety regulations. In addition, variations in the spread of work may be undertaken by mutual consent.

The use of shift work is also provided for in the enterprise agreement, specifically where unimpeded production is required, or for short periods in relation to the production schedules within the context of appropriate regulations and agreements. Provision for the use of overtime is also encompassed in the agreement. The adoption of these new patterns of work has seen the dockyard reduce its core workforce from 2400 to 900 employees supported by up to 900 contractors. The elimination of restrictive work practices, idle time and lines of demarcation and the gearing of the size of the workforce to supply and demand has seen the dockyard increase its productivity by 700 per cent. Lost time has decreased from 10 per cent to 0.1 per cent per annum.

What has emerged from these changes is an increasing realisation of the importance of developing a strategic and integrative approach to the organisation's human resources as a way of improving performance. Underlying the development of these work patterns at the Williamstown Dockyard has been the integration of human resources drawn from both internal and external labour markets. From being described as the 'iron lung', and notorious as the worst worksite in the country, the Williamstown Naval Dockyard has achieved world competitiveness by attracting both national and international contracts. Its achievements have also been acknowledged by its inclusion in the Australian Best Practice Development Program as an Australian Organisation that has achieved World's Best Practice.

Source: Contributed by Peter Holland.

Activities for discussion, analysis and further research

1. What was the catalyst for these dramatic changes at the dockyard?
2. What were the advantages in developing these new work patterns and practices?
3. What factors helped the Williamstown Naval Dockyard develop these work patterns and practices?

REFLECTIVE PRACTITIONER

KIMBERLEY TURNER

This started as me by myself. After that I looked at the other types of people who I would need on board. Because of the lack of experience I had in the aviation industry, I looked at it from a functional perspective and said, I need a pilot, I need an air traffic controller, an engineer and someone with an operations background. So I went around and strategically hand-picked people with different industry backgrounds so that we could provide an all-encompassing service to the aviation industry. And that led to a level of confidence as clients recognised that we had all this expertise available in the technical functional areas. That was my first step of growth in terms of building the team and looking at the structure.

In terms of layers of management, for the first three to four years I had everyone reporting to me. You can do that quite easily when your team is quite small but my role as a manager was triple-hatted. I was the primary subject matter expert, the project manager (for client work) and the business manager. As we grew I needed help to manage these functions, so the second transition was when I employed an office manager, who was really an operations manager, to assist me in keeping on top of things.

The third transition is what we have gone through in the past couple of years by putting that extra layer of management in to take responsibility of the key areas of the business. Everybody kept saying to me: 'Kimberley, you need an operations manager to run the day-to-day so you can focus on running the business.' My perspective was: 'Yes, I know that but we are not there yet in terms of that growth or financial backing to support that requirement. We can't quite sustain that and until I can feel that the business is settled and has reached that growth level, I don't want someone else to run it. I want to run it.' So that third stage of growth in the structure that we have looked at, is myself, my senior executive team which is three of my key staff, and looking at the department structure and putting someone in charge of each department as the manager. Not a director but a hands-on manager.

What works in theory and practice are two different things and that comes down to the people. So, looking at the organisational structure chart, theoretically I have only four people reporting back to me. Some people are multi-hatted and have responsibility for two areas of the business and that works quite well as some areas are still quite small.

Effectively, the structure hasn't changed at all from the time I first envisioned it. It's just a case of building the organisation and filling the positions as the organisation grows. Our fourth stage of growth is keeping and maintaining the company structure but upgrading those management positions into director's positions, where the director of training might have three training managers under them where one runs projects, one runs training development and the third runs training delivery. So that's our next stage of growth and we are working towards that in the next three years.

FOCUS ON PRACTICE

Strategies for improving

1. Consider an organisation which has changed its range of products or services. How does this impact on its structure? Should the organisation change how it manages its processes?
2. Consider what strategies an organisation can use to keep its operational levels to a minimum.
3. What could an organisation do to retain an organic nature when it significantly changes the number or kind of customers it attracts?

Source: Jones et al. (2000).

SUMMARY

MAX YOUR MARKS!
Thirty interactive questions
on *Organisation Structure*
are available now at the
Online Learning Centre that
accompanies this book:
www.mhhe.com/au/bartol4e
(For access to MaxMark
please refer to the front of
this book.)

- Organising is the arranging of work and resources so planned goals can be achieved. Important to the organising function is building organisation structure. This has four main elements: job design, departmentalisation of positions and units, methods of vertical coordination and horizontal coordination. Organisation charts give a graphic depiction of the structure and help employees trace the chain of command.

- There are four main approaches to job design: simplification, rotation, enlargement and enrichment. The job characteristics model guides job enrichment efforts by showing the value of core job characteristics, critical psychological states, and high growth-need strength to job outcomes. A related job design aspect is alternative work schedules, which often help with diverse work-force needs. Major alternative schedules include flexitime, compressed workweek and job sharing.

- Among common departmentalisation forms are functional, divisional, hybrid and matrix. Vertical coordination, or linking activities at the top of the organisation with those at middle and lower levels, can be achieved in five major ways: formalisation, span of management, centralisation versus decentralisation, delegation, and line and staff positions.

- Three particularly useful means to facilitate horizontal coordination are slack resources, information systems and lateral relations. Slack resources give a cushion of resources allowing adaptation to change, while information systems enhance exchange of information. Lateral relations, involving coordinating efforts with peers in other departments and units, has several main forms: direct contact, liaison roles, task forces, teams and managerial integrators. Horizontal coordination helps with innovation as it facilitates the exchange of ideas across organisational units.

QUESTIONS FOR DISCUSSION AND REVIEW

1. Explain the four elements comprising organisation structure. What evidence can you see of them at your college or university?
2. Describe the relationship between an organisation chart and its chain of command. If you were new to an organisation, how could the chart help orient you?
3. Contrast the various major job-design approaches. Use the job characteristics model to explain how you might enrich a particular job.
4. Distinguish between the three main alternative types of work schedule. What changes might be needed to accommodate non-traditional work schedules?
5. Explain the role of formalisation in vertical coordination. Give an example of a policy or rule likely to have a dysfunctional impact on organisational effectiveness. How should things be changed to have a positive effect?
6. Explain the relationship between span of management and the extent to which an organisation is flat or tall. Why are many major organisations flattening their structures? What are the potential problems of downsizing?
7. Contrast the advantages of centralisation and decentralisation, and explain when each is appropriate. Why is delegation important to both?
8. Explain the differences between line and staff positions. Which type would you prefer? Why?
9. Explain slack resources and computer-based information systems as applied to horizontal coordination. Explain how each helps horizontal coordination in organisations.
10. Distinguish between various types of lateral relations. How could they be used in your college or university?

CRITICAL THINKING QUESTIONS

To answer some of these questions you will need to do further research. Useful references are given below each section of the questions.

This chapter reviewed the basic elements of organisational structure. The following questions examine elements of structure within a variety of organisational settings.

Goold and Campbell (2002) assert that the structure of most organisations rarely occurs as the result of systematic and methodical planning. Instead, they suggest structure is generally the product of a series of haphazard events that tend to evolve as events unfold in a continuing series of fits and starts. Further, they suggest it is politics rather than policies which are the chief determinant of structure. Goold and Campbell set out nine practical tests which they believe can assist managers in evaluating the existing organisational structures or designing new ones.

1. The nine tests will hardly be surprising to those who have read the textbook, so what are they?

Goold and Campbell suggest that poor organisational structures can have serious consequences for organisations attempting to make major design changes and these can lead to 'turf wars' and delayed strategic initiatives.

2. How would you go about major design changes in an organisation that has poor structures?

(Material relevant to questions 1 and 2 may be found in Goold, M. and Campbell, A. 2002, Do you have a well-designed organisation?, *Harvard Business Review*, 80, 3, pp. 117–24.)

The costs of an organisational restructure can be massive in both size and scope. This is illustrated in recent moves in Australia's retail sector where the ongoing battle between Coles Myer and Woolworths continues into the arena of information technology and supply-chain management. Coles Myer will invest about $315 million over five years in IT as part of its massive supply-chain revamp, which is expected to return $425 million in annual benefits. However, Woolworths is already well into their organisational restructure. Called 'Project refresh', it entails a $1 billion supply-chain and IT revamp.

3. Why is IT the focus of the restructure of the supply-chain system?

4. What sort of changes would be made by this technology-focused restructure of the supply chains?

(Material relevant to questions 3 and 4 may be found in Mills, K. 2003, Retailer revives supply chain, *Australian*, 30 September, p.C02.)

5. While the big players such as Woolworths and Coles Myer can play around with millions of dollars and take years to achieve a new structure, what happens for the small to medium enterprises (SMEs)?

6. What problems could this focus on traditional organisational structures produce for SMEs in Singapore?

(Material relevant to questions 5 and 6 may be found in Buenas, D. 2003, Bureaucracy still reigns in SMEs: SIM survey; Top managers call the shots, practice approved by most companies surveyed, *Business Times*, Singapore, 9 December.)

Another perspective on organisational structures and the need to remain flexible and adaptive is provided by ongoing events in the global airline industry. Once the single most profitable carrier in the world, Singapore Airlines (SIA) now has to fight the increasing number of budget carriers head-on while still keeping an eye on full-service carriers that are catching up from behind.

After facing near bankruptcy, airlines such as British Airways, United and Qantas have become as 'lean and mean' as SIA, and provide almost classic cases of successful organisational turn-arounds.

7. What are the simple explanations for their turnaround?

While SIA clearly faces competition from the old, established airlines, it also faces the challenge of new players in the industry such as Emirates and Qatar Airways from the Middle East, and China Airlines and Dragon Air in Asia. India is expected to pose a future threat and, most importantly, has the potential to provide four major airport sites in India to compete with SIA's home base, Changi airport, as an alternative stop on the lucrative Europe–Australia route. The impact of SARS is still being felt in the region also and the long-term effect on the travelling public is likely to continue with the outbreak of bird flu made public in early 2004.

8. What changes to its organisational structure and operations do you think SIA will make in response to these challenges?

(Material relevant to questions 7 and 8 may be found in Teo, L. 2003, Dealing with the big boys; Singapore Airlines has also got to watch its full-service rivals, which are becoming as lean and as mean as the national carrier, *Straits Times*, Singapore, 24 December.)

MANAGEMENT EXERCISES

Exercise 1 Management exercise: Designing an innovative organisation
You have landed a job as the administrative assistant to the CEO of Chameleon Technology, a fast-growing high-technology firm. You took the job to learn more about how to manage high-technology firms. Also, you think that, with the company growing rapidly, good career opportunities will open up soon.

Chameleon had great success with its initial product, a small hard-disk drive for personal computers which holds more data and costs less than competitors' products. Recently, the company introduced a high-resolution video screen for personal computers, also selling better than anticipated. As the company is growing rapidly, the CEO is having problems handling long-range planning as well as day-to-day developments in a dynamic environment. For example, recently some sales were made but product were not shipped on time. In another case, production was raised to meet rising demand, but the human resources department was not told of the need for more workers. In both cases, the problems happened because the CEO's office did not coordinate these activities as well as before.

As well, the CEO wants to foster the kind of innovative thinking which leads to improvements in existing products and new offerings. The CEO feels Chameleon is too dependent on its two products and the company is not moving fast enough to improve the disk drive and develop new products.

Because of your recent management studies, the CEO asks you to develop some ideas about how to better coordinate company activities and foster innovation. Chameleon is currently functionally organised, with manufacturing, sales, human resources, finance and accounting, and engineering departments. The company has about 600 employees.

Prepare a proposal for the CEO outlining steps to improve vertical and horizontal coordination and encourage more innovation.

Exercise 2 Skill building: Understanding organisation structure
Managers carrying out the organising function must understand organisation structure concepts. Significant issues about an organisation's structure are in the left column. Match these with examples from the right column (see next page).

Understanding organisation structure		
Organisational issues		**Definition/example**
1. _____ Chain of command	a.	Written policies, procedures (rules for purchasing equipment)
2. _____ Organisation chart	b.	Provide reasons for significant deviations (explain change in production from 40 to 90 units)
3. _____ Job simplification	c.	First, second, third and fourth levels working together (four levels of managers in manufacturing meet to discuss possible new technology)
4. _____ Job rotation	d.	A cushion of resources used to meet unprogrammed requirements (additional trucks to deliver unusual number of orders)
5. _____ Job enlargement	e.	Work four 10-hour days (6 am to 4 pm Monday to Thursday)
6. _____ Job enrichment	f.	Authority related to specific function (pay policy enforced by director of human resources)
7. _____ Flexitime	g.	Authority follows chain of command (CEO decides which three plants will be closed following reorganisation)
8. _____ Compressed workweek	h.	Line of authority (John reports to Sue)
9. _____ Job sharing	i.	Number of reporting units (seven divisions reporting to operations director)
10. _____ Departmentalisation	j.	Adding variety of similar tasks (assume the functions of peer in addition to current job)
11. _____ Vertical coordination	k.	Assigned only a few specific activities (make new files; file papers)
12. _____ Formalisation	l.	Line diagram reflecting structure (organisation has nine SBUs)
13. _____ Span of control	m.	Elastic work hours; core hours (9 am to 5 pm; 6 am to 2 pm; 10 am to 2 pm)
14. _____ Centralisation	n.	Power and authority retained (need permission from headquarters)
15. _____ Authority	o.	Upgrading job task-mix (taking on budgeting, planning and other functions)
16. _____ Accountability	p.	Coordination with other units/departments (engineering, sales and manufacturing working out a problem)
17. _____ Line authority	q.	Two employees/one job (John works mornings, Joe works afternoons)
18. _____ Functional authority	r.	Right to make decisions (can spend up to $75 000 per purchase)
19. _____ Slack resources	s.	Clustering into work groups, units, divisions (assembly team, motors division)
20. _____ Lateral relations	t.	Shifting workers through functions (sales, then human resources, then finance)

Small Business Development Corporation

Small businesses represent over 95 per cent of all firms in Australia, Hong Kong and New Zealand, and over 90 per cent of all businesses throughout the Asia-Pacific Region. However, they have a high rate of collapse, and many firms fail to ever grow in size or turnover.

Since the late 1980s, governments around the region have adopted a number of different strategies to help reduce this level of business failure. In Australia and New Zealand, this has usually been done by the creation of small business enterprise centres and/or development corporations.

Traditionally, small business owner/managers have been reluctant to use government services. They are either unaware of the facilities provided, or else uncomfortable in dealing with the bureaucracy. Yet without access to cheap (or free) advice, assistance and training, many of these firms will never be able to grow or succeed.

One way to overcome this gap has been to focus on community-based solutions. Many towns and regions have either created their own small business development agencies, or else been encouraged to do so by state governments, who then provide some funding, help in finding and training agency staff, and on-going access to information.

For example, in Western Australia the state government began establishing a network of Business Enterprise Centres (BECs) in the late 1980s. By 2004, this had grown to some 37 centres located in small country towns, major regional centres and key parts of the Perth metropolitan area. This means that almost anyone in the state is now within relatively easy reach of help if they want to begin or grow a business. Each centre is headed by a manager and one or two support staff, and provides free advice on any issue relating to business management: human resources, preparing a business plan, marketing, product development, launch of a new invention or innovation, preparing financial statements, intellectual property or recruiting new employees.

Each centre is created as a non-profit, limited-liability incorporated association, overseen by a voluntary management committee drawn from the local business community, government agencies and other interested parties. Each local association is responsible for employing and dismissing the staff in its BEC, raising funds, and overseeing the management of the centre.

However, there is also a formal government agency, the Small Business Development Corporation (SBDC), which is staffed by public service employees and answers to the state's Minister for Small Business. It also offers advice and assistance to business owners, undertakes research into the small business sector, and develops government policy in this area. In addition, the SBDC provides an annual operating grant to each BEC, as well as other support such as training of centre staff, assistance in their recruitment, and passing on of information about various government programs and schemes that might be relevant to small businesses. Between them, these organisations (one a formal government department, the rest a collection of independent community centres) are designed to provide a network of 'one-stop shops' where any current or prospective small business person can find help in running their firm.

Source: Contributed by Michael Schaper.

POWERWEB

International articles related to this topic are available at the Online Learning Centre at **www.mhhe.com/au/bartol4e**

Activities for discussion, analysis and further research

1. Outline the advantages and disadvantages of continuing to run these agencies as separate units. Would you prefer to have them remain separate, or would you merge them together?
2. If you merged the SBDC and BECs together, how would you departmentalise activities: on a functional, divisional, hybrid or matrix basis? Why?
3. If two types of organisations continue to be run separately, what steps can be taken to ensure that there is sufficient vertical coordination?
4. Visit the SBDC website: www.sbdc.com.au. Do you think the site clearly shows visitors how the two organisations work together, and how they are separate? If not, how would you change the website to deal with this issue?

FURTHER READING

Devinney, T.M., Midgley, D.F. and Venaik, S. 2000, The optimal performance of the global firm: Formalizing and extending the integration-responsiveness framework, *Organization Science: A Journal of the Institute of Management Sciences*, November/December 2000, 11, 6, pp. 674–96.

D'Netto, B. and Sohal, A.S. 1999, Changes in the production manager's job: Past, present and future trends, *International Journal of Operations & Production Management*, 19, 2, pp. 157–82.

Gaeta, G. 1995, Hong Kong's financial industry in transition, *Columbia Journal of World Business*, Summer, 30, 2, pp. 42–51.

Kalleberg, A.L. 2001, Organizing flexibility: The flexible firm in a new century, *British Journal of Industrial Relations*, December, 39, 4, pp. 479–505.

Kennedy, J.C. 2002, Leadership in Malaysia: Traditional values, international outlook, *Academy of Management Executive*, August, 16, 3, pp. 15–27.

CHAPTER 9

STRATEGIC ORGANISATION DESIGN

CHAPTER OUTLINE

Designing organisation structures: An overview
Which comes first—strategy or structure?
Factors influencing organisation design

Assessing structural alternatives
Functional structure
Divisional structure
Hybrid structure
Matrix structure
Emerging structures

Weighing contingency factors
Technology
Size
Environment

Matching strategy and structure

Promoting innovation: Using structural means to enhance prospects
Vital roles
Reservations
Differentiation paradox
Transfer process

LEARNING OBJECTIVES

After studying this chapter, you should be able to:

- Summarise current views about the link between strategy and organisation structure.
- Explain functional, divisional, hybrid and matrix types of departmentalisation.
- List the major advantages and disadvantages of each type of departmentalisation, and discuss the basic circumstances in which each is likely to be effective.
- Explain the stages of matrix departmentalisation.
- Identify emerging types of structures.
- Assess how contingency factors, such as technology, size and environment, impact organisation structure.
- Delineate how to match strategy and structure.
- Indicate how structure can enhance prospects for innovation.

Bridge Street farmer

While Pitt and Collins Street farmers are laying claim to the landscape within a Friday night dash of the city, Christine Campbell is a different breed. Her Bridge Street office looks over the bright lights of the Sydney bourse as the stock prices flash across the electronic board. But her stock is cattle, sheep, cotton, grains and, increasingly, water. Christine Campbell lives and breathes rural Australia.

Campbell runs a family company owned by that figure beloved of the media, the reclusive, mysterious, multi-millionaire, John Dieter Kahlbetzer. Kahlbetzer is an Australian who spends much of his time in Argentina, running a brother agribiz operation. Back home, Campbell has effectively been the regent of an agricultural fiefdom, preparing the way for the heirs to what seems destined to be another Australian agricultural dynasty.

A migrant who came to Australia to work on oil rigs and made his pile in oil, Kahlbetzer, 71, has become consumed by land, and his land has been transformed by water. The bush barons are becoming water barons as tradable water rights assume the importance prime beef once held.

Under Campbell's 25-year stewardship, first as financial controller and strategist, the Kahlbetzer family company, Twynam, now owns almost half a million hectares, a giant chessboard of 17 farms that stretch the length if not the breadth of NSW.

The holding was built up through a series of property plays that have made the company one of NSW's biggest landholders, one of its biggest owners of water rights, the nation's biggest cotton farmer and, with a $21.7 million purchase last year of John Elliott's Murrumbidgee River property, Cobran, our biggest rice grower. Twynam owns one of the largest sheep flocks in Australia—170 000 strong—and produces 6000 bales of wool a year.

As well as cotton and rice, wheat, canola and pulses make up the Twynam contribution to national and international shopping baskets, making the company our 10th biggest crop grower over all. It can muster a beef herd of 35 000 beasts and, while its total acreage is well behind that of our biggest land owner, the Queensland and Northern Territory based Stanbroke Pastoral, with 12.7 million hectares, Twynam's realm encompasses prime, diverse NSW land and water packages. Drought has seen Twynam's workforce cut to around 60 per cent of its usual 300, but the geographic and enterprise diversification of its properties buffers it by allowing resources to be shifted between operations.

From her seventh floor office in Bridge Street, Christine Campbell keeps a hand on the chess pieces, but her feet stay firmly on the company ground. In 1986, she became executive director, and when the company took over the then publicly owned Colly cotton group in 1999, she stepped into a new role as chief executive of the vertically integrated business.

In 2002, when Kahlbetzer decided to semi-retire, she became executive chair, and Kahlbetzer's son, Johnny, moved into the chief operating role. (Like his brother before him, Kahlbetzer's younger son, Markus, 22, is studying agricultural economics at university.)

continued

STRIVING FOR EXCELLENCE *continued*

Christine Campbell didn't seem cut out to become a bush baroness. When she left school aged 15 she began a secretarial course. The combination of an inspiring teacher and the right subject grabbed her and set her on a new course—accounting. Working as a secretary, she began a six-year evening course in accounting at her local Bankstown Tech, in Sydney's west. Campbell soon found she needed to be working in the field during the day. 'Recruitment advertisements then were divided into men's jobs and women's jobs. Accounting jobs, even bookkeeping jobs, were men's jobs, so I had to apply for a man's job', she says. 'The mechanical jobs such as typing and comptometrist were women's jobs. All the analytical jobs, and the jobs with a structured career path, were men's jobs.'

So the girl from Bankstown became an assistant to the accountant for a real-estate developer while she finished her accounting qualification. The timing was right. 'Computers were just coming in, so I was able to experience setting up systems for computerisation. That made it possible to move from one industry to another—and to work with interesting people. Then, in the seventies, business deregulation brought another sort of change.'

Source: Richardson, J. (2003).

DESIGNING ORGANISATION STRUCTURES: AN OVERVIEW

As mentioned in Chapter 8, developing organisation structure is called organisation design. In organisation design, what factors must managers consider? According to one study, an important issue is an organisation's strategy.

Which comes first—strategy or structure?

Alfred D. Chandler (1962) studied the development of large US firms. He wanted to see if strategy development came before or came from organisation structure design. Chandler concluded that companies follow a general pattern of developing strategy then changing structure, instead of the reverse.

Chandler's view was that organisations often change strategy to use resources to fuel growth more effectively. Strategy changes lead to management problems as current structures fit new strategies poorly. Unless firms adjust structures, new strategies cannot succeed and inefficiencies will occur.

The structure-follows-strategy thesis was seen as simplistic, as some structures can impact company strategies (Frederickson 1986). For example, CEO of Eastman Kodak, Colby Chandler, estimated between 1981 and 1985 the firm lost $3.5 billion in sales. As Kodak's functional structure did not permit specific strategies needed for its multiple businesses, they were not developed. Colby Chandler restructured the $17-billion-a-year firm into 34 divisions, ranging from colour film to copiers, to operate as strategic business units. In two years, all units developed specific strategies, almost all gained market share, and Kodak's exports grew 23 per cent (Taylor 1989). So causal linkages may work both ways between structure and strategy. Structure may follow strategy first; then new structures may influence new strategy development. In any event, Alfred Chandler's work suggests mismatched strategy and structure can lead to organisational problems.

Factors influencing organisation design

While strategy and organisation structure are linked, the effectiveness of any structural type is influenced by contingency factors, such as dominant technology or organisation size (Nadler & Tushman 1988). Structural means for innovation promotion may also aid strategy implementation and organisational goal attainment. These components and their relationships

FIGURE 9.1 Major components influencing the design of effective organisation structures

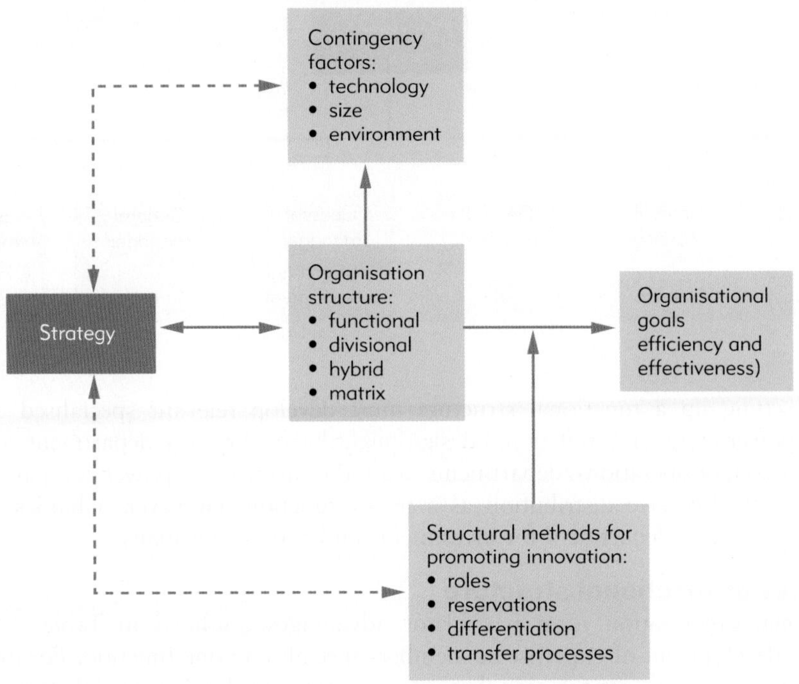

to organisation structure are shown in Figure 9.1. We explore these later in this chapter, but first we examine major types of structure, or departmentalisation, raised in Chapter 8, as they are the main structural alternatives available.

ASSESSING STRUCTURAL ALTERNATIVES

As discussed before, the four most common departmentalisation types are functional, divisional, hybrid and matrix. These are known as organisation structures or designs. Each has major advantages and disadvantages (Duncan 1979; Robey & Sales 1992).

Functional structure

Functional structure is a type of departmentalisation where positions are grouped into functional (or specialisation) area. In other words, positions are combined on the basis of similarity of expertise, skill and work activity.

Common functions

Functional structures have several common specialties (Robey & Sales 1992; Bateman & Snell 2003). For example, production, or operations, combine activities for product manufacture or service delivery. Marketing promotes and sells products and services. Human resources attracts, retains and enhances effectiveness of organisation members. Finance obtains and manages financial resources. Research and development produces unique ideas and methods leading to new and/or improved products and services. Accounting and financial reporting meet internal and external source needs. Finally, the legal function handles legal matters. In organisation structure, the term 'function' (specialised area of expertise) is not the same as in management's major functions (that is, planning, organising, leading and controlling). The functional structure of the Denver-based herbal tea company Celestial Seasonings is shown in Figure 9.2. It includes many functional areas discussed before.

functional structure

Structure in which positions are grouped according to their main functional (or specialised) area

FIGURE 9.2 The functional structure of Celestial Seasonings

A firm setting up a functional structure must develop relevant specialised areas. For example, a power company's functional design might have an energy department comparable to the production, or operations, departments in another firm, as the power company produces energy. It might also have distribution as a major function. However, a bank's functional structure might have a department for investments and another for loans.

Advantages of functional structure

The functional organisation form has major advantages, outlined in Table 9.1. One is encouraging development of expertise as members specialise in one function. For example, as human resources director in a functional structure, you might develop specialists in recruiting, compensation and training. Employees also have clear career paths in their own function, which encourages development of expertise. As well, a functional structure aids efficient resource use, as it is simple to shift staff between projects when they are in the same department. Economies of scale may be available too, as large quantities of work can be managed when people specialise or work volume justifies major equipment. A further benefit is that functional structures ease coordination within departments, since all activities are related (Galbraith & Kazanjian 1986; Jones 2003). Consider where people knowledgable in logistics, finance and sales were in the same functional group, with an electrical engineer as manager. The diverse backgrounds would mean the manager would have difficulty coordinating or assessing activities individually. Finally, functional grouping enhances development of specialised technical competencies for strategic advantage.

TABLE 9.1 MAJOR ADVANTAGES AND DISADVANTAGES OF A FUNCTIONAL STRUCTURE

Advantages	Disadvantages
In-depth development of expertise	Slow response time on multifunctional problems
Clear career path within function	Backlog of decisions at top of hierarchy
Efficient use of resources	Bottlenecks due to sequential tasks
Possible economies of scale	Restricted view of organisation among employees
Ease of coordination within function	Inexact measurement of performance
Potential technical advantage over competitors	Narrow training for potential managers

Disadvantages of functional structure

Functional designs have disadvantages too, shown in Table 9.1. One is that to handle complex problems, cross-functional coordination is needed and this may slow responses, as issues and conflicts move up the chain for resolution. Bottlenecks may also develop when one function waits for another to finish its work. Specialists' orientation may narrow too, and they are less able to understand other functions' needs or overall organisation goals. Furthermore it may be hard to measure one unit's performance as many functions contribute to overall results. Finally, functional structures limit managers' training as they operate within one function and have little knowledge of others.

Uses of functional structure

The functional form is common in small and medium-sized organisations too large to coordinate activities without a formal structure, but too small for cross functional coordination to be hard. Such firms often have a few related products or services or deal with a fairly homogeneous customer or client set. For example, Pizza Hut, which deals mainly in pizza and related food items, has a functional structure, with operations, distribution, and finance and administration as functional departments. The design is useful for large, more diverse organisations, such as insurance companies, operating usually in fairly stable environments where change is slow so functions can coordinate their efforts. A functional structure may be used in large firms where much coordination is needed among products (Child 1984).

The functional structure becomes progressively less effective as environments become less predictable (Schmidt 2003).

CASE IN POINT

Website steers trucker's business

When the Sydney transport company Allied Express went on to the internet nearly three years ago, it wanted its site to be much more than just another pretty face on the web. It intended to exploit internet technology to achieve growth.

In its first phase, the Allied site was essentially a brochure put online, but the company had a much broader aim. General manager Michelle McDowell says: 'The benefit for us was to actually book and track our jobs over the internet'. Allied spent eight months on electronic-commerce development, and opened the next stage for business a year ago. Customers can now book jobs, track parcels and access scanned, proof-of-delivery signatures on the site, all in real time.

McDowell says: 'We wanted it set up so that the minute you book a job with us through the internet it would be straight into our main dispatching system and printed out in one of our vehicles. We saw little point in having an internet booking printed out on paper back at the base'. Internet security issues were an important concern. McDowell says: 'Getting the security right was critical. We did not

want people booking things on other people's accounts or looking up information that wasn't theirs'.

Allied regards its e-commerce strategy as a medium-term investment. It is not looking at the number of internet bookings as the measure of success. It says the real value lies in its potential for competitive advantage and value-added customer services. Hernani Inacio, senior executive in charge of management information systems at Allied, says: 'Over the past year, we have won lucrative contracts with several big customers because of the internet. Our internet services provide reasons for them to trade with us because they can track parcels in real time and do electronic commerce'.

Allied now processes transactions in bulk for customers including Foxtel, using the interface between its web server and its dispatch system. Each morning, for example, Foxtel sends a file with about 1000 bookings directly to Allied's internet server. Dulux is another important internet client; store managers can log on to the Allied website, book jobs, then track the delivery. Allied's internet strategy is the most recent step in a decade-long shift to the emerging field of electronic technology. Allied says that since 1991, when it began to computerise its manual systems, it has invested about $18.5 million in information technology.

Before 1990, Allied had a conventional voice-dispatch system for managing a fleet of 130 vehicles. Its annual revenue was about $9 million. This financial year, the company expects turnover of $78 million, compared with $59 million last year. Its computers process 20 000 jobs a day, helping a national staff of 300 to manage a fleet of more than 1000 vehicles and drivers with depots in four states.

'Our strategy to computerise our manual systems has paid off resoundingly', McDowell says. 'But at the start of the decade, with Australia deep in recession, the company was viewed as a huge gamble. There wasn't a lot of computer savvy around in our industry. Basically, anyone with a mobile phone, a vehicle and a group of mates could form a courier company.' Technology alone does

not account for the rapid growth of Allied—acquisitions have played a big part. In 1996, for example, Allied acquired its airfreight division, Skytrax. It has also bought smaller courier companies and taxi-truck companies.

'We look for businesses that we can simply add to our existing structure, which is built for high-volume sales', McDowell says. 'Without much effort, we can add $100 000 to our turnover. It has generally been quite easy.'

Source: Hanvey, M. (1999).

Activities for discussion, analysis and further research

1. How has Allied used e-technology to improve service to its customers?
2. Recently a staff member was relocated from the US to Australia. She was given a tracking number to track her shipment and see its progress. Try logging on to the Allied system and examine how you could track a removal around the world.

Divisional structure

divisional structure

Structure in which positions are grouped according to similarity of products, services or markets

Divisional structure is a departmentalisation type with positions grouped by product, service or market similarity. Figure 9.3 shows how functional and divisional structures differ. A divisional structure has each division with major functional resources to pursue its own goals without depending on other divisions. For example, Figure 9.4 shows the seven telephone divisions of Bell Atlantic Corporation, a regional firm giving local telephone service in several US states. If functionally organised, telephone operators would all be grouped in a central operations department, and field repair personnel all in a central repair services department. With a divisional structure, by contrast, operators and repair personnel are allocated to divisions so each can operate fairly independently. In this case, divisions operate as separate firms. Divisional structures are called self-contained structures with each division containing all major functions (Patrick 2003).

Forms of divisional structure

There are three major divisional structure forms: product, geographic and customer. A simplified example of each is shown in Figure 9.5. The form used depends on the rationale for division formation.

product divisions

Divisions created to concentrate on a single product or service or at least a relatively homogeneous set of products or services

Product divisions focus on a single product or service or a relatively homogeneous product or service set. This structure is used when large differences in product or service lines make coordination in a functional design slow and inefficient. With a divisional structure, departments have their own functional specialists, such as marketing, manufacturing and personnel, working with their specific division's product only.

geographic divisions

Divisions designed to serve different geographic areas

Geographic divisions serve different geographic areas. This departmentalisation type is often used where products and services must be tailored to different regions' needs. So the Bell Atlantic telephone divisions in Figure 9.4 are organised by geography.

FIGURE 9.3 Functional versus divisional

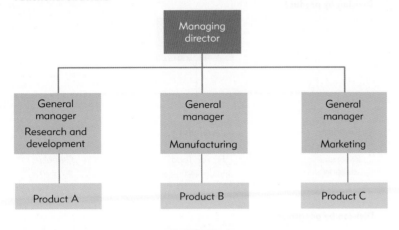

Functional structure

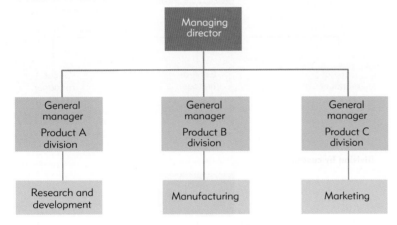

Divisional structure

FIGURE 9.4 Seven divisions of the Bell Atlantic Corporation

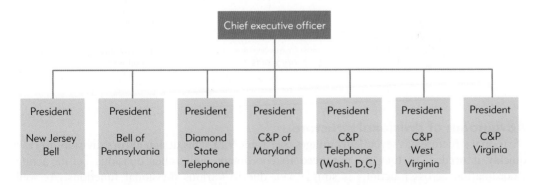

Customer divisions service particular client or customer types. This design is best where there are major differences among customer types, making adequate coordination of customers' various needs within a standard functional structure difficult. With customer divisions, each department has individuals performing functions necessary for a specific type of customer (Albert 1985).

customer divisions

Divisions set up to service particular types of clients or customers

FIGURE 9.5 Major forms of divisional structure

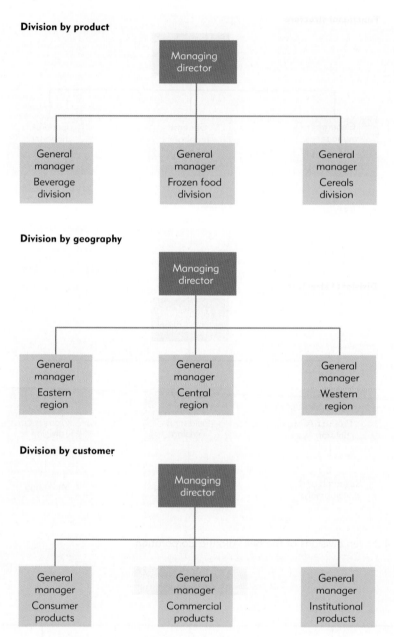

Division by product

Managing director

General manager Beverage division

General manager Frozen food division

General manager Cereals division

Division by geography

Managing director

General manager Eastern region

General manager Central region

General manager Western region

Division by customer

Managing director

General manager Consumer products

General manager Commercial products

General manager Institutional products

Advantages of divisional structure

Divisional structure has several advantages (see Table 9.2). This design allows divisions to react quickly if needed, as they do not need to coordinate with other divisions before acting. Coordination across functions is simple too, due to various divisional functions. As well, functions emphasise division goals. The structure gives a strong customer-service focus. This is due to a focus either on a narrow product or service range (product divisions) or a narrow audience (geographic or customer divisions). A divisional structure allows performance accountability, as results can be connected to a product, service, geographic area or customer type, as applicable. Finally, a divisional structure means managers can develop more general management skills because they deal with multiple functions unlike those in functional

TABLE 9.2 MAJOR ADVANTAGES AND DISADVANTAGES OF A DIVISIONAL STRUCTURE

Advantages	Disadvantages
Fast response to environmental change	Duplication of resources in each division
Simplified coordination across functions	Reduction of in-depth expertise
Simultaneous emphasis on division goals	Heightened competition among divisions
Strong orientation to customer requirements	Limited sharing of expertise across divisions
Accurate measurement of division performance	Restriction of innovation to divisions
Broad training in general management skills	Neglect of overall goals

structures. Corporate-level managers are also more distant from functional-level activities and can develop a more strategic-level view of divisional activities (Jones & Hill 1988; Kinicki & Williams 2003).

Disadvantages of divisional structure

Divisional structure has disadvantages too (see Table 9.2). Divisional organisation can result in duplicated resources. For example, divisions may all have their own computer system (departments can share this in a functional structure) which may be underused. Staff in this structure do not develop the in-depth specialisation that they can in a functional one. For example, if a firm moves from functional to product design, management may assign human resource specialists to product groups. Thus, an individual recruitment specialist may need to deal with compensation and other issues in a product department, as duplicating the whole human resource department may be too costly. Divisions may also become absorbed with their own concerns and compete for resources (Duncan 1979; Robey & Sales 1992). Often expertise and innovation sharing is limited across divisions. If geographical spread is great, customer differences may cause dissatisfaction to emerge (Bounds 1995). Finally, with a divisional structure, employees may focus on the division's immediate goals rather than longer-term organisational goals.

Uses of divisional structure

A divisional structure is likely in larger organisations with major differences in products, services, geographic areas or customers served. Sometimes setting up self-contained units is impossible if the firm needs common resource sharing, such as expensive manufacturing plant.

Hybrid structure

Hybrid structure is a departmentalisation form with both functional and divisional structure elements at the same management level (Daft 1998; Robey & Sales 1992). It combines advantages of both structures. Many large firms have both functional and divisional departments. Functional ones benefit from efficiencies in resource usage, economies of scale, or in-depth expertise. Divisional departments are used when the benefits come from stronger focus on products, services or markets. IBM's hybrid structure is shown in Figure 9.6. At IBM, functional units handle communications, finance, human resources and research—where

hybrid structure

Structure adopting both functional and divisional structures at the same management levels

FIGURE 9.6 IBM's hybrid structure

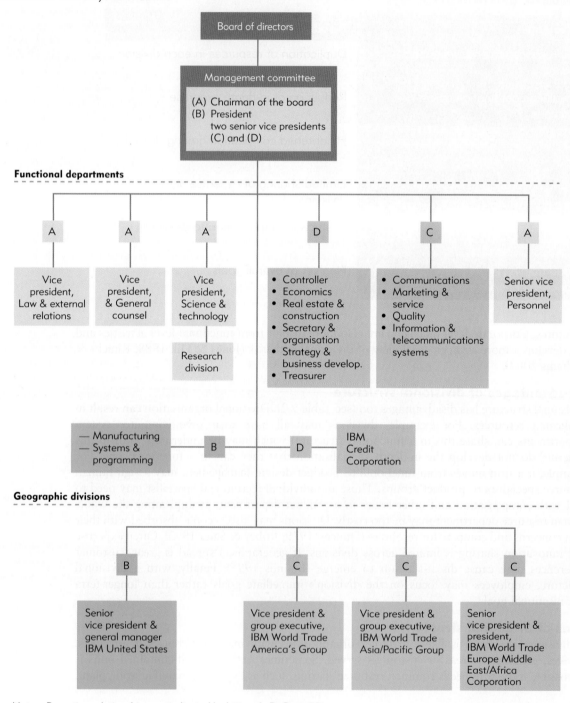

Note: Reporting relationships are indicated by letters A, B, C, and D

in-depth expertise is needed and resources are more effectively used in a functional setup. There are four major product divisions focused on product development in areas needing different expertise and dealing with rapidly evolving technology. IBM chose not to put a sales and service group into each division. Instead, IBM chose to centralise sales and service functions into another division geographically organised. In a hybrid design functional departments are known as corporate departments as they generally have staff authority relative to divisional departments, and authority from the organisation's corporate level.

Advantages of a hybrid structure

A hybrid structure generally has several advantages (see Table 9.3). With a hybrid design, an organisation can have specialised expertise and economies of scale in major functional areas. A partial divisional structure can lead to adaptability and flexibility with diverse product or service lines, geographic areas, or customers. Finally, mixing functional and divisional departmentalisation helps divisional and corporate goal alignment (Rue & Byars 2003).

Disadvantages of hybrid structure

Managers must be alert to hybrid structure's disadvantages to minimise the weaknesses (see Table 9.3). Hybrid organisations tend to develop excessively large staffs in corporate-level functional departments. As corporate departments grow, they may try to take control of divisions, resulting in conflict. Finally, responses of hybrid structures to unexpected situations where coordination is needed between a division and the corporate functional department can be slow. For example, a personnel matter needing a policy exception may be slower to fix with a hybrid structure than with either functional or divisional departmentalisation.

Uses of hybrid structure

A hybrid structure is used when there is much environmental uncertainty best met by a divisional structure but needing functional expertise and/or efficiency. Typically, the approach is kept for medium-to-large firms with resources to justify divisions and some functional departmentalisation.

Matrix structure

A **matrix structure** as a type of departmentalisation superimposes divisional horizontal reporting relationships onto a hierarchical functional structure. Thus the structure is both functional and divisional at once. There are two chains of command, one vertical and one horizontal. A basic matrix structure is shown in Figure 9.7. In this case, vice presidents of operations, marketing, finance, engineering, and research and development represent functional departments, making up the vertical hierarchy. Managers of businesses A, B and C represent divisional units operating horizontally at the same time. Functional and divisional department heads forming the matrix (e.g. vice presidents and business managers in Figure 9.7) are called matrix bosses.

One major characteristic of matrix structure is that staff in the matrix report to two matrix bosses. For example, as Figure 9.7 shows, a marketing researcher might report up the vertical chain to the vice-president of marketing, and across the horizontal to business A's manager. This dual authority system violates the classical unity of command principle (an individual should have only one boss at any time), making a matrix structure complex.

matrix structure

Structure superimposing a horizontal set of divisional reporting relationships onto a hierarchical functional structure

TABLE 9.3 MAJOR ADVANTAGES AND DISADVANTAGES OF A HYBRID STRUCTURE	
Advantages	**Disadvantages**
Alignment of corporate and divisional goals	Conflicts between corporate departments and divisions
Functional expertise and/or efficiency	Excessive administrative overhead
Adaptability and flexibility in divisions	Slow response to exceptional situations

FIGURE 9.7 Matrix organisation structure

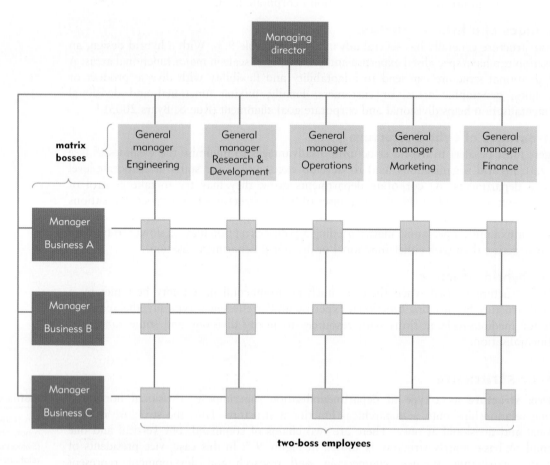

Matrix stages

Organisations adopting a matrix structure go through several structural stages (Davis & Lawrence 1977; Bateman & Snell 2004):

- Stage 1 is a traditional structure, usually functional, following the unity-of-command principle.
- Stage 2 is a temporary overlay, where managerial integrator positions are created to manage specific projects (e.g. project managers), oversee product launches (e.g. product managers), or handle issues of limited time needing coordination across functional departments. These managers often lead or work with temporary interdepartmental teams set up to address the issue.
- Stage 3 is a permanent overlay, where managerial integrators operate permanently (e.g. a brand manager coordinates issues related to a brand on an ongoing basis), often through permanent interdepartmental teams.
- Stage 4 is a mature matrix, in which matrix bosses have equal power.

Though a true matrix has functional and divisional managers with equal power, stages 2 and 3, involving managerial integrators (see Chapter 8), are often called matrix structures.

Each stage has more horizontal integration and administrative complexity (Jerkovsky 1983). Even with managerial integrators, there is dual authority as they work directly with functional department members (e.g. engineers or marketing specialists) assigned to their project. Managerial integrators informally supervise work of staff assigned to their projects, though rarely have direct line authority over them. Typically, the emphasis is on teamwork.

With a mature matrix, there is true dual authority (Galbraith & Kazanjian 1986). Major decisions are all approved by both functional and divisional managers. The mature matrix is used when the functional and divisional dimensions are of prime and equal importance. Dow Corning worked with this design, even adding a third dimension for a simultaneous international focus (Goggins 1974). For international operations the 'Think locally, but act globally' view explains activities of matrix structures (Bartlett & Goshal 1992; Bagwell 2003).

Matrix structures, especially the temporary and permanent overlay forms, operate successfully in many firms. However, a matrix design's advantages and disadvantages must be carefully weighed before adoption (see Table 9.4) (Davis & Lawrence 1977; Adams & Kirchof 1984; Ford & Randolph 1992).

Advantages of matrix structure

With a matrix design, divisional project and functional managers can make decisions. This means upper-level management can focus on long-term strategic issues. Moreover, using the matrix gives projects (or products or brands) strong horizontal coordination beyond that of a functional design alone, and improves chances of success. This aids environmental monitoring for both projects and functional areas, and is used when companies are moving more to international operations (Hill 1997). A matrix structure can also react quickly to change, as decisions can be made at lower levels. Functional specialists can also be added to, or removed from, projects when needed, giving effective human resource use. Finally, support systems, computers, special equipment and software can be assigned to many projects, lowering the system costs.

Disadvantages of matrix structure

As a matrix adds a layer of project managers and support staff to a functional hierarchy, costs grow. With two bosses, workers in a matrix may not be able to see who has authority and is responsible for decisions. The greater communication needed and dual-authority arrangements raise the possibility of conflicts, particularly between project and functional managers. Individuals can focus too much on internal relations, neglecting clients and project goals. Matrix designs can also encourage group decision making until groups make even minor decisions, which can seriously erode productivity. Finally, while a matrix can adapt to change, this can be slow if members have poor interpersonal skills, or senior management tries to keep control.

When to consider a matrix structure

Matrix designs are unsuitable for many companies. For example, Texas Instruments replaced its matrix structure, blaming it for its competitive failure (Katz 1982). Many other firms have found the structure very suitable (*Supervisory Management* 1995; Farnham 1994; Denton

TABLE 9.4 MAJOR ADVANTAGES AND DISADVANTAGES OF A MATRIX STRUCTURE

Advantages	Disadvantages
Decentralised decision making	High administrative costs
Strong project or product coordination	Potential confusion over authority and responsibility
Improved environmental monitoring	Heightened prospects for interpersonal conflicts
Fast response to change	Excessive focus on internal relations
Flexible use of human resources	Overemphasis on group decision making
Efficient use of support systems	Possible slow response to change

1995). The need for horizontal coordination must be high to justify greater administrative complexity at lower levels. Matrix designs are usually valuable under three conditions (Davis & Lawrence 1977):

1. Considerable environmental pressure necessitates a simultaneous strong focus on both functional and divisional dimensions. For example, diverse products may need a product orientation, but increasingly sophisticated engineering technology may argue for a functional orientation.
2. Demands on the organisation are changing and unpredictable, requiring large information-processing capacity and rapid coordination of activities. For example, in the microchip industry, foreign competitors often make technological improvements and lower prices at the same time.
3. There is pressure for shared resources. For example, in competitive markets, organisations may need flexibility in use of functional resources across projects or products.

MANAGERIAL DILEMMAS

Bringing ends together

The message has been around for some time that outsourcing is the way of the future. One Sydney manufacturer, in taking this message to heart, has outsourced his entire labour force. Tripac International (Australia) has adopted a strategy which has turned losses into profits, retained some of the staff which were about to be laid off and boosted productivity.

The story starts with the diversified whitegoods manufacturer, Email, who owned the subsidiary named Muller, a large, long-established car-parts manufacturer in Sydney's south-west. Email had an arrangement with Ford Australia to make air-conditioning parts for Falcons, Fairlanes and LTDs. While apparently a good deal, this made chronic losses for the organisation and Muller was on the

verge of shutting down. Tripac International purchased Muller, introduced a number of efficiencies at the plant and adopted a blanket outsourcing policy. Only top management is actually employed by the company. Everyone else is hired by an 'employee leasing' firm which has the right to hire and fire. Tripac can concentrate on making the plant as efficient as possible as it no longer has to focus on personnel requirements.

EL Consults Employment Processing Outsourcing division, EL Blue, employs and supplies staff as needed by the Tripac factory. Half of them are hired directly on a permanent contract basis while half are casual. This staff structure has given Tripac a flexible workforce that has been financially successful.

Source: Adapted from Tabakoff, N. (1999).

Activities for discussion, analysis and further research

1. What were the imperatives which prompted the changes in structure for Tripac?
2. What might be some of the consequences of this complete outsourcing?
3. Consider the impact on Ford when Email finally decided to off-load the unprofitable business. Ford could not build cars without the component Muller was supplying and they needed continuity. When Email could not be convinced to retain Muller, Ford started to attempt to persuade whoever took over to maintain production. Where are the organisation boundaries for Ford?

There is evidence that matrix designs need an organisation culture change to support the increased need for collaborative decision making (Joyce 1986; *Marketing* 1995; Bateman & Snell 2004). As well, managers and other staff may need special training, especially in interpersonal skills, for effective functioning (Kolodny 1979; 1981). A mature matrix structure is not needed by many firms; however, temporary and permanent overlay stages are more common, particularly as temporary and permanent cross-functional teams.

Emerging structures

Although many different types of organisational structures are possible as organisations try different ways of doing things, two emerging structure types are interesting: the process structure and networked structure, or virtual corporation (Galbraith 1995).

Process structure

A **process structure** is a type of departmentalisation with positions grouped by a complete work flow. The basic idea is that individuals from each function working on a process are grouped into process teams and given beginning-to-end responsibility for the process or identifiable work flow. Under this structure type, divisions are called new product development, order fulfilment or customer acquisition and maintenance—signifying processes they are responsible for. The structure is known as the horizontal organisation, because they tend to be relatively flat. Functional specialties working in a team environment mean most operating decisions are made at low organisation levels by teams (Child 1995).

process structure

Type of departmentalisation where positions are grouped by a complete flow of work

Networked structure

The **networked structure** is a form where functions are contracted out to other firms and coordinated by information technology networks, operating like a single organisation. This structure is the virtual corporation, acting as if it is virtually one corporation (Marcia 1995; *Economist* 1995). For example, the Italian clothing maker Benetton contracts production to about 350 small firms, getting economies of scale by buying materials for all of them. Having small firms do labour-intensive sewing and packing enables Benetton to respond to rapid fashion shifts flexibly. One virtual corporation problem is that proprietary information may have to be exchanged, creating future competitors (Chesborough & Teece 1996; Schmidt 2003b).

networked structure

Form of organising where many functions are contracted out to other independent firms and coordinated by use of information technology networks to operate as if they were within a single corporation

While managers weigh the advantages and disadvantages of various structural alternatives in developing appropriate organisation design—including emerging structures—they must consider how major contingency factors affect structural requirements. We review these next.

MANAGING THE E-CHALLENGE

Implementing the government's on-line policy

How do you define an organisation when organisations are electronically linked?

Boeing proposed allowing their customers to have direct access to Boeing's project databases via an electronic link that would allow customers to tailor the data into reports in any format they required. Customers also had access to Boeing's internal status reports. Another, more complex example is that being confronted by one of our government departments, which we will call GD.

The GD, in common with all Commonwealth departments, has been required by government to change its methods of operation so that all business is conducted 'on-line'. This policy, commonly referred to as the 'Government On-line' policy, was to be implemented by December 2001. There are a number of different on-line applications that have been (or are being) initiated. Coincidental to this policy, and due to the nature of the GD a Memorandum of Understanding had also been signed between the GD, The Consideration Commission (TCC), and The Peak Industry Association (TPIA), part of which was to the effect that:

- the GD and TPIA will endeavour to simplify the administrative requirements for participating general practitioners
- the GD and the TPIA will 'jointly develop initiatives to encourage electronic billing for the GD's services and access by electronic means to the GD's forms'
- 'the GD will, in line with the practices of The Payments Commission (TPC), remove the requirement to submit copies of accounts when electronic billing has been utilised'.

Both The Payments Commission and the GD report to the Minister for the GD; and the President of TCC is also the Secretary of the GD. Another Memorandum of Understanding between the GD, TCC and TPC covers their respective roles and responsibilities in relation to accounts processing (which TPC does on behalf of the GD, for services rendered by service providers, as appropriate, to entitled citizens).

There are also other interested parties, or parties whose interests have to be considered: the developers and providers of practice management software for service providers; the organisation that represents them (The Software Industry Association (TSIA)); the Australian Professional Service Providers Society (APSPS); and the Bigger Government Department.

Some of the tasks confronting the GD are:
- defining the requirements, and a system that will meet them
- engaging the existing processor (TPC) to develop the centralised processing system
- gaining agreement from various software suppliers to modify their practice management software so that it is compatible
- persuading them to do this at their own expense
- encouraging service providers to purchase the updated software, thereby compensating the software suppliers for the expense of modification
- estimating the proportion of service providers who will transfer their operations to the new system
- resolving issues of internet access for the new system; accommodating service providers who do not have access, or regard it as too time-consuming and expensive, and determining how long the current system will have to be maintained to service them
- gaining support from service providers (and their representative organisations such as TPIA and

the APSPS), some of whom feel the proposal has no particular benefit for them but is simply a means of the GD (and thus the Commonwealth Government) saving money at the expense of the service providers, whose practices will bear the cost of doing the manual (data entry) processing formerly done by TPC on behalf of the GD.

The implementation by the GD of the government's on-line policy seems likely to increase costs for the providers of services. It would be reasonable to expect that this would be passed on to the GD by the providers. However, the GD and the providers (through the TPIA) have agreed on the fees to be charged and the reimbursement offered. The arrangements stand until renegotiated, and providers will not be reimbursed for more than the agreed fee.

Individual providers who are unhappy with this may choose to opt out of their agreement with the GD. (They could still provide their services to entitled citizens, who would have to agree to pay the full cost of the service or claim it, as any other citizen can, under government claims systems.) Thus the GD (and the government) will save money. The overall cost to the GD's system is lower, which would seem to be a benefit. However, the cost to the providers, the veterans and another system has increased.

Source: Contributed by Peter Lewis.

Activities for discussion, analysis and further research

1. Which organisation do you think the following would regard themselves as dealing with?
   - the entitled citizens
   - the service providers
   - The Payments Commission
   - the Government Department
2. If you were placed in charge of the development of the proposed system, what are some of the ways you could go about it?
3. What capabilities and skills do you think you would need as the leader of the project to successfully bring about the change to the proposed system?
4. Where would you see yourself situated within the GD, and what authority do you think you would need in order to achieve a successful outcome?
5. Who would define success, and how would you wish your performance to be assessed?

WEIGHING CONTINGENCY FACTORS

Early in the study of management, classical theorists (see Chapter 2) tried to describe an ideal organisation structure. Instead, they found that a structural configuration that was effective for one organisation was less so for another. Contingency theory resulted. This viewpoint argues that appropriate managerial action depends on a situation's parameters (see Chapter 2). The best structure for a firm was seen to depend on contingency factors such as technology, size and environment.

Technology

Different organisations need different structures partly due to **technology**—knowledge, tools, equipment and work techniques an organisation uses to deliver product or service. Technological complexity and interdependence are two critical aspects (Fry 1982; Gome 2003b).

Technological complexity

Research on technology's importance was conducted in the 1950s by a team led by Joan Woodward (1958; 1965). The team were interested in how much classical theorists' management principles were practised by a group of 100 British manufacturing firms.

The researchers were surprised to find no connection between use of classical principle in structuring firms and their success. Actual practices were very varied. Eventually, Woodward found three different technology types often predicted structural firms' practices:

1. In **unit and small-batch production**, products are custom-produced to customer specifications or made in small quantities largely by craft specialists. Examples are diamond cutting in New York's diamond centre and stretch limousine production.
2. In **large-batch and mass production**, products are made in large quantities, often on an assembly line. Examples are most car production, chocolate Easter eggs such as those made by Cadbury's chocolate factory (Cadbury.co.nz) and manufacture of microchips for computers and related products.
3. In **continuous-process production**, products are liquids, solids or gases made through a continuous process. Examples are petroleum, chemical and some food products.

The team noted technologies are increasingly complex to manage, with the least complex being small-batch and unit production and the most complex continuous-process production. Greater complexity comes from more elaborate machinery and its greater work-process role. Technological complexity, in turn, seemed to explain firms' different structural practices (see Table 9.5).

For example, researchers found complexity increased as management levels grew (a taller structure), as there were more staff personnel per line worker, and wider spans of control at upper-management levels. Woodward's results also found higher formalisation and centralisation in large-batch and mass-production technology firms, where many workers' efforts needed standardisation. Formalisation and centralisation, in contrast, were low in companies with unit and small-batch, as well as continuous-process, technologies, where work decisions are made at lower levels.

At first-line supervisor level, spans were greatest with large-batch and mass-production technology, as one supervisor could handle many workers doing fairly routine work. It was smallest for continuous-process where process difficulties can cause major problems (Woodward 1965; Collins & Hull 1986).

Overall, Woodward's research showed structural characteristics of successful firms were close to the median for their particular technology. Subsequent research supports the influence of technological complexity on organisation structure (Fry 1982; Hull & Collins 1987).

technology

Knowledge, tools, equipment and work techniques used by an organisation in delivering its product or service

unit and small-batch production

Type of technology where products are custom-produced to meet customer specifications or are made in small quantities primarily by craft specialists

large-batch and mass production

Type of technology where products are manufactured in large quantities, frequently on an assembly line

continuous-process production

Type of technology where products are liquids, solids or gases made through a continuous process

TABLE 9.5 WOODWARD'S FINDINGS ON STRUCTURAL CHARACTERISTICS AND TECHNOLOGY*

Structural characteristics	Small batch	Mass production	Continuous process
Levels of management	3	4	6
Executive span of control	4	7	10
Supervisory span of control	23	48	15
Industrial workers vs. staff (ratio)	8:1	5.5:1	2:1
Formalisation	Low	High	Low
Centralisation	Low	High	Low

*Data are medians for organisations within each technological category.
Source: Woodward (1965, pp. 52–82).

Technological interdependence

technological interdependence

Degree to which different organisation parts must exchange information and materials to perform required activities

Another technology aspect affecting organising considerations is **technological interdependence**, or how much different organisation parts need to exchange information and materials to perform required activities (Fry 1982). There are three major types of technological interdependence: pooled, sequential and reciprocal (Thompson 1967).

The type with least interdependence is **pooled interdependence**, where units operate independently but individual efforts impact on the whole organisation's success (hence 'pooled'). For example, you go to your bank's local branch and they will rarely need to contact another branch to complete your transaction. If, however, the branch's performance is poor, customers will leave, ultimately affecting the whole bank's health.

pooled interdependence

Relationship in which units operate independently but individual efforts are important to the whole organisation's success

By contrast, in **sequential interdependence**, the task of one unit must be finished before the next unit in the sequence can start. For example, a strike at one General Motors Holden plant may mean workers at other plants have to be temporarily stood down. This happens when the sequentially interdependent assembly means non-striking plants need parts from the striking plant.

sequential interdependence

Relationship in which one unit must complete its work before the next in the sequence can begin work

Finally, the most complex situation is **reciprocal interdependence**, where one unit's outputs are inputs to another unit and vice versa. When a plane lands, the flight crew hand the plane to the maintenance crew. After refuelling, resupplying and other activities, maintenance releases the plane to the flight crew so the aircraft can leave. Thus the flight crew's output is maintenance's input, then the process reverses. Clearly, reciprocal interdependence needs the most horizontal coordination (Gome 2003b). In designing organisation structure, technological interdependence and complexity must be considered. Organisation size may be relevant too.

reciprocal interdependence

Relationship in which one unit's outputs become inputs to another unit and vice versa

Size

Woodward's research also looked at how size and structural aspects were related, but nothing definitive emerged. Research since then has tried to determine how size and structure relate, with some success. The issue is complicated because size is part of the equation. Factors such as environment and technology also affect organisation structure. Also, size can be assessed in many ways, such as by gross sales, profits or even employee numbers (most common), making comparisons hard.

Studies of size effects on structure have identified four trends:

1. As organisations grow, departments and levels are added, and structures grow more complex. With functional forms, this drives a change to divisional structure (Astley 1985; Cullen, Anderson & Baker 1986).
2. Increasing size means the number of staff positions are increased to help top management cope. When critical mass is reached this levels off (Cullen et al. 1986), but it leads to the third trend.

3. Organisational growth requires more rules and regulations. Guidelines help with vertical co-ordination, but can lead to excessive formalisation and lower efficiency (Gooding & Wagner 1985).
4. As organisations grow, decentralisation increases. This is probably due to the rules and regulation guiding lower-level decision making (Robbins 1990).

Due to potential size effects, divisionalised firms may keep subunits small by setting up new divisions when other ones become unwieldy. Johnson & Johnson has over 150 autonomous divisions to reap the advantages of smaller size and encourage innovation (Dumaine 1992). The strategy is backed by research showing larger organisational subunits to be less efficient than smaller counterparts. While size influences structural requirements, environment is also important.

Environment

Burns and Stalker (1961) studied the effects of environment on organisation structure. Studying 20 British industrial firms, they found different structural characteristics, depending on whether the environment was stable with little change or unstable with rapid change and uncertainty.

Mechanistic and organic characteristics

In stable environments firms had fairly **mechanistic characteristics**, highly centralised decision making, many rules and regulations, with hierarchical communication channels. Vertical coordination was emphasised, with little delegation between management levels. Firms operated successfully as environmental change was gradual, and upper management could stay on top of changes.

In highly unstable and uncertain environments by contrast, firms had more **organic characteristics**, decentralised decision making, few rules and regulations, with hierarchical and lateral communication channels. Horizontal coordination was emphasised, with considerable delegation between levels. Firms developed these characteristics as their rapidly changing environments meant that people at many levels had to monitor the environment and decide on a response (McColl 2003b). Mechanistic and organic organisation characteristics are shown in Table 9.6.

Differentiation and integration

Lawrence and Lorsch looked further into the idea of environment influencing organisation structure. They thought organisational environments might affect various units differentially. To test this, they studied three departments—manufacturing, sales, and research and development—in three industries with varied environments—plastics, food processing and containers. They focused on **differentiation**, how organisational units differ in members' behaviours, orientations and formal structures (Lorsch 1976). As expected, differentiation was found. R&D departments focused on new developments, worked fairly informally, and looked for long-term success. Sales departments meanwhile looked to immediate customer satisfaction, operated more formally, and were largely interested in short-term sales. Manufacturing departments were in between, concerned largely with efficiency, operating less formally than sales, but more formally than R&D departments, and in an intermediate-term time frame. Interestingly, departmental differentiation was greatest for the plastics industry, with the most unstable environment, and least in the container industry, with the most stable environment.

Differentiation was just one element. In effectiveness terms, the best firms balanced differentiation with **integration**, how much departments must coordinate efforts by collaboration. Greater departmental differentiation due to environmental instability was

mechanistic characteristics

Characteristics such as highly centralised decision making, many rules and regulations, and mainly hierarchical communication channels

organic characteristics

Characteristics such as decentralised decision making, few rules and regulations, and both hierarchical and lateral communication channels

differentiation

Extent to which organisational units differ from one another in terms of behaviours and orientations of members and their formal structures

integration

Extent to which there is collaboration among departments needing to coordinate their efforts

TABLE 9.6 CHARACTERISTICS OF MECHANISTIC AND ORGANIC ORGANISATIONS

Mechanistic	Organic
Work is divided into narrow, specialised tasks.	Work is defined in terms of general tasks.
Tasks are performed as specified unless changed by managers in the hierarchy.	Tasks are continually adjusted as needed through interaction with others involved in the task.
Structure of control, authority and communication is hierarchical.	Structure of control, authority and communication is a network.
Decisions are made by the specified hierarchical level.	Decisions are made by individuals with relevant knowledge and technical expertise.
Communication is mainly vertical, between superior and subordinate.	Communication is vertical and horizontal, among superiors, subordinates and peers.
Communication content is largely instructions and decisions issued by superiors.	Communication content is largely information and advice.
Emphasis is on loyalty to the organisation and obedience to superiors.	Emphasis is on commitment to organisational goals and possession of needed expertise.

Source: Adapted from Burns & Stalker (1961, pp. 119–22).

matched by greater efforts at integration in successful firms. For example, successful container companies had a functional hierarchy, rules and regulations, for integration. Successful plastics companies, however, used several vertical and horizontal coordinating methods to integrate in the face of high differentiation (Lawrence & Lorsch 1969). Horizontal coordination methods, discussed in Chapter 8 (e.g. teams and managerial integrators) were significant.

MATCHING STRATEGY AND STRUCTURE

Remembering contingency issues, managers must match strategy with structure in achieving effectiveness. Miller (1986; 1988) matched similar strategies to Porter's competitive strategies (see Chapter 6) with appropriate structures. Miller checked four main choices:

Niche differentiation. This strategy distinguishes one's products and services from those of competitors for a narrow target market (equivalent to Porter's focus strategy with differentiation). An example is BMW's introduction of the Mini (Howarth & Thomson 2003b).

Cost leadership. This strategy emphasises organisational efficiency so products and services can be offered at lower prices than those of competitors (equivalent to Porter's cost-leadership strategy). For example, Australian-based airline, Virgin Blue, has just begun flying the cross-Tasman route. The company has offered fares that are much lower than the other low-cost competitors.

Innovative differentiation. This strategy distinguish one's products and services from those of competitors by leading in complex product or service innovations (similar to Porter's differentiation strategy but narrower, particularly to sophisticated innovations). Examples of small innovative companies include a local Dunedin service provided by 'the Ding Man'—a firm supplying roadside repairs of car panels that have been 'dinged' or slightly damaged in carparks. Another example is veterinary companies that provide a total 'at home' care package when a loved pet dies. This includes a funeral service, home burial, photograph and a commemorative plaque for the pet.

Market differentiation. This strategy distinguishes one's products and services from thoses of competitors by advertising, prestige pricing and market segmentation (similar to Porter's differentiation strategy but narrower, particularly to market approaches). Product and service designs may be no better than those of competitors, but offer attractive packaging, good service, location convenience and product or service reliability. The Subway food outlet is an example of a fast-food sandwich maker that offers a variety of different types of bread and fillings, quick service and either 'eat in' or 'take away' food options.

Miller's structure and strategy matches are shown in Table 9.7. In these matches, Miller considered environment appropriateness for strategy–structure combinations, following the logic used in contingency approaches.

The typical organisation with niche differentiation or focus strategy is small or medium sized, with a relatively homogeneous customer and client set, where an appropriate structure is functional. A functional structure supports a cost leadership strategy, even in large firms, with small numbers of related products or services. Similarly, market differentiation strategy may work with a functional structure and a narrow product and service range and can be coordinated effectively across functional units.

Divisional or hybrid structures generally suit market differentiation. A cost leadership strategy can work with these structures while strategy is at division level.

A matrix structure fits with an innovative differentiation strategy. Matrix structures focus on flexibility and collaboration between specialists, conditions useful in new product development.

TABLE 9.7 MAJOR MATCHES OF STRUCTURE AND STRATEGY

Type of departmentalisation	Strategy
Functional	Niche differentiation, or focus
Functional	Cost leadership; possibly market differentiation
Divisional or hybrid	Market differentiation or cost leadership at division level
Matrix, integrators	Innovative differentiation

Source: Compiled from Miller (1986; 1988).

GENDER FACTOR

The Seriously Good Chocolate Company

The Seriously Good Chocolate Company is owned and operated by Jane Stanton, 'Chocolateur'. Jane is an innovative business woman who is passionate about her very successful and expanding enterprise. The Company started operating four years ago and it makes delicious hand-made chocolate truffles in an ever-increasing range of flavours and dark and white chocolate coatings. The key to the continued success is the exotic and innovative range of fillings that includes a variety of New Zealand wine-based fillings, for example, the Alan Scott Riesling

chocolate truffle, and a local beer-based filling, the Speights chocolate truffle. A special citrus truffle with a citrus zing has even been made especially for the Southern Sting—the local women's basketball team—to give them that extra edge in their game!

The company currently employs 12 permanent full-time employees, and several others, including local students, are employed during the holidays and when production is increased. A batch production system is used to make a particular type of chocolate truffle at any one time. Jane recently bought a machine for tempering and rolling the chocolate, and after this was installed production quadrupled. The chocolates are sorted and packed by hand into the distinctive black and red presentation boxes before being stored and distributed. Other product ranges are packed in luxury boxes with ribbons and novelty items, such as a chicken at Easter time. Packaging and production is done in-house with the help of a designer. Specially designed and produced gift boxes are produced for the corporate gift market.

Staff work extra shifts to cope with increased times of demand and to coincide with promotions such as Easter, Christmas and Valentine's Day. A recent marketing campaign included producing a designer T-shirt and chocolate gift package for Mother's Day, which went on sale in the David Jones stores in Australia. Other markets for expansion are being investigated by Jane in Singapore, North America and Germany.

However, despite plans for development and expansion of her business, Jane is keen to 'stick to the knitting' and to the business of making chocolate truffles. She manufactures complementary products such as chocolate sauces, which are also distributed in the food section of department stores in New Zealand and Australia. The factory is based in Southland which has a growing economy and a growing tourism industry. Her factory outlet shop attracts many visitors. Jane receives a great deal of support from other women who are in business. She is part of an active mentoring and support network, both locally and throughout New Zealand, and finds

the support and help of other women essential to her continued success and energy in business. She has developed business relationships with women owners of other businesses, for example, Linden Leaves, a company which produces a range of luxury soaps and bath products. Government agencies such as the Department of Trade and Industry provided start-up support and continuing business advice. Being located in Southland, which has a growing economy and tourism sector, is an important part of the *business*.

Source: Contributed by Elizabeth Hall.

Activities for discussion, analysis and further research

1. What kind of organisational structure do you think is currently used at The Seriously Good Chocolate Company?
2. If the company quadrupled in size in the near future, what kind of organisational design and structure would you suggest that Jane should consider using? How would this affect staffing at the factory?
3. Jane has a very involved and active role in all aspects of the company's day-to-day operation. She frequently travels overseas to explore new markets and business opportunities. What roles do you think she should consider delegating and why?
4. Jane has developed a number of relationships with other women in business. Do you think that she should formalise her relations with other companies? If so, why should she? How should she go about it?

Guidelines for keeping your organisation 'fit'

In today's global environment it is important to keep our structure nimble and able to keep up with the rapid changes which occur. Here are some guidelines.

1. You must continuously analyse the environment, strategy, technology and human resource pool to decide which organisation structure will keep your organisation competitively advantaged.
2. If you decide that it is appropriate to create a more formal structure, then you must define the

parameters of each staff member, ensure that job descriptions are clear and regularly evaluate each member's performance.

3. If, on the other hand, you feel that a more organic structure is required, then you must enlarge and enrich jobs to allow workers to tailor their jobs to meet the needs of the organisation as well as their own growth needs.
4. If your environment is changing and you are diversifying, you may need to examine whether a product structure would allow you to remain

more nimble and flexible. This would help you to keep the structure more organic.

5. In these days of outsourcing, it is important to continuously review your alliances and networks to ensure that they achieve what you originally

intended and help you keep the organisation flat and organic. Review the issues of who controls what and when.

Source: Adapted from Jones et al. (2000).

PROMOTING INNOVATION: USING STRUCTURAL MEANS TO ENHANCE PROSPECTS

Structure's support of strategy can be reinforced to encourage innovation. Innovation is critical to different differentiation strategies (especially an innovative differentiation strategy). In this section, we discuss four means of using organisation structure to facilitate innovation: vital roles for innovation, the need for innovative units or reservations, the differentiation paradox and transfer process (Galbraith 1982).

Vital roles

Successful innovations are rarely just one individual's work. The innovative process is more likely to occur if three vital entrepreneurial roles are filled: idea champion, sponsor and orchestrator. These were discussed in Chapter 1 and are briefly reviewed now.

An idea champion generates a new idea or believes in a new idea's value, supporting it against potential obstacles. These are often entrepreneurs, inventors, creative individuals or risk takers. Generally low in the hierarchy, they find it hard to get innovations accepted without a sponsor. A sponsor, usually a middle manager, sees an idea's significance and helps get needed funding to continue an innovation's development, helping the implementation of the new idea. However, innovations also need an orchestrator's help (Kinicki & Williams 2003). An orchestrator is a high-level manager, who articulates the need for innovation, funds activities, creates middle-manager incentives for sponsoring innovative ideas, and protects ideas people. Orchestrators are vital as innovations upset the status quo and are resisted by those who must adjust to the new ideas. These roles are significant and their effectiveness can be enhanced by creating special units or reservations.

Reservations

Breakthrough ideas are more likely if early efforts are separated from the organisation's operating units (Maidique 1980). This is because most units aim to perform similar recurring tasks efficiently (e.g. produce the millionth automobile, process the millionth cheque or serve the millionth hamburger). Focusing on completing tasks assigned, operating units are not adept at developing new operations. So many firms wanting to encourage innovation set up **reservations**, organisational units devoted to generation of innovative ideas. The aim is to create 'garage-like' atmospheres where new approaches can be tried out. Steven Jobs and Steven Wozniak created the first Apple computer in a garage, which was a reservation. Kevin Roberts, the New Zealand director of the advertising company Saatchi and Saatchi, has a similar philosophy. In a recent interview with CNN he said of his employees, 'And all we need to do is to give them an idea, liberate them, and get the hell out of their way'. The reservations in his company are fun places with comfortable lounge chairs, coffee tables and fruit in baskets to eat (http://edition.cnn.com/TRANSCRIPTS/0102/17/pin.00.html, accessed 3.4.04).

Reservations can be fairly permanent, such as research and development departments. **New venture units** can be set up as separate divisions or specially incorporated companies to develop new products or business ideas and initiatives (Burgelman 1985; Bart 1988).

reservations

Organisational units devoted to the generation of innovative ideas for future business

new venture units

Either separate divisions or specially incorporated companies created to develop new products or business ideas and initiatives

new venture teams

Temporary task forces or teams made up of individuals relieved of normal duties to develop a new process, product or program

differentiation paradox

Idea that although separating innovation efforts from the rest of the organisation increases the likelihood of developing radical ideas, such differentiation also decreases the likelihood radical ideas will be implemented

Reservations can be temporary task forces or teams of people relieved of normal duties to develop a new process, product or program. These are **new venture teams**. Though differentiation, particularly establishing reservations, effectively encourages innovation, there is an associated paradox.

Differentiation paradox

The **differentiation paradox** occurs when separating innovative efforts from the rest of the firm increases chances of radical idea development, but when such differentiation also decreases the likelihood of their implementation. The reason is that new ideas are often viewed as so radical they are threatening or even rejected outright. The paradox is strongest when a radical innovation is introduced to an organisation's operating units. Under these circumstances, the ideas may be rejected. For example, during the 1970s at Xerox's Palo Alto Research Centre, scientists invented the first personal computer, mouse, picture-oriented layout based on icons, and word processing software displaying fonts as they appear on the page. Sadly, the company did not appreciate the inventions' value and Xerox never capitalised on them (Chakravarty 1994). Instead, Apple, Microsoft and others did. The PARC situation at Xerox shows the differentiation paradox and the need for concern about technological transfer.

Transfer process

As the differentiation paradox suggests, the more apart innovators are from the company, the harder moving innovations into marketable products or services becomes. For example, Bell Labs averages around a patent a day since being founded in 1925 to give cutting-edge research support to AT&T. Yet AT&T has largely failed to translate Bell's research into products and services to fuel growth (Schrage 1987).

The effective transfer, or transition, process goes through several stages. In the first stage, an idea generator, or champion, develops an idea in a reservation. If initial results are positive but the idea needs more work, organisation experts hone it. Then, if results are still positive, the next stage tests the idea in an operating division. The final stage implements the innovation. Of course, it may not happen smoothly and may be easier if the innovation involves incremental change. However, to develop and implement significant innovations, efforts must be fostered and new ideas transferred from innovating units to the whole firm.

Organisations can set up separate new venture units and, when they are large enough, bring them into the main structure as separate divisions, lessening transfer problems.

This chapter focused on structure design supporting organisation strategy. In the next, we consider another aspect of the organising function, human resource management.

GAINING THE EDGE

Not so joint retail venture

In September of 2000, Ford Australia embarked on its first exercise in retail joint venture (RJV), in an attempt to coordinate sales and marketing programs and gain economies of scale by merging logistics, training and parts warehousing. This move has had varying degrees of success.

The first RJV in Australasia was set up in 1999, with the merger of six dealerships in Auckland, New Zealand. This was followed by a similar arrangement

with seven dealers, this time in Perth. Then, in Sydney, 19 dealerships were combined into an RJV, creating one of the largest Ford dealerships in the world. The new venture, which had an annual revenue of about $1 billion and 1400 employees, was the result of an agreement between the Ford Investment Enterprises Corporation (FIECo) and the 15 Sydney Ford dealers that held those dealerships. According to Keith Williamson, director of FIECo,

the RJV was meant to be 'a partnership between participating Ford dealers and FIECo ... to create a more effective, consumer-focused way of selling and servicing Ford cars and trucks'.

New vehicle sales for the group were expected to account for 74 per cent of Ford's total sales in metropolitan Sydney. However, the success of the venture was hampered by the refusal of two major dealers to join. Ford also discussed setting up a retail joint venture in Melbourne but due to dealer consolidation already occurring, decided not to continue. The retail joint venture concept was launched in the United States in 1998 by Detroit-based Ford Motor Company, as a way of reducing the retail price of its vehicles by cutting the cost of distribution (which accounts for almost 30 per cent of the retail cost of a car). However, three years later Ford announced that it would quit the retail

business and sell all its holdings in the United States. Ford Australia eventually bought out several partners in Sydney who had various reasons for leaving the venture, and currently has around 80 per cent stake in the distribution network.

Commenting on Ford's strategy, Holden's executive vice president of sales and marketing, Ross McKenzie, reflected that distribution is the last area where car manufacturers are still struggling to reduce costs.

Source: Margaret Tein (details of sources are listed on p. 736).

Activities for discussion, analysis and further research

1. What were the issues in the external environment that Ford Motor Company responded to by starting the concept of the retail joint venture?
2. The concept was less than successful in the United States. Suggest some reasons for this.
3. Do some web searches to discover what the complaints of the Sydney partners were, which caused Ford to attempt to buy them out and acquire an 80 per cent stake in its distribution network.
4. Do an analysis of the Australian motor industry environment and discuss the issues which would impact on the organisation.
5. In what way would involving themselves in a distribution network impact on the structure of Ford Australia?

REFLECTIVE PRACTITIONER

AEROSAFE
RISK MANAGEMENT

KIMBERLEY TURNER

In the next year or two, I want to bolster up our business with a range of regular casual and part-time staff capacity to fill various roles and, once the model is validated, that is where I'll be looking at growing our client base and raising our income to the stage where we can transition at a slow pace into changing those positions from casual or part-time to full-time ones, but the structure won't change at all. With that current structure, we can support growth of about 300 per cent without changing the structure at all.

In the last twelve months we have implemented profit share for some staff. In the last three years, we have had offers to buy out the business but my response has been not yet. We have the infrastructure in place. That will transition out as we grow. At the moment I want to be the business development manager. I want to grow and develop the business. I am kind of floating between all of those things. I don't want to let go of standing in front and delivering. When I stand up and do

things, we get another job out of the group. I still need to do that up-front work and bring someone else in to carry on with things. But we're still in that transition step. The stage between working for the business and owning the business. It is a different mindset. I'd like everyone to be like that but different people are motivated by different things. I know that for one of my staff it is about working for me and it has always been about believing in me.

Strategies for improving

1. In today's environment, it is proposed an organisation should remain organic in nature. Discuss this concept with reference to an organisation which alters the range of products or services it offers.
2. Consider what outsourcing, and therefore establishment of a network organisation, does to an organisation's ability to maintain strict control processes and therefore a mechanistic structure.
3. If an organisation has quality or innovation as part of its key strategies, what can it put into place to ensure that it will stay decentralised?

Source: Jones et al. (2000).

SUMMARY

- Chandler's study of the origins of large US firms helped establish the idea that managers should design structures to support organisation strategy. While structures that are needed to effectively and efficiently reach organisational goals will be influenced by major contingency factors and structural methods for promoting innovation.
- Functional, divisional, hybrid and matrix are four common forms of departmentalisation. Functional structure combines positions based on similarity of expertise, skills and work activities. Divisional structure groups positions by similar products, services or markets. Three major divisional-structure forms are product, geographic and customer. Hybrid structure adopts both functional and divisional structures at the same management level. A mature matrix is a structure that is simultaneously both a functional and a divisional organisation, with two command chains (one vertical and one horizontal). Matrix structures progress through several stages, starting with a traditional structure then moving to a temporary overlay, permanent overlay and, perhaps, mature matrix stage.
- Matrix structures are appropriate when environmental pressure needs a strong focus on both functional and divisional dimensions; changing, unpredictable demands need rapid processing of large amounts of information; and there is pressure for shared resources. Functional, divisional, hybrid and matrix structures all have advantages and disadvantages. Circumstances under which each will be effective differ. Emerging structures include process and networked structures.
- The best organisation structure relies on contingency factors including technology, size and environment. Higher technological complexity and interdependence levels need more horizontal coordination. Increased size leads to more departments and levels, greater specialist numbers, more staff positions and an eventual tendency toward decentralisation. Organisations have relatively mechanistic characteristics in more stable environments, while those in more unstable environments have relatively organic characteristics. Unstable environments are associated with more differentiation among units, increasing the need for integration. Integration is achieved through horizontal coordination.
- Some structure and strategy matches are more likely to be successful: functional structure and niche differentiation, cost leadership or perhaps market differentiation; divisional or hybrid structure and market differentiation or cost leadership at a division level; and matrix structure and innovative differentiation.
- Enhanced organisational prospects for innovation are possible by several structural mechanisms. The vital roles of idea champion, sponsor and orchestrator are important for innovation. Organisations must designate reservations, or units devoted full time to innovation. However, the differentiation paradox must be faced. On one hand, innovation is more likely if innovating units are separated from the organisation physically, financially and/or organisationally. On the other hand, separation makes it hard to transfer innovations to other organisation elements.

QUESTIONS FOR DISCUSSION AND REVIEW

1. Summarise current views on the link between strategy and organisation structure. To what extent can these differing views be reconciled?
2. Contrast functional and divisional departmentalisation types, including their respective advantages and disadvantages. Given your particular career interests, develop a list of advantages and disadvantages for (a) working in a company organised by function and (b) working in a company organised by product.
3. Describe hybrid, or mixed, departmentalisation. How does this structure help incorporate some advantages of both functional and divisional types?
4. Outline matrix departmentalisation's advantages and disadvantages. How do they relate to conditions where it is appropriate to use matrix structures?

5. Contrast the two critical aspects of technology: technological complexity and interdependence. Give examples of small-batch, mass-production and continuous-process technologies. Alternatively, provide examples of three types of technological interdependence.

6. Explain the four trends identified by studies of size effects on structure. Can you give evidence of these trends in familiar organisations?

7. Contrast mechanistic and organic characteristics of organisations. To what extent do you view your college or university as having mechanistic or organic characteristics? Cite examples to support your view. Why might organisations with organic characteristics need more managerial efforts at integration?

8. Outline how strategy and structure could be matched to help enhance organisational success. What implications would this have for subsequent changes in strategy or structure?

9. Explain the notion of a reservation applied to encouraging organisational innovation. How does the differentiation paradox help explain AT&T's difficulties using Bell Labs' innovative ideas in marketable products?

10. Describe the typical stages in an effective innovation transfer process.

CRITICAL THINKING QUESTIONS

To answer some of these questions you will need to do further research. Useful references are given below each section of the questions.

Building on the concepts of organisational structure dealt with in the last chapter, Chapter 9 explains how it is possible that the same structures which make one organisation successful may be completely unsuited to another organisation. The following questions highlight the importance of managers adopting a strategic approach to organisational design, especially in terms of the need to assess alternatives and provide for contingency factors. A key task in this section is to extend traditional notions to current theories on the strategy-structure mix.

According to a recent book by Bartlett and Ghoshal, *Managing Across Borders: The Transnational Solution* (2002), the strategy, structure and systems approach to running an organisation is outdated. They suggest that, instead of thinking of employees as workers, it's time to recast them as volunteer investors—as in people who are voluntarily investing their time and talent in a project. In his review of this book, Head (2002, p. 50) cites Bartlett's view that people 'were termed human resources, then they were assets on a balance sheet. But they're not a balance sheet asset. You can't screw them to the floor'.

The need to reinvent does not stop there, of course. Bartlett believes frontline managers need to become 'entrepreneurial initiators', while middle managers must become developmental coaches, and top managers must assume the role of organisational builders. It is a move away from the traditional focus on strategy and systems to one which emphasises people and purposes—quite a revolution for many in the way they look at their organisation. In fact, Bartlett and Ghoshal believe we are seeing the biggest change in the corporation since the 1920s when 'companies like DuPont, Standard Oil, Sears and General Motors established divisional structures allowing them to diversify'.

1. What are the key features of the divisional structure of most organisations today?

2. What are the major factors influencing the move away from the strategy, structure and systems model described by Bartlett and Ghoshal?

3. What are organisations moving to now and why?

4. There are some very clear issues that must be incorporated into strategic organisational design with these moves. What are some of the most important?

This brings us back to the opening notion of treating staff as 'volunteer investors—people who decide to invest their time, skill and energy into a corporation'. The key to this approach is that organisations will realise that their scarcest resource is intellectual capital. Thus, where not very long ago, managers used to regard shareholders as their most important clients because they supplied the scarce resource of finance, that view is changing as knowledge becomes the new constraining resource. This will bring about the need to recognise employees and treat them with the same respect and importance that managers reserve for the shareholder today.

(Material relevant to questions 1 to 4 may be found in Head, B. 2002, Corporate plays, *Australian Financial Review*, 5 October, p. 50; Bartlett and Ghoshal 2002, *Managing Across Borders: The Transnational Solution*, Hutchinson Business Books, London, England.)

The notion of a changing focus on strategy and structure is reflected in views at the national level regarding Australia's operation in a globalised marketplace. James (2002, p. 48) cites the world's most influential thinker on national economic strategy and company competitiveness, Michael Porter, as saying that, if Australia wants global success, it must learn to exploit its unique local strengths. James believes that Australia does not have a strategy for competing in the global economy and is not doing what is necessary to get one. He believes that sound macro-economic structures are necessary for competitiveness, but they are only part of the equation. Countries that do not know how to exploit their unique advantages will lose economic strength.

A main strategy of national competitiveness is the identification and use of structures that Porter calls industry clusters. These are groupings of companies that are typically world leaders in an industry or product type. They create something similar to critical mass—a collective ability to set the global standard. They come in many forms, from fragmented to highly concentrated, but the common element is high quality business relationships, high levels of trust and collective skills formation.

Porter cites the Australian wine industry as an example of a cluster where a group has been able to attain world-class standards—but, as he points out, this process has taken place over decades. A key feature of a cluster is that it is based on normal, almost everyday interactions that do not necessarily need to be the basis of a contract. As Porter says, 'You are neighbours, you work in the same place. You interact with them on lots of different levels but often you don't need a contract, because there are very strong incentives not to take advantage of people'.

Porter adds, 'if you think about the nature of relationships that firms have, you can think of a spectrum. On one end is the large vertically integrated firm that performs all the functions in-house. It makes its own machines, it makes its own parts and so forth. That is the more traditional old-style structure for an enterprise. At the other end of the spectrum are organisations which outsource everything'. He says: 'You have just the kernel of what you do inside your firm, but then you outsource with all kinds of other players to get all the parts and components and services that you need' (cited in James 2002).

5. Given the information above, what organisation structure would you expect to find in clusters?

6. How can Porter's frameworks explain what is going right as well as wrong in Australia's industrial sectors?

7. What are some of Australia's other possible industry clusters?

(Material relevant to questions 5 to 7 may be found in James, D. 2002, How to kick global goals, *Business Review Weekly*, 28 March, p. 48.)

While textbooks document the process of organisational design as one which is clearly evolving into more flexible and open structures, questions 8 and 9 focus on the challenges a law firm poses. The partnership structure of law firms differentiates them from most other business entities. This difference means the large-scale committee approach used in most organisations that generally works to define goals and culture and provide the basis for a shared vision, is much more difficult to implement in the environment of the law firm. Levin (2003) suggests that law firms are often slower to adopt the critical strategic mind-set needed in organisational redesign. Instead, decisions are usually made by a small committee of partners—partners who feel they have the right to a voice in any solution but are hindered by the realities of billable time, which discourages them from putting time into activities that cannot be charged to a particular case.

8. Why should the involvement of the partners be a crucial component of the organisational design process in a law firm?

9. What actions would you take if you were a consultant working with a law firm on a project to redesign the organisation?

The very distinct culture within the legal profession has meant that some of the issues involved in competition, staff retention and hiring, that have been familiar challenges to most organisations for many years, are relatively new to law firms. The lesson for law firms to learn from others' experience is that ongoing success will require the ability to translate strategic goals into a design strategy. The challenge then is to adopt a mindset which encourages open dialogue within the entire law firm, but especially among the partners, which seeks answers to questions as to the overall vision of the firm today and tomorrow. Armed with this information, Levin (2003, p. 44) believes that the resultant design strategy will truly reflect the goals and aspirations intrinsic to an individual law firm rather that generating preconceived 'solutions'.

(Material relevant to questions 8 and 9 may be found in Levin, A.C. 2003, Design by consensus; Involving the partners is not only necessary, it can actually be done, *Legal Times*, 6 October, p. 44.)

MANAGEMENT EXERCISES

Exercise 1 Management exercise: Developing an organisation structure

The Sun Petroleum Products Company, a subsidiary of Sun Company Inc., is a successful refining company. Its six refineries manufacture three main business products: fuels, petrochemicals and lubricants. The products are sold to Sunmark Industries (another Sun subsidiary), chemical manufacturers, industrial plants, the auto industry and a variety of other customers. The $7 billion company has a workforce of about 5400.

Sun Petroleum currently has a functional organisation structure, with the following positions reporting directly to the CEO: chief counsel; the directors of financial services, technology, planning and administration (including human resources); and operations (to whom the managers of marketing and manufacturing and supply distribution report).

Because of changing markets for the company's main products, Sun Petroleum is thinking about changing its organisation structure to a hybrid design. In the process, the president is considering adding a senior vice-president of resources and strategy to oversee the company's strategic planning.

First, draw an organisation chart depicting Sun Petroleum's current organisation structure.

Second, draw a chart showing the proposed change from Sun Petroleum's current structure to a hybrid organisation structure.

Third, be prepared to discuss the advantages and disadvantages of the proposed new structure and some possible ways of promoting innovation (Ackerman 1982).

Exercise 2 Skill building: Recognising structural strengths and weaknesses

The four basic alternative types of organisation structure are functional, divisional, hybrid and matrix. Each has certain characteristics, advantages and disadvantages. Indicate the structure type the following statements best fit by placing the first letter of that structure type in the blank (see next page).

Functional Divisional Hybrid or Matrix

1. _____ Corporate and divisional goals can be aligned.

2. _____ These organisations can react quickly to changes in the environment.

3. _____ Employees generally have clear career paths.

4. _____ Functional specialists can be added or removed from projects as needed, allowing effective human resource use.

5. _____ These organisations tend to develop excessively large staffs in the corporate functional departments.

6. _____ Goals may conflict with overall organisational goals.

7. _____ These organisations focus on the development of in-depth expertise.

8. _____ Response time on multifunctional problems may be slow because of coordination problems.

9. _____ Line of authority and responsibility may not be clear to individual employees.

10. _____ Specialised expertise and economies of scale can be achieved in major functional areas.

11. _____ Employees work for two bosses.

12. _____ Department performance is easily measured.

END-OF-CHAPTER CASE: ON THE RIM

When structures just don't work

It's hard for organisational members to recognise or admit that their structure is not serving stakeholders as it should. The Faculty of Commerce and Management at Griffith University seemed to be functioning well in 2003, with growing student numbers, widespread satisfaction with courses and a growing research and community profile. Although the 'bottom line' indicators may have been healthy, a more careful analysis revealed a number of problems that were keeping the university from functioning at an optimum level. One problem was that at both international and domestic promotional events, enquiring students were confused as to why the

POWERWEB

International articles related to this topic are available at the Online Learning Centre at **www.mhhe.com/au/bartol4e**

'management experts' had a School of Management, a School of Marketing, a School of Marketing and Management, and a Graduate School of Management. Students also were confused as to why a course of the same name could be so different when taught at the Gold Coast campus as compared to the Nathan or Logan campuses. There was also inefficiency in the use of staff resources, with a common example being that rather than having one convenor designing a course for three campuses, there would be three different convenors designing a course of the same name on three different campuses. Added to this was the development of unhealthy competition between Schools, with each School designing and marketing their own suite of postgraduate programs and competing against each other in trying to attract domestic and international students. The losers in this internal competition struggle would often be students, who found that Schools offered postgraduate programs with only a limited choice of electives as Schools wanted to keep students enrolled in their courses rather than their 'competitors'' courses.

The organisational restructure process was a challenge for Pro-Vice Chancellor Professor John Dewar. The restructure was aligned with the 'Griffith Project' which is the university's strategic directions policy aiming to raise Griffith to a top-10 Australian university. A broadly consultative process was instituted, with activities including the distribution of discussion papers, public forums, special meetings and discussion of individual concerns. The new structure would have to respond to the need for a more cohesive and distinct public profile, the need for better coordinated teaching programs, the continuing growth in numbers of students and staff and the need to preserve areas of strength within the organisation.

The restructure focused on creating the Griffith Business School (GBS) in place of the former faculty structure. The GBS combined the marketing and promotional functions of the former Schools, so that a more united image could be presented to stakeholders and potential students. The new structure also combined teaching areas into departments, with an example being that there was now one Department of Management and one Department of Marketing, rather than a confusing array of overlapping teaching areas. Budgetary control was moved from the internally competing Schools to the GBS level, so that teaching programs could be designed without the influence of internal 'turf wars'. The new department structure preserved the prestige of high-reputation research areas, such as the Department of Politics and Public Policy, in order to build on existing strengths as well as maximising the efficiency potential of combining complementary teaching areas. Quality-control resources were expanded and centralised through the appointment of Associate Deans to help improve areas such as teaching and research.

The restructure has been hailed as a success by most participants and stakeholders. The measure of success of the restructure, however, can only be determined by whether the GBS plays its part in helping the university to reach its strategic goal of becoming a top-10 Australian university.

Source: Contributed by Peter Woods.

Websites:

http://www.gu.edu.au/school/gbs/
http://www.gu.edu.au/about/org_structure.html

Activities for discussion, analysis and further research

1. How did contingency factors influence the restructured shape of the organisation?
2. How did the restructure attempt to resolve evident functional overlaps?
3. How did the organisation's strategy influence its restructured organisational design?

FURTHER READING

Blanning, R.W. 1999, Establishing a corporate presence on the internet in Singapore, *Journal of Organizational Computing & Electronic Commerce*, 9, 1, pp. 83–100.

Chetty, S.K. 1999, Dimensions of internationalisation of manufacturing firms in the apparel industry, *European Journal of Marketing*, 33, 1/2, pp. 121–43.

Ellis, S., Almor, T. and Shenkar, O. 2002, Structural contingency revisited: Toward a dynamic system model, *Emergence*, 4, 4, pp. 51–86.

Lam, A. 1996, Engineers, management and work organization, *Journal of Management Studies*, March, 33, 2, pp. 183–213.

Yeung, H.W-C., Poon, J. and Perry, M. 2001, Towards a regional strategy: The role of regional headquarters of foreign firms in Singapore, *Urban Studies*, January, 38, 1, pp. 157–84.

CHAPTER 10

HUMAN RESOURCE MANAGEMENT

CHAPTER OUTLINE

The human resource management framework
The Harvard Map
The regulatory framework
Australian regulatory framework
New Zealand regulatory framework
Main legislation in Australia and New Zealand

Establishing the employment relationship
Acquiring human resources
Job analysis
Recruitment
Methods of recruitment
Selection

Maintaining the employment relationship
Remuneration and benefits
Training and development
The Karpin Report
Training challenge
Performance management
Performance appraisal
360-degree feedback

HRIS, internet, intranets and extranets

The future of work
Flexible employing organisations
Flexible employees

Terminating the employment relationship

Corporate responsibility

LEARNING OBJECTIVES

After studying this chapter, you should be able to:

* Describe the legislative and business framework within which human resource management is conducted.
* Explain the three phases of the employment relationship (acquisition, maintenance and termination) and their importance to achieving organisational objectives.
* Assess the impact of information technology on human resource management.
* Explain the linkages between socially responsible organisations and human resource policies and practices.

STRIVING FOR EXCELLENCE

Not so crazy, after all

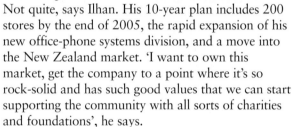

In 1997, when a corner shop came up for sale in Brunswick, Melbourne, John Ilhan snapped it up for $440 000. It was loose change for the owner of the Crazy John's mobile-telephone retail chain, but a pivotal moment in Ilhan's rise from a junior sales position at Ford to Australia's richest self-made person under 40 (worth an estimated $200 million).

It was the tenant, rather than the building, that attracted Ilhan's attention. Strathfield Car Radios had occupied the Sydney Road shop for years, including a period in the late 1980s when Ilhan worked for Strathfield as a salesman. The way he tells it, Ilhan managed to turn the under-performing store into the best in Victoria for the Strathfield chain, but he was not paid a bonus of $1100 that had been owed to him for six months. He left in 1991, set up a mobile-phone shop directly across the road from Strathfield and struggled for several years to stay afloat in the face of fierce competition from his former employer.

There are three other things that Ilhan will never forget. The first is the comment by his sixth-grade teacher at Jacana Primary School in Melbourne's west, who told him he had no potential. He was told the same thing by his boss at his first employer, Ford, when he asked why he had not been promoted for three years. And, even after he was a moderately successful mobile-phone seller, he remembers going to a Telstra function where there was no name tag for him. 'They wrote one for me in Texta and I was really embarrassed—I was a laughing stock, a nobody. Those sort of things give you a drive and you have to prove a point to yourself.'

That point, he says, is to start from nothing and make something of yourself. With more than 30 stores in four states, and leases signed for another 70 stores to open by Christmas—he seems to have made his point.

Not quite, says Ilhan. His 10-year plan includes 200 stores by the end of 2005, the rapid expansion of his new office-phone systems division, and a move into the New Zealand market. 'I want to own this market, get the company to a point where it's so rock-solid and has such good values that we can start supporting the community with all sorts of charities and foundations', he says.

The 10-year plan also includes making Crazy John's the employer of choice in the telecommunications industry, although Ilhan does not use this type of human-resources jargon. Instead, he talks of setting up an in-house creche and a training college for staff, and limiting working hours to 10am-3pm so parents can ferry children to and from school. Ilhan, the father of three young daughters with his wife Patricia, says: 'Is working three hours a day less really going to destroy the business? I don't think so.'

As laudable as these proposed initiatives are, it is clear that Ilhan does not look after his staff merely to be a nice guy. In talking of other examples of staff incentives, such as the bonus pool that is shared among everyone, including receptionists and couriers, Ilhan says: 'If someone works so hard, makes a lot of money for the company, if you look after them, they're going to give you more. Loyalty is very important to me.'

Loyalty is mentioned many times by Ilhan in relation to staff, suppliers, Telstra and customers. Crazy John's has connected its customers exclusively

continued

STRIVING FOR EXCELLENCE *continued*

to Telstra since the chain began, despite, Ilhan says, 'open cheque-book' approaches from Optus, Vodafone and Orange. 'It's not about the money, it's about long-term relationships. The customer wants to see you loyal to one carrier.'

Customer loyalty, more than any other factor, has been the key to Ilhan's success. Early on, Ilhan decided that low margins and high volume was the best business model, at a time when some retailers were making up to $400 on a handset. He claims to have been the first to offer a $1 handset (in 1993) and 'buy one, get one free', much to the fury of the rest of the industry. Again, it was not Ilhan trying to be seen as a nice guy, it was a shrewd strategy.

'My whole aim was numbers of sales and price. I thought: everyone is making huge margins in this area, I'll just drop the margin and the customers will love me, I'll get more sales and the turnover will make up for the lost margins, and repeat business will come back'. Ilhan says that in Victoria, repeat business makes up 90 per cent of his sales, and in the newer stores in other states the figure is about 50 per cent. He expects these figures to rise with the expansion of the company's new call-centre, which rings customers a month before their mobile-phone contract expires.

As well as cheap deals, Ilhan says Crazy John's customers are loyal because they get good service.

'I go shopping today and I'm appalled by the arrogance of other retailers. People have lost the idea of what retail is. The customer is the master and we're the servants. Respect to a customer is very important. I look at a company like Coles Myer, I could run it standing on my head. It's so easy—what are the customers' expectations?'

Those comments highlight another key reason for Ilhan's success: he really believes in himself, and that self-belief makes him an extraordinary salesman. When he opened his first store in 1991, across the road from Strathfield, he could not afford to stock any phones (which then cost several thousand dollars each) so he would persuade customers to buy from a brochure, then close the shop, drive to the phone supplier, pick up the phone and deliver it to the customer's home or office.

Surely it would have been easier for the customer to walk across the road to Strathfield and buy a phone on the spot? Ilhan agrees, but says that many of his first customers followed him from Strathfield and they knew he would do whatever it took to make them happy. 'I'd chase around town to find them a cheaper battery, in the days when batteries cost $150. I'd spend half an hour searching for a box to give a customer for free. They don't forget those sort of things. It's a personal thing.'

Source: Schmidt, L. (2003).

THE HUMAN RESOURCE MANAGEMENT FRAMEWORK

human resource management

Those management functions concerned with attracting, maintaining and developing people in the employment relationship

As detailed in Chapter 1, the generally accepted four basic functions of management are planning, organising, leading and controlling. Another viewpoint identifies a fifth management function, that of staffing. In these terms, **human resource management** is concerned with the staffing function, that is those functions concerned with attracting, maintaining and developing people in the employment relationship. The diagram opposite introduces a basic human resource management (HRM) framework (Fig. 10.1).

This HRM framework places the core functions of HRM within two inter-related contexts.

Within the 'business context', an organisation's plans and objectives influence how it deals with its staff. Small entrepreneurial organisations are more likely to recruit on a needs basis and have informal HRM policies and procedures. Large complex organisations with greater job specialisation are more likely to have formal systems to give structure and accountability for their staff functions. The human resource management functions of acquiring, maintaining and developing human resources will be different for these two types of organisation.

Within the 'regulatory and environment context', organisations are influenced by different forms of legislation, while responding to different environmental influences.

FIGURE 10.1 Human resource management framework

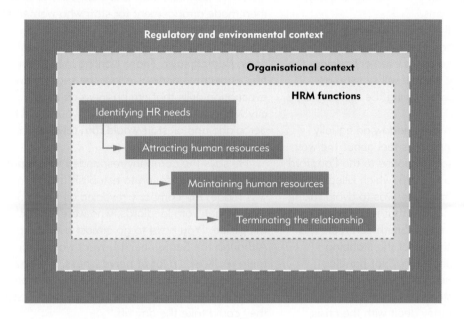

Cool in a crisis

Crisis management has become ever more important in the corporate world for the past two decades. Yet there is still the misconception that workplace catastrophes are most likely to be sudden, one-off accidents that occur only in industries such as transport, construction or aviation.

Ian Smith, the chief executive of the issues management firm Gavin Anderson, says: 'It's easy to understand that you have to deal with crises if your assets can fall out of the sky.' But all businesses are at risk, Smith says, and the recent case of Pan Pharmaceuticals highlights what can happen to companies that suffer from the 'it can never happen to us' syndrome.

The Institute for Crisis Management (ICM) in the United States defines a business crisis as 'any problem or disruption that triggers negative stakeholder reactions and results in potentially damaging public scrutiny'. The ICM's analysis shows that up to three-quarters of all business crises are not one-off, unexpected events but the result of smouldering problems that senior management has ignored, such as fraud, harassment, discrimination or other forms of mismanagement. No business is immune to such controversies. Peter Bartlett, the national chairman of the law firm Minter Ellison, says: 'Any professional services firm these days has to recognise that it can happen and, over a 10-year period, is likely to happen.'

One reason why companies are having to prepare for crises is cost pressures. Workplace injuries are estimated to cost about $20 billion a year. There is also a multiplier effect—five to ten times the initial cost of injury and recovery—when it comes to replacing staff, legal expenses, lower morale, penalties and bad publicity. Even when there is no injury, a $50 000 fine for breaches of occupational health and safety laws can hurt a company's profits and reputation.

The cost of latent problems is harder to estimate. A product recall or a whistleblower's revelations of unethical behaviour will have immediate financial costs, but these can be dwarfed by the long-term damage to a company's reputation and brand. Although these are undoubtedly assets, their intangible nature makes them hard to value.

Smith says: 'You can't put a value on managing a crisis other than to say that if it's managed badly, it can cost companies millions.'

Handling a crisis well can do more than just minimise costs. 'If it's managed well, you're maintaining, and in some cases even enhancing, the value of your brand, and people will see you as having integrity, being safe, having the right ethics, and so on', Smith says.

Reputation costs can overshadow an equally important issue: how employees feel about the way a crisis is managed. Esso's response to the Longford gas explosion in Victoria in 1998, which killed two workers and injured eight others, was to avoid taking responsibility, despite evidence that management had been cutting safety costs. Smith contrasts this with Qantas's recent handling of the stabbing incident en route to Launceston. 'Not handled correctly, it could have seen all sorts of issues created for Qantas.' Instead, pride was shown in the employees and the way they dealt with the crisis, from the quick actions of cabin crew to the supportive response of senior management and the chief executive, Geoff Dixon.

Bartlett says that over the past five years, Minter Ellison has developed sophisticated monitoring of high-risk areas. This includes audit and professional standards committees to analyse conduct and matters of conflict. It also keeps a close eye on information technology security and human resources to prepare for any potential discrimination or harassment claims.

The company's most recent experience of crisis management was in 2001 after the terrorist attacks of September 11. Minter Ellison was the only Australian law firm with an office in New York. Bartlett says the firm's order of priorities was to check that the staff were safe and offices undamaged, then communicate this to next of kin, the firm's partners, staff and clients in Australia. It then made arrangement for staff who wanted to leave New York.

Staff in Australia were also affected by the crisis, Bartlett says. Those working in high-rise offices became nervous about the security and evacuation drills that are business-as-usual for most city workers. 'After September 11, you would hear an aeroplane and all staff would turn towards the window.'

He says the company responded with a policy of regular communication to establish trust. If a threat was made, the company revealed all the information it could get from landlords, who were in touch with the police. 'You have to go almost overboard. Although the September 11 event was so far away, there really was a lot of nervousness. We had one day when there was a threat, and the landlords and the police were dismissing it, but we told all staff they could take the day off.'

Source: McColl, G. (2003).

Activities for discussion, analysis and further research

1. Undertake some research into recent crises that have occurred in your regional area. Find out what plans employers had in place to deal with these.
2. Interview an employee of your acquaintance and discuss the employee's feelings of confidence in the company's ability to handle potential crisis situations which may affect them.
3. Identify the various human resources management issues alluded to in the above case study. Can you think of any more issues which might face an organisation in a crisis situation?

Theories of HRM

With HRM's emergence as a specialist field in the early 1980s, theorists looked at the interplay between these different organisational contexts. Beer and Spector (1985) proposed a set of assumptions underlying HRM policies. These included:

- a shift from reactive activities to proactive, system-wide services emphasising the fit between HRM and strategic planning and cultural change;
- the concept of people as human capital, capable of development instead of being viewed as a straight organisation cost;
- the ability to develop common interest between stakeholders instead of assuming inevitable conflict between stakeholders.

Management's critical task

Fombrun, Tichy and Devanna (1988) suggested management's critical task was to align formal structure with HR systems of selection, appraisal, reward and development to drive the organisation's strategic objectives. In this way, single product, functional organisations could have functional selection processes using subjective criteria and appraisal systems, together with unsystematic reward systems. In contrast, multi-product, multinational organisations could use both functional and generalistic selection criteria, with systematic criteria, impersonal and objective appraisal measures and reward systems based on multiple planned goals.

The Harvard Map

At the Harvard Business School, Beer, Spector, Lawrence, Quinn-Mills and Walton (1984) developed an analytic map of HRM (often referred to as 'The Harvard Map') to describe the relationship between organisational performance and human resource policies. The Harvard Map not only considered the effectiveness of the organisation but also broadly considered the consequences of HRM policy choices for society.

The Harvard Map shows human resource policy can be influenced by two major factors— 'stakeholder interests' and 'situational factors'.

Stakeholder interests include shareholders, management, employee groups, government, community and unions. These groups are seen as potentially influencing choices about human resource policy within an organisation. Ideally these interests will be weighed and considered in total, but in reality organisations can respond to pressure or strong interest groups and ignore other stakeholders. The Harvard Map outlines the consequences of an organisation failing to consider all stakeholder interests.

Situational factors, both internal and external to the organisation, can influence choices about human resource policy and stakeholder interests. These factors include workforce characteristics, business strategy, business conditions, management philosophy, the labour market, unions, technology, laws and societal values.

In this way an organisation will make HR policy decisions about the following:

- the extent of *employee influence* (e.g. participative vs. autocratic decision making)
- the *flow* of human resources (retention, turnover, etc.)
- the *reward system*
- the *work systems*

These HR policy choices will bring about the following outcomes:

- the degree of employee *commitment* to work and the organisation
- the overall *competence* of employees
- the extent to which HR policy choices are *cost effective*
- the degree to which there is *congruence* between the goals of the employees and those of the organisation

Based on these outcomes, the Harvard Map then considers the long-term consequences for individual well-being, organisational effectiveness and societal well-being. These consequences in turn have the ability to influence stakeholder interests, situational factors and HR policy choices. The Harvard Map's benefits are that it provides an analytic framework to consider multiple interacting factors. It reminds those using the model that changes in one part of the framework have the potential to change other parts. Its broad approach in considering more than just financial viability of HR policy choices can be seen in retrospect to be consistent with more recent considerations of the 'balanced scorecard' (Kaplan 2002) approaches to HRM, as well as concerns for organisational social responsibility.

Life wasn't meant to be easy

What is the downside of being a chief executive?

Michael Chaney, Wesfarmers: 'I'm having trouble (answering the question) because I enjoy it so much. (But) receiving some of the accolades, you feel a bit embarrassed; it ignores the efforts of the whole group.'

Wal King, Leighton Holdings: 'I think the downside is that you give up a certain amount of your own private life. You can't absolutely say I have my business life and my private life; they become intermingled.'

John McFarlane, ANZ Banking Group: 'It's such fun being a chief executive. The worst that can happen is you fail and you feel terrible. Then the question is, how do you approach that? The first thing you do is you don't fail. Recognise failure is a possibility but not an option.'

David Murray, Commonwealth Bank: 'When people unfairly question our reputation, people allege we are untrustworthy. We know we make mistakes but when those mistakes are blown out of all proportion ... it ruins everything that gets built.'

Graham Turner, Flight Centre: 'I don't think there's a serious downside as long as you're prepared to take the responsibility. As a chief executive, life wasn't meant to be easy, but it's great to exercise a degree of control over your own future.'

Source: Washington. S. (2002).

Reflection point:

1. Consider the comments from the above CEOs. Can you detect a common theme?
2. What do you think might be some other downsides of being a chief executive officer?
3. Would you want to be a CEO? Why or why not?
4. Do some research on other CEOs around the region and see if you can find articles written about them or transcripts of interviews with them. What feelings do they express about their positions? Are they consistent with the above? How do they differ?

The regulatory framework

Perhaps one of the most important situational factors impacting on human resource policies and choices is that of the regulatory framework within which decisions are made and actions carried out. The regulatory framework is responsible for establishing the industrial relations environment within which the contract of employment is established.

Both Australia and New Zealand have experienced significant change in industrial relations laws and practices. In both countries these systems were deregulated, more recently New Zealand has seen a trend to re-regulate under the Labour National Alliance. Likewise both countries have emerged from periods of declining economic growth incorporating significant organisational change.

Australian regulatory framework

Australian industrial relations is highly influenced by its historical development and its links to the Australian Constitution. Within the Constitution, Section 51(xxxv) allows the federal government to:

> make laws with respect to conciliation and arbitration for the prevention and settlement of industrial disputes extending beyond the limits of any one state (Deery, Plowman, Walsh & Brown 2001, p. 129).

Access to conciliation and arbitration was limited to formally registered bodies, that is, employers (and/or their employer associations) and **unions**. Unions are membership groups formed to represent and advance employees' interests. In wage fixing, they negotiate binding collective agreements with management that spell out pay and work conditions for employees covered by industrial awards.

From the beginning, we can see that Australia developed a centralised, formal and highly regulated system of wage fixation requiring involvement of unions and employer bodies in establishing conditions of work and in resolving disputes about conditions of work.

Prior to the Australian Labor Party (ALP) and the Australian Council of Trade Unions (ACTU) Accords (known as the ALP–ACTU Accords), which began with the election of the Australian Labor Party Government in 1983, the area of industrial relations was often thought to be distanced from human resource management. These Accords had the effect of requiring many organisations to review job structures, pay scales, implement skills-based training and improved career structures as part of the conditions for receiving pay increases (Dabscheck 1989).

The election of a conservative government in 1996 after 13 years of Labor government saw the introduction of the *Workplace Relations Act 1996*. Continuing on with the reforms of the Labor Party, this Act moved quickly to take responsibility for workplace relations (previously termed 'industrial relations') down to the workplace and attempt to replace collectively negotiated agreements with individual contracts named 'Australian Workplace Agreements' or AWAs. It also reduced the power of the Australian Industrial Relations Commission (AIRC) to intervene or to use conciliation and arbitration to settle disputes, unless both parties in dispute are in agreement. However, problems with AWAs become evident when there is unequal negotiating power between parties. Although the legislation assumes equal power to negotiate outcomes, the current system increases the ability of employers to change employees' work conditions and pay.

New Zealand regulatory framework

The New Zealand system had developed a system of conciliation and arbitration similar to Australia. However for some years New Zealand has been going its own way and developing its own style of industrial relations, first through the abolition of compulsory arbitration in 1984 by a Labor Government, followed by the introduction of the *Employment Contracts Act 1991* (the ECA) which decentralised the wage-fixing system and, most recently, with the introduction of the *Employment Relations Act 2000* (the ERA) which has been described by Boxall (Boxall 2001, p. 28) as 'a fundamentally sound rebalancing of rights' that had previously been eroded.

The ECA radically overhauled industrial award agreements, reduced the rights and powers of unions in negotiating collective agreements, and allowed for individual contracts to be negotiated but did not require them to be in a written form. The extent of reform was possible due to the lack of any parliamentary 'house of review' such as exists with the Australian Senate. The legislation significantly shifted the power in industrial relations matters toward employers, away from unions, and reduced the ability of third parties to intervene, as has happened more recently in Australia.

Where the ECA was based on the philosophy that market power should determine all wage and condition outcomes, Labor's ERA:

- promotes collective bargaining
- recognises unions
- ensures union membership is voluntary
- is consistent with International Labor Organisation (ILO) conventions

The ERA recognises that, in the employment contract, parties do not have equal power. This inequality of bargaining power has led to the promotion of collective bargaining as a means of equalising the power dynamics. This is in direct contrast to the Australian government's emphasis on establishing individual work contracts.

unions

Membership groups formed to represent employees and to negotiate collective agreements with management that determine the terms and conditions of employment

'The [NZ] government is mindful of the United Nations Declaration of Human Rights, the International Labour Organisation and New Zealand's *Bill of Rights Act 1990* and the freedom to associate. These allow an employee to join a trade union as well as the freedom not to.' (Anonymous 2002). Summaries of the main features of the ECA can be found on the website of the New Zealand Human Resources Institute (Anonymous 2002).

Boxall (2001) notes that in addition to the changes under the ERA, the following conditions which remain unchanged are still significant:

- Union membership remains voluntary and has not changed.
- Bargaining structure remains largely structured around enterprises and workplaces.
- The personal grievance mechanisms remain the same as under the ECA.
- Collective employment agreements must still be ratified by members.
- There is no return to secondary or second-tier bargaining, which was abolished under the *Labour Relations Act 1987*.
- There is no return to collective bargaining.

Boxall (2001) then lists the changes that are important:
- Union access rights to enter and recruit new members are being improved.
- Union membership confers the right of a member to be covered by a relevant collective agreement.
- Unions regain the sole right to represent their members in collective bargaining, though employers can still negotiate a 'standard individual agreement' with non-union members.
- Collective bargaining must be conducted in 'good faith'.
- Strike laws are much the same but strengthened, applying to both employers and unions.
- Independent contractor status should reflect the real nature of the relationship, not just the wording. Fixed-term contracts are available where genuine reasons exist and if employees are properly advised.
- Individual recruitment and bargaining now have stronger procedural requirements
  Mediation is the compulsory initial process in personal grievances. Grievances may be referred to the Employment Relations Authority.
- Reinstatement returns as the primary remedy for unjustified dismissal cases.

Main legislation in Australia and New Zealand

Other Acts and regulations in both Australia and New Zealand deal with discrimination, equal employment opportunity, human rights, occupational health and safety, environmental management and privacy. All influence the employment contract. Below is a list of some of the main legislation that impacts on the workplace and hence should be considered when establishing HR policies and procedures.

Australian legislation
Employment Services Act 1994
Equal Employment Opportunity (Commonwealth Authorities) Act 1987
Equal Opportunity for Women in the Workplace Act 1999
International Labour Organisation Act 1973
International Labour Organisation (Compliance with Conventions) Act 1992
Judicial and Statutory Officers (Remuneration and Allowances) Act 1984
Long Service Leave (Commonwealth Employees) Act 1976
Maternity Leave (Commonwealth Employees) Act 1973
Occupational Health and Safety (Commonwealth Employment) Act 1991
Privacy Act 1988
Remuneration and Allowances Act 1990
Remuneration and Allowances Alteration Act 1986
Remuneration Tribunal Act 1973
Safety, Rehabilitation and Compensation Act 1988

States Grants (Coal Mining Industry Long Service Leave) Act 1949
Tradesmen's Rights Regulation Act 1946

Employment and Workplace Relations Acts and Bills amending Portfolio Acts:
Employment, Workplace Relations and Small Business Legislation Amendment (Application of Criminal Code) Act 2001
Occupational Health and Safety (Commonwealth Employment) Amendment Bill 2000
Occupational Health and Safety (Commonwealth Employment) Amendment (Employees Involvement and Compliance) Bill 2002
Safety, Rehabilitation and Compensation and Other Legislation Amendment Act 2001

New Zealand legislation
Accident Insurance Act 1998
Accident Insurance (Transitional Provisions) Act 2000
Employment Relations Act 2000
Equal Pay Act 1972
Health and Safety in Employment Act 1992
Holidays Act 1981
Human Rights Act 1993
Minimum Wages Act 1983
Parental Leave and Employment Protection Act 1987
Parental Leave and Employment Protection (Paid Parental Leave) Act 2002
Protected Disclosures Act 2000
Privacy Act 1993
Smoke-free Environments Act 1990
Treaty of Waitangi Act 1975
Volunteers Employment Protection Act 1973
Wages Protection Act 1983

MANAGING THE E-CHALLENGE

Creating a culture that's good for business

In mid-2001 Natalie Carrington started at Wilcom as their 'human resource consultant' reporting directly to the chief executive officer. Wilcom is part of the CEO's group of companies, whose primary business is the provision and support of equipment for embroidery of textiles (e.g. carpets, fabric and clothing).

The CEO of the group (and of Wilcom) is visionary, highly motivated, enterprising and innovative; proud of the achievements of the group and of the staff, of their openness, their enthusiastic dedication and commitment to excellence. He is insistent that the group maintains—and if possible enhances—what he believes to be its current leadership position in their industry. He attributes the performance and cohesiveness of the staff to policies such as:

- flexible work policies
- treating staff with dignity and respect and trusting them to do the right thing
- encouraging openness within the workplace and keeping staff informed, and
- when recruiting, including on the selection panel representatives of the staff with whom new employees will be working, and allowing them a significant input

Wilcom in particular develops, provides and supports software for embroidery machines (both its own and those of major name-brand suppliers). More than half of Wilcom's employees are software engineers, designers and programmers. They are regarded by their peers in the software industry as demonstrating 'world's best practice' in the development of software. The CEO wants to develop

resources etc.) that would enable new employees to be inducted into the Wilcom culture effectively and efficiently. He believes there is potential for this to be refined into a system for developing project management capability that could be marketed on-line to other organisations and to individuals.

One of Natalie's primary responsibilities, in addition to facilitating the establishment of this project management culture within the CEO's group of companies, is to oversee the commercial development and exploitation of the system.

Source: Contributed by Peter Lewis.

Activities for discussion, analysis and further research

1. What theoretical models do the policies practised at Wilcom exemplify?
2. What do you think are the major challenges confronting Natalie?
3. In essence, what is Natalie's role?
4. What do you think Natalie can do to facilitate a change in culture from its present orientation to 'a project management culture'?
5. What skills and capabilities would Natalie require to achieve the desired cultural outcome?

a 'project management culture' within the group. He sees computers, IT and knowledge management as integral to this development. They have for some time now been using project management software on their intranet as they work towards this objective.

The CEO also aims to capture the key elements of this culture and develop a methodology, training packages and resources (CD-ROMs, on-line intranet

ESTABLISHING THE EMPLOYMENT RELATIONSHIP

Having established the respective legal and regulatory frameworks for Australia and New Zealand, the next section deals with the three main phases of the employment relationship: acquiring human resources; maintaining human resources; and terminating the relationship.

Acquiring human resources

human resource planning

Determining future human resource needs in relation to an organisation's business objectives or strategic plan, then devising ways to meet the objectives

All organisations undertake planning for different purposes. **Human resource planning** involves determining future human resource needs in relation to an organisation's business objectives or strategic plan, then devising ways to meet these objectives (Walker 1980; Lengnick-Hall & Lengnick-Hall 1988). This section deals with the first staffing phase—the processes of attracting the 'right' number of people with the 'right' skills at the 'right' time and place. It shows the importance of defining jobs correctly through job analysis, then outlines recruitment and selection methods.

Job analysis

Two friends make surfboards on weekends and demand for their boards is high. They might make a business of their weekend pastime. To turn it into a business they will continue to make surfboards, but more of them. They will face many issues such as marketing, cost control, sales and bookkeeping. As small business operators, they may need to do everything themselves, with little thought as to whether they have the skills or knowledge for these tasks. However, if the business grows and profits allow them to hire someone, they will have to decide who to hire and what the new person is going to do. It is one thing to wait until a surfboard sells to make money. It is different to have to pay someone whether or not any surfboards are sold. Even worse is employing a person who cannot work quickly or accurately enough to meet customer demand.

The staffing issues facing these two friends are similar to those faced by larger organisations. Before an organisation can recruit and select 'the right people' to achieve organisational goals, it has to determine tasks to be grouped together into jobs to achieve business objectives. It will also need to determine the employee specifications required if the job is to be done properly. **Job analysis** is the systematic process of collecting information on a job's task functions and identifying employee specifications for job success (Fig. 10.2). Two outcomes of job analysis are the development of job descriptions (what a job entails) and job specifications (skills, abilities, education and previous work experience required to perform the job).

Job analysis is an important foundation for other human resource management processes. It can improve all of the following:

- **Recruitment and selection**—Job descriptions allow an organisation to accurately describe the job to potential applicants, and job specifications give important decision criteria in candidate selection for the job.
- **Performance appraisal**—Clearly defined tasks and specifications establish performance baselines against which an individual's performance may be measured.
- **Remuneration**—Accurate job descriptions and specifications allow organisations to value the job relative to the market and to other employees in the organisation.
- **Training and development**—Job analysis outcomes allow planning of initial and consequent training requirements and for later development opportunities.
- **Job design and redesign**—The systematic processes in job analysis can ensure jobs meet regulatory requirements (occupational health and safety standards) and can be used to redesign jobs as organisations change.

job analysis

The systematic collecting and recording of information about the purpose of a job, its major duties, the conditions under which it is performed, the required contacts with others and the knowledge, skills and abilities needed to perform it effectively

Recruitment

Recruitment is the finding and attracting of job candidates able to effectively fill job vacancies (Werther & Davis 1989; Schuler & Huber 1990). Recruitment has three objectives within the human resource management function:

- to increase the pool of job applicants at minimal cost
- to ensure the organisation complies with legislative requirements such as equal opportunity or non-discriminatory processes
- to improve the overall selection process by only attracting appropriately qualified and skilled applicants.

recruitment

The process of finding and attracting job candidates capable of effectively filling job vacancies

FIGURE 10.2 Job analysis process

Identification of job functions:		**Identification of person specifications**		**Position description and specifications**
• tasks • work behaviours • functions • equipment • work conditions	+	• knowledge • skills • abilities • competencies	=	

Only one woman in BHP's top 117 managers

On 20 May 1997, Sheryle Bagwell, a journalist with the *Australian Financial Review*, wrote an article with the above heading. Bagwell cited a study commissioned by BHP and carried out by the National Centre for Women at Melbourne's Swinburne University of Technology, which found that management in that organisation was very much a male establishment. Of the 117 top positions in the company at the time of the research, only one was filled by a woman.

In the report, which concluded that 'management ranks remain largely closed to women in BHP', several reasons were proposed for the inequity in the number of males and females holding top positions. First, 'unstated promotion criteria' appeared to favour male Anglo-Australians. Second, management preferred to recruit applicants from English-speaking backgrounds and third, women had left BHP because they found the company to be too inflexible (not because of family reasons, often considered to be a reason that women do not succeed in greater numbers in senior management).

At the time of the research (1995), women represented 9.5 per cent of the full-time workforce at BHP, a slight reduction from the previous year. Yet when all BHP groups were analysed, only 3.9 per cent of positions at other management levels were occupied by women. This figure was reported to be lower than other international companies engaged in similar operations, such as Esso Australia (7.3 per cent), Linfox (10 per cent), Mayne Nickless (15.2 per cent) and IBM Australia (17.6 per cent).

Bagwell reported that BHP had concurred with the findings of the study. The company had expressed concerns about 'its failure to promote women into its senior ranks', and also about their organisational culture, which was perceived to favour Anglo-Australian male employees. The report's conclusions were seen to be a 'scathing indictment of BHP's recruitment and promotion practices'. The organisation was criticised as operating in a 'time warp' with 'employment and

promotional culture locked in the 1960s'. It is interesting to note that despite these findings, the study concluded that the cultural environment at BHP was 'not hostile', because 'most people appeared to be open to change'. The situation reported above is not a unique or outdated case. In 1993, approximately 3 per cent of senior managers in Australia were women, and in 1999 this figure was believed to be between 3 and 5 per cent. Similar figures are also reported in England and America.

In 2001, www.miningaustralia.com.au/articles reported that women made up 7 per cent of the workforce of BHP-Billiton, and average salaries for women were below that of males. Representation of females in senior management positions was lower than for males, and the average turnover of female employees was higher than that of males.

In May 2002 BHP-Billiton were contacted in order to determine the number of women currently in senior management roles. They responded that this information was not available.

Source: Contributed by Glenice Wood; adapted from Bagwell, S. (1997).

Activities for discussion, analysis and further research

1. If you were a member of the human resources department at BHP and a meeting had been called to discuss the findings of this report, what suggestions would you make in terms of:
   - improving the recruitment and selection policy, and procedures for inducting appropriately qualified women into a management pipeline
   - enhancing training, performance appraisals and promotion opportunities for suitably qualified women in management
2. What perceptual biases appear to be operating in the selection process if only one of the 117 available executive positions is held by a woman? Discuss this in terms of 'perceptual shortcuts' commonly made in management practice.

3. What does the above article indicate about the effectiveness of the *Affirmative Action (Equal Employment Opportunity for Women) Act 1986 (Cwlth)*? Review the Act and isolate the step or stage that needs to be the focus of attention (Schuler et al. 1992; Stone 2002) in order to address the disproportionate numbers of male managers at executive levels in BHP.

4. Further information on current practices at BHP may be obtained on the following website: www.bhpbilliton.com/bb/home/home.jsp.

In situations where an existing job becomes vacant, there are some key questions to be asked before committing to the recruitment process:

Does the business need still exist? Work requirements may have changed so that the position is no longer relevant or required. (This should not be confused with downsizing, where an organisation reduces their workforce while expecting the same or more performance outcomes.)

If there is still a business need, is the job description of the vacant position appropriate? A job vacancy gives an opportunity to undertake a quick job analysis, especially where the nature of work has recently changed.

Can the business need be met by redesigning existing jobs? An opportunity exists to consider reallocating tasks between existing jobs or redesigning them to achieve better efficiencies. Managers must be conscious of any industrial relations implications of undertaking major workplace reforms.

If, after these questions have been answered, the position still needs to be filled, then the recruitment process can proceed.

Recruitment can be either internal or external. Each has advantages and disadvantages. For example, banks traditionally recruited new employees at entry level, then promoted internally in conjunction with internal training. While this ensured these employees developed loyalty and strong knowledge of organisational culture, they were less likely to be innovative. In a traditional, stable business environment, this was not a problem, but as the financial market was deregulated and the nature of banking changed, it became important for banks to reassess their recruitment strategies. New forms of retail banking require different skills to traditional banking forms, and thus a change in recruitment strategy.

TABLE 10.1 ADVANTAGES AND DISADVANTAGES OF INTERNAL VS EXTERNAL RECRUITMENT

Advantages	Disadvantages
Internal recruitment	
Improves morale	Closed group; inbreeding
Better assessment opportunity	'Nepotism'
Motivates staff	Infighting for promotion
Maintains organisational knowledge	Induction and training costs
External recruitment	
Fresh blood	Harder to assess
New knowledge and experience	Lowers morale of internal applicants
Gain competitor insights	Adjusting to different work cultures

Methods of recruitment

A number of recruitment methods are available to organisations. These include the following:

- **Internal promotions**—low cost, improves morale but no guarantee of finding right person
- **Advertisements**—able to target local, state or national markets, also able to promote positive image of company; cost increase with increased content and style
- **Employee referrals**—can be low cost, generates loyalty but may be limited talent pool
- **Employment agencies**—useful for low-skilled or temporary fills, but at a cost
- **Executive recruitment ('head-hunters')**—high fee-based search service which 'hunts out' senior management replacements; this method assumes the best person may not be looking to leave their existing job
- **Campus interviews**—large pool of talent in one location, but it is important that academic qualifications are not the only criteria
- **Contractors**—less permanent, reduces on-costs, useful for project work but not good for loyalty

The most recent method of recruitment has been through the internet. Job and career sites give excellent opportunities for people not only to access job opportunities at any time and from any internet site, but also provide the benefit of applicants being able to apply and download their CV directly onto the organisation's database.

Advertising rates on the internet are significantly less than for traditional display advertisements. When coupled with improvements in CV scanning software, organisations can achieve significant efficiencies. However, concerns about this medium of recruitment relate to issues of privacy and of appropriateness. While accessible, they do not guarantee that sufficient numbers of appropriately skilled applicants will be searching the internet for a job.

Selection

selection process

The decision-making system used to identify which job applicants are best suited to the vacant position

The recruitment process provides an organisation with a number of applicants to be considered for a vacant position. The **selection process** is the decision-making system applied to these applicants. As the importance of the vacant position increases, so do the consequences of an incorrect decision as to who should fill the position. The selection process tries to refine the decision-making process to optimise the fit between person and position. It is an attempt to predict who will be most successful in the position and, as with all predictions, it is always possible to get it wrong.

Reliability and validity

reliability

The degree to which the decision process will measure the same thing consistently

Reliability in selection refers to how much the decision process will consistently measure the same thing. Drawing short straws to make a decision is unlikely to give the same result consistently, but a standardised set of questions related to job requirements is likely to give consistent results if repeated.

validity

Whether the decision process actually measures what it sets out to measure

Validity in selection refers to whether the decision process actually measures what it sets out to measure. If the decision process for a vacant position is based on the school the applicant attended, then the organisation should be able to demonstrate the relationship between a particular school and job ability. The same applies to using psychological tests—there must be validated studies demonstrating a particular test is an accurate predictor of what it says it is predicting.

Selection methods

There are several selection methods organisations use, individually or in combination, but there are some standard components which seem to be used universally.

Application forms request job candidate details from applicants and may be as simple as personal contact details (name, address, contact numbers) through to extensive biographical details of qualifications, experience and achievements.

Weighted application forms aim to provide a systematic, objective analysis of different factors, and when weighted appropriately to reflect job-relatedness, can be a valid predictor for those jobs. The difficulty with weighted application forms is they need to be validated for each position, which is costly and time consuming.

Written tests include tests of intelligence, ability, aptitude and interest. Their use has seen a recent resurgence as they become more refined and demonstrate their ability to successfully predict suitable applicants for specific jobs. Some organisations justify their use due to the costs of making incorrect selection choices, but the issue remains one of validity and reliability.

The *selection interview*, in combination with application forms, is a well-established method used for almost any job. Its attractiveness as a selection method is balanced against debate as to its value as a predictor (see, for instance, Arveny & Campion 1982). Its attractiveness in selection may have more to do with people's desire to actually meet the person they choose than whether the interview was a valid or reliable predictor of job performance. However, the interview's validity and reliability can be improved. Clark (1992) reports several measures to improve interviews, including these:

- training of interviewers
- combining interviews with other selection devices
- clearly identifying what is being sought in a candidate
- improving validity by looking for specific items whose relevance have been established
- using interviews to identify disqualifying data rather than qualifying data
- using panel interviews to improve validity over sequential interviews
- using interviews to assess interpersonal motivations and career aspirations, which may be difficult to identify by other means

Assessment centres provide an opportunity to evaluate applicant performance in simulated tests of the tasks related to the position. Trained assessors evaluate candidates as they operate in simulated situations they are likely to face in the position. Activities may be a combination of problem-solving exercises, leadership and team exercises, interviews and business-decision simulations. The ability to predict job performance in management positions well can be attributed to the identification of relevant job tasks, the combination of selection devices used and the training assessors receive. Assessment centres can therefore usually justify the high cost of establishing and conducting them.

MANAGEMENT SKILLS FOR A GLOBALISED ECONOMY

How to conduct an effective interview

You have a job vacancy in your unit and must interview several job candidates. What should you do? There are several steps to take before, during and after the interview to increase the likelihood of getting useful information to make your decision.

Before the interview

Much of the secret of conducting an effective interview is in the preparation. The following guidelines will help.

Determine job requirements. Using the job description and specification, draw up a list of characteristics the person must possess to perform the job. For example, suppose you are a bank manager and have an opening for a teller. Important characteristics would include oral communication skills, willingness to check for errors, ability to get along with others, and a service orientation to handling customers. Once these are identified, you can develop an interview guide.

Prepare a written interview guide. A written guide of what you wish to cover during the interview ensures all major points are addressed with each interviewee. You must plan questions assessing the degree to which candidates possess characteristics you identified as needed for the job.

Since past performance is a good predictor of future performance, a useful method is to frame questions in terms of examples of what a person has done, instead of focusing on generalities or speculations about what they will do in the future. For example, a poor question aimed at assessing how well an individual interacts with customers might be: 'How well do you handle problem customers?' Clearly candidates are unlikely to answer they have difficulty handling problem customers, even if it is true.

An *improved* approach asks questions as to how the individual has dealt with customers previously. For example, you might ask, 'Please describe a time when a customer paid you an especially nice compliment because of something you did. What were the circumstances?' You might follow up by asking, 'Tell me about a time when you had to handle a particularly irritating customer. How did you handle the situation?' Answers to these types of questions give insights into how a candidate is likely to treat customers and handle difficult situations. (If the individual has no job experience, questions can be adjusted; for example, '. . . a time when you had to handle a particularly irritating person'.)

Next, prepare a step-by-step plan of how to present the position to the candidate. Develop a similar plan for points to be made about the work unit and organisation. These plans help you present information in an organised way and ensure you cover all important points.

Review the candidate's application and/or résumé. This familiarises you with the candidate's specific experiences and accomplishments relevant to job requirements. Read these background materials before the interview; otherwise you will be unprepared for the interview. It is easy to miss gaps, discrepancies and relevant experience when background materials are reviewed quickly in front of the candidate.

During the interview

Your carefully prepared questions help maintain control during the interview. Here are additional guidelines.

Establish rapport. Small talk at the start of an interview can help put the candidate at ease. Comment on a résumé item, such as a hobby you have in common or a place you have both lived. Be careful, though, not to let the interview get too far off track with extended discussion of, say, your football team.

Avoid conveying the response sought. Suppose you try to determine a candidate's ability to work with other tellers, all working in a relatively small area. You ask, 'Will you be able to work well with other tellers, especially given our space constraints?' A bright interviewee realises quickly, from your question, the answer you are seeking and replies, 'Of course, no problem'. A better approach would be: 'We all sometimes have unpleasant experiences with co-workers. Tell me about the most difficult time you ever had working with someone else'.

Listen and take notes. Be sure to do a great deal of listening. Experts recommend the interviewer talk for 20 to 30 per cent of the time and allow the interviewee to talk for 70 to 80 per cent. You need to learn as much as you can about the candidate in the available time. So take notes to help remember important points.

Ask only job-relevant questions. Interviewers can stray into asking potentially discriminatory questions. One example is asking a female applicant the type of work her spouse does. Such a question is discriminatory since it is rarely asked of a male candidate and is irrelevant to job requirements or the person's qualifications. The best policy is to ask only questions clearly and directly related to job requirements.

After the interview

Write a short report right after the interview, scoring the candidate on the characteristics you identified as important to effective job functioning. Briefly indicate your rationale, using examples or summaries of responses. By documenting your ratings right after the interview, you will have good data to help your selection decision.

Source: Based on Janz, Hellervik & Gilmore (1986); Jenks & Zevnik (1989); Gatewood & Feild (1990).

In addition to risking the cost of an incorrect choice, organisations must operate within a regulatory context which imposes penalties for not conducting the selection process equitably. Large organisations have to make many selection decisions on a regular basis, and it is in their interest to ensure managers making selection decisions are at least trained and aware of the relative strengths and weaknesses of available selection devices.

MAINTAINING THE EMPLOYMENT RELATIONSHIP

Remuneration and benefits

This section deals with employee pay and benefits. In Australia the pay component of an organisation is referred to as 'remuneration', whereas in the US it is known as 'compensation'. Since compensation in Australia is associated with payment of wages or salaries to workers injured in workplace accidents, we refer to pay as 'remuneration' rather than 'compensation'. **Remuneration**, in this context, is financial payments to employees in return for work.

Having attracted and selected appropriately skilled people, it is necessary to reward them so they will accept the job, but not pay them so much the organisation loses money through weight of salaries and wages paid to employees.

Remuneration links to the regulatory framework, in that pay rates are often determined after negotiations between employer and employee representatives collectively or with the employee directly. Negotiated awards and enterprise agreements specify minimum rates to be paid to workers, as well as conditions within which they work. Individual contracts are legally binding and specify rates of pay and services to be performed for that pay.

Remuneration links to training and development. Organisations can offer lower-than-average wages or salaries if they can offer unique benefits and training or development opportunities otherwise unavailable. Alternatively they may be willing to accept high turnover rates if there are plenty of potential candidates and positions involve low skill-levels. Some call centres and commission pay jobs fall into this category.

As salaries can be more than 60 per cent of an organisation's costs, there should be some form of regularly reviewed salary system. A major purpose of salary systems is to achieve internal and external pay relativity.

Internal relativity comes when salaries or wages are remunerated at levels where employees believe they are being paid a reasonable rate relative to other workers in other jobs within the organisation. External relativity is achieved when wage and salary rates for employees are comparable with rates paid by external organisations.

This does not mean all organisations try to pay the same as everyone else. If an organisation wishes to set up a reputation as a market leader, both in terms of product and service, then it may choose to pay above average wages or salaries to attract and retain suitably skilled employees. Conversely, if an organisation pays below market rates, it would have to accept a high turnover or have a strategy to retain employees (due to non-salary benefits or unique work opportunities).

remuneration

The financial payment to employees in return for their work

Training and development

Organisations must attract and retain an adequate supply of people with skills and competencies to meet organisational objectives. They have three choices in employee selection:

1. They can select employees who already have the skills and competencies necessary to achieve organisational objectives.
2. They can select employees with the ability to acquire necessary skills and competencies.
3. They can have a mixture of the two.

training

The process of equipping people with skills and competencies in a systematic manner

development

To broadly prepare the employee for future opportunities through the acquisition of new knowledge, skills and attitudes

Each option will impact on the amount and type of training offered in the organisation or acquired from external sources. **Training** is the equipping of people with skills and competencies systematically, while **development** aims to broadly prepare employees for future opportunities through acquisition of new knowledge, skills and attitudes. The aim of training is to increase skills, knowledge and competencies to be able to better achieve performance objectives. It is usually structured, and may be formal, informal, on or off the job, during or after work hours. Training is directly related to recruitment and selection, and is linked to performance management and review.

Clark (1992) states that there are three broad strategic rationales for training. They are as follows:

1. *The proactive approach*—This is designed to meet a company's long-term objectives and to anticipate rather than react to organisation needs.
2. *Reactive approaches*—These are usually driven and prompted by immediate problems which could, if not addressed, adversely impact on the achievement of performance objectives.
3. *Enhancement of employee motivation, commitment and retention*—In this way, training is motivational. It is a means whereby employee expectations can be met, of providing career pathways, improving job security and increasing job satisfaction.

The Karpin Report

One of the most significant influences on how training is viewed within Australia has been the Karpin Report. In 1995, David Karpin chaired a task force with a brief to:

- analyse Australia's current situation and performance from a management perspective;
- consider how Australia's performance compared with what was happening in the rest of the world;
- examine current trends and future changes in Australia's business environment;
- consider the inevitable challenges Australia will be facing in the next decade; and
- propose strategies for change to help position Australia for strong international competitiveness by 2010.

Karpin released the task-force report which found that Australian enterprises, training providers and educational institutions are not moving quickly enough to address the new paradigm of management. Many of their counterparts overseas, and especially the leaders in various fields of industry and education, are changing more rapidly and more extensively.

The report identified that by 2010, organisations will be learning organisations, with leaders encouraging learning within the organisation. Likewise, managers will be result-driven MBA graduates who, having completed several overseas job tasks, will need to cope with significant pressure while delegating to an internationally based workforce.

The Karpin Report issued five key challenges that the task force believed would influence development of management skills. They were:

- a positive enterprise-based culture, through education;
- upgrading vocational education and training and business services;
- capitalising on talents of diversity;
- achieving best-practice management development; and
- reforming management education institutions.

The heavy emphasis on management development, education and utilising workforce diversity in these five key challenges for Australian business emphasised the extent to which training and development contributes to organisation success.

Training challenge

Caudron (2000a) reports that one of the biggest challenges organisations face is that, while CEOs are sold on learning, they do not see a link between training and business performance. Training has failed to demonstrate its impact upon the bottom line, been limited by compartmentalised content-based solutions and often operates in isolation, failing to understand core business or to establish links with the core mission. Caudron believes the challenge for organisations is to embed learning into core business processes. This can be achieved by:

- linking training objectives to business strategy, ensuring everyone is pointed in the same direction;
- addressing corporate culture—to create long-lasting organisational change trainers can't ignore the influence of corporate culture;
- focusing on outcomes, not activities;
- de-emphasising 'classroom' training and emphasising learning on the job;
- allowing employees time to process what they've learned; and
- demanding the same strategic change in practices from training suppliers as expected from within the organisation.

When linked to corporate strategy and organisational objectives, training and development can help organisations improve their ability to respond to rapidly changing environments. They can become critical to achievement of an organisation's core business objectives, but must move from an activity-focused event to outcomes-based integrated learning opportunities.

Performance management

Given how much it costs to acquire employees, organisations will want to ensure that the outlay on staff is achieving an appropriate return. Along with rapid organisational change, restructuring, acquisitions and mergers, downsizing and receivership, organisations are looking to align corporate objectives and strategies with individual performance standards and outcomes (Nankervis & Leece 1997).

Performance management can therefore be defined as 'an interlocking set of policies and practices which have as their focus the enhanced achievement of organisational objectives through a concentration on individual performance' (Storey & Sisson 1993, p. 132). The scope of *performance management systems* is therefore broader than that of the *performance appraisal process*, which becomes just one of the tools by which managers determine whether their business objectives are legitimate and if they are aligned internally and externally with business units and markets.

Research by KPMG (2001) indicates that while traditional performance-measurement systems may be suitable for maintaining business as usual—managing day-to-day activities and compiling historic figures for accounting and other purposes—such systems have not measured up to the increasingly complex task of directing organisations in a world of 'continuous inexorable change'. Figure 10.3 presents these differences diagrammatically.

Historically, measurement has focused on *traditional* performance areas, which tend to look at financial, operational or functional efficiency. Traditional measures are generally abundant, precise, internally generated, quantitative in nature, and derived from operational accounting and information systems. In addition, they have generally been historical or lagging in nature. Non-traditional measures, on the other hand, have tended to be less well-defined. They relate to intangibles and *emerging* areas such as an entity's marketplace, stakeholders, strategic implementation and resource management. Ideally, such measures are predictive in nature. However, they are often fed with incomplete, anecdotal and conflicting data that is inconsistently gathered.

Table 10.2 outlines the different types of questions businesses can ask in order to identify what should be measured as distinct from what is being measured.

Performance appraisal

As one of the more obvious components of performance management, **performance appraisal** is the process of appraising the job performance of employees. Clark (1992) identifies five reasons for appraising performance:

performance appraisal

A judgmental process of the job performance of employees

FIGURE 10.3   Traditional and emerging areas of performance measurement

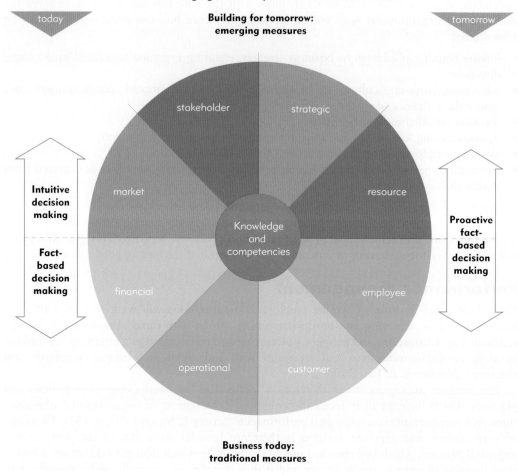

Source: KPMG (2001).

- to mould employee behaviour according to company-determined norms;
- to enhance consistency between employee actions and corporate goals;
- to improve quality of human resource planning, in particular training and succession;
- to improve quality of salary reviews; and
- to provide a record in cases of dismissal, demotion, grievance or appeal.

Traditional appraisals are usually performed by line managers. The human resource department has a role in designing the system, training end-users and collecting and collating data from appraisals (Clark 1992).

Supporters of appraisal argue that it serves as a key link in the human resource management system. Performance appraisal is linked to other human resource functions in the following way:

- Job analysis provides job descriptions and criteria to which jobs are to be performed. These are the criteria by which an employee's performance can be judged.
- Job requirements and employee duties are communicated during the recruitment and selection process. Performance-appraisal processes should align with criteria communicated at the time (unless later reviewed and agreed by employee and manager).
- Performance appraisals may help identify the effectiveness of both job analysis and recruitment and selection processes. Consistent failures in a position may identify weaknesses in either determination of job components or adequacy of applicants chosen to do the job.

TABLE 10.2 BALANCING TRADITIONAL AND EMERGING NEEDS

TRADITIONAL MEASUREMENT NEEDS	
Financial	• Are we focusing on the right financial measures to judge the success of our company/divisions/units? • How much of our value is reflected in our balance sheet? Do we have the right balance between financial and non-financial measures to address key intangible assets beyond the balance sheet?
Operational	• Do we have the right short-term operational measures in place to respond quickly when an activity central to the core business (around sales and delivery to customers) goes awry? • To what extent do we measure both the effectiveness and efficiency of operational processes?
Customer	• How well do we measure and monitor shifts in customer needs and expectations? • Do our operational teams clearly understand their role in fulfilling customer needs, and are they measured and provided incentives accordingly?
Employee	• Have we aligned compensation to our strategic objectives, and how is performance measured, rewarded and recognised? • Do we regularly measure employee satisfaction and take action with the results?
EMERGING MEASUREMENT NEEDS	
Market	• How well does our measurement system track changes in industry and external forces that impact on the continuing relevance of our strategy/business model? • What do we need to measure and monitor on an ongoing basis around existing and emerging competitor activities?
Stakeholder	• Do we understand who our stakeholders are, what their needs and expectations may be, and measure how we are meeting those needs and expectations, as well as trade-offs between stakeholders? Do we fall prey to assuming we know what stakeholders want? • How well do we measure and monitor shifts in stakeholder needs and expectations?
Strategic	• Do our measures align with and facilitate implementation of our strategy? • Has the measurement system been reviewed/updated for recent events including strategic changes, acquisitions or divestitures, leadership changes, and industry or regulatory changes? • Does the measurement system tell us if the vision/mission/strategy is 'alive' and driving behaviour in the organisation?
Resource	• Do we have measures in place to tell us how well we are marshalling resources today and whether we have the right tangible and intangible resources to achieve our strategy? • Do we have the right information to determine where we should be building and acquiring competencies (talent, alliances, distribution channels, software, etc.) for the future?

Source: KPMG 2001, p. 9.

- Performance appraisal gives a rationale for an organisation's remuneration system. In some organisations there is a direct link between performance and pay, performance and promotion or performance and bonuses.
- Performance appraisal links into training and development by identifying skills and knowledge deficits.
- Appraisal outcomes may be the basis of instituting disciplinary action against an employee. If dismissal procedures are instituted, managers must ensure regulatory requirements for appropriate dismissal are followed.

As with methods used in recruitment and selection, performance appraisal methods must be:

- valid—measure what they say they measure
- reliable—consistent and repeatable
- fair and equitable—not disadvantage any group

Critics of performance appraisal point to levels of dissatisfaction with the process by employees and lack of adequate skills of managers to effectively perform fair and equitable appraisals.

Employees are often dissatisfied with performance management system methods and managers are frequently reluctant to engage in a process which communicates levels of dissatisfaction with performance. The process may enforce an unhappy employee's compliance. Problems may also occur if individual appraisals are performed on team members who operate interdependently.

Organisations usually undertake appraisals for two purposes: to identify pay/bonus/promotion opportunities and to provide feedback linked to developmental opportunities. However, these purposes can be counterproductive, which is why it is recommended the two processes be completed separately, with the first to assess any developmental or training needs and the second to assess whether or not performance warrants increased or decreased salary and bonuses. As a result of these criticisms and difficulties, interest is growing in the process of 360-degree feedback.

360-degree feedback

Traditional appraisal systems reinforce a hierarchical approach to organisations—managers appraise supervisors who appraise employees. This approach assumes the more senior person is the only one able to provide feedback. 360-degree feedback begins with the belief that it is useful to receive feedback not only from one's immediate supervisor but from peers and subordinates. The collection of ratings or views from subordinates, peers and supervisors are collated to provide a multi-source means of assessment.

The feedback from different appraiser groups or categories provides different perspectives and insights into how an employee is seen to be performing at different levels in an organisation. Benefits come from having a larger sample of appraisals and opportunity to represent outcomes graphically. Where the employees rate themselves, graphical outcomes give useful starting points in discussing perceived strengths, weaknesses, similarities and differences. There are, however, problems with maintaining anonymity in small groups or teams and ensuring adequate training in the system's use.

HRIS, INTERNET, INTRANETS AND EXTRANETS

An early function of the human resource department was collection and storage of employee details. This data was needed to meet legislative requirements or for use in transaction processing. Originally stored in hard copies on paper files, this data eventually found its way onto computer databases which processed transactions more easily and quickly. Again, reactively, reports could be generated identifying cost breakdowns, cumulative totals and exception reports on issues such as pay, leave entitlements and sick leave taken. It was not until database systems began to manipulate data into quality information linking data to organisational objectives that these computerised systems began to allow human resource management departments to operate strategically.

Information technology's impact on business continues to outpace other forms of organisational change. Access to stored databases and knowledge bases has increased with convergence of the **internet**, **intranets** and **extranets**. The internet is a global connection of computer servers interconnected by telecommunication systems through which individuals can access stored information from their own computer and modem. Intranets are closed networks of information databases and systems within an individual organisation, whereas extranets are closed networks of information systems between a group of organisations.

Coupled with the explosion in the use of email, these changes are significantly impacting on HRM. Organisations are adopting web-based strategies because of benefits of platform independence, access to wide-ranging information and potential to access information-rich multimedia files. The internet is a powerful business tool because it represents a convergence of closed network intranets within an organisation and closed network extranets between organisations. The issue for HR departments is to find how these networks can help them provide improved service provision, cost savings and value-added services.

Networks can deliver the following HR services:

- improved internal communication (speed and consistency of message, collaborative groups, etc.);
- distribution of HR policy, news and information and employee surveys;
- training and development activities on-line;
- recruitment over the internet;
- HR self-service—employees accessing and changing personal details, travel bookings and claims, etc.;
- 360-degree feedback and traditional performance monitoring data input; and
- collaborative work groups independent of location or time zone.

There are also other possibilities. The list only represents forms of transaction processing. To become more flexible and competitive, companies are moving from legacy information systems to integrated business management systems. Companies use enterprise-wide systems (such as PeopleSoft and SAP) to streamline business processes and improve information sharing to compete in the rapidly evolving business world. Human resource management systems are an important component of integrated software. Today, they drive recruiting, payroll systems, employee databases, succession planning, benefits calculations and workflow solutions. But the success of these systems hinges on many complex factors and involves more than the technical expertise of HR and information technology departments. The organisation's historical focus has typically been one of relatively narrow HR and Information Systems (IS) issues, rather than on the larger business context. Without a core platform and a central strategy to drive decisions about hardware, software and work processes, the entire organisation can find itself shackled with automated inefficiency. Organisations must focus on the strategic contribution of the new systems to achieving business objectives, and recognise HR's vital role as an active business partner with senior management and a critical service provider to business units.

Despite its benefits, introducing information technology into HR brings its own challenges. With widespread take-up of email, there is a need to develop clear and comprehensive policies on access, use and misuse of email (see Supplement 3 for Chapter 15). Legal issues arise when employees use email to distribute pornography to unsuspecting recipients or to harass or threaten. Other legal issues emerge if organisations move to dismiss these employees without having established clear policies, communicated them and followed regulatory guidelines for dismissals. Privacy issues arise in terms of access to confidential data. Copyright and intellectual property rights are an issue when material is developed on the internet or when material is used from the internet.

internet

A global connection of computer servers interconnected by telecommunication systems through which individuals can access stored information from their own computer and modem

intranets

Closed networks of information databases and systems within an individual organisation

extranets

Closed networks of information systems between a group of organisations

THE FUTURE OF WORK

Widespread use of flexible working arrangements has enabled organisations to achieve functional and numerical flexibility. In general this has benefited both business and employees still employed, but has led to reduced labour demand in industries applying such practices. There has also been a trend to reduce numbers of core, permanent employees and increase numbers of part-time, casual or temporary employees.

Teleworking

Organisations have also attempted to have a more flexible workforce through teleworking. Teleworking enables workers to work remotely using telecommunications, but it is only one option among others, rather than being the final form of flexible work. Even within teleworkers, there is a difference between skilled managers and professionals with freedom to choose when and where work activities are to be completed, compared to unskilled data-entry or call-centre employees whose work is highly structured, regulated and supervised. The extent to which the employee can control and schedule work, and the degree of variety involved in that work, will influence the level of satisfaction for teleworkers.

Hotdesking

Hotdesking is another way organisations are trying to respond to changing work demands more flexibly and efficiently. The term refers to removal of dedicated individual workspaces and offices, which are replaced by desks booked on demand. Supporting files, facilities and documents are also scheduled and delivered. Some organisations are redesigning workspaces to enable individuals to work collaboratively, combining software solutions with furniture facilitating group or collaborative work.

Temporary and part-time workers

Temporary agency work, short-term hires, regular part-time work, on-call workers and contract workers have been used to deal with workload fluctuations or absences, and these are likely to increase in future. In addition, firms are increasingly using agency-placed contingent and contract workers. This involves the use of contract workers among highly skilled occupational groups such as engineers, computer analysts and architectural services. Other areas also growing include management and public relations, research and development and scientific testing services. Use of personnel supply firms is increasing for lower-skilled workers such as administrative support workers and helpers, with firms relying on temporary help to supply workers in occupations such as office and clerical work, for which firm-specific skills are not usually needed.

Caudron (2000b) reports a consequence of these changes is that traditional jobs are often too rigid for today's workplaces. Job classifications and descriptions, pay structures and promotion charts are disappearing from new-style organisations. Koch Industries and Amazon.com have both abandoned traditional human resource structures. The customary way a person is hired, paid and trained to do a specific job is too rigid for an ever-changing marketplace.

As a result, new work relationships will be established between employer and employee. Traditional employment relationships previously based on exclusivity ('you are my employee', 'this is my job') and on permanence of employment have previously led to situations where those employees remaining from downsizing exercises face an increased workload to cover for missing employees. In the current environment of rapid change, this attitude to job ownership is flawed. Organisations are increasingly required to adapt their employment relationships from one of fixed designated jobs to relationships based on flexible project demands. Employees must embrace a work future closer to an independent contractor than an employee, and employers will have to view their workforce as a dynamic mix of currently required skills and knowledge, not a fixed establishment of dedicated employees.

While this is no different from how some professional service groups operate now, such as IT, engineering and legal services, the challenge for future organisations is to translate this model to the wider workplace. It does not stop employees being engaged in a full-time capacity, but changes the criteria for engaging them.

The biggest hurdle for organisations is in moving from being a traditional employer to a flexible employer of knowledge and services. It requires expertise to successfully transform the organisation and establish new human resource policies and procedures. It also assumes the organisation can accurately forecast its needs and manage the workforce.

Many organisations would like to engage and disengage workers as needed, but are constrained by factors such as limited resources to manage such variable demands, legislative constraints or unionised workforces. Likewise employees may still seek full-time employment for fear of being unable to locate enough 'work on demand' and be unemployed for long periods.

Flexible employing organisations

Companies reducing their workforces as a straight downsizing exercise are unlikely to get medium-to-long term benefits. Downsizing not linked to a strategic plan is likely to result in greater staff hire costs to make up for lost skills. In these circumstances companies need to manage flexible staffing requirements from a strategic, rather than from a cost-minimisation, perspective. Rather than seeking last minute short-term low-skilled employees, successful organisations will form strategic alliances with staffing agencies to guarantee supply of skilled and reliable contract and temporary staff. These agencies will offer one-stop shopping for business solutions and staffing services, and a broader service range including contract and temporary hires, payroll administration, human resource and training services.

Flexible employees

In a climate of scarce full-time jobs, high unemployment and changing job markets, searching for a full-time position with one employer becomes daunting. For many, the only option has been to go into business themselves, either in a small business or as consultants. The difficulty is that traditional employment markets see these people working very long hours for little return. An alternative is for the person to contract themselves to a staffing agency, offering their knowledge, skills and time to major projects on a full-time basis or to multiple small jobs in different companies. This is the same principle as working as a consultant, except they may work as part of a project team supervised by the staffing agency or provide services to multiple, different organisations.

TERMINATING THE EMPLOYMENT RELATIONSHIP

Because the employment relationship is a legal contract between employer and employee, it is important to consider how the relationship is terminated. This section of the chapter deals with both voluntary and involuntary forms of termination and their implications for human resource management.

Voluntary termination

Voluntary termination involves employees giving an agreed minimum notice of intention to leave the employment relationship. Reasons for voluntary termination include resignation and retirement. Resignation may be due to the employee being offered another job, changed personal circumstances allowing or requiring them to leave employment, dissatisfaction with the existing job or as part of a voluntary redundancy offer. Voluntary redundancy involves an employer reducing the workforce size by asking employees to voluntarily leave the employment relationship, usually in return for an improved termination pay package. Retirement involves the employee reaching a specified age where they are eligible to retire and access superannuation savings and/or any relevant pension scheme. Compulsory retirement, once widely practised, is now considered discriminatory and hence illegal.

Involuntary termination

Involuntary termination includes retrenchment, redundancy and dismissal. **Retrenchment** refers to the forced termination of the employment relationship due to financial, technological or organisational circumstances, and often reflects an attempt by an employer to reduce labour costs in order to remain in business. **Redundancy** is also a forced termination of the employment relationship but results from the permanent deletion of specific positions within an organisation due to the positions no longer being required. **Dismissal** is where the employer gives the required notice to terminate the employment relationship. Legal dismissal may be as a result of disciplinary action over time, or may be immediate if due to a serious breach of the employment contract, such as wilful damage to property, significant theft or violent behaviour toward other workers.

The termination phase of the employment relationship raises a number of issues for human resource management. Organisations require sufficient knowledge and skill to be able to determine when dismissal is warranted and how it should be enacted. They also need to be aware of any provisions under existing industrial award or enterprise bargaining agreements dealing with retrenchments and redundancies, as well as the financial cost involved in settling retrenchment and redundancy cases.

From a more general perspective, organisations need to monitor and review the nature and extent of terminations. In addition to maintaining computerised HR systems, organisations often institute exit interviews for voluntary terminations, being the final interview immediately prior to or just after separation from the organisation. The interview is an opportunity to review the reasons for leaving and may also be used to offer counselling or assistance in finding a new job.

Some organisations engage out-placement consultants to provide a range of services to employees who are leaving or are being retrenched. Services may include career counselling, résumé preparation and advice, serviced office facilities and, in some cases, finding alternative employment. The cost involved for organisations undertaking such services can be returned many times over by the good will established with those employees leaving and in their consequent description of the organisation in public.

Finally the rate of employees leaving an organisation will influence the level of activity in other phases of human resource management. When employees leave, an organisation has the choice of either recruiting new replacements or reallocating work within the remaining employees. Either way, if staff turnover is excessive, those remaining are likely to suffer, as is the organisation's ability to achieve its objectives.

retrenchment

The forced termination of the employment relationship due to financial, technological or organisational circumstances, often reflecting an attempt by an employer to reduce labour costs in order to remain in business

redundancy

A forced termination of the employment relationship resulting from the permanent deletion of specific positions within an organisation due to the positions no longer being required

dismissal

The employer giving the required notice to terminate the employment relationship

CORPORATE RESPONSIBILITY

As noted previously, organisations face multiple challenges to survive and thrive. Competition demands faster responses to constantly changing markets. Work systems must become more adaptive. The very nature of the relationship between employer and employee is changing, often blurring the boundaries between employee, contractor and self employed. At one time, success for organisations could be determined by their capacity to provide competitive returns on investment to shareholders. If shares remained high and profits continued to build, the organisation could be deemed to be 'successful'. From a human resource perspective, the challenge was to ensure that employees themselves provided the best return on the organisation's investment.

However, in the last decade there has been a growing realisation that profits alone do not guarantee survival, and that focusing only on improving financial bottom lines can also create challenges and threats for organisations. Organisations must now respond to more than just their shareholders' desire for increased profits. Increasingly, different stakeholders are demanding to be heard on a wide range of issues; for example, unions fighting for fair wages, environmental groups demanding sustainable business practices, government regulators requiring increased compliance in areas such as worker safety, privacy and equal opportunity. This has changed the challenge for organisations who must now balance these often-competing demands.

In a corporate responsibility report recently published in Australia (Reputex 2003), only one company out of the top 100 listed companies—Westpac Banking Corporation—was given the highest rating of 'AAA Outstanding' for corporate responsibility. The report rated each company on four scales (corporate governance, environmental impact, social impact and workplace practices) before determining the overall rating. In order to achieve the highest rating in workplace practices, organisations needed to 'demonstrate a very high level of commitment to creating a workplace that generates excellent value for employees and the organisation through ongoing development of its workforce, management systems, policies and strategies' (Reputex 2003). Organisations were rated on employee involvement, occupational health and safety, fair wages, a commitment to workforce diversity and work/life balance, training and development, and industrial relations policies (Reputex 2003), amongst other criteria. While it might at first seem that returns on investment and corporate responsibility are contradictory, there is a growing awareness that being able to demonstrate corporate responsibility can actually generate shareholder value (Martin 2002).

The human resource challenge therefore changes from maximising return through increased productivity and profit from employee effort to achieving a balance of profit in conjunction with socially responsible practices. Organisations found to be socially responsible will be able to market this when attempting to attract and retain skilled employees. At the same time the human resource policies and procedures will need to be aligned to ensure that employees are recruited, trained and rewarded in ways that maintain socially responsible behaviour and decisions consistent with the organisational goals and objectives.

GAINING THE EDGE

Work in progress

Flatter management and happier workers: that was the promise at Portland. Two decades on, a radical experiment finds the wheel never stops turning.

The young Turks singled out to set up the greenfields aluminium site back in the 1980s could have done it by the book—the one that highlighted distrust, demarcation and dictatorial management. But this group had other ideas about how to run Alcoa's new smelter in the southern Victorian town of Portland.

Osborn and others saw themselves as a new generation of managers, influenced by the radical ideas that had revolutionised Japanese industry. In Australia, despite some attempts to redesign work based on postwar British models, union/employer animosity was high and an adversarial culture was endemic.

Here, the young managers figured, was the opportunity to build a more productive culture by getting rid of hierarchies, introducing multi-skilling,

and experimenting with some dramatic ideas—such as consulting with the workers.

Almost 20 years on, Osborn is managing director of Alcoa Australia and Portland is one of the company's top plants, and one of the three most competitive smelters worldwide. The innovations it spurred have spread throughout Alcoa worldwide, and are credited with enabling the company to increase profits through major workforce changes and improved productivity. And the ideas that seemed so new at Portland are now commonly applied, or at least tried, in many areas of work.

Enter the young Turks. They had no particular role models to guide their approach. But many had attended seminars sponsored by the federal government to introduce manufacturers to Japanese production systems. Just-in-time production—the idea introduced into Japanese companies such as Toyota in the 1970s—was one of the more radical concepts.

JIT meant that you supplied parts for the process only when you needed them. There was also a focus on quality and on treating the next person in the production line as a customer to be served. The worker was the core of the production process, and everything else had to be directed at supporting the core. Managers had to think about how they could facilitate rather than direct work—an approach that led to more autonomy for employees.

'The ethos was that as a manager group we were there to support the people getting the work done to run the smelter', says Osborn.

A strategy was mapped out before hiring and the emphasis was on recruiting younger people, many of whom had never been to a smelter. The idea was that they would be open to change—and perhaps less likely to have an adversarial approach or a strong allegiance to unions. Anaconda Nickel managing director Peter Johnston, who was a manager at Portland during construction, says Alcoa gave the Portland team a lot of leeway: 'We became the yardstick. Alcoa used these principles right through the organisation over time.'

The influx of young families into Portland caused a shortage of childcare, so the smelter built a creche. It also built a gym, set up links with community organisations, and began working on ways to recycle waste rather than dump it in landfill. The smelter is surrounded by bushland but was filling 13 000 cubic metres of it a year in 1989 when it began evaluating all its processes. These days, it creates just two cubic metres of waste a month through improved processes and cleaner production.

Trust was the key

Six years into its operation, Portland management started negotiations for employees to move from eight- to 12-hour shifts, and to a salary rather than wage-based structure. Osborn says trust was the key to the changes: 'They had seen the organisation had really taken risks and been innovative in making them and their families important to the organisation. It was a huge shift to flexibility in work requirements.'

What's changed, and what remains two decades on from that idealistic start?

The early years when the company built a culture around people—and acknowledged their need for a private life—has meant continued focus on work and family policies.

The result was more flexible work arrangements, with each location tailoring the policy to its needs. A follow-up survey in 1999 documented improvements in morale, less absenteeism and improved job satisfaction. But it also showed the company needed to change the workplace culture to attract and retain employees.

One staff member's profile: Marissa Jennings

'Part-time works really well for us.' Jennings, who is in her forties, went to Portland for the high wages and now shares a job as operator in the anode division with another woman. Alcoa has a policy of encouraging women to move into non-traditional roles. About 12 per cent of Portland's employees are female, as are 11 per cent of those on the factory floor.

This is high for the industry. Jennings was the only woman in her area for two years. She says it was tough at first—she felt the men were waiting for her to make a mistake, although that has changed. She began working half-time to support her youngest child in Year 12 and decided to stay part-time. The job is physically tough and she wanted more time with her family.

Source: McCallum, J. (2003).

Activities for discussion, analysis and further research

1. Identify the human resource initiatives which are referred to in the case above. In what ways would these have impacted on the effectiveness of the organisation and its performance?

2. Undertake a comparison between these new management practices and those which are referred to in the text of the case study as 'postwar British models, [in which] union/employer animosity was high and an adversarial culture was endemic'.

3. Access the website of Alcoa, and its Portland facilities in particular. Explore the staff benefits and activities which would make this site an employer of choice.

KIMBERLEY TURNER

AEROSAFE
RISK MANAGEMENT

For us, human resource management incorporates all aspects from recruitment through to termination. I probably do the majority of that work. I am well supported by our office manager in the running of that function. The office manager probably doesn't realise how much she knows about the company and the HR aspects of it. She is very good and her support is significant.

Finding the right people is always going to be the key challenge for any organisation, and of course that's how it is for us. Different things motivate different people and even if you dangle the carrot of significantly large financial packages, that doesn't guarantee performance. In the early days, when I was quite immature in business, I thought that was what everybody was after. I thought that if I paid them at a certain level, they would perform at that level. Expectations were very high. What I have learned is that ultimately I need to have confidence in the people I have around me.

I would say that I have held back from building certain people that I am not as confident in. Now that might be perceived by those staff as I don't let go or I'm not willing to delegate, but really it's a trust and a quality check thing. I guess that to me that staff member hasn't proven themselves or they may not have a full complement of skills that are required in comparison to other staff members where it has actually transitioned quite successfully. I would say that about 30 per cent of my staff have the right capability for their role and have my full trust; about another 30 per cent have the potential to fall into that category; and the other 40 per cent don't have that capacity; and it all falls onto me in the management role deciding who fits in what capacity, and aligning the resources and the effort that is put in and assessing the benefit and the return as to whether it's worth it. I know that sounds a little bit harsh but that's the reality of business. Ultimately it's my company and I'm accountable and it's about reputation and delivery of quality products and services. It's my reputation that's out there in industry and carries the company and I need to do everything possible to enhance that reputation and protect it, rather than compromise on that reputation in order to get another sale. That's not important to me in business.

A few years ago, we set up a process where each staff member has a professional development program designed purely for them into the areas where they'd like to go professionally, and obviously they align with where the business is going as well. That gives me a good idea as to the direction of their thinking and it enables me to harness that and tap into it and allow the business to drive forward. Because the business, by its nature, is focused around our people, it is only as good as the expertise that we've got. So people are really important to me because that is what we sell. We sell our ability to dissect complex problems and provide real practical solutions to the client.

Some of the staff are studying at a masters level to learn more. It's interesting that one of my staff came back to me recently and said, 'I don't feel like I'm actually being stretched or challenged or learning anything new in my post-grad studies, but it's a wonderful validation that we're on track with our work and ahead of the game.' That was a little bit scary and daunting because committing to that staff member's professional development in that area, certainly my expectation was that they would grow and develop and challenge their thoughts so that their ideas would be more refined. So, that's been an interesting observation for me, in that the focus of that professional development hasn't been the right vehicle to stretch or challenge that person.

Finding the right people is critical for every business. I don't know if the bigger you get, the more fudge factor you can absorb and tolerate. But when you are small, every single person needs to be the right person. You can't afford to have the right person at the wrong time in your company. Every person needs to be right because you need to be all pulling together to get that right direction. Staff are always the biggest issue because if you have the right team, you can achieve anything.

FOCUS ON PRACTICE

Strategies for improving

1. Human resource planning processes are the key to maintaining the right skills mix. Consider a position in an organisation of your choice and attempt to plan and analyse the skills which will be required by the person doing this job in 15 years.
2. List the selection criteria and tools you might use to select the appropriate candidate for the job mentioned above in 15 years' time.
3. How would you carry out an informal performance review for the job mentioned above?
4. It is important to treat employees with respect and consideration when giving any manner of feedback after performance appraisal. Consider how you might give negative feedback for unsatisfactory performance in a respectful and considerate manner.

Source: Jones et al. (2000).

SUMMARY

- Human resource management is an integral part of the management of any organisation. In broad terms it involves the management of three phases of the employment relationship: establishing the relationship by acquiring human resources; maintaining the relationship; and managing the termination of the relationship. These functions occur within an organisational context at the same time as interacting with a regulatory and environmental context.

- Industrial relations systems are part of the regulatory context, inputting directly into the way in which the terms and conditions of employment are established. These systems were shown to influence human resource management functions through legislative and regulatory intervention. Other forms of legislation govern aspects of safety, environmental management, discrimination and equal opportunity within an organisation.

- Human resource planning involves determining future human resource needs in relation to an organisation's business objectives or strategic plan, then devising ways to meet these objectives. Job analysis is an important component that helps establish human resource needs and produces position descriptions and specifications. Job descriptions allow an organisation to accurately describe the job to potential applicants, and job specifications provide important decision criteria when making a selection from candidates for the job. Job analysis can be used to improve job design and redesign, performance appraisal, remuneration and training and development. When used appropriately it forms the basis upon which an organisation ensures that organisational objectives are met.

- Recruitment and selection processes ensure that an organisation is able to attract suitable applicants and to then decide which applicants best contribute to organisational objectives. Advantages and disadvantages have been identified in both internal and external recruitment, with the final choice contingent upon the organisational circumstances.

- Maintaining employment relationships involves active processes aimed at aligning employee effort with organisational goals. Human resource management functions in this phase include establishing appropriate remuneration levels that take into account internal and external relativities. Managers need to ensure that the work effort of employees is effectively managed and evaluated and that feedback is provided in an accurate and unbiased manner. Training and development provides an opportunity for an organisation to increase the ability of its employees to perform efficiently and effectively.

- Attempts by organisations to increase the flexibility of their workforce, and hence to increase its effectiveness and efficiency, have greatly influenced the way in which the workforce is defined. Increasing use of part-time and casual employees is changing the nature of the workforce, while trends such as teleworking and hot-desking are additional examples of flexible organisations.

- Information technology impacts on the ability of organisations to harness the knowledge and expertise of its employees. The internet, intranets and extranets are all being utilised to improve organisational knowledge and capacity, while computerised human resource systems are contributing to the strategic capacity of the organisation.

- Organisations need to manage carefully the final phase of the employment relationship. Organisations must have systems in place by which terminations occur effectively and legally. Managers and supervisors require skills to ensure that their own performance as managers does not contribute to staff turnover or place the organisation at risk of prosecution for unfair dismissal.

- Finally, changes in the flow of human resources through an organisation will have an impact on other human resource management functions. Increased turnover rates will have an impact upon those employees remaining, and on the need for increased numbers of new employees. Increased employee recruitment will influence productivity, impact upon resources and may generate additional training demands.

QUESTIONS FOR DISCUSSION AND REVIEW

1. Describe what impact the changes to Australia's industrial relations system since 1987 have had on the relationship between management, unions and employees. How has the election of the Liberal/National Party Coalition in 1996 changed these relationships?
2. Compare and contrast the different approaches of Australian and New Zealand wage-fixing mechanisms.
3. Define job analysis and describe how it relates to other human resource functions, especially recruitment and selection, performance appraisal, remuneration and training.
4. The chapter noted the emergence of internet-based recruitment sites. Outline and discuss the benefits and pitfalls for managers and for applicants of this new form of recruitment.
5. Identify the factors that allow assessment centres to provide good predictions of job performance. Discuss why the process is not used more often.
6. What would be the human resource implications for an organisation that did not maintain internal relativity for its remuneration system? Likewise, what human resource implications would there be for not maintaining external relativity?
7. What can organisations do to better integrate training and learning into core business functions? Discuss what organisational barriers exist to stop this from occurring.
8. Explain the benefits of 360-degree performance feedback over traditional performance appraisal processes.
9. Outline and discuss the impact of intranets and extranets on the three phases of attracting, maintaining and terminating human resources.
10. Debate the extent to which governments should impose conditions upon the termination of the employment relationship.

CRITICAL THINKING QUESTIONS

To answer some of these questions you will need to do further research. Useful references are given below each section of the questions.

The strategic use of humans lies at the core of the ability to enhance the effectiveness of an organisation. Human resource management utilises tools such as human resource planning, staffing, development and evaluation and compensation. This section extends these basic building blocks of HRM to consider some of the challenges facing employers today.

While the validity of the HR function has been accepted within most organisations since the mid 1980s, it is only recently that it has not automatically been the target of budget cuts in times of economic downturn. Traditionally, business decline heralded drastic cuts in 'soft' areas such as human-resources specialists. Those lucky enough to retain positions generally 'focused on what many in management still regarded as their core competency: hiring, and—particularly in tough times—firing' (Mccoll, 2003, p. 70). With over a decade of experience now to draw on, this short-sighted approach reveals a legacy of expensive redundancies and subsequent rehiring difficulties when the business improved.

1. Today, human-resources staff are increasingly becoming a part of the senior management team. Why? What is it they can offer?

2. What are some of the mistakes organisations made in the past that HRM is now able to build on and rectify today?

3. Is the trend to push human-resources responsibilities down to line managers a threat to the growth in human-resources departments' numbers and authority?

4. Mccoll (2003) suggests that the expanding role and authority of the HR manager has also had a very positive impact on career prospects for those working in this area. How and why?

(Material relevant to questions 1 to 4 may be found in Mccoll, G. 2003, Higher responsibilities, *Business Review Weekly*, 8 May, p. 70.)

As the above section outlined, while HRM has been around since the 1930s, it is really only in the last decade that it is being recognised as an integral part of strategic planning at the highest levels of the organisation.

5. What are some of the issues and the changes facing HR managers of today as a result of this acceptance?

The need for HRM to focus on performance management is further borne out in recent research by Human Synergistic International (HIS) in New Zealand and Australia into the cultures of more than 8000 organisations (Birchfield 2003).

Of the employees interviewed:

- 42 per cent did not believe their organisation's objectives were clear and well understood;
- 45 per cent did not understand their organisation's mission and role;
- 57 per cent did not believe their top executive groups had a shared philosophy on what their organisation stands for.

Looking at performance management:

- 47 per cent did not genuinely believe their evaluations were based on real measures of performance and instead believed they were based on favouritism.

In terms of leadership in managing performance:

- 49 per cent said their manager would not even notice when they did good work;
- 63 per cent reported their manager took little or no corrective action when someone was under-performing;
- 36 per cent said they got praised when they performed particularly well;
- 60 per cent reported their managers did not show them how to improve their performance;
- 71 per cent reported their managers did not help them plan how to get their work done at a high level.

The key recommendation from this extensive research resonates with the issues discussed above, that HRM 'practitioners need to shift their focus from planning and appraisal to execution in the hands of everyday managers' (McCarthy, Head of HIS, cited in Birchfield 2003, p. 45).

6. While performance management clearly features as a key item on the HRM agenda, much of the writing in the area of future HRM concerns the fact that demographic changes will be an increasingly important factor in decision making. What are some of these demographic changes and what impact will they have in the future?

(Material relevant to questions 5 and 6 may be found in Birchfield, R. 2003, The Future of HR: What are the critical issues? *New Zealand Management*, 50, 10, November, p. 45.)

7. In a view not often found in university textbooks, Fox (2004) expresses concern that HRM experts have lost their role as champions of the workers. If this is so, why is this loss particularly important, taking into account demographic changes?

8. The management taint and lack of experience many HRM managers have in labour relations may leave many workers sceptical about their ability to represent them in the workplace. However, speaking at a seminar at Griffith University in Brisbane, 2003, HRM and industrial relations specialist Tom Kochan of the Sloan School of Management at MIT in the United States pointed to a growing body of data establishing links between work practices and financial performance. He

concluded that the HRM profession has a chance to take a much greater and more productive role in designing new approaches to the issue (quoted in Fox 2004). How do you think HR professionals will go about this?

(Material relevant to questions 7 and 8 may be found in Fox, C. 2004, Confronting a workplace crisis of trust, *Australian Financial Review*, 13 January, p. 42.)

MANAGEMENT EXERCISES

Exercise 1 Skill building: Linking HRM components with specific activities

Several important components of the human resource management process are listed below. Try to match these components with the 15 specific activities/issues shown. Indicate the appropriate human resource management component by putting the first letter of that component in the appropriate blank.

Linking HRM components with speific activities

Human resource management process components:

Selection	Performance appraisal	Recruitment
Human resource planning	Compensation	Labour relations
Training and development		

1. _____ Employees plan to organise
2. _____ Management by objectives
3. _____ Orientation, technical skill, management development
4. _____ Assessment centre
5. _____ Halo, contrast, leniency, severity, self-serving bias
6. _____ Job descriptions
7. _____ Job posting
8. _____ Skills inventory
9. _____ Replacement planning
10. _____ Interview
11. _____ Needs analysis
12. _____ Internal equity
13. _____ Realistic job preview
14. _____ Promotion
15. _____ Graphic rating scales

Exercise 2 Management exercise: Managing human resources in retail hardware

You have accepted a position as a department head in a large hardware store. The owner, and store manager, likes to involve others in decisions. During your job interviews, he mentioned that if you became a department head, he would seek your views on improving the store's human resource management. He is very interested in your input because he wants to open up other stores. (In fact, you took the job partly because you believe the expansion will help your career.)

The manager said he, with the assistant manager and nine other department heads, is planning to hold strategic planning meetings soon to consider the impact of human resources on expansion plans. He anticipates holding other meetings focusing on different human resource management aspects. He further states he wants to maintain a stimulating, challenging and exciting working environment.

From what you have learned, the store's 18 per cent annual growth and 15 per cent return on investment could be improved. In addition human resource management seems currently to be non-existent.

Questions

1. What issues will you suggest to consider as part of human resource planning?
2. What will you discuss about recruiting and selecting human resources?
3. What suggestions for training, performance appraisal and remuneration will you make?

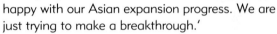

END-OF-CHAPTER CASE: ON THE RIM

Price is all in Singapore

It is easy to be fooled by the gloss of the tiny city-state of Singapore—soaring buildings, glittering shopping centres, queues of BMWs—but at the heart of this most advanced of Asian cities is the traditional Chinese obsession with price, hence the incessant question, 'How much?'.

Money drives Singapore. People, only half jokingly, are said to assess potential partners on the basis of the 'five Cs': car, condominium, credit card, country club and, above all, cash.

For many companies, among them Australian retailer Harvey Norman, making money in this 'How much?' culture is tricky. After more than three years' operation, Harvey Norman's Singapore-listed business, Pertama Holdings, is just beginning to succeed. After-tax profit for the half year to 31 December 2002 was S$2.8 million, up from a nominal S$1000 the year before.

'There are a lot of risks over here, and they are significant', says Martin Dunkerley, Pertama's managing director. 'The retail market is very, very tough, and department stores in general are finding it tough. But even in these times we are showing results.'

Pertama's improved profit—on revenue that was up 23.5 per cent to S$183.3 million—comes in a retail market that grew 6.2 per cent in 2002 after a poor first nine months. The good showing is a relief to Harvey Norman Holdings' chief executive and biggest shareholder, Gerry Harvey, who promised

much when the company ventured into Asia three years ago.

'When you add up the little package of what we are doing up there, we are disappointed we are not further down the track', Harvey says. 'But we are still happy with our Asian expansion progress. We are just trying to make a breakthrough.'

Pertama, which in October 1999 was a struggling chain of six electrical stores, was to be the springboard for an ambitious strategy that would take Harvey Norman into Malaysia, Hong Kong and, eventually, China. The company later bought Electric City, another struggling retail chain. Pertama now operates three Singapore businesses: an exporter of locally made electrical goods; a distributor of Samsung consumer electronic products to Malaysia; and 11 shops in Singapore that trade as Harvey Norman. All three enterprises were profitable in the latest half-year.

The company's biggest setback came in 2001, with the worst recession in 35 years. The economy remained in a trough until growth resumed in the December quarter of 2002. By then, confidence was shaken by layoffs, a slowing of crucial foreign investment and the commoditisation of important Singapore exports such as computer chips.

'It was bad timing', Harvey says. 'Singapore had huge growth all those years, and all of a sudden it

POWERWEB

International articles related to this topic are available at the Online Learning Centre at **www.mhhe.com/au/bartol4e**

didn't. My view is if something is worth doing, you go on and do it. It was bad timing but I would do it again.'

The company arrived when other changes were happening in retailing. Once considered a shoppers' paradise, Singapore has priced itself out of many of its retail interests—including electronic goods. Rich shoppers who used to flock to Singapore now find better shopping elsewhere.

Partly to blame are high retail rents, which even the recession failed to dampen. Singapore's Urban Redevelopment Authority says that, in 2002, the median retail rent in central Singapore fell only 4.8 per cent, to S$677 per square foot per month. Harvey says: 'Singapore is a terribly high-rent place, which makes it very difficult to make money in retailing because the landlords make all the money. You are in a situation where your opposition is not making a lot of money. You are not, and neither are they.'

High rents prevented Harvey Norman achieving its stated aim of closing most of its small electrical stores and concentrating on a few mega-stores. Although some small shops have been shut, only one mega-store (of 7500 square metres) stocking electrical, IT, furniture and bedding has been opened. Martin Dunkerley says: 'Generally speaking, it is a very tough and very competitive place for tenants. But, when space becomes available, it has got to stack up in terms of the rental.'

Not only are rents high, big spaces are rare and coveted. Harvey Norman's Millennia Walk mega-store is something of a compromise but it is certainly no single-level box stuck in the suburbs.

Millennia Walk, in the heart of the Suntec IT office precinct, was struggling until Harvey Norman gutted the shops strung along both sides of the first floor of the two-level mall and refurbished them as a single store. The layout— shared by Harvey Norman's 100 per cent-owned imported-furniture-specialist store Space—is unusual. Dividing the store is a void that soars to a 17-metre-high post-modern ceiling, designed by American architect Philip Johnson. The upmarket look is a good match for the store's stylish displays of furniture and plasma and projection televisions. On the other hand, Pertama's smaller electrical stores have a low-cost, discount feel. Stock is piled in narrow aisles and there is little attempt at display. 'I am not sure if they are targeting the

right customers', says one Singapore analyst.

Harvey Norman faces intense competition in Singapore. At the lower end are thousands of small electrical stores that cater to lower-income groups and the Singaporeans' love for bargaining. At the high end are a stylish Japanese chain, Best Denki, and a British group, Courts. Pertama's small electrical stores compete with family-run stores, but the Millennia Walk store is similar to Courts' mixture of furniture, electrical and IT products.

The Singapore venture has developed along different lines to the Harvey Norman Australian operation. Whereas, in Australia, the stores are in the suburbs, most of the Singapore stores are in prosperous central districts. Most Australians drive to Harvey Norman stores but few Singapore people own cars and the best-performing malls are near railway stations. Another difference is that the 11 Harvey Norman stores in Singapore are owned by the company rather than by franchisees, as is the case in Australia. Buying and distribution in Singapore is centralised; suppliers deliver to a single warehouse rather than to the stores. Small shops and high rents make on-site warehousing in Singapore expensive, so, because the country is tiny, centralisation is cheaper.

Harvey Norman had problems replicating the Australian culture for other reasons. Staff in the early days were not known for good service. They paid little attention to customers and price was take-it-or-leave-it.

Giselle Roux, retail analyst with Salomon Smith Barney, observes that, while Australia's service standards are 'quite poor', Singapore's are 'uniquely poor' and its 'retail staff are considered a particularly low form of life'.

Angelo Augustus, Harvey Norman's first Pertama managing director, says the service problem was tackled by replacing low-level incentives with rewards to salespeople for volumes sold and margins achieved; and senior management were involved in sales training. He says senior staff recently visited Harvey Norman's Australian operations. 'What we are doing more now is satisfying the customers' needs', says Augustus, now a Harvey Norman franchisee in Melbourne's outer-eastern Nunawading. 'We are talking about the benefits of the product and not just its features.'

Dunkerley says the sales incentives have transformed the operation and resulted in a deep commitment to sales and service. He tells of staff who work 80 hours a week and of cables and other items being delivered to customers' homes after hours. 'I love to hear that sort of thing', he says. 'It is very inspiring as an MD to know that people at the sales level are prepared to sacrifice their own time and effort to do that for a customer.'

Augustus says marketing, including the 'Go Harvey Norman' jingle and sponsorship of popular television shows such as Singapore's Wheel of Fortune, helped promote the Harvey Norman name. Customers visited the stores and saw that the range had grown beyond the more downmarket goods offered before the Harvey Norman takeover.

Augustus says repeat customers were telling him: 'Hey, your guys know what they are talking about and they are trying to help me'. Augustus sees little real difference between Singaporean and Australian consumers. He says that, for many Singaporeans, who have far fewer opportunities for leisure than Australians, strolling and eating in shopping malls are the most pleasant pastimes. This means that retail events such as the recent Harvey Norman camera fair can be highly successful; but it also means shoppers are acutely aware of the competition in products and prices.

Another difference is that older Singaporeans shop with cash and always expect a discount. Staff in the early days of Harvey Norman management could not offer discounts. Today they do.

Most younger Singaporeans use credit cards but there is little interest in store credit schemes, which are popular in Australia. Initially, Harvey Norman offered zero-interest instalment cards, but the credit offered was not enough to encourage purchases. In October 2002, the company launched its own 'Go Ezi' credit scheme, making its own creditworthiness assessments.

With a new managing director and the first profit runs on the board, Pertama is considering expanding in Asia. Dunkerley, as he reassesses the company's business plan, is studying its position and prospects. He says there is a strong commitment to moving into new Asian markets. 'It is just a matter of choosing the right time and the right way.' So far, Pertama's results have not added value to the share price, says Salomon Smith Barney's Roux. 'So long as the company doesn't bet the book on it, Asia is a risk worth taking', she says. 'Everyone expects it to be an instant success one year on with no mistakes. Well, they have made their mistakes and they have taken their time to get to know and understand the market.'

The Singapore connection

Harvey Norman controls Pertama Holdings through Harvey Norman Ossia (Asia), a majority-owned joint venture with a leading international sporting-goods distributor, Ossia International. Ossia is controlled by a Singapore businessman, George Goh, head of a powerful business family that controls four listed public companies in Singapore.

Ossia was the largest shareholder in Rebel Sports, which was sold to Harvey Norman Holdings after the formation of the joint venture.

'Anything that is not a significant shareholding we divest', says Goh. 'In Rebel, we had 18 per cent, so we decided to sell to Gerry.'
Source: Roberts, P. (2003).

Activities for discussion, *analysis and further research*

1. Identify the human resource concepts which are referred to in the above case study.
2. What are the fundamental differences between the industrial relations legislation in Singapore and Australia? You can research this by accessing the government department websites in both countries.
3. What differences did Harvey Norman need to adjust to in order to be profitable in the Singapore environment?
4. Access the Harvey Norman website in Australia. Explore the site for information on employee benefits and work conditions.
5. Which of the two Singapore organisations, Pertama or Ossia, would you prefer to work for? Why?

FURTHER READING

Andreason, A.W. 2003, Expatriate adjustments to foreign assignments, *International Journal of Commerce & Management*, 13, 1, pp. 42–61.

Björkman, I. and Xiucheng, F. 2002, Human resource management and the performance of Western firms in China, *International Journal of Human Resource Management*, September, 13, 6, pp. 853–65.

Hassard, J., Morris, J. and Sheehan, J. 2002, The elusive market: Privatization, politics and State–Enterprise Reform in China, *British Journal of Management*, September, 13, 3, pp. 221–32.

Sila, I. and Ebrahimpour, M. 2003, Examination and comparison of the critical factors of total quality management (TQM) across countries, *International Journal of Production Research*, 1/20, 41, 2, pp. 235–69.

Warner, M. 2002, Globalization, labour markets and human resources in Asia-Pacific economies: an overview, *International Journal of Human Resource Management*, May, 13, 3, pp. 384–99.

GRADUATE GLIMPSE

LINDA DUNCOMBE

Linda Duncombe has a Bachelor of Commerce (Management and Marketing) from the University of Western Sydney. She is the regional private banking manager, Sydney East and Canberra, for National Australia Bank Limited.

What does your job entail?

I manage 25 staff within the private bank across Sydney and Canberra. In the private bank we look after high net-worth individuals. I coach and lead the team of bankers that look after these relationships. Part of my role as regional manager is to develop and implement individual training and development programs for each team member, and for the whole of the organisation.

How have your university studies assisted you in your career?

Prior to starting university I was in a support role. Within five months of commencing my university degree I received my first promotion into management. I am now in a senior management role—my fifth level of management. I am able to think more laterally and enjoy a good challenge where the solution is outside the 'status quo'. My development in this area is a direct result of my experiences from completing my degree and has resulted in me being selected to be a part of some very dynamic teams within the National Australia Bank that have looked at group strategies and implementing change.

How do you use your knowledge of management principles in the day-to-day functions of your position?

One of the most important principles that I employ is the implementation of training and development programs. These are unique for each team member, and allow them to develop and grow.

PAUL VORBACH

Paul Vorbach has a Master of Commerce from the University of Sydney and a Master of Business Administration from the University of Technology, Sydney. He has also studied intensive management programs in England at Oxford University and in France at Reims University. Paul is the founder and managing director of AcademyGlobal, a career and personal development training firm.

What does your job entail?

My key roles encompass business, personnel and product development. I am also responsible for overseeing financial, administrative and quality aspects of the business. Whilst I also perform some 'technical' tasks such as consulting and training, our growing number of senior associates are increasingly responsible for delivering these services.

How have your university studies assisted you in your career?

While I have never believed that the answers to all business issues lay in a classroom, my university studies have provided me with the opportunity to challenge a number of assumptions and consider the application of some widely-researched and applied tools and methodologies. UTS has a well-structured curriculum which encourages debate ensuring a sharing of insights across industries and cultures.

What is an important management principle that you draw upon frequently in your role?

A number of the key strategy tools remain helpful. Michael Porter's five forces model remains useful in opportunity evaluation and competitor analysis. The timeless writings of Peter Drucker have an enduring quality, always serving as good source of fundamental thinking.

SATS moves further ahead as Asia's airport services leader

airline and has had an uninterrupted profit record for over twenty years. This enviable success in a tough industry has been driven by exceptional route management, aggressive investment in new aircraft and Singapore's unique advantages as a passenger and freight hub. But another key success factor is the role of SATS.

Singapore Airport Terminal Services (SATS), a subsidiary of Singapore Airlines, has made Singapore's Changi Airport one of the most efficient in the world; and the company has recently internationalised its business by exporting that expertise in airport services management. For most airlines, ancillary services are a cost centre and a cash drain. However, SATS has been profitable since its first day. SATS reported an after-tax profit of S$214.8 million for the 2002/03 financial year, an increase of S$2 million on the previous 12 months. However, SATS announced in 2003 that its management would take a pay cut of between 22.5 per cent and 27.5 per cent. The move is in line with measures being taken to restructure costs with the decline in business demand. The key has been efficient management and quality service to a large client base. Now SATS has taken its expertise and its profitable business formula to new markets. Besides Singapore Changi Airport, it now has ground handling and/or catering facilities at Beijing,

Chek Lap Kok in Hong Kong, Kansai (Osaka), Macao, Maldives, Manila, Taipei, Ho Chi Minh and Madras. It has plans to further develop joint ventures at several airports in the Asia Pacific.'

SATS provides an extremely efficient behind-the-scenes infrastructure that has helped Singapore's airport and its aviation industry to be of world standard. It has earned recognition from the freight industry for its cargo handling, being judged the best airfreight terminal operator in Asia on seven occasions. Changi airport is consistently voted the world's best airport for fastest baggage deliveries. SATS ensures that the first bag unloaded from a flight will be available to passengers within 12 minutes and that the last bag will be available within 29 minutes. SATS believes that if you can't measure it, you can't manage it. That's why SATS constantly monitors 30 key performance indicators on a regular basis. To avoid any conflicts of interest, monitoring is done by an independent department which issues regular management reports. SATS continues to benchmark against leading ground-handling companies in order to ensure that it remains one of the best in the world. Its baggage presentation times, check-in servicing and cargo delivery times are the envy of its competitors. SATS spares no effort nor cost to use the latest technology or IT to further improve our service standards. Singapore Airlines has a policy of continuous investment in, and upgrading of, aircraft and equipment.

SATS believes its most valuable resource is its people and we are continually investing in them. In 2002, training was 21 605 man-days covering everything from product knowledge to language to people skills. One fundamental, but less obvious, reason for SATS' success has been its separate management and independent profit responsibility. The key to SATS' productivity is its people and human resource management programs. Incorporated in 1972, SATS has 11 joint venture operations at other international airports within the Asia-Pacific region, and more than 9000 employees. In 2000 the company spent 3.4 per cent of its payroll on training. On average, each employee was allocated 2.3 training places and received 33.6 hours of training. 'We are regularly called upon to initiate a change or respond to one in our daily work', says Prush Nadaisan, the new chief executive of SATS. 'Our ability to respond to change successfully depends on the quality of our training and the range of skills covered; product knowledge, service, people skills and information technology. Our training programmes are designed to meet these objectives. The cornerstone of SATS' training philosophy is that a well-trained workforce would give us the ability to get ahead in good times and prosper even during difficult ones.' Customers are the reason for the existence of businesses. They are the final judge of how well the organisation is doing its job, and the quality of its products and services. In the face of global competition, organisations need to go beyond delivering high-quality products, and to focus on excellence of service.

Organisations with a customer focus have a passion for achieving customer-driven quality. At SATS, over 75 per cent of staff are in operations. Each year they service about 76 000 flights carrying more than 24 million passengers, prepare 23 million meals, and handle 1.43 million tonnes of cargo. To sustain the passion for service excellence in its staff, SATS uses regular performance reviews to provide critical feedback to enable staff to improve service. Trainee reviews of new staff are carried out monthly, and quarterly reviews are conducted for existing staff.

Trainee reviews are managed through a trainee review and evaluation card (TREC). This serves as a key tool for assessing and monitoring the performance of new customer service agents and officers. It ensures the effectiveness of the three-month induction program and the successful transfer of learning to the workplace.

The key areas assessed are grooming, communication skills and customer-service skills. There is a pool of 92 group trainers who serve as mentors to new staff. After one month of comprehensive classroom and on-the-job training to equip them with these skills, trainees are assigned a mentor for up to two months. At the end of this period, mentors use the TREC to assess trainees' readiness to work independently. For those who are not ready, the mentoring period is extended. For those assigned to work independently, the customer service officer (CSO) group trainer follows up to monitor and assess their performance. The CSO group trainer observes the staff working independently for a period of three weeks. Those who are not ready for confirmation are recommended to have their probation extended. Those deemed ready are recommended for assessment by the customer service supervisor group trainer.

To ensure that excellent customer service is maintained, the performance of existing staff is reviewed on a quarterly basis. These staff development review sessions allow line-trainers and immediate supervisors to jointly assess the performance of existing frontline staff while they are working. Such assessments take place in real-time and immediate feedback is provided for staff to improve their performance. When necessary, staff are provided with refresher training. Among the areas assessed are soft skills, grooming, punctuality, product knowledge, processing time, initiative and many more. To develop mentors and trainers, SATS identifies model employees who have the right attributes for mentoring. They are appointed by customer service managers (CSMs), who head each team. Mentors are identified for three different levels of staff: customer services agents, customer services officers, and customer services supervisors. All selected staff are trained by the CSMs for their roles. They are also briefed by line-trainers on the trainees' performance prior to the mentorship. This allows the mentors to better focus on the needs of their charges. During the mentorship, line-trainers meet up with mentors regularly to gather ongoing feedback.

So, what is the impact of this training system on SATS' business? Through the use of feedback from these reviews, SATS is able to achieve consistency and continuity, delivering excellent customer service that has been recognised through awards and accolades from governments, airlines and passengers. Its awards include the airport services purchasing ground handling 2000 award, the purchasing department supplier of the year award, the most consistent caterer award and the best station award. SATS was selected as security consultant for the Asia Aerospace 2002 Trade Fair in Singapore. SATS Cargo Division was awarded ISO 9001:2000 certification by the Singapore Productivity and Standards Board. As the leading ground-handling and in-flight catering service-provider at Changi airport, SATS has also contributed to Changi being voted the world's best airport for a record 15 consecutive years.

Source: Contributed by John Krasnostein; adapted from *Asian Business Review* (1999).

Activities for discussion, analysis and further research

1. Log on to the websites listed below and develop a list of key performance indicators. Now apply these indicators to SATS. How has SATS been able to develop airline ancillary services into a profitable business and an export earner for Singapore, while other airlines lose money in these activities?

   www.findarticles.com/cf_trvgnt/m0VOU/7_298/59 679876/p1/article.jhtml?term=Singapore+Airlines www.findarticles.com/cf_trvgnt/m0EIN/1998_Oct_ 16/53088754/p1/article.jhtml?term=Singapore+Ai rlines+Key+Performance+Indicators www.findarticles.com/cf_trvgnt/m4PRN/1999_May_ 17/54644528/p1/article.jhtml?term=Singapore+Ai rlines+Key+Performance+Indicators

2. Analyse SATS' staff training program and demonstrate how it is the key to success in delivering world-class service standards. Since all SATS employees are Asian, can you identify any findings from Hofstede's or Trompenaars' work that indicate consistency between Singaporean values and culture, and the training and staff evaluation methods used by SATS? To what extent could an Australian, American or British company achieve the same success in service standards with their own employees?

3. In groups of three or four, develop a five-year strategy for SATS for the period 2004–9. Describe further improvements to service scope and quality that could be made. Identify new international markets for further service extension, and consider the critical issues that are likely to arise in the next five years.

Please insert the CD-ROM that is packaged with this book to view video clips that correspond to this Part theme.

PART 4

LEADING

While planning provides direction and organising arranges resources, the leading function adds the action ingredient. Leading involves influencing others' work behaviour to reach organisational goals. In the process of leading, effective managers become catalysts in encouraging innovation. Thus leaders kindle the dynamic spirit for success.

As CHAPTER 11 notes, an organisation's energy comes from its workers' motivations. Managers can use several motivational approaches focusing on individual needs, the thought processes involved in deciding whether or not to expend effort, and available reinforcements and rewards.

CHAPTER 12 considers the following possibilities in exploring leadership: does leadership depend on inherent traits or can anyone learn and apply effective leader behaviours to various situations? To have influence, leaders must be able to communicate their ideas and visions, and have workable methods of learning about others' thoughts.

CHAPTER 13 discusses the nature of managerial communication, including an exploration of different types of communication and channels involved.

As CHAPTER 14 explains, many managers have realised that groups of teams can be a powerful means of accomplishing organisational goals. Understanding group dynamics and being able to encourage the power inherent in group activities are important to the leading function.

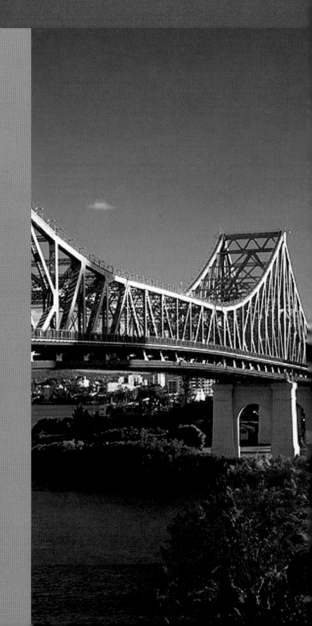

CHAPTER 11

MOTIVATION

CHAPTER OUTLINE

The nature of motivation

Need theories
Hierarchy-of-needs theory
Two-factor theory
ERG theory
Acquired-needs theory
Assessing need theories

Cognitive theories
Expectancy theory
Equity theory
Goal-setting theory
Assessing cognitive theories

Reinforcement theory
Types of reinforcement
Schedules of reinforcement
Using reinforcement theory

Social learning theory
Major components
Using social learning theory

LEARNING OBJECTIVES

After studying this chapter, you should be able to:

- Define motivation and outline the motivation process.
- Compare and contrast major need theories of motivation.
- Describe three major cognitive theories of motivation and explain how they facilitate the motivation process.
- Explain reinforcement theory of motivation and discuss how it can help managers.
- Discuss the social learning theory of motivation.

STRIVING FOR EXCELLENCE

Profile: Warburton the worker

Dick Warburton is a man of contrasts. The former chairman of David Jones (he retired from the position in 2003) and the current chairman of Caltex Australia and the Board of Taxation is a member of Australia's business elite who says he needs to keep the faith with people on the shop floor, where he used to work. He says he dislikes confrontation, preferring to reach consensus on issues, but he has been involved in contentious issues such as competition policy, tax reform and the sale of Australia's wool stockpile.

Warburton is a formidable opponent. He has been a consummate business and political networker for 40 years and is close to Prime Minister John Howard and former federal Opposition Leader Simon Crean. He has worked in industries such as retailing, resources, agriculture, chemicals, plastics, gaming, wine and the law. He has been involved with many industry and professional bodies and is active in philanthropic organisations. He says he has a good working relationship with union leaders such as former ACTU secretary Bill Kelty, but he is also part of the Sydney business establishment. He is a member of O'Connell Street Associates, a group of influential business figures. He was appointed to the board of the Reserve Bank of Australia by Paul Keating in 1992 and reappointed by Howard in 1997. In 2000, Howard asked him to chair the Board of Taxation, which was set up to consult with the community on the development of tax legislation.

Like John Ralph and Stan Wallis, Warburton straddles corporate and government appointments. A senior government source describes him as 'likeable, down to earth, pragmatic and not afraid of getting his hands dirty—the quintessential Australian chairman'.

Warburton rejects the suggestion that governments use him for their political ends. 'Sometimes governments want to use you as a buffer or to whitewash something—I am not interested in that. I won't get involved if I think this is the case', he says. 'Governments want people they can trust, not sycophants. They want people who stand up for what is right. This creates tension, but if they want a whitewash I am not interested.'

Meredith Hellicar, managing director of InTech, met Warburton in the mid-1980s, when they were working on business regulation—she with Esso and he with DuPont. She now sits on two boards that Warburton chairs: AurionGold and HIH Claims Support (established in July 2001 by the Howard Government to administer a support scheme for individuals and small businesses affected by the collapse of HIH Insurance). She describes him as inclusive, collaborative and open-minded. Hellicar says: 'He does not impose his views on the board, but it isn't directionless—you are going somewhere.'

What motivates Warburton? Hellicar says that, although he enjoys the power and the money, he regards his directorships as a full-time job. She says he is not dabbling or in semi-retirement, and takes his portfolio of positions very seriously. Warburton says he works long hours and on weekends.

Warburton says making money is still a key motivator for him. He says that one of the attractions of being on a board of a listed company, as opposed to an unlisted one, is that he can share in the equity of the business. But he also says that he prefers

continued

unlisted companies. 'Listed companies are driven by short-termism. Institutions that have quarterly key performance indicators drive hard when you have long-term interests.' No, he does not mean that unlisted companies are less accountable. 'It is exactly the same level of accountability, but you don't have to argue your case publicly. You always have a master, be it listed or unlisted, but you are not in a fishbowl.'

Source: Based on Skeffington (2002).

motivation

Force energising behaviour, giving direction to behaviour, and underlying the tendency to persist

Motivation is the force energising or giving direction to behaviour. In this chapter, we explore the basic nature of motivation and consider a general model. Next, we examine motivation theories based on individual needs, such as the need for achievement. We also look into motivational approaches emphasising cognitive aspects, focusing on how people think about where to direct effort and evaluate outcomes. We then analyse reinforcement theory, emphasising the power of reward. Finally, we review social learning theory's contemporary extension.

THE NATURE OF MOTIVATION

As motivation is an internal force, we cannot directly measure motivation. Instead, we watch behaviour and infer motivation. For example, we might decide that an engineer friend who works late every evening, works in the office on weekends, and always reads the latest engineering journals has high motivation. Conversely, we might believe that an engineer friend who is first to leave at the end of the day, rarely works extra hours, and spends little time reading about new developments in the field is not motivated to excel.

How well these two handle projects will depend both on their motivation, as shown by their efforts, and on their ability to handle engineering subject matter. Working conditions may impact performance. Many interruptions, extra assignments or cramped offices may negatively affect it. On the other hand, a quiet workplace, assistants' help, and support resources, may positively affect project performance. Actual performance is thus a function of ability, motivation and working conditions, as shown in Figure 11.1 (Campbell & Pritchard 1976).

FIGURE 11.1 The relationship between performance and ability, motivation and working conditions

As a result, managers must hire those able to do what is needed. They must ensure people are motivated to contribute needed inputs, that these inputs are used well or directed to high performance, and that this performance results in workers reaching outcomes desired.

The challenge then is provision of working conditions to nurture and support individual motivation to work to company goals (Ronen 1994).

The main motivation process elements are shown in Figure 11.2. As the diagram shows, our inner needs (food, companionship and growth) and cognitions (knowledge and thoughts about efforts we might put forth, and rewards expected) lead to various behaviours. Assuming these are suitable, they may lead to rewards. In turn the rewards help reinforce our behaviours, fulfil needs and influence cognitions about links between our behaviours and possible rewards. Lack of reward in turn leads to unfulfilled needs, leaves behaviours unreinforced, and influences

FIGURE 11.2 The motivation process

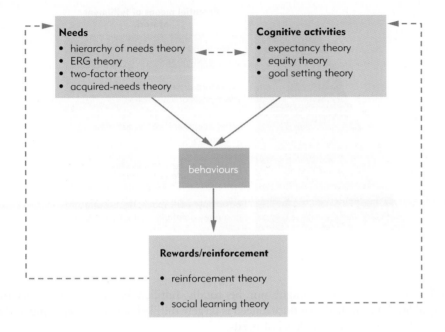

thoughts about where to focus future efforts. As motivation is complex, major motivational theories address various process elements (see Fig. 11.2). To understand the managerial implications of these elements we explore respective theories later in this chapter, beginning with need theories.

NEED THEORIES

Need theories argue that we behave as we do because we are attempting to fulfill internal needs. These content motivation theories specify what motivates people (content of needs). In this section, we explore four theories examining individuals' needs and how these needs work as motivators: hierarchy-of-needs theory, two-factor theory, ERG theory and acquired-needs theory.

Hierarchy-of-needs theory

One motivation theory is **hierarchy-of-needs theory**, developed by Abraham Maslow and popular in the early 1960s. It argues that individual needs form a five-level hierarchy (shown in Fig. 11.3).

According to the hierarchy, survival is the first need, where we focus on basic **physiological needs**, such as food, water and shelter, until these are satisfied. Next, we are concerned with **safety needs**, or the desire to feel safe, secure and free from threat. Once we feel safe and secure, we turn to relationships with others to fulfil our **belongingness needs**, which are the desire to join with and be accepted by others. With this support, we focus on **esteem needs**, which are a two-pronged desire to have a positive self-image and to have our contribution valued and appreciated. Finally, we reach the highest level, **self-actualisation needs**, or the development of our capabilities and attainment of our full potential. We test our creativity, see our ideas put into place, pursue new knowledge and develop our talents (McColl 2003). At this level needs are never fulfilled, for as we develop capabilities, our self-actualisation potential and needs grow. Some work-related ways to fulfil hierarchy needs are shown in Figure 11.3.

hierarchy-of-needs theory

Theory (developed by Maslow) arguing that individual needs form a five-level hierarchy

physiological needs

Survival needs such as food, water and shelter

safety needs

Needs pertaining to the desire to feel safe, secure and free from threats to our existence

belongingness needs

Needs involving the desire to affiliate with and be accepted by others

esteem needs

Needs related to the two-pronged desire to have a positive self-image and to have our contributions valued and appreciated by others

self-actualisation needs

Needs pertaining to the requirement of developing our capabilities and reaching our full potential

FIGURE 11.3 Maslow's hierarchy of needs

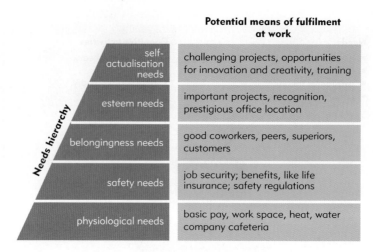

Potential means of fulfilment at work

Needs hierarchy	Potential means of fulfilment at work
self-actualisation needs	challenging projects, opportunities for innovation and creativity, training
esteem needs	important projects, recognition, prestigious office location
belongingness needs	good coworkers, peers, superiors, customers
safety needs	job security; benefits, like life insurance; safety regulations
physiological needs	basic pay, work space, heat, water company cafeteria

Maslow saw that a need might not be totally fulfilled before we move to the next hierarchical level. He argued that once a need is largely fulfilled, it stops motivating and tension starts to build to fulfill the next level of needs.

Maslow's hierarchy stimulated thinking about people's different needs, but it had some flaws. Research shows needs may cluster into two or three categories, not five. Also, the hierarchy may not be the same for all. Entrepreneurs may chase dreams for years despite lower-level needs being relatively deprived. Others seem to work on several needs at once, while some needs may be more important at a particular time (Wahba & Bridwell 1976; Mitchell & Moudgill 1976).

An increasingly global economy means managers will have staff from many countries who may differ in needs they seek to satisfy through work (Ronen 1994; Bateman & Snell 2004). Research has shown variations, with people from Greece and Japan being more motivated by safety needs and those from Sweden, Norway and Denmark by belongingness needs (Adler 1991; Hofstede 1980).

Furthermore, in countries with low living standards, physiological and safety needs will more likely be prime motivators of behaviour. As wealth grows and living standards rise, personal growth and accomplishment needs (such as esteem and self-actualisation) become more important as motivators.

Two-factor theory

Building on Maslow's work, Frederick Herzberg talked with accountants and engineers (Steers, Porter & Bigley 1996). He got them to describe situations where they felt very good about their jobs and others where they felt very bad about them. A pattern emerged. Factors making individuals satisfied with their jobs were associated with job content. These were called **motivators**. On the other hand, factors making individuals dissatisfied were associated with job context. These were called **hygiene factors** (see Fig. 11.4).

Herzberg's **two-factor theory** argues that hygiene factors keep workers from feeling dissatisfied, but motivators help workers feel satisfied and motivated. The implications are clear: (1) provide hygiene factors reducing worker dissatisfaction, and (2) include motivators, as they are the only factors to motivate workers and lead to job satisfaction. The two-factor theory has been criticised because researchers could not get the same results with other study methods (King 1970; Locke 1976). Nevertheless, the theory is significant as it focused attention on the need to provide motivators and improved our understanding of motivation.

motivators

Factors seeming to make individuals feel satisfied with their jobs

hygiene factors

Factors seeming to make individuals feel dissatisfied with their jobs

two-factor theory

Herzberg's theory that hygiene factors are necessary to keep workers from feeling dissatisfied, but only motivators can lead workers to feel satisfied and motivated

FIGURE 11.4 Herzberg's two-factor theory (Jones et al. 2000)

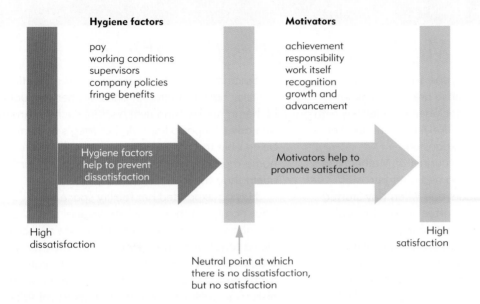

Hygiene factors

pay
working conditions
supervisors
company policies
fringe benefits

Motivators

achievement
responsibility
work itself
recognition
growth and
advancement

Hygiene factors
help to prevent
dissatisfaction

Motivators help to
promote satisfaction

High
dissatisfaction

High
satisfaction

Neutral point at which
there is no dissatisfaction,
but no satisfaction

ERG theory

After criticisms of Maslow's hierarchy-of-needs theory, Clayton Alderfer (1972) proposed an alternative, **ERG theory**. The name comes from combining Maslow's five needs levels into three: existence, relatedness and growth. **Existence needs** include physiological desires, such as food and water, and work-related material wants, such as pay, fringe benefits and working conditions. **Relatedness needs** address relationships with significant others, such as families, friendship groups, work and professional groups. They address our need to be accepted by others, achieve mutual understanding on major matters, and influence those we interact with on a regular basis (Baumeister & Leary 1995). **Growth needs** produce creativity and innovation, and the desire to have impact productively on our surroundings.

According to ERG theory, we concentrate first on existence requirements. When resolved, we have energy to focus on relatedness needs. When relatedness needs are satisfied, we have energy and support to pursue growth needs. Thus ERG theory uses a **satisfaction-progression principle** similar to Maslow's hierarchy, since the satisfaction of one need allows focus on the next.

Aside from using three levels not five, ERG theory differs in three ways from Maslow's hierarchy. First, though the idea of a hierarchy is retained, Alderfer argues we can face more than one category at once. Lower-levels needs need not be well satisfied before we look to others. However, lower-level-need satisfaction lets us attend to higher-level needs. Thus when a worker who is busy solving a problem skips lunch they will get hungry. At some point hunger may interfere with problem-solving efforts. Second, ERG is more flexible, as it recognises that some people's needs occur in an order different to the ERG framework (Nayak & Ketteringham 1986). Third, ERG theory has a **frustration-regression principle**. This states that if we are frustrated trying to satisfy a higher-level need, our concern with that need may cease. We may come to focus more on a concrete and reachable lower-level need. For example, if we cannot get more interesting work, we may seek to build stronger co-worker relationships.

Both Maslow's hierarchy and ERG theory are hard to test, requiring changes to individuals' needs and fulfilment levels to be measured and tracked over time. Limited research on ERG theory has shown support (Steers et al. 1996). If ERG theory is supported and people try to

ERG theory

Alternative (proposed by Alderfer) to Maslow's hierarchy-of-needs theory which argues there are three levels of individual needs

existence needs

Needs including various forms of material and physiological desires, such as food and water, as well as work-related forms such as pay, fringe benefits and physical working conditions

relatedness needs

Needs addressing our relationships with significant others, such as families, friendship groups, work groups and professional groups

growth needs

Needs impelling creativity and innovation, along with the desire to have a productive impact on our surroundings

satisfaction-progression principle

Principle stating that satisfaction of one level of need encourages concern with the next level

frustration-regression principle

Principle stating that if we are continually frustrated in our attempts to satisfy a higher-level need, we may cease to be concerned about that need

Mother Meg's success takes the cake

'I do enjoy the business', she says. 'I love the manufacturing side.' Those are the words with which Kay Wormwell concluded an interview with *The Australian Financial Review* discussing her intended international expansion.

Kay Wormwell is the founder of Mother Meg's Australian Fine Foods, named after her grandmother many years ago when Kay started going around to all the coffee shops she could find to sell her only product of those days—home-made almond bread. This was in the early 90s when Wormwell was operating with a single domestic-sized oven under her home on the Gold Coast.

Kay originally started baking biscuits for corporate morning teas as an extension of her deli business on Queensland's Gold Coast. She later moved to Toowoomba on the Darling Downs where the Mother Meg's Fine Foods product range was developed using traditional recipes and cooking styles handed down from her grandmother. The Mother Meg's range of biscuits, plum puddings and fruitcakes is hand baked with all Australian ingredients, organically grown where possible. The business has secured contracts to supply Mother Meg's products to prominent Australian companies and Kay recently received an emerging exporter award for her success in selling products to the Japanese market.

Since the early days her views and marketing strategy have not altered. She says her products are higher in quality than rival biscuits such as Arnott's upmarket Emposio line. Mother Meg's skills are being able to produce volume and still maintain a home-made recipe. Kay now travels much further afield than the local coffee shops.

Having expanded her facility space in Toowoomba to three times its original size, she has also expanded her customer range to include David Jones and Myers stores. Over the past year, Mother Meg has added Qantas in-flight catering to the suite of customers. However, the brand also sells under other labels such as Royal Albert.

In spite of now having 30 employees, Wormwell still likes to be hands-on. She gladly abandons the executive office for spending time with employees to iron out the glitches with a second-hand packaging machine acquired to wrap biscuits destined for Qantas passengers.

Update: Kay Wormwell sold Mother Meg's in March 2004 in order to spend more time with her family. Kay does, however, still work full time at Mother Meg's and is enjoying spending more time in the kitchen, doing what she loves best—baking. The business side of the company is being looked after by new owner, Ben Baker.

Source: Adapted from Wisentahl (2003); (further details of sources are listed on p. 736–7).

Activities for discussion, analysis and further research

1. Identify the factors which motivate Kay Wormwell in her job.
2. Interview an employee of your acquaintance and discuss the employee's feelings about having a hands on manager.
3. There are a number of web-based references to Mother Meg's products. Track one down and see if you can find the product. Why might a retail organisation add that product to their stock? Why do you think Qantas added it for its passenger service?

fulfil many needs at once, then motivating staff means providing many ways to fulfil needs. With ERG theory's frustration-regression element, managers must allow employees to satisfy growth needs, or they may lose interest. Frustrating growth needs motivated aboriginal Daniel Tucker to move on from a twice-refused apprenticeship to become an indigenous mining company director employing 41 and with an annual turnover of $8 million (Tredgold 2003b).

ERG theory's message for managers is the same as Maslow's. Find out the needs that subordinates try to satisfy at work, ensure outcomes satisfy those needs when they do well, and so help the organisation reach its goals.

Acquired-needs theory

While hierarchy-of-needs and ERG theories see some needs as crucial, David C. McClelland has another view, **acquired-needs theory**. McClelland argues that needs are gained or learned by experience. Though needs come from a range of conditions, a specific event can influence our desires profoundly (Fierman 1987).

McClelland studied three needs: achievement, affiliation and power. He measures these with the Thematic Apperception Test (TAT), where stories are written about deliberately ambiguous pictures. The stories are scored on their achievement, affiliation and power themes. The assumption is that people write on themes significant to them (Spangler 1992). Test results mostly show a blend of achievement, affiliation and power needs, not with one high and the others absent.

Initially McClelland's (1985) work considered the **need for achievement (nAch)**, the desire to accomplish challenging tasks and achieve excellence in one's work. Those with high nAch seek competitive situations, gaining results by their own efforts and getting fairly rapid feedback. They seek moderate goals and take calculated risks, but avoid very hard goals due to the high risk. As high-nAch people seek problems needing innovative, novel solutions, they provide creativity and innovative ideas (Steers 1987).

Of the larger population about 10 per cent is thought to have high nAch. Managers seeking to motivate high achievers must give challenging, reachable goals and give progress feedback at once. High-nAch people, McClelland argues, may find money per se unmotivating (as their main satisfaction comes from achievement). They may still see money as a source of progress feedback (McClelland 1976; 1985).

McClelland also addressed the **need for affiliation (nAff)**, the desire for warm, friendly relationships with others. Those with high-nAff tend to choose professions where interaction with others is needed, such as health care, teaching, sales and counselling. A co-operative, supportive work environment is needed where staff can meet performance expectations and high affiliation needs by working with others. High-nAff staff can be assets if high-level cooperation with and support of others, including clients and customers is needed (Steers 1987).

McClelland came to see the **need for power (nPow)**, the desire to influence others and control one's environment, as a significant organisational motivator. Need for power has two forms, personal and institutional. Individuals needing **personal power** try to dominate others to show they have power. Followers are expected to be loyal to them, not the organisation, which can mean unreached larger goals. Individuals who need **institutional power** work with others to solve problems and reach organisational goals. These people want things done in an organised way. They will sacrifice some of their own goals for the organisation's good (McClelland 1976; 1985). Motivating those with high institutional-power need means providing positions organising others' efforts. Thus the founder of Bloom's cosmetics is delegating and splitting organisation positions, appointing a senior sales manager and an export manager. As well she is drawing up a style book to lay out many of the broad rules only she was aware of previously (Howarth 2003c).

McClelland analysed various needs in relation to managerial effectiveness. He first thought that the best managers would have high achievement need. His work later suggests the focus of high-nAch individuals is their own results, not the development and performance of others. So, high-nAch people are good entrepreneurs. Those with high affiliation need may be weak

acquired-needs theory

Theory (developed by McClelland) stating that our needs are acquired or learned on the basis of our life experiences

need for achievement (nAch)

Desire to accomplish challenging tasks and achieve a standard of excellence in one's work

need for affiliation (nAff)

Desire to maintain warm, friendly relationships with others

need for power (nPow)

Desire to influence others and control one's environment

personal power

Need for power in which individuals want to dominate others for the sake of demonstrating their ability to wield power

institutional power

Need for power in which individuals focus on working with others to solve problems and further organisational goals managerially, seeking good interpersonal links not goal attainment. Managers with personal-power orientations often try to use others' efforts for their own gain (McClelland 1985).

McClelland's work suggests the best managers are those with a high institutional-power need due to their coordination of others' efforts to reach long-term organisation goals (Andrews 1967; McClelland & Boyatzis 1982). Thus the need profile of successful managers in competitive environments includes (1) moderate-to-high institutional power need, (2) moderate achievement need to help in their early career, and a desire for organisation competitiveness as they move to higher levels, and (3) a minimum need for affiliation for them to influence others sensitively. McClelland's later research shows achievement need to be more important than power in small firms and also in large, decentralised ones when they are working like small companies which need to improve and grow cost-efficiently (McClelland 1995).

What if you want to be a manager but don't have the 'right' need profile? McClelland argues it can be developed. He trained individuals and raised their need for achievement. Those trained were promoted faster and made more money than others. Training involved tasks requiring goal achievement, and situations became more challenging as they became more able. Appealing entrepreneurial models were also presented to trainees. The same methods can build need for institutional power (McClelland 1965; 1985; McClelland & Burnham 1976). Other needs, such as affiliation, may be more difficult to develop this way.

Assessing need theories

Needs identified in the four theories are shown in Figure 11.5. It is agreed that higher-level needs are important for motivation. Given demand for new ideas, better quality and increased capacity for implementing change, fostering growth needs is crucial. For example, Hewlett-Packard has an open-stock policy where engineers can take home laboratory stock parts. The policy assumes this fosters original thinking and innovation. In one story, Bill Hewlett, a company founder, found the stock area locked one Saturday and used a bolt cutter on the padlock. He left a note saying, 'Don't ever lock this door again. Thanks, Bill.' (Peters & Waterman 1982). The open-stock policy fosters employee growth, helping Hewlett-Packard's reputation for innovation.

MANAGERIAL DILEMMAS

Stepping out safely

Indonesia has very high unemployment rates. To overcome some of those stresses, it has attempted to expand its overseas labour force. Indonesia will have to work hard to catch up with the Philippines which supplies eight million overseas workers. Over the last five years, Indonesia has exported 1.6 million documented overseas workers who have sent home a cumulative $5 billion.

At the same time as lobbying foreign governments to open their doors to Indonesian workers, the Indonesian government is trying to better prepare workers for life overseas. A three-day course has been designed to equip workers with skills to assert their rights and avoid exploitation.

Source: Adapted from Cohen, M. (2000).

Reflection points

1. If you were an Indonesian unskilled or semi-skilled worker, what might motivate you to go overseas to work?

2. Try to find out why those workers send so much money home.

3. In the Singapore paper *The Straights Times* there are often articles about the treatment of expatriate domestic workers. Undertake a search to identify the risks these workers run in a foreign environment.

Decision points

1. What are the abuses that such a worker might face and how can those be avoided?

2. Consider what the Indonesian government might do to better protect its labour exports.

FIGURE 11.5 Comparison of needs in four theories (adapted from Gordon 1987, p. 92)

Maslow: hierarchy of needs theory	**Alderfer:** ERG theory	**Herzberg:** two-factor theory	**McLelland:** acquired needs theory
physiological	existence	hygiene	
safety and security			
belongingness and love	relatedness		need for affiliation
self-esteem	growth	motivators	need for achievement; need for power
self-actualisation			

COGNITIVE THEORIES

Need theories identify internal desires guiding behaviour, but do not explain the thought processes involved. In contrast, **cognitive theories** work to isolate thinking patterns used in deciding whether or not to act in a certain way. Cognitive theories do not conflict with need theories; rather, they look differently at motivation. As they focus on the thought processes of motivation, cognitive theories are called process theories. The three major cognitive work motivation theories are expectancy, equity and goal-setting.

Expectancy theory

The **expectancy theory** of motivation, proposed by Victor H. Vroom, argues that we consider three main issues before making the effort to perform at a given level. These can be seen in the circles of Figure 11.6, which show expectancy theory's basic components.

Effort-performance expectancy

When considering **effort-performance (E→P) expectancy**, we assess the probability our efforts will lead to needed performance levels. This means assessing our abilities, and considering if contextual factors, such as resource availability, are adequate. To see how effort-

cognitive theories

Theories attempting to isolate thinking patterns we use in deciding whether or not to behave in a certain way

expectancy theory

Theory (proposed by Vroom) arguing that we consider three main issues before we expend effort necessary to perform at a given level

effort-performance (E→P) expectancy

Our assessment of the probability our efforts will lead to the required performance level

FIGURE 11.6 Basic components of expectancy theory

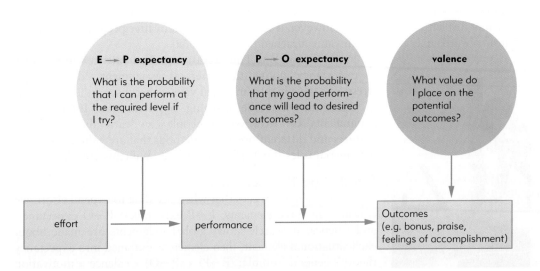

performance expectancy works, imagine your boss asks you to head a major special project. The project is design and implemention of a new computerised system to track customer complaints, enhancing customer service and identify complaint trends quickly. Firstly you consider the probability of being able to reach needed performance levels, given your abilities and other environmental factors. If you feel you lack knowledge about developing such a system, and/or resources are not available, you might assess the probability of success as low. That is, your E→P expectancy for this assignment might be low. Alternatively, if you feel well qualified for the project and resources are available, you might assess the probability of success—the E→P expectancy—as high. However, effort-performance expectancy assessment is only one evaluation aspect.

Performance-outcome expectancy

performance-outcome (P→O) expectancy

Our assessment of the probability our successful performance will lead to certain outcomes

With **performance-outcome (P→O) expectancy**, we assess the probability successful performance will lead to specific outcomes. Major issues are reward potentials (a bonus, promotion, or feeling of success), although we also consider potential negative results (loss of leisure time or family disruption due to extra job hours). In your special-project situation, your boss may have given rewards before, such as recognition and bonuses, to those taking on special projects. If so, you might assess P→O expectancy for taking on the project as high. However, if past experience with special projects shows the boss sometimes arranges rewards but other times forgets, you might view the P→O expectancy as medium (perhaps a 50–50 rewarded probability). Finally, if your boss never rewards extra effort, you might assess P→O expectancy as virtually zero—at least for rewards from the boss.

extrinsic rewards

Rewards provided by others, such as bonuses, awards or promotions

Many potential rewards can be linked to performance. Rewards from others, bonuses, awards or promotions, are **extrinsic rewards**. As well as monetary rewards managers can use non-monetary rewards to raise motivation. On the other hand, rewards related to internal experiences with successful performance, such as feelings of achievement, challenge and growth, are **intrinsic rewards**. Given various possible outcomes (both positive and negative), we assess the probability our performance will lead to desired outcomes. If our assessment of P→O expectancy is high, it builds motivation. If assessment is low, expectancy reduces willingness to perform at a high level. Still, there is another motivational component—the importance of various outcomes.

intrinsic rewards

Rewards related to our own internal experiences with successful performance, such as feelings of achievement, challenge and growth

Valence

valence

Our assessment of anticipated value of various outcomes or rewards

With the **valence** component, we assess various outcomes' anticipated value. Valence is high if rewards available interest us. However, loss of leisure time, family disruption or other negative-value outcomes may offset the reward value. When we attach a high overall valence to a situation, the rewards available will motivate. You might view very positively a special bonus from the boss in the previous special-project example,. But the bonus may be less influential if a rich aunt just left you $3 million. However, if you develop the innovative project, the resulting intrinsic rewards may have a high value attached (Walker 2003a).

Jones, George and Hill (2000) identified valence's importance to expectancy, noting that overseas assignments, despite their stress, can have high managerial valence because of the high levels of autonomy and the learning opportunities. International assignments are attractive as people can learn about different cultures and different operating methods that are valuable skills in managerial roles (Loeb 1995; Kinicki & Williams 2003).

Combining the elements

Expectancy theory argues that when deciding to expend effort, we consider all three elements: E→P expectancy, P→O expectancy, and valence. Research shows global judgments are made about each situational element, then elements combined into expectancy theory's general formula: (E→P) × (P→O) × valence = motivation

(Staw 1984). In the special-project situation, for example, assume all three elements are assessed as high. You will likely be highly motivated about the project: high E→P expectancy × high P→O expectancy × high valence = high motivation. By contrast, any element assessed as zero means the equation equals zero, no matter the other two elements' levels. You will abandon the project if you (1) see a zero (or very low) probability of adequate performance, (2) see zero (or very low) chance successful performance will yield certain outcomes, or (3) give zero (or very low) valence value to possible outcomes. In more mixed situations, where no element has very low ratings, you contrast the situation with others and choose the one with the best chance of valued outcomes. In the special-project situation, you might negotiate with your boss to improve possible outcomes or change assignments to a task with greater motivational potential.

Expectancy theory helped predict if particular naval officers would voluntarily retire; forecast the job an undergraduate would take on graduation; and identified the MBA program a particular graduate would select (Parker & Dyer 1976; Arnold 1981; Wanous, Keon & Lattack 1983; Steers & Porter 1991).

Implications for managers

Expectancy theory has a number of managerial consequences. For one, managers must build high P→O expectancy formation by connecting rewards to high performance. To clarify, consider three scenarios with Alissa, Bob and Christen. In the first, Alissa does well and gets a bonus, concluding high performance leads to valued outcomes (enhanced P→O expectancy). In the second, Bob does well but the boss does not even say 'good job', much less pay a bonus. So Bob sees high performance as not paying, at least organisationally (reduced P→O expectancy). In the third scenario, Christen does little but gets a major annual bonus. Christen will see high performance as unconnected to valued outcomes (reduced P→O expectancy). As a result, Bob and Christen's motivation will be lower in future, while Alissa's motivation will be higher. For Bob, lower P→O expectancy flows from the manager's failure to reward high performance; but for Christen, low performance was rewarded.

Apart from the P→O expectancy, expectancy theory has other managerial implications. Managers must foster high subordinate E→P expectancy. Their high expectancy leads to high success motivation (Kaufman 1995; Walker 2003b). They foster this through clear performance expectations; setting challenging but reachable performance goals; ensuring employees are trained and have the resources to reach required performance levels; and being encouraging. Managers can build motivation through reward opportunities (extrinsic and intrinsic) with high employee valence (Nadler & Lawler 1983).

Managers can also boost expectancy levels and motivation by training subordinates so they have expertise needed for high performance. Then combining training, high expectancy and motivation improves chances of success (Milbank 1995; *Wall Street Journal* 1995a; 1995b).

Expectancy theory gives useful guidelines, however managers' results may not be as expected from their efforts unless employees see outcomes as equitable, an issue equity theory addresses.

Equity theory

J. Stacy Adams (1965) developed equity theory to explain how we identify and react to events we see as inequitable.

According to **equity theory**, we prefer situations of balance, or equity, which exist when we see the ratio of our inputs compared to our outcomes as being equal to that for a comparison other (or others). The comparison chosen depends on what we see as appropriate. For example, in deciding equity of a pay rise, co-workers may be compared to peers in other units, and/or a friend at another firm similarly qualified. We will see equity as relative (compared with another) not absolute (compared with a set standard). To assess our inputs we consider many variables such as education, skills, experience, work hours and results. Outcomes include pay, bonuses, praise, parking, office space, furniture and work assignments. Inputs and outcomes for assessing equity are totally based on our idea of relevance.

equity theory

Theory arguing that we prefer situations of balance, or equity, which exists when we perceive the ratio of our inputs and outcomes to be equal to the ratio of inputs and outcomes for a comparison other

The theory notes that two inequity types produce tension. One is under-reward, when our inputs:outcomes ratio is seen to be less than a comparison other. In the second, over-reward, our inputs:outcomes ratio is seen to be greater than a comparison other. Equity theory research shows we adjust to over-reward conditions quickly—deciding our inputs are worth more than we first thought (Locke 1976; Mowday 1991). Under-reward situations are more difficult to resolve.

Reducing or eliminating inequity

While someone's actions are based on what seems feasible in a situation, Adams suggests maintaining self-esteem is very important. Thus, a person will work to maximise outcomes and resist costly input changes. Changing perceptions of others' inputs and outcomes or trying to alter their side of the equation is better than changing assessment of our own inputs or altering our own side of the equation. Leaving will occur only where inequity is high when other options are unfeasible. Finally, changing the comparison others will be resisted, particularly if they are stable.

Adams' equity approach looked at a situation at one point in time, but it seems inequity perceptions last. Adding time explains why people erupt over small inequities. Previous inequity residues build up until one small incident 'breaks the camel's back' and a strong reaction ensues (Cosier & Dalton 1983; Washington 2003).

Implications for managers

To apply expectancy theory's recommendations, managers must use two-way subordinate communication to understand their perceptions of equity. Subordinates must know the 'rules' of outcome allocation relative to inputs. Also, since an inequity pattern can lead to major problems, managers must have good communication with subordinates, superiors, peers, customers and others associated with the job. Growing workforce diversity can mean increased feelings of inequity due to the varied viewpoints. Many firms have thus set up diversity-management programs to foster mutual understanding and ensure equitable treatment.

Motivation is best when most staff see their treatment as equitable, with balanced inputs and outcomes. The best performers are motivated to continue to perform as they get deserved outcomes. Meanwhile, mediocre contributors and performers see that to increase their outcomes, they must increase inputs.

Goal-setting theory

The value of cross-organisation goal setting, as well as steps involved, are explored in Chapter 6. We summarise goal-setting theory in relation to motivation here. Goal setting, seen once as a technique, has become a motivational theory as researchers seek to explain the cognitive factors impacting its success. It is argued that it works by focusing attention and action, mobilising effort, increasing persistence, and encouraging strategy development to achieve goals. Feedback on results is vital (Locke & Latham 1984; 1990).

Goal setting's success in motivating performance depends on setting goals with the right aspects. They must be specific and measurable, challenging, attainable, relevant to the organisation's major work, and time-limited (i.e. achieved in a defined time). At Intel, maker of microprocessor chips or personal computers' 'brains', goals have cut time needed to develop and produce new chips. The company used to develop new chips every four years. Now Intel's cycles overlap, with development of the next generation two years before the Pentium chip hit markets (Hof 1995). The goal of succession was not addressed at Kozminski's family-owned jewellers, resulting in significant problems (Walker 2003c).

Goal commitment, or the attachment to, or determination to, reach a goal, is vital to goal setting. Expectancy theory's major elements influence goal commitment: effort-performance

Promoting the use of electronic communications for the right purposes

In the early days of electronic communication, staff had to be encouraged to stop sending letters and faxes and to use email instead. Staff were generally allowed to use email for personal messages, in order to motivate them to learn how to use email, to appreciate its potential and gain experience. This was also seen as the best means of getting staff to co-operate in cutting paper use, reducing postage and lowering telephone charges for sending faxes.

E-Advance, the training arm of an Australian university, has progressed to the stage where it uses electronic means of communication wherever possible. Brochures are sent out almost entirely in electronic form. Students are welcome to email their assignments to the tutors. Teaching staff are professionals from all around Australia, giving E-Advance a 'virtual' faculty. While staff have been encouraged to use email, this has not been without its problems. Recently, a staff member became rather secretive about using email and would shut down the computer even while at lunch. While this may be good security practice, it was not consistent with the person's behaviour in relation to other issues of security.

Then the manager of E-Advance, in a chance meeting with a former colleague of the staff member, learned that the person had been asked by a previous employer to refrain from using chat lines during the day. (Chat lines tie up much of the bandwidth into the university.) An investigation took place. First, it was established that management had the right to read messages in university email accounts. An after-hours inspection of that account revealed only work-related messages in the in-box. However, a quick look at 'sent messages' revealed a number that were, to say the least, far from work-related. The person concerned had obviously been mixing business with pleasure! All inward messages had been deleted, but not the outward messages. On some occasions more than ten messages were sent to one person in less than an hour.

These messages were generally of a personal nature, suggesting that the parties were desperately missing each other. There was more than one correspondent—even one in the UK. In a message to the UK correspondent, the staff member had suggested that they should meet, saying that the person had been 'asked' by the university to represent it at an education fair in the UK. (This was news to the management!) In time, the staff member asked for leave and indicated that it was for overseas travel on the university's behalf.

On return, the person was given notice that their contract would not be renewed, and was asked to clean out any personal possessions and leave the premises. Management was concerned that the investigation sent a message to other staff that was contrary to its policy of encouraging electronic communication. They were aware that some companies—especially American companies—monitor staff email and will caution their staff if they detect personal messages that are overly long or contain risqué material. For example, staff in the Brisbane office of an American company received a message from the Houston head office noting that a cartoon of Santa Claus in a compromising position would not be tolerated and that a repeat misdemeanour would lead to dismissal. E-Advance management decided to discuss the issue openly, trusting that staff members would act responsibly and would limit their personal use of email to a reasonable level.

Source: Contributed by Ken Dooley.

Activities for discussion, analysis and further research

1. What do you consider to be reasonable personal use of email at work? Should personal use be tolerated? Should it be banned? Can it be banned?
2. Suggest rules for the personal use of email that might be acceptable to staff and management.

What effect would banning personal use of email at work have on motivation?

3. If staff were not allowed to use email for personal correspondence, how would you motivate them to use email for work?

4. Access the following websites and discuss issues raised in the sites with your colleagues.
www.cse.unsw.edu.au/~waleed/anti-stand/msg00015.html
http://mlis.state.md.us/1997rs/billfile/hb0778.htm#Exbill
http://members.aol.com/emailfaq/emailfaq.html#2a

expectancy (can I reach the goal?), performance-outcome expectancy (will I be rewarded if I reach it?) and valence (do I value available rewards?). Individuals' commitment to goal attainment is greater when their expectations of reaching the goals are high, they see strong links between goal accomplishment and rewards and they value rewards (Locke, Latham & Erez 1988). So expectancy and goal-setting theory fit well.

Research has supported goal setting's value to performance improvement and it is a helpful motivational tool for managers.

Assessing cognitive theories

While they complement each other, each cognitive motivation theory gives a different view. Expectancy theory tells managers to build positive effort-performance expectancies in staff with encouragement and training. It shows how much clear links between performance and outcomes help, as well as the need to offer rewards with positive valence (valence clues come from need theories). Goal-setting theory fits with expectancy theory as it helps pinpoint performance levels related to effort-performance and performance-outcome expectancies. Finally, equity issues influence individual assessment of the value of maintaining motivation equity.

REINFORCEMENT THEORY

reinforcement theory

Theory arguing that our behaviour can be explained by consequences in the environment

The reverse of cognitive theories is the reinforcement motivation approach, which does not explain an individual's behaviour through their thought processes. B. F. Skinner pioneered one **reinforcement-theory** approach, operant conditioning or behaviourism. The theory argues that behaviour can be explained by environmental consequences and not cognitive explanations (Luthans & Kreitner 1975). The theory uses the concept of the **law of effect**, which states behaviours with pleasant or positive consequences are more likely to be repeated than those with unpleasant or negative ones.

law of effect

Concept stating that behaviours having pleasant or positive consequences are more likely to be repeated and behaviours having unpleasant or negative consequences are less likely to be repeated

In reinforcement theory, a stimulus cues a response or behaviour, followed by a consequence. If this is rewarding, we are more likely to repeat the behaviour when the stimulus recurs. If we find it unrewarding, we are unlikely to repeat the behaviour. For example, assume you manage one of a consumer-products company's marketing-research units. Another unit's manager urgently asks for aid with market research data (stimulus). You move some staff from other tasks, even working late to produce needed data (behaviour). If the other manager makes sure your unit is recognised for its efforts (pleasant consequence) you are likely to make extra effort to help again. If the product manager were to complain about a minor error (unpleasant consequence), ignoring the rest of the data or extra effort you made (less than pleasant consequence), you will be unlikely to help again. Using reinforcement theory techniques is **behaviour modification**.

behaviour modification

Use of techniques associated with reinforcement theory

Types of reinforcement

Four reinforcement types influence behaviour in behaviour modification: positive and negative reinforcements, extinction and punishment. A behaviour is increased by positive and negative reinforcements, and decreased by extinction and punishment (see Fig. 11.7). Skinner argued individual growth is helped by positive reinforcement and extinction, with immaturity in individuals being fostered by negative reinforcement and punishment, which in the end contaminates the whole organisation.

Positive reinforcement

Positive reinforcement uses pleasant, rewarding consequences to encourage desired organisationally-useful behaviour. Rewarding outcomes, such as praise, a pay rise, or time off, are positive reinforcers if desired behaviour is repeated. As people's perceptions of pleasant and rewarding differ, managers must check the effect of a reinforcer to see if desired behaviour increases.

New behaviours will not be exactly as desired, so managers shape them. **Shaping** is rewarding behaviours similar to that desired until the desired response occurs. For example, a manager training a new salesperson may compliment their greeting of customers (if this approximates the response desired). The manager may suggest questions to understand customer needs better. The manager then rewards the salesperson's efforts at asking better questions, and makes other suggestions. In this way behaviour is gradually shaped to competency.

Philip Weinman (Gome 2003b), a business angel, or private investor, was unhappy with workers in an online training company he bought into. He came to the office for his customary 9am start to find that the hard working, passionate staff did not see regular office hours as needed in their business. Over the next few weeks he drew up formal rules and expectations on a number of organisational processes. Gradually the people in the organisation came to see that the 'flexible' working hours were not appropriate for an organisation wanting to impress corporate customers.

positive reinforcement

Technique aimed at increasing a desired behaviour, which involves providing a pleasant, rewarding consequence to encourage that behaviour

shaping

Successive rewarding of behaviours closely approximating the desired response until the actual desired response is made

FIGURE 11.7 Types of reinforcement situations according to Skinner

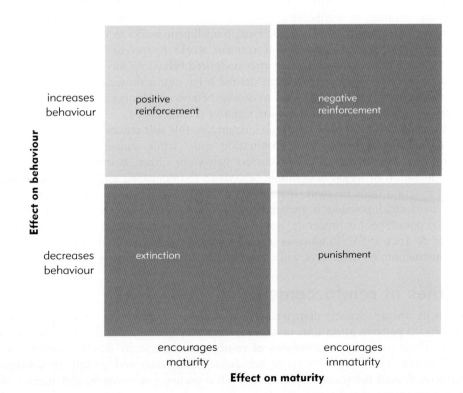

Negative reinforcement

Like positive reinforcement, **negative reinforcement** focuses on increasing desired behaviour, but differently. Negative reinforcement means presenting noxious (unpleasant) stimuli so a person will display behaviour desired to stop the stimuli. Desired behaviour is thus reinforced, but negatively, as the person must show the desired behaviour to stop the unpleasant state. For example, an engineer may work to finish a project on time (desired behaviour) to stop (consequence) the chief engineer's nagging or yelling (noxious stimuli). With negative reinforcement, noxious or unpleasant stimuli are present or likely unless desired behaviour occurs. For instance, the chief engineer may be nagging about the deadline; or he may not be yelling or nagging yet, but the engineer knows from the past that late projects trigger this. In either case, negative reinforcement means the project will be more likely on time.

Negative reinforcement encourages desired behaviour, but the individual may feel negatively toward the provider of the negative reinforcement. Then, they may react by doing only what is required and not giving extra time when needed, or they may even leave the organisation. Whenever possible, positive reinforcement should be used. The work environment becomes unpleasant and organisation culture negative when reinforcement is negative. Nagging, threats and other negative results can make subordinates resentful and they may try to hit back. Negative reinforcement fosters immature behaviour. For example, it may encourage the engineer to finish projects on time only if the boss is in the office.

Extinction

Extinction involves decreasing behaviour by stopping previously positive results from it. For example, when the first few times an employee clowns in a staff meeting, the manager laughs. Laughing reinforces the clowning so it becomes disruptive. If the manager refrained from (withheld) laughing in response, the employee's behaviour would be extinguished.

Punishment

Punishment is giving negative consequences to decrease or discourage a behaviour. Examples are criticising unwanted behaviour as it occurs, suspending a person without pay, denying (or possibly giving) training, or withholding resources such as new equipment. Punishment differs from negative reinforcement in two ways. First, punishment works to decrease or discourage undesired behaviour, where negative reinforcement works to increase or encourage desired behaviour. Second, punishment is applied after undesired behaviour has been shown. Negative reinforcement, conversely, occurs before the desired behaviour is shown. Both punishment and negative reinforcement are negative ways to change behaviour. Skinner argued that their long-term effects on people and organisations are negative (Haigh 2003).

Arguments against using punishment include undesirable side effects (e.g. punisher-focused negative feelings) and behavioural elimination only while punishment is threatened. Punishment does not give a model of correct behaviour either. It may still be useful for dangerous, unethical or illegal undesirable behaviour. Extinguishing undesirable behaviour is impractical if action must be swift. If punishment is needed, it will be most effective if it is controlled by formal policies; if punishment occurs as soon as possible after undesired behaviour; if punishment is moderate, not severe; and if it is consistent (Arvey & Ivancevich 1980; Beyer & Trice 1984). In all cases it must not occur publicly. While punishment can be useful for instruction, consequences will almost always be very negative (Jones 2000)

Schedules of reinforcement

Reinforcement theory argues that positive reinforcement produces desired behaviours. Different reward patterns affect time taken to learn a new behaviour and level of behavioural persistence. These patterns, or **schedules of reinforcement**, specify positive reinforcement's basis and timing. There are two major schedules: continuous and partial. In continuous reinforcement, desired behaviour is rewarded when it occurs. For example, a manager praises a worker performing a task correctly. It is effective during initial learning, but becomes impractical. Further, desired behaviour quickly stops (rapid extinction) unless reinforcement continues. With a partial schedule, desired behaviour is sometimes rewarded. During initial learning, behaviour is often rewarded to encourage repetition, and less so later. The four main partial reinforcement schedules are: fixed interval, fixed ratio, variable interval and variable ratio (see Fig. 11.8).

Fixed interval

In a **fixed-interval reinforcement schedule**, reinforcers are given using a fixed time schedule, assuming behaviour desired has occurred. An example is a plant manager visiting one section every day at the same time, praising efforts to build product quality. Fixed-interval schedules yield uneven responses, with desired behaviour peaking just before reinforcement is due, then dropping until the next is due. With this schedule, extinction is quick if reinforcement is late or stops.

Fixed ratio

In a **fixed-ratio reinforcement schedule**, reinforcers are given after a fixed number of cases of desired behaviour, not on a fixed time schedule. For example, innovation awards might occur after five usable ideas are given. Another fixed-ratio reinforcement is piecework pay systems for making a set number of units. Fixed-ratio schedules give high response rates, but extinguish quickly if reinforcement stops even temporarily.

Variable interval

In a **variable-interval reinforcement schedule**, a reinforcer is given on a variable, or random, time schedule which averages out to a specific frequency. For example, a plant manager visits a section praising efforts to increase product quality on average five times a week, but at varying times. This schedule promotes a high, steady response rate which slowly extinguishes.

Variable ratio

In a **variable-ratio reinforcement schedule**, a reinforcer comes after varying, or random, frequency of desired behaviour (not on a varying time schedule) so the reinforcement pattern averages out to a specified ratio of events per reinforcement. For example, special awards for

fixed-interval schedule of reinforcement

Pattern in which a reinforcer is administered on a fixed time schedule, assuming the desired behaviour has continued at an appropriate level

fixed-ratio schedule of reinforcement

Pattern in which a reinforcer is provided after a fixed number of occurrences of the desired behaviour

variable-interval schedule of reinforcement

Pattern in which a reinforcer is administered on a varying, or random, time schedule which averages out to a predetermined time frequency

variable-ratio schedule of reinforcement

Pattern in which a reinforcer is provided after a varying, or random, number of occurrences of the desired behaviour in such a way the reinforcement pattern averages out to a predetermined ratio of occurrences per reinforcement

FIGURE 11.8 Types of partial reinforcement schedules (adapted from Arnold & Feldman 1986, p. 70)

	FIXED INTERVAL	**FIXED RATIO**
fixed	Reinforcement administered every x minutes	Reinforcement administered every xth occurrence of the behaviour
	VARIABLE INTERVAL	**VARIABLE RATIO**
variable	Timing of reinforcers varies randomly around some average time period	Number of occurrences of the behaviour required to receive reinforcer varies randomly around some average number
	passage of time	number of times behaviour occurs

Spacing or timing of reinforcers

Basis for determining frequency of reinforcement

GENDER FACTOR

The motivating factor

Debbie Duncan has had 23 years experience in the travel industry, and owns her own travel agency in Ballarat, Victoria. Recent dramatic changes in the airline industry necessitated a change of franchise from Traveland to Jetset. Debbie believes the change was a positive one, and she attributes this to the professionalism of her team of senior travel consultants and their ability to deliver outstanding customer service. Debbie's transformational leadership style encourages staff to achieve their individual goals, as well as to operate as an integral part of a close-knit team. Individual strengths and weaknesses are identified, and these are endorsed or accommodated by the entire team. Placement of staff within the office is carefully considered so that personalities can complement each other, and people have the opportunity to learn from the person nearest them.

Above-award salaries are paid, and expectations of absolute excellence in customer service are clearly communicated. When goals are achieved, the whole group celebrate the achievement together. 'I find that 90 per cent of the time it's the happy team environment that they come to work for', says Debbie. In addition, Debbie allows staff to establish preferences or expertise in specialist areas, and to take ownership for that area of the business. She believes her job as a manager is to identify the specific training her staff need in order to achieve to their optimum level of performance and satisfaction. If individual weaknesses are identified, appropriate training and development is made available to enable the weaknesses to become strengths.

Debbie believes that she can best motivate her staff by providing a happy environment and giving them the tools to do their work properly. She has focused on developing a system where people do not feel they need to compete against each other. Her staff have targets they are expected to achieve,

but they seem to recognise their own capabilities and stress levels and do not overachieve in pursuit of additional bonus payments. Debbie believes this proves that money alone is not the primary motivator, at least for this group of people.

A very open communication system ensures that all staff know how the business runs, and what they need to do to achieve the company's goals. Debbie emphatically sees her staff as her most important asset. They are experts in their field and also clearly valued as people, and play an integral part in the success of the business.

Source: Contributed by Glenice Wood (personal interview with Debbie Duncan, 6 May 2002).

Activities for discussion, analysis and further research

1. In what ways do staff learn about appropriate behaviour in this organisation? What learning theory best explains the mechanism that operates in Debbie Duncan's business?
2. How are issues of equity managed in this organisation? Why do you think that Debbie has managed to create a non-competitive environment with her staff? Would a transformational style of leadership be a factor in creating such an environment?
3. What is the major motivator for staff in this organisation? What theory best explains this? A significant amount of literature suggests that there is a difference in the way men and women lead and motivate their employees. Do a literature search using gender and leaders and review four articles to consider the question: 'Do you think that different styles of leadership can impact on the motivation of staff?'
4. Log on to the website: www.jetset.com.au/ or www.jetset.com.au/ballarat. Is the organisation's philosophy explicitly stated in terms of staffing? Would it be appropriate to do so on such a site?

new ideas might be given on a ratio average of one award per five innovative ideas (i.e. after three ideas once, then after seven, etc.). Poker-machine payoffs, giving rewards after a variable number of lever pulls, are a variable-ratio schedule. This gives a high response rate and is the partial reinforcement method that is slowest to extinguish. Variable-ratio reinforcement was

How to get the best out of your people

In spite of all the theories that are studied in this text, motivating people is one of the hardest things to do well and to maintain effectively. This is because at work we see only a part of the individual. There are many factors which impact on workers and work is only one of them. Here are some behaviours which will help you achieve motivated workers.

1. Make sure that workers know what is expected of them as unambiguously as possible. Mixed messages cause confusion and decrease performance.
2. Use extinction rather than punishment to eradicate undesirable behaviour. If you must punish, focus on the behaviour, not the individual. Try not to allow emotion into the situation—keep it straightforward.
3. Ensure that there are good role models for others to observe and ensure that the good role models are visibly rewarded for their achievements.
4. Ensure that rewards are equitable.
5. Make sure that rewards are given for small achievements as well as large ones—some individuals may need small successes to encourage them to greater levels of achievements.

Source: Adapted from Jones et al. (2000).

---

used in the McDonald's Monopoly promotion, where customers were given game pieces with stamps representing a Monopoly game board's properties. While the odds of winning the promotion's top prize were very long, immediate reinforcement came from chances to win instant food prizes at much shorter odds. The promotion was so successful it has been repeated twice.

Using reinforcement theory

Suggestions have been made to help managers use the reinforcement approach. They advise managers to encourage behaviours desired by positive reinforcement and tell subordinates what behaviours will be rewarded. Once desired behaviours are learned, variable-interval and variable-ratio reinforcement patterns are effective approaches to behaviour maintenance. Finally, if punishment is needed, it should be moderately severe, and administered quickly and consistently for best results (Beyer & Trice 1984; Hamner 1991; Rue & Byars 2003).

SOCIAL LEARNING THEORY

On the basis of his work on reinforcement theory, Albert Bandura believed the approach's apparent success could not be explained without allowing for people's cognitive or thinking capacity. Accordingly, he and others developed **social learning theory**, arguing that learning occurs by continuous interaction between our behaviours, personal factors and environmental forces. Individuals influence their environment, which affects how they think and behave. In other words, much behaviour is learnt by observing, imitating and interacting with the social environment. While social learning theory combines cognitive and reinforcement approaches, it is discussed here because it builds on reinforcement theory.

social learning theory

Theory arguing learning occurs through continuous reciprocal interaction of our behaviours, various personal factors and environmental forces

Major components

Social learning theory argues that three cognitively related processes are important to explain behaviour: symbolic processes, vicarious learning and self-control (Bandura 1977; Krietner & Luthans 1991).

Symbolic processes

symbolic processes

Various ways we use verbal and imagined symbols to process and store experiences in representational forms to serve as guides to future behaviour

Social learning theory argues that we depend on **symbolic processes**, or the use of verbal and imagined symbols to process and store experiences (words and images) to guide future behaviour. Using symbols, we solve problems without trying all courses of action. We can visualise a South Pacific holiday spot without ever being there. Desirable future images let us set goals and act toward them. Our symbolic processes have a cognitive component, **self-efficacy**, a belief in one's abilities to complete a particular task. Similar to expectancy theory's effort-performance expectancy element, self-efficacy is focused more on beliefs about our own capacities. It may help explain goal levels we set, as well as task effort and persistence. One study found faculty members who were feeling competent at research and writing wrote more articles and books, which, in turn, raised self-confidence and likelihood of future productivity. Studies of sales performance of life insurance agents gave similar findings (Barling & Beattie 1983; Taylor, Locke, Lee & Gist 1984).

self-efficacy

Belief in one's capabilities to perform a specific task

Vicarious learning

vicarious learning

Our ability to learn new behaviours and/or assess their probable consequences by observing others

Vicarious learning or observational learning is our ability to use observation to learn new behaviours and/or assess outcomes. It is important because, in contrast to reinforcement theory, we do not actually have to perform a behaviour to learn its consequences. Observing and copying others' behaviour is **modelling** (see Fig. 11.9). If you learnt to swim or play tennis by imitating another's behaviour (a skilled friend or instructor perhaps), you were modelling. Modelling has four stages. In the attention stage, we choose a model to observe, due to their skill or success, and we attend to relevant behavioural aspects. In the retention stage, we retain information about behaviour in mental images and words. In the reproduction stage, we work to reproduce a behaviour, but may be only partly successful, needing to adjust our behaviour further, using feedback. In the motivation stage, we are motivated to adopt a model's behaviour. For this stage to lead to actual adoption of behaviour, there must be reinforcement, usually from one of three sources. First, behaviour can be reinforced by consequences similarly to reinforcement theory. Second, reinforcement occurs vicariously by seeing results of others behaving that way. Third, we can self-reinforce by self-control.

modelling

Actually observing and attempting to imitate behaviours of others

Self-control

self-control

Our ability to exercise control over our own behaviour by setting standards and providing consequences for our own actions

Self-control, or self-regulation, is the ability to control our own behaviour by setting standards and providing consequences (rewards and punishments) for our own actions (Boslet 1994). Self-control helps performance when we make self-rewards dependent on reaching high levels of performance (Bandura 1977). Examples are promising ourselves a 15-minute break if we finish an assignment by a set time, giving ourselves a treat when we get an A on an exam, or congratulating ourselves internally on a job well done. Since social learning theory recognises self-reinforcement, it gives more credit for control over our own behaviour than reinforcement theory (Engardio 1994; Shoebridge, 2003).

Using social learning theory

Though social learning theory has much research support, studies have only started to explore organisation implications (Davis & Luthans 1980; Evans 1986). The theory has two major managerial implications beyond other motivational theories. First, giving positive models helps accelerate learning appropriate behaviours, especially with opportunities to try new behaviours in a supportive setting and get feedback (Labate 1993). Modelling can thus be very useful in

FIGURE 11.9 The modelling process

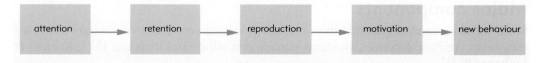

training new workers. Second, vicarious learning shows that employees will draw conclusions about prospects for rewards and punishments, both from their own experiences and that of others (Betts 1992).

As the theories suggest, to promote high motivation, managers should reward members based on performance levels, so high performers get more than low performers (other things being equal) (Lawler 1981; *Newsweek* 1995). Thus social learning theory and other motivational theories raised in this chapter help influence organisational behaviours (Jacob 1995; Norman 1994; Tully 1994). They are critical in effective leadership, to which we turn in the next chapter.

GAINING THE EDGE ... AND LOSING IT!

Small is beautiful

When model-turned-entrepreneur Nanz Chong-Komo established a string of stores known as One.99 shops in Singapore, she revolutionised the highly cut-throat retail world in that affluent society. One.99 shops are discount stores with all kinds of goods targeted at impulse buyers: Japanese confectionery and titbits, stationery, bags, fashion accessories, household items, ceramic kitchenware and knick-knacks. The products, marketed at very low margins, emphasise quality, fun and functionality. Her stores carried more than 3000 product lines, half of them imported from Japan and the rest from Thailand, Hong Kong, Taiwan and China.

Chong-Komo was born in Hong Kong. Her father sewed clothes for a garment factory, while her mother wove wigs in their tiny flat. When she was nine, Chong-Komo's family migrated to Singapore to operate a jewellery business. At seventeen, she began studying for a business diploma at a commerce polytechnic, but her family's financial problems forced her to quit when she was halfway through the course. Then in 1986 a grooming course led her to a modelling agency, and unexpectedly launched her on an international modelling career.

A year later, she jetted off to Hong Kong where she took third prize in a beauty contest. Movie offers started trickling in. However, Chong-Komo did not want to be a public figure with no private life; she decided to give stardom a miss, and chose instead to become a businesswoman.

In 1993, she realised her dream by opening a small boutique selling women's silk work-suits. The business had some success, but Chong-Komo wore herself out trying to be boss, accountant, sales girl and purchasing manager. A year later, she sold the business for A$48 000, pocketed a small profit and

resolved that her next venture would be a whole lot bigger. While looking around for that next venture, Chong-Komo recalled her years of shopping on modelling assignments around the world. A self-proclaimed 'shopaholic', she noticed that clothes, shoes and snack items tended to cost more in Singapore than anywhere else. She also observed the popularity of the one-price stores that were sprouting all over the world. So in 1997 Chong-Komo set up her own chain of discount stores, named them One.99 shops, and invested A$300 000 of the savings she had accumulated from 10 years of modelling. She imported, stored and marketed all the products herself to 'chop out the middleman'.

In one of her numerous interviews with Singapore's daily newspaper, the *Straits Times*, Chong-Komo stressed that the focus of her stores is not on the selling price, but on value; she believed that 'smart shoppers can recognise immediately when something is of value'. In another interview with the magazine *Asian Business* she said, 'if you open a boutique, which I had before in 1993, you have a nice, little boutique… But how do you make an impact in the retail scene and bring a totally different shopping experience? I noticed that in Singapore things are pretty expensive. If they are low priced, the quality is not very good, or perhaps the service is poor. So I wanted to contradict all these things. Sell at a low price, offer good quality and good service, all in an upmarket shopping centre ambience.'

In just four years, Chong-Komo had launched and expanded her One.99 Shop chain, where everything was priced at S$1.99 (A$1.90). Her business, which at the time had 13 stores, grew from A$3.5 million in its first year to A$13 million in its third.

Chong-Komo faced great difficulties in getting the concept off the ground. Landlords of shopping centres were dubious about the viability of her business, and were reluctant to lease her space. Eventually they were won over by her persuasion, and were impressed by some samples of her wares.

A former model with no formal training in business, Chong-Komo credited her success to common sense and the lessons she learned from her parents' retail experience. In 2000, she was named Woman Entrepreneur of the Year by Singapore's Association of Small and Medium Enterprises (ASME).

In 2002, Chong-Komo's One.99 Shop had sales of $14 million but lost $700 000. Debts were also accrued to the value of $3 million which eventually put the firm in receivership. In 2003 Chong-Komo proclaimed bankrupcy and her business folded.
Source: Contributed by Stephen Choo (further details of sources are listed on p. 737).

Websites:

www.sbdc.com.au/ (Small Business and Development Corporation)

This website provides resources that assist micro firms and small firms in Western Australia. It has a link Women in Business that provides useful information devoted to women entrepreneurs.

www.csulb.edu/~sbsluss/Women_and_Business.html (Association of College and Research Libraries Women's Studies Section) This site provides a selective, annotated list of links to Internet resources on women and business.

Activities for discussion, analysis and further research

1. Women are increasingly leaving corporate careers and starting their own businesses. Identify the motivations and challenges facing women who become their own boss. You can begin this exercise by looking at the above websites. Be complete in your answer.
2. Using the findings from question 1, identify the motivations and challenges that relate to Nanz Chong-Komo.
3. What lessons could we draw from Nanz Chong-Komo in encouraging women and men to strike out on their own? Be complete in your answer.
4. Research the web to find out more about Nanz Chong-Komo and the conditions that led to the demise of her business. Could these conditions have been foreseen and avoided? How would you have done things differently?

REFLECTIVE PRACTITIONER

When a staff member leaves or when they are terminated I have almost always seen it as a failure on my part, in that I have not selected correctly or not managed properly. Consequently, I suspect that my management style is quite lenient or quite tolerant of people's lack of performance in that if they leave then it's a failure on my part in the selection process. So I find I tolerate lack of performance in some ways because of that intrinsic link which says that it was my decision and my selection. I have become better in distancing myself from that, in that when you look at the books or the performance in terms of real tangibles, it is easier to make a decision that is more detached. The business plan and the business structure have been great for that because it is black and white, as opposed to thoughts of giving someone a go. I want to give people the opportunity—for me having an opportunity is a real motivator. I thrive and am motivated on opportunities. So, therefore, I tend to think that it will be a motivator to someone else also. I want my staff to think: 'Wow, there are really so many opportunities in this company'. But I don't think everybody realises how much effort it takes to cultivate and turn that opportunity into reality. One of my senior staff said to me recently that I make it look easy and this sometimes may mislead people on their assessment of how much work is actually involved.

I really get a lot of motivation out of finding an opportunity and doing something different that others haven't done. I get great pleasure and reward when opportunities are cultivated. I am an opportunist and nothing frustrates me more than having wasted opportunities. When things are just within reach and you let them go for whatever reason, that really frustrates me. I think that is a sign of lack of discipline.

KIMBERLEY TURNER

Recognition for that of type of work is a good motivator. It's not so much the driving force as much as it's a validation that spurs me on even more. It makes me want to do more and go further. Money isn't a big motivator. The earning capacity of the company is just another opportunity and a means to an end as opposed to an end of itself.

During one of our reviews of the company, we compared ourselves to another consulting business in a similar area whose annual turnover is approximately twice ours. It was easy to see that many of the decisions they had made in terms of staff composition, structure, and activities they undertake were directly linked to financial gain. In contrast, the decisions that we have made within our organisation are more about providing a solid foundation for expertise, a platform to be leaders in the industry, and providing the opportunities to do the type of work we want to be involved in. The whole diversification of our business outside the aviation industry is born out of the motivation to lift up what we have done in aviation and put it into practice in another industry. One of the rewards is the challenge and the results it would bring. This would stretch us by doing something that is way out of our comfort zone. That sort of thing motivates me personally, therefore I know it will motivate us as a company, and that's how I run the business.

I like to think that the things which motivate me will also motivate my staff. I know it hits the mark with a core group of them. Others are motivated through other means. I have tried to get the balance between physical and tangible rewards such as profit share, bonuses, time in lieu, holidays, all the way through growth and expansion, promotion, other opportunities. Some of the staff are motivated purely through the opportunity of working with an airline to design their safety management system because that is all they have ever wanted to do. I can utilise the type of work that we are getting in as a motivating factor for staff. I try hard to find the balance but some people easily lose sight of what they have received. It seems to be difficult to keep the physical rewards at the forefront of people's thinking. After these have been given and have been used, it's in the past and doesn't exist. I find I need to communicate more effectively to staff the total picture of what they have received such as bonuses, sponsorship to conferences, or professional development. It needs to be reiterated as a total package as part of the performance review to be made clearer as a reward process.

FOCUS ON PRACTICE

Strategies for improving

1. Performance will improve when you treat employees with confidence and let them know that you expect successful performance from them.
2. Develop ways to ensure you have the authority to reward employees in the way most likely to gain their commitment to the task.
3. Make sure individuals are aware of the exact value of outcomes required and their priority to the organisation.
4. Give examples of, and contrast, a positive and negative reinforcer for a particular behaviour.

Source: Jones et al. (2000).

SUMMARY

MAX YOUR MARKS!
Thirty interactive questions on *Motivation* are available now at the Online Learning Centre that accompanies this text:
www.mhhe.com/au/bartol4e
(For access to MaxMark please refer to the front of this text.)

- Motivation energises behaviour, directs behaviour, and underlies the tendency to persist. Actual performance comes from ability and working conditions, as well as motivation. Efforts to understand the motivational process have centred on several major elements: needs, cognitive activities, and reward and reinforcement issues.

- Need theories argue that we behave as we do due to internal needs we work to fulfil. These are content theories as they focus on what motivates others. For example, Maslow argues that our needs form a five-level hierarchy, from physiological to self-actualisation needs. Herzberg's two-factor theory contends that hygiene factors keep workers from dissatisfaction, but only motivators lead to feelings of satisfaction and motivation. ERG theory updates Maslow's approach by suggesting three need levels and including a frustration-regression principle and satisfaction-progression explanation of movement among need levels. While hierarchy of needs and ERG theories see some needs as inherent, McClelland's acquired-needs theory argues that needs are acquired or learned from life experiences. His work focused on needs for achievement, affiliation and power, as well as on how they impact managerial success.

- Cognitive theories, or process theories, isolate thinking patterns used in deciding to behave in a particular way. Expectancy theory argues that, in deciding how much effort to use, we consider three issues: effort-performance expectancy (probability our efforts will lead to performance-levels required), performance-outcome expectancy (probability successful performance leads to certain outcomes) and valence (anticipated value of various outcomes or rewards). Equity theory indicates we prefer situations of balance, or equity, which occurs when we see the ratio of our inputs and outcomes is equal to the ratio of inputs and outcomes of a comparison other (or others). Goal-setting theory highlights the importance of goal commitment, specific and challenging goals, and feedback. Goal setting directs attention and action, mobilises effort, raises persistence, and encourages development of strategies to achieve goals.

- Reinforcement theory argues that our behaviour can be explained by environmental consequences. The four major reinforcement types are positive and negative reinforcement, extinction and punishment. Schedules of reinforcement specify the basis for, and timing of, positive rewards. Rewards include fixed-interval, fixed-ratio, variable-interval, and variable-ratio schedules. Social learning theory argues that learning occurs through continuous interaction of behaviours, personal factors and environmental forces. Three cognitively related processes are very important: symbolic processes, vicarious learning and self-control.

QUESTIONS FOR DISCUSSION AND REVIEW

1. Briefly describe the concept of motivation and explain the motivation process. Describe a situation illustrating the idea that performance is a function of ability and working conditions, as well as motivation.

2. Explain the hierarchy-of-needs theory. Assume you are manager of a large fast-food outlet. How could this theory help you motivate various individuals who work for you?

3. Outline the hygiene factors and motivators identified by Herzberg. Why might managers find this theory appealing and useful?

4. Identify the major differences between ERG and hierarchy-of-needs theories. Suppose you are the new manager of a work unit. How could ERG theory assist you assess how to motivate members of your new unit?

5. Describe the acquired-needs theory of motivation. According to McClelland's work on need for achievement, what are some problems in motivating high-nAch individuals? How could you encourage need for achievement in others? How might you encourage need for institutional power?

6. Outline the expectancy theory of motivation. Suppose you are in charge of a group of engineers responsible for completion of various projects. How would you use expectancy theory to motivate them to perform at a high level?

7. Explain equity theory. In part, equity theory argues that our judgments of equity (or inequity) are based on our own perceptions of situations. What difficulties does the perceptual aspect of equity judgments present for managers?

8. Explain four main reinforcement types. For each, identify a situation where you have seen it used and assess the outcome.

9. Contrast four major types of partial reinforcement schedules. Provide an example of each type from your own experience.

10. Explain the social learning theory of motivation. Describe an instance where you obtained important information through vicarious learning. Also describe a situation in which you learned through modelling. To what extent can you identify the modelling process steps in your own situation?

CRITICAL THINKING QUESTIONS

To answer some of these questions you will need to do further research. Useful references are given below each section of the questions.

This chapter of the textbook reviewed the key theories of workplace motivation. An important focus in this task was the emphasis placed on the fact that it is worker motivation which truly creates the energy of an organisation. The challenge for managers is to be able to balance the focus on individual needs with the ability to provide the appropriate reinforcements and rewards available within the organisation. These themes are now developed to examine some of the current issues in motivation

Tora (2002, p. 3) states that employers are trying to find out what 'lights your fire'. And while the word 'motivation' has been around for decades, what she is talking about is 'passion'.

1. Why the change in terminology?

2. Why are organisations encouraging employees not just to be motivated, but also to be passionate?

3. What sort of initiatives would you expect to find in an organisation concerned with promoting 'passion' amongst their employees?

(Material relevant to these questions may be found in Tora, I. 2002, The driving force, *Sydney Morning Herald*, 22 May, p. 3.)

Tora identified workplace surveys as a tool for finding out what really engages and motivates employees.

4. Why are surveys seen as a much more useful tool than other, more traditional methods such as monitoring employee complaints?

5. What is the aim of workplace surveys and what sorts of questions can they realistically deal with that impact on employee motivation?

6. Despite the positive aspects discussed above, there are some dangers in the survey methodology. What are they?

(Material relevant to these questions may be found in Hunter Valley Research Foundation 2001, Beyond the 'squeaky wheel', *Newcastle Herald*, 29 May, p. 38.)

A key focus of this attention to motivation is encouraging staff retention and attracting employees to an organisation. A 2001 survey of 400 Australian CEOs and managing directors by Deloitte Touche Tohmatsu found that employee share or option plans were crucial in Hi-tech companies for attracting and retaining skilled staff. These plans have been widely utilised in Australia in Hi-tech companies to overcome the exodus of local IT professionals to the US or Europe. Respondents to the survey rated the need to attract skilled staff ahead of other concerns such as capital raising, increased competition and new product development. Overall, the Deloitte survey results suggest that share option strategies are critical to employee motivation and trends suggest that 90 per cent of growing technology companies prefer to offer employees share or option plans.

7. Others, however, suggest there may be other motivators which are more popular. What sort of factors might be valued more by Hi-tech workers in particular?

8. Why do you think there may be these national differences between Australia, Europe and the United States?

(Material relevant to these questions may be found in Chapman, S. 2001, Survey shows shares a tool to attract staff, *IDG Data*, 2 July.)

Dwan (2003) provides a brief review of what de-motivates us at work. Using the analogy 'the straw that broke the camel's back' and 'simply the last straw', she concisely conjures up how one small thing can, without warning, topple all that has gone before and produce quite unexpected consequences.

9. With this analogy in mind, what are some of the key de-motivators for managers?

10. What might help keep those straws off the camel's back?

Overall, the issue of motivation always returns to the fact that motivation is personal and internal, arising from within each individual. There are, however, external factors such as working conditions, organisational culture and work norms which are clearly identifiable. An important aspect of the manager's job is to identify the organisational factors which crush the motivation levels of their workgroup—and then to work out how these can be eliminated or minimised.

(Material relevant to these questions may be found in Dwan, S. 2003, Memo to managers: The straw that can break the employee's back, *New Zealand Business*, September, p. 44.)

MANAGEMENT EXERCISES

Exercise 1 Skill building: Learning about reinforcement schedules
Positive reinforcement is particularly significant to both manager and employee. Understanding reinforcement schedules will help selecting correct types to use at particular times. In the table opposite match the type of partial reinforcement schedule with the examples indicated by placing the first letters of titles in the blanks.

Exercise 2 Management exercise: Marketer or entrepreneur
Lee Brown has been a market planning specialist for the Sweet Tooth Company for the last two years. This is her first job following graduation from university, and she is pleased with her progress in the company. She has been given three merit pay rises and expects to be promoted soon to the position of senior market planning specialist. She enjoys her work, and her immediate boss is one of the finest market planners she could ever hope to work with. Her boss gives her autonomy, support and resources when she needs them. Similarly, he seems to know when she needs help and gives it to her in a way which brings out the best in her. Lee frequently wonders how anyone could be happier than she is with her job and company.

Last week she met Jamie Wilson, a former schoolmate, at the local shopping centre. Lee recalled that Jamie, an excellent student who majored in human resource management, had accepted a position as a compensation analyst with a local health-care company. While catching up on their lives over the last two years, Jamie said she had a business proposition she had been considering for some

Learning about reinforcement schedules

Fixed interval	Fixed ratio
Variable interval	Variable ratio

1. _____ Monthly pay cheque

2. _____ Jackpot on a poker machine

3. _____ A free trip for two after making sales of $300 000 in a year

4. _____ The general manager visits the plant on average every two months to let everyone know their efforts are appreciated

5. _____ Lottery

6. _____ Certificate and pin for 25 years of service

7. _____ Monthly attendance award

8. _____ Sports tickets given to employees—usually once or twice a year depending on availability

9. _____ Restaurant waiter/waitress receives an award for serving the chain's half millionth customer

10. _____ Refreshment break every morning and afternoon

11. _____ Boss brings in snacks about every two or three weeks to treat everyone in the work unit

12. _____ $10 each for the first 100, $12 each for the next 30, $15 each for the next 30, and $19 each for all others produced during a work shift

time but did not believe she could pursue alone. She needed a partner and suggested Lee could be that person.

Her proposition was that child-care centres were desperately needed in their area. The city of about 35 000 people had only one small child-care facility, which had a very long waiting list and very high rates. Jamie's research had revealed that three different churches in the area would gladly support additional child-care centres by furnishing their facilities, at little or no cost, provided the centres were managed as separate businesses. Jamie had located a building which could be developed into an excellent child-care centre. Jamie reasoned she and Lee could start the business in one or more of the churches and expand into the building she had found. Financially, the return from operating one child-care centre would not quite equal Lee's current total compensation. However, two or more centres would yield a very nice income for both partners. Jamie had found appropriate licences could be obtained in a few weeks and the financing required to start the business was available at favourable rates. Other materials and supplies were readily available as well.

Lee was intrigued with this proposition and told Jamie she wanted a week to think it over. She intends to discuss her interest in this proposition with Jamie tomorrow.

Requirement
Using expectancy theory, indicate the factors impacting on Lee's decision and strength of her motivation to participate in the proposed business.

Exercise 3 Case study: Managing a seven-day dairy

You are the owner and manager of a successful seven-day dairy. Your shop is open seven days a week from 7 am until 10 pm. A lot of university students live in the area and the shop is on a busy road with constant road and foot traffic. Your busiest times are from 8 am to 10 am, 12 noon to 1.30 pm, 3 pm to 6 pm, and then from 8.30 pm until you shut at 10 pm. One person can manage the shop by themselves, but there are times when customers have to wait for a while when it is busy.

Your current staff are:

Joan   permanent, works from 8.30 am to 5pm, her hourly rate is $10.80.

Gill   permanent, works from 5 pm to 10 pm Monday to Friday, and from 8.30 am to 5 pm on Saturday and Sunday, hourly rate is $12.80 because of the unsocial hours.

You also employ four part-time students who fill in the other hours and work when it is busy. Students are paid $9.35 hour and $10.20 for unsocial hours.

   Your weekly net return varies between $1700 and $2400 (depending upon the time of year and whether or not students are about). Your rent and outgoings are low at $200 per week, as you live in the same building as the shop.

The situation

You are exhausted because of the extra hours that you are working to help out at the busy times. Attention to the management basics has been slipping and sometimes items are out of stock because you haven't had time to regularly go to the wholesalers and purchase them. The other worrying thing is that university exams are coming up soon and two of the students who work part-time have already asked you if they can reduce their hours of work over the exam period. You are not happy about this, as the exam period is busy with increased sales of snack food, cigarettes and other convenience items!

   At the moment, three of your part-timers (Janet, Troy and Elsie) are consistently arriving at work late. None of them have offered any reason for being late and it is causing a problem because the permanent staff members have to stay longer at work to provide cover. The late-comers say they like their job and are happy with their hours of work, and you don't want to dock their wages because you are afraid that they might leave. You have been doing some reading about organisational behaviour and you think that a behaviour modification programme would be the most effective solution.

Questions

1. What management problems are occurring here?
2. What motivation theories might be used to understand the problem of lateness at work?
3. Outline a behaviour modification scheme to encourage attendance at work. Be sure to identify a specific behaviour, an appropriate reinforcement and a reinforcement schedule.

Performance bonus systems: How well do they relate?

Otago Steel Foundry Ltd, a company located in Dunedin in the South Island of New Zealand, has taken a strategic decision to introduce a bonus incentive scheme for the manufacture of a high-quality, high-value product. However, negotiations between management and the New Zealand Engineering, Printing and Manufacturing Union (Engineers' Union) have been prolonged and acrimonious, and are now at an impasse.

Company background

The company in its present form arose out of a merger some six years ago between two smaller companies operating in different markets, essentially dictated by product size. Corstorphine Steel Foundry Ltd produced castings at the bottom end of the weight range, from a few pounds weight to about two tonnes, while Waverly Steel Foundry Ltd focused on the larger size of casting, from one tonne to about twenty tonnes. Typical products are, respectively, rollers for conveyor belts and generators used in the electricity supply industry. Both Corstorphine and Waverly continued manufacturing their own products after the merger. The Otago board of directors located the head office at the Corstorphine works, and promoted its general manager to chief executive of the new company. It also filled other key managerial positions in Waverly from the ranks of its sister operation. Waverly staff saw the tie-up as a take-over of their company, and not a joining of two equal partners.

No redundancies resulted from the merger, even although both markets have experienced some recession. On the other hand a lucrative opportunity has emerged for Waverly in the shape of high-quality fabricated castings.

However, differences in culture, as well as product type, also separated the two companies, in that Waverly's management ran a family-style of operation, whereas Corstorphine executives were in constant conflict with the unions. Their production employees had operated under bonus-incentive conditions for many years, both prior to and since the merger. The Engineers' Union represented the majority of production employees in both works. White-collar staff in both plants are not paid bonuses.

Over the past six years senior management have introduced incentive schemes into all production areas in Waverly, despite much strife. Management frequently pointed out that productivity had increased by 110 per cent, wages had risen by 30 per cent, and no one lost their job, as a result of the changed working practices. While the production employees reluctantly accepted the changes, it was against the advice and wishes of the union delegates, most of whom are skilled craftsmen.

The welding shops

Because of production-process defects, all castings require rectification, achieved through repair welding. The weld is polished by a grinder operator to flush with the rest of the casting.

All repair welders, in common with the other production operators, are paid a basic rate per hour. This excludes bonus payments, and cannot be lowered under the existing collective contract. The top-paid production operators in Otago, in terms of basic rates but not total pay, are the moulders, followed by the furnacemen, and then the repair welders.

A bonus supplements the basic rate, based on the application of an incentive system, known as the 75/100 Straight Proportional Incentive Scheme, in which earnings are directly proportional to results achieved, subject to meeting a bonus starting performance of above 75. (Up to 75 performance, only basic rate is paid). That is, a proportionate increase in performance gives an equal proportionate increase in pay. Table 11.1 below gives more details of the relationship between pay and performance. For the purpose of budgeting and costing of its products, Otago aims that its workforce achieves at least Standard Performance, designated as 100. This rewards the worker with a third bonus (33.33

POWERWEB

International articles related to this topic are available at the Online Learning Centre at **www.mhhe.com/au/bartol4e**

per cent). There is no ceiling limit on the bonus earning potential of employees.

Standard Performance is that level of performance that a qualified worker, suitably trained, following the method and quality specification for the job, taking the appropriate rest, and motivated by an incentive, would achieve over a working shift of eight hours without over-exertion. Personnel department staff, usually ex-craftsmen specially trained in work measurement techniques, determine the time required to work on particular jobs for the achievement of Standard Performance. This 'standard time' includes an allowance for rest and relaxation. From an analysis of the welders' recorded times spent on jobs compared to the work measured times, the personnel department calculates actual performance, which determines pay as shown in Table 11.1.

All existing incentive schemes operate on a small-group basis. Earnings are pooled, with each group member (e.g. welders) receiving an equal money share, irrespective of their own individual performance.

Fabrication welding

In response to a new demand for fabricated products, which are complex shapes and cannot satisfactorily be directly cast but can only be produced by welding castings together, Otago management recently introduced fabrication welding at its Waverly plant. It is a much more intricate skill than repair welding, and requires a very high standard of work.

The company initially selected Waverly repair welders for fabrication duties on the basis of welding tests, resulting in a 60 per cent rejection rate. Those passing the test underwent a 10-week intensive training program, being tested a further three times. This resulted in another 15 per cent failing to satisfy the skill requirements, meaning that only 25 per cent of the original repair crew qualified as fabrication welders.

TABLE 11.1 75/100 STRAIGHT PROPORTIONAL INCENTIVE SCHEME—REPAIR WELDERS

Performance	Total pay as a percentage of basic rate	Repair welders—total pay per hour $
0	100.00 %	15
20	100.00 %	15
50	100.00 %	15
60	100.00 %	15
75	100.00 %	15
80	106.66 %	16
90	120.00 %	18
100	133.33 %	20
110	146.66 %	22
120	160.00 %	24
130	173.33 %	26
150	200.00 %	30

Notes:
(1) In the middle column, basic rate equals 100%, and total pay (including bonus), is expressed as a percentage of it. Bonus payment commences above 75 performance, where the relationship between total pay and performance is calculated by the formula:
Total pay = 1.33 x Performance
For example, a performance of 90 gives total pay of 120%, which comprises 20% bonus and basic rate (100%).
(2) The right-hand column shows the actual total pay per hour in dollars, and includes bonus. Welders' basic rate is $15 per hour. Only the best repair welders achieve performances of 120 and above. Over the past five years the actual average performance achieved by Waverly repair welders was just over 100, which is about 5 per cent lower than the average for Corstorphine.

Late last year Otago provisionally agreed with the Engineers' Union that fabrication welding would carry a temporary fixed-rate pay rate of $20 per hour, irrespective of output, pending work measurement times becoming available for use in the introduction of a 50/100 Geared Incentive Scheme. In this arrangement, earnings are not directly related to results achieved. That is, a proportionate increase in performance gives less than a proportionate increase in pay, subject to a bonus starting performance of above 50 (up to 50 performance only basic rate is paid). Standard Performance (100) gives a third (33.33 per cent) increase in pay. There is no ceiling limit on the bonus earnings potential of employees. Table 11.2 below shows more details about the relationship between performance and pay.

Personnel department carried out fabrication welding time-studies over a period of two months, at the end of which they produced time standards for fabrication welding. Management then announced it wanted to introduce the 50/100 Geared Incentive

Scheme immediately, and that each fabrication welder would earn his own bonus based on performance, that is, dispensing with the small-group arrangement. (All production employees are male in both works.)

There is a good export market for fabrication castings, and an excellent profit possible, provided the rejection rate holds below 2 per cent and the welders achieve at least Standard Performance. Castings will be quality tested in the foundry at various production stages, and also by the customers at their own plants, mainly overseas. Otago Steel itself will meet the cost of fixing returned products: management intend that the fabrication welders would be paid only the basic rate for working on rejected castings.

Management also believed that the performance of 80 recorded during the derivation of time standards by the personnel department, and retrospectively calculated by them, arose because the welders received a temporary fixed rate of $20 per hour, irrespective of actual production achieved.

TABLE 11.2 50/100 GEARED INCENTIVE SCHEME—FABRICATION WELDERS

Performance	Total pay as a percentage of basic rate	Repair welders— total pay per hour $
0	100.00 %	15
20	100.00 %	15
50	100.00 %	15
60	106.66 %	16
75	116.66 %	17.50
80	120.00 %	18
90	126.66 %	19
100	133.33 %	20
110	140.00 %	21
120	146.66 %	22
130	153.33 %	23
150	166.66 %	25

Notes:
(1) In the middle column, basic rate equals 100%, and total pay (including bonus) is expressed as a percentage of it. Bonus payment commences above 50 performance, where the relationship between total pay and performance is calculated by the formula:
Total pay = 0.66 x Performance + 66.66
For example, a performance of 90 gives a total pay of 126.66%, which comprises 26.66% bonus and basic rate (100%).
(2) The right-hand column shows the actual total pay per hour in dollars, and includes bonus. Welders' basic rate is $15 per hour.
(3) Only the best fabrication welders will achieve a performance of 120 and above.

Personnel department stood by the fairness of its work-measured times. Not surprisingly the welders dismissed both of these assertions, and on the contrary claimed that the bonus times were impossible to achieve, and thus they couldn't attain a decent bonus.

There is strong support among the workforce for the Union, perhaps surprising given the success of the *Employment Contracts Act 1991* in reducing union power in New Zealand. The Engineers' Union proved an able negotiator in the past, particularly in the Waverly plant.

Fabrication welders told their union officials they were rejecting the fabrication welding incentive scheme, and instead wanted a fixed rate of $25 per hour. They further commented that all incentive schemes in both works should operate on an individual basis. There is a great demand for their high-quality welding skills in the North Island and Australia. District basic rates for repair welders varied between $12 and $19 per hour.

Unexpectedly, the personnel director informed the Engineers' Union yesterday that he was giving the fabrication welders four weeks' notice of termination of their temporary fixed rate of $20 per hour: they would revert to their basic rate of $15 and not get bonuses until the incentive scheme was up and running. In an immediate reaction, the Engineers' Union called a mass meeting of workers in both plants, which intimated to management that industrial action would commence in all production areas, unless the welders' demands were met.

Source: Alexander Sibbald.

Activities for discussion, analysis and further research

1. How would you resolve the dispute?
2. What are the main personnel issues in the case?
3. Compare the 50/100 and 75/100 incentive schemes, and make any appropriate comments.

FURTHER READING

Beer, M. and Katz, N. 2003, Do incentives work? The perceptions of a worldwide sample of senior executives, *Human Resource Planning*, 26, 3, pp. 30–45.

Gelfand, M.J. and Dyer, N. 2000, A cultural perspective on negotiation: progress, pitfalls, and prospects, *Applied Psychology*, January, 49, 1, pp. 62–100.

Kanter, R.M. and Dretler, T.D. 1998, 'Global strategy' and its impact on local operations: Lessons from Gillette Singapore, *Academy of Management Executive*, November, 12, 4, pp. 60–9.

King, D. 2002, The extra mile, *New Zealand Management*, February, 49, 1, pp. 11–12.

Whyte, R. 2002, Loyalty marketing and frequent flyer programmes: Attitudes and attributes of corporate travellers, *Journal of Vacation Marketing*, December, 9, 1, pp. 17–35.

CHAPTER 12

LEADERSHIP

LEARNING OBJECTIVES

After studying this chapter, you should be able to:

- Outline the major sources of leader power and explain how leaders can use power to encourage subordinate commitment.
- Describe the current state of efforts to identify leadership traits.
- Explain the different findings of Iowa, Michigan and Ohio State studies of leader behaviours and discuss their implications.
- Describe the Leadership Grid approach to leadership and assess the extent to which females and males behave differently as leaders.
- Delineate Fiedler's contingency theory of leadership.
- Contrast the following situational approaches to leadership: normative leadership model, situational leadership theory and path–goal theory.
- Describe transformational leadership and explain its link to innovation.
- Evaluate the extent to which leaders are needed in organisations.

STRIVING FOR EXCELLENCE

Jamieson's new perspective

Brian Jamieson's Minter Ellison business card describes what he is—and what he is not. After his title, managing partner, is an asterisk. At the bottom of the card, the asterisk is explained: 'Non-Lawyer'. The business card is a neat example of the potential tensions for Jamieson in running the Melbourne office of a national law firm. His credentials as a skilful and highly successful professional-services firm manager are unquestioned, after he played a crucial role in building KPMG Australia. But at KPMG he was merely crossing the line from audit practitioner to manager. At Minters, he is managing 65 Melbourne partners, but he has never stood in their shoes.

If any non-lawyer can make a success of managing lawyers, Jamieson can. But it is a tough role. Jamieson does not pretend that the transition from accounting firm to law firm will be easy, but he says there are a couple of similarities that help. First, he is used to a partnership structure, where the shareholders run the business—something that managers from a more traditional corporate structure often find difficult to cope with. 'I know how to deal with partners', he says. 'There are some that are more high-maintenance than others, and some that you never have to worry about, that just get on with their job.'

The other similarity is that the key commercial imperative in accounting and law firms is effective use of time, or billable hours. 'It's all about utilising your people-capacity. Keeping your work in progress and your debtors under control. Profitability and drawings. So slipping across from accounting to here, all of that is very familiar territory.'

There are differences, however. Jamieson says that, generally speaking, accountants are better at letting go of the management of their firm. 'I could get myself into hot water [but] I've found the lawyers, or some of them, still desirous of wanting to be involved in some decision-making. Here, partners, at the end of the day, have the final say, more so than at the big accounting firms.'

Jamieson is at a loss to explain the difference, but one possibility is that accountants see more than lawyers do of the way the commercial world works. 'It's an interesting question as to whether being involved in business decision-making at board and management levels in organisations, that accountants see that and understand it and therefore accept it more in their own partnership.'

Another difference that has struck Jamieson in his first six months at Minters is that client conflicts are a bigger problem for law firms than for accounting firms. Although both types of firms are unlikely to act for two big competitors in the same industry, Jamieson says law firms really have to be careful about who they act for in potentially litigious matters. 'You have to really look ahead as to what the implications of taking on a client might be, because you don't know who else is going to be dragged into it [the litigation] and one of those might be your client as well.'

Part of Jamieson's new role is to develop a thought-leadership role for Minters. He has also prepared a blueprint for developing the firm, which includes creating an office-wide structure in

continued

STRIVING FOR EXCELLENCE *continued*

Melbourne for business development. Instead of having five or six separate practice groups all doing their own thing, Jamieson will bring it all together, with shared databases and marketing initiatives, such as boardroom lunches for chief executives.

At 59, Jamieson could be leading a much quieter life. He says KPMG was keen for him to stay on as chairman of the Victorian office, a role he took in December 2000 when he handed over the chief executive reins to Lindsay Maxsted. As chairman, Jamieson had no direct client work or management responsibilities; his main tasks were promoting KPMG, looking after client issues and mentoring young partners.

When Minters first sounded him out about the Melbourne managing partner role, in April 2001, he was not interested. It was too soon after his chief executive position finished, and he was thinking about pursuing a career as a professional director. Seven months later, Minters asked him again. By then, directorships had lost their appeal and Jamieson realised that he missed having a management role. He also liked the feel of Minters. 'In any partnership, you can't have everyone being best mates, but they do seem to get on well together. There's a good bond.'

Source: Schmidt, L. (2003).

---

leadership

Process of influencing others to achieve organisational goals

In this chapter, we explore methods leaders have to influence others. We consider the possibility leaders have common traits, and review attempts to identify universal leader behaviours to be used in any situation. We then probe efforts to develop situational approaches helping leaders decide when certain types of behaviour are applicable. Next, we examine transformational leadership and its link to innovation. Finally, we consider the question of whether and under what circumstances leaders are needed.

HOW LEADERS INFLUENCE OTHERS

power

Capacity to affect the behaviour of others

Why do people accept a leader's influence? Often they do so because the leaders have power. Yet as Katharine Graham notes, 'Nobody ever has as much power as you think they do' (*Forbes* 1987). In this section, we examine major power sources and ways leaders can effectively use available power.

legitimate power

Power stemming from a position's placement in the managerial hierarchy and the authority vested in the position

Sources of leader power

Power is the capacity to affect others' behaviour (Mintzberg 1983; Pfeiffer 1981). Organisation leaders can rely on some or all six major power types (French & Raven 1959; Raven 1993).

Legitimate power comes from a position's place in the managerial hierarchy and authority vested in the position. When accepting a job, we know we will be directed in our work by an immediate boss and others in the hierarchy. Normally, we accept these directions as legitimate as these people hold positions of authority.

reward power

Power based on the capacity to control and provide valued rewards to others

Reward power is based on the ability to control and provide valued rewards to others (Fierman 1995). Most organisations offer rewards under a manager's control, including pay rises, bonuses, interesting projects, promotion recommendations, a better office, training support, high visibility organisational assignments, recognition, positive feedback and time off.

coercive power

Power depending on the ability to punish others when they do not engage in desired behaviours

Coercive power depends on the ability to punish others if they do not display desired behaviours. Forms of coercion or punishment available to a manager include criticism, reprimands, suspension, warning letters for a personnel file, negative performance appraisals, demotions, withheld pay raises, and terminations.

expert power

Power based on possession of expertise valued by others

Expert power is based on possession of expertise valued by others (Lopez 1994; *HR Magazine* 1994; Pottinger 1994). Managers often have knowledge, technical skills and experience crucial to subordinate success.

Information power comes from access to and control over distribution of information about organisational operations and future plans (Raven & Kruglanski 1970; Grove 1993). Managers usually have more information than subordinates and can decide how much is given to them.

Referent power comes from being admired, personally identified with, or liked by others (Fierman 1995; Bird 1994). When we admire people, want to be like them, or feel friendship toward them, we follow their directions more willingly and are loyal to them.

Effective use of leader power

Although all power types are influential, they lead to different subordinate motivation levels (Yukl 1994; Phillips-Carson, Carson & Roe 1993). Subordinates may react with commitment, compliance or resistance. With commitment, employees are enthusiastic, working hard toward organisational goals. With compliance, employees make minimal effort for average, not outstanding, performance. With resistance, employees seem to comply but do the absolute minimum, possibly even sabotaging organisational goal attainment.

The relationship between a leader's use of different power sources and likely subordinate reactions is shown in Table 12.1. As the table shows, expert and referent power generally lead to subordinate commitment, while legitimate, information, and reward power lead to compliance. Subordinate resistance often results from use of coercive power (Norman 1988; Jackson 1990; Washington 2003). Not surprisingly, effective leaders use little coercive power (Rose 1993).

Empowerment

Many managers integrate an important aspect of power use into their leadership styles: empowering their subordinates. In this subordinates assume some leadership responsibility and authority, including the right to enforce quality standards, check their own work and schedule activities. Empowered subordinates are given the power to make decisions which leaders or supervisors did before.

Empowerment supports leadership in several ways:

* Managerial ability to get things done with support and help from subordinates with special work knowledge is increased.
* Worker involvement, motivation and commitment, and working toward organisational goals are increased.
* Opportunity for managers to concentrate on significant issues is increased and less time is spent on daily supervision (Jones & Hill 1999).

Effective managers see significant benefits from empowerment; ineffective managers try to control decision making and force subordinate agreement. The leadership style of empowering managers develops good decision-making ability in subordinates, as well as guiding, coaching and inspiring them (Burton 1995; Nakarmi 1995; Bateman & Snell 2004).

Effective managers usually use different power types (Rapaport 1993). While power helps explain issues behind leader influence, we must look at other concepts, such as leadership traits and behaviours, to understand leaders' organisational influence.

information power

Power resulting from access to and control over the distribution of important information about organisational operations and future plans

referent power

Power resulting from being admired, personally identified with, or liked by others

TABLE 12.1 MAJOR SOURCES OF LEADER POWER AND LIKELY SUBORDINATE REACTIONS

	Resistance	Compliance	Commitment
Power source	Coercion	Legitimate	Referent
		Information	Expert
		Reward	

SEARCHING FOR LEADERSHIP TRAITS

After discussing effective leadership, army psychologists sought methods of officer selection during World War I and set the stage for postwar research (Stogdill 1948). Early researchers worked to identify traits differentiating effective leaders from non-leaders (Jago 1982). **Traits** are a person's internal qualities or characteristics, such as physical (e.g. height, weight, appearance, energy), personality (e.g. dominance, extroversion, originality), skills and abilities (e.g. intelligence, knowledge, technical competence) and social factors (e.g. interpersonal skills, sociability and socioeconomic position).

Early researchers measured various people's traits, then set up leaderless groups (without formal leaders) to see if some traits would predict who would be seen as leaders. Researchers abandoned the trait approach in the 1950s when no traits separated leaders from non-leaders consistently (Stogdill 1948; Mann 1959).

There are suggestions the trait approach may have been abandoned too soon. Sophisticated statistical methods now allow improved result-assessment across studies. Some traits originally studied are characteristic of those identified as leaders—specifically, intelligence, dominance, aggressiveness and decisiveness (Lord, De Vader & Alliger 1986).

Future research may find some traits predict leaders, at least sometimes. For example, a study at AT&T found oral communication and human relations skills, advancement need or motive, resistance to stress, uncertainty tolerance, energy and creativity predicted managerial advancement (Bray, Campbell & Grant 1974). However, it is still unclear if a set of traits would predict leadership performance. Many think performance is more the things leaders do than their traits. So, recent leadership research has looked at their behaviours.

IDENTIFYING LEADER BEHAVIOURS

Several researchers focused on finding the specific behaviours making some leaders more effective than others (Richman 1988). Traits may be hard to change but, if universally effective behaviours leading to successful leadership were identified, most people could learn these behaviours. In this section, we review efforts at identifying significant leader behaviours. The research grew from work at the University of Iowa, the University of Michigan and Ohio State University. We also explore whether females and males display different leadership behaviours.

Iowa and Michigan studies

At the University of Iowa, Kurt Lewin and colleagues worked to identify effective leader behaviours (Lewin & Lippitt 1938). They considered three leader behaviours or styles: autocratic, democratic and laissez-faire. **Autocratic** leaders make unilateral decisions, dictate work methods, limit worker knowledge of goals to the next step, and give punitive feedback. In contrast, **democratic** leaders involve the group in decision making, let them decide on work methods, make overall goals known, and use feedback for coaching. **Laissez-faire** leaders generally give the group absolute freedom, give materials needed, participate only to answer questions, and avoid giving feedback—in other words, do little.

To determine the most effective leadership style, Lewin's researchers trained adults in the styles then put them in charge of groups in preadolescent boys' clubs. On every criterion they found groups with laissez-faire leaders performed poorly in comparison to both autocratic and democratic groups. Work quantity was equal in groups with autocratic and democratic leaders, while work quality and group satisfaction was higher in democratic groups. Thus it seemed democratic leadership could lead to both good work quantity and quality, with satisfied workers. Perhaps the key to effective leadership had been found.

Unfortunately, further research gave mixed results. Sometimes democratic leadership resulted in better performance than autocratic but other times performance was poorer than or just equal to the autocratic style. Results on follower satisfaction were consistent. Satisfaction

---

traits

Distinctive internal qualities or characteristics of an individual, such as physical characteristics, personality characteristics, skills and abilities, and social factors

autocratic

Behavioural style of leaders who tend to make unilateral decisions, dictate work methods, limit worker knowledge about goals to just the next step to be performed, and sometimes give feedback that is punitive

democratic

Behavioural style of leaders who tend to involve the group in decision making, let the group determine work methods, make overall goals known, and use feedback as an opportunity for helpful coaching

laissez-faire

Behavioural style of leaders who generally give the group complete freedom, provide necessary materials, participate only to answer questions, and avoid giving feedback

levels were higher with a democratic leadership style than an autocratic one (Bass 1981; Rue & Byars 2003).

These results created a managerial dilemma. While a democratic leadership style meant subordinates were more satisfied, performance was not always better, or even equal to performance under an autocratic leadership style. Many managers were also unused to operating democratically. To help resolve this dilemma, especially in decision making, Robert Tannenbaum and Warren H. Schmidt (1973) developed the leader behaviours continuum in Figure 12.1. The continuum has leadership behaviour variations, ranging from autocratic (boss-centred) on the left to democratic (subordinate-centred) on the right. Moving from the autocratic end is a move toward the democratic end and vice versa. With the continuum, the meaning of 'autocratic' softened. It does not necessarily include punitive tendencies or hiding the task's ultimate goal from subordinates. At the continuum's autocratic end, autocratic means that the boss makes the decision and lets others know what they are to do, not involving them in the decision.

According to Tannenbaum and Schmidt, managers, when deciding on a leader behaviour pattern to adopt, must consider forces within themselves (e.g. comfort level with various options), within subordinates (e.g. readiness to take responsibility), and the situation (e.g. time pressures). Short term, managers must be flexible in their leader behaviour depending on the situation. Long term, managers are advised to try to move to the subordinate-centred continuum end, because such leader behaviour increases employee motivation, decision quality, teamwork, morale and employee development.

Other work at the University of Michigan confirmed the usefulness of the employee-centred approach compared with a more job-centred, or production-centred, approach. In an employee-centred approach, leaders build effective work groups dedicated to high performance goals. With a job-centred approach, leaders divide work into routine tasks and closely supervise workers, seeing that specified methods are followed and productivity standards met. However, output varied: an employee-centred approach might give low output and a job-centred approach high output (Bass 1981; Likert 1961; 1979). Further study was needed.

FIGURE 12.1 Continuum of leader behaviours (Tannenbaum & Schmidt 1973, p. 164)

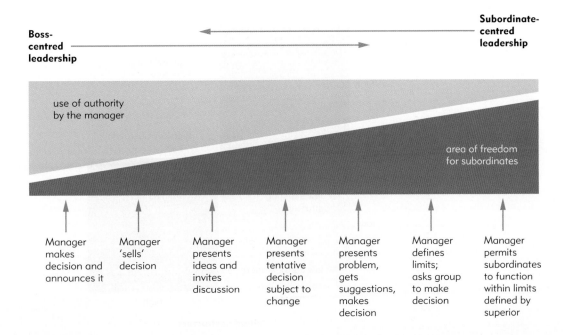

Ohio State studies

A group at Ohio State University had another way to study leadership. First they identified significant leader behaviours. Then they developed a questionnaire to measure different leaders' behaviours and track factors such as group performance and satisfaction to see the most effective behaviours. Several different leader behaviours, or styles, were identified. However, two seemed important: initiating structure and consideration.

Initiating structure is the degree to which a leader defines their own role and those of subordinates in achieving unit goals. It includes basic managerial functions of planning, organising and directing, and focuses mainly on task issues. Initiating structure is similar to the Michigan studies' job-centred leader behaviour, but with a wider range of managerial functions. It emphasises task-related issues (Taylor 1993).

Consideration is how much a leader builds mutual trust with subordinates, respects their ideas and shows concern for their feelings. A consideration-oriented leader will be friendly with subordinates, have good two-way communication, and encourage participative decision making (Gupta 1995; Jacob 1995; *Wall Street Journal* 1994). Consideration parallels the Michigan studies' employee-centred leader behaviour, emphasising people-related issues (King 1995; Kirby 2003).

Departing from both the Iowa and Michigan studies, which saw leadership dimensions falling at opposite ends of a continuum, Ohio State researchers saw initiating structure and consideration as independent (Chester 1979). This meant behaviours occupied separate continuums. A leader could be high on both, low on both, high on one and low on the other, or have gradations of both. The Ohio State two-dimensional approach is shown in Figure 12.2. It is an appealing configuration, as many leaders seem to show both initiating structure and consideration.

The two-dimensional approach led to the idea that a leader could emphasise task issues while producing high subordinate satisfaction levels by showing consideration behaviour simultaneously. Initial studies supported the idea that a leader displaying both high initiating structure and high consideration would be most effective, but the great high-high leader idea was later seen as mythical (Larson, Hunt & Osborn 1976). The high-high approach lost favour

initiating structure

Degree to which a leader defines their own role and the roles of subordinates in terms of achieving unit goals

consideration

Degree to which a leader builds mutual trust with subordinates, respects their ideas and shows concern for their feelings

FIGURE 12.2 Ohio State two-dimensional model of leader behaviours

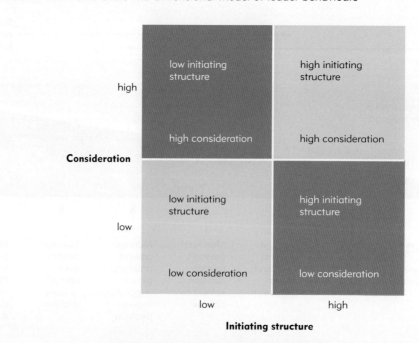

because, like the Iowa and Michigan studies, it was simplistic. Research showed situational elements, such as subordinate expectations and task nature, affected success of leadership behaviours (Kerr, Schriesheim, Murphy & Stogdill 1975; Greene 1979).

CASE IN POINT

Independents' day

It was the basket case of Australian retailing until the South Africans got into the act. Now Metcash's single-minded strategy is paying off. Metcash Trading Ltd chief executive Andrew Reitzer likes to get down and dirty. He likes his managers to do the same. 'I always say to my people, "hold up your hands—is there mud on your hands? If there isn't mud on your hands you are starting to fly a desk and that's not the job".'

Reitzer, 50, has spent the last five years reshaping the group from basket case to, well, basket-full. The $6.7 billion-a-year wholesaler once spurned by the banks, suppliers and customers is a profitable and increasingly powerful force in the Australian supermarket sector, up against the goliaths of Woolworths and Coles.

Luck and persistence have played a part. But its success is also the result of a controversial strategy to unite thousands of independent grocers around the country to get them to act more like a single retail chain: junking 29 different supermarket banners for just two—the Independent Grocers of Australia (IGA) and more recently, FoodWorks.

'Five years ago when we said what we're going to do with brand, market, everyone laughed. They thought, these guys are dreaming. We're now firmly on everyone's radar', says Reitzer.

Just as well for him. The listed Johannesburg-based wholesaler Metro Cash & Carry bought out the near-collapsed David's Holdings business in 1998. But it wanted leaders who were committed.

In a corporate variation on the sixteenth-century Spanish adventurer Hernando Cortes' burning of his ships to prevent retreat, they were told there was no going back if they failed. When the call came, Reitzer had half an hour to consult his family. Within three days he was on a plane to Sydney.

Reitzer had climbed the ranks of Metcash's parent over 20 years. But he wasn't prepared for the mess in front of him. The David's acquisition more than doubled the size of the entire company. Reitzer says he spent the first year gripped by a fear of failure.

'A lot of people have said, "you were so brave and had a lot of vision". I say, "thank you". But it's not the truth. The truth is we were terrified. We didn't realise how difficult it would be. We were more motivated by fear than anything else. My finance director says in those days we used to sleep like a baby—we'd wake every 30 minutes crying.'

Metcash is a highly focused marketing and distribution business that makes its money on high-volume, wafer-thin margins—little more than two cents in every dollar—across three businesses. It wholesales under the IGA banner to 4000 retail outlets around the country, including 1100 franchised supermarkets.

It runs Australian Liquor Marketers, selling to 15 000 customers in Australia and New Zealand, and has another 70 000 customers ranging from sandwich shops to convenience stores through its Campbell's Cash & Carry wholesale outlets.

The company founded by the David family had grown rapidly by acquisition but failed miserably at integrating and streamlining its operations. Before Metcash acquired majority ownership, the corporate

doctors had been called in and started axing thousands of jobs. Reitzer says their medicine only made the company worse.

Reitzer's team swiftly boiled the revival task down to 12 urgent priorities. The most immediate was to reorganise the business from old-fashioned functions to core business lines and drive decision-making back as close to the customer as possible.

Reitzer cleaned out top management and brought in his own team—half of them from South Africa. 'For all the bad things we found', he says, 'the most unbelievable thing was the quality of the people. They were fantastic, really knowledgeable; they understood what they had to do and they were treated despicably. All they needed was a little bit of vision, a bit of direction, and a firm kick in the butt.'

That said, Metcash yields more than double the revenue out of a workforce less than a third its former size—just 4000 staff. In the warehouse, new voice and logistics technology has helped cut costly errors and drive down supply chain costs.

He also argues that leaders have to demonstrate different styles for different times. 'There are times you have to be an absolute democrat and reach a consensus. There are other times when you walk out the door and say, "This is the way it is going to be. I know what I'm doing, follow me".' There are also times for being caring, putting people first, 'but I've yet to meet anyone who doesn't benefit from a firm kick every now and again', says Reitzer.

Source: Hooper, N. (2003).

Activities for discussion, analysis and further research

1. Consider the various theories of leadership you have studied in this chapter. Which theories do you see Reitzer practising?
2. What advice would you give any of his staff who would wish to advance in that organisation?
3. Do a web search on IGA and consider what strategies they have used to try and establish themselves as leaders in the industry.

The Leadership Grid

Blake and McCanse's (1991) Leadership Grid®, emphasises leader behaviours on both task and people issues. Rather than focus on leader behaviours like the Ohio State studies, the grid approach uses parallel leader attitudes—concern for people and concern for production. The grid is shown in Figure 12.3. Depending on concern for people and production levels, a manager can be anywhere on the grid. Blake and McCanse argue the most desirable leadership orientation is 9,9, meaning high concern for both people and production. However, as with the Ohio State studies a 9,9 orientation might not always be best. The grid allows flexible leader behaviours, depending on the assessment of people and production issues.

Managing diversity

Female versus male leader behaviours

Researchers of leadership wondered if female managers behaved as leaders differently to males. Early results showed females as being more focused on interpersonal issues and, therefore, not suitable for leadership positions. Males were seen as more focused on task issues and better candidates for leadership positions (Bass, Krusell & Alexander 1971; Rosen & Jerdee 1978). Both stereotypes are incorrect. Most studies show female and male leaders are similar in the interpersonal and task behaviours shown or that the differences are small. They are just as effective in achieving subordinate job satisfaction and performance (Bartol & Martin 1986; Dobbins & Platz 1986; Powell 1993).

Despite this, few women have top-level positions in major firms (Dunkel 1996). One is Teresa Gattung, chief executive officer of Telecom, New Zealand Ltd, who is one of New Zealand's top business leaders. There have been studies of the 'glass ceiling', which refers to barriers to women's upward organisational mobility. Proposed solutions include workforce diversity programs, expanded traditional executive-recruitment networks, and formal mentoring and career-development programs that prevent channelling women and people from

FIGURE 12.3 The Leadership Grid (reprinted from Blake & McCanse 1991, p. 29)

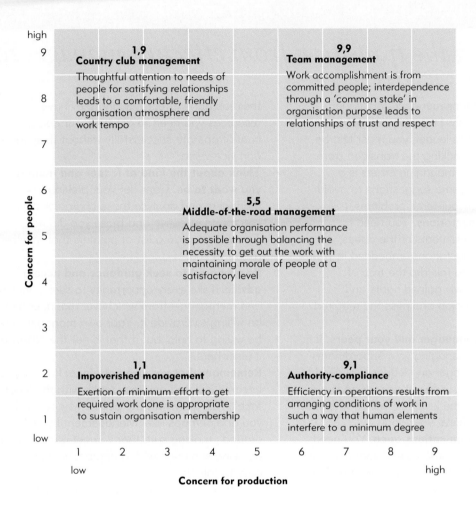

minority groups into positions with low prospects of promotion to executive levels (Redwood 1996; Eagly, Karau & Mukhijani 1995).

Leadership styles across cultures

Leadership styles are shown to vary across countries or cultures. Managers from Europe are more people-focused than either Japanese or American managers. Japanese business culture emphasises the group not the individual, so individual personalities, needs and desires are less important. United States organisations have a profit orientation and downplay individual needs and desires. In contrast, European countries have a more individual focus than Japan and a more humanistic one than the United States, meaning European managers tend to be more people-centred (Calori & Dufour 1995).

Another cross-cultural difference involves time horizons. The time horizons of managers in any country differ and there are cultural differences too. For example, the focus of US firms is short-term profit, so managers' leadership styles value short-term outcomes. The focus of Japanese firms is long-term growth, so Japanese managers' leadership styles value long-term outcomes (Calori & Dufour 1995). The general focus for Australian managers seems also to be short term, but with outcomes of stability and efficiency (James 2003). Research on these and other international leadership aspects is recent, and other cultural differences in managers' leadership styles may emerge.

Making the transition from effective manager to effective leader

Very frequently, the terms manager and leader are used interchangeably. However, before you can become an effective leader, you must first be an effective manager. Making the transition from individual contributor to managing others is a difficult one. Here are some suggestions to avoid the most frequently encountered problems.

1. **Have realistic expectations.** You need to make accurate assessments of the duties, obligations and expectations embedded in your new role. It is easy to fall into the trap of focussing on the newly gained rights and privileges of the new job and miss the required perspective.

2. **Don't forget your manager and your peers.** It is easy to get lost in managing your subordinates. As an effective manager and leader, you need to use your skills with your own manager and your colleagues at the same level, as well as with your subordinates, to achieve your goals.

3. **Keep lateral communications open.** You need to have effective relationships with managers in other sections or departments on the same level as yourself. You have resources they need to get their job done effectively and they have resources you need to achieve your goals. You cannot operate successfully without their support and vice-versa.

4. **Think about the kind of leader and manager you want to be.** Consider your previous managers and analyse those characteristics you found effective and those you did not. This will give you a list of pointers that may be useful to you.

5. **Be prepared to seek guidance and accept advice.** Take every opportunity to seek coaching and mentoring—from whichever manager may be willing to provide it. Your own manager may be willing to help, but if that is not the case, seek it elsewhere.

6. **Remember that you are not alone.** It is easy to become isolated and lose touch with the 'coal face'. Talk daily with the people who report to you and perhaps use 'Management by walking around', making sure that you get a reputation as being someone who is approachable and easy to talk to.

Source: Adapted from Kinicki, A. & Williams, B. (2003).

DEVELOPING SITUATIONAL THEORIES

situational theories

Theories of leadership taking into consideration important situational factors

Although trying to identify leader behaviours effective in every situation, researchers eventually found leader behaviours which worked in one situation could be ineffective in another. As a result, emerging leadership theories involved situational factors. Called **situational theories** due to their focus, they are also known as contingency leadership theories as they hold appropriate leader traits or behaviours to be contingent, or dependent, on situational elements. Since many factors influence leader effectiveness, different approaches have evolved. Among these are Fiedler's contingency model, the normative leadership model, Hersey and Blanchard's situational theory, and path–goal theory. Each gives useful guidance.

Fiedler's contingency model

Situational approach (developed by Fiedler and his associates) which suggests leaders differ in the degrees of their orientation toward the task versus toward the people

Fiedler's contingency model

Fred Fiedler and associates (Fiedler 1967; Fiedler & Garcia 1987) developed a **contingency model** which is a situational approach. The model argues that leaders differ in degree of orientation toward task versus toward people. This makes leaders effective in some situations but not others. Fiedler's contingency model identifies situation types where each is likely to do best.

LPC orientation

The contingency model is based on a leader's **LPC orientation**, a personality trait measured by the least preferred coworker (LPC) scale. The LPC scale has 18 sets of bipolar adjectives. The leader is asked to describe the 'person with whom [he or she] can work least well' by rating them on a range of 1 to 8 points for each set. An example of a set is:

Pleasant	:	:	:	:	:	:	:	:	Unpleasant
	8	7	6	5	4	3	2	1	

LPC (least preferred coworker) orientation

Personality trait indicating the extent to which an individual places a higher priority on task accomplishment than on personal relationships

If a leader describes a least preferred coworker in negative terms on the LPC scale, they are likely to be task-motivated, putting 'business before pleasure'. If they describe the least preferred coworker in relatively positive terms, they are likely to be people-motivated, seeing a close relationship with coworkers as important to team success. The basic idea of the model is that the leader's LPC orientation must match carefully situational factors favouring that type of leader's prospects for success (Rue & Byars 2003).

Assessing the situation

The contingency model identifies three situational factors affecting the degree of favourability or of situational control for a leader:

Leader-member relations is how much support a leader has from group members. It is an important situational variable. To assess this, a leader asks, 'Will the group members do what I tell them, are they reliable, and do they support me?'

Task structure is how clearly specified are a task's goals, methods and performance standards. With vague assignments, it is hard to know what should be done and how to assess one's progress. Low task structure therefore lowers a leader's favourableness, or situational control, while high task structure raises it. To analyse this, a leader asks, 'Do I know what I am supposed to do and how the job is to be done?'

Position power is the amount of power the organisation gives the leader to accomplish tasks needed. It is related to reward and punishment ability. To evaluate this, a leader asks, 'Do I have the support and backing of the "big boss" and the organisation in dealing with subordinates?'

Matching leadership style and situation

The contingency model combines levels of these three situational factors into eight situations, or octants, representing different favourability, or situational control degrees (see Fig. 12.4). For example, a combination of good leader–member relations, high task structure, and strong position power—octant 1—is most favourable. Boxes below the octants show which leader

FIGURE 12.4 Fiedler's contingency model of leadership (adapted from Jago 1982, p. 324)

		Decreasing situational favourability/control →							
Elements of situation	leader–member relations	good				poor			
	task structure	high		low		high		low	
	position power	strong	weak	strong	weak	strong	weak	strong	weak
Octant		1	2	3	4	5	6	7	8
Characteristics of leader	relationship-oriented (high LPC)	mismatch	mismatch	mismatch	match	match	match	match	mismatch
	task-oriented (low LPC)	match	match	match	mismatch	mismatch	mismatch	mismatch	match

Note: Leaders perform best when there exists a match between characteristics of leader and elements of situation

How much can managers manage?

Contemporary trends in management have brought in a new order of cooperation, partnership and consensus which is challenging the very basis upon which management exists—its right to manage, to control corporate destiny.

The conventional wisdom is that good management is all about consultation with workers. However, consultation takes time, and speed and timing are often crucial in today's rapidly changing business environment.

Consider the reflections of Kimberley Turner, managing director of Aerosafe Australia, who is our Reflective Practitioner in this textbook. She has definite ideas about her leadership style and what works for her.

Decision point

1. The shift to more consultative and participative leadership is making organisations more competitive, especially as they will retain staff who are more involved in their organisation. Discuss the leadership characteristics of a manager who can shift between the consultative and the autocratic approach of leadership. Under what other circumstances besides issues of health, safety and product integrity might a manager forgo the consultative approach?

Reflection point

1. Review the leadership theories discussed in this chapter and discuss which might apply to a participative, consultative approach.

type (low LPC or high LPC) matches the situation and will be most effective. According to the contingency model, in situations with either high (octants 1, 2, and 3, on the left) or extremely low favourability (octant 8, on the far right), a low-LPC leader does best; in moderate favourability situations (octants 4 through 7), a high-LPC leader excels.

The logic of the model is that when a situation is very unfavourable, the leader strongly emphasises the need for task accomplishment to move the group toward its goal. Alternatively, when it is very favourable, a task-oriented leader gets the group's cooperation easily in doing what is needed for the task, as they willingly involve themselves. In a moderately favourable situation, either due to poor leader–member relations or an unstructured task, a supportive, relationship-oriented leader emphasises good working relationships across group members or provides support with an unstructured task (Fiedler & Chemers 1976; Rubello 1995).

Fiedler believes managers cannot easily change LPC orientation or management style. As a result, he argues they must understand their leadership style and analyse the degree of favourability, or situational control. If the match is poor, a leader must make changes (e.g. increase task structure) or find a more suitable situation. Fiedler calls this 'engineering the job to fit the manager'.

Analyses of studies of Fiedler's contingency model support its managerial value. However, they suggest other unaccounted factors are at work (Strube & Garcia 1981; Peters, Hartke & Pohlmann 1985; Bateman & Snell 2004). Managers may need to rely on other situational leadership theories, such as the normative leadership model.

normative leadership model

Model helping leaders assess critical situational factors affecting the extent to which they should involve subordinates in particular decisions

Normative leadership model

The **normative leadership model** was designed for a narrow, but important, purpose. It helps leaders assess situational factors affecting how much they should involve subordinates in decisions (Vroom & Jago 1988).

The model has five types of management decision methods for use on group problems (problems where the decision affects more than one subordinate in the work unit). The methods are shown in Table 12.2. Each is designated by a letter and a number. 'A', 'C' and 'G' stand for 'autocratic', 'consultative' and 'group', respectively. Autocratic and consultative methods each have two variations, designated I and II. Methods become more participative when moving from AI (decide yourself) to GI (let the group decide).

To help managers choose the best method, the normative leadership model has eight basic questions about decision problem aspects (see the top of Fig. 12.5). The questions are clear; however, two clarification points may help. First, in question QR 'technical quality' means how much the solution facilitates reaching external objectives (e.g. better quality, lower cost, longer lasting). Second, the structure aspect of question ST (problem structure) relates to the structure issue in Fiedler's contingency theory. With structured problems, it is generally clear where you are, where you want to go, and what to do to get there (e.g. deciding when to schedule manufacture of extra batches of existing product). Unstructured problems are 'fuzzier' in regard to understanding the present situation, formulating goals, and deciding how to achieve them (e.g. deciding what new products to develop).

McDonald's Australia, and elsewhere in the region, is trying to reduce the fuzziness which has emerged in its market. Long clear and focused, their market has become bored with the 'taste' of the fast food giant's offerings. So frequent small innovations are being introduced to change the market's perception of McDonald's food as being high in fat and salt and encouraging

TABLE 12.2 NORMATIVE LEADERSHIP MODEL DECISION STYLES

Symbol	Definition
AI	You solve the problem or make the decision yourself using the information available to you at the present time.
AII	You obtain any necessary information from subordinates, then decide on a solution to the problem yourself. You may or may not tell subordinates the purpose of your questions or give information about the problem or decision on which you are working. The input provided by them is clearly in response to your request for specific information. They do not play a role in the definition of the problem or in generating or evaluating alternative solutions.
CI	You share the problem with relevant subordinates individually, getting their ideas and suggestions without bringing them together as a group. Then you make the decision. This decision may or may not reflect your subordinates' influence.
CII	You share the problem with your subordinates in a group meeting. In this meeting you obtain their ideas and suggestions. Then you make the decision, which may or may not reflect your subordinates' influence.
GI	You share the problem with your subordinates as a group. Together you generate and evaluate alternatives and attempt to reach agreement (consensus) on a solution. Your role is that of chairperson, coordinating the discussion, keeping it focused on the problem, and ensuring critical issues are discussed. You can provide the group with information or ideas that you have, but you do not try to 'press' them to adopt 'your' solution, and you are willing to accept and implement any solution supported by the entire group.

Source: Reprinted from Vroom & Yetton (1973).

FIGURE 12.5 Decision trees for normative leadership model (reprinted from Vroom & Jago 1988, pp. 184–5)

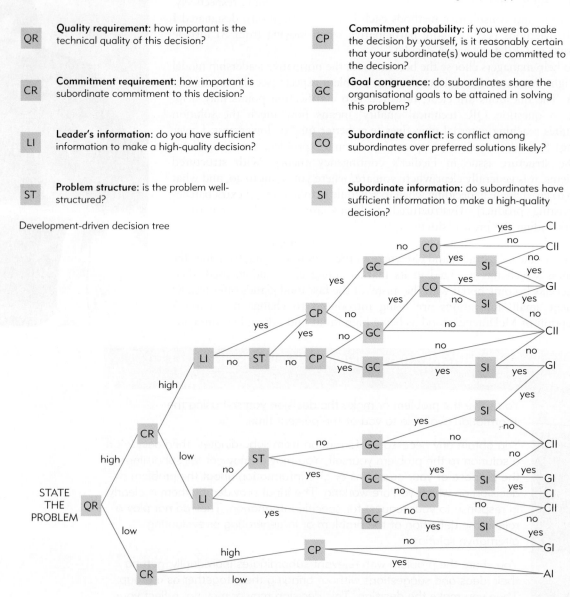

QR	**Quality requirement:** how important is the technical quality of this decision?
CR	**Commitment requirement:** how important is subordinate commitment to this decision?
LI	**Leader's information:** do you have sufficient information to make a high-quality decision?
ST	**Problem structure:** is the problem well-structured?
CP	**Commitment probability:** if you were to make the decision by yourself, is it reasonably certain that your subordinate(s) would be committed to the decision?
GC	**Goal congruence:** do subordinates share the organisational goals to be attained in solving this problem?
CO	**Subordinate conflict:** is conflict among subordinates over preferred solutions likely?
SI	**Subordinate information:** do subordinates have sufficient information to make a high-quality decision?

Development-driven decision tree

unhealthy eating habits to being fresher, low fat/low salt and 'interesting' (Shoebridge 2003b). An example of this is the introduction of the McCafe—a coffee bar incorporated into some of the McDonald's restaurants. In the McCafe, a wide range of salads, low-fat muffins and drinks can be purchased.

The eight questions are used with the two decision trees in Figure 12.5. The development-driven decision tree is used when subordinate development is more important than speed in the decision process. The time-driven decision tree is used when speed is more important than subordinate development.

Situational leadership theory

Another useful contingency theory is **situational leadership theory**, developed by Hersey and Blanchard (1988). It is based on the idea that leader behaviours must change based on one situational factor—follower readiness.

situational leadership theory

Theory (developed by Hersey and Blanchard) based on the premise leaders need to alter their behaviours depending on one major situational factor—the readiness of followers

The situational theory focuses on two behaviours similar to the initiating-structure and consideration behaviours Ohio State researchers identified:

Task behaviour is how much the leader spells out duties and responsibilities of a person or group. It includes telling people what to do, how to do it, when to do it, where to do it, and who is to do it.

Relationship behaviour is how much the leader uses two-way or multiway communication. It includes listening, facilitating and supportive behaviours.

Since these behaviours, like the Ohio State leader behaviours, involve two independent dimensions, a leader can be high on both, low on both, or high on one and low on the other (see the four quadrants in Fig. 12.6).

To determine the combination of leader behaviours for a situation, under situational leadership theory, a leader must assess an interesting factor: follower readiness. This is follower ability and willingness to accomplish a task. *Ability* (job readiness) includes ability, skill, knowledge and experience needed for a specific task. *Willingness* (psychological readiness) consists of confidence, commitment and motivation to complete a task. As can be seen at the bottom of Figure 12.6, the readiness continuum has four levels: low (R1), low to moderate (R2), moderate to high (R3) and high (R4).

The bell-shaped curve running through the four leadership quadrants specifies the leadership style appropriate to a given readiness level:

Telling is used in low-readiness situations, when followers are unable and unwilling or too insecure to be responsible for a given task. The telling style means giving people directions on what to do and how to do it.

Selling is used for low-to-moderate readiness, when followers are unable to take responsibility but are willing or feel confident to do so. The selling style gives specific directions, but supports individual willingness and enthusiasm.

Participating is used for moderate-to-high readiness, when followers can take responsibility but are unwilling or too insecure to do so. Since they can perform, a supportive, participating style emphasising two-way communication and collaboration is most effective.

Delegating is used for high readiness, when followers are able and willing or confident enough to take responsibility. At this point, they need little support or direction; so the delegating style is best.

To apply situational leadership theory, leaders decide task areas they want to influence, assess the person's readiness level, and select the corresponding leadership style. The theory's underlying idea is that leaders should increase followers' task-related readiness quickly by changing their leadership style to move through the cycle from telling to delegating. A comprehensive test of situational theory indicated its best application may be with newly hired staff or those in new jobs. These are likely to benefit most from the telling style's highly structured leadership behaviour (Graeff 1983; Blank, Weitzel & Green 1990; McShane & Travaglione 2003).

Path–goal theory

The last situational leadership theory we consider, **path–goal theory**, explains how leader behaviour can influence subordinates' motivation and job satisfaction (House & Mitchell 1974). It is called path–goal theory as it focuses on how leaders influence subordinates' perception of work goals and paths to achieve both work (performance) and personal goals (intrinsic and extrinsic rewards) (Evans 1970; House 1971; Wofford & Liska 1993).

Path–goal theory is based on expectancy motivation theory. As discussed in Chapter 11, expectancy theory has three main elements: effort-performance expectancy (probability our efforts will lead to performance level required), performance-outcome expectancy (probability our successful performance will lead to certain outcomes or rewards) and valence (anticipated value of outcomes or rewards). Path–goal theory uses expectancy theory to find ways a leader might make work goal achievement easier or more attractive.

path–goal theory

Theory attempting to explain how leader behaviour can positively influence the motivation and job satisfaction of subordinates

FIGURE 12.6   Situational leadership theory® (adapted from Hersey & Blanchard 1993, p. 197)

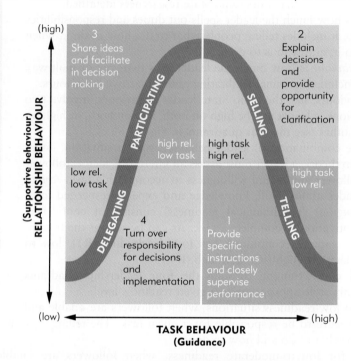

path–goal theory

Theory attempting to explain how leader behaviour can positively influence the motivation and job satisfaction of subordinates

directive

Leader behaviour involving letting subordinates know what is expected of them, providing guidance about work methods, developing work schedules, identifying work evaluation standards, and indicating the basis for outcomes or rewards

supportive

Leader behaviour entailing showing concern for the status, well-being and needs of subordinates; doing small things to make work more pleasant; and being friendly and approachable

participative

Leader behaviour characterised by consulting with subordinates, encouraging their suggestions, and carefully considering their ideas when making decisions

achievement-oriented

Leader behaviour involving setting challenging goals, expecting subordinates to perform at their highest level, and conveying a high degree of confidence in subordinates

Leader behaviours

To affect subordinate perception of paths and goals, path–goal theory identifies four major leader behaviours:

Directive leader behaviour means letting subordinates know what is expected of them, guiding on work methods, developing work schedules, identifying work evaluation standards, and showing the basis for outcomes or rewards. It is similar to task orientation.

Supportive leader behaviour means showing concern for subordinates' status, well-being and needs; doing things to make work more pleasant; and being friendly and approachable. The behaviour is similar to relationship-oriented or consideration behaviour.

Participative leader behaviour is characterised by consultation with subordinates, encouraging their suggestions, and considering their ideas carefully in decision making.

Achievement-oriented leader behaviour means setting challenging goals, expecting subordinates to perform at their highest level, and conveying a high level of confidence in them.

Situational factors

In assessing how the four behaviours enhance subordinates' path–goal motivation and job satisfaction, leaders must consider two situational factor types: subordinate and context characteristics. Subordinate characteristics are subordinates' personality traits, skills, abilities and needs. For example, directive leadership will motivate subordinates with low task-skills, while a participative leader will be appreciated by someone highly skilled.

Context characteristics fall into three categories: task, work group, and the organisation's formal authority system (hierarchical levels, degree of decision centralisation, and nature of formal reward system). For example, supportive leadership may help motivation on a boring task, while achievement orientation may increase motivation on an interesting one.

Choosing leader behaviours

In selecting appropriate leader behaviours with path–goal theory, leaders must diagnose various situational factors' effects on the three expectancy theory elements (the path) and desired end results (the goals). A practical approach involves three steps. First, think in expectancy-theory elements. Second, diagnose situational factors to be changed to improve expectancy-theory elements (to increase motivation). Third, initiate appropriate leader behaviours to change situational factors (Norton 1994; Argus 2003). Several path–goal theory application examples are shown in Figure 12.7.

Since it is a situational leadership approach, path–goal theory argues leadership behaviour effective in one situation is not necessarily so in another. For example, using directive leadership to clarify already clear task demands will have little effect. At worst employees will get frustrated, reducing work's intrinsic valence. Unlike Fiedler's contingency approach, path–goal theory assumes leaders can be flexible, learning to use any of its four leader behaviours as needed (Gabor 1994).

Path–goal theory covers many leader behaviours and situational variables operating simultaneously. Its flexibility gives managers a framework to consider their behaviour's impact on subordinate motivation, goal attainment and job satisfaction (Yukl 1994).

FIGURE 12.7   Examples of path-goal theory (adapted from Yukl 1981, pp. 148, 150)

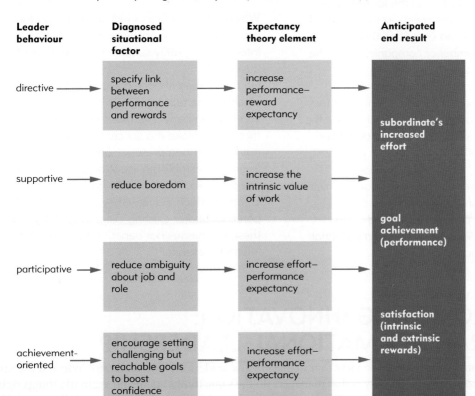

seek.com.au

Looking for a job in Australia? Been through all the newspapers and company websites and having difficulties finding jobs matched to your career path or particular set of qualifications? This is a quandary faced by nearly every person looking for employment within the Pacific Rim. In order to find a job, a job seeker must plough through newspaper advertisements, employment agencies and industry contacts. This search is not only time-consuming but usually is limited to the geographical coverage of a particular newspaper. For the company that is looking to employ, finding a potential employee via advertisements can also be a costly and often 'hit and miss' exercise.

The question which three Australian entrepreneurs asked then was: 'How can we use internet technology to make finding a job or finding employees more efficient?' The answer? seek.com.au.

Launched in March 1998 by Paul Bassat, Andrew Bassat and Matthew Rockman, seek.com.au uses the internet and modern technology to create Australia's leading employment website and the largest source of private-sector job advertisements in the country. In 2004, seek.com.au has had over 65 000 positions advertised, with the number of companies using the service consistently growing.

In addition to this, not only can the potential employee browse these job advertisements, but they can enter their information and dossier and have the database email them jobs which fit their particular requirements. Also, rather than enter the lengthy paper trail of resumes, cover letters and job requirements, applicants can store electronic versions of these documents on the seek.com.au site (accessible through a personal login) and automatically send their information to a potential employer with the touch of a button.

From the perspective of the company advertising for a position, seek.com.au allows the hirer to canvass an entire nation instantaneously, and have their advertisement run every day, all day without the usual 'Wednesday and Saturday' advertising runs of most major national newspapers. The employers also know that, if they are advertising for a particular discipline or skill, those registered with seek.com.au who hold the skill will find a copy of their advertisement in their email inboxes.

This innovative method of employment seeking and advertising has been the pioneer in a new way in which people advertise and look for employment within Australia, with the number of people visiting the site in 2004 estimated at 10 per cent of the overall Australian workforce, and over 55 per cent of the overall Australian job-seeker market.

Source: Contributed by Joel Mendelson.

Activities for discussion, analysis and further research

1. Which other traditional industries do you think could establish an online presence? Is the internet necessarily suitable for every type of business?
2. Go online then choose a successful company and establish the reasons why it is successful as an internet company. Are these the same factors that would make it a successful company if it had not had a strong presence on the internet?
3. In groups, establish a list of organisations which you think would not benefit from being online. Establish which industry they are in, and their potential and/or existing client base. Why would these businesses not benefit from having an internet presence?

PROMOTING INNOVATION: TRANSFORMATIONAL LEADERSHIP

An interesting issue is the view that managers and leaders are not necessarily one and the same (Zalezni 1990). One view is that managers do the same things again and again (do things right), but leaders innovate (do the right things), bring in major changes, and inspire followers to high effort levels (Holloman 1968; Zaleznik 1977). In studying this, Bernard M. Bass and colleagues distinguish between transactional and transformational leaders (Burns 1978; Bass 1985; Hater & Bass 1988).

Transactional leaders motivate subordinates to perform as expected. They do this by helping them recognise task responsibilities, identify goals, become confident about desired performance levels, and understand their needs and desired rewards are linked to goal achievement. As you have seen, transactional leadership is allied to the path–goal leadership theory. Other situational leadership theories in this chapter can be seen as transactional leadership approaches.

In contrast, **transformational leaders** motivate individuals to perform above expectations by inspiring them to: focus on broader missions transcending their own immediate self-interest; concentrate on intrinsic high-level goals (achievement and self-actualisation) not extrinsic low-level goals (safety and security); and be confident in their abilities to achieve the leader's missions (*Dealerscope* 1995; *Wall Street Journal* 1995; Nakarmi 1994).

Transformational leadership does not replace transactional leadership. It supplements it with an add-on effect: performance above expectations (see Fig. 12.8). The logic is that even the most successful transformational leaders need transactional skills to effectively manage day-to-day events forming the broader mission's basis (Hooper 2004).

According to Bass, three factors are significant to transformational leadership: charisma, individualised consideration and intellectual stimulation. Of these, charisma is crucial. **Charisma** is the leader's ability to inspire pride, faith and respect; see what is really significant; and to explain a sense of mission, or vision, inspiring followers (Sprout 1995). Martin Luther King, Mahatma Gandhi, John F. Kennedy, Franklin D. Roosevelt and others have been described as charismatic (House & Singh 1987).

Researchers have tried to identify behavioural elements of charismatic leaders. Their efforts suggest these leaders try to change the status quo, project future goals or idealised visions very different from the present, and behave unconventionally and counter to existing norms. Studies show charismatic leaders rely heavily on referent and expert power, trying to have others share their vision of radical change (Conger & Kanungo 1987).

The second transformational leadership factor, **individualised consideration**, means to delegate projects to enhance follower capabilities, pay attention to each's needs, and treat them

transactional leaders

Leaders who motivate subordinates to perform at expected levels by helping them recognise task responsibilities, identify goals, acquire confidence about meeting desired performance levels, and understand how their needs and the rewards they desire are linked to goal achievement

transformational leaders

Leaders who motivate individuals to perform beyond normal expectations by inspiring subordinates to focus on broader missions transcending their own immediate self-interests, to concentrate on intrinsic higher-level goals rather than extrinsic lower-level goals, and to have confidence in their abilities to achieve the extraordinary missions articulated by the leader

charisma

Leadership factor comprising the leader's ability to inspire pride, faith and respect; to recognise what is really important; and to articulate effectively a sense of mission, or vision, to inspire followers

individualised consideration

Leadership factor involving delegating projects to help develop each follower's capabilities, paying personal attention to each follower's needs, and treating each follower as an individual worthy of respect

FIGURE 12.8 Add-on effect of transformational leadership (adapted from Bass 1985, p. 23)

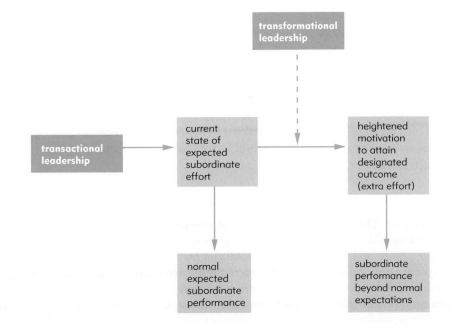

GENDER FACTOR

What female managers bring to IT

At present, relatively few women have made it to the top in the IT industry. However, according to Jan Rosi, a manager in Compaq Computer Australia, women are thought to bring particular skills into management that can add to the success of an organisation. These abilities, including finely-tuned communication skills coupled with a team-based approach, suit the flat organisation structure adopted by many IT organisations. They allow decisions to be made with greater speed, as opposed to the traditional, top-heavy style of hierarchy where decisions were made sequentially and slowly.

Much of IT work relies on the ideas that are brought to problem solving, requirement definition and marketing campaigns. A diversified workforce with skilled employees of different sexes, ages, and cultural backgrounds can greatly enhance the quality of these ideas. The more diversity that is brought to a problem, the more likely it is that an exceptional idea will be conceived. The particular management skills of women can benefit IT organisations by facilitating this process.

Women bring to their teamwork a sense of nurturing, consultation, and an ability to listen to the views of others. Their style is collaborative in nature, and is more concerned with the individual than the wider office politic. Intuition can also be added to this list of skills. Women tend to bring very practical solutions to problem scenarios and do not rely on technical excellence alone, instead coming up with innovative ideas to address problems. This quality is valued as it enhances the business bottom line. Effective communication also facilitates the bottom line of organisations by motivating people to work towards a shared vision. In addition, good communication with key audiences can greatly enhance public relations.

In summary, high levels of interpersonal skills, which are required to facilitate business outcomes, and the ability to communicate appropriately to technical staff to achieve the end result, place women in a good position to succeed in the area of IT. Mentoring is seen as one of the ways women can benefit themselves and at the same time assist the advancement of women in the industry.

Source: Contributed by Glenice Wood; adapted from Yelland (2002).

Activities for discussion, analysis and further research

1. Are the leadership behaviours of the women in this case study different to those of male managers? If so, in what way?
2. Are the female qualities in this case study aligned more with those of transformational leaders or transactional leaders? Explain your views.
3. How closely do you believe the qualities described in the case study fit the definition of charismatic leadership? In groups, discuss how you would feel as employees, working under leadership with the characteristics attributed to women in the IT industry.
4. Go to the website: http://thenew.hp.com/country/au/eng/welcome.html for more information on this company. What does this site tell you about the people who staff this organisation? If women are believed to be so valued in the IT industry, how do you explain the total lack of reference to women in the company?

as worthy of respect. The third factor, **intellectual stimulation**, means to offer new ideas to stimulate rethinking old ways of doing things, encourage followers to look at problems from several vantage points, and foster creative breakthroughs.

Not everyone agrees transformational leaders must have charisma. It seems to be agreed that such leaders must give a vision of a desired future state, mobilise commitment, and generate changes to help followers reach the vision (Howell & Frost 1989; Tichy & Ulrich 1984).

ARE LEADERS NECESSARY?

Some argue that leadership's importance is overrated and in many contexts makes little difference (Yukl 1989). In this section, we explore leadership substitutes, and consider the organisational life-cycle approach to understanding the applicability of different leadership styles.

Substitutes for leadership

An interesting aspect of path–goal theory is that situational factors may make some leader behaviours unneeded and/or ineffective. However, path–goal theory does not specify conditions under which, due to situational factors, leader behaviour may be unneeded. The **substitutes for leadership** approach tries to specify some situational factors likely to make leader behaviours unneeded or negate their effectiveness (Kerr & Jermier 1978; Podsakoff, Niehoff, MacKenzie & Williams 1993).

According to this approach, **neutralisers** are situational factors stopping a leader behaviour influencing subordinate performance and/or satisfaction. In other words, they negate leader behaviour effects. Examples of neutralisers negating the impact of relationship- and task-oriented leader behaviours are subordinates' high need for independence, low subordinate valence for rewards available (see Chapter 12), and physical distance between leader and subordinates. Managers must assess the presence of neutralisers and work to alter the situation, so appropriate leader behaviours can operate. (For instance, a manager may develop new reward choices, such as training, if subordinates have low valence for current rewards.)

On the other hand, **substitutes** are situational factors making the leadership impact impossible or even unnecessary (Kerr & Jermier 1978; Podsakoff et al. 1993). Substitutes for relationship-oriented behaviour include interesting, satisfying work and subordinates with a professional work orientation. Substitutes for task-oriented behaviour include able and experienced subordinates and routine work, with clearly specified methods, and/or feedback. The presence of substitutes for leadership let a leader concentrate their attention on other areas (Brady 1987; Hooper 2004).

Aside from concern about leadership needs of specific subordinates and work groups, managers must also consider the broader perspective of organisational life cycle.

Leadership and the organisational life cycle

The idea of companies having life cycles, or predictable development stages (see Chapter 7), guides the appropriateness of transactional or transformational leadership (see Table 12.3) (Baliga & Hunt 1987). At the entrepreneurial, or beginning, stage, transformational leadership helps create a vision letting the organisation be born and take a few steps. At collectivity stage, other workers join the initial group, and transactional leadership allows management of accelerating growth. By the formalisation-and-control stage, growth needs greater emphasis on transactional leadership to maintain direction and control. By the elaboration-of-structure stage, high formalisation and control may reduce innovation to a low level, so heavy emphasis on transformational leadership is needed again. Though both transactional and

intellectual stimulation

Leadership factor involving offering new ideas to stimulate followers to rethink old ways of doing things, encouraging followers to look at problems from multiple vantage points, and fostering creative breakthroughs in obstacles which seemed insurmountable

substitutes for leadership

Approach attempting to specify some main situational factors likely to make leader behaviours unnecessary or to negate their effectiveness

neutralisers

Situational factors making it impossible for a given leader behaviour to have an impact on subordinate performance and/or satisfaction

substitutes

Situational factors making leadership impact not only impossible but also unnecessary

TABLE 12.3 LEADERSHIP AND THE ORGANISATIONAL LIFE CYCLE	
Organisational life-cycle stage	**Most important leadership emphasis**
Entrepreneurial	Transformational
Collectivity	Transactional
Formalisation and control	Transactional
Elaboration of structure	Transformational

transformational leadership styles can help at every stage of effective organisations, the emphasis differs (Roberts 2003). Managers must understand both leadership approaches to effectively function. Inherent in these approaches is the need to be well versed in organisational communication processes, a subject we turn to in the next chapter.

GAINING THE EDGE

Profile: Busman's holiday

If most of the world's airlines are losing money, how can travel agents be making money? The answer, according to Graham Turner, the founder and managing director of Flight Centre, is that airlines must have a system to distribute their tickets and attract passengers, even if they are running at a loss. That is why he has just spent $122 million acquiring a British travel firm and raised $80 million in fresh capital, causing the stockmarket to hold its collective breath.

True believers, who have made a fortune following Turner, say he can do no wrong. They watched Flight Centre's shares soar from their 95 cent float price in 1995 to a high of $28.84 in June 2002. Disbelievers say Turner has gone a step too far this time. They point to the 37 per cent fall in Flight Centre's share price in the past 10 months (to $18.10 on 4 April 2003) and worry about whether Turner's brilliance can outshine the global aviation slump.

The man himself is in no doubt. 'In six months I think you'll see that the people who took up their rights (in the $80 million capital raising) got a pretty good deal', he says. 'We know that the timing was not brilliant, but when opportunities come up you have to take them.'

His low-key description of Flight Centre's one-for-20 rights issue at $18 a share, and the ambitious acquisition of the London-based Britannic Travel, is typical of Turner's robust approach to life and business. A former Prime Minister, Gough Whitlam, called this style of management 'crash, or crash through'. An even more apt description is the Special Air Service regiment motto: 'Who dares, wins'.

Throughout his business life, Turner has willingly accepted challenges that others decline. Perhaps the best example is a story attributed to Bill James, a former partner in Turner's first enterprise, Top Deck Travel. James told *The Courier Mail* newspaper in April 2000 that a ferry operator refused to let Turner drive a bus on board for the trip from Spain to Morocco. Turner allegedly tossed the fare to the ticket collector and roared up the gangway, squeezing his double-decker on to the ferry, its roof nudging the door and its back platform almost in the ferry's wake.

There are parallels with what is happening at Flight Centre today. All forms of travel around the world have declined dramatically because of the Iraq war, as well as the global economic downturn. Rather than expanding, most travel-related businesses are contracting. Not Turner. He sees tough times as a chance to snatch market share and push his unique business model deeper into overseas markets.

'What people on the outside probably see is bankrupt airlines on one side, and low-cost carriers who don't pay you anything on the other', he says. 'That is our challenge. How do we make money out of airlines that are not healthy, and from airlines that don't pay anything to distribute their product?'

Having put his own question so succinctly, what is his answer? After a short laugh, Turner gives his answer. 'Well, until the airlines actually go out of business it's a matter of protecting their arses', he says. 'Believe it or not, some airlines have actually thought they could do that without a distribution system, or if they had one, then they didn't have to pay for it.'

Turner's view of Flight Centre, which has been one of Australia's most remarkable business success stories of the past 20 years, is of a retailer and product distribution system, and that means distributing more than air tickets. Insurance, accommodation and packaged holidays are also on the menu of the Flight Centre group, which trades under six retail names, seven corporate and three wholesale brands. Strict internal efficiencies, and a 'family culture' in each of the company's 1128 shops, ensure that the group has been able to handle rapid growth in Australia and to expand globally.

All Flight Centre shops are company-owned, but managers can buy equity of up to 20 per cent in their outlet. A generous sales incentive scheme means that staff can easily triple their base wage. One example is a Melbourne employee who turned a $38 000 base into $200 000, with commissions. Shop staff is restricted to between three and seven people. 'This is a manageable size for people to get along and understand each other', Turner says. 'That's what we call a family. We organise along the lines of the hunter-gatherer society.'

For investors, the question is whether Flight Centre can maintain it, and if the Turner magic can survive dramatic changes under way in the travel industry, and at Flight Centre. The aviation industry downturn is one aspect. Another is the rise of the internet as a force in travel product distribution. A third is that Turner is taking a step back from the daily grind and redefining himself as managing director, with growth strategy as his job description.

The Britannic deal is the first example of Turner's new mission, which actually looks much like the old: growth, growth and more growth. Speaking in his modest Brisbane office, the bearded managing director, who could be mistaken for the ageing hippie he almost is, says Britannic is an excellent business, which is very profit-focused.

'If you look at the travel business generally, there are not a lot of good players who are consistently profitable, and who have a good business model', he says. 'We're not that acquisitive, but good opportunities only come up every few years, and in this case you can say that the timing was not brilliant. But, having said that, we did get the deal up, with the support of the investment community, and despite our impeccably bad timing.'

It is a step too far to call Flight Centre a one-man band. Turner has an able team and a superb system. But he also drives Flight Centre as a sole trader would push his business at every opportunity. Although he can clearly see growth ahead, some critics can see issues looming that may be bigger than Turner.

Source: Based on Treadgold, T. (2003).

Activities for discussion, analysis and further research

1. Log onto the Flight Centre's website and do a search on the company's mission and values.
2. How do they reflect Turner's leadership style?
3. How would you categorise Turner's leadership style? Would you work for him? Why?

REFLECTIVE PRACTITIONER

KIMBERLEY TURNER

AEROSAFE
RISK MANAGEMENT

It's about having a healthy organisation. If my staff are happy and satisfied and doing well, obviously, I have had a part to play in establishing an effective work environment. If staff are not happy, then it's probably something I am not doing or that I could be doing. I have not got to the stage of 360 degree feedback, and I don't know if I am actually going to go there. We might get there, but for me it is not quite that important at the moment. I guess I read those signs in the feedback in an informal sense. It's a fine line because to invite staff to review your performance as a company manager or leader there is a real risk. It's not that I am worried about what they might say, it's whether or not I am willing to amend what I do to fit what they say. I certainly acknowledge feedback but in some instances I don't want to change and I won't be changing because that is the way I want to run my business. You can find yourself turning into a real chameleon if you're too responsive to every piece of feedback received from a variety of areas. Everyone will have an opinion on what and how they think you should run things. You can find yourself constantly changing and adjusting, and that does not provide the hook of stability that you need as a leader in a company if you are constantly adapting, changing and accommodating other people's ideas of what you should be like.

I've gone through a period in my business where I actually did that and I found it quite unsettling and I found that when I was unsettled, the whole organisation was unsettled. Before I knew it, I found I had retention issues. In the reflection afterwards, I could only track it back to the lack of stability in the company, and that is directly related to my conduct in the business. The success of the business is directly related to the effort that I put in.

I think that being a leader is about having the ability to influence and motivate others, lead by example, show people how it is done. You are not a leader if people are not following you. I guess that is perhaps the true measure. If you turn around, if there's no-one behind you, then who are you leading? The other thing is whether they are following you out of curiosity or they are really behind you and supporting you in the direction that you're going.

Because of my age, I've tried to utilise a leadership style that is quite consultative, that taps into the expertise of those around me. I know that I am very decisive and know exactly what I want. Whether or not I communicate that depends on how I think I will be received. Sometimes I will alter my style to match those who are around me. When you try to lead and motivate people who are twice your age, the style that you need to adopt is very different to the one you would use if you are leading people who are younger than you or more junior to you in

business experience. So I think I have a box of different leadership styles that I will pull out. Part of my leadership style that is consistent regardless of the situation is the motivational aspect. I want to see people do well, whether it is about motivating a staff member to take on professional development, a client to take on our work, or our encouraging one of our service providers. One of the things that was hard for me was to accept that it was OK for other people to be better than me in aspects of business and our discipline. That was a real turning point for me in my perception of myself as a leader. If I consider my behaviour and my conduct as a manager, it had to be OK for me to encourage development of others to the point that they might leapfrog over me in my subject expertise, or the ability to be a fantastic project manager.

I started in business at nineteen, so my age has been an issue where leadership was concerned. However, being a woman in business has also been interesting. Acting assertively or confidently, which are things that can certainly assist in your leadership, can be taken the wrong way and sometimes it is perceived that women shouldn't be like that. It can come across as being strong willed, or unable to be flexible, while it is just being confident and assertive. I would say that I am quite consultative but I do that to accommodate my environment as opposed to 'that's my style'. Having an autocratic leadership style, being succinct and direct doesn't always go down well if you are trying to lead people who are 25 to 30 years older than you. Whereas if you walk in and say: 'OK, this is where I'd like to take us. I'd like to seek your guidance and your input', it's not that the answer will be any different, it's just the approach which is likely to get you to the outcomes you want.

FOCUS ON PRACTICE

Strategies for improving

1. In a situation where one of your staff was relationship-oriented, how would you ensure the situation would lead to the satisfaction of their need?
2. How might you remove obstacles to success to enable your staff to succeed?
3. How would you enable a subordinate to know how their activities contribute to organisational success?
4. Sharing organisational problems and issues with staff often leads to innovative and creative ideas. Design a process to make this a regular part of the weekly activities.

Source: Jones et al. (2000).

SUMMARY

- Leadership is the process of influencing others to achieve organisational goals. Leaders use six major types of power to affect others' behaviour: legitimate, reward, coercive, expert, information and referent. Leaders must use their power carefully to encourage commitment and increase power, not diminish it. Researchers have identified some common traits distinguishing leaders from non-leaders. General traits include intelligence and dominance; there are some other leadership traits that are only applicable in specific situations.

- Studying leader behaviours gave a more promising research direction. The Iowa, Michigan and Ohio State studies were early efforts identifying effective leadership behaviours, or styles. The Ohio State researchers found two leadership styles, initiating structure and consideration, viewed as independent dimensions not opposite ends of a continuum. Unfortunately, leaders showing both high initiating structure and high consideration did not always get the best results. The Leadership Grid emphasised concern for people and for production. Studies indicate female and male managers are similar in levels of exhibited interpersonal and task behaviours.

- Situational leadership theories grew from realising that leader behaviours working well in one situation are often not as effective in another. Fiedler's contingency model holds that a leader's effectiveness depends on whether the leader's LPC orientation fits the situation as set by leader–member relations, task structure and position power.

- The normative leadership model helps leaders determine how much to involve subordinates in decisions. Situational leadership theory argues leaders must alter their combination of task and relationship behaviours according to follower task readiness. The path–goal leadership theory relies on expectancy motivation theory and attempts to explain how leader behaviour influences subordinate motivation and job satisfaction.

- Transformational leadership can be important in innovation as it motivates individuals to perform above normal expectations, pursuing new visions. It adds-on to transactional leadership, as both are needed.

- There is some evidence leadership may make little or no difference in some contexts. One reason why it may not be so important is that there are substitutes for leadership. Also, the organisational life cycle may affect the emphasis placed on transactional and transformational leadership.

QUESTIONS FOR DISCUSSION AND REVIEW

1. Outline the major power types available to managers. Think of a situation you were a leader in. What power types were available to you? Which ones did you use most? What follower commitment, compliance and resistance did you experience?

2. Explain the status of current research efforts identifying leader traits. What traits can you identify in someone you see to be a good leader? Do other familiar leaders possess any of the same traits?

3. Describe the continuum of boss- (authoritarian) and subordinate-centred (democratic) behaviours. Identify situations in which you have seen a democratic leader in action and situations in which you have seen an authoritarian one. How did followers react? Did situational factors make a difference to followers' reactions?

4. Explain the different findings of Iowa, Michigan and Ohio State researchers investigating leadership. Use the findings to give advice to managers on how to lead more effectively.

5. Outline the basic ideas in Fiedler's contingency leadership model. Analyse a student association or other leadership situation in terms of leader–member relations, task structure and position power. On the basis of Fiedler's model, what type of leader behaviour would the situation need?

6. Describe the normative leadership theory. Consider a leadership situation you have experienced in which a decision had to be made. Use the appropriate decision tree to determine the extent to which the group should have been involved. How closely does the decision tree's recommendation match what was done? What were the results?

7. Explain the basic ideas making up the path–goal leadership theory. Use it to determine how a leader might improve motivation in a familiar group.

8. Contrast transactional and transformational leadership. Identify a transactional leader and a transformational leader. To what extent is each one's leadership emphasis appropriate, given the life-cycle stage of the organisation each manages?

9. Differentiate between neutralisers and substitutes for leadership. Give two examples of each in a familiar organisation.

10. Explain how leadership relates to organisational life cycle. Analyse a familiar organisation in terms of appropriate use of transactional and transformational leadership.

CRITICAL THINKING QUESTIONS

To answer some of these questions you will need to do further research. Useful references are given below each section of the questions.

This chapter of the textbook examined the question of whether leadership is an inherent quality or whether it can be learned. The answers to this debate help in developing an appreciation of the role leadership plays in a successful organisation. Below is a brief review of the work of three current theorists in the area.

Rosabeth Moss Kanter is one of the world's foremost academics in change management and globalisation. In an interview with Stuart Crainer, she described her latest initiative, the 'Change Toolkit'. This is a web-based tool to aid executives in successfully leading change within their organisations.

1. A primary focus of Moss Kanter's Change Toolkit is the fact that it is a web-based format. Why do you think she sees this as an important feature?

2. One of the questions asked of Moss Kanter was whether we have unrealistic expectations of our corporate leaders. What do you think she answered and why?

3. What issues do we need to address to be able to re-think our understanding of leadership?

The interview goes to discuss the Western heroic view of leadership. Moss Kanter dismisses the tough heroic style that once dominated as being no longer very appropriate. Instead, she opts for a view of leadership as more Confucian than cowboy.

4. What do you think she means by this?

5. How should organisations respond to the challenge of rising expectations?

6. In typical Moss Kanter style, she explains one of the major causes of leadership failure as the tendency toward 'putting lipstick on a bulldog' (Crainer 2003, p. 43). What do you think she means by this?

(Material relevant to these questions may be found in Crainer, S. 2004, Rosabeth Moss Kanter—on cowboys and Confucius, *New Zealand Management*, February, p. 43.)

Another perspective on leadership is provided by two experienced consultants in the field. Dahmen and Hammond (2002, p. 25) summarise the key qualities of good leadership as:

- Inspiration—where a good leader looks at their employees as a team and then incorporates the team's aspirations, feelings and values when describing its goals. Dahmen and Hammond believe that this provides inspirational goals as they surpass both the basic needs of the individual and the bottom-line needs of the organisation.
- Credibility—which they see as a mixture of 'courageous judgement plus integrity and consistency'. A leader is not afraid to take risks, as long as the decision to take the risk is underwritten by careful analysis of a given situation.

- Conviction—where a combination of faith and pragmatism are used to meet challenges. Dahmen and Hammond believe that a good leader should welcome challenges, but it is their trust in the team that allows them to face the challenge together.

While all of the above can be found in existing leadership theories, Dahmen and Hammond add the vital element of succession planning into the mix of qualities ascribed to a good leader. Thus, they state (2002, p. 25) 'leaders who are not capable of developing leaders will not be successful anymore'.

7. What do they mean by this last statement and why is it so important today?

The above discussion clearly advocates the notion that leadership can be learned, and Dahmen and Hammond (2002) suggest ways in which this learning process can be articulated within the organisation through meeting three objectives:

- understanding that developing leaders is fundamental to organisational success
- defining what leadership is and what it means to lead
- identifying and rewarding leadership behaviour

8. How would an organisation go about implementing these three objectives?

Overall, the intent behind the strategy of identifying and developing future generations of leaders is to prepare them to lead the organisation in the face of whatever challenges are thrown up by the external environment, and to achieve the organisation's objectives. Dahmen and Hammond (2002) suggest that the key to ensuring organisations achieve these aims is the development of a leadership competency model. This will not only define what leadership means to the organisation but also what it means to lead.

9. Why is this important for an organisation?

10. A key step in the leadership training offered by Andersen, the organisation Dahman and Hammond work for, is 'providing solutions'. This refers to the specific training and business experiences that can enhance a participant's leadership skills. Why do consultancy companies such as Andersen emphasise the importance of this step?

(Material relevant to these questions may be found in Dahmen, C., and Hammond, M. 2002, Developing leaders: An 11-step approach, *Management*, March, pp. 25–7.)

A different perspective on leadership is offered by the results of a recent survey directed by Professor James Sarros of Monash University. Instead of exhortations to jump on the latest management fad or adopt the newest form of technology, the study suggests that 'business leaders need to go back to the drawing board and learn how to get people to trust each other at work.   Trust is in very short supply in Australian business'. (Fox 2001, p. 50) The study found strong correlations between trust and traditional leadership roles such as mentoring, role modelling, caring for staff and motivation. The study also offers interesting developments on the argument as to whether leaders are born or made. The view offered by Sarros is that most leadership skills can be learned, as long as individuals already possess the innate qualities of intelligence, enthusiasm and drive.

11. Fox (2001, p. 50) cites Sarros as stating that the results of the study show that 'promoting trust in the work-place may sound like old-fashioned niceness but it needs to be taught, like other leadership skills' and that 'it's particularly needed at the moment'. Why?

Sarros suggests that trust is the forerunner of loyalty and this message clearly supports the need for organisations to refocus their leadership efforts. The study makes the association between reciprocal trust and respect between workers and leaders and the fact that trust provides 'faith in a leader's capacity to get the job done, plus a conviction that their mission and goals are achievable and representative of everyone's needs. When the leader is walking the talk, trust follows' (cited in Fox 2001, p. 50).

12. Sarros believes that an organisation can create a trusting and loyal work place, just as they can go about developing leadership skills. How would you go about creating this?

13. It is said that leaders in small organisations have an easier task in creating a trusting and loyal work place than those in larger ones—why do you think there might be this difference?

(Material relevant to these questions may be found in Fox, C. 2001, Trust in short supply in Australian office, *Australian Financial Review*, 21 August, p. 50.)

MANAGEMENT EXERCISES

Exercise 1 Self-assessment: Do you have charisma?

Charisma has helped many leaders in accomplishing goals. It may assist you in the future. The following questions will help in identifying your current charisma level.

1. I worry most about:
   (a) my current competitors
   (b) my future competitors

2. I'm most at ease thinking in:
   (a) generalities
   (b) specifics

3. I tend to focus on:
   (a) our missed opportunities
   (b) opportunities we've seized

4. I prefer to:
   (a) promote traditions that made us great
   (b) create new traditions

5. I like to communicate an idea via:
   (a) a written report
   (b) a one-page chart

6. I tend to ask:
   (a) 'How can we do this better?'
   (b) 'Why are we doing this?'

7. I believe:
   (a) there's always a way to minimise risk
   (b) some risks are too high

8. When I disagree with my boss, I typically:
   (a) coax him/her nicely to alter his/her view
   (b) bluntly tell him/her, 'You're wrong'

9. I tend to sway people by using:
   (a) emotions
   (b) logic

10. I think this quiz is:
    (a) ridiculous
    (b) fascinating

Source: Fortune (1996).

Exercise 2 Management exercise: The question of subordinate involvement

Case: Purchasing decision problem

You have just been appointed director (purchasing) for a manufacturing firm. The company has seven plants, all in the eastern states. The company has historically operated in a highly decentralised way with each plant manager encouraged to operate with only minimal control and direction from head office. In the purchasing area, each purchasing executive who reports to the plant manager does the purchasing for their plant. There is little or no coordination among them, and relationships are largely competitive.

Your position was created when it appeared to the chief executive the company could have difficulty securing certain essential raw materials. To protect the firm against this possibility, the present haphazard decentralised arrangement must be abandoned or at least modified to meet current problems.

You were chosen for the position because of your extensive background in corporate purchasing with another firm which operated in a much more centralised way. Your appointment was announced in the last issue of the company house magazine. You are anxious to get started, particularly as the peak buying season is just three weeks away. A procedure must be set up to minimise likelihood of serious shortages, and secondarily achieve economies from the added power of centralised purchasing (Vroom & Jago 1988).

Instructions

Get together with a group designated by your instructor, and use the normative leadership model to determine the degree to which you should involve subordinates in the purchasing decision.

END-OF-CHAPTER CASE: ON THE RIM

Surviving the crisis

Lim Kim Hong, now 53, is a native of Muar in the Malaysian state of Johor. Born to a poor family, he was forced to leave school at 13 to become an apprentice carpenter. By age 14 and dissatisfied with earnings of $2.10 a month, he quit to set up a backyard furniture business. From furniture, he expanded to producing spring mattresses. That was his big break and the rest is history.

He first set up his company, Sumurwang, as a sole proprietorship in 1969. In 1980, Lim converted it into a private limited company, Lim Kim Hong Holdings Sdn Bhd, and renamed it Sumurwang Sdn Bhd in 1984.

Lim saw the potential for spring mattresses in China, given the large population, and started the first Malaysian manufacturing operations in China by opening a mattress factory in Tianjin in 1984. By 1996, the China operations had expanded to 10 plants.

The success in spring mattress manufacturing was capped with Lim taking his company to public

listing on the Kuala Lumpur Stock Exchange as Dreamland Holdings Berhad. Lim then ventured into the stainless steel pipes business in the 1990s and Dreamland Holdings Berhad became Kanzen Berhad.

A rare and golden opportunity came for Lim to realise the true value of the company he has built when an offer was made to buy Kanzen Berhad. With cash in hand, Lim was on the lookout for something to buy and he finally settled for Sanyo Industries (Malaysia) Sdn Bhd, which was his vehicle to venture into the electrical appliances business. He transformed the business, gave it a new image and renamed it I-Berhad. Today it is a leading digital products company renowned for its 'i' brand, which has the distinction of being a Global Malaysian brand with strong attributes of providing leading-edge technology at high value and competitive prices.

POWERWEB

International articles related to this topic are available at the Online Learning Centre at www.mhhe.com/au/bartol4e

Lim is proud of Sumurwang's track record. He built up the Dreamland spring mattress business against the then market leader Dunlop, penetrated the spring mattress market in China, and successfully entered the US market for stainless steel pipe fittings in the early 1990s. However, his pride is balanced with realism. He knows that he cannot fight the big boys head-on. His strategy is to focus on markets such as Islamic countries and China where the government has been promoting Malaysia's image and manufacturing capabilities. It is believed that if Sumurwang can build up a good brand image and knows how to market its products effectively, especially in niche markets like the Middle East, China and Europe, it is likely to be successful.

Over the past 20 years. Lim has developed from a small businessman into a tycoon who has overcome his early handicap of low educational background to overcome many obstacles.

Though Lim has had very little formal education, he has always placed a high importance on learning, attending a number of courses in Taiwan. He also surrounds himself with highly qualified managers and professionals. As a manager, he is said to be direct, straightforward and results-oriented. His philosophy is that he will not ask his employees to do something he would not do himself. He leads by example.

Certainly, Lim is one of a select group of Asian business tycoons who have survived the regional crisis with their fortunes intact. With the benefit of hindsight, reasons for his resilience appear obvious: conservative and focused management, healthy cash surpluses, low gearing and an impeccable sense of timing in sniffing out bargains.

Source: Based on Lee Min Keong (1999).

Activities for discussion, analysis and further research

1. What kind of leader do you think Lim Kim Hong is? Why?
2. What issues must he take into consideration to keep on expanding his business?
3. Find out if Sumurwang Sdn Bhd has a website. If it does, log onto it and look up the company's objectives and mission. See if you can find out anything about Lim Kim Hong's leadership style.

FURTHER READING

Catlette, B. and Hadden, R. 2003, Increasing employee performance, *Security Management*, May, 47, 5, pp. 26–8.

Idris, F., Abdullah, M., Idris, M.A. and Hussain, N. 2003, Integrating resource-based view and stakeholder theory in developing the Malaysian excellence model: A conceptual framework, *Singapore Management Review*, 2nd Half, 25, 2, pp. 91–100.

Krause, T. and Hidley, J. 2003, The role of senior leaders in safety performance, *Industrial Safety & Hygiene News*, February, 37, 2, p. 45.

Nursing Management—UK 2004, Developing nurse leaders for today and tomorrow, February, 10, 9, pp. 8–10.

Sharma, A.K. and Talwar, B. 2004, Business excellence enshrined in Vedic (Hindu) philosophy, *Singapore Management Review*, 1st Half, 26, 1, pp. 1–20.

CHAPTER 13

MANAGERIAL COMMUNICATION

CHAPTER OUTLINE

The nature of managerial communication
Types of communication
Managerial communication preferences
Basic components of the communication
    process

**Influences on individual communication
    and interpersonal processes**
Perceptual processes
Attribution processes
Semantics

Managing diversity: Cultural context
Communication skills

Group communication networks

Organisational communication channels
Vertical communication
Horizontal communication
Informal communication: The grapevine
Using electronics to facilitate
    communication

LEARNING OBJECTIVES

After studying this chapter, you should be able to:

- Explain the major types of managerial communication and discuss managerial communication preferences.
- Outline the basic components of the communication process.
- Describe how perceptual processes influence individual communication.
- Explain the role of attribution processes, semantics, cultural context and communication skills in communication by individuals.
- Assess the usefulness of decentralised group communication networks.
- Distinguish between major organisational communication channels and explain their role in managing effectively.
- Discuss the growing potential of electronics in regard to organisational communication channels.

STRIVING FOR EXCELLENCE

Konichiwa, mate

The president of Toyota Australia, Ken Asano, likes to talk. He likes to talk with suppliers at the monthly lunches he hosts to discuss business conditions; with groups of employees from the shop floor, who spend a few hours in his office each month for an informal chat; with union officials and journalists; and to his sales team and senior management. Asano even likes to talk with his competitors, such as the president of Ford Australia, Geoff Polites. He says it is the key to his management style. 'I must try to understand a person's situation first and then I can try and find a win-win solution.'

For three years, Asano has spent a lot of time talking to executives at the Japanese headquarters of his parent company, Toyota Motor Corporation (TMC), convincing, cajoling and prodding them about the benefits of establishing part of TMC's global research and development (R&D) centre in Australia. On 12 June, Asano's long campaign paid off. TMC announced it would spend $47 million to establish the Toyota Technical Centre Asia Pacific in Melbourne's south-eastern suburbs.

The R&D centre means far more than just a pretty new facility and 90 new jobs. All Australian car makers must justify their existence to their parent companies and Toyota is no different. TMC could easily import vehicles from a lower-cost subsidiary in a country such as Thailand and forget about building cars here; it is up to executives such as Asano to convince TMC that Australia must be part of its global strategy. The R&D investment is a huge vote of confidence in the future of Toyota Australia.

Asano says: 'This is a great opportunity for us. Toyota Australia is a global company now.' TMC's decision to establish the centre in Melbourne will allow Toyota Australia to expand its role in TMC's global value chain. 'Hopefully, this will become a true centre for the Asia-Pacific region.'

However, three years ago, Toyota warned that it might withdraw from Australia unless productivity and competitiveness improved. Since then, Toyota has poured $350 million into developing its new Camry model, announced that it would build a new, $50 million Australian headquarters and snared the $47 million R&D investment. Toyota's long-term future in Australia looks bright.

Toyota Australia employees say Asano has breathed fresh life into the Australian subsidiary. His management style is widely described as open and approachable and his communication skills are strong by car company standards. He regularly addresses workers, visits the shopfloor, and he is open about the company's production, export and sales goals.

Asano worked in Australia from 1990 to 1993 as assistant to the then-president, Bob Johnson. He was disappointed when he returned in 2000. 'I felt there was not so much change within the company.' He says the focus of Toyota Australia was too narrow. Many in the organisation were content with maintaining domestic sales and ignoring the rest of the world. Like many Australian car companies that had grown up behind the safety of tariff walls, Toyota had become complacent.

At his first senior management meeting, Asano wrote two words on the whiteboard: Dog Years. There was stunned silence and then the inevitable question: 'Ken', asked one manager, 'What do you

continued

STRIVING FOR EXCELLENCE *continued*

mean by "dog years"?' Asano says he felt the company had a lot of catching up to do. Like a dog, ageing seven times faster than a human, Toyota had to try to cram seven years of work into every 12 months. 'I told them we need to be seven times quicker.'

Asano also stressed that Toyota Australia had to see itself as a global car company, and warned that without increased production and exports, backed by better domestic sales and market share, Toyota Australia would close.

Asano says that during an assignment in China he made the mistake of believing there were two main styles of doing business: the Western style and the Asian style, best represented by the Japanese. But he soon realised the Chinese style of business—with its heavy reliance on personal relationships and bureaucratic process—was very different. 'After the first couple of years in China, I was defeated. I had lost my confidence. It's a totally different logic in China.'

Eventually, Asano came to understand the Chinese way, but it is little wonder he had initial difficulties. His personal style is not suited to formality and bureaucracy and he clearly prefers the Australian style of business.

One of Asano's achievements is the workplace agreement negotiated with the Australian Manufacturing Workers Union (AMWU) in early 2002. Toyota Australia's industrial record has been poor. As recently as 1993 and 1996, the company had been crippled by strikes that cost up to $10 million a day; and Asano remembers the wildcat strikes that were common during his first stint in Australia between 1990 and 1993. Insiders say relations between management and the unions were tense at best and explosive at worst. An employee says: 'At one stage, I think we had our own car park at the Industrial Relations Commission.'

Under Asano, Toyota has been strike-free for three years and the 2002 workplace agreement was negotiated without a murmur of industrial action. The national secretary of the AMWU vehicle division, Ian Jones, says simply: 'The agreement was a triumph of Asano's leadership.'

Jones agrees that Asano communicates well. In the lead-up to the negotiations, the union established a steering committee of shop stewards and union representatives to liaise with the company about issues that needed to be confronted. Asano immediately joined the committee and still sits in on its monthly meetings, explaining the company's position and helping work through issues before they become problems. Jones says: 'He's got a sense of how Toyota Australia fits into the world and he's great at explaining it.'

Asano says his message about making Toyota Australia into a global company is starting to filter through the organisation. Senior and middle management understand it, and the workers on the shopfloor are coming to grips with it. He says that he will keep spreading the message until every Toyota worker knows that Toyota must become a flexible, fast, global company. 'True power comes from the bottom up.'

Asano is unsure when his posting to Australia may end and says his position depends on continued good results. He's had an impressive start: hauling Toyota Australia into the global market, winning back the trust of its workers and securing its place in Toyota's global value chain. Not bad for a guy who talks too much.

Source: Thomson, J. (2003).

Update: In January 2004 Mr Ken Asano returned to Japan to take on a new role in TMC.

Good organisational communication and interpersonal processes are crucial to organisational effectiveness (Goldhaber 1993). Effective communication is vital to all major management functions; it is especially important to the leading function as it is the channel for interaction with and impact on others. In this chapter, we examine managerial communication and associated interpersonal processes, including different types of communication managers use, their communication preferences, and the basic components of the communication process. We consider factors which either block or enhance people's communication and interactions. We look briefly at group communication networks. Finally, we consider communication channels in organisations, investigate how the use of multiple communication channels promotes innovation, and explore the use of electronics in organisational communication.

THE NATURE OF MANAGERIAL COMMUNICATION

Communication is the exchange of messages between people to reach common meanings (Baskin & Aronoff 1980). Unless meanings are shared, managers cannot influence others.

Communication is critical to every manager's job. In fact managers are estimated to spend about 85 per cent of their day in some communication activity (Adams, Todd & Nelson 1993). Even brilliant strategies and best-laid plans will fail without effective communication (Thomas & Sireno 1980; Hildebrandt, Bon, Miller & Swinyard 1982). When communication is ineffective there will also be many more accidents and potentially risky activities (Winslow 1995; *Wall Street Journal* 1995).

Types of communication

Managers use two major communication types: verbal and non-verbal. Each is important in effective transmission of organisational messages.

Verbal communication

Verbal communication is the written or oral use of words to communicate. Both written and oral communications pervade organisations.

Written communication has a variety of forms, such as letters, memoranda, reports, résumés, written telephone messages, newsletters and manuals. The cost of producing a single letter or memo has risen, and is estimated to have reached $81.90 (Griffin 2000). Further, one of the most common complaints of managers is that poor writing skills are almost endemic. This means that poor writing is not only a financial cost but it may also damage the image or reputation of a company.

Despite the problems that can be caused by poor skills, written communication has advantages over oral. It provides a record of the message, can easily be widely circulated, and the sender can carefully consider their intended message. Written communication does have disadvantages, including preparation expenses, impersonality, potential receiver misunderstanding, and delayed feedback on the message's effectiveness (Lewis 1980).

Oral or spoken communication occurs in face-to-face conversation, meetings and telephone conversations. Oral communication is fast, generally more personal than written communication, and gives rapid feedback from those in the conversation. Oral communication's disadvantages include being time-consuming, sometimes being hard to finish, and the work needed to document communication if a record is wanted (Lewis 1980).

Given the advantages and disadvantages of written and oral communication, it is not surprising managers use both verbal communication types. Later in this chapter we consider managerial preferences for written and oral communication. First, we consider another communication type important to managers.

Non-verbal communication

Non-verbal communication is using elements and behaviours not coded into words. Studies estimate 65 to 93 per cent of what is communicated is non-verbal (Birdwhistell 1972). Of course, verbal communication must be accompanied by some non-verbal communication. Major categories are kinesic behaviour, proxemics, paralanguage and object language.

Kinesic behaviour (or 'body language') is body movements such as gestures, facial expressions, eye movements and posture. In assessing people's feelings on an issue, we draw conclusions not only from their words but also from non-verbal behaviour, such as facial expressions.

Proxemics is the impact of proximity and space on communication. For example, managers may arrange their offices with an informal area where people can sit without feeling the spatial distance and formality of a big desk. Another familiar proxemics example is that it is more likely you will get to know students you sit near in class than those elsewhere in the room.

---

communication

Exchange of messages between people to achieve common meanings

verbal communication

Written or oral use of words to communicate

non-verbal communication

Communication by means of elements and behaviours that are not coded into words

kinesic behaviour

Body movements, such as gestures, facial expressions, eye movements and posture

proxemics

Influence of proximity and space on communication

Paralanguage is the vocal aspects of communication, or *how* something is said rather than *what*. Voice quality and tone, laughing and yawning are in this category.

Object language is use of material things, such as clothing, cosmetics, furniture and architecture, to communicate (Baskin & Aronoff 1980; Nabers 1995; Kinicki & Williams 2003). If you wrote a job résumé lately, you probably thought about layout and paper type. These are object language aspects; you are communicating information about yourself beyond the words on the page. These non-verbal elements are important to managerial messages.

Evidence shows that if verbal and non-verbal elements contradict, receivers see non-verbal communication as accurate (Hayes 1973; Baskin & Aronoff 1980). This means managers must consider both non-verbal and verbal message parts (Schmitt 1997). Furthermore, to understand others' thoughts and feelings better, managers should consider both non-verbal and verbal parts of messages they receive.

Managerial communication preferences

As noted before, managers spend much time communicating in some form. Studies show they prefer oral to written communication, largely as oral communication is more informal and timely (Mintzberg 1973; Kurke & Alrich 1983). One study showed four top managers in four different organisation types spent 74 per cent of their working hours communicating orally, through informal and formal meetings, telephone calls and organisation tours (see Fig. 13.1) (Smeltzer & Fann 1989; Mintzberg 1975). They spent about 50 per cent of their time interacting with subordinates. Most of the rest was spent with the board of directors, peers, trade organisations, clients and suppliers. While the study focused on top-level managers, other levels also prefer spoken over the written word (Lewis 1980; Smeltzer & Fann 1989; Bateman & Snell 2004).

Managers serve as communication centres through the managerial roles presented in Chapter 1 (such as monitor, disseminator and spokesperson). In these roles managers are the basis of the organisation's communication network. If managers and those they interact with communicate ineffectively, the results are serious, not just for their work unit but also for the whole organisation (Petzinger 1997).

On the other hand, efforts to promote effective communication can be the key to an organisation's success.

FIGURE 13.1 Proportion of time top managers spent on various activities (based on Kurke & Aldrich 1983, p. 979)

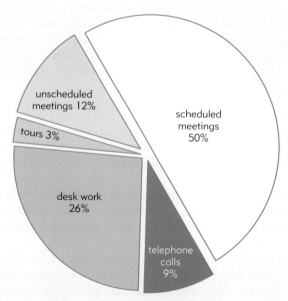

Basic components of the communication process

A look at the communication process's basic components helps us understand how challenging effective organisational communication can be (Krone, Jablin & Putnam 1987; Ihlwan 2003b). It also highlights the point that the only way we interact with others is by communication. The process's components are shown in Figure 13.2.

Sender

The **sender** initiates the message. This is usually in response to an outside stimulus, a question, a meeting, an interview, a problem or report.

Encoding

Before messages can be exchanged, the sender must **encode**, or translate meaning intended into words and gestures. The sender's choice depends on factors such as their encoding skills, assessment of the receiver's ability to understand symbols, judgments about how appropriate certain symbols are, experience in similar situations, job status, education and emotional state.

It is in the encoding stage that many problems occur in international business communications, where one or more participants may be using a language other than their native language (Oldenburg 1989).

Message

The encoding outcome is a **message** of verbal (oral or written) and non-verbal symbols designed to convey meaning to the receiver. The **medium** is how the message is conveyed to the receiver. Examples are written words in a memo, words spoken on the telephone, slide graphics, and gestures in face-to-face situations. The message sender must consider the medium's appropriateness. For example, a telephone call may help conflict resolution on a minor item, but a face-to-face meeting may be better to negotiate a major change.

Receiver

The **receiver** is the person with whom the message is exchanged. If no exchange occurs (i.e. the receiver does not get the message), there is no communication. There may be just one receiver, in a conversation between two individuals, or many, with a report sent to organisation members.

Decoding

When the message is received, the receiver **decodes**, or translates symbols into the message interpreted. With effective communication, sender and receiver reach common meaning. However, the decoding process may give problems if the receiver does not decode the message as intended.

sender

Initiator of the message

encode

Process of translating an intended message into words and gestures

message

Encoding-process outcome, which consists of verbal and non-verbal symbols developed to convey meaning to the receiver

medium

Method used to convey the message to the intended receiver

receiver

Person with whom the message is exchanged

decode

Process of translating symbols into the interpreted message

FIGURE 13.2 Basic components of the communication process (adapted from Lewis 1980, p. 55)

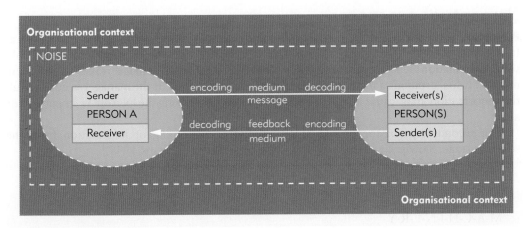

Noise

noise

Any factor in the communication process interfering with exchanging messages and achieving common meaning

Noise is any factor in the process interfering with message exchange and achieving common meaning. Noise includes interruptions during encoding, telephone line static and receiver fatigue (Chase 1998).

Feedback

feedback

Receiver's basic response to the interpreted message

Feedback is the receiver's basic response to the message interpreted. This involves reversing the communication process so receiver and sender swap roles. Feedback gives preliminary information to the sender about the success of the communication.

When communication does not allow feedback, it is **one-way communication**. Examples of one-way communication include memos, newsletters and announcements—at least when not explicitly seeking a reader response. When managers do not build immediate feedback into communication, they risk the receiver misunderstanding the intended message. With one-way communication, mistakes might not be uncovered until too late.

one-way communication

Communication resulting when the communication process does not allow for feedback

When communication specifically includes feedback, as in Figure 13.2, it is **two-way communication**. This communication allows the exchange of accurate common meaning (Chase 1998). Still, effective two-way communication requires careful focus on the process, especially if many organisation layers are involved in transmission. There are two reasons for this. First, each extra link increases the chances that the encoding and decoding processes and/or noise will distort information. Second, subordinates are reluctant to give negative information to upper hierarchical layers as they expect criticism (Kaplan, Drath & Kofodimos 1984; Trinca 2003). So managers must work hard to achieve accurate information even with two-way communication.

two-way communication

Communication resulting when the communication process explicitly includes feedback

As well as normal communication difficulties of encoding, decoding, noise and subordinate reluctance to give negative information, situational stresses may cause communication breakdown.

INFLUENCES ON INDIVIDUAL COMMUNICATION AND INTERPERSONAL PROCESSES

You may have been frustrated by coming to a meeting to find some anticipated participants did not seem to know about it. How is it some people get a particular communication and others do not? While miscommunications may be caused by misdirected mail and lost messages, they may result from individual factors influencing organisational communication. These include perceptual issues, the attribution processes, semantics, the cultural context and communication skills.

Perceptual processes

perception

Process individuals use to acquire and make sense out of information from the environment

Perception is the process of acquiring and making sense of information in the environment. It is complex, with three main stages. The first is *selecting*, or filtering stimuli so only some information gets our attention. For example, suppose a manager takes over a new unit and hears a rumour a member of the unit has a short temper. If the manager is not careful, this information may cause them to focus on situations where the person is impatient or angry.

The second stage of the process is *organising*, or patterning of information from the selection stage. Slowly say each of the following four words (Luthans 1995):

M-A-C-T-A-V-I-S-H
M-A-C-D-O-N-A-L-D
M-A-C-B-E-T-H
M-A-C-H-I-N-E-R-Y

Like many, you may have said the last as 'MacHinery'. This happens because the pattern makes us expect another word with the same type of pronunciation. This exercise shows a perception characteristic: the tendency to organise information into expected patterns. In the example of the person reputed to have a short temper, the manager may organise selectively perceived behaviour into a pattern of incidents where the person was angry.

The third stage is *interpreting*, or giving meaning to selected and organised information. In our example, the manager may begin to (perhaps unfairly) interpret information as showing the person has a short temper.

Many factors affect individuals' perceptions, such as experiences, needs, personality, culture and education. As a result, people's perceptions of situations and messages differ. Several distortions apply to managerial communication and interactions. These are stereotyping, the halo effect, projection and perceptual defence (Gordon 1996; Luthans 1995). Awareness of these can help managers avoid problems the distortions create.

Stereotyping

Stereotyping is the tendency to attribute characteristics to someone on the basis of their group membership. When a manager stereotypes, two steps occur. First, the manager classifies the person as a member of a group seen as having some common characteristics. Second, the manager draws conclusions about an individual's characteristics based on those perceived characteristics, rather than seeking information directly.

Stereotyping is a problem where generalisations are inapplicable or do not apply evenly to all group members or when people generalise about less related matters. Then, managers may convey inappropriate expectations (Mathewson 1988).

Halo effect

The **halo effect** is the use of a general impression, founded on one or a few personal characteristics, to judge other characteristics. For example, a manager may have a general impression based on one thing a worker does, such as compiling reports well or poorly, to judge their ability in other areas, such as customer handling. To avoid the halo effect, interviewers and managers must gather enough data to make reasonable judgments in areas being evaluated (Bateman & Snell 2004).

Projection

Projection is the tendency to assume others share your thoughts, feelings and characteristics. Unfortunately, this encourages managers to use one-way communication, assuming they know how their employees feel on all issues. Using two-way communication to learn how others feel about different issues helps avoid the effects of projection.

Perceptual defence

Perceptual defence is the tendency to block out or distort information one finds threatening or challenging to one's beliefs (Luthans 1995). So managers or workers may be unreceptive to some information. This can lead to the 'shoot the bearer of bad news' syndrome, where the bad-news bearer is 'beheaded' though they did not cause the problem. Thus managers may get angry at employees giving information on serious problems which cannot be ignored, even though the manager must be aware of them.

Attribution processes

Attribution theory is one way to understand how perceptions influence managerial communication and interpersonal processes. **Attribution theory** explains how people make

---

stereotyping

Tendency to attribute characteristics to an individual on the basis of an assessment of the group to which they belong

halo effect

Tendency to use a general impression based on one or a few characteristics of an individual to judge other characteristics of that same individual

projection

Tendency of an individual to assume others share their thoughts, feelings and characteristics

perceptual defence

Tendency to block out or distort information one finds threatening or which challenges one's beliefs

attribution theory

Theory attempting to explain how individuals make judgments or attributions about the causes of the behaviour of another or of their own

LG Electronics

The use of machines to communicate our wants and needs is nothing new. Since Alexander Graham Bell invented the telephone in 1876, people have been using this technology for everything from ordering world war to ordering a pizza. However, with the inception of internet technology and smart devices, it is now possible that much of the information used for making some household decisions—communication that would usually come from another member of the household—could come from the household appliances.

LG Electronics, a pioneer consumer electronics company of South Korea founded in 1958, has developed a range of household appliances that can connect to the internet to assist in making the simplest household task 'easier' for the client. For example, LG has developed an 'internet refrigerator'. This device uses a basic internet connection to alert a service centre about any malfunction or when a service is due. Also, with the addition of a touch screen the refrigerator can monitor when food is likely to expire or when food needs replenishing. With the internet connection it may also be possible to have the refrigerator order new supplies when it senses that they are low. The traditional use of the refrigerator door as a familial notice board has also been taken into consideration. The touch-screen technology and a micro-camera mounted in the screen assembly allow users to record video messages and leave them 'on the fridge' for others in the house to view at a later time. A simple note on the fridge now has an electronic counterpart.

This technology does not stop with the refrigerator. Other appliances such as ducted and split-system air conditioners, microwaves, dryers and washing machines may also be used in a similar way, having their own control as to their most efficient use. Many would say that this proves Stanley Kubrick's vision of a computer-controlled world is becoming eerily true. However, the internet does allow the user an increased degree of control.

In cooperation with a devoted LG website, users can actually 'log in' and control their devices from anywhere on the globe, turning on washing

machines and air conditioners while the user is still sitting in the office.

Although this technology is still in its infancy, the result may be that we can spend less time worrying about our mundane tasks, and leave these to the machines.

Source: Contributed by Joel Mendelson (details of sources are listed on p. 737).

Activities for discussion, analysis and further research

1. Can you see any potential barriers to these type of devices entering the current household appliances market?
2. As a consumer, how do you feel about appliances with access to the internet being able to directly communicate with suppliers to order on your behalf? Does this constitute any 'breakdown' in communication?
3. Log on to the internet and investigate other areas in which devices have control over some decisions within organisations worldwide, and how these devices communicate their decisions with their users. Is this communication effective?

judgments or attributions about causes of the behaviour of another or themselves (Luthans 1995). These judgments form a basis for later actions. The theory predicts we make either dispositional (attributed to internal causes, such as personality traits or a person's own efforts) or situational (attributed to external causes, such as equipment or luck) causal judgments. For example, if Jane fails to complete an assignment on time, should we attribute it to internal factors like lack of effort or ability, or do we decide some work context or issue is to blame? In making these judgments we consider consensus (how much the behaviour resembles how most act in a given situation), consistency (how much the person acts in the same way in this or similar situations at other times), and distinctiveness (the degree to which the person behaves differently in other situations). Thus, if other staff finished the same task on time, Jane has had trouble finishing similar assignments on time before, and she has missed deadlines on other assignment types, we would probably make a dispositional judgment about why the assignment was late. On the other hand, if others were late finishing the assignment, Jane normally finishes on time, and usually finishes other types of assignments by the deadline, we are likely to attribute the problem to situational factors. The attributions influence how we handle the late assignment.

In making causal judgments, managers must consider the **fundamental attribution error**— the tendency to underestimate situational influences and to overestimate dispositional influences to explain behaviour. This error is more likely when explaining behaviour of others. If success and failure is involved, we may succumb to **self-serving bias**. This bias is the tendency to see yourself as responsible for successes and others for failures (Tosi, Rizzo & Carroll 1986; Johns 1996). This sets up communication problems between managers and subordinates. For instance, a manager attributes subordinates' successes to the manager's effective leadership, and failures to subordinates' shortcomings. Subordinates, meanwhile, see successes as coming from their own hard work and ability, and see failures as stemming from bad luck or work environment factors, including areas the supervisor manages (DeGregoria & Gillis 1980; Meyers 1983).

Semantics

Words are symbols, so their meanings differ for everyone. Semantics is the study of meanings and word choice. A **semantic net** is the network of words and word meanings a person has available for recall (Lewis 1980). Everyone has their own net, which overlaps, but does not correspond precisely, with those of others. **Semantic blocks** are blockages or communication difficulties coming from word choices (Munter 1987). Such blocks are common due to the range and shades of meanings people give to words, depending on their semantic net. Receivers decode words and phrases conforming to their own semantic networks, which may differ from the sender's (Axley 1984). The examples presented in Table 13.1 show the potential for semantic blocks between manager and subordinate.

Within organisations, different units can have terminology that has evolved through tradition or is related specifically to the work being done. A common cause of semantic blocks is use of *professional jargon*, or language related to a specific profession but unfamiliar to outsiders. This language must be used carefully as it can bewilder newcomers, customers or visitors. Nevertheless, organisation-specific language builds cohesion among employees, reinforcing corporate culture and, as it does at the Walt Disney Company, supporting a competitive edge (Bormann 1983). It becomes particularly challenging when organisations operate across national boundaries, such as Country Road's less than successful US operations (Lloyd 2003).

At many firms, employees speak a language of their own. Organisations often create their own language, which

fundamental attribution error

Tendency to underestimate the importance of situational influences and overestimate the importance of dispositional influences in explaining behaviour

self-serving bias

Tendency to perceive oneself as responsible for successes and others as responsible for failures

semantic net

Network of words and word meanings a given individual has available for recall

semantic blocks

Blockages or communication difficulties arising from word choices

TABLE 13.1 EXAMPLES OF SEMANTIC BLOCKS IN COMMUNICATIONS BETWEEN MANAGER AND SUBORDINATE

What the manager said	What the manager meant	What the subordinate heard
I'll look into hiring another person for your department as soon as I complete my budget review.	We'll start interviewing for that job in about three weeks.	I'm tied up with more important things. Let's forget about hiring for the indefinite future.
Your performance was below par last quarter. I really expected more out of you.	You're going to have to try harder, but I know you can do it.	If you screw up one more time, you're out.
I'd like that report as soon as you can get to it.	I need that report within the week.	Drop that rush order you're working on and fill out that report today.

Source: Reprinted from Hodgetts & Altman (1979, p. 305).

becomes part of daily communication among employees. In fact, outsiders may need translations. For example:

A hipo, a Wallenda and an imagineer order drinks at a bar. They do a little work—edit a violin, non-concur with a wild duck, take care of some bad Mickey—and then ask for the bill. 'This is on the mouse', says one of them. Who picks up the tab?

In this case, a veteran employee at IBM says a 'hipo' (short for 'high potential') is a designation for an employee who appears to be on the fast track to success. Another IBMer claims an employee seen as having low potential is known as an 'alpo'. This second label become especially pointed if one realises 'alpo' is a brand of dog food in America. IBM employees do not disagree with their bosses; instead, they 'non-concur'. An individual who often non-concurs, but constructively, is known as a 'wild duck'. The 'wild duck' label was a favourite of a former chairman, Thomas Watson Jr, who borrowed it from Kierkegaard.

Corporate slang can be prevalent in publishers, whose employees work with words. At *Newsweek*, top editors are often called 'Wallendas', after the famous family of aerialists. The designation recognises the editors' job vulnerability. Writers at *Newsweek* refer to the weekly's top national story as the 'violin'.

In one move, the Walt Disney Company deliberately set up its own corporate jargon to support its efforts to have employees think of Disney theme parks as stages. At orientation and training sessions, they are taught to say they are 'onstage' when working in the theme park and 'backstage' when in lower areas, where they cannot be seen by the public. They learn to refer to co-workers as 'cast members'. An imagineer is a member of Disney's Imagineering division, the innovative group responsible for dreaming up new ideas and figuring out how to make them work.

Jack Herrman, a former Walt Disney World publicist, remembers co-workers would label anything positive a 'good Mickey' and anything negative (like a cigarette butt on the ground) a 'bad Mickey'. When employees take someone to lunch on the Walt Disney World expense account, they say it is 'on the mouse'. 'You're immersed in the jargon they impose upon you as a way of life', Herrman says. Through such language, the company reminds members constantly of their roles. In this way, Disney uses language to support their competitive edge (Miller 1987).

Managing diversity: Cultural context

Culture also influences communication and interpersonal processes. One means of cultural influence is the importance of the communication context (Hall 1959; 1976; Kennedy & Everest 1991). Context includes situational factors such as participants' roles, existing relationships, and non-verbal communication. **High-context cultures** emphasise establishing and strengthening relationships in communication while exchanging information. High-context culture countries include Mexico, Saudi Arabia, India and China (see Fig. 13.3). For those from these countries, circumstances, or context, and non-verbal communication will be as important as what is said. In **low-context cultures** emphasis is on information exchange and less focused on building relationships by communication. Low-context culture countries include Australia, Canada and the United States. Individuals from low-context countries place more emphasis on spoken words, paying less attention to circumstances or non-verbal communication (Patrick 2003). For example, many Asian cultures show deference to those higher in the social structure by not making eye contact; but someone from a low-context country ignores such subtleties. There are also differences between country and city dwellers in the same country, and genders (Tannen 1995a; 1995b). So those from low-context areas and high-context areas may have problems communicating unless they allow for their differences.

An implication is that, if a low-context supervisor tries to give performance feedback to a high-context subordinate, they will have problems if they focus on objective facts without attending to building trust and the relationship. Strong communication skills can help them adjust more readily to cultural context matters.

Communication skills

To be effective communicators in various settings, managers need strong listening and feedback skills. These are critical because managers spend so much time communicating orally.

Listening skills

As discussed earlier, receivers must ensure they decode and interpret the sender's intended message. As managers rely heavily on information from oral communication, listening skills are crucial (Lewis & Reinsch 1988). Listening experts often differentiate between relatively passive listening, where the listener follows the general gist, and active listening. **Active listening** is where a listener participates actively in trying to grasp facts and the speaker's feelings. Listening actively for both content and feelings is needed to understand the message's total meaning (Gordon 1987). Managers who are poor listeners face problems (Lenzner 1995). For guidelines to enhance listening skills, see 'How to listen actively' in Management skills for a globalised economy.

Feedback

Other important managerial interpersonal communication skills centre on feedback, both giving and receiving it. Effective feedback has several characteristics. It focuses on relevant behaviours or outcomes, not the person. It deals with specific, observable behaviour, not generalities. Perceptions, reactions and opinions are labelled as such, rather than given as facts. Finally, feedback spells out how people can improve (Kaplan et al. 1984). Skilled feedback makes guiding subordinates easier and raises prospects for mutual success.

Receiving feedback is as important as giving it. Most of us have no problem getting positive feedback. Getting negative feedback can be more problematic. However, the way managers and others react to feedback influences how much they get (Kaplan 1984). When receiving negative feedback, it helps to paraphrase what is being said (so you can check your perceptions), seek clarification and examples of any points unclear or with which you may disagree, and avoid defensiveness (Centre for Creative Leadership 1976).

high-context cultures

Cultures where the emphasis in the communication process is on establishing and strengthening relationships in the course of exchanging information

low-context cultures

Cultures where the emphasis in the communication process is on exchanging information and is less focused on building relationships

active listening

Process in which a listener actively participates in attempting to grasp facts and feelings being expressed by the speaker

FIGURE 13.3 Continuum of low-context and high-context cultures

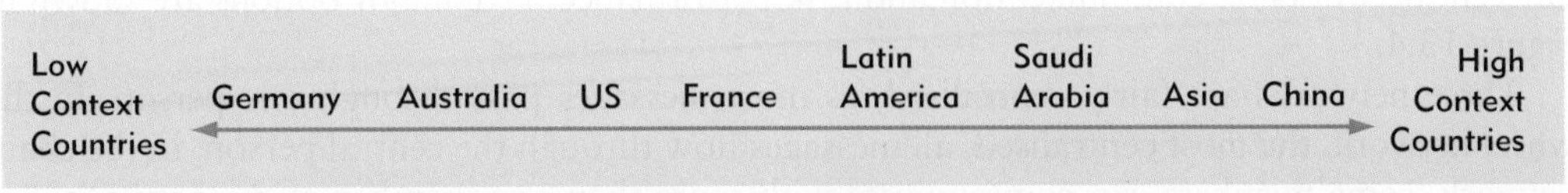

Low Context Countries	Germany	Australia	US	France	Latin America	Saudi Arabia	Asia	China	High Context Countries

How to listen actively

The following guidelines will help you be an active listener:

1. Listen patiently to what the other person has to say, though you may think it is wrong or irrelevant. Indicate simple acceptance (not necessarily agreement) by nodding or injecting an occasional 'um-hm' or 'I see'.

2. Try to understand feelings the person is expressing, as well as intellectual content. Most of us have difficulty talking clearly about our feelings, so careful attention is needed.

3. Restate the person's feelings, briefly but accurately. At this stage, simply serve as a mirror and encourage them to continue talking. Occasionally make summary responses, such as 'You think you're in a dead-end job' or 'You feel the manager is playing favourites'. Keep your tone neutral and try not to lead the person to your pet conclusions.

4. Allow time for discussion to continue without interruption, and try to separate the conversation from more official communication of company plans. That is, do not make the conversation any more 'authoritative' than it already is by virtue of your organisational position.

5. Avoid direct questions and arguments about facts; refrain from saying 'That's just not so', 'Hold on a minute, let's look at the facts', or 'Prove it'. You may want to review the evidence later, but a review is irrelevant to how a person feels now.

6. When the other person touches on a point you want to know more about, simply repeat their statement as a question. For instance, if the person remarks, 'Nobody can break even on their expense account', you can probe by replying, 'You say no one breaks even on expenses?' With this encouragement, they will probably expand on the previous statement.

7. Listen for what isn't said—evasions of pertinent points or perhaps too-ready agreement with common clichés. Such omissions may be clues to a bothersome fact the person wishes were not true.

8. If the other person appears to genuinely want your viewpoint, be honest in your reply. But in the listening stage, try to limit the expression of your views, since these may condition or suppress what the other person says.

9. Focus on message content; try not to think about your next statement until the person is finished talking.

10. Avoid making judgments until all information has been conveyed.

Source: Adapted from Gordon (1987, p. 230).

Organisations have found it pays to get customer feedback, especially from dissatisfied customers. For example, Roger Nunley, industry and consumer affairs manager at Coca-Cola, said studies show one dissatisfied consumer in 50 complains; the rest switch brands. Yet if a complaint is addressed, the individual is likely to stay a customer. So, firms such as Qantas, Coca-Cola, American Express and Mattel have contact numbers for customers to voice complaints (Sellers 1988; Quintanilla & Gibson 1994).

communication network

Pattern of information flow among task-group members

GROUP COMMUNICATION NETWORKS

When tasks need several people's input, managers must look at the **communication network**, the information flow patterns among task-group members. Studies have assessed the impact of different networks on communication and task performance. Five major options are shown in Figure 13.4.

Three networks are fairly centralised, as most messages pass through one person. In the wheel network, the most centralised, all messages flow through the central person. In the chain network, some members can communicate with more than one member of the network, but

FIGURE 13.4 Group communication networks (adapted from Baskin & Aronoff 1980, p. 77)

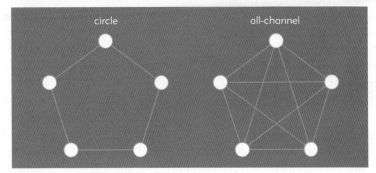

MANAGERIAL DILEMMAS

Manager's use and abuse of modern communication methods

In order to provide leadership, managers must be able to influence their subordinates and they must do this through all means at their disposal. This includes all forms of communication, including many which are relatively new and have very differing characteristics; for example, use of intranets, the internet, email, video streaming, and meetings held via satellite. To make matters more difficult, most of the managers working today were employed and trained prior to the development of these modern communication methods. Further, in their management training and education courses they were provided with principles and practices developed in a pre-electronic age. There are a number of dilemmas that this provides.

Managers who find it more efficient to use email to communicate with staff are often seen as aloof and uncaring. More importantly, unless they learn good 'netiquette' their message may often be

misunderstood or misinterpreted. They must be careful not to provide offence and to think carefully before sending emails which often can cause unnecessary distress to staff. Recently a senior manager advised her junior managers to write emails when they were emotional but never to send them! Writing them would relieve their tension but sending them could cause immeasurable heartache and lead to irreparable damage in relations.

Organisations which see their intranet or the internet as an efficient means of storing and making available policy documents and forms for staff may find that staff are overloaded with information and, while being made aware that such and such a policy is now accessible at some web address, they may never actually access the site. It is very dangerous to assume that providing staff with access to a new policy is the same as making staff aware of, and informed about, a new policy. A manager wishing to be helpful sent a list of all web sites containing their organisation's policy documents—all 17 of them—with a note that said 'this list may be useful!' It only emphasised the impracticality of disseminating important policy information without proper discussion and consultation.

Managers who use video streaming for their presentations will find that staff not actually present in a room where the presentation is taking place are less likely to develop an affinity with the manager and will indulge in distracting activities which they would not do in the presence of the manager. Further they will ask fewer questions than the staff present at the manager's talk. Despite the modern highly developed technology, there are often breakdowns in communication and inevitably the remote centres miss out on some part of the presentation.

Hence, despite the efficiency and attractiveness of using modern communication techniques, managers must consider how effective they are in assisting with their role as leaders. Consider for example how one demonstrates 'directive leader behaviour', or 'participative leader behaviour' via electronic means of communication.

Source: Contributed by Ken Dooley.

Activities for discussion, analysis and further research

1. What are the advantages of using modern communication methods for a manager attempting to provide leadership?
2. What are the disadvantages of using modern communication methods for a manager attempting to provide leadership?
3. For which form of leadership would electronic means of communication be more appropriate—transformational or transactional? Discuss.

the person in the chain's centre emerges as message controller. In the Y network, usually the person at the fork of the 'Y' becomes the central person. The last two networks shown in Figure 13.4 are decentralised, since communication flows readily among members. In the circle network, each can communicate with the person on either side. Finally, in the star network, the most decentralised, each member can communicate with any other.

For fairly simple, routine tasks, centralised networks are faster and more accurate. This is because in centralised networks, the person in the central position (marked with an X in Fig. 13.4) tends to be coordinator, and facilitates routine task completion. In contrast, for more complex tasks, decentralised networks are faster and more accurate, with the star network being best. With complex tasks, free exchange of information in the circle and star facilitates the process and creativity.

It is interesting that morale in the networks was higher for decentralised ones, regardless of task type. This is a managerial dilemma. Centralised networks are best for accurate performance on simple tasks, particularly when time is short. However, morale suffers. For more complex tasks, decentralised networks give both high performance and morale. From a practical standpoint, many organisational tasks are complex (Shaw 1981). If tasks are simple and need more centralised communication networks, managers can boost morale by allowing subordinates to work on more complex tasks, allowing involvement in a more decentralised network.

ORGANISATIONAL COMMUNICATION CHANNELS

communication channels

Patterns of organisational communication flow representing potential established conduits through which managers and other organisation members can send and receive information

One point in assessing organisational communication is the flow of information through the company. When information does not reach individuals and groups needing it, effectiveness and efficiency problems emerge. Organisational **communication** patterns are called **channels** as they are ways managers and other members can send and receive information. In this section, we consider two directions of flow: vertical and horizontal. We also examine an informal communication-flow form, the 'grapevine'. Finally, we consider results of using communication channels for innovation, as well as electronics to facilitate organisational communication.

Vertical communication

Vertical communication is message exchange between two or more organisational levels (see Fig. 13.5). So vertical communication may involve a manager and a subordinate or several hierarchical layers. It can flow down or up. Managers are found to spend about two-thirds of communication time in vertical communication (Porter & Roberts 1976; Rue & Byars 2003).

Downward communication

When vertical communication flows from higher to lower levels, it is **downward communication**. This has many forms, such as staff meetings, company policy statements, newsletters, informational memos and face-to-face contact. Most of the communication involves information in one of five categories: (1) job instructions on specific tasks, (2) job rationales explaining relationships between tasks, (3) organisation procedures and practices, (4) feedback on individual performance and (5) attempts to encourage a sense of mission and organisational goal dedication (Katz & Kahn 1978).

Downward communication across several levels can become distorted. A middle manager survey shows quality of received information is poor (Harcourt, Richerson & Wattier 1991). As shown by Figure 13.6, 80 per cent of top management's message is lost within five levels. Distortion occurs for three main reasons. The first is faulty message transmission due to sender carelessness, poor communication skills, and difficulties encoding a message clearly for members at many levels. Second, managers overuse one-way communication, using memos, newsletters and manuals, with little possible immediate receiver feedback. Third, some deliberately or accidentally filter communications by withholding, screening or manipulating information. Deliberate filtering occurs when a manager enhances personal power by tightly controlling organisational information (Baskin & Aronoff 1980; Lewis 1980).

A way to increase effective downward communication is through multiple channels and repetition (Ansberry 1991). Downward communication can be enhanced too by encouraging feedback by upward communication.

Upward communication

When vertical communication flow is from lower levels to one or more higher organisation levels, it is **upward communication**. Upward communication includes one-to-one meetings with the immediate superior, staff meetings with superiors, memos and reports, suggestion

vertical communication

Communication involving a message exchange between two or more levels of the organisational hierarchy

downward communication

Vertical communication flowing from a higher level to one or more lower levels in the organisation

upward communication

Vertical flow of communication from a lower level to one or more higher levels in the organisation

FIGURE 13.5 Vertical and horizontal organisational communication (adapted from Pace 1983, p. 40)

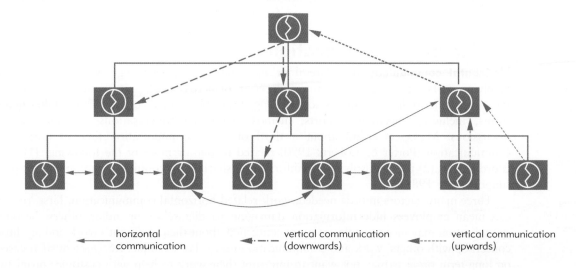

FIGURE 13.6 Levels of understanding as information is transmitted down the organisation (adapted from Lewis 1980; and Scannell 1970)

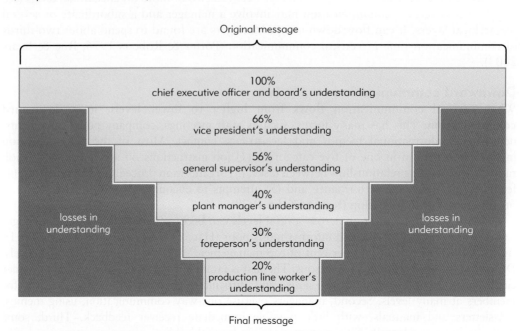

systems, grievance procedures and employee attitude surveys. Information spread through upward communication typically relates to (1) current work project progress, (2) unsolved problems and situations where subordinates need help from superiors, (3) new developments within or affecting the work unit or organisation, (4) improvement and innovation suggestions, (5) employee attitudes, morale and efficiency (Planty & Machaver 1952; Cranwell 1969; Goldhaber 1986).

Distortion typical of downward communication also affects upward communication for two reasons. First, information favourable to the sender will be sent upward, while unfavourable information will be blocked, even when organisationally important. Subordinates will more often filter information when they distrust their superiors, see them as having lots of influence over their careers, and strongly desire to move up (O'Reilly & Roberts 1974). Second, managers discourage upward communication (Aldrich 1986; Atkinson 1996; Roberts 2003b). Encouraging upward communication can foster quality effectively.

Horizontal communication

horizontal communication

Lateral or diagonal message exchange either within work-unit boundaries, involving peers reporting to the same supervisor, or across work-unit boundaries, involving individuals who report to different supervisors

Horizontal communication is lateral or diagonal message exchange within work units, involving peers reporting to the same supervisor, or across work-unit boundaries, involving those reporting to different supervisors (see Fig. 13.5). Horizontal communication takes many forms, including meetings, reports, memos, telephone conversations and face-to-face discussions. Managers spend about a third of their communication time in horizontal communication (Porter & Roberts 1990) related to one or more of the following: (1) task coordination, (2) problem solving, (3) information sharing, (4) conflict resolution and (5) peer support (Pace 1983).

Three major factors impede needed, work-related horizontal communication. First, rivalry can mean employees hide information damaging to themselves or aiding others. Second, specialisation may mean people are more concerned about their own unit's work and are little concerned with others' work and communication needs. For example, R&D scientists focused on long-term projects may not want to interrupt their work to help with customer problems

Girl trouble at Paperworks

Stuart McTavish is a financial manager for Paperworks, a large paper-products distribution company based in the South Island of New Zealand. Seven female employees work with Stuart in the main office, where work tasks are structured around clerical, credit control, pay and customer services activities. As the senior office manager, Stuart is having to deal with an issue that has been festering for a while and, if not resolved, will be taken out of the company's control and into the employment court.

The problem began when five of the female office staff went out together socially on a Friday night. After a few drinks, two of them—Emma and Jo—had a shouting match that ended in a physical fight. Both women were battered and bruised, but neither laid a formal assault complaint or took the incident any further. However, the bad feelings that resulted from this event have spilled over into work, where there is now a hostile atmosphere.

Emma was seen as the instigator of the fight with Jo. A number of Emma's work friendships have changed, and when her colleagues have to work with her, they are now reluctant to do any more than the minimum required of their jobs. The atmosphere in the office is having an effect on customer relations and on productivity.

Stuart has not been actively involved in getting to the bottom of the present disharmony, as he thought it was up to the women to sort it out for themselves. However, just before Christmas the animosity among the women came to a head, and there was a series of meetings with all of the staff to discuss the issue.

Emma became very upset as an outcome of the meetings, and on medical advice she took stress leave for a fortnight. She returned to work after the New Year's holiday break, and things in the office seemed to have returned to normal. Stuart is often out of the office on Thursdays, and the rules are generally bent more on that day than any other workday. However, one Thursday Stuart was in his office all day. Emma sent an email to her counterpart, Linda, who works later hours, telling her 'she was not taking her afternoon tea and would be leaving early, if that was all right'. Upon receiving this email, Linda was infuriated for a number of reasons. First, she thought Emma should speak to her directly, as they shared the same physical office space. Second, she was annoyed that Emma should ask her for permission when she was not in a position to grant or deny the request. Third, she felt that she was always having to carry someone else's work—usually Emma's. Feeling frustrated and tired of having to deal with difficult situations, Linda decided to hand the matter over to Stuart, who was, after all, the manager. She immediately forwarded the email to him.

Stuart responded by calling Emma in to a 10-minute meeting. He told her that this was not the right way to handle a work-related request, and he declined her request to leave at 3.30 p.m. instead of 4 p.m. Emma phoned in sick for the next couple of days.

Now three days later, Emma has laid a formal complaint against Paperworks because she feels that everyone is against her and that she is a victim of workplace harassment. Stuart is about to meet the union delegate and senior managers from Head Office. The other staff members are upset and anxious to know what is happening, yet aware that full disclosure might escalate the current conflict. Stuart grabbed a coffee and sat at his desk bewildered. Why had this happened? Why did he have to deal with it? How was he going to deal with the situation that he was now in?

Source: Contributed by Elizabeth Hall.

Activities for discussion, analysis and further research

1. What strategies can Stuart adopt to deal constructively with the conflict?
2. Explain how active listening facilitates communication.
3. The case focuses on different facets of managerial communication, face-to-face interaction, conflict management, gender differences in communication and email interactions. How does the current situation influence how Stuart ought to think about communicating company policies? How would you advise Stuart to structure communications with employees?

identified by sales. Third, motivation may be low when horizontal communication among subordinates is discouraged or unrewarded. Committees, task forces and matrix structures are ways managers encourage horizontal communication, mainly at work-unit boundaries (see Chapters 8 and 9) (Goldhaber 1986; Tredgold 2003d).

Informal communication: The grapevine

Vertical and horizontal communication patterns are formal patterns, or channels, as communication follows the official hierarchical structure and task requirements. You might see **formal communication** as associated with an organisational position. In contrast, **informal communication**, or the **grapevine**, occurs without reference to hierarchy or task requirements. Informal communication relates to personal, not positional, issues (Pace 1983). For example, personal relationships unrelated to organisational positions exist among employees who ride to work in the same car, attend the same church, or have children in the same school. Grapevine communications stem largely from relationships which may overlap, but may not coincide with hierarchy and task communication requirements.

The term 'grapevine' can be traced to the American Civil War, when telegraph lines strung from tree to tree in grapevine-like patterns gave garbled intelligence messages (Davis 1972). All organisations have grapevines, and the patterns can be both vertical and horizontal. A classic study looked at four configurations for grapevine chains (see Fig. 13.7). In a single-strand chain, communication moves from person A to B to C and so on. In the gossip chain, person A seeks out and communicates with others. When following a probability chain, person A spreads a message randomly, as do individuals F and D. In a cluster chain, person A gives the message to three others, one of these passes it on to two more, then one of them passes it on still further. According to the study, the cluster chain predominates. This finding suggests people who are part of grapevines will be selective about those to whom they relay information and only some of those will pass information further (Davis 1980).

Overall, grapevines are fast, carry large amounts of information, and yield data that is between 50 and 90 per cent accurate (Friedman 1981; Goldhaber 1986; Zaremba 1988). Although the grapevine is seen as inaccurate, the problem comes mainly from misinterpreting incomplete details (Pace 1983; *Wall Street Journal* 1989).

Although not officially set up or sanctioned, grapevines occur in all organisations and cannot be abolished. They create problems when they carry gossip and false rumours, but if managed properly have many good aspects. By dwelling on errors, grapevines can help communicate organisational rules, values, morals, traditions and history. Grapevines give employees time to consider potential changes and can help their organisational goal contributions (March & Sevon 1984; Weick & Browning 1986; Mishra 1990). As well, they foster innovation by building organisation communication.

formal communication

Vertical and horizontal communication which follows paths specified by the official hierarchical organisation structure and related task requirements

informal communication

Communication which takes place without regard to hierarchical or task requirements

grapevine

Another term for informal communication

FIGURE 13.7 Types of grapevine chains (reprinted from Davis, in Ferguson & Ferguson 1980, p. 59)

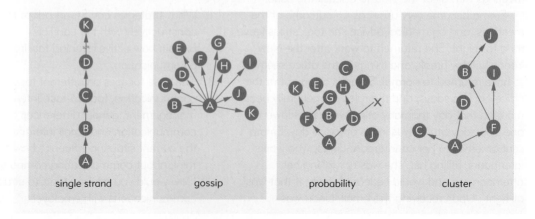

single strand   gossip   probability   cluster

ezydvd.com.au

Gone are the days of having to run down to your local video store to choose which movie to see this Saturday night. A new revolution is here, the DVD—a new medium which enhances the viewing experience, embraces surround sound, gives you director commentary and even lets you take control of the camera and choose from which angle you wish to view the film.

The sale of DVDs has also entered the twenty-first century with many current video retailers extending their current sales and hire functions to include an internet sales face. However, as a contrast to this 'concrete business with internet sales' approach, South Australian Company 'ezydvd.com.au' has opted for the opposite—a primary online business which has only recently opened 'brick and mortar' stores.

Operations of this firm started in 1999, with the establishing of a business that had one clear organisational goal: 'To be a leading retailer of DVDs'. Since then the firm has expanded to become one of Australia's leading DVD retailers, now stocking over 9000 titles, with over 100 new titles being added to the online catalogue every week. This e-commerce success story has been attributed to a dedication, by management, to the continual commitment to meeting the ever-changing demands of Australian and international markets. This means that the company needs to be dynamic and ever-flexible in its operations.

Ezydvd.com.au has utilised the internet, and its high acceptance and use within Australia and the Pacific Rim, as the basis for its primary business operations. The use of technologies, such as advanced e-commerce solutions for payment and account processing, secure servers, innovative and user-friendly webpages, has not only meant that potential customers can easily browse, search or be notified of new releases and specials, but also that they can be sure that their data is safe and confidential. Also, as the webpage and secure servers do not require constant supervision, ezydvd.com.au operates 24 hours a day, 7 days a week regardless of weekends, nights or public holidays.

With the management of the organisation sensing that there was still a market for a traditional 'brick and mortar' retail DVD specialty store, the company opened its first franchised store in Sydney on 31 October 2003, with the goal of having over 60 retail stores around Australia by the end of 2004.

This e-success story demonstrates the way a small company with strong managerial ideals and a commitment to the fulfilment of market requirements can grow into a national leader in its field.

Source: Contributed by Joel Mendelson; www.ezydvd.com.au.

Activities for discussion, analysis and further research

1. How could the managerial communication in a business be helpful in the overall growth from small business to market leader?

2. Consider yourself as a manager of an organisation like ezydvd.com.au. How would your managerial communication styles have to differ between your online and store clients?

3. What sort of communication techniques would you have to use with a store franchisee, in comparison with an online store employee?

Using electronics to facilitate communication

Electronic advances have given managers new communication methods, channels and concerns. Four advances are electronic mail systems and the internet, voice mail, teleconferencing and videoconferencing, and interest in groupware is growing.

electronic mail system

Mail system which allows high-speed exchange of written messages by use of computerised text-processing and communication networks

An **electronic mail system** (email) allows high-speed written messages to be exchanged through computerised text-processing and communication networks. Anyone with a computer terminal can write and send a written message to anyone else with a computer mailbox. In an early study managers said they saved about seven hours per week as their electronic mail system increased decision-making speed (Crawford 1982). Other managers estimated their system saved them about three hours per week by eliminating unreturned phone calls and cutting internal correspondence (Nyce & Groppa 1983). However, a recent study found that, if an employee gets 25 to 30 messages a day and takes an hour or more every day to respond to them, then $300 to $400 a month is wasted replying to poorly written, ambiguous emails and those sent to the wrong people (Griffin 2000). In fact some organisations are even resorting to turning their email off in order to recover their time (Ellis 2003).

There is also evidence that electronic mail leads to information exchange among managers who were not communicating either by mail or telephone, and that they get new types of information (Rice & Case 1983; Kiesler 1986). Electronic mail systems improve vertical and facilitate horizontal communication (Huseman & Miles 1988; *Inc* 1995).

One disadvantage of electronic mail is that it lacks non-verbal cues (facial expressions, body movements and voice tone) that aid face-to-face communication (*Wall Street Journal* 1995). (Of course, regular mail has fewer non-verbal cues than face-to-face messages too.) Another is that the speed and seemingly temporary nature of email may lead people to vent anger (or 'flaming') in an email message they never would have sent had they put it on paper. Accordingly, handling significant misunderstandings on a face-to-face basis when possible is best; be cautious resolving difficulties via email. Still another disadvantage is that the ease of sending mail electronically can cause some to receive excessive amounts of unsolicited or irrelevant mail, commonly called 'spam' (Zachary 1994). A growing concern is that the apparently anonymous nature of the process makes employees feel secure, using the system inappropriately (McMorris 1995; Bryan 2000; Kinicki & Williams 2003).

Electronic mail is the first step to the internet, the global computer network people use to communicate. Over 77 million people in the United States alone use the internet on a regular basis (*CyberAtlas* 2000). It is also estimated that managers in over 21 000 companies communicate this way (Eng 1995). Australia in 1998 had 16 per cent of the population using the internet regularly, with Singapore (24 per cent) and Hong Kong (12 per cent) showing comparable rates. By 2000, penetration had accelerated, with Singapore (75.9 per cent) and Hong Kong (43.4 per cent) showing greatly enlarged internet usage (*Economist Intelligence Unit* 2002)

Managers and companies use the internet for many reasons, such as supplier and contractor communication; between remote offices; between customers and potential customers; for recruitment; communicating with the general public; and finding competitor information (GCC Group 2000).

Internet communication is growing. Nevertheless, there are concerns about security. Ironically, the internet's very purpose, allowing the sharing of vast quantities of information, raises security issues. Experts believe the internet can be made quite secure. However, whether it can be secure enough to be used for many business transactions is unclear.

As well as securing internet communication, managers face other internet problems. When employees surf the Net on company time for fun, costs rise and they may do it inappropriately (Bryan 2000; Kirby 2000).

voice mail

Recording system providing senders with an opportunity to leave messages for receivers by telephone

An allied form of electronic communication is **voice mail**, a recording system where senders can leave telephone messages. With voice mail, non-verbal cues (voice quality and tone) are present. Voice mail is useful with short messages not needing discussion. In another development, voice recognition, computers and telephone technologies have made electronic secretaries possible. This strategy permits people to interact with their voice mail programs more actively (Bulkeley 1995; Wildstrom 1995; Hartnett 1999; Carter 1999).

Another electronic communication form, **teleconferencing**, is simultaneous communication among a group of people by telephone or computer with specially designed software (Laudon & Laudon 1994). The software is called groupware as it aids sharing messages among group members. Groupware allows meetings among group members at different sites. However, it can also facilitate group meetings in one location. In this case, each group member is in front of a computer. Groupware coordinates simultaneous messages and displays them on a special screen all can see. Messages are anonymous, and most communication is done through computers. Sometimes no one speaks a word (Kirkpatrick 1992; Bartino 1992; Bateman & Snell 2004).

Groupware is successful (Rifkin 1995; *Business Week* 1995) when work is group- or team-based, and members are rewarded for group performance, and with top management's full support. Organisation culture must allow a high degree of flexibility, with the program being seen as one tool in the group's best interest. Finally all participants must be trained and comfortable in using the whole system.

A related electronic communication form is **videoconferencing**, or holding meetings with people in two or more locations by closed-circuit television. One creative application of the technology has diners facing a video screen interacting with others apparently engaged in the same process, but some distance away (Ziegler 1995). Teleconferencing use has grown (Hellweg, Frieberg & Smith 1984; Aldrich 1986). Firms with their own private television networks include Optus, Ford, Merrill Lynch and Xerox (Meeks 1988).

As communication occurs with groups, managers find it helpful to have a knowledge of group dynamics. We explore this topic in the next chapter.

teleconferencing

Simultaneous communication among a group of individuals by telephone or via computer using specially designed software

videoconferencing

Holding meetings with individuals in two or more locations by means of closed-circuit television

GAINING THE EDGE

Cool is good for communication

Developing trust between management and staff is essential if a crisis is to be handled properly. This is true of one-off incidents such as a security threat or a workplace accident. But it is even more important for dealing with the problems caused by workplace changes such as a hostile takeover or mass redundancies.

Important workplace change requires trust because it is usually a two-stage process, says T. J. Larkin, a partner of the communications consultancy Larkin Communication. Mass sackings, for example, are usually the result of a merger or the introduction of new technology or work practices. Managers may be simultaneously retrenching 10 to 20 per cent of a workforce and asking those who remain to carry out the changes. 'So at the same time, you're doing something painful and unpopular to them, you're almost always asking them for their support', Larkin says.

Creating a culture of trust is achieved by communicating early and often. 'It's not the downsizing that kills employee morale and

performance, it's the uncertainty about the downsizing,' Larkin says. When communication is delayed—often because managers think they should wait until they have all the facts—the results can be dramatic. In this kind of vacuum, employees will rely on rumours, the media and unions for information. It is better to talk to staff than to remain silent, even when the information is only estimates or likely scenarios. Research shows that performance, job satisfaction and employees' sense of trust all fall by 20 to 25 per cent when managers are slow to communicate. When there is frequent communication, performance is maintained, while satisfaction and trust increase 7 to 14 per cent.

Carolyn Barker, the national director of the Australian Institute of Management, says rumours and leaks maximise the distress and minimise the opportunity for explanation. She says managers should communicate important workplace changes such as mass redundancies to all employees at once, coordinating meetings across locations and time zones if necessary. Face-to-face communication should be backed up by written announcements that people can take away to discuss with colleagues and family.

In the short term, managers should make space available for staff to gather to talk and vent their feelings. These spaces should include internet discussion groups or hotlines. They should also make available psychological and financial counselling for those who need support.

Although good communication will help deal with the immediate crisis, managers should also be sensitive to the medium and long-term consequences. Barker says managers often see a survivor syndrome among employees who remain. 'Managers need to recognise this syndrome [and] make the time to talk about the real or perceived increase in people's workloads.'

She says employees may need training to develop new skills, or short-term contract support to help them reorganise the workflow. 'A surprising outcome of all this is that often people find amazing efficiencies in process because they have to keep

their head above water, and often, in the long term, the productivity increases.'
Source: McColl, G. (2003).

Activities for discussion, analysis and further research

1. Consider the linkages between trust and communications. In what ways does the communication of possible scenarios and estimates build trust, even though the information is only partially complete?
2. Do some research on Telstra and their workforce reduction over the past several years. What do the articles you read say about the way in which Telstra handled the redundancies and what does this tell you about the trust levels which their staff may have felt?
3. How might Telstra have communicated their intent more effectively?
4. Find other examples of both effective and non-effective communications when large organisations alter their staffing arrangements.

REFLECTIVE PRACTITIONER

KIMBERLEY TURNER

AEROSAFE
RISK MANAGEMENT

Looking at the way I communicate with different staff, I think I have a tendency to be very direct and succinct with my male staff. I am quite comfortable with that. With managing female staff, I find I need to be more sensitive or more consultative, or have that more discussionary-type approach. One of the exercises I run when we do Crew Resource Management training is looking at the way people communicate. We ask people to describe the ocean. Some will get quite poetic and describe the colours, the depth, the emotions that the ocean engenders in them. Others say: 'it's blue, wet, salty, fish live in it'. The difference in the ways people communicate is crucial to me. If I talk about the ocean being calm or tempestuous and I'm talking to a salty wet fish person they can't hear me, they can't understand a word I'm saying. I need to know which type I'm talking to. Just understanding such little things affects the way I communicate.

Good management is about adapting. You need to rise over and above idiosyncrasies and it takes effort and work and time.

The communications strategies we have in place utilise some quite formal tools and techniques. This is about getting the flow of information to the right place at the right time to get the right results, to get the right levels of action. We have different opportunities and vehicles for people to share information and communicate that information. We do it both in a documented sense and in a face-to-face situation.

All managers meet with their staff on a daily basis in the mornings. People get into work, get themselves organised and meet with their key staff to confirm tasking, communicate what has happened in the last day or two. This ensures that everyone knows what is going on and what they need to know. Some of us will have a follow-up debrief in the afternoon depending on the level of complexities that arise. So that's the daily communication. We also have a weekly work-in-progress meeting where each department outlines what they have done over the previous week and what is planned for the coming week. That is all tracked and monitored by the office manager so it can be accessed by everyone and everyone can have input into that. I also have weekly meetings with the managers responsible for the various business plans and that is more the month in view. So at every layer of communication, you are looking at the next layer. So the daily meeting looks at the week to come and so forth.

We also have an informal communication network within the company. I think it is important for me to constantly read the body language, the tone, the informal comments that come through either by email or personally. For me another important aspect is communicating with remote staff that we have in Canberra, Newcastle or Brisbane. Also, there's my levels of communication with my staff when I am not in the office. This is where my office manager is very valuable. She's my eyes and ears and also the funnel as to how communication gets back and forth to me. It has been a challenge to transition people from having that daily contact with me directly to moving them to interacting with someone else to get information to me. That has been a protection mechanism for myself as well as a practical issue to control information flows. There was a time when I made myself available 24 hours a day seven days a week. And it would be crazy—at 6.30 on a Sunday morning you're getting a phone call from a staff member because it suits them. So putting some boundaries and guidelines as to who communicates with whom and when, as well as who or what takes precedence, has been important, as this gives people the opportunity to formally communicate while being careful to not stifle the informal aspects.

FOCUS ON PRACTICE

Strategies for improving

1. Draw up a list of criteria to determine whether a communication should be face to face or whether email is adequate.
2. Check with a number of organisations to discover if they have any policy regarding the use of company email for personal use.
3. How would you go about establishing a sense of trust in the organisation to discourage distortion of information along the grapevine?
4. Think about a number of people you interact with. How do their cultural and linguistic differences impact on the meaning of their communications? How do you avoid those problems?

Source: Jones et al. (2000).

SUMMARY

- Effective communication and interpersonal processes are important in gaining and maintaining organisational competitive edge. Communication is the exchange of messages between people to achieve common meanings. In their work, managers use two communication types: verbal (including written and oral) and non-verbal. When elements contradict, the receiver will interpret the non-verbal communication as the true message. Managers tend to prefer oral to written communication, spending about 75 per cent of their working hours communicating orally.

- The communication process has several basic components: sender, encoding, message, receiver, decoding, noise and feedback. When communication gives relatively immediate feedback, it is two-way communication. Without a feedback provision, it is one-way communication.

- Many factors affect individual communication. There are four major types of perceptual distortion: stereotyping, the halo effect, projection and perceptual defence. Attribution theory helps explain how individuals use information communicated to judge the causes of the behaviour of another or of themselves. Semantic blocks can occur because various meanings and shades of meanings individuals attach to words depend on each person's semantic net. An individual's cultural orientation to high or low context can have a major impact on communication and interpersonal processes. Individual communication is facilitated by skill development in areas such as listening, giving feedback and receiving feedback.

- When tasks require input from several people, managers must think about the communication network among task-group members. Centralised networks are the wheel, chain and Y; decentralised networks are the circle and star. For relatively simple, routine tasks, centralised networks are faster and more accurate. When tasks are more complex, decentralised networks are faster and more accurate.

- Managers must be concerned with information flow among the various organisation parts. Formal organisation communication follows channels specified by the official hierarchical organisation structure and related task requirements. It flows in two main directions, vertical and horizontal. When vertical communication flows from a higher level to one or more lower levels, it is downward communication. When it moves from a lower level to one or more higher levels, it is upward communication. Horizontal communication is lateral message exchange. Informal communication, or the grapevine, takes place without regard to hierarchical or task requirements or organisational position. Electronic mail systems, voice mail, teleconferencing, and videoconferencing are examples of the communication aids available to managers through electronics advances.

MAX YOUR MARKS!
Thirty interactive questions on *Managerial Communication* are available now at the Online Learning Centre that accompanies this text: www.mhhe.com/au/bartol4e(For access to MaxMark please refer to the front of this book.)

QUESTIONS FOR DISCUSSION AND REVIEW

1. Explain major communication types managers use, and discuss their communication preferences. For a familiar organisation, identify examples of each type. Classify non-verbal communication examples in terms of kinesic behaviour, proxemics, paralanguage and object language.

2. Outline basic components of the communication process. Identify these in a conversation you witness.

3. Delineate several common tendencies to distort perceptions. Give an example of how each could adversely affect communication.

4. Describe attribution theory, including fundamental attribution error and the concept of self-serving bias. Identify an example of the fundamental attribution error based on a situation you have seen.

5. Explain the idea of semantic blocks. List some words used at your university or college which might cause semantic blocks to outsiders unfamiliar with the terminology.

6. Differentiate between high-context cultures and low-context cultures in terms of the emphasis on the communication process. How could you use the high/low context concept to help you supervise more effectively?

7. Outline major types of centralised and decentralised group communication networks. Explain conditions under which centralised and decentralised networks will give the best performance. Evaluate how well suited they appear to be for the situations involved.

8. Differentiate between vertical and horizontal communication. Identify major methods used in your college or university for downward communication from senior administrators to students and for upward communication from students to senior administrators. What mechanisms are there for horizontal communication among students?

9. Assess organisational implications of the grapevine. What evidence points to the existence of a student grapevine in your department at your college or university?

10. How can managers use electronic mail systems, teleconferencing and videoconferencing to their advantage in communicating? What potential problems exist with each?

CRITICAL THINKING QUESTIONS

To answer some of these questions you will need to do further research. Useful references are given below each section of the questions.

This chapter of the textbook provided an overview of the nature of managerial communication and looked in detail at the varying forms and channels of communication used within organisations today. The following questions examine specific challenges in the communication process and investigate the impact new forms of technology have on communication.

The first questions deal with the problems of communicating in difficult and delicate situations (in this case where medical professionals deal with the terminally ill). Teutsch (2002) reports the case of a Sydney man who has raised money to assist doctors in improving their bedside manner after his terminally ill wife endured rude and arrogant remarks from a number of medical staff. One completely inappropriate comment followed the removal of the woman's ovaries. Evidently, the surgeon told her: 'Well, you can just use a bit of KY Jelly'. Her husband commented: 'To think that someone would be thinking of sex when she'd just had her ovaries removed, as well as her kidney, and a breast: that kind of arrogance and rudeness just defies the imagination' (cited in Teutsch, 2002, p. 7).

A positive outcome of this situation was the founding of the Pam McLean Cancer Communications Centre at Royal North Shore Hospital in Sydney. The Centre is dedicated to teaching doctors how to improve their bedside manner.

1. What are some of the benefits for both patients and medical professionals of this initiative in improving communication?

2. Why do you think the communication discussed above occurred in the first place?

(Material relevant to these questions may be found in Teutsch, D. 2002, Love and anger, *Sun Herald*, 9 June, p. 7.)

The advent of outsourcing has seen a dramatic change in the way some companies communicate with their customers and, for some, call centres are now the major contact point. Bryant (2002, p. 54) reports on an ACA Research survey which found that 'staff in those call centres are bored, disgruntled and inexperienced'. Not surprisingly then, attrition is a major problem faced by call centre operators and poor customer service is a result. While stress and boredom are cited as key reasons why staff leave, Anne de Witt, the RACV's General Manager of Member Call Centres, sees these as symptoms of bigger issues. 'Sometimes there is a gap between what managers believe the issues to be and what staff think they are ... this is where communication with staff, such as employee opinion surveys, is essential to find out what staff really feel' (Bryant 2002, p. 54).

3. The RACV has carried out a number of these employee surveys. What do you think were some of the issues they found?

De Witt advocates the use of clear communication programs to overcome these problems. She believes that regular staff updates on the direction of the company, explaining how this will directly impact the strategies of the call centre and the staff in them, keeps everyone educated and informed. The key is to enhance information flows so all employees understand how and why the business is managed.

4. Given these statements, what sort of initiatives would you expect to see in operation at organisations such as RACV?

(Material relevant to these questions may be found in Bryant, G. 2002, Call centres connect with staff, *Business Review Weekly*, 30 May, p. 54.)

While call centres may be the dramatic new growth area in employment, it is the implementation of new technology which has made this possible. Just as technology is changing the way we work, it is also changing the way we communicate. Some of the ways this has occurred and the impact it is having, and may have, are the subject of a recent book by Ilana Snyder, an associate professor in Monash's faculty of Education. A basic tenet of the book is that institutions who want to remain with print-based literacy practices will have to rethink the ways in which they function.

These developments in technology have produced new types of text and new language practices, and they result in new forms of social interaction. Today, reading and writing are only part of what we need to know to be considered literate.

5. What are the forms communication now takes?

The new system combines words, pictures and sounds in complex ways to create meaning. Information presented on a sheet of paper may be functionally quite different on the computer screen. We may use a completely different set of conventions and skills to successfully communicate in these new mediums.

6. Snyder's view of technology and changing communication focuses on the education sector. What are some of the key issues you would expect her to be raising here?

It is a process that clearly does not end with educational institutions; these students will move on to enter the workforce. Once there, they will present very different expectations to organisations in terms of the type and methods of training.

(Material relevant to these questions may be found in Snyder, I. 2002, *Literacies: Communication, Innovation and Education in the Electronic Age*, Routledge.)

The perspective discussed above is really just one aspect of the much larger change wrought through the global communications landscape as a result of technological innovations in ICT. A key feature of the change is the ability of digitalisation to integrate a variety of forms of communication, such as graphics, text, video, sound and voice, into one interactive service. While this has seen electronics, computers, telecommunication and audiovisual media all integrated, it also increasingly begs the question of what will happen to people without access to this information.

Called the 'digital divide', it is not just an issue of communication within the world of business but one that affects society and nations as a whole. One of the seminal issues within this 'big picture' of the change occurring in communication is the fact that the new digital era is one that is very much dominated by the United States and, therefore, by US culture and even more specifically, American English. It is the power of language as the medium of communicating more than just a transfer of information which these last questions address.

7. Writing from a Malaysian perspective, Majid (2004) raises a number of concerns about a world of mass communication that is firmly rooted in one dominant culture. What do you think some of these concerns are?

8. Given the strength of the US dominance of most forms of communication today, what is the potential for countries, and thus organisations, to retain their national identity?

(Material relevant to these questions may be found in Majid, M. 2004, Rush of American technology, *Straits Times Press*, Malaysia, 4 January, p. 9.)

MANAGEMENT EXERCISES

Exercise 1 Self-assessment: Listening self-inventory

The purpose of this exercise is to gain insight into how well you listen. Please complete the following 15-item questionnaire twice. The first time check the appropriate response (yes or no) for each question. In checking your response, please think in terms of your behaviour in the last few meetings or conversations in which you participated. The second time through the questionnaire, place a plus (+) or a minus (–) in the third column. Mark a plus (+) next to your answer if you are satisfied with that answer, a minus (–) next to the answer if you wish you could have answered that question differently.

Listening self-inventory	Yes	No	+ or –
1. I frequently attempt to listen to several conversations at the same time.			
2. I like people to give me only the facts and then let me make my own interpretations.			
3. I sometimes pretend to pay attention to people.			
4. I consider myself a good judge of non-verbal communications.			
5. I usually know what another person is going to say before he or she says it.			
6. I usually end conversations that don't interest me by diverting my attention from the speaker.			
7. I frequently nod, frown or whatever to let the speaker know how I feel about what they are saying.			
8. I usually respond immediately when someone has finished talking.			
9. I evaluate what is being said while it is being said.			
10. I usually formulate a response while the other person is still talking.			
11. The speaker's delivery style frequently keeps me from listening to content.			
12. I usually ask people to clarify what they said rather than guess at the meaning.			
13. I make a concerted effort to understand other people's point of view.			
14. I frequently hear what I expect to hear rather than what is said.			
15. Most people feel that I have understood their point of view when we disagree.			

Your instructor will provide instructions for tabulating your answers.

Source: Glenn & Pood (1989).

Exercise 2 Management exercise: A question of inferences

Read the story presented below and indicate whether you believe the statements following the story are true (T), false (F) or unknown (?). Then join a group designated by your instructor, and determine as a group whether each statement is true, false or unknown.

Haney test of uncritical inferences
The story
A businessman had just turned off the lights in the store when a man appeared and demanded money. The owner opened a cash register. The contents of the cash register were scooped up, and the man sped away. A member of the police force was notified promptly.

Statements about the story			
1. A man appeared after the owner had turned off his store lights.	T	F	?
2. The robber was a man.	T	F	?
3. The man who appeared did not demand money.	T	F	?
4. The man who opened the cash register was the owner.	T	F	?
5. The store owner scooped up the contents of the cash register and ran away.	T	F	?
6. Someone opened a cash register.	T	F	?
7. After the man who demanded the money scooped up the contents of the cash register, he ran away.	T	F	?
8. While the cash register contained money, the story does not state how much.	T	F	?
9. The robber demanded money of the owner.	T	F	?
10. A businessman had just turned off the lights when a man appeared in the store.	T	F	?
11. It was broad daylight when the man appeared.	T	F	?
12. The man who appeared opened the cash register.	T	F	?
13. No one demanded money.	T	F	?
14. The story concerns a series of events in which only three persons are referred to: the owner of the store, a man who demanded money, and a member of the police force.	T	F	?
15. The following events occurred: someone demanded money, a cash register was opened, its contents were scooped up, and a man dashed out of the store.	T	F	?

Source: Haney (1986).

END-OF-CHAPTER CASE: ON THE RIM

Dealing with the clash of cultures and the law in Pacific Nations

POWERWEB

International articles related to this topic are available at the Online Learning Centre at www.mhhe.com/au/bartol4e

Firms operating in the Pacific Island countries are very keen to provide services in those countries which match those supplied in their home countries—usually developed countries such as Australia, New Zealand, Japan or the USA. However, they need to and /or are required to utilise local labour in their operations. This provides great opportunities but can also pose problems for managers, especially those intent on providing good leadership based on their experiences in their home country. Fijian people are some of the most friendly people on earth and their friendliness is not strained or artificial—it is genuine and natural. They are also for the most part very peaceful. Hence Fijians are great staff to have in tourist and hospitality operations and require no training to provide friendly caring service to visitors.

However, in Fiji staff who are used to the Fijian way of life often have a greater allegiance to their family than to the organisation they are working for. Given access to large amounts of money they can be tempted to steal and to give this money to their family and friends, often keeping very little for themselves. When they are apprehended and turned over to the authorities, the result may be that they are given a minor punishment with a light sentence compared to that which would be handed down in a more developed country. A local Fijian book shop manager who recently misappropriated over A$70 000 from her university was not jailed, and received a fine that was much less than the amount taken. In Australia such an offence would carry at least a jail sentence, even though for a first offence it may be suspended.

Expatriate managers will find this very hard to accept and become very frustrated with their host countrymen and women. Unfortunately there is little that can be done once the crime has been committed. This is because the justice systems are quite different in the manner in which they are applied, having been implemented in very different cultures. Fijian culture is based on a village society where each and every member is cared for by their fellow villagers. If a member is out of work then they are always welcome in their village where they will always have a family home and where they will be provided with meals. If a dispute occurs, for example, if one of the villagers commits a crime, the approach to dealing with the dispute is for the chiefs from the various families to meet, drink Kava and to mull over the situation. This will often result in the perpetrator apologising to their victims and being required to pay some form of compensation. Once that is completed the misdemeanour is forgotten. Note that the values of the villagers are often very different to Westerners. They do not see property as so important. They are also prepared to forgive and forget and do not harbour grudges. Translating this cultural approach to justice into a legal system based on the Westminster system of jurisprudence is not straight forward.

A manager who has discovered fraud or theft in their organisation, reports it to the authorities, and then finds that the perpetrators are treated lightly is faced with a dilemma. Do they complain to the authorities and face possible opposition to their business by government officials disturbed at being criticised by an expatriate? Do they accept the leniency of the system and face the possibility of other staff stealing from the organisation without penalty? Do they continue in business in the Pacific nation, or do they consider withdrawing or taking their business elsewhere? The bookshop manager concerned simply had to accept the court's decision and get on with business. Greater controls were applied and all checks were carried out more frequently. These measures were introduced to at least limit the amounts that could be taken before the thefts are detected.

Source: Contributed by Ken Dooley.

Activities for discussion, analysis and further research

1. Dealing with differing cultures can be seen as a real test of leadership. Why is this so?
2. What leadership theories provide assistance in dealing with staff with differing value systems to management?
3. Are managers from developed countries being too 'precious' when expressing surprise that they experience so much corruption in less developed countries? (Hint: Consider the ethics of Western organisations and management generally.)
4. What lessons learnt in providing leadership in overseas postings can lead to personal growth in a manager?

FURTHER READING

Alleyne, S., Egodigwe, L. and Holmes, T.E. 2004, How to effectively compete in a tough job market, *Black Enterprise*, February, 34, 7, pp. 73–82.

Bamford, J., Ernst, D. and Fubini, D.G. 2004, Launching a world-class joint venture, *Harvard Business Review*, February, 82, 2, pp. 90–101.

Chi-Ya, C.B. 2003, The development of virtual collocation strategies in information technology for small businesses: A Taiwanese case study, *International Journal of Management*, December, 20, 4, pp. 523–35.

Legewie, J. 2002, Control and co-ordination of Japanese subsidiaries in China: Problems of an expatriate-based management system, *International Journal of Human Resource Management*, September, 13, 6, pp. 901–20.

Pan, F. and Zhang, Z. 2004, Cross-cultural challenges when doing business in China, *Singapore Management Review*, 1st Half, 26, 1, pp. 81–91.

CHAPTER 14

MANAGING GROUPS

LEARNING OBJECTIVES

After studying this chapter, you should be able to:

- Differentiate between different workplace group types and explain how informal groups develop.
- Use a systems approach to describe factors influencing the way groups operate.
- Describe major work-group inputs, including group composition, member roles and group size, and explain how they affect teamwork.
- Explain the significance of group-process factors, such as group norms, group cohesiveness and group development.
- Discuss how task forces and teams can be used to promote innovation.

Deloitte's new Mr Fix-it

Giam Swiegers says that the day he wakes up and is not worried about being chief executive of Deloitte Touche Tohmatsu, the smallest of Australia's Big Four accounting firms, will be the day he makes his biggest mistake. 'I think you are a fool if you take a position like this and you don't worry', he says. 'It is a big responsibility looking after the careers of 2600 people.' Swiegers becomes chief executive of Deloitte on 1 June, when the incumbent, Lynn Odland, retires. [Deloitte has subsequently increased its staff to 3400, after deciding to re-integrate its consulting arm, Deloitte Consulting.]

Swiegers has much to worry about. Deloitte is on the bottom rung of the Big Four in Australia in terms of revenue, and it grew by just 1.2 per cent between 2000/01 and 2001/02. This revenue growth rate is comparable with its rivals—apart from Ernst & Young, which absorbed most of Andersen's Australian practice in May 2002—but does not compare well with many mid-tier firms. Swiegers is concerned about this.

In the past 12 months, Deloitte lost three of its biggest audit clients—Brambles Industries, Newmont Mining Corporation and Normandy NFM. This leaves Deloitte auditing just eight of Australia's 100 biggest companies—far fewer than its rivals, PricewaterhouseCoopers (PwC) which has 36, KPMG with 28 and Ernst & Young with 26. Three mid-tier firms each have one, and KPMG and PwC share the auditing role for BHP Billiton.

In addition, Deloitte recently received a demoralising and unprecedented attack over its pricing policies from Tony Harrington, the chief executive of Australia's largest accounting firm, PwC. He accused Deloitte of 'predatory pricing' policies on audit tenders.

On his own assessment, Swiegers is a fix-it man. He says: 'Deloitte has always used me in offices that have problems, to turn them around and then [they] move [me] on to the next spot'. So what is the problem with Deloitte that means the fix-it man is now leading the entire firm? Swiegers says: 'We are undersized in this market, we need to grow, but grow profitably. It is easy to grow, but hard to achieve profitable growth'.

Swiegers has many ideas about how to expand the company by improving the performance of Deloitte's partners and accounting professionals. He believes that creating the right culture of motivation within the firm will attract clients. 'I think professional services firms are more like sports teams than any other business. Speak to any sports psychologist and they will tell you, if the team is not firing on the day [it plays] then it doesn't matter how well you train them. We have our people playing and competing every day. You have to keep them motivated because this is a zero-sum game: you get it all or you get nothing.'

Swiegers will not commit publicly about Deloitte's growth goals, saying these are not set. As part of its annual review of goals, conducted from February to May, Swiegers intends to ditch the firm's old strategies, and develop new ones 'attuned to market and regulatory changes'. Swiegers says: 'I believe you get teams to cut the length of the ruler they are going to be measured by, because when you force goals on to teams they are unhappy to be measured. [But] it will definitely be a "stretch" goal'.

continued

Swiegers believes his weakness lies in detail and implementation, and he needs a team around him with complementary skills. 'I need people who implement well. I am an ideas person; I love running off ideas. If I get left alone, I will run away with some of my ideas. I need someone [on my team] who can test my ideas. I like people who challenge, question and debate.'

Asked if he wants Deloitte to be the number one firm in Australia, Swiegers, who is more than 180

centimetres (six feet) tall, says: 'I used to race mountain bikes, and once a year my wife and I did a 105-kilometre race over two mountains in South Africa. If you have my weight on a mountain bike, you never look at the top of the mountain; you look two metres ahead. That is how you get over mountains. I will look two metres ahead and make sure the wheels keep turning'.

Source: Walters, K. (2003).

In this chapter, we examine group characteristics, including work-group types, informal group development and group operations. Next, we look at inputs and processes affecting group outcomes. We also explore how task forces and teams can foster innovation.

FOUNDATIONS OF WORK GROUPS

What is a group?

group

Two or more interdependent individuals interacting and influencing each other in collective pursuit of a common goal

A **group** is two or more interdependent individuals interacting and influencing each other in collective pursuit of a common goal (Shaw 1981; Alderfer 1987). This definition differentiates a group from a simple gathering of people. Strangers leaving by the same door at a theatre or studying in a library's reference section are not a group. In neither case are the people interdependent, nor are they interacting and influencing each other collectively trying to reach a shared goal. Similarly, groups are different to organisations as the latter involve systematic efforts (such as the four major management functions and a formal structure), and goods or services production. Groups do not use as much systematic effort as organisations and may or may not produce goods or services. Teamwork happens when groups work together efficiently and effectively to reach organisational goals. We discuss teamwork later, focusing on how work groups operate.

Though groups have always been central to organisations, they are seen increasingly as important assets. Organisations using groups and teamwork power come in all sizes (Magnet 1988; Yerak 1994).

Types of work group

There are different types of workplace groups. They fall into two categories: formal and informal. These and some subcategories are shown in Figure 14.1.

Formal groups

formal group

Group officially created by an organisation for a specific purpose

A **formal group** is officially created by an organisation for a particular purpose. There are two types of formal groups: command and task.

command or functional group

Formal group consisting of a manager and all the subordinates who report to them

A **command**, or **functional**, **group** is a formal group made up of a manager and all subordinates reporting to that manager. Each organisation work unit (manager and subordinates) is a command group. For example, if you stay in a large hotel, your room will be cleaned by a housekeeper who reports to a housekeeping supervisor. With other housekeepers reporting to the same supervisor, they are a command group. If you attend a lunch, those who wait on your table and report to a catering supervisor form another command group. Each supervisor reports to a higher-level manager, belonging to the higher-level

FIGURE 14.1 Types of work group

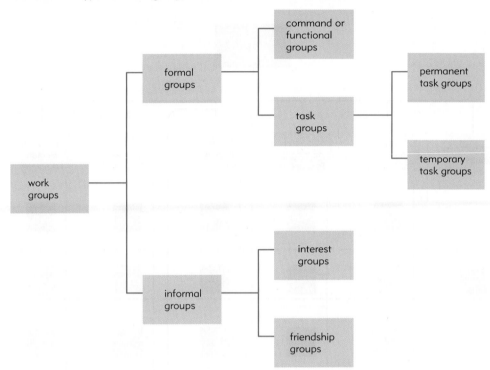

command group. In this way, supervisors link lower-level and higher-level groups. A linking pin is someone who coordinates different command-group levels by acting in a supervisory role in a lower-level group and a subordinate role in a higher one. Organisations are thus made up of command, or functional, groups in a pyramid, with linking pins holding them together.

A **task group** is a formal group set up to supplement or replace work normally undertaken by a command group. Task groups can be permanent or temporary. A permanent task group, or **standing committee** or team, handles recurring issues in a narrow subject-area over an indefinite, generally lengthy, time period. A temporary task group deals with a specific issue in a specific time frame. For example, as part of Heinz's Profitability Improvement program, managers in temporary teams from different departments look for and prioritise major cost-saving projects (Saporito 1985). Temporary task groups, or ad hoc committees, may be called task forces, project groups or teams (Stech & Ratliff 1985). Names vary, so the time frame establishes whether a task group is permanent or temporary. We discuss task forces and teams in more detail later.

Informal groups

An **informal group** is set up by employees, not the organisation, to serve members' interests or social needs. The groups may or may not further organisational goals. An informal group's membership may be the same as a formal group, for example when members of a work group eat together. Bosch Australia found a drift to work and informal groups based on language background (Way 2003c). Other times, an informal group has representatives of one or more formal groups (see Fig. 14.2).

There are two major types of informal groups: interest and friendship.

An interest group is an informal group set up to help employees in common concerns. Interests leading to informal groups can be wide, such as a presently impractical new technology (but which a group of engineers informally study), a sport (e.g. volleyball), or a desire to have the firm change a policy. A friendship group is an informal group existing

task group

Formal group created for a specific purpose, supplementing or replacing work normally done by command groups

standing committee

Permanent task group of individuals charged with handling recurring matters in a narrowly defined subject area over an indefinite, but generally long, time period

informal group

Group established by employees, not the organisation, to serve group members' interests or social needs

FIGURE 14.2 Formal and informal groups in an organisation

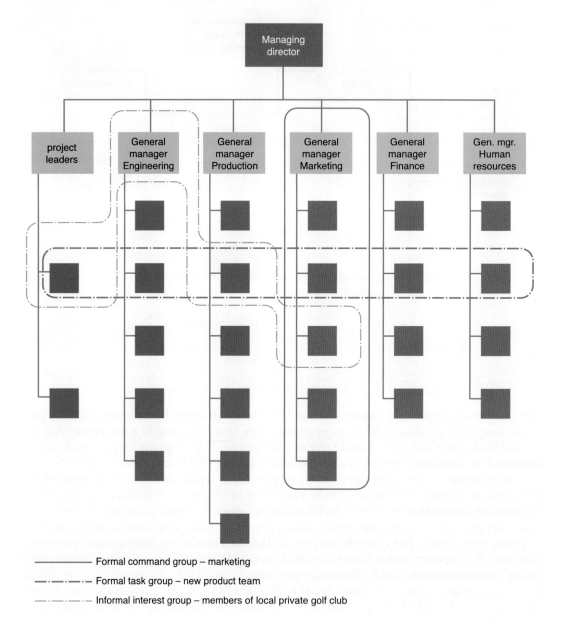

Formal command group – marketing

Formal task group – new product team

Informal interest group – members of local private golf club

because of employee social needs. The groups stem from mutual attraction, based on common characteristics such as similar work, backgrounds and/or values. Informal groups can help by aiding information flow and reinforcing employees' readiness to work together. They can be harmful when group concerns are put above work goals or there is a serious falling out. Managers must understand informal groups due to their potential for impact on organisational effectiveness.

How informal groups develop

George Homans (1950) explained how informal groups come from formal group dynamics. When a formal group is set up, members have required behaviours and sentiments (see Fig. 14.3).

FIGURE 14.3 The informal-group emergence process

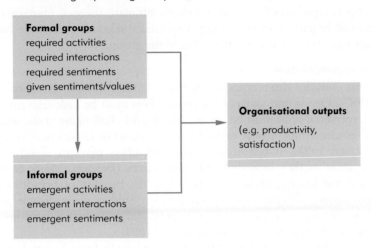

Required activities are behaviours needed to perform job tasks. *Required interactions* are specified dealings with others as part of the job. *Required sentiments* are views and attitudes needed to do the job. Also involved are *given sentiments*, non-required attitudes and values brought to the job (Nayak & Ketteringham 1986; Kinicki & Williams 2003). Homans believes these emergent activities, interactions and sentiments are associated with informal groups and can supplant or supplement required activities, interactions and sentiments.

Most organisations have many formal and informal groups. Because formal groups are created for specific purposes, it is important managers and others ensure they operate effectively. Therefore, this chapter will focus mostly on formal work groups.

How work groups operate

Several factors affect teamwork and formal work-groups' effectiveness. In analysing these, it helps to see groups as systems using inputs, engaging in many processes or transformations, and producing outcomes (see Chapter 2 for a discussion of the systems approach to organisational analysis). Figure 14.4 lists several factors helpful in understanding group interactions and outcomes. These are grouped into input, process and outcome categories. Note important outcomes are not just group performance measures such as quantity, quality and costs, but member satisfaction too. As well, in effective groups, teamwork increases effectiveness and members' readiness to work together again.

FIGURE 14.4 A general model of work-group behaviour

WORK-GROUP INPUTS

For groups to operate, there must be some basic inputs. Some inputs affecting groups and teamwork are group composition, members' roles and group size.

Managing diversity: Work-group composition

As work-group composition bears on a group's ultimate success, managers must consider carefully who will be part of a work group. Two crucial selection factors are potential member characteristics and reasons for their attraction to the group.

Member characteristics

Managers must consider three types of member characteristics in establishing work groups (Hackman 1987). One is that skills of group members must be task-relevant. Another is that members' interpersonal skills must be correct. Finally, for challenging tasks, some diversity (e.g. personalities, gender, ethnic group, attitudes, background or experience) in group makeup is helpful (Blackmon 1998). If too homogeneous, members may get along but be unable to generate new ideas as they lack different perspectives (Jackson, Many & Whitney 1995). Alternatively, if too heterogeneous, members lose the benefits of breadth of talent due to problems coordinating diverse efforts (Way 2003c). Studies show diverse groups are more creative and flexible around changing requirements, and make better decisions (see Chapter 5) (Goodman, Ravlin & Argote 1986; Cox & Blacke 1991).

Managers need to realise they must be patient to benefit from group diversity. A study of culturally homogeneous versus culturally diverse groups (various nationalities and ethnic backgrounds) showed culturally diverse groups performed poorly initially, but over time did better than homogeneous ones in assessing and solving business situations (Watson, Kumar & Michaelson 1993). Managers can improve diversity's benefits by having members trained to function well in groups (Woodruff & Miller 1995). Some firms have diversity training to ensure members understand, appreciate and effectively use individual differences. For example, General Electric developed a vision statement for its diversity program: 'To be recognised as one of the world's most competitive companies due to our ability to value and fully utilise the contributions of all employees from all cultural and social backgrounds' (Capowski 1996, p. 14). Managers can promote diversity benefits by monitoring groups to ensure they develop properly (Blackmon 1998).

Attraction to the group

role

Set of behaviours expected of an individual occupying a particular position in a group

Another consideration in group make-up is the reasons potential members are attracted to the group. While people cannot generally choose their work groups, they may be able to choose some task-group types, such as task forces and committees.

Why do people join or participate in groups? (Shaw 1981). Some may like group members or be attracted to them (Armstrong & Holyoke 1995). Others may enjoy a group's activities, such as looking at new ideas in a technical interest area. Others may value a group's goals or purposes (Engardio 1988). People also join due to affiliation needs. According to McClelland's acquired-needs motivation theory, these will be higher in some people than others, but all have some affiliation need (see Chapter 12). Lastly, individuals may join a group because it helps with a goal beyond the group (e.g. joining a committee to meet people from a work unit one would like to get a job in) (Gome 2003c). People join groups for any or all of these reasons.

Member roles

Why do we expect a committee's chair will call a meeting to order, someone from finance will give relevant financial expertise, and the secretary will take notes? This is because each has a **role**, a set of behaviours expected of someone in a group position. In a work group, individuals have many roles. For example, a person may be an expert in an area, may represent a command group and also be a workforce member interested in the result of some change.

Additionally, the fact that someone is a member of a group brings with it other roles. Common group roles fall into three categories: task, maintenance and self-oriented roles (Allcorn 1985; Bateman & Snell 2004).

Group-task roles help the group develop and reach goals. Among these are the following:

- Initiator-contributor: Proposes goals, suggests ways of approaching tasks, recommends procedures for approaching a problem or task
- Information seeker: Asks for information, viewpoints and suggestions about a problem or task
- Information giver: Offers information, viewpoints and suggestions about a problem or task
- Coordinator: Clarifies and synthesises various ideas to tie together members' work
- Orienter: Summarises, points to departures from goals, and raises questions about discussion direction
- Energiser: Stimulates the group to higher work and better quality levels

group-task roles

Roles helping a group develop and accomplish its goals

Group-maintenance roles do not address the task directly but help foster group unity, positive interpersonal relations among group members, and development of members' ability to work together effectively. Group maintenance roles include:

- Encourager: Expresses warmth and friendliness toward group members, encourages them and acknowledges their contributions
- Harmoniser: Mediates disagreements between members and attempts to help reconcile differences
- Gatekeeper: Tries to keep lines of communication open and promotes participation of all members
- Standard setter: Suggests standards for how the group will operate and checks whether members are satisfied with group functioning
- Group observer: Watches the group's internal operations and gives feedback on how participants are doing and how they might be able to function better
- Follower: Goes along with the group and is friendly but relatively passive

group-maintenance roles

Roles not directly addressing a task itself but, instead, helping foster group unity, positive interpersonal relations among group members and development of their ability to work effectively together

Self-oriented roles relate to group members' personal needs and may negatively influence group effectiveness. These include the following:

- Aggressor: Deflates contributions of others by attacking their ideas, ridiculing their feelings and displaying excessive competitiveness
- Blocker: Tends to be negative, stubborn and resistive of new ideas, sometimes to force the group to readdress a viewpoint already dealt with
- Recognition seeker: Seeks attention, boasts about accomplishments and capabilities, and works to prevent being put in an inferior position in the group
- Dominator: Tries to assert control and manipulates the group or certain group members by flattery, giving orders or interrupting others

self-oriented roles

Roles related to the personal needs of group members and often negatively influencing group effectiveness

Group leaders may assume many task roles. They may also use some maintenance roles to help group progress. However, a leader cannot assume all task and maintenance behaviours needed without assistance from others in the group. In leaderless groups (where no leader is appointed), individuals likely to emerge as leaders (be perceived as leaders) are active participants who adopt task roles (Bass 1990).

Even with a formal leader, other informal leaders may emerge. An **informal leader** is someone, other than the formal leader, who emerges from the group with major influence and is seen as a leader by members. Although some members may try to use informal leadership despite the formal leader's behaviour, emerging informal leaders are most likely when a formal leader has trouble facilitating group progress (Eddy 1985). In addition to roles, another important input factor is group size.

informal leader

Individual, other than the formal leader, emerging from a group as a major influence and perceived by members as a leader

Group size

Research on small groups gives some understanding of the effects of group size. Research has looked at how different numbers affect interactions, and at how group size affects performance (Shull, Debecq & Cummings 1970; Shaw 1981; Rue & Byars 2003).

Size and group interactions

Group numbers affect member interactions. With two-person groups, or dyads, the two will either be very polite, avoiding disagreements, or often disagreeing, straining relations. Adding someone else rarely solves interaction problems as the result is 'two-against-one'. Groups with four or six members often deadlock as groups have equal factions.

In contrast, groups of five or seven have some benefits. One is no deadlocks, due to the odd numbers. Another is that they are large enough for different ideas but small enough to allow participation.

As groups grow beyond seven, particularly above 11 or 12, active participation is harder. Group interaction becomes more centralised, and some have more active roles than others. Disagreements are more common and group satisfaction drops unless members work at group maintenance roles. Interactions may also be drawn out on complex issues (Altier 1986; Schiller 1988).

Size and performance

Does size impact on group performance? This is hard to answer as size effects depend partly on the task's nature. For example, in a group where members work independently (such as waiters in a restaurant) the effects are different from a group where members closely coordinate efforts (such as a rescue team). Generally, though, size effects on group performance form an inverted 'U' (see Fig. 14.5) (Cummings, Huber & Arendt 1974; Goodman et al. 1986; Walker 2003d). Thus, as more people join a group, performance improves; but after a point, as more workers are added performance levels off and may even deteriorate.

Why does performance stabilise, even dropping as group size increases? One reason is **social loafing**, or people's tendency to use less effort working in groups than alone (Gooding & Wagner 1985; Karau & Williams 1995). Effects snowball if other members detect social loafing and reduce their own efforts (Kidwell & Bennett 1993). Individuals engaging in social loafing are called free riders as they benefit from the group's efforts without proportionally sharing in costs (Albanese & Van Fleet 1985). Thus, social loafing is called **free riding**. The evidence shows those who tend to individualism are more likely to free ride as group-size increases than those leaning to collectivism. **Individualism** is where personal interests are given

social loafing or free riding

Tendency of individuals to expend less effort when working in groups than when working alone and to benefit from the group's work without bearing a proportional share of costs involved

individualism

Condition where personal interests are given more weight than the group's interests

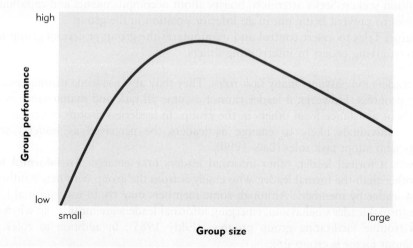

FIGURE 14.5 Effects of group size on performance

more weight than group needs. Individualists are self-oriented and ignore group interests if they conflict with their own. **Collectivism** occurs where group demands and interests are given precedence over individual desires and needs. Collectivists make personal sacrifices for the group's good (Wagner 1995).

Managers can lessen the chances of social loafing (Karau & Williams 1995). Assigning just enough people to do the work is one way. Others are giving each different tasks, making individual work visible, giving individual feedback, having likely loafers work with respected people, setting a standard for group progress measurement, and making rewards depend on both individual and group performance. Finally, since social loafing is less likely with a task-committed group, interesting, challenging tasks must be designed or task-committed group members chosen (Karau & Williams 1995; Jackson & Harkins 1985; Zaccaro 1984).

> **collectivism**
>
> Condition where the demands and interests of group interests are given precedence over desires and needs of individuals

CASE IN POINT

Phone home?

Most employees with access to a company phone have made personal calls in business hours and without the explicit permission of their employer. Indeed, these calls in all but the very few organisations that expressly forbid them are considered, if not exactly as a right, then as a basic privilege of employment. This largely tacit deal between the employer and the employee hinges on notions of what is reasonable in the circumstances. The employer seems to concede that a blanket prohibition on the use of company phones for personal calls would be a mean-spirited and ultimately counterproductive rule to impose. On the other hand, the employee's concession is that calls made will not be too frequent or too long, and they will not be trivial or time wasting.

So it seems that the employment relationship can tolerate the implied terms that are encompassed in the employee making the occasional, short and important personal call from work. But what happens when a large contingent of employees is temporarily located overseas, in a developing country, and with telephone access only to an extremely expensive satellite communications network? Let's see.

In response to one of the world's more recent humanitarian disasters, an international relief effort, including an in-country infrastructure rebuilding program, was undertaken. Aid organisations from all over the world deployed to assist and among these was one group with the responsibility of establishing the backbone of a national telecommunications capability. In light of the devastation of the host country's hard-wire or trunk network, the decision

was made to use expensive but highly efficient and portable satellite communications technology. The equipment utilised effectively act as independent ground stations that communicate through a satellite link and on to permanent facilities, in this case offshore, where calls can be trunked via landline to their eventual destination. Thus a telecommunications capability could be quickly put in place while the longer-term work of rebuilding the network took place.

The first five or six months of the relief effort resulted in a blur of activity. Hours worked were long and hard, but slowly some semblance of order was coming to a country and a society that had suffered years of warfare and terror. Similarly, some order was emerging in the operations of the aid organisations. Now that death from disease, injury or starvation was at least not commonplace for the local population, aid workers could go back to some of the tasks that were put aside or passed over in the rush to save lives. Unfortunately, the paper work was about to catch up with a vengeance.

One of the more pressing post-emergency tasks was to get a clear picture on aid expenditure so far and to begin settling with some very patient creditors. Almost immediately this work began, alarm bells started to ring. Invoices for international telephone calls were way up on estimates. In fact they were hundreds of thousands of US dollars over what was considered appropriate. After itemised accounts were procured, it was revealed that a massive number of calls had been placed to one Pacific Rim country in particular. Of these, so many different numbers had been used that it was obvious that these could not be work related calls to, say, suppliers or parent organisations.

As the investigation began to uncover more of the story, it soon became clear that the numbers called were largely private and centred on one particular urban area. This area was easily identified as the one from which the staff operating the satellite communications equipment had been drawn. Further enquiry revealed that these staff had been making personal calls with sometimes alarming frequency.

Eventually it came to be known that most staff with access to the satellite phone system had made personal calls to their home country. Of these, a small number could be classified as high-order users with one notable for making two or more half-hour calls per day for a total cost equivalent to a reasonable annual salary. Mid-order users, with two or three calls per week, comprised a much larger group; however, it was the low-order users, with an average of one short call each fortnight, that formed the majority.

At this stage, it needs to be pointed out that while management had never given permission for staff to make personal calls, on the other hand it had not been expressly denied either. Additionally, the facts that some managers were themselves making personal calls, and that most managers and supervisors were aware of the practice, need to be considered. Similarly it should be remembered that this was an organisation that quietly acquiesced to personal calls in its home country.

In the fullness of time it was decided to separately bill individuals for all personal calls attributable to them and to issue a written instruction prohibiting all future calls. While pressure had been brought to bear to initiate criminal charges against all users, it was the restraint of the entirely

reasonable low-order users and the fact that calls were common knowledge that argued against this. Unfortunately, in the clamour to lay blame, the magnificent effort of those that resisted temptation day to day while operating in often dangerous and lonely outposts went unacknowledged.

Source: Contributed by Mark Weston Wall.

Activities for discussion, analysis and further research

1. Most of us would probably agree that those who refrained from using the communications system to make personal calls were in the right in this case study. However, what can be said about those who did use the system and in particular the low-order users?

2. From the case study it is clear that managers and supervisors were not only aware of the fact that staff were making personal calls, they were also making their own calls. Does this somehow excuse or at least mitigate the behaviour of the staff?

3. From the perspective of the management of groups, what might be done to ensure that this problem is resolved without causing undue divisiveness in the work teams involved, and retaining the group cohesiveness required in this type of organisation?

4. If itemised international accounts had not been available, what techniques might management have employed to identify the cause of the exorbitant call costs?

5. Reactive management is one thing; however, is there something management might have done to prevent this situation from arising? What might have been reasonable in the circumstances?

WORK-GROUP PROCESSES

positive synergy

Force resulting when combined gains from group interaction are greater than group-process losses

negative synergy

Force resulting when group-process losses are greater than gains achieved from combining the forces of group members

Why do some groups accomplish little, while others with similar inputs, a great deal? The answer lies, in part, in *group processes*, the dynamic, inner workings of the group. As group members work, some energy goes into group development and operations. This is diverted from the task, and is known as process loss, as it is lost energy which could have been devoted to the task (Shepperd 1993; Walker 2003d). Process loss is inevitable, given group members' normal interdependence.

Alternatively, tremendous gains can flow from the combined group-member force, or synergy (Hackman 1987). **Positive synergy** is when combined gains from group interaction (as opposed to individuals alone) are greater than group-process losses. When synergy is positive, the whole (the group's total effect) is greater than the sum of its parts (what tasks members could achieve alone). **Negative synergy** is when group-process losses are greater than gains from combining members' forces. If you have been in a group so ineffective you could have done the job faster alone, then you have seen negative synergy. We next discuss three major group-process factors affecting group synergy and effectiveness: norms, cohesiveness and group development.

Group norms

Norms are expected behaviours sanctioned by a group which regulates and fosters uniform member behaviours (Goodman, Ravlin & Schminke 1987). For a behaviour to be a norm, members must see it as expected for group membership.

Work groups do not use norms to regulate all behaviour. Rather, they develop and enforce norms related to central matters (Goodman et al. 1987; Howarth 2003c). For example, group norms develop about production processes. These norms relate to quality and quantity standards, as well as how the job is done. A work group at the New Zealand Fisher and Paykel factory making 'Dishdrawer' dishwashing machines has national product safety standards to comply with as well as company standards for exceptionally high quality products. Social arrangements are another norm area. That is, groups often set norms about when and where to have lunch; what type of social function, if any, to have when someone leaves; and acceptable socialising at and outside work. Working to assignment deadlines, 'swotting' for exams, and 'hanging out' together at libraries, pubs and cafes are norms for many university students. Finally, work-groups' norms often involve resource allocation, such as materials, equipment, assigned work area (e.g. near a window) and pay (Lubin 1995).

Norms typically develop by one of four mechanisms: explicit statements, critical events, primacy and carryover behaviours (Feldman 1984).

norms

Expected behaviours sanctioned by a group that regulate and foster uniform member behaviour

MANAGERIAL DILEMMAS

Andrew Bartlett

When Andrew Bartlett decided to expand his small plumbing business, he had no idea about some of the people-management challenges that he would eventually have to address.

Based in Perth, Andrew began operating as a sole trader in 1992. However, demand for his skills was strong, and within two months of starting, he employed an assistant. Over the next three years, his staff expanded to include five other full-time plumbers, two apprentices and three office administrators. Always keen to be seen as a 'hands on' man, Andrew made sure that his time was divided equally between office work in the mornings and customer relations and sales on most afternoons. He also spent a lot of time making sure the business team worked together well. On Friday afternoons, for example, his team would meet to review the week's activities, share information about clients, and plan for the week to come. Once every three months, they would review progress against their business plan and then adjourn for a lunch paid for by the firm. In addition, Andrew was also heavily involved in the activities of his industry organisation, the Master Plumbers Association (MPA) of Western

Australia. This provided him with access to the latest industry news and developments, useful contacts and frequent leads to more work.

His staff were recruited on the basis of personal contacts and personal referrals. Most of them were people he had met while doing his own apprenticeship with a larger plumbing firm in the mid-1980s. Andrew could take pride in his team; there had never been a resignation or staff departure. Even after several years, he still had all of his original team. As the 1990s drew to a close, it became apparent that the Perth market was constrained for plumbing firms of Andrew's size. The local market was dominated by a large number of very small plumbing operators, and a few very large firms. There seemed little room for a medium-sized company.

To overcome this, Andrew turned his attention to Bunbury, Western Australia's second city, located about 180 kilometres south of Perth. In 1999 Andrew employed a local plumber, Stephen, whom he had met at a regional meeting of the MPA executive. This experiment seemed to be a success and in late 2001 Andrew and Stephen embarked on their most ambitious move: a dramatic expansion of staff to a total of four plumbers (Stephen, Brett, Janine and Charles). Administration was handled from the Perth office. However, since then there have been a number of serious problems in the Bunbury operation. There were frequent complaints from long-term Bunbury customers, several of whom contacted Andrew directly to voice their concerns. Others had simply stopped dealing with the firm. It was difficult to obtain accurate information; it often took Stephen several days to return phone calls to Andrew. Financial information was often late in coming, and their accountant became concerned about GST liabilities, correct invoicing, and whether or not the southern branch was actually covering its own costs. Recently sales had begun to drop off noticeably.

One afternoon, during their weekly golf game, Andrew's most senior Perth-based plumber raised the issue with him. 'I just don't know what to do. Today I had a phone call from Janine and Charles. They've threatened to leave unless Stephen goes. They claim they don't know what's going on, and that they're always given the hard jobs to do.' Andrew raised an eyebrow, but said nothing. He had heard similar stories before. Charles had already previously phoned him to complain that Stephen and Brett kept a lot of information to themselves; that Stephen was quite dictatorial in his approach to managing the other three; and that he was quick to apportion blame and accuse the others if something went wrong. Much of the limited information that was sent to Perth was only ever seen by Stephen or, occasionally, Brett. The other two had no idea what was going on. They simply did the plumbing jobs assigned to them while Stephen tended to jealously hoard the details about current and future projects.

At the end of the golf game, it was suggested that the issue should be discussed at the Perth team's weekly Friday meeting. Andrew, however, was not so sure. As in all small businesses, the owner of the firm is almost always the manager and chief decision-maker. However, unlike the CEO or senior managers of a large organisation, he had no specialist advisers who could help him sort out this problem. He did not think it appropriate to raise these issues in front of all ten Perth staff, but was unsure what to do next.

Source: Contributed by Michael Schaper.

Weblink:

For more information about the plumbing industry in Western Australia, visit the website of the Master Plumbers Association of WA: www.masterplumbers.asn.au

Reflection points

1. At what stage of group development is:
   the Perth office staff cohort?
   the Bunbury plumbing team?
2. How do you think this impacts on their interactions?
3. What practical steps can be taken to make the Bunbury group work better and more cohesively together?

Decision points

1. Explain the advantages and disadvantages of having one small business split into two parts that are physically separated from each other. Is it desirable that the Perth and Bunbury teams work separately from each other, or should their activities be integrated? If integration is desirable, how should this be done?
2. Visit the Master Plumbers' website. What is the value of joining an organisation such as this? Is it a worthwhile investment of a manager's time?

Explicit statements

Explicit supervisor and coworker statements can inform about group members' expectations. These are a good opportunity for a supervisor to influence group norms. Supervisory statements are very important as a new group is formed or a new person joins (Magnet 1988; *Fortune* 1994).

Critical events

In any group, critical events in a group's history set precedents for the future.

Primacy

Primacy as a source of norms is the tendency for the first behaviour pattern a group displays to set group expectations.

Carryover behaviours

Many norms are carryover behaviours from other groups and organisations. When group members have similar past experiences (such as being on similar company committees), norms are set quickly. Otherwise, they may evolve more slowly (Bettenhausen & Murnighan 1985; Prinzinsky 1996).

Group cohesiveness

Another factor related to group process is **group cohesiveness**, how much members are attracted to a group, are motivated to stay in it, and are influenced by one another. We look at the consequences of group cohesiveness before exploring its determinants (Luthans 1995; Arnold & Feldman 1986).

Consequences of group cohesiveness

Outcomes of group cohesiveness can be very positive for communication and job satisfaction. Members of cohesive groups communicate more often and are more sensitive to each other, and generally are better able to gauge the feelings of other group members. Members of highly cohesive groups are more satisfied with their jobs and team members than those of less cohesive groups (Dobbins & Zaccaro 1986). Group cohesiveness leads to **organisational citizenship behaviours**, discretionary actions not required by the job but helping attain organisational goals (such as assisting a coworker struggling with a task) (Organ & Ryan 1995). Although some negative possibilities exist (such as too much communication among group members), improved communication and job satisfaction from group cohesiveness are organisationally valuable (Kinicki & Williams 2003).

Group cohesiveness influences hostility and aggression levels that one group shows to another. Whether this is an organisational asset or liability depends on where the energy is channelled. For example, cohesiveness may help when there is friendly competition among groups doing the same type of work but not dependent on each other to get work done. Aggressiveness from group cohesiveness can energise a group against external competition (Dallas 1995). Alternatively, when groups depend on each another to reach organisational goals, hostility or aggression results in little cooperation and other negative results, such as missing deadlines, raising costs and frustrating customers.

Another area group cohesiveness influences is performance—in highly cohesive groups, members' performance levels are more similar. Members will avoid disappointing the group by underperforming, sometimes known as 'chiselling', or showing up other members by overperforming or 'ratebusting'.

The impact of cohesiveness on actual performance levels, however, depends both on the group's level of cohesiveness and existing performance norms. This is shown in Figure 14.6. Groups do best when group cohesion and performance norms are high, encouraging all members to perform at the same high level. By contrast, if group cohesion is high and performance norms are low, performance is lower (Seashore 1954; Stogdill 1972). Here, high group cohesion bolsters adherence to low performance norms. Effects can be seen in an example of a former MBA student, whose summer job was in a highly cohesive lawn-care crew with low performance norms. As he raked grass clippings vigorously on his first work day, crew members, even the crew leader, told him to slow down or they would all get tired if they worked at that rate. Then the crew leader showed him how to use a handkerchief to mop his brow while leaning on his rake so it would look like he had been working hard and just stopped to wipe off the resulting perspiration. The handkerchief routine was used if one was caught not working when the supervisor drove up on periodic work-crew checks.

Group cohesiveness can also affect a group's readiness to innovate and change. Change is harder when opposed by a highly cohesive group, but is much easier with the strong backing of such a group (Serwer 1995; Ferguson 2003).

group cohesiveness

Degree to which members are attracted to a group, are motivated to remain in it, and are mutually influenced by one another

organisational citizenship behaviours

Discretionary actions that are not part of job requirements but contribute to attaining organisational goals

GENDER FACTOR

Helen Clark at the helm

Helen Clark has been a member of the Labour Party executive in New Zealand since 1978, and has had wide experience as a minister of large portfolios, as a deputy prime minister, and as leader of the opposition. She has been prime minister since 1999, and currently has responsibility for the portfolios of arts, culture and heritage, the security intelligence service and the ministerial services of New Zealand.

She has been described as a workaholic; a 'hands-on, direct operator'; and 'intelligent, methodical, a planner who knows what has to be done and stays on track once she starts'. In addition, she is thought to keep the 'malcontents and aggrieved' on side as she believes they have an important part to play in decision making. She has a cautious operating style; preferring to test tactical decisions, initiatives and matters of policy within a tight circle of trusted colleagues before moving further afield to build support. She also takes an active role in defining policy, choosing not to accept advice passively: 'I regard all advice with scepticism'.

Helen Clark's management style is described as 'controlling'. She dispenses discipline via 'corrective phone calls' after mistakes have been identified. She is also reported as using humiliation as a tool for controlling meetings in caucus. These techniques are believed to be instrumental in promoting unity in a party that has traditionally been seen as internally destructive, because 'MPs want to win office more than they want to win internal arguments and battles'. Caucus is now considered to be highly disciplined under a leadership style that is conservative and meticulous.

However, Helen Clark's leadership style has been criticised in the past as demonstrating lack of vision and a superficial understanding of Maori ambitions and future needs. Party members have reported being denied the opportunity to think and act quickly in an innovative, future-oriented manner, and having far less regular access to her than to previous prime ministers. In addition, delegation has

been limited, and then only to a highly select, trusted group of individuals. Apparently, Helen Clark is addressing these issues by continuing to 'learn on the job', displaying an impressive capacity to embrace complex issues of policy and economics. Her style is now reported to have become more 'visionary' and 'forward-looking', and she has modified her directiveness with her ministers. It would appear that she is tracking well to achieving her goal of three terms in office.

Source: Contributed by Glenice Wood (details of sources are listed on p. 737).

Activities for discussion, analysis and further research

1. What types of work group operate in Helen Clark's caucus?
2. With Helen Clark's described management style, do you think it is likely that there will be incidents of social loafing or free riding by members of the caucus? Why, or why not?
3. What group norms have been established by Helen Clark and her party? Is there any indication that group norms play a significant part in the operation of the party?
4. Log onto to the website: www.primeminister.govt.nz for biographical details of Helen Clark, speeches and releases.

FIGURE 14.6 Effects of cohesiveness and performance norms on group performance

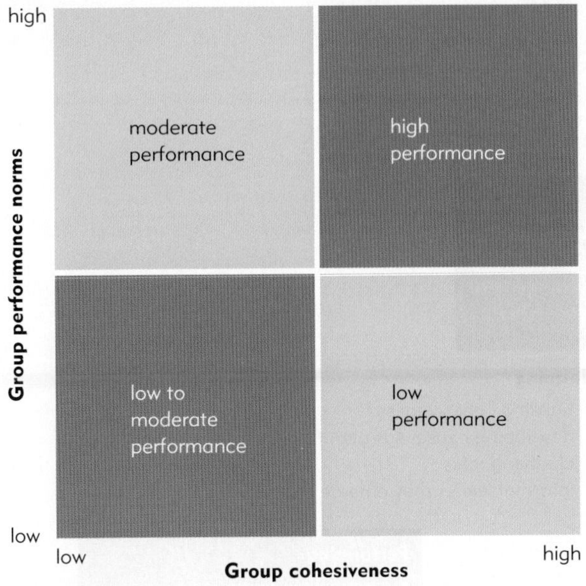

Determinants of group cohesiveness

Many factors positively influence group cohesiveness. For example, similar attitudes and values mean people can communicate, find common ground and develop mutual understandings. External threats, such as fierce external competition or survival challenges, are compelling reasons for a group to act as a cohesive unit. Major successes produce strong positive feelings about group membership, forming links between members (Mullen & Copper 1994). A group that is difficult to join, based on high standards (medical or dental schools at a university), sacrifice (Australian Volunteers Abroad) or difficult training (the Special Air Service) can make a common bond. Finally, group size can be a factor. Cohesiveness is easier for small groups and is harder to achieve and maintain as groups grow (Brown 1988; *Forbes* 1989; Labarre 1995).

Group development

New groups, such as work units, committees and task forces, form constantly. Even established groups change as members leave and new ones join. These changes affect groups' processes.

It is argued that groups pass through fairly predictable developmental stages. Understanding these helps managers effectively participate in groups, assisting those they are responsible for. One approach to analysis of group development identifies five major stages: forming, storming, norming, performing and adjourning (see Fig. 14.7) (Tuckman 1965; Tuckman & Jensen 1977).

New groups may progress through these phases, but, if membership changes, development may briefly regress to earlier stages.

Stage 1: Forming

In the group's **forming** stage, members try to assess task and group interaction ground rules. Members seek information about the task, evaluate how the group could interact to achieve it, and begin to test how valued their input will be. Members may test behaviour acceptability, such as making small talk, joking, sarcasm or leaving to make phone calls. Because of the uncertainty, members may depend on a powerful person, if present, or on existing norms, if commonly known. Due to the need to understand ground rules, groups at this stage often need time to get to know the task and each other before going on.

forming

Stage in which group members try to assess ground rules applying to a task and to group interaction

FIGURE 14.7 Stages of group development

Forming
- orientation to task
- testing interpersonal behaviours
- dependency on power person
- discovering ground rules

Storming
- resistance to task demands
- interpersonal conflicts
- exploring areas of disagreement
- struggle for group leadership

Norming
- building cohesiveness
- developing consensus about norms
- clarifying roles
- informal leader may emerge

Performing
- channelling energy to task
- roles clear and functional
- norms support teamwork
- emerging problem solutions

Adjourning
- goals accomplished
- preparing for disengagement
- dependency on power person
- some regret at disbanding
- termination of group

storming

Stage in which group members frequently are in conflict with each other as they locate and resolve differences of opinion about key issues

norming

Stage in which group members begin to build group cohesion, as well as develop a consensus about norms for performing a task and relating to each other

performing

Stage in which energy is channelled toward a task and in which norms support teamwork

Stage 2: Storming

During the **storming** stage, group members conflict with each other as they find and try to resolve opinion differences on key issues. Issues might involve task needs and possible resistance. Another common conflict area relates to interpersonal relations, how members relate. At this stage, members may struggle for leadership if one has not been not appointed. Listening and trying to resolve major issues are important. Otherwise, the group will be ineffective, not progressing beyond this stage, and may even disband.

Stage 3: Norming

In the **norming** stage, group members start to build group cohesion, reaching a consensus about task performance and relationship norms. Member idiosyncrasies are accepted, and people start to identify with the group. Member roles are clearer, and the group is willing to engage in mutual problem solving. If no leader is appointed or the leader is weak, an informal leader may emerge. At this stage, norm and role clarification, cohesiveness building, and using group resources in problem solving are important.

Stage 4: Performing

The **performing** stage is when energy is channelled toward a task and norms support teamwork. Solutions come from the previous stage's problem solving. Group members' roles clarify, becoming more effective as the group works to positive synergy and group goals. Not all groups reach this stage. Those which do will be effective as long as they work at the task, while maintaining good group relationships.

Stage 5: Adjourning

During the **adjourning** stage, group members prepare for disengagement as the group nears successful goal completion. Members may be pleased with finishing their tasks, but regret impending group dispersal. The adjourning stage applies more often to temporary task groups such as committees, task forces or limited-duration teams. With permanent formal groups, adjournment is less common. However, reorganisations, take-overs and mergers can cause it to occur.

Do all groups have these stages? The five group-development stages mainly apply to new unstructured groups. They are less likely in groups where members work together often or where operating methods or ground rules are well established (Seeger 1983).

Meetings are an important place for group development. Senior executives average 23 hours a week in meetings, and middle managers about 11 hours (Hymowitz 1988). Other members have several hours a week in meetings. Meetings are often seen as poorly run or not giving worthwhile results (Schwartzman 1986). A way to help group development in meetings is by focusing on meeting conduct. Meetings are productive when well organised and operating with agreed ground rules. To learn about effective meetings, see 'How to lead a meeting' in Management skills for a globalised economy.

adjourning

Stage in which group members prepare for disengagement as the group nears successful completion of its goals

MANAGEMENT SKILLS FOR A GLOBALISED ECONOMY

How to lead a meeting

There are three major phases in leading a meeting: preparation, meeting in progress, and follow-up.

Preparation

Preparation is a key element in conducting an effective meeting. The following steps are involved:

1. Ensure the meeting is needed. According to one estimate, it costs about $100 per hour, including overheads, to have a manager attend a meeting. Therefore, a two-hour meeting attended by 10 managers adds up to $2000. Colleagues will appreciate not attending meetings on routine matters which could be handled by a memo.

2. Define the meeting's objectives. An objective might be to involve others in a decision, coordinate major activities, or discuss important information. It is helpful to orient attendees by briefly describing each objective either in a memo announcing the meeting or on the agenda. Be specific when stating objectives. For example, 'Decide between using sales reps or an in-house sales force' is much more helpful than 'Discuss sales'.

3. Identify participants. Limit participation to decision makers, those with expertise needed, and/or are affected by outcomes. As noted, five to seven is ideal for group interaction, but sometimes a meeting must be larger to involve

all participants needed. If too large, however, it will be difficult to manage.

4. Prepare an agenda. When there is time, circulate the agenda before the meeting and get feedback. The agenda should be a short list of main topics for discussion. It helps key participants focus on preparations needed for the meeting and assist in ensuring important topics are covered. Send the final agenda out two or three days in advance.

5. Distribute background information needed. Consider what information participants will need in advance, and send it out with the final agenda. Avoid sending huge reports that are unlikely to be read. It is better to send a summary and note that the full report is available if needed.

Meeting in progress

Good preparation helps the meeting progress more smoothly. Actually running the meeting involves five steps:

1. Review the agenda. Start on time, and review the agenda and major objectives. This helps focus participants on why they are there and needed outcomes. It helps to print the agenda on a blackboard or flip chart for easy reference.

2. Get reports from those with preassigned tasks. This should be done as soon as feasible, although you may have to wait for a particular agenda item to ask for a report or presentation. Getting reports early ensures presenters have enough time and gives recognition for their pre-meeting work. It also gives some background information for other parts of the agenda.

3. Encourage participant input. Group effectiveness and member satisfaction will be greater when all are able to provide input in their areas of expertise. A leader should ensure the meeting is not dominated by one faction or a few members. If someone speaks too much, the leader might say, 'Well, Joan, let me see if I understand what you are saying'. Then, after summarising, the leader might follow with, 'Perhaps others have views on this issue'. If an individual has said little, the leader might say, 'Jim, we haven't heard from you yet. What are your views?'

4. Keep the meeting on track. If discussion wanders, refer to a point made just before the digression to get discussion back on track. If an issue is raised which cannot be resolved due to insufficient information, ask someone to look into it and report back.

5. Summarise and review assignments. Summarise what has been agreed upon or accomplished in the meeting. Also, review what each person has agreed to do and make sure deadlines are set. Review plans for the next meeting if that is appropriate. End the meeting on time.

Follow-up

The meeting leader should follow up on the meeting:

1. Send out a memo summarising the meeting. The memo should summarise the main accomplishments, and it should specify actions each person agreed to take and deadlines set.

2. Follow up on assignments where appropriate. This involves checking with various people about their progress, usually in preparation for a later meeting.

Meeting leadership takes practice. It is usually a good idea for individuals to chair small, lower-level meetings early in their careers to get experience (Jay 1976; Huber 1980; Whetten & Cameron 1998; Bailey 1987; Dressler 1995).

MANAGING THE E-CHALLENGE

Using the internet to educate staff

The advent of the internet and the technology that makes it possible has had a huge effect on the way organisations do their work and are managed. Most organisations, especially those that are project-oriented, use some form of team-based structure to achieve their objectives. Members of project teams need to thoroughly understand the procedures and methods of work being employed. Sometimes these are tailored from the more generic organisational procedures to suit the project's environment, in which case it is very important that everyone on the team not only understands the tailoring and its rationale, but actually follows the tailored procedures. Failure to do this could have severe consequences for the project team and the organisation. Creators of software, for example, often have to comply with Software Capability Maturity Model (CMM) requirements. Those that fail to do so could lose their CMM level accreditation. This could have very severe consequences when it comes to winning new projects.

One reason that procedures are not followed is lack of awareness by team members—particularly new team members. Another is that people tend not to bother reading bulky documents describing procedures, particularly when the project encounters a crisis.

Boeing sought to overcome some of these issues by taking advantage of the internet and its associated technology. They ensured that team members had the required procedures at their fingertips by putting them on-line, with associated work methods supporting the procedures available through hypertext links in the main procedure. For example, if a procedure called on a group to perform requirements analysis, the methods for doing this were available through hypertext links embedded in the procedure. This meant that staff could easily be made aware of the relevant procedure without needing to search for it. Enabling staff members to home in on the procedures required for their current task made adhering to them that much easier.

Source: Contributed by Ravind Baglia.

Activities for discussion, analysis and further research

1. What group work processes do you think are important when considering using technology to enforce work procedures?

2. Does having a system of procedures on-line ensure that the procedures will be followed? Why or why not?

3. How would you manage the issue of individuals interpreting procedures differently, with the result that a project could end up with an inconsistent standard of work?

4. Does a scheme such as this affect the role of a 'team leader', or a 'group leader'? Explain.

PROMOTING INNOVATION: USING TASK FORCES AND TEAMS

Groups are used when organisations can benefit from the experience and ideas of two or more people. Group efforts are increasingly tapped when creativity and innovation are needed for organisational success. In this section, we investigate some special uses of teams.

Task forces

A **task force** is a temporary group formed to recommend on a specific matter (Altier 1986; Guzzo & Dickson 1996). It may be called an **ad hoc** or temporary **committee** (Stech & Ratliffe 1985; Kiechel 1991). Because they deal with issues involving several company parts, task forces often have members from command groups affected by an issue (Markels 1995). These people provide expertise, furnish information about their command groups' needs, and help with creative problem solving or ideas for opportunity taking (Birchard 1995). As task forces promote interaction among members of diverse departments, they suit creativity and innovation fostering.

A task force may also operate on a larger scale, such as New Zealand's Information and Communication Technology (ICT) Task Force, which last year produced a report with the ambitious goal of creating 100 $100 million information technology companies within 10 years. If the target is reached, the task force estimates that information and communication technology will be contributing 10 per cent of New Zealand's GDP. The task force, led by SolNet founder Murray McNae, says one of the keys to hitting the target is encouraging commercialisation skills; in particular, helping New Zealand IT companies to get past the $15 million to $30 million size barrier. That will depend on lifting leadership and international sales and marketing abilities, creating a talent and skills pool and getting access to capital. (http://www.computerworld.co.nz/webhome.nsf/0/74BB3E7AE6AD8B24CC256D63007EEC 4C?opendocument)

task force

Temporary task group formed to recommend on a specific issue

ad hoc committee

Another term for a task force

Teams

A **team** is a temporary or an ongoing task group of members working to identify problems, form a consensus about action, and implement actions needed on a task or organisational area. Two characteristics separate a team from a task force. First, team members typically identify problems in an area (not deal with them after prior identification). Second, they reach a consensus about what is to be done and actually implement decisions as a team (not make recommendations implemented by others; Armstrong & Holyoke 1995). Of course, members (unless top-level managers) usually keep superiors informed, as needed (Roberts 2003). They also need agreement of their superiors on decisions with major implications for others and the organisation.

team

Temporary or ongoing task group with members charged to work together to identify problems, form a consensus about what should be done, and implement necessary actions in relation to a particular task or organisational area

Teams are often, but not always, task groups of individuals across command groups. Temporary teams handle a specific project to completion, where permanent teams have continuing responsibilities in a given area (Updike, Woodruff & Armstrong 1995). Teams may have a fluid membership of those who join when expertise is needed and leave when work is done.

Teams have been very successful in a wide range of firms, such as Heinz, General Motors, Hawker de Havilland, Hewlett-Packard, Xerox and Tenix. Teams have gained attention, especially to foster innovation, increase quality and facilitate change (Reich 1987). By one estimate, 80 per cent of organisations with 100 or more members use teams somehow, and 50 per cent of their employees belong to at least one team (Gordon 1992; Coradetti 1994; Fenn 1995; *Wall Street Journal* 1994). Three important types of teams are entrepreneurial, self-managing and virtual teams.

Entrepreneurial teams

> **entrepreneurial team**
>
> Group of individuals with diverse expertise and backgrounds brought together to develop and implement innovative ideas aimed to create new products or services or significantly improve existing ones

An **entrepreneurial team** is a group with varied expertise and backgrounds assembled to develop and implement innovative ideas for new products or services or improve existing ones significantly (Rosow in Davidson 1986; Brahm 1995; Loeb 1994). Entrepreneurial teams focus on new business by pioneering different endeavours or devising novel products and services fitting with existing business lines (Stevens 1995; Gome 2003d).

Self-managing teams

> **self-managing team**
>
> Work group with responsibility for a task area without supervision, and given authority to influence and control group membership and behaviour

A **self-managing team** is responsible for a task area without supervision and with authority to influence and control group membership and behaviour. They can set pay and bonus levels (Byrne 1995) and are also called autonomous work groups. The Swedish automobile manufacturer A.B. Volvo pioneered these groups at its Kamar plant in the early 1970s. There, autonomous work teams of about 20 workers assemble entire car units, such as the electrical system or engine (Lohr 1987).

Increasingly companies are experimenting with self-managing teams (Dumaine 1990; Tjosvold 1993). One study indicates those in self-managing teams hold more favourable work attitudes, higher job satisfaction and greater organisational commitment than those in traditionally designed jobs. The results of other studies are mixed (Cordery, Mueller & Smith 1991; Guzzo & Dickson 1996).

Even in high-performing teams some people will not measure up, and in self-managing teams disposing of these people is hard for the team (Markels 1995; Parkin 2003). Similarly, evaluating team-member performances and setting members' pay can cause some groups to defer to management (Lublin 1995).

> **virtual team**
>
> Physically dispersed work group using information technology as a means to interact but rarely, if ever, meeting physically

A major block to the success of self-managing team is the tendency to label a work group as a 'self-managing team' without giving the training and support needed. Four steps increase success prospects (Hackman 1987). First, before forming the team, its value must be assessed, as well as deciding tasks and degree of authority to be delegated to it. Second, in forming a team, group composition and necessary resource allocation must be thought through. Third, as

the group moves through group development stages, training in effective team work and guidance in appropriate norm setting are needed. Finally, managers must help by removing performance obstacles and helping the group learn. Experts warn productivity may drop as new self-managing teams develop. In fact it may be 18 months or more before productivity rises (Sims 1995).

Virtual teams

Virtual teams comprise members who rarely if ever meet, interacting through different means of information technology including phones, faxes, email, computer nets and video conferencing. Global organisations with widely dispersed activities are finding virtual teams increasingly important as knowledge becomes further specialised (Townsend, DeMarie & Hendrickson 1998; Kodama 2000a; Bateman & Snell 2004). Virtual teams allow creation of problem-solving or exploration teams, overcoming having members unable to work in the same physical location (Kodama 1999).

Duarte and Snyder (1999) identify factors critical to effective use of virtual teams. They include the following. Firstly, the organisation has established organisationally-appropriate reward systems with acceptable non-traditional work arrangements. Secondly, team members and their organisational community receive continual training opportunities. Thirdly, there are commonly understood and sufficiently flexible team processes. Fourthly, widely available technological support resources are available, with adequate training in their use. Fifthly, there is valued cultural diversity and an overall culture of trust. Sixthly, technology use and high performance levels must be modelled by leaders. Finally, team leaders and members must be experienced in applying technological tools, and comfortable in their virtual environments.

To effectively use this strategy, technological demands of the task must be understood and matched to take full advantage of the relative strengths of rapidly evolving technology (Duarte & Snyder 1999; Vokola, Rezgul & Wood-Harper 2000). As well as this, the impact of both organisational and other cultural levels must also be clearly understood (Rockett, Valor, Miller & Naude 1998; Crowe 2003).

Establishing a virtual team takes six steps (Duarte & Snyder 1999). These are: identification of significant organisational influence or power sources; development of a clear statement of purpose or mission; team participant identification; orchestrated initial contacts across the team; in possibly the only face-to-face contact the team will have, orient members to the virtual-team processes, and set up team-control and management processes (Miesing 1998; Thite 1999).

Virtual teams allow managers to overcome spatial dispersion, setting up teams of people who are knowledgeable, expert and experienced for specific problems or a particular opportunity (Townsend et al. 1998; Cook 1999). Virtual teams' members can come from other organisations; for example, an outsourced supplier (Pape 1997). This team form lets managers move beyond the organisation's traditional boundaries (Holmqvist 1999; Kodama 2000b).

GAINING THE EDGE

Whistle while you work

Not so long ago, while walking down the corridor of my work place, I heard a colleague say to a couple of others: 'Who's laughing in here? Don't you know it is against policy to have fun? The boss might think you're not doing your job!'

On another occasion upon being asked how they were, I hear a colleague saying 'Surviving'. The response to this depressing statement was 'Surviving is good'.

Both of the above are indicative of the culture of this organisation. Responses of this kind are warning signals that something is amiss.

Research has demonstrated that humour is of high benefit in managing work groups. It has been known to lower absenteeism, improve job-satisfaction ratings, lead to higher productivity, promote better retention rates and lower staff

turnover, and even reduce customer-service complaints and problems.

Other benefits in the use of humour as a management tool include a rise in creativity and faster problem solving, as people see solving problems as a way to have fun. When people are having fun, they enjoy doing so together and more effective team-work is often the result.

There is no way to ban humour from the workplace. But it sometimes appears that management tries very hard to ensure that people do not have fun at work. Humour will appear in guerrilla warfare form unless it is part of the culture of the organisation.

As I walk down the corridors of my organisation, I note the cartoons on the glass inserts of staff office doors or the photocopies of comic strips which appear in pigeon holes. Think of the number of emails and faxes you may have received which are bitter-sweet forms of humour taking a dig at something happening in the organisation.

Source: Stauffer, D. (1999); Tein, M. (2003).

Activities for discussion, analysis and further research

1. Develop a number of strategies which might encourage a culture which accepts fun and humour as part of 'the way we behave around here'.

2. Southwest Airlines is famous for its over-the-top having-fun culture. Go into their website and find some examples of the type of activity they engage in which livens up the work day and the workplace.

3. Look up the newsletter *Humour and Health*, whose editor is Joseph Dunn, and find some articles on how to introduce humour in the workplace. Describe the benefits expected from such actions.

REFLECTIVE PRACTITIONER

You will have noticed that I keep referring to we or us when I talk about the company. There are two perspectives to that. On one hand it is something I have trained myself to do. But to me, our company was always going to be more than just me. I have always referred to us even when it was just me. This is what I wanted to make available to industry. I have trained myself to think that way because it provides a good environment and a platform where it is not just about me, it is about the group and how we operate and function together and what we can contribute collectively.

We had an instance not too long ago where a team of three of the managers took on the responsibility and ran through the whole selection process to go and find a staff member that they were after. It was really great to see them step up to the mark and really take ownership in the type of person, be that from a professional perspective or a personal one. They went through the decision-making process, the design of the selection criteria, the recruitment process. They were much more thorough and rigorous than I have ever been. I thought that was a great reflection of the importance they gave to selecting the right person to join the team. That was a good experience letting them manage the whole process from beginning to end. Unfortunately, that person didn't last with the company as they didn't perform as required. But letting them go was the team's decision as well.

KIMBERLEY TURNER

Little things like that demonstrate that in a small evolutionary-type way, I am taking a step back and allowing people to take on more responsibility, and I am slowly letting go.

When you are working with a small-to-medium sized team, when you bring in a new person or lose one person, the whole dynamic of your work environment changes. The organisational culture is readjusted and realigned.

Strategies for improving

1. Assist all group members to understand how they gain from particular goal-oriented activities. How will this benefit the organisation?

2. How do you individually reward individuals whose tasks are interdependent?

3. Develop strategies which will enable a work-team's members to understand linkages between their various roles.

Source: Jones et al. (2000).

SUMMARY

- Increasingly work groups are important to an organisation's competitiveness. The two major work-group types are formal and informal. Formal groups include command, or functional, groups and task groups. Informal groups include interest and friendship groups. The required aspects of formal groups lead to emergent behaviours, interactions and sentiments of informal groups.
- One way to analyse groups is to view them as systems using inputs to engage in processes or transformations and produce outcomes. Important group inputs are group composition, particularly member characteristics and reasons for group attraction; member roles, including task, maintenance and self-oriented; and group size.
- Work-group processes have positive synergy. Important factors influencing group processes are norms, cohesiveness and development. Group norms come from explicit supervisor and coworker statements, critical group-history events, primacy and carryover behaviours. Many factors lead to group cohesiveness. Cohesion, in turn, has major consequences for group communication, satisfaction, performance, hostility and aggression toward other groups, and willingness to innovate and change. New groups have five development stages: forming, storming, norming, performing and adjourning. Size influences group interactions and encourages social loafing or free riders. Those leaning to individualism rather than collectivism are more likely to display social loafing. Important results to consider in evaluating effectiveness are group performance, member need satisfaction and future work-group compatibility.
- Some major organisation mechanisms to tap the creativity and innovative capacity of groups include task forces, or ad hoc committees, and teams, particularly entrepreneurial and self-managing teams.

QUESTIONS FOR DISCUSSION AND REVIEW

1. Outline the major work-group types. Identify several groups at your college or university. Classify them by work-group type.
2. Explain how informal groups develop. Choose a familiar organisation and identify two informal groups. Trace how the groups came to exist.
3. Explain basic inputs groups require to operate. Analyse inputs of a work group you think runs effectively. What member characteristics help it operate successfully? What brings members to the group? What roles do members play? How does the number of members affect group interaction?
4. Explain the significance of norms and cohesiveness in group functioning. Think of a group to which you belong. What are four important group norms? How did they develop? Assess the level of group cohesiveness and its consequences.
5. Explain how groups develop. Trace the development of a group in which you have participated.
6. Describe how size influences group performance and interactions. Include assessment of social loafing and possible effects associated with individualism and collectivism. To what extent have you seen these factors operate in groups?
7. Differentiate between task forces and teams. Explain how each promotes innovation. Identify examples of task forces and teams in the business section of your local paper, in the *Financial Review*, and/or magazines such as *Business Review Weekly* and *Asia Week*.
8. Explain why self-managing teams have been so successful. If you were a manager, why would you like or not like to have them in your organisation?
9. Explain the process of setting up a virtual team. What difficulties might emerge if any one step were overlooked?

CRITICAL THINKING QUESTIONS

To answer some of these questions you will need to do further research. Useful references are given below each section of the questions.

This chapter of the textbook developed the concepts established in Chapters 12 and 13 on leadership and communication to examine how groups can be used by organisations as a powerful tool for achieving organisational goals.

It would be remiss, however, to suggest that collecting people together and calling them a 'team' is always successful. A recent article by Trevor Goddard provides some interesting insights into what can go wrong when implementing teams.

Ford Motor Co, General Motors' (GM) Saturn Division and Procter & Gamble (P&G) can all be cited as high profile adherents of the team-building approach over the last decade, but all are also now experiencing real difficulties. Ford is labouring under increasingly diminishing gaps in development time compared to their Japanese competitors, while GM's teamwork based 'factory of the future' is reverting to the traditional, Detroit-style assembly line. This trend back to the past and away from teamwork is also reflected in P&Gs return to individual accountability for developing and marketing new products.

1. What simple reason could there be for similar failures in the teamwork efforts of these three quite different organisations?

2. Using sporting analogies, Goddard (2004) calls the three types the baseball team, the football team and tennis doubles team. What do you think the characteristics of each are?

3. What do you think the weaknesses of each of the three team types are?

While there are strengths and weaknesses in all three types of team, the main differences arise from the behaviour they require, what each does best, and in what they are inherently unable to do. It is this last point which is particularly important as the one thing that limits all three is that they must remain true to type: 'they cannot be hybrids. One kind of team can play only one way' (Goddard 2004, p. 11). This clearly makes it very difficult to change from one type of team to another.

4. How should change be implemented to move from one type of team to another?

(Material relevant to these questions may be found in Goddard, T. 2004, Identifying different teams, *New Straits Times Press*, Malaysia, 13 January, p. 11.)

One of the main explanations dealt with in this textbook to explain the popularity of group work in organisations was the enormous potential they can unlock from within group participants. Groups can produce results which are far greater than the sum of the individuals themselves; this is commonly known as 'synergy'. A recent newspaper report provides a different perspective on this power. Glendinning (2002) examines the notion of the power of groups within the educational setting through a brief review of the learning initiatives undertaken in one of Sydney's western suburbs state schools, Blacktown Girls High School. In an area generally associated with underprivileged, under-resourced students, the school was the recipient of the 2001 Director-General's award for innovation in girls' education. Central to the changes introduced was the restructuring of classes in ways that created the most effective learning environment for the students. One of the major findings was that the students learned better when given opportunity to form discussion groups. The students are put in learning groups of three or four from year 7 on. These groups are built around differences in personalities and skills, rather than friendships. Surprisingly (or perhaps not, after reading the text), after any initial problems are sorted out in the 'forming' and 'norming' phases, many students choose to stay in their learning team right through their senior years.

5. What would you predict to be some of the results from this group emphasis on education—both for students and for the school?

(Material relevant to this question may be found in Glendinning, L. 2002, Girls' own schools attract attention, foster invention, *Sydney Morning Herald*, 13 June, p. 4.)

The next questions look at the relationship between new technology and groups. Paul Lee (2002, p. 18) a partner at Deloitte Consulting, writes that 'during the past two decades, many organisations have experienced dramatic changes to their operations, driven largely by the perceived need to reap the benefits of the new available technologies'. He suggests that this has occurred in two waves. The first focused on the internal operations of the organisations and how technology could be used to integrate parts of their business operations. The second wave has been externally focused to see how technology can be used to promote linkages with customers and suppliers. Once achieving this 'state-of-the-art technology', organisations find that they must also alter the whole way in which they operate and, even more fundamentally, the way they think about their employees. Lee (2002, p. 18) believes that the focus is essentially on 'collaborative knowledge networks' which should 'allow groups of people to work together outside conventional organisational structures' and 'lead to knowledge-sharing, the acceleration of business processes and a creative approach to solving everyday business problems'.

6. What are some of the reasons why this generally is not occurring in Australia?

The development of the technology networks implemented in the first wave and their operationalisation in the second wave allows a near complete real-time information and communication sharing amongst all elements of an organisation's internal and external environment. Employees, customers, suppliers and strategic partners are brought together in a collaborative knowledge network where better decisions, based on more complete information, can be made more quickly. Before you dismiss these ideas as theoretical only, Lee (2002) provides the example of the Australian mining industry as a sector that is actively pursuing the third wave. It is a surprising example as it is a sector that even Lee admits, is often perceived as 'a model of conservatism and rigidity in its people practices'. Here however, he suggests it is at the cutting edge of allowing 'programs of creativity for their people to operate in informal collaborative networks with responsibility for developing their own solutions'.

7. Given your knowledge of groups, what are some of the challenges to forming these 'collaborative knowledge networks'?

8. Given the likely problems, how have successful organisations such as Xerox, Nippon Roche and the World Bank enabled a knowledge-sharing environment to be successfully nurtured?

(Material relevant to these questions may be found in Lee, P. 2002, Knowledge networks trigger the next big wave of change, *Australian Financial Review*, 16 May, p. 18.)

While the collaborative knowledge networks of Lee's (2002) third wave may still have some way to go before they are the norm in Australian organisations, there is extensive use of self-managing work teams. As a recent study by Kirkman and Shapiro (2001) explains, self-managing work teams assign jobs, plan and schedule work, make decisions and take action on problems, and are consistently linked to increased job satisfaction and increased productivity. However, as their study revealed, there are still important issues which must be addressed in this increasingly conventional form of group work.

Kirkman and Shapiro (2001) set out to investigate indications that national differences are responsible for the lack of success experienced by self-managing work teams in some countries. Their study suggested that the participative management style inherent in these teams may not be suitable in countries such as the Philippines or Russia, which are characterised by a belief in the importance of status and power differences.

9. How might these characteristics circumvent the benefits normally associated with teams?

(Material relevant to this question may be found in Kirkman, B. and Shapiro, D. 2001, The impact of cultural values on job satisfaction and organisational commitment in self-managing work teams, *Academy of Management Journal*, June, 44, 3.)

The last questions look at some unexpected but pleasing developments in the notion of teams and networking within the Australian small business and accountancy sector.

10. What are the pressures for accountants to adopt a team-oriented approach?

11. How could accountants adopt a team-oriented approach?

The fact is that the pressure of change and dangers of specialising in areas that may have a limited life or may change rapidly, means that many organisations, regardless of size, are turning to a team-oriented approach to cope.

(Material relevant to these questions may be found in Stensholt, J. 2001, Teamwork Beats The Tax Trauma, *Business Review Weekly*, 4 October, p. 76.)

MANAGEMENT EXERCISES

Exercise 1 Skill building: Assessing group cohesiveness

Cohesiveness can be a favourable work-group characteristic. This exercise is designed to assist in assessing cohesiveness of a work group you are currently a member of. This could be a group preparing a paper for a class, a group developing a solution to a case or exercise, a group where you work, or any other group effort. If you are not involved in a particular work group, please refer to the most recent work group in which you participated.

Assessing group cohesiveness	Agree Disagree
1. Individual members of the group are respected by the others.	1 2 3 4 5 6 7 8 9 10
2. The group goal is enthusiastically supported by group members.	1 2 3 4 5 6 7 8 9 10
3. The group has established norms quickly to facilitate accomplishing our goal.	1 2 3 4 5 6 7 8 9 10
4. Group members share similar work values.	1 2 3 4 5 6 7 8 9 10
5. The group is able to bring out the best performance from each member.	1 2 3 4 5 6 7 8 9 10
6. Group members' attitudes towards the ultimate goal are positive.	1 2 3 4 5 6 7 8 9 10
7. Group members' goal commitment increases the longer we work together.	1 2 3 4 5 6 7 8 9 10
8. Communications within our group improve steadily as we progress.	1 2 3 4 5 6 7 8 9 10
9. A feeling of 'we' versus 'I' is evident in our group.	1 2 3 4 5 6 7 8 9 10
10. The group pulls together, making the task easier.	1 2 3 4 5 6 7 8 9 10
11. Everyone believes their contribution is important.	1 2 3 4 5 6 7 8 9 10
12. The group seeks input from everyone prior to making decisions.	1 2 3 4 5 6 7 8 9 10
13. The group interaction seems to bring out the best in each member.	1 2 3 4 5 6 7 8 9 10
14. The size of the group helps promote a feeling of mutual support.	1 2 3 4 5 6 7 8 9 10
15. If one member of the group needs help, other members are quick to respond.	1 2 3 4 5 6 7 8 9 10

Your lecturer will tell you how to interpret your score.

Exercise 2 Management exercise: Shipwrecked

Wreck survivors' situation sheet

A private yacht, sailing through an archipelago located between the 10th and 20th parallels in the Pacific Ocean, is caught in a sudden storm and runs aground on a coral reef. The passengers and crew reach the sandy shores of one of the islands. Shortly before impact, they tried a MAYDAY message on the radio with approximate coordinates; it was impossible to repeat the distress message or to receive a reply because of the rush of events. Unfortunately, chances of the message getting through—in view of atmospheric conditions, quality of transmission, and distance—were poor.

The situation can be summarised as follows:

1. The island is small and uninhabited. There is plenty of tropical vegetation, and among the plants abound coconuts, mangoes and bananas. It rains in the afternoon most days, but the climate is mild and does not require heavy clothing. At low tide, fish and shellfish can be seen just offshore.
2. Nobody had time to pick up any supplies from the yacht. Passengers' and crew members' pockets contain some cigarettes, matches, two lighters and a pocket knife. Among them, they have three watches.
3. The lagoon between the beach and reef where the yacht ran aground is about 900 metres in diameter and has an area of deep water.
4. Only a few of the passengers and crew are good swimmers.
5. Most certainly, all equipment aboard the yacht (i.e. radio transmitter, radar, generators) was destroyed on impact.
6. The crew predicts the yacht will be dragged along the reef and will sink at high tide about eight hours later.

The total group has decided the wrecked yacht must be reached before it sinks to recover those items necessary for future survival. The best swimmers will go to analyse the situation on board the yacht and attempt to bring supplies back to the shore. The group needs to prepare a list of those items it considers most valuable for the group, selecting them in priority order. Anticipating this, some crew members have compiled lists of items they think will be needed. Because time is valuable, it is decided the total group's list will include 15 of these items (the most retrievable in the time available), listed in priority order. Each person may suggest one alternative item not on the original list, which they may place on the list of 15 if so desired.

Wreck survivors' individual task sheet

During this task, do not communicate with anyone. Your task is to rank, in priority order, 15 items from the following lists. In addition, you can add one item of your choice which in all probability was left on board the yacht. Next to the number 1 write the name of the item you believe is most important. Continue until you reach number 15, the least important. You will have 15 minutes to complete this task.

These items are the choices of five members of the crew.

Chris	Pat	Dale	Kelly	Robin
axe	bed sheets	suntan lotion	rope	marine charts
hammer and nails	blankets	toilet articles	binoculars	pistol and ammunition
knives	cooking pots	mirror	water tanks	wooden planks
fishing tackle	canned food	condensed milk	large plastic sheet	tool box
transistor radio	beverages	chocolate bars	bottles of rum	flippers and harpoon
plastic buckets	first-aid kit	mosquito netting	life jackets	shark repellent

Wreck survivors' group task sheet

The subgroup members now have to agree on a single list, which they write on newsprint—15 items in priority order, including those items most likely to ensure survival. It is important to remember:

- You must reach a consensus regarding the ranking given to each item.

- 'Consensus' means each subgroup member agrees to the plan, at least to some degree. Coercion and methods of conflict avoidance such as averaging, voting and 'horse-trading' are not recommended.
- The subgroup may organise as it wishes to obtain the best results.

Item of your choice, if any:

Individual ranking

1. _____
2. _____
3. _____
4. _____
5. _____
6. _____
7. _____
8. _____
9. _____
10. _____
11. _____
12. _____
13. _____
14. _____
15. _____

The subgroup has 45 minutes in which to complete this task.

Group ranking

1. _____
2. _____
3. _____
4. _____
5. _____
6. _____
7. _____
8. _____
9. _____
10. _____
11. _____
12. _____
13. _____
14. _____
15. _____

Source: Adapted from Pfeiffer, J. W. (1994).

END-OF-CHAPTER CASE: ON THE RIM

Team-development at Fisher Paykel: The introduction of 'everyday workplace teams'

(This was an historical study carried out before Fisher and Paykel Industries Limited was restructured in 2001.)

The Fisher and Paykel Range and Dishwasher Division, based in Dunedin, New Zealand, is part of the Fisher and Paykel Whiteware and Health-Care manufacturing company. The Range and Dishwasher Division is responsible for the manufacture of all cookware products. The division employs approximately 570 staff, with 400 employees in manufacturing roles and 170 support staff.

Following loss of market share in the wake of removal of export tariffs, the company was determined to succeed through a culture of change and innovation. This culture would be built on skilled and autonomous teams, focused on low cost/no cost improvement activity. The division's responses to the company-wide focus on team working was to establish planning meetings between several key individuals in the division, which were held over several months in 1994/95, and to pilot teamwork sessions.

POWERWEB

International articles related to this topic are available at the Online Learning Centre at
www.mhhe.com/au/bartol4e

Vision of 'everyday workplace teams'

The outcome was a vision of a self-managing team culture with the concept of 'everyday workplace teams' (EDWT) at its heart. While team working already existed to some extent with small work groups managed by supervisors, it needed to be strengthened and formalised. EDWT captured the belief that being a team member should be an integral part of employees' everyday work. The planning team identified that an everyday workplace team would:

- encourage contributions from members
- have a unified vision
- understand and use quality tools
- have a positive focus
- be responsible for plans linked to goals
- have a plan to develop the team, the members and the process

Implementation process

A project team, initially called the 'understanding team' (later called the 'implementation team') was set up, comprising the company accountant, a trainer, a production planner, the maintenance manager and an area leader who had already begun team-training sessions. Their project brief was to ensure that an understanding of EDWT was communicated throughout the division. This team would also identify the boundaries of particular teams, as some measure of restructuring was required, and would also be involved in the start-up of the teams.

Over the years several initiatives had been launched in the company with initial enthusiasm, but had fizzled out. It was feared that many would see EDWT as another management fad that would quickly fade. The challenge was to introduce radical and ongoing change which staff would accept but which would certainly threaten some long-established 'comfort zones'. The aim was to end the mentality of 'leaving your brain at the door' which existed in some quarters in the division, and to develop new expectations of staff which went beyond their manufacturing and assembly roles. Such a change could be expected to meet with some opposition but also promised great opportunities for personal as well as organisational benefit.

The EDWT workbook

Realising the enormity of their task, the team adapted their brief to move further and faster into the implementation process itself. The outcome was the development of an EDWT workbook, which would operate as a standardised team training tool for start-up and for on-going reference. Production would stop for an hour while the team leader (with support initially from the training department) facilitated a team session using the EDWT workbook. This was a significant measure of the company's commitment to the EDWT concept. The highly interactive workbook contained such modules as communication skills, team building, working together and running meetings. The latter part of the workbook was more geared to teams becoming involved in activities to improve the running of their work area. The key aims of the workbook were:

- the development of functional teams
- the development of supporting team skills in individual team members
- linking the team to divisional goals
- prompting the team to direct energy to improvement activities in their work area.

All teams would use the workbook in order to develop a division-wide common understanding of team working. It was expected that it would take approximately twelve months to work through the book. At the completion of the workbook, teams would give a presentation to senior management on their team development and improvement activities.

Cost savings

Team members with limited support from engineering are now able to drive projects, to monitor cycle times and to rebalance workflows as necessary. Downtime and wastage have fallen. Increased control over the work area has led to greater acceptance and implementation of change. Previously, an introduction of a new product line or radically different model would incur high implementation costs and long lead-times to markets. Recently, however, a product design change was accomplished on the range line with no impact on the production schedule, and this is quickly becoming the norm across all assembly areas.

Skill development

Team members have developed skills in addition to the assembly work. Recognition of up-skilling in generic skills such as communication, data collection and analysis, and team skills has been captured (to some extent) by a competency-based pay scale for team members. Linking in the pay scale has been significant in achieving 'buy-in' from team members to this cultural change. However, it has not worked as well for those already at or near the top of the pay scale. How to reward both team performance and individual performance still needs to be further debated.

EDWT is part of the daily practice and language of the company. However, the division's experience suggests cautious use of language, as buzzwords invite reinterpretation, which although humorous can constitute barriers to change. EDWT is popularly

known in the division as 'everyday waste of time' which, in fact, belies the changes that have occurred and the enthusiasm for change in many team members who value the enhanced scope for personal development. There is also a large measure of passive acceptance. Outright resistance is still evident but not dominant.

Approximately 20 per cent of the teams have stalled in their efforts to complete the workbook, due in some cases to time commitment, in others to lack of management support. Some teams, particularly in salaried areas, feel that the workbook is neither necessary nor appropriate for them. Solutions might lie in customising the workbook for certain teams (e.g. engineering) and in providing additional facilitation support.

Team leaders

Perhaps the role that has been most affected by the change is that of the team leader. Previously the team leader (then called charge hand) was the technical expert or senior operator. The role now requires a high level of people-management skills in facilitating team sessions, coaching and developing team members, as well as in developing business plans, monitoring production and daily problem solving. There has been a difficult transition. Several former team leaders have stepped down from the role since the change and returned to the line. Recruitment of predominantly external candidates has filled these vacancies and newly created positions.

Some lessons from implementation

The question begs to be asked whether Fisher and Paykel would drive team development using the same process again. Hindsight has indicated that several factors could have been improved in the implementation process. Many team leaders expressed some concern that the initial development was not done in sufficient consultation with them, which is generally agreed within the division to have been an important oversight. The excitement and challenge of implementing the vision perhaps obscured some of the more detailed planning required. In particular, resistance may have been minimised and 'buy-in' increased had team leaders had training in facilitation skills prior to running the sessions with their teams.

However, it is also interesting to consider what the outcome would have been with increased consultation. The up-skilling of both team leaders and team members has required strong shifts out of comfort zones and into new ways of thinking and working. It could be argued that had the team leaders been part of the development process, the change could have been more watered down, perhaps with team sessions being facilitated by trainers, or even derailed.

This leads to the final point to consider when moving to a cultural shift. However much the change process is driven, the momentum can quickly die when initiating any sort of change in the workplace. There was enormous effort involved in this initiative and there were many low points for its champions when resistance threatened to overwhelm it. Ensuring that the change has full management support and is visibly encouraged would have prevented some of the teams from stalling. Better contingency planning for barriers that could inhibit or stifle change could have been considered more thoroughly before moving into the implementation period.

In summary, the move towards a formal team structure at the Range and Dishwasher Division has provided a platform for growth and spawned up-skilling and improvement activities in teams. As the change becomes further embedded into the environment, it becomes more difficult to remember what the environment was before. Team sessions have become a weekly event in many parts of the division with teams working continually on low-cost/no-cost improvements. Measuring the success has become almost intangible. The focus now turns to where the organisation moves to next, and to constructing a measurement for how team activities are contributing to the bottom line. The division is in the process of reviewing the initiative to date and reflecting on what has been learned about implementation of significant cultural change.

Change begets change and the key challenge for the division now is to keep the momentum going and meet ever-increasing expectations from staff for involvement and for seeing that their input is indeed valued and enacted.

Source: Dr Mary Mallon, Tania Kearney, Fisher and Paykel.

Activities for discussion, analysis and further research

1. Fisher and Paykel encountered some difficulties in reconciling the exciting development of a new vision and culture with the detailed planning required for implementation. How would you ensure these two factors were given appropriate consideration?

2. Why did some people resist the introduction of team working, even though it enabled them to develop more generic skills and encouraged their contribution to change? How could this resistance be overcome?

3. Design a training program for those charge hands now expected to operate as team leaders.

4. When introducing team-working, what other aspects of organisational systems need to be reviewed and potentially changed?

FURTHER READING

Chetty, C. and Campbell-Hunt, C. 2004, A strategic approach to internationalization: A traditional versus a 'born-global' approach, *Journal of International Marketing*, 12, 1, pp. 57–82.

Dose, J.J. 1999, The diversity of diversity: Work values effects on formative team processes, *Human Resource Management Review*, Spring, 9 1, pp. 83–109.

Huff, L. and Kelley, L. 2003, Levels of organizational trust in individualist versus collectivist societies: A seven-nation study, *Organization Science: A Journal of the Institute of Management Sciences*, January/February, 14, 1, pp. 81–91.

Journal of Developmental Entrepreneurship, 2003, Maori entrepreneurship in the contemporary business environment, December, 8, 3, pp. 219–36.

Petersen, D. 2003, Human error, *Professional Safety*, December, 48, 12, pp. 25–33.

GRADUATE GLIMPSE

BOB VAN DE KUILEN

Bob van de Kuilen has a Bachelor of Commerce and a Master of Commerce, both majoring in management. He is the CEO of his own management consulting firm, Novo Management Consulting Ltd.

What does your job entail?

I work for large companies, including Fortune 500 companies, implementing large operational change and improvement projects. We do this by facilitating behaviour change throughout the business at hand. We believe that organisational results stem from the collective behaviours of people within the organisation. We focus on observable behaviours, or in other words what people do and how they act. In turn, we believe these behaviours are created by three key levers: systems, processes, and people (i.e. their knowledge, skills, values, etc). It is these that we use to deliver measurable improvements to a business.

How have your university studies assisted you in your career?

My studies gave me a good grounding in understanding organisations from a number of different perspectives. That has helped me enormously in the field I'm in, because we're constantly being confronted with complex problems that can't be viewed one-dimensionally. Effective managers can't be technical experts alone, they need to have a whole toolkit of skills and abilities.

What is an important management principle that you draw upon frequently in your role?

The fundamentally positive principle that people come to work to do a good job but often they don't have the tools or mandate to do so. Good managers look at how structures or patterns that exist in the organisation shape individual performance, with the premise that if they get those structures and patterns right, they will have high-achieving employees.

MARTINIQUE VISSER

Martinique Visser uses problem-solving, management and communications principles in her job with the New Zealand diplomatic service. She has a Bachelor of Management Studies from the University of Waikato, New Zealand, and is the consular assistant at the New Zealand Embassy in The Hague, Netherlands.

What does your job entail?

The main focus of my job is managing the needs of distressed New Zealand citizens in our seven countries of accreditation: Netherlands, Sweden, Norway, Finland, Estonia, Lithuania and Latvia. This means that if a New Zealander ends up in hospital or jail, I am their first contact. I also assist those who have lost their documentation, or had it stolen, and I am the New Zealand point-of-contact for all information queries.

How have your university studies assisted you in your career?

My degree gave me a strong base in numerous skills which I draw upon daily. I am continuously employing my knowledge and understanding of management, communication, accounting and law. This strong knowledge base has allowed me to continue to adapt these skills to the requirements of my current position.

How do you use your knowledge of management principles in the day-to-day functions of your position?

As I may have to deal with severely distressed individuals, communication and people management skills are essential to my role. A vital part of my job is being able to manage panicked individuals, and calmly guide them through the steps to resolving their dilemmas. Time management also then becomes highly important, as helping New Zealand citizens is my top priority. I then have to juggle all my other responsibilities around the times that I need to dedicate myself solely to helping a distressed New Zealander.

The NGO community

Most of Australia's health, community support and charitable services are provided by NGOs (non-governmental organisations) in our cities, small towns and the bush. While these activities include large, well-known organisations such as The Salvation Army and The Smith Family, the majority of the sector is made up of small and unheralded local community groups. The services and community support they provide are crucial to the well being of communities and even to the smooth and effective running of formal government services. Between them they provide housing, volunteer workers and other forms of support and recreation to communities large and small. The size and impact upon the economy and community life of this sector is often not appreciated. There are approximately 600 000 non-profit organisations in Australia. Between them they employ 6 per cent of the workforce and contributed $26 billion to Australia's GDP. (ABS 1999)

However, this huge sector of Australia's economy has operated in the past with minimal cross-sector organisation, with the result that the sector operated in a fragmented, uncoordinated and unsupported way. The isolation of the many thousands of community groups across Australia's bush, small towns and cities meant that it was difficult to communicate effectively. Consequently, many small community groups were unable to easily access official information with regard to government support and funding. Furthermore, their isolated operations meant that their purchasing of operating supplies and services (such as banking and insurance) placed them at a disadvantage.

Into this vacuum came a commercial organisation in 1999 called 'Our Community Inc.', dedicated to providing a service to the myriad of community organisations scattered across Australia's countryside and cities. 'Our Community' describes itself as 'A one-stop gateway for practical resources, support and linkages between community networks and the general public, business and government—building capacity to strengthen the community in every Australian State and Territory'.

The enterprise was founded upon the firm belief that it would fill a strong and unmet market need since the NGO sector was not being effectively supported in financial, informational and support-service terms.

The enterprise's plan for becoming the major support organisation in this sector was approached with a distinct strategy in mind. First, 'Our Community' would work to overcome the isolation of NGOs by creating a website (www.ourcommunity.com.au) that would provide a central forum for all the tens of thousands of groups around Australia. Second, they would secure their client base with essential support and services that the NGOs were in need of but could not obtain elsewhere. These included regularly updated newsletters detailing municipal, state, federal and philanthropic grants. Additionally, a raft of services intended to provide support to the groups' administration was provided, such as pooled equipment purchasing, and national arrangements for public liability insurance and banking services along with training courses and support for governance boards, management and administration. Thirdly, they provided an intermediary role between business, government and research for the NGO community in order to improve the level of support available for community groups.

In the four years that 'Our Community' has been operating, it has established and consolidated its client base and continued to maintain its competitive advantage by deepening its expertise and relational assets in the sector. It has entered into sector-wide partnerships with government at all levels with the Prime Minister's 'Community Business Partnership' being the most recent example.

However, 'Our Community' now finds itself needing to extend its operations beyond Australia because of the deep interest shown by other countries in their innovative model, and because of the need to form closer links with research expertise from the US., Europe and the UK to inform their business, government and client partners in the enterprise.

'Our Community' continues to expand and in 2004 held its second annual national conference in Melbourne, the largest Australian community conference ever.

Source: Contributed by George Sansbury.

(ABS statistics from *ABS Year Book* 1999, Special Article— Australia's non-profit sector, by Associate Professor Mark Lyons, University of Technology, Sydney.)

Activities for discussion, *analysis and further research*

1. Log on to the 'Our Community' web site (www.ourcommunity.com.au) and examine its approach to providing information and support to the sector that the enterprise services.
2. Consider to what extent the use of web-based technology assisted 'Our Community' in establishing itself in the marketplace.
3. To what extent will 'Our Community' be able to maintain its competitive advantage in the future? What factors do you think may affect its ability to do so?

 Please insert the CD-ROM that is packaged with this book to view video clips that correspond to this Part theme.

CONTROLLING

As we have learned, the planning function gives direction, the organising function arranges resources, and the leading function adds the action element. Still, how does a manager ensure an organisation performs to standard and achieves its intended goals? The controlling function adds the vital regulatory aspect, allowing managers a range of methods to monitor performance and take needed corrective action. Controls must be used flexibly, though, as too much control stifles innovation.

In exploring the controlling function, CHAPTER 15 looks closely at the overall control process, including process steps, major control types, various managerial approaches to implementing controls, and problems attempting to control innovation.

In CHAPTER 16, we examine how managers attempt organisation control by managing conflict caused by change. Conflict must be both controlled and managed. This is a subtle difference many managers do not understand. This chapter explores how organisation members respond to particular situations and how these responses impact on organisational success.

PART 5

CHAPTER 15

CONTROLLING THE ORGANISATION

CHAPTER OUTLINE

Control as a management function
Significance of the control process
Role of controls
Levels of control

The control process
Steps in the control process
Deciding what to control: A closer look

Types of controls
Major control types by timing
Multiple controls
Cybernetic and non-cybernetic control

Managerial approaches to implementing controls
Bureaucratic control
Clan control
Market control
Promoting innovation: Controlling while nurturing innovation

Assessing control systems
Potential dysfunctional aspects of control systems
Overcontrol versus undercontrol
Characteristics of an effective control system

LEARNING OBJECTIVES

After studying this chapter, you should be able to:

- Explain the major control roles in organisations.
- Describe how control responsibilities change with management levels.
- Outline the general process applicable to most control situations.
- Delineate the principal conditions managers need to consider in deciding what to control.
- Explain the major control types based on timing and the use of multiple controls.
- Differentiate between cybernetic and non-cybernetic control.
- Describe basic managerial approaches to implementing controls.
- Outline the potential dysfunctional aspects of control systems and explain the implications of overcontrol and undercontrol.
- Delineate the major characteristics of effective control systems.

STRIVING FOR EXCELLENCE

WAN's *new Law*

Pages per journalist, sales per advertising representative, and personal responsibility for meeting budgets: to anyone familiar with the newspaper industry, these sound like commonsense management efficiency measures. At West Australian Newspaper Holdings (WAN), their introduction as performance indicators by the new chief executive, Ian Law, represents the start of a revolution that may lead the Perth company to expand beyond Western Australia.

In July, Law asked the heads of all sections how they proposed to increase revenue or lower costs. This sent shock waves through a business that for decades has operated as a near-monopoly in WA. For Law, who arrived at WAN in February after a successful career as general manager and editor-in-chief of the regional publishing division of Rural Press, it was an extension of his past method of working.

After the attack on operational efficiency will come the urge to expand. Law knows that this potential move will pit him against a deeply conservative board that has consistently argued that every previous attempt to expand has failed because nothing on offer matches the high margins produced by The *West Australian* newspaper. But Law knows that this is not necessarily true.

In 1998, Rural Press bought *The Canberra Times* newspaper for $160 million, outbidding WAN. Law, who took control of the Canberra daily, knows the results achieved, although he declines to be specific. 'It is in the past', he says. The chairman of Rural Press, John B. Fairfax, has been more outspoken. At the 1999 annual meeting of Rural Press, Fairfax said: 'We are pleased to confirm that the operation was earnings-per-share positive in the first year.' A former Rural Press colleague of Law, who declined to be named, says the turnaround was almost overnight: earnings rose 20 per cent in the first six months.

Squeezing higher profits out of *The Canberra Times* came from Law's adherence to his strict set of newspaper efficiency measures. This is why some stockbrokers have upgraded their investment recommendations for WAN. Robert Gee, an analyst with Paterson Ord Minnett, has changed his rating of WAN from a hold to a short-term buy. He says cost savings from lower newsprint costs and staff redundancies are combining with higher revenue from cover-price increases and a forecast rebound in advertising, to largely counter last year's profit decline. 'Last year was the bottom of the cycle', Gee says. 'The North-West Shelf gas contract with China should prove to be the catalyst for a wide-ranging recovery in the WA economy, with WA Newspapers a major beneficiary.'

Law says his first priority is to focus on WAN's core business. 'That can be achieved by bringing in some cultural changes and by focusing on detail and performance. I am a great believer in measuring all elements of the business, whether manufacturing efficiency, cost per unit in pre-press and printing, (or) sales revenue per person.'

Law declines to say what his efficiency targets are, but says he will know when he gets there. 'All I will say is, I believe we can achieve greater efficiencies.'

continued

As we saw before, the planning function gives direction, the organising function arranges resources, and the leading function adds the action ingredient. But how does a manager ensure an organisation meets standards and actually reaches set goals? The controlling function is the regulatory element, allowing managers to use various ways to monitor performance and take needed corrective action. Controls must be flexible, as too much control smothers innovation.

We devote this chapter its supplements to various aspects of control, the fourth major management function. In this chapter, we consider the significance of control as a management process. We examine the control process itself and discuss how managers decide what to control. We also review major control types and when they are appropriate. We then describe different managerial approaches to implement controls, including how to control without hampering innovation. Finally, we analyse how managers can assess the control systems they use.

During the control process, managers use systems to increase the likelihood of meeting organisational goals. Supplement 1 to Chapter 15 focuses on four of these: quality, financial, budgetary and inventory.

Another major control system is operations management, which is overseeing processes in producing a product or service. As Supplement 2 to Chapter 15 points out, a key operations management element is productivity. Managers must develop operations strategies, develop operating systems, utilise facilities, and promote innovative technology with productivity in mind.

Finally, as Supplement 3 to Chapter 15 shows, information systems are significant control methods. Computer-based systems give managers information to help make decisions for adjusting performance to meet goals. Information systems do not just help improve organisational operating efficiency. They can be used innovatively to provide a competitive edge.

CONTROL AS A MANAGEMENT FUNCTION

controlling

Process of regulating organisational activities so actual performance conforms to expected organisational standards and goals

All managers face issues around the controlling function. **Controlling** is regulation of activities so performance conforms to organisational goals and standards (Newman 1975; Brand & Scanlan 1995; Rose 1995). As this suggests, controlling means managers develop standards, compare performance against them, and ensure needed corrective actions are taken. As organisational activity depends on human behaviour, controlling ensures staff act in support of company goals. So controls highlight behaviours needed and discourage unwanted ones (Merchant 1985; Flamholtz 1996; Fox 2003a). For instance, over their two-year training, management trainees working to become McDonald's franchisees work through a thick guide presenting what to do and what not to do in running a McDonald's outlet (March 1989; *McDonald's Corporation* 1995). To be effective, though, they must do three things: be flexible enough to cope with the unexpected; allow accurate assessment of company events; and provide information as soon as possible (Jones et al. 2000).

Significance of the control process

As expected, the controlling function relates to the other three major management functions: planning, organising and leading. It builds on the planning function by allowing performance monitoring and adjustment so plans can be reached. Controlling ensures resources are used for organisational objectives supporting organising and leading functions (see Fig. 15.1). For example, control feedback might show that reorganisation, increased training, clarified communication, greater leadership influence, or other activities associated with organising and leading functions are needed.

During the control process, managers set up control systems. A **control system** is a set of mechanisms to increase the chances of reaching organisational standards and goals (Flamholtz 1979). Control systems regulate any important area. They may relate to production quantities, resources used, profit margins, product or service quality, client satisfaction, delivery timeliness, or specific activities generating a product or service. For example, to ensure quality McDonald's has a seven-step procedure for workers when cooking and bagging french fries. This is one procedure corporate evaluation teams check in unannounced outlet inspections (Deveny 1986).

control system

Set of mechanisms designed to increase probability of meeting organisational standards and goals

Role of controls

In evaluating the role of controls, consider what can happen with inadequate controls. Daiwa Bank, Japan's tenth-largest bank, was forced to close in the United States when it was revealed that a bond trader in Daiwa's New York office amassed a staggering $1.1 billion in losses and hid them over an 11-year period. In one of several letters to Daiwa's management, Toshihide Iguchi, the trader, told how the New York office did not detect a $100 million discrepancy. Iguchi noted the incident was 'indicative of how dysfunctional [controls] were at Daiwa' (Shirouzu 1995, p. A16). A similar set of lax controls allowed Barings Bank's Tim Leeson to accumulate comparable trading losses in Singapore.

Controls can help managers avoid these problems. Specifically, controls assist managers with five challenges: coping with uncertainty, detecting irregularities, identifying opportunities, handling complex situations and decentralising authority.

Coping with uncertainty

Uncertainty arises as organisational goals are set for future events, based on the best knowledge available at the time, but things may not go to plan. Environmental factors result in changes in customer demand, technology, and raw-material availability. In control-system development, managers watch specific activities, reacting to significant environmental changes rapidly (Fox 2003b). For example, by controlling all manufacturing phases, Italy-based Luxottica Group S.p.A. produced high-quality spectacle frames cheaply. CEO Leonardo Del Vecchio bought out

FIGURE 15.1 Relationship of controls to the other functions of management

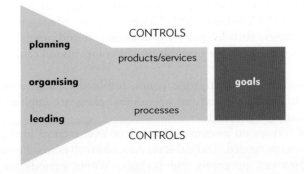

many frame distributors. Thus Luxottica gradually controlled both product manufacturing and distribution. More recently, Luxottica started to gain control over retailing its frames by purchasing the owner of LensCrafters spectacle chain (Kindel 1995).

Detecting irregularities

Controls help detect irregularities such as poor quality, cost overruns or staff turnover. Early detection saves time and money by stopping minor problems becoming major ones (Mitchell 2003). Finding problems early helps avoid difficult-to-fix problems, such as missing deadlines or selling faulty products. For example, Daiwa Bank might have avoided international embarrassment and business losses if it had had better operational control. Among other things, Daiwa did not follow normal financial practice of cross-checking daily trades against monthly summaries and balance statements (Shirouzu 1995).

Identifying opportunities

Controls also identify situations where results are better than expected, alerting management to opportunities (Drucker 1985). At May Department Stores, managers write monthly reports noting well-selling items and money generated. These are then used in developing merchandising strategies for all stores, including what to buy, from whom, and how to display merchandise (Dunkin & O'Neil 1987). Another example is the small massage kiosks being introduced into several Westfield shopping centres to enhance shoppers' experience (Harley 2003).

Handling complex situations

As firms grow, taking on more complex operations and projects, controls aid coordination. They help managers tracking major elements to ensure synchronisation. For example, international operations increase complexity and also increase needs for control as shown by Daiwa's situation.

Decentralising authority

Another major control role is giving managers more latitude. With controls, managers can move decision making lower in the organisation but still monitor progress. Of course, control issues vary by managerial level.

Levels of control

Just as planning responsibilities differ by managerial level (see Chapter 6), each level has parallel control responsibilities (see Fig. 15.2). Strategic, tactical and operational control levels increase chances of realising different level plans (Lorange, Morton & Ghoshal 1986; Schreyoff & Steimann 1987; Simons 1995).

Strategic control means monitoring critical environmental factors to ensure strategic plans are implemented as set, assessing the effects of strategic action, and adjusting plans as needed. Top-level managers, taking an organisation-wide view, exercise strategic-level control. Inherent in strategic control is the need for these managers to be sure that core competencies are developed and maintained to ensure the organisation's ability to pursue its strategic goals (Schreyoff & Steimann 1987; Simons 1995; Hooper 2003b). Managers, for strategic control, focus on long time-frames, such as quarterly, semi-annual and annual reporting cycles, and longer. Although if environments are unstable and/or competition keen, shorter cycles may be used.

While largely concerned with strategic issues, top-level managers may use tactical and operational control to ensure tactical and operational plans are implemented as intended at middle- and lower-management levels.

Tactical control focuses on assessing department-level tactical plans, monitoring results and making corrections as needed. Tactical-level control involves middle managers focusing on department-level objectives, programs and budgets. Within periodic or middle-term time-frames they use weekly and monthly reporting cycles. They test environmental reaction to

strategic control

Control type involving monitoring critical environmental factors that could affect viability of strategic plans, assessing effects of organisational strategic actions, and ensuring strategic plans are implemented as intended

tactical control

Control type focusing on assessing implementation of tactical plans at department levels, monitoring associated periodic results, and taking corrective action as needed

FIGURE 15.2 Levels of control (adapted in part from Lorange, Morton & Ghoshal 1986, p. 12)

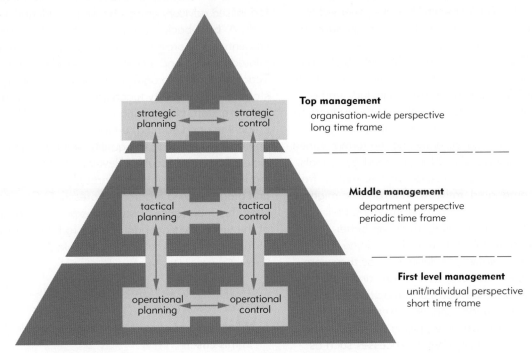

departments' tactical initiatives (Marcom 1991; Hooper 2003b). Concerned with tactical control, middle managers engage in strategic control by giving upper-level managers data on strategic issues. They take part in operational control by checking critical aspects of operating-plan implementation.

Operational control means overseeing operating-plan implementation, monitoring daily results, and adjusting as needed. Lower-level managers' responsibility is largely operating-level control, and they are concerned with schedules, budgets, rules and individuals' specific outputs. Operating control gives rapid feedback on what is being done toward short- and long-term organisational goals.

For effectiveness, control levels—strategic, tactical and operational—must be clearly inter-related, as different level planning systems are integrated.

operational control

Control type involving overseeing implementation of operating plans, monitoring day-to-day results, and taking corrective action as required

Keeping an eye on student experience

Effective management controls play a part in 'keeping it real' when it comes to customer experiences vs. advertising hype. University students are customers of a teaching and learning environment, and their learning experiences play a crucial role in whether they maintain their enrolment, drop out or transfer to another institution. Drop outs and transfers were a dilemma for Professor Ian O'Connor in 2002, when he took the role as Deputy Vice Chancellor (Teaching and Learning) of Griffith University. Like many universities, Griffith's research profile and its ability to attract international students was experiencing healthy growth. The university, however, seemed to have difficulty keeping the students until graduation, a problem commonly referred to as 'student retention'. The control systems that kept watch on student experiences were not giving much insight into this problem. These control systems include end-of-course (or subject) evaluations that invite students to rate their experience and comment on teaching. These were used inconsistently and the format varied between the university's 13 faculties and 40 schools. Other controls focused on collecting information from those who graduated, rather than those who might be considering dropping out or transferring their enrolment. Controls that tried to deliver better teaching such as university teaching training programs were relatively under-utilised as they were optional for new teaching staff. Deans and program convenors who were supposed to monitor the quality of the student learning experience were overwhelmed by their many responsibilities, giving them little time to devote to vital quality control processes such as reviewing course outlines.

Within a broadly consultative framework, Professor O'Connor dealt with the problem by strengthening old controls and implementing new ones. An extensive quality audit process actively sought out the experiences and problems of current students, and this 'one-off' exercise was followed up with more formalised advisory groups between students and staff. A 'buzz-back' website was established, where students could provide feedback on administrative-related matters and receive free chocolates in return! Teaching training programs became compulsory for staff new to university teaching, including sessional teaching staff. New positions for Associate Deans (Teaching and Learning) enabled a more focused approach to ensuring the quality of student learning experiences, and faculties developed consistent and regular course evaluations. Through an integrated and broadly based program, Professor O'Connor has lifted the importance of student experience to the top of the university's agenda in order to fulfil its mission of the 'pursuit of excellence in teaching'.

Source: Contributed by Peter Woods.

Activities for discussion, analysis and further research

1. What types of control by timing can be identified in this case?
2. What managerial approach to control does this university use in improving student learning experiences and why?
3. Identify the characteristics of this control system that would fit the profile of being effective.

THE CONTROL PROCESS

While control systems are tailored to specific situations, they follow the same general process. In this section, we will consider the control process steps, then examine the issues about deciding what to control.

Steps in the control process

The basic process of controlling is shown in Figure 15.3. The process has several major steps.

1 Determine areas to control

Managers must first decide which areas to control. Choices must be made, due to cost, as it is not possible to control every organisational aspect. As well, employees resent too much control. Managers usually base controls on organisational goals and objectives developed in planning. For example, Briggs & Stratton, who make small engines for lawn mowers, closely monitored market share when the company began to have severe Japanese competition. The company boosted advertising budgets, spent more on research and engineering, and cut production costs to regain and maintain their former market share of over 50 per cent (Cook 1986; Croghan 1996; Hanley 2003b).

2 Establish standards

In the control process, standards are essential as they set out specific criteria for evaluating performance and employee behaviours. Often incorporated into goals set in the planning

FIGURE 15.3 Steps in the control process

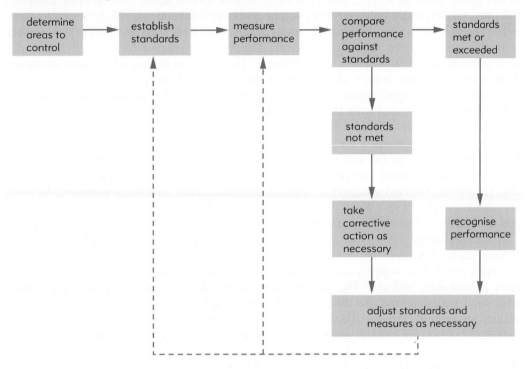

process, they only need restating. Sometimes they must be developed in the control process (Bateman & Snell 2004). When one firm set up its service-improvement program, it found staff on average took 10 minutes to approach a customer. The company set up training programs, sales incentives, and a scheduling program assigning salespeople to areas where they were most needed. They also set a standard of two minutes to approach customers. Each salesperson also had daily sales goals set (Hamilton 1987; Calloway 1990; Richman 1993).

Standards usually have three major purposes for employee behaviour (Merchant 1985). For one, standards mean staff can understand what is expected and the basis for evaluating their work. This helps their effectiveness. For another, standards are a basis for finding job problems related to people's personal limits. These can come from lack of ability, training or experience, or any other job-related deficiency hindering performance. Timely identification means action can occur before difficulties become serious or unresolvable. Finally, standards help reduce the negative effects of goal incongruence. **Goal incongruence** occurs with major differences between a member's goals and those of their organisation. This has many causes, including a lack of support for organisational objectives (e.g. an employee sees a job as temporary and just does the minimum needed), resulting in behaviours incompatible with organisational goal attainment (Pogson 2003).

A common example of goal incongruence is employee theft, such as wasting company resources as well as taking equipment, materials and money (Hollinger & Clark 1983). Wasted resources almost killed one small firm. A new CEO set standards for work hours and expense-account usage. The CEO recalls 'it was a country club. Most employees were arriving to work late, expense account abuse was rampant, and nobody ever thought we owed the stockholders anything. Values around here were really warped' (Behar 1988, p. 70).

goal incongruence

Condition where there are major incompatibilities between goals of an organisation member and those of the organisation

3 Measure performance

Once standards are set, the next step is measuring performance. For a given standard, a manager must decide how to measure performance and how often. One method of setting standards and coordinating performance measurement is management by objectives (see Chapter 5).

The means of measuring performance depend on the standards set. They can include units made, dollar value of service, materials used, defects found, scrap rate, steps or processes followed, profits, return on investment, output quality or stores opened. At American Express, where good service is vital, 12 card operations departments were asked to develop performance standards and measure their achievements. Departments seemed to do well under this arrangement, but overall service did not improve. The firm then developed a system measuring departments' customer impact. The system, or the service tracking report, measures success in processing new card applications within 15 days, replacement of lost or stolen cards in one day, sending errorless bills, and over 100 other tasks (Uttal 1987; Welch 1992).

While quantitative measures are used if possible, many performance aspects are hard to measure this way. Consider a McDonald's drive-through line. It may be easy to measure how long an order takes to fill, but it is harder to decide how polite employees are. Similarly, research and development can be hard to measure quantitatively in the short-term, as it may take years to see the final outcomes of research programs. Then qualitative judgments by peers are often used (Uttal 1987; Welch 1992; Walters 2003b). Most firms combine both quantitative and qualitative performance measures for control.

Once measurement means are chosen, managers must decide the frequency of measurement. In some cases, they must have control data on a daily, hourly or more frequent base (such as air traffic controllers' supervisors). In other cases, weekly, monthly, quarterly, semi-annual or even annual data will do. The measurement period depends on the goal's importance, situational variation, and the difficulty and expense of fixing any problem. Nuclear power plants, for example, have elaborate control systems that constantly give operational data. Extensive controls are needed, given the consequences of a power-plant accident.

4 Compare performance against standards

This step is comparing performance measured in step 3 against standards set in step 2. Managers may base comparisons on reports summarising planned versus actual results. Such reports can be oral, written or computer generated. With computer networks, managers can have up-to-the-minute status reports on many quantitative performance measures.

management by exception

Control principle suggesting managers should be informed of a situation only if control data show a significant deviation from standards

Computer systems suit **management by exception**, a control principle suggesting managers should be told of events only if control data show a major deviation (Newman 1975; Rue & Byars 2003). This principle, with or without computers, aids managers by bringing their attention to those cases needing action. While it can be effective, managers must take care not to focus on problems and ignore subordinates' positive results.

Managers often compare performance and standards by walking around work areas, observing conditions, a practice called management by wandering around. For example, executives of a discount store chain make frequent visits to stores, checking displays, talking with employees and meeting customers (Saporito 1992). Other organisations use 360-degree feedback systems, which give an individual performance ratings from many sources, such as superiors, peers and customers (see Chapter 9).

5a Recognise positive performance

When performance meets or exceeds standards, managers must acknowledge it. Recognition can range from a 'well done' comment for a routine outcome to more valuable rewards, such as bonuses, training or pay rises, for major successes or consistent good work. This fits with motivation theories, such as expectancy and reinforcement approaches, which propose rewards for good performance to sustain it and gain further improvement (see Chapter 11) (Hamilton 1987; Galloway 1990; Howarth 2003d).

5b Take corrective action as necessary

When standards are not met, managers must assess why and take corrective action. They will check standards and other performance measures to see if they are realistic. Managers may decide standards are inappropriate—as conditions have changed—and corrective action to meet standards is undesirable. Often, corrective actions are needed.

The skills option—How to retain control when outsourcing

How to avoid the outsourcing traps:

What to do

- Conduct an internal audit to determine what skills the division you are looking to outsource has or lacks.
- Ensure that there are adequate leadership and management systems to maximise the efficiency of the relationship with service providers.
- Award contracts based on a hard evaluation of service providers, not on a sales presentation that makes unrealistic promises.
- Agree with the service providers on how accountability and outcomes will be measured.

What not to do

- Rush the selection process. Awarding a new contract after a couple of weeks' assessment of candidates is a recipe for failure.
- Make unsustainable financial demands on service providers.
- Contract out a project and then assume the service provider will complete it without further client input.
- Assume every contractor invited to tender will be desperate for the business.

Source: Lloyd, S. (2002) p. 74.

6 Adjust standards and measures as necessary

Control is dynamic. So managers must check standards to ensure that they, and related performance measures, are still relevant. For one thing, they may have been inappropriate or circumstances may have changed. For another, beating a standard may show up unplanned opportunities, the potential to raise standards, and/or a need for major variations to company plans. Finally, even if standards are met, changing conditions, such as higher employee skill levels, may mean standards can be raised in future. Conversely, a manager may see reaching a standard is too costly and decide to cut the standard. Managers use control to track activities, but must review the process to ensure current needs are met.

Deciding what to control: A closer look

Well-developed objectives, strategic plans and supporting goals focus on what is organisationally important. They then suggest control areas. While managers collect data on the achievement of desired ends, they may have to control elements leading to those ends.

One way to help managers decide what to control is the **resource dependence** approach (Green & Welsh 1988; Gome 2003c). This says managers must consider controls where they depend on others for needed resources. In this context resources can be parts, information, service, funding or any other resource needed to reach objectives. However, a dependency does not mean an area must be controlled. Four conditions must be met before a final decision is made. Areas meeting all four conditions are **strategic control points**, performance areas chosen for control as they help meet organisational goals. Conditions and a related decision tree are shown in Figure 15.4.

Four conditions for control

The first two conditions refer to the need for controls. The second two assess whether controls are feasible and practical.

The first condition is relatively *high dependence* on the resource. The more important dependence is and the less the resource is available from other sources, the higher dependence is on the resource. If you are running a McDonald's outlet, you will be highly dependent on

resource dependence

Approach to controls that argues managers need to consider controls mainly in areas in which they depend on others for resources necessary to reach organisational goals

strategic control points

Performance areas chosen for control because they are particularly important in meeting organisational goals

FIGURE 15.4 Resource-dependence decision tree (adapted from Green & Welsh 1988, pp. 287–301)

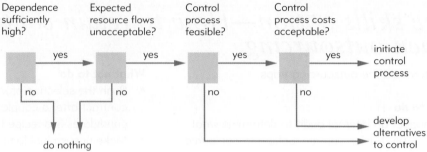

resources such as food, food containers, water, napkins and working equipment. These resources are crucial. Alternatively, if a resource is unimportant or easily substituted (e.g. replacement for a trampled shrub), then elaborate controls are not needed.

The second condition for control is a strong chance that *expected resource flow will be unacceptable*. In other words, a manager anticipates problems with a resource or is unsure. Anticipated problems can relate to any aspect, but are usually linked to resource quantity, certain characteristics (e.g. specifications and quality) and timeliness (Quinlivan 2003). The more a manager feels a resource will give problems, the more control needed. For example, for a McDonald's outlet manager, it is hard to stockpile food (lettuce, hamburger buns and milk) which can spoil. Yet fluid customer patterns affect usage, making food inventory control important. On the other hand, though water is an important resource, supplies are reliable, so a formal control system is not needed.

The third condition influencing the institution of controls is *control-process feasibility*. A basic control process—setting performance standards, measuring performance, comparing performance to standards, feeding back information on discrepancies and taking corrective action—may not be feasible. Typically, this is an issue when specifying performance standards is hard or when it is difficult to measure performance or to do so in a timely way (McShane & Travaglione 2003). For example, McDonald's cannot establish fixed standards on overseas prices. In Japan, McDonald's had a six-week sale, cutting regular hamburger prices from $1.75 (about 224 yen) to $0.83. The promotion was so successful buns ran out. McDonald's in Japan suspended the sale in half of its outlets until more buns were available. In the meantime, it offered medium french fries for $0.83 not the usual $2.00. In this case, price and promotion issues were locally controlled as McDonald's could not assess these issues from headquarters (*New York Times* 1992).

Finally, an important issue influencing whether to institute a control process is *cost acceptability*. Managers must weigh the costs and benefits of control. A control system may cost more than the organisation gains. Again, McDonald's is a good example. Company headquarters could have more control over outlets by setting up a videoconferencing network, and having a two-way video-audio connection to every store (see Chapter 13). At present costs would be too high to do this, given possible gains.

Alternatives to control

What happens if the first two conditions (questions on the left in Fig. 15.4) show controls are needed, but the process is not feasible or too costly? Then managers must develop alternatives.

One way is to change dependence relationships and avoid control. For example, if there are several suppliers, controls are needed less. Because there are few local

Saudi Arabian suppliers, for example, the Saudi Big Mac has Mexican sesame seeds and onions, buns from Saudi wheat, Spanish beef patties and lettuce, American pickles and special sauce, and New Zealand cheese (*McDonald's Corporation* 1994). Managers can also work with a source of dependence to build reliability, cutting control needs. This happened when McDonald's experts helped Thai farmers learn to grow Idaho russet potatoes, the key in McDonald's french fries (Deveny 1986).

Another way is to change the nature of the dependence to make it more feasible and/or cost-effective to control. For instance, redesigning complex jobs to have narrower, simpler tasks reduces dependence on experienced workers. While job simplification has problems (see Chapter 8), it may make control easier if labour is tight (Walker 2003d).

A further approach is eliminating dependence. This can happen by vertical integration, where the firm makes inputs instead of sourcing them outside or replaces a customer role by selling its own outputs (see Chapter 6). McDonald's finally did this after hamburger-bun supplies in Britain became difficult, by building its own plant with two partners (Deveny 1986). Goals and objectives can also be changed to no longer depend on a source. Changing goals is drastic and unlikely until options are exhausted. Still, it may be best sometimes.

CASE IN POINT

Does socially responsible investment pay dividends?

What power does a nun in her 50s have in the corporate world? Very little, except when she leads an organisation whose members represent about $110 billion in investments! Sister Patricia Wolf is the head of the Interfaith Center on Corporate Responsibility (ICCR), a New York-based association of 275 faith-based institutional investors. The Center is a leader in the corporate social responsibility movement and every year its members sponsor more than 100 shareholder resolutions on major environmental and social issues.

Coca Cola was one company where ICCR investors took action. Investors explained to Coca Cola that AIDS was having a significant impact on its operations in Africa, where infection rates topped 20 per cent in some markets. Employees were not receiving any treatment, and the disease was leading to a shrinking workforce and a shrinking market. The World Bank has warned that complete economic collapse will occur if the AIDS pandemic is not arrested in southern Africa. Only 10 000 of the 25 million Africans with the disease are taking antiretroviral medicines. The company responded by agreeing to provide treatment for its workers and to undertake an economic assessment of the impact of HIV. ICCR members are monitoring the fulfilment of this agreement.

The global warming campaign of 2004 saw increased support from shareholders for disclosure by corporations of the impact climate change will have on their operations and revenues. Five of the largest electric utility companies in the United States, which are also among the largest emitters of carbon dioxide in the world, agreed to comply with shareholders' resolutions before the resolutions came up for a vote. The resolutions called for an independent committee of the board of directors to evaluate the utility's response to rising regulatory and competitive pressures to reduce greenhouse gas emissions, and to issue a report to the shareholders of their findings. Each of the companies acknowledged that this was important information for shareholders to receive and it is expected that this will set a precedent forcing similar disclosure from other companies in the electric power sector.

Sister Patricia Wolf argues that socially responsible initiatives make good economic sense, and do not damage share value over the long term. Supporting research has shown that over a five-year period or longer, socially responsible investments do as well or better than normal investments.

Source: Contributed by Peter Woods and the ICCR.

Activities for discussion, analysis and further research

1. What roles could company controls have played in being proactive in the areas of concern raised by ICCR?
2. Suggest the steps in the control process that Coca Cola needs to go through in order to monitor the health of its workers with HIV/AIDS.

TYPES OF CONTROLS

As well as deciding the areas to control, managers must consider the control types to use. In this section, we discuss major control types based on timing, consider multiple control use, and contrast cybernetic and non-cybernetic control types.

Major control types by timing

Using a systems view, one can see an organisation's productive cycle as including inputs, transformation processes, and outputs occurring at different times (see Chapter 2). Thus, controls can be classified based on their timing, or stage in the productive cycle, depending on whether the focus is on inputs, transformation processes or outputs (see Fig. 15.5) (Benjamin 2003). Managers have options about the transformation cycle stage at which they will institute controls. Three types of controls based on timing are feedforward, concurrent and feedback.

Feedforward control

feedforward control

Regulation of inputs to ensure they meet standards necessary for the transformation process

Feedforward control focuses on input regulation to ensure inputs meet standards needed for the transformation process (see Fig. 15.5). Inputs subject to feedforward control include materials, people, finances, time and other organisational resources. The emphasis of

FIGURE 15.5 Major control types by timing

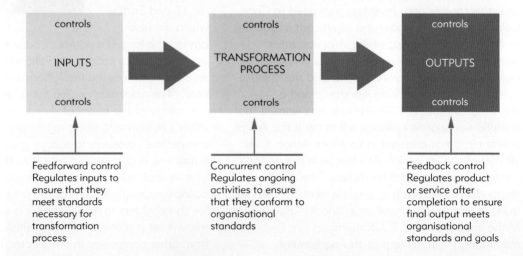

Feedforward control
Regulates inputs to ensure that they meet standards necessary for transformation process

Concurrent control
Regulates ongoing activities to ensure that they conform to organisational standards

Feedback control
Regulates product or service after completion to ensure final output meets organisational standards and goals

feedforward control is on preventing difficulties later in the productive process. It is also called precontrol, preliminary, preventative or steering control.

Though feedforward controls can contribute significantly to organisational effectiveness, they may not cover every possible option (Lippert & Lupo 1988; *Detroit News* 1995). Other control types may be needed.

Concurrent control

Concurrent control involves regulating ongoing activities as part of the transformation process, ensuring they conform to organisational standards. The emphasis is on identifying difficulties in the productive process which could mean faulty output (see Fig. 15.5). Concurrent control or screening or yes-no control often has checkpoints where decisions are made on continuing progress, taking corrective action, or stopping work altogether. As concurrent control means regulating current tasks, it needs clearly specified standards on how activities must be conducted (Ouchi & Maguire 1975; Heathcote 2003).

concurrent control

Regulation of ongoing activities that are part of the transformation process to ensure they conform to organisational standards

Feedback control

Feedback control is regulation exercised after a product or service has been finished to ensure final output meets organisational standards and goals (see Fig. 15.5). Feedback control, or post-action control or output control, has important functions.

For one, it is often used when feedforward and concurrent controls are not feasible or too costly (Bateman & Snell 2004). For example, a sales manager will have a problem using concurrent control to regulate daily activities of salespeople visiting customers. Instead, the sales manager will use feedforward control by carefully selecting new people and then using feedback control comparing sales quotas (standards) with actual sales.

Feedback control is often used when the exact processes involved in producing a product or service (e.g. performing complex surgery) are hard to specify in advance. This control type serves as a final check for previously undetected deviations. Recently, many firms have worked to raise quality so feedback control is not needed or there are few deviations to find and thus little scrap or rework needed (see Chapter 16).

Feedback control also provides data to help planning. Examples are numbers of units made or sold, cost of various production parts, quality measures, return on investment, or clients served. The data helps revise existing plans and formulate new ones. Finally, feedback control provides output information useful for employee performance rewards.

feedback control

Regulation exercised after a product or service has been completed to ensure the final output meets organisational standards and goals

Multiple controls

Typically organisations use **multiple control systems**, combining feedforward, concurrent and feedback control processes, and with several strategic control points. Strategic control points are, as noted, performance areas chosen for control as they are important in meeting organisational goals. Multiple control systems develop due to needing to control various aspects of the productive cycle, including inputs, transformations and outputs.

When organisations lack multiple control systems focused on strategic control points, they often have problems, requiring managers to reconsider control processes (Andrews 2003). Many controls require human discretion. The level of needed discretion is another way to distinguish control system types.

multiple control systems

Systems using two or more of the feedforward, concurrent and feedback control processes and involving several strategic control points

Cybernetic and non-cybernetic control

A basic control process can be cybernetic or non-cybernetic, based on how much human discretion is part of the system. A **cybernetic control system** is self-regulating and, when operating, can monitor the situation and take needed corrective action. A heating system with a thermostat is a cybernetic system. Once set, the self-regulating system keeps the temperature at the level set without intervention. In some computerised inventory systems, cybernetic control places orders when inventory reaches a specified level. Ordering occurs without human discretion, such as managerial approval before the order is placed.

cybernetic control system

Self-regulating control system that, once operating, can automatically monitor the situation and take corrective action when necessary

non-cybernetic control system

Control system relying on human discretion as a basic part of its process

The growing use of computers widens cybernetic control options; however, most organisational systems are non-cybernetic. A **non-cybernetic control system** uses human discretion in the process. By their nature, areas needing control typically fail unpredictably. They are also complex enough to need human discretion to select the needed correction. Strictly speaking, even systems needing little human discretion, such as a computerised inventory system with automatic ordering capacity, produce reports for humans. Typically there are built-in monitoring systems to alert a staff member if things go wrong. Still, computers permit more controls closer to the cybernetic continuum end.

MANAGING THE E-CHALLENGE

Controlling telecommuters

Mike Lazarus rarely visits the office any more. It's not that he's not interested. Rather, he's found over the years that it's possible to do most of his work from home or on the road—and now he makes a living showing other companies how it's done.

Some twenty years ago, Swedish firms were having difficulty attracting good staff to work in the city because they were put off by the traffic, the congestion and pollution. The solution at the time was to contract the rail authorities to set up special carriages that contained computers and phones, allowing these highly-valued executives to commence work from the time they caught the train.

Advances in communications technology have now made this and other options available to many professionals. The Australian Bureau of Statistics reports that about 20 per cent of the workforce in Australia now spends 'some hours' working at home. Staff at the offices of the Department of Public Works in Queensland can elect to work at home. The head of training in the purchasing department operates independently of her office. (The office is 'hot desked' anyway; if all staff were to actually turn up for work on any one day there would not be enough desks for them all.) She uses a mobile phone with phone diversion through to her home phone, and is available at almost any time— in fact, all of the time when she is not in a meeting. She can answer her email from home, or from anywhere where she can use a computer.

Working from home has many advantages from the employee's point of view. Less time is wasted travelling to and from work, and employees can fulfil family responsibilities while still meeting work commitments. From the employer's point of view there are also advantages: lower overheads where less office space is required, satisfied employees

and a more flexible workforce. Flexibility is important, as firms with global links now expect employees to take part in teleconference or video conference meetings at any time of the day or night. Allowing or encouraging staff to set up office at home means that they can attend these meetings with a minimum of disruption to their home life, and without needing to be at work at inconvenient hours. Previously, special security arrangements were needed to allow the staff into the office for teleconference and video conference meetings, and to provide safe travel to and from home.

Organisational structures are being flexed to allow for working from home. In some cases the structure is based on a network, and although the traditional structure applies in the office, the principles of control are changing. Managers are realising that they did not really control what went on in the office anyway, especially after the introduction of email, direct dialling and mobile phones. These new arrangements call for more open forms of control, with staff treated as mature individuals wanting to complete their required tasks and achieving goals for themselves and their employer.

Source: Adapted from Braue (2002).

Activities for discussion, analysis and further research

1. List the advantages and disadvantages of working from home for the employee. Then consider it from the employer's point of view. Try to add to the discussion in the case study. Consider different homes and domestic situations, different workplaces and types of work.

2. Consider how employees are now controlled in the work place and attempt to identify the essential differences between controlling staff in the office and controlling them in their own homes.
3. Identify trends that will affect the growth of working from home. Consider new technology, current social practices and trends in housing.
4. Evaluate the information supplied on the following websites to assist with the management of telecommuting. Who are these sites designed for: management or staff?

www.findarticles.com/cf_dls/m1318/8_53/55215117/p1/article.jhtml

http://boards1.ivillage.com/messages/get/wfWFhmoms143.html

www.kinderstart.com/familydynamics/parentsworkingathome.html

www.msnbc.com/news/645458.asp?cp1=1

www.amazon.com/exec/obidos/ASIN/0874779766/ref=pd_sim_books/002-8596459-3496058

MANAGERIAL APPROACHES TO IMPLEMENTING CONTROLS

As well as the control types they use, managers also have choices about mechanisms to put controls in place. There are three managerial control approaches: bureaucratic, clan and market. It helps to think of them in terms of how control is exercised—whether by bureaucratic rules, the clan or the market. All three will be used to some extent.

Bureaucratic control

Bureaucratic control uses regulation by rules, policies, supervision, budgets, schedules, reward systems and other mechanisms to ensure employee behaviours are as expected and performance standards met. Results of heavy bureaucratic control use are shown in Table 15.1. As shown, control sources are largely external to the person, emphasis is on a fixed narrowly defined task set, and on top-down hierarchical control.

With bureaucratic control, rules and policies develop to handle recurring conditions. When unexpected events or rare exceptions occur, supervisors decide any needed corrective action. Supervisors also check to see people follow rules and other mechanisms (Andrews 2003).

Bureaucratic control helps predictable activities run smoothly, but heavy use has downsides. Bureaucratic control hinders innovation, and inhibits change needed in rapidly changing environments, leading to employee compliance, rather than commitment, by focusing on following regulations others develop (see Chapter 12). For these reasons, organisations try to emphasise clan control.

bureaucratic control

Managerial approach relying on regulation through rules, policies, supervision, budgets, schedules, reward systems and other administrative mechanisms aimed at ensuring employees exhibit appropriate behaviours and meet performance standards

Clan control

Clan control uses values, beliefs, traditions, corporate culture, shared norms and informal relationships to regulate employee behaviour and help with organisational goals. Results of heavy clan control use are listed in Table 15.1. Contrasted with bureaucratic control, clan control emphasises internal motivation, flexible duties and broad tasks, and influence based on relevant information and expertise rather than hierarchical position.

With clan control, groups are emphasised and the focus of responsibility is teams. This control type is common with professionals, where training, norms and group identification replace bureaucratic control's strong emphasis on rules and regulations (Parkin 2003).

Clan control builds commitment to organisational objectives, generally raising employees' willingness to face workplace change. For these reasons, some firms with routine jobs are emphasising clan control. At Corning, for example, teams range from 10 to 25 people, making many operational decisions on a broad task range. Teams monitor their performance on established goals and appraise members for feedback and development. The plant has a skill-

clan control

Managerial approach relying on values, beliefs, traditions, corporate culture, shared norms and informal relationships to regulate employee behaviours and facilitate reaching of organisational goals

TABLE 15.1 CHARACTERISTICS ASSOCIATED WITH BUREAUCRATIC AND CLAN CONTROL

Characteristics	Bureaucratic control	Clan control
Means of control	Rules, policies and hierarchy	Shared goals, values and tradition
Source of control	Mainly external mechanisms	Mainly internal motivation
Job design	Narrow subtasks; doing, rather than thinking	Whole task; doing and thinking
Definition of duties	Fixed	Flexible; contingent on changing conditions
Accountability	Usually individual	Often team
Structure	Tall; top-down controls	Flat; mutual influence
Power usage	Emphasis on legitimate authority	Emphasis on relevant information and expertise
Responsibility	Performing individual job	Upgrading performance of work unit and organisation
Reward emphasis	Extrinsic	Intrinsic
Innovation	Less likely	More likely
Likely employee reactions	Compliance	Commitment

Source: Adapted from Walton (1985, p. 81).

based pay plan, and most employees get pay rises for learning new jobs. Since increased emphasis on clan control, the plant has improved productivity, and reduced defect rates, inventory costs, injury rates, and time to complete a customer order (Liebowitz & Holden 1995). Teams are being used in many businesses, including insurance, automobile, aerospace, electronics, food-processing, paper, steel and financial services industries (see Chapter 14) (Hoerr 1988; 1989; Tang & Crofford 1995–96).

Market control

market control

Managerial approach relying on market mechanisms to regulate prices for certain clearly specified goods and services needed by an organisation

outsourcing

Process of employing an outside vendor to perform a function normally carried on within the organisation

Market control uses market mechanisms to set prices for specified goods and services an organisation needs, saving managers from setting up elaborate cost controls. To use market control, there must be competition in relevant goods or services and needs must be clear (Charlesworth 2003). For example, purchasing departments often set specifications for needed goods, then set up a competitive bidding process. Without specifications and bidding (or at least comparable goods or services sources), purchasing agents would have to decide if specific prices were reasonable on the basis of processes involved. Controlling costs this way is expensive.

The use of market control is increasing due to outsourcing. **Outsourcing** is the process of using an outside vendor to perform a company function. For example, General Motors drove component divisions to become more efficient or lose work to outside sources. Until recently, it made about 70 per cent of components. Decisions about the makers of components are being made through market control by comparing the price and quality of outside suppliers to GM's internal costs and quality (Sedwick 1996; Vlasic 1996). In other areas, information technology services are among the most commonly outsourced organisational activities (Crowe 2003).

Market control often regulates internal operations by setting up profit centres for service units, such as printing or data processing, then charging other company parts for services.

Generally, market control works poorly when precisely specified requirements cannot be set due to uncertain or fluid circumstances (e.g. customer needs) or when little or no competition exists to base pricing on (e.g. R&D projects).

Promoting innovation: Controlling while nurturing innovation

A managerial challenge is to control without blocking creativity and innovation needed for long-term survival. In this section we consider managers' balancing of four strategic control levers to both foster innovation, and regulate organisational activities. We also review the incrementalist approach to controlling innovation.

Four levers for strategic control: A balancing act

Managers have four major levers for use in effective strategic control (Simons 1995). Together the levers build accountability, enable empowerment and allow strategic direction shifts. The four levers, shown in Figure 15.6, are associated with planning (see Chapter 6) but are part of the controlling function of monitoring strategic directions and taking corrective action needed.

1. *Belief systems* are ways managers communicate and reinforce a firm's basic mission and values. Mission statements, credos and slogans inspire and give general direction, guiding organisational efforts and long-term effectiveness. Use of belief systems is strongly linked to clan control.
2. *Boundary systems* define members' acceptable activity domain. Through policies, rules and procedures, organisations work to reduce risks that members will waste or misuse the resources and energies by setting boundaries to operations. Boundary systems are closely linked to bureaucratic control.
3. *Performance management systems* focus on ensuring specific goals are achieved. These systems let managers check progress on specific targets and facilitate evaluation and feedback relative to achieving those targets. Performance management systems are mainly linked to bureaucratic control. Clan control can be an option when end results are specified, but members decide the best means.
4. *Interactive monitoring systems* encourage search and learning so the organisation can identify and adapt to new opportunities. Without a focused effort on new opportunities and developing new strategic competencies, companies may simply pursue earlier plans now made obsolete or suboptimal by changing environmental and competitive circumstances. Such efforts require environmental scanning, internal data collection on

FIGURE 15.6 Four levers of strategic control

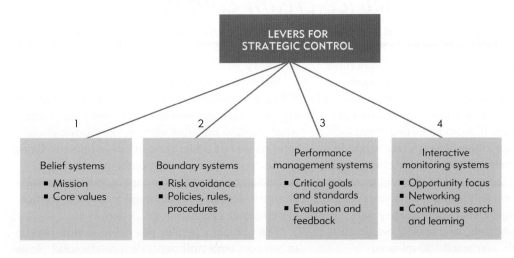

areas doing better than expected, and encouraging organisation members to seize sudden opportunities and deal with problems. Such systems involve members of all organisational levels in continuous challenge and debate about data, assumptions and action plans.

Incrementalist approach

In controlling innovative efforts such as R&D projects, James Brian Quinn (1979; 1985) says the ideal process is 'controlled chaos'. On one hand, it is unpredictable and chaotic. On the other, it can be controlled by mixing reliance on clan control with carefully set up bureaucratic controls. Using the **incrementalist approach** gives control over the process without stifling it. The approach relies on clan control but with phased plans and bureaucratic controls going from a general level, growing more specific as the project goes on. In the incrementalist approach's early stages, managers set general goals, pick key project people, set critical limits (such as spending) and establish decision points to check progress.

At middle stages of projects, technical aspects are better understood and/or market needs are clearer, and managers set more critical performance goals, limits and checkpoints. Still, they let technical group members decide how to pursue goals, within limits and checkpoints, as many questions remain (Fryer 2003).

At later innovation stages, when experiments show many variables clearly, managers may set more concrete controls to accompany more specific planning. Even then, many factors are unknown, and other technical options may still be opened. However, at review points, unsuccessful options are cut. Deciding to kill a project is hard, and managerial judgment is needed as there are still uncertainties. Due to these, managers may retain some less promising options needing fewer resources. Smaller-scale options may give major innovations, while the planned option fails. Sony's Walkman, a miniature stereo cassette player with lightweight earphones, came from an attempt to produce a miniature stereo tape recorder. The idea of putting the miniature player, from one engineering group, with earphones of another came from honorary chairman Masaru Ibuka, Sony's founder. Still, few resources went into the product at first, as the Walkman was viewed largely as a young people's toy (Nyak & Ketteringham 1986).

The incrementalist approach means managers must strike a balance between control approaches to encourage innovation. Otherwise, control systems can block innovation, inhibiting long-term organisational effectiveness.

incrementalist approach

Approach to controlling an innovative project that relies on clan control but also involves a phased set of plans and accompanying bureaucratic controls beginning at a general level and becoming more specific as the project progresses

GENDER FACTOR

ICE—a gourmet ice-cream company

Rosie and her husband John own a small gourmet ice-cream company (ICE) in Dunedin, in the South Island of New Zealand. The business has a number of strengths in the market. First it has a unique product. The ice-cream is made from real cream and organic eggs which makes it unique and different from the competitors. ICE produces over three hundred different ice-cream flavours that range from liquorice to watermelon. The company often makes special batches at the request of different groups of customers; for example, there is a wide range of low calorie, low carbohydrate ice-cream. They also supply local supermarkets, and special events such as school fairs with their small 150 ml-sized containers, as these are ideal impulse-purchase products for people to taste and enjoy at these kinds of events.

Because of its niche in the ice-cream market, ICE is able to sell small volumes at premium prices. High retail prices cover the high production costs, which tend to be larger with so many products on offer as well as under constant development. Being a small business and using batch production technology allows ICE to adapt quickly to market changes without going through traditional control systems and structures.

The company employ five full-time staff and up to ten part-time staff depending on demand. Rosie deals with the customer-demand side of the business as well as the day-to-day employment of the staff. She supervises the production process, deals with government product labelling and other requirements related to the food industry, selects the types of packaging, ensures that high-quality standards are maintained, and also is responsible for marketing the product and managing the paper work.

However, being small also comes with several disadvantages. The current business site is not big enough and staff commonly trip over each other's toes. Ice-cream is also a seasonal product that is traditionally enjoyed over the summer months, and the seasonal demand is hard to predict given the ever-fluctuating New Zealand climate, where in Dunedin it can suddenly snow in mid-summer. Because ice-cream is a perishable product it cannot be manufactured and stored too far in advance of the time of consumption. These factors limit the amount of forward planning that can be done in regards to production.

ICE has an opportunity to export its product to international markets. It has already moved into the Asian market where its green-tea ice-cream is proving to be very popular. Small batches are made in Dunedin and are exported as frozen goods on a weekly basis. ICE already has a large contract with a major airline where the ice-cream is enjoyed by business and first-class customers and is attracting a growing reputation for excellence.

Rosie's husband has experience as a former bank manager and he has well-developed managerial and business skills, but as the hands-on manager Rosie wonders how they will manage to control the business at an operational level if they are to develop their business into new international markets.

Source: Contributed by Elizabeth Hall.

Activities for discussion, analysis and further research

1. Even though this is a small family-owned and operated business, how could TQM principles be applied at ICE?
2. How are the eight strategic dimensions of quality relevant at ICE?
3. How can ICE maximise inventory control given that many of the raw-product inputs are highly perishable?
4. What kinds of operating systems could ICE use as it increases its sales and production?
5. What advice would you give Rosie in regard to future design and utilisation of facilities if a new factory site was chosen?

ASSESSING CONTROL SYSTEMS

Whether controls are supposed to facilitate innovation or for other reasons, managers must assess control systems continually to ensure they get expected results. In this section, we consider the potential dysfunctional aspects of control systems. If any of these are present, the control system needs adjusting. We also examine overcontrol and undercontrol, and finish by checking characteristics of effective control systems.

Potential dysfunctional aspects of control systems

Of course not all control system effects are positive. Poorly designed and/or excessive controls may produce one or more of four major dysfunctional side effects: behavioural displacement, game playing, operating delays or negative attitudes (Merchant 1985; Bateman & Snell 2004).

Behavioural displacement

Behavioural displacement occurs when behaviours encouraged by control and reward systems mismatch organisational goals. In one case, a research laboratory used the number of patents filed as an effectiveness indicator. Sadly, filed patent numbers grew but numbers of successful research projects dropped (Kotter, Schlesinger & Sathe 1979). Displacement has three basic causes: poor analysis of relationship between controls and desired outcomes, overemphasis of control measure quantification when qualitative aspects are important, and emphasising activities rather than end results.

behavioural displacement

Condition in which individuals engage in behaviours encouraged by controls and reward systems though they are inconsistent with organisational goals

Game playing

Game playing with controls occurs when managers improve their standing on performance measures by manipulating resource usage and/or data and not achieving actual performance improvements. Resource usage manipulation means getting more than needed resources so objectives can be easily met or exceeded. Some resource-level slack may be helpful in buffering against unforeseen events; carried too far though, it can weaken an organisation's competitive position through higher costs. Manipulating data means faking performance data or influencing performance results during data reporting.

Operating delays

Operating delays may come from actions needed by feedforward and concurrent controls. If excessive, such controls can cripple goal attainment. This provokes actions undermining the effects of controls (Cornwell & Cave 2003). For example, in a diversified corporation, 74 per cent of general managers reported getting expenditure approvals after money had been spent (Merchant 1984).

Negative attitudes

Controls may lead to negative attitudes, especially if the controls are excessive or poorly designed (Greenberger & Strasser 1986). Professionals particularly will resist controls. Most often, they oppose bureaucratic controls which do not seem to help organisational goal attainment.

Overcontrol versus undercontrol

Excessive control raises the likelihood of negative outcomes, so managers must not overcontrol. **Overcontrol** is cutting job autonomy to the point where it severely limits job performance. However, managers must not go too far the other way, resulting in undercontrol. **Undercontrol** is giving an employee autonomy to the extent that the firm cannot direct efforts to organisational goal achievement. In fact, undercontrol is often cited for organisations not achieving their goals (Jaworski, Stathakopoulos & Krishnan 1993; Merchant 1982; Kinicki & Williams 2003).

Characteristics of an effective control system

Effective control systems have common characteristics (Merchant 1985; Stoner & Wankel 1986). To assess existing or proposed control systems, these can be used as a checklist of essential features.

Future-oriented

Effective control systems must regulate future events, not fix blame for past ones. Well-designed control systems let managers know progress toward unit objectives, showing where future corrective action is needed, and finding unexpected development opportunities—all aids to future action.

Multidimensional

Most control systems must be multidimensional to catch major performance issues. For example, the Campbellfield Ford Motor Corporation plant would be in trouble if it checked quantity without considering quality, scrap rate and overhead.

Cost-effective

The costs of controls are important. One factor controlled at McDonald's is rest-room cleanliness. The company manual specifies rest-room cleaning frequency, and both the outlet manager and company inspection teams check this (Moser 1988). Still, McDonald's could

---

overcontrol

Limiting individual job autonomy to the point where it seriously inhibits effective job performance

undercontrol

Granting autonomy to an employee to the point where the organisation loses its ability to direct individual effort toward achieving organisational goals

control cleanliness more by having one person at all outlets do nothing but ensure this. The costs may be greater than the benefits of more control, as McDonald's reputation for cleanliness is already very good. Control's benefits should outweigh its costs.

Accurate

As controls are a basis of future actions, accuracy is crucial. Inaccurate control data is worse than none, as poor decisions may flow from such data.

Realistic

Control systems should have realistic views about what is achievable. Employees will otherwise see the control system as unreasonable and ignore or sabotage it.

Timely

Control systems give production cycle or process data at a specific time. For example, data may be in a monthly sales report, a weekly project update, a daily production report, or from a production line's quality inspections. For managers and employees to respond to problems promptly, control systems must give information in time for corrective action.

Monitorable

Control systems must be designed for monitoring ease to ensure expected performance. One way to check a control system is to introduce an imperfection, such as a defective part, and see how long the system takes to detect and report it to the correct person. Clearly, the test must be monitored to ensure the imperfection does not cause problems if the control system fails (as in a maintenance-quality test for aeroplanes). Other monitoring control system methods have various kinds of audits.

Acceptable to organisation members

Control systems work best when accepted by affected members. Otherwise, they may override and undermine them. Employees will accept control systems which focus on major issues compatible with organisational goals, which give useful data, when data collected give a fair and accurate picture of employee performance, and when data are used for improvement (as opposed to blaming) (McColl 2003b).

Flexible

As organisations must be flexible to changing environments, control systems must be able to meet new or revised needs. Accordingly, they should be be able to adapt quickly to measure and report new information and track new endeavours.

In the 1990s, Japanese companies had problems due to exchange rates and competitors cutting costs by copying Japanese manufacturing innovations (e.g. total quality management). Losing their advantage, Japanese firms moved to enhance efficiency. Many focused on output controls—goals and budgets—but without stopping innovation. One approach was shifting responsibility for budgets and profit targets to first-line supervisors and workers (Jones 1999). This showed employees the direct impact of their activities on profit. Another approach came from the identification of substantial costs involved buying components. Companies worked with suppliers to cut costs and raise quality. Members from many organisation functions were put into cross-functional teams to cut costs, one strategy being to teach suppliers to effectively use budgets and goals. The focus on output control has been very useful.

GAINING THE EDGE

The Macpac experience

In 1996 the Macpac phenomenon was 10 years along its road towards creating a workplace that was different. The Macpac vision statement at the time said: 'We create outstanding equipment and clothing for people who seek the challenge of the outdoors.'

The purpose of Macpac products is to keep people alive outdoors. Their brand is about quality, performance and innovation. A lot of rhetoric can be heard about these qualities, but Macpac attempts to make them a reality.

Macpac's journey parallels that of Bruce McIntyre, one of the company's founders. As a young man, Bruce had the experience of working as an employee and then doing the same work for himself. He learnt his trade from his grandfather, but at the age of 19 he wanted to make a difference and produce better packs at a cheaper price. Instead of going to work at 8 am to a boring job sewing for his grandfather, he now went to work at 8 am to create products of his own for his own business. Same work, same workplace; but the difference was he was working for himself, not for others. This experience was a driving force for Bruce as he attempted to make Macpac (in the words of Gregory Bateson) 'a difference that makes a difference'.

Bruce then set about growing a business that would be a different workplace for people like him.

The early 1980s saw Macpac go through a series of growth stages and mergers. In 1985 Bruce took a year off from the firm. When he came back, he realised that the organisation he had helped to create was built on structural lines no different from those of other, more traditional workplaces. Bruce recognised that the organisation needed to change if he was to pursue his dream of creating a different form of workplace. He had to stop being a manager and become a leader.

Today, Macpac is a different organisation. It is based on teams of people creating products of value to society. Its purpose statement is 'to inspire people to explore the natural world'.

Bruce, and Macpac, have realised that business is an ecosystem that serves society. To achieve its purpose, Macpac must also satisfy the needs of the three cornerstones of business:
- its customers
- its investors and owners
- and (last but not least) 'us! the staff'.
Macpac has identified that:
- Investors provide capital and trust. In exchange for this they require return on investment and opportunity.
- Staff provide time, expertise and ideas. In exchange for this they require finance, recognition, enjoyment and a meaningful role in society.
- Customers provide opportunity and revenue. In exchange they require expertise and promised performance at [a] fair price.

In order for the teams to function they need feedback on performance. To do this they need measures that reveal how well Macpac is going, in terms of meeting the needs of the three stakeholder groups: 'our customers, investors and ourselves (the staff)'. And they want, in the words of Macpac, 'to provide our teams with feedback (information) on their daily, weekly and monthly performance, enabling your team to self manage and continuously improve the way things are done'. What are team measures? Performance measurement is about measuring the performance of teams and processes, not of the individual. To do this Macpac adapted the performance measurement framework of Cross and Lynch (1995). This adapted framework is summarised in the figure below.

The apex of the framework reflects the goals and values of the organisation. The second layer reflects the key indicators of the three stakeholder groups and is for the management or 'guidance' team. Level three contains the business operating system measures that are used for guidance at this level. Macpac has identified seven operating systems:
- order fulfilment
- production
- new product implementation
- revenue management
- procurement

Performance measurement framework (adapted from Cross and Lynch 1995)

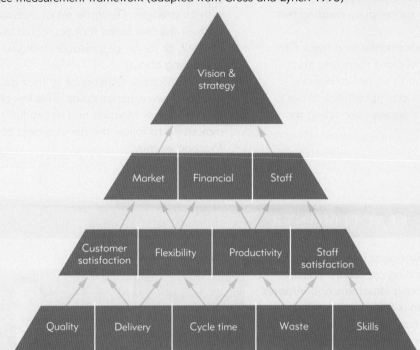

- demand management
- capacity planning.

At the base of the pyramid are the team process measures. These are the measures that the teams of staff can record to provide frequent feedback on how well they are contributing to the goals of the organisation. The five key dimensions of performance are relatively straightforward. The objectives of each team are to increase quality, delivery and member skills while reducing cycle time and waste. In this way Macpac offers its teams the opportunity to manage their own work, and ensured that they had good information to do this well.

Has this changed for Macpac? Let's see how the journey has evolved. Bruce spoke about his journey at the 'Spirit at work' conference in 2001. Bruce's personal journey is leading him into a teaching and healing role. At the time Macpac was experiencing a reasonable international demand and a profitable return for its product. However, as can be experienced, the situation changed quickly. As a result of a 40 per cent rise in the New Zealand dollar exchange rate, competitive overseas markets and an inability to find enough domestic manufacturing staff, by mid 2003 Macpac had lost $1 million and was predicting to lose as much again in the following year. Bruce had to rethink his strategy.

As a result, Macpac has outsourced its manufacturing. The company's backpacks are now made in the Philippines, its clothing and sleeping bags in China and its tents in Vietnam. Has this affected the measures? While the operating systems and teams may have changed, the base measures are still as valid as ever! The objectives of each team no matter where they may be located are still appropriate. To increase quality, delivery and member skills while reducing cycle time and waste are universal principles no matter what the operation.

What does the future hold? During 2004 Macpac headquarters in Christchurch expanded again, the design force had doubled to support the Macpac strategy to constantly improve its products. And more qualified design staff are being sought, but may not be available, as there is a shortage of suitable engineers!

What does this mean? Macpac is now truly a global brand.

Source: Contributed by Ross Milne (figure adapted from Cross, K. and Lynch, R. 1995, *Measure Up ... How to measure corporate performance*, 2nd ed., Blackwell, London).

Activities for discussion, analysis and further research

1. Very early in his life, Bruce McIntyre learned the different experience of working for himself as opposed to working for someone else. He attempted to create this opportunity for the

workers at Macpac. What factors do you consider important in successfully creating this environment?

2. The figure depicts performance as a pyramid containing the objectives and measures that connect an organisation's vision, values and objectives to its day-to-day operations. What is the significance of the arrows connecting the layers?

3. The base of the pyramid provides the pyramid with its strength. Design a set of measures in each of the five areas that you could use for yourself, or for an organisation that you know something about.

4. Visit the Macpac experience at their public website: www.macpac.co.nz. This link provides an overview of Macpac and its products. You may use it to follow the development of the Macpac journey.

REFLECTIVE PRACTITIONER

The control of the organisation occurs mostly through our business planning approach. The difference between adopting structures and informal control in the organisation is fairly important because sometimes you can tip the scales too far in one direction or not far enough in the other.

For me, the internal control of the business has come by putting various structures in place. These structures include our organisational structure, business planning process, development and implementation of a company operations manual which meets ISO9000 requirements, staff performance regime, staff professional development program, department reporting and communication strategy, client management process, time and task management program and, most importantly, achievement and reporting against financial targets.

Any start-up company is all about growing something from nothing, and although in the early days we did not have the structures and internal control or management processes we now have, I'd never say that we have been out of control. Our organisation has been around now for seven or eight years and in this time we have actively focused upon developing internal processes in order to release us to expand, grow and duplicate the provision of services and products. The greatest level of control has been achieved through greater formalisation of things which allows us to manage the organisation in a much more succinct, cost effective and efficient way.

One of the most important areas of management or control in any organisation is that of the finances. In terms of the financial control of the business, we have a full-time account staff member who now

KIMBERLEY TURNER

AEROSAFE
RISK MANAGEMENT

reports back within an agreed reporting framework. This starts with a weekly accounts meeting with the myself and the accounts manager, and is supported by a monthly accounts meeting with our accountant, and a quarterly financial performance meeting between the senior partner of our accountant firm and our company executive team. This executive team consists of the head of each department—the team reports within a framework which makes it easier to monitor how the organisation is going and keep things on track. This provides us with a structure which has enabled us to control the financial performance of the business. The results have been amazing. There is greater efficiency in that part of the business. We have improved our performance with not only accounts receivable and accounts payable but also the company productivity. So it has actually provided us with the results which demonstrate that those controls being in place works.

In the same light, we have put similar structures in place with staff management, from the operational management side of things—such as project work, tasking, scheduling, confirmation of contracts, service and things with client work. All those tools and techniques help us to control the operational running of the business.

Furthermore, structuring the communications side of the organisation provides our team with being on the same network, providing access to the one company planner and a consistent time billing process—these have all contributed a great deal to the organisation's effective running. This may seem very simplistic, but it certainly has seen us grow leaps and bounds. It has eliminated a lot of potential confusion which may have existed or has existed in the past.

Besides the finance and the people, the most important things we need to control are the client expectations, business opportunities, bookings, client interaction, tasking and the allocation and completion of project work. This is about matching our capacity to need and to the work that is available. That has been really good to the point where we have established a balance of setting up those systems with being receptive and responsive to industry needs.

We have progressed our organisation to the stage where all staff are allocated to tasks and client work three to six months in advance which allows me as a manager to monitor productivity and performance against capability and capacity. Managing your internal capability and capacity is critical to business success. The best way to achieve this is by making the most of the capability we have within the company and monitoring this with our controls. Before we had the structured controls in place we were quite reliant on individuals to make sure that all the moving parts fell into place. Whereas now, the framework allows other staff to move the people and the skills around and tie in the work without any input from me.

That structure and framework has allowed me and my team to differentiate between those things that I need to control personally and those that I can delegate to others. The more structure I have in place, the easier it is for me to delegate. I can step back and have confidence in the framework and the process so the formalisation becomes the tool for delegation. I can feel confident that the guidance I would normally give on an informal basis is being given on a structural formal basis.

FOCUS ON PRACTICE

Strategies for improving

1. Design some strategies to evaluate behavioural control systems that enable the organisation to maintain the culture it desires.
2. How do you achieve the right balance of direct supervision and bureaucratic control to monitor progress towards goals?

3. Devise strategies to involve subordinates in any consideration and implementation of corrective action.

Source: Jones et al. (2000).

SUMMARY

- Controlling is regulation of organisational activities so actual performance conforms to set goals and standards. Controls are needed to help managers handle five challenges: coping with uncertainty, detecting irregularities, identifying opportunities, handling complex situations and decentralising authority. Just as planning responsibilities differ by level, control responsibilities exist at strategic, tactical and operational levels.

- The basic control process has several major steps: (1) determine control areas; (2) set standards; (3) measure performance; (4) compare performance to standards; (5a) if standards are met or exceeded, recognise performance; (5b) if standards are not met, take needed corrective action; (6) adjust standards and measures as needed. The resource-dependence approach to controls argues that managers must consider controls in areas where they depend on others for resources to reach organisational goals. Four conditions helping show when controls should be used are: a high dependence on a resource; an expectation that resource flows may be unacceptable without controls; feasibility of instituting a control process; and acceptable process costs.

- There are different control types. Major types based on timing are feedforward, concurrent and feedback. Managers may need multiple control systems using two or more of feedforward, concurrent, and feedback control processes, and involve some strategic control points. Finally, systems can be cybernetic or non-cybernetic, depending on how much human discretion is part of the system.

- Managers have options about approaches to implement controls. The three basic ones are bureaucratic, clan and market. Managers have four strategic control levers to help regulate activities and encourage motivation: belief systems, boundary systems, performance management systems and interactive monitoring systems. The incrementalist approach helps control specific innovation projects. It relies on clan control but involves a phased set of plans and accompanying bureaucratic controls from a general level, becoming more specific as the project progresses.

- Potential dysfunctional aspects of control systems are behavioural displacement, game playing, operating delays and negative attitudes. To decrease chances of these effects, managers must avoid either overcontrol or undercontrol. Effective control systems must be future-oriented, multidimensional, cost-effective, accurate, realistic, timely, monitorable, acceptable to organisation members and flexible.

- This chapter focuses on basic concepts for organisational control systems, and the following supplements examine specific managerial control methods, such as financial and quality control.

QUESTIONS FOR DISCUSSION AND REVIEW

1. Explain the five major control roles. Give three examples from your college or university of controls fulfilling at least one of these roles.

2. Describe three levels of controls in organisations. For a familiar organisation, identify a control at each level.

3. Outline a general process applicable to most control situations. Using this, explain how you would develop a system to control home delivery staff at a local pizza shop.

4. Explain the principal factors, or conditions, managers need to consider in deciding what to control. Use these to assess a control existing at your college or university.

5. Describe the major types of controls by timing. Suppose you are managing a small factory making specialised microchips for a well-known computer manufacturer. Explain how you would use each control type to help maintain adequate control over manufacturing. What strategic control points would you establish?

6. Differentiate between cybernetic and non-cybernetic control. Explain how you might use these two types of control in a managerial position.

7. Explain the three basic approaches to implementing controls. For each approach, give an example based on a familiar organisation.
8. Explain the four strategic control levers. How does development of Sony's Walkman illustrate this approach?
9. Identify the major potential dysfunctional aspects of control systems in organisations. How could overcontrol or undercontrol contribute to these?
10. Delineate the major characteristics of effective control systems.

CRITICAL THINKING QUESTIONS

To answer some of these questions you will need to do further research. Useful references are given below each section of the questions.

This chapter provided a detailed review of the processes involved in the major forms of control and how managers go about implementing them, as well as the difficulties inherent in attempting to control innovation. The following questions will develop several of the themes to provide a different perspective from those offered in the text. We begin with the topical issue of security as a control issue.

The events of 11 September 2001 created a whole new awareness of the need for security control systems to be implemented in organisations. However, as described in an article in the *Security Director's Report* (2004), recent interviews with industry leaders in the United States uncovered a lack of knowledge about organisational security management tools. Some of the issues in the broader context of technology, security and control are proving to be very complex. The issue of effectively eliminating spam in computerised workplaces is one of the most unexpected and difficult to deal with.

1. What are the issues with spam in the workplace?

2. Besides using computer software to screen out material, what other control methods can be put in place?

Another aspect of control that is raised by technology is employer rights of access to staff emails versus individual privacy. Again, the events of September 11 have changed the debate on individual versus organisational security rights in ways that were completely unanticipated. While much of the focus continues to be on unknown outsiders gaining unauthorised access to the organisation, there has also been increased scrutiny of employees and the types of information an organisation has on them. The source article for these questions suggests that the relationship between job dissatisfaction and employee dishonesty is an important area of loss control.

3. What do you think is meant by this?

The article concludes by presenting one very simple control technique which the authors believe would reduce fraudulent internet transactions by up to 80 per cent. Based on requesting that online buyers provide their credit verification value (CVV)—the 3 or 4-digit non-embossed code on credit cards—it seems a surprisingly simple tool to introduce.

4. What reasons could there be for organisations not using CVV identification during internet transactions?

(Material relevant to these questions may be found in Anon 2004, Are you aware of these new security management tools?, *Security Director's Report*, p. 7.)

The article above touched on the vexed issue of monitoring employees as a legitimate control system within organisations. Reylito Elbo, a Philippino management consultant, reports that one of his client companies has decided to record and monitor all employees' telephone conversations with customers, in an effort to establish an objective work appraisal program.

5. What do you think the employees' response to this new computer-telephony integrated (CTI) initiative has been?

6. Given the essentially negative perception by employees, how can electronic monitoring such as CTI possibly increase employee performance?

Overall, the advantages of CTI are very enticing, yet the monitoring of employees does raise several concerns, key among these being the ethical issues.

7. What are they?

The message from Elbo (2003) is very clear: organisations must review what effective communication can do for both them and their employees. While part of management's job is one of regulation, managers must also build cooperation and work with employees to identify employee problems and seek solutions. Similarly, employees have the responsibility to articulate their feelings and perceptions in ways which also help solve problems and resolve conflict.

(Material relevant to these questions may be found in Elbo, R. 2003, Weekender: Labor & management, *Business World*, Philippines, 28 November.)

The next questions examine the big picture of organisational control, looking at the notion of one organisation being able to control an entire industry. As Davidson (2002) reports, the fate of who controls television in Australia is currently being fought between Foxtel, Optus and the free-to-air networks. It is a battle which can be reduced to the level of the set-top box which receives the cable and satellite television signals into our living rooms. Foxtel is part of Rupert Murdoch's empire, News Corporation, and ownership is a vital part of his plan to 'create a vertically integrated media company that owns everything in the entertainment chain from football leagues and sports teams to remote controls' (Davidson 2002, p. 22).

8. Given this, what is the real issue behind ownership and control of the set-top box?

While the pay-TV operators try to reach consensus, the free-to-air networks are also battling with their own problems introduced by the government's moves to make all TV in Australia a digital affair. This requires free-to-air television stations to 'triplecast' their broadcasts—so they must transmit in analog, standard definition digital and high definition digital until enough Australians have digital set-top boxes. The problem is that this triple casting is very expensive and Australians have been very slow in the move from analog to digital. The solution the commercial free-to-air TV stations want is to be allowed to have future, interactive versions of their set-top box rolled into interactive versions of pay-TV set-top boxes. Again, the central issue for the commercial free-to-air TV companies is one of control.

9. What is the control issue between the private pay-TV and commercial free-to-air providers?

The main advantage of digital technology is the vastly increased number and range of services which can be provided—moving from, say, Foxtel's 45 channels to hundreds, as well as providing interactive services. Again, the cost of getting digital set-top boxes to all Australian homes is estimated at around $7 billion and, as Davidson (2002) points out, is a burden no one wants to shoulder alone. While News Corporation managed to outplay its major rival in the UK market (by offering incentives such as heavily subsidised digital set-top boxes), there are other major rivals in the interactive component of the digital system. This is clearly seen in the partnerships which have been forged in the pay-TV sector where Seven is in a joint venture with AOL, Nine has partnered with Microsoft, and Foxtel's other major owner is Telstra. The battle is truly on for who will control the internet component of the set-top box as this is crucial to the interactive services. Why? Because it presents the massive potential for additional revenue.

Davidson (2002, p. 22) cites Warren Lee, a former Foxtel and News Limited executive who now advises clients on media, telecommunications and technology issues, as saying: 'This digital environment, if it ever eventuates, will have some of the most complex business practices and relationships that anyone has ever seen, and to try to regulate in advance for what that might look like is a nightmare'.

(Material relevant to these questions may be found in Davidson, J. 2002, The fate of television and who controls it, *Australian Financial Review*, 18 May, p. 22.)

The next questions focus on how control can move from a monopoly situation with the advent of a new player in the market. De Beers has been the dominant force in the diamond market for nearly seventy years. However, as Treadgold (2002) reports, they are about to change the strict command and control system of the diamond supply pipeline which has been the basis of their organisational structure for 68 years. The cause of this change is Argyle Diamonds, a subsidiary of Rio Tinto. Argyle was part of De Beers' cartel until 1996, when it broke free to sell its diamonds independently—and it immediately began to focus on developing a market for low-grade diamonds in the United States.

For Australia's three diamond producers, Rio Tinto, BHP Billiton, and the new kid on the block, Kimberley Diamond Company (KDC), the change is good news, simply because it should mean increased demand and potentially higher prices. The change for De Beers, however, was much more dramatic and one which heralded a fundamental change in their operations. Lussier, a senior De Beers executive, summarised the situation as one where 'control of supply has served the industry well, but now we must learn how to drive demand. The long and the short of it is that the old weapon of stocking [warehousing diamonds] is being replaced by a new weapon called marketing' (cited in Treadgold 2002).

De Beers' domination goes back to 1934 and was based on controlling production from the key source of the world's supply of diamonds, in those days South Africa, and stockpiling surplus diamonds so they could then control supply. The result was an orderly market which very much favoured De Beers. The discovery of commercial quantities of diamonds in both Russia and Australia about 30 years ago was the first real threat to this domination and their first response was in line with their traditional means of operating—to attempt to secure control of these sources of supply. It was a response that proved almost financially disastrous but it did result in acknowledgement that they needed to change and their present moves are illustrative of this.

The previous example discussed TV changing from analog to digital to open up the potential for massive potential in multichannelling, and the same is now occurring in the diamond industry.

10. What does being a multi-channel business mean in the diamond industry?

With the advent of mines in countries such as Russia, Botswana and Canada, De Beers' share of world diamond production is now down to an estimated 40 per cent and will continue to fall. Australian diamonds were responsible for a new trend in marketing, targeting middle America, where 'the diamond dream' was provided to a cut-price formula—a move which horrified De Beers, which had always sold diamonds as the ultimate luxury product. Falling market share and falling profits forced De Beers to re-evaluate their principal concept of controlling supply in the market.

Another aspect of control illustrated in the Argyle side of this diamond story is the market they targeted—self-purchasing women. Working with major American chains they established a market for diamond jewellery priced between US$99 and US$199. De Beers' Lussier admits that Argyle's strategy worked because women 'weren't buying it because it looked pretty. They were buying it because it was a diamond' (Treadgold 2002).

11. As the monopoly enjoyed by De Beers for so long dissipates, what are some of the changes in control you could expect to see?

(Material relevant to these questions may be found in Treadgold, T. 2002, Diamonds are for everyone, *Business Review Weekly*, 6 June.)

While losing organisational control of the market due to external factors may be put down to bad luck, or even survival of the fittest, losing it due to a lack of proper internal controls often borders on the criminal. One of the best-known examples of this was the 1995 collapse of the 233-year-old

Barings investment bank and, as Bartholomeusz (2002, p. 3) reports, after this very public debacle, it was supposed that it would be impossible for a rogue trader to ever again run amok within the mainstream banking system. The trial that followed Barings' collapse made it very clear that the bank's control and compliance systems had completely failed as detection did not occur until Nick Lesson had made over $2.3 billion in losses and, by then, it was too late to save the bank.

Another of Europe's most respected banks was caught in exactly the same predicament, however, in 2002 when the Allied Irish Bank admitted 'a massive breakdown in its controls' with a 37-year-old trader in Allied's US operations losing nearly $1.5 billion from unauthorised currency trading inside a year. More by luck than planning, the losses may not bankrupt the bank in this case, but they again highlight the vulnerability of 'financial institutions operating globally, or at least in global markets, to reckless or fraudulent activity', and accentuate the need for quality control systems as an integral part of business management (Bartholomeusz 2002, p. 3).

In this latest case, the problem arose in foreign currency trading and where the supposed protection control systems were circumvented by fictitious data being entered artificially into the bank's systems. Bartholomeusz (2002) questions how the massive amounts of trading activity which must have taken place to accumulate this sort of debt could have been hidden in the small and risk-averse operation Allied thought it was running in the US. While the control systems at Barings did not work in Leeson's case, as he had access to all the aspects of the systems that were supposed to oversee his activity, there seems to be no such explanation at Allieds.

12. What are the issues of control which Allied would have been looking at immediately after the situation was discovered?

A real lesson for the global banking system now seems to be that global operations themselves present unique difficulties in control.

13. One similarity in both cases is that one operated out of Singapore, the other out of the US. What might some of the lessons be?

(Material relevant to these questions may be found in Bartholomeusz, S. 2002, Brogue trader—The sequel that wasn't meant to happen, *Age*, 8 February, p. 3.)

The ongoing nature of control issues in the banking sector is taken up again in an article by Coutts (2004), which further develops the problems faced by the National Australia Bank. However, he takes a more direct view of NAB's most recent financial problem with control, suggesting that organisations have 'long known that if something goes wrong, the cause is usually a poorly designed system rather than malevolent workers' (Coutts 2004, p. 61).

14. What does he mean by this?

He goes on to suggest organisations who appear not to trust employees to use their own discretion or allow them to act promptly in the best interest of the customer pay a price—'In these circumstances, an informal organisation grows to circumvent the dictates of management, and workers develop their own ways and means of handling their work, often without the knowledge of management'.

15. How do the events at the National Australia Bank in early 2004, where currency traders had lost $385 million of shareholders' and depositors' funds, suggest that informal organisational control systems had developed in the foreign exchange trading branch of the bank?

16. What are some of the possible numerical targets the currency traders may have been trying to meet which got them into this situation?

In summary, informal organisations can be an invaluable tool within the existing formal structures of a bigger organisation. The fact that they may not be subject to the same control systems can be a powerful mechanism to increase productivity but, as the last two articles make very clear, only when they are the result of managers trusting staff to act in the best interests of their company. However, informal organisations which are the result of resistance to managerial control are a disaster waiting to happen. The challenge for the managers in growing and innovative organisations is to ensure that their managers remain in touch with their workplace so developments are monitored, encouraged and adjusted when required.

(Material relevant to these questions may be found in Coutts, L. 2004, The resistance movement, *Business Review Weekly*, Australia, 19 February, p. 61.)

MANAGEMENT EXERCISES

Exercise 1 Skill building: Timing the use of controls

The timing of control use is very important to organisational goal achievement. Controls at the proper point in development can give valuable information about quality, quantity, whether expectations are met or not, and possible solutions or opportunities. Following are examples of controls concerning timing. Indicate whether the type shown is a feedforward (FF), a concurrent (C) or a feedback (FB) control by placing the appropriate letters in the spaces provided.

Timing the use of controls	
1. ____	Road testing a new car
2. ____	Daily cash flow report
3. ____	Testing components from vendors prior to assembling a final product
4. ____	Ensuring employees are properly trained prior to starting a particular function
5. ____	Constantly checking woollen material for irregularities as it is being produced
6. ____	Certification of doctors prior to allowing them to practise
7. ____	A governor (a mechanical device for automatically controlling engine speed by regulating fuel flow) that controls the speed of a car or truck
8. ____	A final check of a report before it is sent to a client
9. ____	Individual employees check their work to ensure it is correct before passing it to someone else
10. ____	Sampling a batch of pills to ensure the correct amount of proper chemicals is included in them

Exercise 2 Management exercise: Opportunity knocks

You and a friend have what you believe to be the opportunity of a lifetime. You are both graduating this year, and your friend's father has asked whether the two of you would like to buy the air-conditioning and heating business he founded and has operated for the last 30 years. It has been very lucrative for him; today he is a millionaire many times over. His firm is the leader in its field in the area, and you and your friend see the possibility of expanding because many new homes are being built locally.

Your friend's father will finance the buyout through a loan, to be paid off over the next 10 years. Both you and your friend have some degree of expertise in the heating and air-conditioning field, as you have both worked for his father during the past four summers. His father has agreed to be a consultant to the two of you for a year or so in case his advice is needed.

The firm has almost 60 well-qualified employees, a large inventory, 40 service trucks in excellent condition, and a well-established list of clients. At the same time, return on investment has been lower than average for the past three years, labour costs are very high, and the company has attracted only a few new clients during the past two years. In addition, there is an indication the firm is not carrying the most up-to-date heating or air-conditioning equipment, and the four large buildings housing showrooms and service centres badly need refurbishing.

You and your friend are discussing the possibility of buying the firm. In considering the situation, the two of you are reviewing forms of control and control process which should be implemented.

Exercise requirement

Discuss the types of control you and your friend would use and the control process the two of you would implement as new owners of the firm.

END-OF-CHAPTER CASE: ON THE RIM

Controlling factories through your web browser

Controlling a factory in Australia from the US through your web browser may sound like science fiction, but it is a reality for BP Solar Australia's manufacturing operations in Sydney Olympic Park, Australia. BP Solar manufactures a range of solar electric products and systems, and its Australian operation exports over 60 per cent of its

POWERWEB

International articles related to this topic are available at the Online Learning Centre at **www.mhhe.com/au/bartol4e**

production overseas. The company recognised that to improve its product quality and to minimise the manufacturing cycle time, it needed a control system that would allow it to compare production details and product quality among its various global production facilities. Global decision makers with responsibility for managing plants and production needed timely and accurate information on manufacturing processes, plant emissions and facilities management.

To meet these needs, companies like BP Solar use industrial automation and control software systems that link production controls with office software such as web browsers, spreadsheets and databases. The system can warn of malfunctions or failures, set air-conditioning temperatures, create emission logs and even save electricity costs through intelligent energy management controls. A big advantage of using these kind of automated control and monitoring systems is that preventative maintenance can be scheduled with the minimum downtime of expensive machinery. Monitoring downtime also helps decision makers reduce stoppages and improve operational efficiency.

The control system, however, can limit operations unless it continually evolves and develops according to operational needs. The system is developing to include daily production summaries and the monitoring of more plant equipment. The information available to managers is also evolving, with more high-level management information such as automated production reports and charts that will enable managers to optimise line production. All of these automated control systems, however, are enhancements that can never substitute for the intuitive and interpersonal opportunities that arise from management walking through the manufacturing plant, making contact with workers on the 'factory floor'. Management control systems provide information to decision makers, but the skill of managers in exercising control will always depend on their ability to make the right decisions with the information before them.

Source: Contributed by Peter Woods.

Activities for discussion, analysis and further research

1. What characteristics of effective control systems are obvious in the management control system employed by BP Solar in their operations in Sydney Olympic Park?
2. What aspects of management control would not be covered by this type of control system?
3. What cost benefits can BP Solar expect through effective utilisation of this control system?

FURTHER READING

Lau, C-M. and Ngo, H-Y. 2001, Organization development and firm performance: A comparison of multinational and local firms, *Journal of International Business Studies*, 1st Quarter, 32, 1, pp. 95–115.

New Zealand Management 2002, Crime around the collar, May, 49, 4, pp. 11–13.

Selmer, J. and de Leon, C.T. 2002, Parent cultural control of foreign subsidiaries through organizational acculturation: A longitudinal study, *International Journal of Human Resource Management*, December, 13, 8, pp. 1147–67.

Sia, S.K. and Neo, B.S. 1997, Reengineering effectiveness and the redesign of organizational control: A case study, *Journal of Management Information Systems*, Summer, 14, 1, pp. 69–93.

Yanni, Y. and Child, J. 2002, An analysis of strategic determinants, learning and decision making in Sino-British joint ventures, *British Journal of Management*, June, 13, 2, pp. 109–23.

SUPPLEMENT 1 TO CHAPTER 15

MANAGERIAL CONTROL METHODS

MAJOR CONTROL SYSTEMS

Looking at major control systems in organisations such as Telstra, Coca-Cola or American Express, you would probably find the systems shown in Figure 15s1.1 (Flamholtz 1996; Anthony, Dearden & Bedford 1984). Control systems enhance the chances of achieving organisation goals and standards. For example, total quality management helps improve quality of products and services. Financial control systems help track overall financial issues, such as whether the firm is profitable or owes too much. Budgetary control systems provide quantitative tools to monitor revenues of various activities and match costs to plans. Inventory control systems ensure inputs are ready as needed and costs minimised. Operations management means controlling the processes of production. Finally, computer-based information systems help maintain control over information and other functions. We discuss operations management and computer-based information systems in supplements 2 and 3, respectively. (Management by objectives, another control system, is described in Chapter 6.)

For the remainder of this supplement, we look at quality, financial, budgetary and inventory control systems. Before considering each, we explore how they differ by the management level they are oriented to and their timing emphasis.

Managerial level

Control systems differ in how much they are used by different managerial levels (see Fig. 15s1.2). For example, total quality management (TQM) is used across the company, but it must be built into strategic levels to be effective. However, for TQM to operate, all organisation levels must be involved (Bateman & Snell 2004). Financial control systems are mechanisms used by top management as they show overall financial health. Middle managers watch financial matters affecting their own area. Middle- and lower-level managers mainly use budgetary controls. Top

FIGURE 15S1.1 Major organisational control systems

FIGURE 15S1.2 Major control systems by managerial level and timing

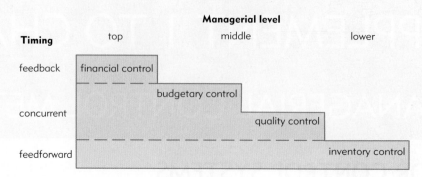

management monitors overall budget performance and deviations. Finally, inventory control rests with lower- and middle-level managers, although upper managers may evaluate costs.

Timing emphasis

Major control systems emphasise time differently. Timing relates to when controls occur, before (feedforward), during (concurrent) or after (feedback) the transformation process yields a product or service (see Chapter 16). Financial control systems are feedback control as data are evaluated at the end of a reporting period. Though too late to make changes affecting particular data, feedback helps plan changes. As computer-based information systems provide financial data, managers have more up-to-date information. In contrast to financial control, budgetary control is concurrent, as it regulates activities so budget levels are met (Howarth 2003d). For example, budgets may be referred to during spending decisions. When budgets are considered only after set periods, budgetary control is closer to feedback control. Total quality management applies to all of the transformation process; it is more a concurrent control, as checks are common during production or service process to ensure quality standards are met. If checks occur after production, when materials are scrapped or rejected if faulty, quality control is feedback. Finally, inventory control is mainly feedforward control, ensuring material and product availability as needed. In the rest of this supplement, we consider these in more detail.

TOTAL QUALITY MANAGEMENT

total quality management (TQM)

Management system integral to an organisation's strategy and aimed at continually improving product and service quality so as to achieve high levels of customer satisfaction and build strong customer loyalty

quality

Totality of features and characteristics of a product or service bearing on its ability to satisfy needs stated or implied

Total quality management (TQM) in some form is quite common (Conference Board 1994a). One major drive toward concern for quality has been fierce global competition from Japanese-based firms offering products and services of higher quality, often at low prices. There are many views of total quality management (and in some cases, names other than TQM are used). For our discussion, we define **total quality management (TQM)** as an organisation-wide management system integral to the company's strategy and aims to improve product and service quality continually, achieving high customer satisfaction levels and building customer loyalty (Bounds, Yorks, Adams & Ranney 1994; Reicheld 1996).

Although quality has been defined in many ways, the American Society for Quality Control offers this definition: **quality** is the totality of features and characteristics of a product or service that bear on its ability to satisfy stated or implied needs (*Quality Progress* 1992; Reeves & Bednar 1994). This definition recognises that quality involves every aspect of product or service, that quality affects a product or service's ability to satisfy needs, and that customer quality needs may not always be explicitly stated or calculated in the same way.

In examining quality and need for quality control issues, we explore the strategic implications of quality, probe major assumptions underlying TQM's philosophy, examine TQM change principles with intervention techniques, and consider issues related to TQM's actual practice.

Strategic implications of quality

David A. Garvin (1987) argues that quality can be used strategically to compete effectively. Choosing an appropriate strategy, though, depends on understanding quality's important dimensions. We therefore explore these before considering how to compete on quality.

Eight dimensions

From a strategic point of view, there are eight important quality dimensions.

Performance involves a product's primary operating characteristics. For a car, performance includes acceleration, braking, handling and fuel use. For service industries, such as fast-food restaurants, airlines, or hotels, performance means prompt service (Hostage 1975; Sherden 1988; White 1988).

Features are supplements to the basic functioning characteristics of a product or service. Examples are free newspapers for hotel guests, extra options on autofocus cameras, or stereo CD players in cars.

Reliability is the likelihood a product will work properly or will not break down in a specific period. As significant use is involved in assessing reliability, this dimension does not easily apply to products and services used immediately.

Conformance refers to how well a product's design or operating characteristics meet established standards. Products and services are developed for standards or specifications (White 1988).

Durability is how much use a product will get before it deteriorates or breaks down to where replacement is more sensible than repair. For instance, home appliance durability varies, ranging from 5.8 to 18 years for washing machines and 6 to 17 years for vacuum cleaners (Yepsen 1987).

Serviceability refers to promptness, courtesy, proficiency and ease of repair. For example, Hoover has a free-call number customers can call when an appliance breaks down. For easy-to-fix items, they can buy parts, mailed with directions.

Aesthetics refers to how the product looks, feels, sounds, tastes or smells—all dependent on personal judgment and preference.

Perceived quality is people's subjective assessments of product or service quality. Information may be incomplete, but customers' perceptions count (Lloyd 2003).

Competing on quality

While some dimensions reinforce each other, others do not. For example, adding features often cuts reliability, and aesthetics may affect durability. Thus, organisations rarely try to compete on very high quality on all eight dimensions at once.

Most companies select a quality niche customers see as important (Yepsen 1987). Of course, another crucial issue is providing intended quality level.

TQM philosophy

Japanese firms are generally credited with pioneering total quality management; however, the concept started in the United States. W. Edwards Deming developed statistical methods to improve quality, but took his concepts to Japan after being ignored (Bateman & Snell 2004). He promoted involvement of employees and organisation units in the quality effort, and presented 14 management points for his philosophy. For Deming's points, see 'Deming's 14 points on how to improve quality'.

Japanese companies, eager to rebuild after World War II, embraced Deming's ideas. In fact, his ideas were so valued they established the Deming prize, an annual quality management award. In the 1950s, J. M. Juran also helped with total quality management efforts. Kaoru Ishikawa is also seen as important (Evans & Lindsay 1996; Juran 1988).

Deming, Juran and Ishikawa saw the company's main aims as to stay in business, aid community stability, have useful products and services meeting customer needs, and foster members' work satisfaction and growth. While there is some variation, these three authorities show TQM's philosophical basis (Hackman & Wagemen 1995).

Good quality costs less than poor work quality. A basic TQM assumption is the costs of poor quality (inspection, rework, scrap rates, lost customers and other factors) greatly exceed the costs of high-quality products and services (training, proper equipment and tools, process improvement and other factors). By one estimate, a factory without TQM spends about 20 to 25 per cent of their budget finding and fixing mistakes (Port 1987).

Employees try to improve quality while they are supported. A second TQM assumption is staff will make quality changes when given the tools and training. Management must also listen to employees' ideas.

Quality improvement needs cross-functional efforts. A third TQM assumption is most quality problems do not fit into one functional area. For example, for high-quality products, design specialists must work closely with manufacturing during the design phase.

Quality improvement needs top management's strong commitment. The reasoning behind this fourth TQM assumption is senior managers control organisational systems designing and producing products and services. Employees' ability to do high-quality work flows directly from the quality of systems managers create.

TQM change principles

According to three TQM authorities, four TQM change principles should guide company quality-improvement interventions. These are as follows (Hackman & Wagemen 1995; Kinicki & Williams 2003):

1. *Focus on work processes.* The quality of products and services ultimately goes back to production processes. It is, therefore, necessary both to specify a need for higher quality, and to train and coach employees to analyse work processes to improve them.
2. *Analyse and understand variability.* The main cause of quality problems, in TQM's view, is process or outcome variation. For example, due to printing technology limitations, a small variation in photo reproduction in a book, like this, is expected (the quality of reproduced photos is important). However, if variation is unacceptable, causes must be found (poorly calibrated printing presses, untrained operators or paper problems). Only when the causes of product or service variability are found, can staff seek better quality.
3. *Manage by fact.* Data must be collected across the problem-solving cycle and from all company levels. Data help identify priority problems, trace causes, then choose and analyse a solution's impact. Although managers emphasise different things, all rely on data collection, statistics, and solution testing before implementation.
4. *Emphasise continuous learning and improvement.* The idea that improvement is vital to long-term organisation health is important. Focusing on continuous improvement means employees always learn and try to improve.

TQM intervention techniques

To implement change principles, TQM offers several techniques. Some common ones are as follows.

The cost of quality analysis helps assess potential cost savings of doing the work right first time. This means identifying the costs of setting quality at a desired level (such as the cost of avoiding quality problems) in comparison with the costs of producing at poor quality. The latter include appraisal costs (constant inspections), internal failure costs (scrap and rework) and external failure costs (customer complaints and returns). Cost of quality analysis helps find where quality changes give savings (Evans & Lindsay 1996).

Quality improvement teams, another TQM technique, are small employee groups solving specific quality and productivity problems, often with stated targets. Typically, teams are responsible for work areas targeted by quality improvement efforts, and are cross-functional. Management or workers may identify problems, and groups compete, then set improvement goals. A survey of manufacturers showed that most used TQM, and about 90 per cent of service firms using TQM had these teams (Gerber 1986; Conference Board 1991). Quality

quality improvement teams

Small groups of employees who work on solving specific problems related to quality and improvement of productivity, often with stated targets for improvement

improvement teams (other names are used) find causes of poor quality and productivity, then correct them. For example, Monsanto set up a team when Ford Motor had trouble with Saflex, a product used in laminated windscreens. The material's dimensions changed before delivery. In two months, the team traced the problem to packaging, designed a prototype, tested it, and set up a new process (Goldbaum 1988).

Training is important to TQM. TQM's philosophy emphasises proper training and tools for workers to produce at high quality and improve continuously. One survey (Conference Board 1991) shows 92 per cent of manufacturing and 75 per cent of service firms using TQM provide training. Almost all senior and middle managers are trained, 80 per cent of first-line supervisors and 50 per cent of non-managerial employees. Another survey found the most common training areas (in descending order) were personal interaction skills, team building, meeting conduct, statistical process control (explained later), supplier qualification training and benchmarking (Olian & Rynes 1991).

Benchmarking is identifying best practices and approaches by comparing one company's productivity with that of others inside and outside the industry (Weatherly 1992). Benchmarking became increasingly common as firms adopted the quality management approach (Main 1992; Rue & Byars 2003).

Collecting customer data systematically is another TQM technique. As TQM aims to satisfy customers and gain loyalty, understanding customer needs and satisfaction is vital. Methods range from focus groups to surveys and complaint monitoring (Hinton & Schaeffer 1994; Rabbitt 1994). One survey found 93 per cent of TQM companies thought customers' expectations would rise in the next three years (Conference Board 1994b).

Working with suppliers is also important to TQM. Benefits of partnering with suppliers were shown by Japanese car manufacturers. Product development is one benefit. Involving suppliers leads to superior products and services. Better financial results and productivity-based supply reliability are other benefits (Conference Board 1994c).

Statistical process control is a method of taking periodic random samples during production to see if quality levels are met or correction is needed. A common TQM technique, it assesses quality during production so problems can be rapidly fixed. As the focus is stopping poor output during the process, this is concurrent control. Most production processes are variable, so statistical process control tests to see when variations fall outside acceptable limits. Variations beyond the range signal a production process malfunction.

TQM: Does it work?

It is hard to answer the question, 'Does TQM work?'. Case studies and reports suggest TQM can provide major benefits (Goldbaum 1988; Houghton 1987; Griffiths 1994).

Sometimes, other changes occurring while TQM is being introduced make it hard to separate out effects strictly attributable to TQM (McCartney 1994). For example, firms starting TQM often increase employee involvement, emphasising employee participation in decisions and moving decisions as low as possible in the organisation (Lawler 1994; Hackman & Wagemen 1995). TQM companies also use teams (see Chapter 14) more than before, making it hard to assess effects of TQM over use of teams.

Some firms put much time and effort into TQM with no noticeable benefits. In fact, one Malcolm Baldrige National Quality Award winner filed for bankruptcy two years later (Fuchsberg 1992; Liebman 1992).

A reason for poor results from TQM programs may be that too much is tried too quickly. It may be better to concentrate on a few significant changes then build on these successes, rather than initiate many changes at once. Another reason for problems with TQM programs occurs when they are introduced with fanfare, but the philosophy, principles and interventions are not taken seriously and/or properly implemented (Brown, Hitchcock & Willard 1994; Houlder 1994). Senior management may not realise the significant organisational culture shift needed (Houlder 1994). Finally, firms may err by focusing on raising quality in unimportant areas and compromise quality in important ones (Greising 1994; Meigs & Meigs 1994).

benchmarking

Process of identifying best practices and approaches by comparing productivity in specific areas within one's own company with that of other organisations both within and outside the industry

statistical process control

Statistical technique using periodic random samples taken during actual production to determine whether acceptable quality levels are being met or production should be stopped for remedial action

As noted earlier, quality is a strategic issue, and quality efforts must be focused on raising customer satisfaction and loyalty (Houlder 1994; Naj 1993; Greising 1994). Overall, TQM efforts can succeed when set up properly, and it is a valuable tool. Quality is not the only issue: financial controls are used too.

FINANCIAL CONTROL

Suppose you are a top-level manager. What financial controls could you use? Here, we review some basic financial control methods, including financial statements, ratio analysis and comparative financial analysis. We also consider how managers can avoid the pitfalls of financial controls.

Financial statements

financial statement

Summary of a major aspect of an organisation's financial status

A **financial statement** summarises a major part of an organisation's financial status. Information in these statements is essential to keep organisational financial control. Two types of financial statement used by business are the balance sheet and income statement (Meigs & Meigs 1993). Financial statements are prepared at the end of reporting periods (quarterly and annually) though computers aid more frequent preparation.

Balance sheet

balance sheet

Financial statement showing an organisation's assets and claims against those assets at a point in time

A **balance sheet** shows an organisation's assets and claims on those assets at a point in time. A balance sheet for The Coca-Cola Company is shown in Table 15s1.1. You may think of a balance sheet as a financial 'snapshot' with two sections. The top half shows current assets, and the bottom half shows claims against assets (Baker 1987).

Assets, or organisation resources, fall into two categories: current and fixed. Current assets are cash and other assets usually converted to cash or used in a year. (Examples are marketable securities, accounts receivable or credit sales not been paid for yet; and inventory.) Fixed assets have a useful life of over a year (such as property, buildings and equipment). In Coca-Cola's case, the balance sheet shows $5.4 billion in current assets, $4.3 billion in investments and other assets, $4.3 billion in fixed assets (after depreciation), and $944 million in goodwill and other intangible assets, for total assets of $15 billion.

The balance sheet's bottom half shows claims, both liabilities and shareholders' equity. Liabilities are claims by non-owners on company assets (in other words, non-owner debts, such as banks). Liabilities fall in two categories: current and long-term. Current liabilities are normally paid in a year (accounts payable, current company bills and short-term loans). Long-term liabilities are usually paid over a period of more than a year (such as bonds). Coca-Cola's current liabilities are $7.3 billion, $1.1 billion long-term debt, $966 million other liabilities, and $194 million of deferred income taxes, a total of $9.6 billion.

Shareholders' equity is claims by owners against assets. As expected, shareholders' equity equals company assets minus liabilities. Shareholders' equity is the organisation's net worth. It is shown on the balance sheet by stock and retained earnings (funds accumulated from organisation profits). In Coca-Cola's case, shareholders' equity is $5.4 billion. As shareholder equity is assets less liabilities, putting assets ($15 billion) on top and liabilities and shareholder equity ($9.6 billion plus $5.4 billion, a total of $15 billion) on the bottom, the sheet 'balances'. Using a comparative sheet with figures from one year to the next (as in Table 15s1.1), trends can be tracked in asset growth, liabilities and current net worth.

Income statement

income statement

Financial statement summarising financial results of company operations over a specified time period, such as a quarter or a year

A balance sheet looks at the company's overall financial worth at one point in time, while an **income statement** summarises company financial results over a specified period, a quarter or year. Income statements show revenues and expenses. Revenues are assets from selling goods and services. Expenses are revenue production costs (such as cost of goods sold, operating expenses, interest expense and taxes). The difference between the two represents profits or losses over a period of time and is referred to as the bottom line.

TABLE 15S1.1 THE COCA-COLA COMPANY AND SUBSIDIARIES
Comparative balance sheet 31 December 1994 and 1995 (in millions of dollars)

Assets	1995	1994
Current assets:		
Cash and cash equivalents	$1 167	$1 386
Marketable securities	148	145
Trade accounts receivable	1 695	1 470
Finance subsidiary receivable	55	55
Inventories	1 117	1 047
Paid expenses and other assets	1 268	1 102
Total current assets	5 450	5 205
Investments and other assets	4 311	3 928
Fixed assets:		
Land, buildings and improvements	2 177	2 035
Machinery, equipment and containers	4 480	4 122
Total fixed assets	6 657	6 157
Less: Accumulated depreciation	2 321	2 077
Net fixed assets	4 336	4 080
Goodwill and other intangible assets	944	660
Total assets	$15 041	$13 873
Liabilities and shareholders' equity		
Current liabilities:		
Accounts payable and accrued expenses	$2 894	$2 564
Loans and notes payable	2 371	2 048
Current maturity of long-term debt	552	35
Accrued taxes	1 531	1 530
Total current liabilities	7 348	6 177
Long-term debt	1 141	1 426
Other liabilities	966	855
Deferred income taxes	194	180
Total liabilities	$9 649	$8 638
Shareholders' equity:		
Common stock, $.25 par value	428	427
Capital surplus	1 291	1 173
Reinvested earnings	12 882	11 006
Unearned compensation related to outstanding restricted stock	(68)	(74)
Foreign currency translation adjustment	(424)	(272)
Unrealised gain on securities available for sale	82	48
	14 191	12 308
Less: treasury stock, at cost	8 799	7 073
Total shareholders' equity	5 392	5 235
Total liabilities and shareholders' equity	$15 041	$13 873

Source: The Coca-Cola Company 1995 Annual Report.

As with balance sheets, income statements for different time periods are often compared. A comparative statement for The Coca-Cola Company is shown in Table 15s1.2. The statement shows net income (revenues less expenses) is about $3 billion, up from about $2.5 billion.

Ratio analysis

ratio analysis

Process of determining and evaluating financial ratios

In assessing financial data's significance, managers may use **ratio analysis**, the process of determining and evaluating financial ratios (Meigs & Meigs 1993). A ratio is a measure of one variable relative to another, given as a percentage or a rate. Ratios are meaningful only when compared with other information. As they are often compared to industry data, ratios help understand company performance relative to competitors and help track performance over time. Four financial ratios are important to managerial control: liquidity, asset management, debt management and profitability. Formulas and data for The Coca-Cola Company for the four ratios are shown in Table 15s1.3.

Liquidity ratios

liquidity ratios

Financial ratios measuring the degree to which an organisation's current assets are adequate to pay current liabilities (current debt obligations)

Liquidity ratios are ratios measuring the degree to which an organisation's current assets can pay current liabilities (current debt obligations). A major liquidity ratio is current ratio, or company ability to meet short-term creditors' claims by current assets. The current ratio in Table 15s1.3 shows Coca-Cola has $0.74 in current assets for every dollar in current liabilities. Coca-Cola's ratio is below the industry average of $0.90 for large beverage firms, but given their long-term success, this may mean good use of funds creating shareholder value.

Asset management ratios

asset management ratios

Financial ratios measuring how effectively an organisation manages its assets management

Asset management ratios (or activity ratios) measure effectiveness of an organisation's asset management. One asset management ratio is inventory turnover.

Inventory turnover measures how well inventory is managed. Low turnover may mean excess or obsolete inventory. High turnover means effective inventory handling relative to sales patterns, as less money is tied up in inventory to be sold. An inventory turnover ratio can be too high. This occurs if sales are lost when items ordered were out of stock. Coca-Cola's inventory turnover of 6.2 (shown in Table 15s1.3) is similar to the industry average of 6.5.

TABLE 15S1.2 THE COCA-COLA COMPANY AND SUBSIDIARIES
Consolitdated statement of income 31 December 1994 and 1995 (in millions of dollars)

	1995	1994
Net operating revenue	$18 018	$16 181
Cost of goods sold	6 940	6 168
Gross profit	11 078	10 013
Selling, administrative, and general expenses	6 986	6 297
Operating income	4 092	3 716
Interest income	245	181
Interest expense	272	199
Equity income	169	134
Other income (deductions)—net	20	(104)
Gain on issuance of stock by Coca-Cola Amatil	74	—
Income before taxes	4 328	3 728
Income taxes	1 342	1 174
Net income	$ 2 986	$ 2 554

Source: The Coca-Cola Company 1995 Annual Report.

TABLE 15S1.3 RATIO ANALYSIS FOR THE COCA-COLA COMPANY AND ITS SUBSIDIARIES

Ratio	Formula		Calculation		Current year	Industry averages
Liquidity ratios						
Current ratio	Current assets		5 450			
	Current liabilities	=	7 348	=	.74x	.90x
Asset management ratios						
Inventory turnover	Cost of goods sold		6 940			
	Inventory	=	1 117	=	6.2	6.5
Debt management ratios						
Debt ratio	Total liabilities		9 649			
	Total assets	=	15 041	=	64.2%	82.2%
Profitability ratios						
Net profit margin	Net income		2 986			
	Net sales*	=	18 018	=	16.6%	7.7%
Return on investment	Net income		2 986			
	Total assets	=	15 041	=	19.8%	6.4%

Source: The Coca-Cola Company 1995 Annual Report & Troy (1995).

*Coca-Cola refers to net sales as net operating revenue in its financial statements.

Debt management ratios

Debt management ratios (or leverage ratios) assess how much an organisation uses debt to finance investments, as well as how well it can meet long-term obligations. The more debt finances needed, the more must be committed to interest and repaying principal. As debts increase, so does the risk the company may not meet its debts and become bankrupt. Thus an important ratio is the debt ratio, the measure of total asset percentage financed by debt (including current liabilities). The higher the percentage, the more assets come from creditors not owners. Coca-Cola's debt ratio of 64.2 per cent (shown in Table 15s1.3) shows creditors supply about 64 cents in every dollar of assets, and the industry average is 82.2 per cent. The lower-than-average debt ratio may be good if they need to take on more debt. Future creditors may give favourable loans due to lower risk of the lower debt ratio.

debt management ratios

Financial ratios assessing the extent to which an organisation uses debt to finance investments, as well as indicating the degree to which it is able to meet its long-term obligations

Profitability ratios

Profitability ratios measure expense control and earnings through organisational resources (Meigs & Meigs 1993). Net profit margin and return on investment are two profitability ratios.

The net profit margin shows how much of each sales dollar is left after deducting all expenses. In Coca-Cola Company's case, net profit margin (shown in Table 15s1.3) is 16.6 per cent. According to this, Coke earns about 16$\frac{1}{2}$ cents on every sales dollar, much better than the industry average of 7.7 per cent. This means Coca-Cola seems to be expanding sales or managing expenses, or both.

The return on investment, or ROI (also called return on assets), measures management's overall effectiveness in gaining profits from assets. The ROI for Coca-Cola (shown in Table 15s1.3) is 19.8 per cent. Given the industry average of 6.4 per cent, Coke's ROI is very good. The ratio suggests the firm makes good investment decisions and ensures benefits are gained from those investments.

Top managers in most companies make strong use of financial controls.

profitability ratios

Financial ratios helping measure management's ability to control expenses and earn profits by use of organisational resources

Comparative financial analysis

Financial statements and ratios help compare data against a standard. Managers must explain variances (positive and negative) so top-level executives can see why they occur and their implications. Three standards managers commonly use to compare data are management goals, historical standards and industry standards.

Management financial goals are set during planning. Then they are standards to compare actual outcomes against during the control process. In The Coca-Cola Company, top management sets goals higher than industry averages on most ratios shown in Table 15s1.3, and for the period shown, they have exceeded industry averages on most (*Fortune* 1995).

In contrast to management goals, which project future standards, historical financial standards are data from past statements or ratios used to contrast current financial performance. The balance sheet and income statement for The Coca-Cola Company illustrate historical standard use as they include the previous year's data for comparison.

Another means of comparison is using industry financial standards, data based on industry averages. Financial ratios for many industries are available. Discussion of The Coca-Cola Company's financial ratios and data in Table 15s1.3 shows use of industry standards.

Financial controls can help top management, but six pitfalls can reduce their value. These are summarised in Table 15s1.4 (Cowen & Middaugh 1988). Managers must consider carefully how they set up and use financial controls to benefit.

TABLE 15S1.4 SIX POTENTIAL FINANCIAL CONTROL PITFALLS

1.   Failing to tailor financial controls to specific organisation requirements

2.   Neglecting to link financial controls to the strategic planning process

3.   Instituting controls which send mixed messages about desired behaviours

4.   Allowing financial controls to stifle innovation and creativity

5.   Forcing the same financial controls on subunits with different control requirements

6.   Implementing financial controls that are too sophisticated for organisational needs

Source: Cowen & Middaugh (1988).

BUDGETARY CONTROL

While financial controls are vital to top management, budgetary controls are important to middle managers. Lower-level managers in turn use budgets to track their own unit's progress. **Budgeting** is the process of stating quantitatively, normally in dollars, planned organisational activities for a given time period. Budgets, the quantitative statements coming from the budgeting process, may include projected income, expenditures and profits. Budgets help as they translate diverse activities and outcomes into a common measure, such as dollars.

Budgets are prepared for the whole company, and for subunits (divisions and departments). For budgetary purposes, organisations call subunits responsibility centres.

Responsibility centres

A **responsibility centre** is a subunit with a manager responsible to achieve one or more goals (Maciariello 1984). Organisations can be seen as a hierarchy of responsibility centres, with small subunits at the bottom and large ones at the top. For example, a Telstra phone store and Telstra's marketing division are different levels of responsibility centre. There are five main types of responsibility centre: standard cost, discretionary expense, revenue, profit and investment. A unit's particular designation for budgetary purposes depends on how much it controls major elements, such as revenues and expenses, that support profits and return on investment.

Standard cost centres

A **standard cost centre** is a responsibility centre where budgetary outcomes depend on goal achievement by working within standard cost constraints. As standard costs are set by engineering methods, this centre type is also an engineered expense centre. With a standard cost

budgeting

Process of stating in quantitative terms, usually dollars, planned organisational activities for a given period of time

responsibility centre

Subunit headed by a manager responsible for achieving one or more goals

standard cost centre

Responsibility centre whose budgetary outcomes depend on achieving its goals by operating within standard cost constraints

centre, managers must control input costs (e.g. labour, raw materials) so preset standards are not exceeded (Waldman 1989; Bohn 1994). A standard cost centre is appropriate only if (1) cost standards of producing a product or service can be estimated fairly accurately and (2) the unit cannot be held responsible for profit levels as it has no significant control over other expenses and/or revenues.

Discretionary expense centres

A **discretionary expense centre** is a responsibility centre where budgetary outcomes are based on achieving goals by operating within expense limits set by managerial judgment or discretion. Discretionary expense centres are departments such as research and development, public relations, human resources and legal units, where it is hard to set standard costs or measure the direct profit impact of a unit's efforts.

Revenue centres

A **revenue centre** is a responsibility centre where budgetary outcomes are measured by ability to generate set revenue levels. Revenue centres include sales and marketing, judged by sales (and revenues) generated in relation to allocated resources (Saporito 1988). Revenue centres are used when the unit is responsible for revenues but has no control over product or service costs, which makes it hard for them to be responsible for profit levels.

Profit centres

A **profit centre** is a responsibility centre where budgetary outcomes are measured by the difference between revenues and costs—in other words, profits. Profit centres are appropriate only when the unit controls both costs and revenues, since these set profit levels (Olins & Waples 1996). The whole firm is also a profit centre.

Investment centres

An **investment centre** is a responsibility centre where budgetary outcomes are based on return on investment. The ROI ratio is not just revenues, but also costs and assets used making the profit. Thus investment centres ensure managers focus on making good investment decisions in facilities and other assets. Of course, this type of centre works best if the unit has some control over investment decisions, as well as over both revenues and expenses (Serman 1989).

Uses of responsibility centres

The uses of responsibility centres depend on organisation structure (see Chapter 8). Standard cost, discretionary expense, and revenue centres are common in functional structures and in functional units in matrix designs. Manufacturing or production units are usually standard cost centres, while accounting, finance and human resources are usually discretionary expense centres. Sales or marketing units are normally revenue centres.

With a divisional organisation design, profit centres can be used because large structural divisions usually control both expenses and revenues associated with profits. Of course, within divisions, departments may operate as other responsibility centre types. Companies with divisions operating as separate, autonomous businesses use investment centres for budgetary purposes.

Budget types

For budgetary control, organisations have a master budget including other budgets which combine to summarise the organisation's planned activities. Two major budget types typically included in the master budget are operating and capital expenditures budgets (Meigs & Meigs 1993).

Operating budgets

An **operating budget** presents the financial plan for each responsibility centre over the budget period and reflects operating activities involving revenues and expenses (Maciariello 1984; Baker 1987). The operating budget lets management assess profit levels after looking at

---

discretionary expense centre

Responsibility centre whose budgetary outcomes are based on achieving its goals by operating within predetermined expense constraints set through managerial judgment or discretion

revenue centre

Responsibility centre whose budgetary outcomes are measured primarily by its ability to generate a specified revenue level

profit centre

Responsibility centre whose budgetary outcomes are measured by difference between revenues and costs—in other words, profits

investment centre

Responsibility centre whose budgetary outcomes are based on return on investment

operating budget

Statement that presents the financial plan for each responsibility centre during the budget period and reflects operating activities involving revenues and expenses anticipated revenues and expenses across responsibility centres. If profits are low, managers can plan to raise revenues (having a marketing promotion to increase sales) and/or cut expenses (lowering proposed travel expenditures or delaying non-essential equipment purchase).

Capital expenditures budgets

A **capital expenditures budget** is a plan for acquiring or divesting major fixed assets, such as land, buildings or equipment. These are capital investments. As these take a long time to be paid for and firms may borrow to cover investments, they are significant organisation decisions. As a result, top-level managers are usually heavily involved, and the decision process often includes the board.

Impacts of the budgeting process

Depending on their use, budgets can positively or negatively impact managerial behaviour. On the positive side, budgets can keep managers up to date on organisational activities, enhance inter-unit coordination, and ensure future investments. They also provide standards to evaluate managers, and a way to adjust if corrective action is needed. Budgets can be negative, if used rigidly and managers are concerned about fair treatment. Poorly run budgetary processes can result in negative managerial behaviours. These include politicking to raise budget allocations, overstating needs to raise allocations, and abandoning possible innovations as the resource fight is too hard (Irvine 1970; Tosi 1974).

INVENTORY CONTROL

Another major type of control system is inventory control. **Inventory** is the material stock used for production or to satisfy customer demand. There are three major inventory types: raw materials, work in process and finished goods (Schroeder 1989; Dilworth 1993).

Raw materials inventory is the parts, ingredients and other inputs to production or service. For example, McDonald's raw materials inventory has hamburgers, cheese slices, buns, potatoes and soft-drink syrup. Raw materials inventory at a bicycle factory includes chains, sprockets, handlebars and seats.

Work-in-process inventory is the items being made into a final product or service. For McDonald's, work-in-process inventory includes hamburgers being assembled, and syrup and soda water being mixed to make a soft drink. A bicycle frame with handlebars and seat attached would be work in process at a bicycle factory.

Finished-goods inventory is the items produced and awaiting sale or transit to a customer. At McDonald's, the finished-goods inventory includes hamburgers on the warmer. Bicycles are the finished-goods inventory at a bicycle factory. Organisations providing largely services, not products, such as hospitals, beauty salons or accounting firms, do not have a finished-goods inventory, as they cannot stockpile finished goods (e.g. operations, haircuts and audits).

Significance of inventory

Inventory has several major organisational purposes (Schroeder 1989; Dilworth 1993). For one, it helps deal with supply and demand uncertainties. For example, having more raw materials may avoid shortages holding up a production process. Having extra finished-goods inventory means customers can be served better. Inventory also allows more economic purchasing, as materials may be cheaper in large amounts. Finally, inventory can help deal with anticipated demand or supply changes, such as seasonal variations or expected shortage. However, change prediction requires caution (Rebello & Burrows 1996).

Inventory costs

Inventory is important to organisations as it is costly. For one thing, there is **item cost**, the item's price (cost of handlebars or seats). Then there is **ordering cost**, the expense of placing an order (paperwork, postage and time). There is also **carrying**, or **holding**, **cost**, the expense

Margin glossary

capital expenditures budget

Plan for acquisition or divestiture of major fixed assets, such as land, buildings or equipment

inventory

Stock of materials used to facilitate production or to satisfy customer demand

raw materials inventory

Stock of parts, ingredients and other basic inputs to a production or service process

work-in-process inventory

Stock of items currently being transformed into a final product or service

finished-goods inventory

Stock of items produced and awaiting sale or transit to a customer inventory

item cost

Price of an inventory item

ordering cost

Expenses of placing an order (paperwork, postage and time)

carrying, or holding, cost

Expenses associated with keeping an item on hand (storage, insurance, theft, breakage)

of keeping an item available (storage, insurance, theft, breakage). Finally, there is **stockout cost**, the economic impact of running out of stock. Stockout costs include lost customer goodwill and sales because an item is unavailable (Rebello & Burrows 1996). Inventory control minimises inventory costs (including stockout costs). An approach to reducing these costs is use of the inventory method called economic order quantity.

Economic order quantity

Economic order quantity (EOQ) is an inventory control method used to minimise ordering and holding costs, and avoid stockout costs. The method uses an equation including annual demand (D), ordering costs (O) and holding costs (H). Assume a bicycle manufacturer estimates annual demand of 1470 bicycle frames for manufacturing, ordering costs at $10 per order, and holding costs of $6 per unit per year. Putting these into the equation shows economic order quantity as 70 frames:

$$EOQ = \sqrt{\frac{2DO}{H}} = \sqrt{\frac{2(1470)(10)}{6}} = 70$$

The EOQ equation helps managers decide what to order, but they also need to know the **reorder point (ROP)**, the inventory level when a new order should be placed. To determine reorder point, managers estimate *lead time (L)*, time from ordering to receiving. In the case of the bicycle manufacturer, lead time for getting frames from a producer is seven days. In the ROP equation, lead time is multiplied by average daily demand (annual demand ÷ 365 days). So, frames should be ordered when just enough frames are on hand to make bicycles until the new frames come. Substituting data for the bicycle manufacturer into the ROP equation shows an order should be placed when stock reaches 29:

$$ROP = (L)\frac{D}{365} = (7)\frac{1470}{365} = 28.19, \text{ or } 29 \text{ (rounded)}$$

The EOQ inventory control system needs continuous inventory monitoring, as shown in Figure 15s1.3. Although it is assumed demand and unit costs are constant, demand may vary and suppliers may give discounts and special offers. Still, EOQ is some help. (We consider more sophisticated inventory issues in Supplement 2.) In using EOQ, a firm often adds fluctuation, or safety, stock. This is kept for unforeseen events like quality problems or reorder delays (McLeavey & Narasimhan 1985). Alternatively, companies may approach inventory control by using 'just-in-time' methods.

Just-in-time inventory control

Just-in-time (JIT) inventory control means materials arrive as needed (Schroeder 1989). The JIT inventory approach is part of a broader JIT manufacturing philosophy. Accordingly, companies must work to eliminate all waste sources, including non-value-adding activities, by having the right part at the right place at the right time. Applying JIT to inventory means having materials arrive as needed, not keeping inventory backup. This means a company can cut holding costs and save space used by inventory waiting in the production area (Burck 1982). In its waste avoidance focus, JIT's philosophy calls for using workers' full capabilities, increasing their responsibility for production processes, and including them in ongoing efforts to improve the production process.

For inventory handling, JIT uses **Kanban** (Japanese for 'card' or 'signal'), a simple parts-movement system using cards and containers to pull parts from one work centre to another. With Kanban, production workstations are given containers and produce enough to fill them. They produce again when they get a card and an empty container from the next workstation, showing more are needed. If the process stops due to breakdowns or quality problems, all

stockout cost

Economic consequences of running out of stock (loss of customer goodwill and sales)

economic order quantity (EOQ)

Inventory control method developed to minimise ordering plus holding costs, while avoiding stockout costs

reorder point (ROP)

Inventory level at which a new order should be placed

just-in-time (JIT) inventory control

Approach to inventory control emphasising having materials arrive just as needed in the production process

Kanban

Simple parts-movement system depending on cards and containers to pull parts from one work centre to another

FIGURE 15S1.3 EOQ inventory control system

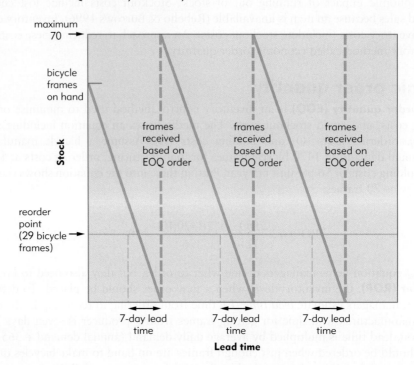

workstations produce only until their containers fill and then stop. The system means identifying sources of production variation is easier (Jones et al. 2000)

With a JIT system, high quality is vital. As suppliers deliver materials or various internal work centres make them just before they're needed, items must be perfect. Otherwise, there is waste and production stops as there is no significant inventory to cover. Due to the high need for coordination and control, JIT inventory systems help develop close relationships between suppliers and customers (Mangelsdorf 1989). Of course, a JIT system takes time to set up, and depends on near-perfect coordination (Pulchalsky 1996). It also means all partners in the process must set up complementary systems to streamline interactions (Jones et al. 2000)

SUPPLEMENT 2 TO CHAPTER 15

OPERATIONS MANAGEMENT

Operations management is part of the controlling function because emphasis is on regulating productive processes critical to reach organisational goals. In looking at operations management, we first explore its basic nature, and examine the productivity link. We next see how operations management can link to overall organisation strategy. We then consider other operations management aspects, such as operating systems, facilities, re-engineering and use of other process technology to promote innovation. Finally, we look at major steps in improving operations management productivity.

DEFINING OPERATIONS MANAGEMENT

Operations management is management of the productive processes converting inputs into goods and services (Chase & Aquilano 1992). Because of its manufacturing association, operations management is also called production-operations management. More recently, the term 'production' is being dropped in favour of 'operations management', which has less manufacturing connotation. The operations management function is carried out by the part of the organisation that produces the primary goods and services.

In a manufacturing organisation the operations management function includes plant managers and all other managers working in factories (e.g. production managers, inventory control managers, quality assurance managers and line supervisors). In a company with a corporate level, operations include manufacturing or operations senior managers, with related corporate operations staff (those primarily concerned with production, inventory, quality, facilities and equipment).

In a service industry such as a hotel, the operations management function includes hotel managers (e.g. housekeeping, food and beverage and general management). Again, if a corporate level exists, operations comprise managers and staff at that level directly involved in actually running hotels (as opposed to managers from other functions, such as marketing and finance). Whether the organisation produces a service, a product, or both, operations managers' focus is productivity.

The productivity–operations management linkage

Productivity is an efficiency concept relating the ratio of outputs to inputs in a productive process (Mahoney 1988). In Chapter 1, we discussed organisational effectiveness and efficiency in performance. Effectiveness is the extent to which performance achieves organisational goals. By contrast, efficiency is resources (inputs) used achieving outcomes (outputs). Productivity is assessing organisational performance efficiency—the ratio of outputs to inputs. As such, productivity helps managers track progress to more efficient resource use in production of goods and services.

Organisational productivity is often measured by this equation:

$$\text{Productivity} = \frac{\text{goods and services produced (outputs)}}{\text{labour + capital + energy + technology + materials (inputs)}}$$

operations management

Management of productive processes converting inputs into goods and services

productivity

Efficiency concept gauging the ratio of outputs relative to inputs into a production process

total-factor productivity

Productivity approach considering all inputs involved in producing outputs

partial-factor productivity

Productivity approach considering the total output relative to a specific input, such as labour

This approach considers all inputs in producing outputs and is called **total-factor productivity**. Managers also use **partial-factor productivity**, an approach considering total output relative to a specific input, such as labour. For example:

$$\text{Productivity} = \frac{\text{goods and services produced (outputs)}}{\text{labour hours (labour input)}}$$

Managers develop particular ratios to assess productivity from specific outputs and inputs. Examples include sales per square metre of floor space, profit per sales dollar, return on investment, claims processed per employee, and tests completed per dollar of labour cost.

While expenses per sales are one measure, they show why managers must consider productivity. If competitors get more output (dollars of sales) from fewer inputs (expenses), they are more profitable and can improve their competitive position. Manufacturing and service firms differ in their influences over productivity.

Manufacturing versus service organisations

Manufacturing and service organisations differ (Schroeder 1993). Manufacturing organisations transform inputs into tangible goods (soft drinks, cars or VCRs). Products can be stored (at least somewhat), and the end consumer is not present during the process. So, manufacturing can be central, and products shipped to customers. Wasted capacity can also be avoided in slack periods by using capacity to produce inventory before future sales. Manufacturing firms can control when and how they will run, and organise for maximum productivity.

Service organisations transform inputs into intangible outcomes (education, health care or transportation). These are produced and consumed almost simultaneously, cannot be stored, and involve the customer. For example, in a service organisation you attend a class, see a doctor, visit a bank, catch a flight or have a haircut. You participate in all of these to receive the service, and none can be stored. Unlike manufacturing, service organisations cannot use idle capacity to produce stored inventory, and may have dispersed operations close to customers, since services cannot be stored and shipped. Compared to manufacturing, service organisations have less control over operations, as they depend on customer volume and needs, which are hard to determine in advance.

As shown in Figure 15s2.1, some organisations (factories, farms and mines) produce largely goods. Others (consulting firms, hospitals or government agencies) produce largely services. Of course, many combine goods and services. For example, as well as cars, Ford and General Motors Holden provide services such as financing, insurance and repairs. Similarly, at a Hungry Jack's/Burger King outlet, you get services in order taking, filling and table availability, and a product in the shape of a cheeseburger.

Organisations can be classified by degree of service by measuring percentage of production process time spent in customer contact (Chase 1978; Chase & Aquilano 1992). A pure goods producer has zero contact with end customers, and a pure service producer 100 per cent. High customer contact lowers efficiency and productivity, since arrival patterns vary and may need customised service. For example, lines are slower at Hungry Jack's/Burger King if non-standard items are ordered, such as a Whopper without pickles.

FIGURE 15S2.1 Continuum of goods and services

pure goods   combination of goods and services   pure services

The operations management process

In transforming inputs into goods and services, operations management has several elements (see Fig. 15s2.2). One is *operations strategy*, operations management's role in formulating and implementing strategies to reach company goals (see Chapter 6). Another is *operating systems*, methods to achieve efficiency and effectiveness in manufacturing and service operations. A third is *facilities*, land, buildings, equipment and other physical assets affecting the ability to deliver goods and services. Finally, *process technology*, used to transform inputs into goods and services, is significant to operations management. We consider each in the next sections.

FORMULATING OPERATIONS STRATEGY

Operations management has different roles in determining strategy, depending on the stage of an organisation's strategic role (Wheelwright & Hayes 1985). The four stages are shown in Figure 15s2.3.

Stage 1: Minimise negative potential. In this stage, top managers try to neutralise negative impacts of internal organisation operations. This is because they see operations management as neutral, or as not affecting organisational competitive success positively. So they use detailed measures and controls to ensure the function does not drift too far before correcting. Top managers generally have minimal involvement in operations. However, major investment decisions concern them (such as new facilities or major equipment purchases) through capital budgeting. Stage 1 is typical of many consumer-products and service companies.

FIGURE 15S2.2 Operations management process

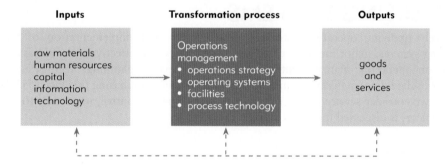

FIGURE 15S2.3 Stages in operations management strategic role (based on Wheelwright & Hayes 1985, pp. 99–109)

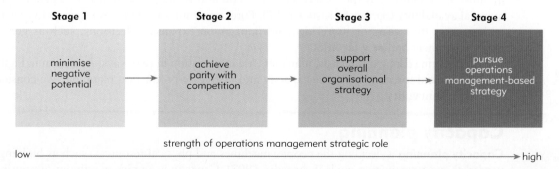

Stage 2: Achieve parity with competition. In this stage, top managers work to have operations management stay up with competitors. Organisations work to maintain equality by adopting industry practices on workforce issues, equipment purchases and capacity upgrades. Typically, they see new equipment and facility investments as good to get ahead of the competition, and economies of scale (quantity production) as the way to efficiency. Traditional manufacturing industries, such as steel and cars, are among firms found in this stage.

Stage 3: Support overall organisational strategy. In this stage, top managers expect operations management to support and strengthen organisation strategy. Operations managers' role is to understand strategy developed by top management and consider innovations to effectively implement strategy. In contrast to those at stage 2, organisations at stage 3 see technological progress as improving competitive position. Nonetheless, at this stage, operations managers help implement and support strategy not formulate it.

Stage 4: Pursue operations management-based strategy. During this stage, top managers see operations management as a strong strategic resource to be used as a basis for developing strategy. They include operations managers in strategy development and formulate one largely on operations capabilities. Operations managers try to anticipate potential technological advances impacting operations, and gain internal expertise before implications are clear. At this stage, organisations try to use innovation to make small strategic jumps ahead of competitors. Stage 4 is characteristic of all world-class manufacturers or service providers. These companies typically emphasise their own innovations, particularly improving processes in producing goods and services.

DEVELOPING AND IMPLEMENTING OPERATING SYSTEMS

Effectively applying operations strategy needs design and implementation of well-set-up operating systems, major methods of achieving efficiency and effectiveness. Primary operating systems in operations management are forecasting, capacity planning, aggregate-production planning, scheduling, materials-requirements planning, and purchasing (see Fig. 15s2.4). In this section, we consider service delivery system aspects. Quality control, important to operations management, is discussed more in Chapter 15.

Forecasting

Forecasting is predicting future conditions and events affecting a company's business. Forecasting methods are set out in Supplement 1 to Chapter 5.

For operations management purposes, forecasting tries to predict demand for goods or services. Demand forecasts can be short- to long-term and depend on quantitative and judgmental methods. Short-term forecasts (up to a year, but often between one and three months) are important as they affect short-run conditions, such as production schedules and material availability (Barrett & Kistka 1987). Forecasting intermediate-term (one to five years) or long-term (five years or more) demand impacts on expansion decisions, such as getting major equipment and new facilities.

After making demand forecasts, managers use information in two ways. As shown in Figure 15s2.4, demand forecasts influence capacity and aggregate-production planning. We consider capacity planning first.

Capacity planning

capacity planning

Process of determining people, machines and major physical resources, such as buildings, necessary to meet production objectives of the organisation

Capacity planning is deciding the people, machines and physical resources, such as buildings, needed to meet production goals (Schroeder 1993). Capacity is a unit's maximum output in a time period. For example, a car wash can handle so many cars per hour due to its physical limits. Common capacity measures by organisation type are shown in Table 15s2.1.

Time horizons

Capacity planning has three time horizons: long-, medium- and short-range. Each involves different capacity issues (Monks 1987; Schroeder 1993; Bolt 2003).

Long-range capacity planning focuses on human, physical and financial resources to reach long-term goals. As increasing long-term capacity needs capital expenditures for facilities and employment, decisions are top management's.

Medium-range capacity planning provides information on facility capacities, as well as how to make some intermediate and short-term changes. These include employee hiring and firing, overtime use and inventory increases.

Short-range capacity planning works to ensure effective use of current major facility capacity in the master production schedule context. Planning in this horizon uses **capacity-requirements planning** to determine needed personnel and equipment to meet short-term production objectives (see Fig. 15s2.4).

Aggregate-production planning

Short-term demand forecasts, and intermediate- and short-range capacity planning, influence aggregate-production planning (Monks 1987; Dilworth 1993). **Aggregate-production planning** is planning how to match supply and product or service demand over a year or so (see Fig. 15s2.4). Although it spans a year, the plan is revised, perhaps monthly. Aggregate planning is balancing market demand with organisation capacity. It is called 'aggregate' because production plans are given in output unit, such as car numbers, steel tonnes, or seat-kilometres, not car models, specific steel products or specific airline flight.

Aggregate planning assumes two things. First, facility capacity, such as plants, retail outlets and major equipment, cannot be quickly changed. Second, short- and intermediate-term demands change due to uncertainty, seasonal variation or other market factors. As a result, operations managers must plan to meet changing demand given fixed facility capacity.

Operations managers can use many strategies to satisfy short- and intermediate-term variable demand. These are summarised in Table 15s2.2.

Scheduling

Aggregate planning is the basis for the next step, creating a master production schedule (see Fig. 15s2.4). The **master production schedule (MPS)** translates an aggregate plan into a formal production plan for specific products or services and capacity needs over a set period.

capacity-requirements planning

Technique for determining what personnel and equipment are needed to meet short-term production objectives

aggregate-production planning

Process of planning how to match supply with product or service demand over a time horizon of about one year

master production schedule (MPS)

Schedule translating the aggregate plan into a formalised production plan encompassing specific products to be produced or services to be offered and specific capacity requirements over a designated time period

TABLE 15S2.1 MEASURES OF CAPACITY ACCORDING TO TYPE OF ORGANISATION

Type of organisation	Capacity measure
Airline	Available seat-kilometres
Brewery	Kegs of beer
University	Classes
Restaurant	Seats and tables
Power company	Megawatts of electricity
Cannery	Tonnes of food
Retail store	Square metres of selling space
Car repair shop	Service bays

FIGURE 15S2.4 Major systems used in operations management

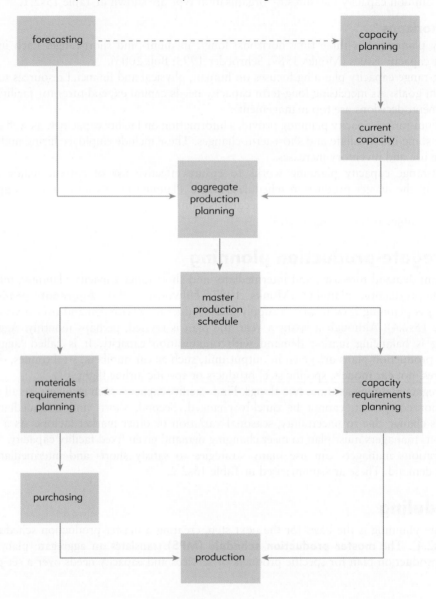

Master scheduling means trial-and-error work and begins with a tentative schedule which is then revised.

Time horizon
A master schedule's time horizon ranges from a few weeks to a year or more, depending on product or service characteristics and lead times for material sourcing. Within a master schedule, activities are often broken down on a weekly basis. Some firms use weekly intervals for 13 weeks (a quarter) and then monthly intervals.

MPS advantages
Using a master production schedule is useful. For one, it helps managers assess different schedules. Many computerised production and inventory control systems let managers simulate proposed production schedules. This lets planners determine materials' lead times and delivery dates from various schedules. Another advantage of the process is it helps determine needed

TABLE 15S2.2 MAJOR APPROACHES TO COPING WITH FLUCTUATING DEMAND

Major approach	Related issues
Pay overtime	Expensive, but cheaper than hiring extra workers who are idle part of the time
Hire temporary workers	Helpful for predictable demand increases of some duration; may be hard to obtain necessary skills
Hire part-time workers	May be more helpful to address demand peaks in service than in manufacturing
Develop multiskilled staff	May involve considerable time and expense, but allows workers to help out where needed
Build inventory	May be good utilisation for slow periods; risks inventory becoming obsolete; increases holding costs; not usually appropriate for service
Take back orders; have customer returns policy	Customers may be dissatisfied and/or go to a competitor; may be effective if time frame is reasonable
Subcontract work to vendors	Expensive; less control over quality
Offer premiums/discounts for customer flexibility	Provide discounts for orders/service during slow periods or charge less for service flexibility (e.g. surface mail)

materials. It does so by giving specific information on products or services to be produced. This ensures materials are bought and delivered to meet scheduled production. Yet another advantage is that MPS gives specific information on immediate needs (such as labour and equipment resources) used in capacity-requirements planning (see Fig. 15s2.4). If needs exceed capacity available, schedule adjustments, such as delaying item or service production, may be needed. Alternatively, capacity underutilisation may mean making some items ahead of schedule or generating demand (with a special promotion). Finally, a master schedule helps share relevant marketing information (such as customer deliveries), inventory and human resource matters (such as staffing needs).

Materials-requirements planning

While master schedule development is important, production cannot occur unless materials needed are in place at the right time for the job. One way to manage these issues is use of materials-requirements planning, which must be closely coordinated with the master production schedule (see Fig. 15s2.4). **Materials-requirements planning (MRP)** is a computer-based inventory system projecting materials needed for goods and services listed in the master schedule and starting actions for getting materials.

MRP systems can handle different inventory types, but are best for **dependent-demand inventory**, or raw materials, components and subassemblies for producing an end product or service. For example, if a business makes wheelbarrows, components such as tyres, wheels and axles are dependent-demand inventory items used in products (wheelbarrows), not end-products themselves. In other words, inventory demand for these is dependent on need for end-products. In contrast, **independent-demand inventory** is end-products, parts for repairs, and other items where demand is tied to market issues. MRP systems are common in manufacturing and are just starting to be applied in service firms. They can yield productivity enhancements in areas such as restaurants, hotels, legal offices and health care.

materials-requirements planning (MRP)

Computer-based inventory system developing materials requirements for goods and services specified in the master schedule, and initiating actions needed to acquire materials when needed

dependent-demand inventory

Type of inventory consisting of raw materials, components and subassemblies used in production of an end product or service

independent-demand inventory

Type of inventory consisting of end products, parts used for repairs, and other items whose demand is tied more directly to market issues than for dependent demand inventory items

Inputs to MRP systems

MRP systems use three inputs: a master production schedule, bill-of-materials information, and inventory status information. The MRP system gets information on products to be made from the master production schedule.

bill of materials (BOM)

Listing of all components, including partially assembled pieces and basic parts, making up an end-product

The system then consults a bill of materials for each product and model to determine materials needed. A **bill of materials (BOM)** lists all components, including partially assembled pieces and basic parts, to make an end-product. The BOM usually has part numbers and needed quantities per product unit. It is often hierarchically arranged to determine basic elements and subassemblies. For example, Figure 15s2.5 shows a product structure tree with BOM levels for a wheelbarrow. As the figure indicates, bars and grips at level 2 are assembled to make the handle assembly in level 1. Similarly, the tyre at level 3 (the most basic) and axle, bearings, and wheel at level 2 make up the level 1 wheel assembly. The top level (0) shows the end product. Bill-of-materials information is kept in computer files for access by the MRP system so materials needed for a proposed master schedule can be found quickly. The more levels to a BOM, the more an MRP system is needed to help manage materials (Finch & Cox 1988). The MRP system uses computerised inventory information to set levels of materials on hand, schedule receipts of ordered materials, and orders released.

In service applications, a bill of activities replaces the bill of materials. Combined with a master production schedule and inventory data, the bill of activities determines activities and personnel needed for service production. If materials are important, a bill of materials may be used. In an application of MRP at an electricity company, connection requests are put into a computer setting out a detailed list of labour, materials and tasks. These are then combined to check capacity. Crews are given work orders from the system. They report back to it as work is completed (Schroeder 1993).

FIGURE 15S2.5 Bill-of-materials levels for a wheelbarrow (reprinted from Monks 1987, p. 444)

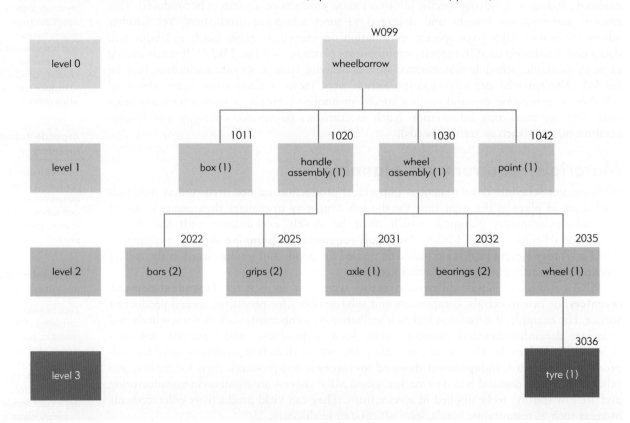

Benefits from MRP systems

MRP systems give four outputs. First, the system triggers material orders. Orders go to purchasing or internal departments for components needed. Second, the system provides data to master production schedulers, identifying difficulties sourcing materials interfering with the master schedule. Third, it provides data to those managing capacity planning. Then they make short-run changes, move equipment and add people (through capacity-requirements planning) or longer-run changes from trends. Fourth, the system provides data on costs, quality and supplier activity.

MRP systems operate differently from the just-in-time (JIT) approach (Chapter 15). Like JIT, MRP cuts inventory costs and keeps the production line supplied with materials. However, MRP does so by planning and using lead times to order as needed on the basis of master production schedules (with a small amount of stock to allow for changes).

Manufacturing-resource planning

Given the success of materials-requirements planning systems, some firms have expanded MRP. **Manufacturing-resource planning (MRP II)**, a computer-based system, combines MRP's production planning and control activities with financial, accounting, personnel, engineering and marketing information. MRP II systems tie operations management information into a system with other functions (Chopra 1982a; 1982b; Dilworth 1993). For example, when an organisation with MRP II makes an item, the system analyses labour and materials costs, captures cash-flow consequences, and notifies marketing that the product is in stock. These activities let operations management coordinate organisation efforts.

While MRP II systems are expensive and take time to set up, results are good (Cockel 1986). Pharmaceutical firms, aerospace and defence contractors, and automotive and parts manufacturers use MRP II systems (Foley 1988; Dilworth 1993). Again, the systems can apply to service firms, but are not widespread.

manufacturing-resource planning (MRP II)

Computer-based information system integrating production planning and control activities of basic MRP systems with related financial, accounting, personnel, engineering and marketing information

Purchasing

In conducting business, most organisations need materials and services they get by **purchasing**, the process of getting needed goods or services in exchange for funds or other payment (Monks 1987; Dilworth 1993). Purchasing needs are identified by materials-requirements planning (see Fig. 15s2.4). Then purchasing occurs. This includes checking vendors' qualifications to provide supplies, seeking substitute sources and negotiating best prices.

purchasing

Process of acquiring necessary goods or services in exchange for funds or other remuneration

Traditionally, purchasing has been seen as clerical, aimed at getting supplies to meet specification, not as technical or managerial tasks. Recently, due to environmental and competitive developments, this has changed (Burt & Soukup 1985; Tully 1995). Four factors contribute to purchasing's growing importance. One is rising costs. Materials and supplies are major costs, and small savings can give major benefits to a company's bottom line.

Another factor is advancing technology. Many products are complex and difficult to assess. Thus, increased technical expertise is needed to make good purchasing decisions. Companies are hiring MBAs with technical focus to manage purchasing in specialist areas. Another factor is needing to get quality materials and services. Without quality input, organisations find it harder to produce the quality outputs to compete effectively.

Finally, rapid technological change increases innovation and shortens lead times. Companies shorten development time and cut expenses by getting more from other vendors and involving them in designing the product or service. For example, General Electric's jet engine division used 16 design teams on aspects of its new commercial engine. Each had members from purchasing so vendors could be part of the design process. GE expects this involvement to lower product development costs by 20 per cent.

The service delivery system

As noted before, service delivery differs from manufacturing in many ways. Services differ as well. A service delivery system aims to maximise customer benefits relative to service provision costs. We first consider service differences by the matrix of service characteristics. We then see how organisations manage customer contact for effective and efficient service (Fitzsimmons & Fitzsimmons 1994; Schneider & Bowen 1995; Hall 2003c).

Matrix of service characteristics

The matrix of service characteristics puts services in four groups based on service complexity and degree of needed customisation (see Fig. 15s2.6). Complexity is based on the level of knowledge needed and skill or capital investment (Dilworth 1993). The customer can perform services shown on the matrix's right side, but needs practice and time. Consumers purchase these to save time and money. Services on the left need more knowledge or equipment than available to the average consumer. Customisation refers to the degree to which a service is tailored to specific customer needs. Services shown in the matrix's top half need much customisation, while those in the bottom are quite standardised.

Services in all quadrants have customer contact, so businesses in all quadrants need workers with good skills for customer interaction. For services in quadrants II and IV, businesses can train workers to needed service levels, but those in quadrant II must be flexible in tailoring services to customers. Services in quadrant I need professionally trained workers. High-level facility and equipment investments are needed for services in quadrant III. Costs of special worker training in this quadrant are often high, but economies of scale help keep individual consumer cost low. For success, quadrant III firms must have a range of attractive services for large customer numbers.

Managing customer contact

Experts say degree of service efficiency is linked to customer contact level. The more contact, the more likely are unusual requests, customer instruction changes, customer desire to chat, and other behaviours cutting service delivery efficiency. By their scope, some services, such as mail service or mail-order catalogue shopping, need lower customer contact levels. Others, such as restaurants and hotels, need moderate levels. Still others, such as doctor's care or counselling, generally need high-level customer contact.

FIGURE 15S2.6 Matrix of service characteristics (adapted from Dilworth 1993, p. 371)

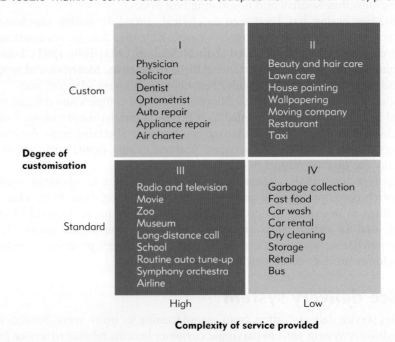

A common way to aid service delivery efficiency is to avoid customer contact with operation parts that do not need customer interaction. In hotels, for example, some functions, such as check-in, bell captain and cashier, demand heavy customer contact and efforts to set a friendly, responsive atmosphere. These are front office functions. Others, such as cleaning rooms, occur without guests as far as possible. These are back office operations. Some operations with front and back offices are shown in Table 15s2.3. Besides limiting customer contact, another aspect of back office operations is that they can be put in inexpensive areas and centralised to achieve economies of scale.

TABLE 15S2.3 EXAMPLES OF SERVICE OPERATIONS WITH FRONT AND BACK OFFICES

Operation	Front office	Back office
Bank	Tellers, customer service	Posting clerks, encoders officers
Stock broker office	Brokers	Transaction clerks, data entry operators
Restaurant	Waiting staff	Chefs, cooks, dishwashers
Library	Reference desk	Purchasing, reshelving
Garage	Reception	Mechanics
Laundry	Pickup counter	Pressers, folders

Source: Reprinted from Dilworth (1993).

DESIGNING AND UTILISING FACILITIES

Facilities are closely tied to capacity planning. **Facilities** are land, buildings, equipment and other physical inputs which determine capacity, take time to change, and need major capital input. Facilities issues for managers include expansion and contraction decisions, facilities location and layout.

facilities

Land, buildings, equipment and other major physical inputs that substantially determine productivity capacity, require time to alter, and involve significant capital investments

Expansion and contraction decisions

Decisions on expanding or contracting facilities relate to long-range capacity planning. Facility decision processes involve four steps (Buffa 1983). First, managers use forecasts of future demand for products or services. As it may take two years or more to build and commission facilities, forecasts must extend beyond this, raising uncertainty.

Second, managers compare capacity and future demand. Current capacity is the maximum possible current output. By comparing this with future demand, managers can see if it is sufficient, inadequate or excessive.

Third, when capacity is insufficient or in excess, managers generate and evaluate alternatives. In many cases, options for facility change are wide. In others, alternatives may be hard to develop. These typically involve location issues, which we discuss below.

Fourth, managers consider risks and decide on a plan, including capacity expansion or contraction, if any. Decisions about facilities are usually high risk as investment in facilities raises fixed costs even if expected demand does not emerge. On the other hand, having insufficient capacity may let competitors attract your customers (Ingrassia & Stertz 1988; Taylor 1992).

Facilities location

Plant, warehouse and service facility location is important to facility decisions. In fact, most decisions on extra facilities are linked to location issues. Most location problems fall in one of four categories: single facility, multiple factories and warehouses, competitive retail outlets and emergency services. Each has different decision criteria for location.

A single-facility location involves a facility that does not need to interact with any others of the organisation. A single factory or warehouse or a single retail shop fits this category. Location decisions for a single facility involve many criteria, such as labour costs, labour supply, raw materials, transportation availability, services and other relevant issues.

Multiple factory and warehouse locations usually mean costs of product distribution are critical. For complex problems with multiple facilities, operations research methods help find locations minimising distribution costs (Ridnitsky 1982; 1987). The use of just-in-time inventory methods also means manufacturing organisations consider sites close to major customers.

Locating competitive retail outlets means the possible revenue obtainable from various locations must be considered. For example, locating a bank, shopping centre, or cinema in relation to both customers and competitors bears on a facility's revenue. Some computer programs use census and other data to aid retailers, such as Woolworths, choose retail outlet locations (Dawson 1988; Dilworth 1993; Hall 2003c).

Emergency services are often located based on response times. For example, police and fire stations must be located to give an acceptable level of service, including short response times for emergencies.

Facilities layout

Another facility aspect is layout, or the processing components (departments, workstations and equipment) placed in the production configuration. There are three main facility layouts: process, product and fixed position (Adam & Ebert 1992; Buffa 1983).

Process layout

process layout

Production configuration in which processing components are grouped according to type of function performed

A **process layout** is a configuration where processing elements are grouped by function. The product or client being served moves between functions depending on specific needs. As a result, function demand is intermittent, as some products or clients may not need a given function. When demand is intermittent, functions can be idle sometimes and overloaded other times. A process layout is best when several products and services are produced or when product or service variations need several functions. See Figure 15s2.7 for process layout examples for a product (machine shop) and a service (medical clinic).

Product layout

product layout

Production configuration in which processing components are arranged in a specialised line along which the product or client passes during the production process

A **product layout** is a configuration where processing elements are put in a specialised line along which the product or client passes during production. With this arrangement, the product or service is produced through a standardised production sequence set specifically to the product or service's characteristics. Product layout examples for a product (a separate assembly line for each of three products) and a service (a driver's licence centre set up for one service) are shown in Figure 15s2.8. Other product layout examples are automatic car washes and cafeteria lines.

Product layouts are used producing a standard large volume product or service. Each needs the same or a similar process, and limited variations.

Fixed-position layout

fixed-position layout

Production configuration in which the product or client remains in one location and tools, equipment and expertise are brought to it, as necessary, to complete the productive process

A **fixed-position layout** is a configuration where the product or client stays in one spot and tools, equipment and expertise are brought to it. This is used where it is not feasible to move the product—due to size, shape or other characteristics—or where it is sensible to take the service to a client. For example, a fixed-position layout is often used building ships, locomotives and aircraft. It can be used for services, such as heating repair (where equipment, supplies and repair expertise are brought to the building) or a mobile CAT scanner (where the unit is taken to different hospitals due to economics). Having facilities is critical to the operations management aspect of process technology.

FIGURE 15S2.7 Process layouts for (top) a machine shop and (bottom) a medical clinic (reprinted from Buffa 1983, p. 32)

PROMOTING INNOVATION: PROCESS TECHNOLOGY

Process technology transforms inputs into goods and services. It includes tools, methods, procedures, equipment and production steps (Schroeder 1993). Increasingly process technology is important for competitive success. One reason is interest in re-engineering, which aims to develop innovative transformations. Another is growing use of sophisticated technology producing goods and services due to computer software, computer-controlled machines, and robot advances. In this section, we explore re-engineering, computer-integrated manufacturing innovations, and use of advanced technology in service organisations.

Re-engineering

Organisations have used re-engineering for advantage in operations and other areas. **Re-engineering** (also called business process redesign or BPR) is analysis and radical business process redesign to achieve breakthroughs from critical performance criteria, such as cost, quality, service and speed (Dixon, Arnold, Heineke, Kim & Mulligan 1994; Teng, Grover & Fiedler 1994). Originally re-engineering relied on information technology for radical change.

re-engineering

Thorough analysis and radical redesign of existing business processes to achieve breakthrough improvements by focusing on critical performance criteria, such as cost, quality, service and speed

FIGURE 15S2.8 Product layouts for (top) a three-product plant and (bottom) a driver's licence processing centre (reprinted from Buffa 1983, p. 33)

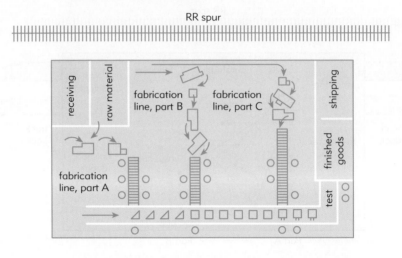

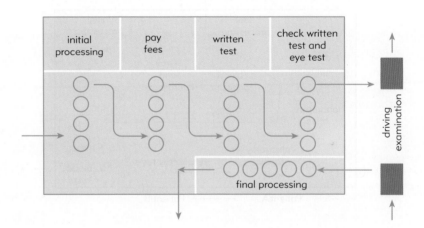

While information technology is influential, a study of 23 re-engineering projects saw major goal change as a key driving force for re-engineering efforts, such as new cost emphasis, quality or cycle-time reduction. Crucially senior management sets goals, and supports re-engineering efforts. Re-engineering efforts also involve cross-functional teams working together to recommend and establish newly designed processes (Dixon et al. 1994; Connors 1996).

Computer-integrated manufacturing

computer-integrated manufacturing (CIM)

Computerised integration of all major functions associated with production of a product

Computer-integrated manufacturing (CIM) is integration by computer of all major production functions. These include product design and engineering, machine instruction, materials handling, inventory control and process direction. Operations using CIM are called 'factories of the future' as they use new technology creating world-class facilities. CIM systems also use sophisticated materials-requirements planning (MRP) systems. They rely on other computerised systems too, such as computer-aided design and manufacturing, as well as flexible manufacturing systems.

Computer-aided design

computer-aided design (CAD)

System using computers to geometrically prepare, review and evaluate product designs

Computer-aided design (CAD) uses computers to prepare, review and evaluate product designs. With CAD, engineers and designers can easily evaluate and alter initial designs. The system takes less time and expense than conventional methods such as physical mock-ups. As design is in an electronic data base, it can be accessed for more work and tests later. CAD systems also let designers test stress tolerance and reliability factors by computer.

Computer-aided manufacturing

Computer-aided manufacturing (CAM) uses computers to design and control production processes. To put products in production, CAM systems access computer-stored information on designs developed by CAD. With CAM, machine set-ups can be changed by computer, as well as materials and work in progress from one machine to another. For simple parts, the process from transmission of CAD materials to manufacture can take half an hour (Bylinsky 1996).

Flexible manufacturing systems

Computer-integrated manufacturing involves another concept, flexible manufacturing systems. **Flexible manufacturing systems (FMS)** use computers for control so many types of parts or product configurations can come from the same production line. Flexible manufacturing uses **group technology**, or classification of parts into families (groups of parts or products similar in manufacture) so members of the same family can be made on the same line. Grouping products allows an FMS to be programmed quickly to set up machines for both very small and large quantities of parts in the same production process (Williams 1994). This flexibility makes it cost-effective to manufacture lots as small as one, and increases manufacturer responsiveness (Nemetz & Fry 1988; Avishai 1989; *PR Newswire* 1995).

Service applications

Advanced technology also gives opportunities for innovation in service industries, though the potential is only just being tapped (Heskett 1986; Hall 2003c).

Super Valu, a grocery wholesaler serving independent supermarkets, has a program called SLASH (Site Location Analysis Strategy Heuristic) to help customers choose good store locations. The program has a CAD system enabling architects to assess over 100 store plans on a screen (Fierman 1990; Hwang 1992; Hirsch 1996). Using advanced technology in service firms requires careful identification of areas where technology can influence services offered and productivity.

IMPROVING PRODUCTIVITY

At 12 noon in Appleton, Wisconsin, all 500-members of staff of the Aid Association for Lutherans (AAL), a fraternal society operating as a large insurance business, piled their belongings on chairs and rolled them to other areas of headquarters. Corridors were jammed as 'organised chaos' reorganised operations. In two hours, the move changed a functionally organised bureaucracy into self-managing teams (see Chapter 14) with fewer supervisor layers. Under the new set up, all policies related to one customer were handled by one team, instead of routing through different departments. Within a year, productivity rose 20 per cent— significant change, particularly for a service company (Hoerr 1988).

These results are only an example of what can be done when productivity improvements are given high priority. Within organisations, productivity improvement—that is, generating more outputs from the same or fewer inputs—relies on a five-step process:

1. *Establish a base point to assess future improvements against.* Managers use a base point such as the number of claims processed daily, dollar income per square metre of selling space, amount produced per day, percentage of output passing inspection, percentage of repaired items returned for more repairs, or customers served per hour. It is important to choose measures focused on important productivity aspects for the organisation or work unit (Naj 1993; Dumaine 1994). The continuous improvement principle of total quality management (see Chapter 15) also can help encourage productivity improvement.

computer-aided manufacturing (CAM)

System using computers to design and control production processes

flexible manufacturing system (FMS)

Manufacturing system using computers to control machines and the production process automatically so different types of parts or product configurations can be handled on the same production line

group technology

Classification of parts into families (groups of parts or products with similarities in how they are manufactured) so members of the same family can be manufactured on the same production line

2. *Set goals to establish desired productivity level.* Many studies in a range of jobs and industries support goal setting's usefulness as a way to raise productivity levels.

3. *Review methods for increasing productivity.* Managers have options to increase productivity. Useful methods include better employee selection techniques, matching people to jobs suited to their qualifications, training staff in job-related skills, redesigning jobs to give workers greater control over their own productivity, giving productivity-linked financial incentives, and using feedback and performance appraisals to let workers know their progress (Guzzo 1988; Ilgen & Klein 1988). Other productivity improvement approaches involve operations management techniques discussed before.

   Managers may overemphasise cutting current process costs, seeing it as best to increase productivity, and not adopt new process technologies giving significant productivity and competitiveness advances (Skinner 1986). Often, rethinking the work process, as suggested by re-engineering, can give breakthroughs.

4. *Select a method and implement.* Managers should choose the method with the best chance of success (Gourlay 1994). Implementation will involve considering how to achieve change (see Chapter 10).

5. *Measure results and modify as necessary.* Further modifications are needed only if productivity does not improve as planned. Met goals, of course, lead to new ones, as productivity increases are a continuing challenge for successful companies (Hammer & Champy 1993).

   The productivity challenge can be met by judicious information technology use, the subject of the next supplement.

SUPPLEMENT 3 TO CHAPTER 15

MANAGEMENT INFORMATION SYSTEMS

COMPUTER-BASED INFORMATION SYSTEMS: AN OVERVIEW

Information technology is causing major changes in how organisations handle and use information. For one, personal computer numbers have increased exponentially. This means managers have available more, better information. To use these opportunities, managers must understand computer-based information systems and their characteristics.

The nature of information systems

Despite the sophistication of information systems, their basic concepts are straightforward. To understand them, it helps to differentiate between data and information, as well as to use a systems view to examine the nature of information processing.

Data versus information

Although 'data' and 'information' are often interchanged, the terms can be distinguished. **Data** are unanalysed facts and figures. For example, when you buy a litre of milk at a supermarket, the cash register linked to a central computer records a litre of milk as sold. However, the data has little direct value.

data

Unanalysed facts and figures

To be useful, the data must become **information**, data analysed or processed into a useful form. For instance, the data on the milk purchase may be processed with other data to produce current store milk inventory figures. This is useful to those in charge of purchasing, delivery and stocking. The data may be processed to develop figures on store sales—broken down by shift for the store manager, day for the district manager, and week for upper management. Thus the milk-purchase data is an analysed element in these and other reports.

information

Data which have been analysed or processed into a meaningful form for decision makers

The difference between data and information is important to managers (Carlyle 1988). To be useful, information must be relevant to their decisions, accurate, timely or available as needed, complete or dealing with areas needing a decision, and concise or giving summary information to the decision maker (Cremillion & Pyburn 1988). With computers, it is easy to generate reports that do not meet managers' needs and harm productivity.

Information processing: A systems view

To get useful information, companies develop information systems. An information system is similar to the systems approach in understanding organisations (see Chapter 2). Information systems involve inputs, transformations and outputs. The elements of an information-processing system are shown in Figure 15s3.1.

In an information system, data collected from the organisation or environment are inputs. The data is transformed, or processed. Processing uses data manipulation and analysis (classifying, sorting, calculating and summarising) to transform data into information. Information-processing systems then use data storage for later retrieval. Outputs are reports, documents and other information sources that decision makers need. Feedback ensures appropriate output that serves intended purposes. Such safeguards can check the system to verify the accuracy (as much as possible) of data and processing, and the usefulness of outputs to users.

FIGURE 15S3.1 Basic components of an information system

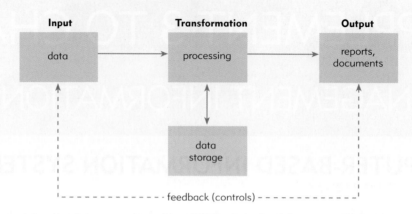

Given this, an **information system** is a set of procedures set up to collect (or retrieve), process, store and disseminate information to support planning, decision making, coordination and control (Laudon & Laudon 1994). Information systems need not be computerised. For example, one could use a hand-made spreadsheet not a computerised one such as Microsoft's Excel (although it is more difficult without the computer). However, we are focusing on **computer-based information systems (CBISs)**. Thus when we discuss information systems, we mean those using computer technology.

Computer-based information system technology

Computer-based information system technology falls into three categories: hardware, software and telecommunications technology (see Fig. 15s3.2).

Hardware

Computer hardware is the equipment used to input, process and output data in a computer-based information system. This includes input devices (keyboards and optical scanners), the computer's central processing unit (main memory and computer-processing section), storage devices (magnetic tape and optical disks), output devices (printers and on-line display terminals), and media connecting these devices.

Electronic information processing used to use mainframe computers in a central data-processing department. Then minicomputers, microcomputers and workstations reduced cost and increased capacity, widening information-processing options. On average, for the past two decades computer processing capacity has doubled, and production cost halved every 18 months or so (Jones et al. 2000). Microcomputers are now so powerful they can be used in organisational networks, linked to others, to telecommunication devices or larger computers. Supercomputers, with their vast speed, have allowed solving of problems needing complex and time-consuming calculations, such as weather prediction. Overall, the trend to more computer hardware power at less expense is eliminating differences between computers.

Software

Computer software is programs and documentation controlling and coordinating a system's hardware elements. Most computers can perform many tasks, such as calculating a person's appropriate pay, tracking a customer's fees or assessing inventory levels. The software gives instructions enabling the computer to perform tasks.

There are many software packages. Among them are word processing packages (e.g. WordPerfect and Word) and spreadsheets (e.g. Excel and Quattro Pro). There are also database packages (e.g. Access and Paradox). A **database** is an efficiently organised set of data in a

---

information system

Set of procedures designed to collect (or retrieve), process, store and disseminate information to support planning, decision making, coordination and control

computer-based information systems (CBISs)

Information systems involving computer technology use

computer hardware

Physical computer equipment, including the computer itself and related devices

computer software

Set of programs, documents, procedures and routines associated with the operation of a computer system which makes hardware capable of various activities

database

Set of data organised efficiently in a central location to serve a number of information-system applications

FIGURE 15S3.2 Basic components of a computer-based information system

central location serving several information system applications. A **database management system** is software letting an organisation build, manage and access stored data (Laudon & Laudon 1994; Sanders 1987). Organisations increasingly use databases for competitive advantage. For example, major catalogue companies, such as Ezibuy, depend heavily on a customer information database (names, addresses, ordering history, current order status, etc.). The database management system helping build the database also gives access to the data for producing mailing labels for catalogues and marketing promotions, processing telephone and mail orders, printing address labels and invoices, various management reports, and quick, efficient customer service.

In addition to commercial packages, unique application software can be developed by the organisation's own specialists. Although custom software is expensive, it can be developed to suit specific needs and may be hard for competitors to copy. Later we revisit this software, and the strategic implications of information systems.

Telecommunications technology

Telecommunications is electronic communication of information over distance. This technology is devices and software connecting computer hardware and enabling transfer of information between locations (Laudon & Laudon 1994; Kinicki & Williams 2003). Telecommunications allows information sharing within and across organisations. For example, Visa International's information network, called VisaInfo, links the credit-card giant's 2500 employees. The network has large amounts of need-to-know information, such as a list of Visa's 19 000 member banks. Visa links member banks with a network of their own. The goal is to reduce the two million pages sent to Visa daily (Thyfault 1996; Gordon & Gordon 1996).

database management system

Software which allows an organisation to build, manage and provide access to its stored data

telecommunications

Electronic communication of information over a distance

Current hardware, software, and telecommunications technology allow information technology to be used in many ways in organisations. This means **information architecture** must be developed: a plan for investing in and organising information technology for goal attainment (Gordon & Gordon 1996; Green 2003a). Designing the information architecture determines how centralised or spread across various locations data and processing will be. It also decides whether microcomputers and workstations will be controlled by a mainframe or minicomputer or whether minicomputers and workstations will be used.

Information needs by organisational level

In designing information systems to enhance information use, it must be realised that information needs differ by level. This is unsurprising, as managerial planning and organising responsibilities differ by level (Gordon & Gordon 1996). Consider the four general levels in Figure 15s3.3. Strategic-level systems serve senior managers' need for long-range planning and control. Tactical-level systems help middle managers plan, make decisions and monitor. Knowledge-level systems assist technical specialists or knowledge workers create and integrate new organisation knowledge. **Knowledge workers** are specialists, engineers, architects or scientists, who design products, services or processes and create new organisation knowledge. They are highly educated professionals. They are supported by **data workers**, who process and disseminate documents, messages and other information. They include secretaries, filing clerks or managers processing and distributing information others create. Operational-level systems support operating personnel and monitor their activities.

Information needs by specialised area

Information needs also generally vary by area, such as manufacturing, finance and human resources. When organisations began to use computers extensively, computer specialists saw a future where the information needs of all areas would be joined in one large system. The realisation has grown that a single system cannot meet all the organisation's information needs,

information architecture

Long-range plan for investing in and organising information technology to facilitate reaching organisational goals

knowledge workers

Specialists, such as engineers, architects or scientists, who design products, services or processes and create new knowledge for organisations

data workers

Individuals who mainly process and disseminate documents, messages and related information

FIGURE 15S3.3 Examples of information systems for various functional areas by management level (reprinted from Laudon & Laudon 1994, p. 36)

	sales	manufacturing	accounting	finance	human resources
Top management	long-term sales trend forecasting	long-term operating plan	long-term budget forecasting	long-term profit planning	human resource planning
	Strategic level systems				
Middle management	sales region analysis	production scheduling	annual budgeting	pricing/ profitability analysis	selection/ retention analysis
	Tactical level systems				
First-line management and operatives	order tracking/ processing	material movement control	accounts payable/ receivable	cash management	employee record keeping
	Operational level systems				
	sales	**manufacturing**	**accounting**	**finance**	**human resources**

especially large ones such as Telstra or General Motors Holden. As well, the information requirements of various organisational parts are dynamic and change rapidly, making one system less likely.

A more likely view is that information system efforts will be more effective if they work to develop systems for needs of specific areas, such as manufacturing and accounting (see Fig. 15s3.3). Data used and information produced are increasingly shared by other systems.

To help share such information, organisations set up **local-area networks (LANs)**, interconnections (usually by cable) to allow communications between computers within a building or located close by. Many firms are setting up **wide-area networks (WANs)**, to allow long-distance communications between computers (Barnes & Greller 1994). Recently, many companies have been developing intranets. This is an internal organisational network using internet technologies so employees can browse and share information. An intranet is a private form of the internet's world wide web and can be accessed only by organisation members or those with permission to use the information, such as customers and suppliers.

TYPES OF INFORMATION SYSTEMS

To serve the needs of all organisation levels, there are six types of information systems: processing transactions, office automation, knowledge work, management information, decision support and executive support (Laudon & Laudon 1994). These system types, the organisational level each is geared to, and examples of each system type for different functional areas are shown in Figure 15s3.4. Of course, these are often used at several levels, though developed for certain types of need.

Transaction-processing systems

A **transaction-processing system (TPS)** is a computer-based information system that executes and records day-to-day transactions in a business. For example, each time you use a credit card at a service station, enrol at college or university, renew a driver's licence, drive on a toll road,

local-area networks (LANs)

Interconnections (usually cable) allowing communications between computers within a single building or in close proximity

wide-area networks (WANs)

Networks providing communications between computers over long distances, usually through telecommunications companies

transaction-processing system (TPS)

Computer-based information system that executes and records routine day-to-day transactions needed to conduct an organisation's business

FIGURE 15S3.4 Types of information systems by level and organisation members served (adapted from Laudon & Laudon 1994, p. 13)

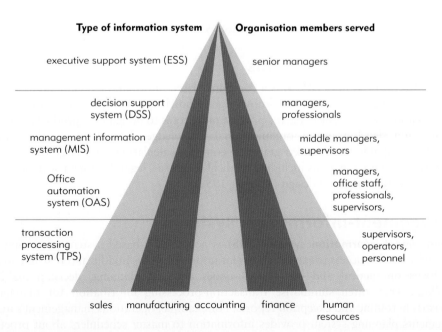

or draw money from a bank account, a computerised transaction-processing system operates. Transaction systems are used for highly structured and repetitive situations when tasks and criteria are clear. The structured nature of the situation makes it possible to write detailed and unequivocal instructions enabling the computer to handle and record transactions properly. A TPS gives help to an organisation's operational level. TPSs produce data used by other types of organisational computer-based information systems.

Office-automation systems

office-automation system (OAS)

Computer-based information system aimed at facilitating communication and increasing the productivity of managers and office workers through document and message processing

An **office-automation system (OAS)** is a computer-based information system helping communication and increasing data workers' productivity by processing documents and messages. Best-known of OASs are word-processing systems, for quick and easy text creation, editing and printing. Increasingly popular OASs are electronic mail (email) systems, which allow high-speed written message exchange through computer text processing and communications networks (see Chapter 13). Other important OASs include the following (McLeod 1986; Laudon & Laudon 1994; Hof 2003a):

Voice mail: a method of recording a telephone message then storing it in secondary computer storage for later retrieval by the receiver

Electronic calendaring: a method of maintaining an electronic appointments schedule

Teleconferencing: simultaneous communication between a group of individuals by telephone or computer using specially designed software

Document retrieval: use of one or more electronic devices to store documents as digitised images or other medium and facilitate the later location and copying of stored images

Facsimile (FAX) transmission: means of sending documents over telephone linkages arriving in printed form at the receiving location

Groupware: software designed to support collaborative efforts among group members, such as scheduling and holding meetings, collaborating on projects and sharing documents

Graphics: means of creating charts and diagrams

Knowledge-work systems

knowledge-work system (KWS)

Computer-based information system that assists knowledge workers in creation of new knowledge for the organisation

A **knowledge-work system (KWS)** is a computer-based information system aiding knowledge workers create new organisational knowledge. Knowledge workers use office automation systems, but knowledge-work systems provide more tools to design new products, services and processes and develop useful organisational knowledge. Knowledge workers may use workstations capable of advanced graphics, complex calculations and large database access. Workstations are used in areas including medical diagnosis, legal document searches, scientific analysis and computer-aided design (Magnet 1992).

Management-information systems

management-information system (MIS)

Computer-based information system that produces routine reports and often allows on-line access to current and historical information needed by managers mainly at the middle and first-line levels

A **management-information system (MIS)** is a computer-based system producing routine reports with on-line access to past and present information for middle and first-line managers. MISs focus on tactical and operational issues and aid planning, decision making and controlling. They often summarise transaction-processing information for managers and supervisors in routine and exception reports. For example, operations management's materials-requirements planning system provides information to master schedulers about procurement problems impacting the schedule. MISs also give capacity planners information on short- or long-run capacity changes needed. As well, they produce first- and middle-level managers' reports on costs, quality and supplier activities.

The term 'management-information systems' broadly describes computer-related systems for management, including the six types of systems discussed here. The term identifies the management field focused on designing and applying computer-based information systems for management. Here we use 'computer-based information systems' or 'information systems' to denote all systems for various management levels. We keep the term 'management-information systems' for the narrower meaning above.

Decision-support systems

A **decision-support system (DSS)** is a computer-based information system supporting managerial decision making in unstructured situations. These systems do not give 'answers' or show optimal decisions for managers. Rather, they work to improve decision-making by providing tools to analyse situations clearly. In essence they assist managers make better non-programmed decisions (Turban 1988).

A DSS is different to an MIS. Compared to an MIS, a typical DSS gives more advanced analysis and greater access to models managers can use to see a situation better. Also a DSS often uses information from external as well as internal sources, largely the domain of the TPS and MIS. Finally, a DSS is more interactive than an MIS. It lets managers communicate directly (often back and forth) with computer programs controlling the system, and see results of various analyses quickly.

One specialised DSS type is a **group decision-support system (GDSS)**, a computer-based information system allowing decision makers to operate together on poorly structured problems. A GDSS focuses on problem solving or decision making, while groupware is more focused on helping communication.

Another specialised DSS type is the **expert system** (Turban & Watkins 1986; Finlay 1994). These are computer-based systems using an expert's knowledge to solve specialised problems. In fact, in such systems, designers work with experts to find information and heuristics, or decision rules, they use with particular problem types (Simon 1987).

Expert systems are a product of **artificial intelligence**, an information technology field aiming to develop computers with human-like capabilities, such as seeing, hearing and thinking (Leonard-Barton & Sviokla 1988). Artificial intelligence is an inquiry area, not an end-product such as an expert system. One development is fuzzy logic, a rule-based approach involving pattern recognition and inferences from incomplete or partially accurate data. For example, Ford Motor Co. is developing a fuzzy logic system for parking a simulated truck, based on a few rules such as 'IF the truck is near jack-knifing, THEN reduce the steering angle'. Computers still cannot conceptualise or reason (Laudon & Laudon 1994; Hof 2003b). Nevertheless, artificial intelligence efforts have been the basis for other developments, such as expert systems.

Executive-support systems

The **executive-support system (ESS)** is a computer-based information system supporting top-level decision making and effective functioning. These are sometimes called executive-information systems (EISs) (Watson, Rainer & Koh 1991).

Unlike more narrowly focused DSS, an ESS has more general computing capabilities, telecommunications, and display options (such as graphs and charts) applicable to different problems. An ESS uses less analytical models than a DSS, gives information from several sources and accepts interactive general queries (Gelfond 1988; Boone 1991).

ESSs are systems tailor-made for executives' needs, often geared to managers' individual work habits. Executive support system characteristics, as well as other major system types, are summarised in Table 15s3.1.

---

decision-support system (DSS)

Computer-based information system supporting the process of managerial decision making in poorly structured situations

group decision-support system (GDSS)

Computer-based information system supporting decision makers working together to solve structured problems

expert systems

Computer-based systems that apply an expert's substantial knowledge to help solve specialised problems

artificial intelligence

Field of information technology aimed at developing computers with human-like capabilities, such as seeing, hearing and thinking

executive-support system (ESS)

Computer-based information system supporting decision making and effective functioning at the top levels of an organisation

TABLE 15S3.1 CHARACTERISTICS OF INFORMATION-PROCESSING SYSTEMS

Type of system	Information inputs	Processing	Information outputs	Users
ESS	Aggregate data; external, internal	Graphics; simulations; interactive	Projections; responses to queries	Senior managers
DSS	Low-volume data; analytic models	Interactive; simulations; analysis	Special reports; decision analyses; responses to queries	Professionals; staff managers
MIS	Summary transaction data; high-volume data; simple models	Routine reports; simple models; low-level analysis	Summary and exception reports	Middle managers
KWS	Design specifications; knowledge base	Modelling; simulations	Models; graphics	Professionals; technical staff
OAS	Documents; schedules	Document management; scheduling; communication	Documents; schedules; mail	Clerical workers
TPS	Transactions; events	Sorting; listing; merging; updating	Detailed reports; lists; summaries	Operations personnel; supervisors

Source: Reprinted from Laudon & Laudon (1994).

PROMOTING INNOVATION: STRATEGIC IMPLICATIONS OF INFORMATION SYSTEMS

During the 1980s, strategic planning experts saw information technology's innovative possibilities and strategy implications (Benjamin, Rockart, Morton & Wyman 1984; Porter & Millar 1985). Before, top managers saw computers as a way to improve internal processes and enhance efficiency. Today information technology is seen as valuable to gain competitive advantage. Many large firms have appointed a chief information officer (CIO), a high-level executive to recommend and oversee information system implementation to enhance an organisation's competitive position.

In considering how information technology can help develop strategies for competitive advantage, managers may use the strategic options matrix in Figure 15s3.5. The matrix is related to Porter's competitive strategy work (see Chapter 6). The matrix uses two dimensions: competitive strategies and strategic linkages (see Fig. 15s3.5) (Neumann 1994; Miller & Dess 1996; Wiseman & MacMillan 1984; Porter 1980).

Competitive strategies

According to the matrix, organisations can combine information technology with three major competitive strategies for competitive advantage. The strategies are differentiation, cost leadership and quick response (see Chapter 6) (Hamm 2003).

FIGURE 15S3.5 Matrix of strategic options related to information technology

Differentiation
The goal of differentiation is either to increase an organisation's differentiation advantages in relation to others (suppliers, customers or competitors) or to decrease differentiation advantages of others relative to the organisation.

Cost leadership
A cost approach works to reduce an organisation's costs in relation to others' costs (suppliers, customers or competitors), helping suppliers or customers reduce their costs so they want to do business with the company, or increasing competitors' costs (Wessel 1987; *The Wall Street Journal* 1987; Brown 1988).

Quick response
The quick response approach focuses on recognising, adapting to, and meeting changing customer needs more rapidly than competitors (Miller & Dess 1996). This is associated with organisation speed in improvement of products or services, or customer responsiveness (Bartholomew 1996).

Strategic linkages
The matrix (see Fig. 15s3.5) suggests three areas where strategic information systems linkages can help competitive advantage. The linkage targets are suppliers, customers and alliances.

Supplier linkages
Suppliers include providers of raw materials, capital, labour or services (Wiseman & MacMillan 1984).

Customer linkages
Customers include organisations that retail, wholesale, warehouse, distribute or use a company's products or services (Datamation 1988).

Alliance linkages
Strategic alliances occur where independent organisations form a cooperative partnership to gain mutual strategic advantage (see Chapter 3) (Miller & Dess 1996; Yoshino & Ranga 1995). Firms can be in the same industry or in different industries. In the context of information technology, organisations with strategic alliances exchange information electronically, trade expertise in information technology or share resources (Santosus 1996; Pastore 1996).

Sustaining competitive advantage

Sustainability is an issue in pursuit of competitive advantage by information technology (Neumann 1994). A competitive advantage is sustainable if it can be maintained long-term despite competitor action or industry factors. In reality, few competitive advantages can be sustained for long without further improvements. One survey suggests strategic information systems' competitive advantage is about 12 to 18 months (Sullivan-Trainor & Maglitta 1990). Potential information technology advantage comes from three factors. The first is a pre-emptive strike—that is, being first with a strategic information system. The second is enhancing the strategic information system in important ways. The third is using strategic information systems to complement and support other competitive advantages (Neumann 1994).

DEVELOPING COMPUTER-BASED INFORMATION SYSTEMS

Developing computer-based information systems can be hard and costly, especially if applications are large and complex. In fact, overrun time and cost is common. One study found only 9 per cent of software projects were on time and budget (Fabris 1996).

Furthermore, systems may give errors causing serious business problems (Port 1988). Due to the scope of such problems, and information technology's strategic value, managers must understand generally what the development of information systems needs.

The systems-development life cycle

**systems-development
life cycle**

Series of stages used in
the development of most
medium- and large-sized
information systems

New information-system development normally follows the **systems-development life cycle** (see Fig. 15s3.6). This is a series of stages used in developing most medium- and large-sized information systems. It is often more informally used in small-scale system development. Typically, development is the responsibility of a project team of managers, users, systems analysts, programmers and other technical personnel.

There are three stages in the life cycle: definition, physical design, and implementation and operation.

Stages in the systems-development life cycle

The *definition stage* aims to evaluate the idea proposed and define system parameters. This stage is significant as, by one estimate, mistakes and omissions not detected until later can cost between 10 and 100 times more to fix than if detected during this stage (Sanders 1987).

FIGURE 15S3.6 The systems-development life cycle

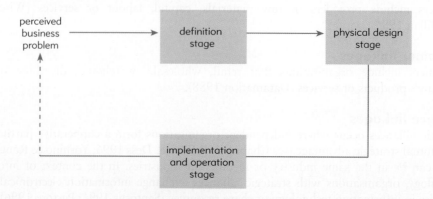

The *physical design stage* takes a project from concept to reality. The stage includes a detailed systems design, conducting necessary programming and debugging, and implementation planning.

The *implementation and operation stage* includes system implementation, effectiveness evaluation and effective operation maintenance. Implementing a typical medium-sized project takes about two years with an expected life span of five to eight years. Continuing maintenance will be needed and operating costs covered (Laudon & Laudon 1994).

Assessing the life-cycle approach

There are benefits to the life-cycle approach. It gives a set of stages and phases to guide major systems-development efforts. It focuses effort on early definition of needed functions and system outputs. Finally, it allows for potential user involvement, especially at the definition stage.

Unfortunately, the life-cycle approach has difficulties. One is that it is costly. Another is that intended users may have problems specifying all needed system functions and outputs early in the life cycle. Yet another is that the life-cycle approach may discourage changes in system definition once the stage is done. Finally, there may be a backlog of projects to enter the cycle.

Overall, the approach seems to be best with very large and/or complex projects or when applications are well structured so parameters can be well defined early in the project. Evidence suggests systems-development efforts that run into difficulty have not followed the life-cycle steps (Licker 1985; Tait & Vessey 1988).

Alternative means of systems development

Given the potential problems of information systems developed through the life cycle, and that a long time-frame is needed for design and implementation, other alternatives have emerged. Among those are applications software packages, prototyping, end-user development and outsourcing (Laudon & Laudon 1995; Gremillion & Pyburn 1988; Hamm 2003).

Applications software packages

Applications software packages are programs available from commercial sources. They are geared to handle specialised areas many organisations need. Many software packages are available for payroll, inventory control, work scheduling, accounts receivable and graphics. Commercial vendors risk the package development costs as they can profit by selling the programs. This means organisations can get commercial packages more cheaply than in-house, custom-developed software.

Commercial packages have disadvantages too. The main one is the generic nature of the packages, which means that they may not cope with unusual circumstances or procedures. However, if savings are great, it may be possible to change organisational practices to comply with the software package's parameters. Another disadvantage of using commercial packages is that it may make it easier for competitors to copy quickly. Finally, packages may have major errors or cause serious problems.

applications software packages

Software programs available for sale or lease from commercial sources

Prototyping

Prototyping is the construction of a rough, working model of all or parts of an information system for preliminary evaluation and further refinement. Unlike a traditional approach, which involves trying to specify all user needs in the early stages, this approach is based on giving a quick response to poorly defined user specifications. The prototype system then has several modifications and enhancements before meeting evolving user needs. Companies using prototyping report that it can cost 25 per cent less than the traditional approach, usable results are quickly produced, and systems are generally more accepted by users because they meet their needs (Gremillion & Pyburn 1988; Arthur 1992).

prototyping

Process of building a rough, working model of all or parts of a proposed information system for purposes of preliminary evaluation and further refinement

User-developed systems

user

Individual, other than an information system professional, engaged in the development and/or management of computer-based information systems

For information systems, a **user** is someone other than an information system professional, engaged in developing and/or managing computer-based information systems. (A user is an **end user**.) End-user computing, development and/or management by users, is an interesting trend (Benjamin 1982).

User-developed systems are created with little help from information-system professionals. The trend to **end-user computing** comes from several sources. First, the popularity of personal computers has meant users have basic computing experience. Second, availability of applications software packages and other user-friendly tools means those who are not computer professionals can tackle information-system development. Third, as many projects have been held up waiting to be developed by information-system departments, users have been forced to take issues into their own hands. Finally, end-users are best placed to identify innovative information system ideas for competitive advantage (Gerrity & Rockart 1986).

end user

Same as a user

However, end-user development may not always be best. Some systems may be too complex for non-professionals. Also systems that have been poorly designed may have undetected errors resulting in much damage. As well, the systems may link poorly to other organisational systems. Finally, if those developing systems do not document program workings, others may have problems when the key person leaves.

end-user computing

Development and/or management of information systems by users

Outsourcing

Outsourcing is using an outside vendor for a normal organisation function (see Chapter 15). For information systems, outsourcing is widespread in computer-centre operations, telecommunications networks, or applications development. For applications development, outsourcing provides specialised expertise, lower costs and flexibility (help can be obtained as needed rather than hiring permanent staff). A disadvantage is that competitive advantage is harder to gain when an external vendor develops the system. They can use the new expertise to develop similar systems for others, or offer them similar services. Thus, outsourcing systems development is best for systems where competitive advantage potential is low, which do not involve handling proprietary information, and do not lose control over systems crucial to company activities (Gordon & Gordon 1996).

Selecting a development approach

Three criteria help determine the best development approach (Gremillion & Pyburn 1988). The first is *commonality*, how likely there is a common need for the type of system in other firms. When this is high, commercial software packages should be considered rather than custom development. Outsourcing may also be possible. For example, organisations outsource payroll processing. The second criterion is *impact*, how much the system affects the firm, the number of people affected, the importance to day-to-day operations, or the potential for competitive advantage. When impact is greater, it is important to have in-house information system professionals involved in development. The third criterion is *structure*, how well the problem and probable solution are understood. When structure is low, prototyping is better, especially for a high impact system.

INFLUENCE OF INFORMATION TECHNOLOGY ON ORGANISATIONS

As computers become commonplace, information technology influences many company aspects. Areas include organisation structure, individual jobs, communication patterns and organisational risk (Davis & Olson 1985).

Organisation structure

As well as organising the information system function, CBISs are influencing the overall structures of organisations. Computers were believed to reduce the need for middle managers, cause top management to be more responsible for innovation and planning, and allow the recentralisation of decision making (Leavitt & Whisler 1958). Indeed, organisations are flattening through middle-management level cuts (Davidow & Malone 1992). This is because top-managers can use computers to get information needed. However, widespread computer use, which was not predicted, means that information is shared and decision making decentralised through horizontal information flows. In terms of organisation structure impact, computers widen managers' structural options. Decision making can be decentralised while control by higher-level managers grows as they keep up-to-date through computer networks (Applegate, Cash & Mills 1988; Malone & Davidow 1992; Hamel & Välikangas 2003).

Individual jobs

Computers influence individual jobs in several ways. Three significant effects are job-design changes, job-related stress and health consequences of computers, and work location options.

Nature of jobs

The impact of personal computers in the workplace has been hard to gauge. For clerical jobs, computers can lead either to very simple jobs requiring little skill, or to jobs needing lots of creativity and skill (Attewell & Rule 1984). For professionals, computers cut routine tasks and increase their ability to communicate with others and use decision-making tools developed for managers. For managers, computers give new aids for decision making, communication and control.

Stress and health consequences

Stress and health issues centre on computers' impact on lower-level white-collar jobs. One issue is the results of **electronic monitoring**, the practice of using computers to continually assess employee performance. For example, computers can monitor telephone and computer use. Critics argue this harms customer service and builds stress (Gelbspan 1987). One study found monitoring lowers the quality of customer service and the work environment. However, it also found that some workers internalised system standards, used data for progress feedback, and were unconcerned by monitoring. Computers may be more effective giving direct, regular feedback to employees, but providing feedback to supervisors less often (Grant, Higgins & Irving 1988).

Prolonged computer use has resulted in health-related problems. Repetitive strain injury (RSI), occurring when muscle groups repeat the same motions frequently, is common. One RSI type is carpal stress injury (CSI), affecting wrist muscles. Over 332 000 RSI-related cases are reported each year. Annual workers' compensation payments for RSI are over $2 billion. Proper posture, stretching often, and ergonomic office furniture help avoid these injuries (Adhikari 1996).

electronic monitoring

Practice of using computers to continually assess employee performance

Location of work

Advances in information technology provide work location options. One is **telecommuting**, working at home using computer technology for contact with the office. Telecommuting may not be satisfactory eventually as some social interaction with coworkers is needed, and there may be problems separating work and home roles. One study found that if people could choose between telecommuting or working in the office, 56 per cent prefer the office, 36 per cent prefer both home and office, and 7 per cent just home (Kotlowitz 1987).

Another option is the **logical office**, with portable computers allowing an office to be where the person is, not restricted to one location. Managers using laptops while travelling have to face problems such as security scrutiny at airports, flat batteries, and poor hotel connection options (but this is improving) (Bulkeley 1990).

telecommuting

Form of working at home made possible by using computer technology to remain in touch with the office

logical office

Concept that portable microcomputers allow an individual's office to be where the individual is, not restricted to a specific location

Communication patterns

Computer-related communications tools, such as email, teleconferencing, groupware and group decision support systems, have increased communication channels and methods (see also Chapter 13) (Barnes & Greller 1994). Information exchange flows within and between organisations have changed. Telecommunications technology means information exchange is easier locally and globally. The technology also allows electronic data interchange (EDI), direct exchange of transaction documents between two organisation's computers (Laudon & Laudon 1994; Green 2003b). EDI has allowed electronic partnerships between suppliers, producers, distributors and retailers.

Ultimately information technology will change organisations' hierarchical nature by building options for employee cooperation and collaboration at different levels (Harris & Foust 1987).

Organisational risk

Despite possible benefits, information technology has some organisation risks. The most significant are possible errors, physical calamities, theft, sabotage and security breaches, invasion of privacy and resistance to major systems.

Errors

With major software, testing for every possible error is impossible. Errors and problems will occur (Keller 1990).

Physical calamities

Physical damage by fire, flood, power failure, earthquake and other factors can disrupt company information flows (Keller 1990; Burgess 1988).

Theft

Theft using computers is over $5 billion per year in the United States alone. Computer theft is often internal. In one incident, employees wired $54 million from the Union Bank of Switzerland's London office to another bank with all codes needed. They were caught when the other bank's computer malfunctioned, and auditors identified the transaction. While a typical bank robber steals about $5000, electronic theft averages $500 000 per incident (Hafner 1988).

Sabotage and security breaches

Sabotage and security breaches are growing. Computer sabotage is deliberate disruption of computer-related activities and/or equipment, software, or data destruction. Computer security breaches include unauthorised entry to computers or computer networks, as well as accessing stored data.

hackers

Individuals who are knowledgeable about computers and who gain unauthorised entry to, and sometimes tamper with, computer networks and files of organisations with which they have no affiliation

computer virus

Small program, usually hidden inside another program, that replicates itself and surfaces at a set time to cause disruption and possibly destruction

Sabotage may be employee or hacker pranks. **Hackers** have a good knowledge of computers and may gain unauthorised entry to, and tamper with, computer networks and organisation files they have no affiliation with. In December 1987, a West German law student used an academic research network to access IBM's 145-country email network, planting an apparently innocuous Christmas tree picture and a holiday message. To clear the greeting, recipients were told to type 'Christmas'. However, they then triggered a program and the greeting was replicated and sent on in chain-letter fashion. Eventually, the system shut down (Burgess 1987; Hafner 1988). The tool in the prank was a **computer virus**, a small program, often hidden in another program, which replicates and surfaces at a set time to cause disruption and possibly destruction. After press reports on a virus called 'Michelangelo', programmed to destroy data on March 6 each year (the Italian Renaissance artist's birthday), many firms have installed programs to detect many virus types. By one estimate, over 7500 viruses are known, four times as many as in 1990, and new ones emerge often. Virus damage worldwide cost $12 billion in 1999 (www.infowar.com), from $996 million in 1995 (Stahl & Violino 1996). Inventive hackers are always trying to beat antivirus programs.

Data security can also be threatened. Crucial databases and software can be compromised. According to a survey of 1290 firms, one in five had actual or attempted computer break-ins. The total may be much higher as only half of the companies were confident attempts would be detected (Violino 1996).

As a result, many companies have increased computer security. They use more elaborate password systems, dial-back systems that check whether an incoming call comes from an authorised number, and encryption hardware that disguises data by coding it to make it hard for others to decipher.

Privacy issues

Widespread information technology use has caused some privacy problems. For one, data security issues described already threaten personal data privacy, including personnel, medical and credit records. For another, organisations can build databases with ease, gathering large amounts of individuals' data (Novack 1995; Green 2003b).

Related to this is the privacy of companies' email and voice mail communications. Courts support employers' right to monitor and retrieve employees' voice and email communications, under published policy. These policies must make it clear that voice, email and other systems (internet access) are company assets, are company property, and should not be seen as private. Policies like this are wise as in some cases company communication facilities have been used for hacking and sexual harassment. (Indeed, employees should note while email messages may be erased, facilities running email can hold copies for some time.) However, the major function of a policy is to guide use of communication facilities to avoid these problems (*1996 Executive File: Hot Employment Issues* 1996). Employers have complained that another area of misuse is employees spending time on computer games or the internet in non-business activities (Weiss 1996).

Resistance

Resources may be put into systems development that managers and subordinates will resist. People may fear senior managers will check and interfere with their work more with the new system. New information technology applications are vital to most organisations' future efficiency and effectiveness.

CHAPTER 16

MANAGING ORGANISATIONS THROUGH CHANGE AND CONFLICT

CHAPTER OUTLINE

Managing change
Diagnosing the need for change
The change cycle

Managing resistance to change
Why individuals resist change
Overcoming resistance to change

Managing conflict
Conflict between individuals and organisations

Causes of conflict
Benefits and losses from conflict
Reducing and resolving conflict
Managing intergroup conflict through resolution

The relationship between change and conflict
Types of intergroup conflict
Changing views on conflict
Stimulating conflict

LEARNING OBJECTIVES

After studying this chapter, you should be able to:

- Identify internal and external factors leading to a need for change.
- Indicate why employees resist change.
- Explain how to overcome resistance to change, including the use of force-field analysis.
- Identify the differences distinguishing conflict between an individual and an organisation from conflict between groups.
- Explain the causes of conflict and how to reduce, resolve and stimulate conflict.
- Explain benefits and losses which can be incurred as a result of organisational conflict.
- Discriminate between different styles of conflict management and describe circumstances where each may be appropriate.
- Explain the relationship between change and conflict.
- Explain how both functional and dysfunctional conflict impact on group behaviour.

STRIVING FOR EXCELLENCE

Nicole Feely, chief executive, St Vincent's Health, Melbourne

It is a long way from being chief of staff in the office of the Prime Minister, John Howard, to running a big Catholic hospital. It is an even longer journey from the tobacco giant Philip Morris to the hospital. But Nicole Feely, who has been chief executive officer of St Vincent's Health in Melbourne for nearly two years, does not think so. She says her past—lawyer, political adviser, a Sydney Olympics role and head of a key business lobby group—has equipped her for the job. 'What I'm finding in this job is that the skills I have picked up along the way are really coming to the fore', she says. 'The only difference lies in the complexity, the size, the multi-faceted nature of running a hospital with a budget of $350 million and a staff of nearly 5000. [At that level] there's no comparison with what I've done in the past. But so far as having the communication skills, understanding the financial-management issues and handling the politics—well, they're all things I bring to the table.'

Women, particularly, rarely get powerful positions without talent. Howard told her in Opposition she could have the chief of staff job in government if she performed. She got the job, despite strenuous—some might say vicious—lobbying inside the Liberal Party to derail her. But the networks remain crucial. And her legal and political careers provide the most telling evidence.

Before Feely went to the bar, she worked for the law firm Freehills (then Freehill Hollingdale & Page) in an industrial relations department used by employers, such as the mining giant Rio Tinto, to help eliminate or minimise union influence in their workplaces. In July 1992, she joined Howard as his press secretary when,

as shadow minister for industrial relations, he was arguing what were then radical proposals to deregulate the labour market.

It is her most recent appointment at St Vincent's Health that reveals the depth and strength of her networks. In her own deliberately chosen words, she was the candidate from left field. 'It was a hard interview process. I had no background in health, had just come from a tobacco company and was relatively young', Feely says. It is worth pondering those negatives. No experience in health—or working with medical staff. Just ask former Mayne Group chief executive Peter Smedley what a handicap that can be. To most in the health industry, the tobacco industry is the devil incarnate. (Feely says one senior person in oncology told her, 'We're happy to have you here but we'll never forgive you for Philip Morris'. He was joking, perhaps.)

Her sense of teamwork, of commitment, of loyalty to the institution, forces the conclusion that Feely has finally found her vocation. Her own words speak volumes. 'Some people talk about [St Vincent's] mission. Some talk about it in spiritual terms. Whatever it is, there is definitely a driving force here to fulfil the work of the Sisters of Charity. A really hard-nosed approach to costs is not at the expense of the work we do for the poor. There is the way we treat each other with respect, whether it be staff or patients. We talk about these values. We talk about how we do things. They're not just as an adjunct.'

Indeed, she insists every executive decision has to consider these values. Take, for example, the decision to buy an MRI (magnetic resonance imaging)

continued

machine. 'It went to board level', she says. 'They asked: 'What else is on the list? We understand we need some new mattresses. How does that fit into spending millions on a MRI?' These thought processes do happen. Senior medical staff were involved. So, too, were the sisters and the executive. Eventually we decided there were real benefits that would come from buying this machine. But it was not a decision taken lightly.'

The icing on the cake is a challenging and rewarding job. A 'landlocked' hospital, to use Feely's terminology, it faces rising costs, greater demand on its services (compounded by the Sisters of Charity's commitment to the poor) and the need to increase revenue. The State Government provides about 75 per cent of its budget. Perhaps more important, in terms of the hospital's historical mission, the average age of the nuns is 65. The order has a finite life, and a way has to be found to transfer its mission to lay people without losing the essential character of the institution. How Feely handles this could, in part, determine the next twist in her career when her contract expires in three years.

Source: Adapted from Way, N. (2004).

As you examine the change process closely, you will identify similarities with the control process discussed in Chapter 15. Change and conflict management must be closely aligned and integrated with all managerial functions.

Successful organisations are not static. In earlier chapters we found the organisation's environment is ever-changing because of many factors. Organisations must therefore change even if all they desire is maintenance of their relative position in a context. If they want to alter or improve their position, change must be greater.

In this chapter we consider change's impact on members and their reactions to it. We examine people's reasons for resistance to change, and conflicts ensuing from this resistance. Further, we explore strategies to overcome change resistance, and to manage and use conflict to support organisational growth and development. Finally, we analyse conflict management within and between groups, discussing ways to reduce or stimulate conflict.

Throughout this chapter, we refer to Chapters 3 and 6. This is because environmental awareness is a basis for effective change management. Further, innovation and any process leading to change may cause organisational conflict. Material presented here will briefly review earlier material as fits with topic development.

MANAGING CHANGE

In today's fluid environment, success demands a competitive advantage. To achieve this, effective managers see change as basic to organisation survival.

Diagnosing the need for change

The competent manager applies the skills discussed before, and scans the internal and external environments. Data is gathered on both internal and external trends. Values, goals and activities are carefully watched to ensure they fit with customer demands and needs. If there is a gap or deficiency, an effective manager works to remedy this (Lessem 1991; Bateman & Snell 2004).

To manage change effectively therefore, one must be aware of a need for change. Many factors influence organisational need for change (Jick 1993; Ross 2003). These can be external and internal (as seen in Fig. 16.1). They result from external and internal environmental trends.

Internal factors

As you saw from Chapter 3, managers must be aware of many internal environment factors. This is a basis for accurate planning, as for accurate control mechanisms. Factors include all aspects of human and industrial relation regulation, balance of cultures and values among organisation staff, and changes of work processes imposed by new technology, just to name a few. Think of a familiar work place and identify changes from internal factors.

External factors

Meanwhile the external environment must be monitored and any changes examined for potential organisation impact. These often demand organisation change, to sustain competitive advantage. Organisations benchmark constantly to keep up with industry developments. They watch competitor, supplier and customer activities. Failing to do so can cause performance problems, threatening organisational survival (Isabella 1993). This is particularly important when operating on a regional basis (James 2003).

In Chapter 6, we discussed planned and reactive change, with the components of organisational change. Figure 16.2 shows a simplified version of the concept, emphasising the

FIGURE 16.1 Internal and external factors causing the need for change in organisations

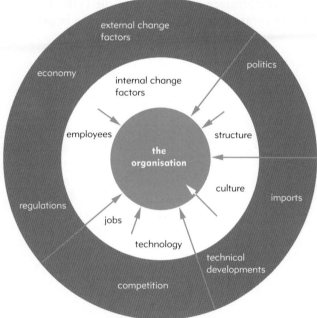

FIGURE 16.2 Factors impacting on organisational activities

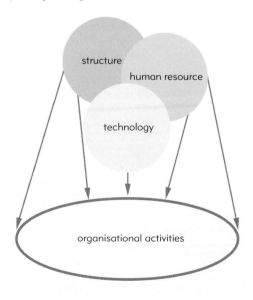

integration of organisational components in an organisation where change can be implemented. No one area can be changed without impacting all other organisation areas.

The change cycle

Effective organisational change is cyclical, starting from the awareness of some organisation aspect being below expected levels. Some indicators signal a need for action (Luthans 1995). Refer to Chapter 15 for control mechanisms to alert managers to this performance gap.

Having identified a performance gap, managers identify a need for change. Then they act, building an environment enabling the organisation to accurately diagnose the problem, develop alternatives for resolution and select the best one. The change cycle requires this alternative to be implemented and more measurement and evaluation to see if the desired outcome is reached (Fisher 1993; Stensholt 2003).

This leads to further performance evaluation and the cycle starts again (see Fig. 16.3). In fact the cycle should be continuous if the organisation is to be proactive, not reactive.

FIGURE 16.3 The change cycle

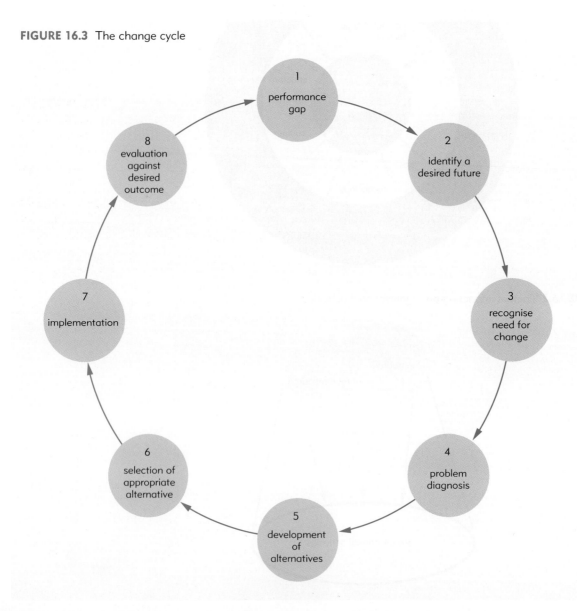

MANAGING RESISTANCE TO CHANGE

Achieving innovation and change takes much managerial planning and skill because people often resist. A change may be opposed even when in the best interests of those affected. In this section, we discuss why people resist change, examining how to overcome such resistance.

Why individuals resist change

Why do people—including ourselves—sometimes resist change? While resistance arises for many reasons, several stand out (Kotter & Schlesinger 1979).

One reason is self-interest. When people hear about a change, they ask, 'How will this affect me?' If the answer is 'adversely', resistance will emerge. How much depends on how strongly

CASE IN POINT

When conflict leads to radical change

The financial year 2002/03 was not a fiscally happy one for the Mayne healthcare group. The company posted a loss, largely due to massive write-downs in its private hospital business. Mayne started off as a parcels delivery company in 1886, and eventually developed to become a multinational logistics and security business. Mayne diversified into healthcare in the late 1980s and gradually acquired hospitals from Hospitals of Australia (HCA) and Australian Medical Enterprises. The company acquired diagnostic, general practice and pharmaceutical businesses, to eventually become Australia's leading provider of health care services. The diagnostic services and pharmaceutical arms of the company have consistently performed well.

The company, however, experienced quite significant conflict with some health professionals who staffed their private hospitals. Mayne and the Australian Medical Association (AMA) often came into conflict over many issues. Nurses also expressed dissatisfaction over perceived lower staffing levels. Relationships between Mayne and health professionals improved due to the implementation of a policy of increased management responsibility. The ongoing conflicts, however, arguably translated to the bottom line, as internal issues with health care professionals affected revenue.

Mayne instituted a number of changes to deal with the problems in 2002/03, including a return of accountability to the local hospital level, rather than focusing on centralised management. This change gave hospital directors and doctors a greater level of involvement in decision making. Mayne also introduced nursing assistants to support registered nurses as a way of coping with the continuing shortage of nursing staff. Mayne also continued its ongoing program of sponsoring medical colleges throughout the year, funding conferences and partnered with key colleges in an attempt to address the shortage of medical practitioners in rural areas.

The company reassessed their interest in running hospitals in the long term, and shifted their focus to a financial turnaround and profitable sale of the hospital businesses. This was largely successful and eventually Mayne sold their remaining hospitals to Affinity Health in December 2003, thus ending conflicts through a major divestment.

Source: Contributed by Peter Woods.

Websites:

http://www.maynegroup.com/
http://www.uow.edu.au/arts/sts/bmartin/dissent/documents/health/mayne.html

Activities for discussion, analysis and further research

1. How would you categorise the major causes of conflict between health professionals and Mayne health?
2. What are the benefits and losses that are apparent from this conflict?
3. What methods did Mayne use to reduce and resolve the conflict?

they feel their self-interests are affected. When integrating their international commercial and investment banking operations Citicorp lost many top investment bankers. The investment banking experts who left saw this as an intrusion on their turf (*Dun's Business Month* 1986).

Another reason for change resistance is misunderstanding and a lack of trust. People are often against change when they don't understand it. As well, low trust levels between managers and employees, common to many firms, increase misunderstandings. From your own experience, you may see it is not always employees who resist change. Managers who mistrust employees and fear power loss can oppose employee involvement in work decisions (Saporito 1986).

Resistance also often comes from assessing the virtues of change differently. Differential assessment is a major reason for innovations lacking support. As innovations involve new concepts, their value may not be clear (Fagan 2003). So people may see a change as useless or even see it as counterproductive.

Finally, individuals' ability to adjust to new situations differs, with some having low tolerance for change (Walters 2003d). They resist change as a result, fearing they will not be able to learn needed new skills and behaviours.

Managers should consider possible reasons for resistance of those involved in a change. This helps managers choose a way to overcome resistance. Otherwise, innovation and change efforts may sink unexpectedly.

Overcoming resistance to change

One approach to deal with resistance, offered by Kurt Lewin, divides the change process into three steps (Lewin 1947; Huse & Cummings 1985). The first step, *unfreezing*, means initial awareness of need for a change is developed. The second, *changing*, focuses on learning needed new behaviours. The third step, *refreezing*, centres on reinforcing new behaviours, usually by positive results, feelings of achievement, and/or rewards from others. Lewin's approach helps managers see that an unfreezing period is needed before people will willingly change. Also to reinforce and maintain changes, refreezing is important (Ferguson 2003).

Managers can adopt several methods to overcome initial change resistance and facilitate unfreezing (Kotter & Schlesinger 1979). Table 16.1 summarises these options, situations where an approach is commonly used, and advantages and disadvantages of each.

One strategy to overcome resistance to change is *education and communication*. This means giving enough information and ensuring the change is clearly communicated to those affected (Kotter & Schlesinger 1979).

Change resistance can be overcome by *participation and involvement*. Lower resistance comes when those affected by change participate in its planning and implementing. At Corning, worker involvement is a key to cost-saving efforts. For instance, a maintenance employee proposed using a flexible tin mould rather than several fixed moulds for wet ceramic material to be baked into automobile catalytic converters, saving $99 000 per year (McComas 1986). Managers often under-utilise participation to overcome resistance to change (Nutt 1986).

Facilitation and support can overcome resistance. When people react to impending change with fear and anxiety, managerial encouragement and help can cut resistance. Other facilitation and support methods include training and providing proper equipment and materials.

Another approach to reducing change resistance is *negotiation and agreement*. Negotiation can be an important strategy when a group sees that change will hurt it and can cause a change effort to fail (Ferguson 2003). If education and participation falter, negotiation may help achieve cooperation (Schlesinger 1987).

Resistance can also be overcome by *manipulation and cooptation*. Manipulation is giving selected change information so potential resisters see it as more attractive or needed. Ethical problems come when use of selective information distorts potential negative aspects of change. In cooptation, a leader or influential person among potential resisters is given a seemingly desirable role to gain their cooperation. The role is usually symbolic, with little influence over

TABLE 16.1 METHODS OF OVERCOMING RESISTANCE TO CHANGE

Approach	Commonly used in situations	Advantages	Drawbacks
Education + communication	Where there is a lack of information or inaccurate information and analysis	Once persuaded, people will often help with implementation of the change	Can be very time-consuming if lots of people are involved
Participation + involvement	Where the initiators do not have all information they need to design the change, and where others have considerable power to resist	People who participate will be committed to implementing change, and any relevant information they have will be integrated into the change plan	Can be very time-consuming if participators design an inappropriate change
Facilitation + support	Where people are resisting because of adjustment problems	No other approach works as well with adjustment problems	Can be time-consuming and expensive and still fail
Negotiation + agreement	Where someone or some group will clearly lose out in a change, and where that group had considerable power to resist	Sometimes it is a relatively easy way to avoid major resistance	Can be too expensive in many cases if it alerts others to negotiate for compliance
Manipulation + co-optation	Where other tactics will not work or are too expensive	It can be a relatively quick and inexpensive solution to resistance problems	Can lead to future problems if people feel manipulated
Explicit + implicit coercion	Where speed is essential and change initiators possess considerable power	It is speedy and can overcome any kind of resistance	Can be risky if it leaves people angry with the initiators

Source: Reprinted from Kotter & Schlesinger (1979, p. 111).

the change. However, it may be good enough to get the person's support. Manipulation and cooptation can backfire if the person realises what is being done and feels manipulated.

Finally, *explicit and implicit coercion* can overcome change resistance. This is use of direct or indirect power to make change resisters conform. Tactics focus on direct or veiled threats of loss of job, promotion, pay and other benefits. People may be transferred or fired. Pressure targets will probably resent coercion even if they yield. Coercion may also escalate resistance (Kirkpatrick 1986; Rue & Byars 2003). If change is unpopular but needs quick implementation, managers may have to use the strategy. Evidence shows managers use coercion more than needed, and fostering subordinates' negative feelings may block future changes (Nutt 1986).

Of course, employees are not the only ones to resist change. Employers can do so too. This happened to B. Thomas Golisano, sales manager for Electronic Account Systems Inc., a small computerised payroll-processing firm. Electronic catered to large companies, but Golisano thought smaller companies might be interested. He put his idea to his bosses, but was not listened to. So he started his own company, Paychex, now the second largest payroll-processing firm in the United States. His former employer says, 'He was right and we were wrong' (Cowan 1986; Meeks 1989; Taylor 1995).

Force-field analysis

force-field analysis

Method involving analysing the two types of forces, driving forces and restraining forces, that influence any proposed change, then assessing how best to overcome resistance

driving forces

Factors pressuring for a particular change

restraining forces

Factors pressuring against a change

To overcome resistance to change, managers can use **force-field analysis**. Developed by Kurt Lewin, this involves analysing two types of forces, driving and restraining forces, that influence proposed change and assessing how to overcome resistance. **Driving forces** are factors pressuring for a change, where **restraining forces** are factors pressuring against a change. The two forces push in opposite directions, giving an equilibrium defining current conditions, or the status quo. To change the status quo to another condition, driving forces can be increased, restraining forces decreased, or both undertaken. Managers generally try to increase driving forces but this, Lewin feels, will produce a balancing increase in resisting forces. Managers can achieve a successful change best if they work to reduce restraining forces (Lewin 1951; Strebel 1994; Tredgold 2003c).

Xerox faced serious overseas competition and worked to halve manufacturing costs at its operations near Rochester, New York. Wiring harnesses were planned to be subcontracted, to lower costs and cut about 150 jobs. Union leaders wanted to save jobs and as company–union relations had been good historically, union leaders met managers to assess ways to keep the harness work in plant.

Figure 16.4 shows a force-field analysis of major driving and restraining forces maintaining the status quo with costs too high for Xerox to effectively compete. The wider the arrow, the stronger the force. In seeking solutions, union leaders suggested relaxing rules so workers could make minor machine repairs rather than wait for maintenance staff to fix them. Union leaders

MANAGERIAL DILEMMAS

Which theory is that?

The principal of a private school in Victoria had the following story to tell me:

'My school has two kindergarten units. Each has its own directress, both of whom are excellent teachers and really terrific with the children. But, for some reason, they just didn't get on. The tension between them had got to the point where the parents of the children were actually commenting on it to me. I really didn't know what to do, but I knew I had to do something. I did not intend to lose either one of them. So I invited them to my office and left instructions that we were not to be disturbed. There they both were seated side by side across the desk from me. I looked at them and said: "I believe the two of you are having some problems?"

Both of them denied that they had any difficulty and looked ready to leave my office. I could not let that happen so I told them that in that case we would just have to sit there until they did have a problem. I picked up a file and started reading,

ignoring my two staff members. Forty-five minutes later, one of them burst into tears and the other followed seconds later. As I passed around the box of tissues, I knew I was going to be successful in my wish and I would be retaining two good staff members.'

Source: Margaret Tein.

Reflection points

1. What strategies did the principal use to resolve conflict between her two staff members? Why did they work?
2. What conflict response did the kindergarten directress display?
3. What conflict management style did the principal use?

Decision points

1. What alternative strategies might have been used to resolve the conflict between those two staff members? What might have been the outcomes?

FIGURE 16.4 Force-field analysis of the forces maintaining high cost level at Xerox plant

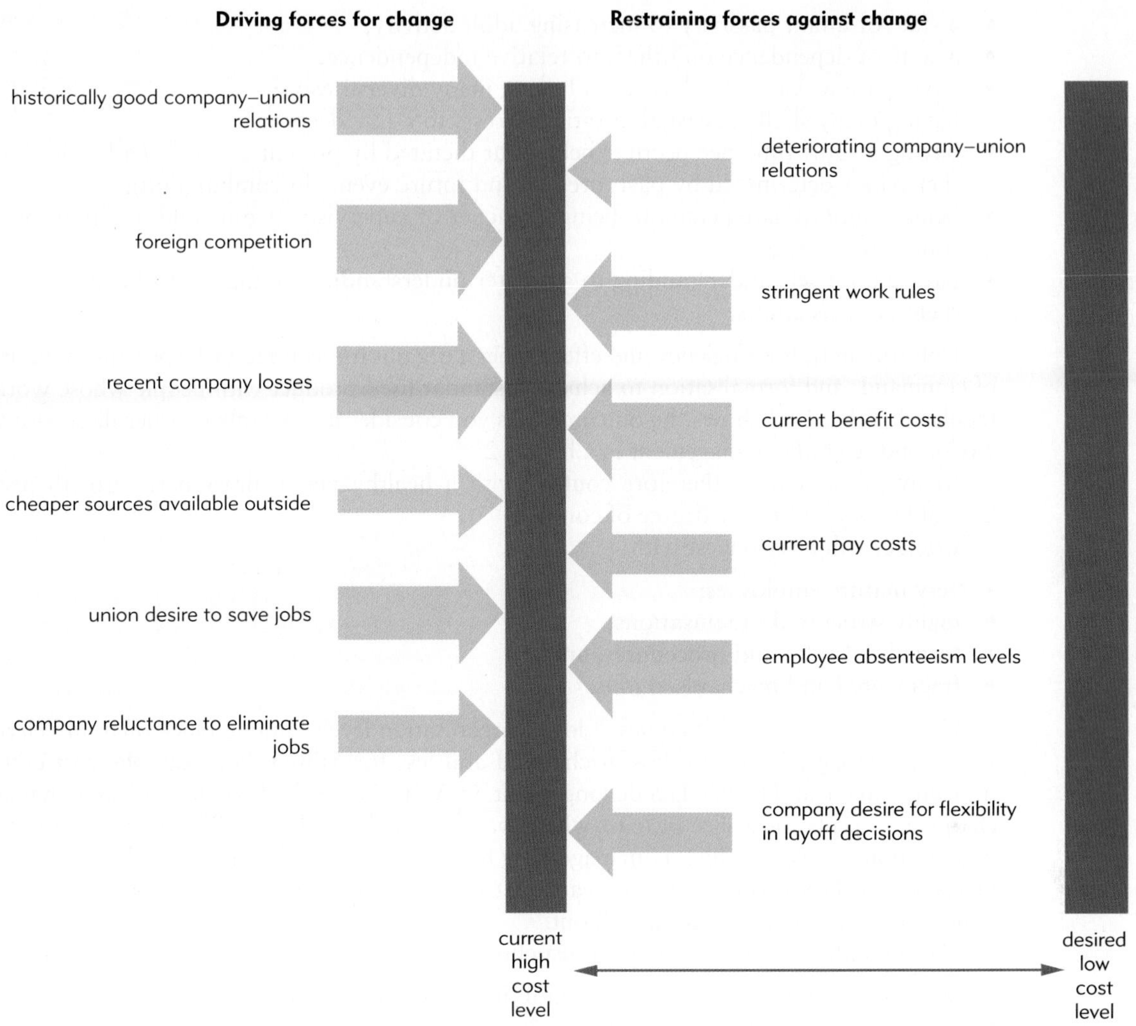

Driving forces for change   **Restraining forces against change**

historically good company–union relations

foreign competition

recent company losses

cheaper sources available outside

union desire to save jobs

company reluctance to eliminate jobs

deteriorating company–union relations

stringent work rules

current benefit costs

current pay costs

employee absenteeism levels

company desire for flexibility in layoff decisions

current high cost level

desired low cost level

and management studied how to save money, finally eliminating six paid days off, making medical insurance cuts, and developing ways to control absenteeism. In return, no layoffs for three years were promised. By working on restraining forces, firm and union could agree on changes leading to lower plant cost levels without contracting wiring harness work out (Kirkpatrick 1986).

MANAGING CONFLICT

Organisational conflicts within and between groups are common. By **conflict** we mean a perceived difference between two or more parties resulting in mutual opposition (Robbins 1974) which may involve three levels: within the person (intrapersonal); between person and organisation; and between organisational groups.

For our purposes we focus on conflict between individual and organisation and between organisational groups. While intrapersonal conflict can be destructive to people and the organisation, it generally leads to conflict between people and their organisation.

conflict

Perceived difference between two or more parties resulting in mutual opposition

Conflicts between individuals and organisations

As people mature, they move from:

- a state of infant passivity to increasing adult activity;
- a state of dependence on others to relative independence;
- having a few ways of behaving to having many diverse ways;
- having many shallow, casual, erratic interests to a few deep ones;
- having a short time-perspective (behaviour dictated by present events) to a longer one (behaviour determined by past, present and future events in combination);
- being a subordinate person to being a teacher or supervisor (from child to parent or trainee to manager);
- having poor self-understanding to a greater understanding of and control over themselves as adults.

Unfortunately, for efficiency and effectiveness, organisations build task specialisation, unity of command, and formalisation to achieve a standardised product with people whose work is regulated. Table 16.2 shows the outcomes. As you consider it, remember earlier discussions of Taylor and scientific management in Chapter 2.

Many job structures therefore conflict with a healthy personality's basic growth needs. Several factors lead to the degree of conflict.

Conflict will be strongest with:

- very mature employees;
- highly structured organisations;
- formalised rules and procedures; and
- fragmented and mechanised jobs.

Hence, strongest conflict comes at lower organisation levels, among blue-collar and clerical workers. Managers' jobs are less mechanised and less formalised. For example, cost cutting measures taken at Heinz's Dandenong plant in Victoria resulted in the cafeteria manager charging 10 cents for a slice of toast which was free of charge before. This impacted only the organisation's rank and file, as management had an executive dining room charging an all-inclusive fee. Production workers' reaction to this change (that was neither discussed nor announced) was an almost total walkout.

When conflict occurs, employees must choose to:

- leave the organisation or work to climb into upper management;
- use defence mechanisms to defend their self-concepts;
- psychologically dissociate from the organisation (e.g. lose interest in their work or cut their standards);
- concentrate on the organisation's material rewards;
- find allies among other workers and all adapt by use of quota restrictions, strikes and sabotage.

While conflict is generally seen as negative, results can be either constructive or destructive. Some destructive ones are well known. For example, conflict means people or groups can become hostile, withhold information and resources, and block each other's efforts. It can delay

TABLE 16.2 CONSEQUENCES OF ORGANISATIONAL STANDARDISATION

Individuals have little control over their work; machines often take over control.

Individuals will be passive, dependent and subordinate.

Individuals will have only short-term work horizons.

Individuals are given repetitive jobs needing minimum skill and ability.

Cameo cars

As the newly appointed credit manager for Cameo Cars, Brenna brought an extensive knowledge of lending processes and practices to this newly created position. Originally a family operation, the car dealership had grown significantly over its 100 years of operation. It now comprised retail vehicle and parts sales, a service workshop, a panel and paint shop and associated auxiliary functions. The company was strongly supported by both customers and staff in the provincial regions where it operated. An examination of the staff composition showed that males dominated the organisation: all of the sales staff were men and only the two administrative office staff were female.

While sales figures were significant, the balance of the debtors' ledger was well outside safe operating margins, and this was having a direct impact on the company's cash flow. Due to the considerable age of much of this debt and the present downturn in the economy, Brenna was concerned that debt recovery would probably be difficult. There were few procedures in place to monitor accounts once charges had been made, and there was no active management of the debtors' portfolio.

After reviewing the operations of the three branches and talking with key personnel, Brenna formulated a plan to implement a new debt collection process. She outlined the plan to top management and then called divisional staff meetings to explain the changes to staff. Department managers were then asked for input to further refine the plan. The managers were strongly resistant to the changes, expressing their misgivings in statements such as: 'we've never done that before', 'that's not the way we do things here' and 'this industry is different'. With approval from top management, Brenna explained the dynamics of the financial minefield that the company was currently in. The department managers had been unaware of these difficulties, considering that if sales were up in their respective departments, they were doing well.

With some fine-tuning the new debtor processes were implemented in phases. Some staff were openly hostile to these changes, and at times deliberately defied the new procedures. Brenna found it frustrating, but persevered with establishing the new debt control system. Application forms were revised and credit checks became the norm for establishing new accounts. Outstanding balances were actively pursued and problems were resolved wherever possible. If no resolution was available, legal action was instigated to recover the outstanding balances. The turning point came when a male staff member allowed a male friend to take a vehicle without ascertaining if account arrangements had been made. He felt that there would be no problems with recovering the debt from his friend.

This did not prove to be the case, and Brenna was required to recover the money at a later date. This situation illustrated the necessity for the new procedures to staff at all levels of the organisation.

In time, with top management support and the participation of staff, resistance to the plan abated and the new debt policies became standard. This resulted in a turnaround of the company's financial position, and saw them rise to become one of the top 10 dealerships in the country.

Source: Contributed by Elizabeth Hall.

Activities for discussion, analysis and further research

1. What theoretical models would be helpful in understanding the resistance to change that these managers demonstrated?
2. Do you think the managers' reactions would have been the same had the new credit manager been a man?
3. Research the phenomenon of occupational segregation in certain types of industry. For example, find answers to the following questions: How many women are employed in the position of credit manager? How many women are graduating with accountancy and finance degrees?

projects, raise costs, and cause valued employees to leave. There can be constructive conflict outcomes. For one, conflict highlights problems and a need for solutions. For another, it promotes change as parties work to resolve the problem. Conflict can raise morale and cohesion, as members deal with concern and frustration. Finally, conflict can stimulate interest, creativity and innovation, encouraging new ideas (Tjosvold 1984). This has led to some interesting strategies for Harvey Norman as it expands into Singapore (Roberts 2003c), such as locating stores close to railway stations, and allowing staff to give discounts to older Singaporean shoppers who tend to shop with cash.

Overall, some conflict is useful, but too much can hurt organisational performance (see Fig. 16.5). Very low conflict levels may mean problems are hidden and new ideas stifled. Too much conflict, in contrast, means much energy is wasted on dissension and opposition. Therefore, managers must understand conflict's causes, how to reduce or resolve it and, as needed, to stimulate it positively.

Causes of conflict

Many factors contribute to conflict (Walton & Dutton 1969; Robbins 1983). Several are discussed below.

Communication factors

Managers blame poor communication for many organisational conflicts. If we define communication as the building of a picture in the receiver's mind exactly the same as the one the sender intended, then perfect communication is rare. So misunderstandings can occur for many reasons. Conflict from unsuccessful communication differs from that of substantive differences, but can still be damaging. For example, a manager communicating unclearly to subordinates whose responsibility it is to perform an unpleasant task in the manager's absence may return to find subordinates in conflict and the task still undone.

Structural factors

Members may experience a feeling of discomfort with how things occur, or processes may seem cumbersome. This may be due to aspects of organisational structure (James 2003b). These may result from unplanned growth.

Size

Reviewing studies relating conflict to organisational size, Robbins (1994) found larger organisations tended to have greater conflict. Size increases were associated with less goal clarity, increased formalisation, specialisation, supervisory levels and opportunity for information to be distorted.

FIGURE 16.5 Effects of conflict on group performance

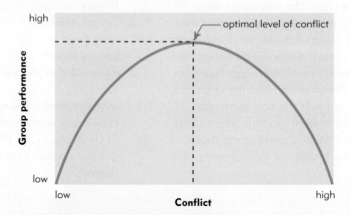

Participation

It seems reasonable to expect greater subordinate participation (for example, in decision making) to lower conflict. From the human relations perspective it is argued that inviting subordinate participation satisfies a drive for involvement. Research, however, shows increased levels of conflict with greater subordinate participation. This is due to increased participation raising awareness of individual differences. However, greater conflict from increased participation does not have to be bad (Barrett 1995; Cotts 1998). If the outcomes, and resulting conflict, improve overall work-unit performance then conflict is productive.

Line–staff distinctions

One often-mentioned source of conflict is the distinction between line and staff units. We have discussed how line-unit tasks are directly related to core organisational activities (Chapter 8). A manufacturing company would have production as a line unit; while a customer-oriented organisation would see a marketing or sales department as line. Staff units support line functions. Research and development, public relations, human resources and industrial relations are examples of staff departments.

Conflict occurs between line and staff groups because of differences in functions, goals, member values and backgrounds. Line groups generally are more operations-focused, while staff groups are more distant from core activities. Line personnel accept their firm more often, while staff personnel criticise company practice. In fact, staff people identify with their professional group over their organisation. Lastly, time horizons of the two groups differ, with staff people focused on long-range matters, and line people on short-term or day-to-day matters. With these differences, it is not surprising line and staff personnel experience a high degree of conflict.

Reward systems

If rewards of one person or group come at another's expense, conflict arises (Kohn 1986, 1987; Gome 2003c). How mutually exclusive reward systems operate may be unclear. For example, staff people are rewarded for being innovative, identifying a need for change. Suggesting and inducing change shows their organisational usefulness. In contrast, line people avoid change as it is disruptive and inconvenient. In fact, line people are rewarded for uninterrupted productive activity.

Resource interdependence

Typically groups compete for organisational resources (Friedkin & Simpson 1985). With greater resources, conflicts may be avoided. However, increased resources are uncommon in organisations. So, lack of coordination and cooperation between groups and conflict are likely (Zachary 1995). Thus task interdependence becomes a conflict source.

Task interdependence

Two types of task interdependence are very prone to conflict. One is sequential interdependence, where one person or work unit relies on another. For example, waiters are more reliant on cooks than the reverse as waiters need cooks to produce good meals in a timely way. The second form of task interdependence is reciprocal, where people or work units are mutually interdependent. For example, purchasing agents want generic specifications to be able to purchase at lowest cost. Users need materials of a particular quality with specific characteristics and find it easier to specify a brand name (Strauss 1964).

Power

Organisational power distribution can also lead to conflict. If a group feels less powerful than it should be, or believes another group holds too much power, it will challenge (Davies 1998a, 1998b; O'Reilly 1997). If departments that are ostensibly equal have different amounts of power, discontent arises. For example, staff people must justify their existence, understand line departments' problems, and work with line personnel. Line personnel do not face these problems, as normally their authority is greater. The imbalance raises tension in a difficult situation.

Personal behaviour factors

Another conflict source is individual differences. People's values or perceptions may generate conflict (Petzinger 1995). To illustrate, a manager values having employees 'pay their dues'. The manager might argue that they spent several years in a mundane low-level organisation position and others can gain from the same experience. Making ambitious subordinates do this leads to serious conflict. Also, managers who hold a particular view of people (for example, inferring laziness or incompetence from little evidence) will produce conflict by their response to some situations. As well, some people enjoy argumentation and combat. Those with especially conflict-prone personal styles find life is a series of hostilities and battles (Siler 1989; Bailey 1990; Ross 2004b).

Communication styles

Conflict may arise from communication problems and interpersonal misunderstandings. For example, linguistic style differences means some men in work teams will talk more, taking more credit for ideas, than women in the teams. Conflict comes when men wrongly assume that women are uninterested or less capable as they participate less, and women incorrectly assume the men are bossy and uninterested in their ideas as they seem to talk more (Jones et al. 2000).

Workforce diversity

Diversity can also produce conflict. An older worker may be uncomfortable or resent reporting to a younger supervisor, an Asian may feel singled out in a group of white workers, or a female top manager may feel her mostly-male top-management team are ganging up when one disagrees with one of her proposalss. Whether justified or not, the feelings cause recurring conflicts.

Differences in goals

As subunits specialise, goals diverge. Production unit goals may include low production costs and few defects. Research and development unit goals may include innovative ideas leading to successful new products. These goals lead to varied member expectations and conflict arises due to these disparate goals. An example of this incompatibility emerged at Heinz's Dandenong plant during the company's adoption of TQM. TQM meant obtaining lowest-priced potatoes for purchasing. For production this meant minimum wastage from bruising and marks on potatoes. Low-cost potatoes were bruised and marked and needed to be removed by hand, raising labour costs and cutting yield. Interaction was intense until the cause of the conflict was found and fixed.

Reward structures

Intergroup conflict is likely when rewards are linked to performance of the individual group rather than the overall organisation. When rewards link to individual-group performance, performance becomes an independent variable, though group performance is very interdependent (Kohn 1986, 1987; Ross 2004b).

Differences in perceptions

Differing world perceptions produce goal differences, and disagreements lead to conflict (Behar 1995). Organisation groups develop different views of reality due to varied goals and time horizons, status incongruence and inaccurate perceptions.

Time perspectives impact a group's perception of reality. Deadlines influence priorities and the importance given to activities. A research worker's time perspective may be several years, while manufacturing engineers operate with time frames up to a year. Upper management will focus on five- to ten-year time periods, while middle managers use shorter spans. Time-horizon differences mean that problems and issues one group sees as critical seem unimportant to another, and conflicts erupt. This may even in some cases be seasonal time (Ross 2004b).

Conflict on groups' relative status occurs and influences perceptions: a firm may have many different status standards, yielding a range of hierarchies (Naughton & Kerwin 1995). For example, conflicts may come from work patterns, such as which group initiates work and which responds. So a production department may see a change as harming its status as it involves work initiated by a salesperson. The salesperson may deliberately aggravate this status conflict.

Inaccurate perceptions can lead groups to stereotype others. Differences may be small; however, groups exaggerate them. When emphasised, differences lead to reinforced stereotypes, deteriorating relationships and developing conflict.

The increased demand for specialists

Conflict between staff specialists and line generalists commonly leads to intergroup conflict. Increased organisational demand for technical expertise expands staff roles and increases conflict. The point is that line and staff people see each other and their roles differently.

Benefits and losses from conflict

As noted before, conflict outcomes can be positive or negative (Ross 2004b). If conflict is eliminated, then the organisation has problems. Conflict is a sign of a vital organisation and is problematic only if excessive. Excessive conflict leads to wasting valuable resources. Harmful, or dysfunctional, conflict is discussed later.

Benefits

Benefits occurring with moderate conflict are as follows:

Productive task focus. When conflict levels are moderate, intragroup differences are minimised, and task focus increases. Natural differences between groups (such as age, education, attitudes and clothing) suit the task. These allow departments to excel at specific tasks.

Cohesion and satisfaction. Cohesion increases with group identification. Members are attracted to a group, being satisfied by belonging. Members cooperate and defer personal goals to achieve departmental goals. Mild intergroup conflict also increases member satisfaction.

Power and feedback. The occasional intergroup conflict balances interdepartmental power relationships, giving feedback on departmental status. Employees' view of their roles and relative importance are often inaccurate, so they expect and demand organisational resources inappropriate to their actual importance. Conflict blunts these excesses as it focuses on organisational problems and reduces intergroup disparities. Feedback lets groups correct these perceptions, and regulates intergroup power or resource balances.

Goal attainment. An organisation's goal-achievement ability is related to energy directed at department level goals. Participants are stimulated to work where competition and conflict is moderate. Cohesion encourages an enjoyable work atmosphere. But complacency can be as bad as too much conflict. So a firm can prosper and achieve its goals only with effective subgroups. Andrews (2004) presents Toyota Australia's approach to melding the output of many diverse groups.

Losses

When conflict is too strong, there may be negative outcomes. Conflict losses are as follows:

Energy diversion. One outcome is diversion of departmental time and effort to winning rather than achieving organisational goals. When the most important factor is defeating other departments, resources are wasted. In extreme cases, information or even vital innovative action can be withheld, or sabotage may occur.

Distorted judgment. A finding from intergroup research is judgment and perception accuracy drops as conflict grows. Then after a group makes a mistake, it may blame perceived opponents instead of realising its own flaws. Conflict participants can also ignore competitors' ideas.

Loser effects. Another interdepartmental conflict aspect is that someone loses. The loser undergoes significant change, tends to deny or distort reality and seeks scapegoats. Cohesion drops as losers display low cooperation and concern for the needs and interests of other departments' members.

Poor coordination. The final problem is emphasis on departmental goal achievement. These goals energise employees, but need not become all-consuming. They must be integrated with organisational goals. Under intense conflict, no integration occurs. Interunit collaboration drops as contact reduces and each group rejects other views. When conflict is intense, departmental goal achievement and enemy defeat are a priority. Compromise is impossible.

MANAGING THE E-CHALLENGE

Getting smart with on-line financing

Have you ever bought a car and had to obtain financing for it? If you have, you have probably had to navigate the maze of proprietary systems where dealers kept a number of computers, each linked to a particular finance company. The dealer often had to deal with several companies and attempt to make a deal with which the customer would be content.

A new development has put an end to all this. SmartLink, developed by Internet Business Systems in Melbourne, claims to reduce the time taken to arrange finance from a day's work to less than a minute, made possible by links with an internet credit reference system. This innovative, ready-made software solution drives productivity and efficiency.

General Motors Acceptance Corporation (GMAC) has decided to use the SmartLink system for its Australian network of 200 Holden and Saab car dealers. In a process which once took up to two days to complete, dealers would deal with GMAC through a personal computer that searched a proprietary system for the purchaser's credit history, taking relayed information from a computerised database. The new software has simplified this: the applicant's details are entered and the credit history is processed instantly. In most instances, a car loan approval can be obtained within a minute.

The system, launched early July 2001, has since been introduced in New Zealand. GMAC is considering expanding into Thailand, Malaysia and eventually into China. This innovation has meant a reform in work processes at GMAC. The use of the internet-based system has eliminated one layer of activity. Previously, information that was forwarded by the dealers to GMAC central processing office in Newcastle was entered by 20 temporary staff, whose services are no longer required. Work at Newcastle is now more productive and information is handled more efficiently.

Source: Based on Kirby (2001) and Broekhuise (2002).

Activities for discussion, analysis and further research

1. In what ways did this innovation alter the work patterns at GMAC?
2. Undertake a web search on Saab Finance and determine how the new system impacts on a car buyer.
3. Discuss the relationship between Internet Business Systems and GMAC. Investigate the potential for this software to be adapted so that it could handle the different leasing situations in the US and Europe, if GMAC decided to transfer this innovation to its operations there.

Reducing and resolving conflict

As managers cannot escape intergroup conflict, they must manage it. Thus we need to examine techniques of resolving dysfunctional intergroup conflicts. Most use exchange between conflicting parties, suggesting that resolution may be facilitated by constructive negotiation.

Changing situational factors. An obvious way to reduce conflict is to change situational factors leading to a problem. So a manager might increase resources, reorganise to reduce inter-dependencies, redesign rewards, or improve communication processes.

Appeal to superordinate goals. If excessive conflict is hard to change managers may be able to refocus people on superordinate goals. These are major common goals needing everybody's support and effort. Examples are ensuring organisational survival and beating highly visible competition. Superordinate goal success is dependent on identifying sufficiently important goals to all parties (Andrews 2004).

Use an interpersonal conflict-handling mode. Aside from a situation change or appealing to superordinate goals, interpersonal modes can help resolve conflict. Managers have five major interpersonal modes to reduce or resolve conflict (Thomas 1977; Reitz 1987).

- **Avoidance** ignores or suppresses a conflict in the hope it will go away or not become too disruptive.
- **Accommodation** solves conflicts by allowing the other's desires to prevail. In essence the manager voluntarily allows the other to have their way instead of continuing the conflict.
- **Competition** attempts to win a conflict at the other party's expense. In other words, one party wins and one loses.
- **Compromise** resolves conflict by having all parties lose some desired outcomes to get others. Compromise can involve bargaining by parties and needs a situation offering all a chance to improve their position or at least be no worse off after resolving the conflict. With compromise each wins some major issues and loses others.
- **Collaboration** resolves conflicts by devising solutions allowing all parties to reach outcomes desired. In other words the solution lets both parties win at least their major issues. Collaboration often needs much creativity developing solutions suited to conflicting parties' needs.

While collaboration is good in conflict handling as both sides may be satisfied, other approaches may work too. Table 16.3 summarises where each conflict-handling mode applies, as reported by 28 chief executives.

Though it is tempting to see some conflict management styles as more effective than others (for example, collaborating versus avoiding), each will work best in some situations.

Managing intergroup conflict through resolution

As managers must live with intergroup conflict, they must confront its management. Thus we must examine methods of resolving dysfunctional intergroup conflict. Most involve exchange between conflict parties, suggesting resolution may be aided by constructive negotiation.

Problem solving

The confrontation problem-solving method lowers tension by face-to-face meetings between groups in conflict, the purpose being to identify conflicts and resolve them. Groups openly debate issues and gather all relevant information until a decision is reached. Effective problem solving needs conflicting parties to be willing to work collaboratively to an integrative solution satisfying needs of all concerned. Problem solving helps increase solution commitment by incorporating everyone's concerns into a consensus.

While problem solving is a desirable approach to conflict resolution, implementing it effectively can be difficult. The greatest obstacle is the win–lose mentality characteristic of conflicting groups. Unless parties involved rise above this, problem solving is likely to fail.

---

avoidance

Conflict-handling mode involving ignoring or suppressing a conflict in the hope it will go away or become less disruptive

accommodation

Conflict-handling mode focusing on solving conflicts by allowing the other party's desires to prevail

competition

Conflict-handling mode involving attempting to win a conflict at the other party's expense

compromise

Conflict-handling mode aiming to solve issues by having each party give up some desired outcomes to get other desired outcomes

collaboration

Conflict-handling mode striving to resolve conflicts by devising solutions allowing both parties to achieve desired outcomes

TABLE 16.3 SITUATIONS IN WHICH TO USE THE FIVE CONFLICT-HANDLING MODES, AS REPORTED BY CHIEF EXECUTIVES

Conflict mode	Situation
Competing/forcing	1. When quick, decisive action is vital; e.g. emergencies 2. On important issues where unpopular actions need implementing; e.g. cost cutting, enforcing unpopular rules, discipline 3. On issues vital to company welfare when you know you're right 4. Against people who take advantage of non-competitive behaviour
Collaborating	1. To find an integrative solution when both sets of concerns are too important to be compromised 2. When your objective is to learn 3. To merge insights from people with different perspectives 4. To gain commitment by incorporating concerns into a consensus 5. To work through feelings which have interfered with a relationship
Compromising	1. When goals are important, but not worth the effort or potential disruption of more assertive modes 2. When opponents with equal power are committed to mutually exclusive goals 3. To achieve temporary settlements to complex issues 4. To arrive at expedient solutions under time pressure 5. As a backup when collaboration or competition is unsuccessful
Avoiding	1. When an issue is trivial, or more important issues are pressing 2. When you perceive no chance of satisfying your concerns 3. When potential disruption outweighs the benefits of resolution 4. To let people cool down and regain perspective 5. When gathering information supersedes immediate decision 6. When others can resolve the conflict more effectively 7. When issues seem tangential or symptomatic of other issues
Accommodating	1. When you find you are wrong, to allow a better position to be heard, to learn, and to show your reasonableness 2. When issues are more important to others than to yourself, to satisfy others and maintain co-operation 3. To build social credits for later issues 4. To minimise loss when you are outmatched and losing 5. When harmony and stability are especially important 6. To allow subordinates to develop by learning from mistakes

Source: Reprinted from Thomas (1977, p. 487).

Expansion of resources

As already noted, a major cause of intergroup conflict is limited resources. What one group gets is at another group's expense. The scarce resource may be a position, money, space and so on. Expanding resources successfully resolves conflicts as it means almost everyone can be satisfied. However, resources cannot always easily expand.

Smoothing

Smoothing emphasises common interests of conflicting groups and de-emphasises differences. The belief is that stressing shared viewpoints helps in goal attainment. If intergroup differences are serious, smoothing—like avoidance—is a short-term answer. Smoothing may lead to low-quality decisions whose full implications are not realised.

Bureaucratic authority

Bureaucratic authority means rules, regulations and formal authority are used to resolve or suppress conflict. This technique does not change attitudes and treats only the immediate problem. It is effective short-term when agreement cannot be reached on a conflict solution.

Limited communication

Encouraging small amounts of communication between departments stops development of misperceptions. When conflict is severe, controlled interaction helps resolution. Often interaction is limited to issues where departments have a common goal. Having a common goal means departments must talk and cooperate to achieve the goal. The technique is most effective when decision making and interaction rules are clear. It may not help with attitude change.

Confrontation and negotiation

Confrontation occurs when conflicting parties deal with each other directly on differences. Negotiation is the bargaining process during confrontation, allowing parties to reach a solution. Both techniques bring parties' representatives together.

Confrontation and negotiation are risky, as discussion may not focus on the conflict and emotions may get out of hand. However, if members can resolve conflict through face-to-face discussions, they will find new respect for each other and this aids future collaboration. Relatively permanent attitude change can be achieved through negotiation.

Confrontation succeeds when managers develop a 'win–win' strategy. This means both groups adopt a positive attitude, to resolve conflict to the benefit of both. If negotiations deteriorate into a win–lose strategy (each group trying to defeat the other), confrontation is ineffective.

Intergroup training

Another conflict reduction strategy is intergroup training. When other techniques are inappropriate for the organisation, individuals may need special training. For this, members attend a workshop away from regular work problems. The technique is expensive, but can achieve attitude change.

MANAGEMENT SKILLS FOR A GLOBALISED ECONOMY

The challenge of dealing with change

Change has been called the one constant in current times and organisations. Dealing with it is both challenging and difficult. Here are some clues.

Allow room for failure. If something does not work, it must be OK to say so. Not every idea is successful. Managers who press on with a change after it is obvious that it will not have the benefits expected lose the respect of their employees.

Give one consistent explanation for the change. In times of change, rumours abound. The only way to get real support is to explain honestly the need for the changes and directions which are being sought. Employees react negatively to conflicting stories. Be consistent.

Look for opportunities. Encourage people to be unconventional. Many 'new' products and services are really variations of others and not true innovations. While these may be acceptable, the best changes are usually when perspectives are unconventional.

Have the courage to follow your ideas. Convincing others that your ideas are worthwhile is not always easy. You may need to invest effort in gaining support from colleagues. You may also need to be prepared to act alone if you cannot gain allies.

Source: Adapted from Kinicki, A. & Williams, B. (2003).

Intergroup training involves the following steps:

1. Conflicting groups come to a training setting with the stated goal of exploring perceptions and relationships.
2. Conflicting groups are then separated and each discusses and lists its perceptions of both groups.
3. Groups come together again and group representatives describe perceptions while members listen. The objective is to report accurately to the other group each group's private images.
4. Before exchange occurs, groups return to private sessions to consider the information; reports generally show a gap between self-image and the other group's report. The next session seeks to analyse causes of discrepancies, which makes each group review its behaviour to the other and possible consequences of that behaviour, regardless of intention.
5. Representatives of each group publicly share discrepancies identified and possible reasons for them, focusing on actual, observable behaviour.
6. After this, the two groups explore the now-shared goal of identifying reasons for perceptual distortion.
7. Exploration of how to manage future relations to minimise conflict recurrence then takes place. After this process, understanding is improved and leads to improved working relationships.

THE RELATIONSHIP BETWEEN CHANGE AND CONFLICT

Change is a process and has several stages which occur in sequence if it is to succeed; however, we are often unaware of the stages. Sometimes they are not overt and we are uncomfortable with change.

As you can see from the two flow diagrams in Figure 16.6, how we feel about change depends largely on the part we play in it. Whether change is welcome or not, it is almost always a case of going from the known to the unknown and therefore a state of apprehension is created. This inevitably leads to conflict.

Types of intergroup conflict

Organisational conflict is inevitable. As intergroup conflict can be both positive and negative, management should not work to eradicate all conflict, only conflict disruptive to efforts to attain organisational goals. Some conflict types or degrees may be beneficial if used for change or innovation. Thus the critical issue is not conflict itself but its management (Heathcote 2004). Using this approach, we can define conflict in terms of organisational effect. In this respect, we discuss both functional and dysfunctional conflict.

Functional conflict

A functional conflict is a confrontation between groups that enhances and benefits organisational performance. Without this type of conflict, there would be little commitment to change, and groups would stagnate.

FIGURE 16.6 Personal responses to change

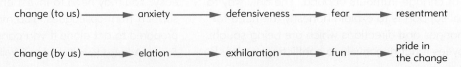

change (to us) ⟶ anxiety ⟶ defensiveness ⟶ fear ⟶ resentment

change (by us) ⟶ elation ⟶ exhilaration ⟶ fun ⟶ pride in the change

Dysfunctional conflict

A dysfunctional conflict is confrontation or interaction between groups that is harmful to the organisation or blocking goal achievement. Management must work to eliminate this conflict. Beneficial conflict can become bad conflict, but generally, when functional conflict becomes dysfunctional cannot be identified precisely (Schmidt 2004). Certain stress and conflict levels may help healthy and positive movement to goals in one group. The same levels may be disruptive and dysfunctional for another (or at a different time for the first group).

Behavioural scientists have spent 30 years researching and analysing how dysfunctional intergroup conflict affects those experiencing it. They found groups in conflict situations react predictably. We now examine a number of changes occurring within, and between, groups resulting from dysfunctional intergroup conflict.

Types of changes in groups in dysfunctional conflict

Changes occurring during intergroup conflict are as follows:

1. Group identification is strong when members share a common mission or purpose. Members see their group as separate and distinct from others. Pride develops and there are signs of the 'we feelings' characterising an in-group.
2. The presence of another group invites comparison and members prefer the in-group to the out-group.
3. A group perceiving conflict with another group becomes more tightly knit. Members present a solid front to defeat the other group. The group tends to become more formal and accepting of a leader's autocratic behaviour.
4. Members tend to see other groups as enemies not neutral objects.
5. Members feel superior, overestimating their own strengths and achievements.
6. Intergroup communication decreases. If it does occur, it is characterised by hostile negative statements, with group members not listening or giving credibility to the other group.
7. Members lose cohesion when a group loses a conflict. Member tension and conflict increases in the group and a scapegoat is sought to blame for the failure.

Conflict, changes in perception, and hostility are not abnormal. They are natural, occurring when members are healthy and well adjusted.

Changing views on conflict

The image of conflict has changed. Up to the mid-1940s, it was seen as harmful and unnecessary. Its existence was seen as a sign of a needed correction. According to this view, conflict had no useful purpose, distracting managers and sapping energy and resources. Conflict therefore was to be avoided. Conflict was also thought to come from poor management and trouble-makers. With effective management techniques and removal of trouble-makers, conflict could be eliminated and optimal performance achieved.

Recently, the view of conflict has shifted. Today, it is seen as inevitable and necessary for high organisational performance. That conflict can be harmful is undeniable, but some forms of conflict encourage development of new tactics and strategies, helping overcome stagnation and complacency. Conflict as an effort motivator can be desirable. This focus of the contemporary view is successful conflict management, not its elimination.

Successful conflict management involves maintaining a specific conflict level and selecting a conflict-reduction strategy. Managers may also consciously create conflict. Where creativity or development of alternatives is needed (as when resisting groupthink), conflict stimulation is advisable.

Conflict is inherently neither desirable nor undesirable. Its value can only be assessed by its performance effects.

It is not simple to identify an optimal conflict level for a situation. It needs good understanding of those involved and their tasks. A manager also must creatively determine strategies and tactics to change conflict levels. Simply raising conflict when this is thought necessary will not foster creativity; it must be channelled and directed. Maintaining conflict at an optimal, or 'Goldilocks', point is a major managerial challenge.

Stimulating conflict

As too little conflict leads to apathy, lethargy and poor performance, managers may need to stimulate conflict. This must be done positively and carefully, to avoid destructiveness. Constructive conflict in a group can be raised in many ways (Robbins 1983). Including people from diverse backgrounds is one. Another is causing members to discuss the need for change by communicating information. Still another means is encouraging internal competition (Peters 1988). Of course, in stimulating conflict, managers must carefully monitor and control the situation.

Management of change and conflict can be classified as part of organisational coordination processes. Managers must stimulate cooperation among people and work groups of many sizes. To resolve conflicts and differences they take part in negotiations. To do this, managers use competencies in the Focus on Others cluster (Boyatzis 1982). Some have been mentioned before. One is self-control. For effectiveness in a conflict-resolution role, the manager must beware of personal involvement in the issue. To retain some objectivity self-control must be shown. This leads to another competency in that cluster—perceptual objectivity. This means the manager's view is not limited by too much subjectivity or personal biases or perspectives. Managers unable to achieve this as needed lose subordinates' respect rapidly. Managers must be able to view an event from many perspectives at once, and distance themselves from emotional involvement.

GAINING THE EDGE

Managing organisations through change and conflict—Fremantle Port

In today's constantly changing environment, success requires that effective managers recognise change in terms of organisational survival. Whether change is desired or feared, expected or unexpected, it is generally accompanied by a degree of discomfort that often brings about a measure of conflict. The manner in which the process of change is managed often makes the difference between success and failure.

Refer again to the changes led by the CEO, Kerry Sanderson, of Fremantle Port introduced in Chapter 1, The Challenge of Management (p. 22). The maritime industry is characterised by a strongly held culture entrenched over decades. Understanding how this culture developed and was reinforced is crucial when planning and managing change. A century-old tradition of 'worker versus boss' is a tough place to improve effectiveness, efficiency and customer focus.

The port has metamorphosed from a loss-making, inertia-clogged government agency to a profitable and innovative organisation. Even in an organisation where improvement can be measured so dramatically, there is a cost. Sanderson notes that the toughest part has been the human toll, admitting that 'a lot of people have lost jobs in the changes… changes were achieved by voluntary redundancies but each still represents a loss'. She acknowledges that you do no one a favour by retaining inefficiencies (Treadgold 1996).

Part of the sweeping changes at Fremantle included dramatic restructuring and downsizing of the workforce, over two major reorganisations. Employment numbers were dramatically reduced with the survivors working under a leaner, flatter management structure. Port services were privatised, sold or streamlined. Other operations such as security and mooring operations were restructured (Treadgold 1996).

Recall that Sanderson advocates an 'inclusive' style of management—including the claims of all stakeholders to build competitive advantage. This new approach to managing required a complex series of interactions between the leader, followers and the situation. It is one thing to know about these pressures but another to manage them and turnaround a port.

A critical issue to management success is the ability to manage and develop a network of interdependent relationships with a wide and diverse range of stakeholders. Managing in the twenty-first century is about managing diverse people and knowledge. Today, Fremantle Port is one of Australia's fastest growing general cargo ports and continues to build a reputation for successfully working to meet the needs of its customers. Fremantle Ports, as strategic port manager, wins the praise of think-tanks such as the Bureau of Industry and Economics and the Australian Quality Council. Fremantle Port recognises its responsibilities as a key to the state achieving its goals.

Visit www.fremantleports.com.au to gain an understanding of the dynamic nature of the business. The strategic planning section of this website gives you a guide to their current values.

Source: Contributed by Allison James (details of sources are listed on p. 737).

Activities for discussion, analysis and further research

1. Identify the driving forces for change and the restraining forces against change faced by Fremantle Port.
2. Identify and briefly explain why employees resist change. Where relevant, identify which of these would have applied to Fremantle Port.
3. How might resistance to change be overcome? Provide examples from Fremantle Port.
4. What techniques are available to resolve dysfunctional intergroup conflicts? To guide your thinking consider the reaction of employees to the announcement of the restructure and dramatic downsizing of the workforce at Fremantle Port.

REFLECTIVE PRACTITIONER

The change in our business at some periods has been quite radical and at some others has been very subtle. At the moment, our business is prone to a lot of subtle change. This is more in terms of improvement rather than fundamental structural changes in the business or in terms of massive changes in personnel or positions or roles and job specs. In the early days the changes were far more rapid, as we were in that start-up phase where you make do with what you've got until you have the opportunity to take a breath and then allow the development process to catch up. If this change is managed well you will generally get where you want quite quickly.

This has the power or potential to instigate conflicts. I think that now, I have taken a much more balanced approach to instigating change. Given that I have now been in business for almost eight years, I have probably become more relaxed in my sense of urgency to bringing change about. In the early days, everything had to be done now, and it had to be

KIMBERLEY TURNER

AEROSAFE
RISK MANAGEMENT

done just so. Whereas now, it is not that daunting or scary to say 'well if this takes two years to implement, that's OK'. My approach is now to make very sure that the changes that are brought in contribute to enhancing the company and building it. It's about making the company more stable and really strengthening the foundations of the business, as opposed to quickly filling the gap of this great perceived deficiency that is already in place.

Consequently I have seen a lot of refinement, a lot of improvement. One of the greatest frustrations or potential areas of conflict in our business over the last few years has been the perception of duplication in change. So, for example, a system has been implemented through a bit of a knee jerk to immediately fill an identified gap with a solution that might have been a 75 per cent solution. Later on down the track, when we have thought it through, it is obvious that we want to fix this properly and we will start to design something new. Staff may react with comments such as: 'Don't we already have that in place? What's wrong with the way that we did it? Is it not working? Isn't that duplication?' That can really create some uncertainty. It really makes people not feel settled and at ease, and then they will question if they can really do it that way; is it really that important?

In the past, if this was not introduced properly, people have missed the mark and misused the things that have been designed to enhance what they have done, and I have found that it has only held them back and created more disruption.

One example of that is our weekly 'work in progress' meetings. These were designed to be purely a snapshot of the current jobs that people have on their plate. That should only take 15 minutes a week to update, then be submitted once a week, reviewed and discussed at the staff meetings. Some staff have taken that so seriously that it takes them two and a half hours a week to update their work in progress and that has missed the mark with the intended purpose. They use it as a pseudo task list when all it is meant to be is a tool to give the rest of the staff a snapshot of what is going on. It can be a signal of needing some help or offering help to others who may be overloaded at the time.

When we instigated that process, we thought it was really very minimal but we probably didn't think it through sufficiently in the implementation phase.

I found that it is quite easy to design the new thing that you want to introduce, you then almost perceive that you have done it. So it is easy to miss taking on that follow-on step which is the implementation process, the thinking through, the walking through it, the communication, and the giving people time for transition. I have learned that the implementation phase is the most important in getting the system up and running.

In my part, it takes a lot of discipline to follow through on implementation. Once I have stated that something is required, and I have informed the appropriate person, I feel like I have set it in motion and therefore it is going to happen. It is much harder to then check back regarding progress of how it is going. That discipline in implementation is really important. The other potential for conflict is when someone has been the owner of a process either through assignment or by default through their own interest. Then, if there is a need to change that process, if you don't do it carefully, you might undermine someone's work for the past two years. So there needs to be discipline to think about the implications of implementation—and impact on people is often more important than the financial costs in a small company like ours.

Another area of conflict which affects our organisation is the area of personal conflict between staff. I like to take a hands-off approach in those cases but sometimes I can't get away with that. I find it amazing that sometimes I have had to counsel staff who are the same age as my parents and that just emphasises for me that 'Hey I am the manager and as such it is my job, my role to do such things'. It does not matter what age I am and if I have children or not. These things get escalated to me and I have to handle them.

The last aspect is when there are decisions made which have not had the agreement of other staff. In the early days, in particular, other people were brought on board because of their experience who could advise or guide me. Sometimes the decisions I made were in conflict with the manner in which that staff member would have dealt with the situation. That in itself has brought conflict. This can shake you up and cause a divide.

It has taken me time to reach that balance between being consultative and just making decisions as the boss, and differentiating that line which says, ' Thank you so much for your input, it is really valued and now I have three different ways of looking at it, but this is the way I want this done'. Generally the staff will stand by my decision even if they don't agree with it and I think that is a sign of good growth and maturity within the company.

In the early days, I probably did not give enough feedback as to the value of their input. However, now on some occasions I sometimes give too much justification regarding the reasons and background for my decisions. Consultative decision making invites people into your decision-making cycle, which is not always, in my view, healthy, as it can give people the impression that they are free to step into decision cycles that they are not invited to step into.

FOCUS ON PRACTICE

Strategies for improving

1. Determine the differences between compromise and collaboration as conflict-handling styles. Which one fits you best? Why? Under what circumstances?
2. How would you go about ensuring workers understood the constraints and pressures of other jobs in the organisation, thus reducing conflict?
3. How would you determine whether conflict is due to structure or culture in a given organisation?

Source: Jones et al. (2000).

SUMMARY

- Although they may be forced to react to unpredictable situations, effective managers try to plan for major change and innovation using a six-step model that includes perceiving an opportunity or a problem, diagnosing the situation and generating ideas, presenting a proposal and adopting change, planning to overcome resistance, implementing change and monitoring results. Planning to overcome resistance to change implemention needs a knowledge of reasons why people resist change. Major reasons are self-interest, misunderstanding and lack of trust, different assessments, and low change tolerance. Managers must know ways to overcome resistance to change, including education and communication, participation and involvement, facilitation and support, negotiation and agreement, manipulation and cooptation, and explicit and implicit coercion. Force-field analysis helps understand driving forces and restraining forces producing the status quo. It is then more effective to reduce restraining forces than to increase driving forces for change.

- Managing conflict is an important group skill. Causes of conflict include task interdependence, scarce resources, goal incompatibility, communication failures, individual differences, and poorly-designed reward systems. Methods of reducing or resolving conflict include changing situational factors, appealing to superordinate goals, and using interpersonal conflict-handling modes. In addition, managers may need to simulate conflict to encourage creativity and innovation.

- Conflict between organisation groups is inevitable, and it may be positive or negative, depending on the impact of organisational goal attainment. Functional conflict helps and benefits organisational performance, while dysfunctional conflict hinders organisational goal achievement. While most managers try to eliminate conflict, the evidence is that organisational performance is benefited by an optimal level of conflict benefits. Dysfunctional conflict produces changes to and between groups. A group will increase cohesiveness, develop autocratic leadership and a task focus, as well as emphasise member loyalty. Changes between groups result in distorted perceptions, negative stereotypes and decreased communication.

- One difficult managerial task is conflict diagnosis and management. Techniques for intergroup conflict resolution include problem solving, resource expansion, avoidance, forcing, smoothing, compromise, and changing people or organisation structure. Each is useful at different times. Conflict management techniques also exist for situations where conflict levels are too low. Conflict stimulation techniques include using communication channels, bringing in new members and changing organisational structure. The point is that to be effective, conflict management must involve both resolution and stimulation.

MAX YOUR MARKS!
Thirty interactive questions on *Managing Organisations Through Change and Conflict* are available now at the Online Learning Centre that accompanies this text: www.mhhe.com/au/bartol4e (For access to MaxMark please refer to the front of this book.)

QUESTIONS FOR DISCUSSION AND REVIEW

1. Consider the university or college you are currently studying at and list internal and external factors which might help its administration identify need for change.
2. Explain why the change process is cyclical and not a straight line.
3. Outline the main reasons why employees resist change.
4. Explain the major approaches for overcoming resistance to change. Suppose you are a manager in a small manufacturing plant   facing increased competition from foreign-made products and needing to increase productivity. Design a plan to overcome employees' resistance to changes and innovations needed to increase productivity. What is your preferred strategy? What is your least preferred strategy?
5. Explain force-field analysis. Suggest three situations where it might be useful to help analyse a change situation.
6. Explain Lewin's model for overcoming resistance to change and link those steps to a situation you have experienced.

7. Managers often believe putting rules and regulations into place will help overcome if not eliminate conflict. What are the consequences of such an approach? Why?
8. What are the major causes of conflict in organisations? Can you make links between causes of conflict and the conflict management styles managers adopt?
9. Discuss strategies managers can use to overcome conflict situations in organisations. Give an example from your own experience.
10. If there is a proven relationship between conflict and change, how can managers best manage change to minimise the possibility of dysfunctional conflict?

CRITICAL THINKING QUESTIONS

To answer some of these questions you will need to do further research. Useful references are given below each section of the questions.

This chapter focused on a key aspect of organisations today—how managers exercise control in times where change creates conflict. An important message of this chapter was the positive way in which conflict can be used to successfully implement change.

The following questions look at some important implications of workplace conflict and how organisations have responded to the challenges of dealing with conflict and change.

1. Why is understanding conflict so important for managers today?

Beagrie (2004) believes organisations who manage conflict in a timely and professional manner win on two fronts—by averting negative outcomes and through receiving the respect and trust of employees. Conversely, failure to adequately deal with conflict can undermine managerial authority and be disastrous to an individual manager's career.

2. What is the first thing a manager should do to resolve workplace conflict?

3. Having worked through this and deciding that action must be taken, what are the next logical steps?

4. What role should HR play in helping other managers manage their conflict situations?

Gautrey (cited in Beagrie 2004, p. 25) provides three top tips for conflict resolution:

- Be honest with yourself and others—generally, it is the last thing the antagonist expects.
- Act quickly—seize the initiative and sort it out.
- Stand firm—stand up for your rights as an individual to express your feelings.

(Material relevant to these questions may be found in Beagrie, S. 2004, Expert's view: Colin Gautrey on managing conflict, *Personnel Today*, 27 January, p. 25.)

Niratpattanasai (2004) cites Thomas and Kilman's seminal work on conflict which suggests that while there are five main ways of coping with conflict, individuals tend to adopt one preferred method.

5. What are the five ways to deal with conflict?

6. What are the strengths and weaknesses of each style?

Niratpattanasai (2004) concludes his article with an important insight into the cultural dimension of conflict-handling styles when he notes that most Thais prefer a style of less confrontation and spend a lot of their time in a conflict situation trying to preserve a relationship.

(Material relevant to these questions may be found in Niratpattanasai, K. 2004, From competing to avoiding, each approach has its pros and cons, *Bangkok Post*, 9 February.)

A central debate in conflict management has been over conflicts of interests. We return to the banking industry with a brief overview of The Australian Securities and Investments Commission's findings of an industry surveillance review it conducted in 2003. The review dealt with a critical issue within the conflict management debate, the independence of research analysts' reports and deficiencies in compliance matters relating to the management and disclosure of conflicts of interest within the investment banking industry in Australia.

7. What do you think these deficiencies were?

8. What can be done to address the conflict of interest concerns ASIC has with Australia's banking industry?

Overall, it seems the conflict of interest debate could easily be stifled by bureaucratic and meaningless policies that lack enforcement value. At first reading, the ASIC review seems to be a paper tiger in that it concludes with ASIC agreeing to undertake extensive consultation with government, industry and other regulators to develop an appropriate policy establishing 'high-level principles' and guidance for Australian Financial Services (AFS) licensees generally about managing conflicts of interest, and more detailed guidance for providers of research reports. However, the seriousness attached to the issue of conflict of interest in the workplace is reinforced by the federal government developing policies in response to a new conflicts management obligation on all AFS licensees that are being introduced as part of their major reforms in the area.

At the end of the day, workplace conflict, in all its forms, is a challenge organisations cannot ignore if they are to remain viable in the long term.

(Material relevant to these questions may be found in Anon 2003, ASIC review of analysts identifies compliance issues, *RWE Australian Business News*, 22 August.)

MANAGEMENT EXERCISES

Exercise 1 **Management exercise: Force-field analysis**
Specification
Think about a situation where you would like to make a change or institute an innovation, but you face resistance. (The situation might involve getting a better grade in a course, instituting an innovative project in a student organisation, overcoming a challenge at work, or improving a relationship with a peer or friend.) Write a sentence or two describing the status quo. Then write a brief description of the situation as you would like it to be if you could change it.

Analysis
List the major driving forces, the factors pressuring for change, and then list the major restraining forces, the factors pressuring against change. Draw a force-field analysis diagram like the one in Figure 16.4. Remember, the wider the arrow, the stronger the force.

Solution
Select two or three restraining forces in your diagram and develop a means for reducing the degree of resistance. Be prepared to explain your diagram and solutions to another class member, who will act as your consultant (Lewin 1951).

Exercise 2 **Skill building: Diagnosing resistance to change**
Understanding why people resist change is the key to implementing new structures, procedures, methods and technologies. Five major reasons people resist change are shown in the following table. Typical comments associated with the reasons are listed. Indicate the reason normally associated with each comment.

Diagnosing resistance to change

Self-interest   Different assessments   Tolerance (low) for change
Misunderstanding   Lack of trust

1. _____   I don't want to take the job because my family will have to move again.

2. _____   We've done it that way for years.

3. _____   I still have trouble following the explanation about why we need this new complicated machine.

4. _____   Management thinks it's an improvement; I have a different view.

5. _____   Upper management won't admit it, but this merger will cost us jobs.

6. _____   Their explanation wasn't very clear regarding how working with them is going to help our unit.

7. _____   The last time they asked us to make a change like this, our conditions ended up being reduced.

8. _____   It appears producing buggy whips is not what our organisation should be doing in two years.

9. _____   I just perfected using this method, and now there's another change to cope with.

10. _____   I can't see where that job will help my career.

11. _____   I'm not sure my manager has been candid about the likely impact of the new procedure.

12. _____   Marketing believes we need field representatives, but engineering doesn't believe they are required, and production wants to control costs. Are they really necessary?

END-OF-CHAPTER CASE: ON THE RIM

Slop, slip, zoom

Australians can thank Philip Rossi's father for the terry-towelling hat. In the early 1950s, Theo Rossi saw new migrants working along the road with handkerchiefs around their heads. 'Dad and his dad had been in the hat trade for decades, manufacturing hatbands', Rossi says. 'So dad made up some hats that were easily washable, went in the back pocket and soaked up the sweat. Once they hit the major department stores, they took off.'

Philip Rossi's strategy was as follows: Improve customer service. Move into exporting. Increase production to 24 hours a day, seven days a week. Investigate emerging markets for new opportunities. Use research and development to create new products. Invest in state-of-the-art equipment. Buy the competition and close it down.

Rossi learnt a valuable lesson: copycats move very quickly. Soon his father's business could not compete as other companies produced a similar product. Rossi learnt that it is imperative to build in economies of scale, have a competitive advantage and stay one step ahead. 'I learnt a lot working with my father.'

Tapex was one of many parts of a fourth-generation family business that began in 1881 and was known as Rossi and Villa, after two Italian migrants   who sold goods from their wagon in rural areas. Rossi, who suffers dyslexia, joined the family business when he left school at 18. Tapex was then manufacturing and selling polypropylene twine to the agricultural market for baling.

In 1982, after Theo Rossi read a story on the legal costs of people falling down manholes, the company began manufacturing flexible plastic safety fences.

POWERWEB

International articles related to this topic are available at the Online Learning Centre at **www.mhhe.com/au/bartol4e**

By 1989, after reading about the high cost to utilities of people digging in the wrong spot, Philip Rossi invented a marking tape to warn people where fibre-optic pipes were buried.

Rossi was twenty-nine when he bought the business from his father. 'I had nine brothers and sisters, so I got no discount.' His father financed the acquisition and Rossi repaid the money with interest over the next eight years. Competition in tape and twine was growing. 'I told staff, 'Let's take on the market'. He immediately increased production to 24 hours a day, seven days a week.

He also divided the company into areas of expertise, developing strategies and explaining to staff and customers where the company was going. 'It used to be seat-of-your pants stuff when the margins were there. You could be sloppy. That changed in the early 1990s.' Rossi continued the family tradition of looking for opportunities in emerging markets. 'Part of our risk strategy is to have a portfolio of businesses.' Using government research grants, Rossi discovered new ways to manufacture sports yarn for synthetic surfaces. 'Our yarn was more resilient but looked like real grass.' Existing technology was also adapted for other uses. For example, he sold twine to power companies to be used as packing inside power cables.

But it was not enough. In 1996, revenue slid to $17 million from $20 million. 'Global competitors were taking market share. We got harsh and spent several years consolidating.' Unprofitable products and environmentally unfriendly products were jettisoned as Tapex focused on producing higher volumes of synthetic yarn and improving the technology.

In 1998, Rossi decided to move into the emerging market of water filtration and developed a biological treatment. 'We invested heavily in the yarn and water filtration divisions, buying state-of-the-art equipment. You can't go into emerging markets as a me-too.' It was not until 1999 that Rossi began to export. 'That was a big mistake. We should have started exporting three to four years earlier, but were too busy looking after our local customers', he says.

In 2002, Rossi bought the Melbourne company Kinnears, his biggest twine competitor, and shut the factory. As part of the sale, Kinnears retrenched 130 workers, some of whom were taken on by Tapex. 'It was hard but it was a tremendously successful move and we are selling a lot more twine', he says. Now Tapex is exporting water filtration products, yarn and agricultural products to the United States, Asia and the Middle East. Yarn brings in 20 per cent of revenue, water filtration products 10 per cent, construction and safety products 20 per cent, agricultural products 25 per cent, and industrial products 25 per cent.

Rossi, forty-two, has a five-year revenue goal of $70 million. 'Will it go to five generations? I have three kids and that would be fantastic.'

Source: Gome (2004).

Activities for discussion, analysis and further research

1. List the advantages of running a company that has been in the family for four generations.
2. How does Rossi protect his company from the risk involved in investing in changing technologies?
3. Find the Tapex website and explore the various activities that the organisation has undertaken and track their international ventures. What evidence can you find that Tapex might have started exporting earlier than they did ? What impact might that have had on their current situation?

FURTHER READING

Andrews, T.G. and Chompusri, N. 2001, Lessons in 'cross-vergence': Restructuring the Thai subsidiary corporation, *Journal of International Business Studies*, 1st Quarter, 32, 1, pp. 77–94.

Buchel, B. 2003, Managing partner relations in joint venture, *MIT Sloan Management Review*, Summer, 44, 4, pp. 91–6.

Oxman, J.A. and Smith, B.D. 2003, The limits of structural change, *MIT Sloan Management Review*, Fall, 45, 1, pp. 77–83.

Pan, F. and Zhang, Z. 2004, Cross-cultural challenges when doing business in China, *Singapore Management Review*, 1st Half, 26, 1, pp. 81–91.

Zain, M., Richardson, S. and Adam, M.N.K. 2002, The implementation of innovation by a multinational operating in two different environments: A comparative study, *Creativity & Innovation Management*, June, 11, 2, pp. 98–107.

GRADUATE GLIMPSE

Carolyn Dickie has a Master of Commerce (management) degree from Curtin Business School at the Curtin University of Technology. She received the Curtin Business School West Australian Chamber of Commerce and Industry Medal for the academically-best graduating student and also the School of Management Prize for the best master's degree student. Carolyn is administrator at the Australian Opera Studio. She is also a sessional lecturer at Curtin University of Technology within the Curtin Business School.

What does your job entail?

At the Australian Opera Studio I am responsible for the overall management of the Studio with duties including contract negotiation, publicity, marketing and sponsorship management, event negotiation and management, budgeting and account keeping, and teaching the young performers basic business skills.

At Curtin University of Technology I lecture in a variety of areas within the School of Management.

How have your university studies assisted you in your career?

My university studies have given me the opportunity to negotiate the various role changes throughout my career, and through this the levels of responsibility, activity and flexibility within my daily work life have expanded enormously. I have also had the opportunity to participate in a number of research projects in my particular area of interest (cross-cultural studies) as well as be involved in a number of academic and industry conferences.

What is an important management principle that you draw upon frequently in the workplace?

It is very difficult to name just one important principle—I use a number of them often. I consider communication, teamwork, motivation and ethics to be critical and I use them on a daily basis.

Mark Simpson has a Bachelor of Business Studies from Charles Sturt University (Wagga Wagga). This is a flexible degree allowing students the choice of a wide range of business subjects. While studying for his degree, he chose to focus on management and international management subjects. Mark is now a branch manager at the ANZ Bank, a position he achieved after completing a graduate traineeship with the bank.

What does your job entail?

I ensure that the branch is run as a successful, customer-focused, profitable business. My responsibilities involve balancing regulatory, compliance and security issues with customer-focused sales and service and the challenges of managing a group of people.

How have your university studies assisted you in your career?

My university studies have been of great assistance to my career. They facilitated me in achieving my current position, for which I was chosen from a pool of around 11 000 applicants. Along with the technical knowledge I gained at university, the communication and problem-solving skills I learned have been invaluable.

How do you use your knowledge of management principles in the day-to-day functions of your position?

I find that every situation is unique and generally requires a new solution, and most certainly some creativity. My knowledge of management principles provides a sound base from which to form ideas and solve the problems that inevitably occur in the day-to-day functions of my role.

Down but not out: Salim Group poised for a comeback

After the Asian currency and economic crises hit Indonesia—like the tidal waves so familiar in the islands—it looked as if the giant Salim Group might implode under the weight of mounting debt and government nationalisations. How could this once-great Chinese family conglomerate fall from favour so swiftly?

The Salim Group was founded by Liem Sioe Liong, an industrious entrepreneur from Fukien province in China, a region famous for its business emigrants. He arrived penniless in Dutch-controlled Indonesia in 1937, and by 1990 he had built an empire with annual sales of US$8 billion. Like so many overseas Chinese tycoons, he created a family conglomerate based on the famous 'golden diamond' principles. This business logic requires a balanced corporate portfolio to stand on four legs: raw materials and staple commodities; manufacturing; property and real estate; and banking and finance. Wholesale and retail trade and distribution also constitute a key component of the golden diamond.

Mr Liem's shrewdest move was to supply peanut oil and other staples to the Indonesian army in the 1950s, during its fight for independence from the Dutch. He struck up a close personal friendship with a young Lieutenant Suharto, who would go on to become President of Indonesia for several decades.

Liem was adept at using his contacts and negotiating skills to build a network of unrelated businesses that would dwarf all other Indonesian industrial groups. Indeed, Salim Group comprised 5 per cent of the GDP of Indonesia, which was once forecast to become the world's fourth largest economy by 2030.

Liem invited friends and family members of Suharto and himself, and a few top-ranking military figures, to become key investors and shareholders. Liem was quick to spot lucrative market niches and market imperfections, and was able to exploit opportunities to buy out or block competition and to secure government-guaranteed monopolies and protection from losses through substantial government equity infusions.

The Salim Group comprised over 350 companies that were operationally separate. About one hundred were centrally administered, while the rest were passive investments. The Group's development was accidental, through opportunistic growth rather than strategic design. Liem himself influenced operations through resource allocation, information and connections. He achieved informal control by rotating a small number of close and loyal managers around the different companies. Such trust and personal relationships allowed subsidiaries to be decentralised while cash flow was allocated centrally.

Until the 1960s Liem focused on raw materials such as cloves, coffee, rubber and soybeans. In the 1970s he capitalised on import-substitution industries, which the Indonesian government was then promoting with long-term profit guarantees and price fixing. This resulted in an expansion into cement, steel, assembly and distribution of foreign cars, and banking. Further diversification into forestry, chemicals, agribusiness and, later, real estate development, followed.

The next phase of development came in the 1980s, when Liem began setting up offshore holding companies to grow investments outside Indonesia as a means of reducing country risk exposure. Perhaps Liem sensed a growing uneasiness about the vulnerability of Indonesia's Chinese minority, where 3 per cent of the population controlled up to 70 per cent of the country's wealth. He set up his First Pacific Group in Hong Kong, and invested in banking and property in Hong Kong, real estate in Singapore, drugstores in the Philippines, a US Savings and Loan, a Dutch Trading House and an Australian communications company.

First Pacific Group was 65 per cent owned by Liem investors, and was run by Manuel Pangilinan, an American-educated Filipino who had come from American Express.

Liem also diversified into chemical production, industrial parks, and manufacturing of tableware, soft drinks and wire harnesses. Salim companies moved into East Germany and the United States with varied success; a number of ventures in these countries failed.

Then Liem's son Anthony took the reins from his ageing father and began a process of reform, modernisation and professionalisation. Anthony Liem recognised the need to transform the Salim Group into a modern corporation, with competitive advantage based on distinctive competencies. He envisaged a company that would be able to compete with multinationals in the changing environment of the Asia-Pacific region, as the cold winds of globalisation penetrated every economy. He set out to streamline the Group's holdings, to consolidate the family's control at the expense of the other Liem investors, and to strengthen the company's balance sheets. He was known as a very astute and capable manager and negotiator, who had extensive international contacts and knowledge. He wanted to use new, non-Indonesian holding companies as acquisition and growth entities. He actively engaged global consultants such as PricewaterhouseCoopers, Jardine Fleming, Goldman Sachs and Citibank to provide independent professional advice. He favoured employing non-family, professional managers with business school qualifications.

By the 1990s the Salim Group had grown from being an Indonesian family conglomerate to become an Asian company with European and North American businesses. However, the Group's capital was being stretched to the limits by a relentless acquisition program. Instead of pausing to consolidate, all divisions were searching for new growth opportunities. The year 1998 was a turning point for the Salim Group, whose very growth and profitability had been underpinned by the patronage of President Suharto, his family and friends. When Suharto was swept from power, Salim lost its protection and sponsorship. Many of its companies eventually wound up in the new Indonesian government's hands. When friends ask Anthony Liem how he is doing these days, he gives a one-word reply: 'surviving'. 'Mr Anthony's fall and rise partly reflect the resilience of Asia's ethnic Chinese

business clans', noted the *Asian Wall Street Journal*. 'Facing anti-Chinese riots and politicians (opposed to the Salim Group's links with former President Suharto) eager to see a fire sale of its assets, Mr Anthony frantically juggled businesses from California to the Netherlands to stay afloat.' But it also highlights the balance between reform and pragmatism that Indonesian policy makers have had to strike to return the nation to a solid footing. Faced with economic crisis and worries that ethnic Chinese money might never return, Indonesia and the International Monetary Fund ultimately decided Salim Group was too important to dismember.

Salim Group's strategy to cope with its financial troubles was to sell stakes in its business to foreign firms. But the Group's companies are not used to having foreigners with controlling stakes and most are likely to try and keep it that way. Basically they want to keep control in sophisticated industries like the automobile industry, in which Salim is likely to let the Japanese take over Indomobil. Based on research on 200 Salim firms out of its 500 firms in Indonesia, foreigners only hold an average of 5.4 per cent, according to the Castle Group, a business advisory services firm.

In June 2002, Salim-controlled First Pacific planned to sell its key Philippines assets for more than US$600 million, and to use the proceeds to stage a comeback. Under the plan, First Pacific would sell its stake in Philippines Long Distance Telephone Company (PLDT) and a property business to a new joint venture company that is 66.7 per cent owned by Chinese Filipino businessman, John Gokongwei. To do this, First Pacific needed to overcome opposition from PLDT's president and chief executive, Manuel Pangilinan. A trusted Salim Group executive for 20 years, Mr Pangilinan became a thorn in Anthony Liem's side as he disagreed with the proposed sale and tried to block it.

First Pacific announced in June 2002 that it will use some of the sale proceeds to pay shareholders a special dividend. It will also reduce its debt by US$187 million and book a one-time gain of about

US$200 million from the planned sale. Then Anthony Liem plans to go back onto the investment offensive. His future plans differ markedly from those of his father. He views investment in such markets as Singapore, Malaysia, Australia and China as a positive way of diversifying country risk and of lowering currency exposure. Noticeably absent from the list are Indonesia, Europe and North America.

Consumer goods businesses may be more likely targets than property or telecommunications. One possible target is the Chinese noodle-making unit of Asia Food and Properties Ltd. Salim already owns the world's largest maker of instant noodles, P.T. Indofood Sukses Makmur. Another could be part of Singapore beverage-maker Fraser and Neave Ltd. There will be a preference for successful consumer goods and well-known brands.

Meanwhile, unlike other tycoons, Anthony Liem reached an agreement with the Indonesian Bank Restructuring Agency (IBRA) to repay his group's debts, and he has stuck by it. He pledged stakes in more than one hundred companies to IBRA as security for debts of 52 trillion rupiah (US$5.83 billion). IBRA has been selling many of the pledged assets. 'Salim Group has recouped its position quite well', said Umer Juoro, an economist. 'Salim Group is one of the companies with the best chance of regaining economic power.'

Source: Contributed by John Krasnostein (details of sources are listed on p. XXX).

Activities for discussion, *analysis and further research*

1. What economic and political conditions in Indonesia allowed the Salim Group to grow and prosper? Explain the pattern or sequence of growth at Salim. Explain Mr Liem's rationale or logic in putting together his business portfolio. What does each business contribute to the group?

2. In groups of three or four, conduct a SWOT analysis of the Salim Group when it was at its peak. What risks and threats does the Salim Group face in the future? What emerging opportunities should the group address? Now develop a rational and profitable growth strategy for the future, based on core strengths and sustainable competitive advantage.

3. Log on to the websites: http://asia.cnn.com/2002/BUSINESS/asia/01/11/indonesia.bca/, www.atimes.com/se-asia/DA09Ae01.html and www.inq7.net/bus/2002/may/31/bus_1-1.htm. Investigate the activities relating to the sale of shares of Bank Central Asia and Philippine Long Distance Telephone Company and analyse the impact of these developments for Anthony Liem's plans and decisions in 2002. What difficulties still remain before Anthony Liem will be able to turn his group around and begin its new growth strategy? If you were Anthony Liem, what strategies and tactics would you consider at this critical juncture?

Please insert the CD-ROM that is packaged with this book to view video clips that correspond to this Part theme.

ACROSS ALL FUNCTIONS

Previous parts of this book introduce management and examine its four major functions: planning, organising, leading and controlling. Now, in Part 6, we see how these various functions apply in the significant management situation of conducting business in the international arena.

Managers need an increasingly world-wide view, CHAPTER 17 focuses on strategic issues and different structures to conduct business across national boundaries. Essential to the international manager is adapting to cultural differences and dealing with special social and ethical concerns which arise in international areas.

More recently concern has grown with regional communities which comprise countries with shared trade, economic and political interests. These include groupings such as the European Economic Community and the North American Free Trade Area. The region of most interest here is the Asia Pacific Region, or the South-East Asia Region.

CHAPTER 18 considers the region, looking at the role and nature of key members. It also discusses the role of Australia in the region and the continuing impact the region has on the global community.

PART 6

CHAPTER 17

INTERNATIONAL MANAGEMENT

LEARNING OBJECTIVES

After studying this chapter, you should be able to:

- Explain the concept of a multinational corporation and describe four major orientations to international management.
- Delineate several elements important in assessing the international environment.
- Explain the concept of competitive advantage of nations and its link to innovation.
- Outline the major methods of entry into international business.
- Contrast four major strategies for multinational corporations.
- Enumerate the main structural alternatives for conducting international business.
- Explain the principal issues related to assignment policies and recruitment, selection, training and repatriation of managerial personnel.
- Describe adjustments in leadership style needed due to cultural differences.
- Delineate the major social responsibility and ethics issues related to international management.

STRIVING FOR EXCELLENCE

China: One man's trade effort

Ask James Liang about opportunities in China for Australian exporters and he smiles: the Chinese market, though competitive, he says, is so big there is room for everyone. Liang, who runs an import/export business, Panausino, between China and Australia, migrated from Shanghai to Sydney 15 years ago when he was thirty-four. He had been climbing the public service ladder as a director of foreign affairs, working in Shanghai in the Ministry of Foreign Economic Relations and Trade, when he decided he did not fit that bureaucratic culture. 'I had visited Australia twice and liked the people', he says. 'They are honest and straightforward.'

On arrival, he decided to spend a month studying the market to see the type of business he might start. During that time, he was approached by one of China's largest stainless steel companies, Shanghai Light Industrial Group. In 1990, he imported his first container of stainless steel products, including kitchenware. Initially, he brought in one container at a time, then five, then 10—and, last year, he imported 60 containers. His customers include David Jones and Target.

Panausino has nine employees. The export side of Liang's business took off three years ago when a friend, a property developer from Shanghai, asked him to find a good Australian architect to design a residential project on a 27-hectare site in Shanghai to suit China's burgeoning middle class, which demands modern, creative designs. Liang says: 'Chinese architects are still very traditional and they need Western ideas.'

Liang contacted the Royal Australian Institute of Architects and was given three names. He visited

three offices and chose one, TMG Design Group, in North Sydney.

Initially, TMG's partners told him they were not sure about China because of uncertainty about payment and working styles, but later, after more discussions, they expressed a very strong interest in the country.

In 2000, TMG designed 2000 homes for the Lakeside development in Shanghai. After a year of working together, TMG and Liang formed an alliance and opened an office in Shanghai to look for more work. Liang says: 'I was on a hello trip to China and visited a classmate who holds a senior position in the city of Wuhu, west of Shanghai. Wuhu is a medium-size city of four million people and they wanted a city plaza, which includes an office building, opera house, museum and library. We got the project, the biggest project since 1949 in that city.'

The mayor of neighbouring Maanshan saw the designs and, not to be outdone, wanted the same. That project started in November 2001. Liang is working on another residential development for 1700 homes in Shanghai, again for middle-class people seeking a contemporary look. He is also signing another $100 million project, to design a 60 000-square-metre shopping centre in Shanghai. Liang says the export side of his business shows the greater promise.

However, he will not be tendering for work associated with the Olympics. 'Everyone is looking at that', he says, 'but we decided we want to work on big, high-profile projects and have clients who

continued

are good at paying. With the Olympics, sometimes there are strings attached. The projects go for three or four years and you have to contribute to other things'.

He says that, in the next five years, China will need many more architects. The country also needs building products and building materials such as sliding doors and timber floors, which Australia can provide.

'I have just started exporting water heaters to China', Liang says. He also says that products developed to suit the harsh weather in Australia would be very useful in China. For example, he has been exporting Pascol paints, made by Wattyl, to China since 1996 in response to a Shanghai developer looking for a durable exterior paint

Source: Gome (2003).

It is argued that organisations must adopt a global view of planning and other activities. By viewing the whole world as their operating area, managers can tap into world-wide markets and be active where conditions support organisational goals. Main (1989) argues that a world-wide outlook is needed to effectively compete in many industries, such as cars, banking, consumer electronics, entertainment, pharmaceuticals, publishing, travel services and washing machines.

Managers can engage in international business, face competition from international organisations or deal with them as suppliers or customers. This means managers must grasp international management issues firmly. Accordingly, here we explore the basic nature of international management, building on coverage of international management issues across this text. We also probe environmental factors affecting managerial international success, and consider the idea of the competitive advantage of nations and its relationship to innovation. We then examine strategic issues associated with international management and consider structural alternatives for conducting international business. We next investigate how to adapt to cultural differences. Finally, we address ethical questions from organisations across the world.

THE NATURE OF INTERNATIONAL MANAGEMENT

international business

Profit-related activities conducted across national boundaries

international management

Process of planning, organising, leading and controlling in organisations engaged in international business

multinational corporation (MNC)

Organisation engaging in production or service activities through its affiliates in several countries, maintaining control over policies of those affiliates, and managing from a global perspective

If you inventoried your belongings, you would find items demonstrating international activity. For example, shoes from Italy or Brazil, a Japanese television and VCR, and a shirt made in China. Even items with brand names of companies based in one country may have been made in another through international business. **International business** is profit-related activities across national boundaries. These include supplies from other countries, products or services sold to customers abroad, and fund transfers to subsidiaries in other countries. **International management** is planning, organising, leading and controlling in organisations engaged in international business (Auerback 1987).

Organisations engaging in international management

Organisations engaging in international management vary in the size and extent that their business activities cross national boundaries. One organisation type involved in international management is the multinational corporation. Although definitions vary, a **multinational corporation (MNC)** is a firm engaged in production or service activities through affiliates in other countries, controlling their policies, and managing from a global perspective (Root 1984; Rugman & Hodgetts 1995; Pacelle 1996). With this perspective, top managers allocate resources and coordinate activities to take the best advantage of business conditions.

It may be hard to identify multinational corporations from the outside, in terms of how much control management has over affiliate policies or whether they use a global perspective.

Going my way?

Since the 1970s, engineers and IT specialists from Taiwan, India and China have been going to the United States to work in the Silicon Valley. However, the past two or three years have seen a changing trend. Engineers are still going but then, so are venture capitalists. These Asian investors have been a growing source of funds for start-ups and at the same time are brokering a special process of two-way trade. On one hand, they're building bridges to Asia for the valley's latest dot.com innovations, but on the other hand they are helping their region's own entrepreneurs take a foothold in this highly competitive market.

Source: Hiebert, M. (2000).

Reflection points

1. What are the issues these young investors must consider as they make their move?
2. They are obviously welcome and significant sources of funds for start-ups. What factors should the recipients of those investments be considering as they accept this support?

Decision point

1. Locate the web sites for Acer Technology and Asia Tech and see what you can find out about how they make their decisions on where to park their venture capital funds.

As a result, an arbitrary percentage (25 per cent of sales from foreign sources) distinguishes multinational corporations from other business types. However, no single universal foreign sales percentage separates multinational corporations from others (Rugman & Hodgetts 1995). The 25 largest multinational corporations are listed in Table 17.1.

While multinational companies tend to be large and engage in many activities across borders, an increasing number of middle-sized and small companies conduct international business. By one estimate about 10 per cent of companies with 100 or fewer employees export (Aley 1995). Regardless of size, their managers hold a basic view of international management.

Orientations toward international management

Top-level managers in firms expanding internationally (particularly in multinational corporations) take one of four orientations about how much operating methods are influenced by headquarters or by members in other parts of the world. These are ethnocentric (home-country oriented), polycentric (host-country oriented), regiocentric (region oriented) and geocentric orientations (world oriented) (Perlmutter 1969; Balagi, Chakravarthy & Perlmutter 1985; Morrison, Ricks & Roth 1991). A home country is where an organisation's headquarters is located, while a host country is a foreign country an organisation does business in.

An **ethnocentric** (or home-country) **orientation** is where executives assume that practices working in the headquarters or home country must work elsewhere (Trachtenberg 1986; *Financial Times* 1996; Fernandez & Barr 1994). An ethnocentric orientation is often a phase organisations go through when they enter the international arena, and it can be hard to eradicate.

A **polycentric** (or host-country) **orientation** is an approach where executives believe company parts located in a given host country should be staffed by locals as much as possible. Locals—sometimes called nationals—are seen to know their own culture, mores, work ethics and markets best. So, subsidiaries in different countries operate under direction of locals and are tied to the parent firm by financial controls. The parent company may have a low public profile relative to the subsidiary.

A **regiocentric** (or regional) **orientation** is an approach where executives believe geographic regions have commonalities making a regional focus worthwhile and that regional company problems are best solved by people from the region. Typically, regional headquarters coordinate efforts among local subsidiaries in the region, while world headquarters manage

ethnocentric orientation

Approach to international management where executives assume practices that work in the headquarters or home country must necessarily work elsewhere

polycentric orientation

Approach to international management where executives believe the parts of the organisation located in a given host country should be staffed by local individuals to the fullest extent possible

regiocentric orientation

Approach to international management where executives believe geographic regions have commonalities that make a regional focus advantageous, and that company problems related to the region are generally best solved by individuals from the region

TABLE 17.1 THE WORLD'S LARGEST 25 MULTINATIONAL CORPORATIONS					
Rank					
2002	**1999**	**1995**	**Company**	**Headquarters**	**Industry**
1	4	12	Wal-Mart Stores	USA	General merchandisers
2	1	4	General Motors	USA	Motor vehicles
3	8	9	Exxon	USA	Petroleum refining
4	11	10	Royal Dutch/Shell Group	Britain/Netherlands	Petroleum refining
5	19	—	BP Amoco	England	Petroleum refining
6	3	7	Ford Motor	USA	Motor vehicles
7	2	—	DaimlerChrysler	Germany	Motor vehicles
8	10	8	Toyota Motor	Japan	Motor vehicles
9	9	20	General Electric	USA	Electronics
10	7	1	Mitsubishi	Japan	Trading
11	5	2	Mitsui	Japan	Trading
12	23	—	Allianz	Germany	Insurance
13	16	—	Citigroup	USA	Finance
14	—	—	Total	France	Petroleum
15	—	—	ChevronTexaco	USA	Petroleum
16	18	15	Nippon Telegraph & Telephone	Japan	Telecommunications
17	—	—	ING Group	Netherlands	Insurance
18	6	3	Itochu	Japan	Trading
19	14	18	International Business Machines	USA	Computers
20	17	24	Volkswagen	Germany	Motor vehicles
21	22	25	Siemens	Germany	Electronics
22	13	5	Sumitomo	Japan	Trading
23	12	6	Marubeni	Japan	Trading
24	—	—	Verizon Communications	USA	Telecommunications
25	—	—	American International Group	USA	Insurance

Source: Adapted from *Fortune* (23 July 2003).

geocentric orientation

Approach to international management where executives believe a global view is needed in both the headquarters of the parent company and its various subsidiaries and the best individuals, regardless of host- or home-country origin, should be utilised to solve company problems anywhere in the world

overall issues, such as global strategy, basic research and development, and long-term financing (Moran, Harris & Stripp 1993; Bateman & Snell 2004). For example, forming a more unified multination European Union by 'harmonising' national rules (e.g. adopting common standards for electric plugs) provides new opportunities for a regional focus. Previously, manufacturers in Europe often set up plants in host countries serving the specific needs of the host country and perhaps of small neighbours. The plant produced the full product range sold in the particular host country. With a more unified European Union, economies of scale can be achieved with different products from regional factories. Products are then shipped over a broad geographical area to customers (Morrison et al. 1991).

The **geocentric** (or world) **orientation** is an approach where executives believe a global view is needed in both parent company headquarters and subsidiaries, and the best people, regardless of home- or host-country origin, should be used to solve company problems. Major issues are viewed globally by both headquarters and subsidiaries, which pose questions such as 'Where in the world shall we raise money, build our plant, conduct R&D, and develop and launch new ideas to serve our present and future customers?' (Perlmutter 1969, p. 13). The geocentric approach is hardest to achieve as managers must acquire both local and global knowledge.

A geocentric approach helped Boeing save its 737 aeroplane. When sales slowed in the early 1970s, a group of engineers saw they had not attended to a potential market, developing regions. Through visits, the engineers found that runways in developing countries were too short for the 737 and were mainly asphalt, which is softer than concrete. They then redesigned the wings for shorter landings on soft pavement and changed the engines for quicker takeoffs. New landing gear was developed and low-pressure tyres installed. Boeing began with small orders for the 737 from developing countries, and later larger Boeing planes due to the experiences with the 737. The 737 became the best-selling commercial jet in aviation history and still sells well (Kupfer 1988; Holmes 1995; Cole 1996). The Boeing approach shows the value of understanding the international environment.

ASSESSING THE INTERNATIONAL ENVIRONMENT

While international management opens great opportunities, the challenge becomes trying to understand a broader set of environmental factors than met in a strictly domestic business. In this section, we explore various elements of the effects of the international environment and a broader concept, the competitive advantage of nations.

Environmental elements

The idea of a general environment, or mega-environment, helps us understand the nature of international management. The general environment is the external environment segment of broad societal conditions and trends where an organisation operates (see Chapter 3). Major general environment elements, including economic, legal-political, sociocultural and technological factors, help us describe the international area more fully.

The economic element

Various countries' economic systems are addressed in Chapter 3. Other economic factors influencing companies' ability to operate internationally are the level of economic development in a country, presence of adequate infrastructure, the country's balance of payments, and exchange rates.

Countries (other than Communist ones) fall into two groups based on level of economic or industrial development. The first group, known as **developed countries**, with high levels of economic or industrial development, includes Australia, New Zealand, Singapore, Canada, the United States, Western Europe and Japan. The second group is the **less developed countries (LDCs)** or developing countries (often called the 'third world'), and consists of relatively poor nations with low per capita income, little industry and high birth-rates. Within LDCs, countries emerging as major exporters of manufactured goods are referred to as **newly industrialised countries (NICs)**, including such nations as Malaysia, Taiwan and South Korea.

We may believe multinational corporations operate across the world. In fact, about 95 per cent are based in developed countries with about 75 per cent of foreign investment channelled to developed countries. However, the rising prosperity of many LDCs (particularly the NIC group) has great potential for market expansion (Mendenhall, Punnett & Ricks 1995; James 2003b).

Deciding to conduct business in a given area also depends on adequate infrastructure. **Infrastructure** refers to highways, railways, airports, sewage facilities, housing, educational

developed countries

Group of countries that is characterised by a high level of economic or industrial development and includes Australia, the United States, Western Europe, Canada, Australia, New Zealand and Japan

less developed countries (LDCs)

Group of non-communist countries, often called the 'third world', consisting primarily of relatively poor nations characterised by low per capita income, little industry and high birth-rates

newly industrialised countries (NICs)

Countries within LDCs emerging as major exporters of manufactured goods, including such nations as Taiwan and South Korea

infrastructure

Highways, railways, airports, sewage facilities, housing, educational institutions, recreation facilities, and other economic and social amenities signalling the extent of an area's economic development

balance of payments

Account of goods and services, capital loans, gold, and other items entering and leaving a country

balance of trade

Difference between a country's exports and imports

exchange rate

Rate at which one country's currency can be exchanged for another's

political risk

Probability of occurrence of political actions resulting in either loss of enterprise ownership or significant benefits from conducting business

expropriation

Seizure of a foreign company's assets by a host-country's government

indigenisation laws

Laws which require that citizens of a host country hold a majority interest in all firms operating within the country's borders

tariff

Type of trade barrier in the form of a customs duty, or tax, levied mainly on imports

import quota

Type of trade barrier in the form of a limit on the amount of product that may be imported over a period of time

administrative protections

Type of trade barrier in the form of various rules and regulations making it more difficult for foreign firms to conduct business in a particular country

institutions, communications networks, recreation facilities, and other economic and social amenities signalling an area's level of economic development. Due to information technology's growing importance, infrastructure for communications and information is most critical. According to an Asian Development Bank estimate, countries in the region must spend $150 billion over the next 10 years to upgrade telecommunications infrastructure. Another $300 billion will be needed for regional transportation, power and water systems. Hence, building infrastructure to support economic development is expensive (Marchand 1996).

Another economic variable is a country's **balance of payments**, the account of goods and services, capital loans, gold and other items entering and leaving the country. **Balance of trade**, the difference between a country's exports and imports, is a critical determinant of a country's balance of payments. Constant trade deficits means a country's wealth is exported, and trade surpluses enhance a country's ability to expand and conduct more international trade (Knowlton 1988; Rugman & Hodgetts 1995; Skotnicki 2003).

This relates to the **exchange rate**, the rate at which one country's currency can be exchanged for another's currency. As exchange rates affect relative prices of goods from various countries, changes can influence a firm's ability to engage in international business (Melloan 1988; Magnusson 1992; Rose 1996).

The legal-political element

Both legal and political conditions affect a firm's ability to conduct business in other countries. Considerations include level of political risk of operating in a country, and governmental trade barriers.

Corporations must assess the political risk of setting up in a given country (Micallef 1981). **Political risk** is how likely political actions will result in loss of ownership or benefits (Hofheinz 1994). A host-country's government seizure of a foreign company's assets is **expropriation**. Countries including Cuba, Zambia and Iran have expropriated foreign-owned companies' assets within their borders. Iran seized many commercial assets, valued at over $5 billion, when Ayatollah Khomeini assumed power in Iran during 1979. Since 1960, 76 nations have expropriated over 1535 firms (Jodice 1980). A related risk is presence of **indigenisation laws**, requiring host-country citizens to hold a majority interest in firms operating inside the country's borders (such as Malaysia). Other risks are less severe but make business harder or more expensive in a host country.

Another legal-political environment aspect is trade control, which uses barriers or limitations on goods entering or leaving a country (Rugman & Hodgetts 1995; Kinicki & Williams 2003). These are often used so domestic goods can compete with foreign sources. The most common barrier type is a **tariff**, a customs duty, or tax, on imports. For example, Ford Motor Company's efforts in Russia are restricted by high import tariffs. A combination of tariffs, excises and value-added taxes doubles Ford's prices (Serenyi 1996). Another barrier is an **import quota**, a limit on the amount of a product to be imported over a time period. Import quotas can protect a domestic market by limiting availability of foreign competitors' product (Daniels & Radebaugh 1989).

As tariffs and quotas provoke direct reprisals from countries with affected products, the more subtle approach of **administrative protections** may be used. These rules and regulations make it hard for foreign firms to operate in a country. In one case, Japanese video recorders had to pass through French customs at a small facility at Poitiers, to be inspected individually. This caused great delays, and recorder importation slowed to a trickle. Japanese manufacturers eventually agreed to a 'voluntary export quota', limiting recorders shipped to France (*New York Times* 1983).

The sociocultural element

The sociocultural environmental element includes attitudes, values, norms, beliefs, behaviours and associated demographic trends characteristic of a geographic area. Comparing people in different nations, it is common to speak about cultural differences.

Geert Hofstede developed a framework to study societal culture's effects on individuals (Jackofsky, Slocum & McQuaid 1988; Hofstede 1980, 1984). He researched values and beliefs of over 100 000 IBM employees in 40 countries across the world. Hofstede's approach uses five cultural dimensions to analyse societies: power distance, uncertainty avoidance, individualism–collectivism, achievement–nurturing orientation, and long-term–short-term orientation. Each is a continuum from high to low.

Power distance is how much individuals in a society see power distribution differences as reasonable and normal. In low-power-distance societies (Sweden, Denmark and Israel) those from different backgrounds often interact, and members of lower-status groups easily move to higher-status positions. In contrast, in high-power-distance societies (China, the Philippines and India) high-status people have little interaction with lower-status individuals, and raising one's status is hard. These differences affect the level of collaboration between subordinates and bosses. If power distance is high, managers will more likely tell subordinates what to do, not consult them. By contrast, managers and subordinates are more likely to collaborate in a low-power-distance society.

The second dimension in Hofstede's framework, **uncertainty avoidance**, is the extent to which a society's members are uncomfortable with and try to avoid situations seen as unstructured, unclear or unpredictable. For example, in low-uncertainty-avoidance countries (Australia, Sweden and Great Britain) firms have fewer written rules and regulations. This develops generalists (knowing many different areas) rather than specialists (knowing a great deal on a narrow area) and encourages managerial risk taking. Companies in high uncertainty-avoidance countries operate in reverse (Japan, Peru and France).

Individualism–collectivism, the third dimension, is how much individuals focus on their own and their immediate families' interests as opposed to the larger group's interests. In cultures valuing individualism (e.g. New Zealand, Great Britain and Canada) managers will change companies easily, feel less responsible for employee welfare, and rely on individual rather than group decision making. In contrast, in cultures valuing collectivism (e.g. Venezuela, Taiwan and Mexico) managers focus on team outcomes not individual ones and emphasise employee welfare, viewing the organisation as a family.

The fourth dimension, **achievement–nurturing orientation**, is how much a society emphasises values such as assertiveness, competitiveness and material success, rather than passivity, cooperation and emotions. In competitive societies (e.g. Japan, Italy and Mexico) employees believe jobs should provide recognition, growth and challenge. In more nurturing societies, (e.g. the Netherlands, Sweden and Finland) emphasis is more on good working conditions, security, feelings and intuitive decision making. Competitive societies have different roles for men and women. Thus, women's opportunities in organisations are limited.

The final of Hofstede's dimensions is orientation to life and work. A society with a **long-term orientation** values thrift (saving) and goal persistence (e.g. Singapore, Hong Kong and Taiwan). In contrast a society with a **short-term orientation** is more concerned with living in the here-and-now and maintaining personal stability or happiness (e.g. Australia, the United States and France); members spend more and save less.

The technological element

The technological element is important in the international environment as technology levels in various countries affect market nature and companies' ability to do business. In fact, much technology transfer occurs during international business. **Technological transfer** is transmission of technology from those possessing it to those who do not. Technology can be goods or processes such as components or machinery, or intangible know-how, such as advanced road-building techniques (Kavanagh 2003c). For example, after buying Tungsram, a state-owned bulb maker in Budapest, Hungary, to build its European position, General Electric overhauled Tungsram's technology and computer systems (Levine 1990; Syrett & Kingston 1995; Perlez 1994).

power distance

Cultural dimension involving the degree to which individuals in a society accept differences in power distribution as reasonable and normal

uncertainty avoidance

Cultural dimension involving the extent to which members of a society feel uncomfortable with and try to avoid situations they see as unstructured, unclear or unpredictable

individualism–collectivism

Cultural dimension involving the degree to which individuals concern themselves with their own interests and those of their immediate family, as opposed to the larger group's interests

achievement–nurturing orientation

Cultural dimension involving the extent to which a society emphasises values such as assertiveness, competitiveness and material success, rather than values such as passivity, cooperation and feelings

long-term–short-term

Cultural dimension involving the degree to which members of a society value thrift and goal persistence rather than living in the here-and-now and maintaining personal stability or happiness

technological transfer

Transmission of technology from those who possess it to those who do not

MANAGING THE E-CHALLENGE

B2B

The business-to-business segment is Asia's fastest growing area of e-commerce. Demand for software to automate supply chains and manage sales and inventories is rising fast. The pressure on businesses to go online is mounting daily. Taiwan wants 50 000 companies on line by 2001. Thailand recently passed a law requiring all export and import documents to go online before 2000.

Building this new model isn't going to be easy. The supply chains and networks of East Asian companies often stretch from Taiwan to mainland China to the Philippines—and to other countries with their own currencies, laws, languages and business practices. Asian business people also prefer dealing face-to-face and relying on relationships cultivated over years rather than through intermediaries they have never met.

Many entrepreneurs are taking the risk that these attitudes will change and setting up ventures to break down cultural and geographic barriers for thousands of small Asian manufacturers.

Western software and equipment makers are arriving in droves hoping to persuade Asian companies to outsource back-office functions such as billing, email, customer databases, accounting and shipping, using the web.

The sort of activities that are expected require a large change in mindset, especially for family-owned companies accustomed to secrecy. The reluctance to outsource such important functions as accounting and billing is a big obstacle. Supply-chain management requires users to open their inventory and procurement processes to suppliers and customers.

Source: Adapted from Moore & Einhorn (1999).

Activities for discussion, analysis and further research

1. New ways of doing business which have been accepted more or less easily by Western organisations are going to be more difficult for Asian firms to accept. Discuss the reasons.
2. What changes to attitudes and practices are required for e-business to work in Asia?

Promoting innovation: The competitive advantage of nations

competitive advantage of nations

Concept that environmental elements within a nation can foster innovation in certain industries, thereby increasing prospects for the success of home-based companies operating internationally within those industries

In considering the impact of environmental factors on organisations, Michael E. Porter (1990a, 1990b) developed the idea of the competitive advantage of nations. The **competitive advantage of nations** holds that a nation's environmental elements foster innovation in some industries, building the prospects of success of home-based companies operating internationally in those industries. These firms' competitive success has positive national prosperity consequences too.

Porter's idea is based on the view of companies gaining competitive advantage by innovation. The innovations may be radical breakthroughs or small incremental improvements (see Chapter 11), so long as firms innovate continually to stay ahead of the competition. Innovation's incidence among companies in particular industries is influenced by national characteristics where they are based.

The diamond of national advantage

To explain why some firms consistently innovate, Porter identifies four national attributes which alone and together set the diamond of national advantage (see Fig. 17.1).

Factor conditions are production components, such as skilled labour or infrastructure, needed to compete in an industry. Factors influence competitive success most when they are

FIGURE 17.1 Determinants of national competitive advantage (Porter 1990)

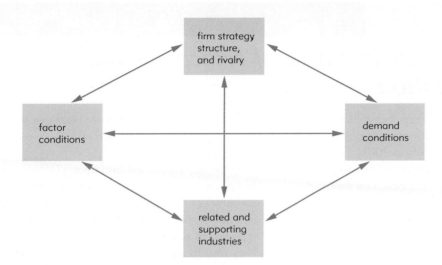

highly specialised, need ongoing heavy investment, and relate directly to industry needs. For example, Holland's research institutes in flower cultivation and shipping build expertise, making the country the world's principal exporter of flowers.

Demand conditions are domestic demand characteristics for an industry's products and services. When domestic buyers are sophisticated and exacting, companies must innovate and meet high standards. For example, environmental concerns in Denmark have made firms there develop world-class water-pollution control equipment and windmills.

The attribute of *related and supporting industries* refers to availability of supplier and other related industries competing effectively internationally. Such industries give cost-effective inputs and latest developments rapidly to home-based firms. Companies can become test sites for potential supplier breakthroughs, speeding innovation.

Firm strategy, structure and rivalry are national major conditions affecting how firms are created, organised and managed, as well as the nature of domestic rivalries. For example, internationally successful firms in Italy tend to be small- or medium-sized, privately owned and functioning as extended families. This suits industries where Italian firms tend to succeed, such as lighting, furniture, footwear and woollen fabrics—needing strategies with customised products, fast change and flexibility. German companies, meanwhile, are likely to be hierarchical and have top managers with strong technical backgrounds. The German approach has been successful in industries needing strong technical and engineering expertise, such as optics, chemicals and complex machinery. Porter sees domestic rivalry as vital because it makes all local industry members innovate and upgrade their efforts. For example, rivalry between Swiss drug firms (Hoffman-La Roche and Novartis) enhances their global positions.

Implications for organisations and their managers

According to Porter, companies must act on factors in the diamond of national advantage and recognise the 'central role' innovation plays in competitive advantage. International business dealings should be expanded selectively, enabling the firm to tap other nations' advantages, including sophisticated buyers or research (Skrzycki 1987; Thomson 2003b). Porter's issues show the importance of long-range planning and strategic management to international business.

GENDER FACTOR

The gender business of relocation and expatriation

Recent Australian research has found that male managers relocate nationally more frequently than their female counterparts (Wood 2001). Survey responses from 507 Australian middle managers (351 males and 156 females) indicated that a significantly greater proportion of male managers (76 per cent) relocated as a result of a request from a superior, compared to 56 per cent of female managers.

When respondents were asked why they thought this was the case, the qualitative responses suggested a belief that organisations perceive men as the head of the family and breadwinner and hence are more appropriate and available for relocation. Women were assumed to be constrained by responsibilities for nurturing and caring for their families, and therefore likely to be reluctant to be relocated.

Such attitudes result in fewer female managers being invited to participate in relocation experiences. Only 33 per cent of female managers had been asked to relocate, compared to 62 per cent of male managers. However 56 per cent of women who were asked did relocate, suggesting that when female managers are given the opportunity to further their careers through relocation, most are willing to do so.

Female managers are also missing out on the international relocation opportunities offered to their male counterparts (Brett & Stroh 1999). In one study of 686 major American and Canadian organisations, women comprised only 3 per cent of the managers who were given foreign assignments (Chan & Smith 2000). In Australia, research estimates that only 6.4 per cent of overseas appointments from the Australian private sector are women (Still & Smith 1998).

According to Smith and Still (1996), the primary barrier to female managers taking up overseas assignments is not a deficiency in either their qualifications or their experience, but organisational and cultural factors. Gender has also been reported as a major obstacle (Linehan, Scullion & Walsh 2001), as it is assumed that women will face negative local values in different cultures that will impair their ability to function effectively as managers.

However, Westwood and Leung (1994) report that problems relating to gender and the cultural environment did not occur in their sample of female expatriates, nor did they create any significant impediment to effective managerial performance. They also found that the majority of female expatriate managers they interviewed had made completely independent decisions to take up managerial positions off-shore, suggesting a very positive attitude towards international assignments. According to Cari Dominguez, Chair of the US Equal Employment Opportunity Commission, women express similar levels of interest in taking on global assignments as their male counterparts. Furthermore, she believes the biggest barriers to women taking up overseas assignments are not cultural barriers in international locations, but barriers imposed from within their own organisation (Dominguez 2003).

Source: Contributed by Glenice Wood (details of sources are listed on p. 738).

References for papers cited (see question 1 below):

Brett, J.M. and Stroh, L.K. 1999, Women in management: How far have we come and what needs to be done as we approach 2000?, *Journal of Management Inquiry*, 8 (4), pp. 392–8.

Chan, B. and Smith, M. 2000, Should we send a woman?, *Charter* (September), pp. 48–50.

Dominguez, C. 2003, Global Diversity: The next frontier in human capital management. Diversity & the bar, EEOC, November/December.

Linehan, M., Scullion, H. and Walsh, J.S. 2001, Barriers to women's participation in international management, *European Business Review*, 13 (1), pp. 10–19.

Smith, C.R. and Still, L.V. 1996, Breaking the glass border: Barriers to global careers for women in Australia, *International Review of Women and Leadership*, 2 (2), pp. 60–72.

Still, L.V. and Smith, C.R. 1998, Global career opportunities for women managers: The company perspective, Discussion paper series, The University of Western Australia, ISSN 1320–1980.

Westwood, R.I. and Leung, S.M. 1994, The female expatriate manager experience: Coping with gender and culture, *International Studies of Management & Organization*, 24 (3), pp. 64–85.

Activities for discussion and further research

1. This exercise could be conducted over a week to allow for sufficient reading and preparation time. Form four or five groups, and allocate to each group one of the papers given as references to the above case study, to be read and discussed by group members. Each group should address the question: 'What are the overt reasons organisations give to explain the lack of female managers being given international expatriate experiences?' and 'What does your group believe are the covert reasons?'

2. Given the transformational leadership style attributed to women in recent research (see Chapter 12, Gender factor, What female managers bring to IT), do you feel these particular characteristics and attributes would equip women very well to take up international assignments? Expand on your reasons.

3. What role do you think stereotyping and discrimination play in excluding more female managers from taking up these relocation experiences?

4. The Karpin report on the Australian Industry Task Force on Leadership and Management Skills (1995) found that globalisation was the most significant environmental trend affecting Australian managers. The report highlighted the need for managers of the future to acquire international experience, cross-cultural management opportunities and an understanding of cultural nuances pertaining to social, economic and political relationships overseas (Boston Consulting Group 1995). Working as a group, research current numbers of female managers who do have the opportunity to experience expatriate management appointments. Log on to the website: www.abs.gov.au/ausstats and explore in the industry classifications the number of expatriates listed under the various employers. Is there a significant difference today to the number of female expatriates (6 per cent) reported in 1996 by Smith and Still (1996)? Is this what you would have expected? Consider the implications for women in management who wish to attain a senior management position.

GAUGING INTERNATIONAL STRATEGIC ISSUES

Many international business firms, especially multinationals, engage in long-range planning. Their planning period usually has a three-, five- or seven-year frame. Studies of multinationals show much planning occurs at headquarters, with some subsidiary involvement (Steiner & Cannon 1966; Negandhi & Welge 1984).

While most international business firms use long-range planning, initial efforts at operating in other countries focus on narrower goals than becoming a fully-fledged multinational corporation. So, we consider major international entry methods then the strategic approaches of multinational corporations

Methods of international entry

The four main methods organisations can use to expand into other countries are exporting, licensing, establishing strategic alliances, and operating wholly owned subsidiaries (Schnitzer, Liebrenz & Kubin 1985; Rugman & Hodgetts 1995).

Exporting

For manufacturing companies, **exporting**, making a product in the home country and sending it overseas, is a common way of entry to international markets. Exporting requires little capital if the product does not need modification. It is low risk, particularly if the product is shipped after payment is guaranteed.

Exporting has potential disadvantages. For one, tariffs, taxes and transportation costs are involved. In addition, the exporter may find it hard to promote products in other countries. If a product succeeds, local competition may emerge. To minimise the disadvantages, companies may get foreign sales representatives, locals who understand product and market needs and whose activities may deter competition emerging.

Licensing

Licensing is an agreement where one organisation gives limited rights to another to use assets, such as expertise, patents, copyrights or equipment, for a fee or royalty. Typically, this allows the licensee to use assets in a certain territory for a specified time. Licensing's main advantage is that a firm can make a profit and not spend large sums to conduct business directly. Since licensees usually come from the country involved, they are familiar with its culture and business methods.

Licensing has disadvantages, however. Most important is that the licenser usually is not allowed to conduct business with the licensed product or service in a territory for 5, 10 or even 20 years. If the product or service succeeds, the licenser will miss more profits from directly doing business. Another disadvantage is the licenser may establish a potential future competitor, since licensees may be able to produce an equivalent product or service after the licence expires. Finally, the licensee may not perform as desired, lessening licensing revenues and long-term potential business.

Strategic alliances

A **strategic alliance** is where two or more independent firms set up a cooperative partnership to gain mutual strategic advantage. In this arrangement no organisation is owned by another alliance member. Often this is a joint venture. A joint venture is where two or more firms arrange to produce a product or service through a jointly owned enterprise (see Chapter 3) (Miller & Dess 1996; Yoshino & Rangan 1995; Inkpen 1995).

According to estimates, about 20 per cent of direct investments are joint ventures (Christelow 1987; Ono 1993; Thomson 2003b). Many companies seek to hold majority interest in joint ventures, to maintain operational control.

One advantage of strategic alliances is the access given to countries where full equity is not permitted. Other advantages include lower risk for introducing new products, keeping up with new technology, and combining the home-country partner's technical expertise and capital with the host-country partner's local knowledge. Among the disadvantages are losses if the venture fails, expropriation, and disagreements among partners which are difficult and time-consuming to resolve.

Wholly-owned subsidiaries

A **wholly-owned subsidiary** is an operation on foreign soil owned and entirely controlled by a firm headquartered outside the host country. Wholly-owned subsidiaries are, like joint ventures, direct investments, with one firm owning the productive facilities. They can come from acquisition (buying an existing company in the host country) or a start-up (building a firm from scratch) (Kinicki & Williams 2003).

There are benefits to wholly-owned subsidiaries. For one, the parent firm has sole management authority over the subsidiary under the host-country laws where it is located. Similarly, the parent firm controls the technology and expertise. As well, profits need not be shared. Moreover, the subsidiary may aid the parent company's ability to service world-wide customers. The major disadvantage, apart from substantial costs, is facilities and expertise—a substantial investment and located within foreign borders—risking expropriation if the political environment shifts.

Multinational corporation strategies

As firms expand internationally, they must develop suitable strategies. Multinational corporations, and to a lesser extent other companies operating internationally, must weigh two factors: the need to make optimum global economic decisions, and the need to be responsive to host-country differences. Thus, multinationals have four strategy options: world-wide integration, national responsiveness, regional responsiveness and multifocal emphasis.

World-wide integration

A **world-wide integration strategy, or globalisation** (or globalism), aims to develop standardised products with global appeal, while rationalising global operations. Rationalising operations, or **rationalisation**, means assigning activities to the organisation part, no matter where it is, that is best suited to delivering the desired results and then selling the finished products where profits will be best. A multinational might therefore consider costs, expertise, raw materials and available capacity, in deciding where to do work. Rationalisation uses economies of scale by using world-wide organisational resources effectively (Rennie 2003).

Globalisation is based on the idea of products used around the globe with little specification change. Coca-Cola, sold in over 160 countries, demonstrates a global product needing only small formula alterations. Few products and situations suit full globalisation.

National responsiveness

A **national responsiveness strategy** gives subsidiaries latitude in adapting products and services to suit host countries' specific needs and political realities. This strategy loses many advantages of world-wide integration. Subsidiaries may operate virtually as national firms, and retain many benefits of affiliation with a multinational company, such as shared financial risks and access to global R&D resources. A national responsiveness strategy may help if globalisation is impossible due to national differences (Hooper 2004b).

Parker Pen Ltd used a national responsiveness strategy with about 500 pen styles from 18 plants. In about 150 countries, local offices created packaging and advertising suited to local tastes. Company officials then saw a *Harvard Business Review* article highlighting advantages of globalisation. The article argued that technology creates vast global markets for standardised consumer products and 'different cultural preferences, national tastes and standards, and business institutions are vestiges of the past' (Levitt 1983, p. 96).

Taking the argument to heart, Parker officials consolidated pen styles to 100 choices from eight plants. They designed one advertising campaign and translated it into several languages. Profits dropped when local managers resisted the single advertising approach, which failed. After losing $12 million in 1985, Parker was sold to a group of British managers. Profits came when a national responsiveness strategy was re-established (Lipman 1988; Koselka 1994). So, managers must carefully evaluate the situation, testing for a global market before moving to develop an international strategy.

Regional responsiveness

A **regional responsiveness strategy** gives regional offices great latitude in coordinating local subsidiaries and adapting products and services to suit their region's needs and political realities. This sacrifices some potential advantages of world-wide integration, but keeps others because regions cover large areas, such as Europe, Africa or the Asia-Pacific region (Hill 2003). Regional offices can get some economies of scale and adjust to regional tastes, but retain many benefits of affiliating with a multinational firm, such as shared financial risks and access to global R&D resources. For example, France-based Thomson Consumer Electronics Inc., a major television-set manufacturer, switched from a national to a regional responsiveness strategy. To do so, Thomson set up four factories in Europe to assemble specific set types for the European market. For instance, the German facility makes high-feature large television sets for the whole European region, while the Spanish factory produces low-cost, small-screen sets (Morrison et al. 1991).

world-wide integration strategy, or globalisation

Strategy aimed at developing relatively standardised products with global appeal, as well as rationalising operations across the world

rationalisation

Strategy of assigning activities to parts of the organisation, regardless of their location, that are best suited to produce desired results, and then selling finished products where they will yield the best profits

national responsiveness strategy

Strategy of allowing subsidiaries to have substantial latitude in adapting products and services to suit the particular needs and political realities of countries they operate in

regional responsiveness strategy

Strategy of allowing regional offices to have substantial latitude in coordinating the activities of local subsidiaries and adapting products and services to suit the particular needs and political realities of the regions in which they operate

multifocal strategy

Strategy aimed at
achieving the advantages
of world-wide integration
where possible, while still
attempting to be
responsive to important
national needs

Multifocal emphasis

A **multifocal strategy** aims to achieve advantages of world-wide integration where possible, while trying to respond to national needs. Thus the strategy includes both world-wide integration and national responsiveness. Organisations with multifocal strategies are harder to manage as they are concerned with two dimensions at once.

ORGANISING INTERNATIONAL BUSINESS

As well as strategic issues, managers in international business must choose an organisation structure, appropriate to the firm's global pursuits. Most organisation design research has looked at multinational corporations. The tendency is to adopt one of five structure types: world-wide functional divisions, world-wide product divisions, international division, geographic regions and global matrix (Robock & Simmonds 1989).

World-wide functional divisions

With world-wide functional divisions, the parent company's top-level functional executives have world-wide responsibility for functions, including manufacturing, marketing and finance (see Fig. 17.2). Thus a foreign subsidiary's functional units report directly to the parent company's functional units. This structure gives strong functional expertise to foreign subsidiaries in manufacturing and engineering. However, as actions require coordination across functional units, the structure limits reaction speed to events in different countries and to competition where products are diverse. The structure works best with a few related products sold in a fairly uniform world-wide market and with few foreign subsidiaries.

World-wide product divisions

With world-wide product divisions, top-level executives manage product areas world-wide (see Fig. 17.3). In this structure type, the parent company emphasises coordinating product-related decisions but lets foreign subsidiaries run other business aspects. Due to the product focus, the structure is most effective with products that are technologically complex, highly diverse or subject to rapid change. It fits with a world-wide integration strategy with several diverse products to consider.

International division

With an international division structure, a division is created and all foreign subsidiaries report to it. Figure 17.4 shows a multinational company with domestic product divisions and an international division. (An international division could be added to a functional structure, but is less common (Daniels, Pitts & Tretter 1985).) The international division structure allows representation of geographic and product interests at the same level. However, the arrangement

FIGURE 17.2 World-wide functional divisions structure

FIGURE 17.3 World-wide product divisions structure

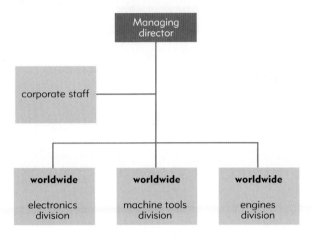

FIGURE 17.4 International division structure

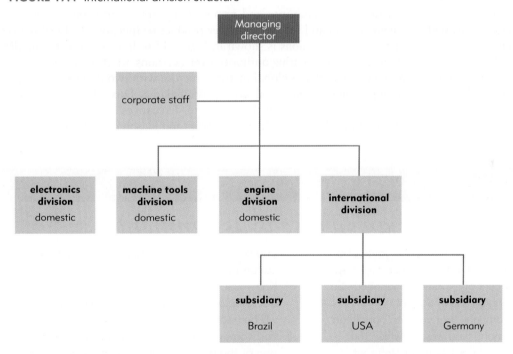

means that coordinating information between domestic product divisions and the international division is difficult. One study of 37 large multinationals showed the international division was most common (Robock & Simmonds 1989).

Geographic regions

In this organisation design, the world is split into regional divisions, with subsidiaries reporting to an appropriate one by location (see Fig. 17.5). This structure helps regional information flow in regions but inhibits information exchange across them. As a result, it caters to regional and national differences, supporting a regional or national responsiveness strategy. A geographic regions structure is often used by European multinationals (Robock & Simmonds 1989; Edmondson 2003).

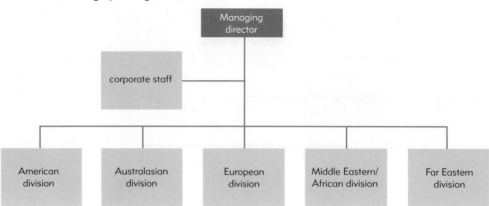

FIGURE 17.5 Geographic regions structure

Global matrix

In a global matrix structure, equal authority and responsibility are assigned on at least two dimensions, with one being region and the second either product or function. A global matrix with region and product as the dimensions is shown in Figure 17.6. In this structure, middle-level executives report to two bosses sharing authority over decisions affecting a region and a business product area. Some argue that a global matrix structure with two dimensions (region and product) is needed in pursuit of a multifocal strategy (Prahalad & Dox 1987). However 93 multinationals studied showed only one with this structure. Executives say they prefer other mechanisms to deal with multifocal issues, such as task forces and liaison positions (see Chapter

MANAGEMENT SKILLS FOR A GLOBALISED ECONOMY

Preparing for an overseas assignment

The following applies to expatriate candidates of both genders but it must be noted that women make up only roughly 15 per cent of expatriate managers. So focus on the following skills is important.

1. Persuade your company that you can handle an overseas assignment. Find ways in which the company will benefit from your appointment overseas. You must be sure that your family will support you in this endeavour. Their support will be important to your organisation if your family is to travel with you. If you are a female, suggest that this can be an advantage in some parts of the world where family issues are held in high regard.

2. Familiarise yourself with the host country. This knowledge will demonstrate the respect with which you hold your host country. Learn the rituals and traditions, especially in exchanging business cards. Know how to dress appropriately

and be aware of standards of behaviour and cultural values.

3. Know what you are talking about. If you know your discipline and act with courtesy and respect, you will be treated similarly regardless of your gender.

4. For women—realise that you cannot always be one of the boys. Gender equality is not always a reality overseas. You may have your colleagues' respect during work hours but may still not be invited to participate in certain after-hours social activities that are a male-only prerogative.

5. Become skilled in the language. Whichever country you may be in, it is useful to know some key phrases. There is no adequate substitute for a knowledge of the country and the local language. The fact that you have bothered to learn the language will earn you the respect of local staff.

Source: Adapted from Kinicki and Williams (2003).

FIGURE 17.6 Global matrix structure

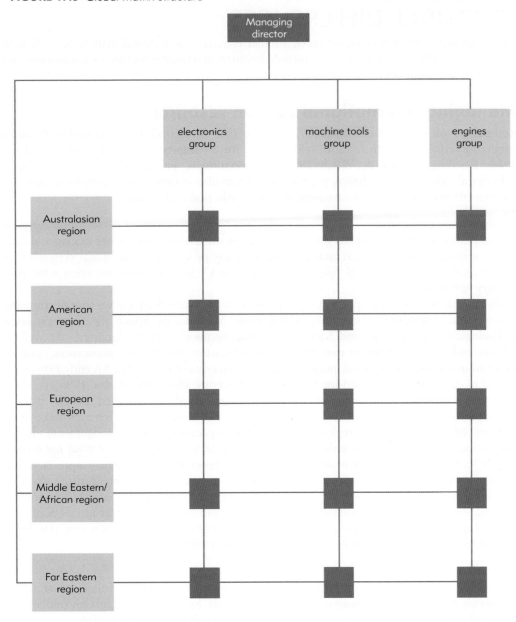

7) (Pitts & Daniels 1984). Greater global information infrastructure of telecommunications and computer companies makes the global matrix more feasible in future.

Networked structure

The networked structure is an organisation form where functions are contracted to independent firms, coordinated through information technology networks to operate as if in one company. This is called the virtual corporation as it acts as if there is one corporation (see Chapter 8). With rapid growth of sophisticated telecommunications capacity, this structure is feasible for those wanting to engage in international business who need great flexibility and to be able to contract out functions but still control core competencies of their competitive advantage.

MANAGING DIVERSITY: ADAPTING TO CULTURAL DIFFERENCES

Structural issues are important; however, another effective international management element is adapting to different cultures. Issues include international human resources management and leadership style adjustment.

Managing international human resources

Researchers on international management argue that firms operating internationally must emphasise strategic human resource management for a competitive international edge (Tung 1984; Dowling, Schuler & Welch 1995). Multinationals, particularly, need a developed managerial talent pool to function effectively. Particular concerns are assignment policies, recruitment approaches, and managerial personnel selection and training.

Assignment policies

An international organisation has four policy options on staff sources for key managerial slots in overseas operations: local nationals, parent company personnel, international personnel, or mixed sources. With the local option, each subsidiary's key positions are filled with host country nationals.

With a parent company option, a representative in each subsidiary knows overall company policies and procedures. They may know more than locals about the parent's latest technological developments and have good communication with headquarters. As well as salaries and benefits, expenses may include car, education and housing allowances, cost-of-living adjustments, international medical coverage, and costs of relocation. Recently firms have moved to cut expenses, emphasising frugality and lowering allowances (Lohse 1995).

With a regional option, significant positions are filled by qualified people from a geographical region. The idea is that regional commonalities and major differences make those experienced in a particular region suited to fill important regional assignments. In an international option, multinationals assign the best person to a job, no matter what nationality or job location. This helps a multinational foster a geocentric management approach and develop multinational managers able to apply a world-wide integration strategy. Multinationals tend to follow a mixed option, putting host-country nationals in foreign subsidiaries, home-country nationals in headquarters, and developing a managerial pool with regional and/or global experience to fill higher-level positions needing a broader view (Hodgetts & Luthans 1991; Morrison et al. 1991; Dowling et al. 1995).

Recruitment

Regardless of assignment policy, evidence suggests firms operating internationally must recruit competent people for key overseas positions. For example, locally-educated foreign students are underutilised in sourcing management talent for foreign subsidiaries (Tung 1984).

Women are also an under-used source of managerial talent. One 1980s study found that only 3 per cent of expatriate managers were women; however, women now own or run increasing numbers of SMEs (*Business Asia* 2003). **Expatriates** are people who are not citizens of host countries where they work. According to a follow-up 1980s study of firms, international personnel managers felt women face major barriers with overseas assignments in contrast to domestic ones (Adler 1984). For example, they identified prejudice, and company reluctance to put women into foreign assignments. Interestingly when the same researcher interviewed 52 female expatriate managers, almost all were successful. Almost half reported that being female helped their assignments, largely due to high visibility (Jelinick & Adler 1984). The situation is changing quickly. By one estimate, women will make up over 20 per cent of expatriates by the year 2005.

As many marriages now involve dual-career couples, posting employees abroad is increasingly complex. Foreign assignments may be declined over concern about negative impact

expatriates

Individuals who are not citizens of countries in which they are assigned to work

on the spouse's career. To get suitable candidates for foreign assignments, firms must help with job-seeking for 'trailing' spouses. Without help it is likely the trailing spouse will become depressed and experience other health problems, limited engagement with the new community, and need emotional support from the working expatriate spouse (Harvey 1995).

Selection and training

Failure rates of expatriates is high, ranging from 25 to 40 per cent. Failures are expensive in the direct costs of early return and replacement. There are other costs, including loss of self-esteem and resulting subsidiary problems (Mendenhall & Oddou 1985; Bateman & Snell 2004). Part of the high expatriate failure rates is probably due to serious inadequacies in selection and training.

Multinational corporations use technical skills as the main criteria to select people for overseas assignments. While technical skills are needed for success, an expatriate's *relational skills*, their ability to relate and communicate effectively with host nationals, must be considered. Communication skills needed include willingness to use the host national's language; confident communication; ability to engage in local small talk such as anecdotes, jokes, and comment on movies and sports; and desire to understand and relate to host nationals (Mendenhall & Oddou 1985). Showing needed flexibility, Australian Ben Lochtenberg, once chairman of Great Britain's Imperial Chemical Industries' (ICI) American subsidiary and now ICI's Australian subsidiary, had to adjust communication style even where there was a common language. For example, in England, his direct Australian manner caused problems, so he learned the indirect British approach. He would say 'Perhaps you ought to think about this a little more' to mean 'You must be mad—forget it'. In the United States, though, when Lochtenberg used the same British approach the subordinate interpreted him literally and the project proceeded after a little thought (Main 1989; Kearns 1995).

Unfortunately, expatriate preassignment training is often poor. The reasons are that human resource administrators believe training is ineffective, expatriate trainees are often dissatisfied with their training, there is often a shortage of time to train before departure, and some assignments are too short to need expensive training (Mendenhall & Oddou 1985). Poor training does lead to problems, as an American manager found. Arriving in France, he rented a luxury apartment and invited all staff to a large party. He had not realised it is uncommon for French employees to visit a superior's home. At the party were people from all company levels, with their spouses, who would not normally have mixed socially. This was a bad start, from which the manager never recovered (Copeland & Griggs 1986; Heathcote & Kirby 2003).

Repatriation

Another area for effective human resource management is **repatriation**, the return to one's home country after a host country assignment (Rugman & Hodgetts 1995; Adler 1991). Normally expatriates' foreign assignments are two to three years. Major reasons for return are (1) the end of the agreed-upon foreign assignment period, (2) desire for children's further education to be in home-country schools, (3) unhappiness with the foreign assignment, and (4) ineffectiveness in the foreign assignment.

Adjustment problems during repatriation are common, as adjusting to returning home may be hard. For one, authority and status may be lower in the home office than in the foreign assignment. Moreover, the returned expatriate may see their foreign experience as undervalued at the home office. They may find their old job has changed and/or their technical expertise is obsolete.

It can take months, even a year, for a returning manager to become effective again. To ease repatriation and reduce anxiety, promising a home-country position at least equal to the one the person left to accept the foreign assignment can be developed. Other steps include renting or maintaining the person's home during the foreign assignment, appointing a mentor to help maintain their career during foreign assignment and repatriation, and communicating with expatriates to keep them linked to home-office activities (Finney 1996).

repatriation

Process of returning to one's home country after an assignment in a host country

Adjusting leadership styles

It is argued that similarity of organisation behaviour across nations is increasing; however, managers overseas may have to adjust leadership styles due to cultural factors (Adler, Dokter & Redding 1986; Kelley, Whatley & Wothley 1987). It is difficult to isolate the effects of culture from differences in economic development and resources of different countries. Much is to be learned about effective leadership in different nations and cultures.

From his study of an American multinational (IBM), Hofstede (1980) believes managers must particularly consider the power-distance index to decide leadership styles appropriate to various countries. Where power-distance is high (e.g. Mexico, the Philippines and India), people accept large power-distribution differences. Subordinates accept superiors acting autocratically, being paternalistic, being subject to different rules to subordinates, and enjoying privileges unavailable to them. Where power-distance is medium (e.g. Australia, Japan and Italy), subordinates expect to be consulted but accept some autocratic behaviour. They expect laws and rules to apply to all, but accept some degree of privilege and status symbols for superiors that are unavailable to subordinates. Where power-distance is low (e.g. Sweden, Denmark, and Israel), subordinates expect consultation on most issues, prefer participative democratic leadership, and rebel or strike if superiors seem to overstep their authority. Typically, laws and rules are seen as applicable to all employees, and privileges and status symbols for superiors as unacceptable. Hofstede's research provides a frame to consider leadership issues across cultures, such as needing to adjust leadership styles. Organisational social responsibility and managerial ethics are other areas needing special consideration for firms operating internationally.

CASE IN POINT

The cost of being an expatriate

One effect of the increasing Asian focus for Australian business is that more and more Australians spend time working overseas. These international workers soon discover they face complex issues and there are costly pitfalls to be avoided that have little to do with their direct job performance.

Since the early 1980s when a few companies posted a small number of senior executives overseas, matters have altered considerably. These days, large companies with well-established international operations are sending large numbers of staff overseas. One example is BHP Petroleum which has an average of 70 to 80 Australians on posting overseas at any given time.

These individuals need to be cautious about arranging their affairs back home if they wish to avoid unnecessary complications regarding investments, superannuation, the value of their family home, to name just a few.

More recently, being an expatriate has had safety implications as political unrest has plagued certain parts of the world.

These are issues which expatriates must consider in conjunction with other aspects of their overseas assignments.

Source: Adapted from Kavanagh, J. (1996).

Activities for discussion, analysis and further research

1. What might an organisation that posts an employee overseas do to support that individual in the effectiveness of their posting?
2. Should they assist that employee in sorting out their local affairs before departure? Why?
3. Log on to the DFAT website and examine the warnings this site gives to individuals travelling to foreign countries. In what ways is this important to organisations that post staff abroad?
4. Recently China Airlines in Taiwan has recruited a large number of ex-Ansett pilots. In what ways does this kind of situation differ from an expatriate posting by an Australian organisation? What areas should these pilots consider when accepting such an opportunity?

Culture and management in New Zealand

Managers do not operate in a vacuum or in isolation. Four intermeshing systems impinge upon managers at their work—technical, political, economic and cultural (Skinner 1964). The behaviour of managers is obviously influenced by technological developments and characteristics of business, the attitudes and policies of government, and the type and level of economic development in the country. Culture also has a large impact on a manager's behaviour.

Thompson and Van Houten (1970) defined culture as 'generally taken to mean those beliefs, values, and techniques for dealing with the environment which are shared among contemporaries and transmitted by one generation to the next'.

Hofstede (1980) states: 'Culture is not a characteristic of the individual; it encompasses a number of people who were conditioned by the same education and life experience. When we speak of a culture of a group, a tribe, a geographical region, a national minority, or a nation, culture refers to the collective mental programming that these people have in common; the programming that is different from that of other groups, tribes, regions, minorities or nations.'

Hofstede goes on to identify three characteristics of a culture. It is (i) something that is shared by all or almost all members of some social group, (ii) something that the older members of the group try to pass on to the younger members, and (iii) something (as in the case of morals, laws, or customs) that shapes our behaviour or structures our perception of the world. People's culture helps to shape their lives. It influences their processes of planning and organising of resources, decision-making, leading and controlling of the environment. A culture dictates what we learn, how we learn and how we will react to it.

Cultures carry out many functions. One function is to provide guidelines for which a society may operate and deal with its problems in its own way. Terpstra and David (1985) identify several problems which every culture must address in order to operate a civilised, progressive society. They are problems of:

- acquiring food, clothing and shelter
- providing protection from human enemies and natural disasters
- regulating sexuality
- child-raising and instruction in socially approved useful behaviour
- division of labour among humans
- sharing and exchanging the product of human work
- providing social controls against deviant behaviour
- providing incentives to motivate persons to want to do what they have to do
- distributing power and legitimising the wielding of power to allow setting of priorities, making decisions, and coordinating actions that obtain social goals
- providing a sense of priorities and an overall sense of worth to social life

Although the principles of management may have a universal outlook, their application in any organisation is influenced by the culture of the society in which they are practised. Without question, 'Western-style management' is the most widely accepted practice in New Zealand today. However, because of the economic, social and ethical attractions offered by alternative management styles, the power and influence of traditional Maori practices which are being widely used by Maori managers in New Zealand organisations today, should not be ignored.

Traditional management practices

Management emphasis in traditional Maori economies was somewhat different to that of today's Western-style organisations. The very existence of the pre-European Maori society depended on the commitment of the people as a whole to their whanau (family) and their community.

Economic planning was dependent on environmental constraints such as the weather and seasonal change. The organisation of labour and time was assigned according to expertise and family occupations. The main criteria for leadership was primogeniture (generally male), and proven ability. The very nature of leadership and decision-making was a communal affair.

Although the rangatira (chief) of the tribe carried the mantle, power and authority came from the community. The monitoring of economic activities and social control was exercised directly by the rangatira and kaumatua (elders), and reinforced by public opinion. The community, unlike in Western practices, exerted great influence upon individuals in the maintenance and keeping of accepted   norms.

Maori managing in today's business environment

Maori today, although struggling in most areas of social, economic and financial development in comparison with their non-Maori counterparts, consistently prove themselves as able and charismatic leaders. Unlike in previous years, more and more Maori are realising their leadership and management potential and making a career in corporate niches in Western business organisations.

The return to Maori of significant resources and the further development of strategic investments have also created a demand within Maori society for highly trained, professional managers to manage the rapidly expanding Maori asset base and Maori enterprises. Many of these business organisations are collectively owned (sometimes having up to 30 000 beneficial owners) and operate under traditional management systems, requiring the managers to have an additional set of managerial skills to that of a manager operating in a solely Western-style business.

With the steadily increasing number of Maori in management positions, both in Western and in Maori businesses, it is inevitable that Maori 'traditional management practices' will be more commonly used and that problems will occur as the two cultures clash.

Victoria University of Wellington's Maori Business staff have identified five areas of management as having the greatest potential for conflict between Western and Maori management styles in New Zealand business organisations today. They are: the way in which managers from the differing cultures make decisions; the use of specific communication channels; the importance of meeting and greeting visitors, business associates and potential clients; the resolution of conflicts; and the style of management that managers from each culture decide to adopt.

Decision-making

The way in which many traditional societies made decisions, and the way in which those in traditional Maori society made decisions, have been well documented. Generally, Maori attitudes towards decision-making call for a consensus agreement to be reached by all parties involved or affected by the outcome of the decision. Participation is highly valued and members of the parties concerned are given every opportunity to influence the affairs of the community or organisation. The consensual approach to decision-making was, and in many instances still is, preferred by individuals and various organisations. Discussions will last for as long as it takes to reach a consensus and decisions are delayed until consensus is reached. Time (in traditional terms) is of secondary importance, and the priority is winning the understanding and support (tautoko) of the group. Once a project or proposal receives the assent of the people, management issues of implementation, development and control then became a collective responsibility.

Maori managers often see themselves as representatives of their people, of which they are a part. Their job is as spokesperson for the group, not as sole authority. Ultimate responsibility lies with those they work with, not necessarily with their immediate superior.

This collective decision-making process is viewed by many who are ignorant of traditional practices as a lack of management ability and/or shirking the responsibilities of making tough decisions. This, however, is not the case.

Maori managers see decision-making by consensus as an integral part of their management style. Gaining communal approval and trust is vital before decisions can be made. This does not mean that they do not have the capacity to make decisions themselves, nor does it mean that they are undermining the responsibility of management entrusted in them. On the contrary, in order to manage effectively, they must gain total support and respect from their group.

Oral communication

There is a strong belief that Maori managers are, on the whole, more comfortable and more willing to use oral communication as a means of control and motivation than many of their non-Maori counterparts. Oratory skills, used in so many Maori situations, particularly on the marae, provide a solid grounding for the Maori manager.

When on a marae, one is often called upon to speak and answer questions in front of large numbers of people. This, in turn, helps to develop not only public-speaking skills, but also debating skills, leadership skills, persuasive bargaining skills, motivational skills, and the ability to argue for or against a belief while also being able to handle criticism from around them.

The ability to communicate orally is seen by many as a real strength. It can often bridge the gap between senior management and junior staff, which in many organisations is widening rather than diminishing.

Written modes of communication such as inter-office memos, appraisals and report structures are often not favoured by Maori managers, especially if these are used as the primary means of communication. Many prefer to resolve problems and communicate by kanohi ki te kanohi (face-to face-mode) with their staff. This mode takes on significant importance if managers are responsible for large numbers of Maori employees, especially older Maori staff.

Meeting and greeting people

Perhaps the most identifiable trait of a manager who espouses and uses traditional Maori ways of managing is the belief in using traditional Maori practices when controlling meetings and/or when greeting people. Many Maori indicate a strong desire to retain and practice the traditional forms of greeting visitors and chairing meetings/gatherings, even those who work within a Western business structure.

Traditionally, meetings start with a karakia (prayer) usually given by a kaumatua who may be brought in especially for this purpose. Then the mihimihi (welcome) begins followed by the meeting itself. At the close of the meeting, the kaumatua is called upon again for karakia and to bless those at the gathering, the ideas discussed and to officially close it.

While many Maori managers use this practice regularly, most are aware that in some circumstances it may be deemed inappropriate. Although Maori issues and protocols are becoming more accepted today, managers still need to tread with caution when employing certain kawa (protocols) in unreceptive environments.

When greeting people, Maori managers often run into conflict with Western organisational norms and values, due to the fact that they are expected to cater for and look after the well being of their visitors, usually by way of powhiri (welcome) and manaakitanga (hospitality and entertainment). Often this means entertaining and feeding visitors. A common complaint from non-Maori senior managers is that their Maori employees are often 'entertaining' rather than working. This is often resented by non-Maori staff and seen as an excuse to stop work and socialise. To the Maori, however, it is an integral part of their managerial duties.

Resolution of conflicts

The way in which Maori managers resolve conflicts has also been identified as an area that may differ to that of the non-Maori manager. In general, because of their ability to speak and debate issues, Maori managers tend to like to resolve conflicts in a direct manner through face-to-face communication rather than through less direct means such as letters, faxes or telephone calls. Many non-Maori who are not used to this form of conflict resolution are uncomfortable with this style and may see it as an intimidatory act or confrontational.

Open management styles

The final area in which there is a significant difference between Maori and non-Maori management practices is in the management styles Maori tend to adopt. Maori generally tend to adopt a more 'open management' style than their non-Maori counterparts. An open-door policy, sharing of ideas, consensus decision-making, and a genuine concern for overall staff well being are characteristics of an open management style. Many managers in Western society do not choose to adopt this style as it can be misinterpreted as weak management. However, managers who do adopt this style must know when and where to draw the line, especially those who are entrusted with confidential information.

Although open management styles are often well received by employees, there are disadvantages. First, managers using this style take on more responsibility for junior staff members, so a larger part of their time is consumed with 'minor' problems and issues.

Secondly, because of the time taken resolving conflicts and problems that could have been delegated to other management staff, less time is available for the senior managers to complete their work, often to the detriment of the organisation.

Third, open management styles make policy making, discussing ideas, and decision making more complex, time consuming and involved than they would normally be.

The difficulty of balancing two cultures

Maori are often in the dilemma of having to balance two cultures, abiding to two sets of values, and readjusting their positions in the social order. While a manager may have status and respect within their organisation, leadership in Maoridom and on the marae is through ascribed means, not necessarily through what someone has achieved.

Having to fulfil obligations to their iwi (people/tribe) and the organisation for which they work, often means living dual lives. Values and systems often conflict within the two cultures, making managers choose between a natural and conditioned response. While this can be extremely challenging for those who succeed, the conflicts often prove too demanding for others.

Those Maori who are able to balance the pull and expectation of Maoridom and the demands of employer organisations, are a valuable asset to New Zealand business management.

HANDLING SOCIAL RESPONSIBILITY AND ETHICAL ISSUES

Organisational social responsibility and managerial ethics were addressed in Chapter 4. Here we examine several concerns of relevance to international management.

International social responsibility

Many social responsibility issues compound when a company has much international business. This is because of increased social stakeholders (customers and communities in different countries, etc.; see Chapter 4), especially if a business uses subsidiaries in other countries. Over the 1970s, multinational corporations were criticised for harmful activities in developing nations. Concerns involved exhausting natural resources, diverting wealth to developed nations, and manipulating LDC governments. Criticisms have abated, for several reasons. These include stronger LDC governments, multinationals emerging based in developed countries, emerging LDC multinationals, more smaller multinationals, greater multinational adaptation to local conditions, and increased environmental concern (Rugman & Hodgetts 1995; Smith 1994; *Economist* 1994). Still, controversy continues, such as concern about 'sweatshops' that followed evidence that clothing was being made by 13- and 14-year-olds working 18-hour days in Honduran factories (Strom 1996). There is still debate about the benefits versus harm wrought by large, powerful companies, particularly in LDCs (Paul & Barbato 1985; Haour 1996).

questionable payments

Business payments raising significant ethical questions of right or wrong either in the host country or in other nations

Questionable-payments issue

A pervasive international ethical issue involves **questionable payments**, payments with ethical questions of right or wrong either in host or other countries (Frederick, Davis & Post 1992; Mahoney 1995). Difficulties come with differences in countries' customs, ethics and laws regarding different payment types. The most common questionable payments are:

- political payments—usually funds to support a political party or candidate
- bribes—money or valuables given to a powerful person to influence decisions in favour of the giver
- extortion—payments made to protect a business against a threatened action, such as cancellation of a franchise
- sales commissions—payments of a percentage of a sale, which become questionable if paid to a government official or political figure or if unusually large
- expediting payments—normally, money given to lower-level government officials to ensure cooperation and prompt routine transaction handling

Cohen (2003) discusses a range of questionable activities flowing from Vietnam's growing numbers of industrial parks.

Many payment types are considered legal and acceptable in many parts of the world, but in general are viewed as unethical and/or illegal.

Service for sale

A growing emphasis on service industries is a feature of the Australian economy. New styles of management, strategy and employment are emerging that are supporting new industries. Service businesses sell their time and expertise instead of products and materials. The economy still requires basic industry, but the complexity of modern technology has created a need for the specialised services that the new industries provide.

Alek Safarian is the founder and chief executive of Novotech, a Sydney service provider to the pharmaceutical and biotech industries. Novotech is an example of the many contract research organisations that have sprung up around the world to support the pharmaceutical industry, and it illustrates the sort of work that these companies do in many industries.

Safarian says: 'It's not like you are making widgets at a factory where, once the production line is up and running, the general manager might have time to sit back and think about growth. In a service company, everyone is involved in generating revenue by using their time. If you are successful, you quickly get to a stage where you are so overrun with client work that you don't have time to think about the strategy for the business.'

The challenge in selling a service rather than a product is that the marketplace is the world. Novotech derives nearly 90 per cent of its revenue from companies in North America, mainly from doing clinical trials of pharmaceuticals. Safarian says the companies he competes with are often well

known in the United States, where Novotech is almost unknown.

Novotech's success has been tied to the growth of the industry it services. The company provides specialised skills that once would have been seen as proprietary sources of competitive advantage for pharmaceutical companies. Safarian says the pharmaceutical industry has realised that outsourcing key activities—such as clinical trials for drugs, or negotiating through the maze of regulatory processes—is more financially efficient than doing them in-house.

Safarian's background is in managing regulatory affairs for large pharmaceutical companies, the service that was Novotech's original business. Over time, he has added services in the way a manufacturing company would add extensions to its product line. 'We look at the size of the market, the availability of specialists who can provide that service, and whether the services travel well.'

Clinical trials for drug companies can usually be performed anywhere as long as the data quality is high. But regulatory advisory services are always going to be country-specific. Novotech can help foreign companies to follow Australian regulations, but has less to offer on US or European regulations.

Safarian has stepped back from working in the ranks to focus on managing the business. The recent rise in the value of the Australian dollar has reduced margins dramatically. An increase in prices would be one way to deal with the problem, he says, but low prices compared with the rest of the world gave his company its advantage in the first place.

He is considering the wider use of currency hedging and has already set up currency risk-sharing deals with some of his business partners overseas. 'For long-term contracts, there are opportunities to agree on a fixed exchange rate for the duration of the project.'

Activities for discussion, analysis and further research

1. Comment on the following statement: 'Service companies now perform processes that were once guarded by manufacturers as trade secrets never to be revealed.' How does a service company overcome this?
2. Develop some strategies in which managers of fast-growing service companies can distance themselves from day-to-day work so they can focus on strategy and management.
3. Service industries can lend themselves to supplying world markets. Explore the ways in which this has advantages in scope and *disadvantages in competition*.

Source: Roberts (2004).

REFLECTIVE PRACTITIONER

Our organisation is just starting to expand into international markets. To date we have provided services to organisations in the United Kingdom, Canada, Singapore, Hong Kong, Taiwan and New Zealand.

In our five-year business plan, expansion into the international arena is certainly on the horizon. During our quarterly company planning days this topic is regularly on the agenda, demonstrating that concepts are turning into application. We do, however, need to get ourselves ready for this; we need to identify and validate the opportunities. We need to assess our capabilities and capacity to deliver. With our current structure, I would probably be more inclined to give our staff opportunities overseas than I would here in Australia.

I know this sounds strange. We may not necessarily have the standing and the reputation yet, and that would be a really good opportunity to allow our staff to create that standing and reputation in a new market, rather than have it be Kimberly Turner. When we step further out into an international market place, that is how I would like it to be—my aim is for our organisation to become broader than just me. It is about developing brand awareness

KIMBERLEY TURNER

and brand confidence—this will need to be instigated by the team and followed from start to finish.

We need to set ourselves up from the perspective of trading and finance and tax. We have done all the research for that area—the issues of exporting and importing and any grants from the government. We have had that information for about three years. We have done the preparatory phase but have not yet initiated the next phase—the going out and seeking and positioning.

One of the things that has become obvious is that our name 'Aerosafe Risk Management' is the potential limitation in other non-aviation and non-defence markets. While I love our aviation work and it is always going to be the heart of what we do, we have a growing number of clients who would like to engage our organisation and tap into our risk management services and support. In response to this demand and in line with a logical progression with growth and diversification , we have recently registered a parent company called 'Global Risk Alliance'. The strategy in selecting that name was to reflect that the global approach was really important

to us, that it is more than just Aerosafe in Sydney. This is part of our preparatory phase for really launching into new industries and markets. We have developed our branding and are in the process of making decisions as to how this will operate the two companies with the one team.

We have our first staff member in the Philippines—an expat who lives there. We have a couple of teaming agreements and alliances in place with an organisation in the UK. We are exploring one in Canada at the moment so I guess we are venturing out very slowly. We are doing this from a very low-risk perspective—start out with the alliance and we don't have to set up major structures initially, yet still have a representative there who can work on our behalf.

The technology in existence makes having someone overseas feasible—that person could tap into our network and our corporate knowledge and be part of the team long-distance. They can break down barriers and still be integrated into the team. But that brings us at least five years out.

FOCUS ON PRACTICE

Strategies for improving

1. Consider how conditions are changing in relation to neighbouring countries and consider how those changes may impact on the way your organisation might conduct business there.

2. Develop a plan to successfully manage the changes across the region, which will enable your organisation to continue to expand internationally.

Source: Jones et al. (2000).

SUMMARY

- International management is the planning, organising, leading and controlling in companies operating internationally. Considerable international business is conducted by multinational corporations. These engage in production or service activities through affiliates in several countries, control those affiliates' policies, and manage from a global perspective. Multinationals and other firms engaged in international business typically display one of four basic orientations, or philosophies, to international management: ethnocentric, polycentric, regiocentric and geocentric.

- Many international environment elements affect organisations' ability to engage in business beyond national borders. The economic element includes economic development level in a country, presence of adequate infrastructure, a country's balance of payments, and monetary exchange rates. Major legal-political element issues are the degree of political risk associated with a country and degree to which governments erect trade barriers. Within the sociocultural element, Hofstede identified five major dimensions related to cultural values: power distance, uncertainty avoidance, individualism–collectivism, achievement–nurturing, and long-term–short-term. The technological element includes technological transfer methods, an important international business aspect. The concept of competitive advantage of nations holds that elements in a nation can foster innovation in certain industries, increasing chances for success of home-based firms operating internationally within those industries. Elements comprising the diamond of national advantage include factor conditions, demand conditions, related and supporting industries, and firm strategy, structure and rivalry.

- Organisations have four entry methods for expansion into other countries: exporting, licensing, establishing strategic alliances, and wholly owned subsidiaries. Multinational corporations' strategies include world-wide integration, national responsiveness, regional responsiveness, and multifocal emphasis. Organisation structures for multinational corporations are world-wide functional divisions, world-wide product divisions, international division, geographic regions and global matrix.

- Adapting to cultural differences requires careful management of international human resources, including assignment policies, recruitment approaches, personnel selection and training, and repatriation. Although scholars argue that leadership issues are converging across nations, effective leadership styles are likely to be different in various cultures.

- Conducting international business raises complex issues regarding social responsibility, international value conflicts, and questionable payments.

QUESTIONS FOR DISCUSSION AND REVIEW

1. Explain the concept of a multinational corporation. Identify several major companies which are probably multinationals. Give reasons for your selections.

2. Describe four major orientations towards international management. Find a newspaper or magazine article about a firm engaged in international business. Which orientation best depicts the company's approach to international management?

3. Outline several elements helpful in international environment assessment. How could you use these to help give advice to a foreign company interested in doing business in your own country?

4. Explain the concept of competitive advantage of nations. Use the concept to assess to what extent conditions in your own country can foster innovation among home-based firms in an industry of your choice. What suggestions do you have to improve conditions?

5. Enumerate the principal methods of entry into international business. Explain the advantages and disadvantages of each. Which would you use if you were running a small firm with few resources but a product with potentially broad international appeal? Would you use a different approach if running a large company with considerable available funds? Give your reasons.

6. Explain four major strategic options for conducting international business. For each, recommend a business type likely to succeed if it adopted that strategy.

7. Describe five main organisation structures used by international businesses. Identify a type of business you would like to manage internationally, and explain the structure you believe would be most appropriate. Explain your reasoning.

8. Discuss the principal issues related to assignment policies and recruitment, selection, training and repatriation of managerial personnel for international assignments. What recommendations would you make to companies just beginning their international expansions?

9. Assess adjustments to leadership style that managers may need to make because of cultural differences. What advice might you give to members of a local company about to set up a wholly-owned subsidiary in the Philippines? How would your advice differ if the subsidiary was to be in Denmark?

10. Explain social responsibility and ethical issues that international managers may confront. What steps would you, as a manager, take to prevent subordinates from making questionable payments while engaged in international business for your firm?

CRITICAL THINKING QUESTIONS

To answer some of these questions you will need to do further research. Useful references are given below each section of the questions.

This chapter examined the impact of globalisation on the role of the manager. The essential skills of the international manager revolve around the ability to able to adapt to cultural differences as well as being sensitive to social and ethical concerns.

China is one of the most recent entrants into the global marketplace. Many Chinese state-owned organisations are having to make adjustments in the way they have traditionally been managed.

1. What do you think some of these changes are?

2. Given the fundamental shifts in management thinking required by these changes, how can managers in China go about implementing them?,

3. Despite the seeming similarity with management of change efforts we are familiar with in the West, McKinsey's experience suggests that the models will not be applied in quite the same way in China. Why? (Note: more detail about McKinsey can be found at http://www.mckinsey.com/.)

4. The opening up of China's markets to overseas competitors has also brought about another change in management thinking—the ability of organisations to raise capital from international markets by issuing of new shares. While clearly a great opportunity for organisations, it also again poses some very interesting management challenges. What are some of these challenges?

(Material relevant to these questions may be found in Hong-fu, L. 2004, Changing a firm for the better amid fierce competition, *Business Daily Update*, 11 February, p. 11.)

What impact do national differences have on the day-to-day level of operations of an organisation? The following questions examine the problem of language—or more precisely, how speaking the same language doesn't necessarily mean we understand each other.

An example of this is provided by a Japanese-born middle-level manager from a major financial services organisation who is living in Australia. She very clearly expressed the view that the Japanese, Singaporean and American managers she dealt with all had very different management styles.

5. What do you think these differences were?

6. What differences in management expectations in Japan and Australia may lead to different management styles?

7. How might modern communication technologies, such as emailing and teleconferencing, add to the problems of cross-cultural misunderstandings in business?

8. What are possible solutions to these communication problems?

(Material relevant to these questions may be found in Lawson, M. 2003, It's not what you say, *Australian Financial Review*, 5 December, p. 58.)

To conclude, we will review thoughts from two eminent scholars (Professor Michael Enright, from the University of Hong Kong and Associate Professor Julian Birkinshaw, from the London Business School), on Australia's place in the globalised world. Much of Australia's domestic industry is large domestic public companies (oligopolies), and both Enright and Birkinshaw believe this type of organisation does not adapt well to the demands of globalisation.

9. Why are oligopolies slow to adapt?

Foreign ownership in Australia is high by international standards. While it was previously discretely hidden in national operations so as to avoid tariff boundaries, the current situation of the deregulated international environment means can 'place parts of their global operations in whichever country provides the greatest advantage' (cited in James 200, p. 86).One result is that the 'country manager' of multinational corporations is becoming redundant and global commerce is transforming corporations into world 'value chains' who strategically locate aspects of their operation in various countries.

The message from Enright is that Australia is not doing well in this move, with foreign investment continuing to go north, directed at countries with the largest GDP. While this may seem good news for the Asia-Pacific region, Enright believes that the movement will not be evenly distributed and will move from South-East Asia towards the north-east.

10. What are the historical reasons behind the changing relationships in Pacific Rim region?

Enright's study of investment flows predicts that current production chains based in South-East Asia (Singapore, Malaysia, Thailand and Indonesia) will be moved in their entirety into China. As James (2001) reports, this massive move from the south to the north of Asia has 'regional security implications, and it reduces Australia's value as a potential 'gateway to Asia'. Australia might be in the right time zone, but it is a long way from North Asia.'

11. Enright explains that the traditional reliance on national economic statistics to judge how well (or poorly) a country is performing is being made redundant with globalisation because of the new realities in the way global organisations operate. What does he mean by this and what are the repercussions?

James' (2001) interview with Birkinshaw takes a different focus, reflecting his special interest in the shape of international organisations and how their subsidiaries can achieve by being innovative. It is a specialty based on the challenge faced by global companies where their strategies of size and dominance of world markets is associated with centralisation and a loss of flexibility required to remain competitive in local markets.

12. What are some of the international strategies an organisation can pursue to deal with this problem?

13. Unlike Enright, Birkinshaw does not see Australia's high level of foreign ownership as a problem, as ownership itself becomes a blurred concept in the global economy. What are some of the reasons for this?

(Material relevant to these questions may be found in James, D. 2001, Gurus of a new world, *Business Review Weekly*, 9 June, p. 86.)

MANAGEMENT EXERCISES

Exercise 1 Management exercise: Going international

You have spent many years working on a revolutionary combination automatic washer and dryer, which went into production for the first time last year. It has been an astounding success in Australia, and you are considering going international with your new product. You have had numerous inquiries and offers from businesses around the world but believe you will concentrate on business in Canada, Great Britain, Western Europe, Australia and New Zealand for the near future. You are going to meet with your director of marketing tomorrow to discuss expanding your business into New Zealand. You recognise several options are available to you, including exporting, licensing, strategic alliances and wholly-owned subsidiaries. In addition, you must consider your philosophy of international management, select a strategy, decide on a structure, determine how to select and train your managers, and determine the appropriate leadership style to use.

Consider the above issues. Then, with two other classmates, discuss how you would proceed with the possibility of conducting business in New Zealand. You want to expand internationally and believe this is the place to start. Explain your rationale for the decisions you make, pointing out the advantages and disadvantages of each of your choices.

Exercise 2 Skill building: Identifying international management orientations

Senior managers normally adopt an ethnocentric, polycentric, regiocentric or geocentric orientation or philosophy to deal with the overseas parts of their organisations. Examples of these orientations follow. In each example indicate the orientation exhibited.

Identifying international management orientations

ethnocentric   polycentric
regiocentric   geocentric

1. _____ The best people are selected from all organisation parts across the world.
2. _____ Basic market decisions are made by local employees.
3. _____ The system used at the multinational headquarters is always best.
4. _____ This firm attempts to develop managers who excel in a particular part of the world.
5. _____ The firm is run by host-country nationals.
6. _____ The corporate goal is to produce a product used in many countries globally.
7. _____ The organisation is focused on the western European approach to management.
8. _____ Home-country managers are given the best jobs and promoted ahead of their peers, regardless of their performance.
9. _____ The subsidiary is highly visible to the local population, while the multinational headquarters is relatively invisible.
10. _____ The multinational considers the world as the base for money, resources, suppliers and customers.

END-OF-CHAPTER CASE: ON THE RIM

Too good to be true

An unsolicited email to a Melbourne businessman, Dan Drum, from a prospective software distributor in Canada was the start of a 12-month saga of false promises, unpaid bills, allegedly pirated software, hijacked trademarks, copied web sites, expensive lawyers, and a string of confused and angry retailers.

Drum, the founder, managing director and 52-per-cent-owner of Hardcat, a medium-size software company, says he was duped. His experience highlights a real challenge for small Australian companies: choosing partners and distributors who can be trusted. The risk is multiplied when the business relationship is with a person or company overseas, and distance and time zones are barriers to communication.

Drum says his Canadian misadventure cost him US$25 000 in expenses and as much as US$3 million in lost sales. But he has learnt valuable lessons about protecting his company and its reputation when dealing through third-party distributors or retailers.

Drum is not alone. Peter Harrison, the group team leader for information technology, biotechnology and health at Austrade, says many small companies are so excited by export opportunities that they become less diligent than they otherwise would be. 'Often when companies go overseas they forget the basic principles of doing business as they would do it in Australia.' Harrison says it is critical to go through a full process of due diligence, to check the company's reputation and obtain third-party referrals from trusted sources.

Nothing seemed out of the ordinary when a Canadian company, Titan Software Sales, of Kitchener, Ontario, contacted Drum by email in September 2002. The chief executive, Jim Reid, expressed interest in marketing and selling Hardcat's asset management software in Canada and the east coast of the United States. Drum says the proposal seemed genuine and most of his retailers—he has 18 worldwide—first contacted him

by email. Only much later did he learn that in 1993 Reid was sentenced in Canada to 19 months' jail for fraud.

Drum says: 'He was smart, affable and knew all the right people. We went along with him because of the excitement of what he was proposing.'

Drum's first mistake was allowing Reid to bypass the standard set of checks and balances that Hardcat applies when assessing new retailers. Usually the company charges retailers US$5000 upfront, to cover the set-up costs of marketing material and training, and to weed out potential retailers who are not serious about the work. Reid never paid the fee.

Drum's second mistake was to not trust his instincts. Harrison says: 'Nothing is better than getting over there and sitting down and talking to people. Often people's gut reactions are a very important part of a business deal. Can I do business with this person or can't I? Do I like him or not?'

Drum met Reid in the US and in Australia, and his gut reaction was that Reid was trouble. On 1 December 2002, Drum emailed three words to his technical director and the co-owner of Hardcat, Rod Dalton: 'I smell something!' Four days later, despite his reservations, Drum signed two retailer contracts with Reid. One was for exclusive rights to sell Hardcat software in Canada; the other to allow Reid to set up a network of retailers in the eastern part of the US. Drum soon found himself and his company entangled in a mess of miscommunication between Reid, Hardcat, potential customers and other retailers in North America and Britain.

Drum says Reid hijacked his business and began acting as though he was an official representative of the Hardcat parent company, not just one of many third-party retailers. Reid registered a company in Canada called Hardcat America, even though his contract did not give him permission to use the name. He also registered an internet domain name without Drum's permission. Most disturbingly, Reid appears to have left a trail of broken promises to retailers and customers. He signed up at least four retail companies in the US, charging them each a set-up fee of US$10 000. By June last year, the retailers were writing to Drum demanding to know why Hardcat America had not provided all the proper marketing material in return for the fee.

Brandon Vermaak, a broker with NCI, a credit insurance and debt collection company, says proper due diligence should include credit checks. This can help to tag businesses that may cause problems with late payments or debts. Vermaak says: 'You need to check whether your agent is more than just a desk and a fax machine, whether he could disappear at a moment's notice.' Credit insurance, although expensive, can protect against losses caused by bad debts and unpaid bills.

Harrison from Austrade warns against exclusive, countrywide deals, because they concentrate risk. 'All of a sudden companies find they have signed away the whole of America for ever. We encourage companies to think of regional and local markets rather than exclusive national markets. And we definitely recommend companies include sunset clauses, review periods, performance targets and milestones in their agreements.'

Drum did not do his due diligence on Reid well enough. Reid provided references and a resume, but Drum did not verify them. He says: 'Most people are honest so you tend to believe them.'

By the middle of last year, Drum knew that somehow he had to extricate himself from the contracts he had signed with Reid. On 24 June, he sent a formal letter to Reid stating that he considered Titan Software Sales' use of the Hardcat name as a breach of contract. Both parties started to communicate through lawyers. The relationship turned very sour.

It took until 16 October—after countless emails, letters, faxes and phone calls—before Hardcat managed to officially sever ties with Reid's company. Reid eventually sent an email to his staff announcing that, 'We [Titan Software Sales] are not engaged in any Hardcat product sales or support or associated with Hardcat Australia'. A week later, he sent a note to Drum's lawyer, handing back the passwords to the Hardcat America website. That was Drum's last contact with Jim Reid.

BRW attempted unsuccessfully to contact Jim Reid; his last known phone number has been disconnected.

Drum, an eternal optimist, sees a silver lining. He says the fact that Reid picked Hardcat is evidence that the product is of high quality and has great potential in North America. But his expansion plans for Canada and the US have been delayed by at least a year. 'We're running [that market] from here until we work out how to sort it out', Drum says. 'We still require a presence over there.' Hardcat is considering opening its own offices in North America rather than finding new retailers and risking more trouble. Existing agreements with retailers on the US west coast remain in place.

It is hard to protect a company completely from a determined fraudster, but putting in a full due diligence effort at the beginning of a business relationship can show up potential hazards. Harrison says: 'Any business deal is a risk and the worst-case scenario is that you will lose everything you put into it. Companies need to take as long as they need to satisfy themselves they have addressed all the risks and learnt all there is to know.'

Source: Roberts (2004).

Activities for discussion, analysis and further research

1. Consider the following statements of advice given to people who want to set up international enterprises.
   Trust no one
   (a) Have policies and processes in place to evaluate potential business partners. Do not make exceptions because a deal looks good at face value.
   (b) Follow up references and do background checks. Get third-party referrals from trusted sources.
   (c) Meet potential business partners. Observe them at work in their own markets. Talk to their customers and suppliers to determine whether they are good people to do business with.
   (d) Avoid exclusive national contracts; they concentrate risk. Include a review period and a sunset clause in contracts that give you a way out if needed.

(e) Protect your products, trademarks and brand names by registering them internationally.

(f) Keep records of meetings, phone calls and correspondence in case a relationship turns sour and lawyers get involved.

What do you think of this advice?

2. In what ways could Drum have avoided the things that happened if he had done due diligence as advised in the list above?

3. In what ways can the study of 'unsuccessful' examples assist in management education? Find other examples of this and explore what students may learn by studying such examples.

FURTHER READING

Caligiuri, P. and Lazarova, M. 2002, A model for the influence of social interaction and social support on female expatriates' cross-cultural adjustment, *International Journal of Human Resource Management*, August, 13, 5, pp. 761–73.

Child, J. and Möllering, G. 2003, Contextual confidence and active trust development in the Chinese business environment, *Organization Science: A Journal of the Institute of Management Sciences*, January/February, 14, 1, pp. 69–81.

Malhotra, N., Ulgado, F. and Agarwal, J. 2003, Internationalization and entry modes: A multitheoretical framework and research propositions, *Journal of International Marketing*, 11, 4, pp. 1–32.

Zeng, M. and Williamson, P. 2003, The hidden dragons, *Harvard Business Review*, October, 81, 10, pp. 92–100.

Gregory, G. 1982, *Comparative: The logic of Japanese enterprise*, Sophia University Institute of Culture, Tokyo, Japan.

Hawkins, S. 1983, How to understand your partner's cultural baggage, *International Management*, European edition, September, pp. 48–51.

Hofstede, G. 1980, *Culture's consequences: International Differences in Work-Related Values*, Sage Publications, Beverley Hills, California, USA.

Robbins, S.P. and Mukerji, D. 1990, *Managing Organisations: New Challenges and Perspectives*, Prentice Hall, Australia.

Skinner, C.W. 1964, Management of international production, *Harvard Business Review*, 42, 5, September–October, pp. 125–36.

Terpstra, V. and David, K. 1985, *The Cultural Environment of International Business*, 2nd edition, South Western Publishing Company, Cincinnati, Ohio, USA.

Thompson, J.D. and Van Houten, D.R. 1970, *The Behavioural Sciences: An Interpretation*, Menlo Park, California, Addison-Wesley Publishing Company.

Webber, R.A. 1969, *Management: Culture and Management*, Richard D Irwin Inc., Homewood, Illinois, USA.

CHAPTER 18

THE REGIONAL CONTEXT

CHAPTER OUTLINE

Focus on Singapore
Issues confronting Singaporean managers
Directions for the future
Relationship with Australia

Focus on New Zealand
Economic reforms
Issues confronting New Zealand
    managers
Growth and influence of Maori in the
    economic sector
Relationship with Asia
Relationship with Australia

Focus on Indonesia
Issues confronting Indonesian managers
Directions for the future
Relationship with Australia

Focus on Malaysia
Issues confronting Malaysian managers
Directions for the future
Relationship with Australia

Focus on Thailand
Issues confronting Thai managers
Relationship with Australia

Japan's impact on the region
Relationship with Australia

Focus on China
Issues confronting Chinese managers
Directions for the future
Relationship with Australia

Australia's position within South-East Asia

LEARNING OBJECTIVES

After studying this chapter, you should be able to:

- Identify the geographic and economic regions your current country of residence fits into and reasons for the positioning.
- Demonstrate an awareness of similarities between philosophical approaches to management existing in the South-East Asia region.
- Demonstrate an understanding of differences in management practices between ASEAN countries.
- Understand the development of your own country's management practices and factors impacting upon it.
- Identify factors affecting future relationships between trading partners of the South-East Asia region.

In this chapter we will examine driving forces and changes in the East-Asian Pacific region. It is a region which, over the last two decades or so, has become a significant force. In this chapter, we will track some changes in specific countries and draw conclusions on issues managers operating regionally must consider.

THE REGIONAL CONTEXT

This chapter is always difficult to develop. For the third edition of this book, aggregated trade statistics reached to the first part of 1998. The 'Asian crisis' became much more apparent in trade and other figures from late 1997. The problem for scholars and writers was that we were aware of subsequent events, which were unclear by the middle of 1998.

This meant that what the statistics showed as a small drop in trade growth, ultimately became a much more significant regional force. This force changed trading, borrowing and other financial patterns in the region, some very long-term. Some regional economies suffered much more from the 'crisis' than others.

However, as the American President J.F. Kennedy said, 'When written in Chinese, the word "crisis" is composed of two characters—one represents danger and one represents opportunity'.

Thus the 'Asian crisis' proved to be both a danger to regional economies and an opportunity for many structural changes. In the past few years, investment funds flowed into Asian countries. Some, such as Hong Kong, Korea, Singapore and Taiwan, known as Newly Industrialised Countries (NICs), have shown their ability to change to the world.

Many multinational companies invested heavily in Asian countries and transferred technologies there, only to discover it is harder to transfer management techniques. It is only after making the financial investment and commitment that organisations find management conformity is more difficult to transfer.

As discussed in Chapter 17, understanding views and practice of management in countries where investment is planned is vital to establish and manage enterprises there.

More recently, the emergence of Sudden Acute Respiratory Syndrome (SARS) and avian (bird) flu continue to stress the regional environment in unexpected and unpredictable ways. SARS meant one complete tourism season was lost and avian flu has resulted in the culling of millions of birds across the region, as well as a number of deaths. Both of these issues point to the increasingly close linkages across the region.

Brunei Darussalam, Cambodia, Indonesia, Laos, Malaysia, Myanmar, the Philippines, Singapore, Thailand and Vietnam form the group known as ASEAN (Association of South-East Asian Nations). Debate has continued as to whether Australia legitimately belongs to such a grouping. Membership of this group would benefit Australia, and Australia's government is pursuing the issue.

Companies seeking to establish themselves in another country already know the significant cultural elements of much of the local population's lives. Two reference points are that the major religions such as Christianity, Buddhism, Islam and Hinduism are represented in most Asian countries; and that the majority are politically called 'democratic'. Managers must also realise that over half the world's population is in Asia and this region has cultural and traditional roots far stronger than the Western world's in their influence over various aspects of life, including management practice.

FOCUS ON SINGAPORE

Singapore's turning point was its 1965 withdrawal from the Malaysian federation. American, Japanese, German, French and British multinational investors then flooded in, with their own management systems, often with expatriates as operational heads. Singapore was ideally located and low labour costs meant management could see workers as an extension of the foreign investors' imported machinery (Wong 1991). Singapore became an assembly centre for home-based technologies and production, then fed an international marketing network.

TABLE 18.1 AUSTRALIA'S TRADE WITH ASEAN IN 12 MONTHS ENDING MARCH QUARTER 2003 (A$ MILLION)

Country	Exports	Imports
Brunei Darussalam	53	687
Cambodia	16	3
Indonesia	3070	4586
Laos	19	1
Malaysia	2181	4175
Myanmar	16	18
Philippines	1102	832
Singapore	4826	4312
Thailand	2495	3329
Vietnam	484	2546
Total ASEAN	14262	20489

Source: ABS Catalogue No 5422.0.

TABLE 18.2 AUSTRALIA'S TRADE WITH ASEAN BY COMMODITY GROUP IN 12 MONTHS ENDED MARCH QUARTER 2003 (A$ MILLION)

Commodity grouping	Exports	Imports
Food and live animals	2654	968
Beverages and tobacco	148	38
Crude materials, inedible, except fuels	1090	315
Mineral fuels, lubricants and related materials	2358	6683
Animal and vegetable oils, fats and waxes	18	111
Chemical and related products	871	947
Manufactured goods classified chiefly by material	2046	1736
Machinery and transport equipment	1468	6042
Miscellaneous manufactured articles	466	1753
Commodities and transactions not classified elsewhere	3142	1896
Total trade with ASEAN	14262	20489

Source: ABS Catalogue No 5422.0.

A tripartite body of employer groups, unions and government representatives was formed in 1972 as the The National Wages Council (NWC). Their goals were to:

- recommend annual wage increases;
- ensure orderly wage determination to promote economic and social development; and
- assist in development of incentive schemes to improve national productivity.

The NWC played a major part in keeping industrial relations harmonious. However, poor personnel practices led to job-hopping rather than training and staff development. Organisations offered better pay to poach staff shamelessly.

To encourage upgrading workers' skills and increase productivity, the Singaporean government set up the Skills Development Fund (SDF) in 1979 (Wong 1991). Then in 1981 the National Productivity Council (NPC) was formed, emphasising higher worker productivity by skills upgrading.

Productivity growth is often seen as the driver of economic growth. This is very true in Singapore where productivity gains allowed economic expansion to continue. In fact, by NPC's figures, between 1981 and 1991, two-thirds of the 7.1 per cent average growth in gross domestic product (GDP) came directly from higher productivity. Had productivity stagnated, GDP would have been 36 per cent below the actual level (NPC 1991).

This is important as the only other source of GDP increase would have been employing more workers. Singapore's tight labour market stops this being a major source of future economic growth. Since 1997 GDP growth has see-sawed (Table 18.3) as the Singaporean economy was buffeted by waves of regional turmoil (Statistics Singapore 2004).

Issues confronting Singaporean managers

Over the next decade Singapore faces many issues. These will impact multinational corporations and Singaporean enterprises.

Economic restructuring

Global competition is accelerating. Singapore was one of the first Asian countries to undergo significant economic and technological change, and now other Asian countries face these changes (Dodd 2000). Therefore it is vital Singapore continue economic restructuring and adopting high technology and value-adding industries. In part, this is shown by the government's continuing drive to encourage multinational corporations to set up regional headquarters in Singapore.

Tight labour market

The speed of industrialisation has produced an acute labour shortage, escalating wage costs and job-hopping. To overcome this, employers source workers from across the region. The Singaporean government has tried to discourage this by setting high permit fees. These workers also tend to job-hop, playing employers off against each other, lacking company loyalty and a feeling of belonging.

Human resource development and management

Many Singaporean workers are still unskilled. Though the general Singaporean educational level is rising, many manufacturing workers only have basic primary education (Wong 1991). Human resource management and development is crucial to Singapore. This means innovative personnel practices must be developed and introduced to use employees effectively.

TABLE 18.3 SINGAPORE GDP FIGURES, 1997–2003

Year	GDP
1997	8.1
1998	−0.9
1999	6.9
2000	9.7
2001	−1.9
2002	2.2
2003	1.1

Source: Statistics Singapore 2004

Productivity and quality of work-life

With higher educational levels come expectations of higher standards of living and work-life quality. Thus Singaporean workers want to be more involved in workplace decision-making processes, and increasingly are interested in consultative management approaches.

The tight labour market means wage escalation lowers competitiveness, especially for businesses with slim profits. Increased productivity is the key organisational objective. Efficiency gains can come from job redesign and task flexibility.

Directions for the future

Singapore's past determination is clear in its leader's plans. Singapore's vision, of being 'the intelligent island', sees every Singaporean home, office, school and factory linked by computer (Dodds 2000). Their commitment matches their vision, and much infrastructure is in place. Further, this vision is not simply an ideal way to establish national competitive advantage and to enhance its citizens' lives.

Four strategic thrusts are to (Birch 1993):

- develop a global hub to turn Singapore into a highly efficient traffic-switching centre;
- boost the economic engine towards greater value-adding manufacturing;
- improve quality of life and increase discretionary time; and
- enhance individuals' potential as skills, creativity and knowledge are increasingly important.

Singapore's political environment supports this vision. This is because the political leadership has been key to the island country's remarkable 25 years of growth and development. Conformity and compliance is expected and enforced in Singaporean society. This has produced some attributes the country's leaders are trying to eliminate.

One of these is *kiasu*, a Hokein word for 'fear of losing out'. It is best summed up in a phrase popularised by a cartoon character, Mr Kiasu, in Singlish (the local idiom): 'Better grab first, later no more'.

This trait means Singaporeans have an unfortunate reputation abroad, and can be seen as risk-aversive. With a government promoting expansion of Singapore's overseas business activities, the *kiasu* syndrome, deterring risk-taking, is seen to be an obstacle to home-grown entrepreneur development (Stewart 1993).

An enterprising spirit is seen as crucial for the future. Despite economic success, Singapore has not nurtured widespread entrepreneurship or enterprising spirit, and now needs to develop these skills.

The island republic's prosperity can be traced to a relentlessly far-sighted government, not individual deal makers. As noted, Singaporeans are risk-aversive and conservative. State-controlled companies expand slowly internationally, and private enterprise is reluctant to back risky enterprises (Bromby 1993). There are even private investors who look for government compensation when their investments do not make a profit. This does not fit with the increasingly sophisticated, knowledgeable, well-travelled and cosmopolitan Singaporean.

Relationship with Australia

Singapore's government wants business to invest overseas to grow beyond their domestic market. Following support offered to offshore investors, interest in Australia is growing as firms diversify under the republic's plan for establishing external economic arms (Chong 1993).

Traditionally Singapore has invested heavily in Australian property. Singapore companies are the third largest hotel and tourism investors after the United States and Japan.

In trade, Singapore is Australia's sixth largest export partner (ABS Catalogue 5422.0). However, many exports to Singapore are re-exported to other South-East Asian countries. For example, Indonesia often imports capital equipment from Australia via Singapore due to customs duty differences (Chong 1993).

Australian businesses investing in Singapore import Australian-made capital equipment to outfit their plants. For example, Goodman Fielder imported bakery equipment for its bakery in Singapore. Cladding-material producer Permasteel-ISA brings 40 per cent of its product (glass and aluminium) from Australian factories to assemble in its two Singapore plants.

Singapore and Australia's relationship is long-term, dating from the early 1960s, with projects including Changi Airport construction and land-reclamation. The relationship is moving to a strategic alliance, and eventually will see Singapore becoming Australia's competitor rather than business partner. Either way, the relationship will expand. One step in this process was the Singapore–Australia free trade agreement signed during 2003 (Burrell 2004). In the 12 months ending in the March quarter 2003, Australia's exports to Singapore were A$4826 million and imports from Singapore were A$4312 million.

FOCUS ON NEW ZEALAND

From 1984 New Zealand undertook significant economic reform moving from a heavily controlled country to a far more liberal one (Bollard & Mayes 1993). The process needed managers (in private and public sectors) to consider all operational aspects. The major changes are summarised below, based on the task-environment model (Chapter 3).

Economic reforms

Customers and clients

Reduction in trade restriction and deregulation of the foreign exchange market provided more options for New Zealand firms to find international customers. Domestically, regulatory limit changes (e.g. shop-trading hours and liquor sales) meant firms' responsiveness to customers, and their expectations, grew.

Competitors

Greater competition (particularly in finance, transport and energy) was seen as crucial to making New Zealand business more competitive internationally. Entry restrictions, price controls, monopolies and other existing advantages (banks and airlines) were removed. Government monopolies such as Telecom and Air New Zealand competed with new entrants Clear and Ansett. For other businesses, the competition was international. Removal of trade barriers and protection freed up imports, and domestic producers had to meet international quality and price standards to survive. Not all of these new competitors were well attuned to the changed environment.

Suppliers

Deregulating finance, transport and energy sectors gave more choice (with greater complexity and risk) to New Zealand firms. Local and international companies now own, wholly or in part, government services (rail transport, natural resources and electricity supply). Phasing out import licensing and changed tariff structures allowed managers greater flexibility sourcing overseas material (and put competitive pressure on local import-substitute manufacturers).

Labour supply

The strength of New Zealand labour unions let them restrict labour supply (e.g. by compulsory membership and blanket coverage), and lift wages to uncompetitive levels. The *Employment Contracts Act 1991* (ECA) swung the power balance back to employers. Unions lost the monopoly right to represent workers, and some union membership benefits (access to legal unfair dismissal remedies) became universal—even chief executives could use the Employment Court for personal grievances and disputes. The implication for managers was that they had to communicate more with their workforce, and develop an employment strategy tailored to organisational needs; they no longer had a rigid pay award set by unions and employer representatives in Wellington. Unions, unable to restrict labour supply, had to build demand for their membership to use their power for higher wages. As a result, they emphasised productivity bargaining, workplace reform, and performance agreements (*National Business Review* 1993).

Issues confronting New Zealand managers

Skill levels
During the last recession, few firms (including public sector apprentice employers) took on new trainees. When firms expanded, skilled technical staff were in short supply and affected companies had to find employees offshore. Workforce planning with staff training and development can help avoid such limits to growth.

Labour relations
The ECA required greater manager skills to reach agreements with workers. If unemployment is high, employers' bargaining position is strong, and some exploit this. However, where demand is high or supply limited, employees are powerful (*National Business Review* 1993).

Workplace reform
Labour market deregulation let New Zealand companies create more flexible work practices. The Council of Trade Unions supported the trend to greater employee involvement in decisions affecting them at work; for example, job design and teamwork strategies set out in Chapters 8 and 14 (New Zealand Council of Trade Unions 1992). Managers must use these to maintain quality and productivity levels.

Social problems
These reforms caused pain for many. While some benefits are clear (lower home-loan interest rates and taxes, improved business confidence), community sectors can suffer. Unemployment is still high, and user-pays policies limit tertiary education access. There are concerns over the impact of corporatisations (business structure creation) in government-funded health service delivery. Unless these issues (especially unemployment) are overcome, the government will be pressured to become more interventionist.

Growth and influence of Maori in the economic sector
The past decade has seen Maori become a major player in the New Zealand economy. The return to Maori of major assets through Treaty of Waitangi settlements, the upskilling and retraining of the Maori workforce following the 1980s economic reforms, and the development of strategic investments have enabled Maori to take a leading role in developing their substantial resource base which has, in the past, been inaccessible to Maori.

With an asset base of over NZ$10 billion, Maori collectively represent New Zealand's third largest business entity. Strategic partnerships with both local and international organisations have seen many Maori organisations grow from small, locally owned and managed enterprises into large, multinational corporates. While the commercial and business practices have had to change within these Maori organisations, the traditional values and philosophies of collective ownership, resource sustainability and consensus decision-making have not. The result has often seen conflict arise within the partnership due to these different philosophies.

With the Maori population expected to grow from 13 per cent of the total New Zealand population in 2004 to 20 per cent of the population by 2050, the role and influence of Maori in the New Zealand economy will grow accordingly.

TABLE 18.4 NEW ZEALAND'S MAIN EXPORT MARKETS IN THE YEAR ENDED DECEMBER 2003 (NZ$ MILLION)

Country	Value
Australia	6 120.6
USA	4 117.1
Japan	3 122.3
China	1 372.4
UK	1 362.5
South Korea	992.2
Germany	745.8
Taiwan	624.8
Belgium	624.1
Hong Kong	558.9

Source: Trade New Zealand 2004.

Relationship with Asia

Asia is an increasingly significant New Zealand market, and the government actively supports business initiatives. East Asian and Japanese exports have grown since 1970, most rapidly since 1990. Now, six Asian countries are among New Zealand's top 10 export customers (see Table 18.4).

Agriculture and forestry products form the backbone of New Zealand exports; however, exports of clothing, software, domestic appliances and machinery are growing.

Ministry of Foreign Affairs and Trade figures for the year ended December 2003 show Japan to be New Zealand's third largest import source (behind Australia and the USA). China and Taiwan are in sixth and seventh places, with Korea, Malaysia and Singapore appearing in the top 15.

Asian investment in New Zealand is significant, particularly in forestry, property and tourism. Most main Auckland hotels belong to Asian investors (Smith 1993) and other investments include retail operations and golf courses. New Zealand and Asian joint ventures are planned or underway in projects such as Asian television broadcasting (Hudson 1993), beer brewing in China (Morrison 1993), and telecommunications in Vietnam (*National Business Review* 1993).

Relationship with Australia

Australia is New Zealand's biggest export market and import source, while New Zealand is Australia's fourth largest export market. The two economies have close cultural, sporting and economic ties and these, coupled with the closer economic relationship agreement (CER) between the two countries, facilitate trade in goods and services.

Recent New Zealand reforms have led to reduced business costs and some manufacturing operations being moved from Australia to New Zealand. This includes manufacture of appliances by PDL, toiletry products by Gillette, powder detergent by Unilever PLC and toothbrushes by Johnson and Johnson (Doman 1993). These shifts highlight why managers must pay close attention to the international environment; changing a company's mega-environmental political and economic fields can alter its competitiveness significantly, and mean its strengths, weaknesses, opportunities and threats must be reassessed.

TABLE 18.5 AUSTRALIAN TRADE WITH NEW ZEALAND (A$BILLION)		
Year	Exports	Imports
2002–03	8.00	4.97
2001–02	7.43	4.74
2000–01	6.87	4.57
1999–00	6.74	4.37
1998–99	5.75	3.88
1997–98	7.47	4.03
1996–97	6.21	3.69
1995–96	5.61	3.59
1994–95	4.79	3.55
1993–94	4.01	3.20
1992–93	3.37	2.79
1991–92	2.83	2.40
1990–91	2.54	2.15
1989–90	2.61	2.17
1988–89	2.22	1.97
1987–88	2.18	1.73
1986–87	1.77	1.43
1985–86	1.51	1.45
1984–85	1.54	1.10
1983–84	1.39	0.91
1982–83	1.16	0.69
1981–82	1.03	0.73
1980–81	0.92	0.64
1979–80	0.86	0.55
1978–79	0.74	0.42

Source: ABS 5410.0 and Trade New Zealand 2004.

FOCUS ON INDONESIA

The Republic of Indonesia is a product of Asia's post–World War II decolonisation. The territory which was known as the Netherlands Indies became a state of its own. Ki Hadjar Dewantara, founder of the Indonesian educational system, set out three basic characteristics of the Indonesian leadership style in the following quotation:

> *Ing ngarso sung tulodo,*
> *Ing madya mangun karso,*
> *Tut sari handayani.*
>   Ki Hadjar Dewantara

Ing ngarso sung tulodo means leaders must build themselves up by changing their attitudes and practices to become exemplary models to subordinates. *Ing madya mangun karso* means leaders must be able to motivate and generate a spirit of self-help and creativity in subordinates.

Tut sari handayani means leaders must be able to persuade their subordinates and be brave enough to become forerunners in bearing responsibilities (Widyahartono 1991).

The above describes what many management students feel is the essence of management practice. It is congruent with the Indonesian state philosophy stated in its constitution's preamble. It comprises the Five Pillars (principles) known as *Panca Sila*, *panca* meaning five, and *sila* meaning principles.

1. Belief in God the Almighty, hence communism is totally rejected. There is no one state religion. All religions are equally fostered.
2. Humanism, that is treating people as human beings, being kind to them and respecting and helping each other.
3. Nationalism, that is putting the nation above all self-interest. The country's welfare and progress are the primary goals of individuals, institutions and organisations.
4. Sovereignty, that is the rights of the people are cared for and respected.
5. Justice, that is fairness in rendering justice to all, regardless of status differences.

The above principles are built into every Indonesian organisation and reflected in the principles and practices of management in every aspect of Indonesian society.

Issues confronting Indonesian managers

The relevance of management to Indonesian society

Indonesia is a country with a range of cultural settings. One managerial style cannot apply to all and distinctive cultural flavours prevail. Thus people from Central Java will close their minds and remain silent about their disagreement, while those from North Sumatra will only respond to an authoritative tone. The resulting tendency is for managers to adopt an American or European methodology. The challenge for Indonesia, currently a developing country, is to develop a style of its own and not mimic Western, Chinese or Japanese styles. In many Indonesian organisations, conflict therefore is cultural, between modernity and tradition (Widyahartono 1991).

Indonesian society is still quite traditionally hierarchical and honour-oriented, almost feudalistic. It prescribes the structuring and maintenance of relations between people. Conflict must be prevented at all cost. Subordinates will therefore only comment on what they believe their superior will like to hear. Unlike most Western value systems, Indonesian society is in general not materialistic.

In overtly Western organisations people work to achieve organisational objectives but in a harmonious manner, operating within Indonesian communication patterns. For example, the Javanese 3A philosophy demonstrates this. The first A is *Asuh* or taking care of others; the second A is *Asah* or improving others' capabilities; the third A is *Asih* or love for each other. Indonesian society is traditionally geared to consultation, agreement and solidarity, with a strong hierarchical orientation (The Expatriate Web Site Association 2000).

In Indonesian organisations work is the way to achieve objectives but also establish and guarantee harmony. The manager's main aim is therefore to achieve and maintain this harmony while accumulating power and authority. It must be noted though that the concept of power and authority in this context is different to the Western view. It is not based on contract or appointment. It is a status embodied in the manager based on their age, class, expertise and so on. An Indonesian manager then uses organisational assets to achieve the goal of harmony.

Indonesians of Chinese origins also apply teachings of Confucius to their dealings. These are the five principles of filial piety, fidelity, obedience, kindness, and loyalty to one's superior.

While these two philosophies may appear different, their similarities give Indonesia a philosophical homogeneity rare in Western countries.

Directions for the future

Indonesia, the world's fourth most populous state with 212.9 million people, showed impressive growth until the last couple of years. Once the relative pauper of South-East Asia,

Indonesia stood poised to become the region's newest industrialised power. As recently as 1976, half of Indonesia's population lived in what the World Bank designated as developing-world poverty. Until 1997 that number reduced dramatically, but after then the economic outlook became considerably less favourable. Until 1997 year-on-year growth averaged 8 per cent, on much the same economic formula as its ASEAN neighbours; after a severe drop in 1998, it has since recovered to 4.2 per cent (Business Monitor International 2004).

The gross national product per person was just US$60 in 1967, growing to US$600 in 1993, and was targeted to US$1000 by the turn of the century. Instead it was US$45 in 1999, recovering to US$213 in 2000.

Indonesia is responding to these and other challenges. One area to be addressed is telecommunications infrastructure to deliver business-integration and rebuilding solutions. Indonesia is a sprawling country and development requires linkages with Jakarta.

This would be a move from its labour-intensive areas of electronics, clothing, textiles, footwear and furniture industries. In fact one World Bank Review expected the manufacturing sector to continue as the main engine of growth, but it would be difficult to change without assured funding.

Other areas needing development are railways, power generation and distribution. This is due to the change in the Indonesian economy from an agriculture and resource base, to one with higher technology levels. This means training and industrial relations will again be important to managers in the country over the next decade.

Relationship with Australia

The Australian view of Indonesia is changing. Previously the Indonesian market was misunderstood. Indonesian economic reform saw changes in taxation, banking and customs procedures. However, there was little information about different business cultures in interpersonal relationships, corporate structures and business customs.

This point is evidenced by involvement of the 'big five' chartered accounting firms in Indonesia. For them, Indonesia was seen as a major expansion area with strong growth in joint ventures, mining, manufacturing and infrastructure projects. Note was made of increased interest in Indonesia by Australian companies due to proximity and market potential, particularly in food processing and distribution, construction and engineering services, mining and textiles (Jay 1993). After the Australian involvement in East Timor, most business interactions slowed or halted; however, they are starting to grow again.

Ultimately, for Australia, a return to growth means an increase in trade opportunities. The issue Australian companies will have to remember as they seek these opportunities is that Indonesia must be judged by Indonesian standards and not Western ones.

FOCUS ON MALAYSIA

Malaysia is a multiracial nation with a population of over 20 million. The population of Malaysia consists of Malays (about 58 per cent of the population), Chinese (about 26 per cent), Indians (about 7 per cent) and other minor racial groups (about 9 per cent). By the time Malaysia gained its independence in 1957, a situation had evolved where the general livelihood of the three main racial groups was segregated largely according to economic calling. Economic returns from small agricultural holdings and wages derived from estate working were small, which meant Malays (Bumiputras—sons of the soil) were not as financially well off as were the Chinese population who tended to be in business.

The Second (1971–75) and Third (1976–80) Malaysia Plans concentrated on two objectives:

- eradication of poverty among the population irrespective of race, and
- restructuring society to eliminate identification of race with economic function.

These objectives were promulgated to influence national planning and development for the 20-year period from 1971 to 1990 (Thong 1991). Through social engineering, it was planned

TABLE 18.6 AUSTRALIAN TRADE WITH INDONESIA (A$ MILLION)

Year	Exports	Imports
2002–03	3070	4586
2001–02	3163	4095
2000–01	3119	3277
1999–00	2248	2701
1998–99	2101	3487
1997–98	3390	2266
1996–97	3233	1753
1995–96	2720	1340
1994–95	2110	1040
1993–94	1910	1220
1992–93	1720	1240
1991–92	1635	995
1990–91	1462	784
1989–90	1030	441
1988–89	734	419
1987–88	595	587
1986–87	528	310
1985–86	522	209
1984–85	431	363
1983–84	375	299
1982–83	384	561
1981–82	416	515
1980–81	358	416
1979–80	293	241
1978–79	217	99

Source: ABS 5410.0 and 5422.0.

that by 1990, as a general guideline, 30 per cent of Malaysian companies would be owned by Bumiputras, 40 per cent by Chinese and Indians, and the other 30 per cent by foreign investors. The intention was to make employment of Bumiputras at various levels of private enterprise representative of the country's racial composition.

Issues confronting Malaysian managers

Multiculturalism

Due to Malaysian encouragement of foreign investments since the early 1970s, management's professionalisation has increased. Many Malaysians have been trained in overseas head offices, and there has been considerable in-plant training by foreign consultants and trainers, integrating motivation programs used on sites in other countries.

Programs such as management by objectives (MBO), critical path methods (CPM), just in time (JIT), and quality control circles (QCC) have been implemented. These were often introduced by chief executives who brought them back from training periods overseas. The crucial issue to all of these approaches has been that the method's success depends on the facilitator's ability to transfer concepts to local operations.

This is complicated by the Malaysian tendency to use an indirect approach. For example, first-time contact is often made through an intermediary. This person takes an informal role of guarantor of trustworthiness and goodwill of the party seeking the contact. This, of course, reflects on the intermediary's future credibility. While this takes time, the degree of success is much greater than a direct approach.

Considerable importance is also placed on 'face'—observance of courtesy and sensitivities to what is right and wrong. A win–win situation must always be maintained for a transaction to be successful.

Malaysia's multiracial composition means foreign managers must be constantly aware of issues specific to each racial group. For example, Malays, being Muslims, will not eat pork, and will not use crockery contaminated by pork. All meat must be slaughtered according to a specific religious ceremony. As well, Indian Hindus will not eat beef, and may be vegetarian. Managers should be aware of these issues, and firms with canteen facilities must cater to these needs (Thong 1991). Finally, as religion plays such an important part in Malaysian life, staffing at some times of the year will need to take religious calendars into consideration.

Decision-making practices

Malaysian managers may seek second opinions consistently when faced with an important decision, by consulting astrology and occult science experts. Meanwhile many Chinese also believe in *feng shui* or geomancy (Thong 1991). An example of this is that it is generally believed that even placement of a building's front door will bring an organisation either good or bad luck.

While these practices may seem odd to Western management students, they are a matter of belief; and in Malaysia many successful managers and businessmen take them very seriously. They may not openly advocate them, and may even have been educated and trained in Western management, but they can still effectively integrate the two styles.

Directions for the future

Vision 2020 aims to give Malaysians affluence that is now only widely available in leading Western economies. This vision has as its goal an industrialised Malaysia where citizens will have the purchasing power available to the average American citizen today. This required doubling of national income every 10 years, so that by 2000, an eightfold increase would have been achieved (Doraisami 1993). The challenge in achieving this vision has become much greater recently. Firstly, it became harder to maintain the economy's momentum as it slowed during the regional crisis. Then other challenges came from transformation of relatively fragile manufacturing sectors and destinations of manufactured exports within the region.

Malaysia's manufactured-export performance has been influenced by its competitiveness relative to neighbouring South-East Asian countries. Malaysia was successful in drawing from Taiwanese and South Korean investments as their currency appreciated, labour costs rose and their preferential treatment by the United States was lost, forcing them to seek off-shore bases.

However, as the cycle continues, labour markets will tighten up and wage rises will produce a new generation of lower-cost producers to undercut Malaysia. This is important, for while manufactured exports account for about 70 per cent of total exports, the Malaysian manufacturing base is very narrow (Doraisami 1993).

Malaysia is working overtime to promote development of medium- and small-scale industries. This needs upgrading of its generally low-level technology, particularly if Malaysia is to achieve newly-developed country status soon.

Malaysia has shortages of both skilled and unskilled indigenous labour as production grows. Concern is growing around environmental issues, and temporary acceleration in economic growth will force exhaustion of forestry and petroleum reserves. These difficulties are then coupled with little attention being given to occupational health and safety standards, waste disposal and environmental hazards due to irresponsible investors.

Malaysia currently plays a leading role in fostering greater economic cooperation in the region through ASEAN. This cooperation is increasingly the critical path to prosperity. As a part of the process, growth triangles are being set up to take advantage of complementary conditions between neighbouring countries, due to growing gaps between labour costs, capital flows and technology levels.

Relationship with Australia

The past few years have seen an encouraging broadening of the business base—from Australia's perspective—in Malaysia. Many small to medium-sized companies have won contracts in a wide range of areas, specifically in construction and development industry service sectors (Chong 1993). For example, the architectural firm Davenport Campbell was involved with a $200 million Tampoi Retail Centre in Johore, and John Holland won a contract to build a 12-storey apartment building in Kuala Lumpur. In addition, one of Australia's largest current investment plans is a petrochemical refinery worth more than $1 billion which BHP has proposed to build in Sarawak, although this is still not proceeding due to financial limitations.

While Australia's investment base is off a low base, Australia's trade with Malaysia is modest compared with other Asian countries, due to Malaysia's reduced raw material imports. This is expected to change as Malaysia needs technology transfer. Traditionally, Australian companies have been better at this transfer than Japanese firms, for example. Furthermore, Australian technology is robust and operates under a range of climatic conditions suited to Malaysian conditions. To illustrate, Nilson's Transformers, Melbourne based, won a $12 million contract with Tenaga Nasional Berhad, Malaysia's electricity-generating body.

While opportunities exist and will increase for Australian investments and developments in Malaysia, the challenge for Australian managers and their organisations will be adjusting to a very different culture.

FOCUS ON THAILAND

Thailand's population is 60 million, of whom 14 per cent are of Chinese origin and 95 per cent are Buddhists. The most pervasive characteristic of Thai society is a love of freedom, and this basic value has greatly affected the development of the country, which is richly endowed with natural resources. Thai businessmen are mostly engaged in commodity production and manufactured goods importation, and most financial institutions have been built on trading activities. While currently the more influential businessmen are traders, manufacturers are a new social group.

Belief and value systems in Thai society are deeply rooted in Buddhism. The Buddhist approach to life and understanding of human behaviour is exemplified by Buddha's passive and contemplative way of dealing with the problems of life. The following are tenets for consideration by Buddhists (Siengthai & Vadhanasindhu 1991):

1. Self-realisation—know who you are, and what your strengths and weaknesses are.
2. Knowing others—know whom you have to deal with and how to deal with them.
3. Causality—know about the cause and effect of what you are doing.
4. Appropriate timing—know the appropriate time for dealing with problems or confronting them.
5. Appropriate place—know where to do things appropriately.
6. Knowing potentiality—know your ability and your limitations.

If you compare these tenets with those of Western society, which is conflict-resolution oriented, Thai society is geared to conflict avoidance. As Western society has developed values and institutions requiring people to deal with others in a particular way, so has Thai society.

The difference is Thai society has a strong desire to keep relationships peaceful and on an even keel. There is a tendency to shrug off small frustrations and disagreements, preventing anger surfacing. To achieve this, relationships must be kept under control. This often leads to social relationships with Westerners staying superficial and leads to involvement avoidance (Siengthai & Vadhanasindhu 1991).

Traditionally an agrarian community, Thailand has developed rapidly to combine a multi-faceted society with technology. In fact it hopes to exploit its geographic advantage as a central point in Asia to compete with established aviation hubs, Singapore and Hong Kong. Thailand has one natural advantage in this, as it is a few flying hours closer to Europe than most established stopovers.

Issues confronting Thai managers

Incompatible business law

Unlike many regional countries, Thailand was never colonised by the British as were Singapore and Malaysia. As a result, Thai business law has little similarity to the common law heritage of Australia's other Asian trading partners. Thai business law seems largely dependent upon a system of discretion, favours and patronage (Castellari 1993).

Demand for infrastructure

Thailand's middle class is demanding better infrastructure, creating opportunities in the country but also stressing the government to provide incentives to satisfy those demands through foreign investments and imports. Many projects are still on hold; however, some resources are becoming available.

An under-educated workforce

While 90 per cent of the workforce is literate, their education level is only primary school. So, Thailand has needed to import thousands of engineers and technicians to satisfy its needs.

Cheap labour base

Thailand's competitive advantage rests heavily on a combination of cheap labour, foreign money and foreign technology. Many Thai industries such as textiles could easily migrate to lower-wage countries if a competitive economic environment is not maintained.

TABLE 18.7 AUSTRALIAN TRADE WITH THAILAND (A$ MILLION)		
Year	Exports	Imports
2002–03	2495	3329
2001–02	2329	2778
2000–01	2219	2780
1999–00	1517	2282
1998–99	1286	1765
1997–98	1651	1332
1996–97	1690	1080
1995–96	1780	1010
1994–95	1560	877
1993–94	1280	767
1992–93	1215	756
1991–92	816	647
1990–91	665	505

Source: ABS.

A critical issue currently facing Thailand is whether it has the infrastructure to move from low-cost producer dependent on foreign investment to an economy supported by domestic and high-value-added production. This is urgent as other countries with lower wage costs covet Thailand's markets and may prove to be attractive to offshore manufacturing (Edwards & Edwards 1993).

Fuelled by a labour shortage, shopfloor wages in greater Bangkok have doubled to between A$10 and A$12 a day. This is over three times higher than in Vietnam and double that of China. The result is that Japanese, Taiwanese and Hong Kong investments in light industry, which lead Thailand to see itself as Asia's newest industrialised economy, are being lured away.

Relationship with Australia

Thailand in the 2000s was Australia's fourteenth largest export market. In the 2002–03 year, Australia sold A$2.5 billion worth of goods, mostly gold, dairy products, wool and crude petroleum (ABS 5422.0). Australia's relationship with Thailand has traditionally been very friendly. Of all 10 ASEAN members, it is Thailand which seems most enthusiastic about Australia's thrust into Asia.

In 1993 a Thai Australian Chamber of Commerce was established in Melbourne, to provide information to companies interested in exploring business opportunities in Thailand. With infrastructure needs, support for continuing manufacturing growth, and increased services in areas like quality control and training, Thailand offers many opportunities to Australian organisations as its economy continues to recover.

JAPAN'S IMPACT ON THE REGION

Japan's economy traditionally depends on raw material importation and high-value-added goods exportation. Japan's export dependency on the United States is very high, matched only by the aggressively export-oriented economies of Malaysia, Thailand and China.

To maintain its export capacity, Japan has set up facilities and assembly plants in South-East Asian countries. The pattern is to put expatriate Japanese managers in charge, with technology and managerial skills transfer not occurring readily. However, many of this decade's new management practices have come from Japan. Quality circles and just in time, for example, are Japanese management developments.

Since World War II, the Japanese economy and industrial infrastructure's restructuring has given birth to the second largest economy in the world. It has brought with it a generally stable work environment for Japanese workers. Lifetime employment, the seniority system and in-house labour unions were the three major system features. Company loyalty was assumed, while promotion involved years of rotation through many departments and locations. Talent was a negligible asset and generalists ruled. Women had equal opportunity so long as their work involved a supporting role to male managers.

In the 1990s changes started. Presently, Japan is in the midst of a transformation. While the new Japan will still have a vast economic structure, deregulation will produce new dilemmas such as unemployment. Deregulation is urgently needed. For example, to open a small business, some 250 forms are needed to satisfy local governmental regulations.

The themes of the new Japan are liberation of the economy from rigid regulation, liberation of consumer and worker from industry's interests, and dismantling of the iron triangle—the collusion between politicians, bureaucrats and industrialists (Hartcher 1993). This will provide a freer Japan but probably a less passive one too. Japan is realising its impact on the world and appears to be increasingly determined to influence world politics and trade and the systems through which they are conducted. Traditionally, Japan has been content to do business in its own way, interacting remotely with its trading partners. The next decade may see changes to this practice. One recent example of this increasing confidence is the decision to contribute military personnel to those in Iraq.

Relationship with Australia

Japan's relationship with Australia has been one of the basic development foundations for Australia's broader relationships with East Asia. In the last few years, dynamic growth has turned East Asia into a market which, in 2002, absorbed 60 per cent of Australia's trade, over six times the value of Australia's exports to the United States (Australian Bureau of Statistics 2003).

Australia is a large commodities trader and as such has a huge direct stake in Asia-Pacific economic diplomacy, supporting an open, non-discriminatory global trading system. Furthermore, Australia has an indirect stake in the open trading system which has been critical to the region's development.

In the past, bilateral dialogue between Australia and Japan focused on the strategic-energy and raw-materials trade relationship between the two countries. Australia supplies about half the raw materials Japan uses for steel production as well as large volumes of coal and natural gas for energy.

Japan is by far Australia's largest trading partner and has been its largest export market since the late 1960s, and its second largest source of imports since the early 1970s. Japan has also become Australia's most important source of tourism revenue, and by 1993 was the largest direct foreign investor in the Australian economy. Australia's manufactured exports to Japan are now larger than its total exports to the United Kingdom (Drysdale & Yamazawa 1993).

Social, cultural and educational contacts and exchanges are growing, bringing with them greater cooperation between both governments on a wide range of international affairs. Also many Australian students undertake Japanese language studies with a view to their future.

In short, Australia's Asia-Pacific partnership with Japan promises great practical economic benefits. Time will, however, demonstrate it to have enormous political significance as well.

TABLE 18.8 TRADE BETWEEN AUSTRALIA AND JAPAN IN 12 MONTHS ENDING MARCH QUARTER 2003

Bilateral trade $38.26 billion
Australian exports to Japan $22.09 billion
Australian imports from Japan $16.17 billion

Main exports to Japan	$ million	Main imports from Japan	$ million
Coal	5272	Road vehicles	8234
Metalliferous ores and metal scrap	2936	General industrial machinery and equipment, and machine parts	892
Non-ferrous metals	1661	Telecommunications and sound equipment	845
Meat and meat preparations	1618	Office and automatic data processing machines	808
Petroleum	1177	Machinery specialised for particular industries	649

Source: ABS May 2003.

FOCUS ON CHINA

China is a land of opportunity and an untapped mine of investment opportunities for foreign investors. With a population over 1.3 billion, it has potentially the biggest consumer market in the world. More importantly, its economy has grown faster than that of any other place in the world over the past 20 years. The growth rate remained high even during the Asia financial crisis, reaching 7.8 per cent in 1998 and 7.5 per cent in 2003, despite suffering heavy floods and SARS in those years. It is predicted China will be the world's second largest economy by 2010 and world's largest by 2030.

Despite the opportunities, undertaking business in China presents its risks and obstacles. Traditional management and decision-making methods fitting other countries may not work in China or may need extensive adjustment. Some reasons include China's embryonic legal structure and immature economic market and banking system, as well as different cultures.

As China develops it will do so not with a US-based business model or way of thinking, and not with a European one, and not even a Japanese one; it will, however, be influenced by all of these, while developing its own distinct philosophies, experts and experiences of business and management.

Issues confronting Chinese managers

Chinese managers face many problems with the very fast development of their economy.

Economic reform

China's economy is only partially reformed, with the state-owned banking system dominating the financial sector. Other state-owned enterprises (SOEs) dominate capital-intensive industrial production, employing the vast majority of urban workers. The government relies on SOEs to keep the urban peace by providing workers with social benefits such as housing, health care and pensions, as the fiscal system at present is far too inefficient to allow the government itself to fund a large-scale social welfare system. What is needed is a simultaneous reform of China's capital markets, industrial ownership structure, social welfare system, and fiscal system, since each constitutes an integral component of the total political-economic system (Oksenberg et al. n.d).

It is hard to attract and retain talented managers. One survey by management-consulting firm Hewitt Associates found that each year 43 per cent of senior managers and leaders in China voluntarily leave their organisations, in contrast to just 5 per cent in Singapore and 11 per cent in Australia. 'I have had five managers in our Shanghai office in the last two years', says a Japanese shipping company executive with 120 employees in China. 'There is no end in sight to this, and it is hard to establish business relationships when you are constantly dealing with new people.' (Wozniak 2001)

The role of leadership

Leadership and authority in China are different to the West. Western leadership tends to be task-focused and straightforward. In contrast, Chinese managers tend to be more focused on determining who is awarded a role or task. In China, personal relationships determine who gets to do what.

In traditional Chinese culture the boss is all-powerful and the organisational hierarchy is a critical element of managing an organisation or business—it is the key mechanism to run the business. The boss is expected to have all the answers and provide clear direction. People expect to be instructed and led at all times, and staff will wait for instruction and be heavily dependent on the boss. This means those lower in the organisation tend to take less initiative and ownership, a behaviour viewed by some Western managers as responsibility avoidance.

Over population

Since 1972, China's population has grown by over 400 million people. Annually 15 million additional laborers enter the urban and rural workforce. This leads to dramatic cuts in rural poverty rates and growing employment opportunities. However, urban unemployment rates are growing rapidly.

Quality of the workforce

The number of workers in China is vast, but the quality is often low. For decades, China's per capita expenditures on primary schools have ranked among the lowest in the world, and the dissolution of communes has led to an erosion in school financing and attendance in many villages. University faculty meanwhile have not fully recovered from the Mao years and, as with other agencies, dependent on government funding, are expected to launch their own enterprises and to secure foreign support to sustain their educational offerings. Low workforce quality leads to problems for Chinese managers including safety and product quality.

Directions for the future

Legal environment
The Chinese legal system is weak and some managers take advantage of this. With the amendment and redevelopment of the legal system, this phenomenon should be reduced in future.

Human resources
China's economic growth also will be restrained by inadequate human resources. In fact, China is a major importer of human talent. It is estimated over 50 000 Hong Kong citizens and 200 000 Taiwanese serve in managerial, professional and technical positions on the mainland. This situation reflects Beijing's inability to attract over 150 000 Chinese graduate students sent abroad and yet to return home.

This leads to inadequate supply of technically proficient staff in managerial, engineering and scientific areas. Shortages are clear in the brain drain from rural and impoverished areas, where skilled labour is particularly important but wages and working conditions are not competitive, and urban firms' difficulty keeping skilled personnel. Eventually, a free labour market and expanded higher education will overcome these problems, but for the foreseeable future, China's growth rate will be affected.

Corruption
Due to historical and political issues, corruption is common in China. Managers at all levels enjoy the personal advantages of their power. The Chinese government continues to battle corruption and hopefully will win.

Bureaucracy
While Chinese firms lack highly-educated, intelligent, competent top managers, they do contain many middle-level managers. The result is that decision making becomes more bureaucratic and inefficient. The government structure makes this situation even worse. Further political and economic reform should lead to reduced bureaucracy.

Relationship with Australia
Diplomatic relations between China and Australia were set up on 21 December 1972, and by and large bilateral relations have developed smoothly. The two governments agreed to develop diplomatic relations, friendship and cooperation on the basis of principles of mutual respect for sovereignty and territorial integrity, mutual non-aggression, non-interference in each other's internal affairs, equality and mutual benefit, and peaceful coexistence.

The relationship between Australia and China is substantial and well established—this year marks 32 years of diplomatic relations. It extends well beyond burgeoning economic and political links to include an array of cultural, educational and extensive people-to-people contacts.

On 24 July 1973, the governments of the People's Republic of China and Australia concluded a Trade Agreement, granted each Most Favoured Nation Status and set up a joint trade committee. China is presently Australia's third largest trading partner (Hong Kong Special Administrative Region excluded) while Australia is China's ninth largest trading partner. China is Australia's 13th largest source of foreign investment, and Australia is in the same position for China. Australian firms have a significant and growing presence, in Beijing, Shanghai and Guangzhou, and in other parts of China. New trade and investment sectors take advantage of Australia's strengths in banking, insurance, accounting and legal services.

In August 2002, China chose the Australian Liquefied Natural Gas Corporation (ALNG) as the resource supplier for the Guangdong LNG project. This deal is worth some $17.5 billion.

The result of these powerful economic trends is that the relationship matters for both Australia and China, and will matter more in future. The outlook for better economic links is thus promising. Two-way trade between the nations is worth over $15 billion a year, with Australia primarily exporting energy and raw commodities, such as iron ore, and importing low-cost manufactured goods.

'China has made tremendous progress toward establishing a fully-fledged, market-based economy and has emerged as an important regional and global economic player. Our commercial relationship with China is expanding more rapidly than with any other major trading partner. Australia–China two-way merchandise trade has almost trebled since 1996–97 to be worth in excess of $22 billion in 2002–03', said Australian Trade Minister Mark Vaile on 24 October 2003 at the signing of the Australia–China Trade and Economic Framework. This is another important stage in the Australia–China relationship. The Framework sets a clear agenda for bilateral trade and economic relationship, including a commitment by both governments to undertake a joint study into the feasibility and benefits of a free trade agreement (FTA) between Australia and China. The Framework also covers many activities aiming to improve commercial and policy linkages. These cover sectors such as energy and mining, agriculture, textiles, clothing and footwear, services, investment, education, ICT, and policy issues including food safety, health, customs cooperation and intellectual property rights (Doman 2003).

AUSTRALIA'S POSITION WITHIN SOUTH-EAST ASIA

Traditionally, Australia's heritage and culture place it squarely in the Western nation category. Historically, its closest relationships have been with Great Britain and Europe and then the United States. The corollary to this overwhelmingly Western orientation has been the tyranny of distance. The importance of this orientation was emphasised by World War II and it was not until the Whitlam years with the end of the 'white Australia policy' that Australia ended its self-imposed cultural quarantine (Tye 1993). When Britain joined the European Economic Community in the 1970s the resulting severing of trade ties with Australia gave real impetus to the exploration of our closest neighbours for trade purposes.

Though economics may seem to be the spur, the Hawke government in the 1980s was guided by a need to espouse a regional viewpoint which saw where Australia's strategic interests lay. Under the Colombo Plan, Australia opened its doors to Asian scholars; through the Five Power Defence Arrangement, it helps maintain regional stability along with New Zealand, Great Britain, Singapore and Malaysia. History shows Australia pursued geo-political interests before it pursued an economic agenda in the region. Then over the past decade Australia's involvement, both political and economic, in South-East Asia has grown. It is therefore no surprise Australia's position and sense of belonging within the region is an important issue.

There is a strong difference of opinion, both on the part of Australians and non-Australians, as to Australia's legitimate membership of Asia. Consider the headline 'Wish as hard as we like, we cannot become part of Asia' (Davidson 1993, p. 15). Davidson quotes Mr Paul Cheng, president of the Hong Kong General Chamber of Commerce as saying, 'Asians may be very polite publicly, saying sure, sure we welcome you. But privately you're not part of Asia— ethnically, culturally, geographically...To keep on the [Keating] policy and keep saying "We are part of Asia"—to me it jars. It's not being realistic'.

This debate will continue. Economically and politically, Australia cannot afford not to be a part of Asia. Australia's economic importance to the region is receding in some areas as the growing supply sources and industrial sophistication of Asian countries mean the importance of Australia's commodity exports is diminishing (Davidson 1993), while service exports including education are growing. The real question for Australia is not whether we are part of Asia or not. Our geographic location on the edge of the Asian continental shelf is not at issue in any form. The issue is whether Australia will develop the cultural maturity to be its own country and enter into equal partnership with our neighbours for the benefit of all.

CRITICAL THINKING QUESTIONS

To answer some of these questions you will need to do further research. Useful references are given below each section of the questions.

This chapter of the text dealt with the bigger picture of management within the Pacific Rim. It examined the role of each of the key nation members as well as reviewing the operation of Australia within the region and within the global economy. The following questions examine some emerging trends and some projections about what may occur.

Australia's smallness economically and its geographical remoteness impose some harsh realities. According to James (2004, p. 64), it is this 'harsh' business climate which makes Australian companies so adept at responding to local conditions. A good example of this is how they have responded to declining foreign investment. The period 1985 to 1995 saw Australia identified as an attractive nation in which to invest, but rates of foreign direct investment (FDI) have fallen from those heady days (when it attracted 3.4 per cent of global FDI), to a level of about 1 per cent. While this lower figure may be more in line with Australia's share of world GDP, some of its neighbours are now the target of investment.

1. Which nations do you think these are and why?

2. What reactions would you expect from Australian companies in response to declining overseas investment?

James (2004) suggests that the fact that much of Australia's domestic industry is run by oligopolies can spell trouble.

3. Why?

4. What options can Australian companies pursue if they want to grow to match the size of their domestic market?

In conclusion, James (2004, p. 64) suggests that a decade of a national market characterised by a few dominant oligopolies and many small businesses and a few medium-sized businesses has seen Australia become a 'camel economy' (two-humped). The challenge for the oligopolies now is how to continue to grow—before the good times run out.

(Material relevant to these questions may be found in James, D. 2004, Perfectly adapted, *Business Review Weekly*, Australia, 1 April, p. 64.)

Kavanagh (2004) focuses on what is happening in the Asian market. She suggests that, while China is the investor's darling, other Asian markets offer promise too.

5. Which countries do you think investors are being encouraged to look at and why?

6. Despite all the glowing results, some investors are warning of problems in China. What do you think they are?

(Material relevant to these questions may be found in Kavanagh, J. 2004, Good value in Asia, *Business Review Weekly*, 15 January, p. 49.)

The notion of Asia emerging as an equal partner or even a prospective leader in the world economy can be expected to have a much wider impact on business dealings within the Asia Pacific region. We examine one small aspect of this in our last questions: the issue of remuneration. Callick (2004, p. 29) reports a senior Asian diplomat's astonishment at the 2004 salary National Australia Bank boss Frank Cicutto was being paid —about A$3.27 million—an amount less than one-third of his resignation

MAX YOUR MARKS!

Thirty interactive questions on *The Regional Context* are available now at the Online Learning Centre that accompanies this text: www.mhhe.com/au/bartol4e (For access to MaxMark please refer to the front of this text.)

payout later that year. 'It's crazy', said the diplomat. 'So much more than your Prime Minister!' (who is on A\$248 000 a year, leaving aside the decreasingly 'super' superannuation package).

The much smaller gap between the average white-collar worker and CEOs in Asian economies is generally explained in part as the result of the lack of options packages at the senior level.

7. Why have stock options not been as readily adopted in Asian nations as they are in Australia?

8. Remuneration packages to executives vary widely across Asia, and many of the variations are the result of cultural differences. What do you think the major differences are?

Despite this general pattern of greater equality in Asian economies, Austrade chief economist Tim Harcourt suggests that emerging demographic trends may influence patterns of greater economic inequality in the future.

9. What do you think Harcourt means?

It has also been documented that there is some movement, in Japan in particular, from traditional systems of base remuneration towards substantial merit-based executive bonuses. This is exactly what occurred in Honda in 2003, and others in the region now watch with interest to see if such moves are indicative of a trend which will be taken up throughout the region.

(Material relevant to these questions may be found in Callick, R. 2004, Income gap a reflection of culture, *Australian Financial Review*, 21 February, p. 29.)

FURTHER READING

Industry Week 2004, Asia yesterday's fast followers, today's global leaders, February, 253, 2, pp. 22–9.

Richardson, J. 2000, Expatriate academics in a globalized era: The beginnings of an untold story? *Asia Pacific Business Review*, Autumn, 7, 1, pp. 125–51.

Schwarz, A. and Villinger, R. 2004, Integrating Southeast Asia's economies, *McKinsey Quarterly*, 1, pp. 36–48.

Shister, N. 2004, Managing global relationships in the extended supply chain, *World Trade*, January, 17, 1, pp. 14–18.

Yonekura, H. 2004, The Japanese economy, *Vital Speeches of the Day*, 1/15, 70, 7, pp. 213–19.

Country Profiles

Background Notes on Countries of the World 2003, Australia, November, pp. 1–12.

Background Notes on Countries of the World 2003, Brunei Darussalam, August, pp. 1–10.

Background Notes on Countries of the World 2003, Hong Kong Special Administrative Region, December, pp. 1–9.

Background Notes on Countries of the World 2003, Kingdom of Thailand, August, pp. 1–11.

Background Notes on Countries of the World 2003, New Zealand, December, pp. 1–11.

Background Notes on Countries of the World 2003, Republic of Indonesia, October, pp. 1–16.

Background Notes on Countries of the World 2003, Republic of Singapore, December, pp. 1–10.

Background Notes on Countries of the World 2003, Socialist Republic of Vietnam, July, pp. 1–13.

Background Notes on Countries of the World 2001, Japan, September, pp. 1–11.

Background Notes on Countries of the World 2001, People's Republic of China, September, pp. 1–14.

Background Notes on Countries of the World 2001, Philippines, September, pp. 1–11.

Background Notes on Countries of the World 2001, South Korea, September, pp. 1–15.

Background Notes on Countries of the World 2000, Laos People's Democratic Republic, September, pp.1–11.

Background Notes on Countries of the World 2000, Malaysia, October, pp. 1–11.

Background Notes on Countries of the World 2000, People's Republic of Korea, October, p. 1.

Background Notes on Countries of the World 2000, Taiwan, October, pp. 1–11.

GRADUATE GLIMPSE

BEN DE BEYER

Ben de Beyer has a Bachelor of Commerce (Hons) from the University of Sydney, and a Master of Philosophy in management studies from Cambridge University. He is an industrial relations manager for Qantas Airways Limited.

What does your job entail?

My role as industrial relations manager involves providing strategic industrial advice to portfolio businesses, and acting as the primary interface between Qantas and relevant unions for portfolio businesses.

How have your university studies assisted you in your career?

My university studies have given me a solid grounding across a range of subjects that have been essential in my career—industrial relations, commercial law, accounting, finance and international human resource management. The further I progress in my career, the more evident it is to me that you need a range of competencies in order to remain adaptable in a work environment where the only constant is change.

What is an important management principle that you draw upon frequently in your role?

The work I reviewed for my honours and masters theses—particularly principles around how managers and organisations manage change, as well as the body of work on cultural management coming out of the UK and US in the mid-90s—have had a strong influence on how I seek to manage others and in the analysis of and response to the management styles of my colleagues, senior managers and union counterparts.

CLAIRE BESANVALLE

Claire Besanvalle has a Master of Human Resource Management from Monash University. She is a human resources advisor for Quix Convenience Stores.

What does your job entail?

I manage the recruitment process for the majority of Quix Convenience stores nationally. I also deal with any industrial relations and performance management issues.

How have your university studies assisted you in your career?

I gained valuable work experience at Network Recruitment Services while at university. I studied part-time and worked in recruitment as I felt I would gain the necessary skills for a career in human resources. The research skills I gained at university have allowed me to conduct research with my clients in recruitment, to develop relationships with those clients and to develop skills in strategic analysis. I also studied industrial relations, which is extremely pertinent for human resource professionals today and in my position at Quix.

What is an important management principle that you draw upon frequently in your role?

The most important management principle for me is change management. Organisations are constantly looking for an advantage in the workplace, and this necessitates constant change. My knowledge of change management allows me to guide my internal and external customers through the process of change.

GRADUATE GLIMPSE

JAMES GRAY

James Gray has a Bachelor of Commerce (Hons) in management from Monash University. He is a labour relations specialist for Ford of Australia Limited.

What does your job entail?

In general, the labour relations office is involved in negotiations with the unions regarding terms and conditions of employment for Ford's employees. My role involves close interaction with a range of stakeholders including senior management, union representatives, suppliers, contractors, and Ford employees at different levels of the organisation. This often requires an understanding of 'best practice' in the industry.

How have your university studies assisted you in your career?

My university studies taught me to be conscientious, hard working and eager to learn, and allowed me to build my presentation, team working, communication and negotiation skills. I have found that these attributes and skills have been essential to my role at Ford, and I continue to strive to strengthen these skills.

What is an important management principle that you draw upon frequently in your role?

My career so far has required an understanding of various facets of management, including change management, industrial relations, employee relations and industrial arbitration. In particular, my understanding of industrial relations (awards, enterprise bargaining, conciliation and arbitration) has been an essential requirement of my current role.

Smart move for Motorola

In September 1999, Motorola Inc and Nanjing Public Transit IC Card Co Ltd signed a cooperative agreement to design and implement an integrated smart card system called the Nanjing Public Transit Automated Fare Collection (AFC) project. This was to be Phase 1 of a multiphased effort to implement smart cards as a form of payment for the entire public transport network in Nanjing, including buses, ferries and the metro subway system. Phase 1 of the project was intended to enhance bus services in the city by providing a cutting-edge smart card as a convenient and easy way for users to pay for public transport. With the new system, riders would buy and reload their smart cards at stationary ticketing machines located around the city. Nanjing Public Transit funded the system in an effort to improve the way its riders pay for public transport and in order to consolidate and improve the efficiencies of its fare collection system. 'We are making an effort to help Nanjing residents enjoy a better life', said Zhu Qiang, director of the Nanjing Public Utility Bureau. 'We expect that our public utility will grow vigorously in the twenty-first century and we believe that cooperation with Motorola is a good beginning.'

Smart cards, like memory cards, are based on a chip: a microprocessor chip rather than a memory-only chip. A smart card is a computer and contains an operating system, a central processing unit and an internal memory. They are, however, inert; they operate only after a special read/write device provides them with power and exchanges coded commands with their operating systems. Information stored in smart cards is highly secure. The smart card industry is relatively young but growing rapidly. In 1992 worldwide production amounted to 400 million cards, worth US$266 million. Memory card production was expected to grow 34 per cent over the four years from 1991 to 1994 in the European market. Some industry analysts foresaw one smart card per person in Europe by 2000.

Four French companies had a combined world market share of 60 per cent: Gemplus,

Schlumberger, Sligas and Bull. Also competing in this growing market are two German, one British, one American and three Japanese producers. Motorola was an aggressive player in this industry. It saw China as a rapidly growing market for public transport applications of smart cards. With a population of 1.3 billion people and a rapidly emerging middle class in its coastal cities, China cannot contemplate car ownership at the same rate as America's 1.7 persons per car. Issues of fuel supplies, air quality, congestion, parking and road infrastructure all mean that the majority of Chinese will use public transport. This requires highly efficient mass transit systems that are safe and reliable, and can move vast numbers of people in the shortest possible time. In order to achieve rapid station throughput of people, a system of fast fare validation is necessary. Hong Kong's Mass Transit Authority (MTA) and Singapore's Mass Rapid Transit (MRT) are among the best models in the world. They use a smart card developed by ERG Company in Perth, Western Australia. These stored-value cards can simply be waved over the turnstile sensor to gain admission, even if buried deep within a handbag, purse or wallet.

During Phase 1 of the Nanjing project, Motorola designed and implemented a smart card system for all three bus companies operating in Nanjing, providing more than 2000 bus validators and issuing 400 000 Motorola M-Smart Mercury contactless smart cards to riders. Once the system was implemented, riders waved their cards in front of a validator to board the bus. The system design, integration, implementation, training and system maintenance was managed on behalf of Motorola by Huamin Smart Card Systems Co Ltd—a joint venture established by Motorola and Huaxu Golden Card Co Ltd.

Motorola is a global leader in providing integrated communication solutions and embedded electronic solutions. Sales in 1998 were US$29.4 billion. Motorola's Worldwide Smart Card Solutions Division is a global leader in providing complete smart card solutions, including smart card systems, products and application development, systems integration and smart and operations management capability. Its M-Smart smart card product platforms of cards, card operating systems, readers and application development workbenches allow organisations to quickly deploy and build value-added smart card applications in such areas as transport, access control, government identification and healthcare. Smart cards are only one aspect of Motorola's business activities in China. Motorola China's previous four-point strategy helped it to become the largest foreign investor in China's electronics industry. Sales reached US$4.9 billion in 2001, replacing Germany's Volkswagen as No. 1 among the top 500 foreign-invested companies in China for the first time in nine years. In 2002, Motorola China had total sales of US$ 5.7 billion; total exports of US$ 3.6 billion; local sourcing of US$ 2.6 billion; total employment of $12 000. It received awards for the largest foreign investor in China's electronics industry; largest foreign company in China, in terms of sales; best in long-term commitment; most innovative; best adapted to the Chinese market; and best employer in China. Motorola's handset business enjoyed the No. 1 position for three consecutive years. Its Global System for Mobile Communications (GSM) and Code Division Multiple Access (CDMA) infrastructure has expanded strongly in China. Its two-way radios and networks set up the first Social Emergency System and established the first iDEN trunking system in Shanghai. It was also active in software, semiconductors and broadband.

Great changes in the business and social environment have taken place since China's entry into the World Trade Organisation, Beijing's successful bid for the 2008 Olympics and the successful reforms of China Telecom and China Netcom. These macro developments spurred Motorola China's management to adopt a new five-year, 2+3+3 strategy in June 2002. The '2' in this strategy refers to building China into a worldwide manufacturing and R&D base. The first '3' refers to three new growth areas (semiconductors,

broadband and digital trunking systems). The second '3' refers to three US$10 billion goals: annual production value to reach US$10 billion by 2006; accumulated inputs in China to reach US$10 billion by 2006; and local purchasing to reach US$10 billion in China within the next five years. Motorola's total investment in China in 2001 was RMB238 billion (US$35.6 billion), with China enjoying an annual growth rate of 100 per cent in the mobile phone network and paging market. Measures have been taken by all sectors to implement the 2+3+3 strategy. Motorola has adjusted its worldwide manufacturing capacity and has shifted some production to China. The company also decided to hire 4000 more engineers and researchers, and add US$1 billion in R&D to the existing 18 R&D centres. A new software centre was completed in Chengdu in May 2002. The energy systems group plans to establish its Asian design and procurement headquarters in Shanghai.

Motorola has made major commitments for investment in research, development and manufacturing in China. It clearly sees China as a significant centre for research and manufacturing, as well as a growing market.

Source: Contributed by John Krasnostein (details of sources are listed on p. 738).

Activities for discussion, *analysis and further research*

1. What macro (country) and micro (specific industry/sector) political risks does Motorola face in China? What strategies can the company use to manage these risks? How can effective international negotiating skills be of value to the company in reducing its political risk and increasing its competitive advantage in China?

2. In groups of three or four, undertake the following project. Visit the China site in the CIA world factbook at the website: www.odci.gov/cia/publications/factbook/ch.html. This site provides a comprehensive overview of the political and economic environment in China. Browse through this site and determine if the

information provided changes your view on the viability of a Western company successfully doing business in China.

3. Analysts expect that the US spy plane incident in 2001 will be only one of a number of crises and conflicts between China and the United States. Explain how the aftermath of tension between the two governments could impact directly on strategy formulation and implementation at Motorola. How much risk does Motorola face because of industry or sectoral sensitivity (communications and electronic technology)? Now develop several scenarios for Motorola, in terms of its options, responses, alternatives and decisions if various political developments were to occur. For example, if the US and China went to war over Taiwan, or if China moved to control the internet or mobile phone industries, what steps should Motorola take to protect its assets, technology and employees?

 Please insert the CD-ROM that is packaged with this book to view video clips that correspond to this Part theme.

GLOSSARY

acceptance theory of authority Theory arguing authority does not depend as much on 'persons of authority' who give orders as on the willingness to comply of those who receive the orders

accommodation Conflict-handling mode focusing on solving conflicts by allowing the other party's desires to prevail

accountability Requirement to provide satisfactory reasons for significant deviations from duties or expected results

achievement–nurturing Cultural dimension involving the extent to which a society emphasises values such as assertiveness, competitiveness and material success, rather than values such as passivity, co-operation and feelings

achievement-oriented Leader behaviour involving setting challenging goals, expecting subordinates to perform at their highest level, and conveying a high degree of confidence in subordinates

acquired-needs theory Theory (developed by McClelland) stating that our needs are acquired or learned on the basis of our life experiences

acquisition Purchase of all or part of one organisation by another

active listening Process in which a listener actively participates in attempting to grasp facts and feelings being expressed by the speaker

activity Work component to be accomplished

ad hoc committee Another term for a task force

adjourning Stage in which group members prepare for disengagement as the group nears successful completion of its goals

administrative management Approach focusing on principles used by managers to co-ordinate the organisations' internal activities

administrative protections Type of trade barrier in the form of various rules and regulations making it more difficult for foreign firms to conduct business in a particular country

aggregate-production planning Process of planning how to match supply with product or service demand over a time horizon of about one year

alternative work schedules Schedules based on adjustments in the normal work schedule rather than in the job content or activities

amoral management An approach that is neither immoral nor moral, but ignores or is oblivious to ethical considerations

anchoring and adjustment Tendency to be influenced by an initial figure, even when the information is largely irrelevant

anti-freeloader argument An argument holding that since businesses benefit from a better society, they should bear part of the costs by actively working to bring about solutions to social problems

applications software packages Software programs available for sale or lease from commercial sources

artificial intelligence Field of information technology aimed at developing computers with human-like capabilities, such as seeing, hearing and thinking

asset ratios Financial ratios measuring how effectively an organisation manages its assets management

attribution theory Theory attempting to explain how individuals make judgments or attributions about the causes of another's or their own behaviour

authority Right to make decisions, carry out actions, and direct others in matters related to the duties and goals of a position

autocratic Behavioural style of leaders who tend to make unilateral decisions, dictate work methods, limit worker knowledge about goals to just the next step to be performed, and sometimes give feedback that is punitive

autonomy Amount of discretion allowed in determining schedules and work methods for achieving required output

availability Tendency to judge the likelihood of an occurrence on the basis of the extent to which other like instances or occurrences can easily be recalled

avoidance Conflict-handling mode involving ignoring or suppressing a conflict in the hope it will go away or become less disruptive

balance of payments Account of goods and services, capital loans, gold, and other items entering and leaving a country

balance of trade Difference between a country's exports and imports

balance sheet Financial statement showing an organisation's assets and claims against those assets at a point in time

BCG growth-share matrix Four-cell matrix (developed by the Boston Consulting Group) comparing various businesses in an organisation's portfolio on the basis of relative market share and market growth rate

behaviour modification Use of techniques associated with reinforcement theory

behavioural displacement Condition in which individuals engage in behaviours encouraged by controls and reward systems though they are inconsistent with organisational goals

behavioural science Approach emphasising scientific research as the basis for developing theories about human behaviour in organisations, that is used to establish practical guidelines for managers

behavioural viewpoint Perspective on management emphasising the importance of attempting to understand various factors affecting human behaviour in organisations

belongingness needs Needs involving the desire to affiliate with and be accepted by others

benchmarking Process of identifying best practices and approaches by comparing productivity in specific areas within one's own company with that of other organisations both within and outside the industry

bill of materials (BOM) Listing of all components, including partially assembled pieces and basic parts, making up an end product

boundary spanning Creating roles within the organisation interfacing with important elements in the

bounded rationality Concept suggesting the ability of managers to be perfectly rational in making decisions is limited by factors such as cognitive capacity and time constraints

brainstorming Technique encouraging group members to generate as many novel ideas as possible on a given topic without evaluating them

break-even analysis Graphic model helping decision makers understand relationships between sales volume, costs and revenues in an organisation

budgeting Process of stating in quantitative terms, usually dollars, planned organisational activities for a given period of time

buffering Stockpiling either inputs into or outputs from a production or service process to cope with environmental fluctuations

bureaucratic control Managerial approach relying on regulation through rules, policies, supervision, budgets, schedules, reward systems and other administrative mechanisms aimed at ensuring employees exhibit appropriate behaviours and meet performance standards

bureaucratic management Approach emphasising the need for organisations to operate in a rational manner rather than relying on owners' and managers' arbitrary whims

business-level strategy Type of strategy concentrating on the best means of competing within a particular business while also supporting corporate-level strategy

capacity argument An argument stating that the private sector, because of its considerable economic and human resources, must make up for government cutbacks in social programs

capacity planning Process of determining people, machines and major physical resources, such as buildings, necessary to meet production objectives of the organisation

capacity-requirements planning Technique for determining what personnel and equipment are needed to meet short-term production objectives

capital expenditures budget Plan for acquisition or divestiture of major fixed assets, such as land, buildings or equipment

capitalist economy Economy in which economic activity is governed by market forces and the means of production are owned by individuals

carrying, or holding, cost Expenses associated with keeping an item on hand (storage, insurance, theft, breakage)

centralisation Extent to which power and authority are retained at the top organisational levels

ceremonial System of rites performed in conjunction with a single occasion or event

chain of command Unbroken line of authority ultimately linking each individual with the top organisational position through a managerial position at each successive layer in between

change Any alteration of the status quo

charisma Leadership factor comprising the leader's ability to inspire pride, faith and respect; to recognise what is really important; and to articulate effectively a sense of mission, or vision, to inspire followers

clan control Managerial approach relying on values, beliefs, traditions, corporate culture, shared norms and informal relationships to regulate employee behaviours and facilitate reaching of organisational goals

classical viewpoint Perspective on management emphasising finding ways to manage work and organisations more efficiently

closed system System doing little or no interacting with its environment and receiving little feedback

code of ethics A document prepared for the purpose of guiding organisation members when they encounter an ethical dilemma

coercive power Power depending on the ability to punish others when they do not engage in desired behaviours

cognitive theories Theories attempting to isolate thinking patterns we use in deciding whether or not to behave in a certain way

collaboration Conflict-handling mode striving to resolve conflicts by devising solutions allowing both parties to achieve desired outcomes

collectivism Condition where the demands and interests of group interests are given precedence over desires and needs of individuals.

command or functional group Formal group consisting of a manager and all the subordinates who report to them

communication channels Patterns of organisational communication flow representing potential established conduits through which managers and other organisation members can send and receive information

communication Exchange of messages between people to achieve common meanings

communication network Pattern of information flow among task-group members

competition Conflict-handling mode involving attempting to win a conflict at the other party's expense

competitive advantage of nations Concept that environmental elements within a nation can foster innovation in certain industries, thereby increasing prospects for the success of home-based companies operating internationally within those industries

competitive advantage Significant edge over competition in dealing with competitive forces

competitors Other organisations either offering or with a high potential of offering rival products or services

complacency Condition in which individuals either do not see signs of danger or opportunity or ignore them

compressed work-week Work schedule whereby employees work four ten-hour days or some similar combination, rather than the usual five eight-hour days.

compromise Conflict-handling mode aiming to solve issues by having each party give up some desired outcomes to get other desired outcomes

computer hardware Physical computer equipment, including the computer itself and related devices

computer software Set of programs, documents, procedures and routines associated with the operation of a computer system which makes hardware capable of various activities

computer virus Small program, usually hidden inside another program, which replicates itself and surfaces at a set time to cause disruption and possibly destruction

computer-aided design (CAD) System using computers to geometrically prepare, review and evaluate product designs

computer-aided manufacturing (CAM) System using computers to design and control production processes

computer-based information systems (CBISs) Information systems involving computer technology use

computer-integrated manufacturing (CIM) Computerised integration of all major functions associated with production of a product

concentration Approach focusing on effecting growth of a single product or service or a small number of closely related products or services

conceptual skills Skills related to the ability to visualise the organisation as a whole, discern interrelationships among organisational parts, and understand how the organisation fits into the wider context of the industry, community and world

concurrent control Regulation of ongoing activities which are part of the transformation process to ensure they conform to organisational standards

conflict Perceived difference between two or more parties resulting in mutual opposition

consideration Degree to which a leader builds mutual trust with subordinates, respects their ideas and shows concern for their feelings

contingency planning Development of alternative plans for use in the event that environmental conditions evolve differently than anticipated, rendering original plans unwise or unfeasible

contingency theory Viewpoint arguing that appropriate managerial action depends on the particular parameters of the situation

continuous-process production Type of technology where products are liquids, solids or gases made through a continuous process

control system Set of mechanisms designed to increase probability of meeting organisational standards and goals

controlling Process of regulating organisational activities so actual performance conforms to expected organisational standards and goals

controlling The process of regulating organisational activities so that actual performance conforms to expected organisational standards and goals

convergent thinking Effort to solve problems by beginning with a problem and attempting to move logically to a solution

co-opting Absorbing key members of important environmental elements into an organisation's leadership or policy-making structure

corporate culture Term sometimes used for organisational culture

corporate philanthropy Corporate contributions for charitable and social responsibility purposes

corporate social responsibility A term used in reference to the concept of organisational social responsibility as applied to business organisations

corporate social responsiveness A term used in reference to the concept of organisational social responsiveness as applied to business organisations

corporate-level strategy Type of strategy addressing what businesses the organisation will operate, how strategies of those businesses will be co-ordinated to strengthen the organisation's competitive position, and how resources will be allocated among businesses

cost leadership strategy Strategy outlined by Porter involving emphasising organisational efficiency so overall costs of providing products and services are lower than those of competitors

creativity Cognitive process of developing an idea, concept, commodity or discovery viewed as novel by its creator or a target audience

crisis problem A serious difficulty requiring immediate action

critical path Path in the network taking the longest to complete

customer divisions Divisions set up to service particular types of clients or customers

customers and clients Individuals and organisations purchasing an organisation's products and/or services

cybernetic control system Self-regulating control system which, once operating, can automatically monitor the situation and take corrective action when necessary

data Unanalysed facts and figures

data workers Individuals who mainly process and disseminate documents, messages and related information

database management system Software which allows an organisation to build, manage and provide access to its stored data

database Set of data organised efficiently in a central location to serve a number of information-system applications

debt ratios Financial ratios assessing the extent to which an organisation uses debt to finance investments, as well as indicating to management the degree to which it is able to meet its long-term obligations

decentralisation Extent to which power and authority are delegated to lower levels

deciding to decide Response in which decision makers accept the challenge of deciding what to do about a problem and follow an effective decision-making process

decision making The process by which managers identify organisational problems and try to resolve them

decision-support system (DSS) Computer-based information system supporting the process of managerial decision making in poorly structured situations

decision tree Graphic model displaying structure of a sequence of alternative courses of action and usually showing payoffs associated with various paths and probabilities associated with potential future conditions

decode Process of translating symbols into the interpreted message

dedundancy A forced termination of the employment relationship resulting from the permanent deletion of specific positions within an organisation due to the positions no longer being required

defensive avoidance Condition in which individuals either deny the importance of a danger or an opportunity or deny any responsibility for taking action

defensive strategies Strategies focusing on the desire or need to reduce organisational operations, usually through cost and/or asset reductions

delegation Assignment of part of a manager's work to others, along with both responsibility and authority necessary to achieve expected results

Delphi method Structured approach to gaining judgments of a number of experts on a specific issue relating to the future

democratic Behavioural style of leaders who tend to involve the group in decision making, let the group determine work methods, make overall goals known, and use feedback as an opportunity for helpful coaching

departmentalisation Clustering of individuals into units and of units into departments and larger units to facilitate achieving organisational goals

dependent demand inventory Type of inventory consisting of raw materials, components and subassemblies used in production of an end product or service

descriptive decision-making models Models of decision making attempting to document how managers actually make decisions

developed countries Group of countries that is characterised by a high level of economic or industrial development and includes Australia, the United States, Western Europe, Canada, Australia, New Zealand and Japan

development To broadly prepare the employee for future opportunities through the acquisition of new knowledge, skills and attitudes

devil's advocates Individuals assigned the role of making sure negative aspects of any attractive decision alternatives are considered

dialectical inquiry Procedure in which a decision situation is approached from two opposite points of view

differentiation Extent to which organisational units differ from one another in terms of behaviours and orientations of members and their formal structures

differentiation paradox Idea that although separating innovation efforts from the rest of the organisation increases the likelihood of developing radical ideas, such differentiation also decreases the likelihood radical ideas will be implemented

differentiation strategy Strategy outlined by Porter involving attempting to develop products and services viewed as unique in the industry

direct contact Communication between two or more persons at similar levels in different work units to co-ordinate work and solve problems

directive Leader behaviour involving letting subordinates know what is expected of them, providing guidance about work methods, developing work schedules, identifying work evaluation standards, and indicating the basis for outcomes or rewards

discretionary expense centre Responsibility centre whose budgetary outcomes are based on achieving its goals by operating within predetermined expense constraints set through managerial judgment or discretion

dismissal The employer giving the required notice to terminate the employment relationship

distinctive competence Unique strength competitors cannot easily match or imitate

divergent thinking Effort to solve problems by generating new ways of viewing a problem and seeking novel alternatives

diversification Approach entailing effecting growth through development of new areas clearly distinct from current businesses

divestiture Strategy involving an organisation's selling or divesting of a business or part of a business

divisional structure Structure in which positions are grouped according to similarity of products, services, or markets

domain shifts Changes in product and service mix offered so an organisation will interface with more favourable environmental elements

downsizing Process of significantly reducing middle-management layers, increasing spans of control, and shrinking workforce size

downward communication Vertical communication flowing from a higher level to one or more lower levels in the organisation

driving forces Factors pressuring for a particular change

econometric models Systems of simultaneous multiple regression equations using several predictor variables used to identify and measure relationships or interrelationships that exist in the economy

economic element Systems of producing, distributing and consuming wealth

economic order quantity (EOQ) Inventory control method developed to minimise ordering plus holding costs, while avoiding stockout costs

effectiveness The ability to choose appropriate goals and achieve them

efficiency The ability to make the best use of available resources in the process of achieving goals

effort-performance (E_P) expectancy Our assessment of the probability our efforts will lead to the required performance level

electronic mail system Mail system which allows high-speed exchange of written messages by use of computerised text-processing and communication networks

electronic monitoring Practice of using computers to continually assess employee performance

encode Process of translating an intended message into words and gestures

end user Same as a user

end-user computing Development and/or management of information systems by users

enlightened self-interest argument An argument holding that businesses exist at society's pleasure and that, for their own legitimacy and survival, businesses should meet the public's expectations regarding social

entrepreneurial team Group of individuals with diverse expertise and backgrounds brought together to develop and implement innovative ideas aimed to create new products or services or significantly improve existing ones

environmental bounty Extent to which the environment can support sustained growth and stability

environmental complexity Number of elements in an organisation's environment and their degree of similarity

environmental dynamism Rate and predictability of change in the elements of an organisation's environment

environmental uncertainty Condition in which future environmental circumstances affecting an organisation cannot be accurately assessed and predicted

equity theory Theory arguing that we prefer situations of balance, or equity, which exists when we perceive the ratio of our inputs and outcomes to be equal to the ratio of inputs and outcomes for a comparison other

ERG theory Alternative (proposed by Alderfer) to Maslow's hierarchy-of-needs theory which argues there are three levels of individual needs

escalation situations Situations signalling a strong possibility of escalating commitment and accelerating losses

esteem needs Needs related to the two-pronged desire to have a positive self-image and to have our contributions valued and appreciated by others

ethics audits Systematic efforts to assess conforming to organisational ethical policies, aid understanding of those policies, and identify serious breaches requiring remedial action

ethics committee A group charged with helping to establish policies and resolve major questions involving ethical issues confronting organisation members in the course of their work

ethics hot line A special telephone line established to enable employees to bypass the normal chain of command in reporting grievances and serious ethical problems

ethnocentric orientation Approach to international management where executives assume practices which work in the headquarters or home country must necessarily work elsewhere

exchange rate Rate at which one country's currency can be exchanged for another's

executive-support system (ESS) Computer-based information system supporting decision making and effective functioning at the top levels of an organisation

existence needs Needs including various forms of material and physiological desires, such as food and water, as well as such work-related forms such as pay, fringe benefits and physical working conditions

expatriates Individuals who are not citizens of countries in which they are assigned to work

expectancy theory Theory (proposed by Vroom) arguing that we consider three main issues before we expend effort necessary to perform at a given level

expected value Sum of payoffs times respective probabilities for a given alternative

expert power Power based on possession of expertise valued by others

expert systems Computer-based systems that apply an expert's substantial knowledge to help solve specialised problems

explanatory, or causal models Models attempting to identify major variables related to or causing particular past conditions and then using current measures of those variables (predictors) to predict future conditions

exporting Process of making a product in the home country and sending it overseas

expropriation Seizure of a foreign company's assets by a host-country's government

external environment Major forces outside the organisation with potential to influence significantly a product or service's likely success

extinction Technique involving withholding previously available positive consequences associated with a behaviour to decrease that behaviour

extranets Closed networks of information systems between a group of organisations

extrinsic rewards Rewards provided by others, such as bonuses, awards or promotions

facilities Land, buildings, equipment and other major physical inputs that substantially determine productivity capacity, require time to alter, and involve significant capital investments

feedback control Regulation exercised after a product or service has been completed to ensure the final output meets organisational standards and goals

feedback Degree to which the job provides for clear, timely information about performance results

feedback Information about results and organisational status relative to the environment

feedback Receiver's basic response to the interpreted message

feedforward control Regulation of inputs to ensure they meet standards necessary for the transformation process

Fiedler's contingency model Situational approach (developed by Fiedler and his associates) which suggests leaders differ in the degrees of their orientation toward the task versus toward the people

financial statement Summary of a major aspect of an organisation's financial status

finished-goods Stock of items produced and awaiting sale or transit to a customer inventory

first-line managers/ supervisors Managers at the lowest level of the hierarchy who are directly responsible for the work of operating (non-managerial) employees

five competitive forces model Porter's approach to analysing the nature and intensity of competition in a given industry in terms of five major forces

fixed-interval schedule of reinforcement Pattern in which a reinforcer is administered on a fixed time schedule, assuming the desired behaviour has continued at an appropriate level

fixed-position layout Production configuration in which the product or client remains in one location and tools, equipment and expertise are brought to it, as necessary, to complete the productive process

fixed-ratio schedule of reinforcement Pattern in which a reinforcer is provided after a fixed number of occurrences of the desired behaviour

flat structure Structure with few hierarchical levels and wide spans of control

flexible manufacturing system (FMS) Manufacturing system using computers to control machines and the production process automatically so different types of parts or product configurations can be handled on the same production line

flexitime Work schedule specifying certain core hours when individuals are expected to be on the job and then allowing flexibility in starting and finishing times as long as individuals work the total number of required hours per day

focus strategy Strategy outlined by Porter entailing specialising by establishing a position of overall cost leadership, differentiation or both, but only within a particular portion, or segment, of an entire market

force-field analysis Method involving analysing the two types of forces, driving forces and restraining forces, that influence any proposed change then assessing how best to overcome resistance

forecasting Process of making predictions about changing conditions and future events that may significantly affect the business of an organisation

formal communication Vertical and horizontal communication which follows paths specified by the official hierarchical organisation structure and related task requirements

formal group Group officially created by an organisation for a specific purpose

formalisation Degree to which written policies, rules, procedures, job descriptions and other documents specify what actions are (or are not) to be taken under a given set of circumstances

forming Stage in which group members try to assess ground rules applying to a task and to group interaction

framing Tendency to make different decisions depending on how a problem is presented

frustration-regression principle Principle stating that if we are continually frustrated in our attempts to satisfy a higher-level need, we may cease to be concerned about that need

functional authority Authority of staff departments over others in the organisation in matters related directly to their respective functions

functional managers Managers with responsibility for a specific, specialised area of the organisation who

functional structure Structure in which positions are grouped according to their main functional (or specialised) area

functional-level strategy Type of strategy focusing on action plans for managing a particular functional area within a business in a way that supports business-level strategy

fundamental attribution error Tendency to underestimate importance of situational influences and overestimate the importance of dispositional influences in explaining behaviour

futurists Individuals who track significant trends in the environment and attempt to predict their impact on the organisation

Gantt chart Specialised bar chart developed by Henry L. Gantt showing current progress on each major project activity relative to necessary completion dates

general managers Managers with responsibility for a whole organisation or a substantial subunit including most of the common specialised areas

geocentric orientation Approach to international management where executives believe a global view is needed in both the headquarters of the parent company and its various subsidiaries and the best individuals, regardless of host- or home-country origin, should be utilised to solve company problems anywhere in the world

geographic divisions Divisions designed to serve different geographic areas

goal commitment One's attachment to, or determination to reach, a goal

goal Future target or end result an organisation wishes to achieve

goal incongruence Condition where there are major incompatibilities between goals of an organisation member and those of the organisation

government agencies Agencies providing services and monitoring compliance with laws and regulations at local, state or regional, and national levels

grand strategy Master strategy providing the basic strategic direction at corporate level

grapevine Another term for informal communication

group cohesiveness Degree to which members are attracted to a group, are motivated to remain in it, and are mutually influenced by one another

group decision-support system (GDSS) Computer-based information system supporting decision makers working together to solve structured problems

group-maintenance roles Roles not directly addressing a task itself but, instead, helping foster group unity, positive interpersonal relations among group members and development of their ability to work effectively together

group technology Classification of parts into families (groups of parts or products with similarities in how they are manufactured) so members of the same family can be manufactured on the same production line

group Two or more interdependent individuals interacting and influencing each other in collective pursuit of a common goal

group-task roles Roles helping a group develop and accomplish its goals

groupthink Tendency of cohesive groups to seek agreement about an issue at the expense of realistically appraising the situation

groupware Software designed to support collaborative efforts among group members, such as scheduling meetings, holding meetings, collaborating on projects and sharing documents

growth needs Needs impelling creativity and innovation, along with the desire to have a productive impact on our surroundings

growth strategies Grand strategies involving organisational expansion along some major dimension

growth-need strength Degree to which an individual needs personal growth and development on the job

hackers Individuals who are knowledgeable about computers and who gain unauthorised entry to, and sometimes tamper with, computer networks and files of organisations with which they have no affiliation

halo effect Tendency to use a general impression based on one or a few characteristics of an individual to judge other characteristics of that same individual

hand of government A view arguing that the interests of society are best served by having the regulatory hands of the law and the political process, rather than the invisible hand, guide the results of corporations' endeavours

hand of management A view stating that corporations and their managers are expected to act in ways that protect and improve society's welfare as a whole as well as advance corporate economic interests

harvest A strategy entailing minimising investments while attempting to maximise short-run profits and cash flow, with the long-run intention of exiting the market

Hawthorne effect Possibility that individuals singled out for a study may improve their performance simply because of the added attention received from researchers, rather than because of any specific factors being tested

Hawthorne studies Group of studies conducted at the Hawthorne plant of the Western Electric Company during the late 1920s and early 1930s, the results of which ultimately led to the human relations view of management

hierarchy-of-needs theory Theory (developed by Maslow) arguing that individual needs form a five-level hierarchy

high-context cultures Cultures where the emphasis in the communication process is on establishing and strengthening relationships in the course of exchanging information

horizontal communication Lateral or diagonal message exchange either within work-unit boundaries, involving peers reporting to the same supervisor, or across work-unit boundaries, involving individuals who report to different supervisors

horizontal coordination Linking of activities across departments at similar levels

human resource management Those management functions concerned with attracting, maintaining and developing people in the employment relationship

human resource planning Determining future human resource needs in relation to an organisation's business objectives or strategic plan, then devising ways to meet the objectives

human skills Skills associated with a manager's ability to work well with others, both as a member of a group and as a leader who gets things done through others

hybrid structure Structure adopting both functional and divisional structures at the same management levels

hygiene factors Factors seeming to make individuals feel dissatisfied with their jobs

hypercompetition State of rapidly escalating competition in which competitors make frequent, daring, and aggressive moves cumulatively creating conditions of continual disequilibrium and change in the industry

idea champion An individual who generates a new idea or believes in the value of a new idea and supports it in the face of numerous potential obstacles

immoral management An approach not only lacking ethical principles but actively opposed to ethical behaviour

import quota Type of trade barrier in the form of a limit on the amount of product which may be imported over a period of time

income statement Financial statement summarising financial results of company operations over a specified time period, such as a quarter or a year

incremental model Model stating managers make the smallest response possible to reduce the problem to at least a tolerable level

incrementalist approach Approach to controlling an innovative project that relies on clan control but also involves a phased set of plans and accompanying bureaucratic controls beginning at a general level and growing more specific as the project progresses

independent demand inventory Type of inventory consisting of end products, parts used for repairs, and other items whose demand is tied more directly to market issues than for dependent demand inventory items

indigenisation laws Laws which require that citizens of a host country hold a majority interest in all firms operating within the country's borders

individualised consideration Leadership factor involving delegating projects to help develop each follower's capabilities, paying personal attention to each follower's needs, and treating each follower as an individual worthy of respect

individualism Condition where personal interests are given more weight than the group's interests

individualism–collectivism Cultural dimension involving the degree to which individuals concern themselves with their own interests and those of their immediate family, as opposed to the larger group's interests

informal communication Communication which takes place without regard to hierarchical or task requirements

informal group Group established by employees, not the organisation, to serve group members' interests or social needs

informal leader Individual, other than the formal leader, emerging from a group as a major influence and perceived by members as a leader

information architecture Long-range plan for investing in and organising information technology to facilitate reaching organisational goals

information Data which have been analysed or processed into a meaningful form for decision makers

information power Power resulting from access to and control over the distribution of important information about organisational operations and future plans

information system Set of procedures designed to collect (or retrieve), process, store and disseminate information to support planning, decision making, co-ordination and control

infrastructure Highways, railways, airports, sewage facilities, housing, educational institutions, recreation facilities, and other economic and social amenities signalling the extent of an area's economic development

initiating structure Degree to which a leader defines their own role and the roles of subordinates in terms of achieving unit goals

innovation A new idea applied to initiating or improving a process, product or service

innovation New idea applied to initiating or improving a process, product or service

inputs Various human, material, financial, equipment and informational resources required to produce goods and services

institutional power Need for power in which individuals focus on working with others to solve problems and further organisational goals

integration Extent to which there is collaboration among departments needing to co-ordinate their efforts

intellectual stimulation Leadership factor involving offering new ideas to stimulate followers to rethink old ways of doing things, encouraging followers to look at problems from multiple vantage points, and fostering creative breakthroughs in obstacles which seemed insurmountable

internal environment General conditions existing within an organisation

international business Profit-related activities conducted across national boundaries

international element Developments in countries outside an organisation's home country with potential to influence the organisation

international management Process of planning, organising, leading and controlling in organisations engaged in international business

internet A global connection of computer servers interconnected by telecommunication systems through which individuals can access stored information from their own computer and modem

intranets Closed networks of information databases and systems within an individual organisation

intrapreneurs Individuals who engage in entrepreneurial roles inside organisations

intrapreneurship The process of innovating within an existing organisation

intrinsic rewards Rewards related to our own internal experiences with successful performance, such as feelings of achievement, challenge and growth

inventory Stock of materials used to facilitate production or to satisfy customer demand

investment centre Responsibility centre whose budgetary outcomes are based on return on investment

invisible hand A view holding that the entire social responsibility of a corporation can be summed up as 'make profits and obey the law'

iron law of responsibility A law stating that 'in the long run, those who do not use power in a manner that society considers responsible will tend to lose it'

issues management The process of identifying a relatively small number of emerging social issues of particular relevance to the organisation, analysing their potential impact and preparing an effective response

item cost Price of an inventory item

Japanese management An approach focusing on aspects of management in Japan that may be appropriate for adoption in other countries

job analysis The systematic collecting and recording of information about the purpose of a job, its major duties, the conditions under which it is performed, the required contacts with others and the knowledge, skills and abilities needed to effectively perform it

job characteristics model Model developed to guide job-enrichment efforts including consideration of core job characteristics, critical psychological states, and outcomes

job depth Degree to which individuals can plan and control work involved in their jobs

job design Specification of task activities associated with a particular job

job enlargement Allocation of a wider variety of similar tasks to a job to make it more challenging

job enrichment Process of upgrading the job-task mix in order to increase significantly potential for growth, achievement, responsibility and recognition

job rotation Practice of periodically shifting workers through a set of jobs in a planned sequence

job scope Number of different tasks an employee performs in a particular job

job sharing Work practice in which two or more people share a single full-time job

job simplification Process of configuring jobs so job-holders have only a small number of narrow activities to perform

joint venture Agreement involving two or more organisations arranging to produce jointly a product or service

judgmental forecasting Type of forecasting relying mainly on individual judgments or committee agreements regarding future conditions

jury of executive opinion Means of forecasting in which organisation executives hold a meeting and estimate, as a group, a forecast for a particular item

just-in-time (JIT) inventory control Approach to inventory control emphasising having materials arrive just as needed in the production process

Kanban Simple parts-movement system depending on cards and containers to pull parts from one work centre to another

kinesic behaviour Body movements, such as gestures, facial expressions, eye movements and posture

knowledge-work system (KWS) Computer-based information system which assists knowledge workers in creation of new knowledge for the organisation

knowledge workers Specialists, such as engineers, architects or scientists, who design products, services or processes and create new knowledge for organisations

labour supply Individuals potentially employable by an organisation

laissez-faire Behavioural style of leaders who generally give the group complete freedom, provide necessary materials, participate only to answer questions, and avoid giving feedback

large-batch and mass production Type of technology where products are manufactured in large quantities, frequently on an assembly line

lateral relations Co-ordination of efforts through communicating and problem solving with peers in other departments or units, rather than referring most issues up the hierarchy for resolution

law of effect Concept stating that behaviours having pleasant or positive consequences are more likely to be repeated and behaviours having unpleasant or negative consequences are less likely to be repeated

leadership Process of influencing others to achieve organisational goals

leading indicators Variables tending to be correlated with the phenomenon of major interest but also to occur in advance of that phenomenon

leading The process of influencing others to engage in the work behaviours necessary to reach organisational goals

legal-political element Legal and governmental systems within which an organisation must function

legitimate power Power stemming from a position's placement in the managerial hierarchy and the authority vested in the position

less developed countries (LDCs) Group of non-communist countries, often called the 'third world', consisting primarily of relatively poor nations characterised by low per capita income, little industry and high birth-rates

liaison role Role to which a specific individual is appointed to facilitate communication and resolution of issues between two or more departments

licensing Agreement in which one organisation gives limited rights to another to use certain of its assets, such as expertise, patents, copyrights or equipment, for an agreed-upon fee or royalty

life cycles Predictable stages of development organisations typically follow

line authority Authority following the chain of command established by the formal hierarchy

linear programming (LP) Quantitative tool for planning how to allocate limited or scarce resources so a single criterion or goal (often profits) is optimised

liquidation Strategy entailing selling or dissolving an entire organisation

liquidity ratios Financial ratios measuring the degree to which an organisation's current assets are adequate to pay current liabilities (current debt obligations)

local-area networks (LANs) Interconnections (usually cable) allowing communications between computers within a single building or in close proximity

logical office Concept that portable microcomputers allow an individual's office to be where the individual is, not restricted to a specific location

long-term–short-term Cultural dimension involving the degree to which members of a society value thrift and goal persistence rather than living in the here-and-now and maintaining personal stability or happiness

low-context cultures Cultures where the emphasis in the communication process is on exchanging information and is less focused on building relationships

LPC (least preferred value on coworker) orientation Personality trait indicating the extent to which an individual places a higher priority on task accomplishment than on personal relationships

management by exception Control principle suggesting managers should be informed of a situation only if control data show a significant deviation from standards

management by objectives (MBO) Process through which specific goals are set collaboratively for the organisation as a whole and every unit and individual within it; the goals are then used as a basis for planning, managing organisational activities, and assessing and rewarding contributions

management-information system (MIS) Computer-based information system that produces routine reports and often allows online access to current and historical information needed by managers mainly at the middle and first-line levels

management information systems Field of management focused on designing and implementing computer-based information systems for use by management

management science Approach aimed at increasing decision effectiveness through use of sophisticated mathematical models and statistical methods

management The process of achieving organisational goals by engaging in the four major functions of planning, organising, leading and controlling

managerial ethics Standards of conduct and moral judgment used by managers of organisations in carrying out their business

managing diversity The planning and implementing of organisational systems and practices that maximise the potential of employees to contribute to organisational goals and develop their capabilities unhindered by group identities such as race, gender, age or ethnic group

manufacturing-resource planning (MRP II) Computer-based information system integrating production

planning and control activities of basic MRP systems with related financial, accounting, personnel, engineering and marketing information

market control Managerial approach relying on market mechanisms to regulate prices for certain clearly specified goods and services needed by an organisation

master production schedule (MPS) Schedule translating the aggregate plan into a formalised production plan encompassing specific products to be produced or services to be offered and specific capacity requirements over a designated time period

materials-requirements planning (MRP) Computer-based inventory system developing materials requirements for goods and services specified in the master schedule, and initiating actions needed to acquire materials when needed

matrix structure Structure superimposing a horizontal set of divisional reporting relationships onto a hierarchical functional structure

mechanistic characteristics Characteristics such as highly centralised decision making, many rules and regulations, and mainly hierarchical communication channels

medium Method used to convey the message to the intended receiver

mega-environment The broad conditions and trends in societies in which an organisation operates

merger Combining of two or more companies into one organisation

message Encoding-process outcome, which consists of verbal and non-verbal symbols developed to convey meaning to the receiver

middle managers Managers beneath the top levels of the hierarchy who are directly responsible for the work of managers at lower levels

mission statement Broad declaration of the basic, unique purpose and scope of operations distinguishing the organisation from others of its type

mission The organisation's purpose or fundamental reason for existence

modelling Actually observing and attempting to imitate behaviours of others

moral management An approach that strives to follow ethical principles and precepts

motivation Force energising behaviour, giving direction to behaviour, and underlying the tendency to persist

motivators Factors seeming to make individuals feel satisfied with their jobs

multifocal strategy Strategy aimed at achieving the advantages of world-wide integration where possible, while still attempting to be responsive to important national needs

multinational corporation (MNC) Organisation engaging in production or service activities through its affiliates in several countries, maintaining control over policies of those affiliates, and managing from a global perspective

multiple control systems Systems using two or more of the feedforward, concurrent and feedback control processes and involving several strategic control points

national responsiveness strategy Strategy of allowing subsidiaries to have substantial latitude in adapting products and services to suit the particular needs and political realities of countries they operate in

natural selection model Term sometimes used for the population ecology model

need for achievement (nAch) Desire to accomplish challenging tasks and achieve a standard of excellence in one's work

need for affiliation (nAff) Desire to maintain warm, friendly relationships with others

need for power (nPow) Desire to influence others and control one's environment

negative entropy Ability of open systems to bring in new energy, in the form of inputs and feedback from the environment, to delay or arrest entropy

negative reinforcement Technique, aimed at increasing a desired behaviour, that involves providing noxious stimuli so an individual will engage in the desired behaviour to stop the noxious stimuli

negative synergy Force resulting when group-process losses are greater than gains achieved from combining the forces of group members

network A set of co-operative relationships with individuals whose help is needed in order for a manager to function effectively

network diagram Graphic depiction of interrelationships among activities

networked structure Form of organising where many functions are contracted out to other independent firms and co-ordinated by use of information technology networks to operate as if they were within a single corporation

neutralisers Situational factors making it impossible for a given leader behaviour to have an impact on subordinate performance and/or satisfaction

new venture teams Temporary task forces or teams made up of individuals relieved of normal duties to develop a new process, product or program

new venture units Either separate divisions or specially incorporated companies created to develop new products or business ideas and initiatives

newly industrialised countries (NICs) Countries within LDCs emerging as major exporters of manufactured goods, including such nations as Hong Kong, Taiwan and South Korea

node, or event Indication of beginning and/or ending of activities in the network

noise Any factor in the communication process interfering with exchanging messages and achieving common meaning

nominal group technique Technique integrating both individual work and group interaction within certain ground rules (NGT)

non-crisis problem An issue requiring resolution but without the simultaneous importance and immediacy characteristics of a crisis

non-cybernetic control system Control system relying on human discretion as a basic part of its process

non-programmed decisions Decisions for which predetermined decision rules are impractical due to novel and/or ill-structured situations

non-rational escalation Tendency to increase commitment to a previously selected course of action beyond the level expected if the manager followed an effective decision-making process; also called escalation phenomenon

non-rational models Models suggesting information-gathering and processing limitations make it difficult for managers to make optimal decisions

non-verbal communication Communication by means of elements and behaviours that are not coded into words

normative decision-making models Models of decision making attempting to prescribe how managers should make decisions

normative leadership model Model helping leaders assess critical situational factors affecting the extent to which they should involve subordinates in particular decisions

norming Stage in which group members begin to build group cohesion, as well as develop a consensus about norms for performing a task and relating to each other

norms Expected behaviours sanctioned by a group that regulate and foster uniform member behaviour

not-for-profit organisation An organisation whose main purposes centre on issues other than making profits

object language Communicative use of material things, including clothing, cosmetics, furniture and architecture

office-automation system (OAS) Computer-based information system aimed at facilitating communication and increasing the productivity of managers and office workers through document and message processing

one-way communication Communication resulting when the communication process does not allow for feedback

open system System operating in continual interaction with its environment

operating budget Statement that presents the financial plan for each responsibility centre during the budget period and reflects operating activities involving revenues and expenses

operational control Control type involving overseeing implementation of operating plans, monitoring day-to-day results, and taking corrective action as required

operational goals Targets or future results set by lower management that address specific measurable outcomes required from the lower levels

operational plans Means devised to support implementation of tactical plans and achievement of operational goals

operations management Function or field of expertise primarily responsible for managing production and delivery of an organisation's products and services

operations management Management of productive processes converting inputs into goods and services

operations research Another name used for management science

opportunity problem A situation offering strong potential for significant organisational gain if appropriate actions are taken

orchestrator A high-level manager who explains the need for innovation, provides funding for innovating activities, creates incentives for middle managers to sponsor new ideas, and protects idea people

ordering cost Expenses of placing an order (paperwork, postage and time)

organic characteristics Characteristics such as decentralised decision making, few rules and regulations, and both hierarchical and lateral communication channels

organisation chart Line diagram depicting broad outlines of an organisation's structure

organisation design Process of developing an organisation structure

organisation structure Formal pattern of interactions and co-ordination designed by management to link the tasks of individuals and groups in achieving organisational goals

organisation Two or more persons engaged in a systematic effort to produce goods or services

organisational citizenship behaviours Discretionary actions that are not part of job requirements but contribute to attaining organisational goals

organisational culture System of shared values, assumptions, beliefs and norms uniting members of an organisation

organisational development (OD) Change effort planned, focused on an entire organisation or a large subsystem, managed from the top, aimed at enhancing organisational health and effectiveness, and based on planned interventions

organisational problems Discrepancies between a current state or condition and what is desired

organisational social responsibility The obligation of an organisation to seek actions protecting and improving society's welfare along with its own interests

organisational social responsiveness A term referring to the development of organisational decision processes where managers anticipate, respond to, and manage areas of social responsibility

organisational termination Process of ceasing to exist as an identifiable organisation

organising The process of allocating and arranging human and non-human resources so that plans can be carried out successfully

outputs Products, services and other outcomes produced by the organisation

outsourcing Process of employing an outside vendor to perform a function normally carried on within the organisation

overconfident Tending to be more certain of judgments regarding the likelihood of a future event than one's actual predictive accuracy warrants

overcontrol Limiting individual job autonomy to the point where it seriously inhibits effective job performance

panic Reaction in which individuals become so upset they frantically seek a way to solve a problem

paralanguage Vocal aspects of communication that relate to how something is said rather than to what is said

partial-factor productivity Productivity approach considering the total output relative to a specific input, such as labour

participative Leader behaviour characterised by consulting with subordinates, encouraging their suggestions, and carefully considering their ideas when making decisions

path–goal theory Theory attempting to explain how leader behaviour can positively influence the motivation and job satisfaction of subordinates

payoff Amount of decision-maker value associated with a particular decision alternative and future condition

payoff table or decision matrix Two-dimensional matrix allowing a decision maker to compare how different future conditions are likely to affect respective outcomes of two or more decision alternatives

perception Process individuals use to acquire and make sense out of information from the environment

perceptual defence Tendency to block out or distort information one finds threatening or which challenges one's beliefs

performance appraisal A judgmental process of the job performance of employees

performance-outcome (P_O) expectancy Our assessment of the probability our successful performance will lead to certain outcomes

performing Stage in which energy is channelled toward a task and in which norms support teamwork

personal power Need for power in which individuals want to dominate others for the sake of demonstrating their ability to wield power

physiological needs Survival needs such as food, water and shelter

plan Means devised for attempting to reach a goal

planned change Change involving actions based on a carefully thought-out process anticipating future difficulties, threats and opportunities

planning staff Small group of individuals who assist top-level managers in developing various components of the planning process

planning The process of setting goals and deciding how best to achieve them

policy General guide specifying broad parameters within which organisation members are expected to operate in pursuit of organisational goals

political risk Probability of occurrence of political actions resulting in either loss of enterprise ownership or significant benefits from conducting business

polycentric orientation Approach to international management where executives believe the parts of the organisation located in a given host country should be staffed by local individuals to the fullest extent possible

pooled interdependence Relationship in which units operate independently but individual efforts are important to the whole organisation's success

population ecology model Model focusing on populations or groups of organisations and arguing that environmental factors cause organisations with appropriate characteristics to survive and others to fail

portfolio strategy approach Method of analysing an organisation's mix of businesses in terms of both individual and collective contributions to strategic goals

positive reinforcement Technique, aimed at increasing a desired behaviour, which involves providing a pleasant, rewarding consequence to encourage that behaviour

positive synergy Force resulting when combined gains from group interaction are greater than group-process losses

power Capacity to affect the behaviour of others

power distance Cultural dimension involving the degree to which individuals in a society accept differences in power distribution as reasonable and normal

procedure Prescribed series of related steps to be taken under certain recurring circumstances

process layout Production configuration in which processing components are grouped according to type of function performed

process structure Type of departmentalisation where positions are grouped by a complete flow of work

product divisions Divisions created to concentrate on a single product or service or at least a relatively homogeneous set of products or services

product layout Production configuration in which processing components are arranged in a specialised line along which the product or client passes during the production process

product/market evolution Fifteen-cell matrix (developed by Hofer) in which businesses are plotted according to the business unit's business strength, or competitive position, and the industry's stage in the evolutionary product/market life-cycle matrix

productivity Efficiency concept gauging the ratio of outputs relative to inputs into a production process

profit centre Responsibility centre whose budgetary outcomes are measured by difference between revenues and costs—in other words, profits

profitability ratios Financial ratios helping measure management's ability to control expenses and earn profits by use of organisational resources

program Comprehensive plan co-ordinating a complex set of activities related to a major non-recurring goal

program evaluation and review technique (PERT) Network planning method for managing large projects

programmed decisions Decisions made in routine, repetitive, well-structured situations by use of predetermined decision rules

project managers Managers with responsibility for co-ordinating efforts involving individuals in several different organisational units all working on a particular project

project Plan co-ordinating a set of limited-scope activities which do not need to be divided into several major projects to reach a major non-recurring goal

projection Tendency of an individual to assume others share their thoughts, feelings and characteristics

prospect theory Theory positing that decision makers find the prospect of an actual loss more painful than giving up the possibility of a gain

prototyping Process of building a rough, working model of all or parts of a proposed information system for purposes of preliminary evaluation and further refinement

proxemics Influence of proximity and space on communication

public affairs department A permanent department that co-ordinates various ongoing social responsibilities and identifies and recommends policies for new social issues

punishment Technique involving providing negative consequences to decrease or discourage a behaviour

purchasing Process of acquiring necessary goods or services in exchange for funds or other remuneration

quality teams Small groups of employees who work on solving specific problems related to quality and improvement of productivity, often with stated targets for improvement

quality Totality of features and characteristics of a product or service bearing on its ability to satisfy needs stated or implied

quantitative forecasting Type of forecasting that relies on numerical data and mathematical models to predict future conditions

questionable payments Business payments raising significant ethical questions of right or wrong either in the host country or in other nations

queuing, or waiting-line, models Mathematical models describing operating characteristics of queuing situations, in which service is provided to persons or units waiting in line

ratio analysis Process of determining and evaluating financial ratios

rational model Model suggesting managers engage in completely rational decision processes, ultimately make optimal decisions, and possess and understand all information relevant to their decisions at the time they make them

rationalisation Strategy of assigning activities to parts of the organisation, regardless of their location, that are best suited to produce desired results, and then selling finished products where they will yield the best profits

rationing Providing limited access to a product or service in high demand

raw materials inventory Stock of parts, ingredients and other basic inputs to a production or service process

reactive change Change occurring when one takes action in response to perceived problems, threats or opportunities

receiver Person with whom the message is exchanged

reciprocal interdependence Relationship in which one unit's outputs become inputs to another unit and vice versa

recruitment The process of finding and attracting job candidates capable of effectively filling job vacancies

re-engineering Thorough analysis and radical redesign of existing business processes to achieve breakthrough improvements by focusing on critical performance criteria, such as cost, quality, service and speed

referent power Power resulting from being admired, personally identified with, or liked by others

regiocentric orientation Approach to international management where executives believe geographic regions have commonalities which make a regional focus advantageous, and that company problems related to the region are generally best solved by individuals from the region

regional responsiveness strategy Strategy of allowing regional offices to have substantial latitude in co-ordinating the activities of local subsidiaries and adapting products and services to suit the particular needs and political realities of the regions in which they operate

regression models Equations expressing fluctuations in the variable being forecast in terms of fluctuations in one or more other variables (predictors)

reinforcement theory Theory arguing that our behaviour can be explained by consequences in the environment

relatedness needs Needs addressing our relationships with significant others, such as families, friendship groups, work groups and professional groups

reliability The degree to which the decision process will measure the same thing consistently

remuneration The financial payment to employees in return for their work

reorder point (ROP) Inventory level at which a new order should be placed

repatriation Process of returning to one's home country after an assignment in a host country

representativeness Tendency to be overly influenced by stereotypes in making judgments about the likelihood of occurrences

reservations Organisational units devoted to the generation of innovative ideas for future business

resource dependence Approach to controls which argues managers need to consider controls mainly in areas in which they depend on others for resources necessary to reach organisational goals

resource dependence model Model highlighting the organisation's dependence on the environment for resources and arguing that organisations attempt to manipulate the environment to reduce dependence

responsibility centre Subunit headed by a manager responsible for achieving one or more goals

responsibility Obligation to carry out duties and achieve goals related to a position

restraining forces Factors pressuring against a change

restructuring Process of making a major change in organisation structure often involving reducing management levels and possibly changing components of the organisation through divestiture and/or acquisition, as well as shrinking workforce size

retrenchment The forced termination of the employment relationship due to financial, technological or organisational circumstances, often reflecting an attempt by an employer to reduce labour costs in order to remain in business

revenue centre Responsibility centre whose budgetary outcomes are measured primarily by its ability to generate a specified revenue level

revitalisation Renewal of innovative vigour of organisations

reward power Power based on the capacity to control and provide valued rewards to others

risk The possibility a chosen action could lead to losses rather than intended results

rite Relatively elaborate, dramatic, planned set of activities intended to convey cultural values to participants and, usually, an audience

role An organised set of behaviours associated with a particular office or position

role Set of behaviours expected of an individual occupying a particular position in a group

routing, or distribution, models Quantitative models assisting managers in planning the most effective and economical approaches to distribution problems

rubbish-bin model Model stating managers behave in virtually a random way in making non-programmed decisions

rule Statement spelling out specific actions to be taken or not taken in a given situation

safety needs Needs pertaining to the desire to feel safe, secure and free from threats to our existence

sales-force composite Means of forecasting used mainly to predict future sales and typically by obtaining views of various salespeople, sales managers, and/or distributors regarding the sales outlook

satisfaction-progression principle Principle stating that satisfaction of one level of need encourages concern with the next level

satisficing model Model stating managers seek alternatives only until they find one which looks satisfactory, rather than seeking an optimal decision

scenario analysis Approach that addresses a variety of possible futures by evaluating major environmental variables, assessing likely strategies of other significant actors, devising possible counter-strategies, developing ranked hypotheses about the variables, and formulating alternative scenarios

schedules of reinforcement Patterns of rewarding that specify the basis for and timing of positive reinforcement

scientific management Approach emphasising the scientific study of work methods to improve worker efficiency

selection process The decision-making system used to identify which job applicants are best suited to the vacant position

self-actualisation needs Needs pertaining to the requirement of developing our capabilities and reaching our full potential

self-control Our ability to exercise control over our own behaviour by setting standards and providing consequences for our own actions

self-efficacy Belief in one's capabilities to perform a specific task

self-managing team Work group with responsibility for a task area without supervision, and given authority to influence and control group membership and behaviour

self-oriented roles Roles related to the personal needs of group members and often negatively influencing group effectiveness

self-serving bias Tendency to perceive oneself as responsible for successes and others as responsible for failures

semantic blocks Blockages or communication difficulties arising from word choices

semantic net Network of words and word meanings a given individual has available for recall

sender Initiator of the message

sequential interdependence Relationship in which one unit must complete its work before the next in the sequence can begin work

shaping Successive rewarding of behaviours closely approximating the desired response until the actual desired response is made

simulation Mathematical imitation of reality

single-use plans Plans aimed at achieving a specific goal which, once reached, will most likely not recur in the future

situational leadership theory Theory (developed by Hersey and Blanchard) based on the premise leaders need to alter their behaviours depending on one major situational factor—the readiness of followers

situational theories Theories of leadership taking into consideration important situational factors

skill variety Extent to which the job entails a number of activities requiring different skills

slack Latitude about when various activities on the non-critical paths can be started without endangering the entire project's completion date

slack resources Cushion of resources that facilitates adaptation to internal and external pressures, as well as initiation of changes

smoothing Taking actions aimed at reducing the impact of fluctuations, given the market

social audit A systematic study and evaluation of the social, rather than economic, performance of an organisation

social forecasting The systematic process of identifying social trends, evaluating the organisational importance of those trends, and integrating these assessments into the organisation's forecasting program

social learning theory Theory arguing learning occurs through continuous reciprocal interaction of our behaviours, various personal factors and environmental forces

social loafing or **free riding** Tendency of individuals to expend less effort when working in groups than when working alone and to benefit from the group's work without bearing a proportional share of costs involved

social scanning The general surveillance of various elements in the task environment to detect evidence of impending changes affecting the organisation's social responsibilities

socialist economy Economy in which means of production are owned by the state and economic activity is co-ordinated by plan

sociocultural element Attitudes, values, norms, beliefs, behaviours and associated demographic trends characteristic of a given geographic area

soldiering Deliberately working at less than full capacity

span of management or **span of control** Number of subordinates who report directly to a specific manager

sponsor A middle manager who recognises the organisational significance of an idea, helps obtain the necessary funding for development of the innovation, and facilitates its actual implementation

stability strategy Strategy involving maintaining the status quo or growing in a methodical, but slow, manner

standard cost centre Responsibility centre whose budgetary outcomes depend on achieving its goals by operating within standard cost constraints

standing committee Permanent task group of individuals charged with handling recurring matters in a narrowly defined subject area over an indefinite, but generally long, time period

standing plans Plans providing ongoing guidance for performing recurring activities

statistical process control Statistical technique using periodic random samples taken during actual production to determine whether acceptable quality levels are being met or production should be stopped for remedial action

stereotyping Tendency to attribute characteristics to an individual on the basis of an assessment of the group to which they belong

stockout cost Economic consequences of running out of stock (loss of customer goodwill and sales)

storming Stage in which group members frequently are in conflict with each another as they locate and resolve differences of opinion about key issues

story Narrative based on true events, which may be embellished to highlight intended value

strategic alliance Arrangement where two or more independent organisations form a co-operative partnership to gain mutual strategic advantage

strategic alliance Where two or more independent organisations set up a co-operative partnership to gain mutual strategic advantage

strategic business unit (SBU) Distinct business, with its own set of competitors, which can be managed relatively independently of other businesses within the organisation

strategic control Control type involving monitoring critical environmental factors which could affect viability of strategic plans, assessing effects of organisational strategic actions, and ensuring strategic plans are implemented as intended

strategic control points Performance areas chosen for control because they are particularly important in meeting organisational goals

strategic goals Broadly defined targets or future results set by top management

strategic management Process through which managers formulate and implement strategies geared to optimising strategic goal achievement, given available environmental and internal conditions

strategic plans Detailed action steps mapped out to reach strategic goals

strategies Large-scale action plans for interacting with the environment to achieve long-term goals

strategy formulation Process of identifying mission and strategic goals, conducting competitive analysis, and developing specific strategies

strategy implementation Process of carrying out strategic plans and maintaining control over how those plans are carried out

substitutes for leadership Approach attempting to specify some main situational factors likely to make leader behaviours unnecessary or to negate their effectiveness

substitutes Situational factors making leadership impact not only impossible but also unnecessary

sunk costs Costs which, once incurred, are not recoverable and should not enter into considerations of future courses of action

supervisors Mainly individuals with expertise and training in an area

suppliers Organisations and individuals supplying resources an organisation needs to conduct its operations

supportive Leader behaviour entailing showing concern for the status, well-being and needs of subordinates; doing small things to make work more pleasant; and being friendly and approachable

SWOT analysis Method of analysing an organisation's competitive situation involving assessing organisational strengths (S), weaknesses (W), environmental opportunities (O) and threats (T)

symbol Object, act, event or quality serving as a vehicle for conveying meaning

symbolic processes Various ways we use verbal and imagined symbols to process and store experiences in representational forms to serve as guides to future behaviour

synergy Ability of the whole to equal more than the sum of its parts

system Set of interrelated parts operating as a whole in pursuit of common goals

systems-development life cycle Series of stages used in the development of most medium- and large-sized information systems

systems theory Approach based on the idea that organisations can be visualised as systems

tactical control Control type focusing on assessing implementation of tactical plans at department levels, monitoring associated periodic results, and taking corrective action as needed

tactical goals Targets or future results usually set by middle management for specific departments or units

tactical plans Means charted to support implementation of the strategic plan and achievement of tactical goals

tall structure Structure with many hierarchical levels and narrow spans of control

tariff Type of trade barrier in the form of a customs duty, or tax, levied mainly on imports

task environment Specific outside elements with which an organisation interfaces in the course of conducting its business

task force Temporary task group formed to recommend on a specific issue

task group Formal group created for a specific purpose, supplementing or replacing work normally done by command groups

task identity Degree to which the job allows completion of a major identifiable piece of work, rather than just a fragment

task significance Extent to which a worker sees job output as having an important impact on others

team Temporary or ongoing task group with members charged to work together to identify problems, form a consensus about what should be done, and implement necessary actions in relation to a particular task or organisational area

technical skills Skills reflecting both an understanding of and a proficiency in a specialised field

technological element Current state of knowledge regarding production of products and services

technological interdependence Degree to which different organisation parts must exchange information and materials to perform required activities

technological transfer Transmission of technology from those who possess it to those who do not

technological, or qualitative forecasting Type of forecasting aimed primarily at predicting long-term trends in technology and other important, environmental aspects

technology Knowledge, tools, equipment and work techniques used by an organisation in delivering its product or service

telecommunications Electronic communication of information over a distance

telecommuting Form of working at home made possible by using computer technology to remain in touch with the office

teleconferencing Simultaneous communication among a group of individuals by telephone or via computer using specially designed software

Theory Z Concept combining positive aspects of American and Japanese management into a modified approach aimed at increasing managerial effectiveness while remaining compatible with the norms and values of American society and culture

time-series methods Methods using historical data to develop future forecasts

top managers Managers at the very top levels of the hierarchy who are ultimately responsible for the entire organisation

total quality management (TQM) Management system integral to an organisation's strategy and aimed at continually improving product and service quality so as to achieve high levels of customer satisfaction and build strong customer loyalty

total quality management Approach highlighting collective responsibility for product and service quality, and encouraging individuals to work together to improve quality

total-factor productivity Productivity approach considering all inputs involved in producing outputs

trade associations Organisations composed of individuals or firms with common business concerns

training The process of equipping people with skills and competencies in a systematic manner

traits Distinctive internal qualities or characteristics of an individual, such as physical characteristics, personality characteristics, skills and abilities, and social factors

transactional leaders Leaders who motivate subordinates to perform at expected levels by helping them recognise task responsibilities, identify goals, acquire confidence about meeting desired performance levels, and understand how their needs and the rewards they desire are linked to goal achievement

transaction-processing system (TPS) Computer-based information system which executes and records routine day-to-day transactions needed to conduct an organisation's business

transformation processes Organisation's managerial and technological abilities used to convert inputs into outputs

transformational leaders Leaders who motivate individuals to perform beyond normal expectations by inspiring subordinates to focus on broader missions transcending their own immediate self-interests, to concentrate on intrinsic higher-level goals rather than extrinsic lower-level goals, and to have confidence in their abilities to achieve the extraordinary missions articulated by the leader

turnaround Strategy designed to reverse a negative trend and restore the organisation to appropriate levels of profitability

two-factor theory Herzberg's theory that hygiene factors are necessary to keep workers from feeling dissatisfied, but only motivators can lead workers to feel satisfied and motivated

two-way communication Communication resulting when the communication process explicitly includes feedback

uncertainty A condition in which the decision maker must choose a course of action with incomplete knowledge of consequences following implementation

uncertainty avoidance Cultural dimension involving the extent to which members of a society feel uncomfortable with and try to avoid situations they see as unstructured, unclear or unpredictable

undercontrol Granting autonomy to an employee to the point where the organisation loses its ability to direct individual effort toward achieving organisational goals

unions Membership groups formed to represent employees and to negotiate collective agreements with management that determine the terms and conditions of employment

unit and small-batch production Type of technology where products are custom-produced to meet customer specifications or are made in small quantities primarily by craft specialists

upward communication Vertical flow of communication from a lower level to one or more higher levels in the organisation

user Individual, other than an information system professional, engaged in the development and/or management of computer-based information systems

valence Our assessment of anticipated value of various outcomes or rewards

validity Whether the decision process actually measures what it sets out to measure

variable-interval schedule of reinforcement Pattern in which a reinforcer is administered on a varying, or random, time schedule which averages out to a predetermined time frequency

variable-ratio schedule of reinforcement Pattern in which a reinforcer is provided after a varying, or random, number of occurrences of the desired behaviour in such a way the reinforcement pattern averages out to a predetermined ratio of occurrences per reinforcement

verbal communication Written or oral use of words to communicate

vertical communication Communication involving a message exchange between two or more levels of the organisational hierarchy

vertical coordination Linking of activities at the top of the organisation with those at the middle and lower levels to achieve organisational goals

vertical integration Approach involving effecting growth through production of inputs previously provided by suppliers or through replacement of a customer role by disposing of one's own outputs

vicarious learning Our ability to learn new behaviours and/or assess their probable consequences by observing others

videoconferencing Holding meetings with individuals in two or more locations by means of closed-circuit television

virtual team Physically dispersed work group using information technology as a means to interact but rarely, if ever, meeting physically

voice mail Recording system providing senders with opportunity to leave messages for receivers by telephone

whistle-blower An employee who reports a real or perceived wrongdoing under the control of their employer to those able to take appropriate action

wholly owned subsidiary Operation on foreign soil totally owned and controlled by a company with headquarters outside the host country

wide-area networks (WANs) Networks providing communications between computers over long distances, usually through telecommunications companies

work agenda A loosely connected set of tentative goals and tasks that a manager is attempting to accomplish

work specialisation Degree to which work necessary to achieve organisational goals is broken down into various jobs

work-in-process inventory Stock of items currently being transformed into a final product or service

world-wide integration strategy, or globalisation Strategy aimed at developing relatively standardised products with global appeal, as well as rationalising operations across the world

REFERENCES

Abrahamson, E. and Fombrun, C.J. 1994, Macrocultures: Determinants and consequences, *Academy of Management Review*, 19, pp. 728–55.

Ackerman, L.S. 1982, Transition management: An in-depth look at managing complex change, *Organizational Dynamics*, Summer, pp. 46–66.

Adair, J.G. 1984, The Hawthorne effect: A reconsideration of the methodological artifact, *Journal of Applied Psychology*, 69, pp. 334–45.

Adam, Jr, E.E. and Ebert, R.J. 1992, *Production and Operations Management*, Prentice-Hall, Englewood Cliffs.

Adams, J.R. and Kirchof, N.S. 1984, The practice of matrix management, in D.I. Cleland (ed.), *Matrix Management Systems Handbook*, Van Nostrand Reinhold, New York.

Adams, J.S. 1965, Inequity in social exchange, in L. Berkowitz (ed.), *Advances in Experimental Social Psychology*, 2, Academic, New York.

Adhikari, R. 1996, Do vendors feel your pain?, *Information Week*, 4 March, pp. 44–7.

Adler, N.J. 1984, Expecting international success: Female managers overseas, *Columbia Journal of World Business*, Fall, pp. 79–85.

Adler, N.J. 1991, *International Dimensions of Organizational Behavior*, P.W.S.-Kent, Boston.

Adler, N.J., Dokter, R. and Redding, S.G. 1986, From the Atlantic to the Pacific century: Cross-cultural management reviewed, *Journal of Management*, 12, pp. 295–318.

Alabanese, R. and Van Fleet, D.D. 1985, Rational behavior in groups: The free-riding tendency, *Academy of Management Review*, 10, pp. 244–55.

Albert, A. 1985, Citicorp shuffles units to emphasize management of institutional assets, *American Banker*, 5 July, p. 1.

Aldag, R.J. and Fuller, S.R. 1994, Beyond fiasco: A re-appraisal of the groupthink phenomenon and a new model of group decision processes, *Psychological Bulletin*, 113, pp. 533–52.

Alderfer, C.P. 1972, *Existence, Relatedness, and Growth: Human Needs in Organizational Settings*, Free Press, New York.

Alderfer, C.P. 1987, An intergroup perspective on group dynamics, in J.W. Lorsch (ed.), *Handbook of Organizational Behavior*, Prentice-Hall, Englewood Cliffs.

Aldrich Jr, N.W. 1986, Lines of communication, *INC.*, June, pp. 140–44.

Aldrich, H. and Herker, D. 1977, Boundary spanning roles and organization structure, *Academy of Management Review*, 2, pp. 217–30.

Aldrich, H.E. 1979, *Organizations and Environments*, Prentice-Hall, Englewood Cliffs.

Aley, J. 1995, New lift for the U.S. export boom, *Fortune*, 13 Nov., pp. 73–8.

Allcorn, S. 1985, What makes groups tick, *Personnel*, September, pp. 52–8.

Alster, N. 1989, Unlevel playing field, *Forbes*, 26 June, pp. 53–7.

Altier, W.J. 1986, SMR forum: Task forces—an effective management tool, *Sloan Management Review*, Spring, pp. 69–75.

Amabile, T.M. 1983, *The Social Psychology of Creativity*, Springer-Verlag, New York.

Amabile, T.M. 1988, A model of creativity and innovation in organizations, *Research in Organizational Behavior*, 10, pp. 123–67.

American Society for Quality Control 1992, Quality glossary, *Quality Progress*, Feb., p. 26.

Amit, R. and Livnat, J. 1988, A concept of conglomerate diversification, *Journal of Management*, 14, pp. 593–604.

Ancona, D.G. and Caldwell, D.F. 1992, Demography and design: Predictors of new product team performance, *Organization Science*, 3, pp. 321–41.

Anderson, E. 1990, Two firms, one frontier: On assessing joint venture performance, *Sloan Management Review*, Winter, pp. 19–26.

Andrews, B. 2003, Know when to fold 'em, *Business Review Weekly*, 25 September–1 October, pp. 64–5.

Andrews, J.D.W., The achievement motive and advancement in two types of organizations, *Journal of Personality and Social Psychology*, 6, pp. 163–68.

Andrews, K.R. 1968, Introduction to the thirtieth-anniversary edition of Chester I. Barnard, *The Function of the Executive*, Harvard, Cambridge.

Annual Report 1998, Harvey Norman Holdings Limited.

Ansberry, C. 1991, Utah's Geneva steel, once called hopeless, is racking up profits, *Wall Street Journal*, 20 Nov., p. A1.

Anthony, R.N., Dearden, J. and Bedford, N.M. 1984, *Management Control Systems*, Irwin, Homewood.

Applegate, L.M., Cash, Jr, J.I. and Mills, D.Q. 1988, Information technology and tomorrow's manager, *Harvard Business Review*, Nov.–Dec., pp. 128–36.

Argus, D. 2003, Certainly can do, *Business Review Weekly*, 11–17 December, p. 52.

Arlow, P. and Gannon, M.J. 1982, Social responsiveness, corporate structure, and economic performance, *Academy of Management Review*, 7, pp. 235–41.

Armstrong, L. and Holyoke, L. 1995, NASA's tiny camera has a wide-angle future, *Business Week*, 6 March, pp. 54–5.

Arnold, H.J. 1981, A test of the validity of the multiplicative hypothesis of expectancy-valence theories of work motivation, *Academy of Management Journal*, 24, pp. 128–41.

Arnold, H.J. and Feldman, D.C. 1986, *Organizational Behavior*, McGraw-Hill, New York.

Arthur, L.J., Quick and dirty, *Computerworld*, 14 Dec., p. 4.

Arveny, R.D. and Campion, J.E. 1982, The employment interview: A summary and recent review of recent research, *Personnel Psychology*, Summer, pp. 281–322.

Arveny, R.D. and Ivancevich, J.M. 1980, Punishment in organizations: A review, propositions, and research suggestions, *Academy of Management Review*, 5, pp. 23–132.

Ashmos, D.P. and Huber, G.P. 1987, The systems paradigm in organization theory: Correcting the record and suggesting the future, *Academy of Management Review*, 12, pp. 607–21.

Astley, W.G. 1985, Organizational size and bureaucracy, *Organization Studies*, 6, pp. 201–28.

Atherton, T. 2003, Passion in action, *Business Review Weekly*, 28 August–3 September, p. 48.

Atkinson, B. 1996, USF&G turning 100, a gleam in its eye, *Sun* (Baltimore), 24 March, p. 1E.

Attewell, P. and Rule, J. 1984, Computing and organizations: What we know and what we don't know, *Communications of the ACM*, December, pp. 1184–92.

Auerback, S. 1987, America, the 'diminished giant', *Washington Post*, 15 April, pp. A1, A18.

Aupperle, K.E., Carroll, A.B. and Hatfield, J.D. 1985, An empirical examination of the relationship between corporate social responsibility and profitability, *Academy of Management Journal*, 28, pp. 446–63.

Avishai, B. 1989, A CEO's common sense of CIM: An interview with J. Tracy O'Rourke, *Harvard Business Review*, Jan.–Feb. pp. 110–17.

Avishai, B. and Taylor, W. 1989, Customers drive a technology driven company, *Harvard Business Review*, Nov.–Dec., pp. 107–14.

Axley, S.R. 1984, Managerial and organizational communication in terms of the conduit metaphor, *Academy of Management Review*, 9, pp. 428–37.

Babbage, C. 1963, *On the Economy of Machinery and Manufactures*, Knight, London, 1832, reprinted by Kelly, New York.

Bagwell, S. 2003, Surf's up in Europe, *Business Review Weekly*, 14–20 August, pp. 60–2.

Bahree, B. 1995, BP comes back even as oil prices sink, *Wall Street Journal*, 8 Sept., p. A6.

Baig, E. 1995, Taking care of business—without leaving the house, *Business Week*, 17 April, pp. 106–7.

Bailey, G. and Sherman, D. 1988, Downsizing: The alternatives may be cheaper, *Management Review*, April, pp. 54–5.

Bailey, G. and Szerdy, J. 1988, Is there life after downsizing?, *Journal of Business Strategy*, Jan.–Feb., pp. 8–11.

Bailey, J. 1987, The fine art of leading a meeting, *Working Woman*, Aug., pp. 68–70, 103.

Bailey, J. 1990, Ousted chairman of Abbott accuses company in filing, *Wall Street Journal*, 6 June, p. A6.

Baker, H.K. 1987, *Financial Management*, Harcourt Brace Jovanovich, San Diego.

Baliga, B.R. and Hunt, J.G. 1987, An organizational life cycle approach to leadership, in J.G. Hunt, B.R. Baliga, H.P. Dachler and C.A. Schriesheim (eds), *Emerging Leadership Vistas*, Heath, Boston.

Bamford, J. and McHenry, S. 1995, The Working Woman 50 top women business owners, *Working Woman*, May, p. 37.

Banagham, M. 1999, Fast food down to the wire, *Business Review Weekly*, 21 May, p. 103.

Bandura, A. 1977, *Social Learning Theory*, Prentice-Hall, Englewood Cliffs.

Bandura, A. 1986, *Social Foundations of Thought and Action: A Social Cognitive Theory*, Prentice-Hall, Englewood Cliffs.

Banerjee, N. 1995, For Mary Kay sales reps in Russia, hottest shade is the color of money, *Wall Street Journal*, 30 Aug., p. A8.

Banks, H. 1994, Superjumbo, *Forbes*, 24 Oct., pp. 180–6.

Barbash, F. 1995, Barings executives blamed for fall, *Washington Post*, 19 July, p. F3.

Barkdull, C.W. 1963, Span of control: A method of evaluation, *Michigan Business Review*, 15, pp. 25–32;

Barling, J. and Beattie, R. 1983, Self-efficacy beliefs and sales performance, *Journal of Organizational Behavior Management*, 5, pp. 41–51.

Barnard, C.I. 1968, *The Functions of the Executive*, Harvard, Cambridge.

Barnes, S. and Greller, L.M. 1994, Computer-mediated communication in organizations, *Communication Education*, 43, pp. 129–42.

Barnett, W.P. 1990, The organizational ecology of a technological system, *Administrative Science Quarterly*, 35, pp. 31–60.

Barney, J.B. 1986, Organizational culture: Can it be a source of sustained competitive advantage? *Academy of Management Review*, 11, pp. 656–65.

Barney, J.B. 1995, Look inside for competitive advantage, *Academy of Management Executive*, 9, 4, pp. 49–61.

Barney, J.B. and Griffin, R.W. 1992, *The Management of Organizations*, Houghton Mifflin, Boston.

Barrett, P. M. 1995, How a young lawyer is making his mark at a Washington firm, *Wall Street Journal*, 15 Feb., pp. A1, A11.

Barrett, R.B. and Kistka, D.J. 1987, Forecasting system at Rubbermaid, *Journal of Business Forecasting*, Spring, pp. 7–9.

Barron, F.H. 1985, Payoff matrices pay off at Hallmark, *Interfaces*, July–Aug., pp. 20–5.

Bart, C.K. 1988, New venture units: Use them wisely to manage innovation, *Sloan Management Review*, Summer, pp. 35–43.

Bartholomew, D. 1996, Boost to response time, *Information Week*, 19 Feb., p. 73.

Bartino, J. 1992, At these shouting matches, no one says a word, *Business Week*, 11 June, p. 78.

Bartlett, C.A. and Ghoshal, S. 1992, *Transnational Management*, Irwin, Homewood.

Bartol, K.M. and Martin, D.C. 1986, Women and men in task groups, in R.D. Ashmore and F.K. Del Boca (eds), *The Social Psychology of Female-Male Relations*, Academic, Orlando.

Baskin, O.W. and Aronoff, C.E. 1980, *Interpersonal Communication in Organizations*, Scott, Foresman, Santa Monica.

Bass, B.M. 1981, *Stogdill's Handbook of Leadership*, Free Press, New York.

Bass, B.M. 1983, *Organizational Decision Making*, Irwin, Homewood.

Bass, B.M. 1985, *Leadership and Performance Beyond Expectations*, Free Press, New York.

Bass, B.M., Krusell, J. and Alexander, R.A. 1971, Male managers' attitudes toward working women, *American Behavioral Scientist*, 15, pp. 221–36.

Baucus, M.S. and Near, J.P. 1991, Can illegal corporate behavior be predicted? An event history analysis, *Academy of Management Journal*, 34, pp. 9–36.

Baum, L. 1987, Delegating your way to job survival, *Business Week*, 2 Nov., p. 206.

Baumeister, R.F. and Leary, M.R. 1995, The need to belong: Desire for interpersonal attachments as a fundamental human motivation, *Journal of Applied Psychology*, 117, pp. 497–529.

Bazerman, M.H. 1986, *Judgment in Managerial Decision Making*, Wiley, New York.

Beckhard, R. 1969, *Organizational Development: Strategies and Models*, Addison-Wesley, Reading.

Beer, M. 1980, *Organization Change and Development: A Systems View*, Goodyear, Santa Monica.

Beer, M., Spector, B., Lawrence, P.R., Quinn-Mills, D. and Walton, R.G. 1984, *Managing Human Assets*, Free Press, New York.

Beer, M. and Spector, B. 1985, Corporate wide transformations in human resource management, in R.E. Walton and P. R. Lawrence (eds), *Human Resource Management, Trends and Challenge*, Harvard Business School Press, Boston.

Beer, M., Spector, B., Lawrence P.R., Quinn-Mills, D. and Walton, R.G. 1984, *Managing Human Assets*, Free Press, New York.

Begley, S. 1998, The boss feels your pain, *Newsweek*, 12 Oct., p. 74.

Behar, R. 1988, How the rich get richer, *Forbes*, 31 Oct., p. 70.

Behar, R. 1995, Stalked by Allstate, *Fortune*, 2 Oct., pp. 128–42.

Bell, D. 1987, The world and the United States in 2013, *Daedalus*, Summer, pp. 1–31.

Ben & Jerry's 1995, Annual Report.

Benjamin, C. 2003a, Enduring wisdom, *Business Review Weekly*, 25 September–1 October, p. 68.

Benjamin, C. 2003b, Take counsel, early and often, *Business Review Weekly*, 2–8 October, p. 57.

Benjamin, R.I. 1982, Information technology in the 1990s: A long-range planning scenario, *MIS Quarterly*, June, pp. 11–31.

Benjamin, R.I., Rockart, J.F., Morton, M.S.S. and Wyman, J. 1984, Information technology: A strategic opportunity, *Sloan Management Review*, Spring, pp. 3–10.

Benne, K. and Sheats, P. H. 1948, Functional roles of group members, *Journal of Social Issues*, 4, pp. 41–9.

Bennet, J. 1993, A stronger yen is hurting sales of Japan's cars, *New York Times*, 5 Nov., pp. A1, C2.

Bennett, J.K. 1994, The 12 building blocks of the learning organization, *Training*, June, p. 41.

Bernstein, A. 1992, Teaching business how to train, *Business Week/Reinventing America*, 23 Oct., pp. 82–90.

Berry, M.M.J. and Taggart, J.H. 1994, Managing technology and innovation: A review, *R&D Management*, 24, pp. 341–53.

Berton, L. 1995, It's audit time! Send in the clowns, *Wall Street Journal*, 18 Jan., pp. B1, B6.

Bettenhausen, K. and Murnighan, J.K. 1985, The emergence of norms in competitive decision-making groups, *Administrative Science Quarterly*, 30, pp. 350–72.

Betton, J. and Dess, G.G. 1985, The application of population ecology models to the study of organizations, *Academy of Management Review*, 10, pp. 750–7.

Betts, M. 1992, Big things come in small buttons, *Computerworld*, 3 Aug., p. 30.

Beyer J.M. and Trice, H.M. 1984, A field study of the use and perceived effects of discipline in controlling work performance, *Academy of Management Journal*, 27, pp. 743–64.

Bhambri, A. and Sonnenfeld, J. 1987, The man who stands alone, *New Management*, Spring, pp. 29–33.

Bhambri, A. and Sonnenfeld, J. 1988, Organization structure and corporate social performance: A field study in two contrasting industries, *Academy of Management Journal*, 31, pp. 642–62.

Birchard, B. 1995, Power to the people, *CFO*, March, pp. 38–43.

Bird, L. 1994, Lazarus's IBM coup was all about relationships, *Wall Street Journal*, 26 May, pp. B1, B7.

Bird, L. and Jereski, L. 1996, Warnaco may buy authentic fitness corp., *Wall Street Journal*, 7 June, p. A2.

Birdwhistell, R. 1972, *Kenesics and Context*, University of Pennsylvania, Philadelphia.

Blackmon, D.A. 1998, A factory in Alabama is the merger in microcosm, *Wall Street Journal*, 5 May, pp. B1, B10.

Blake, R.R. and McCanse, J.S. 1991, *The Managerial Grid*, Gulf, Houston.

Blank, W., Weitzel, J.R. and Green, S.G. 1990, A test of the situational leadership theory, *Personnel Psychology*, 43, pp. 579–97.

Blomberg N. 1999, Bill-paying becomes focus of online war, *Taiwan News*, 13 Aug., p. 15.

Bluedorn, A.C. (ed.) 1986, Special book review section on the classics of management, *Academy of Management Review*, 11, pp. 442–64.

Blumenstein, R. 1996, Ohio strike that is crippling GM plants is tied to plan to outsource brake work, *Wall Street Journal*, 12 March, pp. A3, A4.

Bohn, R.E. 1994, Measuring and managing technological knowledge, *Sloan Management Review*, 22 Sept., p. 61.

Bongiorno, L. 1996, The Pepsi regeneration, *Business Week*, 11 March, pp. 70–3.

Boone, M.E. 1991, Computers reshape Phillips 66, *Industry Week*, 1 July, p. 12.

Booth, C. 1992, Against the time, *Time*, 17 Feb., pp. 54–6.

Bormann, E.G. 1983, Symbolic convergence: Organizational communication and culture, in L. Putnam and M.E. Pacanowsky (eds), *Communication and Organizations: An Interpretive Approach*, Sage, Beverly Hills.

Boslet, M. 1994, Metal buttons toted by crop pickers act as mini databases, *Wall Street Journal*, 1 June, p. B3.

Boulding, K.E. 1956, General systems theory—the skeleton of science, *Management Science*, 2, pp. 197–208.

Bounds, G., Yorks, L., Adams, M. and Ramney, G. 1994, *Beyond Total Quality Management: Toward the Emerging Paradigm*, McGraw-Hill, New York.

Bounds, W. 1995, Kodak reorganizes its sales force at imaging group, *Wall Street Journal*, 24 Jan., p. B3.

Bourgeois, L. J. 1981, On the measurement of organizational slack, *Academy of Management Review*, 6, pp. 29–39.

Bowen, E. 1987, Looking to its roots, *Time*, 25 May, pp. 26–9.

Bower, J.L. and Christensen, C.M. 1995, Disruptive technologies: Catching the wave, *Harvard Business Review*, Jan.–Feb., pp. 43–53.

Boxall, P. 2001, Evaluating continuity and change in the Employment Relations Act 2000, *New Zealand Journal of Industrial Relations*, February, 26, 1, pp. 27–44.

Boyatzis, R.E. 1982, *The Competent Manager: A Model for Effective Performance*, Wiley, New York.

Boyd, B.K., Dess, G.G. and Rasheed, A.M.A. 1993, Divergence between archival and perceptual measures of the environment: Causes and consequences, *Academy of Management Review*, 18, pp. 204–26.

Brady, K. 1987, The power of positive stress, *Working Woman*, July, pp. 74–7.

Brahm, J. 1995, High-tech tools speed, *Machine Design*, 26 Jan., pp. 36–40.

Bramel, D. and Friend, R. 1981, Hawthorne, the myth of the docile worker, and class bias in psychology, *American Psychologist*, Aug., pp. 867–78.

Brand, D.C. and Scanlan, G. 1995, Strategic control through core competencies, *Long Range Planning*, 28, 2, pp. 102–14.

Bray, D.W., Campbell, R.J. and Grant, D.L. 1974, *Formative Years in Business: A Long Term AT&T Study of Managerial Lives*, Wiley, New York.

Brealey, R.A. and Myers, S.C. 1991, *Principles of Corporate Finance*, McGraw-Hill, New York.

Breeze, J. 1986, Paul Devinat's scientific management in Europe—A historical perspective, in D.A. Wren and J.A. Pearce II (eds), *Papers Dedicated to the Development of Modern Management*, Academy of Management.

Brief, A.P., Dukerich, J.M., Brown, P.R. and Brett, J.F. 1996, What's wrong with the Treadway commission report? *Journal of Business Ethics*, Feb., pp. 183–98.

Brockner, J. 1992, The escalation of commitment to a failing course of action: Toward theoretical progress, *Academy of Management Review*, 17, pp. 39–61.

Brown, B. 1988, James Bildner's spectacular rise and fall, *Wall Street Journal*, 24 Oct., p. B1.

Brown, C. 1995, The body-bending business, *Forbes*, 11 Sept., pp. 196–204.

Brown, M.G., Hitchcock, D.E. and Willard, M.L. 1994, *Why TQM Fails and What to Do about It*, Irwin, Burr Ridge.

Brown, P.B. 1988, The anti-marketers, *INC.*, March, pp. 62–72.

Brown, W. 1988, Electronic pulses replacing paper in workplace, *Washington Post*, 2 Sept., pp. F1, F2.

Brown, W. 1991, Perrier's market share fizzles in the aftermath of its recall, *Washington Post*, 4 Jan., p. F3.

Browning, E.S. 1990, Long-term thinking and paternalistic ways carry Michelin to top, *Wall Street Journal*, 5 Jan., pp. A1, A8.

Browning, E.S. 1992, Nestl? appears to win battle to acquire Source Perrier, *Wall Street Journal*, 24 March, p. A13.

Browning, E.S. 1993, Perrier tries to rejuvenate stodgy image, *Wall Street Journal*, 2 Sept., p. B1.

Browning, E.S. 1994, Computer chip project brings rivals together, but the cultures clash, *Wall Street Journal*, 3 April, pp. A1, A8.

Brull, S.V. and Gross, N. 1996, Sony's new world, *Business Week*, 27 May, pp. 100–8.

Bryan, M. 2000, Every step you take, every move you make, *Australian Financial Review*, 4–5 March, p. 27.

Bryant, G. 1999, Be part of the e-boom, *Business Review Weekly*, 21 May, p. 162.

Budescu, D.V. and Weiss, W. 1987, Reflection of transitive and intransitive preferences: A test of prospect theory, *Organizational Behavior and Human Decision Processes*, 39, pp. 184–202.

Bulkeley, W.M. 1990, When laptop computers go on the road, the hassles can cancel out the benefits, *Wall Street Journal*, 16 May, pp. B1, B4.

Bulkeley, W.M. 1995, Will ultimate voice mail make secretaries obsolete? *Wall Street Journal*, 20 Oct., pp. B1, B5.

Bulkeley, W.M. and Stecklow, S. 1994, Harvard's president, citing exhaustion, is going on leave during fund drive, *Wall Street Journal*, 29 Nov., p. B7.

Burck, C.G. 1982, Can Detroit catch up? *Fortune*, 8 Feb., pp. 34–9.

Burgelman, R.A. 1985, Managing the new venture division: Research findings and implications for strategic management, *Strategic Management Journal*, 6, pp. 39–54.

Burgess, J. 1987, Prankster's Christmas greeting generates few ho-ho-hos at IBM, *Washington Post*, 18 Dec., pp. F1, F10.

Burgess, J. 1988, Searching for a better computer shield, *Washington Post*, 13 Nov., p. H1.

Burgess, J. 1992, IBM finishes one race, starts another, *Washington Post*, 31 March, p. C1.

Burne, J.A. 1994, The pain of downsizing, *Business Week*, 9 May, p. 61.

Burns, J.M. 1978, *Leadership*, Harper and Row, New York.

Burns, T. and Stalker, G.M. 1961, *The Management of Innovation*, Tavistock, London.

Burrough, B. 1987, Broken barrier: More women join ranks of white-collar criminals, *Wall Street Journal*, May 29, p. 29.

Burrow, S. 2003, The price of success, *Business Review Weekly*, 28 August–3 September, p. 52.

Burt, D.N. and Soukup, W.R. 1985, Purchasing's role in new product development, *Harvard Business Review*, Sept.–Oct., pp. 90–7.

Burton, T.M. 1995, Visionary's reward: Combine 'simple ideas' and some failures; result: Sweet revenge, *Wall Street Journal*, 3 Feb., pp. A1, A5.

Business Asia 2003, Call to women to increase exports, August, 11, 7, p. 29.

Business Review Weekly 1999, 100 fastest-growing private companies, 15 March, p. 54.

Business Review Weekly 2000, Race to be first and best makes instant managers, 31 March, p. 36.

Business Week 1983a, The antibribery act splits executives, 19 Sept., p. 16.

Business Week 1983b, The shrinking of middle management, 25 April, p. 56.

Business Week 1984a, After its recovery, new headaches for Tylenol, 14 May, p. 137.

Business Week 1984b, The new breed of strategic planner, 17 Sept., pp. 62–8.

Business Week 1988, Public service, 11 Jan., p. 156.

Business Week 1989, Why a big steelmaker is mimicking the minimills, 27 March, p. 92.

Business Week 1995a, Groupware requires a group effort, 26 June, p. 154.

Business Week 1995b, Prejudice: Still on the menu, 3 April, p. 42.

Bylinsky, G. 1987, Trying to transcend copycat science, *Fortune*, 30 March, pp. 42–6.

Bylinsky, G. 1996, To create products, go into a cave, *Fortune*, 5 Feb., pp. 80A–D.

Byrne, H.S. 1995, Lifting off, *Barron's*, 27 March, pp. 17–18.

Byrne, J.A. 1987, Culture shock at Xerox, *Business Week*, 22 June, pp. 106–10.

Byrne, J.A. 1992a, Here's what to do next, Dow Corning, *Business Week*, 24 Feb., p. 33.

Byrne, J.A. 1992b, The best laid ethics programs, *Business Week*, 9 March, pp. 67–9.

Byrne, J.A. 1995, Virtual B-schools, *Business Week*, 23 Oct., pp. 64–8.

Byrne, J.A. 1996a, Gross compensation? *Business Week*, 18 March, pp. 32–3.

Byrne, J.A. 1996b, How high can CEO pay go? *Business Week*, 22 April, pp. 100–6.

Cahill, P. 1999, Video Ezy holds course for Asia, *Business Review Weekly*, 11 June, p. 54–5.

Calori, R. and Dufour, B. 1995, Management European style, *Academy of Management Executive*, 9, 3, pp. 61–70.

Cameron, K.S., Whetten, D.A. and. Kim, M.U. 1987, Organizational dysfunctions of decline, *Academy of Management Journal*, 30, pp. 126–38.

Caminiti, S. 1992, The payoff from a good reputation, *Fortune*, 10 Feb., pp. 74–7.

Campbell, J.P. and Prichard, R.D. 1976, Motivation theory in industrial and organizational psychology, in M.D. Dunnette (ed.), *Handbook of Industrial and Organizational Psychology*, Rand McNally, Chicago.

Campion, M.A. and McClelland, C.L. 1993, Follow-up and extension of the interdisciplinary costs and benefits of enlarged jobs, *Journal of Applied Psychology*, 78, pp. 339–51.

Campion, M.A., Cheraskin, L. and Stevens, M.J. 1994, Career-related antecedents and outcomes of job rotation, *Academy of Management Journal*, 37, pp. 1518–42.

Cane, A. 1994, From a caterpillar to butterfly, *Financial Times*, 27 May, p. 11.

Capowski, G.S. 1993, Designing a corporate identity, *Management Review*, June, p. 37–8.

Capowski, G.S. 1996, Managing diversity, *Management Review*, June, pp. 13–19.

Carey, A. 1967, The Hawthorne studies: A radical criticism, *American Sociological Review*, June, pp. 403–16;

Carley, W.M. 1995, Salesman's treatment raises bias questions at Schering-Plough, *Wall Street Journal*, 31 May, p. A1, A8.

Carlisle, H.M. 1974, A contingency approach to decentralization, *Advanced Management Journal*, July, pp. 9–18.

Carlyle, R.E. 1988, Managing IS at multinations, *Datamation*, 1 March, pp. 54–66.

Carnevale, A.P. and Stone, S.C. 1994, Diversity: Beyond the golden rule, *Training & Development*, Oct., pp. 22–39.

Carnevale, M.L. 1994, Marketing and media: FCC would allow higher charges as cable TV systems add channels, *Wall Street Journal*, 24 Oct., p. B12.

Carroll S.J. and Tosi, H.L. 1973, *Management by Objectives: Applications and Research*, Macmillan, New York.

Carroll, A. 1989, *Business and Society: Ethics and Stakeholder Management*, South-Western, Cincinnati.

Carroll, A.B. 1979, A three-dimensional conceptual model of corporate performance, *Academy of Management Review*, 4, pp. 499–500.

Carroll, A.B. 1987, In search of the moral manager, *Business Horizons*, March–April, pp. 7–15.

Carroll, S.J. and Gillen, D.J. 1987, Are the classical management functions useful in describing managerial work?, *Academy of Management Review*, 12, pp. 38–51.

Carson, P.P., Carson, K.D. and Roe, C.W. 1993, Social power bases: A meta-analytic examination of interrelationships and outcomes, *Journal of Applied Social Psychology*, 23, pp. 1150–69.

Carton, B. 1994, Muscled out? At Jenny Craig, men are ones who claim sex discrimination, *Wall Street Journal*, 29 Nov., pp. A1, A7.

Carton, B. 1995, Gillette faces wrath of children in testing on rats and rabbits, *Wall Street Journal*, 5 Sept., p. A1.

Carver, C.S., DeGregoria, E. and Gillis, R. 1980, Field-study evidence of an attribution among two categories of observers, *Personality and Social Psychology Bulletin*, 6, pp. 44–50.

Castrogiovanni, G.J. 1991, Environmental munificence: A theoretical assessment, *Academy of Management Review*, 16, pp. 542–65.

Caudron, S, 2000a, Learning revives training, *Workforce*, Jan., 79, 1, pp. 34–7.

Caudron, S, 2000b, Jobs disappear when work becomes more important, *Workforce*, Jan., 79, 1, pp. 30–2.

Chakravarthy, B.S. and Perlmutter, H.V. 1985, Strategic planning for a global business, *Columbia Journal of World Business*, Summer, pp. 5–6.

Chakravarty, S.N. 1994, Back in focus, *Forbes*, 6 June, pp. 72–6.

Chandler, A.D. 1962, *Strategy and Structure*, M.I.T., Cambridge.

Charlesworth, R. 2003, Skills, training and a plan, *Business Review Weekly*, 25 September–1 October, p. 50.

Chase, M. 1986, Robot apprentices, *Wall Street Journal*, 16 Nov., p. D16.

Chase, M. 1998, HMOs send doctors to school to polish

bedside manners, *Wall Street Journal*, 13 April, p. B1.

Chase, R.B. 1978, Where does the customer fit in a service operation?, *Harvard Business Review*, Nov.–Dec., pp. 137–42.

Chase, R.B. and Aquilano, N.J. 1992, *Production & Operations Management*, Irwin, Homewood.

Chatman, J.A. and Jehn, K.A. 1994, Assessing the relationship between industry characteristics and organizational culture: How different can you be? *Academy of Management Journal*, 37, pp. 522–53.

Cheng, A.T. 1999, Leaps of faith, *Asia Inc.*, Aug., pp. 54–5.

Chesanow, N. 1987, Quick, take this memo, *Washington Post*, 7 Sept., p. C5.

Chesbrough, H.W. and Teece, D.J. 1996, Organizing for innovation, *Harvard Business Review*, Jan.–Feb., pp. 65–73.

Child, C. 1995a, GMAC reorganizes field staff for better service, *Automotive News*, Dec. p. 8.

Child, C. 1995b, Olds hires new brand manager from cereal maker, *Automotive News*, Dec. 25, p. 5.

Child, J. 1984, *Organization: A Guide to Problems and Practice*, Harper and Row, London.

Chong, C.K. 2000, Seven hurt in rush for Hello Kitty, *Straits Times*, 14 Jan., p. 3.

Chopra, V. 1982a, Productivity improvement through closed loop MRP (Part one), *Production and Inventory Management Review and APCIS News*, March, pp. 18–21.

Chopra, V. 1982b, Productivity improvement through closed loop MRP (Part two), *Production and Inventory Management Review and APCIS News*, April, pp. 49–51.

Christelow, D.B. 1987, International joint ventures: How important are they? *Columbia Journal of World Business*, Summer, pp. 7–13.

Clancy, B. 2003, High cost is a spanner in the works, *The Weekly Times*, 3 December, pp. 104–5.

Clark, R. 1992, *Human Resource Management*, McGraw Hill, Sydney.

Clemons, E.K. 1995, Using scenario analysis to manage the strategic risks of reengineering, *Sloan Management Review*, Summer, pp. 61–71.

Clifford, M.L. 1999, Daewoo boss is playing a dangerous game, *Business Week*, 16 Aug., p. 18.

Cockel, B. 1986, Textronix, *Distribution*, Aug., p. 54.

Cohen, M. 2000, Breaking the chains, *Far Eastern Economic Review*, 16 March, p. 28.

Cohen, M. 2003, Costly dreams, *Far Eastern Economic Review*, 23 October, p. 52.

Cohen, M.D., March, J.G. and Olsen, J.P. 1972, A garbage can model of organizational choice, *Administrative Science Quarterly*, 17, pp. 1–25.

Cohn, D.V. 1995, Workers double up to get a job done, *Washington Post*, 23 Jan., p. D5.

Cole, J. 1995, Boeing teaches employees how to run small businesses, *Wall Street Journal*, 7 Nov., pp. B1, B2.

Cole, J. 1996, Boeing will offer a luxury 737 as entry to business-jet market, *Wall Street Journal*, 2 July, p. B4.

Collins, G. 1995, Ten years later, Coca-Cola laughs at 'New Coke', *New York Times*, 11 April, p. C4.

Collins, P. D. and Hull, F. 1986, Technology and span of control: Woodward revisited, *Journal of Management Studies*, March, pp. 143–64.

Collins, R. and Schmenner, R. 1996, Pan-regional manufacturing: The lessons from Europe, *Financial Times*, 2 Feb., p. 8.

Conference Board 1991, *Employee Buy-in to Total Quality*, New York, 1991.

Conference Board 1994a, *Linking Quality to Business Results*, New York.

Conference Board 1994b, *Quality Outlook*, New York.

Conference Board 1994c, *TQM and Supplier Relationships*, New York.

Conger, J.A. and Kanungo, R.N. 1987, Toward a behavioral theory of charismatic leadership in organizational settings, *Academy of Management Review*, 12, pp. 637–47.

Connors, M. 1996, Baxter's big makeover in logistics, *Fortune*, 8 July, pp. 106C–N.

Contractor 1995, Roto-Rooter continues growth as residential service giant, April, p. 8.

Cook, J. 1986, We are the market, *Forbes*, 7 April, pp. 54–5.

Cook, J. 1989, We're the low-cost producer, *Forbes*, 25 Dec., pp. 65–6.

Cook, P. 1999, I heard it through the grapevine: Making knowledge management work by learning to share knowledge, skills and experience, *Industrial and Commercial Training*, 31, 3, pp. 101–5.

Copeland, L. and Griggs, L. 1986, Getting the best from foreign employees, *Management Review*, June, pp. 19–26.

Coradetti, W.R. 1994, Teamwork takes time and a lot of energy, *HRMagazine*, June, pp. 74–7.

Cordery, J.L., Mueller, W.S. and Smith, L.M. 1991, Attitudinal and behavioral effects of autonomous group working: A longitudinal field study, *Academy of Management Journal*, 4, pp. 464–76.

Cornell, A. and Cave, M. 2003, What they didn't teach you in business school, *AFR Boss*, July, pp. 64–8.

Cornish, E. 1990, A short list of global concerns, *Futurist*, Jan.–Feb., pp. 29–36.

Cosier, R.A. and Dalton, D.R. 1983, Equity theory and time: A reformulation, *Academy of Management Review*, 8, pp. 311–19.

Costa, G. 2003, ACCC targets imported 'local' goods, *The Age* (http://www.theage.com.au/articles/2003/08/19/1061261154731.html (accessed 3/12/2003).

Cotts, C. 1998, Starr has left, but K&E is fine, *Wall Street Journal*, 31 Aug., p. A6.

Court, M. 1994, Removing macho management lessons from the field of education, *Gender Work and Organisation*, 6,1, pp. 33–249.

Cowan, A.L. 1986, Getting rich on other people's pay checks, *Business Week*, 17 Nov., pp. 148–9.

Cowan, D.A. 1986, Developing a process model of problem recognition, *Academy of Management Review*, 11, pp. 763–76.

Cowen, S.S. and Middaugh II, J.K. 1988, Designing an effective financial planning and control system, *Long Range Planning*, 21, pp. 83–92.

Cox Jr, T. 1994, *Cultural Diversity in Organizations: Theory, Research & Practice*, Berrett-Koehler, San Francisco.

Cox, T.H. and Blacke, S. 1991, Managing cultural diversity: Implications for organizational competitiveness, *Academy of Management Executive*, Aug., pp. 45–56.

Cranwell, J.R. 1969, How to have a well-informed boss, *Supervisory Management*, May, pp. 5–6;

Crawford, A.B. 1982, Corporate electronic mail—a communication-intensive application of information technology, *MIS Quarterly*, 6, pp. 1–14.

Cringeley, R.X. 1993, *Accidental Empires*, Harper Business, New York.

Croghan, L. 1996, Why it's time for local 7232 to make peace with Briggs & Stratton, *Financial World*, 30 Jan., p. 30.

Cronin, M.J. 1997, Intranets reach the factory floor, *Fortune*, 17 June, p. 122.

Cronin, M.J. 1998, Ford's intranet success, *Fortune*, 30 March, p. 158.

Crowe, D. 2003, Outsourcing, *AFR Boss*, July, p. 24.

Cullen, J.B., Anderson, K.S. and Baker, D.D. 1986, Blau's theory of structural differentiation revisited: A theory of structural change or scale? *Academy of Management Journal*, 29, pp. 203–29.

Cummings, L.L., Huber, G.P. and Arendt, E. 1974, Effects of size and spatial arrangements on group decision making, *Academy of Management Journal*, 17, pp. 460–75.

D'Aveni, R.A. 1995, *Hypercompetitive Rivalries*, Free Press, New York.

Dabscheck, B. 1989, *Australian Industrial Relations in the 1980s*, Oxford University Press, Melbourne.

Daft, R.L. 1998, *Organization Theory and Design*, West, St Paul.

Daft, R.L., Sormunen, J. and Parks, D. 1988, Chief executive scanning, environmental characteristics, and company performance: An empirical study, *Strategic Management Journal*, 9, pp. 123–39.

Dallas, S. 1995, Rock bottom restaurants: Brewing up solid profits, *Business Week*, 22 May, p. 74.

Dalton, D.R. and Mesch, D.J. 1990, The impact of flexible scheduling on employee attendance and turnover, *Administrative Science Quarterly*, 35, pp. 370–87.

Daniels, J.D. and Radebaugh, L.H. 1989, *International Business*, Addison-Wesley, Reading.

Daniels, J.D. Pitts, R.A. and Tretter, M.J. 1985, Organizing for dual strategies of product diversity and international expansion, *Strategic Management Journal*, 6, p. 301.

Datamation 1988, Ocean freighters turn to high tech on the high seas, 1 March, pp. 25–6.

David, F.R. 1987, *Concepts of Strategic Management*, Merrill, Ohio.

David, F.R. 1989, How companies define their mission, *Long Range Planning*, 22, pp. 90–7.

Davidson, J.P. 1986, A way to work in concert, *Management World*, March, pp. 9–12.

Davies, C. 1995, Growing elderly population prompts rise in businesses catering to seniors, *Warfield's*, 14 July, pp. 9, 13.

Davies, E. 1998a, Management style on trial, *Fortune*, 11 May, pp. 30–2.

Davies, E. 1998b, Dad! Billy keeps suing me! *Fortune*, 20 July, pp. 16–18.

Davis, G.B. and Olson, M.H. 1985, *Management Information Systems: Conceptual Foundations, Structure, and Development*, McGraw-Hill, New York.

Davis, K. 1972, *Human Behavior at Work*, McGraw-Hill, New York.

Davis, K. 1980, Management communication and the grapevine, in S. Ferguson and S.D. Ferguson (eds), *Intercom: Readings in Organizational Communication*, Hayden, Rochelle Park.

Davis, K.R. and McKeown, P. G. 1984, *Quantitative Models for Management*, Kent, Boston.

Davis, S.M. and Lawrence, P. R. 1977, *Matrix*, Addison-Wesley, Reading.

Davis, T.R.V. and Luthans, F. 1980, A social learning approach to organizational behavior, *Academy of Management Review*, 5, pp. 281–90.

Davison III, W.N. and Worrell, D.I. 1988, The impact of announcements of corporate illegalities on shareholder returns, *Academy of Management Journal*, 31, pp. 195–200.

Dawson, C. 2000, Pioneer's uncharted territory, *Far Eastern Economic Review*, 9 March, pp. 48–9.

Dawson, D. 1988, Place for a store, *Marketing*, 7 April, pp. 35–6.

de Bono, E. 1968, *New Think*, Basic Books, New York.

De Cordoba, J. 1995, Mellon heir's labor of love for Haitians survives his death, *Wall Street Journal*, 30 Jan., pp. A1, A8.

Deal, T.E. and Kennedy, A.A. 1982, *Corporate Cultures: The Rites and Rituals of Corporate Life*, Addison-Wesley, Reading.

Deery, S., Plowman, D., Walsh, J. and Brown, M. 2001, *Industrial Relations: A Contemporary Analysis*, 2nd ed., McGraw Hill, Sydney.

Delbecq, A.L., Van de Ven, A.H. and Gustafson, D.H. 1975, *Group Techniques for Program Planning*, Scott, Foresman, Glenview.

Dembo, R.S., Chiarri, A., Martin, J.G. and Paradinas, L. 1990, Managing Hidroel?ctrica Espa–ola's hydroelectric power system, *Interfaces*, Jan.–Feb., pp. 115–35.

Demetrakes, P. 1995, Food plants: Apt to adapt, *Food Processing*, March, p. 52.

Deming, W.E. 1986, *Out of the Crisis*, M.I.T., Center for Advanced Engineering Study, Cambridge.

Dennis, A.R. and Valacich, J.S. 1994, Group, sub-group, and nominal group idea generation: New rules for a new media? *Journal of Management*, 20, pp. 723–36.

Denton, D.K. 1995, Process mapping trims cycle times, *HRM Magazine*, Feb., p. 56–9.

Dess, G.G. and Beard, D.W. 1984, Dimensions of organizational task environments, *Administrative Science Quarterly*, 29, pp. 52–73.

Dess, G.G., Gupta, A., Hennart, J-F. and Hill, C.W.L. 1995, Conducting and integrating strategy research at the international, corporate, and business levels: Issues and directions, *Journal of Management*, 21, pp. 357–93.

Detroit News 1995, Ford-Mazda to cut white-collar jobs, 23 May, p. B1.

Deutsch, C. 1999, Working wide of the mark, *Business Review Weekly*, 30 July, p. 48.

Deveny, K. 1986a, Bag those fries, squirt that ketchup, fry that fish, *Business Week*, 13 Oct., p. 86.

Deveny, K. 1986b, McWorld? *Business Week*, 13 Oct., pp. 79–86.

Dewar, R.D. and Simet, D.P. 1981, A level specific prediction of spans of control examining the effects of size, technology, and specialization, *Academy of Management Journal*, 24, pp. 5–24;

Dilworth, J.B. 1993, *Production and Operations Management*, McGraw-Hill, New York.

Discount Store News 1996, Expansion abroad outpaces domestic growth. The power retailers: Toys 'R' Us, 5 Feb., p. 52.

Dixon, J.R., Arnold, P., Heineke, J., Kim, J.S. and Mulligan, P. 1994, Business process reengineering: Improving in new strategic directions, *California Management Review*, 36, Spring, pp. 9–31.

Dobbins, G.H. and Platz, S.J. 1986, Sex differences in leadership: How real are they? *Academy of Management Review*, 11, pp. 118–27.

Dobbins, G.H. and Zaccaro, S.J. 1986, The effects of group cohesion and leader behavior on subordinate satisfaction, *Group and Organizational Studies*, 11, pp. 203–219.

Dodds, T. 2000, Singapore paddles in the global ocean, *Australian Financial Review*, Thurs. 27 April, p. 16.

Donaldson, T. and Preston, L.E. 1995, The stakeholder theory of the corporation: Concepts, evidence, and implications, *Academy of Management Review*, 20, pp. 65–91.

Donovan, J.J. 1994, *Business Re-engineering with Information Technology*, Prentice-Hall, Englewood Cliffs.

Dorfman, J.R. and Gupta, U. 1995, Choice positions for four black mask problems, *Wall Street Journal*, 3 Feb., pp. B1, B2.

Dow Jones Newswires 2000, Service comes with the wash, *Australian Financial Review*, 22 Feb., p. 13.

Dowling, P. J., Schuler, R.S. and Welch, D.E. 1995, *Human Resource Management*, Wadsworth, Belmont.

Dozier, J.B. and Miceli, M.P. 1985, Potential predictors of whistle-blowing: A prosocial behavior perspective, *Academy of Management Review*, 10, pp. 823–36.

Dressler, C. 1995, We've got to stop meeting like this, *Washington Post*, 31 Dec., p. H2.

Drucker, P. F. 1954, *The Practice of Management*, Harper, New York.

Drucker, P. F. 1967, *The Effective Executive*, Harper and Row, New York.

Drucker, P. F. 1974, *Management: Task Responsibilities and Practices*, Harper and Row.

Drucker, P. F. 1985, A prescription for entrepreneurial management, *Industry Week*, 29 April, pp. 33–4.

Dubashi, J. 1987, Through a glass lightly, *Financial World*, 19 May, pp. 20–9.

Dumaine, B. 1990, Who needs a boss? *Fortune*, 7 May, pp. 52–60.

Dumaine, B. 1992, Is big still good? *Fortune*, 20 April, pp. 50–60.

Dun's Business Month 1986, Citicorp loses top investment talent abroad, November, p. 21.

Duncan, R. 1979, What is the right organization structure? Decision tree analysis provides the answer, *Organizational Dynamics*, Winter, pp. 59–80.

Duncan, W.J. 1989, *Great Ideas in Management*, Jossey-Bass, San Francisco.

Dunegan, K.J. 1993, Framing, cognitive modes, and image theory: Toward an understanding of a glass half full, *Journal of Applied Psychology*, 78, pp. 491–503.

Dunkel, T. 1996, The front runners, *Working Woman*, April, pp. 30–5.

Dunkin, A. and O'Neal, M. 1987, Power retailers, *Business Week*, 21 Dec., pp. 86–92.

Dwyer, P. 1992, Air raid: British Air's bold global push, *Business Week*, 24 Aug., pp. 54–61.

Economist 1988, Japan makes a bid for the merger business, 17 Sept., pp. 85–6.

Economist 1992, Survey of the car industry, 17 Oct., pp. 13–15.

Economist 1993, The price is high, 14 Aug., p. 63.

Economist 1994, The war between the sexes, 5 March, pp. 80–1.

Economist 1995a, An ex-swordsman ploughs into the peace business, 23 Sept., p. 59.

Economist 1995b, The uncommon good, 19 Aug., p. 55.

Economist 1995c, The outing of outsourcing, 25 Nov., p. 27.

Economist 1996, In praise of the blue suit, 13 Jan., p. 59.

Economist Intelligence Unit 2002, Country monitor, 20 May, X, 19.

Eddy, W.B. 1985, *The Manager and the Working Group*, Praeger, New York.

Edgardio, P. 1994, A new high-tech dynasty? *Business Week*, 15 Aug., pp. 90–1.

Edmondson, G. 2003, This SUV can tow an entire carmaker, *BusinessWeek*, 22 December, pp. 22–3.

Eichenwald, K. 1992, Two sued by S.E.C. in bidding scandal at Salomon Bros., *New York Times*, 3 Dec., p. A1.

Eisen, A. 1978, The meanings and confusions of Weberian 'rationality', *British Journal of Sociology*, March, pp. 57–70.

Eisenhardt, K.M. and Brown, S.L. 1998, *Competing on the Edge*, Harvard Business School Press, Boston.

Elbing, A. 1978, *Behavioral Decisions in Organizations*, Scott, Foresman, Glenview.

Eldridge, E. 1996, Ben & Jerry's gears up for CEO search, *USA Today*, 30 Sept., p. 58.

Elegant, S. and Hibert, M. 2000, Tech Mecca, *Far Eastern Economic Review*, 16 March, p. 48–50.

Elkin, G. 1999, based on course work by Kesh Gilmore, University of Otago.

Elkin, G. with acknowledgment to the *Otago Daily Times*, 28 July 1997.

Elkin, G.R. 2000, adapted from Tremaine, M. Different ways of making a difference, in J. Sayers, and M. Tremayne (eds) 1994, *The Visions and the Reality: EEO in the New Zealand Workplace*, Dunmore Press, Palmerston North.

Eller, D. 1995, Motorola trains VPs to become growth leaders, *HRMagazine*, June, pp. 82–7.

Employment Relations Bill 2002—Part 1 Identifying the Legal Repercussions.

Ellis, R. 2003, A sensible e-mail strategy can still bring huge benefits, *Computer Weekly*, 30 September, p. 25.

Eng, P. M. 1995, Big business on the net? Not yet, *Business Week*, 26 June, pp. 100–1.

Engardio, P. 1988, The Peace Corps' new frontier, *Business Week*, 22 Aug., pp. 62–3.

Engardio, P. 1994, A hothouse of high-tech talent, *Business Week/21st Century Capitalism*, p. 126.

Epstein, S. 1998, *Constructive Thinking*, Praeger, Westport.

Erlick, J.C. 1995, IKEA bites the big apple, *HFN The Weekly Newspaper for the Home Furnishing Network*, 18 Sept., p. 6.

Ettorre, B. 1995, GE brings a new washer to life, *Management Review*, Sept., pp. 33–8.

Ettorre, B.A 1996, A conversation with Charles Handy, On the future of work and an end to the 'century of the organization', *Organizational Dynamics*, 25, 1, Summer, pp. 15–26.

Evans, J.R. and Lindsay, W.M. 1996, *The Management and Control of Quality*, West, Minneapolis/St Paul.

Evans, M.G. 1986, Organizational behavior: The central role of motivation, *Journal of Management*, 12, pp. 203–22.

Executive File: Hot Employment Issues 1996a, Whose mail is it anyway?, Smith Publishers, Nashville.

Executive File: Hot Employment Issues 1996b, Defensive driving on the information superhighway, July, Smith, Nashville.

Expat Web Site Association 2000, *Business Across Cultures*, www.expat.or.id/business/e-mail.html

Fabris, P. 1996, Ground control, *CIO*, 1 April, pp. 40–5.

Fagan, D. 2003, Reputations on trial, *Business Review Weekly*, 10–16 April, pp. 54–6.

Fagley, N.S. and Miller, P. M. 1987, The effects of decision framing on choice of risky vs. certain options, *Organizational Behavior and Human Decision Processes*, 39, pp. 264–77.

Fallon, J. 1994, Joan & David debuts London flagship, signature line, *Footwear News*, 12 Sept., p. 5.

Farnham, A. 1994, America's most admired company, *Fortune*, 7 Feb., pp. 50–4.

Featherstone, T. (ed.), 1999, *Shares*, Business Review Weekly Media, Hannanprint Victoria, Victoria.

Feldman, D.C. 1984, The development and enforcement of group norms, *Academy of Management Review*, 9, pp. 47–53.

Fenn, D. 1995a, Service teams that work, *INC.*, Aug., p. 99.

Fenn, D. 1995b, When to go pro, *INC. 500*, p. 72.

Ferguson, A. 2000, The next Internet peak looks like serious business, *Business Review Weekly*, 21 Feb., p. 34.

Ferguson, A. 2003a, Kunkel: So much more to do, *Business Review Weekly*, 10–16 April, pp. 38–41.

Fergusson, A. 2003b, Lloyd's, *Business Review Weekly*, 17–23 July, pp. 38–9.

Ferguson, A. and De Clercq, K. 1999. Boss cocky, *Business Review Weekly*, 5 Nov., p. 60–5.

Ferguson, D.H. and Selling, T.I. 1985, Probability analysis: A system for making better decisions, *Cornell H.R.A. Quarterly*, Aug., pp. 35–42.

Fiedler, F.E. 1967, *A Theory of Leadership Effectiveness*, McGraw-Hill, New York.

Fiedler, F.E. and Chemers, M.M. 1976, *Improving Leadership Effectiveness: The Leader Match Concepts*, Wiley, New York.

Fiedler, F.E. and Garcia, J.E. 1987, *New Approaches to Effective Leadership: Cognitive Resources and Organizational Performance*, Wiley, New York.

Fierman, J. 1987, The entrepreneurs: The best of their class, *Fortune*, 12 Oct., p. 144.

Fierman, J. 1990, Fidelity's secret: Faithful service, *Fortune*, 7 May, pp. 86–92

Fierman, J. 1995, Winning ideas from maverick managers, *Fortune*, 6 Feb., pp. 66–80.

Financial Times 1996, Lessons from doing business in Japan, 12 April, p. 10.

Finch, B.J. and Cox, J.F. 1988, Process-oriented production planning and control: Factors that influence system design, *Academy of Management Journal*, 31, pp. 123–53.

Finlay, P. 1994, *Introducing Decision Support Systems*, NCC Blackwell, Manchester.

Finn Jr, E.A. 1987, Megatort mania, *Forbes*, 1 June, pp. 114–20.

Finney, H.C. and Lesieur, H.R. 1982, A contingency theory of organizational crime, *Research in the Sociology of Organizations*, 1, pp. 255–99.

Finney, M.I. 1996, Global success rides on keeping top talent, *HR Magazine*, April, pp. 69–72.

Fisher, A.B. 1992, Welcome to the age of overwork, *Fortune*, 30 Nov., pp. 64–71.

Fisher, A.B. 1995, Making change stick, *Fortune*, 17 April, pp. 121–8.

Fisher, L.M. 1996, Chip index dips for 6th month in row, *New York Times*, 10 May, p. D3.

Fitzsimmons, J.A. and Fitzsimmons, M.J. 1994, *Service Management for Competitive Advantage*, McGraw-Hill, New York.

Flamholtz, E. 1979, Behavioral aspects of accounting/control systems, in S. Kerr (ed.), *Organizational Behavior*, Grid, Ohio.

Flamholtz, E.G. 1996, *Effective Management Control: Theory and Practice*, Kluwer, Boston.

Fleming, J.E. 1981, Public issues scanning, in L. Preston (ed.), *Research in Corporate Social Performance and Policy*, 3, JAI, Greenwich, pp. 154–74.

Flint, J. 1995, Can you tell applesauce from pickles, *Forbes*, 9 Oct., pp. 106–8.

Flint, J. with Heuslein, W. 1989, An urge to service, *Forbes*, 18 Sept., pp. 172–6.

Flynn, J. and Del Valle, C. 1992, Did Sears take its customers for a ride? *Business Week*, 3 Aug., pp. 24–5.

Flynn, J. and Nayeri, F. 1995, Continental divide over executive pay, *Business Week*, 3 July, pp. 40–1.

Foley, M.J. 1988, Post-MRPII: What comes next? *Datamation*, 1 Dec., pp. 24–36.

Fombrun, C. Tichy, N.M. and Devanna, M.A. 1984, *Strategic Human Resource Management*, Wiley, New York.

Footwear News 1995, The innovators: Designs aside, these are the preeminent minds and personalities that have spearheaded the footwear industry, 17 April, p. S36.

Forbes 1987a, It's tough up there, 13 July, pp. 145–60.

Forbes 1987b, The top 25, 15 June, p. 151.

Forbes 1995, Swatch out!, 5 June, pp. 150–2.

Ford, R.C. and Randolph, W.A. 1992, Cross-functional structures: A review and integration of matrix organization and project management, *Journal of Management*, 18, pp. 267–94.

Fortune 1995, A conversation with Roberto Goizueta and Jack Welch, 11 Dec., pp. 96–102.

Fortune 2003, The world's largest corporations, 148, 2, p. 106.

Fowler, E.M. 1988, Management participation by workers, *New York Times*, 27 Dec., p. D6.

Fox, C. 2003a, Clicking together, *AFR Boss*, October, pp. 26–7.

Fox, C. 2003b, The truth about buying and selling, *AFR Boss*, October, pp.30–6.

Frank, R. 1995, Coca-Cola is shedding its once-stodgy image with swift expansion, *Wall Street Journal*, 22 Aug., pp. A1, A5.

Frederick, W.C., Davis, K. and Post, J.E. 1992, *Business and Society: Corporate Strategy, Public Policy, Ethics*, McGraw-Hill, New York.

Frederickson, J.W. 1986, The strategic decision process and organizational structure, *Academy of Management Review*, 11, pp. 280–97.

Freeman, S.J. and Cameron, K.S. 1993, Organizational downsizing: A convergence and reorientation framework, *Organization Science*, Feb., pp. 10–29.

French, J.R.P. and Raven, B. 1959, The bases of social power, in D. Cartwright (ed.), *Studies in Social Power*, Institute for Social Research, Ann Arbor.

French, W.L. and Bell Jr, C.H. 1978, *Organization Development: Behavioral Interventions for Organizational Improvement*, Prentice-Hall, Englewood Cliffs.

Friedland, J. 1995, Did IBM unit bribe officials in Argentina to land a contract? *Wall Street Journal*, 11 Dec., pp. A1, A5.

Friedman, M. 1962, *Capitalism and Freedom*, University of Chicago, Chicago.

Friedman, S. 1981, Where employees go for information: Some surprises, *Administrative Management*, 42, pp. 72–3.

Fry, L.W. 1976, The maligned F. W. Taylor: A reply to many of his critics, *Academy of Management Review*, 1, pp. 124–9.

Fry, L.W. 1982, Technological-structure research: Three critical issues, *Academy of Management Journal*, 25, pp. 532–52.

Fryer, B. 2003, What's the story, *AFR Boss*, July, pp. 61–3.

Fuchsberg, G. 1992, Total quality is termed only partial success, *Wall Street Journal*, 1 Oct., pp. B1, B9.

Fuhrman, P. 1988, The workers' friend, *Forbes*, 21 March, pp. 124–8.

Fuhrman, P. 1992, Jewelry for the wrist, *Forbes*, 23 Nov., pp. 173–8.

Fuld, L.M. 1988, *Monitoring the Competition*, Wiley, New York.

Fuld, L.M. 1989, How to get the scoop on your competition, *Working Woman*, Jan., pp. 39–42.

Funk, D. 1996, Insurance industry on rebound after recent wave of consolidations, *Warfield's Business Record*, 3 June, pp. 9, 12.

Gabor, A. 1994, The making of a new-age manager, *Working Woman*, Dec., pp. 18–22.

Gaither, N. 1986, Historical development of operations research, in D.A. Wren and J.A. Pearce II (eds), *Papers Dedicated to the Development of Modern Management*, Academy of Management.

Galbraith, J.K. 1962, *The New Industrial State*, University of Chicago, Chigago.

Galbraith, J.K. 1975, *The Age of Uncertainty*, Houghton-Mifflin, Boston.

Galbraith, J.R. 1977, *Organization Design*, Addison-Wesley, Reading.

Galbraith, J.R. 1982, Designing the innovating organization, *Organizational Dynamics*, 10, Winter, pp. 5–25.

Galbraith, J.R. 1995, *Designing Organizations*, Jossey-Bass, San Francisco.

Galbraith, J.R. and Kazanjian, R.K. 1986, *Strategy Implementation: Structure, System, and Process*, West, St Paul.

Gallagher C.A. and Watson, H.J. *Quantitative Methods for Business Decisions*, McGraw-Hill, New York.

Galloway, P. 1990, Counterattack, *Chicago Tribune*, 19 Dec., p. C1.

Gallupe, R.B., Cooper, W.H., Gris?, M-L. and Bastianutti, L.M. 1994, Blocking electronic brainstorms, *Journal of Applied Psychology*, 79, pp. 77–86.

Gargan, E.A. 1994, For a furniture maker, a taste of a global future, *New York Times*, 17 March, pp. C1, C3.

Garland, S.B. 1998, Finally, a corporate tip sheet on sexual harassment, *Business Week*, 13 July, p. 39.

Garran, R. 2000, Hackers breach treasury site, *Australian*, 20 March, p. 3.

Garvin, D.A. 1987, Competing on the eight dimensions of quality, *Harvard Business Review*, Nov.–Dec., pp. 101–9.

Gatewood, R.D. and Carroll, A.B. 1991, Assessment of ethical performance of organization members: A conceptual framework, *Academy of Management Review*, 16, pp. 667–90.

Gavin, M.B., Green, S.G. and Fairhurst, G.T. 1995, Managerial control strategies for poor performance over time and the impact on subordinate reactions, *Organizational Behavior and Human Decision Processes*, 63, pp. 207–21.

Geber, B. 1986, Quality circles: The second generation, *Training*, Dec., pp. 54–61.

Gelbspan, R. 1987, Keeping a close watch on electronic work monitoring, *Washington Post*, 13 Dec., p. H4.

Gelfond, S.M. 1988, The computer age dawns in the corner office, *Business Week*, 27 June, pp. 84–6.

Genasci, L. 1995, That was the workweek that was, *Washington Post*, 15 Oct., p. H4.

Gentile, M.C. 1994, *Differences That Work: Organizational Excellence Through Diversity*, Harvard Business School Press, Boston.

George Jr, C.S. 1972, *The History of Management Thought*, Prentice-Hall, Englewood Cliffs.

George, J.M. 1997, AIDS/AIDS-related complex, in L. Peters, B. Greer, and S. Youngblood (eds), *The Blackwell Encyclopedic Dictionary of Human Resource Management*, Blackwell, Oxford.

Gerrity, T.P. and Rockart, J.F. 1986, End-user computing: Are you a leader or a laggard? *Sloan Management Review*, Summer, pp. 25–34.

Gersick, C.J.G. 1991, Revolutionary change theories: A multilevel exploration of the punctuated equilibrium paradigm, *Academy of Management Review*, 16, pp. 10–36.

Gibbons, P. 2000, Privacy: Senate searchlight on web, *Business Review Weekly*, 4 August.

Gibbs, B. 1994, The effect of environment and technology on managerial roles, *Journal of Management*, 20, pp. 581–604.

Gibson, R. 1994, General Mills tries to cook up fix for restaurant unit, *Wall Street Journal*, 16 Nov., p. B4.

Gilbreth, L.M. 1921, *The Psychology of Management*, Sturgis and Walton, 1914, reissued by Macmillan, New York.

Gittler, H. 1985, Decisions are only as good as those who can change them, *Wall Street Journal*, 7 Oct., p. 22.

Glain, S. 1995, Samsung is spending billions to diversify, *Wall Street Journal*, 10 Feb., p. B6.

Glenn, E.C. and Pood, E.A. 1989, Listening self-inventory, *Supervisory Management*, Jan., pp. 12–15.

Goggins, W.C. 1974, How the multidimensional structure works at Dow Corning, *Harvard Business Review*, Jan.–Feb.

Goldbaum, E. 1988, How quality programs win respect and get results, *Chemical Week*, 5 Oct., pp. 30–3.

Goldhaber, G.M. 1993, *Organizational Communication*, Brown, Iowa.

Goldsmith, C. 1995, British Airways' new CEO envisions a marriage of travel and amusement, *Wall Street Journal*, 6 Nov., p. B11.

Goleman, D. 1998, *Working with Emotional Intelligence*, Bantam Books, New York.

Golembiewski R.T. and Proehl, C.W. 1978, A survey of the empirical literature on flexible workhours: Character and consequences of a major innovation, *Academy of Management Review*, 3, pp. 837–53.

Gome, A. 1999, The brand that fell to earth, *Business Review Weekly*, 11 June, pp. 98–103.

Gome, A. 2000, A counsel of elders, *Business Review Weekly*, 24 March, pp. 70–3.

Gome, A. 2003a, Head start, *Business Review Weekly*, 11–17 September, pp. 56–7.

Gome, A. 2003b, Like pulling teeth, *Business Review Weekly*, 14–20 August, pp. 58–9.

Gome, A. 2003c, China demands service, *Business Review Weekly*, 10–16 April, pp. 48–50.

Gome, A. 2003d, Profits grow in fresh pastures, *Business Review Weekly*, 27 March2 April, p. 54.

Gome, A. 2003e, Russian raider, *Business Review Weekly*, August 21-27, p.58.

Gome, A. 2003f, Corks pop in China, *Business Review Weekly*, 17–23 April, p. 51.

Gomez-Mejia, L.R., McCann, J.E. and Page, R.C. 1985, The structure of managerial behaviors and rewards, *Industrial Relations*, Winter, pp. 147–54.

Gomory, R.E. 1989, From the ladder of science to the product development cycle, *Harvard Business Review*, Nov.–Dec., pp. 99–105.

Goodling, R.Z. and Wagner III, J.A. 1985, A meta-analytic review of the relationship between size and performance: The productivity and efficiency of organizations and their subunits, *Administrative Science Quarterly*, 30, pp. 462–81.

Goodman, P. S., Ravlin, E. and Schminke, M. 1987, Understanding groups in organizations, *Research in Organizational Behavior*, 9, pp. 121–73.

Goodman, P.S., Ravlin, E.C. and Argote, L. 1986, Current thinking about groups: Setting the stage for new ideas, in P.S. Goodman and associates (eds), *Designing Effective Work Groups*, Jossey-Bass, San Francisco.

Goodpaster, K.E. and Matthews Jr, J.B. 1982, Can a corporation have a conscience? *Harvard Business Review*, Jan.–Feb., pp. 134–41.

Gordon, J. 1987, Learn how to listen, *Fortune*, 17 Aug., pp. 107–8.

Gordon, J. 1992, Work teams—how far have they come? *Training*, 29, pp. 59–65.

Gordon, J.R. 1987, *A Diagnostic Approach to Organizational Behavior*, Allyn and Bacon, Boston.

Gordon, J.R. 1996, *Organizational Behavior: A Diagnostic Approach*, Allyn and Bacon, Boston.

Gordon, S.R. and Gordon, J.R. 1996, *Information Systems: A Managerial Approach*, Dryden, Fort Worth.

Gosling, J. and Mintzberg, H. 2004, The five minds of a manager, *The Weekend Australian Financial Review*, 31 December–4 January, pp. 64–5.

Gourlay, R. 1994, Back to basics on the factory floor, *Financial Times*, 4 Jan., p. 12.

Graeff, C.L. 1983, The situational leadership theory: A critical view, *Academy of Management Review*, 8, pp. 285–91.

Grandori, A. 1984, A prescriptive contingency view of organizational decision making, *Administrative Science Quarterly*, 29, pp. 192–209.

Grant, R.A., Higgins, C.A. and Irving, R.H. 1988, Computerized performance monitors: Are they costing you customers? *Sloan Management Review*, Spring, pp. 39–45.

Gray, B. and Ariss, S.S. 1985, Politics and strategic change across organizational life cycles, *Academy of Management Review*, 10, pp. 707–23.

Gray, D.H. 1986, Uses and misuses of strategic planning, *Harvard Business Review*, Jan.–Feb., pp. 89–97.

Green, H. 2003a, Companies that really get it, *BusinessWeek*, 25 August, p. 102.

Green, H. 2003b, Bugging the world, *BusinessWeek*, 25 August, pp.65–6.

Green, S.G. and Welsh, M.A. 1988, Cybernetics and dependence: Reframing the control concept, *Academy of Management Review*, 13, pp. 287–301.

Greenberger, D.B. and Strasser, S. 1986, Development and application of a model of personal control in organizations, *Academy of Management Review*, 11, pp. 164–77.

Greene, C.N. 1979, Questions of causation in the path-goal theory of leadership, *Academy of Management Journal*, 22, pp. 22–41.

Greenwald, A.G. and Banaji, M. 1995, Implicit social cognition: Attitudes, self-esteem, and stereotypes, *Psychological Review*, 102, pp. 4–27.

Greenwood, R.G. 1981, Management by objectives: As developed by Peter Drucker, assisted by Harold Smiddy, *Academy of Management Review*, 6, pp. 225–30.

Greenwood, R.G. and Wrege, C.D. 1986, The Hawthorne studies, in D.A. Wren and J.A. Pearce II (eds), *Papers Dedicated to the Development of Modern Management*, Academy of Management.

Greenwood, R.G., Bolton, A.A. and Greenwood, R.A. 1983, Hawthorne a half century later: Relay assembly participants remember, *Journal of Management*, 9, pp. 217–31.

Greising, D. 1994, Quality: How to make it pay, *Business Week*, 8 Aug., pp. 54–8.

Gremillion, L.L. and Pyburn, P.J. 1988, *Computers and Information Systems in Business: An Introduction*, McGraw-Hill, New York.

Griffin, C.E. 2000, Bad words, *Entrepreneur Magazine*, February, p. 34.

Griffin, R.W. 1991, Effects of work redesign on employee perceptions, attitudes, and behaviors: A long-term investigation, *Academy of Management Journal*, 34, pp. 425–35.

Griffiths, J. 1994, Europe's manufacturing quality and productivity still lag far behind Japan's, *Financial Times*, 4 Nov., p. 11.

Gross, N. 1989, A wave of ideas, drop by drop, *Business Week*, Innovation 1989 issue, 16 June, pp. 22–30.

Grossman, R.J. 1996, Damaged, downsized souls, *HR Magazine*, May, pp. 54–62.

Grove, A. 1993, How Intel makes spending pay off, *Fortune*, 22 Feb., pp. 56–61.

Guest, R.H. 1956, Of time and the foreman, *Personnel*, 32, pp. 478–86.

Gupta, A.K. and Govindarajan, V. 1984, Build, hold, harvest: Converting strategic intentions into reality, *Journal of Business Strategy*, March, pp. 34–47.

Gupta, U. 1995, Starting out; how much? Figuring the correct amount of capital for starting a business can be a tough balancing act, *Wall Street Journal*, 22 May, p. R7.

Gupte, P. 1988, Merge in haste, repent in leisure, *Forbes*, 22 Aug., p. 85.

Guyon, J. 1988a, GE to acquire Borg-Warner's chemical lines, *Wall Street Journal*, 17 June, 1, p. 3.

Guyon, J. 1988b, GE chairman Welch, though much praised, starts to draw critics, *Wall Street Journal*, 4 Aug., pp. 1, 8.

Guzzo, R.A. 1988, Productivity research: Reviewing psychological and economic perspectives, in J.P. Campbell, R.J. Campbell, and associates, *Productivity in Organizations*, Jossey-Bass, San Francisco.

Guzzo, R.A. and Dickson, M.W. 1996, Teams in organizations: Recent research on performance and effectiveness, *Annual Review of Psychology*, 47, pp. 307–38.

Hack, M. 1989, Harvard project manager serves pros, casual users, *InfoWorld*, 30 Jan., pp. 54–5.

Hackman, J.R. 1987, The design of work teams, in J.W. Lorsch (ed.), *Handbook of Organizational Behavior*, Prentice-Hall, Englewood Cliffs.

Hackman, J.R. and Oldham, G.R. 1980, *Work Redesign*, Addison-Wesley, Reading.

Hackman, J.R. and Wagemen, R. 1995, Total quality management: Empirical, conceptual, and practical issues, *Administrative Science Quarterly*, 40, pp. 309–42.

Haefele, J.W. 1962, *Creativity and Innovation*, Reinhold, New York.

Hafner, K.M. 1988, Is your computer secure, *Business Week*, 1 Aug., pp. 64–72.

Haigh, G. 2003, Grow your own, *Business Review Weekly*, 11–17 September, pp. 66–7.

Hall, E.T. 1959, *The Silent Language*, Doubleday, New York.

Hall, E.T. 1976, *Beyond Culture*, Anchor Press/Double Day, Garden City.

Hall, R.H. 1996, *Structures, Processes, and Outcomes*, Prentice-Hall, Englewood Cliffs.

Hambrick, D.C., MacMillan, I.C. and Day, D.L. 1982, Strategic attributes and performance in the BCG matrix: A PIMS-based analysis of industrial product businesses, *Academy of Management Journal*, 25, pp. 510–31.

Hamel, G. and Välikangas, L. 2003, The resilient corporation, *AFR Boss*, November, pp.56–61.

Hamilton, J.O'C. 1987, Why rivals are quaking as Nordstroms heads east, *Business Week*, 15 June, pp. 99–100.

Hamm, S. 2003, Just turn on the data, *Business Week*, 25 August, pp. 63–4.

Hammer, M. and Champy, J. 1993, *Reengineering the Corporation*, Harper Business, New York.

Hamner, W.C. 1991, Reinforcement theory and contingency management in organizational settings, in R.M. Steers and L.W. Porter (eds), *Motivation and Work Behavior*, McGraw-Hill, New York.

Haney, W.V. (ed.), 1986, *Communication and Interpersonal Relations*, Irwin, Homewood.

Hanley, M. 2003, Way to go, *AFR Boss*, October, pp. 64–7.

Hannah, J. 1996, GM workers agree to end strike, *Bryan–College Station Eagle*, 23 March, p. A12.

Hannan, M.T. and Freeman, J. 1977, The population ecology of organizations, *American Journal of Sociology*, 82, pp. 929–64.

Hanvey, M. 1999, Web site steers trucker's business, *Business Review Weekly*, 21 May, p. 51.

Haour, G. 1996, Environmental concerns: Are they a threat or an opportunity? *Financial Times*, 15 March, p. 4.

Harcourt, H. 2003, Its too early to tell..., *Business Review Weekly*, 27 November–3 December, p. 67.

Harcourt, J., Richerson, V. and Wattier, M. 1991, A national study of middle managers' assessment of organizational communication quality, *Journal of Business Communication*, 28, pp. 348–65.

Hardy, Q. 1999, Ask ehow to turn knowledge into power, *Business Review Weekly*, 8 Oct., p. 55.

Harley, R. 2003a, Re-imagining the mall, *AFR Boss*, October, pp. 40–3.

Harmsen, P. 2000, Going solo pays off for foreign firms in China, *Business Times*, 11 Jan., p. 10.

Harrigan, K.R. 1985, Vertical integration and corporate strategy, *Academy of Management Journal*, 28, pp. 397–425.

Harris, C.L. and Foust, D. 1987, An electronic pipeline that's changing the way America does business, *Business Week*, 3 Aug., pp. 80–2.

Harrison, E.F. 1981, *The Managerial Decision-Making Process*, Houghton Mifflin, Boston.

Harvard Business Review 1985, Managing innovation: Controlled chaos, May–June, pp. 73–84.

Harvard Business School Press 1995, *Mary Parker Follett–Prophet of Management: A Celebration of Writings from the 1920s*, Boston.

Harvey, M.G. 1995, The impact of dual-career families on international relocations, *Human Resource Management Review*, 3, pp. 223–44.

Hater, J.J. and Bass, B.M. 1988, Superiors' evaluations and subordinates' perceptions of transformational and transactional leadership, *Journal of Applied Psychology*, 73, pp. 695–702.

Haveman, H.A. 1992, Between a rock and a hard place: Organizational change and performance under conditions of fundamental environmental transformation, *Administrative Science Quarterly*, 37, pp. 48–75.

Hayes, M.A. 1973, Nonverbal communication: Expression without word, in R.C. Huseman, C.M. Logue, and D.L. Freshley (eds), *Readings in Interpersonal and Organizational Communication*, Holbrook, Boston.

Hays, L. 1995a, IBM's helmsman indicates that bulk of layoffs is over, *Wall Street Journal*, 6 Jan., p. B3.

Hays, L. 1995b, The outsider's new in crowd: Five IBM lifers, *Wall Street Journal*, 12 Jan., p. B1, B8.

Hays, L. 1995c, IBM chief unveils top-level shake-up, consolidating sales arm, software line, *Wall Street Journal*, 10 Jan., p. B6.

Head, A. 1999, Wake in fright on January 1, *Business Review Weekly*, 22 Oct., p. 62.

Head, A. 2000, Small business should log on and write off, *Business Review Weekly*, 24 March, p. 56.

Heathcote, A. and Kirby, J. 2003, India is keen for more jobs, *Business Review Weekly*, 1–7 May, p. 22.

Heartly, J.R. 1992, *Concurrent Engineering*, Productivity Press, Cambridge.

Hellweg, S., Freiberg, K. and Smith, A. 1984, The pervasiveness and impact of electronic communication technologies in organizations: A survey of major American corporations, paper presented at a meeting of the Speech Communication Association, Chicago.

Helm, L. and Edid, M. 1994, Life on the line: Two auto workers who are worlds apart, *Business Week*, 30 Sept., pp. 76–8.

Hersey, P. and Blanchard, K.H. 1988, *Management of Organizational Behavior: Utilizing Human Resources*, Prentice-Hall, Englewood Cliffs.

Herzberg, F. 1966, *Work and the Nature of Man*, World Publishing, Ohio.

Heskett, J.L. 1986, *Managing in the Service Economy*, Harvard Business School, Boston.

Hiebert, M. 2000, Two way vision, *Far Eastern Economic Review*, 17 Feb., p. 51–2.

Hildebrant, H.W., Bon, F.A., Miller, E.L. and Swinyard, A.W. 1982, An executive appraisal of courses which best prepare one for general management, *Journal of Business Communication*, Winter, pp. 5–15.

Hill, C.W.L. 1994, *International Business: Competing in the Global Economy*, Irwin, Homewood.

Hill, C.W.L. 1995, The computer industry: The new industry of industries, in C.W.L. Hill and G.R. Jones (eds) *Strategic Management: An Integrated Approach*, Houghton Mifflin, Boston.

Hill, C.W.L. 1997, *International Business*, Irwin, Homewood.

Hill, C.W.L. and Jones, G.R. 1997, *Strategic Management: An Integrated Approach*, Houghton Mifflin, Boston.

Hill, S. 2003, Korean film industry takes on Hollywood, *Business Asia*, 11, 9, pp. 22–5.

Hinton, T. and Schaeffer, W. 1998, *Customer-Focused Quality: What to Do on Monday Morning*, Prentice-Hall, Englewood Cliffs.

Hirsch, J.S. 1996, A high-tech system for sending the mail unfolds at Fidelity, *Wall Street Journal*, 20 March, pp. A1, A5.

Hodgetts, R.M. and Luthans, F. 1991, *International Management*, McGraw-Hill, New York.

Hoerr, J. 1988, Work teams can rev up paper-pushers, too, *Business Week*, 28 Nov., pp. 64–72.

Hoerr, J. 1989, The payoff from teamwork, *Business Week*, 10 July, pp. 56–62.

Hof, R. 2003a, Why tech will bloom again, *BusinessWeek*, 25 August, pp. 36–41.

Hof, R. 2003b, The quest for the next big thing, *BusinessWeek*, 25 August, pp. 58–62.

Hof, R.D. 1992, From dinosaur to gazelle, *Business Week/Reinventing America*, 23 Oct., p. 65.

Hof, R.D. 1995a, How to kick the mainframe habit, *Business Week*, 26 June, pp. 102–4.

Hof, R.D. 1995b, Intel: Far beyond the Pentium, *Business Week*, 20 Feb., pp. 88–90.

Hofer, C.W. and Schendel, D. 1978, *Strategy Formulation: Analytical Concepts*, West, St Paul.

Hofstede, G. 1980, Motivation, leadership, and organization: Do American theories apply abroad? *Organizational Dynamics*, Summer, pp. 42–63.

Hofstede, G. 1984, The cultural relativity of the quality of life concept, *Academy of Management Review*, 9, pp. 389–98.

Hollinger, R.D. and Clark, J.P. 1983, *Theft by Employees*, Lexington Books, Lexington.

Hollingshead, A.B. and McGrath, J.E. 1995, Computer-assisted groups: A critical review of the empirical research, in R.A. Guzzo and E. Salas, *Team Effectiveness in Organizations*, Jossey-Bass, San Francisco.

Holloman, C.R. 1968, Leadership and head: There is a difference, *Personnel Administration*, July–Aug., pp. 38–44.

Holloran, T.J. and Burn, J.E. 1986, United Airlines station manpower planning system, *Interfaces*, Jan.–Feb., pp. 39–50.

Holmes, S. 1995, Politics key to Boeing sales in China? *Seattle Times*, 10 April, p. A1.

Holmes, S.L. 1978, Adapting corporate structure for social responsiveness, *Business Horizons*, Fall, pp. 47–54.

Holmqvist, M. 1999, Learning in imaginary organisations: Creating interorganizational knowledge, *Journal of Organizational Change Management*, 12, 5, pp. 419–38.

Homans, G. 1950, *The Human Group*, Harcourt, Brace, New York.

Hooper, N. 2003, Independents' day, *AFR Boss*, October, pp. 54–7.

Hooper, N. 2004, Call me irresistible, *AFRBoss*, January, pp. 38–42.

Horton, N.R. 1988, Restructurings and dismemberments, *Management Review*, March, pp. 5–6.

Hostage, G.M. 1975, Quality control in a service business, *Harvard Business Review*, July–Aug., pp. 98–106.

Houghton, J. 1987, For better quality, listen to the workers, *New York Times*, Forum, 18 Oct., section 3, p. 3.

House, R.J. and Mitchell, T.R. 1974, Path-goal theory of leadership, *Journal of Contemporary Business*, 3, pp. 81–97.

House, R.J. and Singh, J.V. 1987, Organizational behavior: Some new directions for I/O psychology, *Annual Review of Psychology*, 38, pp. 669–718.

Howarth, B. 1999, Information is the key, *Business Review Weekly*, 8 Oct., p. 90.

Howarth, B. 2000, E-commerce dabblers create a new market, *Business Review Weekly*, 7 April, p. 12.

Howarth, B, 2003, Remember the customer, *AFR Boss*, November, p. 49.

Howarth, B. 2003a, To market or to manage, *Business Review Weekly*, 21–7 August, pp. 60–2.

Howarth, B. 2003b, A new bloom, *Business Review Weekly*, July 17–23, p. 55.

Howarth, B. 2003c, MasterCard's big swipe, *Business Review Weekly*, April 24–30, p. 86.

Howarth, B. and Thomson, J. 2003, Nostalgia drive, *Business Review Weekly*, 14–20 August, p. 72–3.

Howell, J.M. and Frost, P. J. 1989, A laboratory study of charismatic leadership, *Organizational Behavior and Human Decision Processes*, 43, pp. 243–69.

HRMagazine 1994, Maverick: The success story behind the world's most unusual workplace, April, pp. 88–9.

Huber, G.B. 1993, *Managerial Decision Making*, Scott, Foresman, Glenview.

Hull, F.M. and Collins, P.D. 1987, High-technology batch production systems: Woodward's missing type, *Academy of Management Journal*, 30, pp. 786–97.

Huse, E.F. and Cummings, T.G. 1985, *Organization Development and Change*, West, St Paul.

Huseman, R.C. and Miles, E.W. 1988, Organizational communication in the information age: Implications of computer-based systems, *Journal of Management*, 14, pp. 181–204.

Hwang, S. 1992, Getting personal, *Wall Street Journal*, 6 April, p. R19.

Hymowitz, C. 1988, A survival guide to the office meeting, *Wall Street Journal*, 21 June, p. 41.

Hymowitz, C. 1995, How a dedicated mentor gave momentum to a woman's career, *Wall Street Journal*, 24 April, p. B1, B3.

Ihlwan, M. 2003a, Who needs the Chaebol anyway, *BusinessWeek*, 8 September, pp. 24–5.

Ihlwan, M. 2003b, Monsters on the high seas, *Business Week*, 13 October, p. 30.

Ihrcke, J. 2000, The key to corporate success, *Economic Bulletin*, Jan., pp. 13–16.

Ilgen, D.R. and Klein, H.J. 1988, Individual motivation and performance: Cognitive influences on effort and choice, in J.P. Campbell, R.J. Campbell, and associates, *Productivity in Organizations*, Jossey-Bass, San Francisco.

INC. 1989, Thriving on order, Dec., pp. 47–62.

INC. 1992, Can you afford to be ethical?, Dec., p. 16.

INC. 1996, Apprentices make the grade, Feb., p. 98.

Ingersoll, B. 1989, Generic-drug scandal at the FDA is linked to deregulation drive, *Wall Street Journal*, 13 Sept., pp. A1, A14.

Ingrassia, P. and Stertz, B.A. 1988, Ford's strong sales raise agonizing issue of additional plants, *Wall Street Journal*, 26 Oct., pp. A1, A10.

Inkpen, A. 1995, *The Management of International Joint Ventures*, Routledge, London.

Irvine, V.B. 1970, Budgeting: Functional analysis and behavioral implications, *Cost and Management*, March–April, pp. 6–16.

Ivancevich, J.M. and Lyon, H.L. 1977, The shortened workweek: A field experiment, *Journal of Applied Psychology*, 62, pp. 34–7.

Jackofsky, E.F., Slocum Jr, J.W. and McQuaid, S.J. 1988, Cultural values and the CEO: Alluring companions? *Academy of Management Executive*, 11, pp. 39–49.

Jackson, J.M. and Harkins, S.G. 1985, Equity in effort: An explanation of the social loafing effect, *Journal of Personality and Social Psychology*, 49, pp. 1199–206.

Jackson, L. 1990, Steel zeal, *Detroit Free Press*, 12 March, pp. 1E, 5E.

Jackson, S.E. and Associates 1992, *Diversity in the Workplace: Human Resources Initiatives*, Guilford Press, New York.

Jackson, S.E., May, K.E. and Whitney, K. 1995, Understanding the dynamics of diversity in decision-making teams, in R.A. Guzzo and E. Salas (eds), *Team Effectiveness and Decision Making in Organizations*, Jossey-Bass, San Francisco.

Jacob, R. 1992, The search for the organization of tomorrow, *Fortune*, 18 May, pp. 93–4.

Jacob, R. 1995a, Corporate reputations, *Fortune*, 6 March, pp. 54–64.

Jacob, R. 1995b, How one red hot retailer wins customer loyalty, *Fortune*, 10 July, pp. 72–9.

Jaffe, A.M. 1994, At Texaco, the diversity skeleton still stalks the halls, *New York Times*, 11 Dec., sec. 3, p. 5.

Jago, A.G. 1982, Leadership: Perspectives in theory and research, *Management Science*, 28, pp. 315–36.

James, D. 1999, We are empowering you to deal with change–better get used to it, *Business Review Weekly*, 8 Feb., p. 55–6.

James, D. 2000, Build a funky business with attitude, *Business Review Weekly*, 31 March, p. 70–4.

James, D. 2003a, Middle-class kingdom, *Business Review Weekly*, 10–16 April, pp. 72–4.

James, D. 2003b, Charisma v. performance, *Business Review Weekly*, 17–23 April, pp. 72–4.

James, D. 2003c, The challenge for China, *Business Review Weekly*, 11–17 December.

James, D. 2003d, Home ground advantage, *Business Review Weekly*, 11–17 December, pp. 64–7.

Janis, I.L. 1982, *Groupthink*, Houghton Mifflin, Boston.

Jaworski, B.J., Stathakopoulos, V. and Krishnan, H.S. 1993, Control combinations in marketing: Conceptual framework and empirical evidence, *Journal of Marketing*, 57, pp. 57–69.

Jay, A. 1976, How to run a meeting, *Harvard Business Review*, March–April, pp. 120–34.

Jefferson, D.J. 1990, Dream to nightmare: When growth gets out of hand, *Wall Street Journal*, 23 Jan., p. B2.

Jegers, M. 1991, Prospect theory and the risk-return relation: Some Belgian evidence, *Academy of Management Journal*, 34, pp. 215–25.

Jelinek, M. and Adler, N.J. 1988, Women: World-class managers for global competition, *Academy of Management Executive*, 11, pp. 11–19.

Jereski, L. 1988, I'm a bad manager, *Forbes*, 8 Feb., pp. 134–5.

Jerkovsky, W. 1983, Functional management in matrix organizations, *IEEE Transactions on Engineering Management*, May, pp. 89–97.

Jiang Jingen 1999, First shots fired in cross-straits war of the Web, *China Daily*, 14 Aug., p. 2.

Jodice, D.A. 1980, Sources of change in third world regimes for direct investment, *International Organization*, Spring, pp. 177–206.

Johns, G. 1996, *Organizational Behavior*, HarperCollins, New York.

Johnston, W.B. 1991, Global work force 2000: The new world labor market, *Harvard Business Review*, March–April, pp. 115–27.

Jones, D. 1995, On-line surfing costs firms time and money, *USA Today*, 8 Dec., pp. A1, A2.

Jones, G.R. 1998, *Organizational Theory: Text and Cases*, Addison-Wesley, Reading.

Jones, G.R. and Hill, C.W.L. 1988, Transaction cost analysis of strategy–structure choice, *Strategic Management Journal*, 9, pp. 159–72.

Jones, G.R., George, J.M. and Hill, C.W.L. 2000, *Contemporary Management*, McGraw-Hill, New York.

Jones, J.E. and Pfeiffer, J.W. 1975, *The 1975 Annual Handbook for Group Facilitators*, University Associates, La Jolla.

Jones, P. 2003, Crowded kingdom, *Business Review Weekly*, 14–20 August, pp. 34–8.

Joyce, W.F. 1986, Matrix organization: A social experiment, *Academy of Management Journal*, 29, pp. 536–61.

Judge, P. C. 1996, Is it rainforest crunch time? *Business Week*, 15 July, pp. 70–1.

Juran, J.M. 1988, *Juran on Planning for Quality*, Free Press, New York.

Kadlec, D. 1996, Here's the scoop on Ben & Jerry's, *USA Today*, 31 Jan., p. 4B.

Kanter, R.M. 1982, The middle manager as innovator, *Harvard Business Review*, July–Aug., pp. 95–105.

Kanter, R.M. 1983, *The Change Masters*, Simon and Schuster, New York.

Kanter, R.M. 1988, When a thousand flowers bloom: Structural, collective, and social conditions for innovation in organizations, *Research in Organizational Behavior*, 10, pp. 169–211.

Kanter, R.M. 1989, The new managerial work, *Harvard Business Review*, Nov.–Dec., pp. 85–92.

Kaplan, R.E., Drath, W.H. and Kofodimos, J.R. 1984, *Power and Getting Criticism*, Center for Creative Leadership Issues and Observations.

Kaplan, R.S. 2002, Lead and Manage Your Organization with the Balanced Scorecard, *Balanced Scorecard Report*, July–August, Harvard Business School Publishing Corporation.

Karau, S.J. and Williams, K.D. 1995, Social loafing: Research findings, implications, and future directions, *Current Directions in Psychological Science*, 4, October, pp. 134–40.

Karpin, D. 1995, *Enterprising Nation: Renewing Australia's Managers to Meet the Challenges of the Asia-Pacific Century*, AGPS, Canberra.

Kast, F.E. and Rosenzweig, J.E. 1972, General systems theory: Applications for organization and management, *Academy of Management Journal*, 15, pp. 447–65.

Kast, F.E. and Rosenzweig, J.E. 1974, *Organization and Management: A Systems Approach*, McGraw-Hill, New York.

Katz, D. and Kahn, R.L. 1978, *The Social Psychology of Organizations*, Wiley, New York.

Katz, R.L. 1974, Skills of an effective administrator, *Harvard Business Review*, Sep.–Oct., pp. 90–102.

Katz, S. 1982, An about-face in TI's culture, *Business Week*, 5 July, p. 77.

Kaufman, J. 1995, How Cambodians came to control California doughnuts, *Wall Street Journal*, 22 Feb., pp. A1, A8.

Kavanagh, J. 1996, Postings overseas can end up as costly affairs, *Weekend Australian*, 14–15 Sept., p. 63.

Kavanagh, J. 2003, A little Homebush in Huangpu, *Business Review Weekly*, December 11–17, pp. 22–4.

Kearns, L. 1995, Australia: Imperial chairman, *Age* (Melbourne), 28 Jan., p. C1.

Keinan, G. 1987, Decision making under stress: Scanning of alternatives under controllable and uncontrollable threats, *Journal of Personality and Social Psychology*, 52, pp. 639–44.

Keller, J.J. 1990, Software glitch at AT&T cuts off phone service for millions, *Wall Street Journal*, 16 Jan., pp. B1, B4.

Keller, J.J. 1995, High anxiety: AT&T breakup jolts managers, *Wall Street Journal*, 21 Nov., pp. B1, B10.

Kelley, B. 1994, A day in the life of a card shark, *Journal of Business Strategy*, Spring, pp. 36–9.

Kelley, H.H. Attribution theory in social psychology, *Nebraska Symposium on Motivation*, 15, pp. 192–238.

Kelley, L., Whatley, A. and Worthley, R. 1987, Assessing the effects of culture on managerial attitudes: A three-culture test, *Journal of International Business Studies*, Summer, pp. 17–31.

Kennedy, J. and Everest, A. 1991, Put diversity in context, *Personnel Journal*, Sept., pp. 50–4.

Keren, G. 1996, Perspectives of behavioral decision making: Some critical notes, *Organizational Behavior and Human Decision Processes*, 65, pp. 169–78.

Kerr, S. and Jermier, J.M. 1978, Substitutes for leadership: Their meaning and measurement, *Organizational Behavior and Human Performance*, 22, pp. 375–403.

Kerr, S., Schriesheim, C.A., Murphy, C.J. and Stogdill, R. 1975, Toward a contingency theory of leadership based on the consideration and initiating structure literature,

Organizational Behavior and Human Performance, May, pp. 62–82.

Kesner, I.F. and Johnson, R.B. 1990, An investigation of the relationship between board composition and stockholder suits, *Strategic Management Journal*, 11, pp. 327–36.

Keys, J.B., Denton, L.T. and Miller, T.R. 1994, The Japanese management theory jungle—revisited, *Journal of Management*, 20, pp. 373–402.

Kidwell Jr, R.E. and Bennett, N. 1993, Employee propensity to withhold effort: A conceptual model to intersect three avenues of research, *Academy of Management Review*, 18, pp. 429–56.

Kiechel III, W. 1982, The big presentation, *Fortune*, 26 July, pp. 98–100.

Kiechel III, W. 1991, The art of the corporate task force, *Fortune*, 29 Jan., pp. 104–5.

Kilbridge, M.D. 1960, Reduced costs through job enrichment: A case, *Journal of Business*, 33, pp. 357–62.

Kilmann, R.H. 1985, Five steps for closing culture-gaps, in R.H. Kilmann, M.J. Saxton, R. Serpa, and associates (eds), *Gaining Control of the Corporate Culture*, Jossey-Bass, San Francisco.

Kilmann, R.H., Saxton, M.J. and Serpa, R. 1986, Issues in understanding and changing culture, *California Management Review*, 28, pp. 87–94.

Kindel, S. 1988, The 10 worst managed companies in America, *Financial World*, 26 July, pp. 28–39;

Kindel, S. 1995, Eye-opening management: Luxottica Group S.p. A., *Hemisphere Magazine*, Aug., pp. 31–4.

King, N. 1970, Clarification and evaluation of the two-factor theory of job satisfaction, *Psychological Bulletin*, 74, pp. 18–31.

King, T. 1995, How a hot ad agency, undone by arrogance, lost its independence, *Wall Street Journal*, 11 April, pp. A1, A5.

Kirby, J. 2000, The heavies hit back, *Business Review Weekly*, 25 Feb., pp. 60–7.

Kirby, J. 2003, The lone ranger, *Business Review Weekly*, May 8–14, p. 36.

Kirkwood, J. and Ruwhiu, D. 2003, Growth at Hubbards Foods, *Journal of the Australian and New Zealand Academy of Management*, 9, 2, pp. 47–57.

Kirkpatrick, D. 1986, What givebacks can get you, *Fortune*, 24 Nov., p. 61.

Kirkpatrick, D. 1992, Here comes the payoff from PCs, *Fortune*, 23 March, pp. 93–102.

Kirkwood, J and Ruwhiu, D. 2003, Growth at Hubbards Foods, *Journal of the Australian and New Zealand Academy of Management*, 9, 2, pp. 47–57.

Kleinfield, N.R. 1989, Wanted: CFO with 'Flair for funk,' *New York Times*, 26 March, p. D5.

Knowlton, C. 1988a, Making it right the first time, *Fortune*, 28 March, p. 48.

Knowlton, C. 1988b, The new export entrepreneurs, *Fortune*, 6 June, pp. 89–102.

Knox, A. 1992, The downside and dangers of downsizing, *Washington Post*, 15 March, p. H2.

Kodama, M. 1999, Community management support through community-based information networks, *Information Management & Computer Security*, 7, 3, pp. 140–50.

Kodama, M. 2000a, Business innovation through customer-value creation, *Journal of Management Development*, 19, 1, 49–70.

Kodama, M. 2000b, Strategic business applications and new virtual knowledge-based business through community-based information networks, *Information Management & Computer Security*, 7, 4, pp. 186–99.

Koepp, S. 1987, Having it all, then throwing it all away, *Time*, 25 May, pp. 22–3.

Koh, L. 2000, Fruits on the net, *Straits Times*, 11 Jan., p. 35.

Kohn, A. 1987a, *No Contest: The Case against Competition*, Houghton Mifflin, Boston.

Kohn, A. 1987b, Art for art's sake, *Psychology Today*, Sept., p. 54.

Kohn, A. 1987c, It's hard to get left out of a pair, *Psychology Today*, Oct., pp. 53–7.

Kolodny, H.F. 1979, Evolution to a matrix organization, *Academy of Management Review*, 4, pp. 543–53.

Kolodny, H.F. 1981, Managing in a matrix, *Business Horizons*, March–April, pp. 17–24.

KPMG 2001, Achieving measurable performance improvement in a changing world: the search for new insights, KPMG Assurances and Advisory Centre.

Koriat, A., Lichtenstein, S. and Fischoff, B. 1980, Reasons for confidence, *Journal of Experimental Psychology: Human Learning and Memory*, 6, pp. 107–18.

Koselka, R. 1994, It's my favorite statistic, *Forbes*, 12 Sept., pp. 162–76.

Kotlowitz, A. 1987, Working at home while caring for a child sounds fine—in theory, *Wall Street Journal*, 30 March, p. 21.

Kotter, J.P. 1979, Managing external dependence, *Academy of Management Review*, 4, pp. 87–92.

Kotter, J.P. 1982a, *The General Managers*, Free Press, New York.

Kotter, J.P. 1982b, What effective general managers really do, *Harvard Business Review*, Nov.–Dec., pp. 156–67.

Kotter, J.P. 1995, Leading change: Why transformation efforts fail, *Harvard Business Review*, March–April, pp. 59–67.

Kotter, J.P. and Heskett, J.L. 1992, *Corporate Culture and Performance*, Free Press, New York.

Kotter, J.P. and Schlesinger, L.A. 1979, Choosing strategies for change, *Harvard Business Review*, March–April, pp. 106–14.

Kotter, J.P., Schlesinger, L.A. and Sathe, V. 1979, *Organization: Text, Cases, and Readings on the Management of Organizational Design and Change*, Irwin, Homewood.

Kraar, L. 1994, The overseas Chinese: Lessons from the world's most dynamic capitalists, *Fortune*, 31 Oct., pp. 91–114.

Krietner, R. and Luthans, F. 1991, A social learning approach to behavioral management: Radical behaviorists 'Melowing out', in R.M. Steers and L.W. Porter (eds), *Motivation and Work Behavior*, McGraw-Hill, New York.

Krone, K.J., Jablin, F.M. and Putnam, L.L. 1987, Communication theory and organizational communication: Multiple perspectives, in F.M. Jablin, L.L. Putnam, K.H. Roberts, and L.W. Porter (eds), *Handbook of Organizational Communication: An Interdisciplinary Perspective*, Sage, Newbury Park.

Kruglanski, A.W. 1986, Freeze-think and the challenger, *Psychology Today*, Aug., pp. 48–9.

Kumpecb, T. and Bolwijn, P. T. 1988, Manufacturing: The new case for vertical integration, *Harvard Business Review*, March–April, pp. 75–81.

Kuntz, M. 1995, Reinventing the store, *Business Week*, 27 Nov., pp. 84–96.

Kupfer, A. 1988, How to be a global manager, *Fortune*, 14 March, pp. 52–8.

Kurke, L.B. and Alrich, H.E. 1983, Mintzberg was right! A replication and extension of the nature of managerial work, *Management Science*, 29, pp. 975–84.

Kurylko, D.T. 1995, Opel says empowerment was factor in wrongdoing, *Automotive News*, 17 July, pp. 1, 36.

Kusumoto, S. 1991, We're not in Honshu anymore, *Across the Board*, June, pp. 49–50.

LaBarre, P. 1994, Management tools must be managed, *Industry Week*, 5 Sept., pp. 78–82.

LaBarre, P. 1995, Patagonia comes of age, *Industry Week*, 3 April, p. 42.

Labate, J. 1993, Deal those workers in, *Fortune*, 19 April, p. 26.

Labich, K. 1995, Winners in the air wars, *Fortune*, 11 May, pp. 68–79.

Lachman, R. 1985, Public and private sector differences: CEOs' perceptions of their role environments, *Academy of Management Journal*, Sept., pp. 671–80.

Laderman, J.M. 1988, The family that hauls together brawls together, *Business Week*, 29 Aug., pp. 64–8.

Lai, F. 2000, McDonald's acts on throwaway burgers, *Straits Times*, 11 Jan., p. 42.

Landro, L. and Sease, D.R. 1987, General Electric to sell consumer electronics lines to Thomson S.A. for its medical gear business, cash, *Wall Street Journal*, 23 July, p. 3.

Landy, F.J. 1992, Hugo MŸnsterberg: Victim or visionary, *Journal of Applied Psychology*, 77, pp. 787–802.

Langlois, C.C. and Schlegelmilch, B.B. 1990, Do corporate codes of ethics reflect national character? Evidence from Europe and the United States, *Journal of International Business Studies*, 21, pp. 519–39.

Larson, E. 1988, Forever young, *INC.*, July, pp. 50–62.

Larson, L.L., Hunt, J.G. and Osborn, R.N. 1976, The great hi-hi leader behavior myth: A lesson from Occam's razor, *Academy of Management Journal*, 19, pp. 628–41.

Latham, G.P. and Wexley, K.N. 1981, *Increasing Productivity through Performance Appraisal*, Addison-Wesley, Reading.

Laudon, K.C. and Laudon, J.P. 1994, *Management Information Systems*, Macmillan, New York.

Lawler III, E.E. 1981, *Pay and Organization Development*, Addison-Wesley, Reading.

Lawler III, E.E. 1994, Total quality management and employee involvement: Are they compatible?, *Academy of Management Executive*, 8, 1, pp. 68–76.

Lawrence, P. R. and Lorsch, J.W. 1969, *Organization and Environment*, Irwin, Homewood.

Leana, C.R. 1985, A partial test of Janis' groupthink model: Effects of group cohesiveness and leader behavior on defective decision making, *Journal of Management*, 11, pp. 5–17.

Leana, C.R. 1986, Predictors and consequences of delegation, *Academy of Management Journal*, 29, pp. 754–74.

Leavitt, H.J. 1964, Applied organization change in industry: Structural, technical, and human approaches, in W.W. Cooper, H.J. Leavitt, and M.W. Shelly II (eds), *New Perspectives in Organization Research*, Wiley, New York.

Leavitt, H.J. and Whisler, T.L. 1958, Management in the 1980s, *Harvard Business Review*, Nov.–Dec., pp. 41–8.

Lee, C. 1994, The feminization of management, *Training*, Nov., pp. 25–31.

Lee, M.K. 1999, A hoarder ready to spring, *Asia Inc.*, Aug., pp. 10–11.

Lee, S.M., Luthans, F. and Olson, D.L. 1982, A management science approach to contingency models of organizational structure, *Academy of Management Journal*, 25, pp. 553–66.

Lee, T.W., Locke, E.A. and Latham, G.P., 1989, Goal setting theory and job performance, in L.A. Pervin (ed.), *Goal Concepts in Personality and Social Psychology*, Erlbaum, New Jersey.

Leibman, M.S. 1992, Getting results from TQM, *HR Magazine*, Sept., pp. 34–8.

Leibowitz, M.R. 1988, Clash of the high speed titans, *High Technology Business*, July, pp. 50–1.

Lengnick-Hall, C.A. 1992, Innovation and competitive advantage: What we know and what we need to learn, *Journal of Management*, 18, pp. 399–429.

Lenzner, R. 1995, The reluctant entrepreneur, *Forbes*, 11 Sept., pp. 162–7.

Leonard, J.W. 1986, Why MBO fails so often, *Training and Development Journal*, June, pp. 38–9;

Leonard-Barton, D. and Sviokla, J.J. 1988, Putting expert systems to work, *Harvard Business Review*, March–April, pp. 91–8.

Lesly, E. 1995, Are these 10 stretched too thin? *Business Week*, 13 Nov., p. 78.

Levine, J. 1992, Beer barrel blues, *Forbes*, 22 June, pp. 98–100.

Levine, J.B. 1990, GE carves out a road east, *Business Week*, 30 July, pp. 32–3.

Levine, J.B. and Byrne, J.A. 1986, Corporate odd couples, *Business Week*, 21 July, pp. 100–5.

Levitt, T. 1983, The globalization of markets, *Harvard Business Review*, May–June, p. 96.

Lewin, K. 1947, Frontiers in group dynamics: Concept, method, and reality in social science, *Human Relations*, 1, pp. 5–41.

Lewin, K. 1951, *Field Theory in Social Science: Selected Theoretical Papers*, Harper, New York.

Lewin, K. and Lippitt, R. 1938, An experimental approach to the study of autocracy and democracy: A preliminary note, *Sociometry*, 1, pp. 292–300.

Lewis, M.H. and Reinsch Jr, N.L. 1988, Listening in organizational environments, *Journal of Business Communication*, Summer, pp. 49–67.

Lewis, P.V. 1980, *Organizational Communication: The Essence of Effective Management*, Prentice-Hall, Englewood Cliffs.

Lichtenstein, S., Slovic, P., Fischhoff, B., Layman, M. and Combs, B. 1978, Judged frequency of lethal events, *Journal of Experimental Psychology: Human Learning and Memory*, 4, pp. 551–78.

Licker, P.S. 1985, *The Art of Managing Software Development People*, Wiley, New York.

Lieber, R.B. 1996, The fight to legislate incompetence out of the cockpit, *Fortune*, 5 Feb., p. 30.

Liebowitz, S.J. and Holden, K.T. 1995, Are self-managing teams worthwhile? A tale of two companies, *SAM Advanced Management Journal*, 22 March, p. 11.

Likert, R. 1961, *New Patterns of Management*, McGraw-Hill, New York.

Likert, R. 1979, From production- and employee-centeredness to systems 1–4, *Journal of Management*, 5, pp. 147–56.

Linden, D.W. 1995, The mother of them all, *Forbes*, 16 Jan., pp. 75–6.

Lipman, J. 1988, Marketers turn sour on global sales pitch Harvard guru makes, *Wall Street Journal*, 12 May, pp. 1, 13.

Lipner, M. 1991, Ben & Jerry's: Sweet ethics evince social awareness, *COMPASS Readings*, July, pp. 22–30.

Lippert, J. and Lupo, N. 1988, A not-so-happy birthday, *Detroit Free Press*, 28 Aug., pp. F1, F2;

Lloyd, S. 1999a, Amway says hello to profit growth, *Business Review Weekly*, 8 Oct., pp. 76–9.

Lloyd, S. 1999b, No pride without lions, *Business Review Weekly*, 25 Aug., pp. 44–5.

Lloyd, S. 2000, The culling game, *Business Review Weekly*, Ap. 7, pp. 96–9.

Lloyd, S. 2003, Country Road fills its potholes, *Business Review Weekly*, 14–20 August, pp. 66–7.

Locke, A., Shaw, K.N., Saari, L.M. and Latham, G.P. 1981, Goal setting and task performance, *Psychological Bulletin*, 90, pp. 125–52.

Locke, E.A. 1976, The nature and causes of job satisfaction, in M. Dunnette (ed.), *Hand book of Industrial and Organizational Psychology*, Rand McNally, Chicago.

Locke, E.A. 1982, The ideas of Frederick W. Taylor: An evaluation, *Academy of Management Review*, 7, pp. 14–24.

Locke, E.A. 1994, The nature and causes of job satisfaction, H.C. Triandis, M.D. Dunnette, and L.M. Hough (eds), *Handbook of Industrial and Organizational Psychology*, Consulting Psychologists Press, California.

Locke, E.A. and Latham, G.P. 1984, *Goal Setting: A Motivational Technique That Works*, Prentice-Hall, Englewood Cliffs.

Locke, E.A. and Latham, G.P. 1990, *A Theory of Goal Setting and Task Performance*, Prentice-Hall, Englewood Cliffs.

Locke, E.A., Latham, G.P. and Erez, M. 1988, The determinants of goal commitment, *Academy of Management Review*, 31, pp. 23–39.

Locke, E.A., Shaw, K.N., Saari, L.M. and Latham, G.P. 1982, Goal setting and task performance: 1969–1980, *Psychological Bulletin*, 90, pp. 125–52.

Lockheed Martin 1992, *Gray Matters: The Ethics Game Manual*, pp. 9, 25, and 29.

Loeb, M. 1994, How to grow a new product every day, *Fortune*, 14 Nov., pp. 269–70.

Loeb, M. 1999, Ten commandments for managing creative people, *Fortune*, 16 Jan., pp. 135–6.

Lohner, B.T., Noe, R.A., Moeller, N.L. and Fitzgerald, M.P. 1985, A meta-analysis of the relation of job characteristics to job satisfaction, *Journal of Applied Psychology*, 70, pp. 280–9.

Lohr, S. 1987, Manufacturing cars the Volvo way, *New York Times*, 23 June, pp. D1, D5.

Lohse, D. 1995, For foreign postings, the accent is on frugality, *Wall Street Journal*, 23 June, p. 1C.

Lopez, J.A. 1994, A better way? Setting your own pay— and other unusual compensation plans, *Wall Street Journal*, 13 April, p. R6.

Lorange, P., Morton, M.F.S. and Ghoshal, S. 1986, *Strategic Control Systems*, West, St Paul.

Lord, R.G., De Vader, C.L. and Alliger, G.M. 1986, A meta-analysis of the relation between personality traits and leadership perceptions: An application of validity generalization procedures, *Journal of Applied Psychology*, 71, pp. 402–10.

Lorsch, J.W. 1976, Contingency theory and organization design: A personal odyssey, in R.H. Kilmann, L.R. Pondy, and D.P. Slevin (eds), *The Management of Organization Design: Strategies and Implementation*, 1, North-Holland, New York.

Lorsch, J.W. 1979, Making behavioral science more useful, *Harvard Business Review*, March–April, pp. 171–80.

Lorsch, J.W. 1986, Managing culture: The invisible barrier to strategic change, *California Management Review*, Winter, pp. 95–109.

Lovdal, M.L., Bauer, R.A. and Treverton, N.H. 1977, Public responsibility committees on the board, *Harvard Business Review*, May–June, pp. 41–64.

Lublin, J.S. 1994a, It's shape-up time for performance reviews, *Wall Street Journal*, 3 Oct., pp. B1, B2.

Lublin, J.S. 1994b, Turning the tables: Underlings evaluate bosses, *Wall Street Journal*, 4 Oct., pp. B1, B14.

Lublin, J.S. 1995, My colleague, my boss, *Wall Street Journal*, 12 April, pp. R4, R12.

Lublin, J.S. 1996, AT&T outplacement manager's phone rings nonstop, *Wall Street Journal*, 25 Jan., pp. B1, B5.

Lubman, S. 1995, Hubris and ambition in Orange County: Robert Citron's story, *Wall Street Journal*, 18 Jan., pp. A1, A8.

Lubove, S. 1995a, New-tech, old-tech, *Forbes*, 17 July, pp. 58–60.

Lubove, S. 1995b, Salad in a bag, *Forbes*, 23 Oct., pp. 201–3.

Luthans, F. 1973, The contingency theory of management, *Business Horizons*, June, pp. 67–72.

Luthans, F. 1988, Successful vs. effective real managers, *Academy of Management Executive*, 2, no. 2, pp. 127–32.

Luthans, F. 1995, *Organizational Behavior*, McGraw-Hill, New York.

Luthans, F. and Kreitner, R. 1975, *Organizational Behavior Modification*, Scott, Foresman, Glenview.

Machan, D. 1991, Eager pupils, *Forbes*, 16 Sept., p. 118.

Maciariello, J.A. 1984, *Management Control Systems*, Prentice-Hall, Englewood Cliffs.

Macintosh, N.B. 1995, *The Social Software of Accounting Information Systems*, Wiley, New York.

Magnet, M. 1988, The resurrection of the rust belt, *Fortune*, 15 Aug., pp. 40–8.

Magnet, M. 1992, Who's winning the information revolution, *Fortune*, 30 Nov., pp. 110–17.

Magnusson, P. 1992, Grabbing new world orders, *Business Week, Reinventing America*, 23 Oct., pp. 110–18.

Mahoney, J. 1995, Gifts, grease and graft—business ethics, *Financial Times*, 8 Dec.

Mahoney, T.A. 1988, Productivity defined: The relativity of efficiency, effectiveness, and change, in J.P. Campbell, R.J. Campbell, and associates, *Productivity in Organizations*, Jossey-Bass, San Francisco.

Mahoney, T.A., Jerdee, T.H. and Carroll, S.J. 1965, The job(s) of management, *Industrial Relations*, February, pp. 97–110.

Maidique, M.A. 1980, Enterpreneurs, champions, and technological innovation, *Sloan Management Review*, Winter, pp. 59–76.

Maier, N.R.F. 1963, *Problem-Solving Discussions and Conferences: Leadership Methods and Skills*, McGraw-Hill, New York.

Maier, N.R.F. 1989, Assets and liabilities in group problem solving: The need for an integrative function, in M.T. Matteson and J.M. Ivancevich (eds), *Management and Organizational Behavior Classics*, BPI/Irwin, Homewood.

Main, J. 1989, How to go global—and why, *Fortune*, 28 Aug., pp. 70–6.

Main, J. 1992, How to steal the best ideas around, *Fortune*, 19 Oct., pp. 102–6.

Malone, M. and Davidow, W. 1992, Virtual corporation, *Forbes ASAP*, 7 Dec., pp. 103–7.

Management Review 1995, Flower power: A talk with Jim McCann, March, pp. 9–12.

Mangelsdorf, M.E. 1989, Beyond just-in-time, *INC.*, Feb., p. 21.

Mann, R.D. 1959, A review of the relationships between personality and performance in small groups, *Psychological Bulletin*, 56, pp. 241–70.

March, J.G. and Sevon, G. 1984, Gossip, information, and decision making, in L.S. Sproull and P. D. Larkey (eds), *Advances in Information Processing in Organizations*, 1, JAI, Greenwich.

Marchand, D. 1996, The information infrastructure— Promises and realities, *Financial Times*, 5 Jan., p. 8.

Marcia, J. Just doing it, *Distribution*, Jan., pp. 36–40.

Marcom Jr, J. 1991, Blue blazers and guacamole, *Forbes*, 25 Nov., pp. 64–8.

Marcus, A.A. 1988, Responses to externally induced innovation: Their effects on organizational rerformance, *Strategic Management Journal*, 9, pp. 387–402.

Markels, A. 1995, A power producer is intent on giving power to its people, *Wall Street Journal*, 3 July, pp. A1, A12.

Marketing 1995, P&G divides to rule, 23 March, p. 15.

Marketing News TM 1995, Lynn Shostack receives AMA services award, 2 Jan., p. 22.

Marsh, B. 1989, Going for the golden arches, *Wall Street Journal*, 1 May, p. B1.

Martin, J. 1992, *Cultures in Organizations: Three Perspectives*, Oxford University Press, New York.

Martin, R.L. 2002, The Virtue Matrix: Calculating the Return on Corporate Responsibility, *Harvard Business Review*, March.

Maruca, R.F. 1994, The right way to go global: An interview with Whirlpool CEO David Whitwam, *Harvard Business Review*, March–April, pp. 135–45.

Maslow, A.H. 1943, A theory of human motivation, *Psychological Review*, 50, pp. 370–96.

Maslow, A.H. 1954, *Motivation and Personality*, Harper and Row, New York.

Mathews, J. 1994, Increasingly, coffee isn't our cup of tea, *Washington Post*, 4 Nov., p. C3.

Mathews, J. 1995, Utensile strength: Rubbermaid's relentless innovation gains success, respect, *Washington Post*, 2 April, p. 1H.

Mathewson, W. 1988, Shop talk, *Wall Street Journal*, 30 Sept., p. 29.

Mathis, R.L. and Jackson, J.H. 1994, *Human Resource Management*, West, St Paul.

Max, R.R. 1985, Wording it correctly, *Training and Development Journal*, March, pp. 50–1.

McCall Jr, M.W. and Lombardo, M.M. 1983, What makes a top executive? *Psychology Today*, February, pp. 26–31.

McCallum, J. 2003, Work in progress, *AFR Boss*, June, pp. 42–6.

McCartney, S. 1994, Compaq borrows Wal-Mart's idea to boost production, *Wall Street Journal*, 17 June, p. B4.

McClelland, D.C. 1965, Achievement motivation can be developed, *Harvard Business Review*, Nov.–Dec., pp. 6–25.

McClelland, D.C. 1976, Power is the great motivator, *Harvard Business Review*, March–April, pp. 100–10.

McClelland, D.C. 1985, *Human Motivation*, Scott, Foresman, Glenview.

McClelland, D.C. 1995, Retrospective commentary, *Harvard Business Review*, Jan.–Feb., pp. 138–9.

McClelland, D.C. and Boyatzis, R.E. 1982, Leadership motive pattern and long-term success in management, *Journal of Applied Psychology*, 67, pp. 737–43.

McClelland, D.C. *Human Motivation*, Scott, Foresman, Glenview.

McColl, G. 2003a, Diversity deficit, *Business Review Weekly*, 7–13 August, p. 76.

McColl, G. 2003b, Cool in a crisis, *Business Review Weekly*, 7–13 August, p. 76–8.

McColl, G. 2003c, People who count, *Business Review Weekly*, June 19–25, pp. 68–9.

McColl, G. 2003d, Workers' playtime, *Business Review Weekly*, April 24–30, pp. 88–90.

McComas, M. 1986, Cutting costs without killing the business, *Fortune*, 13 Oct., pp. 70–8.

Mcgee, S. 1995, Garish jackets add to clamor of Chicago pits, *Wall Street Journal*, 31 July, p. C1.

McGregor, D. 1960, *The Human Side of Enterprise*, McGraw-Hill, New York.

McGuire, J.B., Sundgren, A. and Schneeweis, T. 1988, Corporate social responsibility and firm financial performance, *Academy of Management Journal*, 31, pp. 854–72.

McKean, K. 1985, Decisions, *Discover*, June, pp. 22–31.

McLeavey, D.W. and Narasimhan, S.L. 1985, *Production Planning and Inventory Control*, Allyn and Bacon, Boston.

McLeod Jr., R. 1986, *Management Information Systems*, Science Research Associates, Chicago.

McLeod, P. L. 1996, An assessment of the experimental literature on electronic support of group work: Results of a meta-analysis, *Human-Computer Interaction*, 7, 3, pp. 257–80.

McMenamin, B. 1995, Diversity hucksters, *Forbes*, 22 May, pp. 174–6.

McMorris, F.A. 1995, Is office voice mail private? Don't bet on it, *Wall Street Journal*, 28 Feb., p. B1.

Mecham, M. 1995, Instant success fuels Korean air expansion, *Air Transport*, 143, p. 28.

Meeks, F. 1988, Live from Dallas, *Forbes*, 26 Dec., pp. 112–13.

Meeks, F. 1989a, The man is the message, *Forbes*, 17 April, pp. 148–52.

Meeks, F. 1989b, Tom Golisano and the red tape factory, *Forbes*, 15 May, pp. 80–2.

Meeks, F. 1992, We all scream for rice and beans, *Forbes*, 30 March, p. 20.

Mehrabian, A. 1972, *Silent Messages*, Wadsworth, Belmont.

Meigs W.B. and Meigs, R.F. 1993, *Accounting: The Basis for Business Decisions*, McGraw-Hill, New York.

Meising, P. 1998, Using electronic networks in management and executive learning, *Journal of Workplace Learning*, 10, 6/7, pp. 324–7.

Melloan, G. 1988, Caterpillar rides the economic policy bumps, *Wall Street Journal*, 5 April, p. 37.

Mendenhall, M. and Oddou, G. 1985, The dimensions of expatriate acculturation: A review, *Academy of Management Review*, 10, pp. 39–47.

Mendenhall, M., Punnett, B.J. and Ricks, D. 1995, *Global Management*, Blackwell, Cambridge.

Mentzer, J.T. and Cox, J.E. 1984, Familiarity, application and performance of sales forecasting techniques, *Journal of Forecasting*, 3, pp. 27–36.

Merchant, K.A. 1982, The control function of management, *Sloan Management Review*, Summer, pp. 43–55.

Merchant, K.A. 1985, *Control in Business Organizations*, Pitman, Boston.

Metcalf, H.C. and Urwick L. (eds), 1940, *Dynamic Administration: The Collected Papers of Mary Parker Follett*, Harper and Row, New York.

Micallef, J.V. 1981, Political risk assessment, *Columbia Journal of World Business*, Summer, pp. 47–52.

Michaelsen, L.K., Watson, W.E. and Black, R.H. 1989, A realistic test of individual versus group consensus decision making, *Journal of Applied Psychology*, 74, pp. 834–9.

Milbank, D. 1995, Long viewed as kaput, many European firms seem to be reviving, *Wall Street Journal*, 14 Feb., pp. A1, A8.

Milkovich, G.T. and Glueck, W.F. 1985, *Personnel/Human Resource Management: A Diagnostic Approach*, Business Publications, Texas.

Miller, A. and Dess, G.G. 1996, *Strategic Management*, McGraw-Hill, New York.

Miller, A. and Dess, G.G. 1996, *Strategic Management*, McGraw-Hill, New York.

Miller, D. 1986, Configurations of strategy and structure: Toward a synthesis, *Strategic Management Journal*, 7, pp. 233–49.

Miller, D. 1988, Relating Porter's business strategies to environment and structure: Analysis and performance implications, *Academy of Management Journal*, 31, pp. 280–308.

Miller, D. and Friesen, P.H. 1982, Structural change and performance: Quantum versus piecemeal-incremental approaches, *Academy of Management Journal*, 25, pp. 867–92.

Miller, D. and Shamsie, J. 1996, The resource-based view of the firm in two environments: The Hollywood film studios from 1936 to 1965, *Academy of Management Journal*, 39, pp. 519–43.

Miller, J. 1978, *Living Systems*, McGraw-Hill, New York.

Miller, J.R. and Feldman, H. 1983, Management science—theory, relevance, and practice in the 1980s, *Interfaces*, Oct., pp. 56–60.

Miller, M.W. 1987, At many firms, employees speak a language that's all their own, *Wall Street Journal*, 29 Dec., p. 17.

Mintzberg, H. 1980, *The Nature of Managerial Work*, Prentice-Hall, Englewood Cliffs.

Mintzberg, H. 1983, *Power in and around Organizations*, Prentice-Hall, Englewood Cliffs.

Mintzberg, H., Raisignhani, D. and Theoret, A. 1976, The structure of 'unstructured' decision processes, *Administrative Science Quarterly*, 21, pp. 246–75.

Mishkoff, H.C. 1986, The network nation emerges, *Management Review*, Aug., pp. 29–31.

Mishra, J. 1990, Managing the grapevine, *Public Personnel Management*, Summer, pp. 213–28.

Mitchell, S. 2003, Roger Corbett's other Big W, *AFR Boss*, October, pp. 48–52.

Mitchell, T.R., Daniels, D., Hopper, H., George-Falvy, J. and Ferris, G.R. 1996, Perceived correlates of illegal behavior in organizations, *Journal of Business Ethics*, April, pp. 439–55.

Mitchell, V.F. and Moudgill, P. 1976, Measurement of Maslow's need hierarchy, *Organizational Behavior and Human Performance*, 16, pp. 334–49.

Mizruchi, M.S. 1983, Who controls whom? An examination of the relation between management and boards of directors in large American corporations, *Academy of Management Review*, 8, pp. 426–35.

Mohrman Jr, A.M., Mohrman, S.A., Ledford Jr, G.E., Cummings, T.G., Lawler III, E.E. and associates 1989, *Large-Scale Organizational Change*, Jossey-Bass, San Francisco.

Monks, J.G. 1987, *Operations Management*, McGraw-Hill, New York.

Montgomery, C.A., Thomas, A.R. and Kamath, R. 1984, Divestiture, market valuation, and strategy, *Academy of Management Journal*, 27, pp. 830–40.

Moore, J. and Einhorn, B., 1999, A Biz-to-biz e-boom, *Business Week*, 25 Oct., pp. 26–7.

Moore, T. 1987, Goodbye, corporate staff, *Fortune*, 21 Dec., pp. 65–76.

Morais, R.C. 1995, If you stand still, you die, *Forbes*, 30 Jan., pp. 44–5.

Moran, R.T., Harris, P. R. and Stripp, W.G. 1993, *Developing the Global Organization*, Gulf, Houston.

Morgenthaler, E. 1989, A 19th-century firm shifts, reinvents itself and survives 100 years, *Wall Street Journal*, 9 May, pp. A1, A16.

Morris, B. 1987, Shaking things up at Coca-Cola Foods, *Wall Street Journal*, 3 April, p. 36.

Morrisey, G.L. 1988, Who needs a mission statement? You do, *Training and Development Journal*, March, pp. 50–2.

Morrisey, G.L. 1996, *A Guide to Long-Range Planning*, Jossey-Bass, San Francisco.

Morrison, A.J., Ricks, D.A. and Roth, K. 1991, Globalization versus regionalization: Which way for the multinational? *Organizational Dynamics*, Winter, pp. 17–29.

Moser, P. 1988, The McDonald's mystique, *Fortune*, 4 July, pp. 112–16.

Moskowitz, M.R. 1989, Company performance roundup, *Business and Society Review*, Winter, pp. 72–8.

Moss, L. 1998, Disney ups Sweeney to Laybourne's old post, *Multichannel News*, 24 Aug., p. 10.

Moutkheiber, Z. 1995, I'm just a peddler, *Fortune*, 17 July, pp. 42–3.

Mowday, R.T. 1991, Equity theory predictions of behavior in organizations, in R.M. Steers and L.W. Porter (eds), *Motivation and Work Behavior*, McGraw-Hill, New York.

Muczyk, J.P. 1979, Dynamics and hazards of MBO application, *Personnel Administrator*, May, pp. 51–61.

Mueller, R. 1979, Criteria for the appraisal of directors, *Harvard Business Review*, 57, pp. 48–56.

Mullen, B. and Copper, C. 1994, The relation between group cohesiveness and performance: An integration, *Psychological Bulletin*, 115, pp. 210–27.

Mullen, B., Anthony, T., Salas, E. and Driskell, J.E. 1994, Group cohesiveness and quality of decision making: An integration of tests of the groupthink hypothesis, *Small Group Research*, 25, pp. 189–204.

Munter, M. 1987, *Business Communication: Strategy and Skill*, Prentice-Hall, Englewood Cliffs.

Muris, T., Scheffman, D. and Spiller, P. 1992, Strategy and transaction costs: The organization of distribution in the carbonated soft drink industry, *Journal of Economics and Management Strategy*, 1, pp. 77–97.

Murray, K. 1994, A cool commander for Murdoch's assault on cable, *New York Times*, 7 Aug., p. 14.

Myers, D.G. 1983, *Social Psychology*, McGraw-Hill, New York.

Myers, R.N. 1992, At Martin Marietta, this board game is lesson in ethics, *Wall Street Journal*, 25 Sept., p. B7A.

Nabers, W. 1995, The new corporate uniforms, *Fortune*, Nov., 13, pp. 132–56.

Nadler, D. and Tushman, M. 1988, *Strategic Organization Design*, Scott, Foresman, Glenview.

Nadler, D.A. and Lawler III, E.E. 1983, Motivation: A diagnostic approach, in J.R. Hackman, E.E. Lawler III,

and L.W. Porter (eds), *Perspectives on Behavior in Organizations*, McGraw-Hill, New York.

Nakarmi, L. 1995, A flying leap toward the 21st Century? Pressure from competitors and Seoul may transform the chaebol, *Business Week*, 20 March, pp. 78–80.

Narisetti, R. 1995, Manufacturers decry a shortage of workers while rejecting many, *Wall Street Journal*, 8 Sept., pp. A1, A4.

Nash, L. 1988, Mission statements—mirrors and windows, *Harvard Business Review*, March–April, pp. 155–6.

Nash, L.L. 1981, Ethics without the sermon, *Harvard Business Review*, Nov.–Dec., p. 81.

National Business Employment Weekly 1987, A question of ethics, Special Edition, *Managing Your Career*, Spring 1987, p. 4.

National Law Journal, 1995, Verdicts, 6 Feb., Supplement, C2.

Naughton, K. and Kerwin, K. 1995, At GM, two heads may be worse than one, *Business Week*, 14 Aug., p. 46.

Nayak, P. R. and Ketteringham, J.M. 1986, *Break-Throughs*, Rawson Associates, New York.

Neale, M.A., Huber, V.L. and Northcraft, G.B. 1987, The framing of negotiations: Contextual versus task frames, *Organizational Behavior and Human Decision Processes*, 39, pp. 228–41.

Near, J.P. and Miceli, M.P. 1995, Effective whistle-blowing, *Academy of Management Review*, 20, pp. 679–708.

Neff, R. 1995, They fly through the air with the greatest of ... Ki? *Business Week*, 23 Jan., p. 60.

Negandhi, A.R. and Welge, M.K. 1984, *Beyond Theory Z*, JAI, Greenwich.

Nemetz, P. and Fry, L.W. 1988, Flexible manufacturing organizations: Implications for strategy formulation and organizational design, *Academy of Management Review*, 13, pp. 627–38.

Neumann, S. 1994, *Strategic Information Systems*, Macmillan, New York.

New Steel 1994, Birmingham steel will build new bar and rod mill in Ohio, November, p. 12.

New York Times 1983, Japan to curb VCR exports, 21 Nov., p. D5.

New York Times 1992, Buns run out at McDonald's, 10 Oct., p. 39.

New York Times 1995, Little IKEA in Manhattan, 7 Sept., p. 5C.

New Zealand Human Resources Institute, http://www.hrinz.org.nz/info/knowledge_base.

New Zealand Human Resources Institute 2002, Employment Relations Bill - Part 1 Identifying the Legal Repercussions, http://www.hrinz.org.nz/info/knowledge_base; accessed 1 Nov. 2003.

Newman, B. 1995, Global chatter, *Wall Street Journal*, 22 March, pp. A1, A15.

Newman, W.H. 1975, *Constructive Control*, Prentice-Hall, Englewood Cliffs.

Newman, W.H. and Logan, J.P. Strategy, *Policy, and Central Management*, South-Western, Cincinnati.

Newsweek 1995, The risky new bonuses, 16 Jan., p. 42.

Nienstedt, P. and Wintermantel, R. 1987, Motorola restructures to improve productivity, *Management Review*, Jan., p. 47.

Nienstedt, P.R. 1989, Effectively downsizing management structures, *Human Resource Planning*, 12, pp. 155–6.

Noble, D.F. 1977, *America by Design: Science, Technology and the Rise of Corporate Capitalism*, Knopf, New York.

Norman, J.R. 1988, A hardheaded takeover by McLouth's hardhats, *Business Week*, 6 June, pp. 90–1.

Norman, J.R. 1994, Choose your partners, *Forbes*, 21 Nov., pp. 88–9.

Nossiter, V. 1979, A new approach toward resolving the line and staff dilemma, *Academy of Management Review*, 4, pp. 103–6.

Novack, J. 1995a, Lender's best friend, *Forbes*, 18 Dec., pp. 198–9.

Novack, J. 1995b, What if the guy shoots somebody? *Forbes*, 4 Dec., p. 37.

Nutt, P. C. 1984, Types of organizational decision processes, *Administrative Science Quarterly*, 29, pp. 414–50.

Nutt, P. C. 1986, Tactics of implementation, *Academy of Management Journal*, 29, pp. 230–61.

Nyce, E.H. and Groppa, R. 1983, Electronic mail at MHT, *Management Technology*, May, pp. 65–72.

O'Neal, M. 1988, Gould is so thin you can hardly see it, *Business Week*, 29 Aug., p. 74.

O'Neill, M. 1999, Industry faces day of reckoning over entry, *South China Morning Post*, 9 Nov., p. 4.

O'Reilly III, C.A. and Roberts, K.H. 1974, Information filtration in organizations: Three experiments, *Organizational Behavior and Human Performance*, 11, pp. 253–65.

O'Reilly, B. 1997, The curse of the Koch brothers, *Fortune*, 17 Feb., pp. 112–16.

O'Toole, J. 1985, *Vanguard Management: Redesigning the Corporate Future*, Doubleday, New York.

Oldenburg, D. 1989, What do you say? *Washington Post*, 23 Aug., p. C5.

Olian, J.D. and Rynes, S.L. 1991, Making total quality work: Aligning organizational processes, performance measures, and stakeholders, *Human Resource Management*, Fall, pp. 303–33.

Olins, R. and Waples, J. 1996, Cunard sails into unknown waters, *Times* (London), 10 March, Business, p. 1.

Onsman, Harry 1999, Workplace: the secret of a happy office, *Business Review Weekly*, 11 June.

Ono, Y. 1993, 'King of Beers' wants to rule more in Japan, *Wall Street Journal*, 28 Oct., p. B1.

Ono, Y. and Brauchli, M.W. 1989, Japan cuts the middle-management fat, *Wall Street Journal*, 8 Aug., p. B1.

Organ, D.W. and Ryan, K. 1995, A meta-analytic review of attitudinal and dispositional predictors of organizational citizenship behavior, *Personnel Psychology*, 48, pp. 775–802.

Ortega, B. 1994, Nearing 80, founder of Dillard stores seeks to keep on growing, *Wall Street Journal*, 11 May, pp. A1, A5.

Ortega, B. 1995, Broken rules, conduct codes garner goodwill for retailers but violations go on, *Wall Street Journal*, 3 July, pp. A1, A4.

Osborn, A.F. 1963, *Applied Imagination*, Scribner, New York.

Otten, A.L. 1986, Ethics on the job: Companies alert employees to potential dilemmas, *Wall Street Journal*, 14 July, p. 21.

Ouchi, W.G. and Maguire, M.A. 1975, Organizational control: Two functions, *Administrative Science Quarterly*, 20, pp. 559–69.

Pace, R.W. 1983, *Organizational Communication: Foundations for Human Resource Development*, Prentice-Hall, Englewood Cliffs.

Papalia, D.E. and Olds, S.W. 1988, *Psychology*, McGraw-Hill, New York.

Pape, W.R. 1997, Group insurance, *INC.* (Inc. Technology Supplement), 17 June, pp. 29–31.

Parets, R.T. 1995, Payout, *Investor's Business Daily*, 23 Aug., p. A6.

Parker, D.F. and Dyer, L. 1976, Expectancy theory as a within person behavioral choice model: An empirical test of some conceptual and methodological refinements, *Organizational Behavior and Human Performance*, 17, pp. 97–117.

Parker, L.D. 1984, Control in organizational life: The contribution of Mary Parker Follett, *Academy of Management Review*, 9, pp. 736–45.

Parkin, D. 2003, Teams need room to grow, *Business Review Weekly*, 25 September–1 October, p. 51.

Pastore, R. 1996, Great expectations, *CIO*, 15 Jan., pp. 46–50.

Patrick, A. 2003, House proud, *Business Review Weekly*, August 14–20, pp. 46–8.

Patrick, F., 1994, IBM one day, Lexmark the next, *Management Review*, Jan., pp. 38–44.

Patterson, A. 1995, Target 'Micromarkets' its way to success; no 2 stores are alike, *Wall Street Journal*, 31 May, pp. A1, A9.

Paul, K. and Barbato, R. 1985, The multinational corporation in the less developed country: The economic development model versus the north–south model, *Academy of Management Review*, 10, pp. 8–14.

Pavett, C.M. and Lau, A.W. 1983, Managerial work: The influence of hierarchical level and functional specialty, *Academy of Management Journal*, 26, pp. 170–7.

Pearce II, J.A. and David, F. 1987, Corporate mission statements: The bottom line, *Academy of Management Executive*, 1, pp. 109–16.

Pearce II, J.A. and Harvey, J.W. 1990, Concentrated growth strategies, *Academy of Management Executive*, 4, 1, pp. 61–8.

Pearce II, J.A. and Robinson Jr, R.B. 1988, *Strategic Management: Strategy Formulation and Implementation*, Irwin, Homewood.

Pearson, A.E. 1988, Tough-minded ways to get innovative, *Harvard Business Review*, May–June, pp. 99–106.

Pereira, J. and Lublin, J.S. 1995, A new CEO for Cherry Garcia's creators, *Wall Street Journal*, 2 Feb., p. 1B.

Pereira, J. and Rebello, J. 1995, Production problems at generic-drug firm lead to serious claims, *Wall Street Journal*, 2 Feb., p. A1.

Perlmutter, H.V. 1969, The tortuous evolution of the multinational corporation, *Columbia Journal of World Business*, Jan.–Feb., pp. 9–18.

Perrow, C. 1961, The analysis of goals in complex organizations, *American Sociological Review*, 26, pp. 854–66.

Peters, L.H., Hartke, D.D. and Pohlmann, J.T. 1985, Fiedler's contingency theory of leadership: An application of the meta-analysis procedures of Schmidt and Hunter, *Psychological Bulletin*, 97, pp. 274–85.

Peters, T.J. and Waterman, R.H. 1982, *In Search of Excellence*, Harper and Row, New York.

Petrozzello, D. 1998, Sweeney heads Disney/ABC cable, *Broadcasting & Cable*, 24 Aug., p. 47.

Petzinger Jr, T. 1995, All happy businesses are alike, but heirs bring unique conflicts, *Wall Street Journal*, 17 Nov., p. B1.

Petzinger, T. 1997, Dave Hurley gets a lesson in business, *Wall Street Journal*, 14 March, p. B1.

Pfeffer, J. 1981, *Power in Organizations*, Pitman, Boston.

Pfeffer, J. and Salancik, G. 1978, *The External Control of Organizations*, Harper and Row, New York.

Pfeiffer, J.W. 1994, *The 1994 Annual: Developing Human Resources*, University Associates, California.

Phalon, R. 1989, Roto-Rooter's new drill, *Forbes*, 11 Dec., pp. 176–8.

Pinchot III, G. 1985, *Intrapreneuring*, Harper and Row, New York.

Pinney, W.E. and McWilliams, D.B. 1982, *Management Science: An Introduction to Quantitative Analysis for Management*, Harper and Row, New York.

Pitman, J. 1997, Kicking the kickbacks, *Australian*, 13 June, p. 27.

Pitts, R.A. and Daniels, J.D. 1984, Aftermath of the matrix mania, *Columbia Journal of World Business*, Summer, pp. 48–54.

Planty, E. and Machaver, W. 1952, Upward communications: A project in executive development, *Personnel*, 28, pp. 304–18.

Podsakoff, P.M., Niehoff, B.P., MacKenzie, S.B. and Williams, M.L. 1993, Do substitutes for leadership really substitute for leadership? An empirical examination of Kerr and Jermier's situational leadership model, *Organizational Behavior and Human Decision Processes*, 54, pp. 1–44.

Pogson, P. 2003, Endnote, *AFR Boss*, October, p. 74.

Pollock, E.J. 1995, Workers want more money, but they also want to control their own time, *Wall Street Journal*, 28 Nov., pp. B1, B12.

Pongvutitham, A. 2000, Small firm thrives on honesty, *Nation*, 14 Feb., p. B1.

Port, O. 1987, The push for quality, *Business Week*, 8 June, pp. 130–6.

Port, O. 1988, The software trap: Automate—or else, *Business Week*, 9 May, pp. 142–54.

Porter, L.W. and Roberts, K. 1976, Communication in organizations, in M.D. Dunnette (ed.), *Handbook of Industrial and Organization Psychology*, Rand McNally, Chicago.

Porter, L.W. and Roberts, K. 1990, Communication in organizations, in M.D. Dunnette and L.M. Hough (eds), *Handbook of Industrial and Organization Psychology*, Consulting Psychologists Press, California.

Porter, M.E. 1980, *Competitive Strategy: Techniques for Analyzing Industries and Competitors*, Free Press, New York.

Porter, M.E. 1985, *Competitive Advantage: Creating and Sustaining Superior Performance*, Free Press, New York.

Porter, M.E. 1990a, The competitive advantage of nations, *Harvard Business Review*, March–April, pp. 73–93.

Porter, M.E. 1990b, *The Competitive Advantage of Nations*, Free Press, New York.

Porter, M.E. and Millar, V.E. 1985, How information gives you competitive advantage, *Harvard Business Review*, July–Aug., pp. 149–60.

Posner, B.G. 1989, If at first you don't succeed, *INC.*, May, pp. 132–4.

Posner, B.Z. and Schmidt, W.H. 1984, Values and the American manager: An update, *California Management Review*, 26, pp. 202–16.

Post, J.E. and the Foundation for Public Affairs 1993, The state of corporate public affairs in the United States, *Research in Corporate Social Performance and Policy*, 14, pp. 81–91.

Post, J.E., Frederick, W.C., Lawrence, A.T. and Weber, J. 1996, *Business and Society: Corporate Strategy, Public Policy, Ethics*, McGraw-Hill, New York.

Post, J.E., Murray Jr, E.A., Dickie, R.B. and Mahon, J.F. 1983, Managing public affairs: The public affairs function, *California Management Review*, Fall, pp. 135–6.

Pottinger, J. 1994, Brazilian maverick reveals his radical recipe for success, *Personnel Management*, Sept., p. 71.

Potts, M. 1987, Bic stock dives after report about lighters, *Washington Post*, 11 April, p. D10.

Potts, M. 1989, Toys 'R' US and McDonald's take on Japanese toy market, *Washington Post*, 27 Sept., p. B1.

Powell, G.N. 1993, *Women and Men in Management*, Sage, Newbury Park.

Powers, T.L. 1987, Breakeven analysis with semi-fixed costs, *Industrial Marketing Management*, 16, pp. 35–41.

PR Newswire 1995a, Rockwell marks 10-year anniversary of Allen-Bradley purchase, 20 Feb., pp. 1–3.

PR Newswire 1995b, Tennant reveals fourth quarter results, 8 Feb.

Prahalad, C. K. and Dox, Y.L. 1987, *The Multinational Mission: Balancing Local Demands and Global Vision*, Free Press, New York.

Preble, J.F. 1984, The selection of delphi panels for strategic planning purposes, *Strategic Management Journal*, 5, pp. 157–70.

Prinzinsky, D. 1996, New bar mill guaranteed fast start, *Crain's Cleveland Business*, 5 Feb., p. 3.

Pritchard, R.D., Jones, S.D., Roth, P. L., Stuebing, K.K. and Ekeberg, S.E. 1988, Effects of group feedback, goal setting, and incentives on organizational productivity, *Journal of Applied Psychology*, 73, pp. 337–58.

Pritchard, R.D., Roth, P. L., Jones, S.D., Galgay, P. J. and Watson, M.D. 1988, Designing a goal-setting system to enhance performance: A practical guide, *Organizational Dynamics*, Summer, pp. 69–78.

Puchalsky, A. 1996, GM recouping ground lost in strike, *Wall Street Journal*, 24 June, p. B2.

Pyatt Jr, R.A. 1986, AAA's lesson for Fairfax, *Washington Post*, 3 Oct., pp. F1–F2.

Queenan, J. 1988, Juice men, *Barrons*, 20 June, pp. 37–8.

Queenan, J. 1989, Purveying yuppie porn, *Forbes*, 13 Nov., pp. 60–4.

Quinlivan, B. 2003, Million-dollar smile, *Business Review Weekly*, 21–7 August, p. 59.

Quinn, J.B. 1979, Technological innovation, entrepreneurship, and strategy, *Sloan Management Review*, Spring, pp. 19–30.

Quinn, J.B., Anderson, P. and Finkelstein, S. 1996, Managing professional intellect: Making the most of the best, *Harvard Business Review*, March–April, pp. 71–80.

Quintanilla, C. and Gibson, R. 1994, 'Do call us': More companies install 1-800 phone lines, *Wall Street Journal*, 20 April, p. B1.

Rachlin, H. 1989, *Judgment, Decisions, and Choice*, Freeman, New York.

Rahim, M.A. and Magner, N.R. 1995, Confirmatory factor analysis of the styles of handling interpersonal conflict: First-order factor model and its invariance across groups, *Journal of Applied Psychology*, 80, pp. 122–32.

Raia, A.P. 1974, *Managing by Objectives*, Scott, Foresman, Glenview.

Ramanujam, V. and Varadarajan, P. 1989, Research on corporate diversification: A synthesis, *Strategic Management Journal*, 10, pp. 523–51.

Ramaprasad, A. 1983, On the definition of feedback, *Behavioral Science*, Jan., pp. 4–13.

Rapaport, R. 1993, To build a winning team: An interview with head coach Bill Walsh, *Harvard Business Review*, Jan.–Feb., pp. 111–20.

Raven, B.H. 1993, The bases of power: Origins and recent developments, *Journal of Social Issues*, 49, pp. 227–51.

Raven, B.H. and Kruglanski, A.W. 1970, Conflict and power, in P. Swingle (ed.), *The Structure of Conflict*, Academic, New York.

Rebello, J. 1995, Radical ways of its CEO are a boon to bank, *Wall Street Journal*, 20 March, pp. B1, B3.

Rebello, K. and Burrows, P. 1996, The fall of an American icon, *Business Week*, 5 Feb., pp. 34–42.

Redwood, R. 1996, Giving credit where credit is due: The work of the federal glass ceiling commission, *Credit World*, May–June, pp. 34–6.

Reeves, C.A. and Bednar, D.A. 1994, Defining quality: Alternatives and implications, *Academy of Management Review*, 19, pp. 419–45.

Regan, M.B. 1995, Shattering the AFL-CIO's glass ceiling, *Business Week*, 13 Nov., p. 46.

Reibstein, L. 1986, A finger on the pulse: Companies expand use of employee surveys, *Wall Street Journal*, 27 Oct., p. A31.

Reich, R.B. 1987, Entrepreneurship reconsidered: The team as hero, *Harvard Business Review*, May–June, pp. 77–83.

Reichheld, F.F. 1996, Learning from customer defections, *Harvard Business Review*, March–April, pp. 56–69.

Reiste, K.K. and Hubrich, A. 1996, Work-team implementation, *Hospital Management Quarterly*, Feb. pp. 47–53.

Reitman, V. 1995, Toyota names a chief likely to shake up global auto business, *Wall Street Journal*, 11 Aug., pp. A1, A4.

Reitz, H.J. 1987, *Behavior in Organizations*, Irwin, Homewood.

Rennie, P. 2003a, Reach for the skies, *Business Review Weekly*, 27 November–3 December, p. 74.

Rennie, P. 2003b, Rio rides China's boom, *Business Review Weekly*, 13–19 February, pp. 34–6.

Rensberger, B. 1987, Lessons of the VCR revolution: How U.S. industry failed to make American ingenuity pay off, *Washington Post*, 13 April, pp. 1, 10.

Reputex 2003, http://www.reputex.com.au/pdfs/RepuTex_DPS_9.pdf , accessed 1 November.

Reuter Textline El Pais 1993, *Spain: Fewer Operators in Spain's Restructured Electricity Sector*, June 8, p. 1.

Reuters 2000, E-jobs boom in China, *Straits Times*, 12 Jan. p. Life 6.

Reynolds, E.V. and Johnson, J.D. 1982, Liaison emergence: Relating theoretical perspectives, *Academy of Management Review*, 7, pp. 551–9.

Rice, B. 1982, The Hawthorne defect: Persistence of a flawed theory, *Psychology Today*, Feb., pp. 70–4.

Rice, F. 1994, How to make diversity pay, *Fortune*, 8 Aug., pp. 78–86.

Rice, R.E. and Case, D. 1983, Electronic message systems in the university: A description of use and utility, *Journal of Communication*, 33, pp. 131–52.

Richards, M.D. 1986, *Setting Strategic Goals and Objectives*, West, St Paul.

Richman, R. 1993, Christmas: Science of the sell, *Chicago Sun Times*, 5 Dec., p. 14.

Richman, T. 1988, In the black, *INC.*, May, pp. 116–20.

Riechheld, F.F. 1996, Learning from customer defections, *Harvard Business Review*, March–April, pp. 56–69.

Rifkin, G. 1994, Don't ever judge this consultant by her cover, *New York Times*, 1 May, p. 5.

Rifkin, G. 1995, A skeptic's guide to groupware, *Forbes ASAP*, pp. 76–91.

Rigdon, J.E. 1991, PepsiCo's KFC scouts for blacks and women for its top echelons, *Wall Street Journal*, 13 Nov., p. A1.

Robbins, S.P. 1990, *Organization Theory: The Structure and Design of Organizations*, Prentice-Hall, Englewood Cliffs.

Roberts, C. 2003a, Brake-through technology, *Business Review Weekly*, 17–23 April, pp. 52–3.

Roberts, C. 2003b, Link loads up, *Business Review Weekly*, 27 November–3 December, pp. 56–7.

Roberts, C. 2003c, Paper tigers, *Business Review Weekly*, 2–8 October, pp. 56–7.

Roberts, C. 2003d, Seek's best day's work, *Business Review Weekly*, 20 August–3 September, pp. 56–7.

Roberts, C. 2003e, Link loads up, *Business Review Weekly*, 27 November–3 December, pp. 56–7.

Roberts, C. 2003f, Pass the parcel, *Business Review Weekly*, 7–13 August, p. 68.

Roberts, C. 2003g, Great products are not enough, *Business Review Weekly*, 20 August–3 September, p. 56.

Roberts, C. 2003h, Price is all in Singapore, *Business Review Weekly*, 10–16 April, pp. 14–16.

Robinson, G. and Dechant, K. 1997, Building a case for business diversity, *Academy of Management Executive*, 3, pp. 32–47.

Robock, S.H. and Simmonds, K. 1989, *International Business and Multinational Enterprises*, Irwin, Homewood.

Rockett, L., Valor, J., Miller, P. and Naude, P. 1998, Technology and virtual teams: Using globally distribute groups in MBA learning, *Campus-Wide Information Systems*, 15, 5, pp. 174–82.

Rodes, L. 1988, At the crossroads, *INC.*, Feb., pp. 66–76.

Rodgers, R. and Hunter, J.E. 1991, Impact of management by objectives on organizational productivity, *Journal of Applied Psychology*, 76, 2, pp. 322–36.

Romanelli, E. and Tushman, M.L. 1994, Organizational transformation as punctuated equilibrium: An empirical test, *Academy of Management Journal*, 37, pp. 1141–66.

Ronen, S. 1994, An underlying structure of motivational need taxonomies: A cross-cultural confirmation, in H.C. Triandis, M.D. Dunnette, and L.M. Hough (eds), *Handbook of Industrial and Organizational Psychology*, Consulting Psychologists Press, California.

Ronen, S. and Primps, S.B. 1981, The compressed work week as organizational change: Behavioral and attitudinal outcomes, *Academy of Management Review*, 6, pp. 61–74.

Root, F.R. 1984, *International Trade & Investment*, South-Western, Cincinnati.

Rose, R.L. 1993, After turning around Giddings and Lewis, Fife is turned out himself, *Wall Street Journal*, 22 June, p. A1.

Rose, R.L. 1996, Caterpillar's profit is surprisingly strong, *Wall Street Journal*, 19 Jan.

Rosen, B. and Jerdee, T.H. 1978, Perceived sex differences in managerially relevant characteristics, *Sex Roles*, 4, pp. 837–43.

Ross, E. 2003, The body cleansers, *Business Review Weekly*, 10–16 April, pp. 86–7.

Ross, E. 2004, Towards an office ceasefire, *Business Review Weekly*, 10–16 January, pp. 78–80.

Ross, J. and Staw, B.M. 1993, Organizational escalation and exit: Lessons from the Shoreham nuclear power plant, *Academy of Management Journal*, 36, pp. 701–32.

Rowland, M. 1988, Creating a plan to reshape a business, *Working Woman*, Aug., pp. 70–4.

Rubel, C. 1996, Treating coworkers right is the key to Kinko's success, *Advertising Age*, 29 Jan., p. 5.

Rubin, J.Z. 1980, Experimental research on third party intervention in conflict: Toward some generalizations, *Psychological Bulletin*, 87, pp. 379–91.

Rudnitsky, H. 1982, How Sam Walton does it, *Forbes*, 16 Aug., pp. 42–4.

Rudnitsky, H. 1987, Play it again, Sam, *Forbes*, 10 Aug., p. 48.

Rue, L.W. and Holland, P.G. 1989, *Strategic Management: Concepts and Experiences*, McGraw-Hill, New York.

Rugman, A.M. and Hodgetts, R.M. 1995, *International Business: A Strategic Management Approach*, McGraw-Hill, New York.

Russell, G. 1987, Rebuilding to survive, *Time*, 16 Feb., p. 44.

Ryan, C. 2003, The reputation wars, *AFR Boss*, November, pp. 24–30.

Sadker, M., Sadker, D, and Klein, S. 1986, Abolishing misconceptions about sex equality in education theory and practice, 25, p. 4.

Sager, I. and Cortese, A. 1995, IBM: Why the good news isn't good enough, *Business Week*, 23 Jan., pp. 72–3.

Salpukas, A. 1994, Hurt in expansion, airlines cut back and may sell hubs, *New York Times*, 1 April, pp. A1, C8.

Sampson, H. 1988, The army's Clausewitz of the meeting room, *Army*, Jan., pp. 49–50.

Sandberg, J. 1995, Internet's popularity in North America appears to be soaring, *Wall Street Journal*, 30 Oct., p. B2.

Sanders, D.H. 1987, *Computer Concepts and Applications*, McGraw-Hill, New York.

Santamaria, S. 2000, Long queues for cutie Kitty collectibles, *Straits Times*, 7 Jan., p. 3.

Santosus, M. 1996, Tactical maneuvers, *CIO*, 1 April, pp. 54–6.

Saporito, B. 1985, Heinz pushes to be the low cost producer, *Fortune*, 24 June, pp. 44–54.

Saporito, B. 1986, The revolt against 'Working smarter,' *Fortune*, 21 July, pp. 58–65.

Saporito, B. 1988, The tough cookie at RJR Nabisco, *Fortune*, 18 July, pp. 32–46.

Saporito, B. 1992, A week aboard the Wal-Mart express, *Fortune*, 24 Aug., pp. 77–84.

Saporito, B. 1993, This Bud's for them, *Fortune*, 9 Aug., pp. 12–14.

Sathe, V. 1983, Implications of corporate culture: A manager's guide to acting, *Organizational Dynamics*, Autumn, pp. 5–23.

Sawaya Jr, W.J. and Giauque, W.C. 1986, *Production and Operations Management*, Harcourt Brace Jovanovich, San Diego.

Saywell, T. and Yan, Z. 2000, Ready for the deluge, *Far Eastern Economic Review*, 23 March, pp. 44–5.

Schein, E.H. 1992, *Organizational Culture and Leadership*, Jossey-Bass, San Francisco.

Schilit, W.K. 1987, An examination of the influence of middle-level managers in formulating and implementing strategic decisions, *Journal of Management Studies*, May, pp. 271–93.

Schiller, Z. 1988, The marketing revolution at Procter & Gamble, *Business Week*, 25 July, pp. 72–6.

Schine, E. 1995, The fall of a timber baron, *Business Week*, 2 Oct., pp. 85–92.

Schlesinger, J.M. 1987, Plant-level talks rise quickly in importance; Big issue: Work rules, *Wall Street Journal*, 16 March, p. A16.

Schmidt, L. 1999a, Harvey Norman, a structured success, *Business Review Weekly*, pp. 72–5.

Schmidt, L. 1999b, She who dares, wins, *Asia Inc.*, Aug., pp. 52–3.

Schmidt, L. 2003a, Card tricks, *Business Review Weekly*, 14–20 August, p. 24.

Schmidt, L. 2003b, No so crazy after all, *Business Review Weekly*, 4–10 September, pp. 44–5.

Schmitt, R.B. 1997, Judges try curbing lawyers' body-language antics, *Wall Street Journal*, 11 Sept., pp. B1, B7.

Schneider, B. and Bowen, D.E. 1995, *Winning the Service Game*, Harvard Business School Press, Boston.

Schnitzer, M.C., Liebrenz, M.L. and Kubin, K.W. 1985, *International Business*, South-Western, Cincinnati.

Schoemaker, P.J.H. 1993, Multiple scenario development: Its conceptual and behavioral foundation, *Strategic Management Journal*, 14, pp. 193–213.

Schoemaker, P.J.H. 1995, Scenario planning: A tool for strategic thinking, *Sloan Management Review*, Winter, pp. 25–40.

Schofield, M. and Arnold, D. 1988, Strategies for mature businesses, *Long Range Planning*, 21, pp. 69–76.

Schonberger, R.J. 1984, An assessment of just-in-time implementation, in *Readings in Zero Inventory*, APICS

27th Annual International Conference proceedings, Las Vegas, Oct. 9–12, p. 57.

Schrage, M. 1987, Bell labs is long on genius but short in the marketplace, *Washington Post*, 1 March, pp. H1, H4.

Schreyoff, G. and Steinmann, H. 1987, Strategic control: A new perspective, *Academy of Management Review*, 12, pp. 91–103.

Schriesheim, C.A. and Bird, B.J. 1979, Contributions of the Ohio state studies to the field of leadership, *Journal of Management*, 5, pp. 135–45.

Schroeder, M. 1991, Charity doesn't begin at home anymore, *Business Week*, 25 Feb., p. 91.

Schroeder, R.G. 1989, *Operations Management*, McGraw-Hill, New York.

Schuler, R.S. and Huber, V.L 1990, *Personnel and Human Resource Management*, West, Minnesota.

Schwartzman, H.B. 1986, The meeting as a neglected social form in organizational studies, *Research in Organizational Behavior*, 8, pp. 233–58.

Schwenk, C. and Valacich, J.S. 1992, Effects of devil's advocacy and dialectical inquiry on individuals versus groups, *Organizational Behavior and Human Decision Processes*, 59, pp. 210–22.

Schwenk, C.R. 1990, Effects of devil's advocacy and dialectical inquiry on decision making: A meta-analysis, *Organizational Behavior and Human Decision Processes*, 47, pp. 161–76.

Scott, R.S. 1996, The mandate is still being honored: In defense of Weber's disciples, *Administrative Science Quarterly*, 41, pp. 163–71.

Seashore, S. 1954, *Group Cohesiveness in the Industrial Work Group*, Institute for Social Research, Ann Arbor.

Sedwick, D. 1996, Competitive brake market at strike's root, *Automotive News*, 18 March, pp. 1, 50.

Seeger, J.A. 1983, No innate phases in group problem solving, *Academy of Management Review*, 8, pp. 683–9.

Segal, T. 1992, Saving our schools, *Business Week*, 14 Sept., pp. 70–8.

Sellers, P. 1988, How to handle customers' gripes, *Fortune*, 24 Oct., pp. 88–100.

Sellers, P. 1998, The 50 most powerful women in American business, *Fortune*, 12 Oct., pp. 76–98.

Senge, P. 1990, *The Fifth Disciple: The Art and Practice of the Learning Organization*, Doubleday, New York.

Serenyi, P. 1996, Ford opens office to boost sales, *Moscow Times*, 29 March, p. 1.

Serwer, A.E. 1994, McDonald's conquers the world, *Fortune*, 17 Oct., pp. 103–16.

Serwer, A.E. 1995, An odd couple aims to put Lionel on the fast track, *Fortune*, 30 Oct., p. 21.

Sharpe, R. 1994, Women make strides, but men stay firmly in top company jobs, *Wall Street Journal*, 29 March, pp. A1, A8.

Shaw, M.E. 1981, *Group Dynamics: The Psychology of Small Group Behavior*, McGraw-Hill, New York.

Shaw, W.H. and Barry, V. 1995, *Moral Issues in Business*, Wadsworth, Belmont.

Shellenbarger, S. 1994, Reviews from peers instruct–and sting, *Wall Street Journal*, 4 Oct., pp. B1, B4.

Shensholt, J. and Gome, A. 2003, *Business Review Weekly*, Chain of deception, 28 August–3 September, pp. 18–20.

Shepard, J.M. 1971, On Alex Carey's radical criticisms of the Hawthorne studies, *Academy of Management Journal*, March, pp. 23–32.

Shepperd, J.A. 1993, Productivity loss in performance groups: A motivational analysis, *Psychological Bulletin*, 113, pp. 67–81.

Sherden, W.A. 1988, Gaining the service quality advantage, *Journal of Business Strategy*, March–April, pp. 45–8.

Sherman, S.P. 1989, Inside the mind of Jack Welch, *Fortune*, 27 March, pp. 39–50.

Shirouzu, N. 1995, Daiwa bank's oversight is called lax in letter by trader who hid losses, *Wall Street Journal*, 12 Dec., p. A16.

Shleifer, A. and Vishny, R.W. 1994, Takeovers in the 1960s and 1980s: Evidence and implications, in R.P. Rumelt, D.E. Schendel and D.J.Teece (eds) *Fundamental Issues in Strategy*, Harvard Business School Press, Boston.

Shoebridge, N. 2003a, Misdirected dollars, *Business Review Weekly*, 29 May–4 June, p. 62.

Shoebridge, N. 2003b, The arches shine again, *Business Review Weekly*, 11–17 December, p. 63.

Shoebridge, N. 2003c, The shock of the new, *Business Review Weekly*, 21–7 August, p. 63.

Shull Jr, F.A., Delbecq, A.L. and Cummings, L.L. 1970, *Organizational Decision Making*, McGraw-Hill, New York.

Siler, C. 1989, The goal is 0%, *Forbes*, 30 Oct., pp. 95–8.

Siler, J.F. 1989a, A warning shot from the king of beers, *Business Week*, 18 Dec., p. 124.

Siler, J.F. 1989b, The slippery ladder at Abbott Labs, *Business Week*, 30 Oct., pp. 136–7.

Siler, J.F. and Atchison, S. 1991, The Rx at work in Utah, *Business Week/Quality*, 25 Oct., p. 113.

Simon, H.A. 1955, A behavioral model of rational choice, *Quarterly Journal of Economics*, 69, pp. 99–118.

Simon, H.A. 1956, Rational choice and the structure of the environment, *Psychological Review*, 63, pp. 129–38.

Simon, R. 1987, The morning after, *Forbes*, 19 Oct., pp. 164–8.

Simons, R. 1995, *Levers of Control: How Managers Use Innovative Control Systems to Drive Strategic Renewal*, Harvard Business School Press, Boston.

Sims Jr, H.P. 1995, Challenges to implementing self-managing teams—part 2, *Journal for Quality & Participation*, March, pp. 24–31.

Sinclair, A. 2003, Endnote, *AFRBoss*, June, p. 74.

Siwolop, S. and Eklund, C. 1986, The capsule controversy: How far should the FDA go? *Business Week*, 3 March, p. 37.

Skinner, W. 1986, The productivity paradox, *Harvard Business Review*, July–Aug., pp. 55–9.

Skotnicki, T. 2003, The challenge for China, *Business Review Weekly*, 11–17 December.

Skrzycki, C. 1987, How some firms become foreign success stories, *Washington Post*, 15 Nov., p. H1.

Skrzycki, C. 1989, Just who's in charge here, anyway? *Washington Post*, 29 Jan., pp. H1, H8.

Sloan Jr, A.P. 1964, *My Years with General Motors*, Doubleday, New York.

Slovic, P. 1995, The construction of preference, *American Psychologist*, 50, pp. 364–71.

Smallwood, W.N. and Jacobsen, E. 1987, Is there life after downsizing? *Personnel*, Dec., pp. 42–6.

Smart, T. 1995, A lot of the weaknesses Carbide had are behind it, *Business Week*, 23 Jan., pp. 83–4.

Smeltzer, L.L. and Fann, G.L. 1989, Comparison of managerial communication patterns in small, entrepreneurial organizations and large, mature organizations, *Group and Organization Studies*, 14, pp. 198–215.

Smircich, L. 1983, Concepts of culture and organizational analysis, *Administrative Science Quarterly*, 28, pp. 339–58.

Smith, A. 1910, *The Wealth of Nations*, Dent, London.

Snow, C. 2003, Southcorp's wine fine, *Business Review Weekly*, 27 November–3 December, pp. 14–15.

Society for Human Resource Management 1995, *Mosaics*, March, p. 1.

Soloman, R.C. 1992, *Ethics and Excellence*, Oxford University Press, New York.

Sonnenfeld, J.A. 1985, Shedding light on the Hawthorne studies, *Journal of Occupational Behavior*, 6, pp. 111–30.

Sounder, W.E. 1988, Managing relations between R&D and marketing in new product development projects, *Journal of Product Innovation Management*, 5, pp. 6–19.

Southerland, D. 1994, They want the card-carrying customer, *Washington Post*, 19 Oct., p. G1.

Spangler, W.D. 1992, Validity of questionnaire and TAT measures of need for achievement: Two meta-analyses, *Psychological Bulletin*, 112, pp. 140–54.

Sparks, D. 1999a, Partners, *Business Week*, 25 Oct., pp. 72–5.

Sproull, L. and Kiesler, S. 1986, Reducing social context cues: Electronic mail in organizational communication, *Management Science*, 32, pp. 1492–512.

Sprout, A.L. 1995, The internet inside your company, *Fortune*, 27 Nov., pp. 161–8.

Stahl, S. and Violino, B. 1996, Viruses still pose a threat, *Information Week*, 4 March, p. 30.

Stalk, G. and Hout, T.M. 1990, *Competing Against Time*, Free Press, New York.

Standard & Poor's Industry Surveys 1993, Autos—auto parts, 24 June.

Statistics New Zealand 2002. Ethnic groups: 2001 census of population and dwellings. Statistics New Zealand: Wellington.

Stauffer, D. 1999, Workers just like to have fun productively, *Business Review Weekly*, 29 Oct., pp. 56–7.

Staw, B.M. 1984, Organizational behavior: A review and reformulation of the field's outcome variables, *Annual Review of Psychology*, 35, pp. 627–66.

Stech, E. and Ratliffe, S.A. 1985, *Effective Group Communication: How to Get Action by Working in Groups*, National Textbook, Lincolnwood.

Stecklow, S. 1994a, Chief prerequisite for college president's job: Stamina, *Wall Street Journal*, 1 Dec., pp. B1, B10.

Stecklow, S. 1994b, Harvard's president, too slow to delegate, got swamped in detail, *Wall Street Journal*, 9 Dec., pp. A1, A10.

Steers, R.M. 1987, Murray's manifest needs theory, in R.M. Steers and L.W. Porter (eds), *Motivation and Work Behavior*, McGraw-Hill, New York.

Steers, R.M. and Porter, L.W. 1991, *Work and Motivation*, McGraw-Hill, New York.

Steers, R.M., Porter, L.W. and Bigley, G.A. 1996, *Motivation and Leadership at Work*, McGraw-Hill, New York.

Steiner, G. and Cannon, W.M. 1966, *Multinational Corporate Planning*, Macmillan, New York.

Stensholt, J. 2003, Golf needs a star driver, *Business Review Weekly*, 10–16 April, pp. 64–70.

Stepanek, M. 1999, How fast is Netfast?, *Business Review Weekly*, 1 Nov., pp. 30–2.

Stepp, L.S. 1991a, In search of ethics: Alcoa pursues a corporate conscience through emphasis on 'core values', *Washington Post*, 31 March, pp. H1, H4.

Stepp, L.S. 1991b, New test of values, *Washington Post*, 4 Aug., pp. H1, H4.

Stern, R.N. and Barley, S.R. 1996, Organizations and social systems: Organization theory's neglected mandate, *Administrative Science Quarterly*, 41, pp. 146–62.

Stevens, A. 1995a, Boss's brain teaser: Accommodating depressed worker, *Wall Street Journal*, 11 Sept., p. B1.

Stevens, A. 1995b, Lawyers and clients, *Wall Street Journal*, 19 June, p. B7.

Stevens, T. 1995, Where the rubber meets the road, *Industry Week*, 20 March, pp. 14–18.

Stevenson, H.H. and Gumpert, D.E. 1985, The heart of entrepreneurship, *Harvard Business Review*, March–April, pp. 85–94.

Stewart, R. 1982, A model for understanding managerial jobs and behavior, *Academy of Management Review*, 7, pp. 7–13.

Stogdill, R.M. 1948, Personal factors associated with leadership: A survey of the literature, *Journal of Psychology*, 25, pp. 35–71.

Stogdill, R.M. 1972, Group productivity, drive, and cohesiveness, *Organizational Behavior and Human Performance*, 8, pp. 26–43.

Stogdill, R.M. 1974, *Handbook of Leadership*, Free Press, New York.

Stoner, J.A.F. and Wankel, C. 1986, *Management*, Prentice-Hall, Englewood Cliffs.

Straits Times 2000a, Pride and hope to profit, 7 January, p. 21.

Straits Times 2000b, X-mas trees recycled in Ikea's green scheme, 11 Jan, p. 37.

Strand, R. 1987, A systems paradigm of organizational adaptations to the social environment, *Academy of Management Review*, 8, pp. 93–4.

Strauss, G. 1964, Work flow frictions, interfunctional rivalry, and professionalism: A case study of purchasing agents, *Human Organization*, 23, pp. 137–49.

Strebel, P. 1994, Choosing the right change path, *California Management Review*, 36, pp. 29–51.

Strom, S. 1996, A sweetheart becomes suspect; Looking behind those Kathie Lee labels, *New York Times*, 27 June, p. D1.

Strube, M. and Garcia, J. 1981, A meta-analysis investigation of Fiedler's contingency model of leadership effectiveness, *Psychological Bulletin*, 90, pp. 307–21.

Studer, M. 1992, SMH leads a revival of Swiss watchmaker industry, *Wall Street Journal*, 20 Jan., p. B4.

Sugawara, S. 1996, Japan Inc. finds a way to keep the lid on layoffs, *Washington Post*, 12 March, p. D11.

Sullivan, R.L. 1995, Lawyers ^ la carte, *Forbes*, 11 Sept., p. 44.

Sullivan-Trainorm, AM.L. and Maglitta, J. 1990, Competitive advantage fleeting, *Computerworld*, 8 Oct., p. 28.

Supervisory Management 1995, After reengineering what's next? May, p. 1.

Switzer, P. 2000, There's bread in them thar loaves, *Australian*, 24 Jan., p. 37.

Syrett, M. and Kingston, K. 1995, GE's Hungarian light lwitch, *Management Today*, April, p. 52.

Tabakoff, N. 1999a, The go-between, *Business Review Weekly*, 8 Oct., pp. 82–4.

Tabakoff, N. 1999b, Workers second-class labor, says union, *Business Review Weekly*, 8 Oct., p. 84.

Tait, P. and Vessey, I. 1988, The effect of user involvement on system success: A contingency approach, *MIS Quarterly*, March, pp. 91–108.

Talbott, S.P. 1994, Peer review drives compensation at Johnsonville, *Personnel Journal*, Oct., pp. 126–32.

Tang T.L-P. and Crofford, A.B. 1995-96, Self-managing work teams, *Employment Relations Today*, Winter, pp. 29–39.

Tannen, D. 1995a, The power of talk, *Harvard Business Review*, Sept.–Oct., pp. 138–48.

Tannen, D. 1995b, *Talking from 9 to 5*, Avon Books, New York.

Tannenbaum, R. and Schmidt, W.H. 1973, How to choose a leadership pattern, *Harvard Business Review*, May–June, pp. 162–80.

Tanzer, A. 1987, Create or die, *Forbes*, 6 April, p. 57.

Taylor III, A. 1989, The U.S. gets back in fighting shape, *Fortune*, 24 April, pp. 42–8.

Taylor III, A. 1992, U.S. cars come back, *Fortune*, 16 Nov., pp. 52–85.

Taylor III, A. 1993, Why GM leads the pack in Europe, *Fortune*, 17 May, pp. 83–6.

Taylor III, A. 1994, The auto industry meets the new economy, *Fortune*, 5 Sept., pp. 52–60.

Taylor, A. 1995, Boeing—sleepy in Seattle, *Fortune*, Aug., pp. 92–8.

Taylor, F.W. 1985, *The Principles of Scientific Management*, Hive, Easton.

Taylor, M.S., Locke, E.A., Lee, C. and Gist, M. 1984, Type A behavior and faculty research productivity: What are the mechanisms?, *Organizational Behavior and Human Performance*, 34, pp. 402–18.

Taylor, R.N. 1984, *Behavioral Decision Making*, Scott, Foresman, Glenview.

Teng, J.T.C., Grover, V. and Fiedler, K.D. 1994, Business process reengineering: Charting a strategic path for the information age, *California Management Review*, 36, Summer, pp. 93–108.

Thackray, J. 1985, Planning an Avon turnaround, *Planning Review*, Jan., pp. 6–11.

Therrien, L. 1989, The rival Japan respects, *Business Week*, 13 Nov., pp. 108–18.

Thite, M. 1999, Identifying key characteristics of technical project leadership, *Leadership and Organization Development*, 20, 5, pp. 253–61.

Thomas, E.G. 1987, Flextime doubles in a decade, *Management World*, April–May, pp. 18–19.

Thomas, J. and Sireno, P. 1980, Assessing management competency needs, *Training and Development Journal*, 34, pp. 47–51.

Thomas, K.W. 1977, Toward multi-dimensional values in teaching: The example of conflict behaviors, *Academy of Management Review*, 2, pp. 484–90.

Thomas, T. 1999a, Loan arranger prefers the solo practice life, *Business Review Weekly*, 29 Oct., pp. 130–1.

Thomas, T. 1999b, Nursery firm looks after the littlies until they grow big, *Business Review Weekly*, 21 May, pp. 98–9.

Thompson Jr, A.A. and Strickland III, A.J. 1987, *Strategic Management: Concepts and Cases*, Business Publications, Texas.

Thompson, J. 2003c, No minor parts, *Business Review Weekly*, 2–8 October, p. 24.

Thompson, J.D. 1967, *Organizations in Action*, McGraw-Hill, New York.

Thomson, J. 2003a, The corporate entrepreneur, *Business Review Weekly*, 20 August–3 September, p. 50.

Thomson, J. 2003b, Made in China, *Business Review Weekly*, 8–14 May, p. 20.

Tredgold, T. 2003a, Sweet success, *Business Review Weekly*, 6–12 November, p. 21.

Tredgold, T. 2003b, Busman's holiday, *Business Review Weekly*, 10–16 April, pp. 32–4.

Tredgold, T. 2003c, Hipster lobster, *Business Review Weekly*, 17–23 April, pp. 52–3.

Trinca, H. 2003a, Simplicity theory, *AFR Boss*, November, pp. 66–8.

Trinca, H. 2003b, The matchmaker, *AFR Boss*, June, pp. 34–7.

Thyfault, M.E. 1996, The intranet rolls in, *Information Week*, 29 Jan., pp. 15, 76–8.

Tichy, N. and DeRose, C. 1995, Roger Enrico's master class, *Fortune*, 27 Nov., pp. 105–6.

Tichy, N.M. and Ulrich, D.O. 1984, The leadership challenge—a call for the transformational leader, *Sloan Management Review*, Fall, pp. 59–68.

Tjosvold, D. 1984, Making conflict productive, *Personnel Administrator*, June, pp. 121–30.

Tjosvold, D. 1993, *Teamwork for Customers*, Jossey-Bass, San Francisco.

Tomsho, R. 1990, U-Haul patriarch now battles offspring in bitterest of feuds, *Wall Street Journal*, 16 July, pp. A1–A6.

Torrington, D. and Weightman, J. 1987, Middle management work, *Journal of General Management*, 13, pp. 74–89.

Tosi Jr, H.L. 1974, The human effects of budgeting systems on management, *MSU Business Topics*, Autumn, pp. 53–63.

Tosi Jr, H.L. and Slocum Jr, J.W. 1984, Contingency theory: Some suggested directions, *Journal of Management*, 10, pp. 9–26.

Tosi, H.L., Rizzo, J.R. and Carroll, S.J. 1986, *Managing Organizational Behavior*, Pitman, Marshfield.

Towne, H.R. 1886, The engineer as an economist, *Transactions of the American Society of Mechanical Engineers*, 7, pp. 428–32;

Townsend, A.M., DeMarie, S.M. and Hendrickson, A.R. 1996, Are you ready for virtual teams? *HRMagazine*, Sept., pp. 122–6.

Townsend, A.M., DeMarie, S.M. and Hendrickson, A.R. 1998, Virtual teams: Technology and the workplace of the future, *Academy of Management Executive*, 12, 3, pp. 17–29.

Toy, S. 1989, Waiter, a magnum of your best Portland champagne, *Business Week*, 11 Dec., pp. 92–4.

Trachtenberg, J.A. 1986, They didn't listen to anybody, *Forbes*, 15 Dec., pp. 168–9.

Trade New Zealand 2000, *New Zealand Country Profile*, www.tradenz.govt.nz/nz/nz.html

Treadgold, T. 1999, From the bottom drawer, a top dollar money manager, *Business Review Weekly*, 29 Oct., p. 59.

Trevino, L.K. 1986, Ethical decision making in organizations: A person–situation interactionist model, *Academy of Management Review*, 11, pp. 601–17.

Trice, H.M. and Beyer, J.M. 1993, *The Cultures of Work Organizations*, Prentice-Hall, Englewood Cliffs.

Trost, C. 1985, Bhopal disaster spurs debate over usefulness of criminal sanctions in industrial accidents, *Wall Street Journal*, 7 Jan., p. 18.

Trost, C. 1992, To cut costs and keep the best people, more concerns offer flexible work plans, *Wall Street Journal*, 2 Feb., p. B1.

Tuckman, B.W. 1965, Developmental sequence in small groups, *Psychological Bulletin*, 63, pp. 384–99.

Tuckman, B.W. and Jensen, M.A.C. 1977, Stages of small-group development revisited, *Group and Organization Studies*, 2, pp. 419–27.

Tuckey, Bill 1999, Debt struck Daewoo buys into the small car war, *Business Review Weekly*, 29 Oct., p. 46.

Tuleja, T.F. 1985, Beyond the bottom line: How business leaders are turning principles into profits, *Facts on File*, New York.

Tully, S. 1994, Why to go for stretch targets, *Fortune*, 14 Nov., pp. 145–58.

Tully, S. 1995, Purchasing's new muscle, *Fortune*, 20 Feb., pp. 75–83.

Tung, R.L. 1984, Strategic management of human resources in the multinational enterprise, *Human Resource Management*, 23, pp. 129–43.

Turban, E. and Watkins, P.R. 1986, Integrating expert systems and decision support systems, *MIS Quarterly*, June, pp. 121–38.

Turner, G. 1986, Inside Europe's giant companies: Daimler-Benz goes top of the league, *Long Range Planning*, 19, pp. 12–17.

Tushman, M. and Nadler, D. 1986, Organizing for innovation, *California Management Review*, 28, pp. 74–92.

Tushman, M.L. and Anderson, P. 1986, Technological discontinuities and organization environments, *Administrative Science Quarterly*, 31, pp. 439–65.

Tushman, M.L. and Scanlan, T.J. 1981, Boundary spanning individuals: Their role in information transfer and their antecedents, *Academy of Management Journal*, 24, pp. 289–305.

Ulrich, D. and Barney, J.B. 1984, Perspectives in organizations: Resource dependence, efficiency, and population, *Academy of Management Review*, 9, pp. 471–81.

Ulvila, J.W. 1987, Postal automation (ZIP 14) technology: A decision analysis, *Interfaces*, March–April, pp. 1–12.

Updike, E.H., Woodruff, D. and Armstrong, L. 1995, Honda's civic lesson, *Business Week*, 18 Sept., pp. 71–6.

USA Today 1992, *Low Grade Government*, 3 Sept., 1992, p. A1.

Uttal, B. 1985, Behind the fall of Steve Jobs, *Fortune*, 5 Aug., pp. 20–4.

Uttal, B. 1987, Companies that serve you best, *Fortune*, 7 Dec., pp. 98–116.

Van de Ven, A.H. 1986, Central problems in the management of innovation, *Management Science*, 32, pp. 590–607.

Van de Ven, A.H. and Delbecq, A.L. 1974, The effectiveness of nominal, delphi, and interacting group processes, *Academy of Management Journal*, 17, pp. 605–21.

Van Fleet, D.D. 1983, Span of management research and issues, *Academy of Management Journal*, 26, pp. 546–52.

Van Velsor, E. and Leslie, J.B. 1995, Why executives derail: Perspectives across time and cultures, *Academy of Management Executive*, 9, pp. 62–72.

Vecchio, R.P. 1987, Situational leadership theory: An examination of a prescriptive theory, *Journal of Applied Psychology*, 72, pp. 444–51.

Verity, J.W. and Hof, R. 1995, Bullet-proofing the net, *Business Week*, 13 Nov., pp. 98–9.

Violino, B. 1996, Internet insecurity: Your worst nightmare, *Information Week*, 19 Feb., pp. 34–6.

Vlasic, B. 1996, Can the UAW put a brake on outsourcing? *Business Week*, 17 June, pp. 66, 70.

Vlasic, B. and Kerwin, K. 1996, GM's man in merging traffic, *Business Week*, 4 March, p. 38.

Vokola, M., Rezgul, Y. and Wood-Harper, T. 2000, The Condor business process re-engineering model, *Managerial Auditing Journal*, 15, 1, pp. 42–6.

von Bertalanffy, L. 1951, General systems theory: A new approach to the unity of science, *Human Biology*, Dec., pp. 302–61.

von Bertalanffy, L. 1962, General systems theory—a critical review, *General Systems*, 7, pp. 1–20.

Vroom, V.H. and Jago, A.G. 1988, *The New Leadership: Managing Participation in Organizations*, Prentice-Hall, Englewood Cliffs.

Wagner III, J.A. 1995, Studies of individualism—collectivism effects on co-operation in groups, *Academy of Management Journal*, 28, pp. 152–72.

Wahba, M.A. and Bridwell, L.G. 1976, Maslow reconsidered: A review of research on the need hierarchy theory, *Organizational Behavior and Human Performance*, 16, pp. 212–40.

Wakizaka, A. 1995, Faxes, e-mail, help the deaf get office jobs, *Wall Street Journal*, 3 Oct., pp. B1, B5.

Waldman, P. 1989, New RJR chief faces a daunting challenge at debt-heavy firm, *Wall Street Journal*, 14 March, pp. A1, A19.

Waldon, H. 1985, Putting a new face on Avon, *Planning Review*, July, pp. 18–25.

Walker, G. 2003, An institution failed, *Business Review Weekly*, 18–24 September, pp. 68–9.

Walker, J. 2003a, Business primer, *Business Review Weekly*, 7–13 August, p. 70.

Walker, J. 2003b, Brief entrepreneurs, *Business Review Weekly*, 17–23 June, p. 54.

Walker, J. 2003c, Quitness achiever, *Business Review Weekly*, 3–9 August, pp. 65–7.

Walker, J. 2003d, A man and his mower, *Business Review Weekly*, 21–7 August, pp. 56–7.

Walker, J. 2003e, Franchises to bloom, *Business Review Weekly*, 18–24 September, p. 54.

Walker, J. 2003f, A man and his mower, *Business Review Weekly*, 21–7 August, pp.56–7.

Walker, N. 2003, Brief entrpreneurs, *Business Review Weekly*, 17–23 July, p. 54.

Wall Jr, J.A. and Callister, R.R. 1995, Conflict and its management, *Journal of Management*, 21, pp. 515–58.

Wall Street Journal 1989a, How you play the game says whether you win, 18 April, p. B1.

Wall Street Journal 1989b, Out of sight, not out of mind, 20 June, p. B1.

Wall Street Journal 1994a, Staples taps Hanaka from Lechmere inc. to become its CEO, 29 July, p. B2.

Wall Street Journal 1994b, Team selling catches on, but is sales really a team sport?, 29 March, p. A1.

Wall Street Journal 1995a, E-mail etiquette starts to take shape for business messaging, 12 Oct., p. A1.

Wall Street Journal 1995a, Motorola inc.: Company is chosen to build cellular system in Calcutta, 5 Jan., p. B4.

Wall Street Journal 1995b, Formosa plastics corp.: Company says pretax profit doubled in the first quarter, 28 April, p. A1.

Wall Street Journal 1995b, Motorola inc. plans to increase business with Chinese ventures, 13 Feb., p. B11.

Wall Street Journal 1995c, Glass ceiling is a heavy barrier for minorities, blocking them from top jobs, 14 March, p. A1.

Wall Street Journal 1995d, Life is good for telecommuters, but some problems persist, 3 Aug., p. A1.

Wall Street Journal 1995e, Miscommunications plague pilots and air-traffic controllers, 22 Aug., p. A1.

Wall Street Journal 1995f, Wanted: Middle managers, audition required, 28 Dec., p. A1.

Wall Street Journal 1995g, Diversity is up, 'Goal-setting' is down in workplace-training programs, 21 March, p. A1.

Wall Street Journal 1995h, Chevron settles claims of 4 women at unit as part of sex bias suit, 22 Jan., p. B12.

Wall Street Journal 1996, New GM rules kerb wining and dining, 4 June, p. B1.

Walters, K. 1999a, Rag traders get some help from an experienced hand, *Business Review Weekly*, 12 November, p. 77.

Walters, K. 1999b, When a deal goes out of its tree, *Business Review Weekly*, 21 May, pp. 45–6.

Walters, K. 1999c, Freight innovator no longer running on empty, *Business Review Weekly*, 29 Oct., p. 61.

Walters, K, 2003a, Governance gripes, *Business Review Weekly*, 3–9 April, p. 79.

Walters, K. 2003b, The figures which count, *Business Review Weekly*, 21–7 August, pp. 70–2.

Walters, K. 2003c, 'Difficult' types, *Business Review Weekly*, 27 November–3 December, p. 70.

Walters, K. 2003d, Big four, big worry, *Business Review Weekly*, 10–16 April, pp. 50–3.

Walton, R.E. 1985, From control to commitment in the workplace, *Harvard Business Review*, March–April, pp. 77–84.

Walton, R.E. and Dutton, J.M. 1969, The management of interdepartmental conflict: A model and review, *Administrative Science Quarterly*, March, pp. 73–84.

Wanous, J.P., Keon, T.L. and Latack, J.C. 1983, Expectancy theory and occupational/organizational choices: A review and test, *Organizational Behavior and Human Performance*, 32, pp. 66–86.

Want, J.H. 1986, Corporate mission: The intangible contributor to performance, *Management Review*, August, pp. 46–50.

Wartick, S.L. and Cochran, P.L. 1985, The evolution of the corporate social performance model, *Academy of Management Review*, 10, pp. 758–69.

Washington, S. 2003a, Smart moves, *Business Review Weekly*, 7–13 August, pp. 44–6.

Washington, S. 2003b, Flying by instruments, *Business Review Weekly*, 8–14 May, pp. 28–30.

Washington, S. and Way, N. 2003, Mystery flight, *Business Review Weekly*, 18–24 September, pp.44–9.

Washington Post 1995, Leeson sentenced to 61/2 years for causing Barings collapse, 2 Dec., p. 1F.

Waterman Jr, H. 1988, The power of teamwork, *Best of Business Quarterly*, Spring, pp. 17–25.

Watson, H.J., Rainer Jr, R.K. and Koh, C.E. 1991, Executive information systems: A framework for development and a survey of current practices, *MIS Quarterly*, March, pp. 13–30.

Watson, W.E., Kumar, K. and Michaelsen, L.K. 1993, Cultural diversity's impact on interaction process and performance: Comparing homogeneous and diverse task groups, *Academy of Management Journal*, 36, pp. 590–602.

Way, N. 1999, Juggling and struggling, *Business Review Weekly*, 22 Oct., pp. 69–75.

Way, N. 2000, The kings of culture, *Business Review Weekly*, 7 April, pp. 100–4.

Way, N. 2003a, Divided they fall, *Business Review Weekly*, 14–20 August, p. 27.

Way, N. 2003b, Bosch minds its language, *Business Review Weekly*, 27 March–2 April, pp. 70–3.

Weatherly, J.D. 1992, Dare to compare for better productivity, *HR Magazine*, Sept., pp. 42–6.

Weber, J. 1991, Meet Du Pont's 'In-house conscience', *Business Week*, 24 June, pp. 62–5.

Webster's New World Dictionary 1984, College Edition, Simon & Schuster, New York.

Weick, K.E. 1995, *Sensemaking in Organizations*, Sage, Thousand Oaks.

Weick, K.E. and Browning, L.D. 1986, Argument and narration in organizational communication, *Journal of Management*, 12, pp. 243–59.

Weiner, S. 1987, Taking the pledge, *Forbes*, 29 June, pp. 41–2;

Weisman, K. 1989, Safe harbor, *Forbes*, 4 Sept., pp. 58–62.

Weiss, E. 1996, Employees: Stop goofing off on net, *Warfield's Business Record*, 11 March, p. 18.

Weiss, R.M. 1983, Weber on bureaucracy: Management consultant or political theorist? *Academy of Management Review*, 8, pp. 242–8.

Welch, J.F. 1992, Service quality measurement at American Express traveler's cheque group, *National Productivity Review*, 22 Sept., p. 463.

Welles, C. 1988, What led Beech-Nut down the road to disgrace, *Business Week*, 22 Feb., pp. 124–8.

Werther Jr, W.B. and Davis, K. 1989, *Personnel Management and Human Resources*, McGraw Hill, New York.

Wessel, D. 1987, Computer finds a role in buying and selling, reshaping business, *Wall Street Journal*, 8 March, pp. 1, 10.

Wheeler, D.D. and Janis, I.L. 1980, *A Practical Guide for Making Decisions*, Free Press, New York.

Wheelwright, S.C. and Hayes, R.H. 1985, Competing through manufacturing, *Harvard Business Review*, Jan.–Feb., pp. 99–109.

Wheelwright, S.C. and Makridakis, S. 1989, *Forecasting Methods for Management*, Wiley, New York.

Whetten, D.A. and Cameron, K.S. 1998, *Developing Management Skills*, Scott, Foresman, Glenview.

White, J.B. 1988, U.S. car-parts firms form Japanese ties, *Wall Street Journal*, 12 April, p. 6.

White, J.B. 1989, Toyota wants more managers out on the line, *Wall Street Journal*, 2 Aug., p. A10.

White, J.B. 1997, Chrysler's intranet: Promise vs. reality, *Wall Street Journal*, 13 May, pp. B1, B6.

Whyte, G. 1989, Groupthink reconsidered, *Academy of Management Review*, 14, pp. 40–56.

Wildstrom, S.H. 1987, A risky tack for Democrats, *Business Week*, 20 July, p. 71.

Wildstrom, S.H. 1995, This 'secretary' really listens, *Business Week*, 24 April, p. 19.

Wilkes, M.V. 1992, Charles Babbage—The great uncle of computing?, *Communications of the ACM*, March.

Willoughby, J. 1987, The last iceman, *Forbes*, 13 July, pp. 183–204.

Winberg, N. 1996, Shaking up an old giant, *Forbes*, 20 May, pp. 68–80.

Winslow, R. 1995, Hospitals' weak systems hurt patients, study says, *Wall Street Journal*, 5 July, pp. B1, B6.

Wiseman, C. and MacMillan, I.C. 1984, Creating competitive weapons from information systems, *Journal of Business Strategy*, Fall, pp. 42–9.

Wokutch, R.E. and Spencer, B.A. 1987, Corporate saints and sinners: The effects of philanthropic and illegal activity on organizational performance, *California Management Review*, 29, pp. 62–77.

Wolff, W.F. 1996, Japan study team probes management of R&D, *Research-Technology Management*, March–April, pp. 4–5.

Wood, R.E., Mento, A.J. and Locke, E.A. 1987, Task complexity as a moderator of goal effects: A meta analysis, *Journal of Applied Psychology*, 72, pp. 416–25.

Woodman, R.W., Sawyer, J.E. and Griffin, R.W. 1993, Towards a theory of organizational creativity, *Academy of Management Review*, 18, pp. 293–321.

Woodruff, D. and Miller, K.L. 1995, Mercedes' maverick in Alabama, *Business Week*, 11 Sept., pp. 64–5.

Woodward, J. 1958, *Management and Technology*, Her Majesty's Stationery Office, London.

Woodward, J. 1965, *Industrial Organisations: Theory and Practice*, Oxford University, London.

World Airlines News 1995, Product news, 9 Jan., p. 1.

Worthy, F.S. 1989, When somebody wants a payoff, *Fortune*, Pacific Rim issue, Fall, pp. 117–22.

Wrege, C.D. and Perroni, A.G. 1974, Taylor's pig tale: A historical analysis of Frederick W. Taylor's pig iron experiment, *Academy of Management Journal*, 17, pp. 6–27.

Wrege, C.D. and Stotka, A.M. 1978, Cooke creates a classic: The story behind F. W. Taylor's principles of scientific management, *Academy of Management Review*, 3, pp. 736–49.

Wren, D.A. 1979, *The Evolution of Management Thought*, Wiley, New York.

Wren, D.A. 1986, Years of good beginnings: 1886 and 1936, in D.A. Wren and J.A. Pearce II (eds), *Papers Dedicated to the Development of Modern Management*, Academy of Management.

Wright, P. M. and Kacmar, K.M. 1994, Goal specificity as a determinant of goal commitment and goal change, *Organizational Behavior and Human Decision Processes*, 29, pp. 242–60.

Wyman, L. 1996, Rugs roll at IKEA; Latest theme at Manhattan store, *HFN The Weekly Newspaper for the Home Furnishing Network*, 8 April, p. 11.

Wysocki Jr, B. 1995, Some companies cut costs too far, suffer 'Corporate Anorexia,' *Wall Street Journal*, 5 July, p. A1.

Yerak, B. 1994, Castite owner lets dream have its way, *Plain Dealer*, 1 June, p. 1C.

Yoshino, M.Y. and Ranga, U.S. 1995, *Strategic Alliance: An Entrepreneurial Approach to Globalization*, Harvard Business School, Boston.

Young, J. 1996, Digital octopus, *Forbes*, June 17, pp. 102–106.

Yukl, G. 1989, Managerial leadership: A review of theory and research, *Journal of Management*, 15, pp. 251–89.

Yukl, G. 1994, *Leadership in Organizations*, Prentice-Hall, Englewood Cliffs.

Zaccaro, S.J. 1984, Social loafing: The role of task attractiveness, *Personality and Social Psychology Bulletin*, 10, pp. 99–106.

Zachary, G.P. 1989, Software makers get a chill from Microsoft's Windows, *Wall Street Journal*, 10 Oct., pp. B1, B8.

Zachary, G.P. 1994, It's a mail thing: Electronic messaging gets a rating—ex, *Wall Street Journal*, 22 June, p. A1.

Zachary, G.P. 1995a, Can unions organize low-paid workers? Watch this woman, *Wall Street Journal*, 23 Oct., pp. A1, A10.

Zachary, G.P. 1995b, Some unions step up organizing campaigns and get new members, *Wall Street Journal*, 1 Sept., pp. A1, A2.

Zaheer, S. 1995, Overcoming the liability of foreignness, *Academy of Management Journal*, 38, pp. 341–63.

Zaleznik, A. 1977, Managers and leaders: Are they different? *Harvard Business Review*, May–June, pp. 47–60.

Zaleznik, A. 1990, The leadership gap, *Academy of Management Executive*, 4, pp. 7–22.

Zaltman, G., Duncan, R. and Holbek, J. 1973, *Innovations and Organizations*, Wiley, New York.

Zaremba, A. 1988, Working with the organizational grapevine, *Personnel Journal*, July, pp. 38–42.

Zemke, R. 1988, Putting the SQUEEZE on middle managers, *Training*, Dec., pp. 41–6.

Ziegler, B. 1995a, IBM fires three Argentine executives amid investigation of bank contract, *Wall Street Journal*, 15 Sept., p. A6.

Ziegler, B. 1995b, Virtual power lunches will make passing the salt an impossibility, *Wall Street Journal*, 28 June, p. B1.

Zinger, B.J. and Madique, M.M. 1990, A model of new product development: An empirical test, *Management Science*, 36, pp. 867–83.

ADDITIONAL REFERENCES AND FURTHER READING FOR NEW CASES

Chapter 1

Striving for excellence, Erica King: CEO Focus Dental Management: Gome, A. 2003, Like pulling teeth, *Business Review Weekly*, 14–20 August, pp. 58–9.

Gaining the edge, The challenge of management—Fremantle Port: Boone, M. 2002, Interactive management, *Executive Excellence*, 19, 5, pp. 12–5; Drucker, P., 1967, *The Effective Executive*, Harper & Row, New York; Duffy, E., 1999, Inclusivity, *Management Today*, June, pp. 4–5; fremantleport.com.au; Pierce, D.F., 2000, Safety in the emerging leadership paradigm, *Occupational Hazards*, June; Treadgold, T., 1996, The port, the storm, the calm, *The Qantas Club*, August, pp. 29–31.

Managing the e-challenge, Technology and fraud: Belson, K. 2000, Like stealing plastic from a baby, *Business Week*, 11 December.

Chapter 2

Striving for excellence, Kirsty Dunphey—Director, M & M Real Estate: Gome, A. and Ross, E. 2003, Missing action, *Business Review Weekly*, 24-30 July, p. 41.

Gender factor, Tall poppy: Awards National Australia Day Council, Poppy King, 1995, www.nadc.com.au/article.php?articleid=96; Poppy King, an Australian success story, www.geocities.com/Athens/8161/poppyking.html; Lawyers suggest mediation for Poppy King dispute, 13 August 1998. www.liv.asn.au/news/media/19980813_poppy.html; Fiona Byrne, 2002, News & views with sting, *Sunday Herald Sun*, 10 February; Laura Kendall, 2001, Poppy grows back, *The Advertiser*, 14 July; Jenny Wills, 2002, 'Lippy King', *Sunday Telegraph*, 14 April.

Managing the e-challenge, Web on menu at McDonald's: McDonald's New Zealand 2001, Dunedin leads the way with Cyber Café, press release, 7 June; http://mccms.mcdonalds.co.nz/rexconductor/files_download.asp?id=100000050&x=1; McDonald's New Zealand 2001,'New Zealand website one of global best', press release, 13 December; http://mccms.mcdonalds.co.nz/rexconductor/files_download.asp?id=100000074&x=1; Munro, B. 2002, Cyber Cafe nets praise', *The Star* (Dunedin), 7 March, p. 1; Reuters 2001, Big Macs and Google—at McDonald's, *ZD Net News*, 7 May; http://zdnet.com.com/2102-1105-900811.html

On the Rim, Hills finds millions in the backyard: www.hills.com.au—Hills Industries website; Corporate Research Foundation 2002, *The Best Companies to Work for in Australia*, 2nd ed., Harper Collins, Sydney.

Chapter 3

Striving for excellence, Vince Gauci, chief executive, MIM Holdings: Based on Treadgold, T., 2003, The blue collar CEO, *Business Review Weekly*, April 3–9, p. 30.

Managing the e-challenge, Keeping up with the game(s): Howarth, B. 2002, Serious fun, *Business Review Weekly*, 14–20 March, pp.60–3; www.brw.com.au/stories/20020314/13666.asp (This site is accessible only by paid subscription.).

Gender factor, Pumpkin Patch: Abridged from Sye, A. 1999, Mail order business, *Her Business*, September/October, 25, pp. 8–9. http://www.pumpkinpatch.co.nz/patch_help.cfm

Chapter 4

Striving for excellence, Andrew Liveris: James, D. 2003, Profile: Andrew Liveris, *Business Review Weekly*, 3–9 July, p. 26.

Managing the e-challenge, Rural women claim the internet: Bollinger, T. 2002, Not just gumboots and scones, *Communities Online Series*, Department of Internal Affairs, Government of New Zealand, 26 March; www.dia.govt.nz/Pubforms.nsf/URL/CommunitiesOnline7.pdf/$file/CommunitiesOnline7.pdf; Cook, M. 2000, Rural web site goes international, *Otago Daily Times* (Dunedin), 12 April, p. 13; Elliott, A. 2000, Creating an internet-based information network for rural women, *Computers in New Zealand Schools*, 12(1), pp. 41–4, 48, www.notjust.org.nz/Gumboots_and_Scones.pdf; Not just gumboots and scones, www.notjust.org.nz/

Gaining the edge, Meeting the challenge of labour shortage: An innovative and socially responsive approach: Washington S., and Morris, J. 2003, Who'll do the work? More retirees and fewer recruits present business with a big problem, *Business Review Weekly*, February 13–9, pp. 70–3; Jackson, R., and Osmond N. 2003, How to recruit and retain older staff, *People Management*, 15 May, pp. 46–7; Online magazine of the Chartered Institute of Personnel and Development, www.peoplemanagement.co.uk

Going global, From gifts to wishes: Aldred, J. 2000, Wishlist proves its worth, *Australian Financial Review*, 29 November; Roman,T. and Robbins, P. 1999, Better staff relations? It's a gift really, *Business Review Weekly*, 21, 5, 15 February; Bartholomeusz, S. 2001, $10m new equity shows dot-com wishes still come true, *The Age*, 20 February; Higgins, D. 2001, Wishlist hot to trot with $10m top-up, *The Sydney Morning Herald*, 15 February.

Gender factor, Christine Nixon is the force: Adapted from Silvester, J. 2002, *The Age*, 20 April.

Chapter 5

Striving for excellence, The regular guy: Durie, J., 2003, *Australian Financial Review Boss*, 13 June, pp. 24–7.

Managerial dilemmas, Tough decisions in a time of crisis: www.oamps.com.au, OAMPS company website; www.hihroyalcom.gov.au, HIH Royal Commission website; Corporate Research Foundation 2003, *The Most Promising Companies in Australia*, Harper Collins: Sydney.

Chapter 6

Striving for excellence, Catherine Livingstone, chairman, CSIRO: Ross, E. 2003, Profile: A master strategist, *Business Review Weekly*, 27 March–2 April, pp. 26–8.

Managing the e-challenge, Doctor Global plans a possible future: www.doctorglobal.com; New Zealand 2002 census data for New Plymouth, at: The World Gazetteer, www.gazetteer.de/d/d_nz_tn.htm; Vaughan, G. 2002, NZ's global doctor seeks US break, *The Independent* (New Zealand), 24 April, p. 16; Wright, H. 2002, Dr. Global eyes huge deal, *NZ Infotech Weekly*, 17 June, p. 2.

Chapter 7

Striving for excellence, Success is skin deep: Emily Ross 2003, In person: Dennis Paphitis, Success is skin-deep, *Business Review Weekly*, 17 November (With additional research by Cassandra Bos).

Gender factor, Happy Hens: *The Otago Entrepreneur* 1993, Happy Hens—an industry that fits the buzzwords, July, pp. 2–3.

Chapter 8

Striving for excellence, Clear the decks: Based on Condon, T. 2002, Profile: Clear the decks, *Business Review Weekly*, 29 August–4 September, p. 46.

Case in point, Franchising: A structure for success: http://www.brw.com.au/; Schmidt, L. 1999; Featherstone, T. (ed.) 1999; *Annual Report 1998*, Harvey Norman Holdings Limited; http://businesssunday.ninemsn.com.au/; www.comsec.com.au

Managerial dilemmas, Structural disease can be deadly: www.ey.com.au, Ernst and Young Australia; www.accenture.com; Accenture Corporate Research Foundation 2002, *The Best Companies to Work for in Australia*, 2nd ed., Harper Collins, Sydney.

Chapter 9

Striving for excellence, Bridge Street farmer: Richardson, J. 2003, Bridge Street farmer, *Australian Financial Review Boss*, 12 September, pp. 45–8.

Gaining the edge, Not so joint retail adventure: Sydney Ford dealers form joint venture, *Australasian Transport News*, 2000; www.trucknbus.com.au/atn/index.cfm?cp=archivelist.cfm&arch=august2000; Tuckey, Bill 2001, Ford deals with it, *Business Review Weekly*, 20 July, p. 36.

Gender factor, The Seriously Good Chocolate Company: Interview with Jane Stanton, Friday 30 May 2004; http://www.choctruffles.co.nz/; http://www.nzte.govt.nz/article/0,1973,SectionID%253D11897%2526ContentID%253D5821,00.html

Management skills for a globalised economy, Guidelines for keeping your organisation 'fit': Jones, G.R., George, J.M. and Hill, C.W.L. 2000, *Contemporary Management*, McGraw-Hill, New York.

Chapter 10

Striving for excellence, Not so crazy, after all: Schmidt, L. 2003, Mobile wealth: Not so crazy after all, *Business Review Weekly*, 4–10 September, pp. 22–3.

Case in point, Cool in a crisis: McColl, G. 2003, Cool in a crisis, *Business Review Weekly*, 7–13 August, pp. 76–8.

Managerial dilemmas, Life wasn't meant to be easy: Washington. S. 2002, Life wasn't meant to be easy, from For Fun and Profit, *Business Review Weekly*, 29 August–4 September, p. 64.

Gender factor, Only one woman in BHP's top 117 managers: Adapted from Bagwell, S. 1997, *Australian Financial Review*, 20 May, p. 7.

Gaining the edge, Work in progress: McCallum, J. 2003, Work in progress, *Australian Financial Review* Boss, June, pp. 42–6.

On the Rim, Price is all in Singapore: Roberts, P. 2003, Pricing is all in Singapore, *Business Review Weekly*, 10–6 April, pp. 14–6.

Going global, SATS moves further ahead as Asia's airport services leader: Adapted from *Asian Business Review* 1999, SATS moves further ahead as Asia's airport services leader, May, pp. 58–9; www.workforceone.org.sg/pd/part2f.html; www.sats.com.sg/sats/newlook1/index.html

Chapter 11

Striving for excellence, Profile: Warburton the worker: Based on Skeffington, R. 2002, Profile: Warburton the worker, *Business Review Weekly*, 19 September.

Case in point, Mother Meg's success takes the cake: Adapted from Wisentahl, S. 2003, Mother Meg's success takes the cake, *Australian Financial Review*, 28 October, p. 57; http://www.dpi.qld.gov.au/news/newsreleases/13614.html, Enterprising women showcase food, fibre and agritourism businesses (Toowoomba), accessed 24 September and 28 November 2003.

Gaining the edge, Small is beautiful: SPH asiaone (http://newpaper.asiaone.com.sg/top/story/0, 4136, 22670, 00.html)

Chapter 12

Striving for excellence, Jamieson's new perspective: Schmidt, L. 2003, Jamieson's new perspective, *Business Review Weekly*, 24–30 April, pp. 92–3.

Case in point, Independents' day: Hooper, N. 2003, Independents' day, *Australian Financial Review* Boss, 12 October.

Gender factor, What female managers bring to IT: Adapted from Phillipa Yelland 2002, *The Age*, 23 April.

Gaining the edge, Profile: Busman's holiday: Treadgold, T. 2003, Profile: A busman's holiday: Graham Turner, chief executive of Flight Centre, *Business Review Weekly*, 29 April, pp. 32–4.

Management skills for a globalised economy, Making the transition from effective manager to effective leader: Adapted from Kinicki, A. and Williams, B. 2003, *Management: A Practical Introduction*, McGraw-Hill, New York.

Chapter 13

Striving for excellence, Konichiwa, mate: Thomson, J. 2003, Konichiwa, mate, *Business Review Weekly*, 21–7 August, pp. 25–8.

Case in point, LG Electronics: Are you talking to your fridge?, Rachel Lebihan 2002, ZDNet Australia, 14 May, http://www.zdnet.com.au/news/communications/0,2000061791,20265246,00.htm;

How wired do you want it?, Rob Waugh 2003, February, http://www.smarthouse.com.au/ArticlesByTopic/KitchensAndAppliances/1224Digital home network, 2004, 12 July, http://www.infolink.com.au/articles/da/0c0125da.asp; LG Website, http://au.lge.com/about/corporate/html/ company_overview.jsp

Gaining the edge, Cool is good for communication: McColl, G. 2003, Cool in a crisis, *Business Review Weekly*, 7–13 August, pp. 76–8.

Chapter 14

Striving for excellence, Deloitte's new Mr Fix-it: Walters, K., 2003, Deloitte's new Mr Fix-it, *Business Review Weekly*, 17–22 April, pp. 62–3.

Gender factor, Helen Clark at the helm: Adapted from James, C. 2001, Riding the learning curve, *Management*; James, C. 1999, Commander in Chief Clark, *New Zealand Management*; Clifton, J. 2002, National emergency, *New Zealand Listener*, 6–12 April.

Chapter 15

Striving for excellence, WAN's new Law: Treadgold, T. 2002, Strategy: WAN's new Law, *Business Review Weekly*, 29 August–4 September, p. 40.

Management skills for a globalised economy, The skills option—How to retain control when outsourcing: Lloyd, Simon 2002, Agency Angst, *Business Review Weekly*, 29 August–4 September, p. 74.

Managing the e-challenge, Controlling telecommuters: Braue, D. 2002, Home and away, *Bulletin*, 26 March, pp. 62–3.

Chapter 16

Striving for excellence, Nicole Feely, chief executive, St Vincent's Health, Melbourne: Adapted from Way, Nicholas 2004, *Business Review Weekly*, 12 May.

Managing the e-challenge, Getting smart with on-line financing: Based on Kirby, J. 2001, GMAC accelerates car loans, *Business Review Weekly*, 20 July, p. 77; Broekhuise, P. 2002, Weinstock targets sloppy nets, *Australian*, 12 March.

Management skills for a globalised economy, The challenge of dealing with change: Adapted from Kinicki, A., and Williams, B. 2003, *Management: A practical introduction*, p. 317.

Gaining the edge, Managing organisations through change and conflict—Fremantle Port: Brown, W. A. 2002, Inclusive governance practices in non-profit organisations and implications for practice, *Non-profit Management & Leadership*, 12, 4, Summer, pp. 369–85; Boone, M. 2002, Interactive management, *Executive Excellence*, 19, 5, pp. 12–5; Duffy, E. 1999, Inclusivity, *Management Today*, June, pp. 4–5; Kotter, J. 1996 in At the Helm video, Leadership (various contributors), Electronic Media Association, Australia; Fremantle Port, fremantleport.com.au; Pierce, D. F. 2000, Safety in the emerging leadership paradigm, *Occupational Hazards*, June; Tallack, R. 1996, Commercial management for shipmasters: a practical guide, The Nautical Institute; Treadgold, T. 1996, The port, the storm, the calm, *The Qantas Club*, August, pp. 29–31.

On the Rim, Slop, slip, zoom: Gome, A. 2004, Slop, slip, zoom, *Business Review Weekly*, 11–7 March, p. 59.

Going global, Down but not out: Salim Group poised for a comeback: Adapted from Lasserre, P., and Schutte, H.S.

1999, *Strategy and Management in Asia Pacific*, McGrawHill, Berkshire; Borsuk, R., Webb, S. and Mapes, T. 2002, Salim deal paves way for comeback, *Asian Wall Street Journal*, XXVI, 195, 7–9 June; http://www.aftaonline.com/aol%20archives/company/97%20-%2000/salim_grp.htm

Chapter 17

Striving for excellence, China: One man's trade effort: Gome, A. 2003, China: One man's trade effort, *Business Review Weekly*, 27 March–2 April, p. 56.

Gender factor, The gender business of relocation and expatriation: Wood, G.J. 2001, Perception: A contributing factor in the different career advancement outcomes of female managers, unpublished doctoral dissertation, Monash University, Melbourne, Victoria, Australia.

Management skills for a globalised economy, Preparing for an overseas assignment: Adapted from Kinicki, A., and Williams, B., 2003, *Management: A practical introduction*, p. 111. McGraw-Hill, New York.

Gaining the edge, Service for sale: Roberts, C. 2004, Service for sale, *Business Review Weekly*, 11–7 March, p. 58.

On the Rim, Too good to be true: Roberts, C. 2004, Too good to be true, *Business Review Weekly*, 11–7 March, pp. 56–7.

Chapter 18

Going global, Smart move for Motorola: Adapted from Lasserre, P. and Schutte, H.S. 1999, *Strategy and Management in Asia Pacific*, McGraw-Hill, Berkshire; www.motorola.com/LMPS/

CREDITS

Details of sources are provided in the References. Following are further details requested by copyright holders.

Abbreviations used below: **CP:** Case in Point; **Ex:** Exercise; **Fig:** Figure; **GE:** Gaining the Edge; **GF:** Gender Factor; **GG:** Going Global; **MD:** Managerial Dilemma; **ME:** Management Exercises; **ME-C:** Managing the E-Challenge; **MSGE:** Management Skills for a Globalised Economy; **OR:** On the Rim; **SE:** Striving for Excellence; **Tab:** Table

Part 1 Opener: Melbourne, photo supplied by Photolibrary.com/George Hall.

Chapter 1: SE: Gome, A. (2003) Like pulling teeth, *Business Review Weekly*, 14–20 August, pp. 58–9, photo courtesy of Focus Dental Management; **Tab 1.1,** Mintzberg, H. (1980) *The Nature of Managerial Work*, Prentice-Hall, Englewood Cliffs. Reprinted by permission of Pearson Education, Inc., Upper Saddle River, NJ; **GF:** Photo courtesy of Second Skin Pty Ltd; **MSGE:** Deming, W.E. (1986) *Out of the Crisis*, MIT Press, Cambridge, p. 23–4. Reprinted by permission of MIT Press, Cambridge, MA; **GE:** Photo courtesy of Fremantle Port; **ME-C:** Belson, K. (2000) Like stealing plastic from a baby, *Business Week*, 11 December.

Chapter 2: SE: Gome, A. & Ross, E. (2003) Missing action, *Business Review Weekly*, 24–30 July, p. 41, photo courtesy of Kirsty Dunphey and M&M Real Estate; **ME-C:** Photo courtesy of McDonald's Restaurants New Zealand Ltd; **GE:** Photo courtesy of Ford Australia.

Chapter 3: SE: Treadgold, T. (2003) Blue collar CEO, *Business Review Weekly*, 3–9 April, p. 30, photo supplied by Newspix/Patrick Hamilton; **GE:** Photo courtesy of Turbosoft; **ME-C:** Howarth, B. (2002) Serious fun, *Business Review Weekly*, 14–20 March, pp. 60–3; **OR:** Photo courtesy of Fuzzyeyes Studio Pty Ltd; **CP:** Logo courtesy of Customer Service Institute of Australia.

Chapter 4: SE: James, D. (2003) Profile: Andrew Liveris, *Business Review Weekly*, 3–9 July, p. 26, photo courtesy of The Dow Chemical Company; **GF:** Photo courtesy of Victoria Police; **GG:** Photo courtesy of Wishlist Holdings Ltd; **Tab 4.3** © 1996 by Dow Jones & Co. Inc. Reproduced with permission of Dow Jones & Co. Inc. via Copyright Clearance Center; **MSGE:** Nash, L.L. (1981) Ethics without the sermon, *Harvard Business Review*, Nov–Dec, p. 81. Reprinted by permission of *Harvard Business Review*; **ME: Ex** 1 Skill building, Lockheed Martin (1992) *Gray Matters: The Ethics Game Manual*, pp. 9, 25 and 29. Reprinted by permission of Lockheed Martin Corporation.

Part 2 Opener: Sydney, photo supplied by Ben Rushton/Fairfaxphotos.

Chapter 5: SE: Durie, J. (2003), *AFR Boss*, 13 June, pp. 24–7, photo courtesy of BHP Billiton Ltd.

Chapter 6: SE: Ross, E. (2002) A modest master strategist, *Business Review Weekly*, 27 March–2 April, pp. 26–8, photo courtesy of CSIRO; **CP:** Photo courtesy of Ventracor Ltd; **Tab 6.2** Drucker, P.F. (1974) *Management: Task, Responsibilities & Practices*, Harper & Row, with permission from Elsevier; **Tab 6.3** Locke, E.A. and Latham, G.P. (1984) *Goal Settings: A Motivational Technique That Works*, Prentice-Hall, pp. 171–2. Reprinted with permission of the author; **Tab 6.5** Porter, M.E. (1980) *Competitive Strategy Techniques for Analyzing Industries and Competitors*, Free Press: New York, pp. 3–28. Adapted with

the permission of The Free Press, a Division of Simon & Schuster Adult Publishing Group © 1980, 1998 by The Free Press. All rights reserved; **MSGE:** Locke, E.A. and Latham, G.P. (1984) *Goal Settings: A Motivational Technique That Works*, Prentice-Hall. Reprinted with permission of the author.

Chapter 7: SE: Ross, E. (2003) In person: Dennis Paphitis, success is skin-deep, *Business Review Weekly*, 13 November, photo courtesy of Aesop; **CP:** Switzer, P. (2000) There's bread in them thar loaves *The Australian*, 24 January, p. 37. Reprinted with permission of the author; **Fig** 7.1 Ihrcke, J. (2000) The key to corporate success, *Economic Bulletin*, Jan, p. 14. Reprinted with permission of the author; **OR:** Dawson, C. (2000) Pioneer's unchartered territory, *Far Eastern Economic Review*, 9 March, pp. 48–9; **MSGE:** Pinchot III, G. (1985) *Intrapreneuring*, Harper and Row, New York. Reprinted with permission of the author.

Part 3 Opener: Auckland, photo supplied by Photolibrary.com/Warren Jacobs.

Chapter 8: SE: Condon, T. (2002) Clear the decks, *Business Review Weekly*, 29 Aug–4 Sept, p. 46, photo supplied by Newspix/Andrew MacColl; **CP:** Photo supplied by Newspix/Lannon Harley; **GF:** Photo courtesy of Nola Nails; **Fig** 8.3 Hackman, J.R. & Oldham, G.R. (1980) *Work Redesign*, Addison-Wesley, Reading, p. 90. Reprinted by permission of Pearson Education, Inc., Upper Saddle River, NJ; **Fig** 8.4 Robbins, S.P. (1990) *Organization Theory: The Structure and Design of Organizations*, Prentice-Hall, Englewood Cliffs, p. 88. Reprinted by permission of Pearson Education, Inc., Upper Saddle River, NJ.

Chapter 9: SE: Richardson, J. (2003) Bridge Street farmer, *AFR Boss*, 12 Sept, pp.45–8, photo courtesy of The Twynam Agricultural Group; **CP:** Hanvey, M. (1999) Web site steers trucker's business, *Business Review Weekly*, 21 May. This article first appeared in *Business Review Weekly*, 21 May 1999. Reprinted with the permission of the author, Michael Hanvey; **GE:** Photo courtesy of Ford Australia; **MD:** Photo courtesy of E.L. Consult/Tripac International; **OR:** Photo courtesy of Griffith University; **Tab** 9.5 Woodward, J. (1965) *Industrial Organisation: Theory and Practice*, Oxford University Press, pp. 52–82. By permission of Oxford University Press.

Chapter 10: SE: Schmidt, L. (2003) Not so crazy after all, *Business Review Weekly*, 4 Sept–1 Oct, pp. 44–5, photo courtesy of Crazy John's; **CP:** McColl, G. (2003) Cool in a crisis, *Business Review Weekly*, 7–13 August; **MD:** Washington, S. (2002) Life wasn't meant to be easy (For fun and profit), *Business Review Weekly*, 29 Aug–4 Sept, p. 64; **GG:** Photo courtesy of Singapore Airport Terminal Services Ltd. (SATS); **GE:** McCallum, J. (2003) Work in progress, *AFR Boss*, 13 June, pp. 42–6; **ME-C:** Photo courtesy of Wilcom International Pty Ltd; **OR:** Roberts, P. (2003) Price is all in Singapore, *Business Review Weekly*, 10–16 April, pp. 14–6. Reprinted with permission of the author; **Fig** 10.3 Sourced from Building for tomorrow: emerging measures from Achieving measurable performance improvement in a changing world: The search for new insights, *KPMG White Papers 2001*. Reproduced courtesy of KPMG LLG, the US member firm of KPMG International; **Tab** 10.2 Sourced from Building for tomorrow: emerging measures from Achieving measurable performance improvement in a changing world: The search for new insights, *KPMG White Papers 2001*, p. 9. Reproduced courtesy of KPMG LLG, the US member firm of KPMG International.

Part 4 Opener: Brisbane, photo supplied by D.W. Stock Picture Library/F. Fell.

Chapter 11: SE: Skeffington, R. (2002) Warburton the worker, *Business Review Weekly*, 19 Sept, p. 58, photo courtesy of Dick Warburton/Caltex; **CP:** Photo supplied by Newspix/Jim Trifyllis.

Chapter 12: SE: Schmidt, L. (2003) Jamieson's new perspective, *Business Review Weekly*, 24–30 April, pp. 92–3, photo courtesy of Minter Ellison; **CP:** Hooper N. (2003) Independents' day, *AFR Boss*, 10 October. Reprinted with permission of the author, photo supplied by Newspix/Lindsay Moller; **GE:** Treadgold, T. (2003) Busman's holiday, *Business Review Weekly*, 10 April, p. 32–4; **Fig** 12.1 Tannenbaum, R. & Schmidt, W.H. (1973) How to choose a leadership pattern, *Harvard Business Review*, May–June, pp.162–180. Reprinted by permission of *Harvard Business Review*; **Fig** 12.3 Blake, R.R. & McCanse, A.A. (1991) *Leadership Dilemmas-Grid Solutions*, Gulf, Houston, p. 29; **Tab** 12.2 Vroom, V.H. & Yetton, P.W. (1973) *Leadership and Decision Making*, University of Pittsburgh Press. Reprinted by permission of the University of Pittsburgh Press. © 1973 by University of Pittsburgh Press; **Fig** 12.5 Vroom, V.H. & Jago, A.G. 1988, *The New Leadership: Managing Participation in Organizations*, Prentice-Hall, Englewood Cliffs, pp. 184–5. Reprinted by permission of Pearson Education, Inc., Upper Saddle River, NJ; **ME: Ex** 1 Sellers, P. (1996) What Exactly is Charisma?, *Fortune*, 15 January. © 1996 Time Inc. All rights reserved.

Chapter 13: SE: Thomson, J. (2003) Konichiwa, mate, *Business Review Weekly*, 21–7 August, pp. 25–8, photo courtesy of Toyota Australia; **Fig** 13.1 Reprinted by permission, Kurke, L.B. & Aldrich, H.E. (1983) Mintzberg was right! A replication and extension of the nature of managerial work, *Management Science*, Vol 29, pp.975–984. The Institute of Management Sciences, now the Institute for Operations Research and the Management Sciences (INFORMS), 901 Elkridge Landing Road, Suite 400, Linthicum, Maryland 21090-2909, USA; **CP:** Photo courtesy of LG Electronics; **Tab** 13.1 Hodgetts, R. M. & Altman, S. (1979) *Management: Theory Process and Practice*, W.B. Saunders Company, Philadelphia, PA, p. 305; **MSGE:** Gordon, J. R. (1987) *A Diagnostic Approach to Organizational Behavior*, Allyn and Bacon, Boston, p. 230. Adapted by permission of Pearson Education, Inc., Upper Saddle River, NJ; **Fig** 13.7 Types of grapevine chains from K. Davis Management Communication & the Grapevine published within *Organizational Communication*, 2nd Edition (eds. Ferguson, Stewart and Ferguson, Sherry Devereaux), Transaction Publishers, 1987, p. 59; **ME-C:** Photo courtesy of EzyDVD.com.au; **GE:** McColl, G. (2003) Cool in a crisis, *Business Review Weekly*, 7–13 August, pp. 76–8; **ME: Ex** 1 Reprinted from Listening self-inventory by Glenn, E.C. & Poole E.A. published in *Supervisory Management*, January 1989, pp. 12–5. Copyright © 1989 American Management Association. Published by the American Management Association International New York, NY. Used by permission of the publisher. All rights reserved. www.amanet.org.

Chapter 14: SE: Walters, K. (2003) Deloitte's new Mr Fix-it, *Business Review Weekly*, 17–22 April, pp. 62–3, photo courtesy of

Deloitte Touche Tohmatsu; **GF:** Photo courtesy of the Office of the Prime Minister, New Zealand.

Part 6 Opener: Perth, photo supplied by APL/Andre Maurer.

Chapter 15: SE: Treadgold, T. (2002) WAN's new law, *Business Review Weekly*, 29 Aug–4 Sept, p. 40, photo supplied by Newspix/ Ross Swanborough; **MD:** Photo supplied by Newspix/Lyndon Mechielsen; **CP:** Photo courtesy of the Interfaith Center on Corporate Responsibility (ICCR); **MSGE:** Lloyd, S. (2002) Agency angst, *Business Review Weekly*, 29 Aug–4 Sept, p. 74.

Chapter 15 Supplements: Tab 15S1.4 Cowen, S.S. & Middaugh II, J.K. (1988) Designing an effective financial planning and control system, *Long Range Planning*, 21, pp. 83–92. Reprinted with permission from Elsevier; **Fig** 15S2.3 Wheelwright, S.C. & Hayes, R.H. (1985) Competing through manufacturing, *Harvard Business Review*, Jan–Feb, pp. 99–109. Reprinted by permission of *Harvard Business Review*; **Fig** 15S2.7 Buffa, E. (1983) *Modern Production/Operations Management*, John Wiley & Sons, New York, p. 32; **Fig** 15S2.8 Buffa, E. (1983) *Modern Production/Operations Management*, John Wiley & Sons, New York, p. 33; **Fig** 15S3.3 Laudon, K.C. & Laudon, J.P. (1994) *Management Information Systems*, Macmillan, New York, p. 36. Reprinted by permission of Pearson Education, Inc., Upper Saddle River, NJ; **Tab** 15S3.1 Laudon, K.C. and Laudon, J.P. 1994, *Management Information Systems*, Macmillan, New York. Reprinted by permission of Pearson Education, Inc., Upper Saddle River, NJ.

Chapter 16: SE: Way, N. (2004) Church and state, *Business Review Weekly*, 13–9 May, Photo courtesy of St. Vincent's Health; **Tab** 16.1 Kotter, J.P. & Schlesinger, L.A. (1979) Choosing strategies for change, *Harvard Business Review*, March–April, p. 111. Reprinted by permission of *Harvard Business Review*; **Tab** 16.3 Thomas, K.W. (1977) Toward multi-dimensional values in teaching: The example of conflict behaviours, *Academy of Management Review*, p. 487. © 1977 by Academy of Management. Reproduced with permission of Academy of Management via Copyright Clearance Center; **GE:** Photo courtesy of Fremantle Port; **OR:** Gome, A. (2004) Slop, slip, zoom, *Business Review Weekly*, 11–7 March, p. 59, photo by Peta Di Palma/supplied courtesy of Tapex.

Part 6 Opener: Singapore, Photo supplied by APL/Macduff Everton.

Chapter 17: SE: Gome, A. (2003) One man's trade effort, *Business Review Weekly*, 27 March–2 April, p. 56, photo courtesy of Panausino; **MD:** Hiebert, M. (2000) Two-way vision, *Far Eastern Economic Review*, 17 February, pp. 51–2; **Fig** 17.1 Porter, M.E. (1990) The competitive advantage of nations, *Harvard Business Review*, March–April. Reprinted by permission of *Harvard Business Review*; **GE:** Roberts, C. (2004) Service for sale, *Business Review Weekly*, 11–7 March, p. 58, photo by Paul Jones/supplied courtesy of Novotech; **OR:** Roberts, C. (2004) Too good to be true, *Business Review Weekly*, 11–7 March, pp. 56–7, photo courtesy of Hardcat Pty. Ltd.

Notes:
All Reflective Practitioner photo source lines are: Courtesy of Aerosafe Risk Management Pty. Ltd.

Cover Image source line is: Photo supplied by Getty Images/The Image Bank/George Lepp.

INDEX

2